The Big Serious Guitar Book

1st Edition

ISBN: 978-1-4675-8642-9
Written by Geoff Stockton, © 2013, All rights reserved
1st Edition independently published 2013

CONTENTS:	PAGE
Introduction	3
Getting Started	5
Basic Guitar Technique	11
Music Reading – An Introduction	14
Fretboard Mapping - Part 1: The Essentials	20
Rhythm – Part 1: Simple Words	22
The Major Scale	25
Rhythm – Part 2: Rests	31
The Cycle Of 5ths	33
Fretboard Mapping - Part 2: Major Scale Positions	34
Music Reading - Part 2: The Fret Board in All Keys	35
Diatonic Harmony - Part 1: Triads	36
Chord Progressions - Part 1: Major I – IV – V Changes	40
The Chord-Tone Pattern	42
Diatonic Harmony - Part 2: Transposition and Bar Chords	46
Recognizing Tonality	52
The Natural Minor Scale	55
Diatonic Harmony – Part 3: Power Chords	61
The Pentatonic Scale	65
Rhythm – part 3: Other Simple Time Signatures	74
Essential Techniques	76
Chord Progressions – part 2: Diatonic Chord Substitution	87
Melodic Patterns – part 1	91
Basic Triad Inversion	131
Diatonic Harmony – Part 4: Four Note Chords	134
Triad Pairs	148
The Modes of the Major Scale	161
Arpeggios – Part 1: Chords of the Major Scale	194
Chord Progressions – Part 3: The 12-Bar Blues	219
Rhythm – Part 4: Syncopation	236
Chord Progressions – Part 4: Interval Patterns	240
Diatonic Harmony – Part 5: Chords of the Harmonic Minor Scale	243
Harmonic Minor Scale Positions	245
The Modes of the Harmonic Minor Scale	246
Harmonic Minor Chord Pairs	258
Symmetrical Harmony – Part 1: Simple Math	264
Rhythm – Part 5: Odd Subdivisions	266
Melodic Patterns – Part 2: Musical Applications	272

Non-Diatonic Harmony – Part 1: Secondary Dominant Chords	277
Chord Progressions – Part 5: Using Secondary Approaches	279
The Melodic Minor Scale	281
The Modes of the Melodic Minor Scale	292
The Melodic Craft – Part 1: Properties of Melody	313
Rhythm – Part 6: Compound Time Signatures	323
Diatonic Harmony – Part 6: Extended Chords	334
Arpeggios – Part 4: Triad Pairs of the Melodic Minor Scale	342
Chord Progressions – Part 6: Key Modulation	353
Navigating Modulations and Non-Diatonic Chords	364
Melodic Patterns – Part 3: Advanced Diatonic Motion	366
Non-Diatonic Harmony – Part 3: Tri-Tone Substitution	386
The Melodic Craft – Part 2: Chromaticism	388
Non-Diatonic Harmony – Part 3: More Chromatic Chords	403
Symmetrical Scales	408
Symmetrical Harmony – Part 2: Hidden Triad Families	421
Melodic Patterns – Part 4: Non-Harmonic Patterns	428
Jazz Licks – Over a IIm7-V7-Imaj7 Context	440
Diatonic Harmony – Part 7: Quartal Harmony	451
The Melodic Craft – Part 3: Motive Development	455
Harmonization	463
Background Writing – The Art of the Counter-Melody	474
About the Author	477
Music Notation to Fretboard Guide	478

This book is dedicated to my wife Sheri, my sons Julian, Gavin and Parker, my stepson Connor and my parents, Don and Patty. Your love and support has pulled me through this rather daunting task. Thank you!

GREETINGS!

Thank you for picking up this book. It was a five year project! The aim was to write a comprehensive guide for the creative guitarist. I've been teaching guitar students full-time for a little over a decade and this book represents the material that I work through with my serious students. By that, I mean those who have a desire to free themselves on a creative level and develop the ability to compose and improvise original music in the styles of their choice. This is what I call achieving the level of the grand communicator.

Music is a language. It's the language of human emotion and thought. It's universal in the sense that all cultures perceive consonance, dissonance and rhythm in a similar way. The minor chord sounds dark or sad to all who hear it. With that being said, music is a language that most people learn only to the extent of knowing how to quote things that others have said, without understanding what they meant or being able to say anything in response. This is because most people, even many of those who made it through music theory 101, don't see the big picture of music and how its language works.

What I set out to do, in writing this book, was to offer what I wish I had when I was an eager sixteen year-old guitar player aspiring to achieve a professional level of skill. I started playing when I was 11 but my real quest for the raw knowledge of music started when I was 16. This book chronicles everything I've discovered in the twenty years since. If I would have had a book like this at that point, I can't imagine what I would have accomplished. I've been through about a hundred songbooks, ten music theory books, three of which were used college textbooks I bought for fifty cents each, as well as books about playing in various styles. I've played hundreds of gigs in various styles and I've written, arranged and produced at least a couple hundred songs.

I've learned important musical lessons from every style in which I've immersed myself. Even styles made entirely electronically have taught me more than most guitarists would ever imagine. Once you've learned enough about the raw elements of music, you begin to learn by osmosis. Imagine learning all kinds of valuable things about music just by listening. One of the major aims of this book is to get you to that point, where you consciously hear and understand every musical part within a recording or a performance.

Let's talk about a couple things that are going to be very important for you to keep in mind, on your path.

PERSEVERANCE:

The most important factor in reaching your goals is sticking to it. There's something that you need to have if you want perseverance and that's self-confidence. If you don't fully believe that you can achieve it with enough work, whatever it is, what's to keep you trying? When you're really new to it, you really need some one on one guidance from someone who knows what they're doing. Most people who don't get this in their first year usually wind up dropping out. The first hump is the hardest to get over but things really start to roll when you've gotten past it so hang in there. The more music you learn, the quicker you learn it until eventually you start learning it as soon as you hear it, as long as no short-cuts are taken.

Practicing And Playing:

There's a big difference between these two things. Playing is when you're doing something that you're already pretty good at. Practicing is when you're working on something that you're not good at yet. The guitarists and other musicians out there who've played for plenty of years but manage to remain mediocre are the ones who spend a few weeks practicing and the rest of their years playing. The musicians who've played for less time and accomplished a lot more are typically the ones who kept what they call the "student's mind". You have to be willing to continuously humble yourself by working on things that are out of your confidence zone. This means you have to spend at least an hour every day in slow-motion. That's why privacy is a real plus when you're practicing. Play in front of anyone. Practice in front of no one.

Hours

Mastering anything in life takes a little self-sacrifice. You need to put in at least an hour a day. A lot of the legends would play and practice for eight hours and more a day. I try to play and practice intensely for two hours a day and study or write and record for another two hours. I don't put four hours in every time but that's what I shoot for and sometimes I'll have an eight-hour day of music. Sometimes I'll go a few days without playing much at all and it never makes me feel too great the next time I pick up the guitar. Daily playing and practice keeps you sharp and it keeps you moving forward. Sell your video game system and make some valuable use of any down time you have. You'll be glad you did as those hours start to add up!

Improvisation:

Daily improvising is your most valuable education as a musician. It's through experience that we most readily gain knowledge and understanding. To improvise is to get your hands dirty, learning through trial and error. That doesn't mean that you have to walk into it blind. This book will offer you a lot of preparation and background that will help give you the self-confidence to go for it. Everything that you learn when you improvise applies directly to written music so record yourself improvising, any chance you get. We'll be covering this more in the first section.

Try to progress through this book in a linear manner, even if you think you already have a particular section covered. You'll never know what knowledge you were lacking until you learn it. This has proven itself to me over and over again. I can't tell you how many times I thought I had a concept covered only to find out that I was barely scratching the surface. Seek out help from a guitarist or a guitar teacher any time you get hung up in a particular section. I have a collection of guitar lessons available on Youtube, where you can find plenty more willing teachers.

There's always a solution to whatever musical problem you're having. Just, move forward, be relentless and never fear knowledge.

Geoff Stockton

Getting Started

This first section is mainly intended to help out those of you, who are brand new to the guitar and/or music in general. It'll be useful also, if you teach guitar or ever plan on teaching it. First off, let's make sure we have what we need.

Checklist:
1) Guitar - amplifier and cable if you're playing an electric
2) Strap
3) Picks
4) Tuner
5) Metronome
6) Recording Device
7) Guitar strings
8) Music Dictionary
9) Supplemental Material

Guitars

If you're reading this book, there's a good chance you already have a guitar sitting next to you. You need to be sure it's in a playable condition. This means it should be properly intonated and set up and its neck should be well aligned. If yours has not already been given the stamp of playability by someone who knows guitars well, I would recommend finding someone who can do that. Any problems with necks and bridges are relatively cheap to fix and VERY worth it. If you're trying to learn on a guitar that's not all the way playable, you're bound to wind up pulling out your hair.

If you can afford a top of the line guitar, buy it and take good care of it. If you can't afford one, don't despair because a guitar doesn't have to have a $1,500.00 price tag on it to sound really good. As long as your guitar is in playable condition you can make it sound great. If you're new to this, it's a good idea to ask someone who can play well to play your guitar for you. This way you get an idea of your instrument's potential and you won't wind up thinking that the problem is your guitar when it's really YOU! Make the acquisition of guitars secondary to your acquisition of guitar skills and musical understanding and you'll be better off. Buy the really nice guitar once you have the really nice skills to match. The last thing anybody wants to be is a poser!

My best advice is to spend some time in guitar stores and pawn shops getting a solid idea about what kinds of guitars appeal to you and talk with as many guitar players as you can about guitars. They can help you get an idea about what types of guitars are best suited to certain types of music over others and offer you lots of valuable advice. Ask the sales people at the guitar stores if they have some guitar catalogues available. These are almost always free and some of them are a great read with lots of info for people just getting into the wide world of guitars. Also, there are a lot of books about guitars that you can find at the local library or bookstore.

Electric Guitar Anatomy

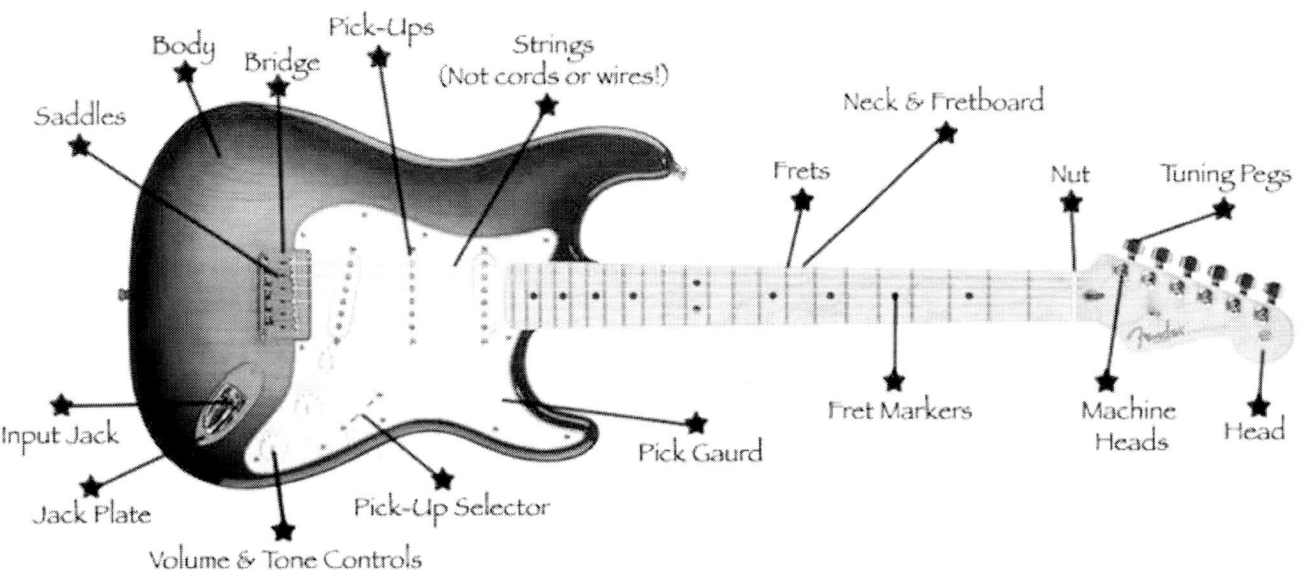

Acoustic Guitar Anatomy

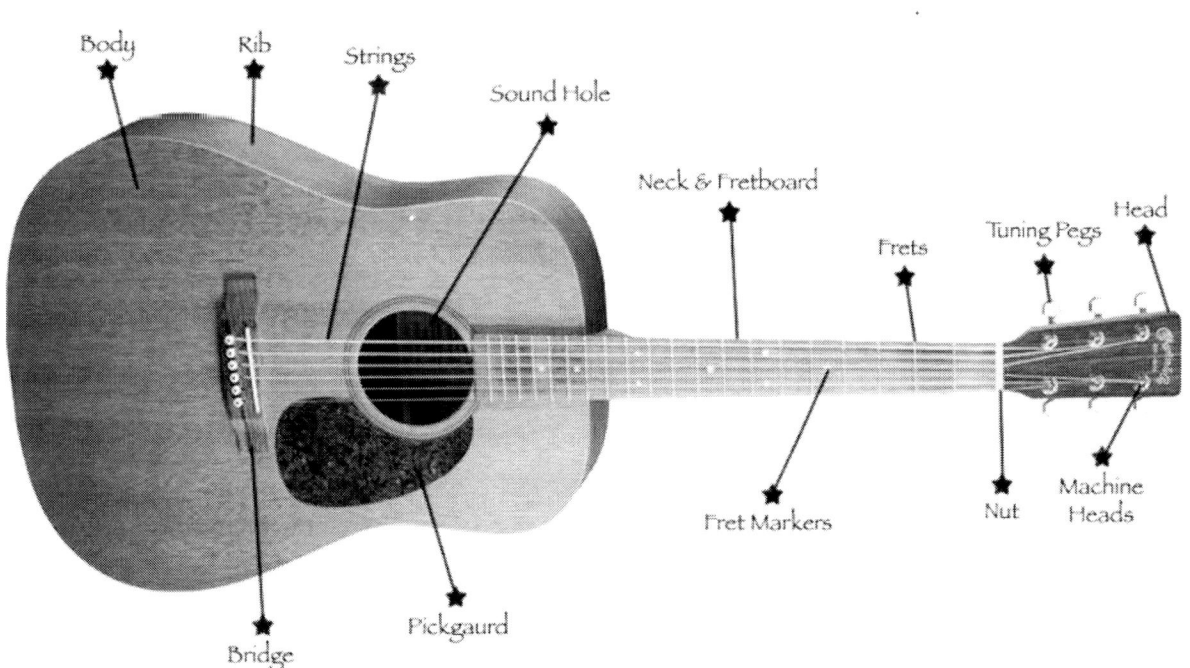

STRAPS

Finding a good guitar strap is important if you're planning on doing a lot of your playing standing up. Most nylon straps feel about as cheap as they are. They aren't very comfortable and you wouldn't want to play for an extended period using the typical nylon strap. If you have a very lightweight guitar, it won't bug you as much, but if your guitar tips the scales somewhere in the middleweight to heavyweight range, the nylon strap will eventually start digging into your shoulder muscles which is never good when you're performing.

Most serious guitar players find it to be worth spending the extra twenty or thirty dollars to get a nice comfortable strap. Some straps are made out of a quilted nylon with lots of padding. Some people really like these but I find them to be a bit too cumbersome and sweaty. I prefer using a good old-fashioned quilted leather strap. It's strong and flexible and distributes the weight evenly enough to keep me comfortable. The backside of the strap, that is the side touching my body, is brushed suede, which lets my shoulder and back breathe a little more. Try out some different straps and see what feels comfortable to you.

Strap height is another important consideration. By strap height, I'm referring to the difference in between having your guitar hanging down to your knees or having it hiked up to your armpits to go with your pocket protector. The prior option is considered, how do they say it, "cool" in some circles. I think playing with your back hunched over so your strumming hand can reach your knee-height guitar looks a bit desperate. That's my humble opinion, of course. The main downfall to this method is that you're really cutting off your fretting finger's ability to stretch apart. Developing a good stretching range for the fretting hand is very important. Whenever you play the guitar, chimpanzee style, you really do cut off about half of that range. There's a healthy medium between the Chimpanzee and nerd methods. I keep my guitar strap adjusted so the guitar rests the same whether I'm sitting or standing. It keeps my approach consistent and that helps keep my technique reliable.

AMPS

If you're playing an electric guitar you will need an amplifier or "amp," if you don't already have one. If you're a beginning guitar student or a living-room jammer, a small practice amp will handle your needs just fine. Make sure it has a distortion channel built into it. This may be called distortion, drive, overdrive, gain, lead, etc. If you're unfamiliar with what this is, it's the fuzzy and/or chunky guitar sound in a typical rock or metal recording; though almost all guitar players use some amount of overdrive or distortion even if it's just a tiny bit, like you would hear in a modern country guitar solo.

If you already have your amp and it has no "dirty" channel, you'll have to make a trip to your local guitar shop and have them show you some distortion and overdrive pedals. They can help you find a pedal that matches your taste in guitar sounds. Bring along a CD that features a dirty guitar sound that you like. This will be a great help to the sales person in helping you choose the right pedal. They can range in price from about $50.00 all the way up to $5000.00 so let them know what kind of budget you're working with.

If you're planning on playing gigs with a band in the near future I would recommend an amp with a couple 10" or 12" speakers, preferably a tube amp with at least 50 watts of power. If it's not a tube amp, you're going to need at least 100 watts of power. This will be as loud as a 50-watt tube amp but it won't sound quite as warm. Go to the local guitar shop and listen to a couple of solid-state amps and then listen to a couple tube amps and you will hear a marked difference in the tube amps. A much more vibrant, lively, rich and full tone compared to the solid-state amps with their passive, plain sounding signal. Advances have been made in tube emulation technology with solid state amps and software and the advances will continue until tube amps will more than likely become obsolete (many will hate me for saying it) but until that day comes, I prefer using tube amps.

As cool as they look in concert films and videos, I would recommend against buying a half stack (a cabinet with four 10" or 12" speakers plus a separate "head" stacked on top) or a full stack (the same, except with two cabinets, for a total of eight speakers) unless you can pay a couple roadies to haul it around for you.

You will never need an amp that's this loud. If you were playing a venue large enough to where you might actually make use of that much volume, your amp would have a microphone in front of it, sending the signal to the much larger PA speakers. So unless you're highly concerned with the classic, textbook rock & roll image, (and I'm not knocking it if you are, it's an art) there's never a need for a stack or even a half-stack.

PICKS

There are a few basic types of picks to choose from. Each of these picks typically come in three or four different gauges; light or thin, (very flexible) medium (somewhat flexible) and heavy (thicker and very stiff) and the occasional extra heavy. I'd recommend buying yourself one of each and start trying them all out. This will give you some ideas about what you like and dislike and what type of pick suites what type of task.

Tri-Pick   Standard Pick   Jazz Picks   Thumb Pick

I'll tell you about my personal preferences but don't take it as gospel. This is just what works for me. Experiment for your own sake. I've come to prefer the standard and jazz pick styles. I do too much alternate picking (up and down) to get away with a thumb pick and the tri-pick design feels very awkward and cumbersome to me. The gauge of pick I use depends on what type of playing I'm doing in a particular song.

If I'm doing a lot of wide strumming and I want to blend in, I use a thin standard pick. Its flexibility makes it so even if I strum harder; I'm not going to get much louder because the pick just bends more to the strings.
When you're using a thin pick on an acoustic guitar, the flapping of the plastic gives you a more percussive sound which can be very desirable for certain types of "strummy" songs.

If I'm doing more intricate picking (one note at a time) and/or I want to cut through, I prefer a heavy standard or jazz pick. Since it doesn't bend, I can get much more predictability from it. This allows me to get more control, not only over which string I'm picking but how loud the note I'm picking is going to be. The tighter I hold the pick, the louder the notes become.

If I'm playing a song where I'm doing some strumming and also doing some picking, I reach for a medium gauge standard pick. This way, I have of little a both basic advantages and I'm not feeling especially awkward in one section of the song or another.

Sometimes I don't use a pick at all. It depends on the needs of the song. As I mentioned above, with enough experimentation you'll find your own personal preferences. There's no right way or wrong way in general whereas there are right and wrong ways for one person in particular. We all have different hands and all types of hands have their advantages and disadvantages.

TUNERS

A tuner is a device, which tells you whether your instrument is in tune and visually guides you to the correct pitches. Having a diverse tuner is very handy. There are a couple different types of tuners. There is the basic guitar or guitar/bass tuner. These only check the pitches of your open strings in standard tuning. I'd recommend against this type of tuner unless it has a flat function that will allow you to add one to four flats to any note. I say this because many songs are played in alternate tunings and a basic guitar tuner won't provide all the required. The other type tuner is the chromatic tuner. It will allow you to tune any string to any pitch. This is what I prefer. Make sure to read the instructions clearly. It's best to have someone with some experience walk you through it, the first couple times. Practicing on an out-of-tune guitar is not going to do you any favors. It's really frustrating to be playing something right and still have it sound wrong. If you own a good smart-phone a tuner can be downloaded for little or no money. If you go this route, make sure it's one with rave reviews.

METRONOMES

A metronome is a device which keeps time with a steady click. The speed or tempo, which is measured in BPM, (beats per minute) can be adjusted. The range of the tempo options should be pretty wide. 40 BPM is usually the slowest tempo and 250 BPM is usually the fastest. The idea is to practice something steadily at a particular tempo and gradually increase the tempo in comfortable increments until you can play it up to speed. This helps you to develop a very solid and reliable "meter" as it's called. In music, meter refers to the ability to hold a tempo steady without any unintended speeding up or slowing down. Holding a tempo is always more challenging than it sounds and the regular use of a metronome in your practice sessions will help build this very important skill. Not only that, but it'll move you ahead at a quicker rate because you're consciously and clearly outdoing yourself, day after day, which encourages you to play more and so begins the begins the cycle of progress. Just like with the tuner, metronome apps can be downloaded for smart-phones

RECORDING DEVICES

There's quite a wide range of recording devices out there and anything will work as a practice tool. You could go to the nearest electronics store and buy a simple little mini-cassette recorder with a built in mic, but these days, without spending a whole lot more, you can get a small digital multi-track recorder, which will allow you to layer guitar parts, one over another. This can be a lot of fun and a whole lot of education. Some of these come with built in drum machines and programmable bass sounds. You could record complete songs and turn them into mp3s. There's plenty of recording software on the market for both PCs and Macs. Depending on your computer's features, you may need to buy an *audio interface* in order to record yourself. Regardless of what sort of device you choose to use it will be a handy tool in your musical growth.

Strings

It's this simple: the thinner the string, the thinner the tone and likewise, the thicker the string, the thicker the tone. The advantage to the thin string is that it's easy to push down. The disadvantage is that the string moves more and becomes more difficult to rapidly pick. In turn, the advantage to the heavy string (aside from the thicker, louder tone) is that it stays more stationary. This allows you too more easily execute fast picking. The disadvantage is that the strings are tougher to push down and manipulate. Honestly, any physical disadvantage a string gauge presents can be overcome by practice so it really comes down to what kind of tone you want. Jimi Hendrix used heavy strings and so did Stevie Ray Vaughn. Tony Iommi from Black Sabbath uses very thin string. (His is a story worth looking into for those of you who don't know.) Listen to your favorite guitarists and find out what their choice of string gauge is. This way, you can get a clear idea of which gauge creates what effect. Personally, I prefer a medium gauge unless I'm playing straight-ahead jazz where I use heavy strings.

Try and put on a fresh set of strings at least once a month. After a few weeks strings start to lose their bounce and liveliness of tone. You can prolong the life of your strings by wiping them down with a string cleaner before and after playing. It also helps to wash your hands before playing.

Music Dictionary

Having a music dictionary is a good idea for any musician in general but especially if you're planning on learning about music from books. If you have internet access, than you don't really need the book, but it's not a bad idea to have one because you never know when you might really need one. I've tried to cover everything in this book, but I realized it would take me a decade to even come close. A simple music dictionary should fill in any gaps you may find between this book and your own prior understanding.

Supplemental Material

As much as I'd like to, I just can't include everything in one book. If you happen to be a beginning level player, I'd strongly advise finding a competent instructor who can handle working you through the material at least until you feel you have your own momentum. I would suggest stocking your bookshelf with books written specifically about the styles of music that you're interested in playing. Get on the internet and look at the massive wealth of video lessons for any styles that you're interested in. We'll be touching on lots of styles since this is book. It's a broad-spectrum analysis of music and guitar playing, but like I said, I can't fit it all in the book. I recommend picking up any songbooks that contain songs that you're interested in. The more music that you learn the more you'll be able to directly connect the knowledge that you'll gather from this book.

Now that we have what we need it's time that we begin our journey.

Basic Guitar Technique

Posture

This is pretty simple. Keep a relatively straight spine and stay relaxed. These two factors make a big difference in your ease of playing. Make sure to keep the guitar flat against your body. The more you let it slide so the face of the guitar is looking up toward the ceiling, the harder it is to reach most of the notes. Try and situate your guitar strap so whether you're standing or sitting, you're holding the guitar at the same level in relation to your body. Keep in mind that you want to be able to comfortably stretch your fingers apart on your lowest (sounding) string. If this feels like more of a strain on your hand than when you're sitting down, you may have your hanging too strap too low.

Picking:

This picture demonstrates the standard method of holding a pick. The tightness of your grip should depend on how loud you want the note to be. The stiffer your grip, the louder the note you'll sound.

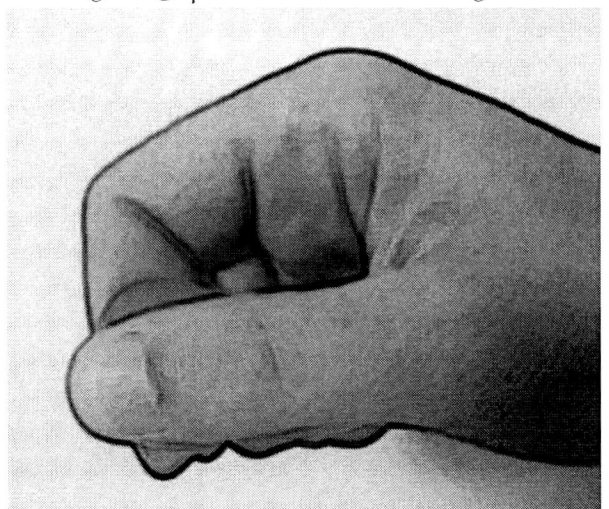

When you're picking a series of individual notes, especially when you're switching from string to string, it's a good idea to keep your hand anchored to the guitar. Some people plant their picking hand pinky on the pick guard. I prefer two other methods. The first of which is resting my palm on the bridge. Sometimes I'll let a little bit of my palm touch the strings where they meet the bridge. More on this, later. My other preferred method is a two-part process. When I'm playing on the higher (sounding) strings, I'm resting my palm on the lower strings. When I'm playing on the lower strings, I have my unused fingers curled inward and resting on the upper strings. The reason I like this technique is because I can pick anywhere on the string from the bridge to the neck while staying anchored. Staying anchored gives me more picking precision. Anchoring on unused strings keeps your electric guitar from howling with string feedback. Having the freedom to move between bridge and neck gives me a greater variety of sounds.

Another consideration is picking direction. For the time being, practice these two things: 1) Pick a long, unbroken, perfectly even series of downstrokes. 2) Pick in a strictly alternating down/up/down/up motion and try to make these notes sound as even as your downstrokes. By "even" I mean that you want all the notes to be of equal length and equal volume. This sounds pretty simple but it actually take quite a bit of practice so put in some hours on it. They will be boring but rewarding hours. Also very important, don't pick too hard. It makes your notes ring flat.

FRETTING

Without frets, your guitar would only have six available notes that you could play. It would get pretty boring. By pressing the string all the way down against a fret, you're cutting off a certain portion of the string, raising the pitch of the note. This makes it a different note. As a result, any note can be found on any string. We'll be getting into the specifics of this, later on. For the time being it's important that you learn proper fretting technique.

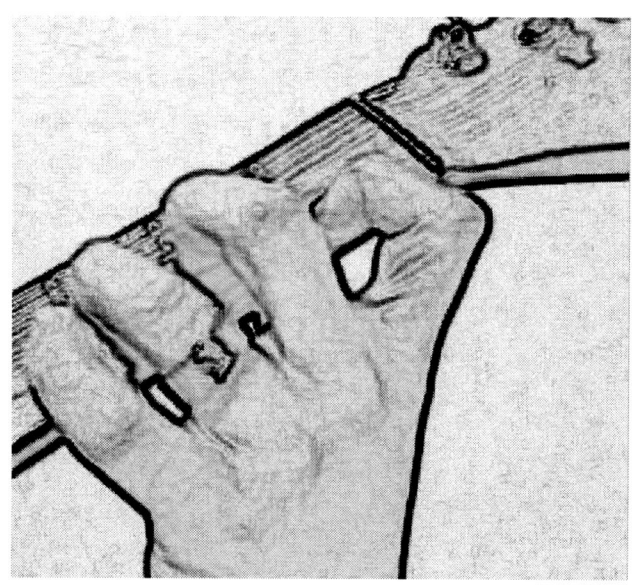

The metal lines separating the spaces are the actual frets, although when somebody says "put your finger on the 1st fret of the highest (sounding) string", they're really telling you to press your finger down on the string somewhere between the nut and the first fret. So in guitar lingo "on the third fret" really means behind the third fret, or between the second and third frets, closer to the third. Be clear in your understanding of fret numbers. The higher the fret number, the higher the sound of the note. The high frets are the ones that would shorten your strings more and produce higher sounding notes. Whether you're talking about strings or frets on the guitar, up looks like down. It sounds like up and that's what counts.

When you first start trying to fret notes on your strings you may hear some buzzing in your notes. This happens because the string isn't being pressed all the way down to the fret. It's common with beginners. Just keep trying to press harder and keep your fingers curved like a claw with the end section of your fingers straight up and down so they form a 90° angle with the string. This gives you the most leverage and takes a lot of the burden off of your weaker finger muscles. If the string continues to buzz no matter how hard you press it down, you may be picking too hard or you may need a neck adjustment. Have someone who knows guitars take a look at it. This is an easy thing to fix.

Eventually, you'll be playing chords. A chord is a group of notes played simultaneously. It's especially important to keep your fingers in "claw" mode when you're playing chords so you don't inadvertently block off adjacent strings with either side of your fretting fingers. Sometimes we have to mute a string that sits between two other strings that we're fretting. We can mute the middle string by letting the pad of the finger that's playing the lower string hang over onto it gently. Make sure to not accidentally press the middle string down in these situations. Some times you'll need to lay a finger flat across two or more strings at once. Take time to practice this, using all your fretting fingers, on any strings and any frets. It will be difficult but it's worth putting some in hours. If you do, it won't remain difficult.

Thumb positioning is also very important. When your thumb is laid flat against the back of the neck, you'll have about half of your finger's natural range of motion from side to side. Ideally you want to be pivoting on the pad of your straightened left hand thumb as shown in the diagram to the right. This will allow your left hand fingers to stretch quite a bit further apart, a very handy guitar skill.

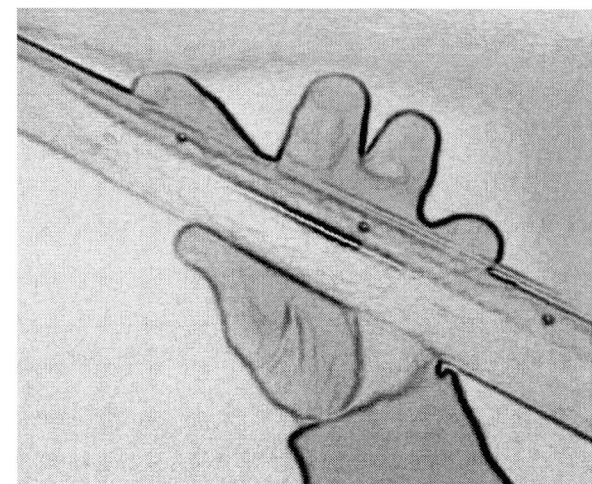

STRUMMING

Strumming simply refers to brushing your pick against multiple strings at a time. This is the broad up and down motion you usually see guitar players employing. Generally we strum chords and pick melodies. Though you can pick the notes of a chord individually, you really can't strum a melody unless it's what we call a chord melody. Below are a few good things to bear in mind when you're practicing your strumming.

This is an **E minor** chord:

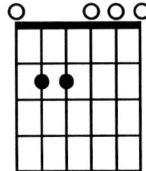

When you first try playing this chord try picking the strings individually, from lowest to highest. This way you can make sure you're successfully pressing down the fretted strings and you're not accidentally blocking off any open strings. Adjust your left hand until all six strings are ringing clearly. Once you've achieved that much, it's time to start strumming.

When you strum, go for quick and light motions. A nice solid strum sounds like all the notes happened at once. You don't want it to sound like a staggered series of notes. This is known as raking, which is a special effect that we'll be talking about later. Keep your pick slanted to run smoothly over the strings. When you switch from an upstroke to a downstroke switch the slant of the pick by turning your wrist as if you were turning a car off, using the key in the ignition. Work to achieve the same goals with your strumming that you're working on with picking: dynamically and rhythmically even, alternating ups and downs. Also, try breaking the strings into two sets: the upper and lower sets. Try strumming only one set or the other. This will help you develop valuable picking hand control.

MUSIC READING - Part 1: An Introduction

Guitar Tablature

There are two forms of written music from which a guitar player can learn. The easiest to learn, right off the bat, is what we call guitar tab. Since this proves to be a useful learning aid for those just getting familiar with music we will start off with an explanation of it before moving on to what we call standard notation, which is the more universal written language of music.

Here is a very basic example of guitar tab:

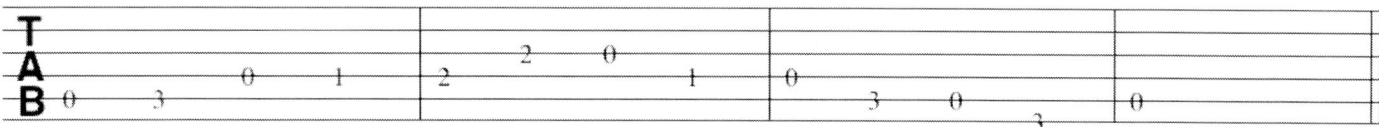

Here are the five things to understand, in order to properly and successfully read guitar tab:

1) Each horizontal line represents a string. Guitar tab, as a result, has six lines.

2) The lowest (sounding) string is represented by the lowest (looking) line. The highest string therefore represents the highest line.

3) The numbers on the lines indicate which fret you're pressing down on that particular string before picking.

4) If it's a zero, it's an open note, meaning you don't have to press anything down. Just pick the string.

5) You read it, just like the English language, from left to right. Stacked notes indicate notes that are played simultaneously. There is, of course, a possibility of up to six notes at a time.

Try reading and playing through the example above. All the notes in this written melody are of equal length, except for the final note, which is longer.

Most professionally transcribed guitar tab will include rhythmic information attached to the notes in the form of what we call stems and beams. The stems are thin vertical lines, either above or below the staff. Beams are the thicker horizontal lines that connect certain stems. As for which stems and why, we'll be covering that as soon as we go over some basic fretboard knowledge. The following is an example of guitar tab with rhythmic notation included.

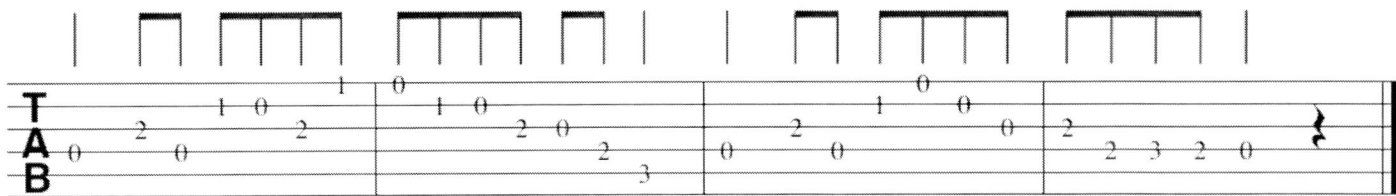

Standard Notation

Being able to read standard notation has many benefits. For one thing, your learning isn't limited by what music is available in guitar tab. This means that you have access to every classical piece, every transcribed jazz solo for every instrument, every fiddle tune, etc. No matter what your personal style is, diving into these things and taking the elements you learn that you find attractive will turn you into a much stronger and more unique musician.

Also, you have a very effective means to communicate your own musical ideas to every other type of instrumentalist. If you write a song and have something you want a violin player to perform on it, you can simply right it down. These same musicians can easily communicate their own ideas right back to you without the painful process of having to walk you through it like a child. In bands and other musical situations where everyone reads the same language, a great deal more gets done a whole lot quicker.

Below is a transcription of the melody used in the tab example above, now in standard notation.

In the standard notation form, there are only five lines and four spaces. Each line and each space represents a particular pitch. We label these pitches with letters of the musical alphabet. These letters; A, B, C, D, E, F and G represent what would be the white keys of the piano. These white keys are known as "natural notes" or simply "naturals".

You will find a *clef* of some kind at the beginning of every piece of sheet music. Standard notation for guitar is typically written in *treble* clef. The treble clef is what you see at the beginning of the example above. It's a stylized G, indicating that the note going the middle of the lower loop is the G below what we call middle C.

For most other instruments that read treble clef music, this same G on the staff would sound as a G above middle C. Guitar music is transposed down an octave in order to fit the bass register of the guitar. Guitar has bass and treble registers, like a piano. The range of the piano has wider range by about octaves, one lower and one higher. (For those, unfamiliar with the term *octave*, a traditional scale has seven tones. The eighth tone to be counted is the octave, which is the same note as the first or root. The distance from the root note to the following root note in either direction is referred to as an octave)

Piano players read music on the grand staff, which is a stack of two staffs (or staves), one being treble clef and the one below being bass clef. Since the guitar doesn't have quite the range from low to high as a piano, guitar players are relegated to the single yet adjusted staff.

Considering the wide range of the guitar, there is no way we can fit it all on this one staff. The staff (as we are aligned with it) covers the middle register of the guitar. As a result, we need to add on temporary extra lines and spaces above and below the staff. These extra lines are called ledger lines. Ledger lines allow instruments of all types to access their whole ranges on a single five line staff.

Here's a diagram showing the entire range of the modern electric guitar. Following the diagram I'm going to take you through the grand tour, which will make for some redundant reading but very worthwhile. You may want to read through it once for now, revisit it after having covered the Fretboard Mapping Part I section and read it repeatedly.

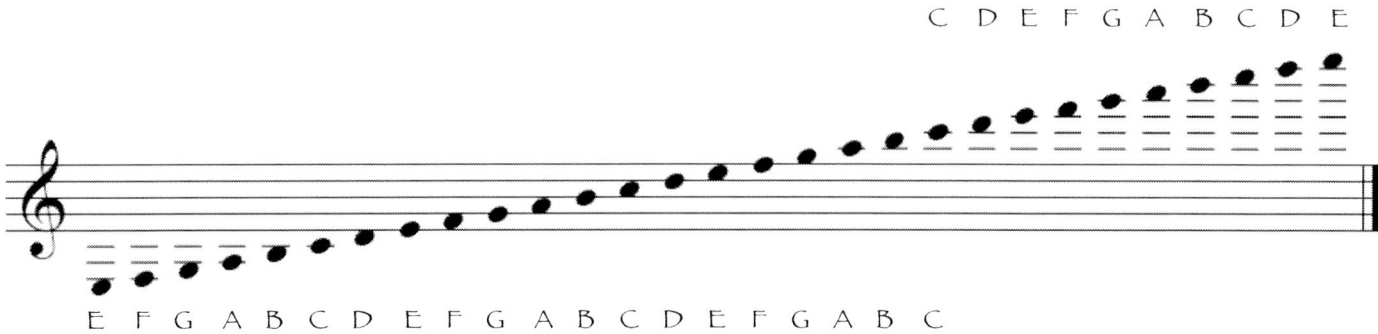

(Note: the official job title of the little black dot that goes on the staff is the note head)

Here is the grand tour of the relationship between the guitar and the staff, from left to right. The information contained here will very likely seem a bit daunting. This is a complete look at the entire staff and guitar, totally unfiltered. We will be breaking this information down to its logical components over the course of the book. While going through this, you may be wondering how I know where all these notes are located in the first place. We will be covering this. For the time being, the locations for these notes can be found and confirmed by the use of the fretboard chart in the following section. (These note locations are as they relate to a guitar in standard tuning.)

1) The low E on the guitar is beneath the third ledger line.
The open low E string is the only location for this note.

2) The low F on the guitar is on the third ledger line below the staff.
The 1st fret of the low E string is the only location for this note.

3) The low G on the guitar is beneath the second ledger line.
The 3rd fret of the low E string is the only location for this note.

4) The low A on the guitar is on the second ledger line below the staff.
Possible locations for this note are the 5th fret of the low E string or on the open A string.

5) The low B on the guitar is beneath the first ledger line.
Possible locations for this note are the 7th fret of the low E string or on the 2nd fret of the A string.

6) The low C on the guitar is on the first ledger line below the staff. Possible locations for this note are the 8th fret of the low E string or on the 3rd fret of the A string.

7) The lower-middle D on the guitar (in standard tuning, the guitar doesn't have a low D) is below the bottom line.
Possible locations for this note are the 10th fret of the low E string, on the 5th fret of the A string or on the open D string.

8) The lower-middle E on the guitar is on the bottom line of the staff.
Possible locations for this note are the 12th fret of the low E string, on the 7th fret of the A string or on the 2nd fret D string.

9) The lower-middle F on the guitar is in the bottom space.
Possible locations for this note are the 13th fret of the low E string, on the 8th fret of the A string or on the 3rd fret of the D string.

10) The lower-middle G on the guitar is on the second line from the bottom.
Possible locations for this note are the 15th fret of the low E string, the 10th fret of the A string, the 5th fret of the D string or on the open G string.

11) The lower-middle A on the guitar is below the middle line of the staff.
Possible locations for this note are the 17th fret of the low E string, the 12th fret of the A string, the 7th fret of the D string or on the 2nd fret of the G string.

12) The lower-middle B on the guitar is on the middle line of the staff.
Possible locations for this note are the 19th fret of the low E string, the 14th fret of the A string, the 9th fret of the D string, the 4th fret of the G string or on the open B string.

13) The lower-middle C on the guitar is above the middle line of the staff.
Possible locations for this note are the 20th fret of the low E string, the 15th fret of the A string, the 10th fret D of the string, the 5th fret of the G string or on the 1st fret of the B string.

14) The upper-middle D on the guitar is on the second line from the top of the staff.
Possible locations for this note are the 22nd fret of the low E string, the 17th fret of the A string, the 12th fret D of the string, the 7th fret of the G string or on the 3rd fret of the B string.

15) The upper-middle E is in the top space of the staff.

Possible locations for this note are the 19th fret of the A string, the 14th fret D of the string, the 9th fret of the G string the 5th fret of the B string or on the open high E string.

16) The upper middle F on the guitar in on the top line of the staff.
Possible locations for this note are the 20th fret of the A string, the 15th fret D of the string, the 10th fret of the G string the 6th fret of the B string or on the 1st fret of the high E string.

17) The upper middle G on the guitar is above the top line of the staff.
Possible locations for this note are the 22nd fret of the A string, the 17th fret D of the string, the 12th fret of the G string, the 8th fret of the B string or on the 3rd fret of the high E string.

18) The upper-middle A on the guitar is on the fist ledger line above the staff.
Possible locations for this note are the 19th fret D of the string, the 14th fret of the G string, the 10th fret of the B string or on the 5th fret of the high E string.

19) The upper-middle B on the guitar is above the first ledger line (above the staff).
Possible locations for this note are the 21st fret D of the string, the 16th fret of the G string, the 12th fret of the B string or on the 7th fret of the high E string.

20) The upper-middle C on the guitar is on the second ledger line above the staff.
Possible locations for this note are the 22nd fret D of the string, the 17th fret of the G string, the 13th fret of the B string or on the 8th fret of the high E string.

21) The upper middle D on the guitar is above the second ledger line above the staff.
Possible locations for this note are the 19th fret of the G string, the 15th fret of the B string or on the 10th fret of the high E string.

22) The high E on the guitar is on the third ledger line above the staff.
Possible locations for this note are the 21st fret of the G string, the 17th fret of the B string or on the 12th fret of the high E string.

23) The high F on the guitar is above the third ledger line.
Possible locations for this note are the 22nd fret of the G string, the 18th fret of the B string or on the 13th fret of the high E string.

24) The high G on the guitar is on the fourth ledger line above the staff.
Possible locations for this note are the 20th fret of the B string or on the 15th fret of the high E string.

25) The high A on the guitar is above the fourth ledger line.
Possible locations for this note are the 22nd fret of the B string or on the 17th fret of the high E string.

26) The high B on the guitar is on the fifth ledger line above the staff.
The 19th fret of the high E string is the only location for this note.

27) The high C on the guitar is above the fifth ledger line.
The 20th fret of the high E string is the only location for this note.

28) The high D on the guitar is on the sixth ledger line above the staff.
The 22nd fret of the high E string is the only location for this note.

Sharp and flat symbols can be placed before the note heads to indicate the black keys that lie between the white keys. These black keys are known as "accidentals". When written out in standard notation, the accidental precedes the note head. When written out in text form, the accidental mark follows the note name.

♭ = flat (The black key directly to the left of the natural note, or one *semitone* lower than the natural note)

= sharp (The black key directly to the right of the natural note, or one semitone higher than the natural note)

In both guitar tab and standard notation, you'll notice vertical lines (unattached to any note heads or numbers) that separate the staff into sections. These sections are called measures and the lines dividing the measures are called barlines. The term "bar" has come to be a common slang term for a measure plus its following barline.

When an accidental mark is applied to a particular line or space of the staff, any note within the same measure, on that line or space will continue to be altered. If the required note, following the accidental is a natural note, a G following a G#, for instance, a natural symbol must be applied to the left of the note head.

♮ = Natural (returns an accidental to natural pitch before the end of the same measure where the accidental took place)

Below is an example of how these symbols will look when applied to the staff. Don't worry about reading and playing it at this point.

FRETBOARD MAPPING – Part 1: The Essentials

Understanding the layout of your notes on the fretboard is something that will save you a lot of time and turmoil as a guitarist. This understanding is relatively simple to accomplish. It starts by knowing the tuning of your open strings. The diagram below will lend you some help. This is how the strings are tuned in what we call standard tuning, which will be our focus throughout this book.

OPEN STRING:	Note Sounded:
1st string (the skinny one)	E
2nd string	B
3rd string	G
4th string	D
5th string	A
6th string (the fat one)	E

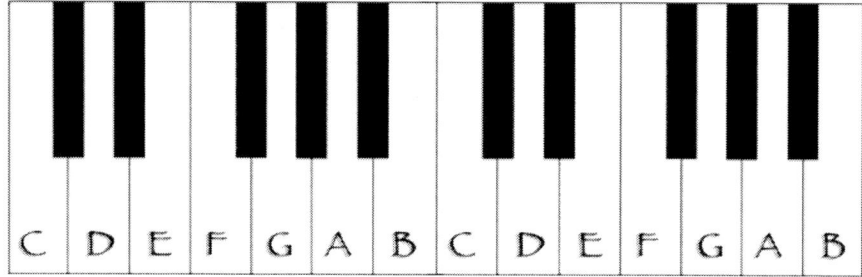

The other factor is the understanding of the natural note cycle. This is displayed above in the form of a keyboard. Think of the keyboard as the universal instrument on which all competent musicians can relate to one another.

Notice that not all natural notes (white keys) have accidentals (black keys) between them. It's a whole step (on the guitar: skip one fret) between all neighboring natural notes except B to C and E to F.
B to C and E to F are half steps apart (on the guitar: directly one fret away)

The tone between A and B will either be an A# (A sharp) or a Bb (B flat) depending on which key you're in or which direction the notes are moving. So, is the case with the tone between C and D, etc.

Between understanding the note cycle, how it translates to the fretboard and what pitches your strings are tuned to, you have all you need to map out the fretboard.

Start on your open E string and think of what comes after E. It's a half step from E to F. That puts F on the first fret. Then what? E, F, G. It's a whole step from F to G. That puts G at the third fret. Then it's a whole step to A at the 5th fret, another whole step to B at the 7th fret and a half step to C at the 8th. This continues all the way to the end of the fret board. It works starting from any open note. Just follow the circle of ABCDEFG. Since the half steps are always between B and C as well as E and F, they will occur at different points on each string.

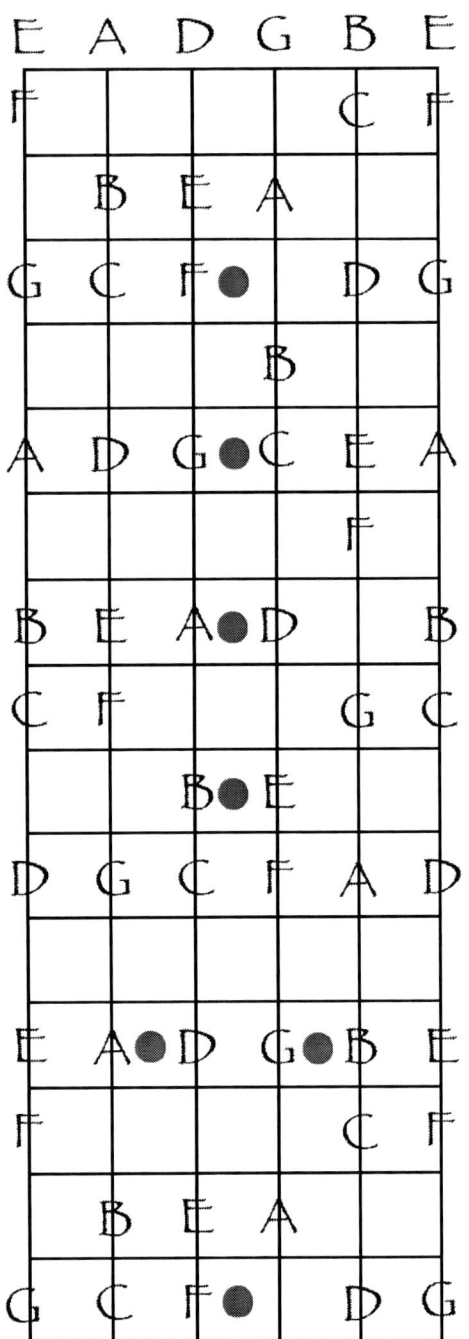

If you achieve a very solid and direct understanding of the (slightly warped) patterns the fret board offers, you develop the ability to play anything, anywhere on the guitar. To the left is a diagram showing the locations of all seven natural notes. (Finding the sharps and flats is as easy as counting one fret away.) I recommend studying this in great detail.

A good starting exercise is to find and play every A within a five fret range then move five frets up, play all those A notes and repeat the process all the way up the neck. Do the same thing with the other six natural notes.

Guitar players break their note and scale memorizing into positions, which we'll be discussing later. For now, as you read ahead, spend lots of time on the exercise mentioned above. It'll serve as an excellent preparation and give you a good general idea about how strings and frets relate to each other. Do this a lot and you'll develop really keen musical instincts.

* *Notice the difference in the physical distances between the notes of the G and B strings compared to those of any string pair. This is because the distance between each string is 2 steps except for the G and B strings which are only two whole steps apart.*

RHYTHM – part 1: Simple Words

Once the layout of notes on the guitar is making logical sense to you, the concept of rhythm is a good thing to explore because it is at the heart of every single element of music. Even the concepts of tonality and harmony are just rhythm on a much faster timeframe. Think of rhythm simply as being the division and organization of time. This is what makes music move forward. We will start at the concept of the pulse, the heartbeat of music. The pulse is made up of a series of beats. The beat is the common unit of time measurement in music. In most modern music we hear the beat stated rather clearly. It's known as the pulse of music. No beat is longer or shorter than the beat it follows unless the music is speeding up or slowing down.

In what we know of as "common time," the beats of this pulse are grouped in fours. Each group of four beats is known as a measure or a "bar". Each of these four beats represents an equal portion, one quarter in this case, of the overall time that makes up the measure. This is where the term quarter note comes from. The quarter note is the footstep of music.

The term "quarter note" is an example of what we call a "note value." In other words, a note value is the duration or length of the note and these durations are measured as equal divisions of a larger chunk of time, namely, the measure.

Note Values:

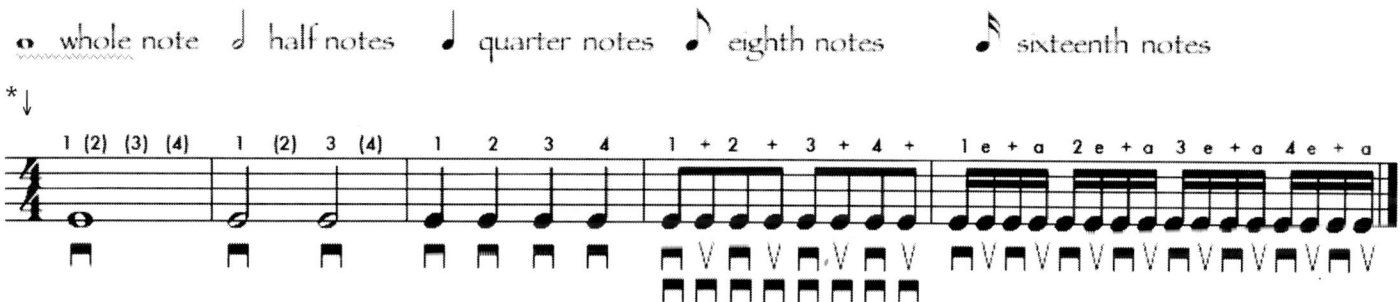

◻ : Downstroke

V : Upstroke

The numbers directly above the staff indicate the means by which we count the notes and/or the time elapsing between two notes.

*↓:

$\frac{4}{4}$ A time signature tells us how many beats are in each measure and what type of note represents the beat. Common time is known as 4/4. The first 4 represents how many beats per measure and the second 4 indicates that each beat equals one quarter note. The second or bottom number of the time signature can only be 2 (half note) 4 (quarter note) 8 (eighth note) and if you're really crazy 16 (sixteenth note). For the time being we will be dealing with 4/4 and 3/4. These are the most common time signatures.

It's a huge advantage for any musician to be able to comfortably read and write rhythmic notation. At this point you may be thinking that this will be difficult. Here's the secret: if you have a simple way of looking at it, it becomes a simple process. If you think of the way in which you read words, you'll note that you don't have to sound out every word that crosses your vision. You already know a fair amount of them. You glance at it and recognize it as a symbol. You're doing it right now.

Reading rhythmic notation is the same process. We have a relatively small vocabulary of rhythmic devices or "words" to learn. Once we have these well understood we can read long streams of them, seamlessly. This will come quicker than you'd expect as long as you allow your self to work past the initial hump. Getting your feet wet can be the hardest part. As with everything you learn and practice, you'll gain speed at an increasing rate.

Below is a chart illustrating four very common rhythmic words. The middle four columns represent two beats worth of time, divided into eighth note sections. The far right column offers you some 'sounds-like' words by which you can remember each of these rhythms. Make sure to follow the picking indications above the chart. They key is keeping your downstrokes on the beats.

Table 1: Basic Quarter/Eighth Note Rhythmic Words

Rhythmic Word:	Beat 1 or 3	"and"	Beat 2 or 4	"and"	Sounds Like These Words:
1: ♩ ♩	♩		♩		aardvark, switchblade, old-school, bike-ride
2: ♫♫	♪	♪	♪	♪	alligator, jalapeño, Alabama, terminator
3: ♩ ♫	♩		♪	♪	grasshopper, coal-miner, gold-digger, ant-eater
4: ♫ ♩	♪	♪	♩		elephant, peppermint, heart-attack,

These rhythms look very similar when they're moving twice as fast against the beat. The note value for each note is cut in half. In other words, the quarter notes become eighth notes and the eighth notes become sixteenth notes. This means that if you add an extra beam to the top of these rhythms, they move twice as fast. I've presented the same chart, using the same 'sounds like' words so you can directly compare. Also, make sure to compare by listening.

Table 2: Basic Eighth/Sixteenth Note Rhythmic Words

Rhythmic Word:	Beats 1, 2, 3, or 4	"ee"	"and"	"uh"	Sounds Like These Words:
1: ♪♪	♪		♪		aardvark, switchblade, old-school, bike-ride
2: ♬♬	♪	♪	♪	♪	alligator, jalapeño, Alabama, terminator
3: ♬♪	♪		♪	♪	grasshopper, coal-miner, gold-digger, ant-eater
4: ♪♬	♪	♪	♪		elephant, peppermint, heart-attack,

We can combine these basic rhythmic words to make larger rhythmic phrases. Here we can see all the possible one-measure combinations of these quarter/eighth rhythms. I've done the same with the eighth/sixteenth rhythms to make half-measure phrases. These two tables directly correspond to each other. For example, 1a is the same rhythm in both tables. It's just moving at two different speeds, in relation to the beat.

Basic One-Measure Quarter/Eighth Note Rhythms:

1a: ♩ ♩ ♩ ♫	1b: ♩ ♩ ♫ ♩	1c: ♩ ♫ ♩ ♩	1d: ♫ ♩ ♩ ♩
2a: ♩ ♩ ♬♬	2b: ♩ ♬♬ ♩	2c: ♬♬ ♩ ♩	2d: ♫ ♩ ♫
3a: ♩ ♫ ♬♬	3b: ♫ ♩ ♬♬	3c: ♬♬ ♩ ♫	3d: ♬♬ ♫ ♩

Basic Half-Measure Eighth/Sixteenth Note Rhythms:

1a: ♫ ♬♬	1b: ♫ ♬♬	1c: ♬♬ ♫	1d: ♬♬ ♫
2a: ♫ ♬♬♬	2b: ♬♬♬ ♫	2c: ♬♬♬ ♫	2d: ♬♬ ♬♬
3a: ♬♬ ♬♬♬	3b: ♬♬ ♬♬♬	3c: ♬♬♬ ♬♬	3d: ♬♬♬ ♬

THE MAJOR SCALE – The Worlds Most Common Family Of Notes

Introduction:

This is the most important tool any musician has, whether they know it or not. Just about any musician or singer you can think of operates in the realm of the major scale. It has many disguises but it's almost always there, one way or another. If you were never to learn a thing about scales and relied on nothing but the discernment of your ears, with enough experience, you'd eventually wind up a master of this scale.

You may wonder why you'd bother spending time reading about it when you could learn it all by ear. It's a question I initially asked and this is the answer I arrived at, a few years into it. By directly learning about this scale you develop the insight and ears to become a solid, creative musician at a much quicker rate. Not only do you get there quicker but you wind up with a much stronger ability to communicate ideas to fellow musicians regardless of instrument.

Knowledge is power. It comes down to the choice of being conscious of what you're learning when you learn a song and being able to easily apply it, creatively, in your own music as opposed to driving around blindfolded, hoping you don't run into stuff, until you get to know the town.

The Basics – Whole Steps and Half Steps:

There are some very flimsy definitions of scales in textbooks and music dictionaries. Here is my best shot at effectively defining the word "scale." A scale is a family of tones that function together to create music. The major scale has seven tones. The root note is the tonal center. Each of the other six tones serves a specific function, in relation to the root note. The major scale naturally occurs as a result of harmony. (More on this ahead.)

The major scale is such a common and naturally occurring family of notes that the design of the piano keyboard is entirely based on it. It's built around the key of C major, which contains all of what we call the natural notes. These are notes that aren't sharp (#) or flat (b) and on a piano, they are the white keys. The gaps between the notes of the C major scale are filled in with black keys, known as accidentals or sharps and flats. The black key between A and B could be called A# or Bb, depending on the musical context. You'll learn what that means further into the book.

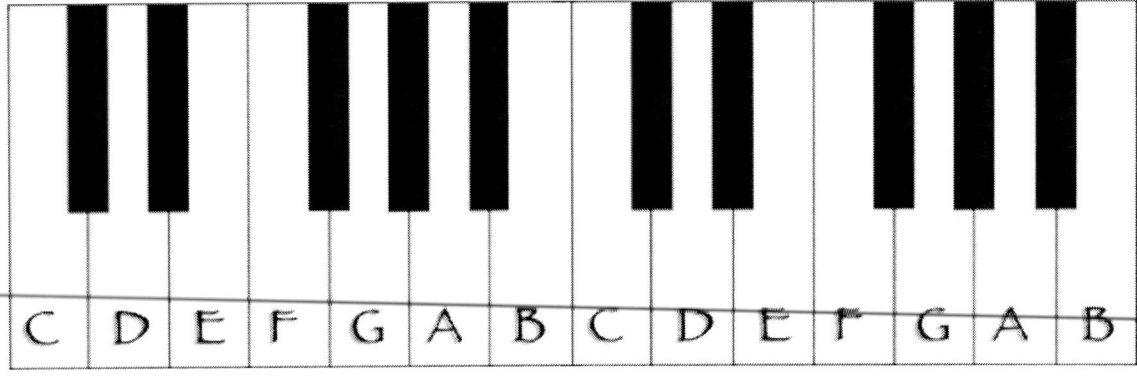

These gaps between the scale-tones are known as whole steps. When there is no gap between two notes, such as between B and C, it's a half step between the two. Whole steps and half steps are the basic units of measurement between notes in music and we add them up to measure larger distances between notes. For instance, it's 3½ steps from C up to G but only 2½ from C down to G. Check my math on the keyboard diagram from the previous page and make sure you're following me. These relationships are known as *intervals*.

Understanding and recognizing these intervals is even more important than knowing the names of the notes because it's the relationship between two notes that creates musical characteristics and qualities that effect us. In other words: C can sound like hundreds of different things to us depending on what notes it's combined with and it doesn't bring a whole lot to mind when we hear it, by itself. On the other hand two notes that are two whole steps apart will always create the same basic effect no matter which two notes they are.

I'll be explaining exactly how to apply the major scale to the guitar in the fretboard mapping sections but in order for you to process this next section, you're going to need to have a least one means of playing these notes. This will get us through until we get on to the fretboard mapping section.

C Major Scale, Open Position:

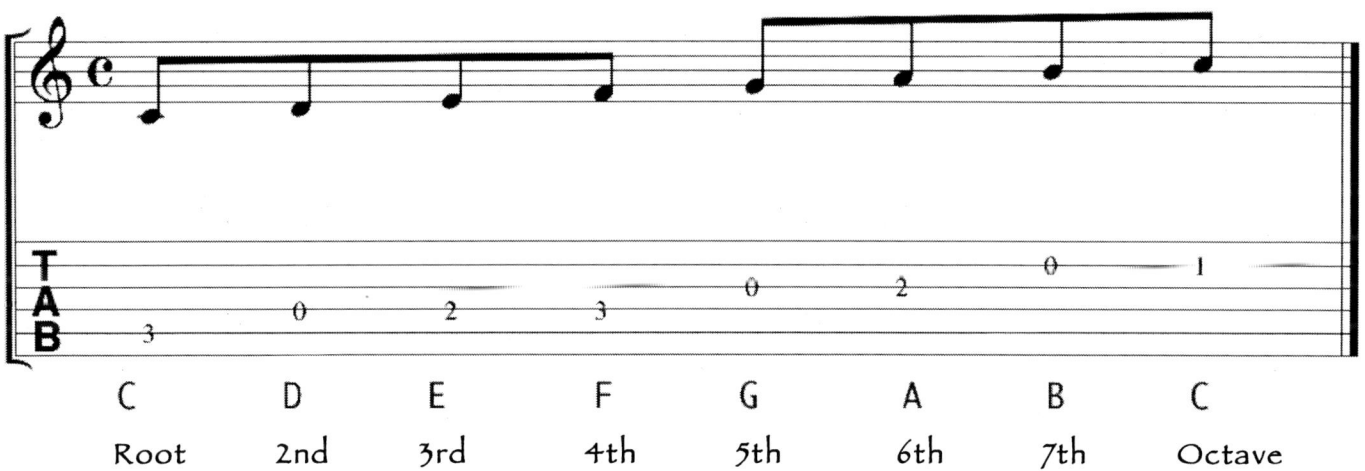

Soon, we'll get into why this major scale is naturally occurring but first you're going to need an understanding of what we call harmonic overtones. Let's take a page to talk about this before we delve deeper into the major scale.

Harmonic Overtones On the Guitar

Every naturally produced pitch, from any voice or instrument, contains what we call harmonic overtones. These are tones that ring above the actual pitch that we're hearing, which we call the fundamental. They are perfectly harmonized with the fundamental and as a result, they blend in to the point where we don't hear them with the naked ear.

We can isolate these overtones on stringed instruments in order to hear them clearly. Guitar players typically call this playing harmonics. In order to do this you touch your finger to the string (without pressing the string down) right over the fret and pick the note. Your finger needs to be on the line between the fret that's written and the next fret. For instance, if the harmonic is on the 12th fret you touch your finger to the string right over the line separating the 12th and 13th frets. Really, the line itself is the fret but most guitar players tend to think of the space between as being the fret.

Below, are the harmonics on the low E string. This same pattern of fret locations applies to the other five strings the same way. The notes that are played as harmonics are written with the abbreviation; *harm.* above them. When one note after the other is played as a harmonic, you'll usually see a dotted bracket as seen below. Sometimes the notes on the staff will be diamond shaped, but not always. Here it is:

Harmonic Overtones

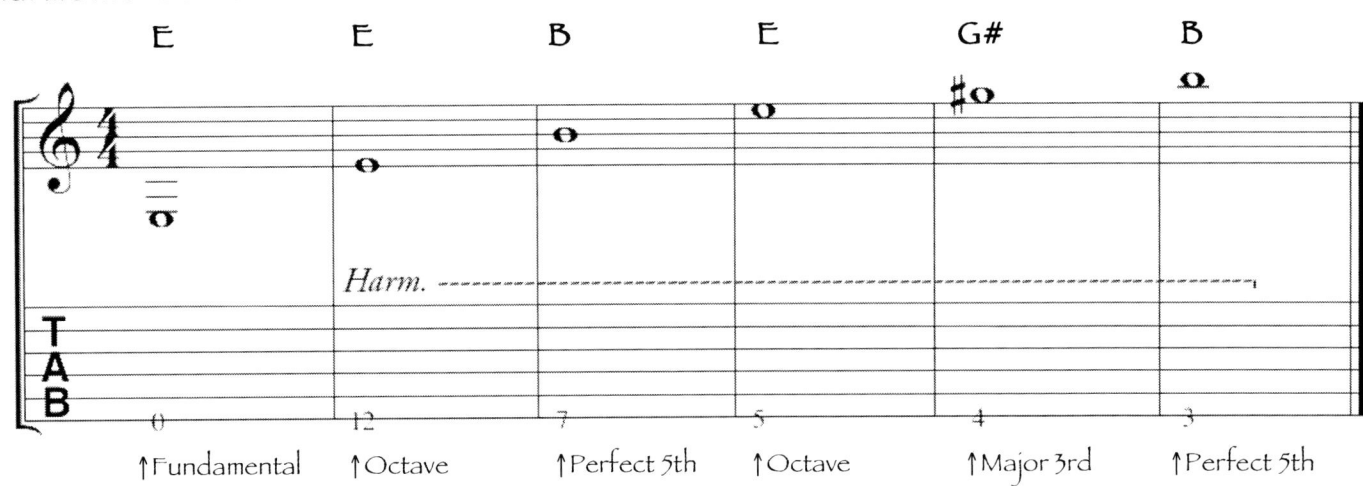

(The names given below the tab will make sense after reading ahead.)

There are more distant overtones that ring above these primary overtones. When we combine these overtones we wind up with another seven-note scale known as the overtone dominant scale. You'll be learning more about this in future sections.

Origins Of The Major Scale

Here's how it works:
It starts with one pitch. This pitch, like all others, has a series of overtones that ring above it. The naked ear doesn't hear these overtones because they are tuned to harmonize perfectly with the fundamental tone.

The overtone closest to the fundamental is 3½ steps above. This tone is known as the perfect 5th because it is the 5th note of the major scale. This note, when sounded against the fundamental, creates our most consonant type of harmony. This means it sounds settled and unified.

The next overtone is 2½ steps above the perfect 5th. 2½ steps + 3½ steps = 6 whole steps, which brings us to our fundamental (root note) one octave higher. The next over tone is 2 whole steps above the octave. This distance is known as the major third (again, named for its place within the final resulting scale.)

When the fundamental is sounded along with the perfect fifth and the major third, we hear a major triad, the first and most basic and stable unit of harmony. The root, 3rd and 5th are the red, yellow and blue of music. As explained here, these notes are contained within the fundamental tone. If this tone were C, than it would have an E and a G contained within it resulting in a C major chord.

C Major Triad

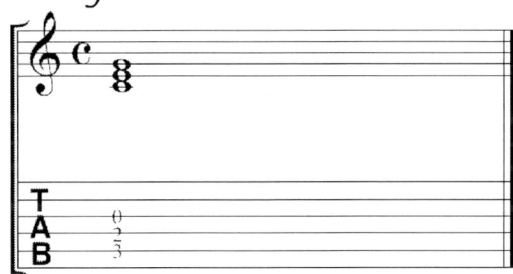

This is why these notes sound consonant when sounded against C: Because they are in tune with C's overtones. When I sound a G above C, the G produces its own set of overtones. These provide the pitches to form a G major chord: G, B and D. If the C is serving as a perfect fifth of an F below, F provides its own overtones: F, A and C. Keep in mind that C is in the middle of this equation with F 3½ steps below and G 3½ steps above.

The resulting combination of notes is a C major scale:
C, D, E, F, G, A and B. We arrived at these notes by way of the primary overtones provided by C and its closest related neighbors G and F.

Also, if we stack 7 notes in perfect 5ths, (3 steps apart) starting at the fourth we wind up with this: F C G D A E B, the notes of the C major scale. No other scale bares this natural significance. This is what makes the major scale the scale our ears naturally gravitate towards, regardless of our social or cultural backgrounds.

The Functions Of Scale-Tones:

The traditional way of looking at the major scale is when it's written out from one root note, up one octave and ending at that point. This however isn't the clearest way of viewing it when you're trying to understand the roles of the scale tones.

This is a good way to look at the major scale. Look at this from the center, outwards.

Root	2nd	3rd	4th	5th	6th	7th	Root	2nd	3rd	4th	5th	6th	7th	Root
C	<u>D</u>	E	<u>F</u>	G	<u>A</u>	B	<u>C</u>	D	<u>E</u>	F	<u>G</u>	A	<u>B</u>	C
	Super-Tonic		Sub-Dom		Sub-Med		Tonic		Mediant		Dominant		Leading-Tone	

*Labels beneath correspond to underlined notes above.

C, the note in the center is the **tonic**. It's also known as the root. This note is the equivalent to the sun in the solar system. It's called the tonic because it's the tonal center.

G, the 5th is the **dominant** because it is the closest related note above C. This is because it is the first overtone in the C note aside from the repeated C. Because of this, it's our most consonant harmony when sounded with C.

F, the 4th is our **sub-dominant**, so called because it's the same distance down to the 4th as it was up to the 5th: 3 steps. C relates to F the same way G relates to C.

E, our 3rd is the **mediant** because it's the halfway point between the tonic and dominant.

A, our 6th is the **sub-mediant** because it's the halfway point between the tonic and sub-dominant.

D, the 2nd is known as the **super-tonic** simply because it's located one step above the tonic.

B, the 7th is the **leading tone**. It's the tensest scale-tone with a strong tendency to move one half step up to resolve at the root.

Train Your Ears!
Each note has a very unique roll and a recognizable effect within the context of the key. These effects only become immediately recognizable through playing with the notes while keeping in mind the names and roles of each note. It would be fairly safe to say the average person could spend a half hour to an hour a day doing this and within a year, have a pretty strong ear. Two advantages to having a good ear:

1: You have much more immediate access to your own musical creativity including a more natural ability to improvise and compose.
2: When you recognize the relationships between the notes you're hearing, every time you listen to music you learn directly from it and this reflects in what you play and write.

Scale Tone Activity

The root, 3rd and 5th of the scale are known as inactive tones. This is because these notes sound settled, rested and resolved. The notes in between these, the 2nd, 4th, 6th and 7th are active tones. Since these notes are not members of the C chord, they sound more tense and unsettled and they gravitate towards our active tones. It's the interplay between tension and release that makes music.

Here's a visual representation: (Underlined notes are inactive and arrows indicate the tendency of the active tones. W and H marks indicate whole steps and half steps.)

```
              W       W       H       W       W       W       H
   Root   ←2nd→    3rd    ←4th    5th    ←6th    7th→    R
    C      ←D→     E      ←F      G      ←A      B→      C
```

The 4th is more inclined to move down to the 3rd because it's a shorter distance and creates a more natural resolution. Some active tones are more active than others. In other words, some notes carry more tension.

very active: ← 7th 4th 6th 2nd → less active

very inactive: ← Root 4th 6th 2nd → less inactive

The most natural way for these notes to behave is for the inactive tones to be emphasized by being placed on the strong beats of the measure and for the active notes to be used as stepping stones, between the beats or on weak beats, from one inactive tone to the next. When a melody behaves this way, it feels very stable and settled. When we treat these tones in a contrary manner, the melody becomes less predictable and builds more tension. Keep in mind that these are just the basic tendencies of the scale tones. They don't always need to have their way.

This is something I call the "chord-tone pattern" which we'll apply to all the scales and positions eventually in order to develop a solid sense of tension and release within keys and eventually modes.

Chord-Tone Pattern

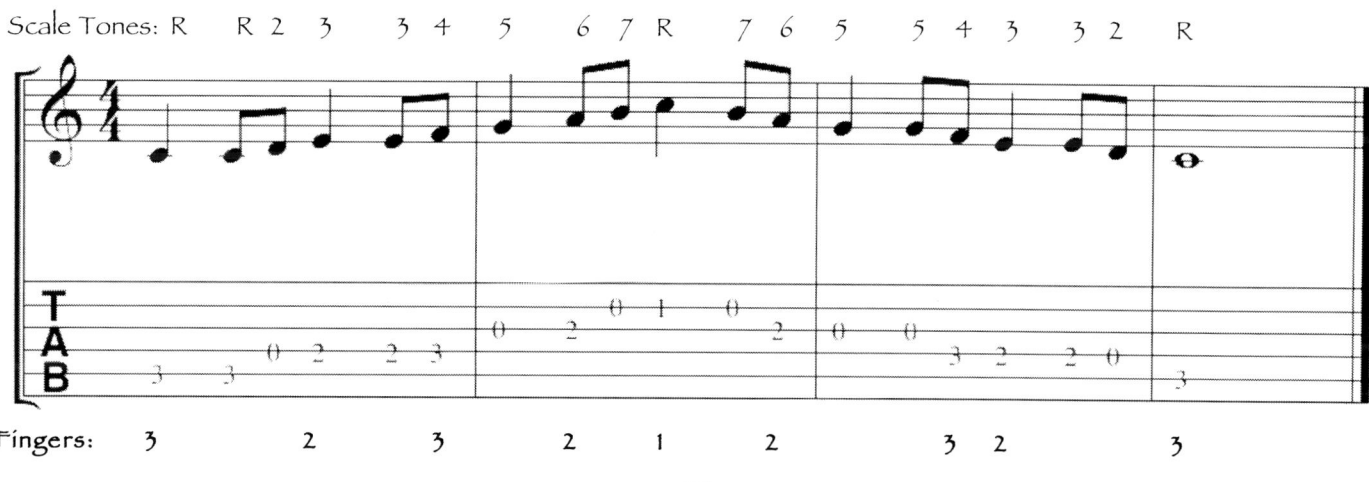

RHYTHM – Part 2: Rests

So far, you've learned about the basic note values and how we form phrases out of them. Most music however, isn't a constant stream of notes. We usually have what we call rests placed here and there. Each note value has a corresponding rest.

In this diagram, the rests are the symbols to the right of each note. Employing rests is easy enough if you can think of the rests as notes that you're not playing. We can begin to get a grip on it by taking some rhythms that we've already learned and replacing some of the notes with rests.

The best way to really solidify these skills is to look closely at accurate transcriptions of your all-time favorite vocal melodies. Just think of your favorite songs that you can sing without hearing and compare how it goes with what the rhythmic notation looks like.

Rhythm Etude - #1

Rhythm Etude #2

THE CYCLE OF 5THS

The cycle (or circle) of 5ths is also known as the cycle of 4ths because 4ths and 5ths are invertible. For instance F is the 4th of C but in the same regard C is the 5th of F. This will likely become more clear by the end of this section. The important thing to understand, for now, is that the cycle of 5ths is a pattern by which we can learn all of our "keys" or "key signatures". The key is effectively the same as the scale. If you're in the key of C major, that means that you're basing your music on the notes of the C major scale. So in effect, the cycle of 5ths will teach us what notes belong in which scales.

We know that a major scale is constructed by basing this pattern: WWHWWWH from the root note. So far we have only done this in the key of C because that pattern, starting from C, gives us all our natural notes. To continue the cycle of 5ths, we would base our next scale on the 5th note of C major, G, and we would use the same pattern of distances, WWHWWWH. This would give us G, whole step to A, whole step to B, half step to C, whole step to D, whole step to E, whole step to F# and finally a half step back to G.

G Major Scale: W W H W W W H
                G A B C D E F#

You may remember that the black keys have two possible names. In this case we opted to call the black key between F and G; F# because we already had a G but didn't yet have an F. Each major scale needs one of each letter whether it's sharp, flat or natural. Those letters should appear in logical order: ABCDEFG, starting from wherever. Here is the entire cycle of 5ths:

Root	W	2nd	W	3rd	H	4th	W	5th	W	6th	W	7th	H
C		D		E		F		G		A		B	
G		A		B		C		D		E		F#	
D		E		F#		G		A		B		C#	
A		B		C#		D		E		F#		G#	
E		F#		G#		A		B		C#		D#	
B		C#		D#		E		F#		G#		A#	
Gb		Ab		Bb		Cb		Db		Eb		F	
Db		Eb		F		Gb		Ab		Bb		C	
Ab		Bb		C		Db		Eb		F		G	
Eb		F		G		Ab		Bb		C		D	
Bb		C		D		Eb		F		G		A	
F		G		A		Bb		C		D		E	

Notice how the 4th note of the C scale is raised a half step when it becomes the 7th note of the G scale. This is a result of the extra whole step that occurs in the later half of the step-pattern. Notice how the same thing happens with C in the G and D scales. C becomes C# the same way F became F#. This continues all the way through the cycle. The fourth of the last scale becomes the 7th of the new scale and is raised one half step. Also, take note that the F remains sharp in the D scale. All the sharps stick around until they become flats. In the key of the G flat we're forced to call B by the name of Cb. Again, this is because we want one of each letter and we need to keep the step pattern uniform. We could have called Gb "F#" in the first place but we would have had to call E "Fb". We can call the first note by F# or Gb, since it's not already bound to any other notes. I prefer calling Gb to balance out the overall ratio of sharps and flats in the cycle

FRETBOARD MAPPING – Part 2: Major Scale Positions

At this point, we've mapped out the fretboard in the key of C major. We've also come to understand the cycle of 5ths. If you've made the connection that there are eleven other major keys to map out you may feel a bit daunted right now. If you have only a vague understanding that there's an equal amount of minor keys, you probably feel doubly daunted. I wouldn't blame you. That is, if this were really the case. Lucky for us, guitar players, since all frets are the same, the positions for each key are identical to those of any other key, major or minor.

Here, we have every major scale shape you'll ever need to learn. These five positions cover the entire fretboard in all keys. Not only are these the positions for every key, but they serve as positions for every *mode*. Each major scale has seven modes, which give you a range of moods from extremely bright to extremely dark. Memorize these shapes like your life depended on them. I'd recommend spending a week focusing on the root position and then spend a week on each of the following positions.

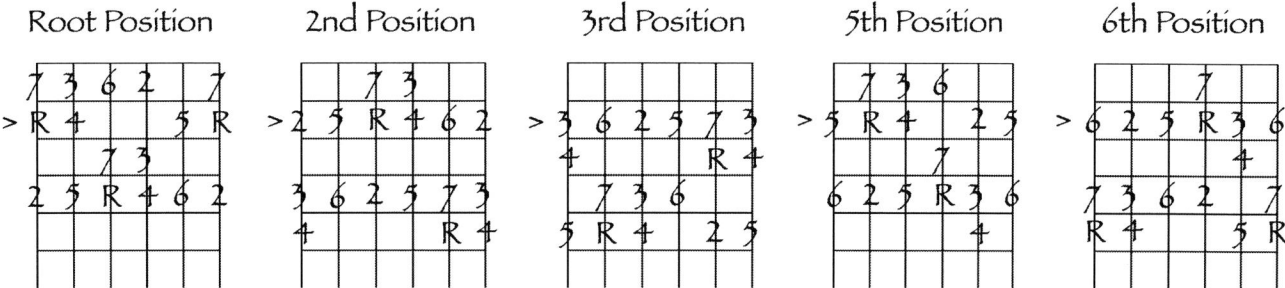

The table below tells you at which fret to plant each position for each major key. The labels at the top of each column represent the key you're playing in. The labels at the beginning of each row represent which position you're using. The numbers within the columns and rows represent at what fret each position, in each key, belongs. Here's the process:

1) Match the position name of one of the box diagrams, above, to the corresponding position name in the far left column of the table.
2) Line up the ">" next to the box diagram with the fret number in the column belonging to the key and position you desire.

	C	G	D	A	E	B	Gb	Db	Ab	Eb	Bb	F
Root Pos:	8	3	10	5	12	7	2	9	4	11	6	13
2nd Pos:	10	5	12	7	2	9	4	11	6	13	8	3
3rd Pos:	12	7	2	9	4	11	6	1	8	3	10	5
5th Pos:	3	10	5	12	7	2	9	4	11	6	13	8
6th Pos:	5	12	7	2	9	4	11	6	13	8	3	10

I'll walk you through an example. I'm playing in E and I want to be stationed on or near the 5th fret. So I look in the E column and decide that the 4th fret is close enough and I follow that row (the one with the 4 in the E column) to the left and find out that it's the 3rd position. Then, I play in that position with its ">" located at the 4th fret.

MUSIC READING – Part 2: The Fret Board in All Keys

The challenging thing about reading music on the guitar is coping with the numerous positional possibilities for any given key. There are no shortcuts around the experience required to become comfortable with all of this information. One thing I can offer you is the process that's allowed me to become more comfortable with reading in all keys and positions.

Before I became the competent (but slow) music reader that I am today, I had played and studied long enough that I understood the fretboard mapping concepts covered in the previous section. So my first step was to do the heavy lifting, so to speak. This involved figuring out how these positions line up with the staff and writing out staff to tab conversion charts in each key.

My next step was to gather up sheet music of things that I wanted to play on my guitar and translate these melodies to guitar tab, including the stems, beams and rests. If the music I happened to be translating contained material that I wanted to work into my improvisational vocabulary, I would transcribe it every position in its original register and an octave lower or higher. By the time I would accomplish this, the bulk of the material would become easy to use in any key.

This would get a lot of the thinking out of the way for me for to focus on step three, learning the material in what I found to be a more direct and simple format. I felt that it allowed me to learn more quickly since I spent less time feeling frustrated with my instrument in my hands, the whole time developing more and more familiarity with the relationship between the staff and the fretboard.

After a couple of years of doing this I started to grow less dependent on the process. To this day, if I'm tackling some music that proves very demanding, I still use this process.

The first step has been taken care of for you. The appendix of this book contains the five basic major/natural minor scale positions displayed in every key, in all areas of the fretboard. This truly is a lot of information but if you use it as a reference over the next couple hundred hours of music reading time, you'll eventually lose the need for such a reference.

The position appendix with all of our keys begins in what we call the open position. These open position scale shapes are in a class of their own, because each one is it's own unique shape that can only be used in that key or very closely related keys to it. The open position is used more heavily by folk, country, bluegrass and rock guitarists than it is by most jazz, blues, and harder rock and metal guitarists.

That's not to say that these players entirely avoid the open position. With jazz and blues players, it's a matter of keeping their vocabulary movable to different keys on the fretboard and the open positions aren't easily movable. Licks, chords and melodies that contain certain functional open strings are specific to the key in which they're being played, in order to achieve the intended effect.

DIATONIC HARMONY - Part 1: Triads

A triad is a three-note chord. A chord is a group of notes that you play simultaneously. They provide the emotional background to the melody. If we base the root- 3rd - 5th formula (from the "Scale Tone Activity" section) on the other notes in the scale, we wind up with the family of chords that function inside the key. The distance between the chord tones is what determines which chords are major and which are minor. Major chords have 2 whole steps between the root and third with a 1 steps between the 3rd and 5th. Minor chords are the opposite. This is why the distance of 2 whole steps is known as a major 3rd and 1½ steps is known as a minor third. Here is how it lays out:

Interval:	Root:	Distance Between	3rd:	Distance Between	5th:	Chord:
I:	C	2w	E	1½	G	C
II:	D	1½	F	2w	A	Dm
III:	E	1½	G	2w	B	Em
IV:	F	2w	A	1½	C	F
V:	G	2w	B	2w	D	G
VI:	A	1½	C	2w	E	Am
VII:	B	1½	D	1½	F	B diminished

The chord progressions of many songs are made up entirely of this family of chords. The I, IV and V chords can be thought of as the primary colors of harmony, since it was the tonic, subdominant and dominant tones that provided the family of overtones of our major key. As you may assume, these chords are emphasized in most of the music we hear.

Each minor chord relates very closely to two of these three primary major chords. For instance: The root and third of the VI chord are also contained in the IV chord as the third and 5th. At the same time, the third and fifth of the VI chord are contained in the I cord as the root and third. Below is a complete picture of this concept:

IV:	F	A	C		I:	C	E	G		V:	G	B	D	F	
	VI:	A	C	E		III:	E	G	B		II:	D	F	A	
		I:	C	E	G		V:	G	B	D		IV:	F	A	C

*One chord is not represented in this equation and that's the B diminished triad. This chord is avoided because it lacks a natural 5th, which is the stabilizing factor in a harmonic unit. It is heard as an incomplete G7 chord. For this reason, Bdim is replaced with G7. This rounds things out nicely. If you have questions about this G7 chord, they will be answered further ahead. This chord structure of a major I, IV and V with a minor II, III and VI and the excluded VII dim triad is true of all major keys. Just write down the notes of the key you want to use, put an m next to the 2nd, 3rd and 6th notes and put a dim next to the 7th note and you have the primary chords in that key.

Basic Open Position Triads in the Key of C Major

These shapes are a good place to start when it comes to learning chords. Since these chords all exist together in one key, they will be very easy to experiment with. These open position voicings are the most common to guitar players. This doesn't mean they're physically the easiest to play. You'll find that in the following section, though there's a lot more voicings for one chord, they're much more simple shapes to play. These voicings have lots of extra roots, 3rds and/or 5ths. This makes them sound very full and therefore, especially usable when you're playing alone or in a small group setting.

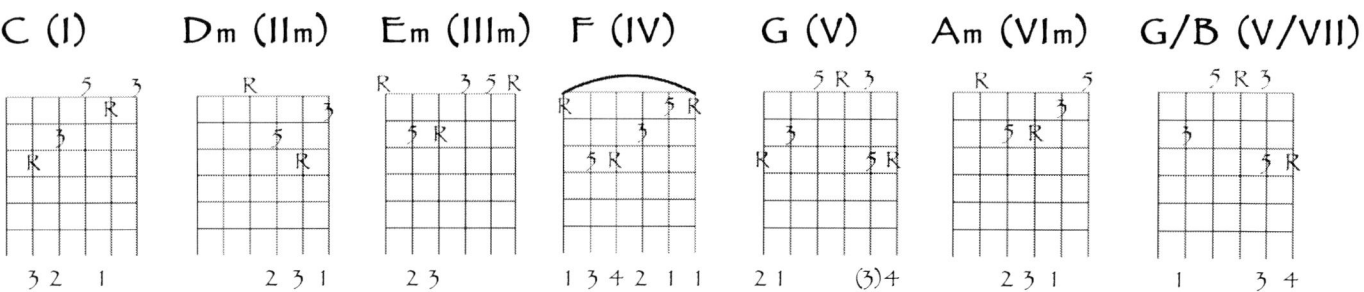

The F-Bomb

The most difficult of these shapes is going to be the F chord. If you glance at the fingering numbers beneath the F diagram, you'll notice that the first finger is supposed to press three different strings down. You'll also notice an arch going across the top of the stings. This tells us that we need to lay the first finger flat across all six strings. This technique is known as "barring" and this voicing of an F major is a "bar" chord because you're using you finger like a bar.

When you first attempt this chord, it seems impossible. My best advice is to show an experienced guitar player how you're trying to play it to make sure you're on the right track. When you're sure you've got the right idea, spend ten minutes a day trying to play it. Before long it'll become possible, shortly thereafter, it'll become tolerable and finally, out of the blue, it'll be so easy, that you don't even think about it.

A Healthy Alternative To The VII chord

Another thing worth noting, here, is the absence of the VIIdim chord. As was stated earlier, the VII chord is not a very stable sounding chord. Typically, when we hear the VII of the key in the chord progression, we're hearing the V chord with it's 3rd, the VII of the key, in the bass. To play this chord in the key of C major, we play a normal G chord, minus the lowest (sounding) string. The label for this chord would be "G/B". If you were to say that out loud, you would say "G over B".

It's a good idea to stay away from the next section until you can play each of these chords clearly and without much thought. Feel free to read on to any section not having to do with chords while you practice and perfect these. You're hands will always learn at a slower rate than your head, unless your playing 4+ hours everyday. It's fine to let your brain move on, even if your fingers are still busy learning how to do something.

Suspended Triads

The 3rd of a chord is the factor that determines whether a chord is major or minor. If the chord has a natural 3rd (2 whole-steps above the root) it will be a major chord. If the chord has a b3rd, (1½ above the root) it will be a minor chord. As we've established, major chords generally sound happy and minor chords generally sound sad. If we replace this governing 3rd with a scale-tone on either side of it, we have a suspended chord.

If we replace the 3rd of a major or minor triad with a 2nd, we have a suspended 2nd (or sus2) chord. If we were to replace the 3rd with a 4th, the result would be a suspended 4th (or sus4) chord. The 2nd and 4th are both neutral tones, common to both the major and minor scale. Because of that, sus2 and sus4 chords have a very neutral, almost Zen quality when played as a static chord. Because the 4th is a greater dissonance than the 2nd, sus4 chords have a much greater tendency to resolve to whatever chord it replaced. The sus2 chord stands on its own, more easily. Though plenty of songs and music make use of static suspended chords, the most common application for these chords is as fleeting embellishments on major or minor chords.

Below is a table illustrating the sus2 chords that we can derive, diatonically from the key of C major. It's worth noting that there are a couple intervals at which we can't build a sus2 chord. The reason we can't build a sus2 on the III chord is that there is no natural 2nd in relation to the III as the following scale-tone is a half-step up, which would be a b2nd. Also, we can't build a sus2 on the VII chord because it has no natural 5th not to mention that it also has no natural 2nd available. All other intervals can successfully produce a sus2 chord.

Diatonic Suspended 2nd Chords in the Key of C Major

Interval:	Root:	Distance Between	2nd:	Distance Between	5th:	Chord:
I:	C	w	D	2½	G	Csus2
II:	D	w	E	2½	A	Dsus2
III:	E	½	F (Yuck!)	3w	B	X
IV:	F	w	G	2½	C	Fsus2
V:	G	w	A	2½	D	Gsus2
VI:	A	w	B	2½	E	Asus2
VII:	B	½	C (Yuck!)	1½	F (Yuck!)	X

If you have a keyboard instrument handy, play these combinations of notes to get a sense of how they should sound before you go on to learn to play these chords in different ways on the guitar. Learning to play chords on a piano or any other type of keyboard instrument is far easier and will allow you to jump right in and experiment with new types of chords.

The following table, I've presented our diatonically derived family of sus4 triads, again in the key of C major. Notice that this time we also have two intervals at which we can't build a sus4 chord. This time, it's the IV and the VII. In the case of the IV, we don't have a perfect 4th interval (2½ steps) from the root of the chord as the tone that sits three scale-tones up from it is a #4th (3 whole-steps). All the other intervals in the scale will produce sus4 triads.

Diatonic Suspended 2nd Chords in the Key of C Major

Interval:	Root:	Distance Between	2nd:	Distance Between	5th:	Chord:
I:	C	2½	F	w	G	Csus4
II:	D	2½	G	w	A	Dsus4
III:	E	2½	A	w	B	Esus4
IV:	F	3w	B (Yuck!)	½	C	X
V:	G	2½	C	w	D	Gsus4
VI:	A	2½	D	w	E	Asus4
VII:	B	2½	E	½	F (Yuck!)	X

Open Position Voicings for Suspended Chords in the Key of C Major:

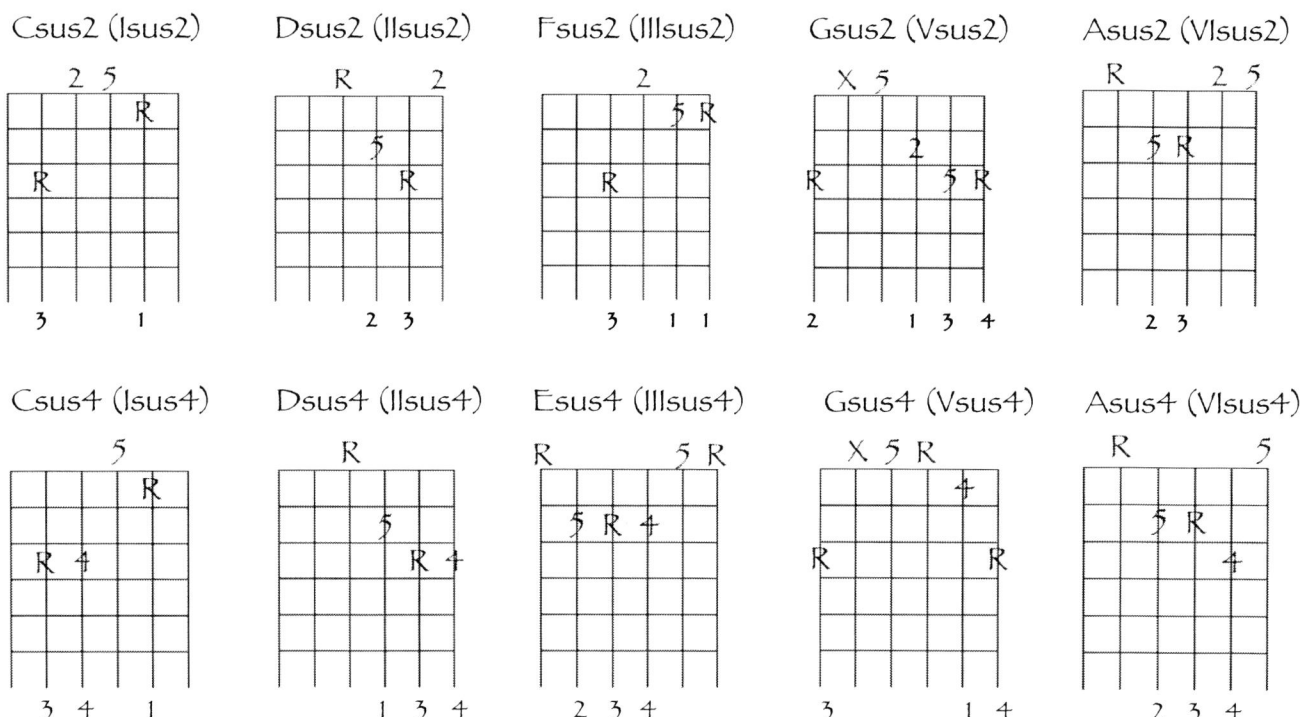

Notes: Don't make the mistake of thinking that these fingerings are arbitrary. They're strategically thought out to work smoothly with corresponding chords. Some of these chords require that you mute you're a string (notated by an X). This involves letting the finger in charge of fretting the bass-note to hang over onto the A-string just enough to mute it.

CHORD PROGRESSIONS – Part 1: Major I – IV – V Changes

A chord progression is nothing more than a series of chord changes. The most basic of these progressions are ones that involve the three major chords in the major key, the I, IV and V. We can put these three chords in every possible order and wind up with quite a list of very usable chord progressions. The vast majority of songs are based around these three chords with the occasional *substitutions*. We'll be covering all our various substitution options, later on. For now, let's lay down a strong foundation in the primary colors.

When you play and listen to these progressions, notice how the I chord sounds perfectly resolved, whereas the IV sounds slightly tense and the V sounds more tense. Listen very closely to the different effects of having the I chord at the beginning, in the middle or at the end of the progressions. This is a big part of training your ears. Really, the only way to train your ears to recognize what you hear is to spend a lot of time listening in a very conscious way. You need to know what you're hearing and think directly about it as you listen.

This first table provides all the possibilities for these three chords in three spaces. Learn the examples and then strum through these, in long whole notes. This will give you the time to switch from one chord to the next. Focus on these six progressions until they start coming naturally to you. The changes in table 2 will come much quicker as a result.

Table 1:

Beginning On I	Ending On I	Centered On I
I – IV – V	IV – V – I	IV – I – V
I – V – IV	V – IV – I	V – I – IV

In that framework, there's a limited amount of possibilities. By adding one more space in which we can repeat one of the three chords, we find quite a few more possibilities, yet it's still a manageable amount of progressions. Keep the spaces uniform with these changes. If one space is a half-measure, the rest of the spaces should each be a half-measure

Table 2:

	Original	1st Permutation	2nd Permutation	3rd Permutation
1A:	I – I – IV – V	I – IV – V – I	IV – V – I – I	V – I – I – IV
1B:	I – IV – IV – V	IV – IV – V – I	IV – V – I – IV	V – I – IV – IV
1C:	I – IV – V – V	IV – V – V – I	V – V – I – IV	V – I – IV – V
2A:	I – I – V – IV	I – V – IV – I	V – IV – I – I	IV – I – I – V
2B:	I – V – V – IV	V – V – I – IV	V – I – IV – V	I – IV – V – V
2C:	I – V – IV – IV	V – IV – IV – I	IV – IV – I – V	IV – I – V – IV
2A:	I – IV – I – V	IV – I – V – I	I – V – I – IV	V – I – IV – I
3B:	I – IV – V – IV	IV – V – IV – I	V – IV – I – IV	IV – I – IV – V
3C:	I – V – IV – V	V – IV – V – I	IV – V – I – V	V – I – V – IV

CHORD SHIFTING

If you're really new to the guitar, it may take a few weeks or even months, with lots of practice to get these changes feeling automatic. This comes from doing it a lot and paying attention to which finger is going where. Once you're shifting quickly, try using any strumming rhythms you like, beginning with simple rhythms, then building. Start off by playing each chord for two measures then cut that in half to allow one measure per change. Follow this up with half measure changes (two beats per chord) and finally try mixing the chord lengths up a bit.

COMPOSING

When you're building chord progressions for a song, one thing you never want to say is this: "Well, that one's already been taken." The truth is that they've all been used hundreds, if not thousands, of times. I'll put it this way. If music were nothing more than chord progressions, there wouldn't be much of a chance for an original musical idea. Luckily there are plenty of other factors to manipulate artistically. This isn't to say you can't make a unique chord progression. It just means that however unique it is, if you're listening close enough, you're bound to hear fragments of chord progressions from pre-existing songs.

You may have noticed how there's a considerably larger amount of possibilities when we go from table 1 to table 2. This is only because of the addition of one extra space to place one of the three pre-existing chords. If you string together any two progressions from table 2, you wind up with over 1,200 possible chord progressions. So this much can be said: the longer of a phrase your progression is, the more likely you'll have a unique set of changes, even when dealing with the most basic and common chords.

The simplest place to start, when you're composing your first chord progressions is to piece smaller progressions like these together and work in even numbers of measures and beats. At first you want to get used to the more common two, four, eight and sixteen bar phrases. Eventually we'll learn sneaky ways to tack on or leave off a measure, here and there, for an added level of uniqueness to our progressions.

Try coming up with a couple of repeatable chord progressions of any simple length (2, 4, 8 or 16 bars) and try periodically switching between the two. This would be a basic verse/chorus form. We'll be delving further into the concept of song forms further in. For now, just have fun and write down anything you discover that you like. Here's a good way to write out chord progressions.

Example Progression:

```
C        G  F     G         F  C
||  /  /  /  |  /  /  /  /  |  /  /  /  /  |  /  /  /  /  |

F        C        G         F     G
|  /  /  /  |  /  /  /  /  |  /  /  /  /  |  /  /  /  /  ||
```

The Chord-Tone Pattern:

Melody, by definition, is a linear (one note at a time) series of notes. A melody has three basic elements: 1: rhythm, 2: tonality (what key it's in) and 3: contour (the up and down motion). Scale patterns are a good way to get to know the melodic potential of scales while at the same time, building up lots of technical skill on your instrument. These scale patterns will be transcribed in all positions, in the key of C. Given that you studied the "Fretboard Mapping (part 2: Thinking Positionally)" section, it will be easy enough to transpose these to all other keys.

We caught a glimpse of this first pattern in the "Scale Tone Activity" section. It's what I simply call the "Chord-Tone Pattern". We've already looked at it in the open position so let's take a look at it in the five movable positions. I'd recommend spending at least a couple hours with each of these, as boring as they may sound for the time being. Learning these patterns in all positions is going to help you develop really strong instincts.

Root Position:

Second Position:

Third Position:

Third Position, Continued:

Fifth Position:

Sixth Position:

Sixth Position, Continued:

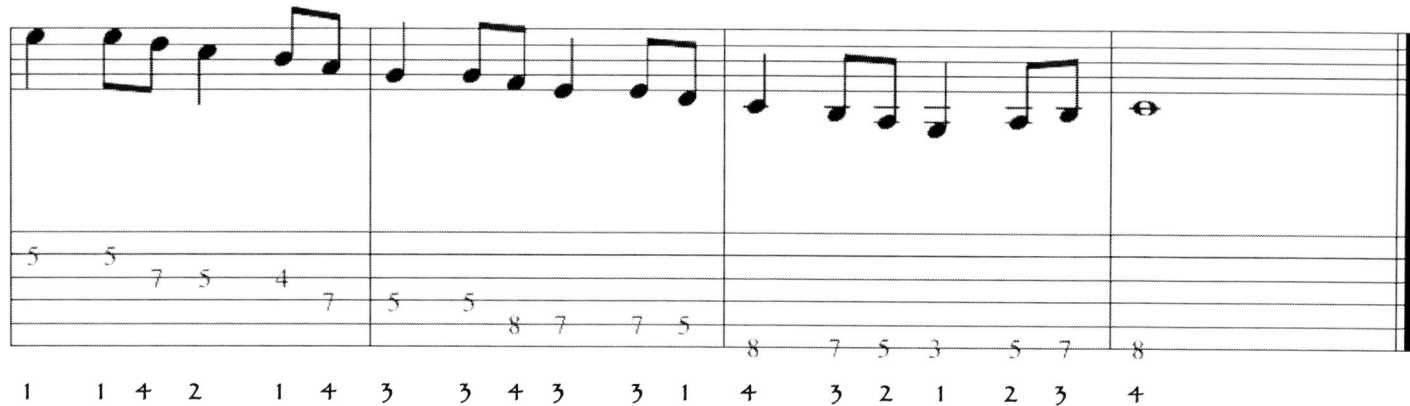

We'll be revisiting this pattern with other scales and modes further down the road to mastery. For the time being, devote a third of your practice time to getting these to become second nature. Make it a goal to eventually play these at 240 BPM. A realistic starting point may be around 60 BPM. Keep increasing your tempo by 5 BPM each time you get totally comfortable with the tempo you're at. Before you know it, you'll breeze through them as if they weren't even there. By this point you will know every point of tension and release in every position of the major scale. This will immediately improve your ability to improvise in any major scale oriented music, which is the majority of the music in the world.

When you know these patterns well, start moving them around on the fretboard to play them in different keys. Stay conscious of what key you're in. That means use the table in the fretboard mapping part 2 section, for as long as you need. Make sure you keep in mind how the root notes line up on the fretboard from position to position. Everything is literally connected to everything else on the fretboard. This knowledge becomes more and more clear with every hour spent on your guitar. This pattern is one of the most intensive and time effective ways that you can build up that knowledge and those instincts.

DIATONIC HARMONY - Part 2: Transposition and Bar Chords

To transpose something is to move it. In this case we're moving everything we've learned about diatonic harmony so far, to a new key. Remember that all major keys contain the same sequences of half steps and whole steps. In other words, every key is identical in its structure, which makes our job here much easier. Notice, in the chart below, how all the chords in the I column are major, all the chords in the II column are minor and so forth. If you know the notes of your major scales well, along with your major diatonic harmony formula, it's easy enough to figure out which chords belong in any key.

I	W	IIm	W	IIIm	H	IV	W	V	W	VIm	W	VIIdim	H
C		Dm		Em		F		G		Am		Bdim	
G		Am		Bm		C		D		Em		F#dim	
D		Em		F#m		G		A		Bm		C#dim	
A		Bm		C#m		D		E		F#m		G#dim	
E		F#m		G#m		A		B		C#m		D#dim	
B		C#m		D#m		E		F#		G#m		A#dim	
Gb		Abm		Bbm		Cb		Db		Ebm		Fdim	
Db		Ebm		Fm		Gb		Ab		Bbm		Cdim	
Ab		Bbm		Cm		Db		Eb		Fm		Gdim	
Eb		Fm		Gm		Ab		Bb		Cm		Ddim	
Bb		Cm		Dm		Eb		F		Gm		Adim	
F		Gm		Am		Bb		C		Dm		Edim	

No matter what you learn about harmony, it will apply to all keys in a uniform matter. The only real differences between these keys are those of a physical nature. In other words, it will lay out differently on your fretboard, from one key to another. You'll see the same shapes in every key. They'll just be located at different frets.

It is worth noting that chords in every key are still going to be located the same distances apart from one another. In other words, the IV chord and the V chord will always be a whole step apart and the II chord and V chord will always be 2½ steps apart. You'll eventually come to easily recognize these distances on the fret board, from string to string.

There are a lot of ways to play any one major or minor chord, many of these we'll be getting into, but for now, you can get by on these four movable chord shapes. I have the fingerings listed directly beneath the note locations. You'll notice that there are two fingering positions for the major A form bar chord. Quite honestly I prefer the lower option. If you're still fairly new to playing the guitar, you may find these chord shapes really difficult. Just spend a quarter to a half hour every day trying your best. You can keep moving along in the book, just keep devoting time to these chord shapes because they're very useful.

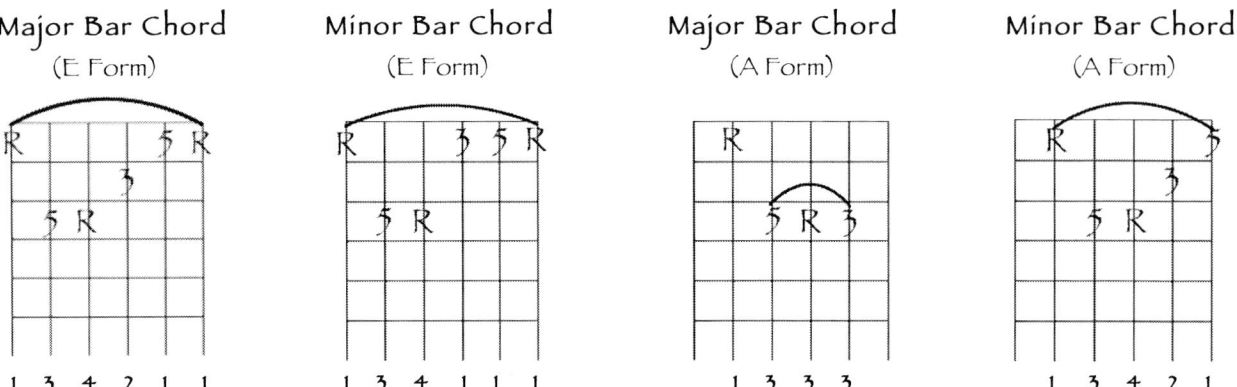

These four shapes give you two ways to play any major chord and two ways to play any minor chord. You have a minor shape with your bass note on the E string and one with your bass note on the A string. The bass note of each of these four shapes is the root of the chord. Find the note you need for the root of your chord on the low E string or A string and use the corresponding chord shape.

Let's say you need a Bb minor chord. You can find Bb on the 6th fret of the low E string so you can place the minor E-form bar chord at the 6th fret. You can also find Bb on the 1st fret of the A string so you could place the A form at the 1st fret. More specifically, you're placing the bass note of the chord shape at the given fret. Here are a couple of examples of how you could play a I-V-VI-IV progression in Bb Major.

Example: Bb   F   Gm   Eb

Bb   F   Gm   Eb

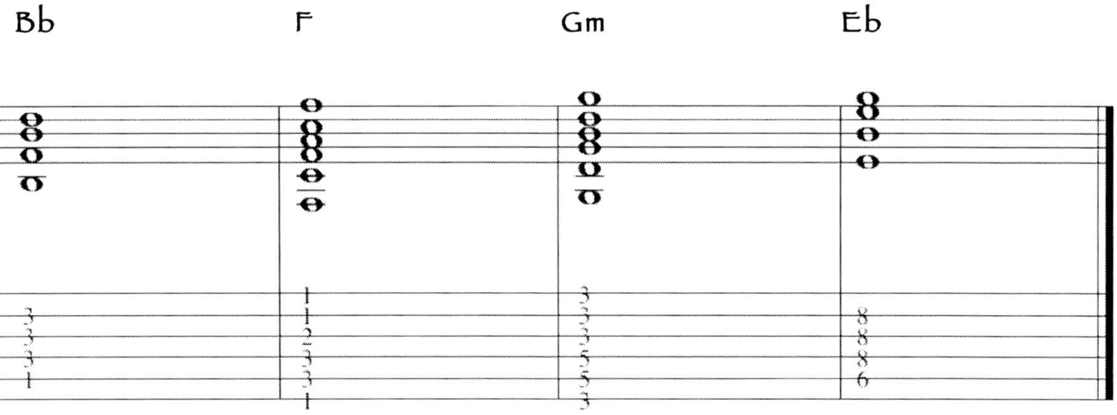

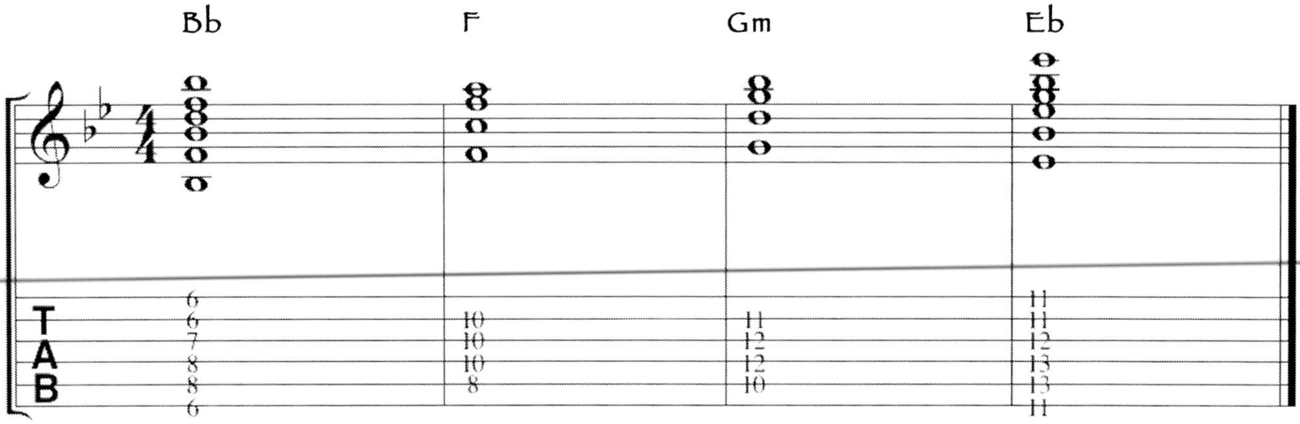

Even when your playing entirely diatonic progressions in the open position, you're going to run into at least one bar chord in even the most natural of keys. As I hope you remember, we started our exploration of chords with the diatonic family of triads in the key of C major, in open position. The standard tuned guitar is designed to be most naturally playable in the most natural key and as we have learned, C major fits the bill. And still we run in to a bar chord as soon as we arrive at the IV. No matter what key you choose to play open position chords, it will always be some combination of open chord shapes and bar chord shapes. The more distant the required or chosen key is, the more you will find bar chords dominating the open position landscape.

The following pages present open position diatonic triad families in all twelve major keys. This includes the key of C major, which we've already covered. It's redundant placement was purely done as a courtesy to those who need to reference it and don't want to be forced to flip back and forth. I'm not including the sus2 and sus4 triads in this expedition because I'd be doing you a greater service in forcing you to find the 2nds and 4ths on your own in order to replace the 3rds of these chords. I can't overstate the importance of being aware which notes are serving which role in the key in anything that you learn and play.

One way that you might want to make use of these pages is to pick any given progression and practice it in all twelve keys, as presented and repeat the process with other progressions that you enjoy. After a good twenty hours working with these chords, your rate for learning songs will increase quite noticeably. Most popular music is made up of diatonic triads but not all of it. In jazz, triads are treated almost as a novelty and show up rarely in performance. We have much to learn yet about chords but this section promises to serve as a hearty foundation.

Basic Open Position Triads in the Key of C Major:

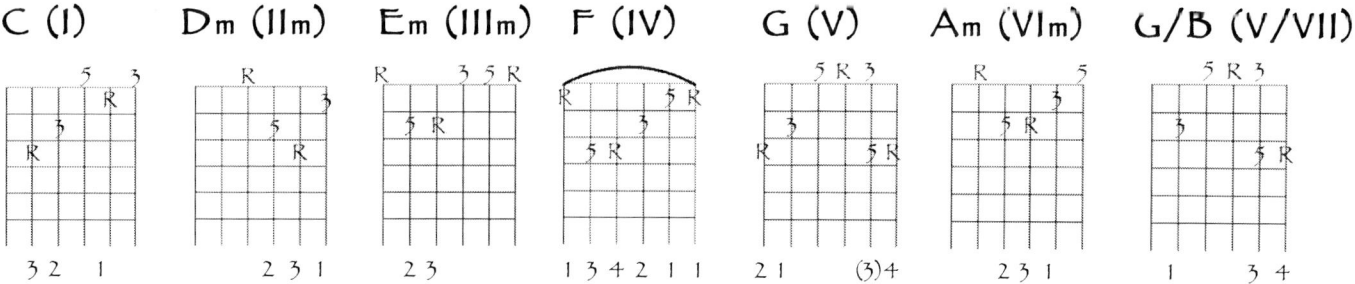

Basic Open Position Triads in the Key of G Major:

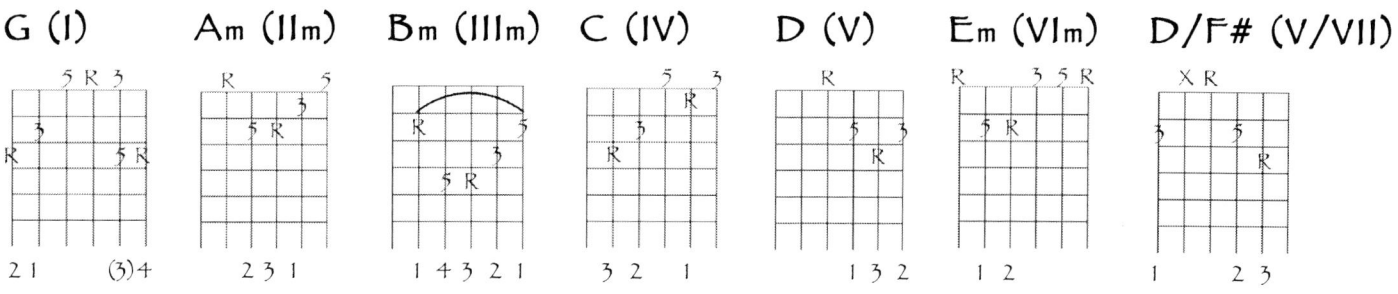

Basic Open Position Triads in the Key of D Major:

D (I)　　Em (IIm)　　F#m (IIIm)　　G (IV)　　A (V)　　Bm (VIm)　　A/C# (V/VII)

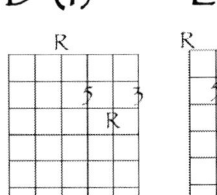 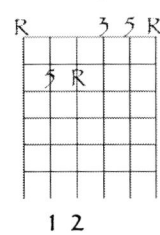 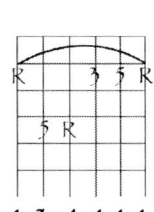 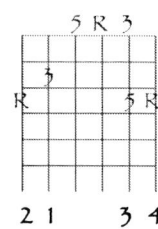 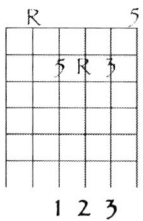 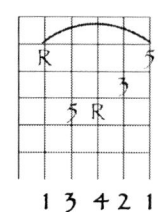 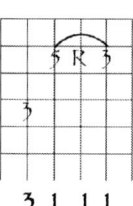

1 3 2　　1 2　　1 3 4 1 1 1　　2 1　3 4　　1 2 3　　1 3 4 2 1　　3 1 1 1

Basic Open Position Triads in the Key of A Major:

A (I)　　Bm (IIm)　　C#m (IIIm)　　D (IV)　　E (V)　　F#m (VIm)　　E/G# (V/VII)

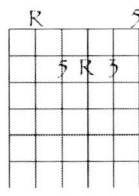 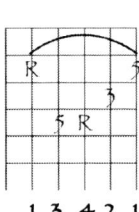 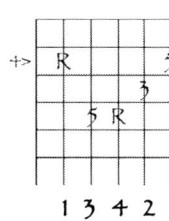 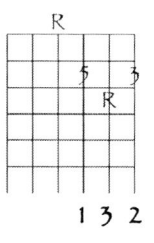 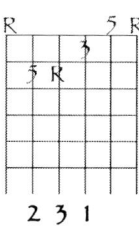 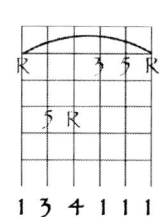 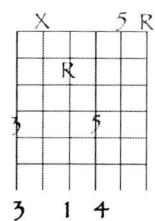

1 2 3　　1 3 4 2 1　　1 3 4 2 1　　1 3 2　　2 3 1　　1 3 4 1 1 1　　3 1 4

Basic Open Position Triads in the Key of E Major:

E (I)　　F#m (IIm)　　G#m (IIIm)　　A (IV)　　B (V)　　C#m (VIm)　　B/D# (V/VII)

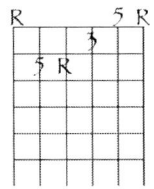 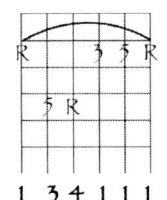 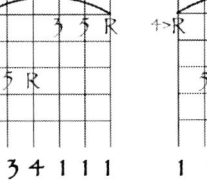 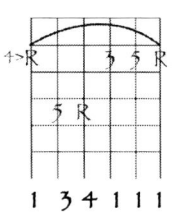 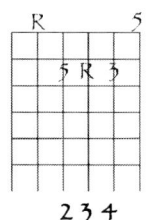 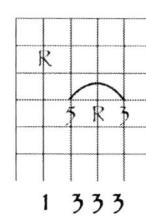 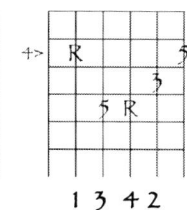 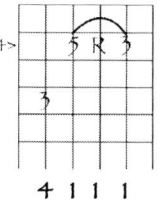

2 3 1　　1 3 4 1 1 1　　1 3 4 1 1 1　　2 3 4　　1 3 3 3　　1 3 4 2　　4 1 1 1

Basic Open Position Triads in the Key of B Major:

B (I)　　C#m (IIm)　　D#m (IIIm)　　E (IV)　　F# (V)　　G#m (VIm)　　F#/A# (V/VII)

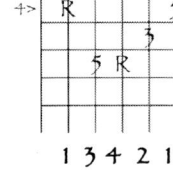 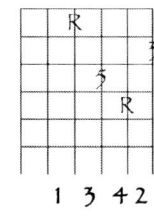 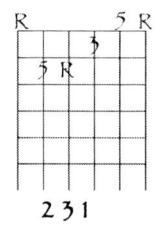 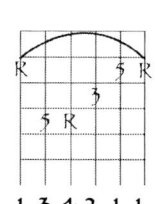 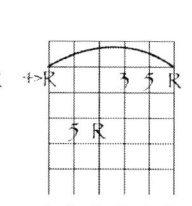 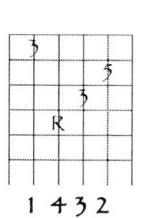

1 3 3 3　　1 3 4 2 1　　1 3 4 2　　2 3 1　　1 3 4 2 1 1　　1 3 4 1 1 1　　1 4 3 2

Basic Open Position Triads in the Key of Gb Major:

Gb(I)　　Abm(IIm)　Bbm(IIIm)　Cb(IV)　　Db(V)　　Ebm(VIm)　Db/F(V/VII)

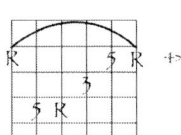 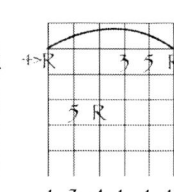 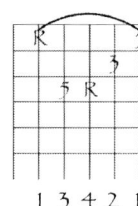 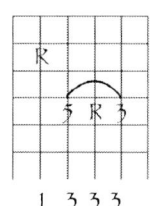 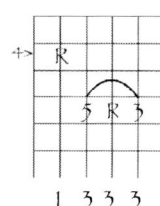 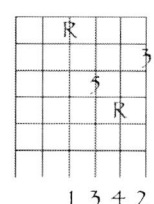 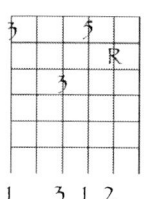

1 3 4 2 1 1　　1 3 4 1 1 1　　1 3 4 2 1　　1 3 3 3　　1 3 3 3　　1 3 4 2　　1　3 1 2

Basic Open Position Triads in the Key of Db Major:

Db(I)　　Ebm(IIm)　Fm(IIIm)　Gb(IV)　　Ab(V)　　Bbm(VIm)　Ab/C(V/VII)

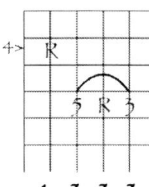 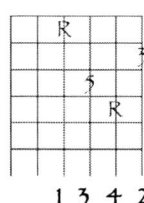 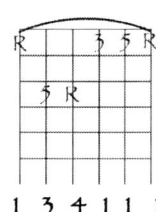 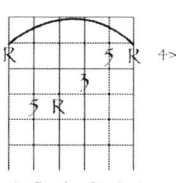 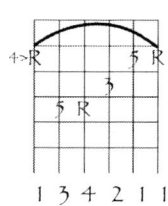 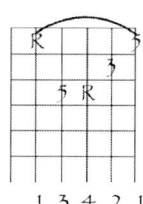 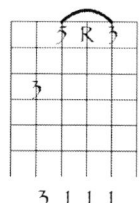

1 3 3 3　　1 3 4 2　　1 3 4 1 1 1　　1 3 4 2 1 1　　1 3 4 2 1 1　　1 3 4 2 1　　3 1 1 1

Basic Open Position Triads in the Key of Ab Major:

Ab(I)　　Bbm(IIm)　Cm(IIIm)　Db(IV)　　Eb(V)　　Fm(VIm)　Eb/G(V/VII)

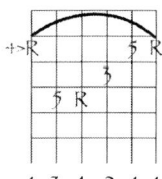 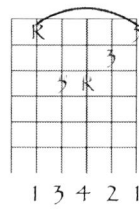 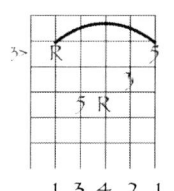 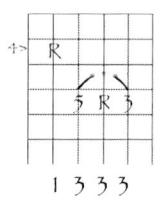 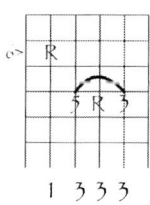 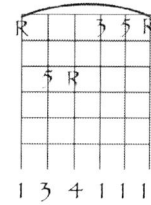 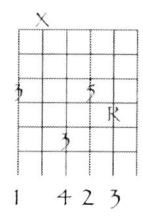

1 3 4 2 1 1　　1 3 4 2 1　　1 3 4 2 1　　1 3 3 3　　1 3 3 3　　1 3 4 1 1 1　　1　4 2 3

Basic Open Position Triads in the Key of Eb Major:

Eb(I)　　Fm(IIm)　Gm(IIIm)　Ab(IV)　　Bb(V)　　Cm(VIm)　Bb/D(V/VII)

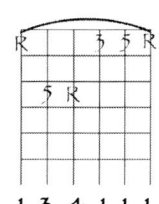 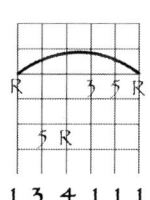 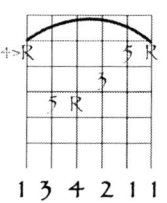 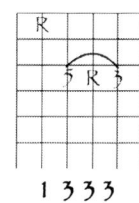 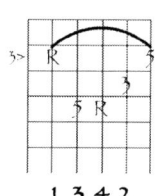 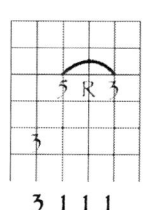

1 3 3 3　　1 3 4 1 1 1　　1 3 4 1 1 1　　1 3 4 2 1 1　　1 3 3 3　　1 3 4 2　　3 1 1 1

Basic Open Position Triads in the Key of Bb Major:

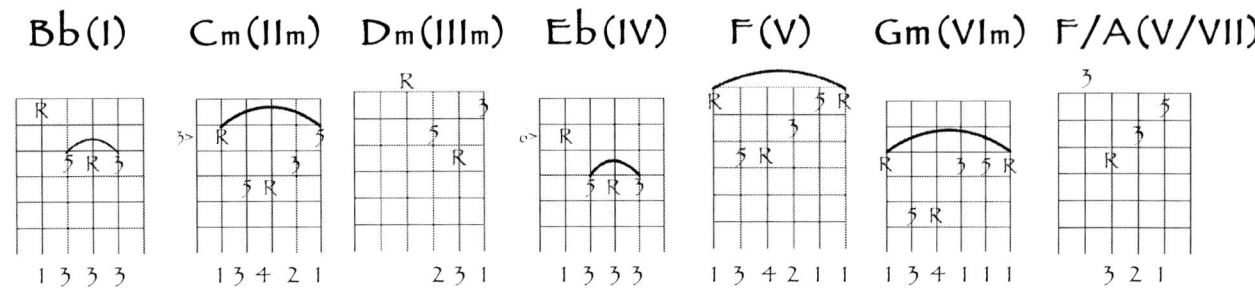

Basic Open Position Triads in the Key of F Major:

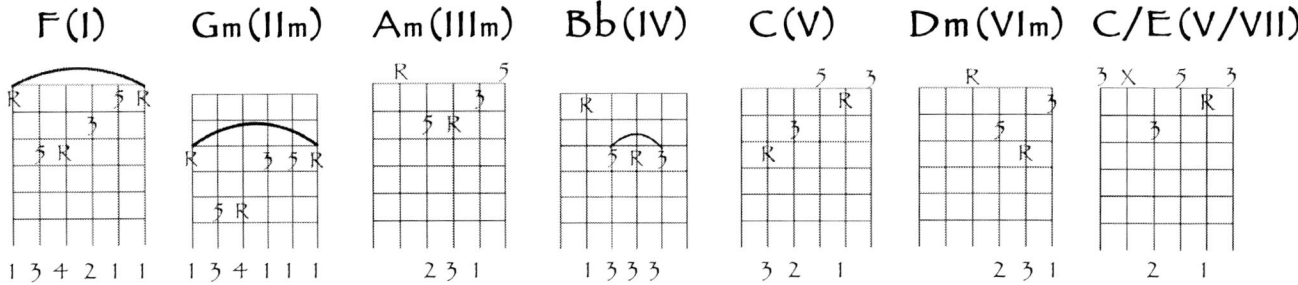

The Capo:

Simply put, a capo allows you to use the exact same voicings from one key, in a different key by clamping onto a given fret, making the notes at that fret, your new open string notes. This gives people with less experience and chord voicing knowledge the ability to play songs in keys otherwise unavailable to them. However, there are some rather expert players who use capos for musical/aesthetic reasons. Below is a chart that tells you which capo clamped frets will produce which keys, using the four most common diatonic open chord families.

Major Key:	C Family	G Family	D Family	A Family
C	0	5	10	3
G	7	0	5	10
D	2	7	0	5
A	9	2	7	0
E	4	9	2	7
B	11	4	9	2
Gb	6	11	4	9
Db	1	6	11	4
Ab	8	1	6	11
Eb	3	8	1	6
Bb	10	3	8	1
F	5	10	3	8

RECOGNIZING TONALITY

Tonality simply refers to the key that the music is in. In a creative musical environment, you'll be called on frequently to create melodic figures based on specific chord progressions. This means that if you want to work efficiently, you need the ability to recognize the key from which the progression is derived. Sometimes you only have a pair of chords, alternating back and forth, to clue you in to which scale or scales will fit the context. This two-chord scenario is known as a *chord vamp* or more simply, *a vamp*. If you can identify the key of a vamp or a progression, you can quickly begin experimenting with the appropriate family of notes. This cuts out a lot of wasted time in stumbling around discovering which notes *don't* work.

There are a couple of concepts that you need to have solidly memorized before tackling this process. First of all, you need to know the distances between the notes in the major scale. This doesn't only refer to the distance between the tones directly next to each other, but also the compound distances from the root to the 4th or from the 3rd to the 5th and so on. Secondly, you need to know which chords in the key function as major and which chords function as major.

Below is a table demonstrating these chord types and distances. It's used in a manner similar to a multiplication table. The numbers in the body of the table represent the distances between chords. Both the distances up and down from one chord to the next are provided, indicated by arrows. The far left column represents the chord you're coming from, whereas the top row represents the chord at which you're arriving. The box that intersects at the column and row of the two chords in question contains the distance, up or down, between the two chords in whole-steps.

	I	IIm	IIIm	IV	V	VIm	VII°
I	↑6 ↓6	↑1 ↓5	↑2 ↓4	↑2½ ↓3½	↑3½ ↓2½	↑4½ ↓1½	↑5½ ↓½
IIm	↑5 ↓1	↑6 ↓6	↑1 ↓5	↑1½ ↓4½	↑2½ ↓3½	↑3½ ↓2½	↑4½ ↓1½
IIIm	↑4 ↓2	↑5 ↓1	↑6 ↓6	↑½ ↓5½	↑1½ ↓4½	↑2½ ↓3½	↑3½ ↓2½
IV	↑3½ ↓2½	↑4½ ↓1½	↑5½ ↓½	↑6 ↓6	↑1 ↓5	↑2 ↓4	↑3 ↓3
V	↑2½ ↓3½	↑3½ ↓2½	↑4½ ↓1½	↑5 ↓1	↑6 ↓6	↑1 ↓5	↑2 ↓4
VIm	↑1½ ↓4½	↑2½ ↓3½	↑3½ ↓2½	↑4 ↓2	↑5 ↓1	↑6 ↓6	↑1 ↓5
VII°	↑½ ↓5½	↑1½ ↓4½	↑2½ ↓3½	↑4 ↓2	↑4 ↓2	↑5 ↓1	↑6 ↓6

Third of all, you need to know which white keys have no black keys in between them. Remember that on the piano, there are no black keys between E and F or between B and C. As long as you know this, you can always calculate the distance between any two notes, in whole-steps and half steps. It also helps to know what these distances look like on the guitar, on one string, from one string to the next and skipping one string. This gives you a couple ways of calculating the distance between two chords.

Fourth and finally, you need to know your cycle of 5ths. By that, I mean that you should know which notes serve which roles, in which keys. For example, you should know that Eb is the 5th of the Ab major scale. If you don't know your keys in that solid of a matter yet, you'll just have to do a little page-flipping back to the Cycle of 5ths section.

I've boiled it down to 4 steps, each one in question form, to figuring out which key any given two-chord vamp originates. I'll start by outlining the four questions and then I'll explain how to answer each question.

1) What types of chords are they?
2) How far apart are they?
3) Where in the key does that occur?
4) What key is X the Y of?

Hypothetical Vamp:

                Ab   Bb
||: / / / / | / / / / :||

What types of chords are they? In this case we're looking at two major chords. This is one of four major/minor triad possibilities: 1: Major – Major, 2: Minor – Minor, 3: Major – Minor or 4: Minor – Major. If a diminished triad would have been present, it would give itself away as the VII chord because the VII is the only diminished triad in the key. There are three major chords in a key and so far, we don't know which two major chords they are. That's where the next question comes in.

How far apart are they? In this case, it's a whole step up from the first to the second chord. If we combine what we've learned from the last two questions, we know that we have two major chords, one whole-step apart from one another on our hands. This brings us to the next logical question.

Where in the key does that occur? It doesn't occur between the I and II because the II is minor. It couldn't occur between the VII and I because not only are they a half-step apart but the VII chord is diminished. The only place in the key where you get two major chords, one whole-step apart from each other, is on the IV and V. Bb is a whole step above Ab and the V is a whole step above the IV. This means that Ab is the IV and Bb is the V. That leaves us with our final question.

What key is Ab the IV of? To figure this out, we simply count down to the I chord by the appropriate whole-steps and half-steps. It's a half-step down to the IIIm, which would give us Gm, followed by a whole-step down to the IIm, which would give us Fm, followed by another whole-step down to the I, which would be Eb. If Eb is our I chord, it's pretty safe to say that we're in the key of Eb. I could have asked myself "what key is Bb the V of?" as well. In that case I would have probably counted in whole-steps and half-steps up the scale rather than down just because it's a shorter distance that way.

If visual aids will help you out at first, use the last couple of tables presented in the book. This begins as a pretty strenuous mental exercise but as you repeat the process, over and over, you'll become very comfortable and quick with it. If you continue using this logic, it eventually becomes almost instantaneous. On the following page, I've laid out a worksheet full of these two-chord vamps. Use the process above to discern from which keys the vamps originate. Check your answers against the answers provided at the very bottom of the page.

When you're certain you have all the right answers, record yourself playing the vamps for a couple minutes each, in any style and then spend some time improvising with the corresponding major scales, using any positions you choose.

Notice how quickly good things start coming together!

0) Ab   Bb   IV V in Eb
‖: / / / / | / / / / :‖

1) C   Bb   __ __ in __
‖: / / / / | / / / / :‖

2) Cm   Dm   __ __ in __
‖: / / / / | / / / / :‖

3) Am   D   __ __ in __
‖: / / / / | / / / / :‖

4) E   F#   __ __ in __
‖: / / / / | / / / / :‖

5) Bbm   Abm   __ __ in __
‖: / / / / | / / / / :‖

6) E   Bm   __ __ in __
‖: / / / / | / / / / :‖

7) F   Eb   __ __ in __
‖: / / / / | / / / / :‖

8) F#m   G#m   __ __ in __
‖: / / / / | / / / / :‖

9) Db   Cb   __ __ in __
‖: / / / / | / / / / :‖

10) Fm   Gm   __ __ in __
‖: / / / / | / / / / :‖

11) Em   A   __ __ in __
‖: / / / / | / / / / :‖

12) F   G   __ __ in __
‖: / / / / | / / / / :‖

13) Bm   Am   __ __ in __
‖: / / / / | / / / / :‖

14) F   Cm   __ __ in __
‖: / / / / | / / / / :‖

15) G   A   __ __ in __
‖: / / / / | / / / / :‖

16) Bm   C#m   __ __ in __
‖: / / / / | / / / / :‖

*17) Am   C   __ __ in __ or __ __ in __
‖: / / / / | / / / / :‖

(This last one could belong to two possible keys. When this situation arises try playing with each key and one of them will sound more correct than the other.)

Answers:

1: V - IV in F; 2: IIm - IIIm in Bb; 3: IIm - V in G; 4: IV - V in B; 5: IIIm - IIm in Gb; 6: V - IIm in A; 7: V - IV in Bb; 8: IIm - IIIm in E; 9: V - IV in Gb; 10: IIm - IIIm in Eb; 11: IIm - V in D; 12: IV - V in C; 13: IIIm - IIm in G; 14: V - IIm in Bb; 15: IV - V in D; 16: IIm - IIIm in A; 17: IIm - IV in G or VIm - I in C.

54

The Natural Minor Scale

Where as you can consider the major scale your basic shade of happy, in the same sense, you can consider the natural minor scale your basic shade of sad. This doesn't mean that all songs in minor keys sound sad. Other factors play a big part in the mood of the music. Most minor key songs that are up-tempo sound more impassioned rather than sad. If we take the notes that make up the key of C major and treat A as the root note, we have the A minor scale. Music made from this scale is in the key of A minor. A, C and E would become your inactive (resolving) notes and B, D, F and G become your active (tense) notes.

C Major
```
   W   W   H   W   W   W   H
R:  2:  3:  4:  5:  6:  7:
C   D   E   F   G   A   B
```

A Minor
```
   W   H   W   W   H   W   W
R:  2:  3:  4:  5:  6:  7:
A   B   C   D   E   F   G
```

Now what happens if we start this minor scale pattern on C instead of A?

C Minor
```
   W   H   W   W   H   W   W
R:  2:  3:  4:  5:  6:  7:
C   D   Eb  F   G   Ab  Bb
```
Now, compare that to C major.
```
C   D   E   F   G   A   B
```

So in 'parallel' relation to the major scale, the minor scale has a flat third, flat sixth and flat seventh.
In 'relative' relation to the major scale, it's the same family of notes but the major key's root is the minor key's third. If we flip that around, the minor key's root is the major key's sixth. This is a hint at the basic concept of the modes, which we'll soon be exploring.

Since the natural minor scale is simply a mode of the major scale, (same notes, newly designated root) it employs all the same positional shapes as the major scale. The names of the positions and the roles of the scale tones change but the shapes physically remain the same. Below, you can see how these shapes relate to the minor scale:

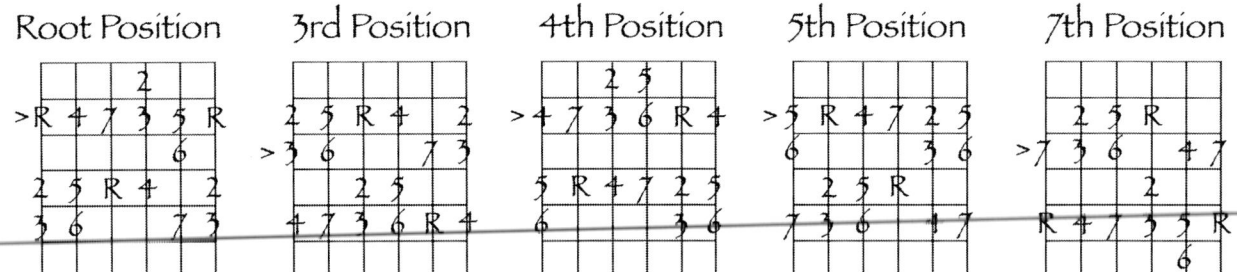

Root Position   3rd Position   4th Position   5th Position   7th Position

Next, is a chart indicating which position will be found at which fret, depending on what minor key the music is in. It functions exactly the same as the similar chart in the "Fretboard Mapping (Part 2: Thinking Positionally)" section.

	Am	Em	Bm	F#m	C#m	G#m	Ebm	Bbm	Fm	Cm	Gm	Dm
Root Pos:	5	12	7	2	9	4	11	6	13	8	3	10
3rd Pos:	8	3	10	5	12	7	2	9	4	11	6	13
4th Pos:	10	5	12	7	2	9	4	11	6	13	8	3
5th Pos:	12	7	2	9	4	11	6	13	8	3	10	5
7th Pos:	3	10	5	12	7	2	9	4	11	6	13	8

It's important to be able to readily bring to mind all your major and minor scale relationships. Being that we know that the 6th of the major scale is the root of its relative minor scale, it's easy enough to do the math. Here is a chart that will help you get familiarized with these positions:

RELATIVE MAJOR	RELATIVE MINOR
C Major	A Minor
G Major	E Minor
D Major	B Minor
A Major	F# Minor
E Major	C# Minor
B Major	G# Minor
Gb Major	Eb Minor
Db Major	Bb Minor
Ab Major	F Minor
Eb Major	C Minor
Bb Major	G Minor
F Major	D Minor

Diatonic Harmony In Natural Minor:

Everything that you've learned about diatonic harmony in the major key applies directly to the relative minor key. The roles of each chord simply move over by two scale tones. For example, the VIm of the major key becomes the Im of the minor key. The I of the major key becomes the bIII of the minor key. Here is how it converts, in the natural, relative keys of C major and A minor:

Relative Minor	Im	IIdim	bIII	IVm	Vm	bVI	bVII
A minor/C major	Am	B dim	C	Dm	Em	F	G
Relative Major	VIm	VIIdim	I	IIm	IIIm	IV	V

Solidify your knowledge of this by writing out a table of the diatonic chords in all minor keys. It can be boiled down to this: the I, IV and V are minor chords, the bIII, bVI and bVII are major chords and the II is a diminished triad.

The Natural Minor Chord-Tone Pattern:

It's a good idea to do everything that you did with the major scale-tone pattern, with the natural minor chord-tone pattern. Even though you're using the exact same shapes, they behave quite differently in the minor mode. As you run through the root position, you'll find this very apparent. Listen closely for how these notes respond in a new way. This will shed a lot of new light on these shapes and you'll start to get a real idea of how important they are.

Root Position:

3rd Position:

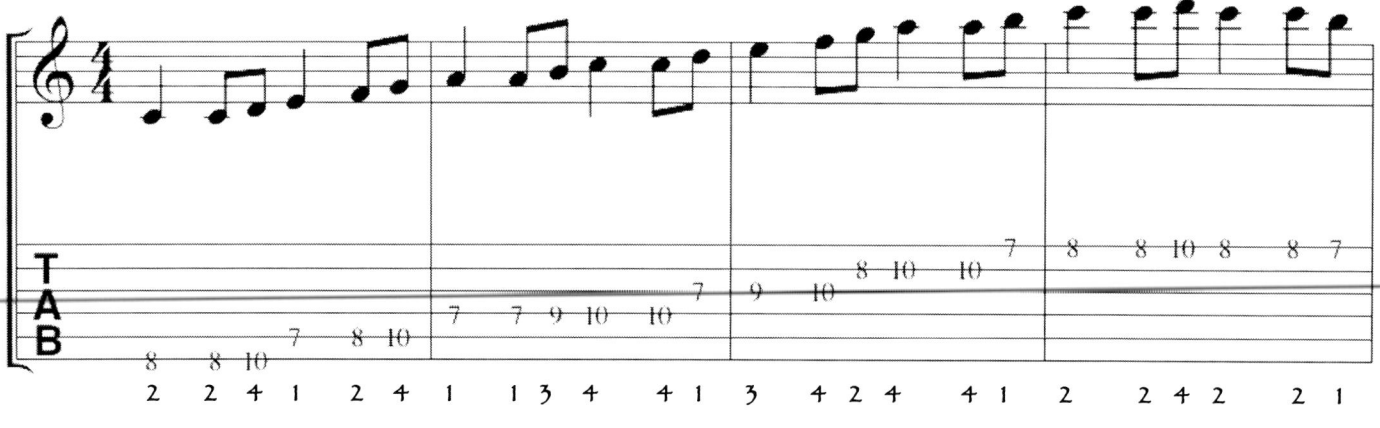

3rd Position, continued:

4th Position:

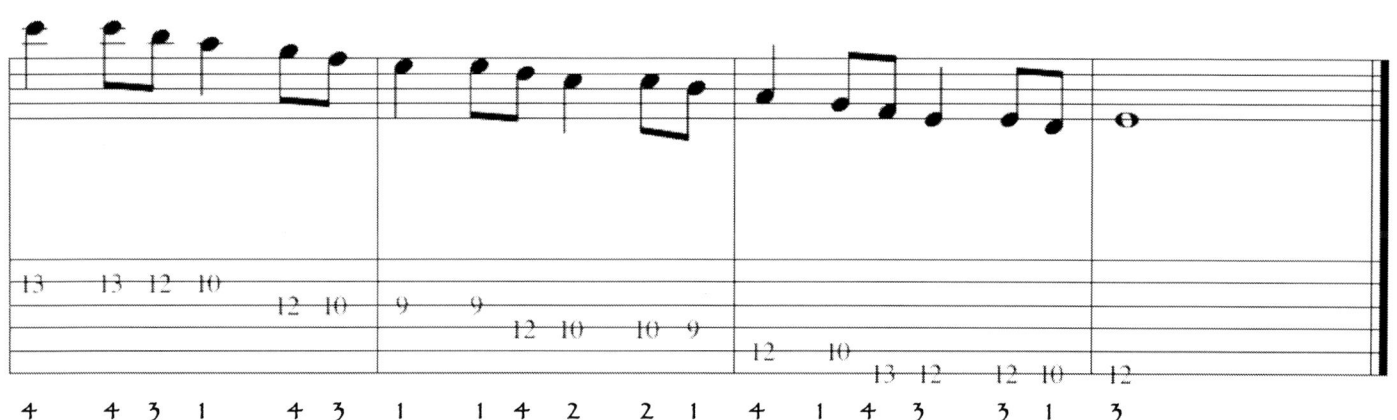

5th Position:

This one jumps one note out of position when we reach the very top. Make sure to pay special attention to the fingerings in this passage because this illustrates how we eventually negotiate shifts from one position to another.

7th Position:

This one also jumps out of position but this time it happens at the very bottom of the position. In this case, we work our way down to the open position and then back up to the root. Again, watch those fingerings closely! The key to gaining a strong command over these boxes is to consistently use the same fingerings. By doing this, you're going to build up speed and confidence much more quickly than if you were to use different fingerings each time.

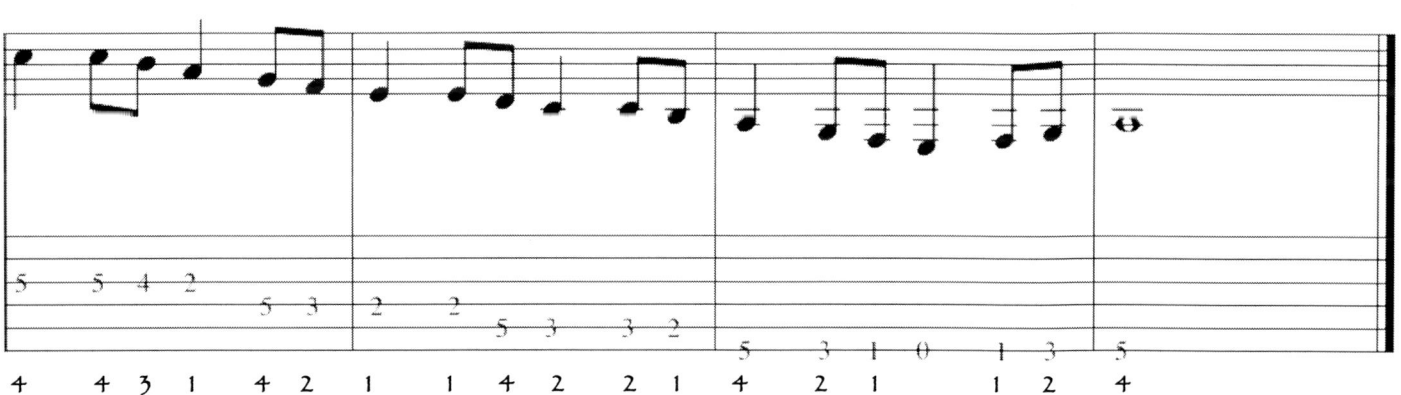

DIATONIC HARMONY – Part 3: Power Chords

Power chords are simply chord voicings comprised of roots and 5ths. By eliminating the 3rds from chord voicings, you wind up with chords that function equally as well in either the major or minor context. That's because it's the 3rd that provides the major or minor color to the chord. Your root and 5th are the same, whether it's a major or minor chord. These notes can be played in any arrangement with multiple roots and 5ths or as a simple root-5th voicing. Below are some common guitar voicings for an E power chord.

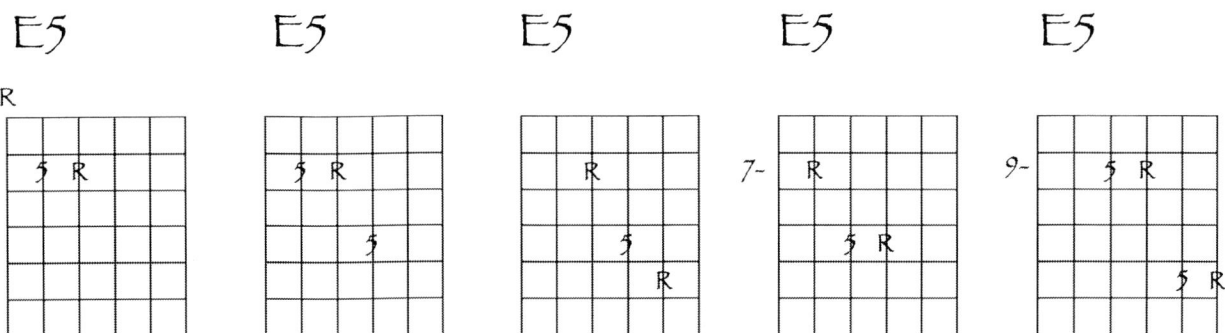

To transpose these voicings, simply align the root note of the voicing with the root note of the chord you desire on the fretboard. If you need an Eb, find Eb on the fretboard. Find it on the string where you want to play the root. Lay down the chord voicing where the root note lines up with that Eb.

Here are a couple very basic ways that we could voice a I-IV-V progression in C major. Practice these in a regular, even fashion and then practice them with the edge of your palm against the strings at the bridge. You want your palm's edge on the first inch of string and no further from the bridge than that. This is known as palm muting and it gives you a distinct effect. It's used in country, blues, rock, funk and metal. Palm muting is not effective on long notes so make sure to lift up your palm when you arrive at the final chord.

The first example is what I would consider the most common arrangement of I, IV and V, where the IV and V are a whole-step apart, located above the I chord.

Example 1:

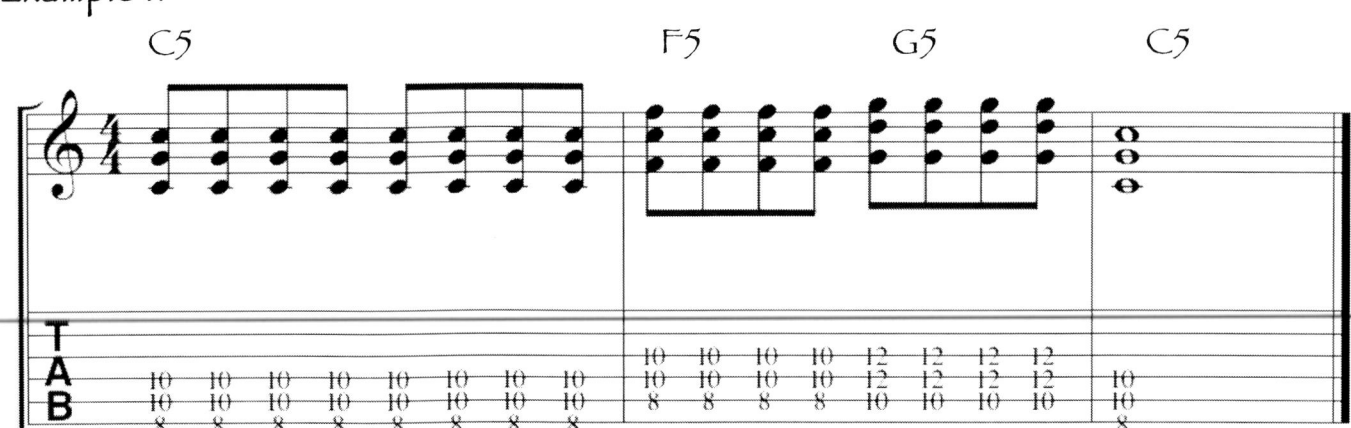

The second example is also a very common scenario. Here we have the IV and V still a whole-step apart, but now located below the I chord.

Example 1:

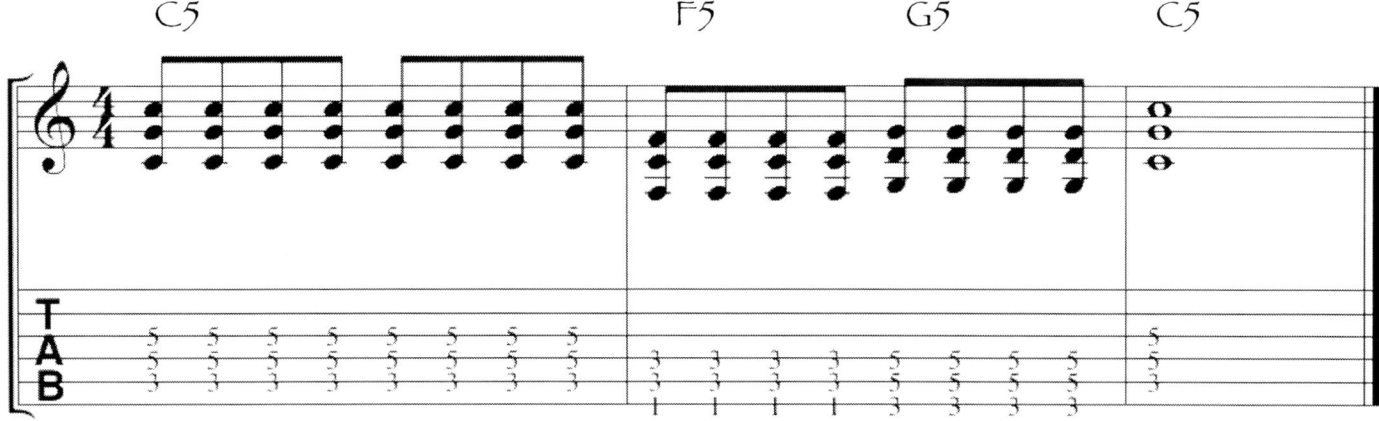

In these next examples, palm mute the single notes and lift your palm off the strings when you play the chord accents. Notice the open A notes between the chords to facilitate smooth, seamless changes. This is a very common technique in rock guitar riffs.

Example 2:

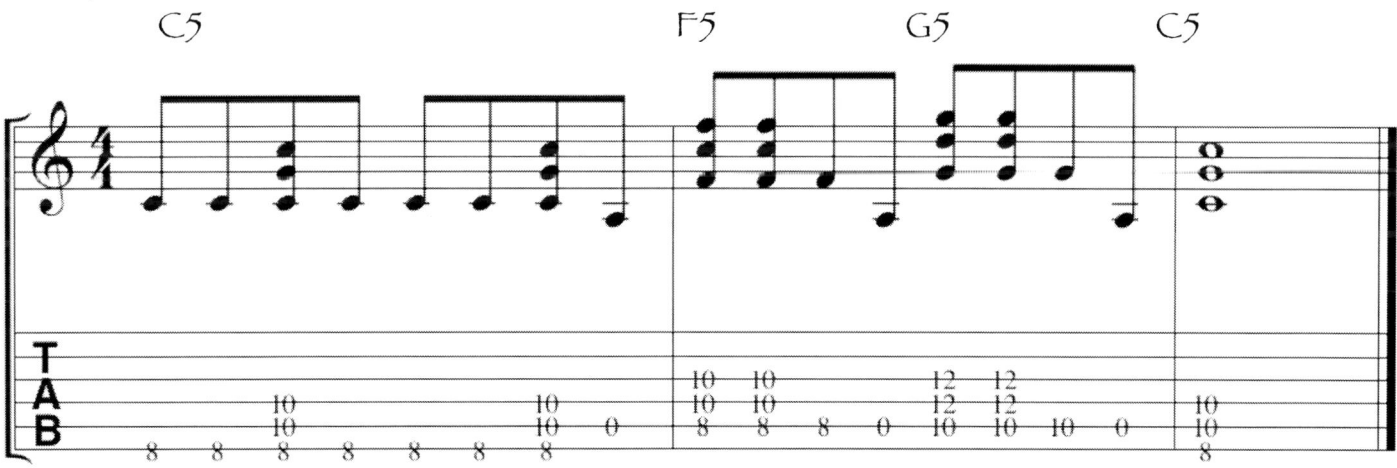

For some effective minor key rock progressions, you can replace the C power chord for an A power chord. This will give you a Im, bVI, bVII situation which is used in a lot of songs including "All Along The Watchtower" by Bob Dylan or Jimi Hendrix, "Don't Fear the Reaper" by the Blue Oyster Cult, "Sultans Of Swing" by the Dire Straits, "A Favor House Atlantic" by Coheed & Cambria and the solo section of "Stairway to Heaven" by Led Zeppelin.

Example 3:

Example 4:

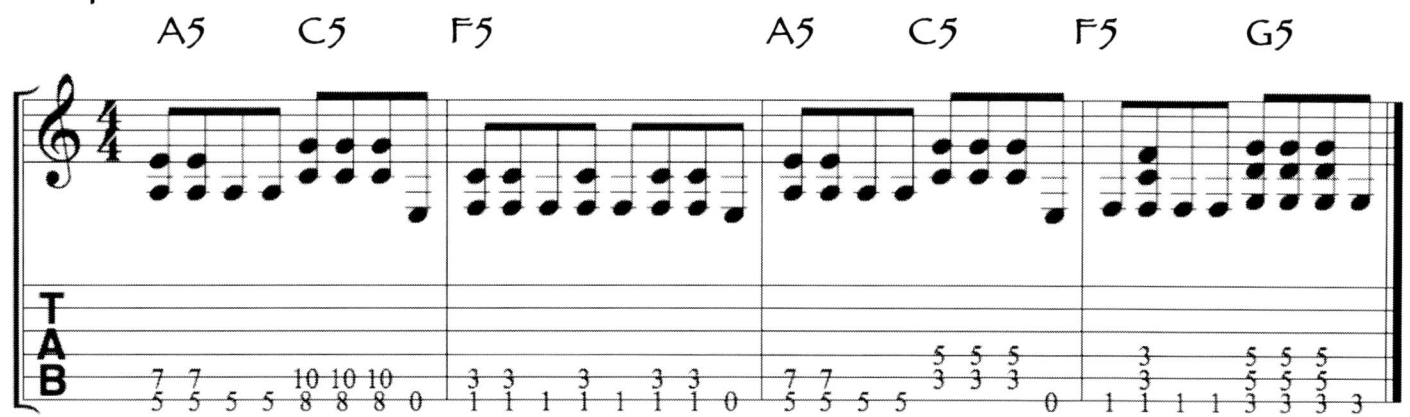

Example 5:

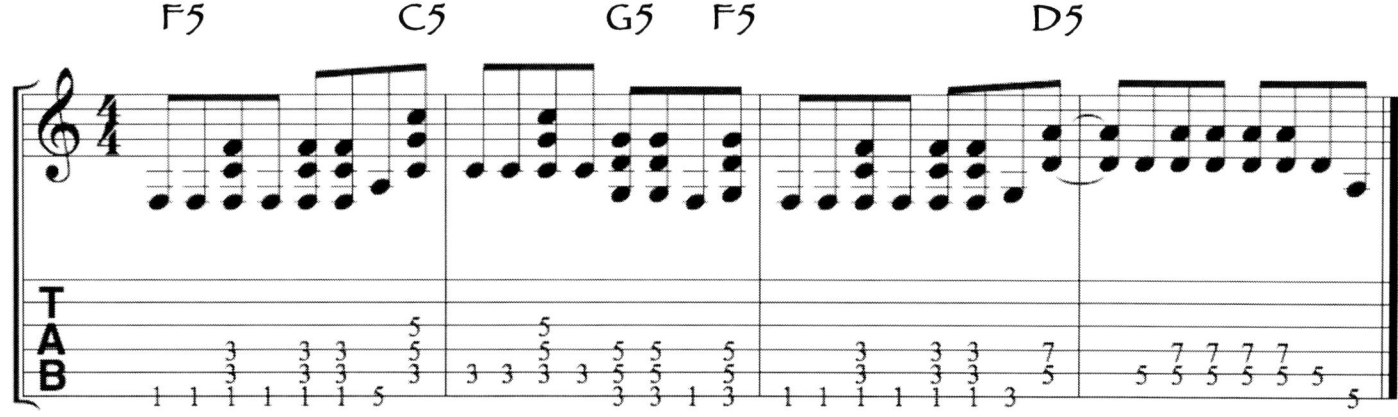

Example 6:

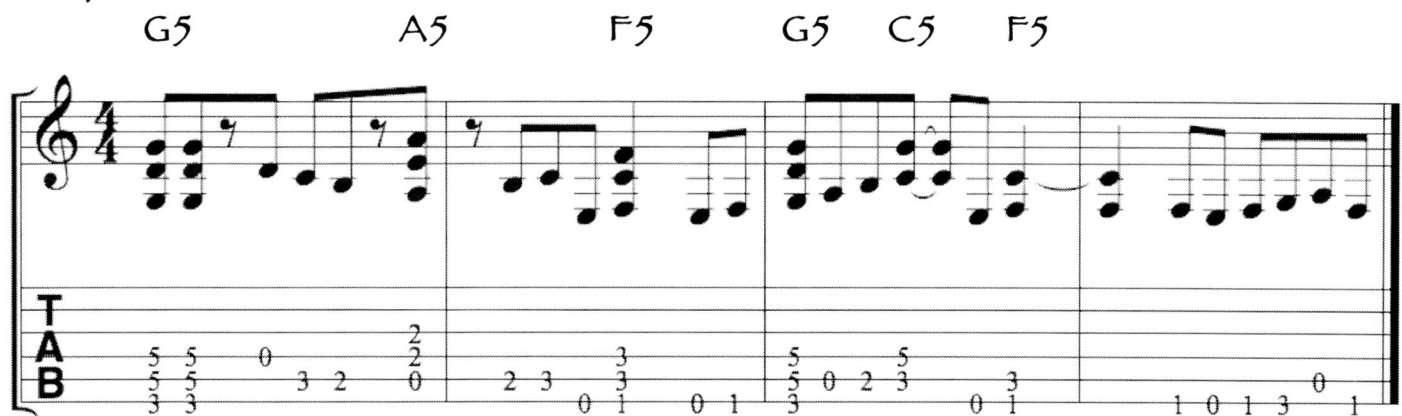

Example 7:

In this last example, during the C5 chord, use your ring finger (fretting the low C) to block off the D-string.

Example 8:

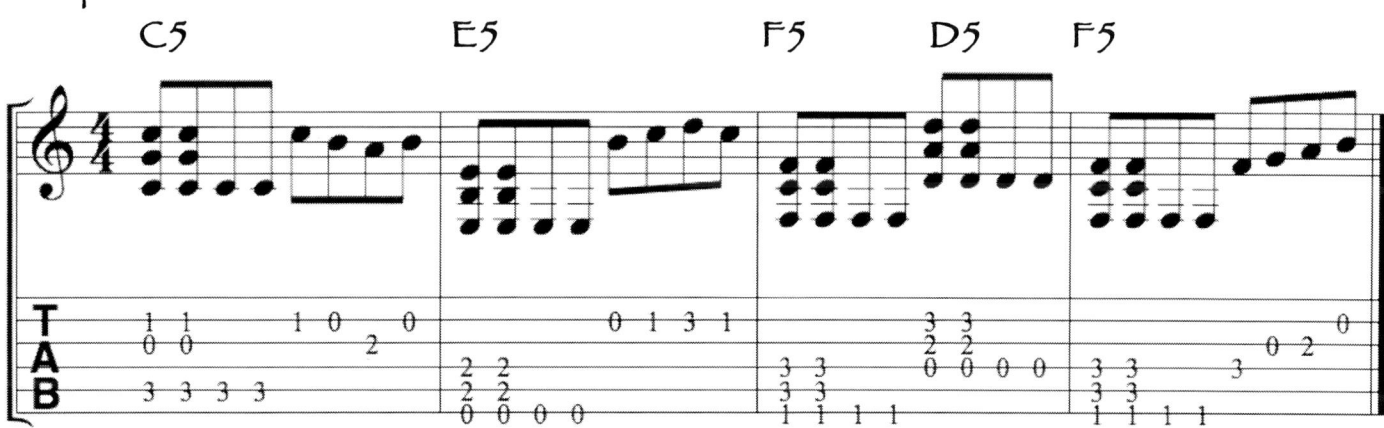

The Pentatonic Scale

Pentatonic, as you may have already assumed, means five-tone. There are many types of pentatonic scales but, by far, the most common of them are the major and minor pentatonic scales. These, just like the major and minor scales, are contained within each other. Whereas the major and minor scales are the most common raw material for building chords and progressions, the major and minor pentatonic scales are, arguably, the most common raw material for building melodies.

One place where we can clearly see the pentatonic scale is on the black keys of the piano. The black keys make up the Gb major pentatonic or the Eb minor pentatonic scales. You can also think of the major pentatonic scale as a major scale without a 4th or a 7th. In turn, you can think of the minor pentatonic as a minor scale without a 2nd or a b6th. In both cases, we're removing the two notes of the corresponding major or minor scale that are one tri-tone apart. Whether you were in C major or A minor, you would be removing B and F.

Below are the positions for both the major and minor pentatonic scales. Remember that these major and minor shapes are identical to each other and that the only real differences are the roles that the notes serve. These positions map out on the fretboard different keys the same way that the diatonic scales you've learned so far do. This means you can reference the tables on pages 29 and 44 for the major and minor modes, respectively. Make note that we number the scale tones as if the omitted tone were still present. This means the scale-tone numbers that you already know still apply to these new scales.

Major Pentatonic Positions:

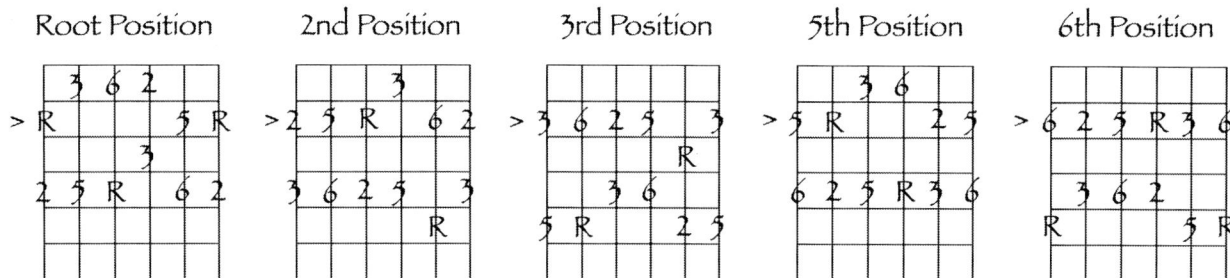

Minor Pentatonic Positions:

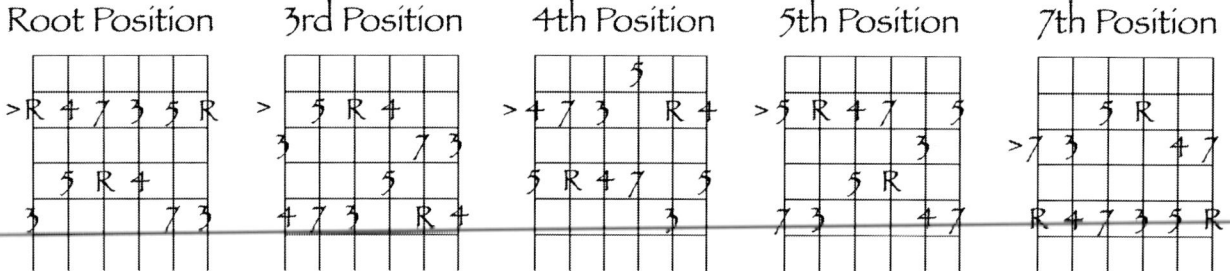

Upon first impression to the western ear, the major pentatonic scale has a country sort of quality to it and the minor pentatonic scale carries with it a blues vibe. This is only upon first impression. These scales have some very jazzy applications, which you'll be finding out about down the road. For now I'll present some typical "core" melodic usage of these two scales. I transcribed all of these licks in the same relative position so you can clearly see the difference in the treatment of the scale-tones.

Major Pentatonic Licks:

Major Pentatonic Lick 1:

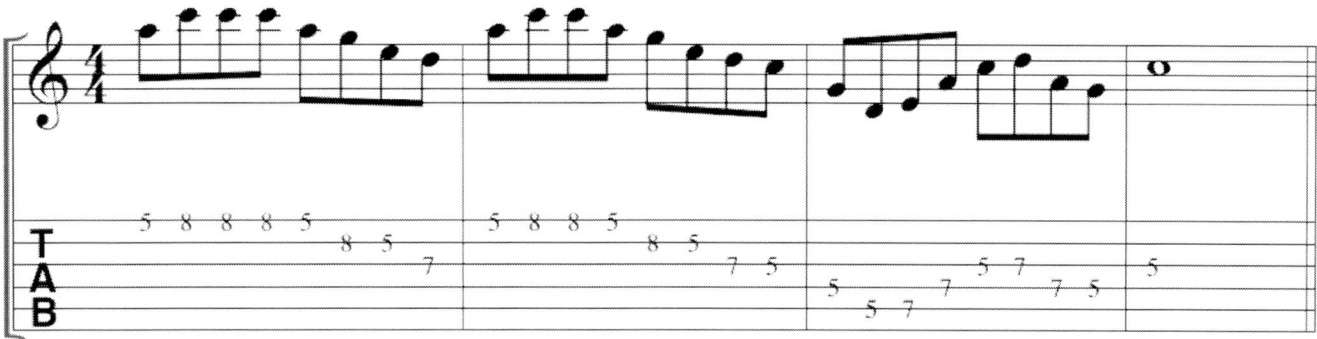

Major Pentatonic Lick 2:

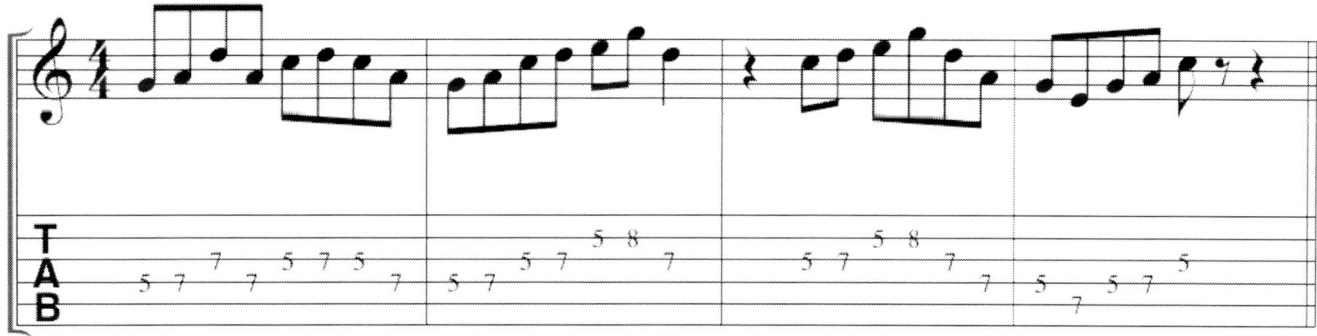

Major Pentatonic Lick 3:

Major Pentatonic Lick 4:

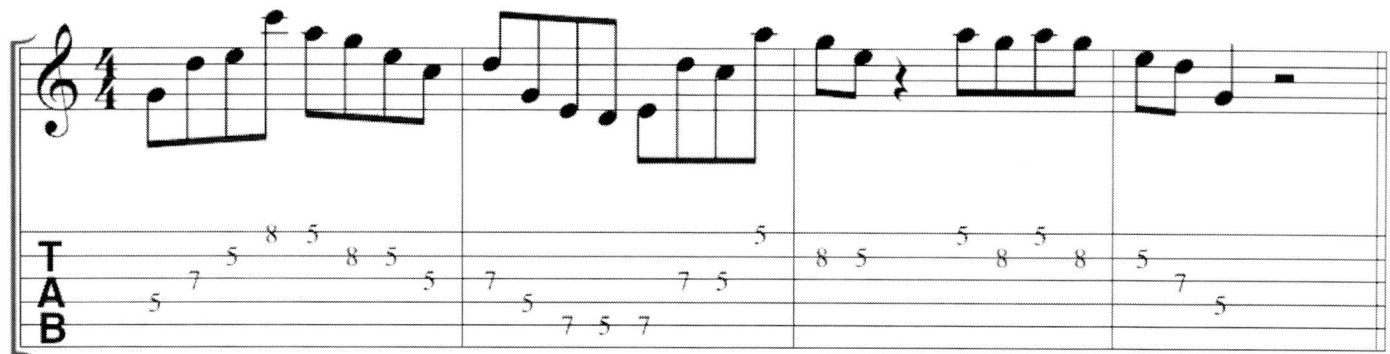

Major Pentatonic Lick 5:

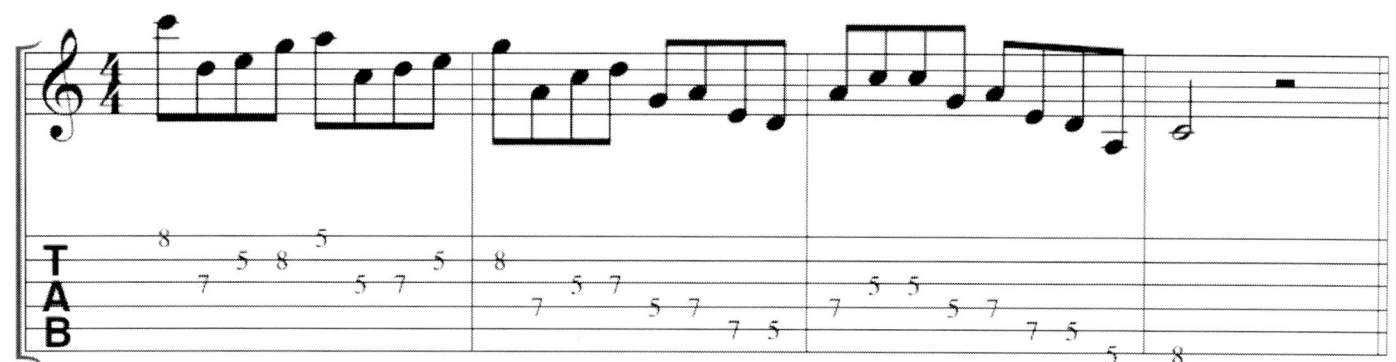

Major Pentatonic Lick 6:

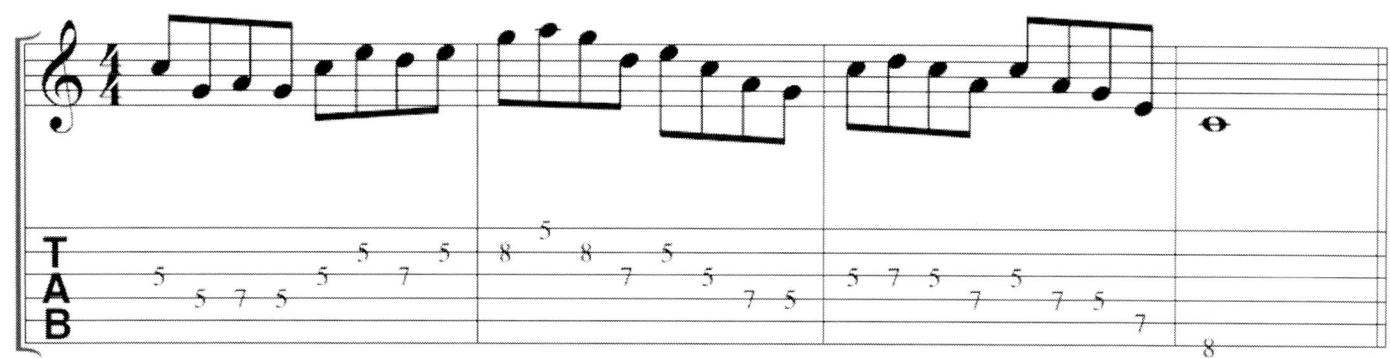

Major Pentatonic Lick 7:

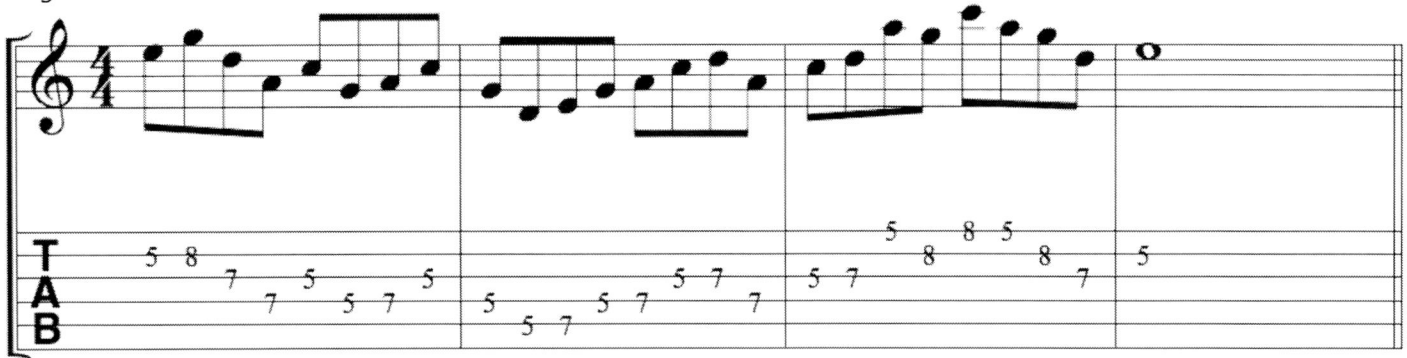

Major Pentatonic Lick 8:

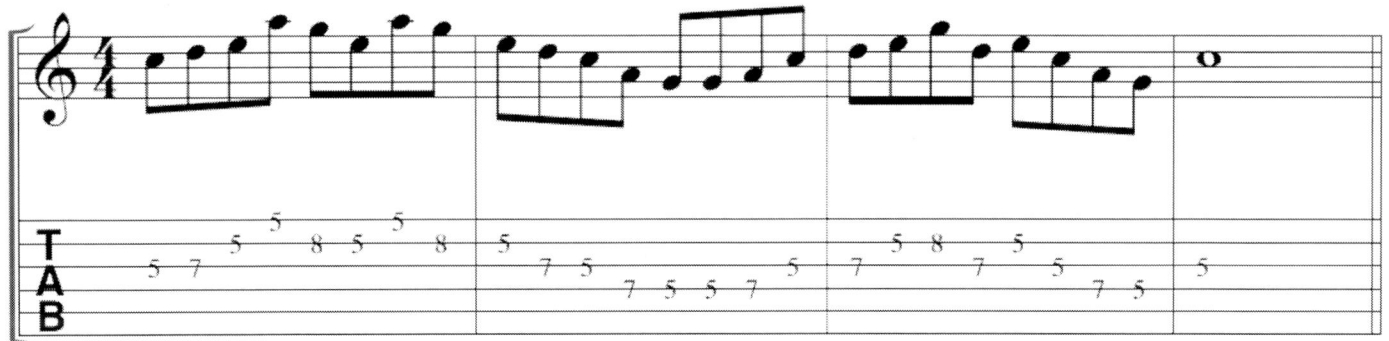

Major Pentatonic Lick 9:

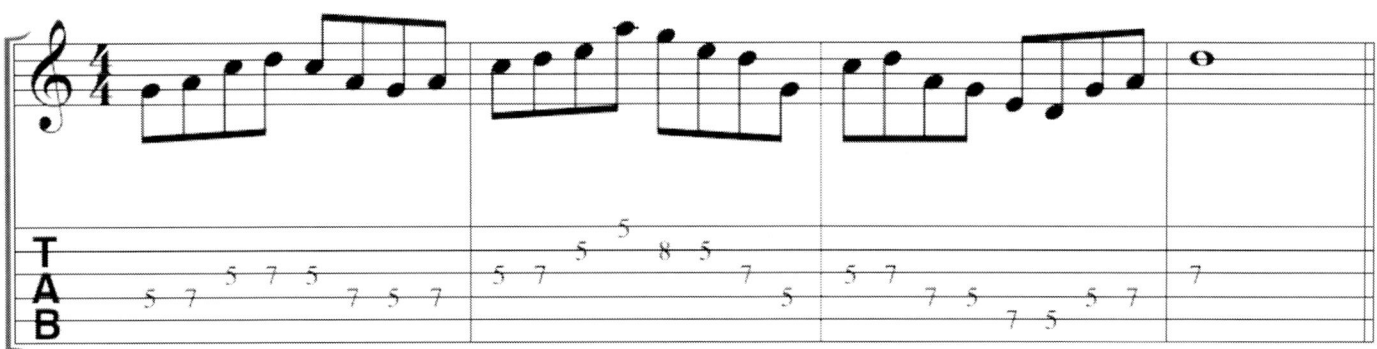

Major Pentatonic Lick 10:

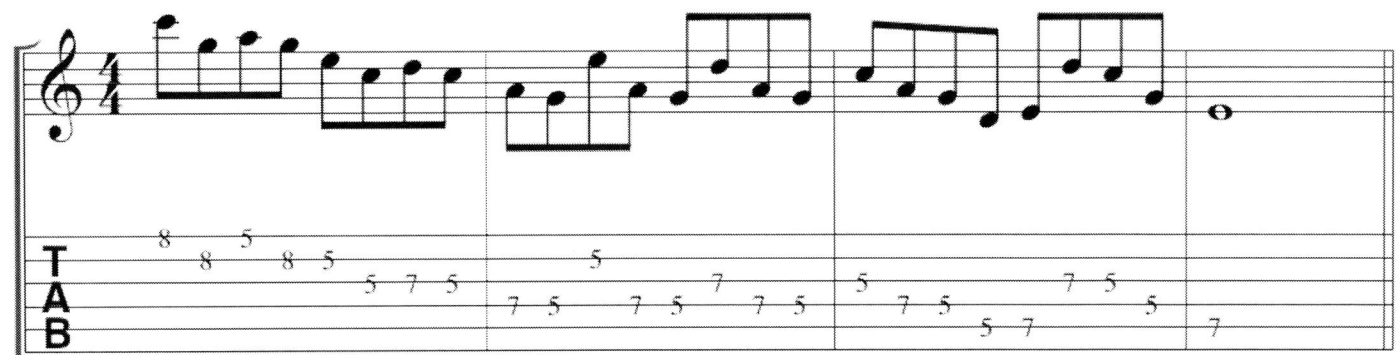

Major Pentatonic Lick 11:

Major Pentatonic Lick 12:

Minor Pentatonic Licks:

Minor Pentatonic Lick 1:

Minor Pentatonic Lick 2:

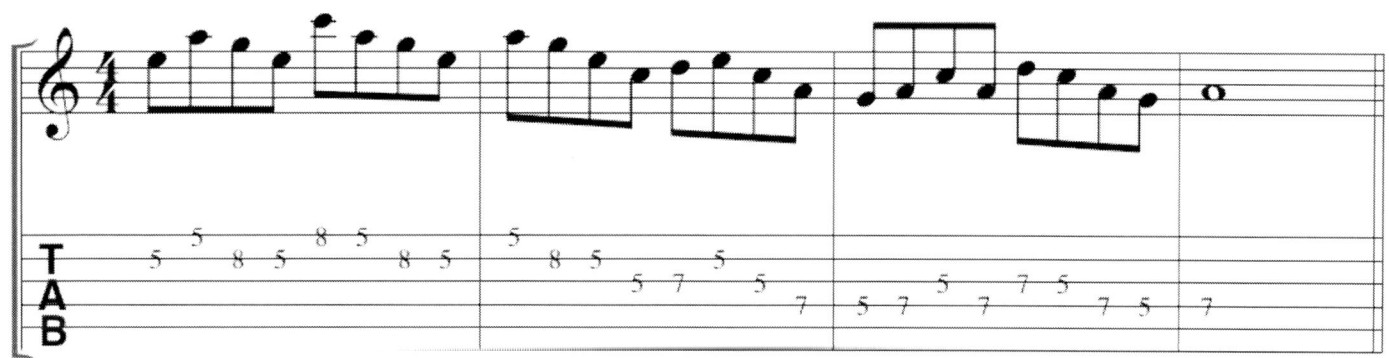

Minor Pentatonic Lick 3:

Minor Pentatonic Lick 4:

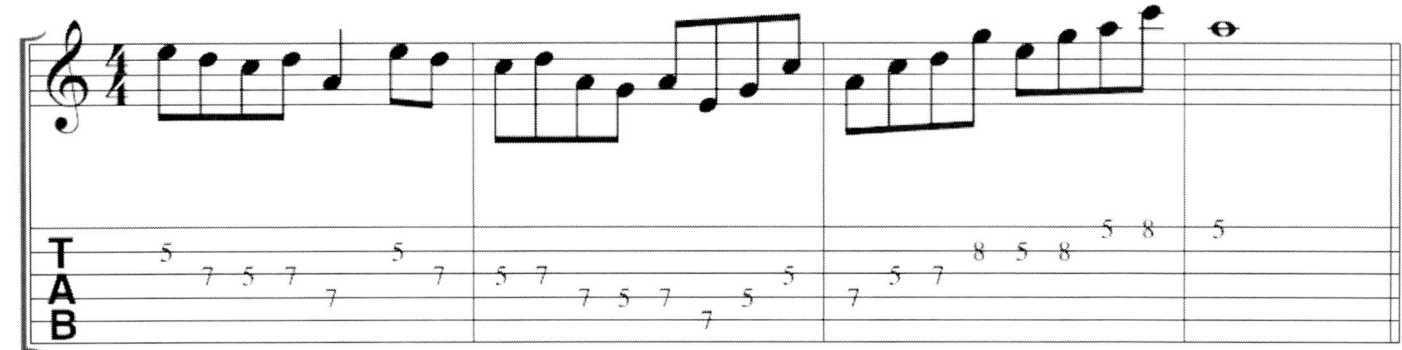

Minor Pentatonic Lick 5:

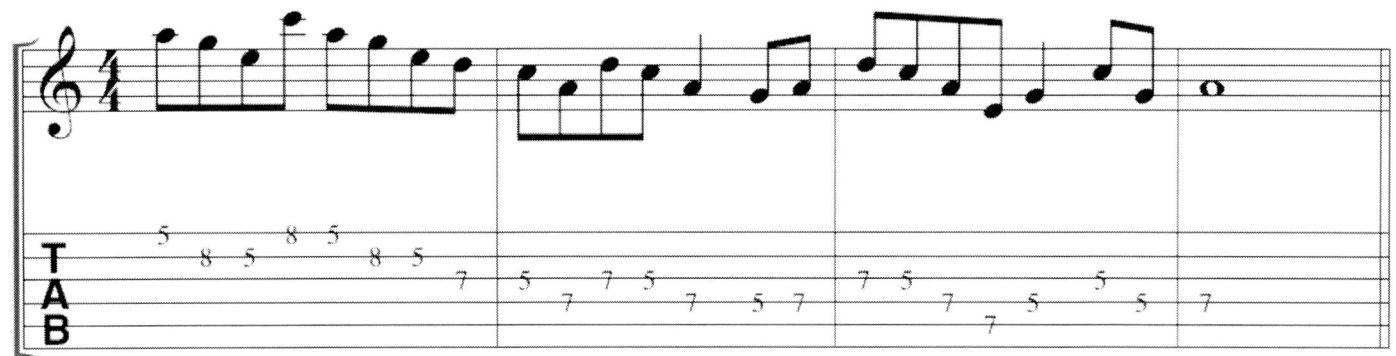

Minor Pentatonic Lick 6:

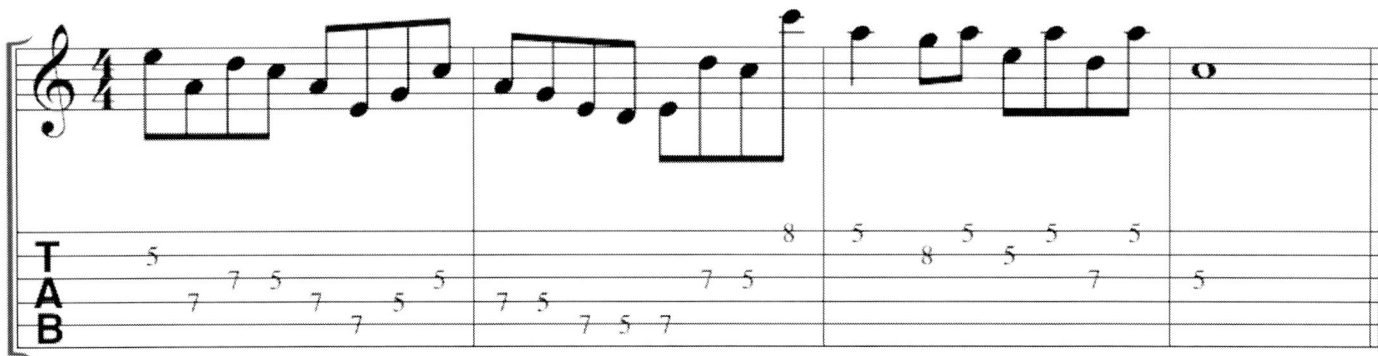

Minor Pentatonic Lick 7:

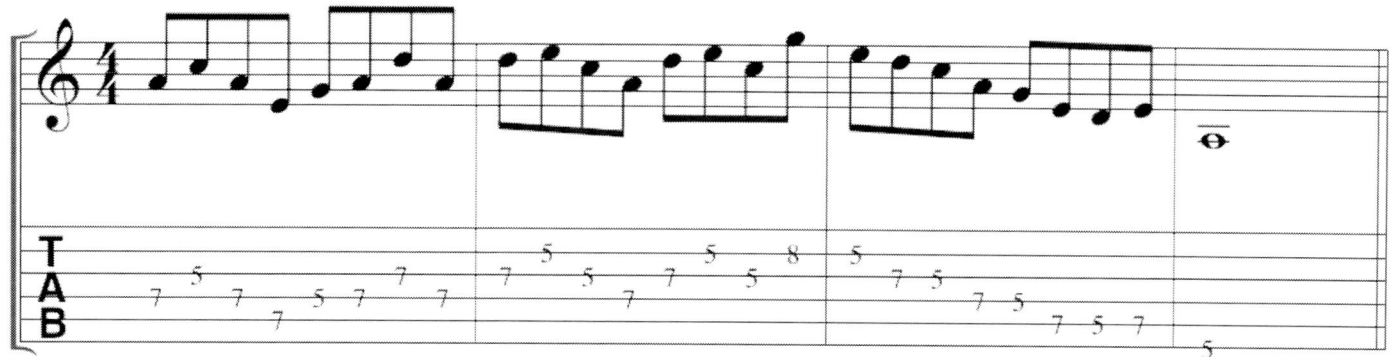

Minor Pentatonic Lick 8:

Minor Pentatonic Lick 9:

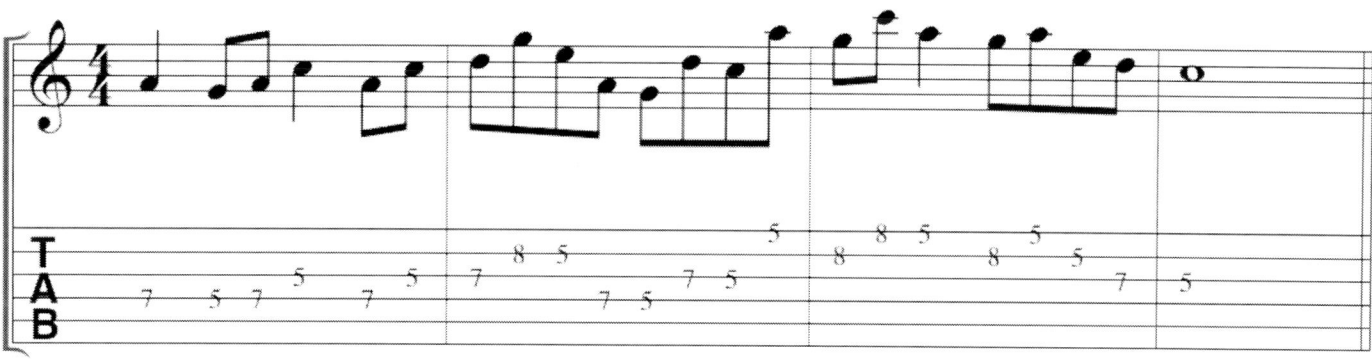

Minor Pentatonic Lick 10:

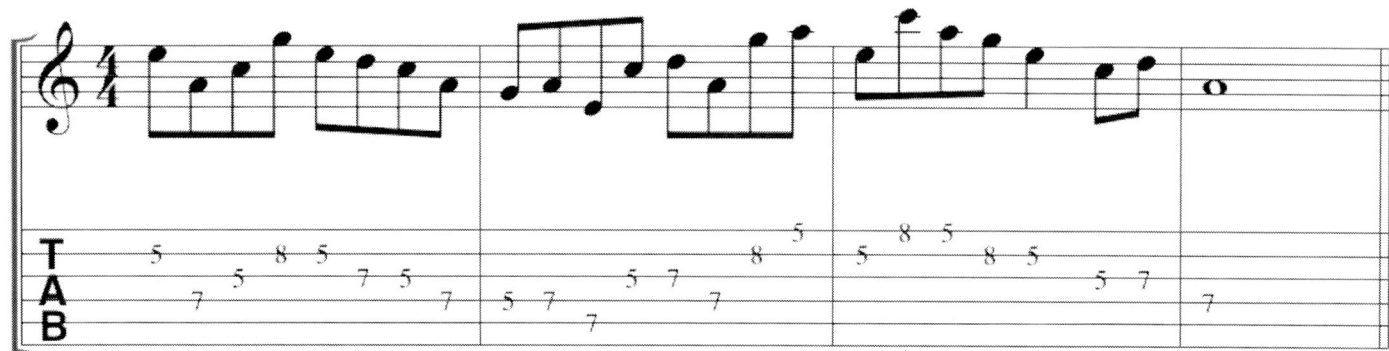

Minor Pentatonic Lick 11:

Once you can play these example licks comfortably, try experimenting with the scale and see what you can find. You'll notice that lots of very common melodic devices will naturally emerge from the scale, major or minor. Further into the book, we'll be looking at some interesting ways to super-impose the pentatonic scale. For the time being, there's plenty of down-to-earth melodic material to be discovered from it.

The scale-tone pattern doesn't work on the pentatonic scale (not enough notes) but all the other scale patterns that you'll learn about in following chapters will apply directly to it. The resulting melodic material is very common guitar soloing material. Make sure to tab out any scale patterns that you learn, using both the major and minor pentatonic scales.

Another thing worth mentioning is that each of these licks will work in most of the 5 available pentatonic scale positions. Experiment with each of these licks in other positions. When you hit a position that doesn't quite accommodate the particular lick that you're working with, see if you can devise a way to slide into the next available position to reach the notes that lie outside the box. Some of these positions will require you to move either the whole lick or part of it up or down an octave. If you spend plenty of time with these licks in this fashion, you'll wind up with a very strong pentatonic vocabulary.

RHYTHM – part 3: Other Simple Time Signatures

Up to this point, all musical examples have been written in a 4/4 time signature. That is to say that all measures of music have been four quarter notes long. Rhythms in 4/4 sound very natural because four is so easily divisible. While music grouped in fours is rhythmically the most natural, it's not the only common rhythmic canvas, so to speak.

3/4

3/4, or three quarter notes per measure is also a common time signature. If you've ever danced a waltz or even saw someone waltzing on TV, then you've heard music in 3/4. Happy Birthday and Silent Night are both in 3/4. So is Blood Brothers by Iron Maiden to give you an idea about the broadness of its application. A basic 3/4 count goes follows: 1 & 2 & 3 & 1 & 2 & 3 & etc.

3/4 Rhythms

6/8

This is another common time signature. It has sixth eighth notes per measure. You may be thinking to yourself that six 8th notes and three quarter notes would leave you with measures of the same length. Good job if you were, because it's true! So, what's the difference between 3/4 and 6/8 time signatures? It's how they are divided and grouped. 3/4 is divided in twos and grouped in threes whereas 6/8 is the opposite. It's divided into threes and grouped in twos. 6/8 has only two dotted quarter-note beats per measure. A dotted quarter note divides into three eighth. Your basic 6/8 count goes 1 & a, 2 & a, 1 & a, 2 & a etc with each note being of equal length.

6/8 Rhythms

9/8

This time signature is probably the least simple of the "simple" time signatures. Nonetheless, it classifies as simple because it's equally grouped and divided. 9/8 is both divided and grouped in threes. That's three dotted quarter notes per measure, each one dividing into three eighth notes. It's three groups of three. The basic 9/8 count goes 1 and a 2 and a 3 and a 1 & a, 2 & a, 3 & a, etc.

9/8 Rhythms

12/8

12/8 is simple and bouncy. It has four dotted quarter note beats. Each beat divides into three eighth notes. Its count goes like so: 1 & a, 2 & a, 3 & a, 4 & a, 1 & a, 2 & a, 3 & a, 4 & a, etc. It sounds the same as 6/8 but sometimes 12/8 is easier for writing purposes.

12/8 Rhythms

Essential Techniques

In this section, we're going to look at some different techniques common to guitar playing, some of which are of a very practical nature and will help you immensely in being able to tackle much of the melodic material within this book. Some of these techniques, such as string-bending, hammer-ons, etc are intended for you to apply at will to the material within the book. In this way, you can shape yourself stylistically in a completely different way than someone else who studies and practices out of this very same book. I have no interest in shaping your style. My only interest is in informing the reader.

Finger Rolling

This is a technique that applies to situations where you have a string of notes all on one fret, moving from string to string. Upon ascending it simply entails beginning on the very tip of your finger for the first note in the sequence and then rolling on to the pad of your finger for the following string. Upon descending it's a little more challenging because you have to start on the right part of the pad of your finger in order to land on the very tip of your finger when you roll over.

Your only other options in this situation are to 1: bar the notes and wind up with overlapping notes (sounding more like a chord), 2: hop on one finger and get a very broken effect with little gaps between the notes or use a series of different fingers and wind up out of position just in time for whatever follows. This technique allows you to play a smooth, legato string of notes on one fret.

With your first, second and third fingers, you should be able to roll across three strings, at least. That's three notes with one finger, each note with a separate part of the finger. With your 4th finger, you'll probably only be able to roll across a couple strings. It will take some practice to get comfortable with it and you may even find it to be especially difficult at first but I can assure you, from the experience of the hundreds of people whom I've taught this technique, everybody eventually gets comfortable with it.

Below is a pentatonic lick that you can use as an exercise. It will help you grow accustomed to this technique.

Rolling Pentatonic Lick, Ascending:

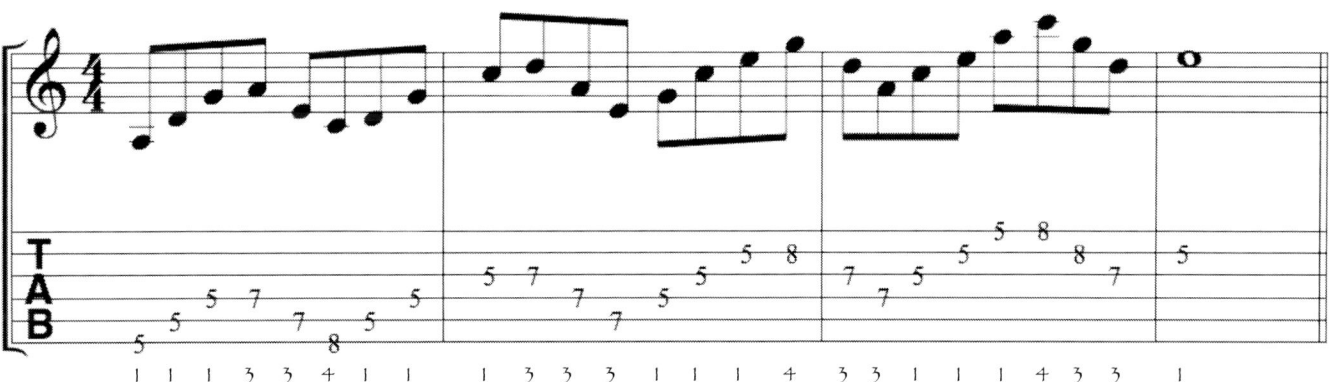

Rolling Pentatonic Lick, Descending:

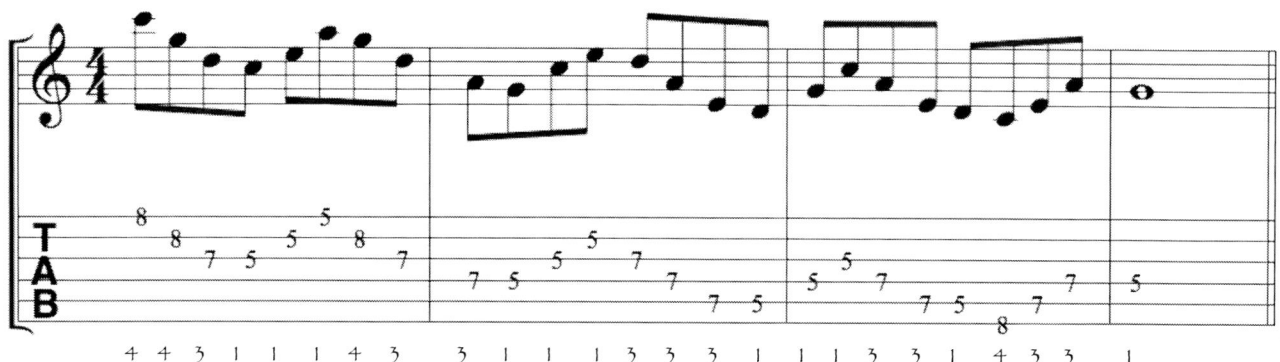

Sweep Picking

This technique is very handy for any run where you play one note per string, moving in either direction. The idea is very simple. Play multiple notes within one picking motion, allowing your pick to follow through to the next string. We use down-strokes for ascending notes and up-strokes for descending notes. The actual physical act tends to take people a great deal of practice until they can do it with any degree of ease. The practice is certainly worth it. Having a strong sweeping ability will allow you to play some very rapid strings of notes with very little effort and with a smooth and graceful sound. The exercise below is the same as the previous exercise, this time with picking indications set up to allow us to sweep at every given opportunity. The fingering is the same as the previous exercise.

Rolling Pentatonic Lick with Sweep Picking, Ascending:

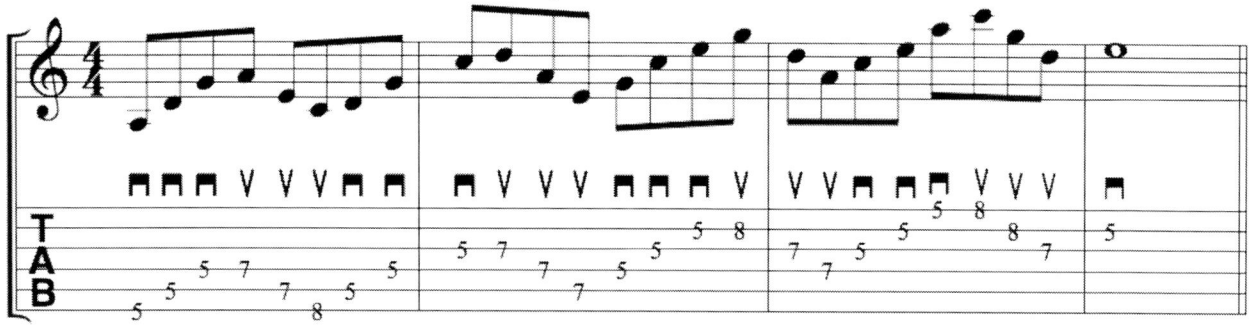

Rolling Pentatonic Lick with Sweep Picking, Descending:

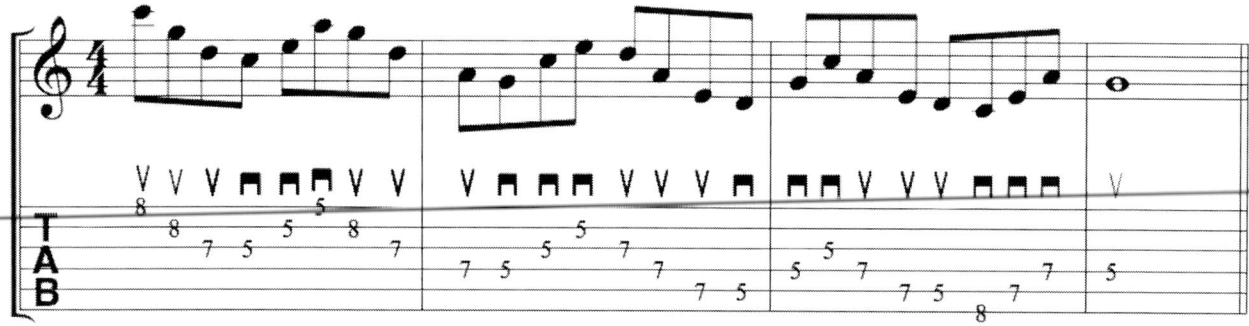

Economy Picking

This is a cross between traditional alternate picking and sweep picking. The idea is to alternate pick on any given string but to follow the pick through to the next string upon changing strings. In terms of basic ascending and descending, you use any odd number of notes per string in order to continue in your current direction and use any even number of notes on a string in order to switch directions.

Below are some economy picking exercises that will help you develop this skill. I can't stress enough how important it is to practice things like this at a very slow tempo, preferably to a metronome. Build the speed very slowly and you will minimize mistakes, which is good, since mistakes can easily become habits. Pay close attention to the picking indications.

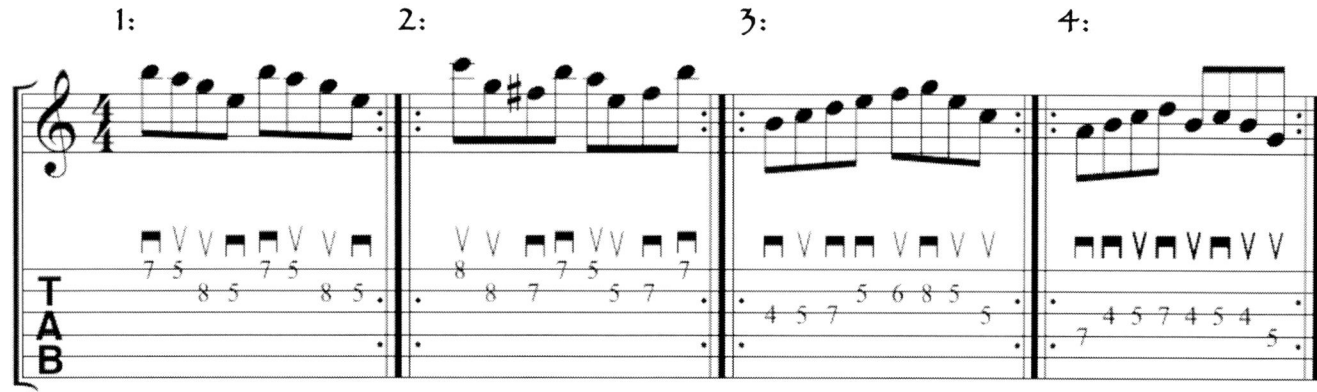

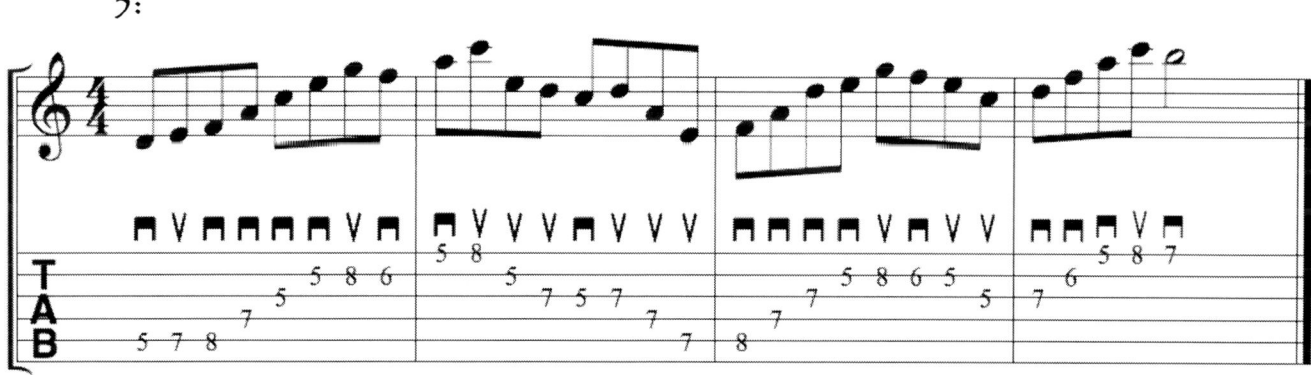

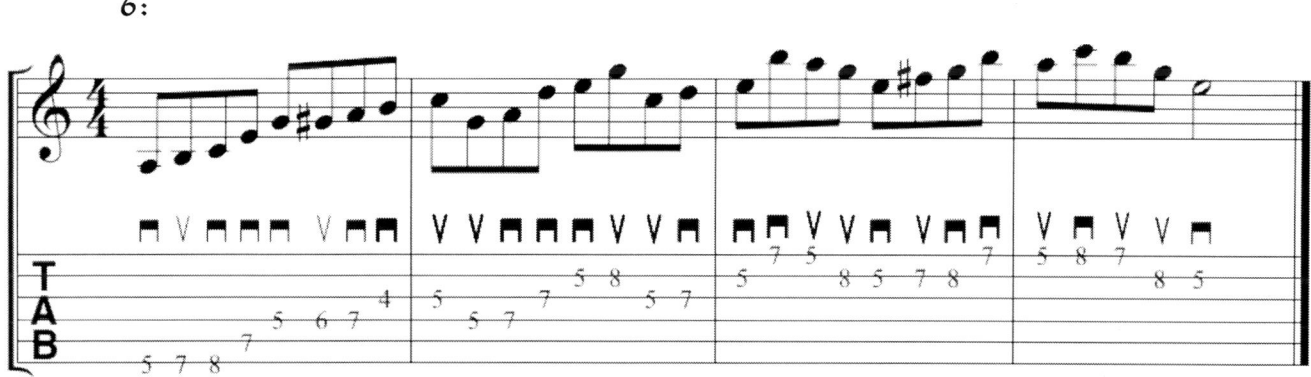

Hammer-Ons and Pull-Offs

A hammer-on occurs when you pick a note and then while the note is still ringing, hammer your finger down onto a higher note on that same string, without picking a second time. This higher, second note has a slightly smoother and softer sound to it than the previous, picked note. It creates a variety of tone to the overall phrase, and it also saves your picking hand a trip. In order get the second note to ring loudly enough, you need to bring your hammering finger down with plenty of force. You can also hammer on to any note from an open string.

A pull-off is the reverse of a hammer-on. This occurs when you pick a higher note, with a larger finger waiting on a fret beneath and then pulling your smaller finger away with some resistance to reveal and sound the lower note, without picking again. You can also pull off with any finger, to an open string.

The exercise below provides hammer-ons and pull-offs in half-step, whole-step, 1½-step and 2-step intervals. It's important to practice both of these techniques with all pairs of fretting fingers. For this exercise, use fingers one and two for your half steps, fingers one and three for your whole steps, with fingers one and four for the larger steps.

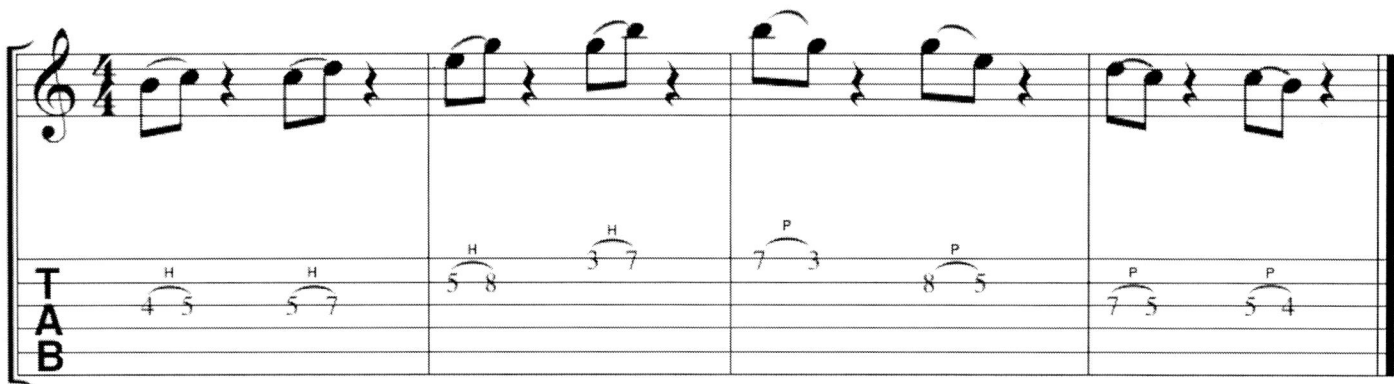

This exercise incorporates multiple hammer-ons and pull-offs to create one smooth legato phrase. Since you're only picking twice per measure, it's easily playable in downstrokes. Start slow and build speed.

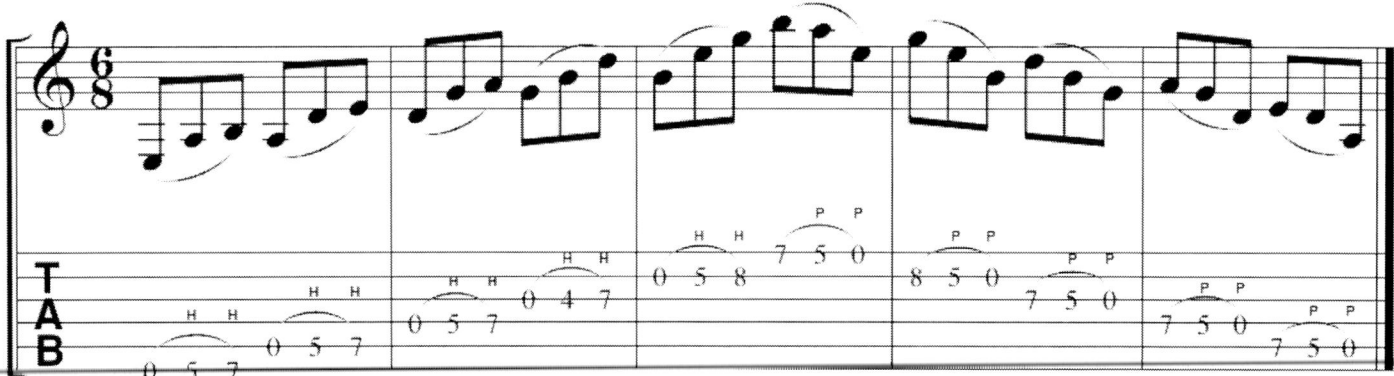

String Bending

Bending or string bending is just what it sounds like it would be. You pick a fretted note and while it's ringing, bend the string in order to tighten it, therefore, raising the pitch of the note. The most common bends are half step and whole step bends, although they can be narrower (quarter step) or wider (1½ steps or more). This requires you to build up some finger strength and a lot of muscle memory.

I would advise practicing half step and whole step bends, using your first, second and third fingers. To do this effectively, start by sliding a note up one or two frets, depending on which type of bend you're working on. While you have this sound fresh in your ears, go back to the note you slid from and try to bend up to the same pitch. Repeat this process until you effortlessly execute this bends with a stunning rate of accuracy. This will take ten of practice hours at the least.

Let's look at some common types of string bends. The light grey numbers on the TAB staff indicate the pitch that you're aiming for with your bent note. The first bend is a garden-variety whole-step bend. The second bend is known as a downward bend, also known as a pre-bend-release. This is achieved, by bending the string and holding it in place, before picking it. You begin to release the note after picking. This takes some serious muscle memory to know that you've got the string bent to the right point before sounding the note. In this case the number in parenthesis is the fret that you're actually fingering. The preceding number is the fret that it sounds like before you release it. Different people notate this differently and this is a common one but not universal.

The third bend is known as a unison bend. Simply hold the higher note in place with your first finger, while pressing the lower note down with your third finger. As soon as you pick the two notes together, bend the lower note to where it's pitch matches the other note. The final bend being a partial chord bend, AKA harmony bend, which is the same concept, except that the note your higher string isn't the same note as the one your bend.

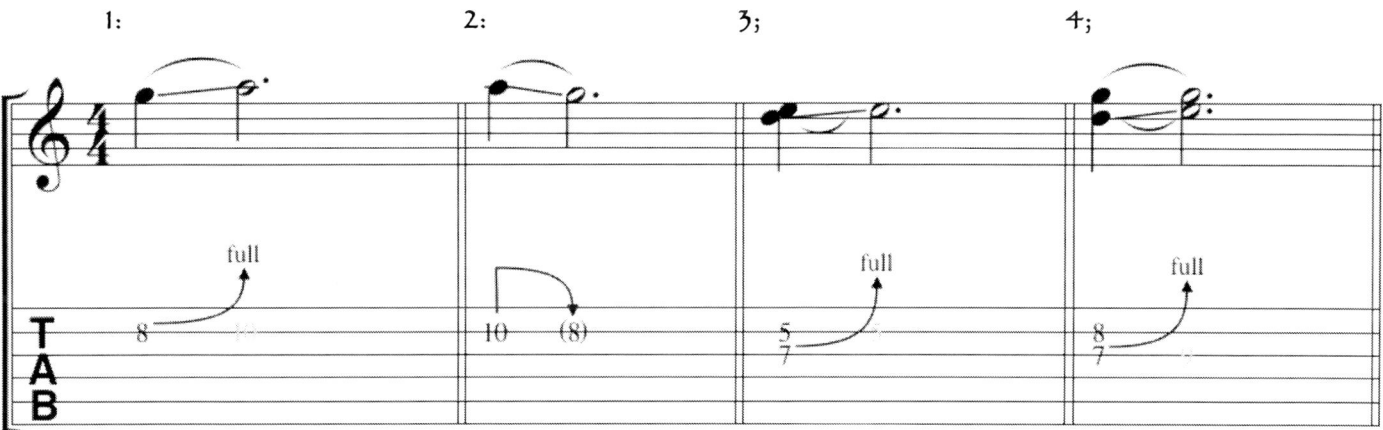

Some Words On the Following Examples

One thing that commonly causes confusion among newer players is the mistake of thinking of a bend as it were one note that been bent. Physically speaking, of course it's true, but sheer mechanics matter very little to the listener. (Unless they're a big guitar nerd!) The only thing that ultimately matters is how it sounds to the ear. When the ear hears a bend, it registers as two notes that have been joined. Number 5 illustrates clearly (in the real staff) how the ear hears it. When playing a bend written in this fashion, make sure to treat both the note that you're bending from and the note that you're bending towards as their own eighth notes.

An exception to this is shown in number 6. This type of bend employs a grace note. Notice the itty bitty note that has an upward stem with a slash through it. A grace note can be put anywhere in a measure with out subtracting from the available rhythmic space because it's only sounded for a tiny fraction of the length of the measure's shortest note. Whatever time that *is* taken up by the grace note is simply borrowed from the previous or following note and if it's a well executed grace note, it will be hard to tell from which side you're borrowing. The grace note bend can clearly be seen in the TAB staff where the bend curve is much steeper than that of number 5.

Number 7 employs a half-step bend. One thing to bear in mind is that there are few things in life that sound worse than an over-shot half-step bend. Try and make it sound as exact (pitch-wise) as if you were sliding up a fret. This one also employs a release following the bend. It's a really good idea to get in the habit of using your picking hand palm to keep the extra strings quiet because in order to release the bend, (especially whole-step bends) you're fingers will "unstick" from the strings physically above the string that you're bending.

Number 8 has a very vocal effect. You start off in position for a half-step pre-bend. Remember, the 6th fret F is the sound. The 5th fret note in parenthesis is the fret that you're playing. For this example, you only need to pick the very first and very last.

Before proceeding to the rest of these examples, make sure to be mindful of bend distances and directions, and rhythmic content of each one. Also, don't forget about muting unused stings out with your palm.

Half-Step Bending Licks

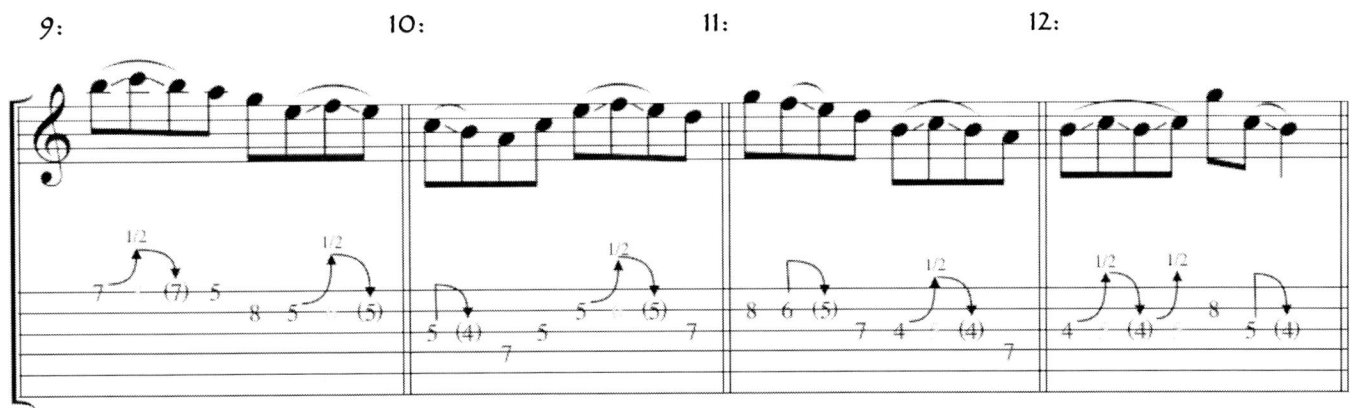
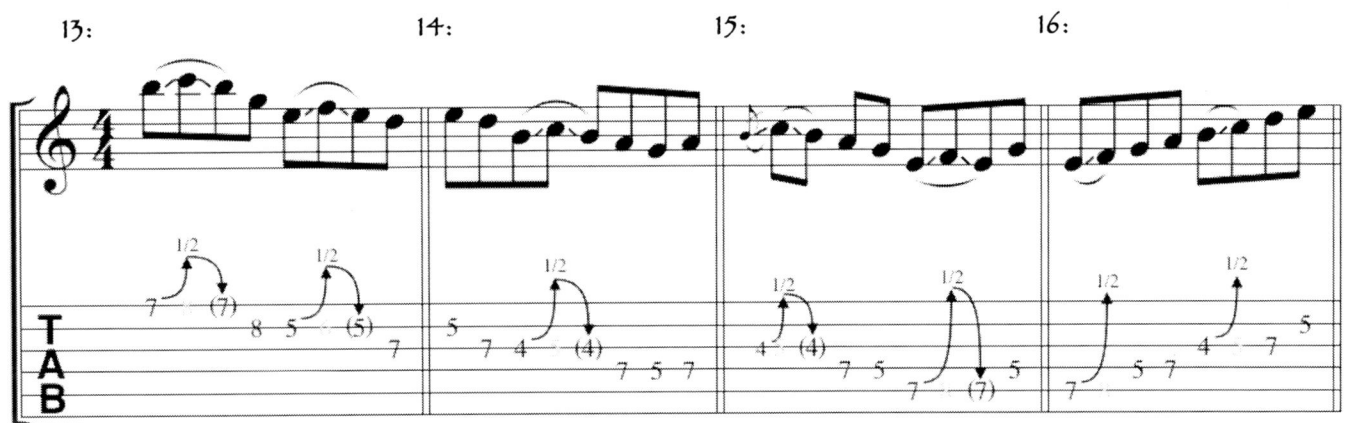
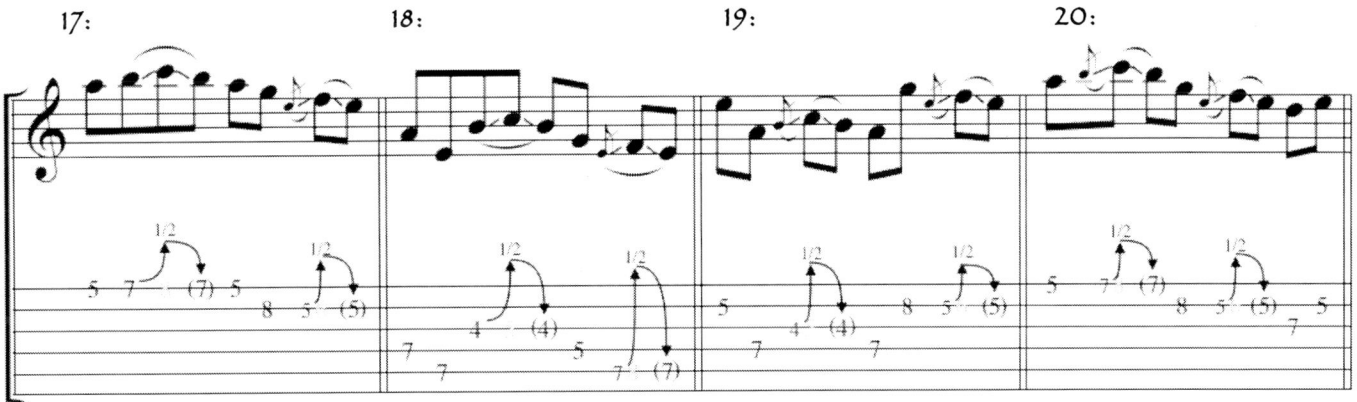

Whole-Step Bending Licks

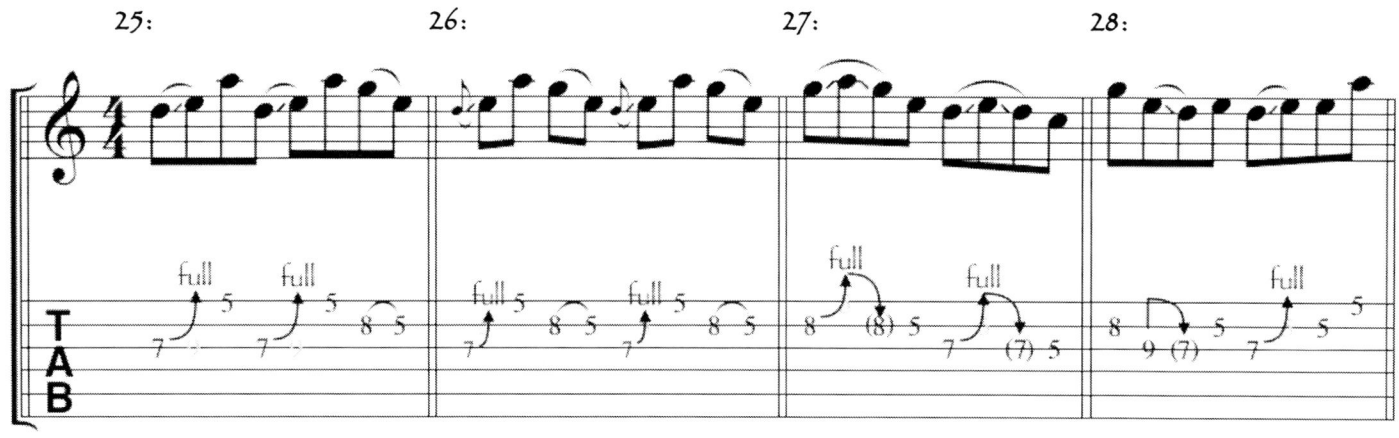

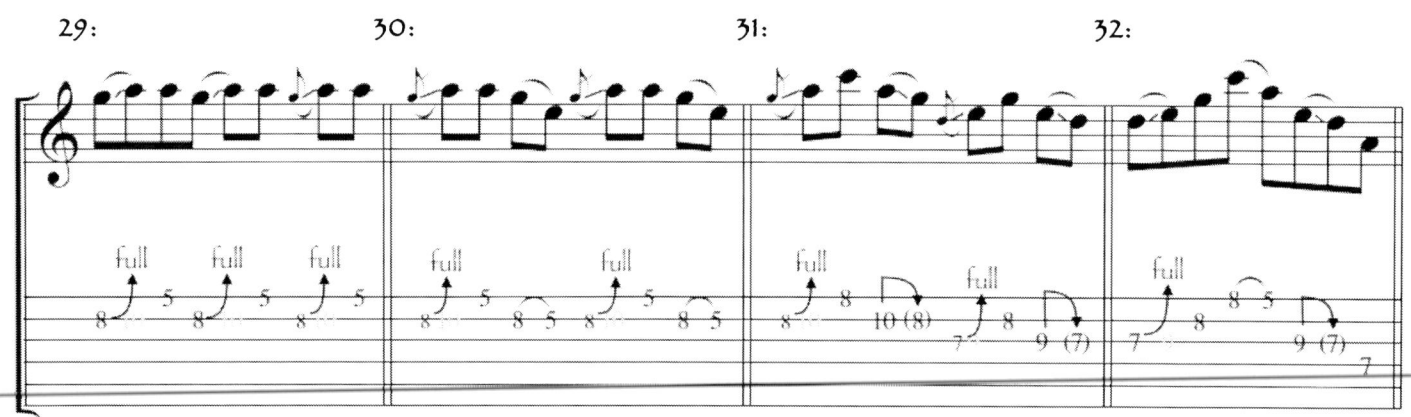

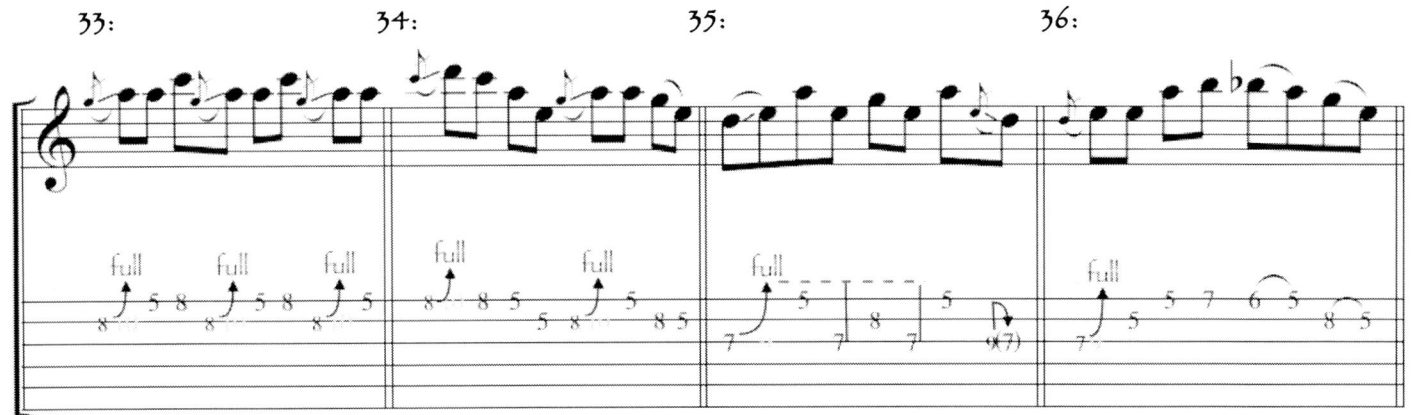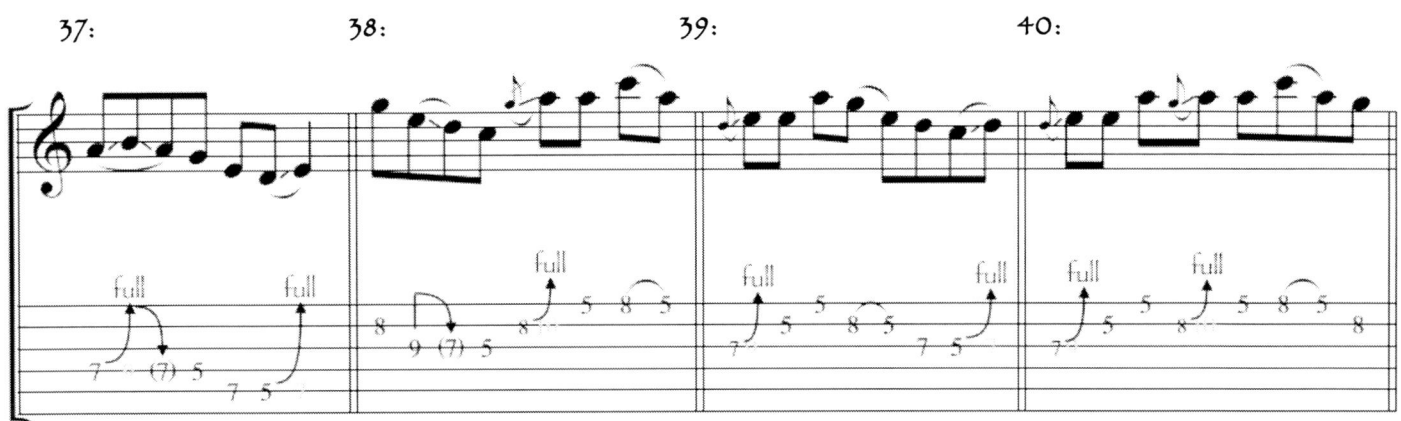

Combined Examples:

Example Phrase 1: This one starts with a very commonly used pattern and moves towards a less typical ending. Make sure not to take too long on these grace-note bends. You should hardly hear the note from which you're bending.

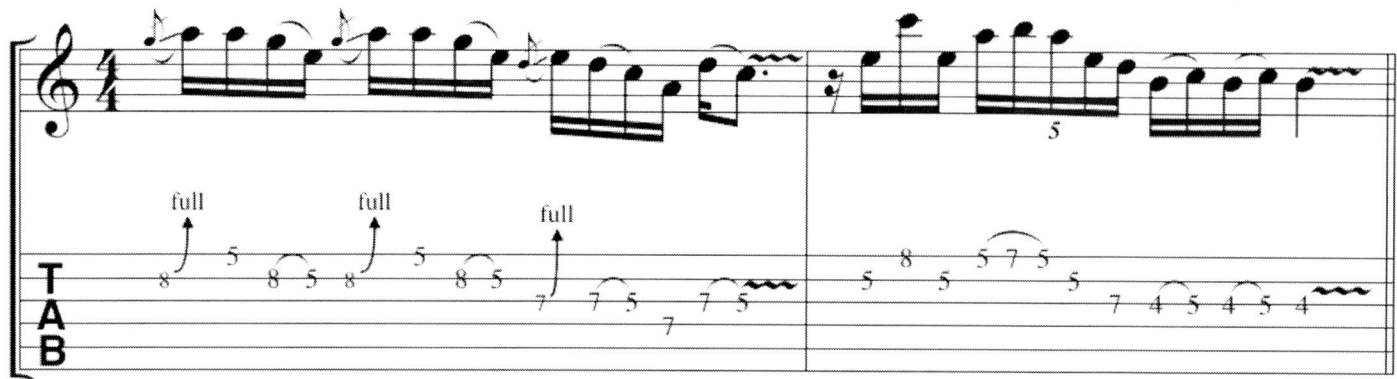

Example Phrase 2: This phrase really straddles the line between blues and pop in its style of melodic delivery. This one could be tricky on the rhythmic side of things so make sure to differentiate grace-note bends from the 16th-note bends. If your last note isn't landing on the beat, then you went wrong somewhere.

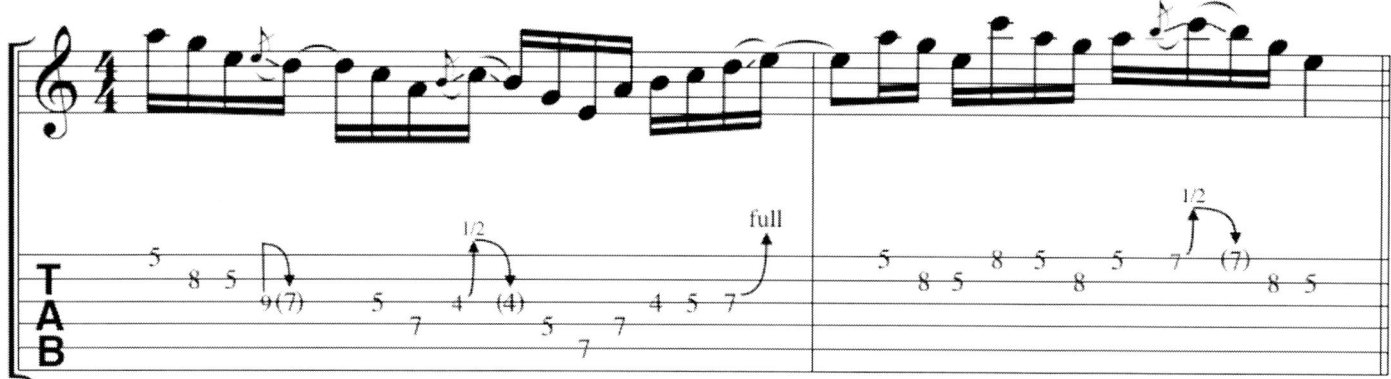

Example Phrase 3: This is a solid little line that has a good blend of elements. The advice that was given in relation to Example 2 remains valuable for this lick.

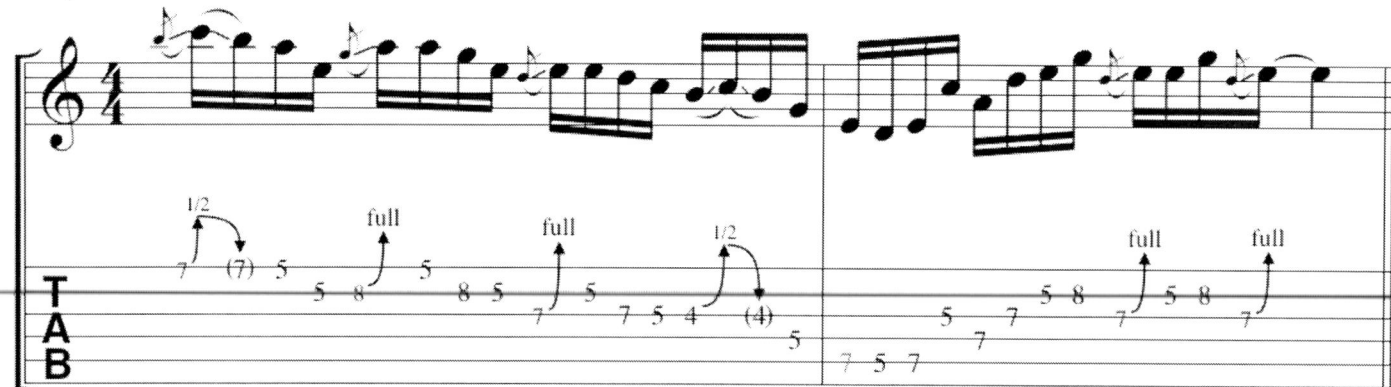

Example Phrase 4: There are a couple of challenging things happening in this particular run. The first of which is the whole step bend from C on the high E-string up to D and back down. As you get used to string bending this may sound simple enough but for whatever reason, these whole-step bend and release maneuvers can prove difficult to sound nice and clean. It's worth the effort to spend a lot of time getting this to sound right because it sounds awful to fall a little short on this particular bend, from the b3rd to the 4th, in a minor mode.

The next obstacle comes one beat later when you bend your B-string G up a whole-step and while holding that one in place, you're grabbing your high E string C with your pinky and pulling it off to where you just pre-positioned your index finger, at the 5th fret.

The other big challenge is another b3rd to 4th bend, this time an octave lower. Due to the position we're working in, this one proves more challenging because you're left with one option and that's to bend the note with your index finger. When you're bending with this finger, it has to go it alone, without the reinforcement of an extra finger or two. If you cramp up while working on this one, you should take a short break and shake your left hand. This will assure that you don't do any muscle damage to your hand.

Example Phrase 5: This lick illustrates some of the techniques used in country string bending licks. In a lot of cases, the bent note will be used as a pedal tone. (A pedal tone is a pitch that is frequently returned to between the other notes in the melody) When coupled with the use of downward bends, this gives the guitar a certain capability to take on characteristics of a pedal-steel. The dotted lines here indicate where you want to hold the bent note in place and pick it in between the other notes.

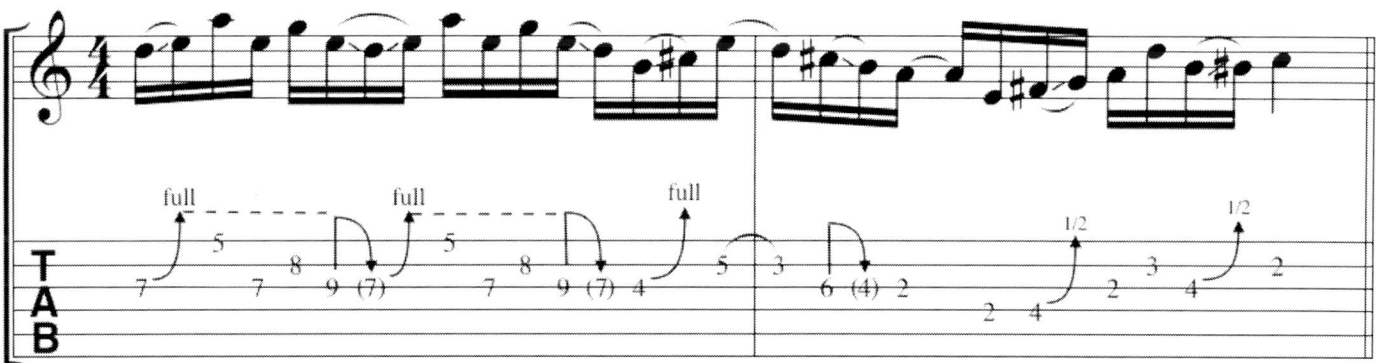

CHORD PROGRESSIONS – part 2: Diatonic Chord Substitution

We've talked about I-IV-V progressions, which do make up a lot of music that we hear but not all of it. The next step is to look at how we can take the basic I-IV-V progressions that you've learned to build and substitute the original chords with the VIm, IIm and IIIm chords. This adds a whole new layer of depth to our chord progressions because we're now working with both bright and dark shades. The substitution principle is pretty simple.

Let's refer back to our color diagram from Diatonic Harmony – part 1, this time without the color names:

IV:	F	A	C			I:	C	E	G			V:	G	B	D	F	
	VI:	A	C	E			III:	E	G	B			II:	D	F	A	
		I:	C	E	G			V:	G	B	D			IV:	F	A	C

Do you remember how each major chord shared two notes in common with the minor chord two steps away, in either direction? Well, it's true, with the exception of the V chord. Two notes above the V chord lies the VIIdim triad. For that reason, and because the V chord is so commonly extended to its 7th (Root 3rd 5th 7th), we can use the IIm as a substitution above the V. With all the other chords, it's simply a matter of two chords, two notes apart, sharing the majority of their notes in common and therefore work easily as substitutions.

This diagram puts it in pretty clear terms.

Lower Substitution	Original Chord	Upper Substitution
VIm	←I→	IIIm
IIm	←IV→	VIm
IIIm	←V→	IIm

OK, great! So that's the concept. Let's put it to some musical use. The graph below starts with the most basic I-IV-V progression I could muster in the top row. The following rows illustrate some possible derivative progressions. I arrived at these simply by picking and choosing which chords to replace and which substitutions to use. This barely scratches the surface of possibility but notice how different of an effect the progression has by the time we get to the end of this short little list.

Diatonic Substitutions

Original	I	I	IV	V
Alternate 1	I	IIIm	IV	V
Alternate 2	I	VIm	VI	V
Alternate 3	I	VIm	IIm	V
Alternate 4	VIm	IIIm	VIm	V
Alternate 5	IIIm	VIm	IIm	V

I've decided to get a little more in-depth and present a wider range of substitution possibilities on a longer, two-phrase progression, complete with some descriptions of the logic used and the effects achieved as a result. These progressions can be played in a style or any multitude of styles, time signatures and tempos that suit your own personal taste. You can also employ any chord voicings that you already know on any of these progressions. You'll want to revisit these progressions when you learn more chord voicings and arpeggios.

Original: A very simple progression built from the primary colors of harmony, made up of two phrases. The effect is one of a question being asked in bar 1, followed by a more urgent question being asked in bar 2, and finally, an answer being stated in bars 3 and 4.

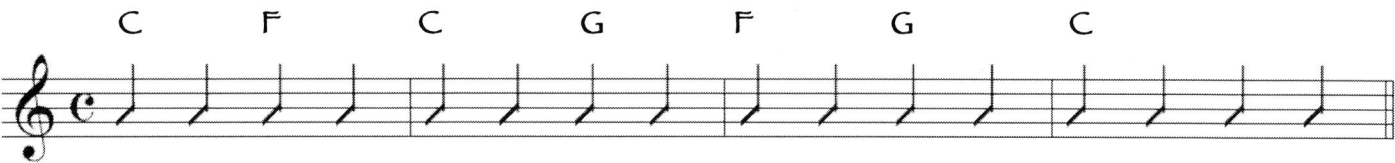

Variation 1: Here, we replace a couple I chords with VIm chords, resulting in a notable difference in mood. The progression seems to have taken on more depth and a broader range of emotional qualities. However, bear in mind that the tempos and rhythms ultimately associated with a progression will dramatically alter its emotional content.

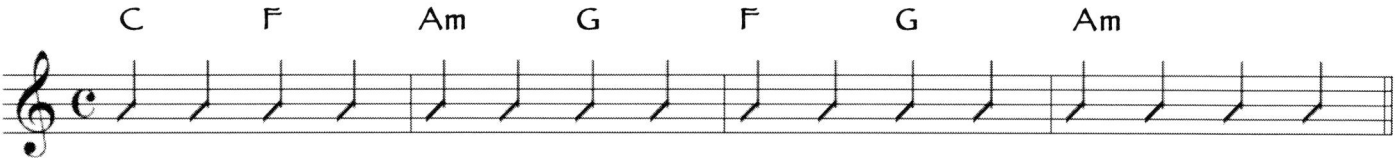

Variation 2: In this one, the final chord is changed to a IIIm, which gives us a useful non-resolving phrase. The IIIm chord and its corresponding mode are greatly associated with mystery in most cultures, worldwide. The IIIm seems to covey a deeper kind of pondering than that which the V conveys.

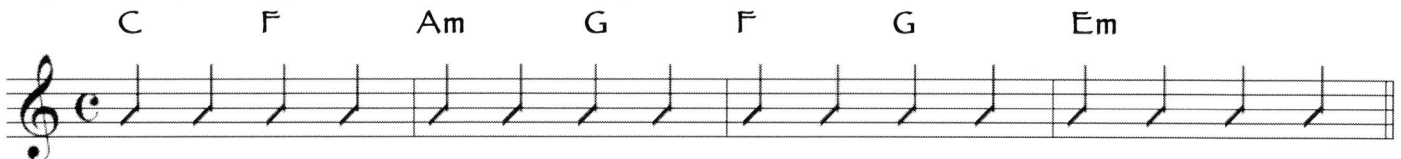

Variation 3: This one ends with the ever-affirmative classic IIm-V-I phrase. You'll soon be learning why this change flows in such a natural manner. For now, you can at least be assured that it doesn't have anything to do with mere convention. IIm-V-I has been predictable since the dawn of vibration.

Variation 4: The IIIm-IV-I at the beginning of this one has a very pleasing effect and the VIm at the end is a somber subversion of our ear's expectations. The reason for this is the aforementioned natural tendency of IIm-V to lead us to the I chord.

Variation 5: This one leans heavily to the A minor tonality. It's worth noting here that I have yet to replace the second I chord with a IIIm. This isn't by accident. The change from IIIm to V is one of my personal least favorite harmonic movements. It seems to serve as a dud and is only occasionally used, and merely tolerated by the listener.

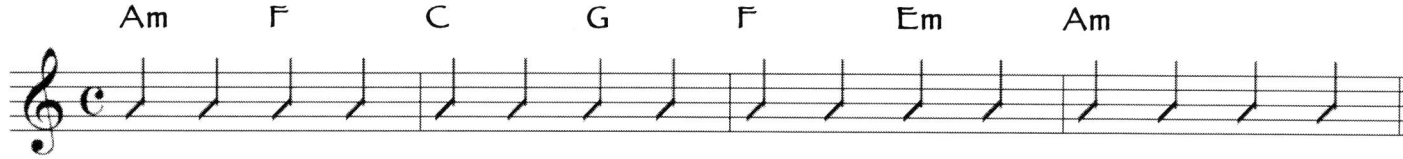

Variation 6: The effect of starting far off in minor territory and working toward a big bright major end creates a really pleasing effect. This progression could be thought of as an A natural minor IVm-Vm-Im followed by a C major IV-V-I, with the G serving as a bridging chord. This is similar to the workings of a pivot chord, which we'll be discussing further in.

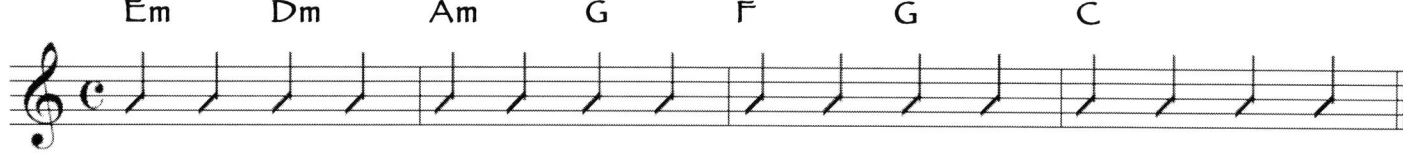

Variation 7: This progression gives the ears a strikingly different type of effect, due to an entirely different harmonic rhythm. This was achieved by using one chord suited to replace two differing chords in each measure. Another thing that makes this one sound far off from our original idea is that it consists entirely of minor chords, which were not at all present in the original.

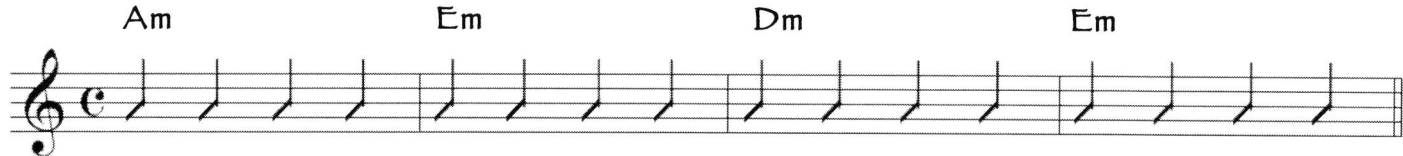

Variation 8: Here is another possible harmonic rhythm scheme that we could achieve by the same basic means as the previous variation. In this case we achieve two phrases of equal rhythmic value. It has a melancholy sound to it as both rhythmic resting points happen to be minor chords.

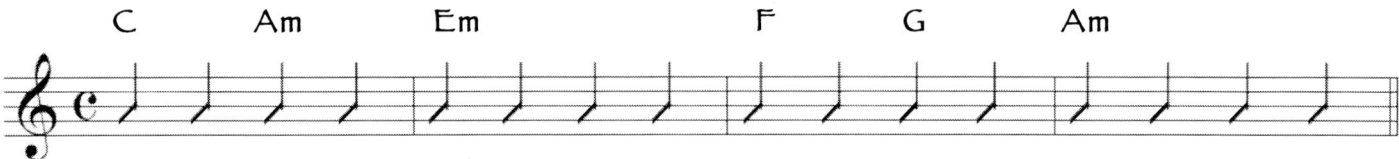

Variation 9: In this next example, we achieve a measure and a half of a VIm chord which seems to make the 2-beat V chord seem shorter than it otherwise would. The resulting harmonic rhythm has a very nice effect to it. In turn, it serves as a very common harmonic rhythm in most styles, modern and ancient.

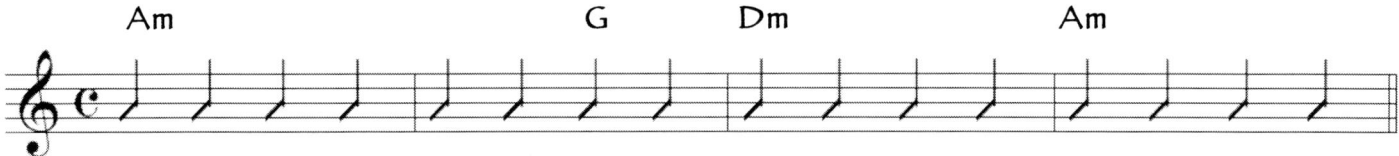

Variation 10: This variation has some serious ascending tendencies. The truth is that every progression can be arranged with voicings that would send it in either direction. But as a result of the stepwise motion of each of the first two measures and the continuous stepwise motion of the final two bars, it would take some hard work to send these chord changes downward.

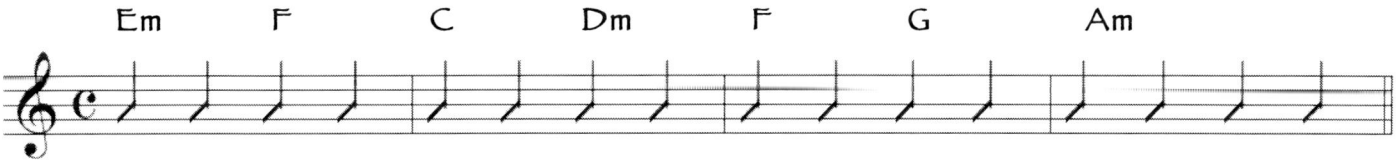

Variation 11: The palendromic nature of this harmonic rhythm seems to have a meaningful effect. This variation is another one that ends with the "pondering of mystery" offered by the IIIm chord.

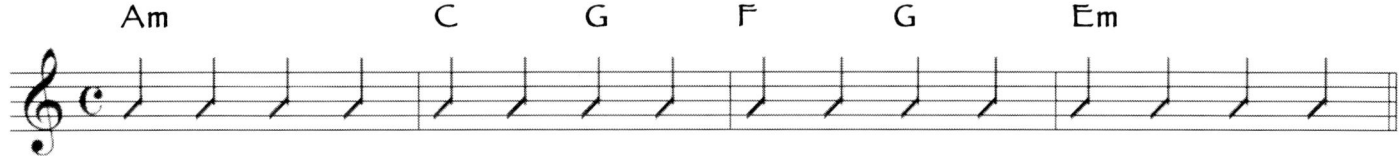

Variation 12: This final variation starts with some drama but is neatly sealed at the end with our original IV-V-I.

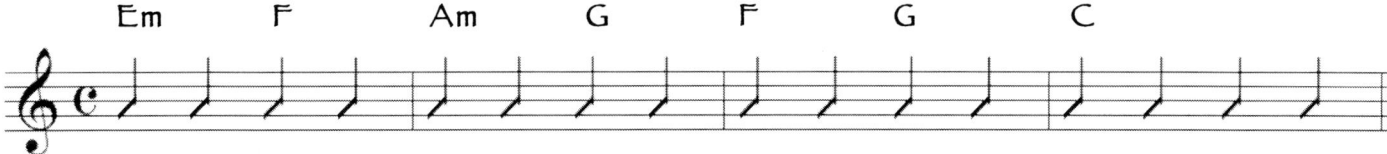

MELODIC PATTERNS – part 1

So far we've only discussed one melodic pattern. It's what I call the scale-tone pattern. It will be a useful pattern for getting to know any seven-note scale or mode and the functions of its scale-tones. The musical application of this pattern, however, is limited. The benefit of most melodic patterns is their rather limitless musical application. In other words: they can really beef up your improvising vocabulary as well as your compositional arsenal.

Here's an introduction to some common melodic patterns. Once you've learned these patterns move them to the other eleven keys. As you learn more scales and modes, apply these patterns to them in all positions. This task is best tackled on paper at first. It gets a lot of the thinking out of the way. When you're feeling ready to apply these patterns to other scales, photocopy a large stack of the blank tab and/or standard staff paper in the back of this book and transcribe them within evenly spaced measures, making sure to pay attention to the spacing of your notes.

Once you have them transcribed, spend some time finding your most sound choice of fingerings and then you're ready to practice that pattern scale without any hinderance. Be mindful of what scale tone you are on at ALL times. Otherwise you will be drilling mindlessly which will only earn you the ability to use this vocabulary blindly.

This first one is commonly called the changing tone pattern after the way every other note is approaching the next scale-tone in line. Ascending, in scale degrees, the pattern goes as follows.

R 3 2 4 3 5 4 6 5 7 6 R 7 2 R

For our purposes, we'll call it Basic Thirds because of the interval of a scalewise 3rd that exists between each group of two notes. We will be looking at some other thirds based patterns so the word basic will distinguish this one. I've taken a lot of time to closely examine how I finger these patterns and in the course of doing that, I learned some nice alternatives. I've written fingerings that work as a very solid four-finger strategy. The final position would work with a three-finger strategy in this particular key but my goal was to lay them out for universal use. I will leave it up to you to come up with your own three-finger strategies for application at higher (smaller) frets.

It should be said that these are fingerings that work well for me, with my particular hands and that we do all have different hands. I don't have very large hands and I've had large-handed students who do much better with fingerings that don't work for me. For this reason, I won't be bothering with a lot about fingerings for the rest of the book. By now, you should be capable of deciding on and sticking to a good fingering strategy for any material you practice.

With that said, on the following page is the pattern in all five positions of the C major/A minor scale with finger numbers provided beneath.

Basic Thirds In A Minor, 7th Position/C major, 5th Position, Ascending:

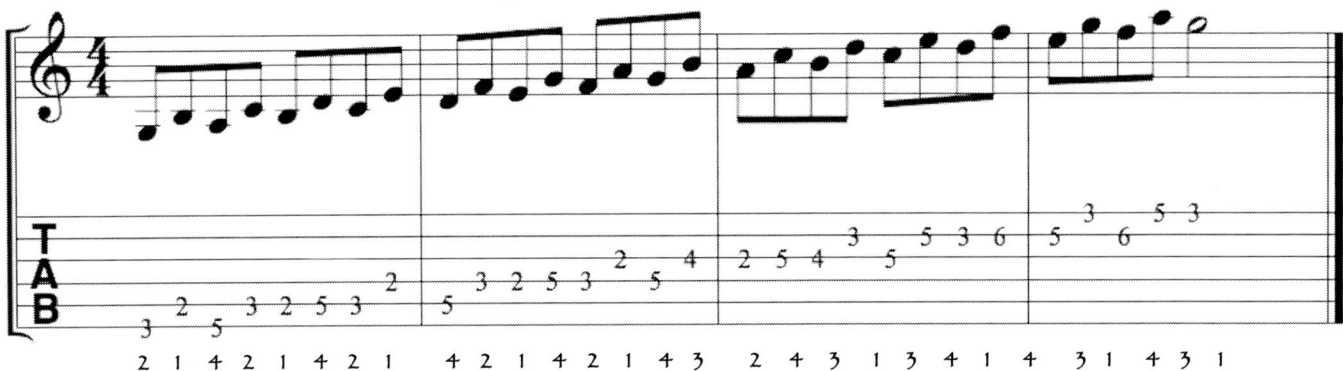

Basic Thirds In A Minor, 7th Position/C major, 5th Position, Descending:

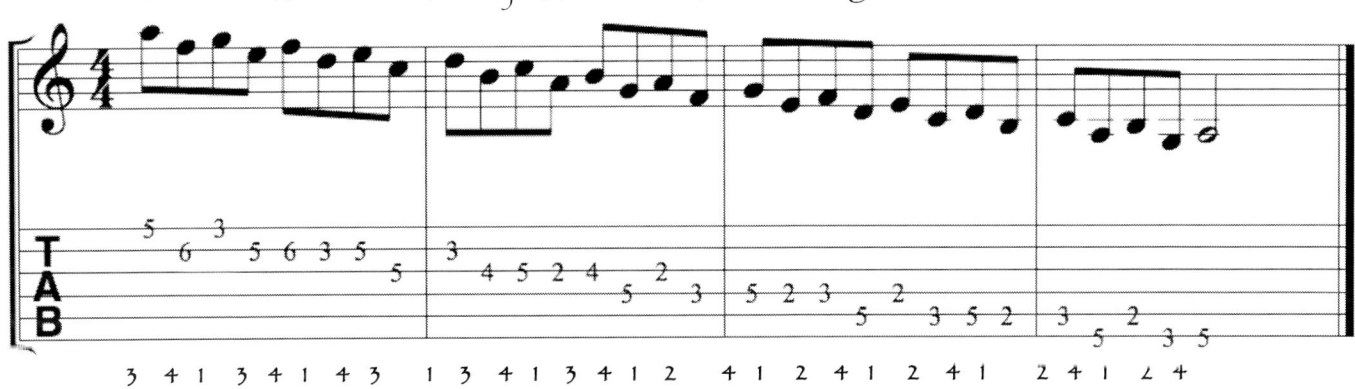

Basic Thirds In A Minor, Root Position/C major, 6th Position, Ascending:

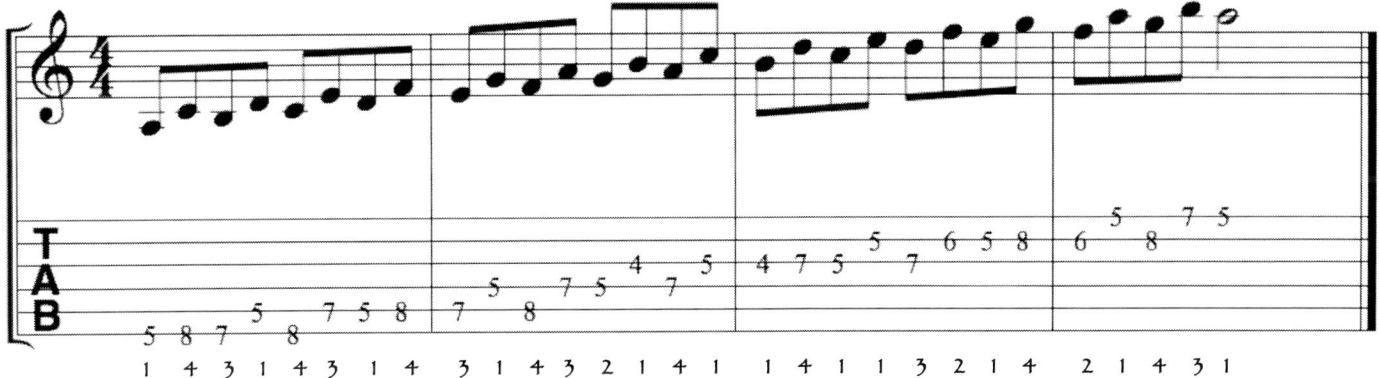

Basic Thirds In A Minor, Root Position/C major, 6th Position, Descending:

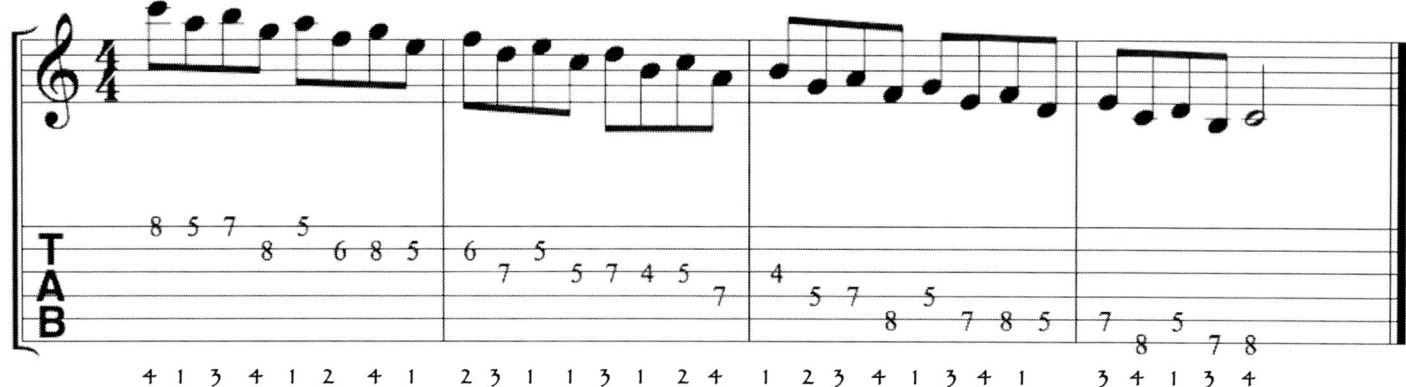

Basic Thirds In A Minor, 3rd Position/C major, Root Position, Ascending:

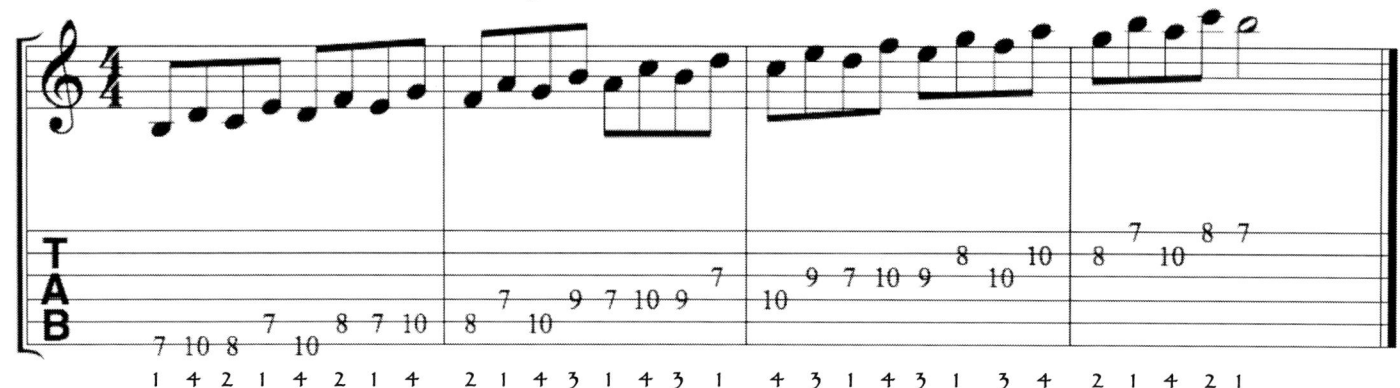

Basic Thirds In A Minor, 2nd Position/C major, Root Position, Descending:

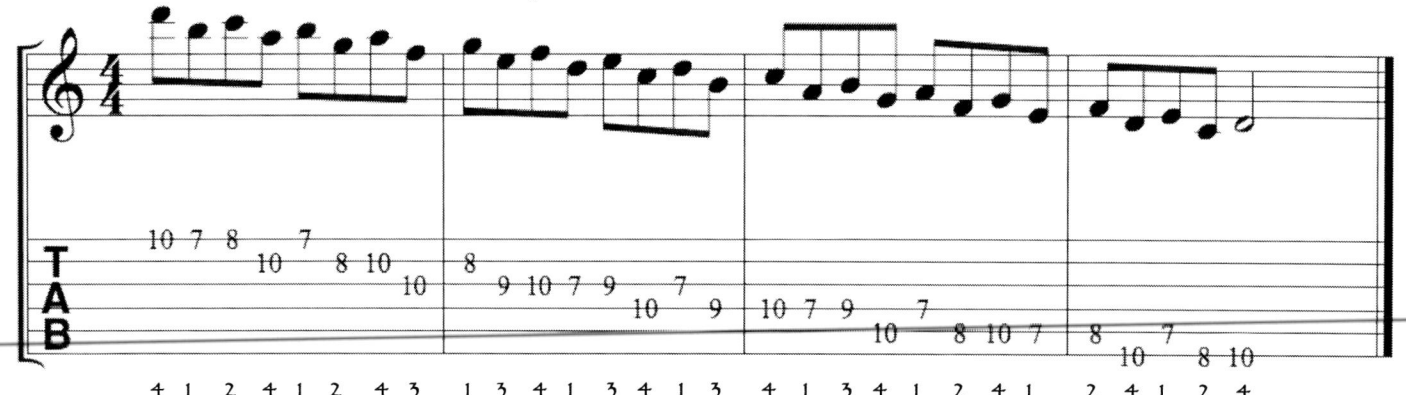

Basic Thirds In A Minor, 4th Position/C major, 2nd Position, Ascending:

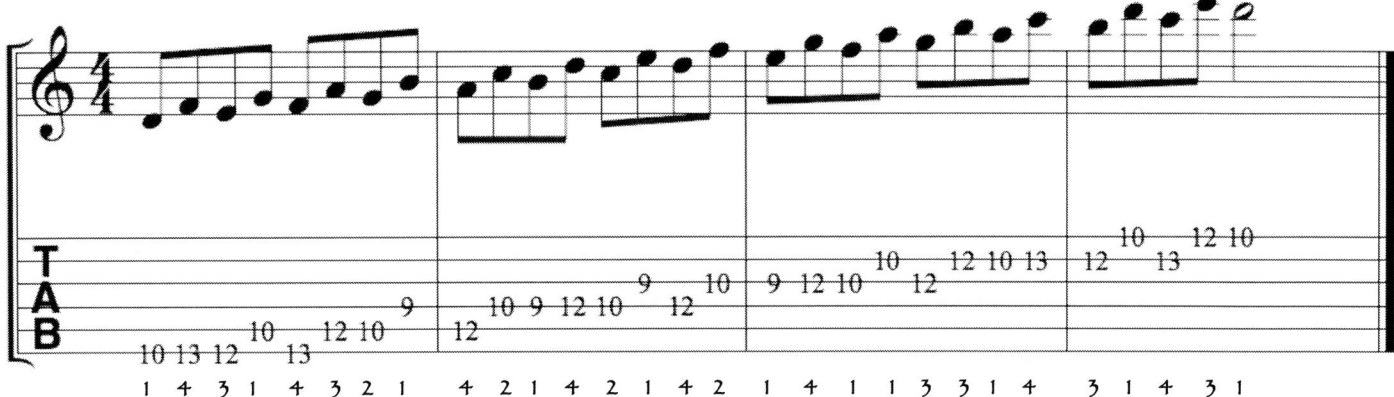

Basic Thirds In A Minor, 4th Position/C major, 2nd Position, Descending:

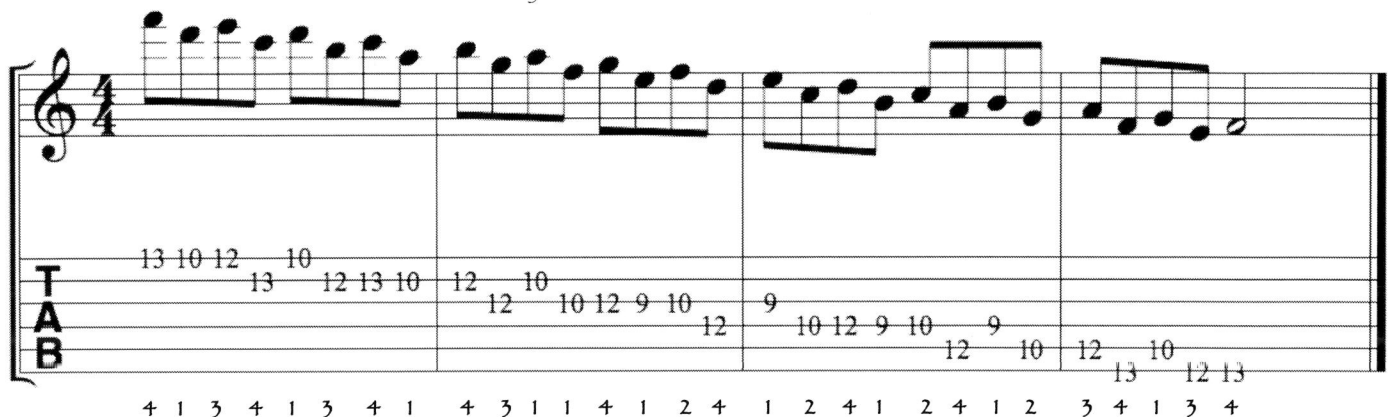

Basic Thirds In A Minor, 5th Position/C major, 3rd Position, Ascending:

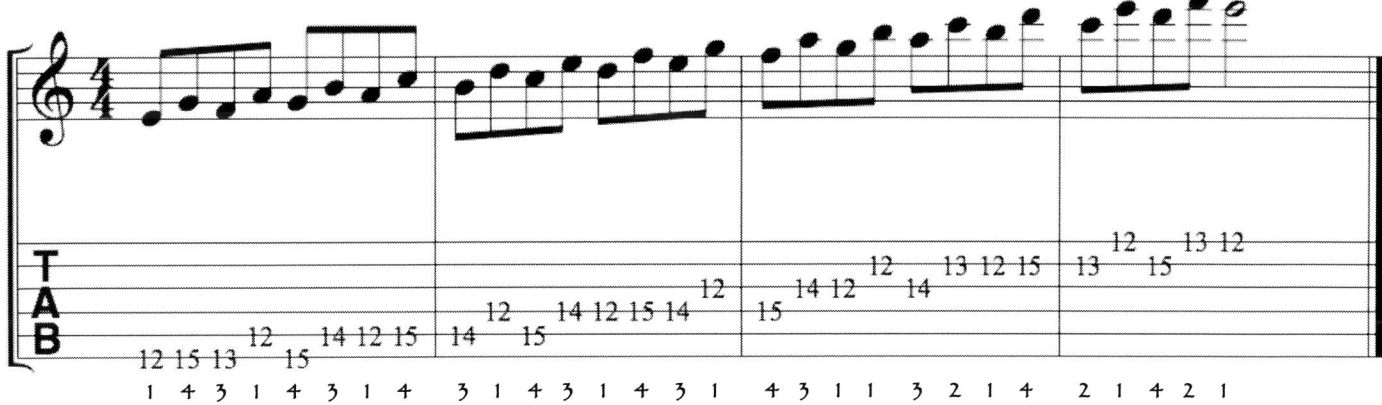

Basic Thirds In A Minor, 5th Position/C major, 3rd Position, Ascending:

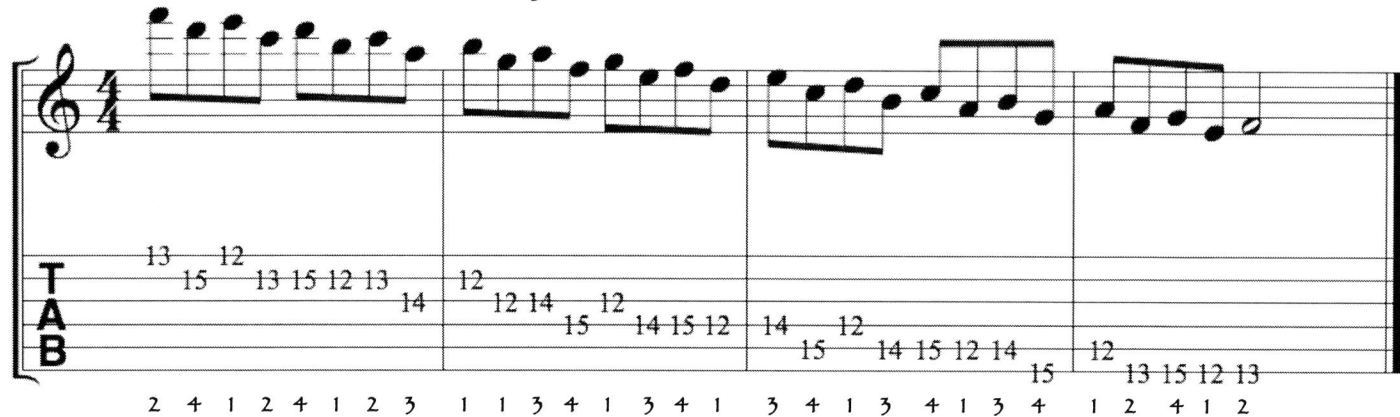

There's a simple method for pulling a new melodic pattern from this basic thirds pattern by flipping every other group backwards. This is what I call the weaving thirds pattern. Here it is in all five positions in the same key. This time you're on your own with the fingerings.

Weaving Thirds In A Minor, 7th Position/C major, 5th Position, Ascending:

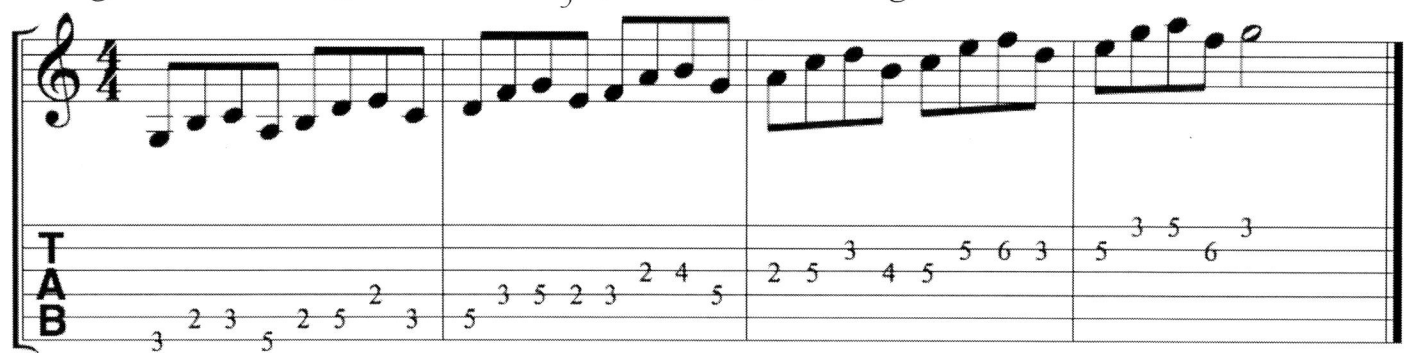

Weaving Thirds In A Minor, 7th Position/C major, 5th Position, Descending:

Weaving Thirds In A Minor, Root Position/C major, 6th Position, Ascending:

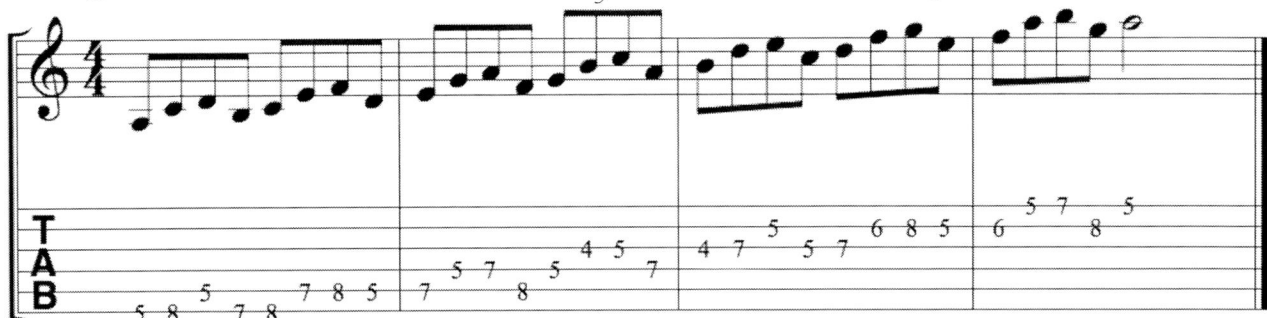

Weaving Thirds In A Minor, Root Position/C major, 6th Position, Descending:

Weaving Thirds In A Minor, 3rd Position/C major, Root Position, Ascending:

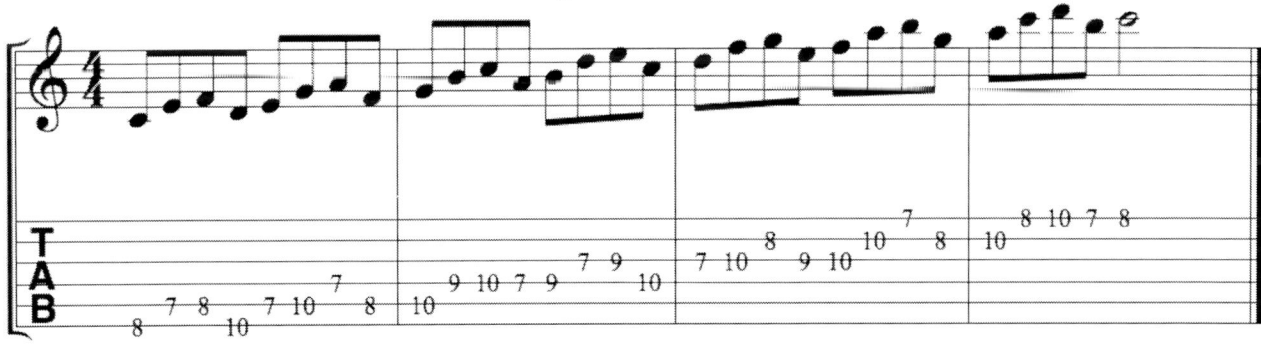

Weaving Thirds In A Minor, 3rd Position/C major, Root Position, Descending:

Weaving Thirds In A Minor, 4th Position/C major, 2nd Position, Ascending:

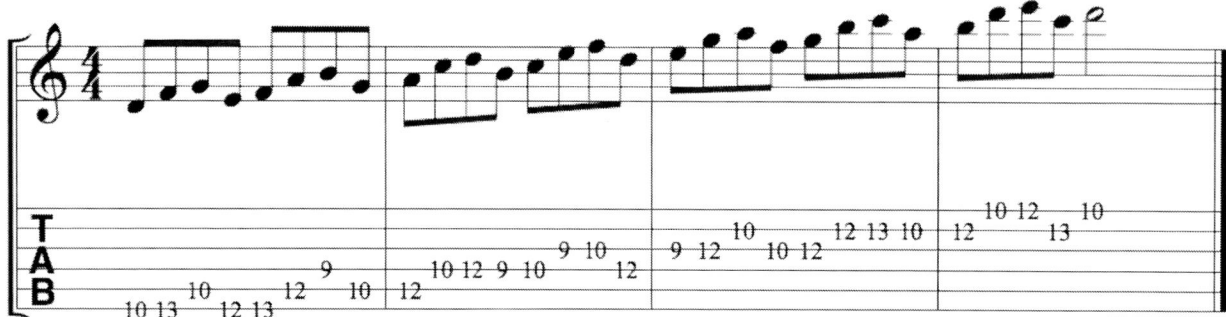

Weaving Thirds In A Minor, 4th Position/C major, 2nd Position, Descending:

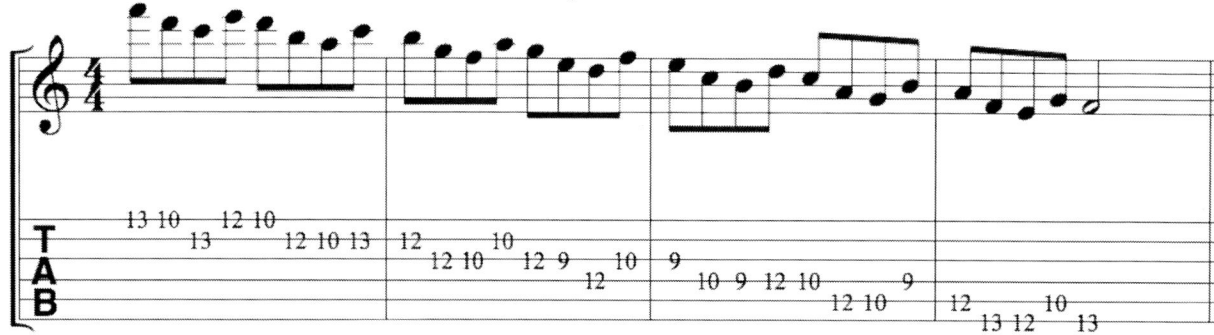

Weaving Thirds In A Minor, 5th Position/C major, 3rd Position, Ascending:

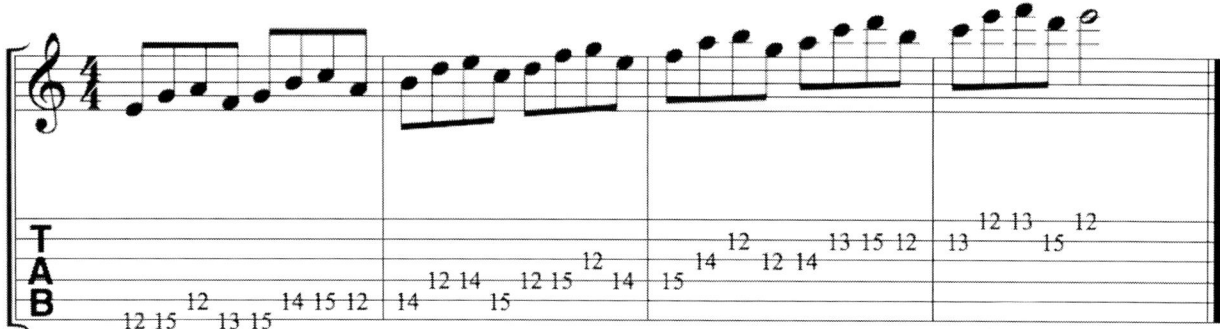

Weaving Thirds In A Minor, 5th Position/C major, 3rd Position, Descending:

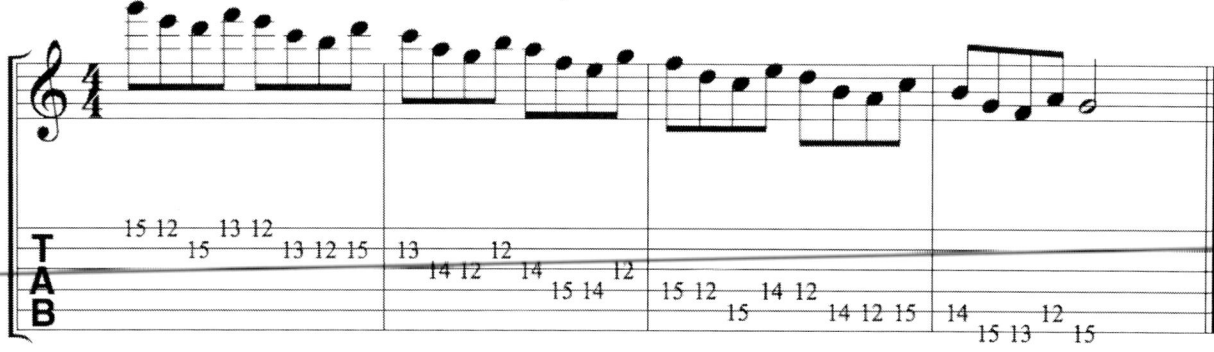

Another thing that we can do is take the basic thirds pattern, flip the first two notes and flip every other group of two from there. I call this the inverse weaving 3rds pattern. Here it is in all five positions:

Inverse Weaving Thirds In A Minor, 7th Position/C major, 5th Position, Ascending:

Inverse Weaving Thirds In A Minor, 7th Position/C major, 5th Position, Descending:

Inverse Weaving Thirds In A Minor, Root Position/C major, 6th Position, Ascending:

Inverse Weaving Thirds In A Minor, Root Position/C major, 6th Position, Descending:

Inverse Weaving Thirds In A Minor, 3rd Position/C major, Root Position, Ascending:

Inverse Weaving Thirds In A Minor, 3rd Position/C major, Root Position, Descending:

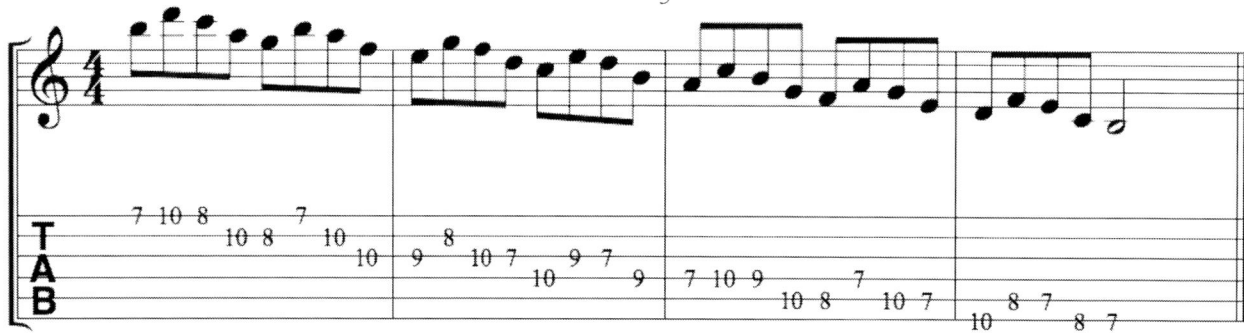

Inverse Weaving Thirds In A Minor, 4th Position/C major, 2nd Position, Ascending:

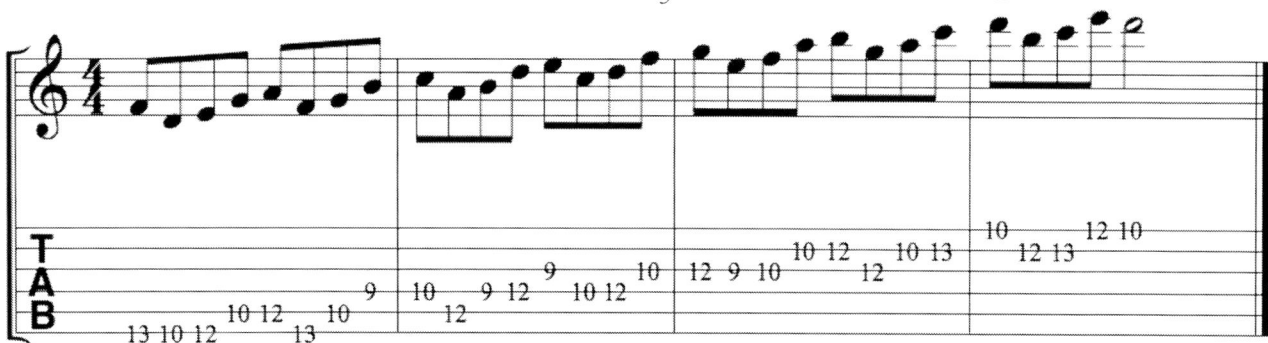

Inverse Weaving Thirds In A Minor, 4th Position/C major, 2nd Position, Descending:

Inverse Weaving Thirds In A Minor, 5th Position/C major, 3rd Position, Ascending:

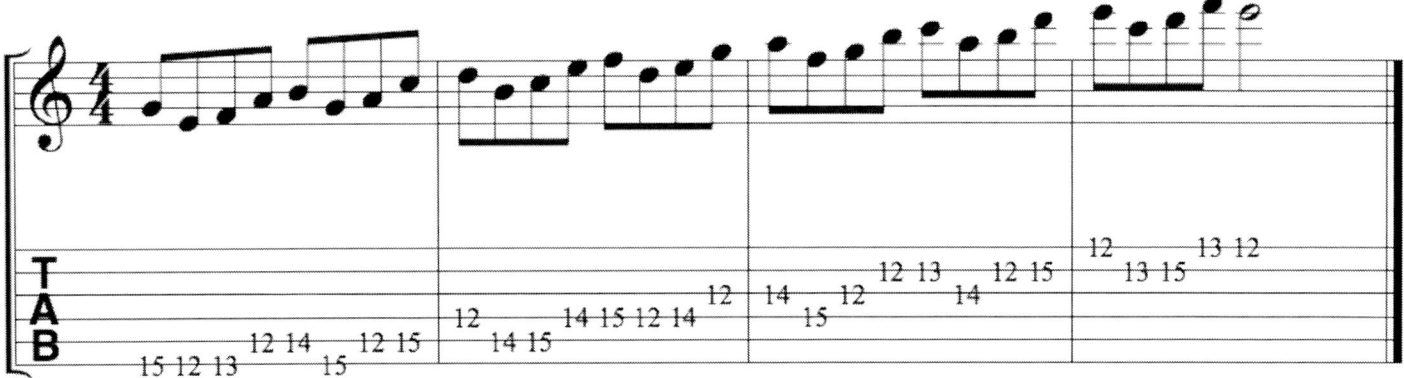

Inverse Weaving Thirds In A Minor, 5th Position/C major, 3rd Position, Ascending:

We can apply these same three modes of movement (basic, weaving and inverse weaving) to any diatonic interval. Here are the basic, weaving and inverse weaving 4ths, 5ths, 6ths and 7ths patterns in all five positions:

Basic Fourths In A Minor, 7th Position/C major, 5th Position, Ascending:

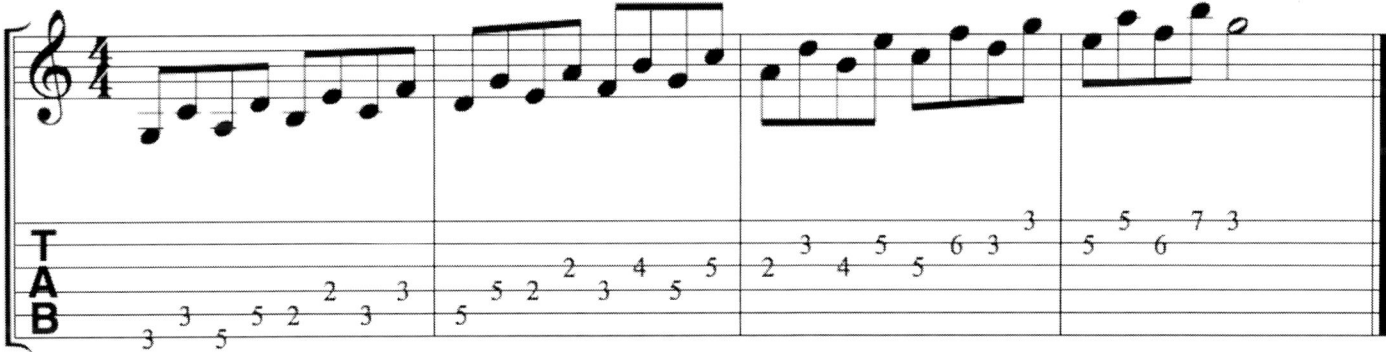

Basic Fourths In A Minor, 7th Position/C major, 5th Position, Descending:

Basic Fourths In A Minor, Root Position/C major, 6th Position, Ascending:

Basic Fourths In A Minor, Root Position/C major, 6th Position, Descending:

Basic Fourths In A Minor, 3rd Position/C major, Root Position, Ascending:

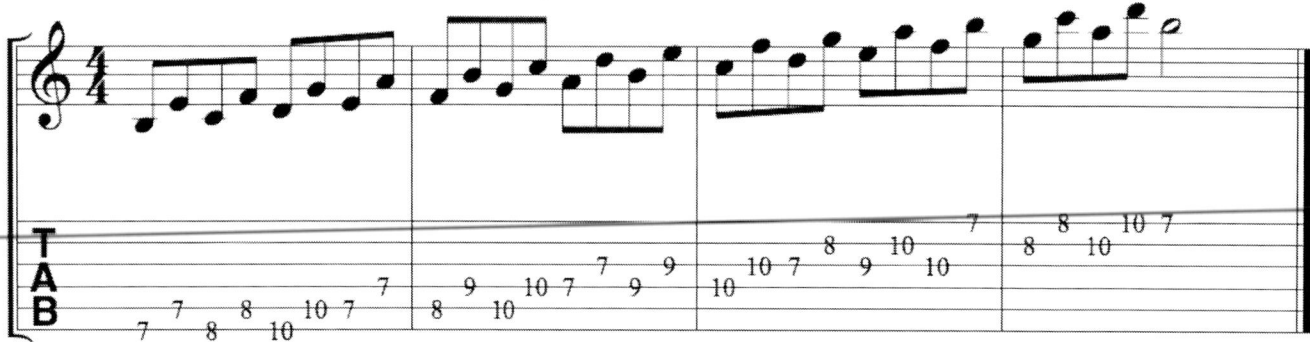

Basic Fourths In A Minor, 3rd Position/C major, Root Position, Descending:

Basic Fourths In A Minor, 4th Position/C major, 2nd Position, Ascending:

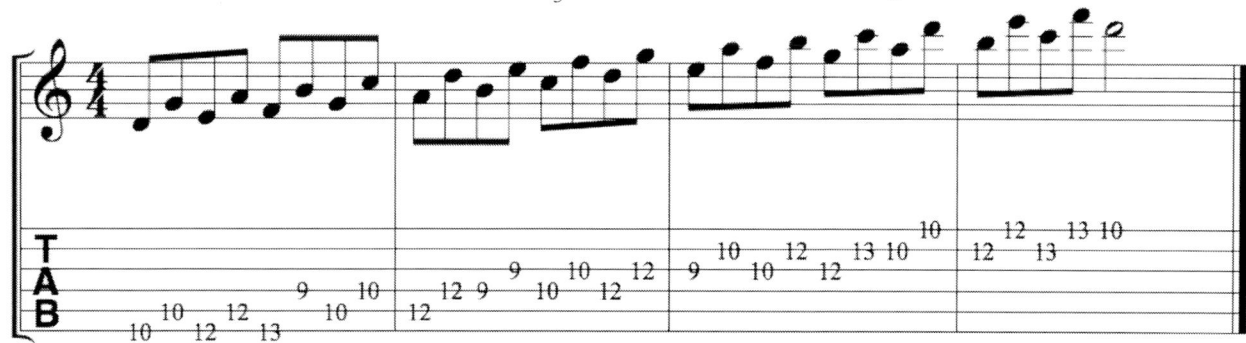

Basic Fourths In A Minor, 4th Position/C major, 2nd Position, Descending:

Basic Fourths In A Minor, 5th Position/C major, 3rd Position, Ascending:

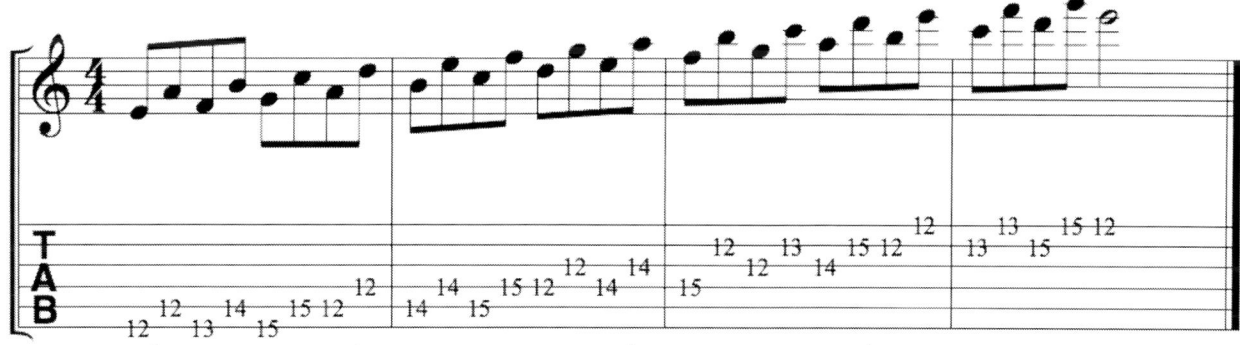

Basic Fourths In A Minor, 5th Position/C major, 3rd Position, Descending:

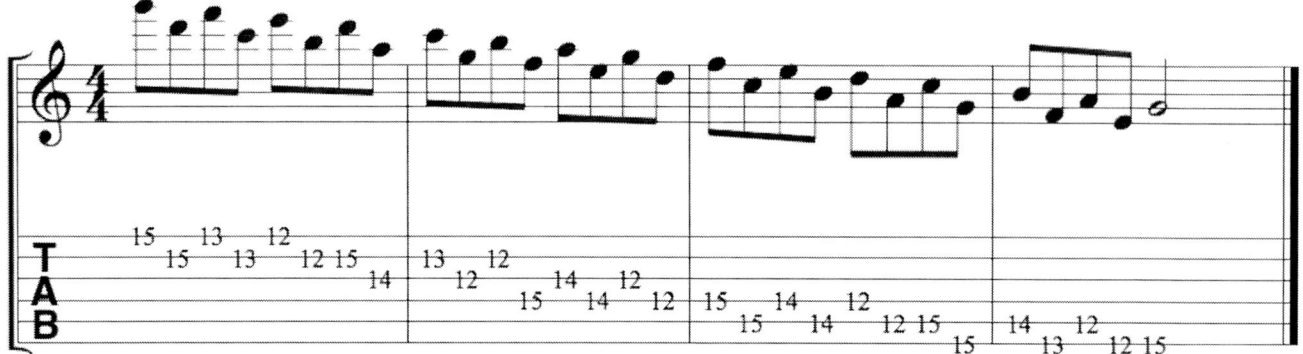

Weaving Fourths In A Minor, 7th Position/C major, 5th Position, Ascending:

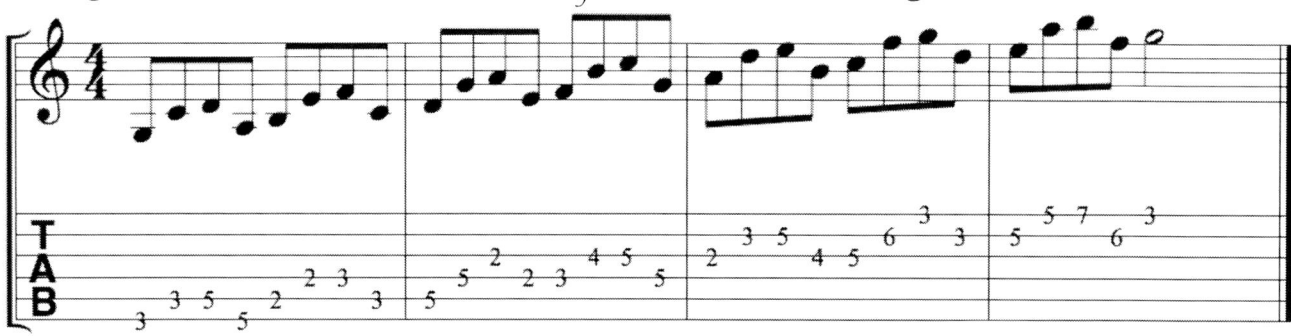

Weaving Fourths In A Minor, 7th Position/C major, 5th Position, Descending:

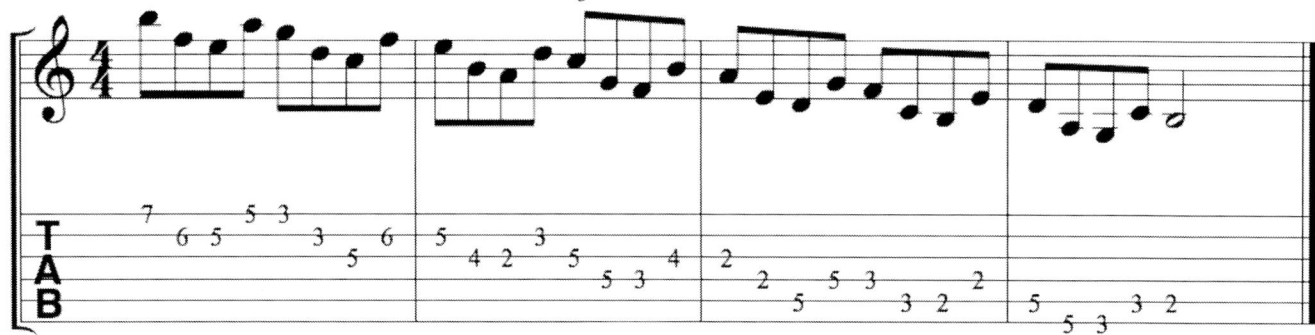

Weaving Fourths In A Minor, Root Position/C major, 6th Position, Ascending:

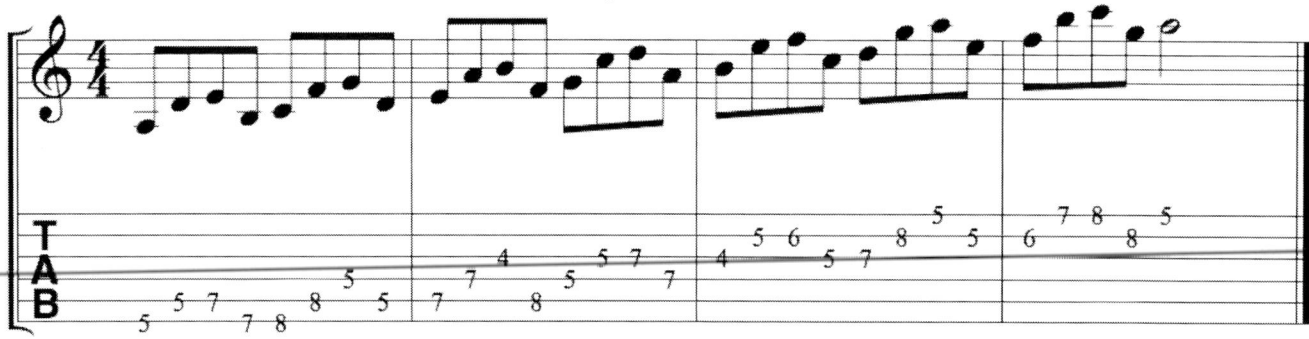

Weaving Fourths In A Minor, Root Position/C major, 6th Position, Descending:

Weaving Fourths In A Minor, 3rd Position/C major, Root Position, Ascending:

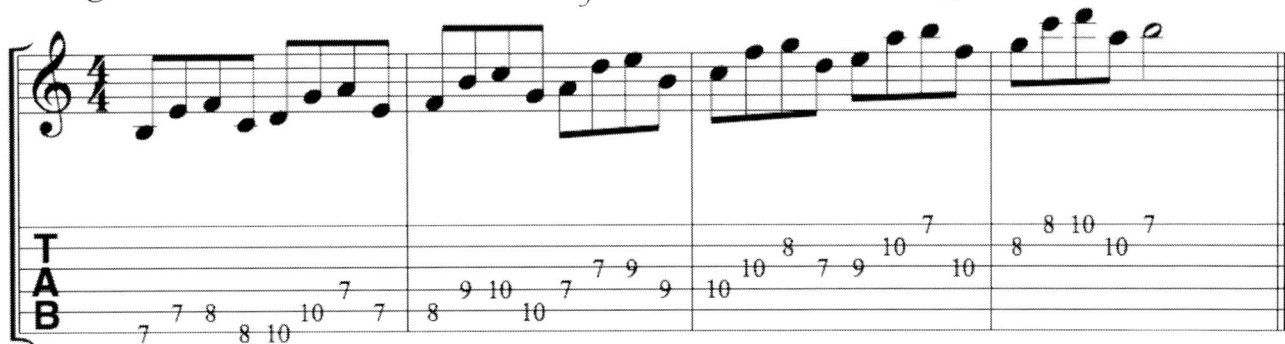

Weaving Fourths In A Minor, 3rd Position/C major, Root Position, Descending:

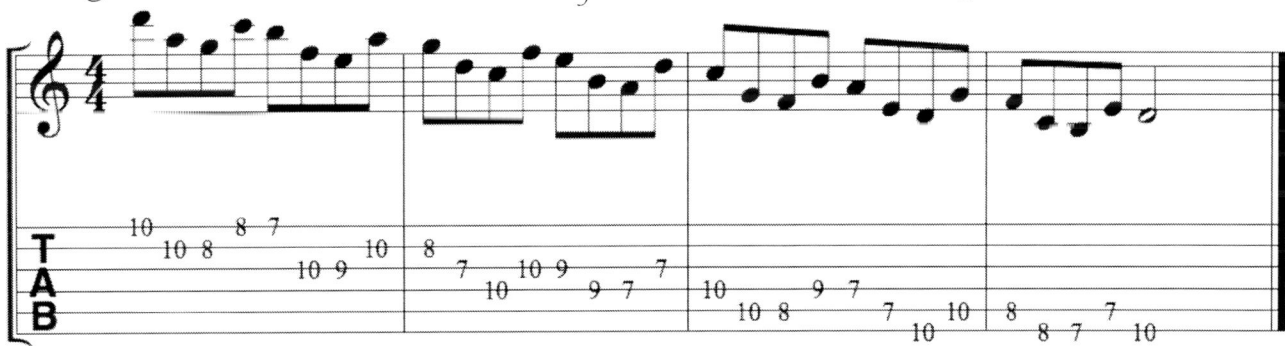

Weaving Fourths In A Minor, 4th Position/C major, 2nd Position, Ascending:

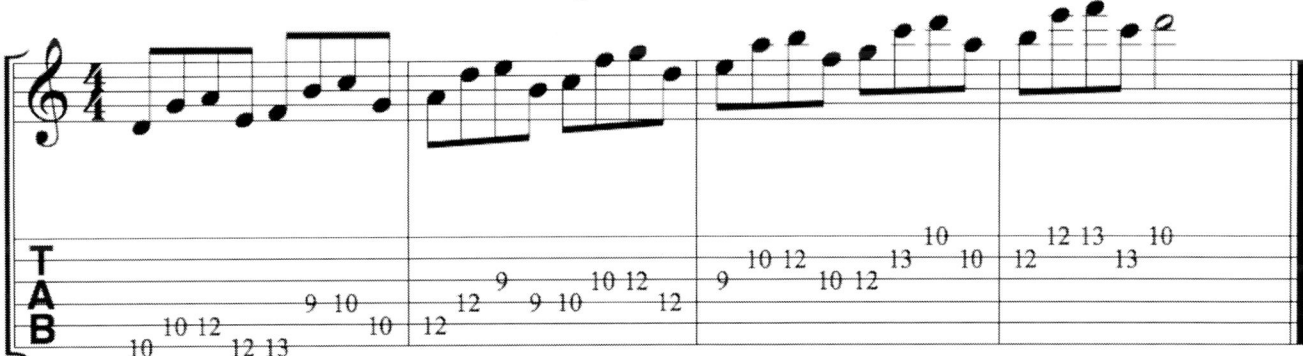

Weaving Fourths In A Minor, 4th Position/C major, 2nd Position, Descending:

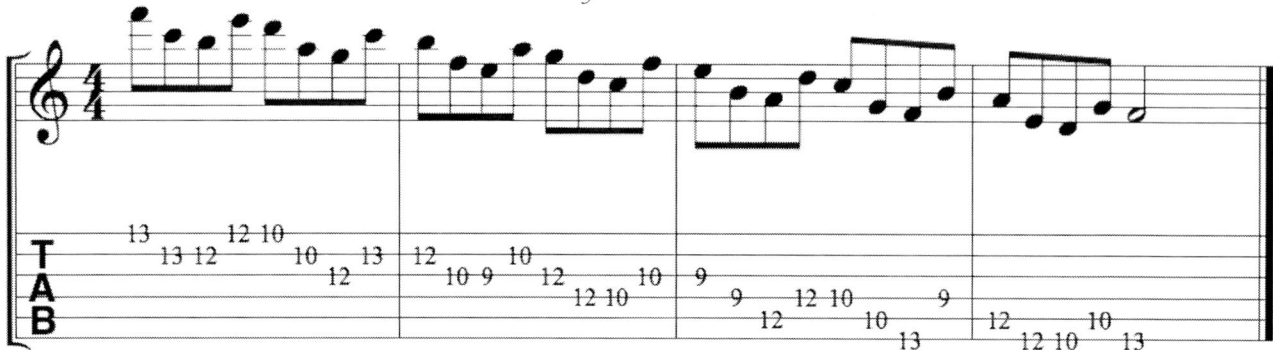

Weaving Fourths In A Minor, 5th Position/C major, 3rd Position, Ascending:

Weaving Fourths In A Minor, 5th Position/C major, 3rd Position, Descending:

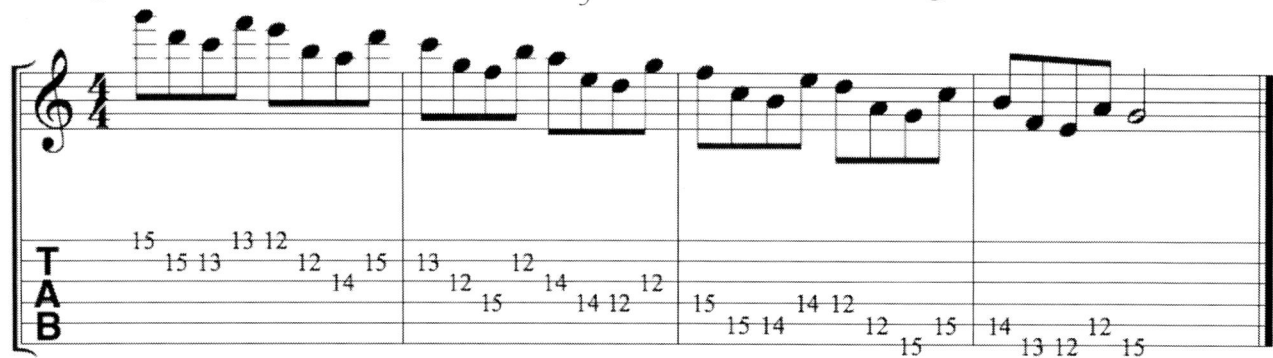

Inverse Weaving Fourths In A Minor, 7th Position/C major, 5th Position, Ascending:

Inverse Weaving Fourths In A Minor, 7th Position/C major, 5th Position, Descending:

Inverse Weaving Fourths In A Minor, Root Position/C major, 6th Position, Ascending:

Inverse Weaving Fourths In A Minor, Root Position/C major, 6th Position, Descending:

Inverse Weaving Fourths In A Minor, 3rd Position/C major, Root Position, Ascending:

Inverse Weaving Fourths In A Minor, 3rd Position/C major, Root Position, Descending:

Inverse Weaving Fourths In A Minor, 5th Position/C major, 3rd Position, Ascending:

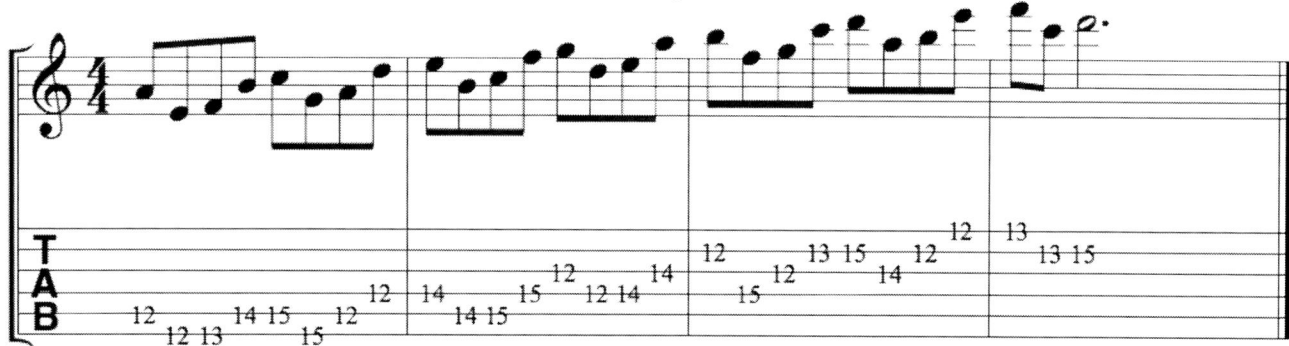

Inverse Weaving Fourths In A Minor, 5th Position/C major, 3rd Position, Descending:

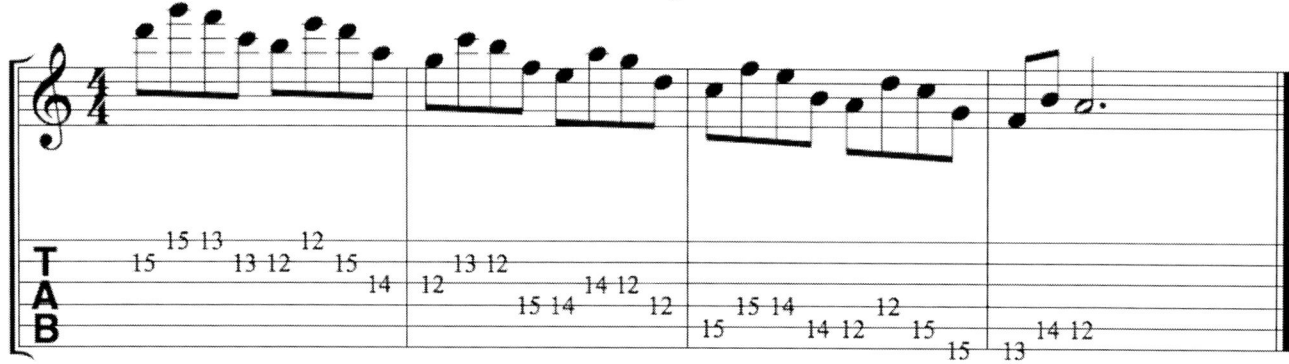

Basic Fifths In A Minor, 7th Position/C major, 5th Position, Ascending:

Basic Fifths In A Minor, 7th Position/C major, 5th Position, Descending:

Basic Fifths In A Minor, Root Position/C major, 6th Position, Ascending:

Basic Fifths In A Minor, Root Position/C major, 6th Position, Descending:

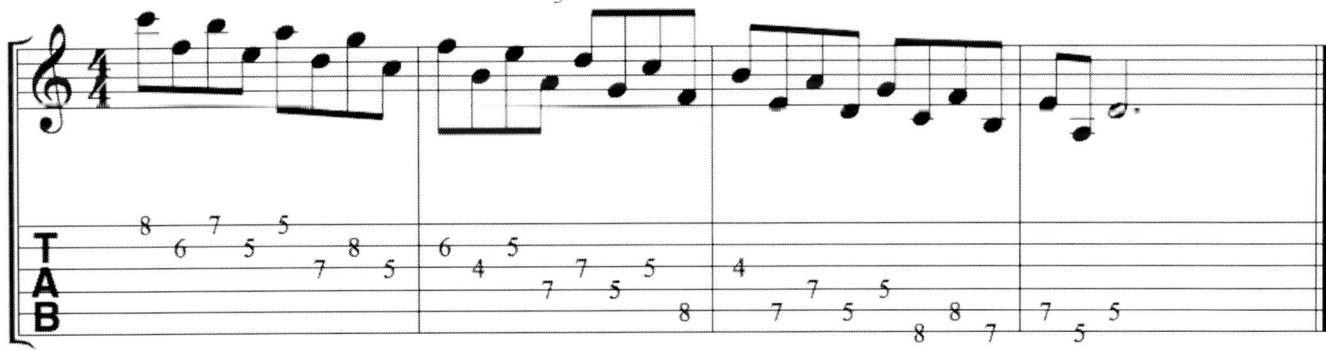

Basic Fifths In A Minor, 3rd Position/C major, Root Position, Ascending:

Basic Fifths In A Minor, 3rd Position/C major, Root Position, Descending:

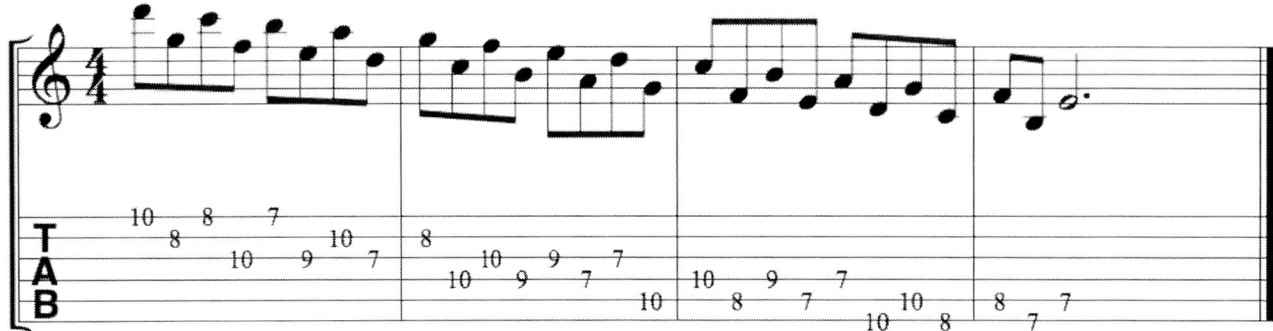

Basic Fifths In A Minor, 4th Position/C major, 2nd Position, Ascending:

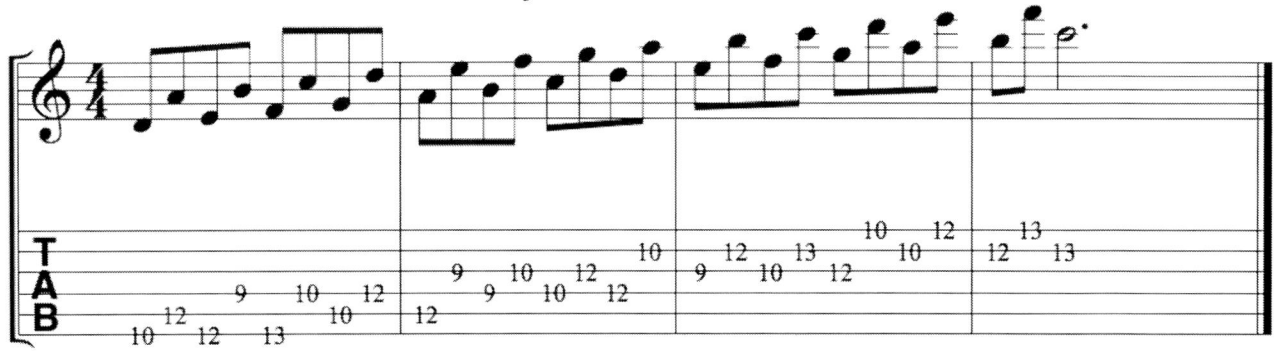

Basic Fifths In A Minor, 4th Position/C major, 2nd Position, Descending:

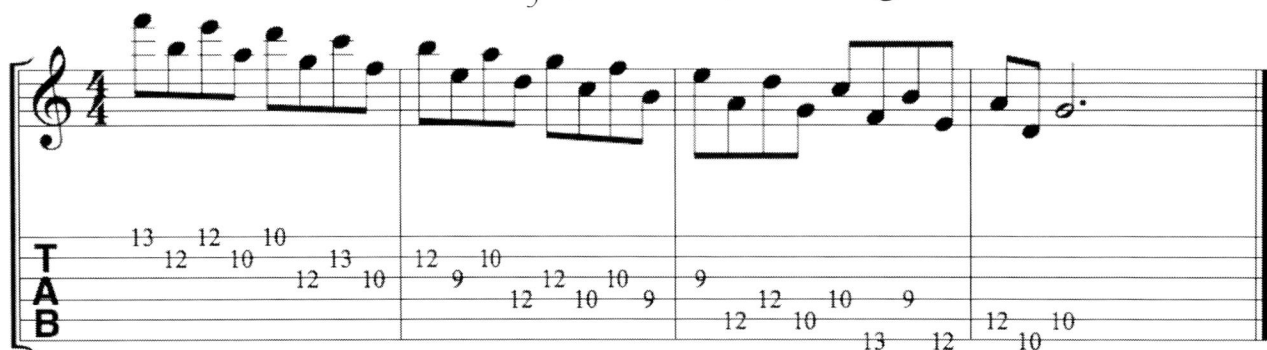

Basic Fifths In A Minor, 5th Position/C major, 3rd Position, Ascending:

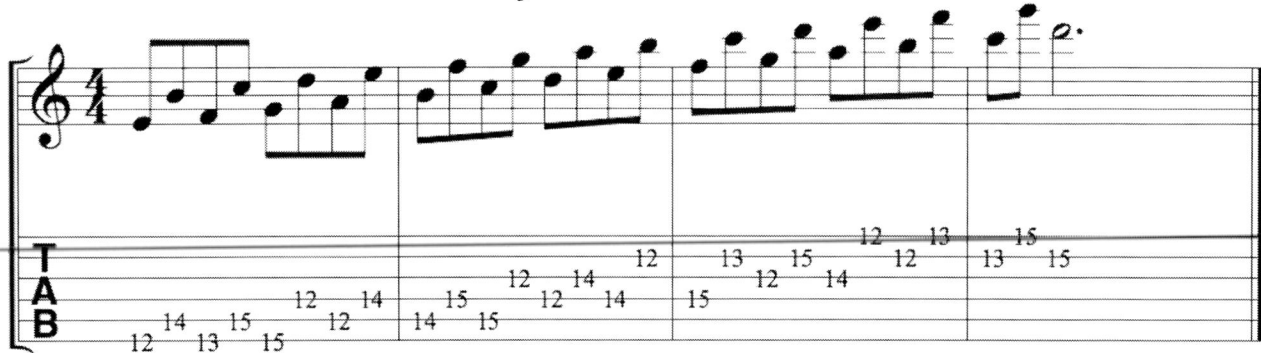

Basic Fifths In A Minor, 5th Position/C major, 3rd Position, Descending:

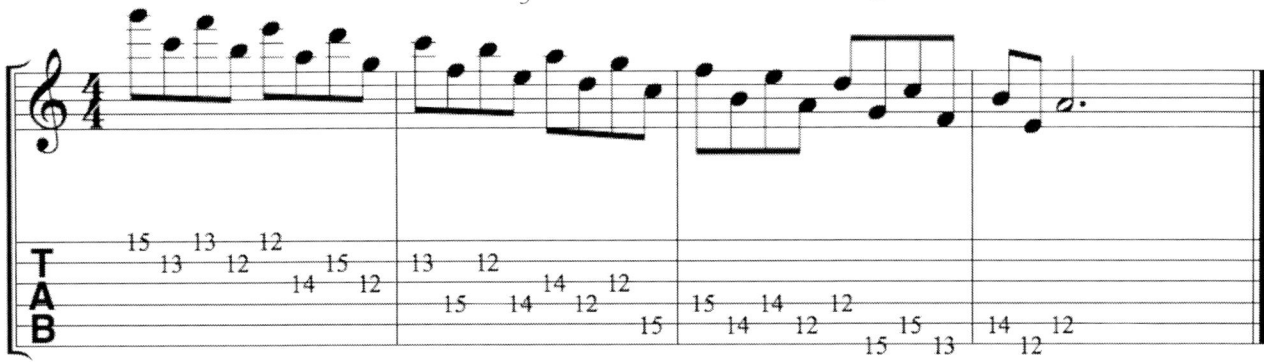

Weaving Fifths In A Minor, 7th Position/C major, 5th Position, Ascending:

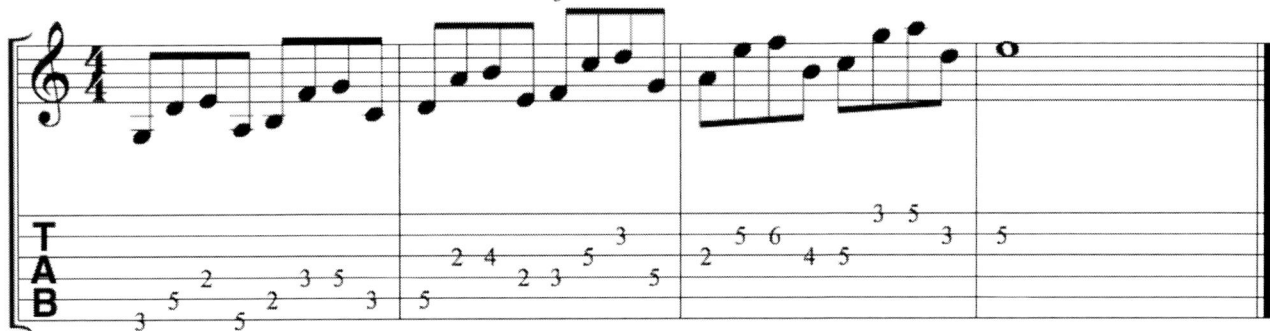

Weaving Fifths In A Minor, 7th Position/C major, 5th Position, Descending:

Weaving Fifths In A Minor, Root Position/C major, 6th Position, Ascending:

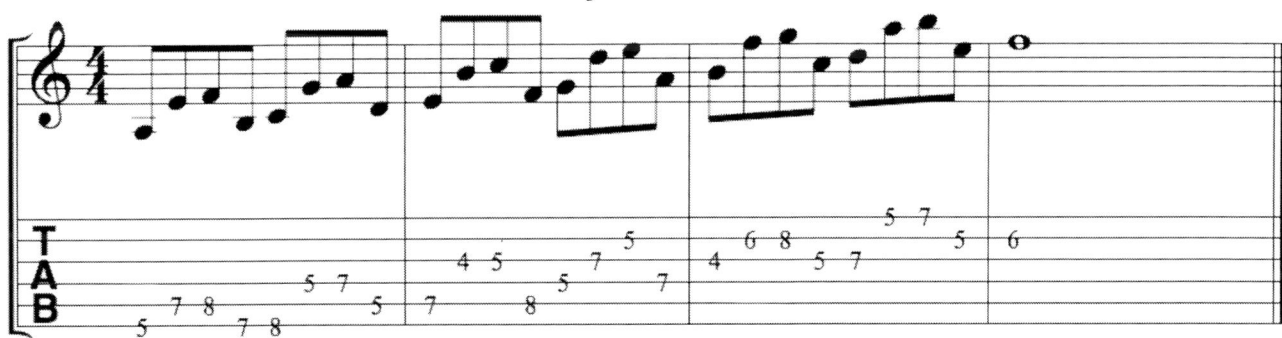

Weaving Fifths In A Minor, Root Position/C major, 6th Position, Descending:

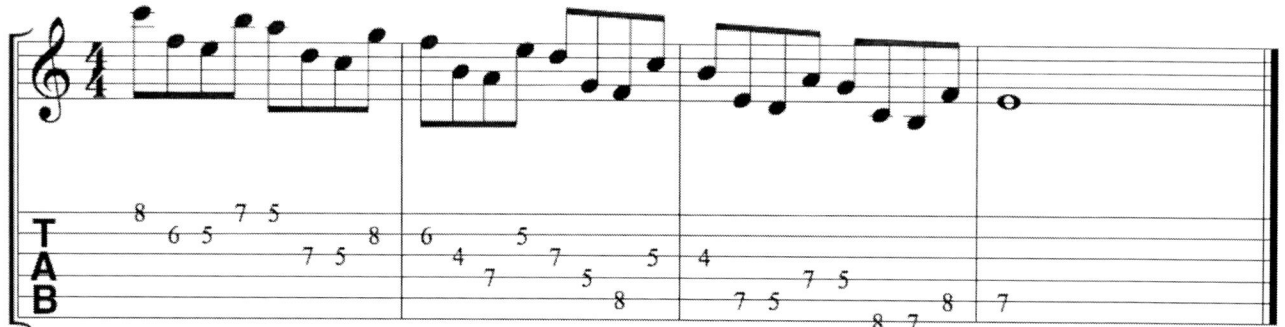

Weaving Fifths In A Minor, 3rd Position/C major, Root Position, Ascending:

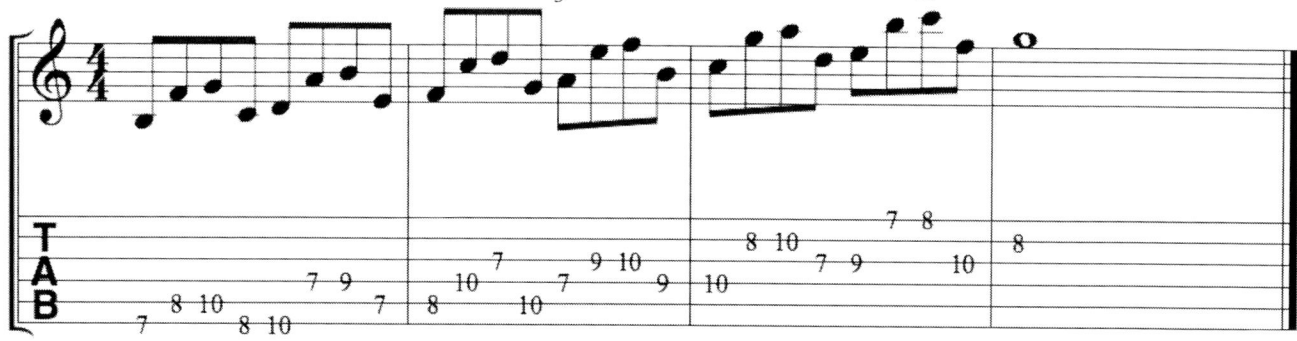

Weaving Fifths In A Minor, 3rd Position/C major, Root Position, Descending:

Weaving Fifths In A Minor, 4th Position/C major, 2nd Position, Ascending:

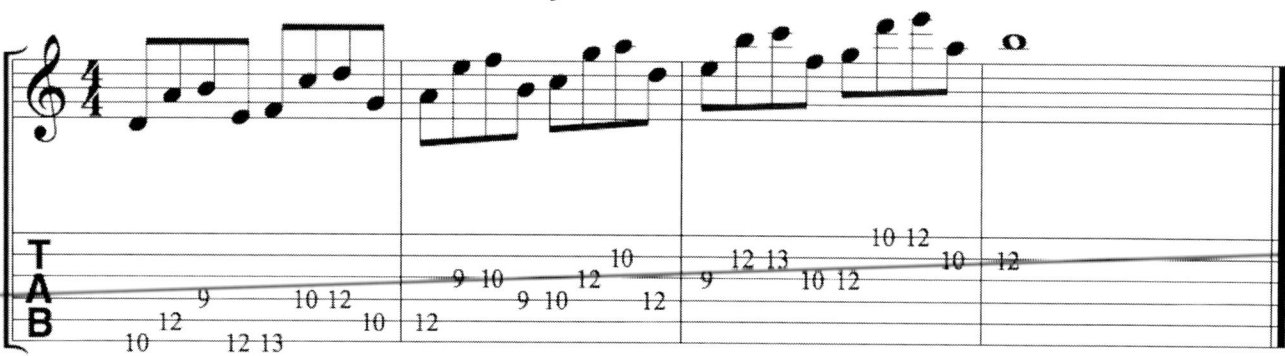

Weaving Fifths In A Minor, 4th Position/C major, 2nd Position, Descending:

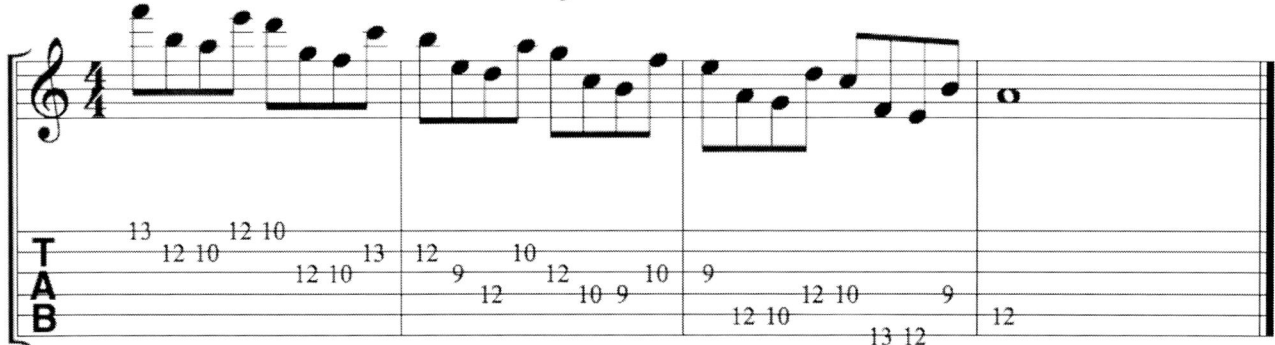

Weaving Fifths In A Minor, 5th Position/C major, 3rd Position, Ascending:

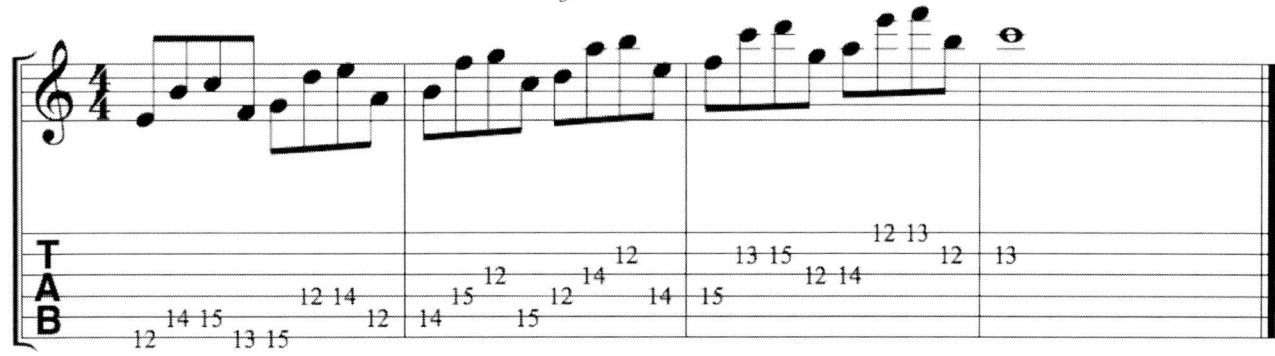

Weaving Fifths In A Minor, 5th Position/C major, 3rd Position, Ascending:

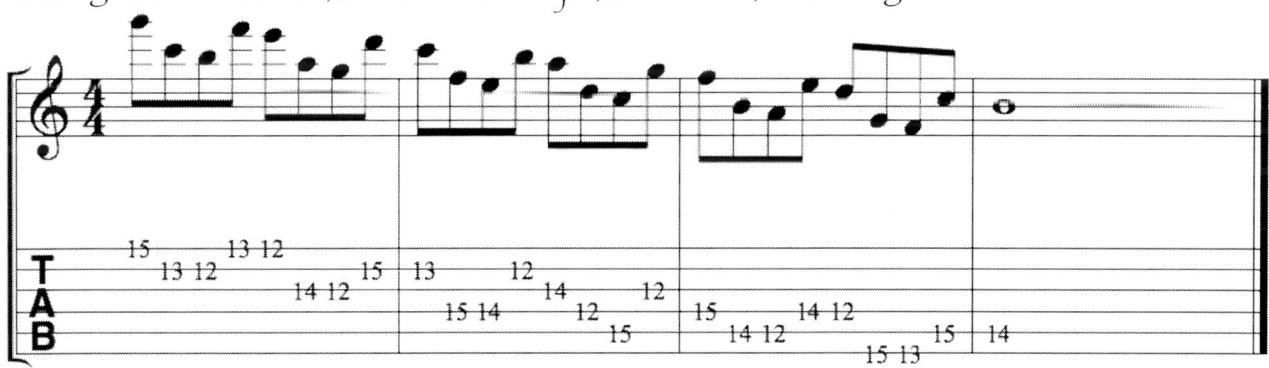

Inverse Weaving Fifths In A Minor, 7th Position/C major, 5th Position, Ascending:

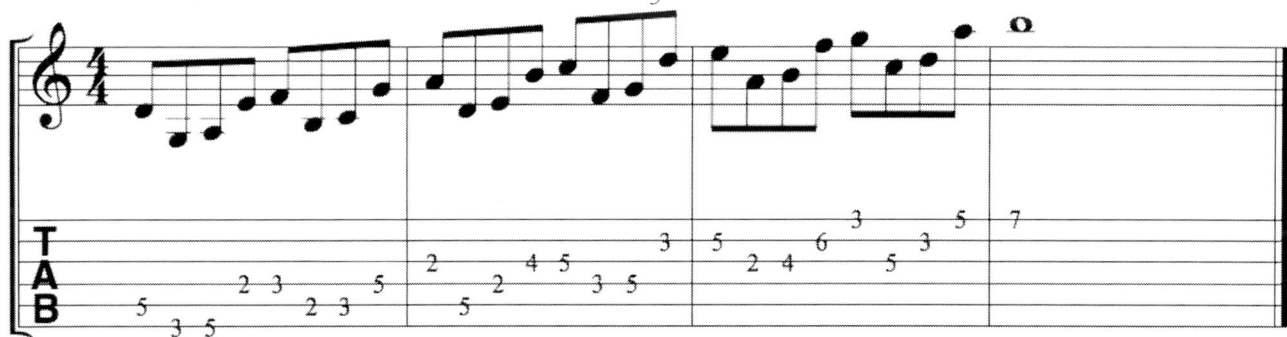

Inverse Weaving Fifths In A Minor, 7th Position/C major, 5th Position, Descending:

Inverse Weaving Fifths In A Minor, Root Position/C major, 6th Position, Ascending:

Inverse Weaving Fifths In A Minor, Root Position/C major, 6th Position, Descending:

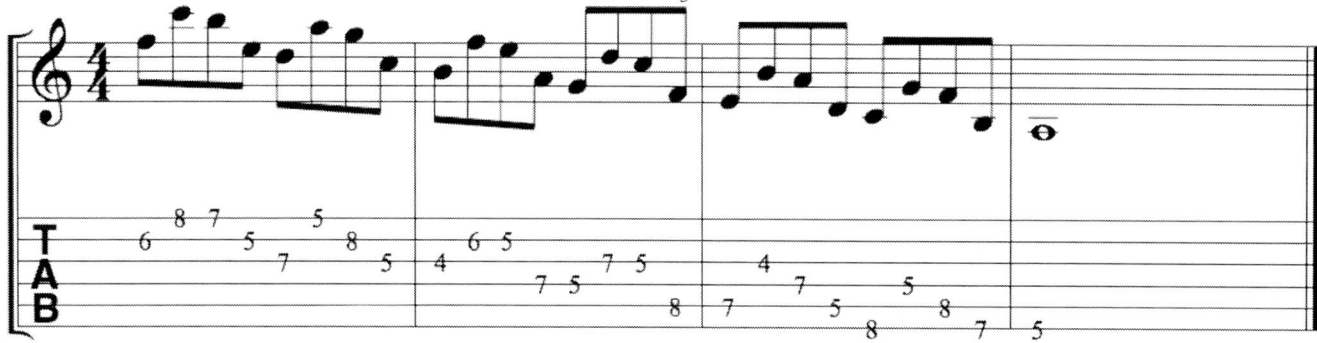

Inverse Weaving Fifths In A Minor, 3rd Position/C major, Root Position, Ascending:

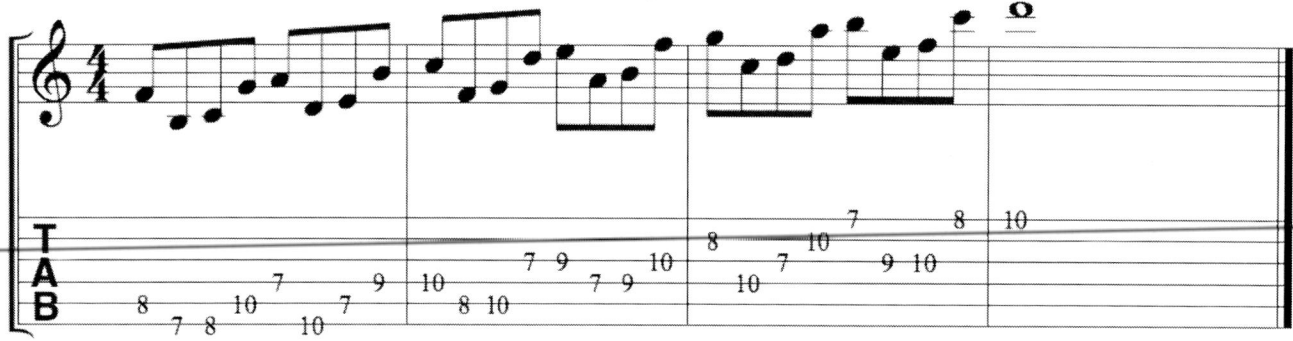

Inverse Weaving Fifths In A Minor, 3rd Position/C major, Root Position, Descending:

Inverse Weaving Fifths In A Minor, 4th Position/C major, 2nd Position, Ascending:

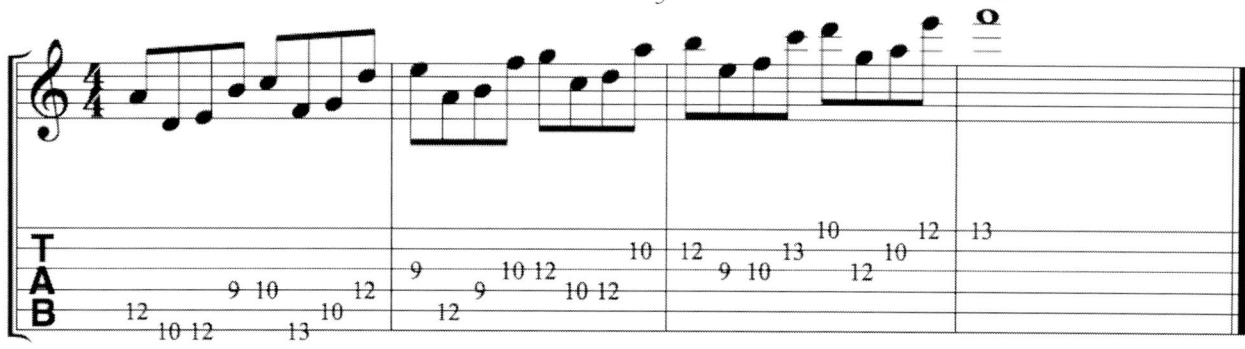

Inverse Weaving Fifths In A Minor, 4th Position/C major, 2nd Position, Descending:

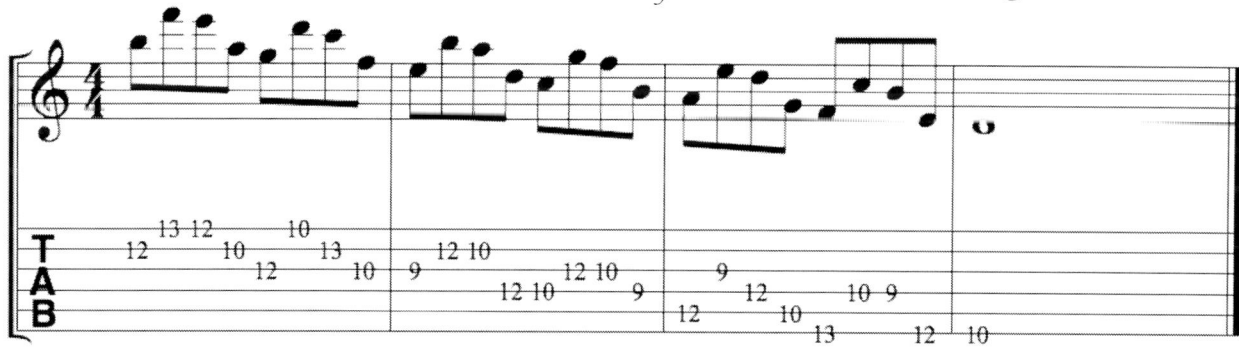

Inverse Weaving Fifths In A Minor, 5th Position/C major, 3rd Position, Ascending:

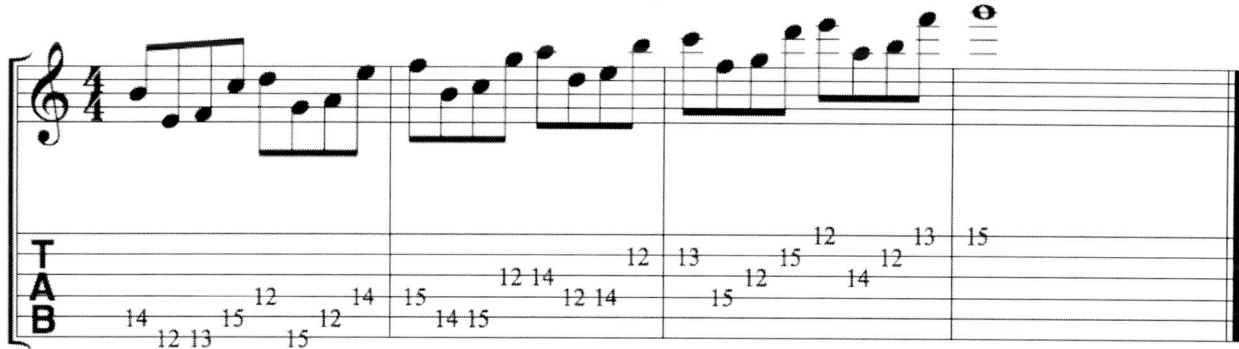

Inverse Weaving Fifths In A Minor, 5th Position/C major, 3rd Position, Descending:

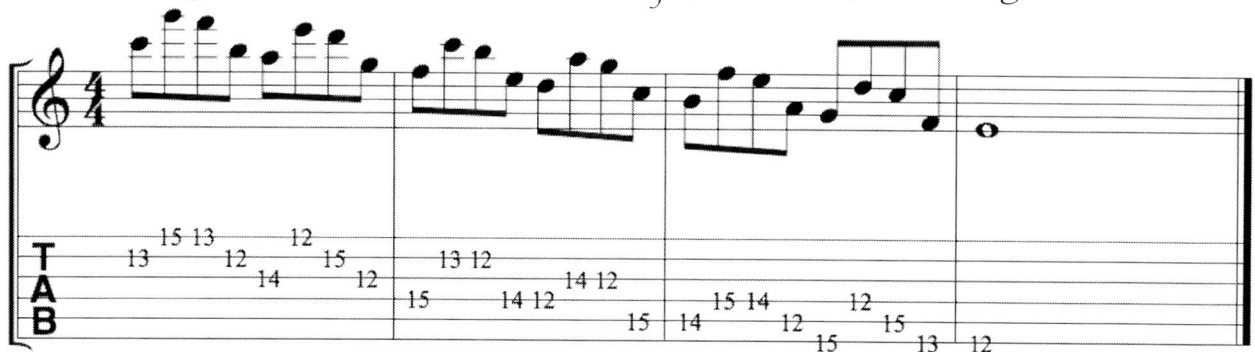

Basic Sixths In A Minor, 7th Position/C major, 5th Position, Ascending:

Basic Sixths In A Minor, 7th Position/C major, 5th Position, Descending:

Basic Sixths In A Minor, Root Position/C major, 6th Position, Ascending:

Basic Sixths In A Minor, Root Position/C major, 6th Position, Descending:

Basic Sixths In A Minor, 3rd Position/C major, Root Position, Ascending:

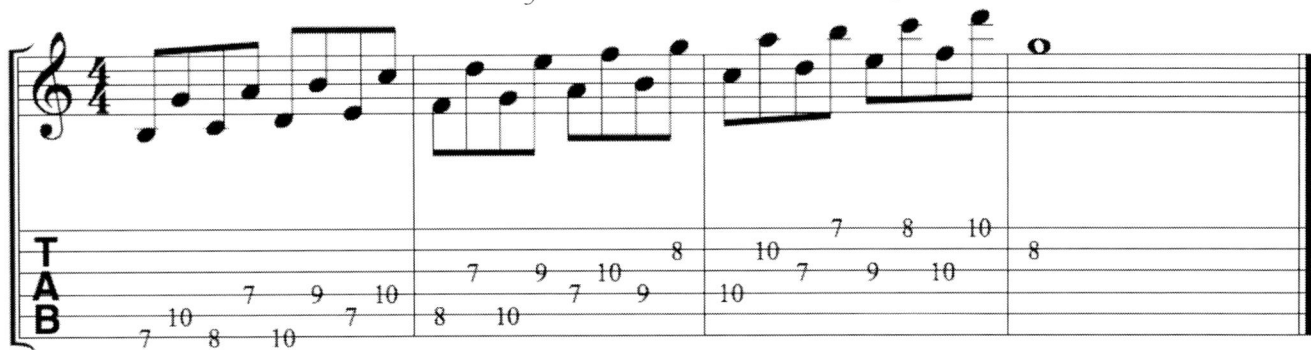

Basic Sixths In A Minor, 3rd Position/C major, Root Position, Descending:

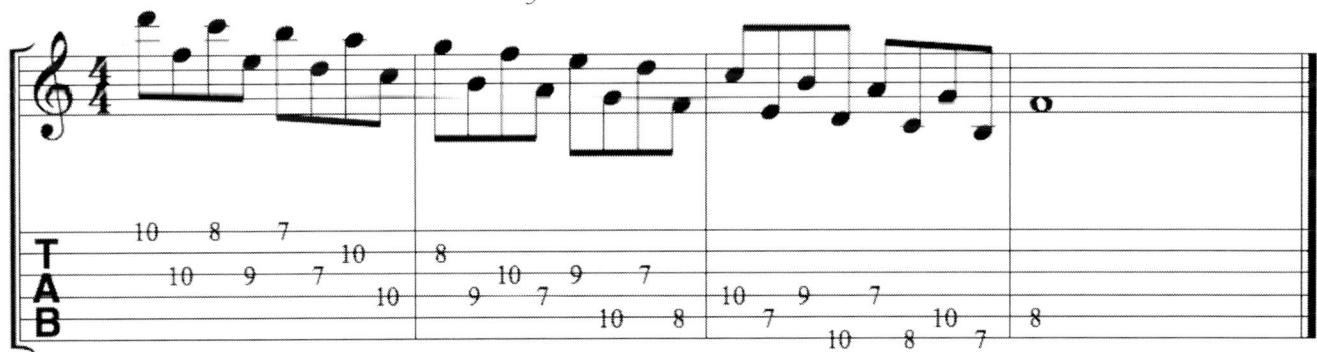

Basic Sixths In A Minor, 4th Position/C major, 2nd Position, Ascending:

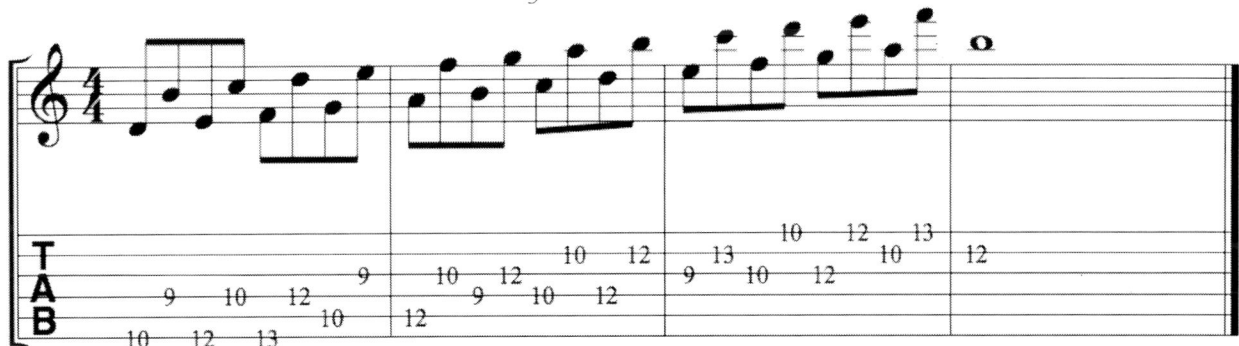

Basic Sixths In A Minor, 4th Position/C major, 2nd Position, Descending:

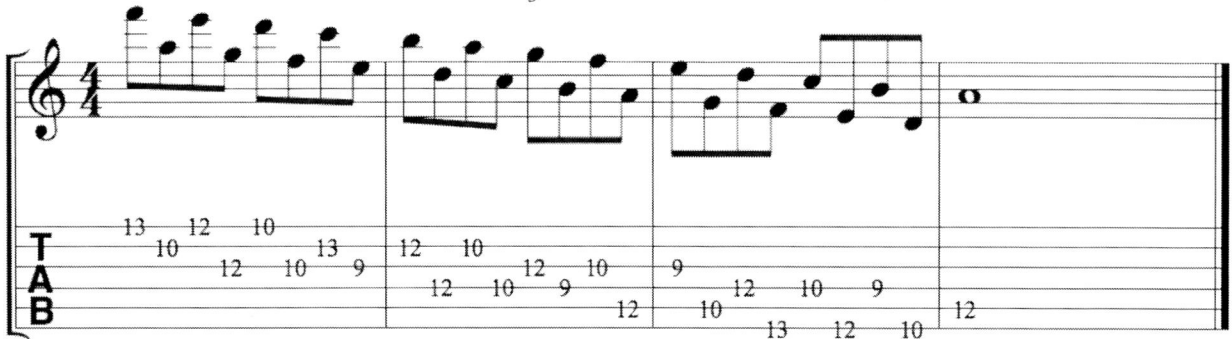

Basic Sixths In A Minor, 5th Position/C major, 3rd Position, Ascending:

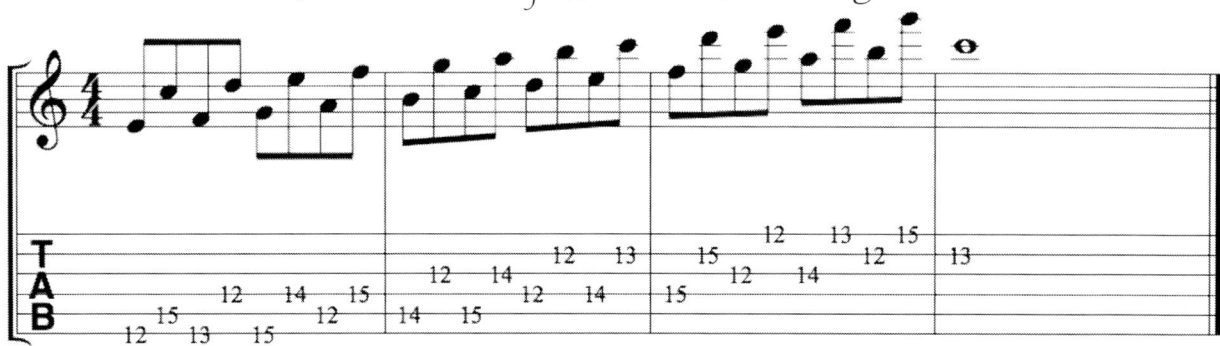

Basic Sixths In A Minor, 5th Position/C major, 3rd Position, Descending:

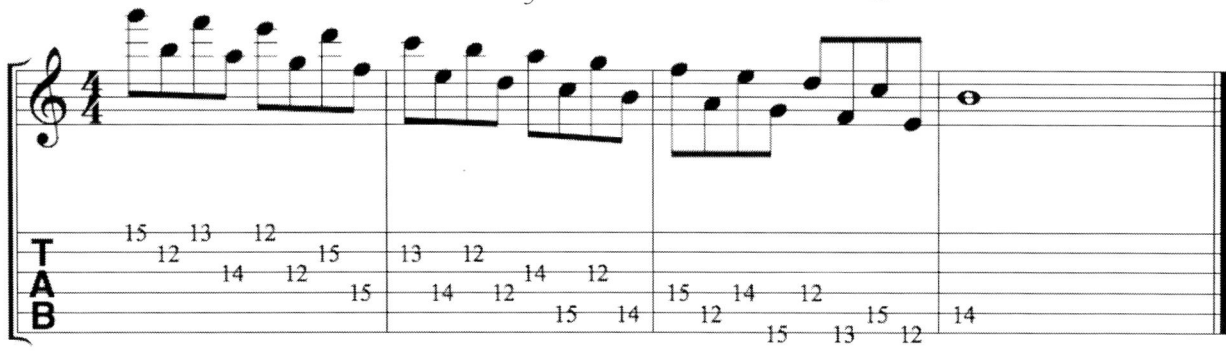

Weaving Sixths In A Minor, 7th Position/C major, 5th Position, Ascending:

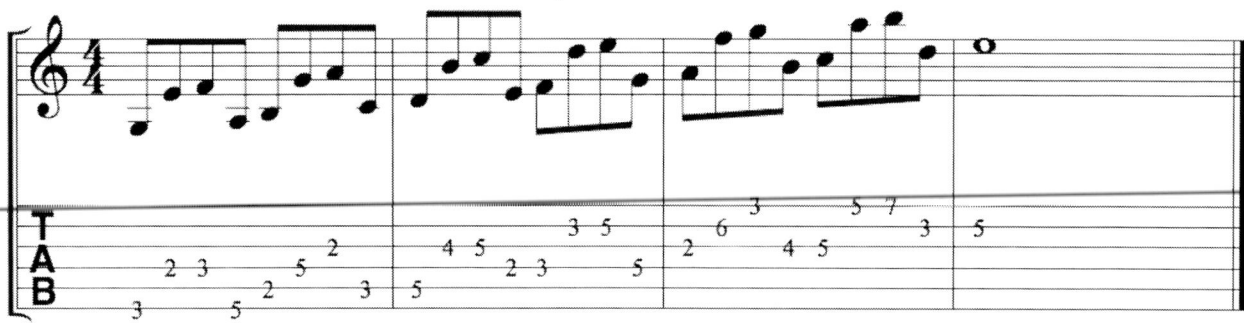

Weaving Sixths In A Minor, 7th Position/C major, 5th Position, Descending:

Weaving Sixths In A Minor, Root Position/C major, 6th Position, Ascending:

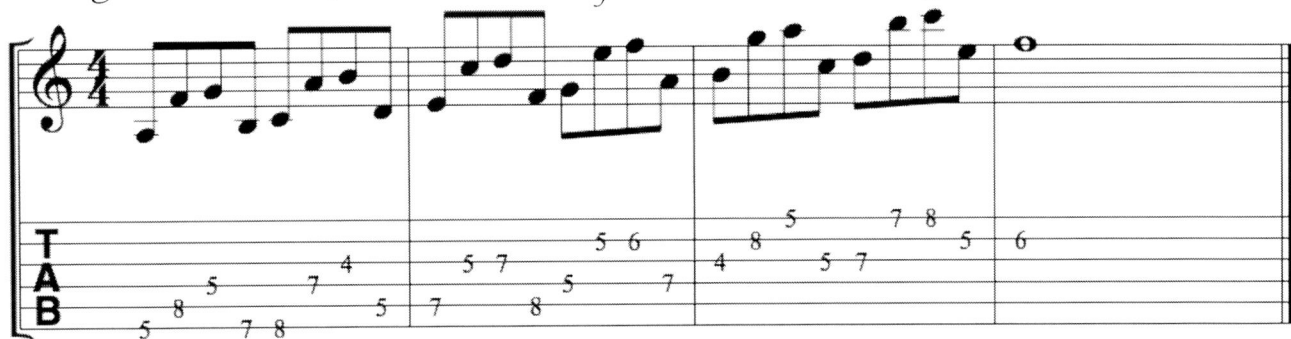

Weaving Sixths In A Minor, Root Position/C major, 6th Position, Descending:

Weaving Sixths In A Minor, 3rd Position/C major, Root Position, Ascending:

Weaving Sixths In A Minor, 3rd Position/C major, Root Position, Descending:

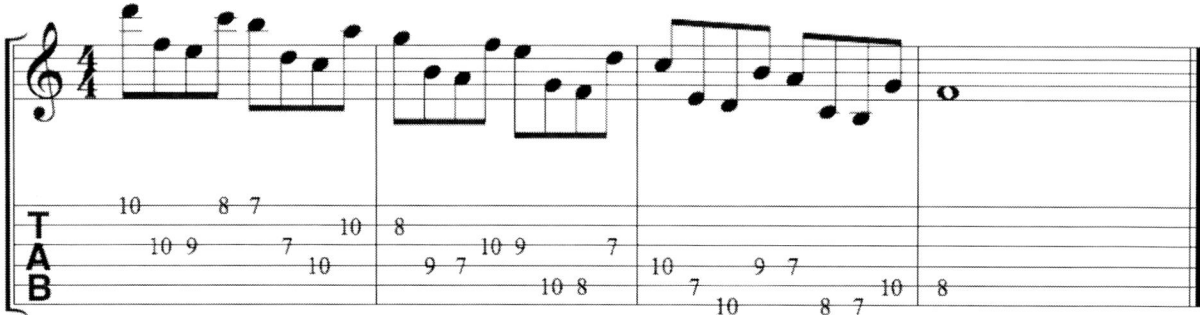

Weaving Sixths In A Minor, 4th Position/C major, 2nd Position, Ascending:

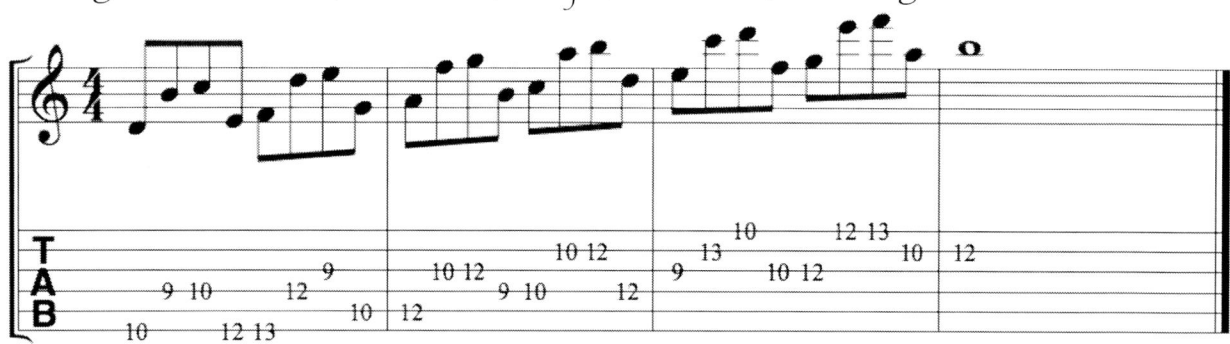

Weaving Sixths In A Minor, 4th Position/C major, 2nd Position, Descending:

Weaving Sixths In A Minor, 5th Position/C major, 3rd Position, Ascending:

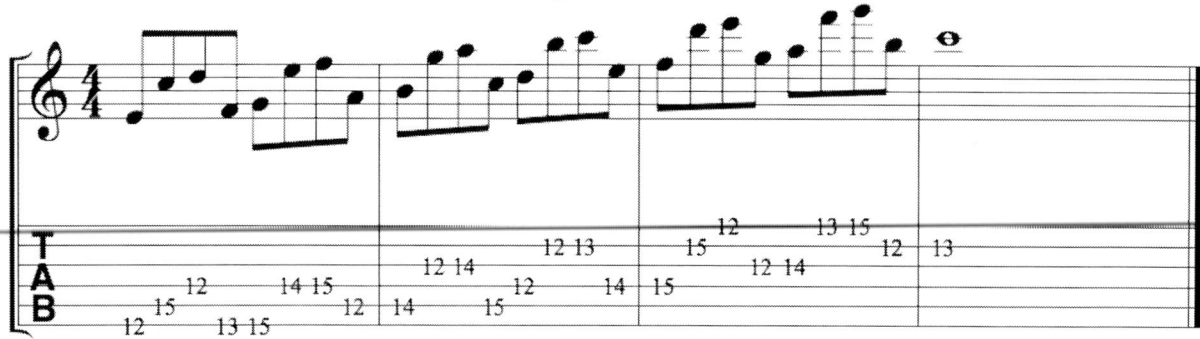

Weaving Sixths In A Minor, 5th Position/C major, 3rd Position, Descending:

Inverse Weaving Sixths In A Minor, 7th Position/C major, 5th Position, Ascending:

Inverse Weaving Sixths In A Minor, 7th Position/C major, 5th Position, Descending:

Inverse Weaving Sixths In A Minor, Root Position/C major, 6th Position, Ascending:

Inverse Weaving Sixths In A Minor, Root Position/C major, 6th Position, Descending:

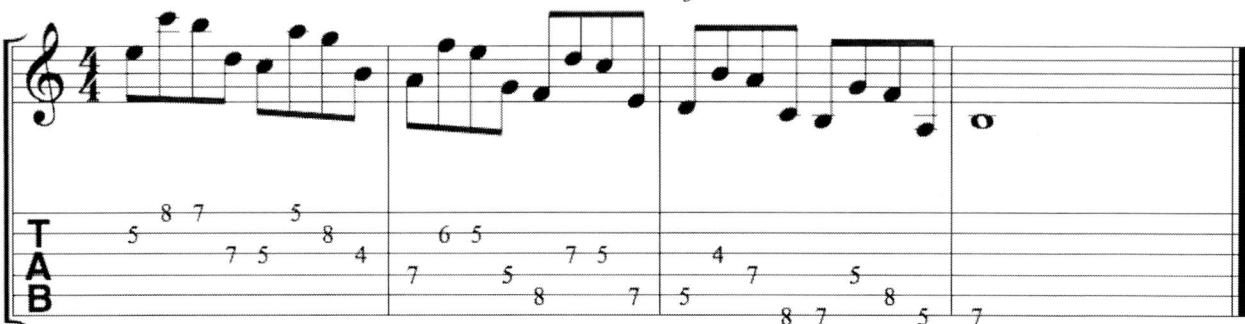

Inverse Weaving Sixths In A Minor, 3rd Position/C major, Root Position, Ascending:

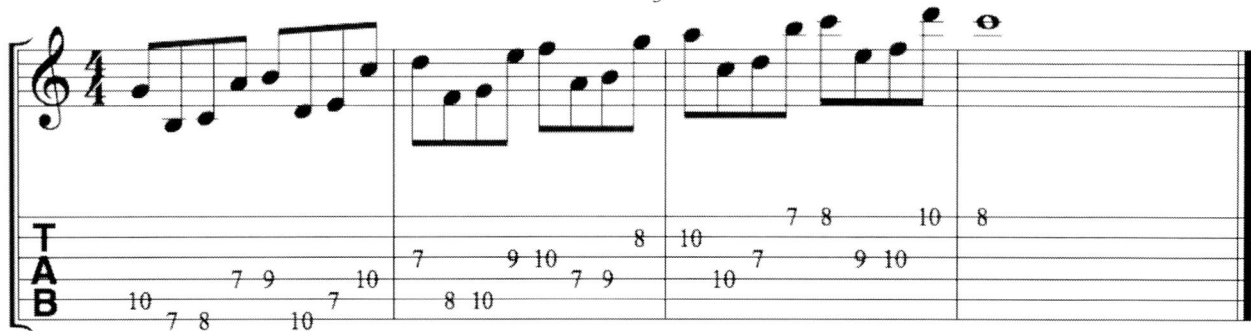

Inverse Weaving Sixths In A Minor, 3rd Position/C major, Root Position, Descending:

Inverse Weaving Sixths In A Minor, 4th Position/C major, 2nd Position, Ascending:

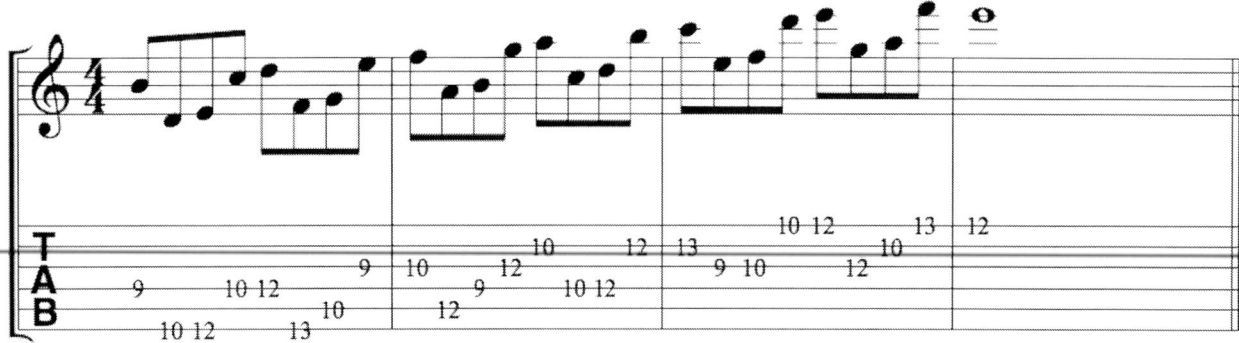

Inverse Weaving Sixths In A Minor, 4th Position/C major, 2nd Position, Descending:

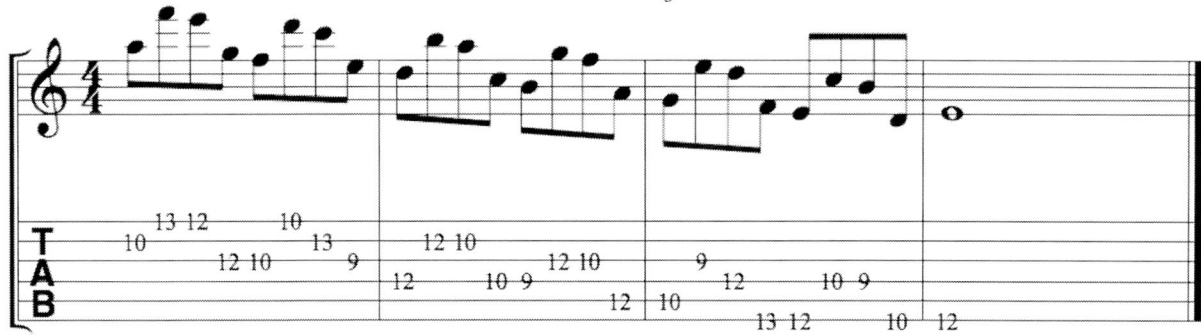

Inverse Weaving Sixths In A Minor, 5th Position/C major, 3rd Position, Ascending:

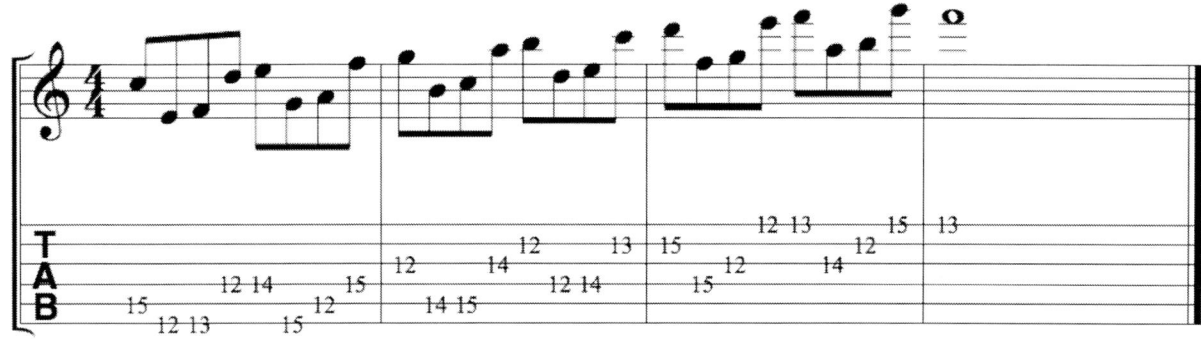

Inverse Weaving Sixths In A Minor, 5th Position/C major, 3rd Position, Descending:

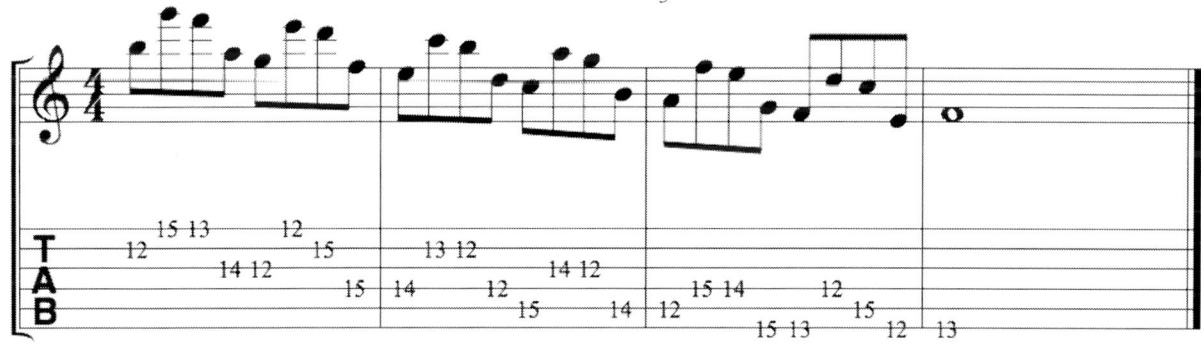

Basic Sevenths In A Minor, 7th Position/C major, 5th Position, Ascending:

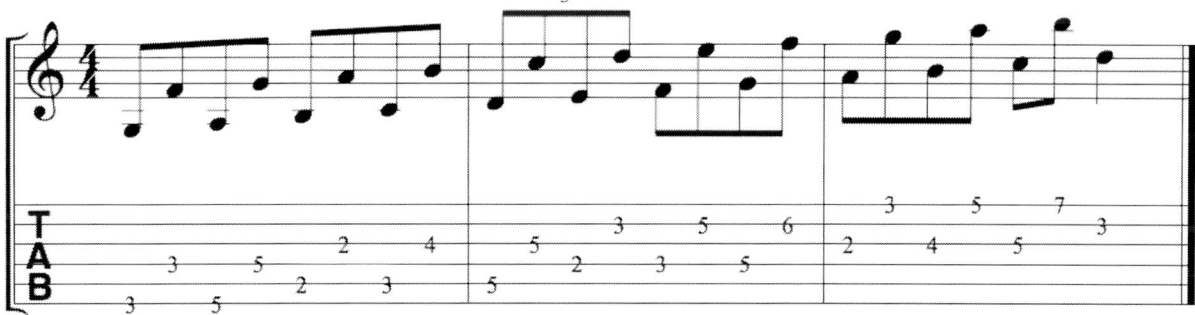

Basic Sevenths In A Minor, 7th Position/C major, 5th Position, Descending:

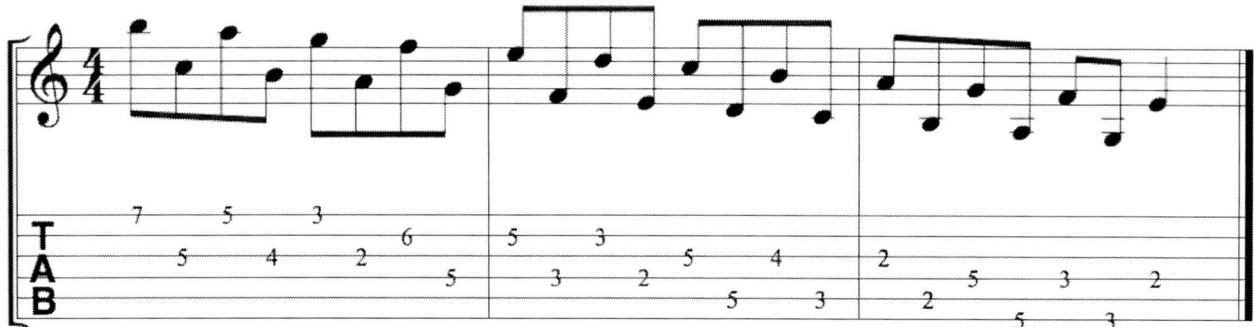

Basic Sevenths In A Minor, Root Position/C major, 3rd Position, Ascending:

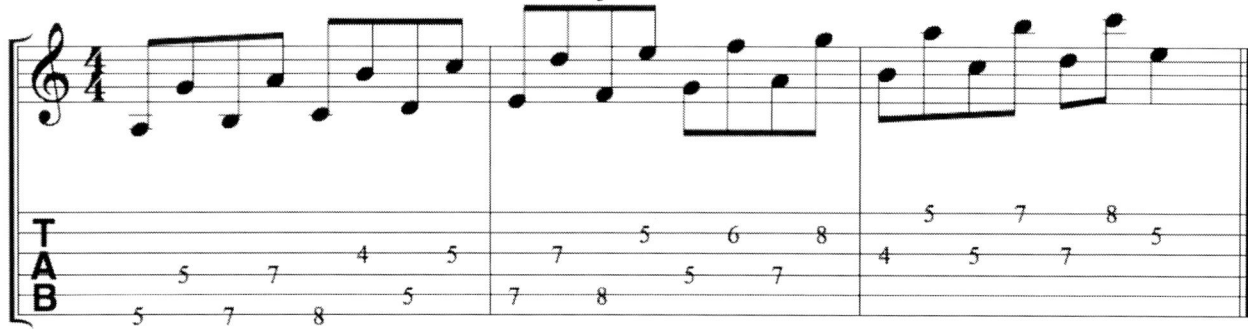

Basic Sevenths In A Minor, Root Position/C major, 3rd Position, Descending:

Basic Sevenths In A Minor, 3rd Position/C major, Root Position, Ascending:

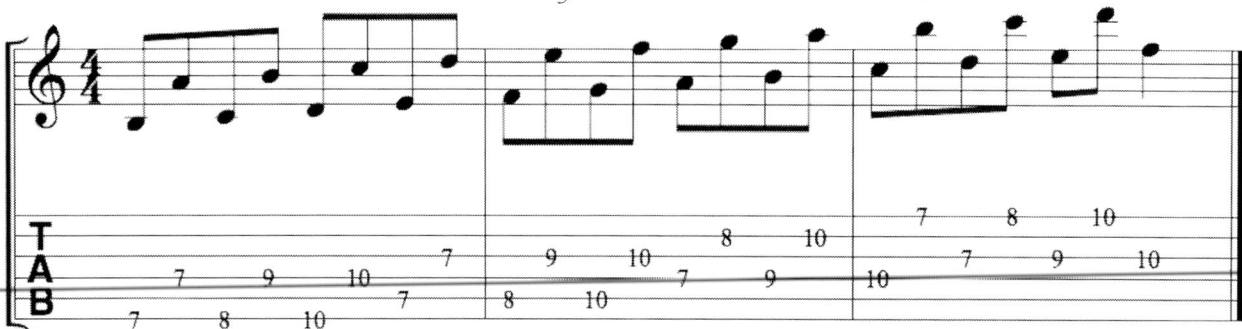

Basic Sevenths In A Minor, 3rd Position/C major, Root Position, Descending:

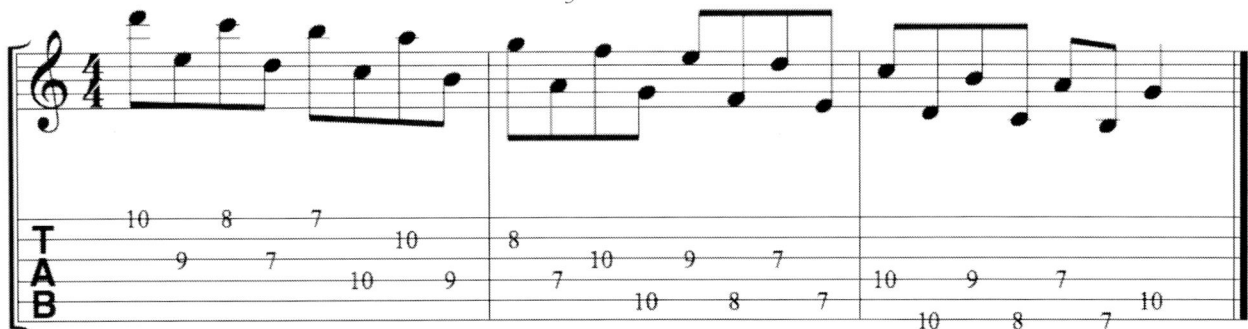

Basic Sevenths In A Minor, 4th Position/C major, 2nd Position, Ascending:

Basic Sevenths In A Minor, 4th Position/C major, 2nd Position, Descending:

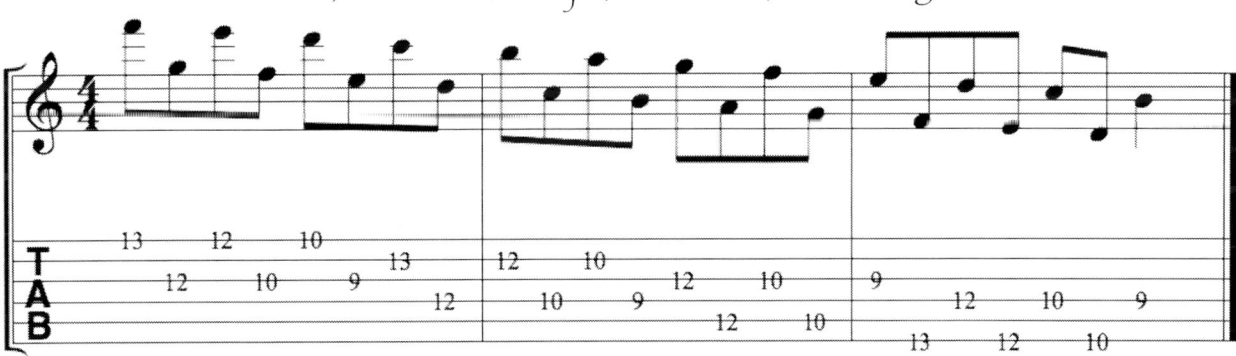

Basic Sevenths In A Minor, 5th Position/C major, 3rd Position, Ascending:

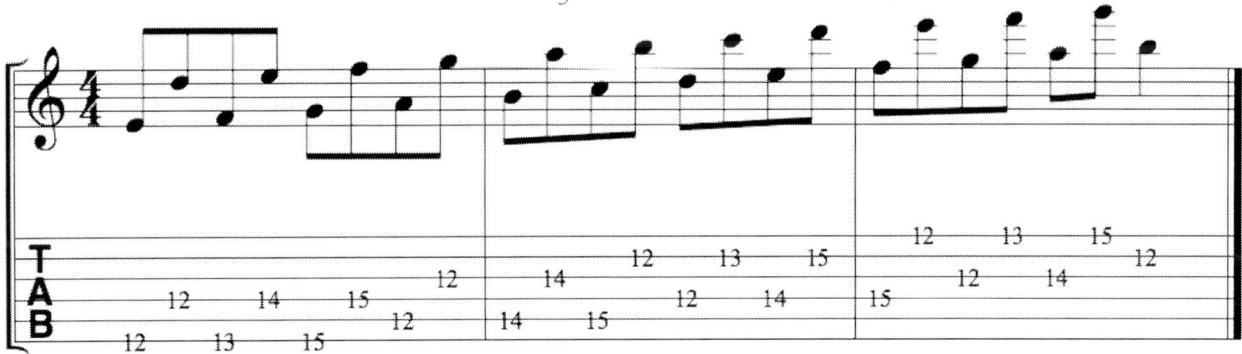

Basic Sevenths In A Minor, 5th Position/C major, 3rd Position, Descending:

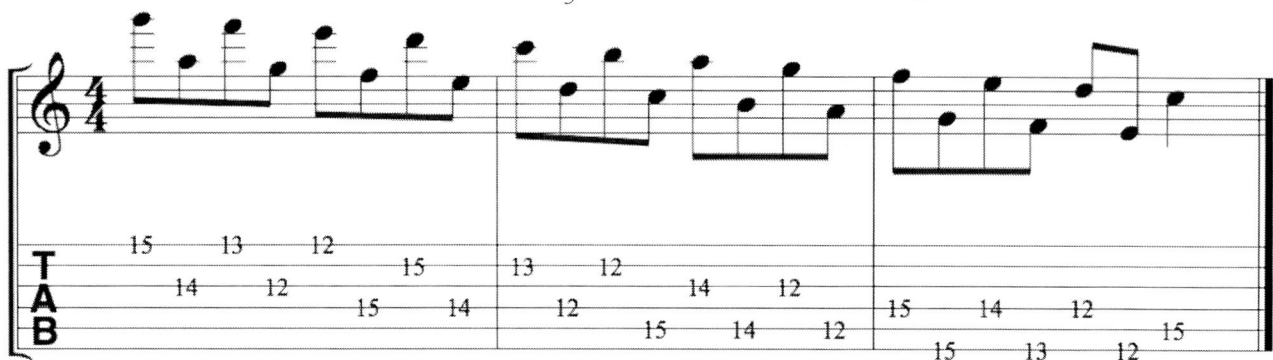

Weaving Sevenths In A Minor, 7th Position/C major, 5th Position, Ascending:

Weaving Sevenths In A Minor, 7th Position/C major, 5th Position, Descending:

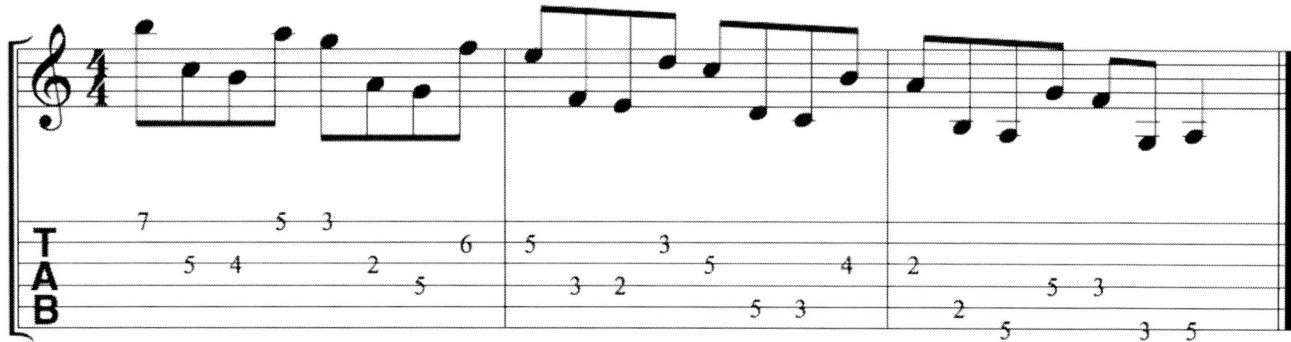

Weaving Sevenths In A Minor, Root Position/C major, 3rd Position, Ascending:

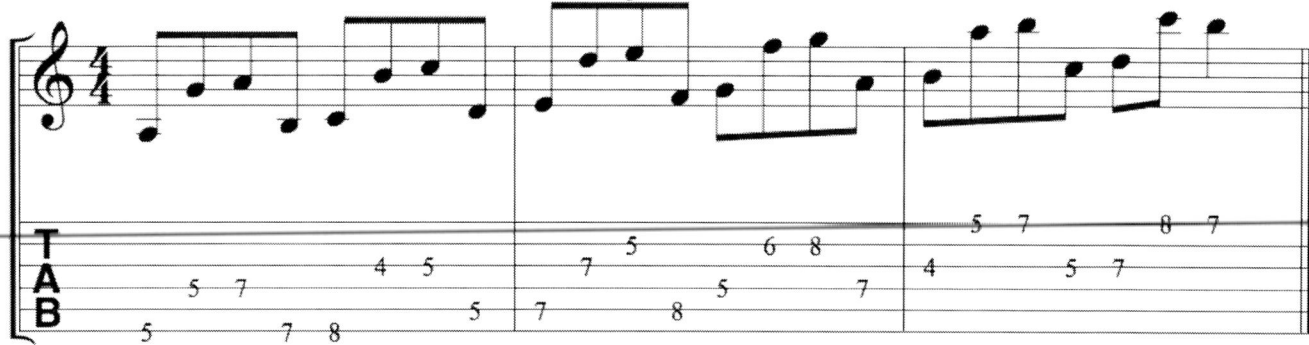

Weaving Sevenths In A Minor, Root Position/C major, 3rd Position, Descending:

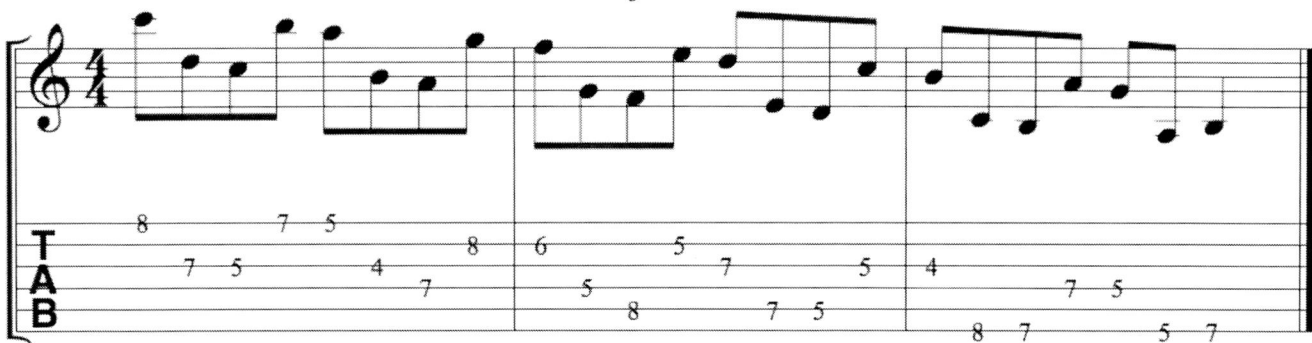

Weaving Sevenths In A Minor, 3rd Position/C major, Root Position, Ascending:

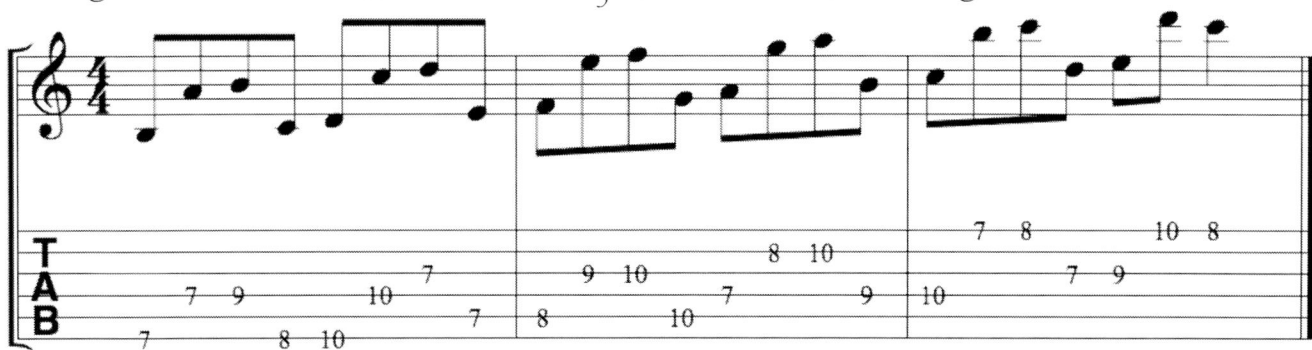

Weaving Sevenths In A Minor, 3rd Position/C major, Root Position, Descending:

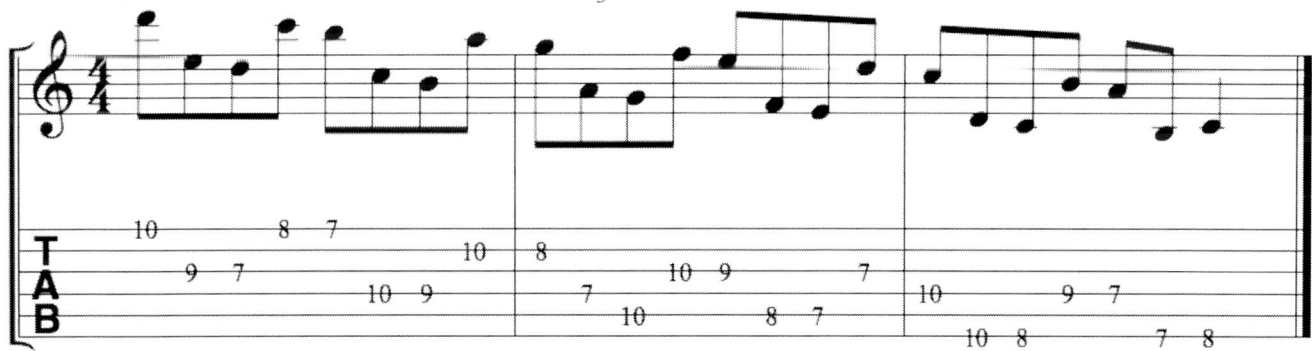

Weaving Sevenths In A Minor, 4th Position/C major, 2nd Position, Ascending:

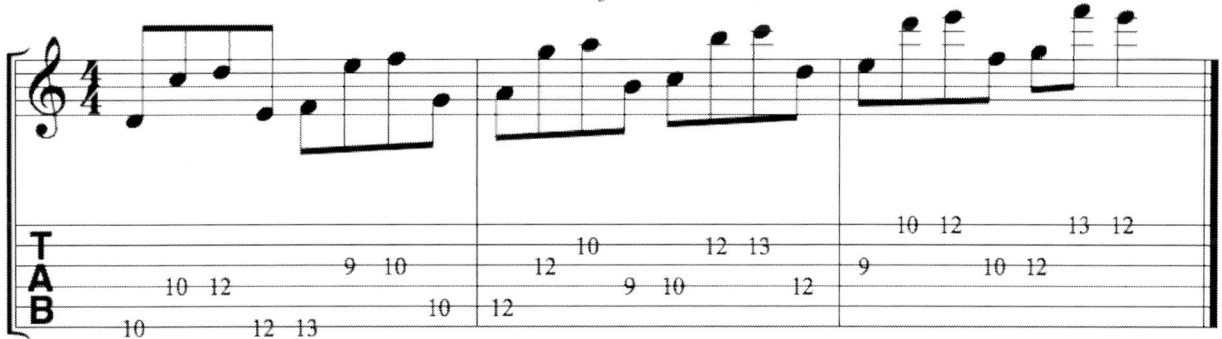

Weaving Sevenths In A Minor, 4th Position/C major, 2nd Position, Descending:

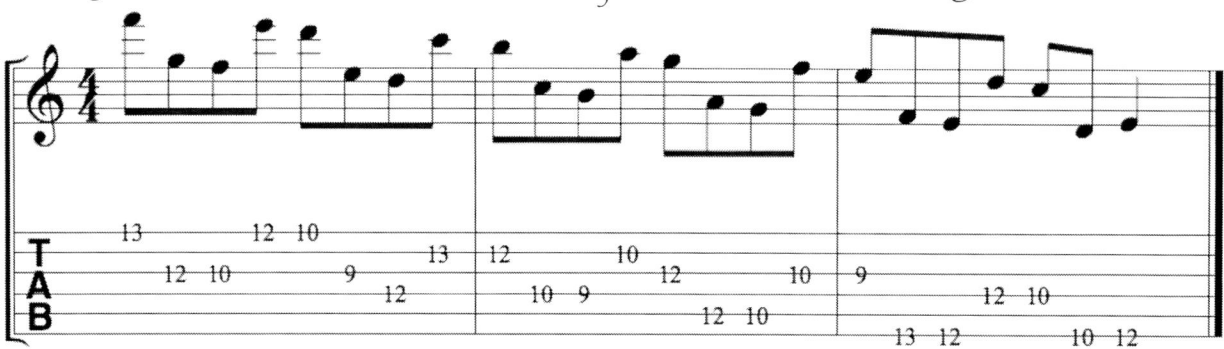

Weaving Sevenths In A Minor, 5th Position/C major, 3rd Position, Ascending:

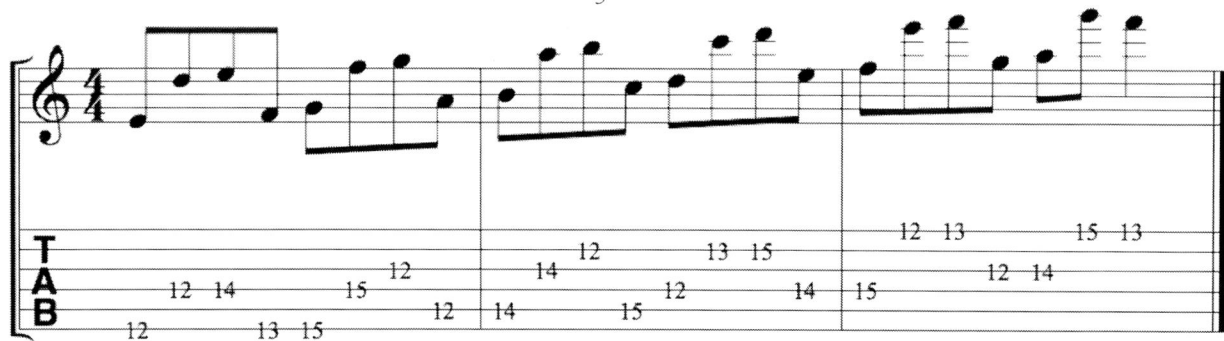

Weaving Sevenths In A Minor, 5th Position/C major, 3rd Position, Descending:

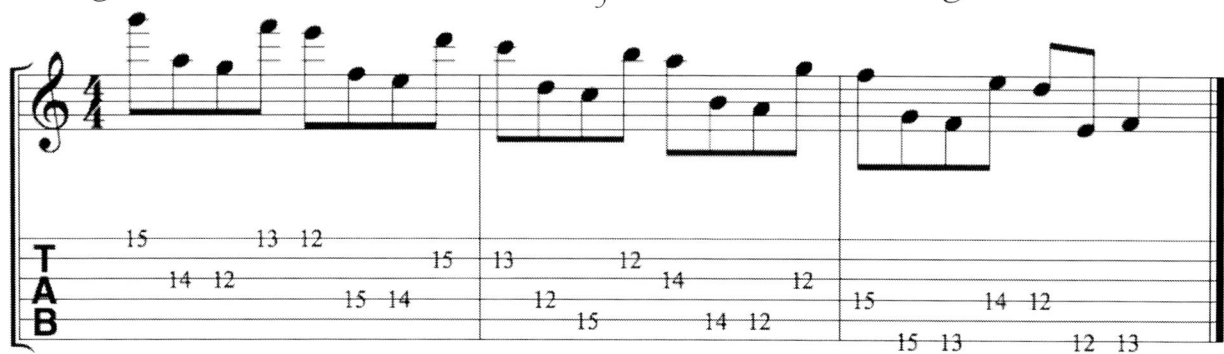

Inverse Weaving Sevenths In A Minor, 7th Position/C major, 5th Position, Ascending:

Inverse Weaving Sevenths In A Minor, 7th Position/C major, 5th Position, Descending:

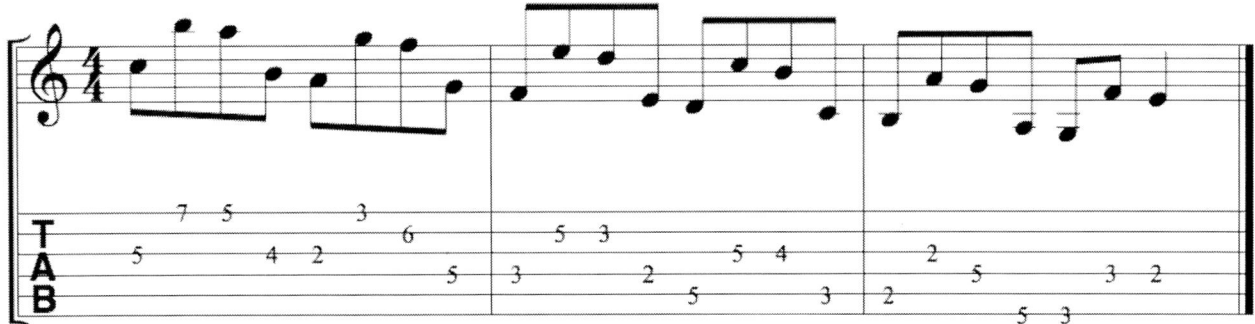

Inverse Weaving Sevenths In A Minor, Root Position/C major, 3rd Position, Ascending:

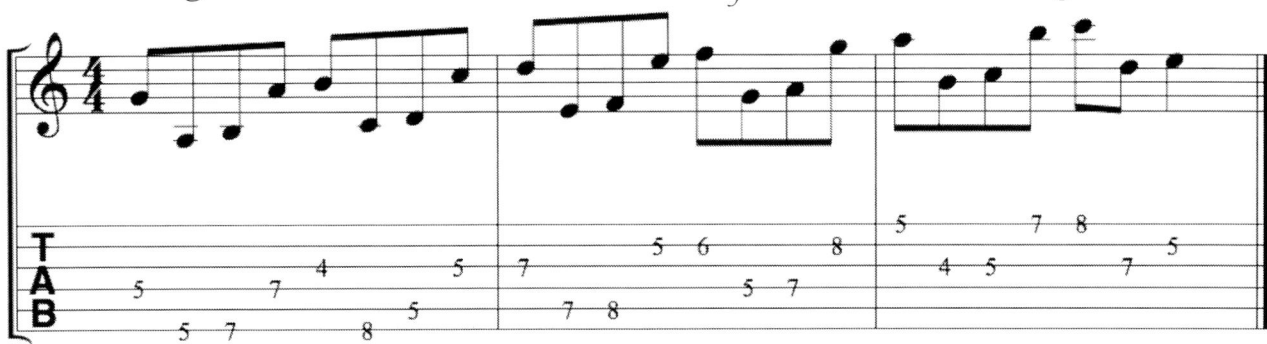

Inverse Weaving Sevenths In A Minor, Root Position/C major, 3rd Position, Descending:

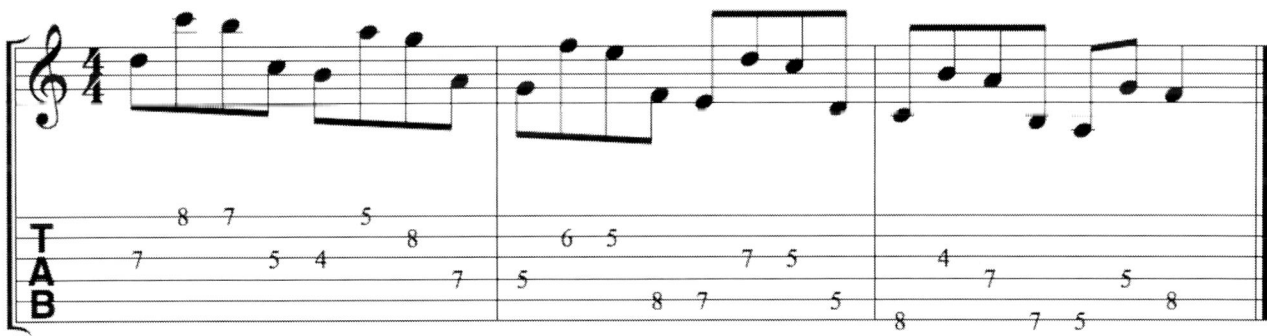

Inverse Weaving Sevenths In A Minor, 3rd Position/C major, Root Position, Ascending:

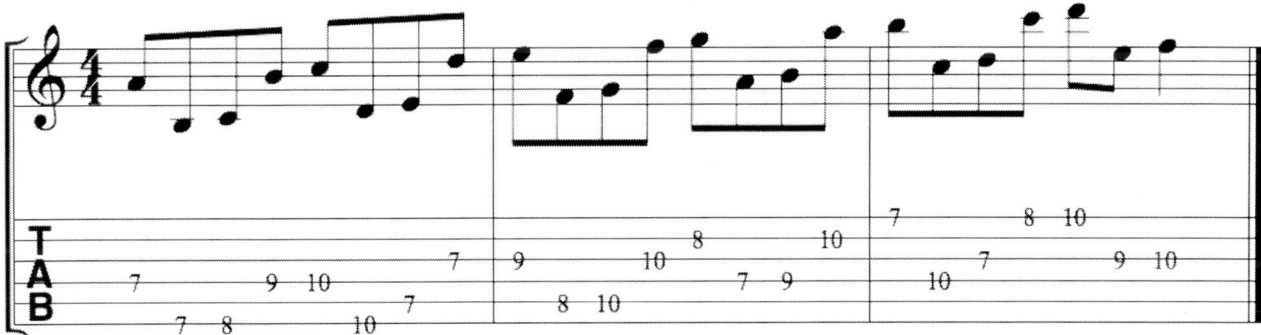

Inverse Weaving Sevenths In A Minor, 3rd Position/C major, Root Position, Descending:

Inverse Weaving Sevenths In A Minor, 4th Position/C major, 2nd Position, Ascending:

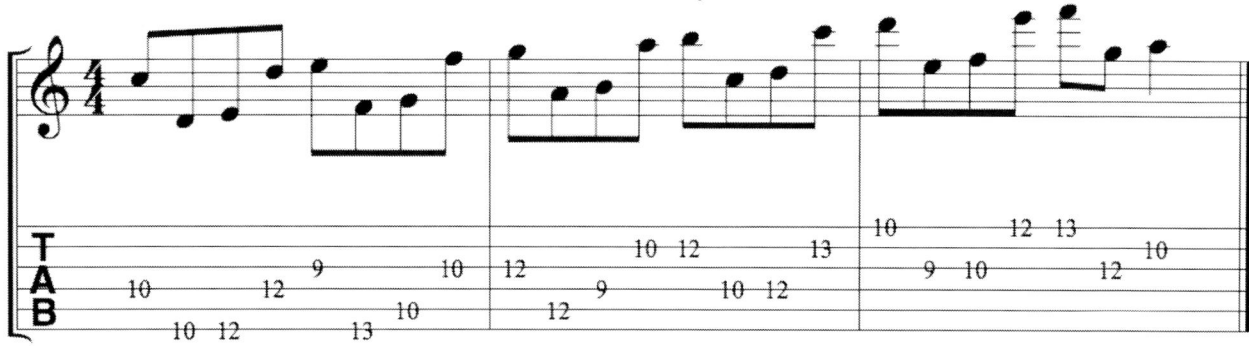

Inverse Weaving Sevenths In A Minor, 4th Position/C major, 2nd Position, Descending:

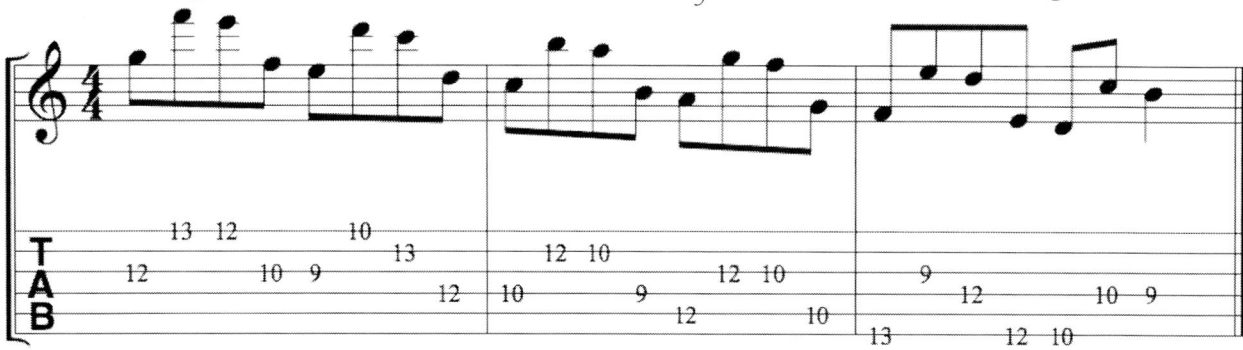

Inverse Weaving Sevenths In A Minor, 5th Position/C major, 3rd Position, Ascending:

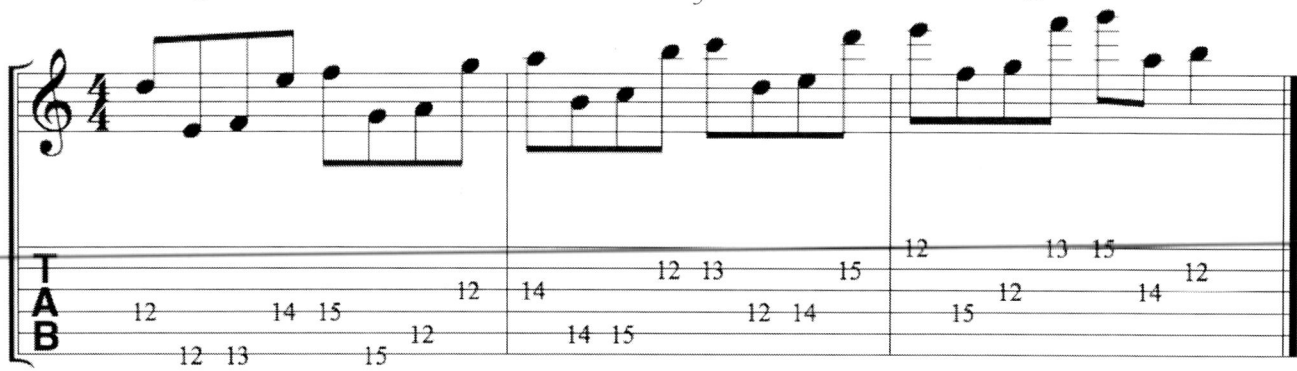

Inverse Weaving Sevenths In A Minor, 5th Position/C major, 3rd Position, Descending:

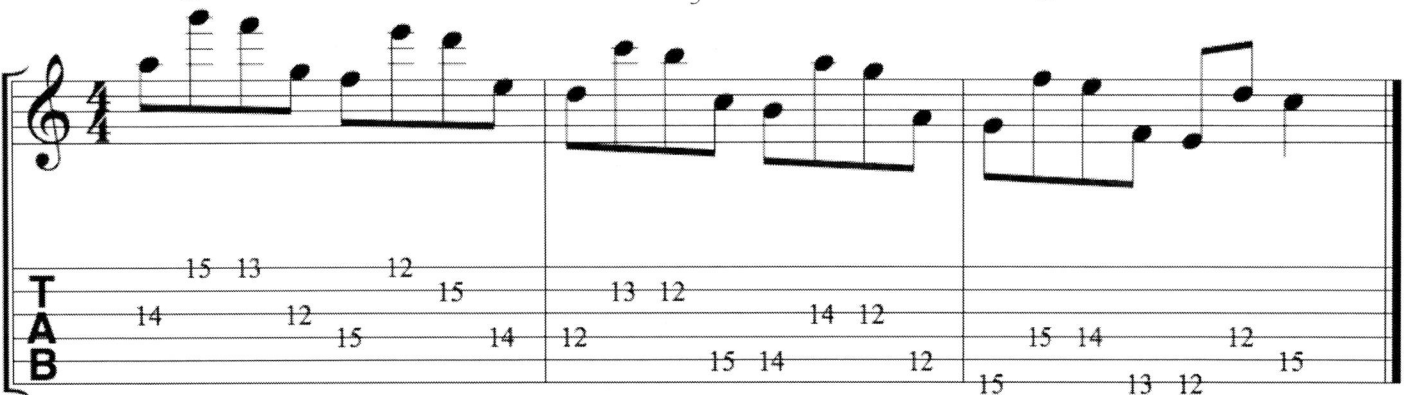

It may seem as though I've presented a wealth of melodic patterns over the course of this section. In reality, we are barely scraping the surface when it comes to melodic patterns. Beneath, I've included a short list of various diatonic melodic patterns, displayed in scale-tone numbers. These patterns can be applied to all scales and positions. I recommend transcribing these patterns in all positions of the scales provided through-out this book and setting up a serious practice regiment to start internalizing this material. The simple, yet extensive act of doing this will expand your improvising vocabulary a hundred-fold by the time you've completed the task. Be warned, this should take you at least a year. If you were doing nothing but melodic patterns for four hours per day, it would still take you a few months to get through all of it.

Note: The underlined scale-tones are there as an indicator of contour. Any underlined scale tone is a scale tone that you are approaching from above, moving downward. Scale-tones without an underline represent scale-tones that you're approaching from below, moving upward

Some Other Melodic Patterns:

1) R67R, 27R2, 3R23, 4234, 5345, 6456, 7567
2) R543, 2654, 3765, 4R76, 52R7, 632R, 7432
3) R7R, 2R2, 323, 434, 545, 656, 767
4) R43, 254, 365, 476, 5R7, 62R, 732
5) R7R3, 2R24, 3235, 4346, 5457, 656R, 7672
6) 5R7R, 62R2, 7323, R434, 2545, 3656, 4767
7) R534, 2645, 3756, 4R67, 527R, 63R2, 7423
8) R453, 2564, 3675, 47R6, 5R27, 623R, 7342
9) R235, 2346, 3457, 456R, 5672, 67R3, 7R24
10) R253, 2364, 3475, 45R6, 5627, 673R, 7R42
11) R7R32R, 2R2432, 323543, 434654, 545765, 656R76, 7672R7
12) R5432R, 265432, 376543, 4R7654, 52R765, 632R76, 7432R7
13) R253, 2364, 3475, 45R6, 5627, 673R, 7R42
14) R67R43, 27R254, 3R2365, 423476, 5345R7, 64562R, 756732
15) R5343R, 264542, 375653, 4R6764, 527R75, 63R2R6, 742327

Basic Triad Inversion

You can find an open-position chord glossary containing all open chord shapes in the back of this book. I suggest photocopying these, in order to save you some flipping back and forth. Rather than wasting space regurgitating these open position chords, I'll make sure you have the ability to figure out these plus countless other voicings. When that's out of the way, I'll share with you how to boil that down to some movable shapes that you can use in all keys.

Say you need an E major chord. E major is made up of E, G# and B. Anywhere on the fretboard that you can play a combination of those three notes is a valid voicing. You can have two or more of one particular note in the chord as long as you have at least one of each. Below, I have transcribed a couple common full-bodied voicings for the E chord along with three-note voicings that are very useful for group playing.

There are three types of these three-note voicings:

Voicing:	Low:	Mid:	High:
Root Position	Root	3rd	5th
1st inversion	3rd	5th	Root
2nd Inversion	5th	Root	3rd

Now we'll look at groups of these three note triad voicings in the key of C, one position at a time. Here we are in the open position, on the first set of 3 strings:

I: C 2nd inv.   II: Dm 2nd inv.   III: Em 1st inv.   IV: F 1st inv.   V: G 1st inv.   VI: Am root pos.

Now on the second set:

I: C 1st inv.   II: Dm 1st inv.   III: Em root pos.   IV: F root pos.   V: G 2nd inv   VI: Am 2nd inv.

Now on the third set:

I: C root pos.   II: Dm root pos.   III: Em 2nd Inv.   IV: F 2nd inv.   V: G 2nd inv.   VI: Am 2nd inv.

And finally on the fourth set:

I: C 2nd inv.   **II: Dm** 2nd inv.   **III: Em** 1st inv.   **IV: F** 2nd inv.   **V: G** root pos.   **VI: Am** root pos.

Now let's observe a couple sets in the 6th position of the same key. That puts us roughly, at the 5th fret.

I: C 1st inv.   **II: Dm** root pos.   **III: Em** root pos.   **IV: F** 2nd inv.   **V: G** 2nd inv.   **VI: Am** 1st inv.

I: C 2nd inv.   **II: Dm** 2nd inv.   **III: Em** 1st inv.   **IV: F** 1st inv.   **V: G** 1st inv.   **VI: Am** root pos.

To make a long story short, these shapes can be mapped out in any key, in any position and on any set of strings. I'd highly recommend doing the legwork. The better you know your triads and scale positions, the easier things will be, so keep wood-shedding them and using them in all keys.

133

DIATONIC HARMONY - Part 4: Four-Note Chords

Triads provide the basic colors of harmony where as 7th chords provide the more sophisticated shades. A seventh chord occurs when we extend up to the 7th from the root, only using odd numbers: Root, 3, 5 and 7. Four different types of 7th chords occur in the major key: Major 7th (maj7), minor 7th (m7), dominant 7th (7) and minor 7th flat 5th (m7b5). The I and IV are maj7, the II, III and VI are m7, the V is dominant 7th and the VII is min7b5.

INTERVAL	Root	Distance	3rd	Distance	5th	Distance	7th	CHORD
I	C	2w	E	1½	G	2w	B	Cmaj7
II	D	1½	F	2w	A	1½	C	Dm7
III	E	1½	G	2w	B	1½	D	Em7
IV	F	2w	A	1½	C	2w	E	Fmaj7
V	G	2w	B	1½	D	1½	F	G7
VI	A	1½	C	2w	E	1½	G	Am7
VII:	B	1½	D	1½	F	2w	A	Bm7b5

Each 7th chord can be thought of as a triad, one scale-wise third above the bass note. In other words: Cmaj7 contains C, E, G and B. The E, G and B can be thought of as an Em triad. Cmaj7 = Em/C

This is a handy thing to know when soloing over seventh chords.

7TH CHORD:	TRIAD/BASS NOTE:
Cmaj7	Em/C
Dm7	F/D
Em7	G/E
Fmaj7	Am/F
G7	Bdim/G
Am7	C/A
Bm7b5	Dm/B

Seventh Chord Voicings

Here are some basic moveable 7th chord shapes, organized by chord type and chord form, with finger numbers included beneath the fret boxes. I've included a couple chords that we derive from scales we haven't yet talked about; the minor natural 7th chord and the diminished 7th chord. Get to know these as we'll soon be going over the musical applications for these chords. It's worth noting that I didn't use Xs to denote avoided strings with the exception of muted strings in between the other chord tones because these strings, you will have to physically mute with some part of your fretting hand finger, typically the finger playing the bass-note. You'll also see some chord tones in parenthesis. These are merely reference notes to help you place the chord but in some cases can be treated as optional notes to add, most likely after deleting another note from the chord.

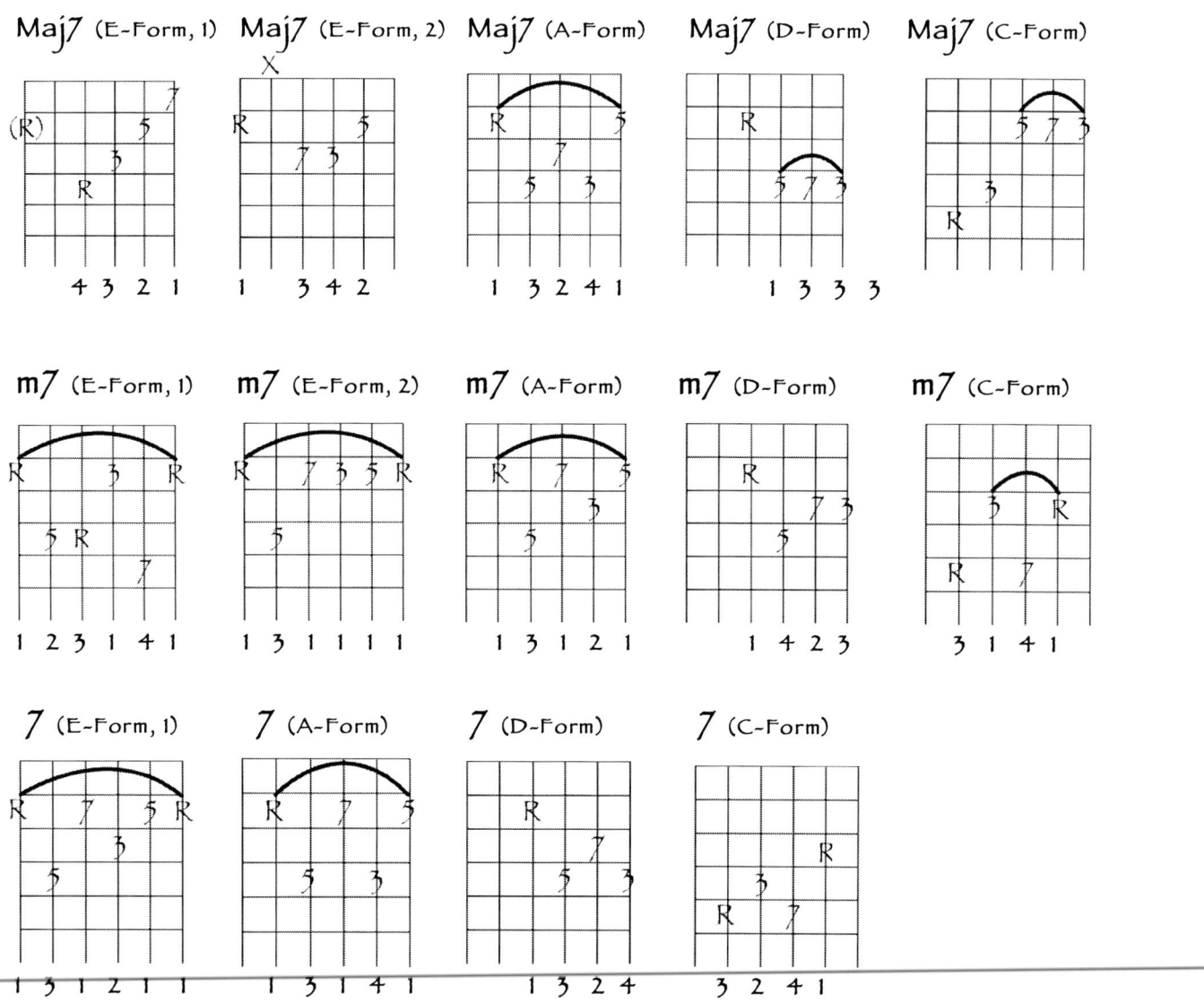

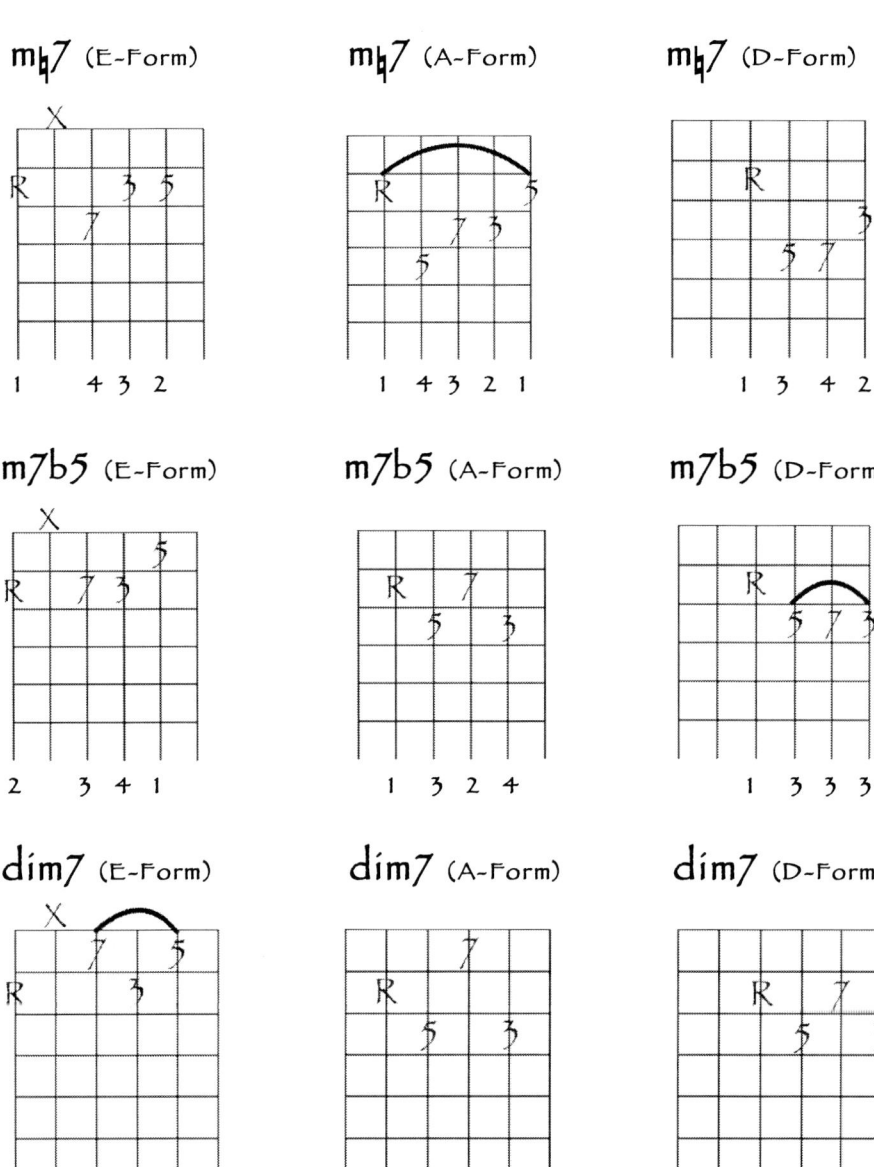

Any of these voicings can be turned into open chords by orientating the lowest used frets of the voicings at the open strings and adjusting your finger choices to accommodate the easier shape left on the frets. For instance an open position Bbdim7 would be (from low to high strings, in fret numbers) X1202 and in this case we can include 0 on the high E-string since E is a member of Bbdim7. This could more easily be fingered by the first, second and third fingers.

These next shapes are what we call shell voicings. These are stripped down to have only one of each note and exclude the 5th. We can justify excluding the fifth on two accounts. First, it's already a very strong overtone contained in the root note, and secondly, it's the same note whether it's a major, minor or dominant chord and therefore doesn't contribute to the overall color and character of the chord.

The idea with stripping chord voicings down to the bare minimum is to make room for other instruments or added tensions and color tones. You'll be learning more about this soon. At the end of this Four-Note Chords section, I've included a standard progression in full voicings and shell voicings in every key.

6th Chords

If we play first inversions of 7th chords, the resulting chords are 6th chords. For instance, if we invert a Cmaj7 chord, you arrive at an Emb6 chord. Minor b6th chords are the least common type of 6th chord which is fine, given that chord voicings for them on the guitar are rather difficult. However, both major and minor sixth chords are very popular devices. Major 6th chords come about by inverting a m7 chord up a chord-tone. Minor 6th chords come about by inverting a m7b5 chord up a chord-tone. The graph below, upon observation, should offer some clarification of what I'm saying if your head is starting to ache.

INTERVAL	Root	Distance	3rd	Distance	5th	Distance	6th	CHORD
I	E	1½	G	2w	B	½	C	Emb6
II	F	2w	A	1½	C	1w	D	F6
III	G	2w	B	1½	D	1w	E	G6
IV	A	1½	C	2w	E	½	F	Amb6
V	B	1½	D	1½	F	1w	G	X
VI	C	2w	E	1½	G	1w	A	C6
VII:	D	1½	F	2w	A	1w	B	Dm6

6th chords typically substitute the diatonic relative chord of the same bass-note. For instance, a C6 would serve as a replacement for a C or Cmaj7 chord. In pop and rock music, they can be written into the progression. Sometimes they are written into a jazz progression but they're usually used as an on the spot substitute for a maj7 by the improvising accompanist. They have a softer quality then that of a 7th chord and their subtlety can prove very useful in songwriting. They can be found in many Beatles and Beatles-inspired songs. The place where they are found most prominently is in the area of early jazz and western swing. Some experimentation with these chords should give you some idea of how they will be creatively useful to you, as long as you really thoroughly explore the contextual possibilities. (The surrounding chords.)

An advantageous feature that major 6th chords have is the lack of a 7th to define whether they are major (I, IV) or dominant (V). This allows them to replace a maj7 chord just as easily as a 7 chord. You could look at a 6th as being a suspension of the 7th, creating a more neutral sounding major chord. The same holds true of the m6 chord in relation to the m7 and m♭7 chords.

Below, you'll find common voicings for major and minor 6th chords, presented in E, A, D and C forms. Take your time with them as some will at first prove difficult. Practice switching between them and any other chords.

6th Chord Voicings

6 (E-Form)   6 (A-Form)   6 (D-Form)   6 (C-Form)

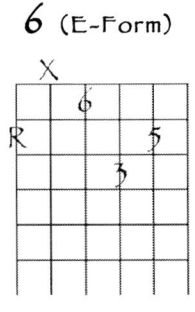

m6 (E-Form)   m6 (A-Form)   m6 (D-Form)   m6 (C-Form)

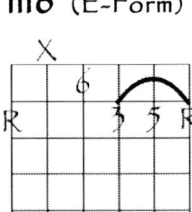 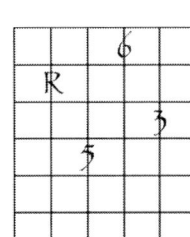 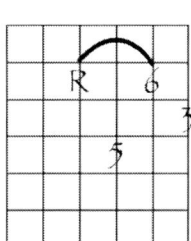 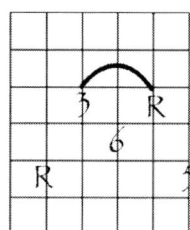

add9 Chords

The add9 chord is a nice alternative when you want a four-note chord in place of a triad but 6th and 7th chords are sounding to jazzy for your needs.

INTERVAL	Root	Distance	3rd	Distance	5th	Distance	9th	CHORD
I	C	2w	E	1½	G	3½	D	Cadd9
II	D	1½	F	1½	A	3½	E	Dmadd9
III	E	1½	G	2w	B	3w	F	X
IV	F	2w	A	2w	C	3½	G	Fadd9
V	G	2w	B	1½	D	3½	A	Gadd9
VI	A	1½	C	2w	E	3½	B	Amadd9
VII:	B	1½	D	1½	F	3½	C	X

add9 (E-form)
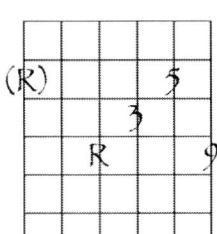

add9 (A-form)
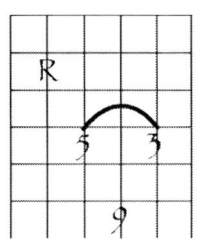

add9 (G-form)
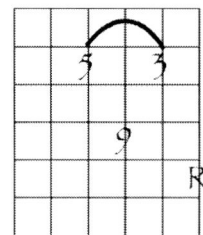

add9 (C-form)
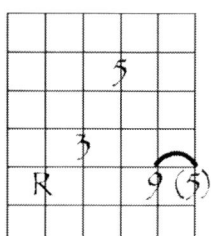

madd9 (E-form)
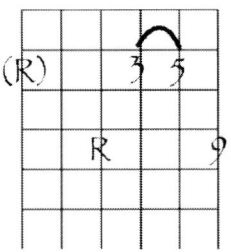

madd9 (A-form)
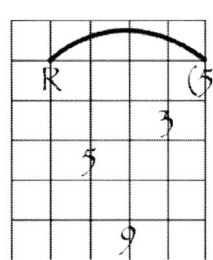

madd9 (G-form)
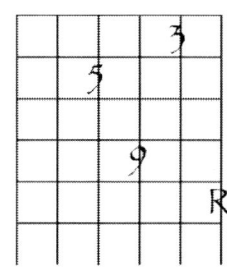

madd9 (C-form)
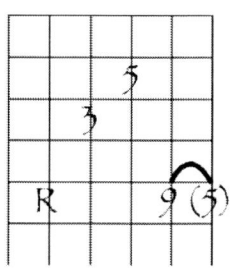

A Standard 7th Chord Progression In All Keys

C Major/A Minor, Full Voicings:

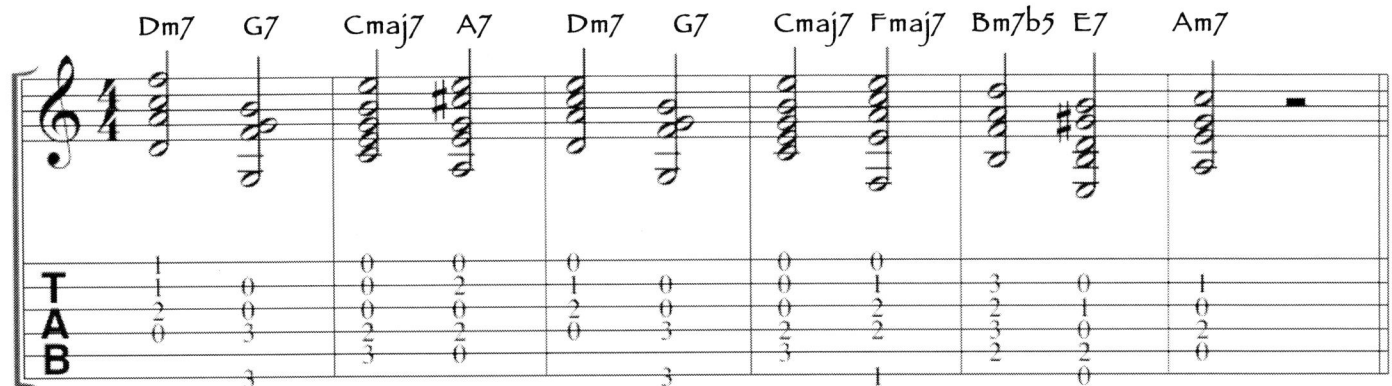

C Major/A Minor, Shell Voicings:

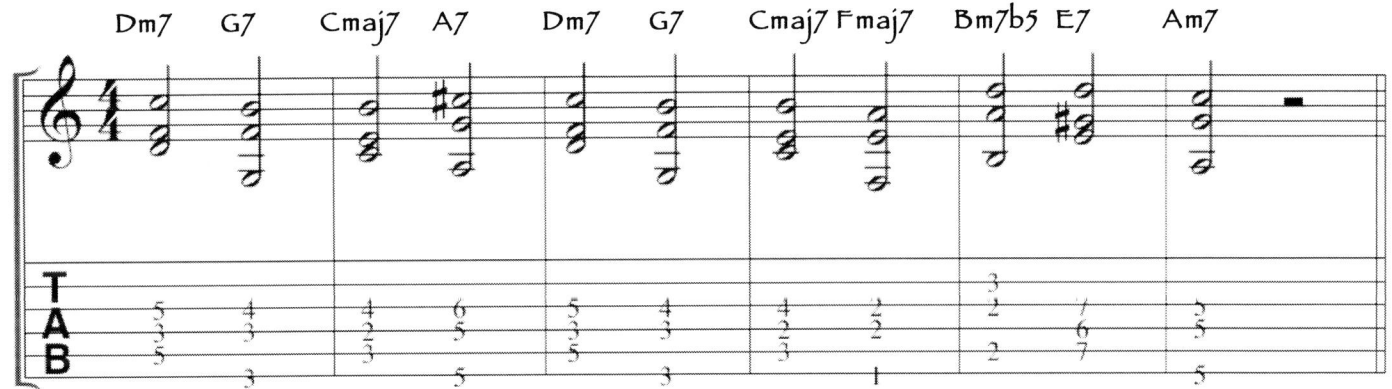

F Major/D Minor, Full Voicings:

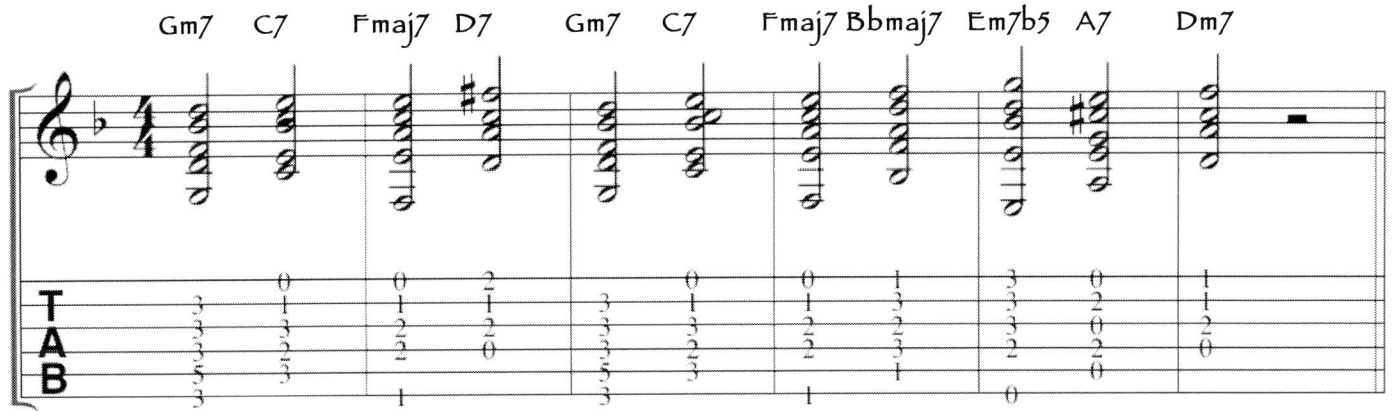

F Major/D Minor, Shell Voicings:

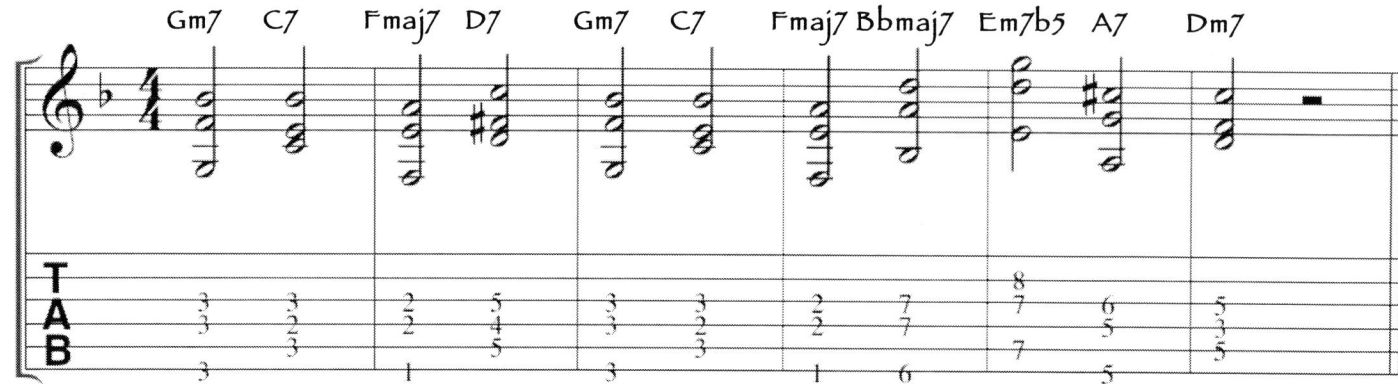

Bb Major/G Minor, Full Voicings:

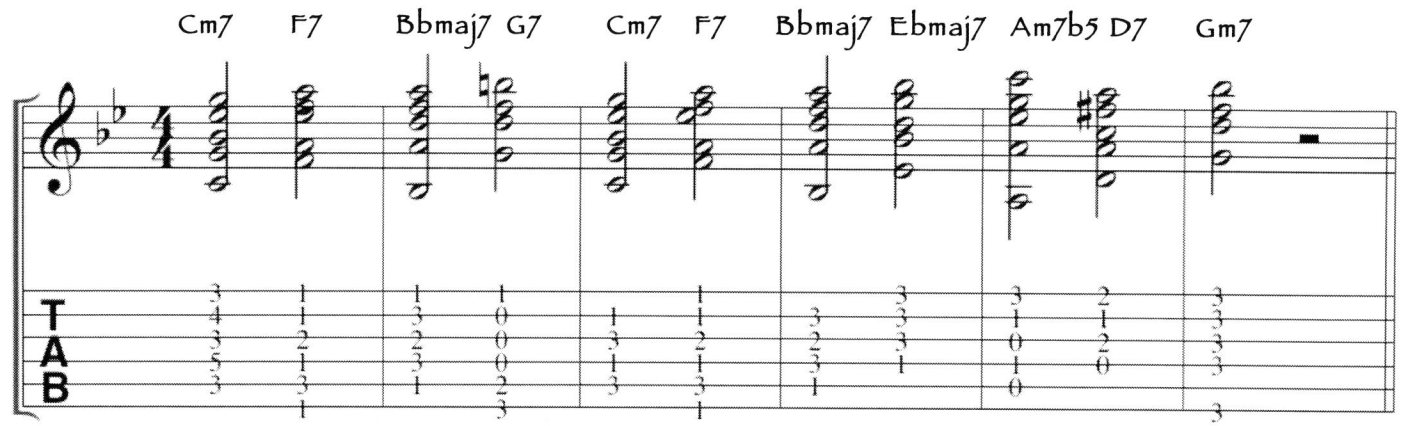

Bb Major/G Minor, Shell Voicings:

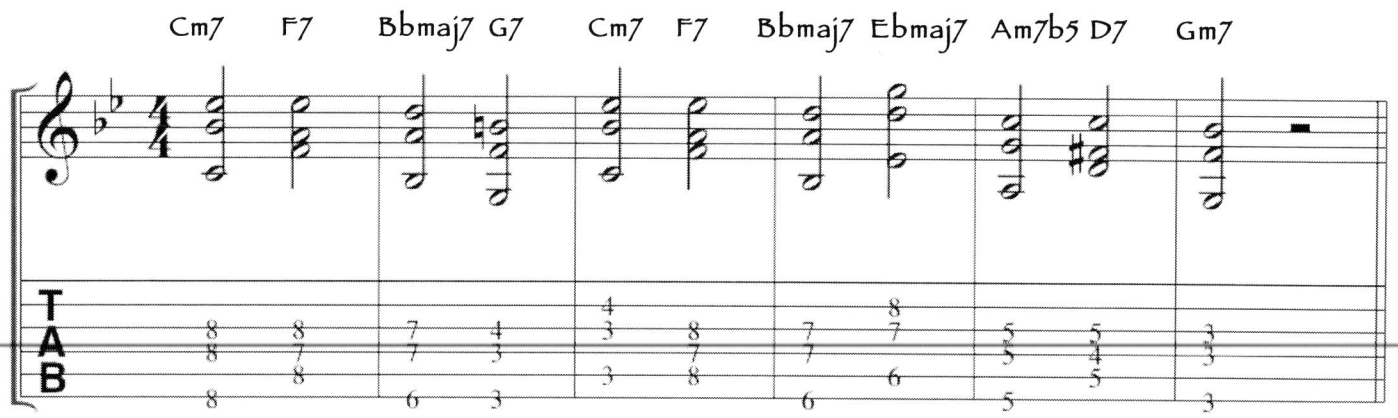

Eb Major/C Minor, Full Voicings:

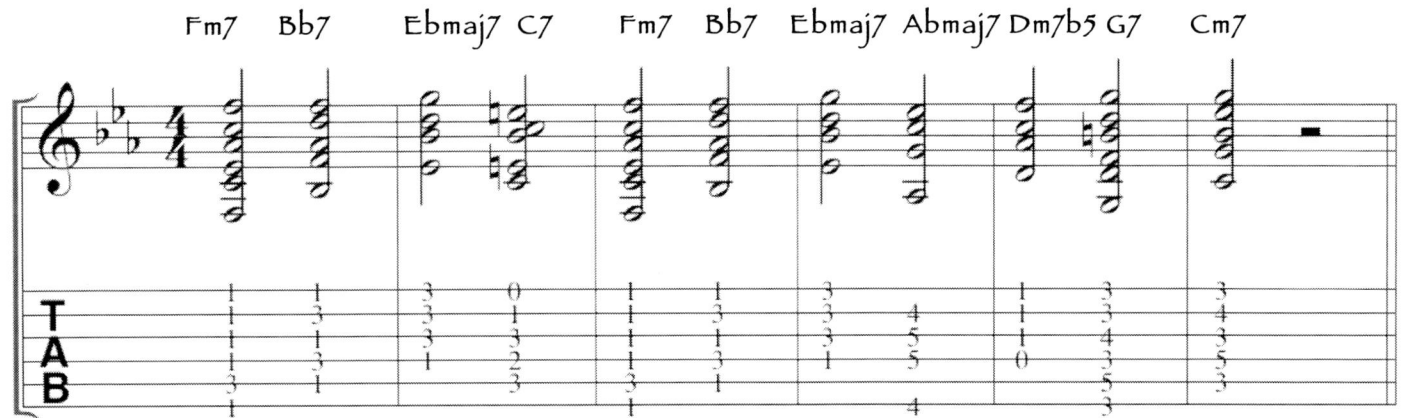

Eb Major/C Minor, Shell Voicings:

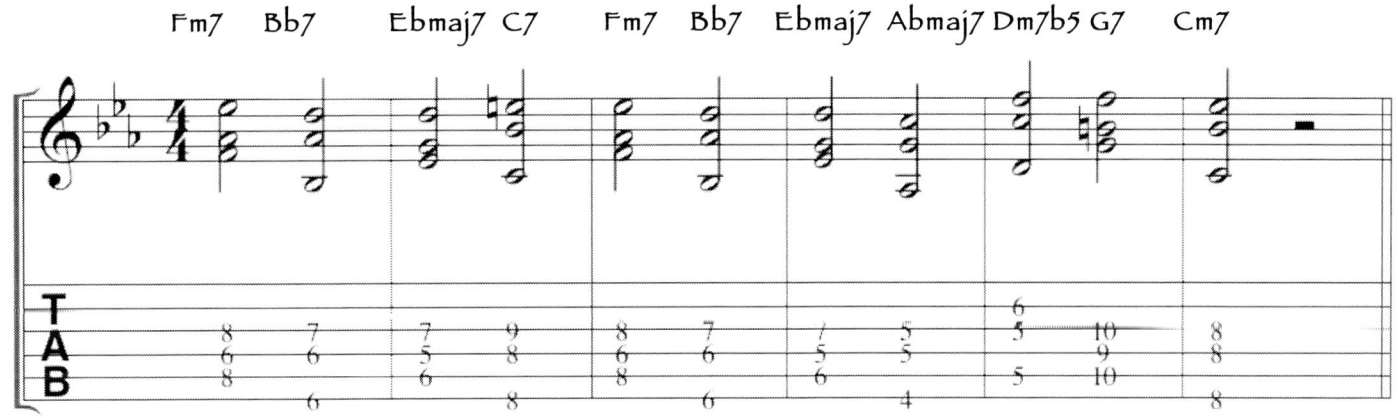

Ab Major/F Minor, Full Voicings:

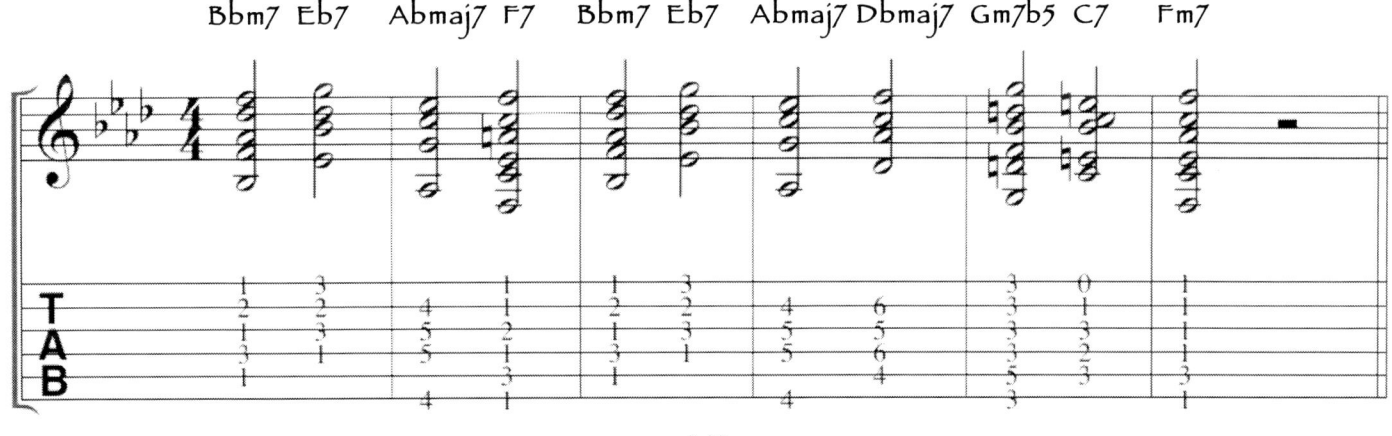

Ab Major/F Minor, Shell Voicings:

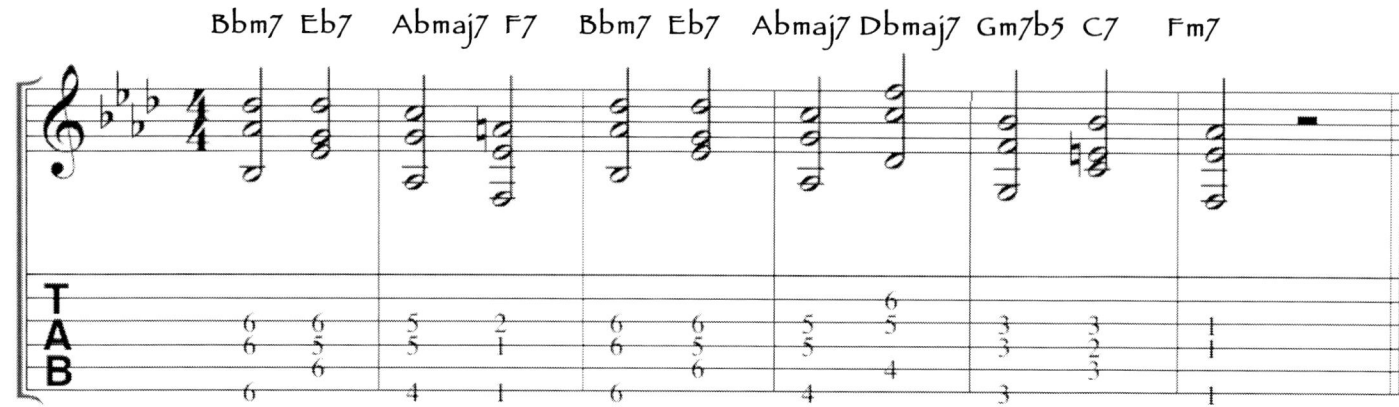

Db Major/Bb Minor, Full Voicings:

Db Major/Bb Minor, Shell Voicings:

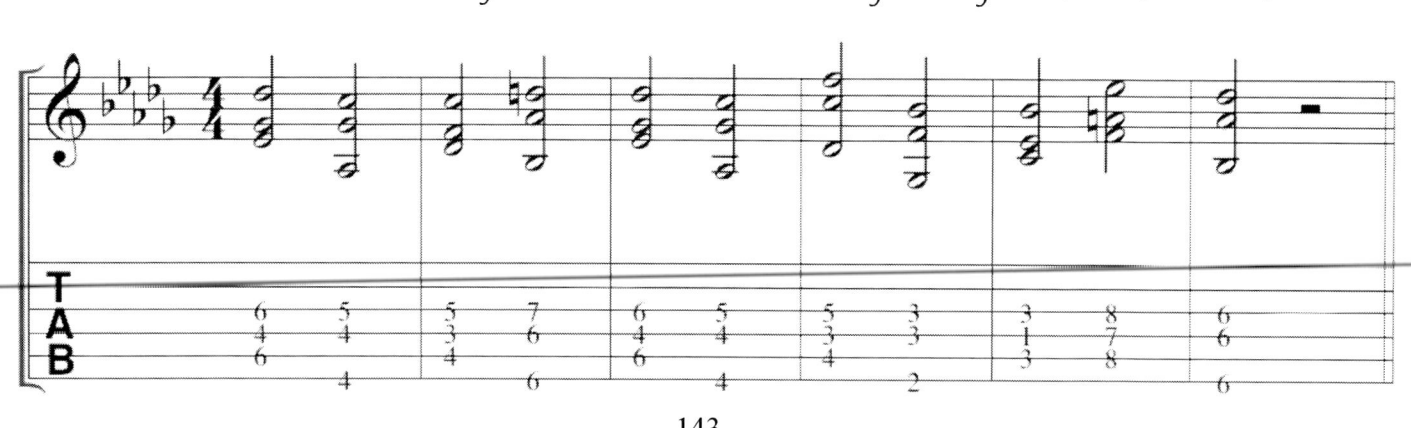

Gb Major/Eb Minor, Full Voicings:

Gb Major/Eb Minor, Shell Voicings:

B Major/G# Minor, Full Voicings:

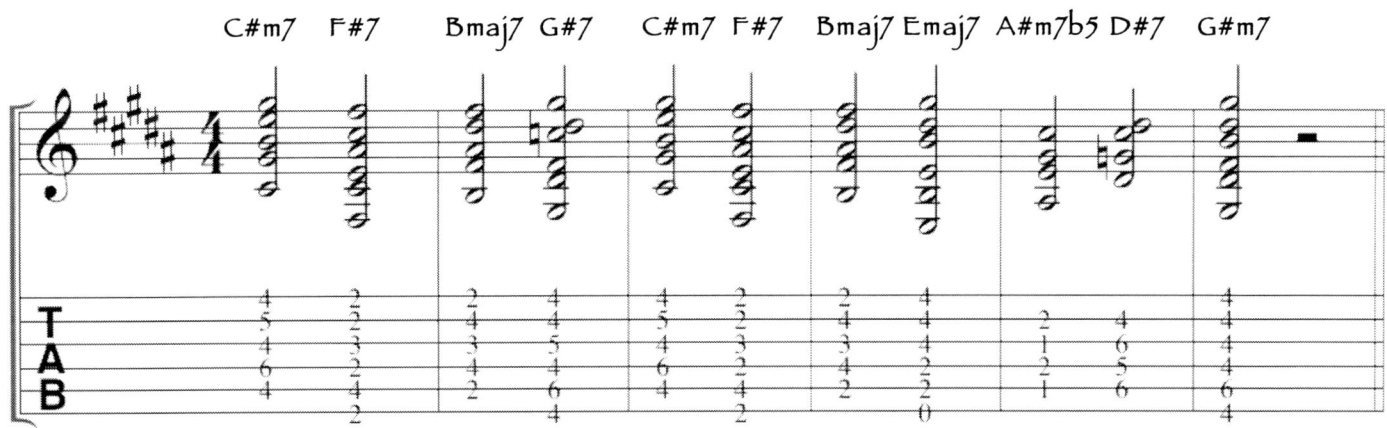

B Major/G# Minor, Shell Voicings:

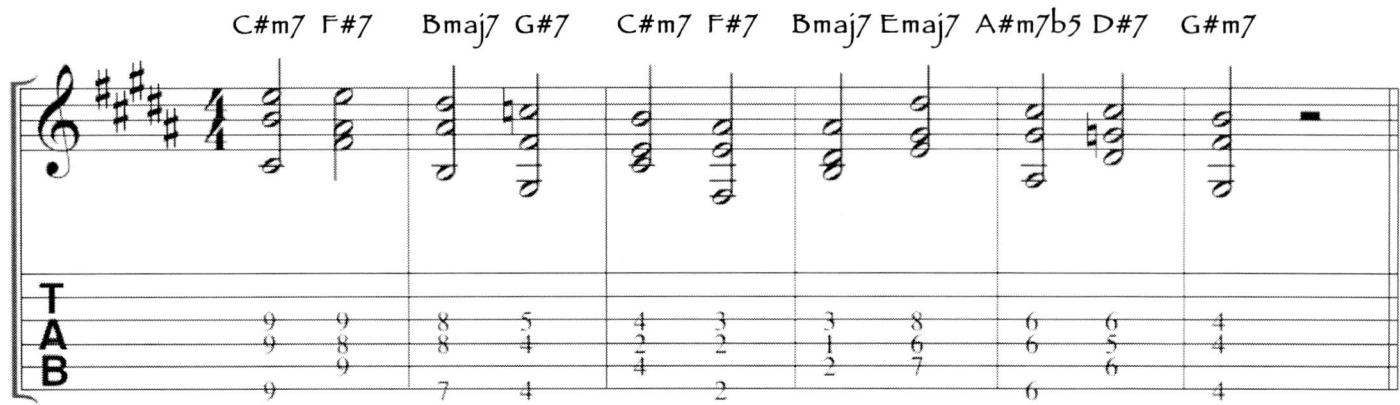

E Major/C# Minor, Full Voicings:

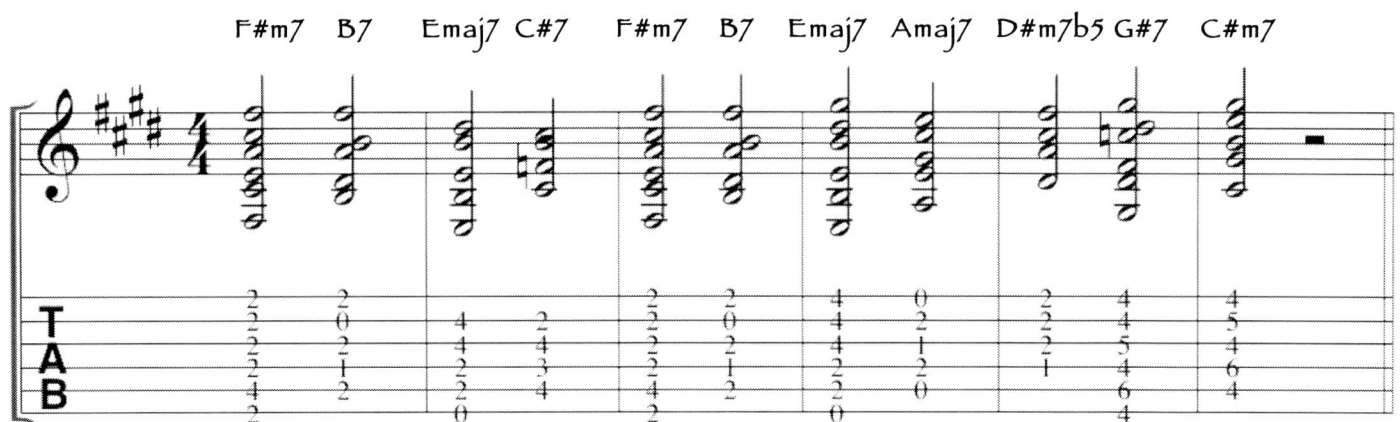

E Major/C# Minor, Shell Voicings:

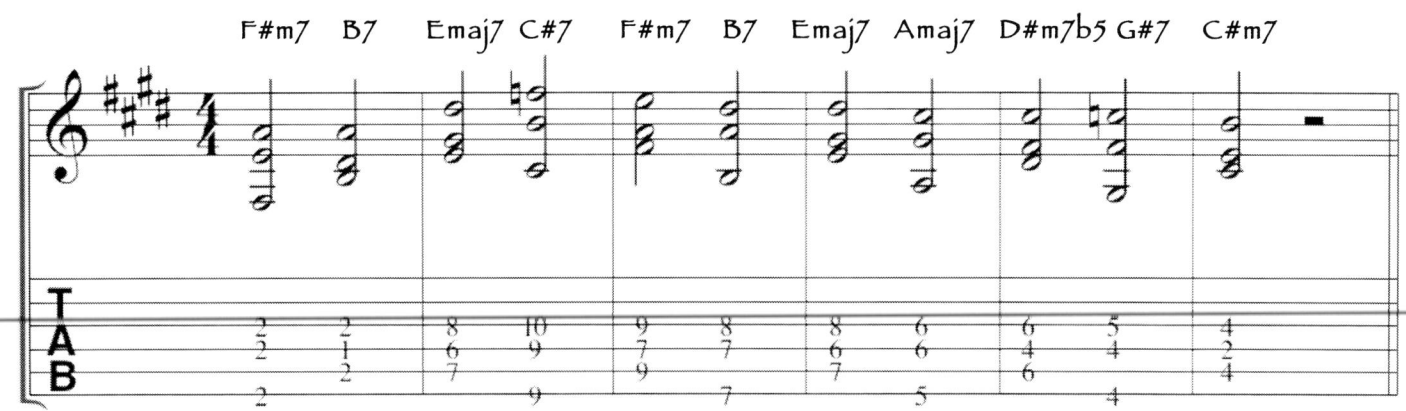

A Major/F# Minor, Full Voicings:

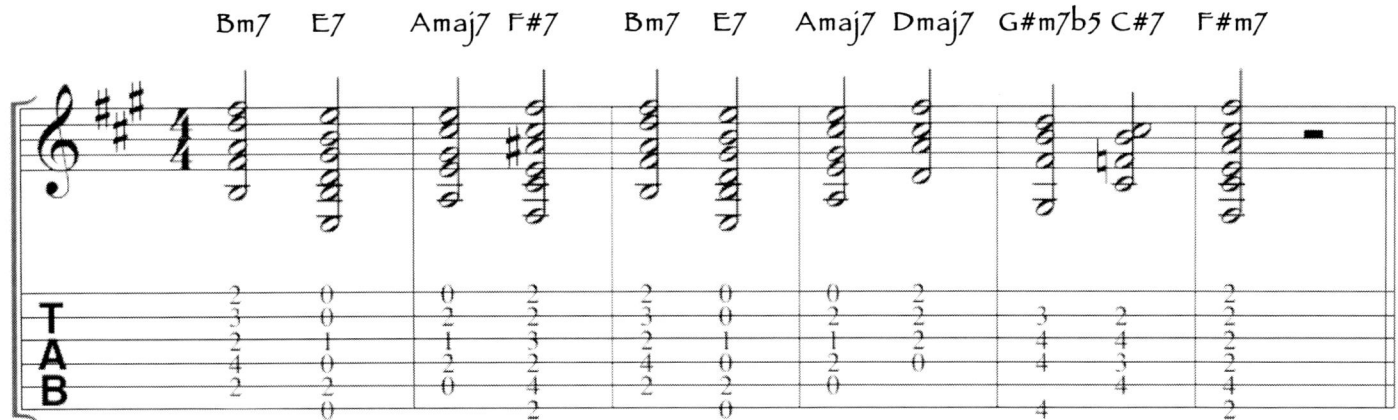

A Major/F# Minor, Shell Voicings:

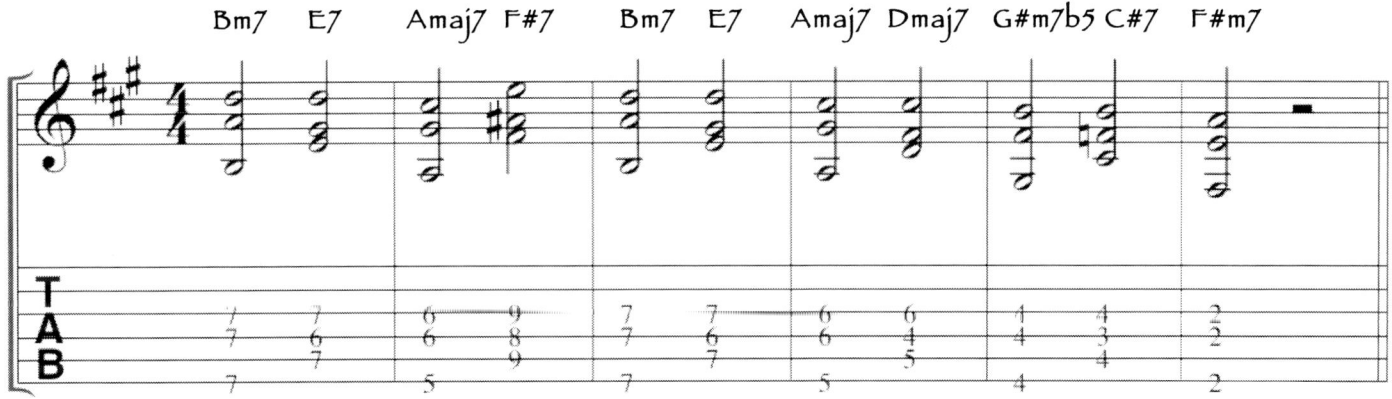

D Major/B Minor, Full Voicings:

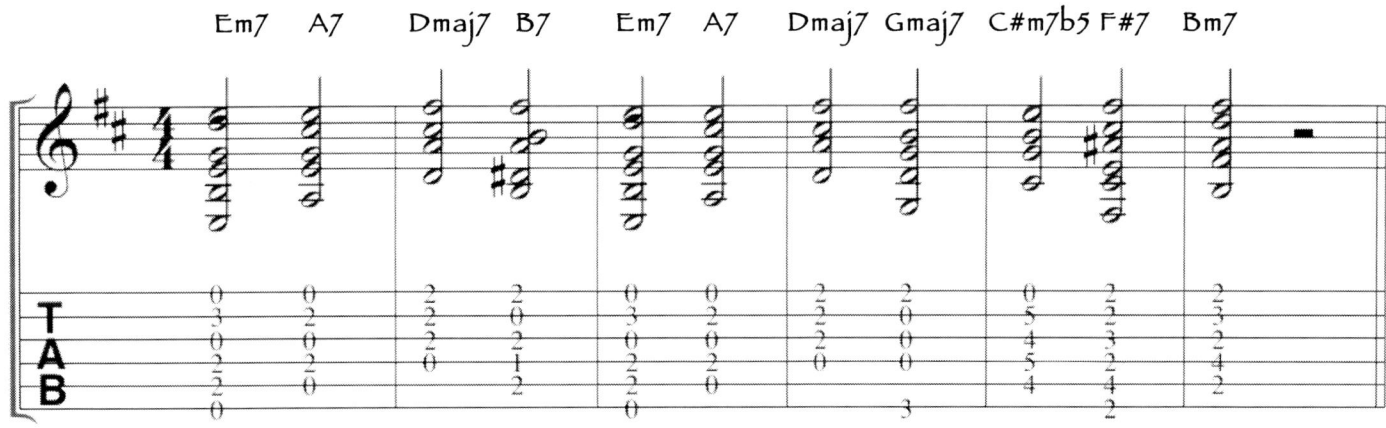

D Major/B Minor, Shell Voicings:

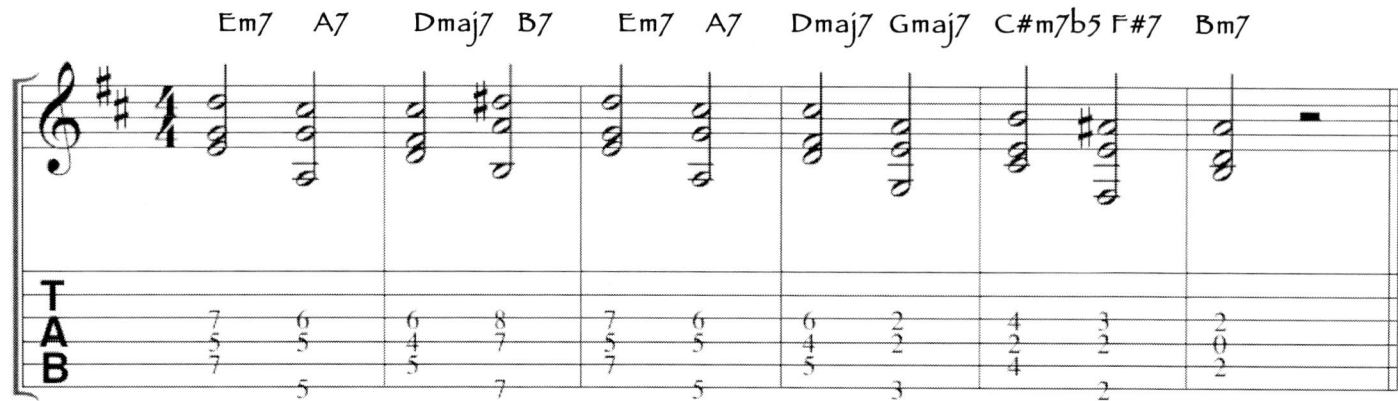

G Major/E Minor, Full Voicings:

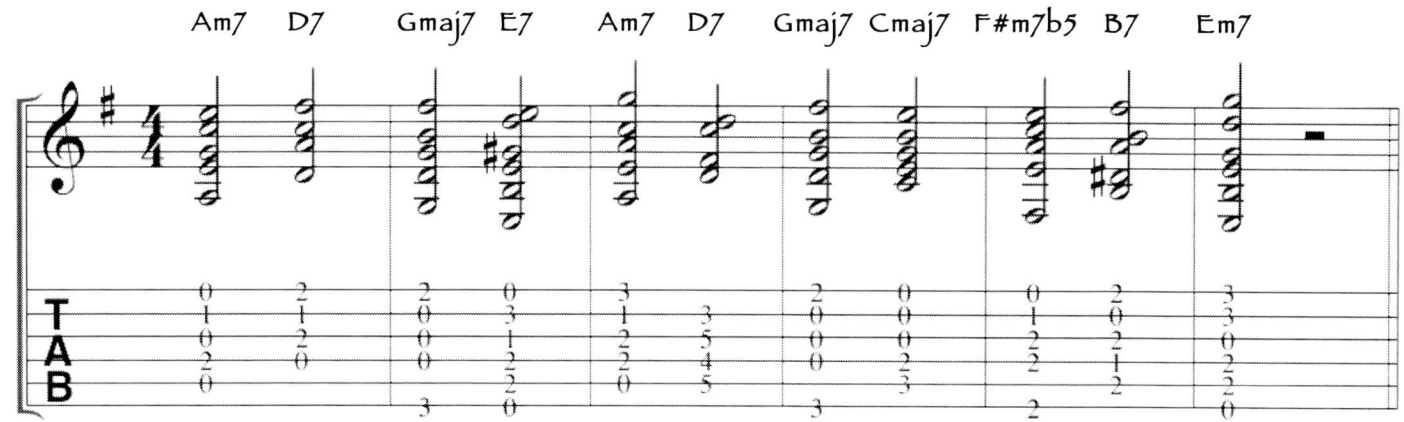

G Major/E Minor, Shell Voicings:

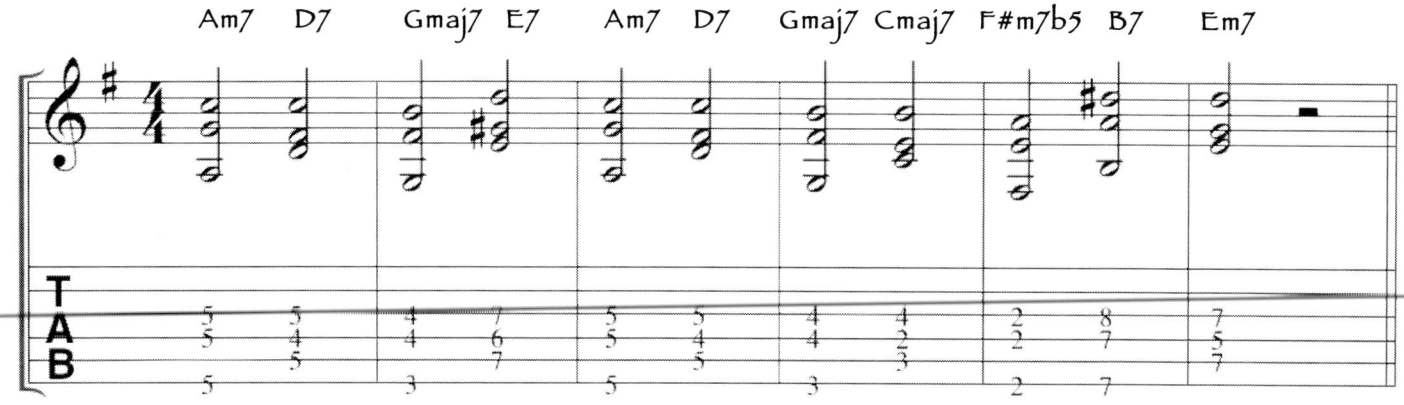

Triad Pairs

This is where all these triad voicings become very useful. Two-chord vamps serve as a very common harmonic backdrop and the usefulness of these triad pairs is pretty obvious in that context. If you're playing rhythm guitar or comping over a vamp that shifts between two chords, a solid knowledge of these combinations will allow you to move anywhere on the fretboard with ease and grace. This allows you to duck and weave out of the way of a vocalist, soloist or keyboardist, which will lend a much more concise overall sound to the band.

Another less obvious application for these combinations is the use of them over one static chord. This will provide you with some very evenly distributed active and inactive tones as they relate to the given chord. This can allow you to create some nice counter-melodic figures built entirely from chords or even to harmonize the given main melody with much ease. Keep this concept in mind if you ever have to write vocal harmonies for any type of modern pop or rock song.

These examples are all written in the key of C major (or A natural minor). Once you are comfortable with all of them in these keys, work out where the same shapes will fall on the fretboard in all your other keys. I'd strongly recommend following through the cycle of 5ths. With each triad pair, we'll look at them on each set of three adjacent strings followed by positional sets where we cross over from one string set to the next.

The first triad pair we'll look at is that of the IV and V chords. When these are played against a static IV chord, the notes of the IV chord serve as inactive (resolving) tones and the notes of the V chord serve as the active tones. When played against the V chord, the reverse is true. This pair will also work nicely against a static IIm7 chord where the IV triad would be mostly inactive and the V triad would be mostly inactive.

The only diatonic note of the key to which you wouldn't have instant access would be the 3rd. If you were harmonizing a melody where the 3rd was involved, you could simply swap the IV triad with the VIm triad, which has the 3rd of the key as its 5th. You could also swap the V triad with the IIIm triad, which has the 3rd of the key as its root. If there is no specific melody to harmonize, a complete absence of the 3rd will in no way detract from the musical effect.

F-G, Set 1:

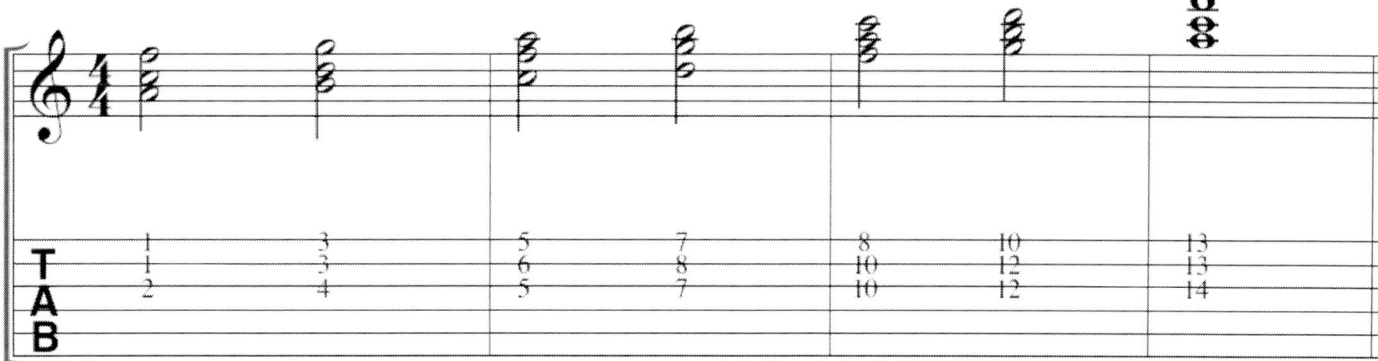

F-G, Set 2:

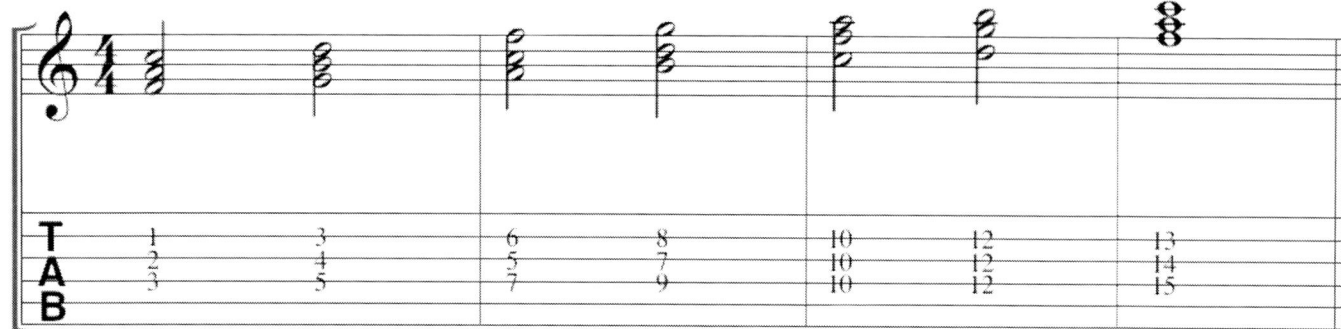

F-G, Set 3:

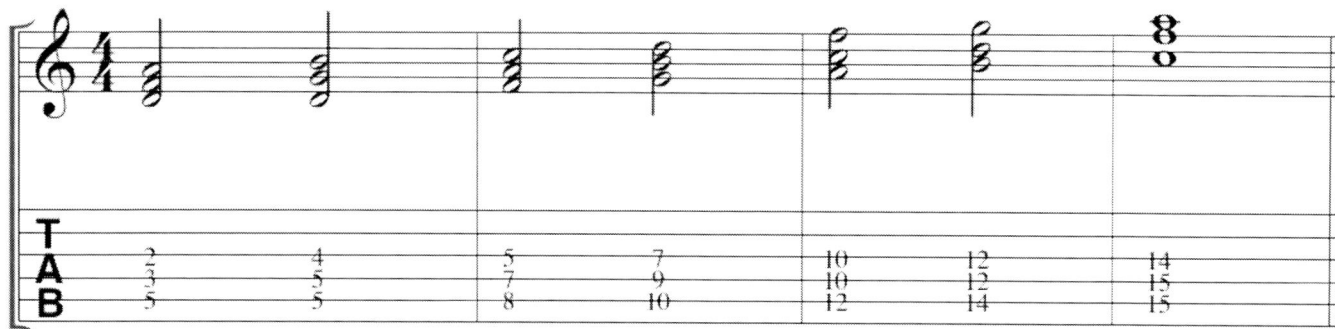

F-G, Set 4:

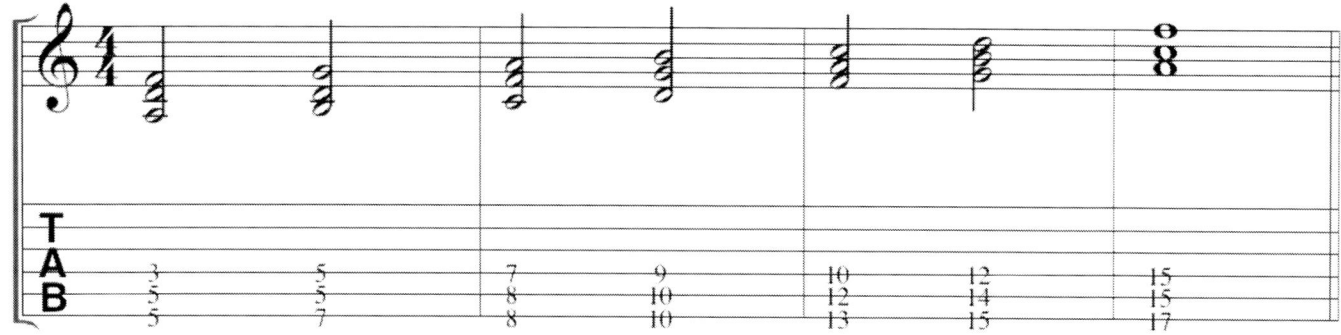

F-G, Crossover 1:

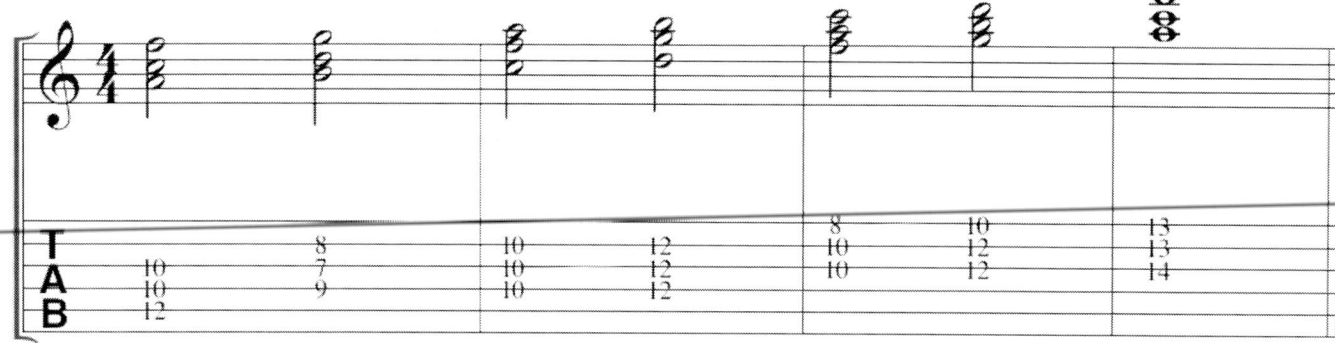

F-G, Crossover 2:

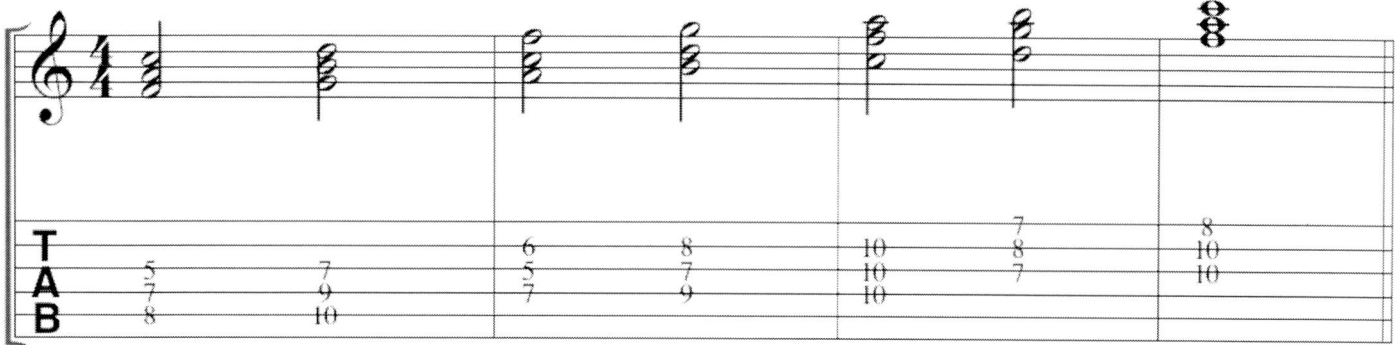

F-G, Crossover 3:

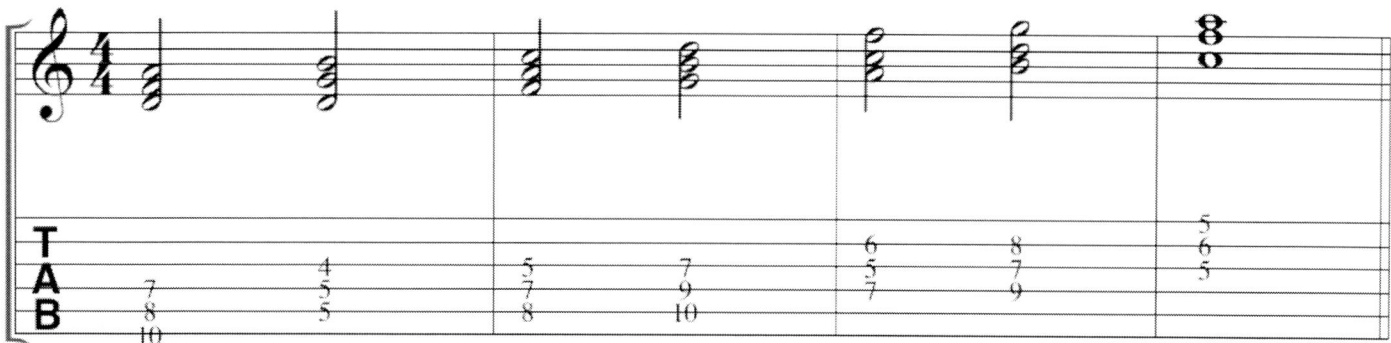

F-G, Crossover 4:

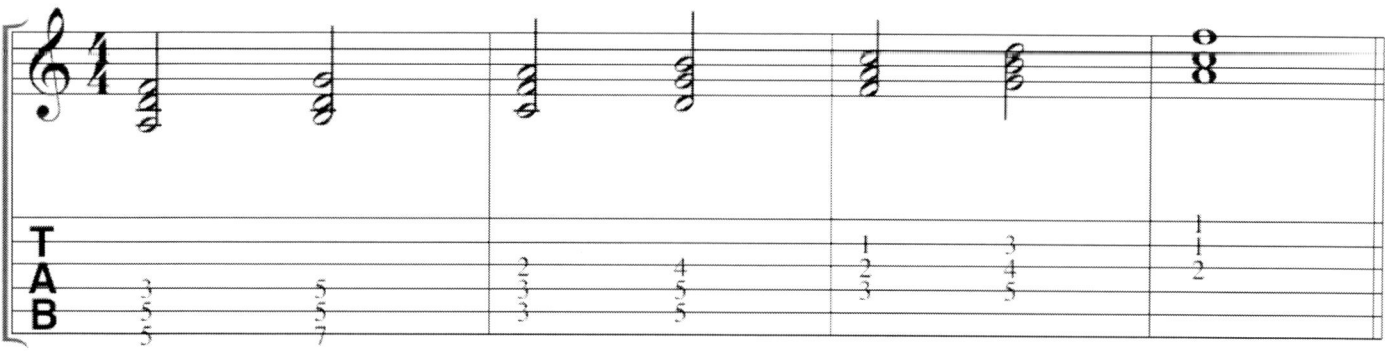

This next pair, made up of the IIm and I triads, will work over either chord as a static harmony but could also work over a non-diatonic chord known as the bVIImaj7. In the key of C, this would be a Bbmaj7. 7th chords are covered further on in this book. Upon studying 7th chords, the logic of this application will become clear. For the time being, put your efforts into getting the basic mechanics of these transitions under your fingers with confidence that you'll have multiple ways of applying these triads as your harmonic knowledge continues to expand.

Being that the study of these triads is being limited to opposing triads (they share no common tones between them), you will always be short one note in the key that you happen to be playing. In the case of this pair, you're without the 7th of the key. If this note is needed for melodic purposes, briefly trade in the I triad for the IIIm triad, since the majority of these notes are common to both chords. The 5th of the IIIm triad is the 7th of the key.

Dm-C, Set 1:

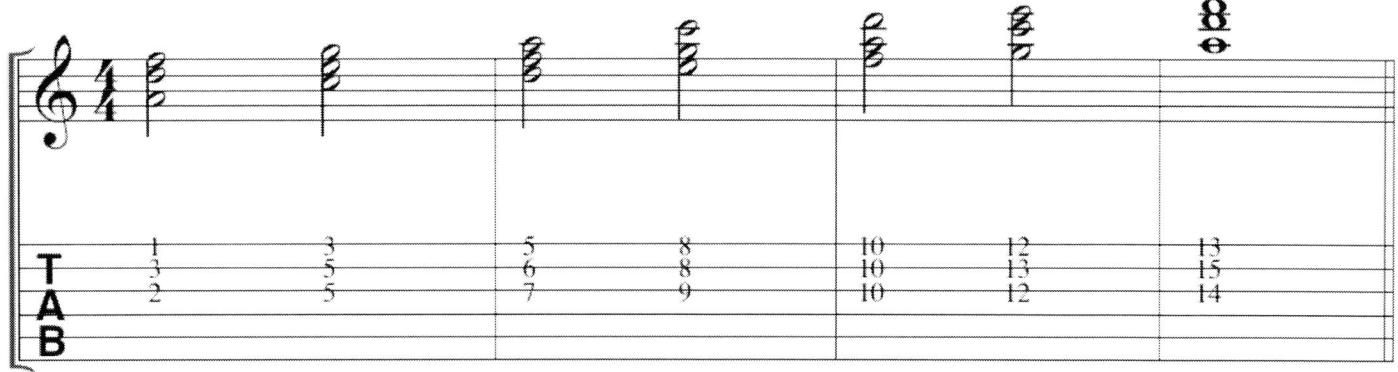

Dm-C, Set 2:

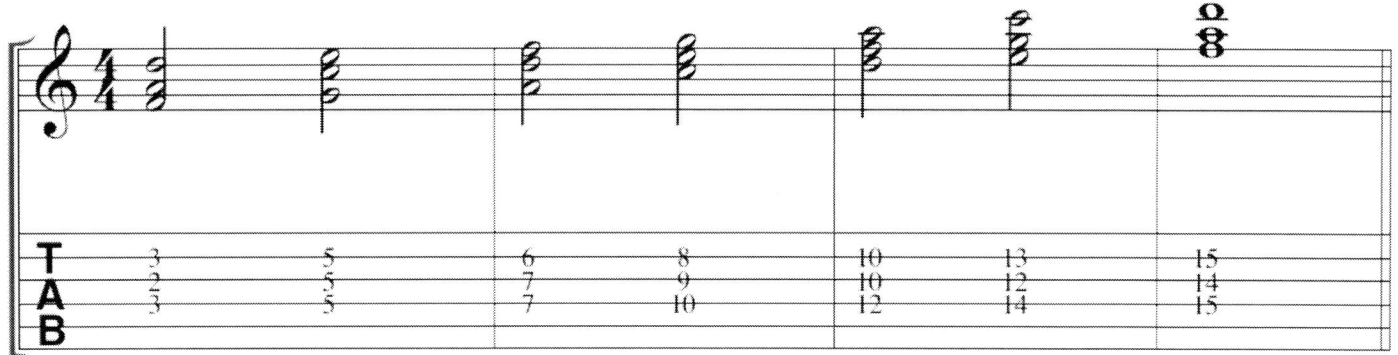

Dm-C, Set 3:

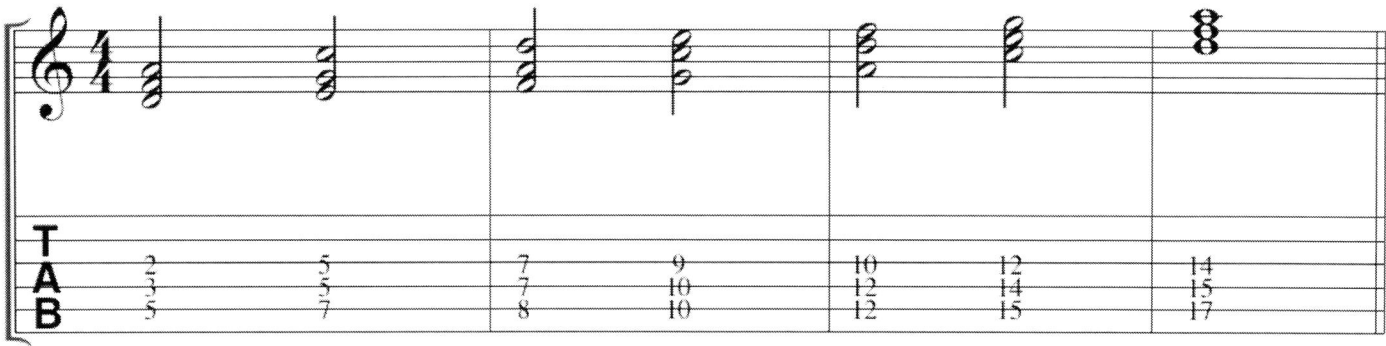

Dm-C, Set 4:

Dm-C, Crossover 1:

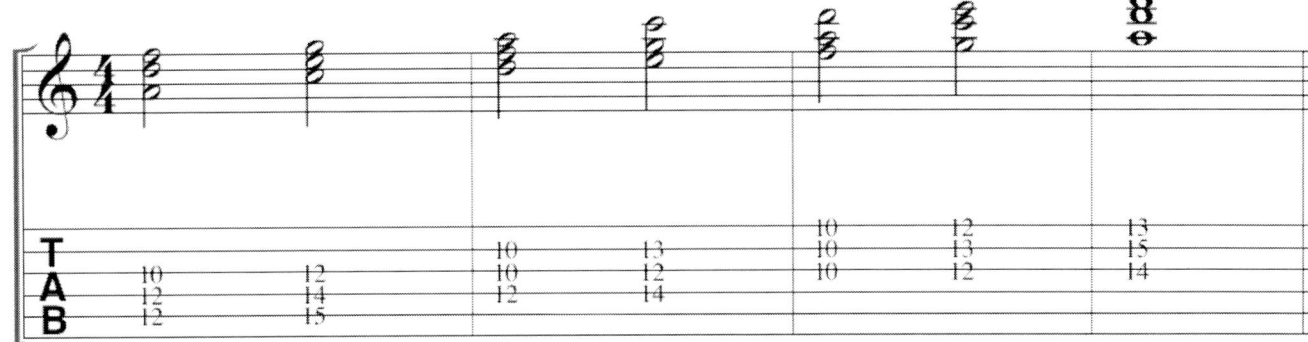

Dm-C, Crossover 2:

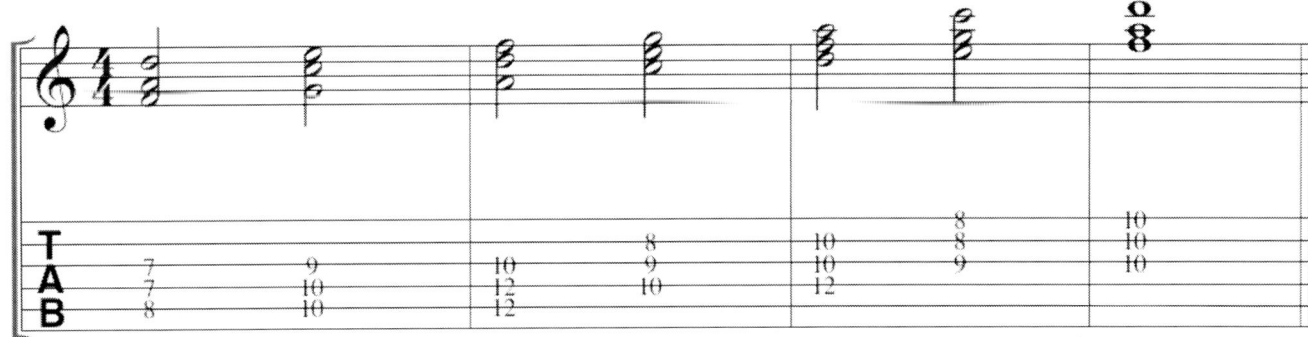

Dm-C, Crossover 3:

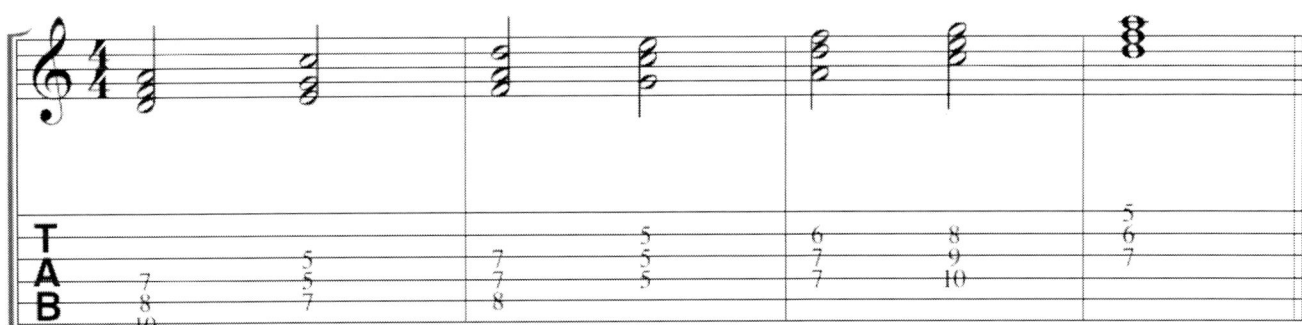

Dm-C, Crossover 4:

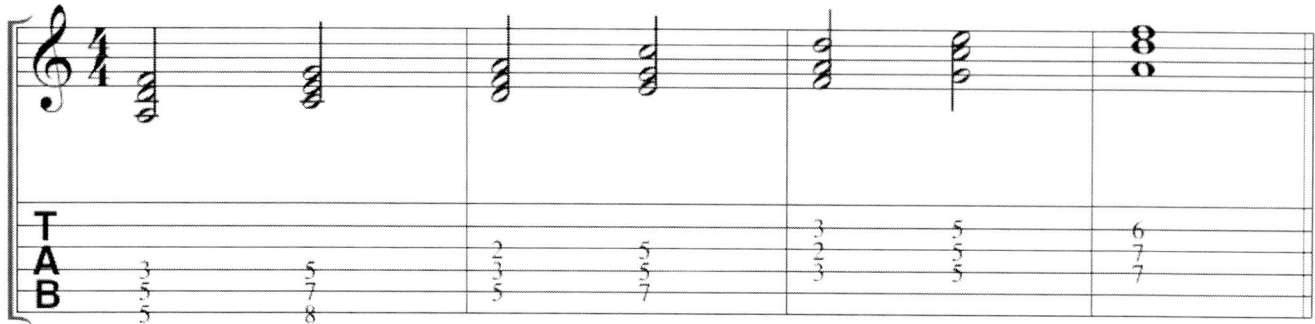

This following pair, made up of the IIIm and IV triads, will work over either chord as a static harmony but could also work over a Imaj7 or a V7 for a sunny, somewhat jazzy sound. Again, 7th chords haven't yet been introduced at this point in our journey so make a note to revisit this section as you cover further sections on harmony. Most rock, pop, folk and country applications for these triad pairs are of a simpler nature. Jazz is where we find the more advanced relationships between these triad pairs and extended chords.

Your missing scale tone in this case happens to be the 2nd. If you need the 2nd as a melodic tone, replace the IV triad with the IIm triad, whose root note is the 2nd of the scale. The 3rd and 5th of the IIm also serve as the root and 3rd of the IV chord. As with other similar substitutions, it only needs to take place for the duration of the needed melody note.

Em-F, Set 1:

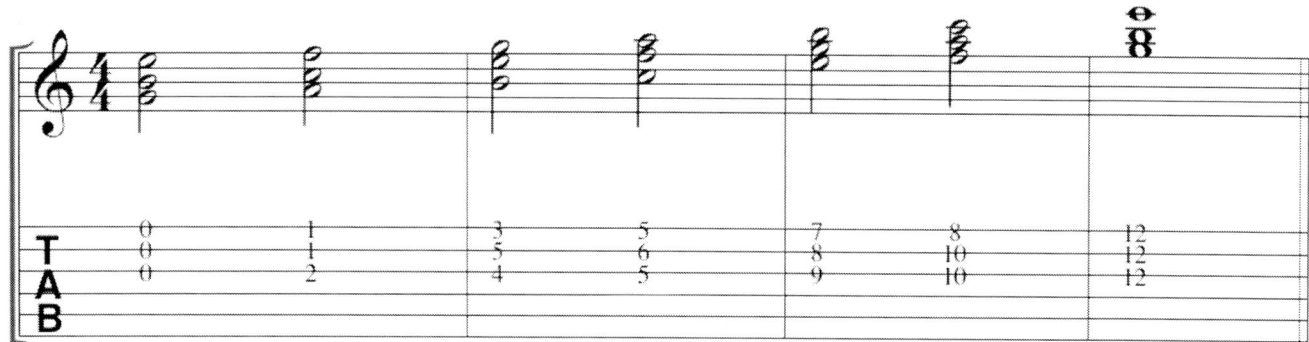

Em-F, Set 2:

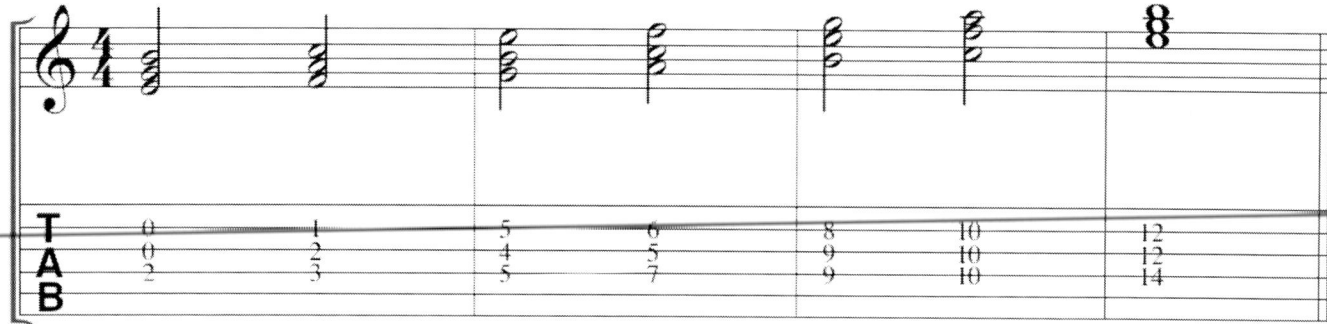

Em-F, Set 3:

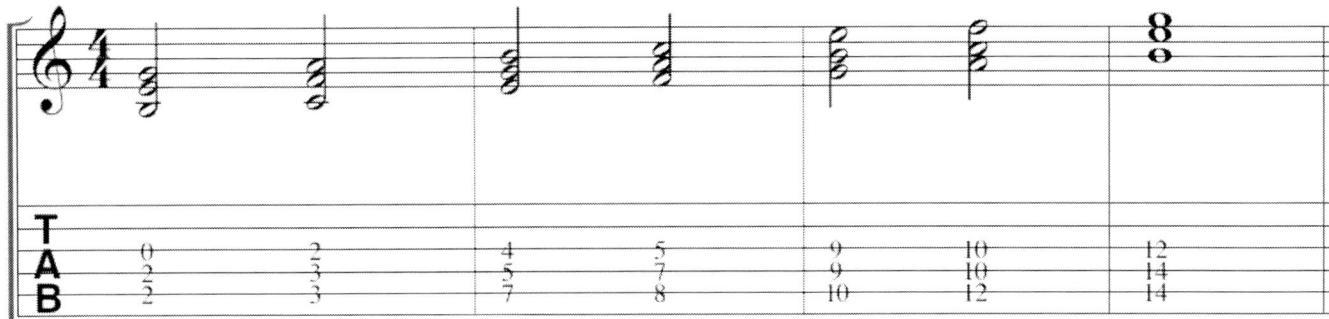

Em-F, Set 4:

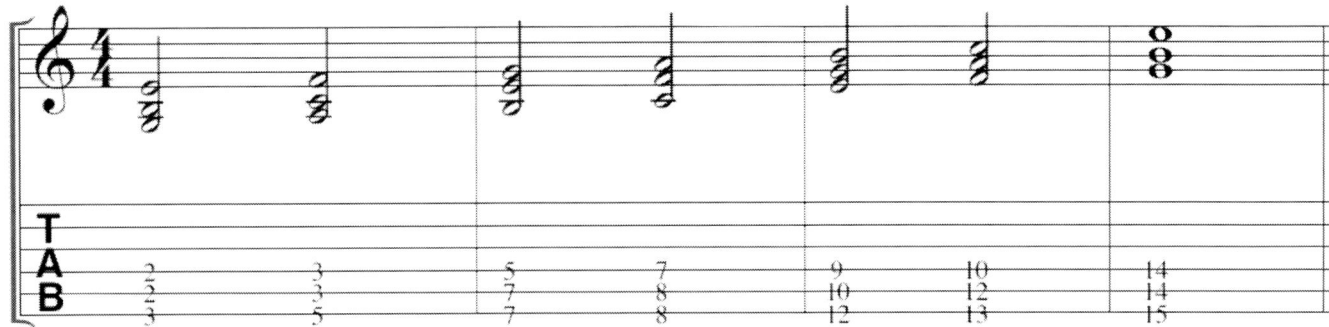

Em-F, Crossover 1:

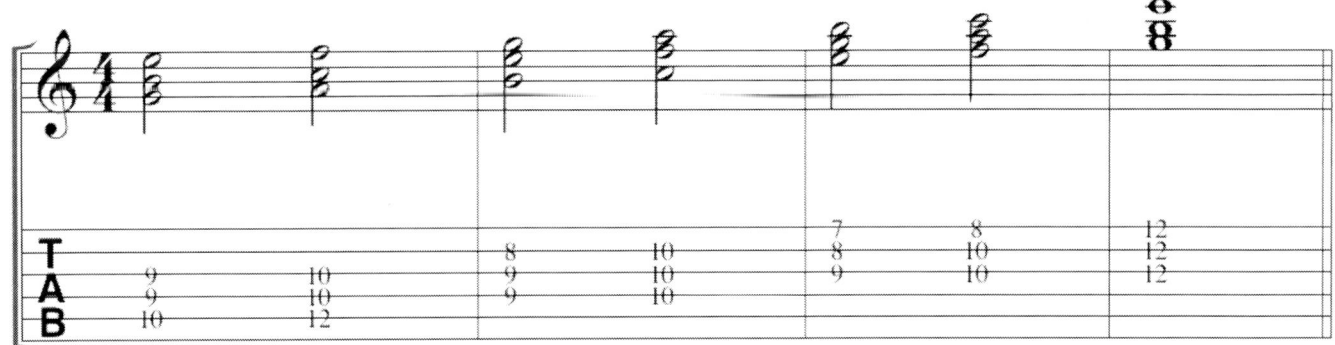

Em-F, Crossover 2:

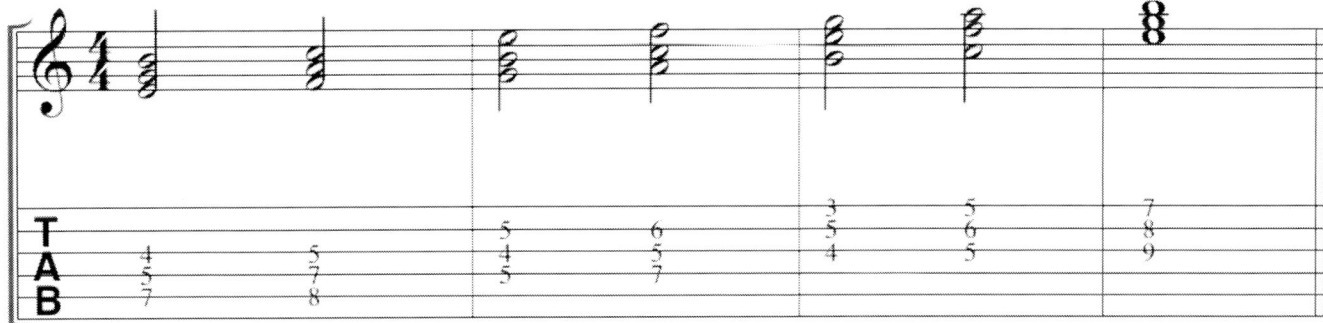

Em-F, Crossover 3:

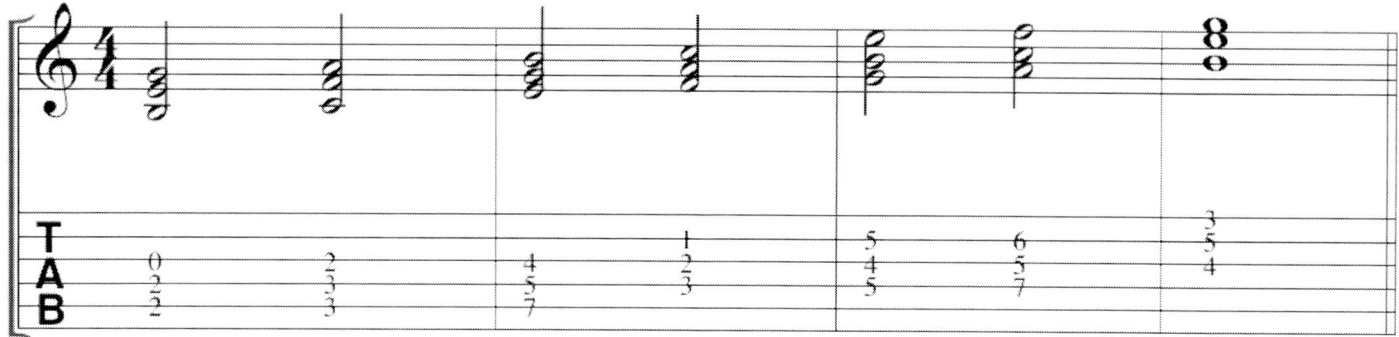

Em-F, Crossover 4:

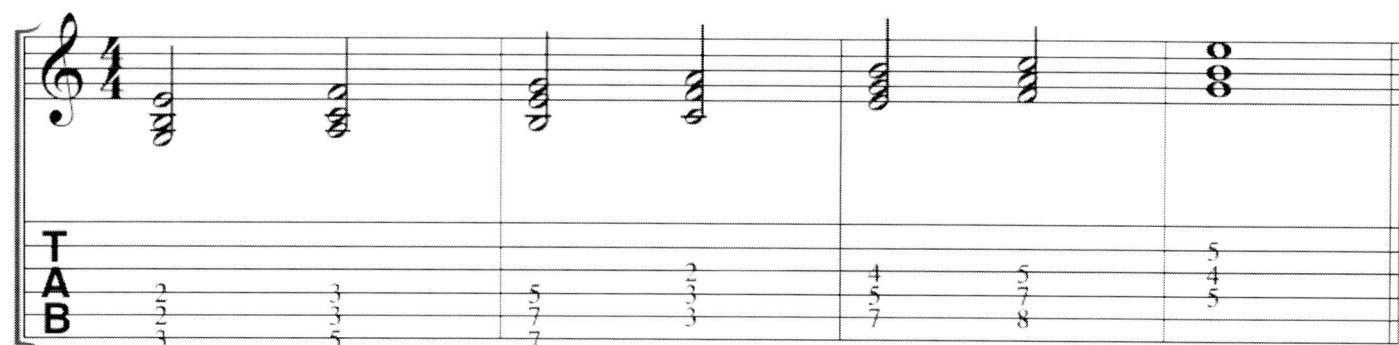

This pair, made up of the IIm and IIIm triads, will work over either chord as a static harmony but could also work over Imaj7, V7 or a IVmaj7. It's worth noting that with some of the triad pairs, certain notes are going to serve as better resolving tones than others and upon further study of harmony it will become a matter of personal and stylistic taste. With that said, much experimentation should be done with them over an audible background of the given static chord.

Dm-Em, Set 1:

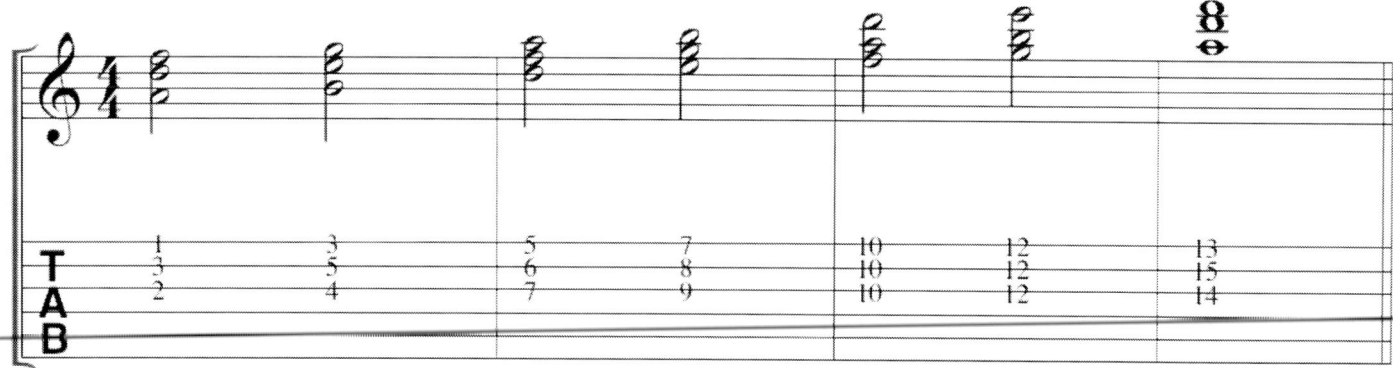

Dm-Em, Set 2:

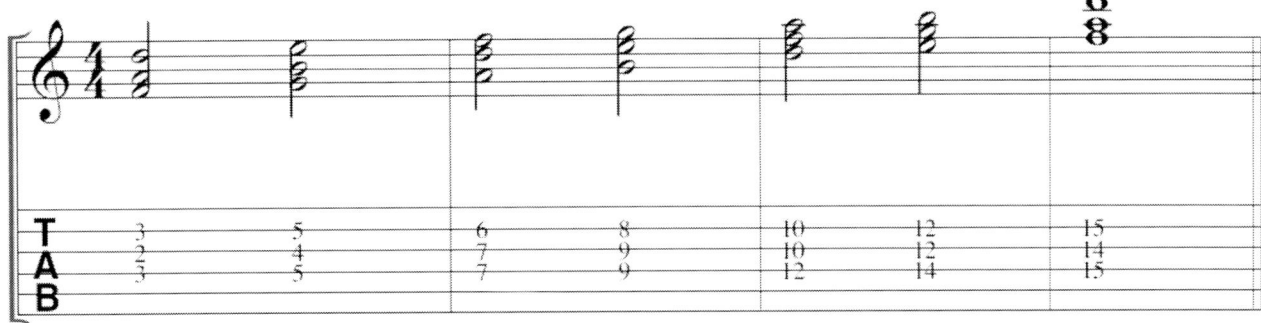

Dm-Em, Set 3:

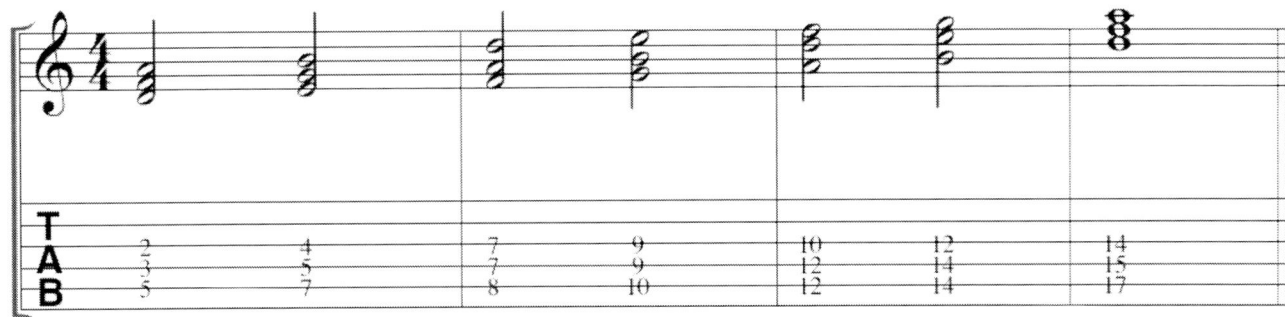

Dm-Em, Set 4:

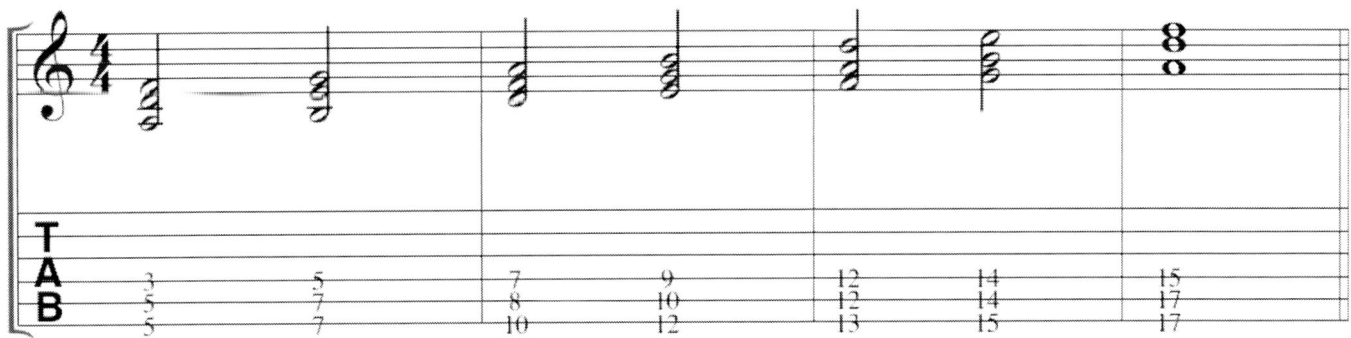

Dm-Em, Crossover 1:

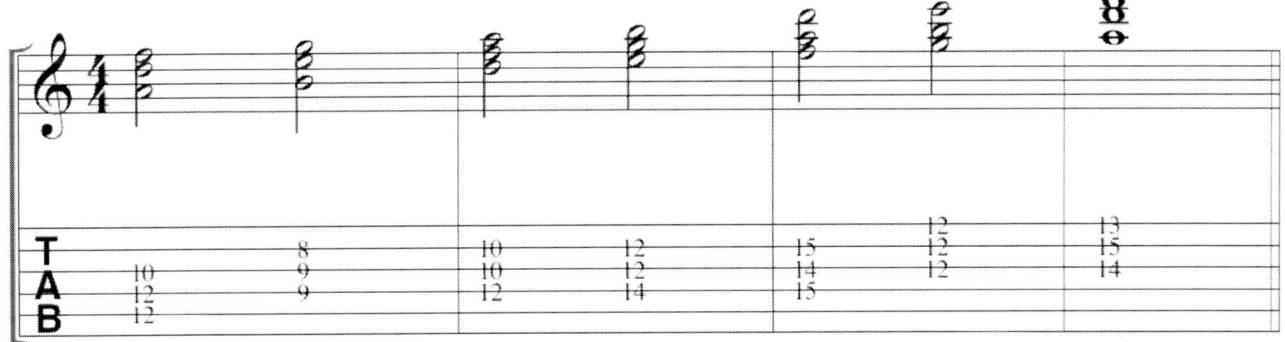

Dm-Em, Crossover 2:

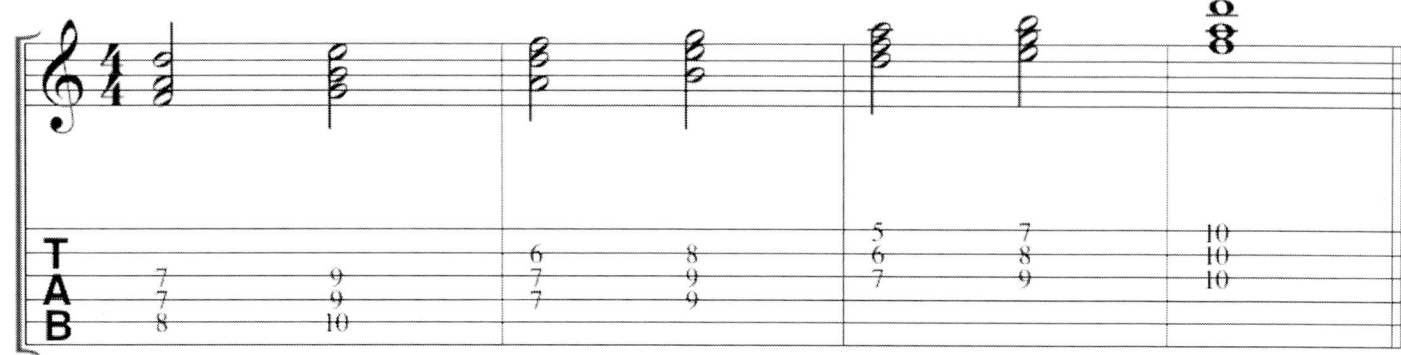

Dm-Em, Crossover 3:

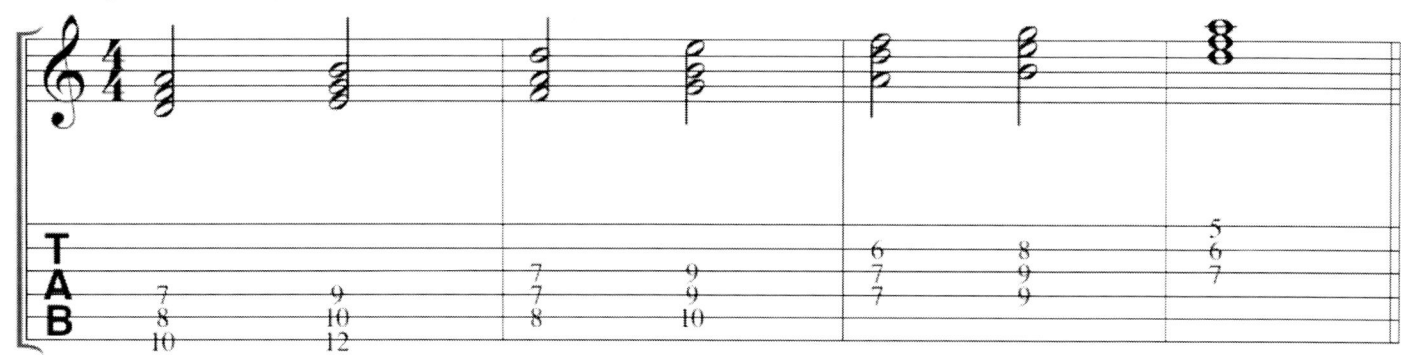

Dm-Em, Crossover 3:

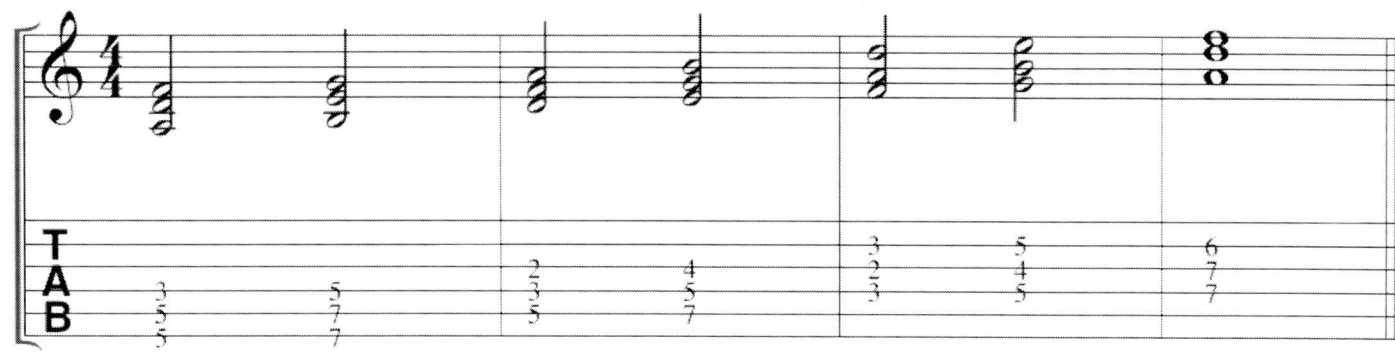

This last pair, made up of the VIm and V triads, will work over either chord as a static harmony but could also work over a Imaj7, IVmaj7 or a IIm7.

In this case, you're left without a 4th in the given key. If a 4th is needed for melodic purposes, replace the VIm triad with the IV triad. Again, the majority of the notes in these two triads (VIm and IV) are common to one another. The root of the IV chord is, of course, the 4th of the parent key.

Am-G, Set 1:

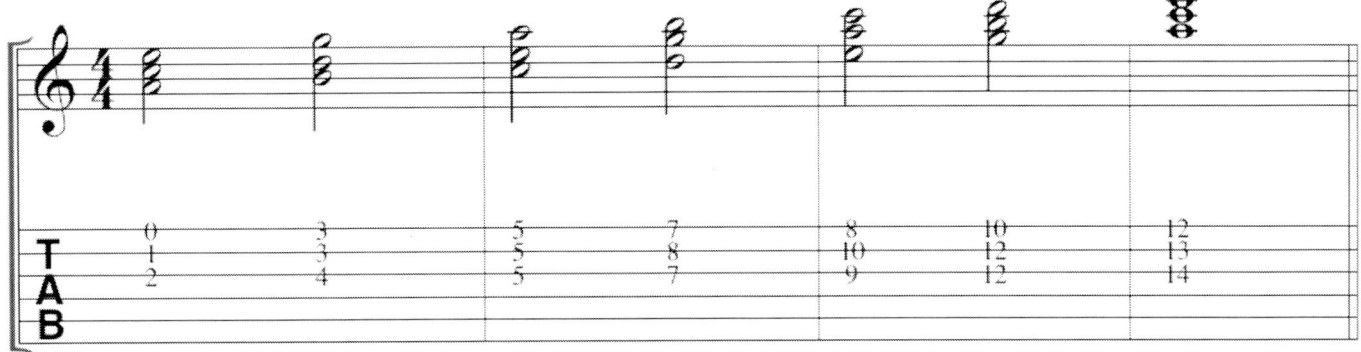

Am-G, Set 2:

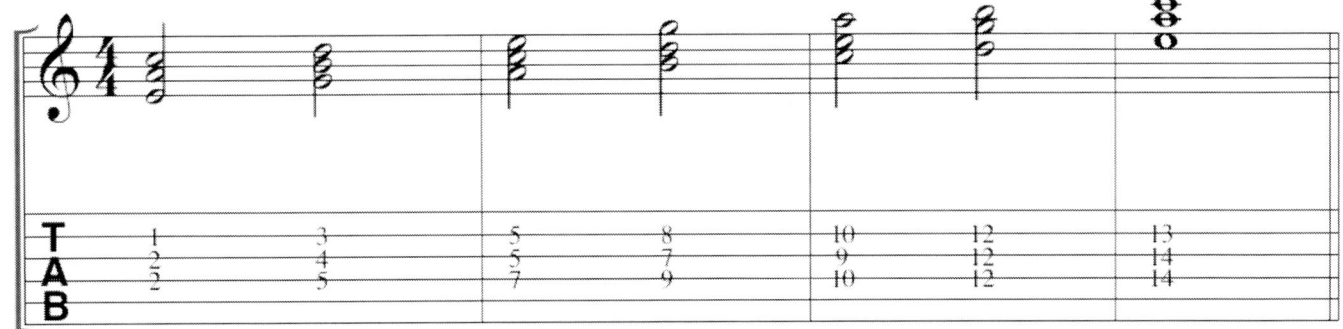

Am-G, Set 3:

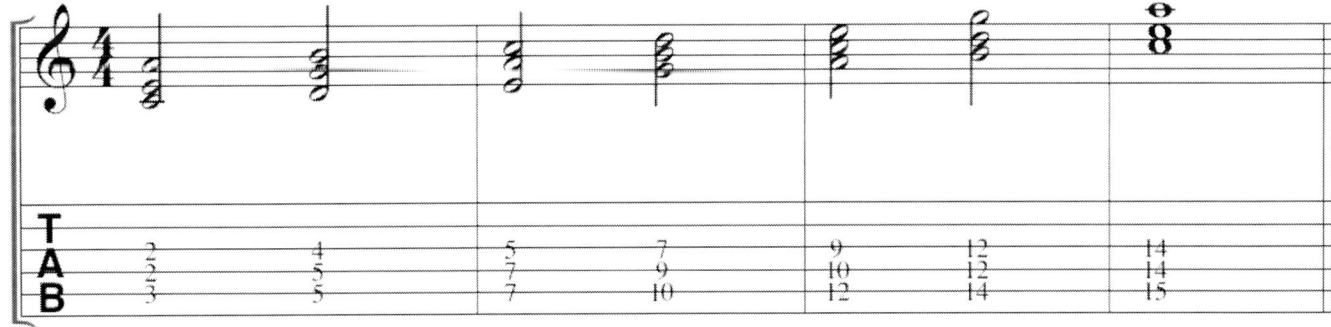

Am-G, Set 4:

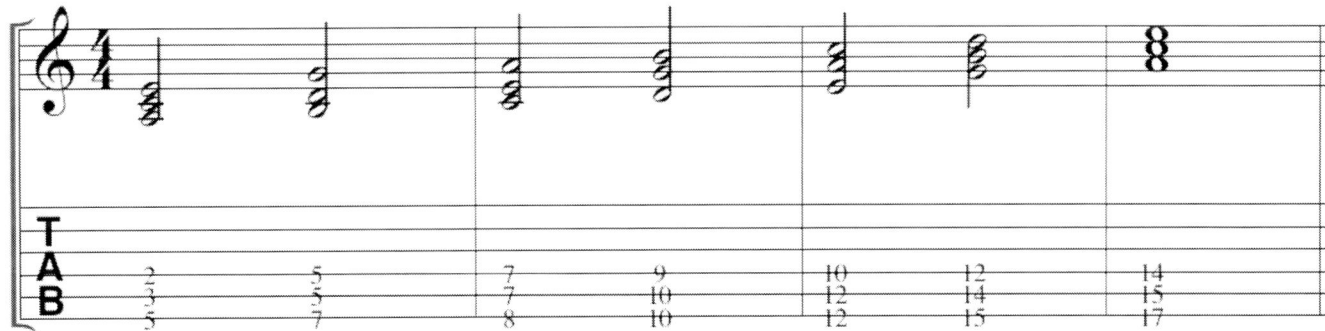

Am–G, Crossover 1:

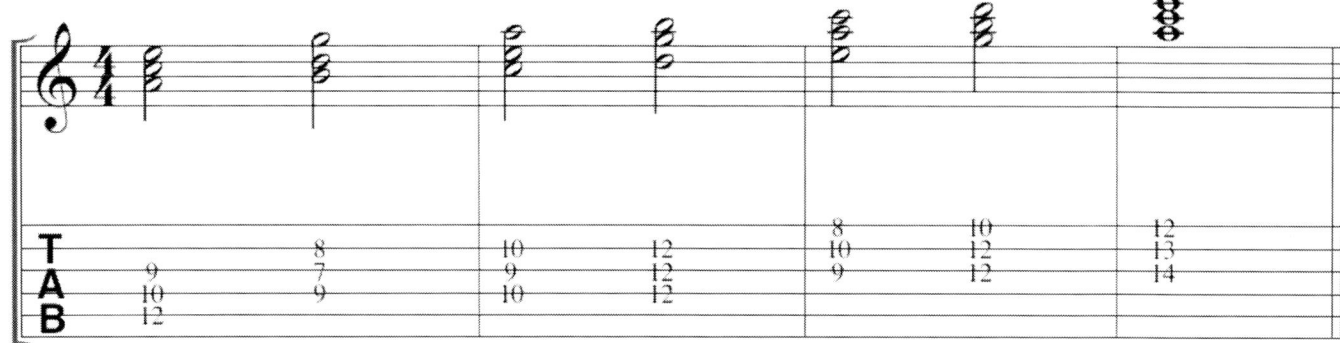

Am–G, Crossover 2:

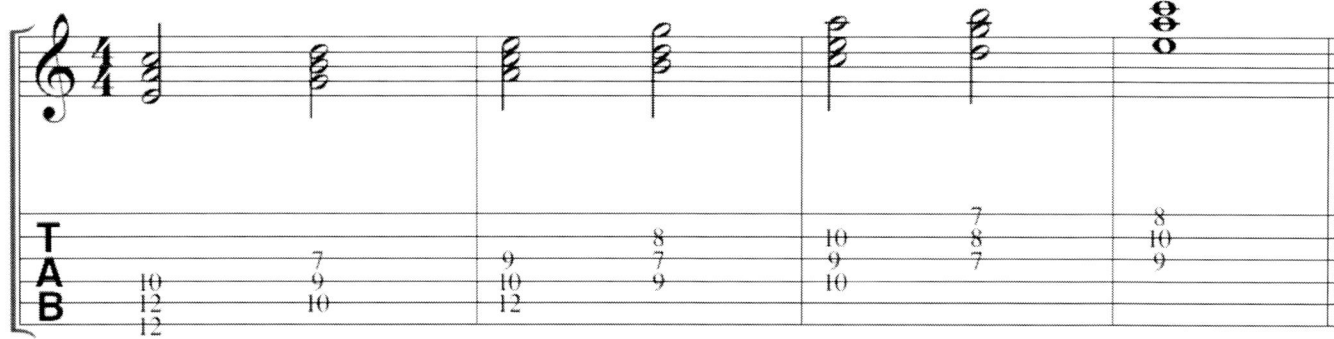

Am–G, Crossover 3:

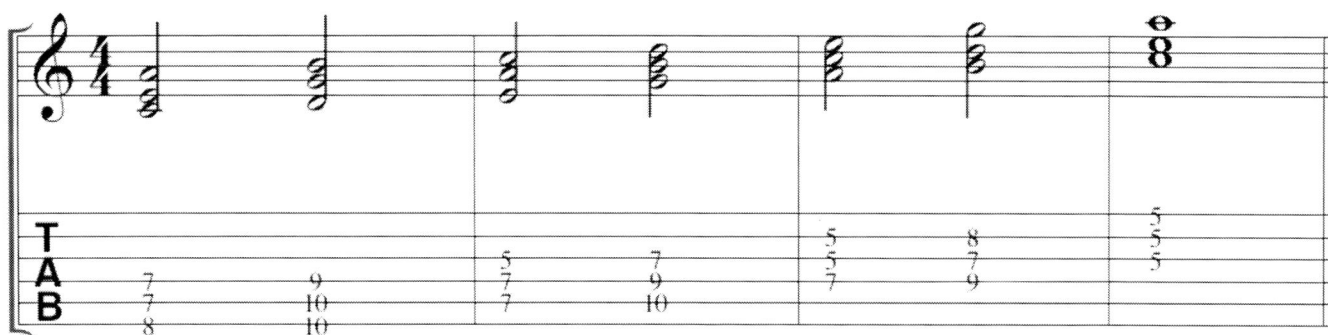

Am–G, Crossover 4:

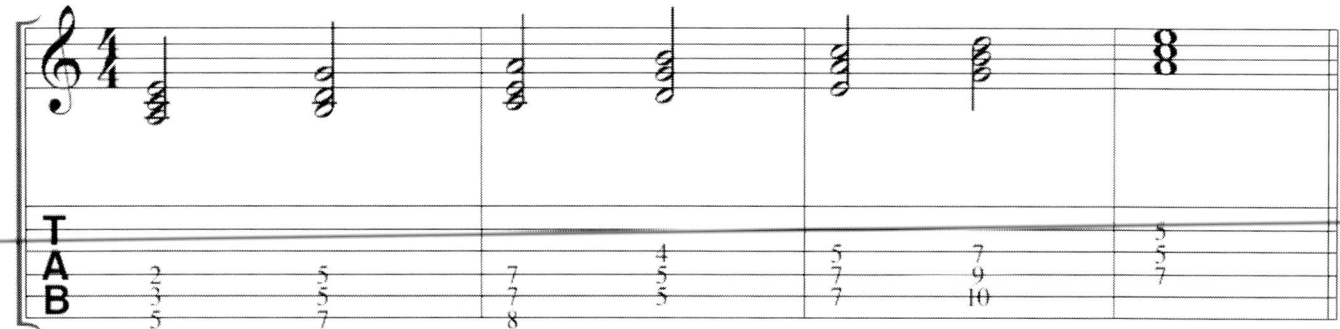

Some Possible Ways To Practice and Apply Triad Pairs:

1) Play through the written ascending pattern, then play backwards through the same line in order to descend.

2) Alternate the triads in rhythmic increments of 4, 2, 1 and eventually ½ beats.

3) Try any conceivable rhythm as a strumming pattern to apply to the triads.

4) Arpeggiate the triads with and without letting the notes cascade (ring over one another).

5) Arpeggiate, using even note values as well as any rhythm and rhythmic feel of your liking.

6) Play over recordings of all the possible chord contexts. In most cases, a steady bass note on the root of the implied chord will be enough, between that and the super-imposed triads.

7) Play the first triad and skip to the third triad which will be an inversion of the first triad. Then play the triad that was skipped (the second triad) and skip one forward from there. Continue this process though the whole range of the guitar.

THE MODES OF THE MAJOR SCALE

Here's my personal definition of modes: A mode occurs when the roles of the notes in a scale shift. If we still have the family of notes that make up a C major scale; C D E F G A B, but instead of C being considered the root, we make D the root, E the 2nd and so forth, this would be the second mode of C major.

If a Dm chord is being sounded, the D note is now going to behave as the root note and the other scale tones roles will shift as well. In other words, a mode is the way the notes of a scale are going to behave over a particular harmonic context, the II chord or V chord, etc.

There are seven modes, one for each note in the scale. Each one has a name given to it by our old pal from math class, Pythagoras. (This guy was actually quite the hipster.) Below are the 7 major scale modes and their names.

The Modes of the C Major Scale (Relative)

Mode:	R		2		3		4		5		6		7	
C Ionian	C	w	D	w	E	h	F	w	G	w	A	w	B	h
D Dorian	D	w	E	h	F	w	G	w	A	w	B	h	C	w
E Phrygian	E	h	F	w	G	w	A	w	B	h	C	w	D	w
F Lydian	F	w	G	w	A	w	B	h	C	w	D	w	E	h
G Mixolydian	G	w	A	w	B	h	C	w	D	w	E	h	F	w
A Aeolian	A	w	B	h	C	w	D	w	E	h	F	w	G	w
B Locrian	B	h	C	w	D	w	E	h	F	w	G	w	A	w

Each of these modes can be played using any major scale position. These defining factors determine which mode you're playing: 1) the emphasis of certain scale tones and/or 2) the chord you're playing over.

Chords and modes relate directly to one another so make sure to mentally drill the chord numerals to their corresponding modes. This will help you identify much more quickly with their sounds and names. The names are incidental but they're a standard, so it's good to know them. Most importantly though, is the mental connection between the modes, the chord and the scale. Associating colors always helped for me.

Chord:	Imaj7	IIm7	IIIm7	IVmaj7	V7	VIm7	VIIm7b5
Mode:	Ionian	Dorian	Phrygian	Lydian	Mixolydian	Aeolian	Locrian
Color:	Red	Green	Purple	Yellow	Blue	Orange	Turquoise

The seventh mode is much like the VII chord, useless. This is because it doesn't have a natural 5th, which serves as the stabilizing factor in any chord or scale. A natural 5th occurs when there's 3½ steps between the root and 5th. This is the case on chords I through VI and in modes I through VI but not the case in the last chord/mode. No songs are written in the Locrian mode.

There are two ways of getting to know your modes and their functions. The previous table represents what's known as the "relative" system, meaning that each mode relates to the next out of the same parent major scale. Another approach, which I think is especially important, is the "Parallel" system, where we look at all seven modes starting from the same note, so that each mode belongs to a different parent major scale. When we set out to learn their relationships in this respect, we typically start at the brightest sounding mode and gradually work our way to the darkest sounding mode by lowering one scale tone at a time.

In the following table, each mode will begin on C. This way we can easily tell which modes contain which altered tones. In the case of C, if the note we're looking at is natural, than it's natural in relation to the major scale. This wouldn't be the case in the key of E, for instance. G# wouldn't be a sharp third. It would be a natural third because G# is two whole steps above E. This is important because we're going to compare each mode directly to its parallel major scale.

The Modes of the C Major Scale (Parallel)

Mode:	R		2		3		4		5		6		7	
C Lydian	C	w	D	w	E	w	F#	h	G	w	A	w	B	h
C Ionian	C	w	D	w	E	h	F	w	G	w	A	w	B	h
C Mixolydian	C	w	D	w	E	w	F	w	G	h	A	w	Bb	w
C Dorian	C	w	D	h	Eb	w	F	w	G	w	A	h	Bb	w
C Aeolian	C	w	D	h	Eb	h	F	w	G	h	Ab	w	Bb	w
C Phrygian	C	h	Db	w	Eb	w	F	w	G	h	Ab	w	Bb	w
C Locrian	C	h	Db	w	Eb	w	F	h	Gb	w	Ab	w	Bb	w

A modes brightness or darkness is relative to its sharp or flat scale-tones in comparison to the major scale or Ionian mode. For instance, Lydian is one shade brighter than Ionian because it's just like Ionian except for its sharp fourth. In the same respect, Mixolydian. This will all be obvious to your ear during/after the following exercises.

IMPORTANT!
Notice that from row to row, one note changes at a time. The last note to be altered remains altered for the rest of the progression through the modes. The next note to be altered is always a fourth away from the last altered note. If this doesn't remind you of anything, go back and study your cycle of 5ths and try following it backwards. You'll find the same pattern.

Remember that since each of these modes are beginning on the same note as one another, they each belong to a different major scale or key. Let's look at C Lydian for example. Lydian is the fourth mode of the major scale, so it stands to reason that all we ask ourselves is this: Which major scale does C serve as the 4th? The 4th is always 2½ steps above its major scale root, regardless of key. C is 2½ steps above G, which means C is the 4th of G major. By this logic, we know that C Lydian belongs to the key of G major. Read that through again if you have a question mark over your head. I swear it makes sense.

Here's a table that equates each of these parallel modes to the major key to which they belong:

Parallel Mode:		Parent Major Key
C Lydian	(IV)	G Major
C Ionian	(I)	C Major
C Mixolydian	(V)	F Major
C Dorian	(II)	Bb Major
C Aeolian	(VI)	Eb Major
C Phrygian	(III)	Ab Major
C Locrian	(VII)	Db Major

Notice that from row to row, the parent major keys are moving in fourths. If you were to start at the darkest mode and work your way to the brightest parallel mode, the parent major keys would be moving in 5ths. So, not only do modes bear a strong relationship to our diatonic chord structure, but they also bear a very real and practical relationship to our cycle of 5ths.

If we were to continue this process of lowering one note at a time beyond this point, the next note that we would flat would be the root. This would land us in B Lydian, exactly one half step lower than where we started. We could keep following this cycle, one half step lower each time and eventually arrive exactly where we started. Music, like the universe itself, contains lots of smaller cycles within larger cycles, within even larger cycles. Do you feel like you're staring off the edge of a cliff yet? Yeah, I still get that too, sometimes.

Before we get into these much-anticipated exercises, it would be a good idea to look at these modes in bare scale tones. This is the real raw material of it.

The Modes of the Major Scale (Parallel)

Mode:	R		2		3		4		5		6		7	
Lydian	R	W	2	w	3	w	#4	h	5	w	6	w	7	h
Ionian	R	w	2	w	3	h	4	w	5	w	6	w	7	h
Mixolydian	R	h	2	w	3	w	4	w	5	h	6	w	b7	w
Dorian	R	w	2	h	b3	w	4	w	5	w	6	h	b7	w
Aeolian	R	w	2	h	b3	h	4	w	5	h	b6	w	b7	w
Phrygian	R	h	b2	w	b3	w	4	w	5	h	b6	w	b7	w
Locrian	R	h	b2	w	b3	w	4	h	b5	w	b6	w	b7	w

Identifying and Mapping the Modes

Now that we can see the ways in which the modes relate to one another, it might be good to talk about each mode on an individual basis. We'll discuss the general moods and some common examples of the major scale modes. I'm going to try to do my best, representing a broad base of styles, but there's quite a bit of music out there so bear with me.

IONIAN

The Ionian mode is the most commonplace of all the modes. It sounds bright, happy and positive. Be mindful that modality is only one aspect of what gives a piece of music its basic feeling. Other major factors are tempo, rhythm, contour and choice of sounds. So, throughout this following section when I refer to the general moods, feelings and concepts associated with each mode, bear in mind that these aspects are mutable and alterable through the manipulation of the other factors.

Ionian has a very "well-balanced" effect because the I chord is a major triad and the chords 2½ steps and 3½ steps above and/or below are also major chords. This feature is what makes this mode so easily accessible to even the most unsophisticated ear and it's partly what earned it the spot as the primary mode. You can hear it in old classics such as "Old McDonald" or "Oh Susannah". It can be found in pop, classic rock, modern rock, folk, bluegrass, country, classical, jazz, reggae, traditional African music, and yes, even in metal, sometimes.

Any note can be treated as a resolving tone within this mode aside from the fourth. However, resolving to any tones other than the root, 3rd and 5th is going to bear a rather jazzy effect so, unless that's part (or all) of the sound you're going for, try and be careful about that.

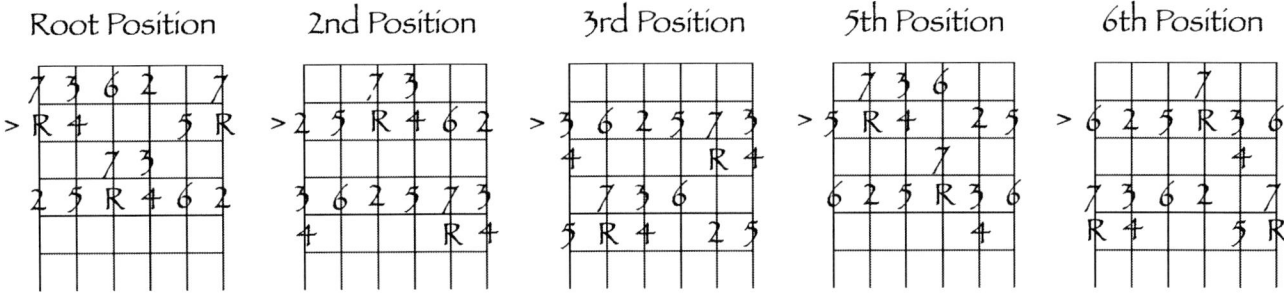

	C	G	D	A	E	B	Gb	Db	Ab	Eb	Bb	F
Root Pos:	8	3	10	5	12	7	2	9	4	11	6	13
2nd Pos:	10	5	12	7	2	9	4	11	6	13	8	3
3rd Pos:	12	7	2	9	4	11	6	1	8	3	10	5
5th Pos:	3	10	5	12	7	2	9	4	11	6	13	8
6th Pos:	5	12	7	2	9	4	11	6	13	8	3	10

The following licks are built diatonically (within the scale) in the C Ionian Mode.

C Ionian Lick 1:

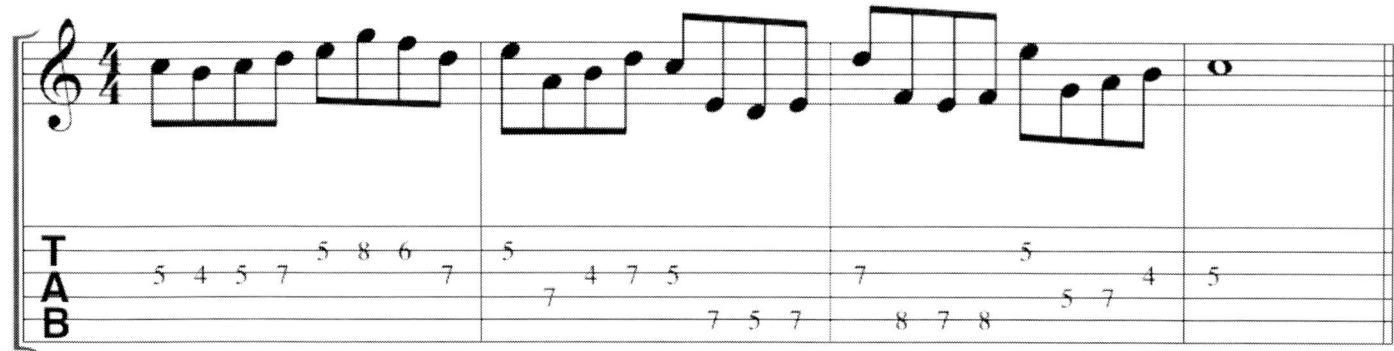

C Ionian Lick 2:

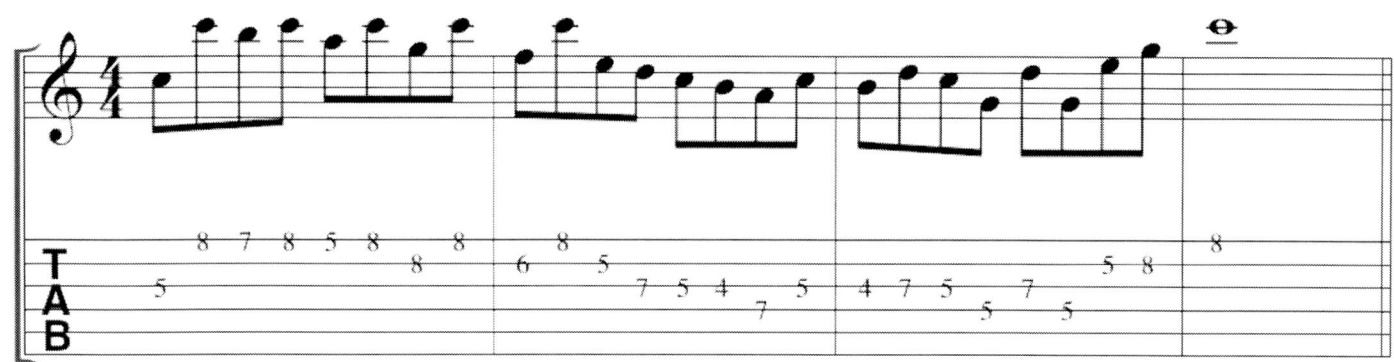

C Ionian Lick 3:

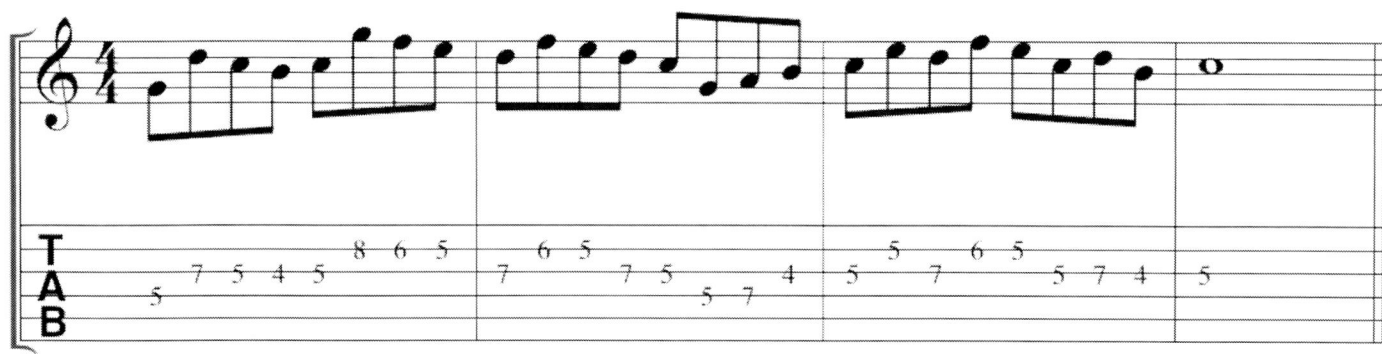

C Ionian Lick 4:

C Ionian Lick 5:

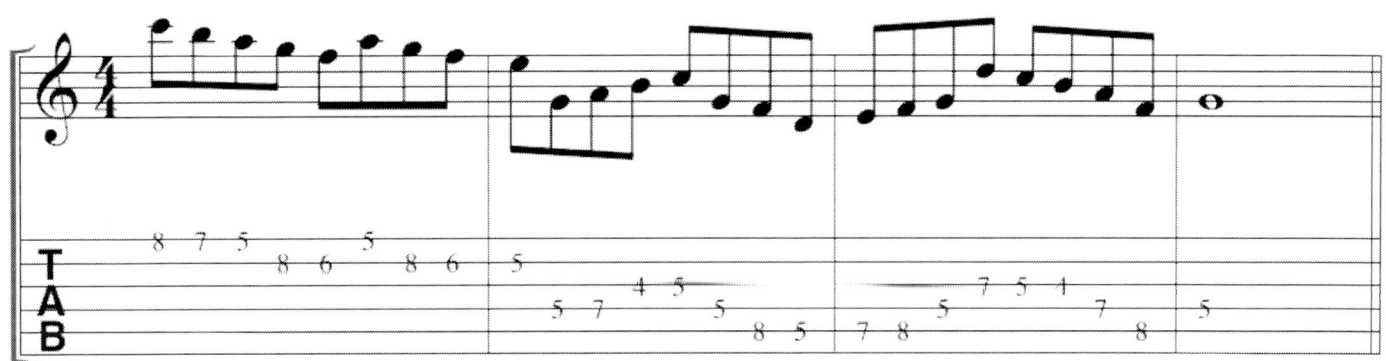

C Ionian Lick 6:

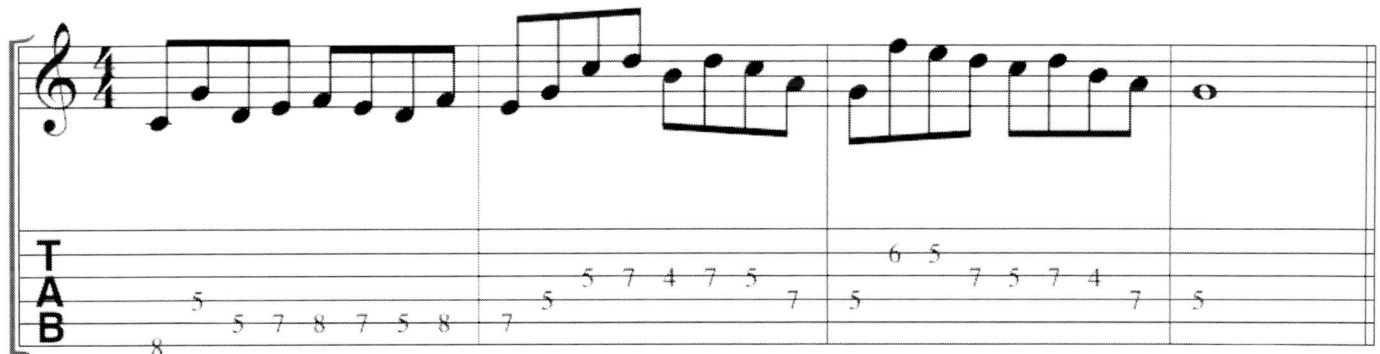

C Ionian Lick 7:

C Ionian Lick 8:

C Ionian Lick 9:

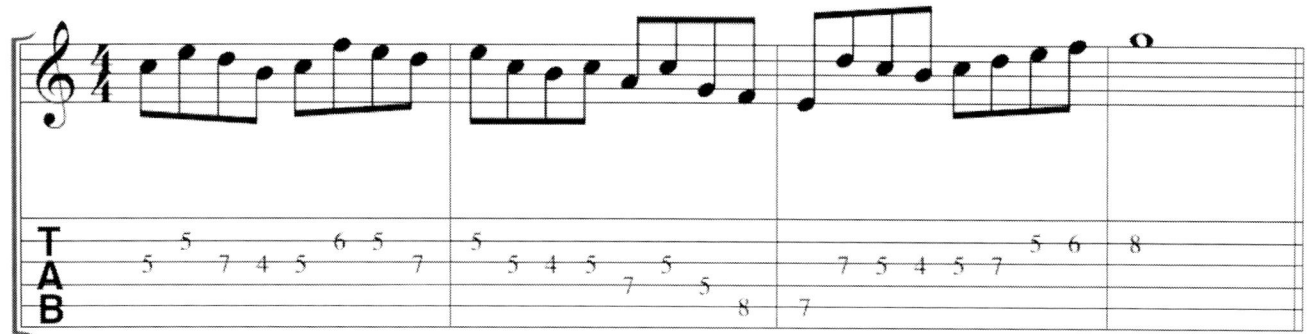

C Ionian Lick 10:

DORIAN

The Dorian mode is one shade brighter than the natural minor scale, and the note that represents this lighter shade is the natural 6th. This natural 6th shows up as the major third of the V chord in our parent key, or the IV of Dorian. This gives the Dorian mode its special sound, which is associated with adventure, the natural world, sexuality and the heroic. This mode is the smoothest of the minor modes. When we cover extended harmony, we'll be looking closer at why this is the case. By "smooth", I mean that you can treat any note as if it were a chord tone. In other words: you can land anywhere you want!

This mode can be applied in a couple distinct ways, which we may as well refer to as Traditional and Modern. In the Traditional fashion, the chords are centered on the parent II chord and so is the melody. The melody makes a point of emphasizing the resolving tones of the mode, which in this case, are the 2nd, 4th and 6th of the parent key. This usage is common in rock, metal, folk, country, world and sometimes in jazz.

In Modern use, the chords are still centered on the parent II, but the melody is written or improvised to sound like it relates directly to the parent I chord, which causes it to sound as if it floats above the chords, rather than interacting directly with them. To be clear, in a D Dorian chord progression, the melody would make very strong reference to the C, E & G notes of the parent I, the C chord. Sometimes this effect is heightened by playing major blues licks relating to the parent I chord. These effects can be heard mostly in R&B, soul and occasionally pop and jazz.

Both applications are good to know and understand and both are fun to use. If you have guts as a musician, you'll discover cool new sounds by placing an idea you'd commonly find in one kind of music and working it into a less likely style. That's what innovators are usually up to.

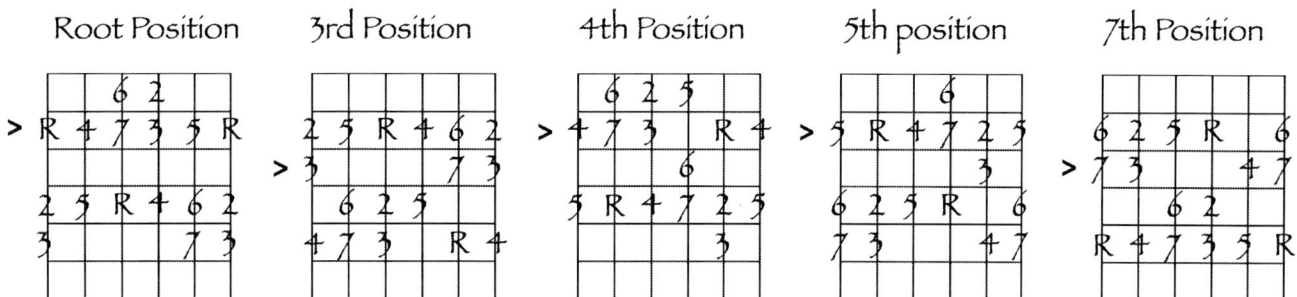

	D	A	E	B	F#	C#	Ab	Eb	Bb	F	C	G
Root Pos:	10	5	12	7	2	9	4	11	6	13	8	3
3rd Pos:	13	8	3	10	5	12	7	2	9	4	11	6
4th Pos:	3	10	5	12	7	2	9	4	11	6	13	8
5th Pos:	5	12	7	2	9	4	11	6	13	8	3	10
7th Pos:	8	3	10	5	12	7	2	9	4	11	6	13

Here are some diatonic D Dorian mode licks. (Throughout all of the following diatonic modal licks, you'll notice that they're all in the same position. Try translating as many of these as you can to some or all of your other positions.

D Dorian Lick 1:

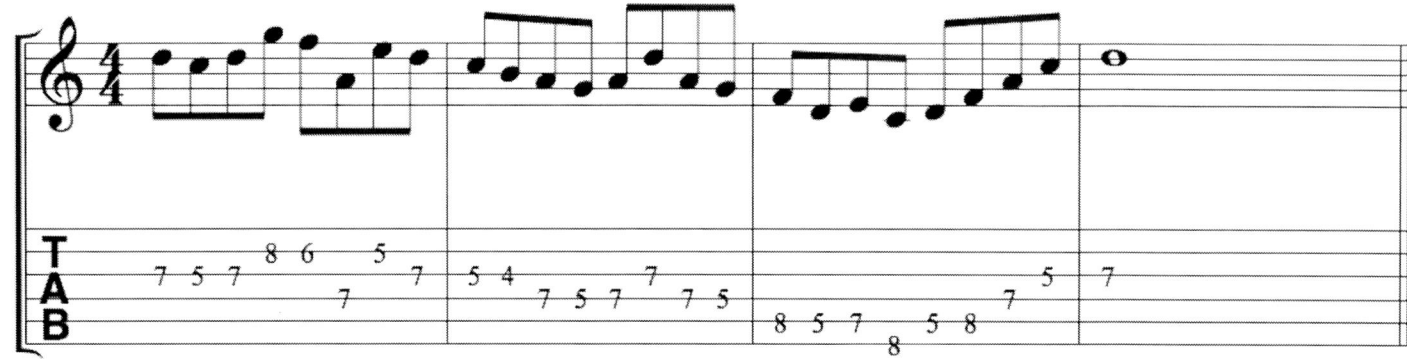

D Dorian Lick 2:

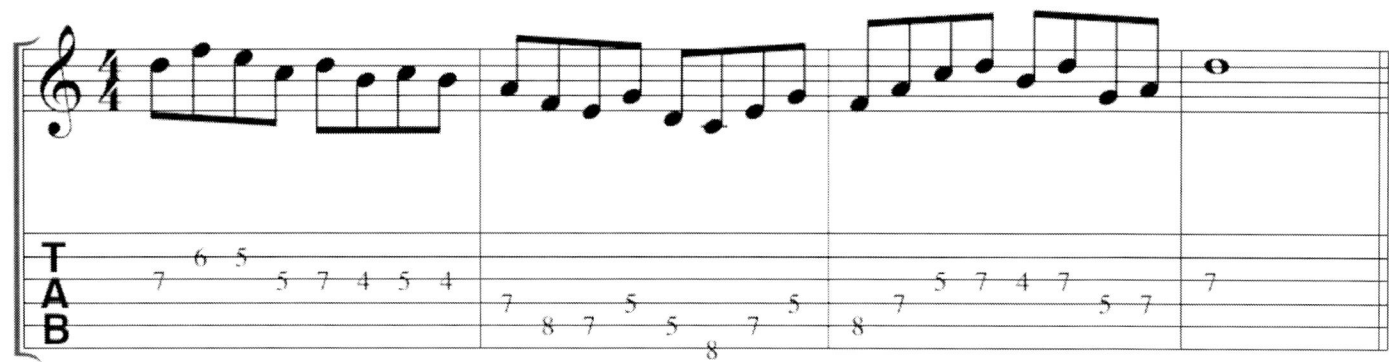

D Dorian Lick 3:

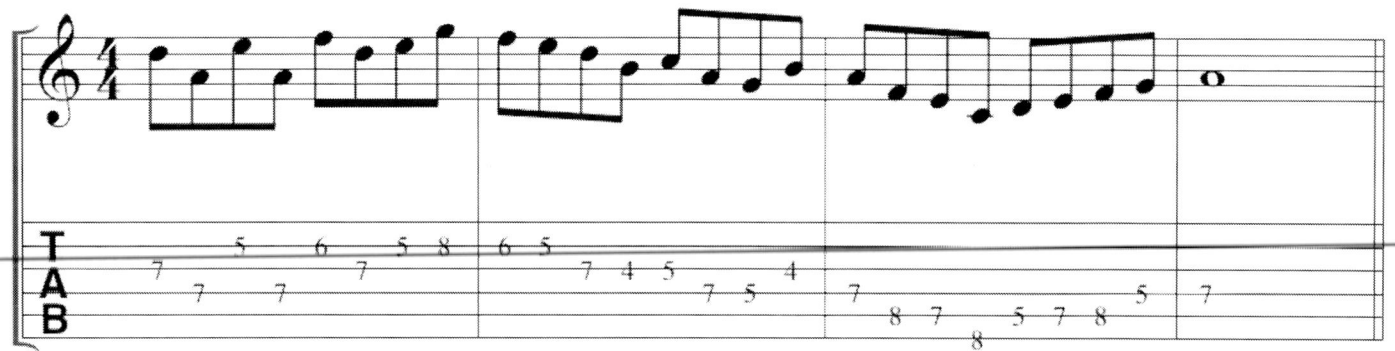

D Dorian Lick 4:

D Dorian Lick 5:

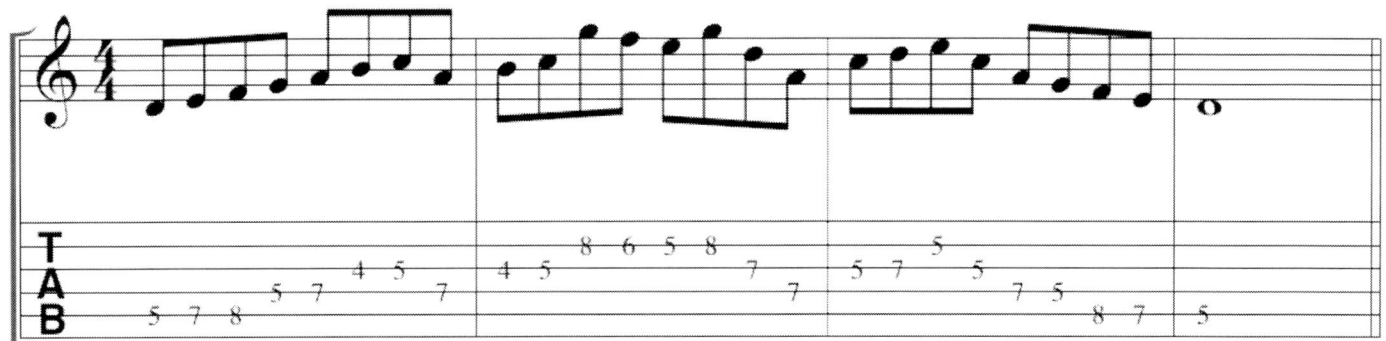

D Dorian Lick 6:

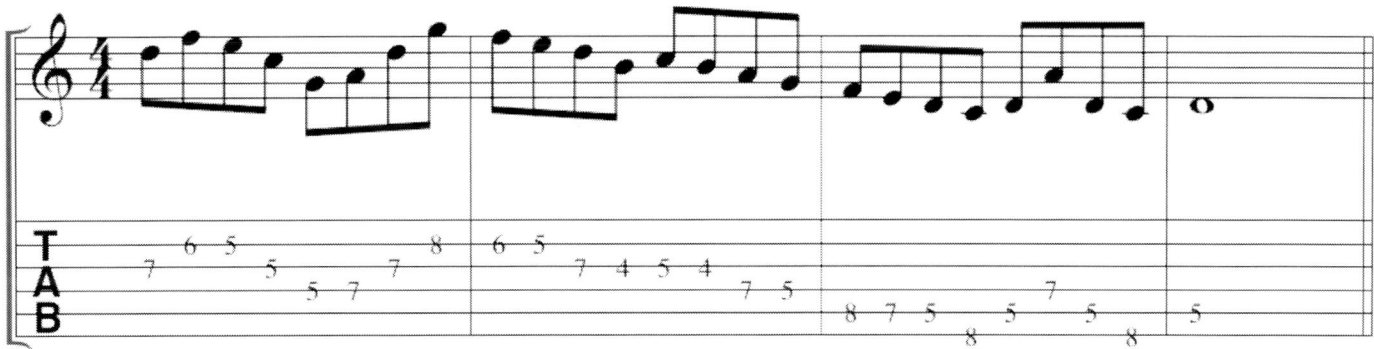

D Dorian Lick 7:

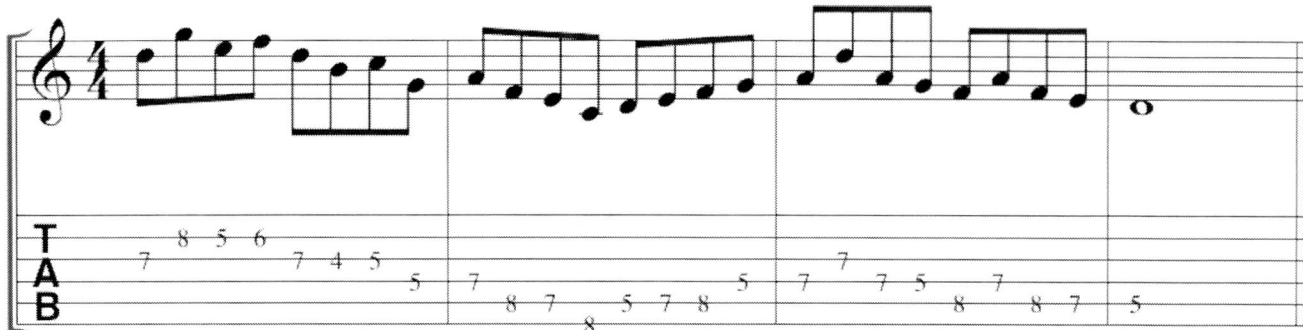

D Dorian Lick 8:

D Dorian Lick 9:

D Dorian Lick 10:

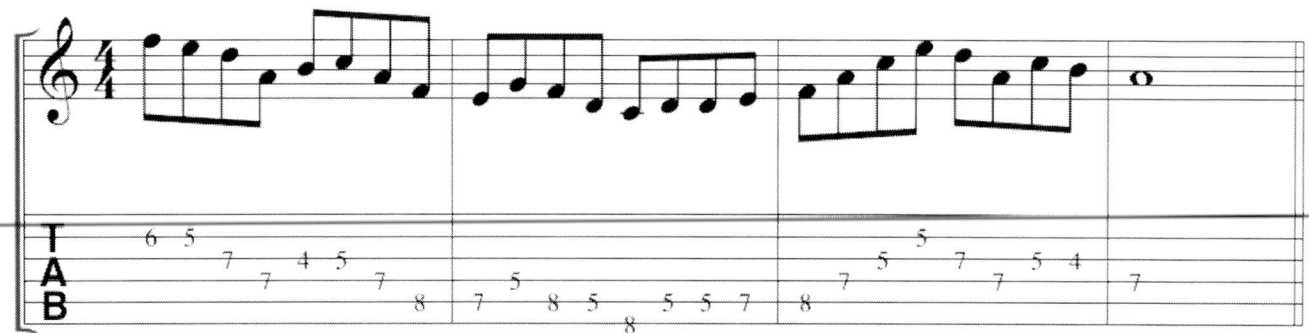

Phrygian

Phrygian, being one shade darker than the natural minor scale, has a sound that is associated with humanity's darker emotions: anger, revenge, loss, violence, but also the more ambiguous themes of mystery, the ancient, nightfall and the desert. Whereas the Dorian was a smooth mode, in the sense of being able to treat any note as a chord tone (or resolving tone), the Phrygian mode is a little more restricted. Most of your scale tones can be treated as chord tones but not all of them. The b2nd and the b6th can only be treated as non-chord tones. In other words, don't land on these two notes. They can only be used as passing tones. I could explain this further but it's something you'll learn best by experimentation.

As a guitar teacher I find myself demonstrating the sounds of the modes pretty regularly. Most students tend to associate this mode with bullfighting, which makes perfect sense because the music most commonly associated with bullfighting is flamenco and flamenco music makes heavy use of the Phrygian mode. It's a common mode in most styles. You won't hear much of this mode in the blues, in jazz, classical or in country. It's an especially common mode in heavy metal, flamenco, Carnatic and Hindustani music. Some great metal and rock examples are Metallica's "Harvester of Sorrow" main riff, Coheed & Cambria's "Apollo I: The Writing Writer" main riff and Megadeth's "Symphony Of Destruction" verse riff.

The modern application of modes that was referred to in the Dorian section isn't going to work as simply in the Phrygian mode because of the two tones that can't serve as any sort of chord tone. As a result, the traditional application is the way to go for this mode.

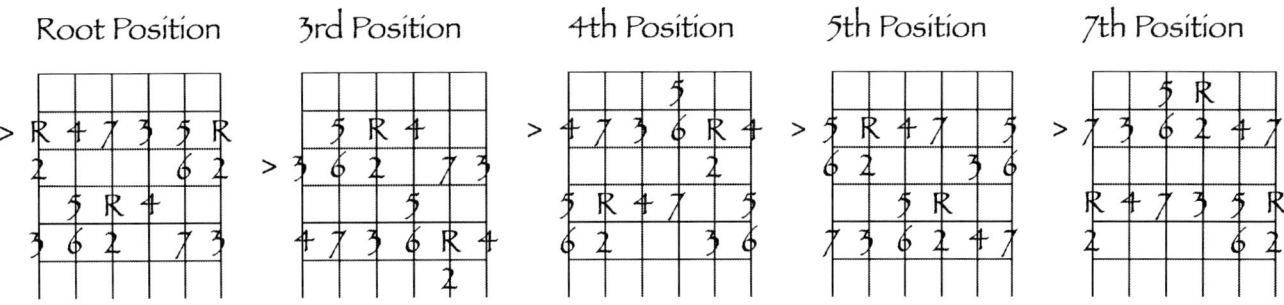

	E	B	F#	C#	G#	D#	Bb	F	C	G	D	A
Root Pos:	12	7	2	9	4	11	6	13	8	3	10	5
3rd Pos:	3	10	5	12	7	2	9	4	11	6	13	8
4th Pos:	5	12	7	2	9	4	11	6	13	8	3	10
5th Pos:	7	2	9	4	11	6	13	8	3	10	5	12
7th Pos:	10	5	12	7	2	9	4	11	6	13	8	3

Now for some diatonic E Phrygian mode licks.

E Phrygian Lick 1:

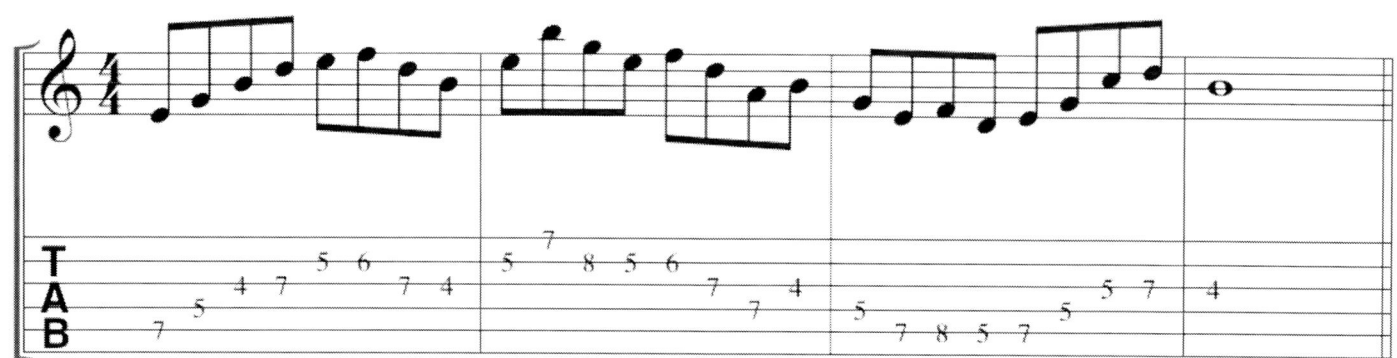

E Phrygian Lick 2:

E Phrygian Lick 3:

E Phrygian Lick 4:

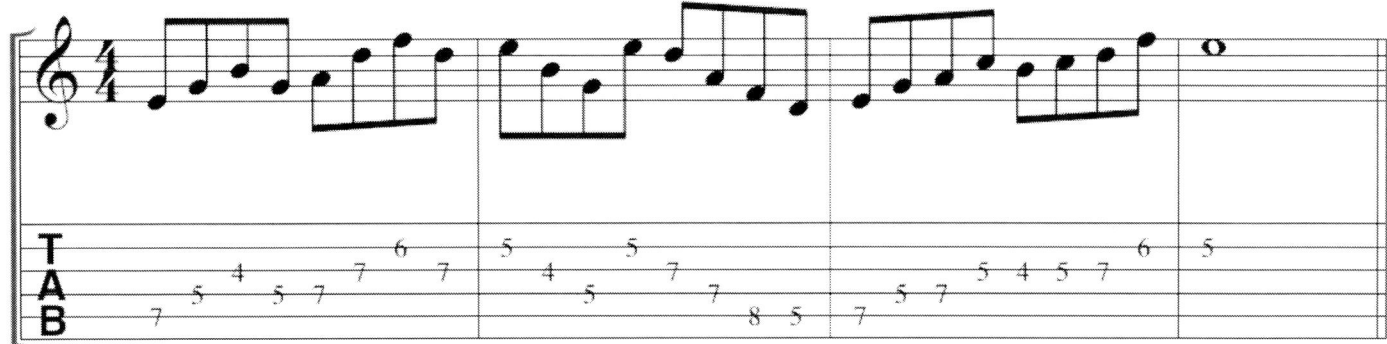

E Phrygian Lick 5:

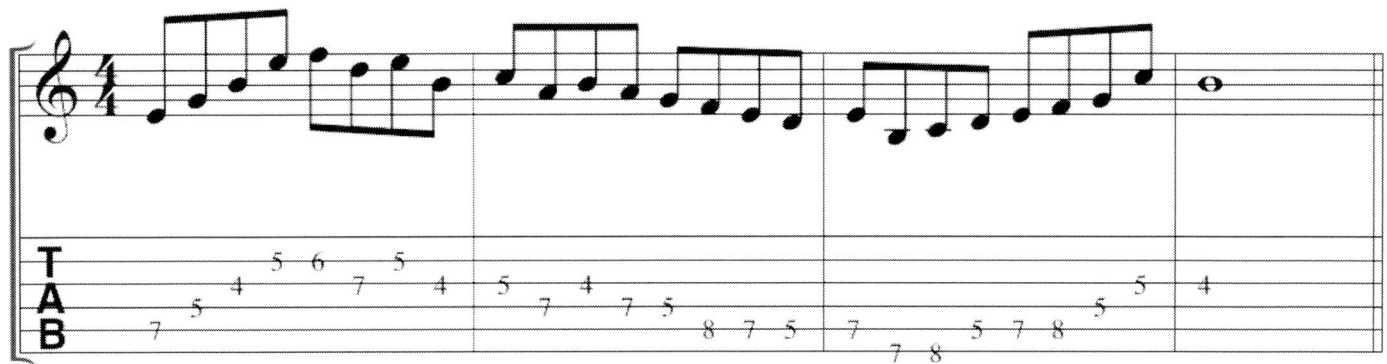

E Phrygian Lick 6:

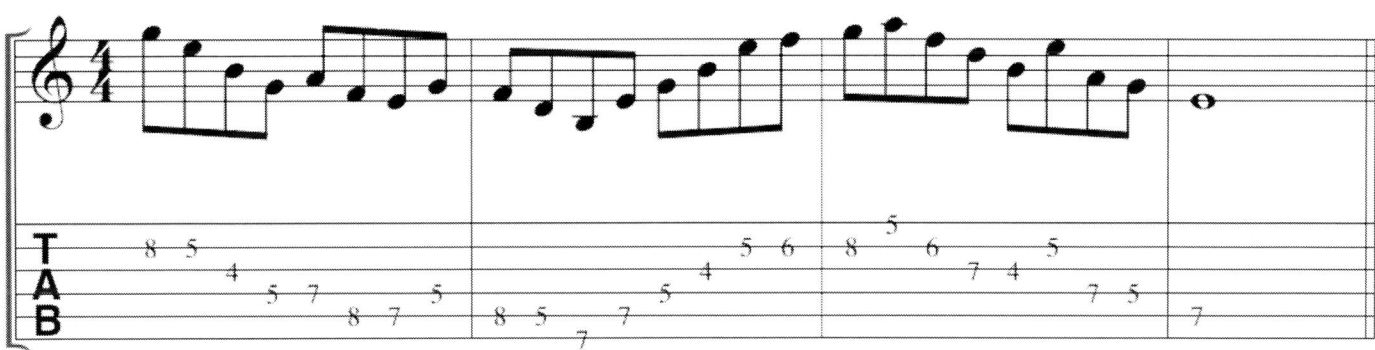

E Phrygian Lick 7:

E Phrygian Lick 8:

E Phrygian Lick 9:

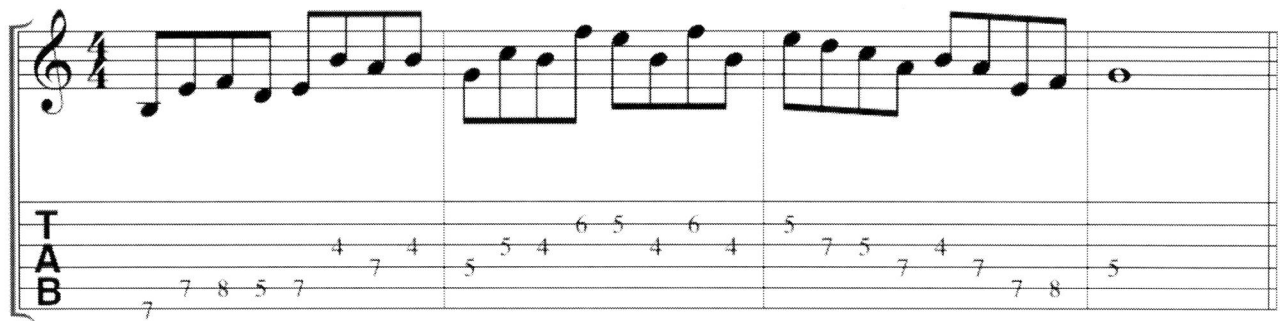

E Phrygian Lick 10:

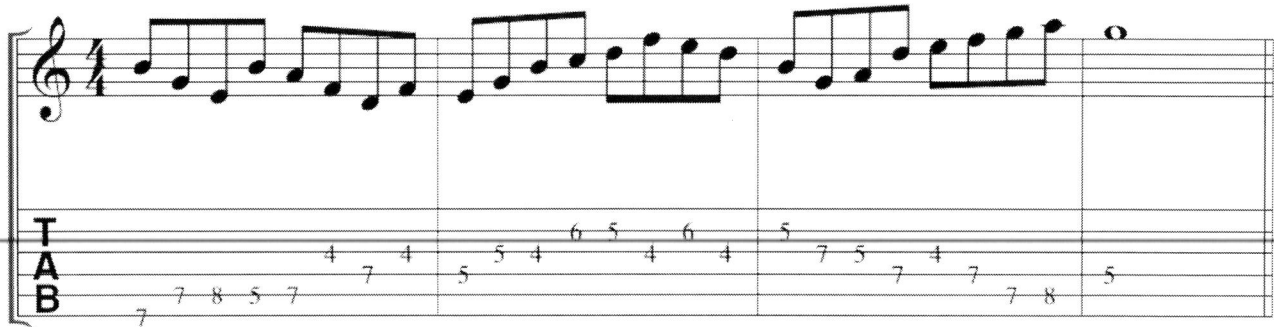

LYDIAN

Lydian serves as the brightest diatonic mode. It's essentially a major scale with a sharp 4th. Since it bears such a bright quality, it's commonly associated with enlightenment, elevation, discovery and positive drive. The Lydian mode was one shade brighter than the major scale. This makes Lydian a close cousin to the Dorian mode, because Dorian is one shade brighter than the natural minor. Another way of thinking of this is that Lydian and Dorian share the same relationship with one another that Ionian shares with Aeolian.

Lydian, like Dorian, is a smooth mode. Any note can be treated as a resolving chord tone. Some resolves will sound more distant than others, but all of your scale tones, as they relate to this mode, can be perceived as a resolving tone. This means that both traditional and modern usage will work fine. The notes you choose to treat as resolving tones are dictated by where you want to be in terms of what I like to call Melodic Altitude.

Allow me to explain Melodic Altitude. Imagine the melody that you're writing or improvising as a little dancing character and the chords behind the melody serve as the stage. We'll call our dancing character Rockhouse. When you land on a root, 3rd or 5th of the underlying mode, Rockhouse settles in a landing posture on the stage for the length of time that you hold the note. If you land on a note other than the root, 3rd or 5th, Rockhouse settles, suspended in mid-air by an invisible plank. If the tone you landed on doesn't function as any type of chord tone, the plank breaks and he falls on his butt. If you land on a tone not within the scale, he gets shot through the roof of the theater and usually doesn't make a very speedy recovery. In the case of Lydian, all the planks are sturdy.

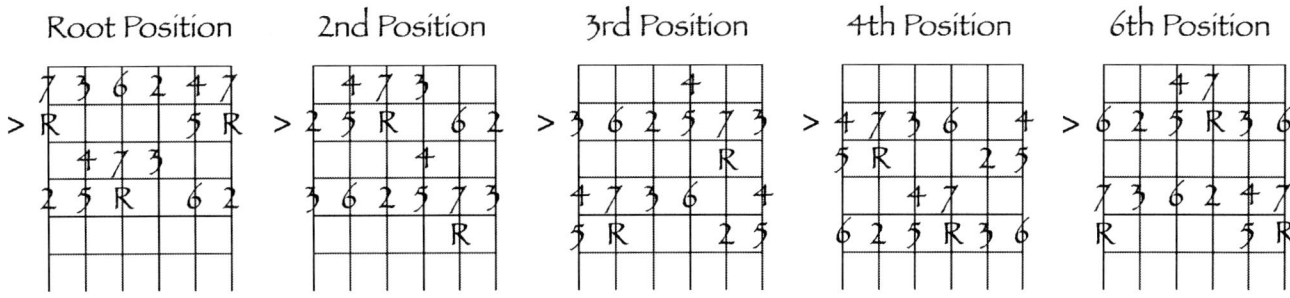

	F	C	G	D	A	E	Cb	Gb	Db	Ab	Eb	Bb
Root Pos:	13	8	3	10	5	12	7	2	9	4	11	6
2nd Pos:	3	10	5	12	7	2	9	4	11	6	13	8
3rd Pos:	5	12	7	2	9	4	11	6	13	8	3	10
4th Pos:	7	2	9	4	11	6	13	8	3	10	5	12
6th Pos:	10	5	12	7	2	9	4	11	6	13	8	3

Here are some diatonic F Lydian modal licks.

F Lydian Lick 1:

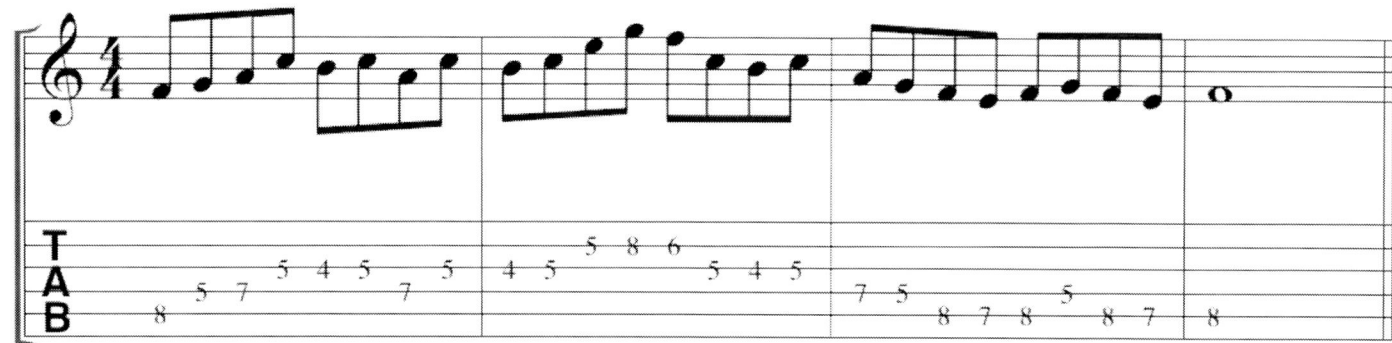

F Lydian Lick 2:

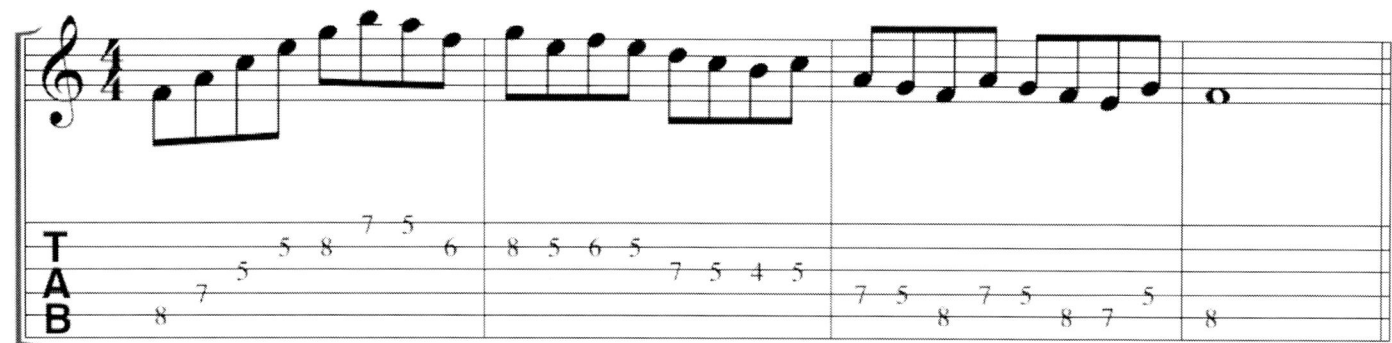

F Lydian Lick 3:

F Lydian Lick 4:

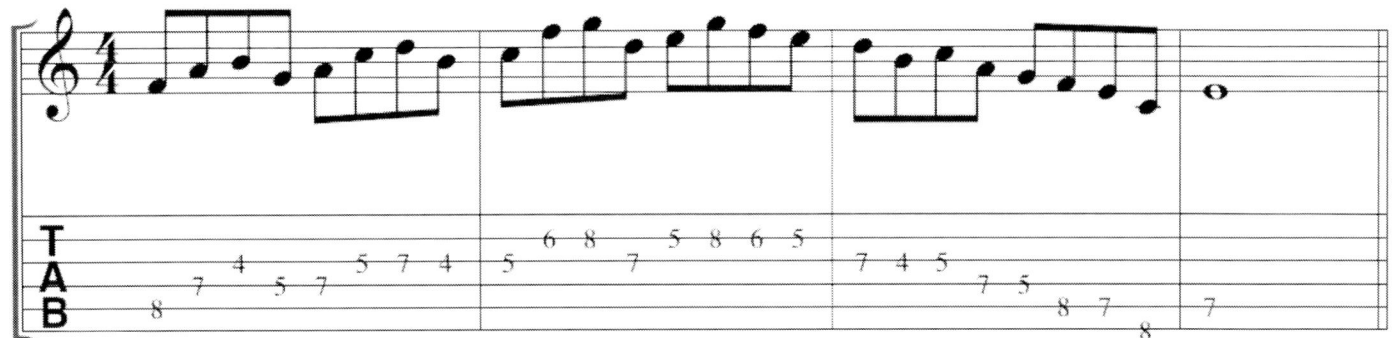

F Lydian Lick 5:

F Lydian Lick 6:

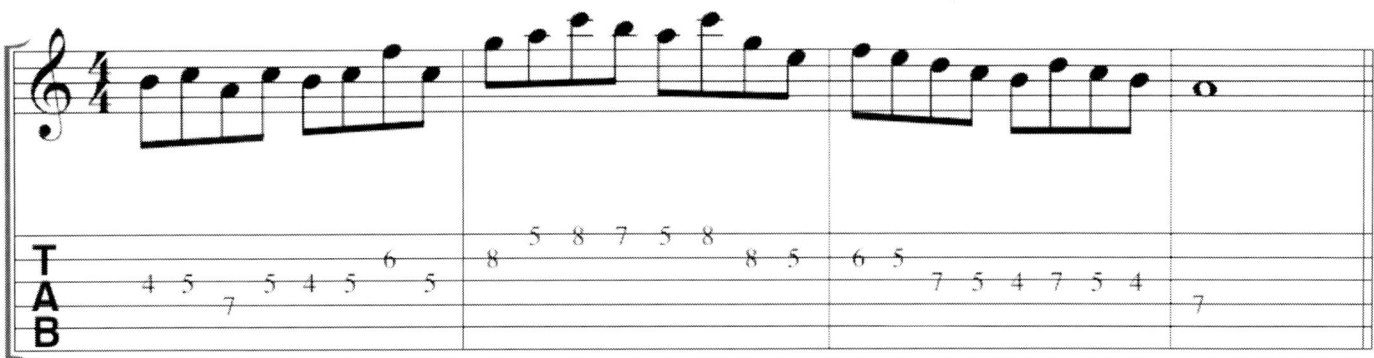

F Lydian Lick 7:

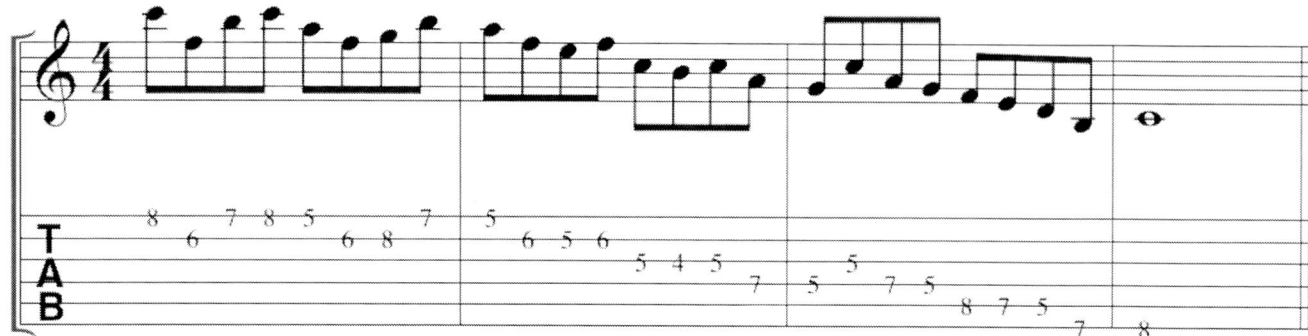

F Lydian Lick 8:

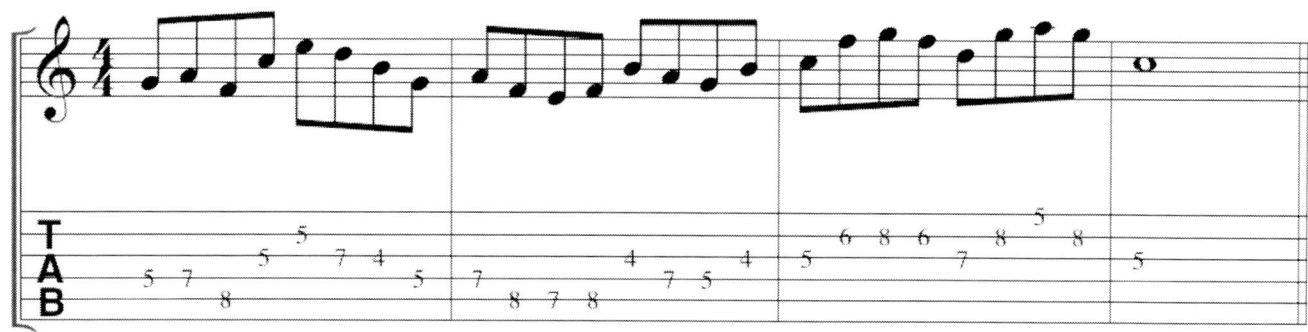

F Lydian Lick 9:

F Lydian Lick 10:

Mixolydian

Mixolydian is the darkest of the three major modes. The interval between the major third and flat 7th is a tritone, (3 whole steps) which is an especially dissonant interval. This creates an unavoidable element of tension within this mode. Fear not though, because this tension is exactly what gives Mixolydian its unique identity.

Even though this mode doesn't extend in the same smooth fashion as Dorian and Lydian, it can still, for the most part, be treated the same way thanks to the desired degree of tension. If there is any note worth avoiding as a 'landing' tone, it would be the 4th of the mode (or root of the parent scale) due to the fact that there would be a resulting half-step clash between your 4th and the major 3rd of the chord. This can easily detract from the effect of the 3rd, which is the most important tone in the chord.

Because of this, modern application of this mode doesn't work all that easily. The types of melodic phrases that will work well in that situation are going to be limited. Some jazz players enjoy melodically super-imposing the related Dorian mode over a Mixolydian context.

This mode has a playful sort of quality and is mostly associated with festiveness, wit and mischief. Its combination of major and minor elements makes it the most commonly employed mode in the blues. It's also very present in rock, pop, jazz, country, bluegrass, Celtic, Latin, funk, Carnatic, Hindustani, reggae, etc.

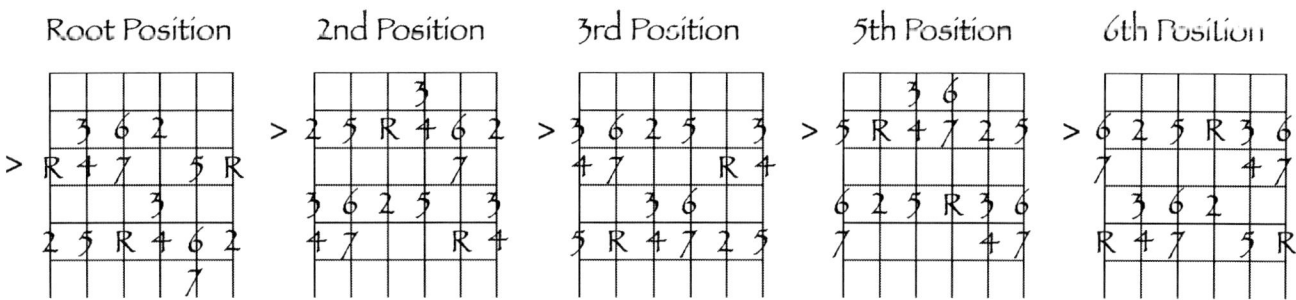

	G	D	A	E	B	F#	Db	Ab	Eb	Bb	F	C
Root Pos:	3	10	5	12	7	2	9	4	11	6	13	8
2nd Pos:	5	12	7	2	9	4	11	6	13	8	3	10
3rd Pos:	7	2	9	4	11	6	13	8	3	10	5	12
5th Pos:	10	5	12	7	2	9	4	11	6	13	8	3
6th Pos:	12	7	2	9	4	11	6	13	8	3	10	5

And now for some G Mixolydian modal licks.

G Mixolydian Lick 1:

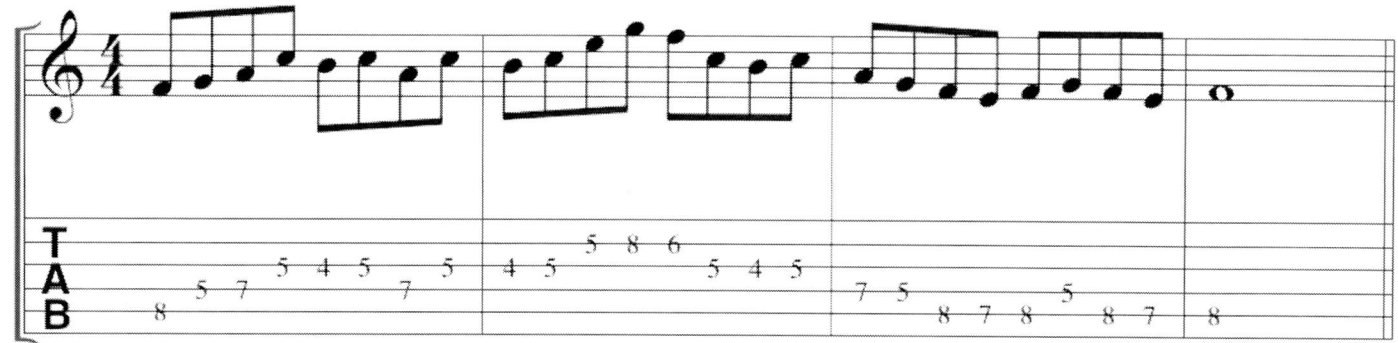

G Mixolydian Lick 2:

G Mixolydian Lick 3:

G Mixolydian Lick 4:

G Mixolydian Lick 5:

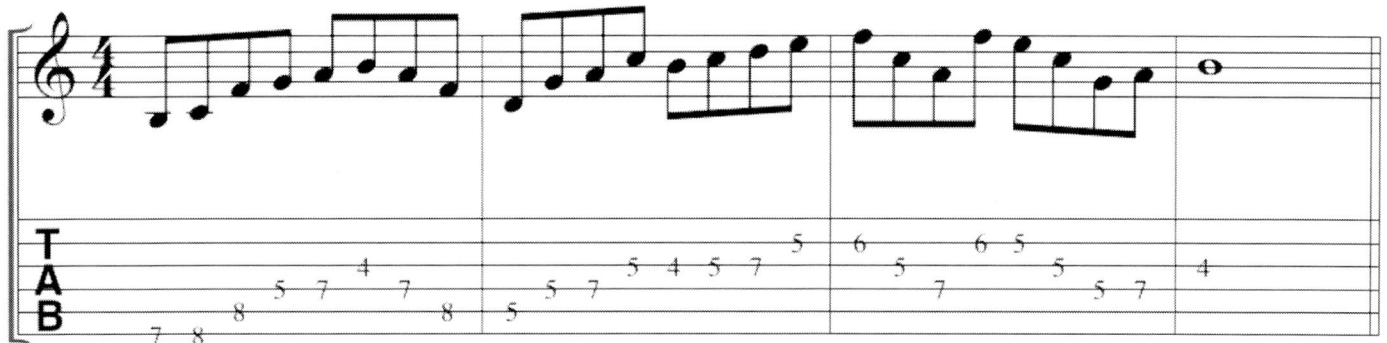

G Mixolydian Lick 6:

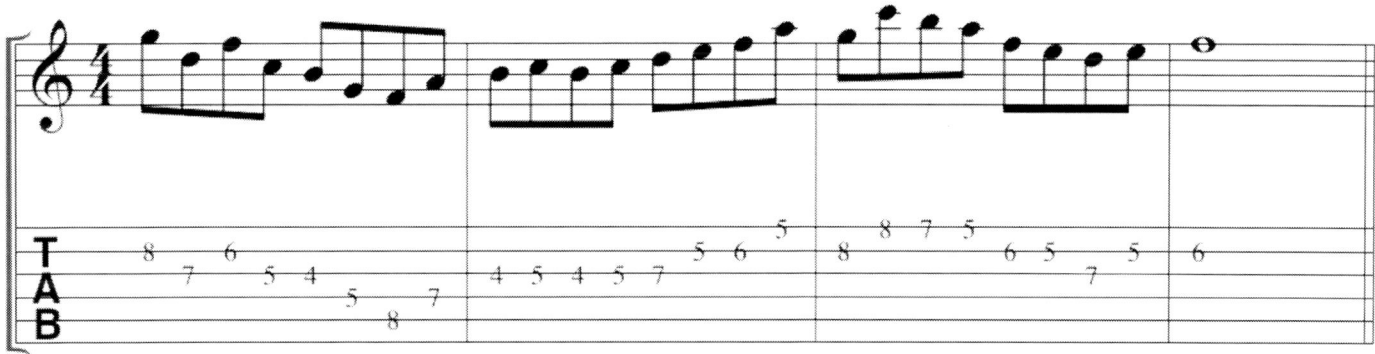

G Mixolydian Lick 7:

G Mixolydian Lick 8:

G Mixolydian Lick 9:

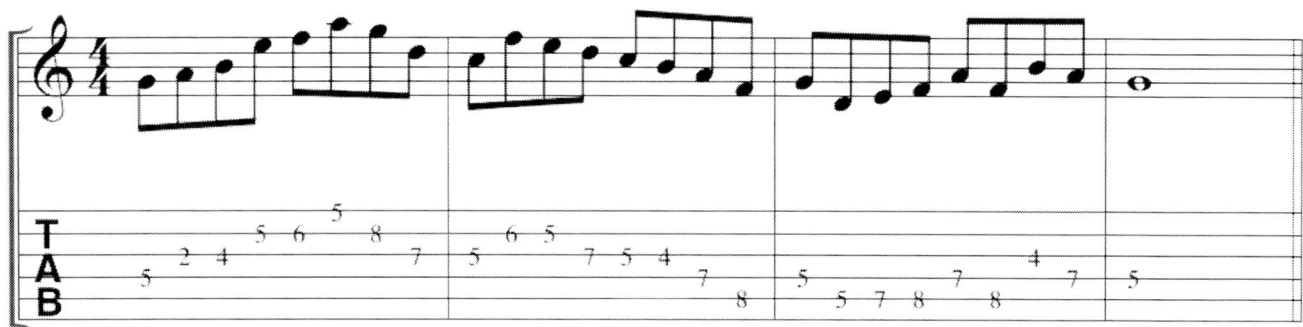

G Mixolydian Lick 10:

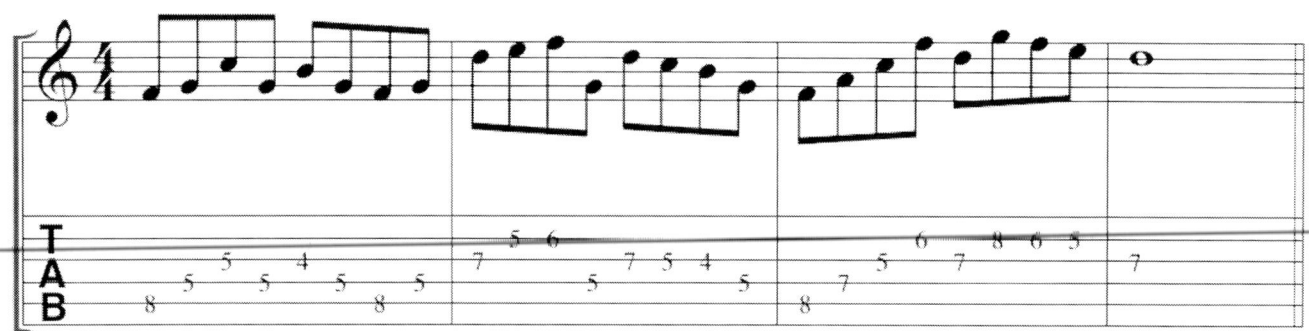

AEOLIAN

Aeolian is the new Ionian. I say this half jokingly. For much of human history, Ionian has been the most common mode for music. As I write this in 2013 AD, in my experience as a guitar teacher and close follower of popular music, in this last decade, we've seen Ionian take a backseat to Aeolian as the most popular mode. It's not this way across the board but Aeolian serves currently as the most popular mode in modern rock, modern R&B, dance music and rap. With these styles dominating the pop charts, we've been hearing a whole lot more of the Aeolian mode than anything else. So needless to say, it's worth knowing.

We have one tone worth avoiding as a point of resolve in this mode and that's its b6th (or the 4th of the parent key). This note can't function as a chord tone but all other notes can. The b6th can only be treated as a dissonance that will, sooner or later, need to be resolved. You're probably starting to really wonder why this is the case. Again, you're going to have to take my word on it until we delve into extended harmony.

After doing some hard thinking I've come to the conclusion that the only style of music I can think of where Aeolian isn't all that common is Jazz. It still finds occasional use there but the Dorian mode and the melodic minor scale are preferred over it for reasons we'll eventually be going over.

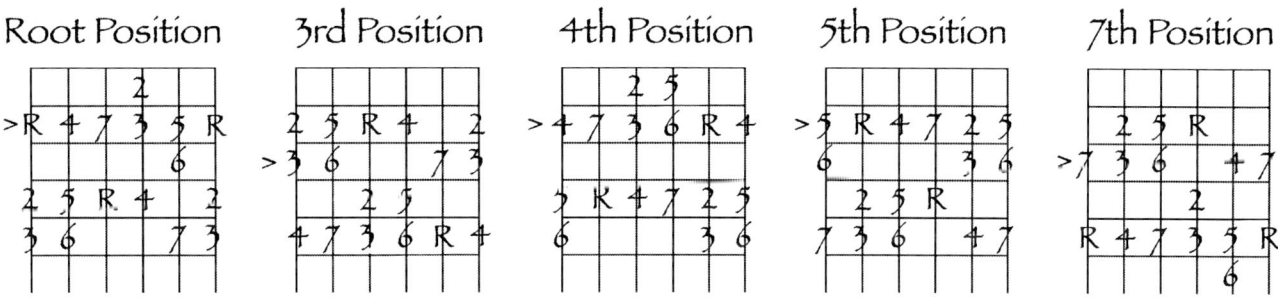

	A	E	B	F#	C#	G#	Eb	Bb	F	C	G	D
Root Pos:	5	12	7	2	9	4	11	6	13	8	3	10
3rd Pos:	8	3	10	5	12	7	2	9	4	11	6	13
4th Pos:	10	5	12	7	2	9	4	11	6	13	8	3
5th Pos:	12	7	2	9	4	11	6	13	8	3	10	5
7th Pos:	3	10	5	12	7	2	9	4	11	6	13	8

Aeolian licks, Aeolian licks...I got Aeolian licks here!

Aeolian Lick 1:

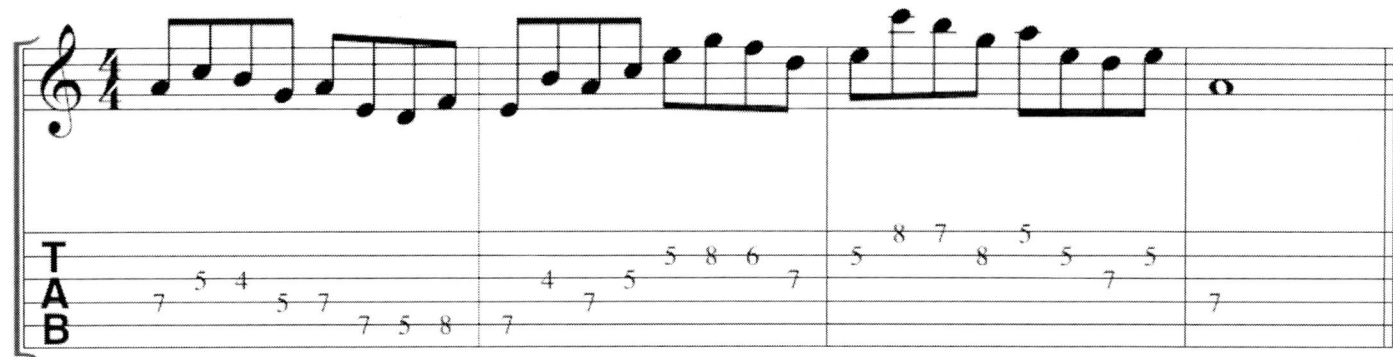

Aeolian Lick 2:

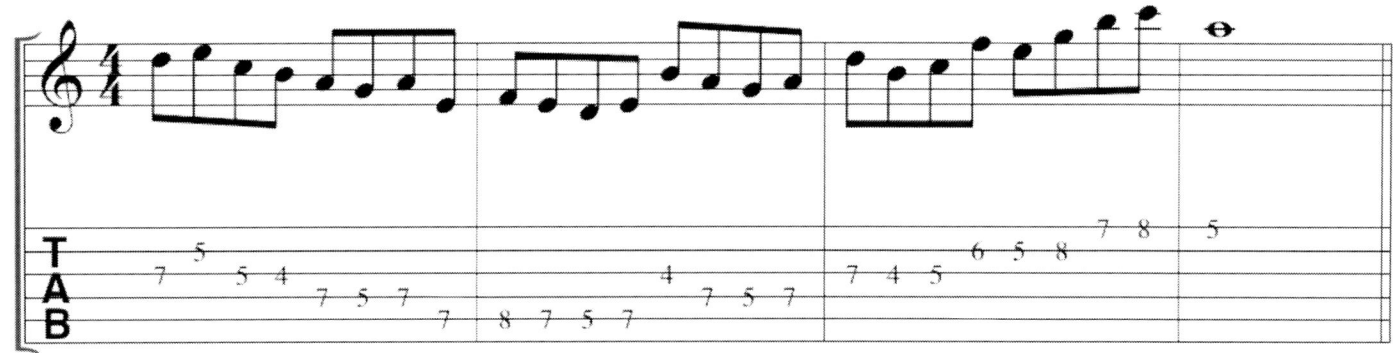

Aeolian Lick 3:

Aeolian Lick 4:

Aeolian Lick 5:

Aeolian Lick 6:

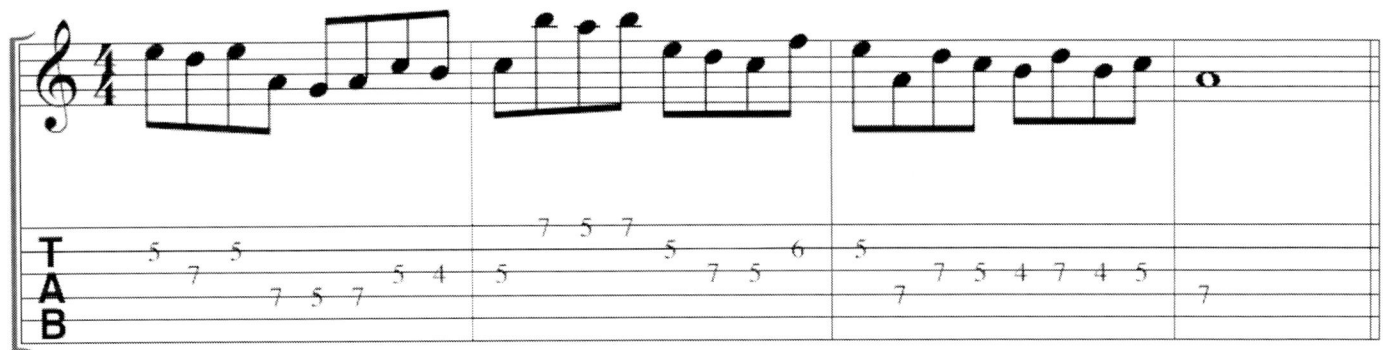

Aeolian Lick 7:

Aeolian Lick 8:

Aeolian Lick 9:

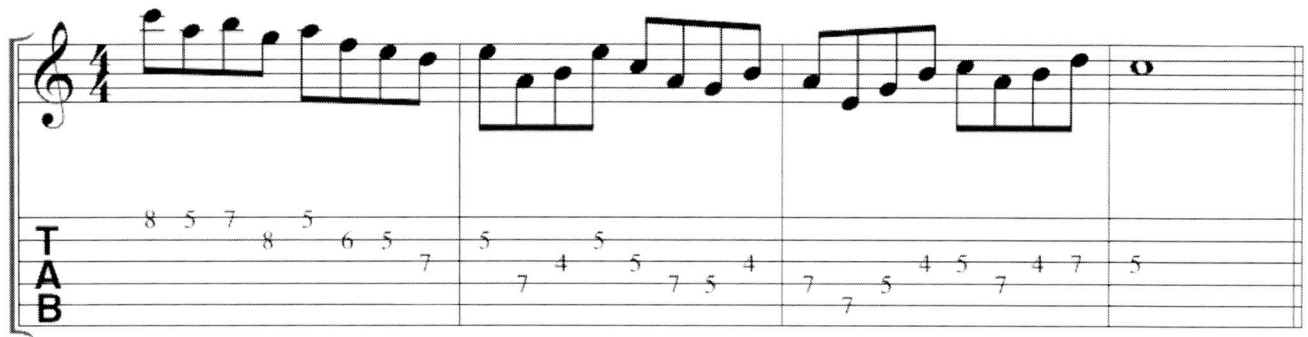

Aeolian Lick 10:

The Scale-Tone Pattern and the Modes

This is where this pattern really becomes handy. You can't exactly practice up and down a mode treating all of the notes equally. Remember that you have five scale positions and contained within each position are all seven modes. You need to be able to hear what the intended root note of the mode is and there's nothing like the scale-tone pattern to help your ears get a handle on what mode you're in. As you listen and play through these exercises, you hear what I mean. When you're playing this pattern properly, it would be imposable to hear the root anywhere other than where you're intending it to be.

I've presented these exercises in my favorite position, the 6th position of the major scale. It's the root position of the relative minor scale. (I got my start playing metal!) This time I dispensed with the fingerings, because I'm assuming you spent some time with the previous scale-tone patterns. If you find your self stopping to try and decide which finger to use for a certain note, that definitely means you haven't spent enough time on the major and natural minor scale. Go back and drill those into your dome some more if you feel like need to do so.

As always, it would be a really good idea to work these out in your other four movable positions as well as your open positions in all twelve keys. Obviously this will be an ongoing project. Just take it one step at a time. Going through all these modes in one position is a really good start. Once you get through these and you have them moving nice and smoothly, break out that blank tab paper and get to work on the root position. Repeat that process with each position. Make this a regular effort. Work on it at least a couple times each week at the very least.

The first mode, Ionian is synonymous with and identical to the major scale, itself. That means that this first exercise is a redundancy from the first section on the scale tone pattern. I've included it here, simply for the sake of direct comparison. In this mode, our inactive (resolving) tones are C, E and G.

C Ionian Scale-Tone Pattern

The second mode, Dorian is a personal favorite. For reasons, which you'll directly understand later, this is a very easy mode in which to improvise. The strong or inactive notes of any conventional diatonic mode (aside from one that you'll learn about, later) are always the root, 3rd and 5th. To clarify, I'm referring to the root, 3rd and 5th of that mode and not of its parent major scale. So in this case, our inactive tones are D, F and A. these are the notes that resolve.

√ **Track 43:** D Dorian Scale-Tone Pattern

In our third mode, Phrygian, the inactive notes are E, G and B. Notice that these are the notes that make up our IIIm chord in this key. It's the same way that the notes of the IIm chord are the inactive notes of Dorian, our second mode. This is the case with all of the modes.

√ Track 44: E Phrygian Scale-Tone Pattern

Here's our fourth mode, Lydian. In our current key, C major, our inactive tones are F, A and C. These notes make up the F major chord, of course. This is another very easy mode in which to improvise, at least, once you get used to the general sound of it. It's very bright!

√ Track 45: F Lydian Scale-Tone Pattern

The fifth mode, Mixolydian is one shade darker than Ionian and is also a very common mode. One thing worth noting is that we're consistently beginning these exercises on whatever the lowest reachable inactive tone, regardless of whether it's the root, 3rd or 5th. In this position, we begin on the 3rd. Make a mental note on the starting chord tone of each of these. It helped me, for some time, to call out the roots thirds and 5ths to my self while playing through each mode.

√ Track 46: G Mixolydian Scale-Tone Pattern

The sixth mode is synonymous with the natural minor scale. Therefore, this next eight-measure phrase is a redundancy from the Natural Minor Scale-Tone Pattern section of the book and it's only here for the sake of complete continuity.

√ Track 47: A Aeolian Scale-Tone Pattern

And finally our dark neighbor, Locrian.

√ Track 48: B Locrian Scale-Tone Pattern

Before we move away from the topic of the modes, I'd like to present a good way of organizing them in your mind. Below, I've divided our modes into two families, each containing three modes.

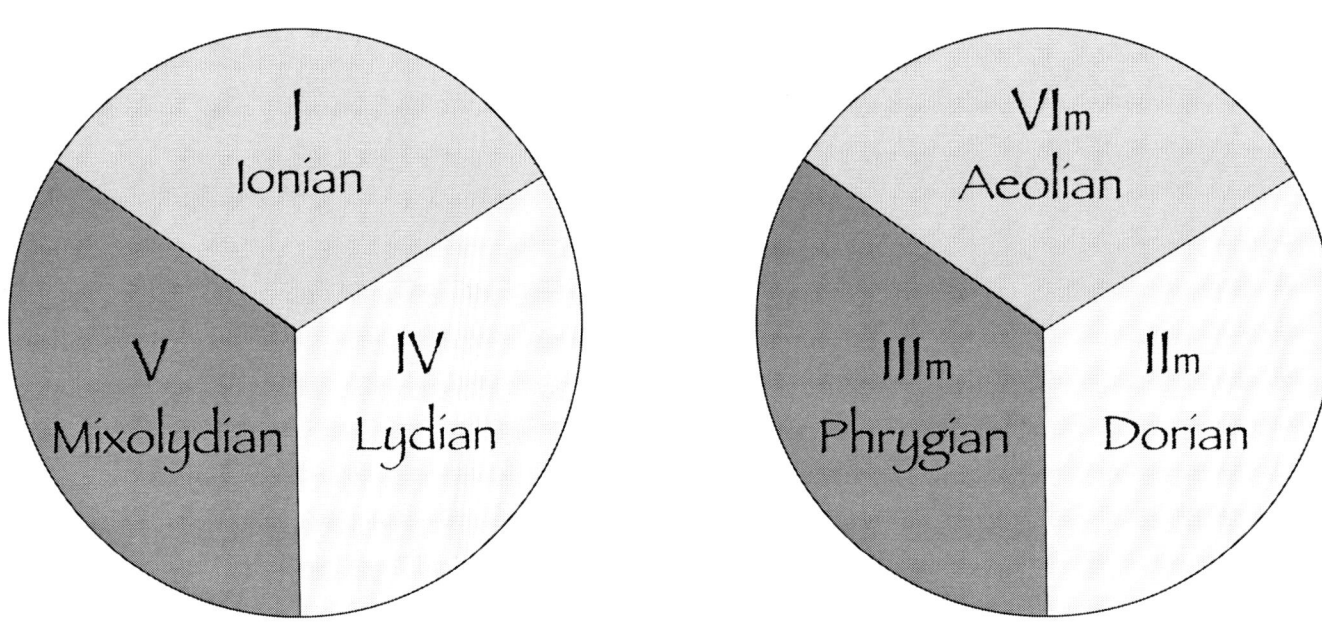

Arpeggios – Part 1: Triads Of The Major Scale

An arpeggio is simply a chord used melodically rather than harmonically. In other words, we play one note at a time as opposed to all of them at once. Upon entering the subject of arpeggios, it's going to be helpful for you to bear in mind what you've learned about modes, chords and scale-tone activity. If you feel weak on any of these subjects, revisit those sections of this book.

You may recall that modes correspond directly to the diatonic family of chords. For example, Dorian is the second mode of the major scale, so the II chord would be home base for the Dorian mode. Furthermore, the three notes that make up the II chord would be the inactive (or resolving) tones of the mode. As a result of this, learning diatonically related arpeggios is a big help in mastering the tension and release of each mode. I'd recommend comparing these to the full positions of the modes.

As for the melodic usage of arpeggios, we can boil it down to two types of uses: 1) Traditional, where the arpeggio corresponds directly to the chord that's being voiced in the accompanying music and 2) Modern, where the arpeggio is superimposed over a contrasting chord to serve as upper chord tones or 'upper extensions', which we'll be covering soon. Classical music, bluegrass and country music lean much more toward Traditional usage, whereas jazz and soul music really lean toward Modern use. Modern rock music, in the broad sense (starting in the late '60s) uses a wide array of balances between modern and traditional arpeggio use.

One thing is for certain and that's that the use of arpeggios is widespread in all styles of music, old and new. Learn these shapes and learn them well if you want to be able to improvise concise melodies over chord changes. That's a skill useful in any style. Not only do you want to know the shapes themselves, but you need a clear understanding of how they relate to one another within a given key.

In this section, I cover five positions for each chord in the major diatonic family. Accompanying the diagrams for each group of arpeggio shapes is a chart indicating what fret each shape will be located at for each key. The columns correspond to the similar charts displayed in previous sections, in the sense that the far left column relates to C major and it works to the right through the cycle of 5ths. This means that in whatever key you work these shapes out, you're going to follow the same column from one chord to the next.

Until we delve into extended harmony we're going to limit our study of these arpeggios to the traditional uses. This doesn't really limit us that much, because there's a whole lot that can be done with them on those terms. Practice playing from the bottom note to the top note (and back down to the bottom) of each of these arpeggios, in steady streams of 8th notes, 16th notes and triplets. For now, work with strict alternate picking but we'll be looking at some other options further in. Also keep your notes from ringing together which means you're going to have to let go of the previous note with your fretting hand right as you pick the next note. Try to make them sound like they're being played on a one stringed guitar.

THE I CHORD:

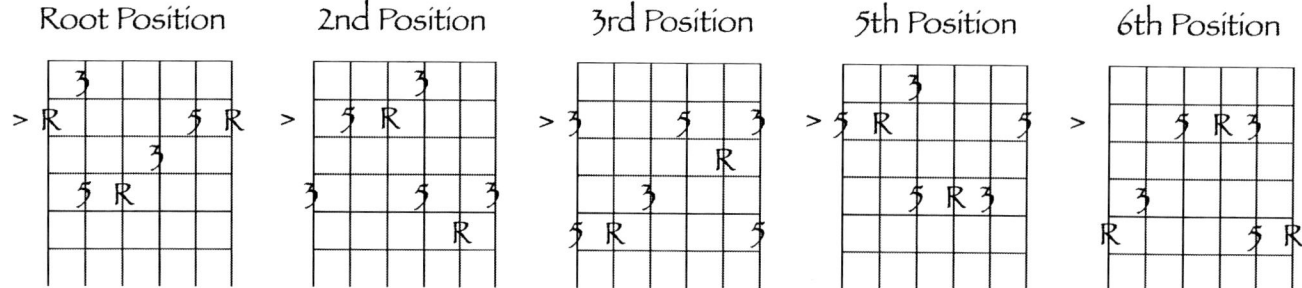

I CHORDS	C	G	D	A	E	B	Gb	Db	Ab	Eb	Bb	F
Root Pos:	8	3	10	5	12	7	2	9	4	11	6	13
2nd Pos:	10	5	12	7	2	9	4	11	6	13	8	3
3rd Pos:	12	7	2	9	4	11	6	1	8	3	10	5
5th Pos:	3	10	5	12	7	2	9	4	11	6	13	8
6th Pos:	5	12	7	2	9	4	11	6	13	8	3	10

THE II CHORD:

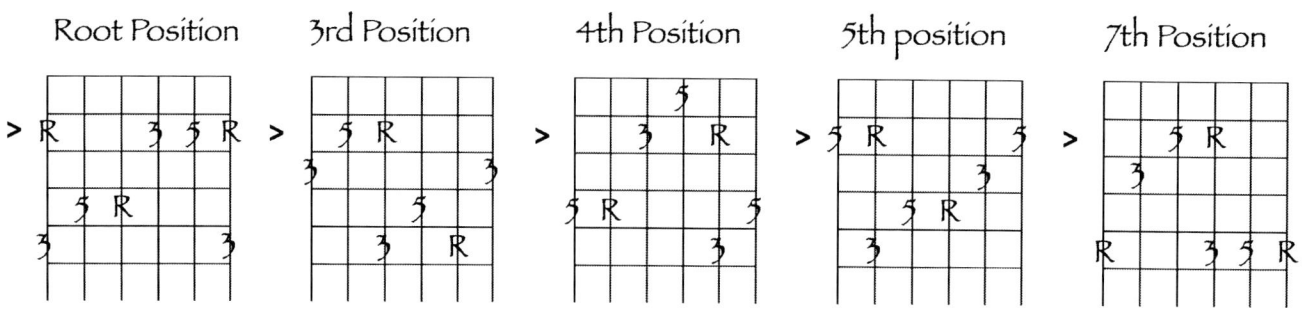

II CHORDS	Dm	Am	Em	Bm	F#m	C#m	Abm	Ebm	Bbm	Fm	Cm	Gm
Root Pos:	10	5	12	7	2	9	4	11	6	13	8	3
3rd Pos:	13	8	3	10	5	12	7	2	9	4	11	6
4th Pos:	3	10	5	12	7	2	9	4	11	6	13	8
5th Pos:	5	12	7	2	9	4	11	6	13	8	3	10
7th Pos:	8	3	10	5	12	7	2	9	4	11	6	13

THE III CHORD:

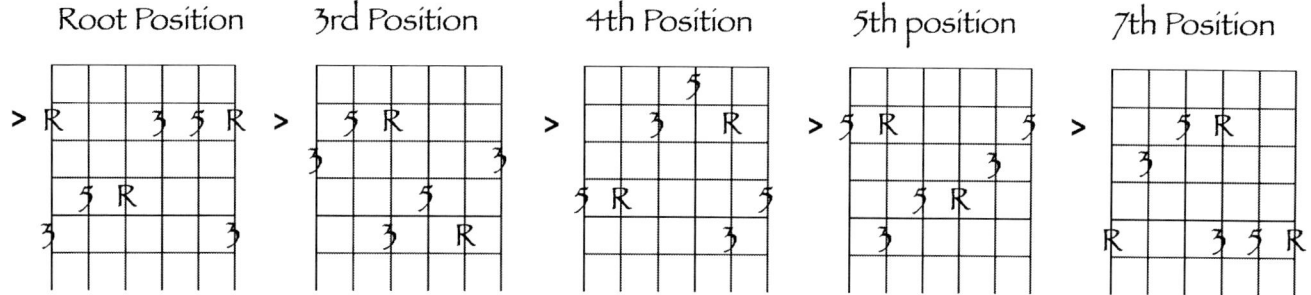

III CHORDS	Em	Bm	F#m	C#m	G#m	D#m	Bbm	Fm	Cm	Gm	Dm	Am
Root Pos:	12	7	2	9	4	11	6	13	8	3	10	5
3rd Pos:	3	10	5	12	7	2	9	4	11	6	13	8
4th Pos:	5	12	7	2	9	4	11	6	13	8	3	10
5th Pos:	7	2	9	4	11	6	13	8	3	10	5	12
7th Pos:	10	5	12	7	2	9	4	11	6	13	8	3

THE IV CHORD:

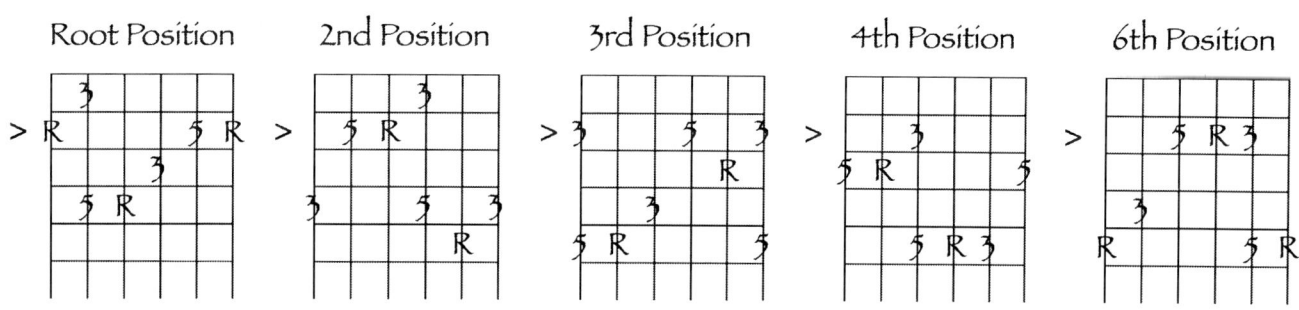

IV CHORDS	F	C	G	D	A	E	Cb	Gb	Db	Ab	Eb	Bb
Root Pos:	13	8	3	10	5	12	7	2	9	4	11	6
2nd Pos:	3	10	5	12	7	2	9	4	11	6	13	8
3rd Pos:	5	12	7	2	9	4	11	6	13	8	3	10
4th Pos:	7	2	9	4	11	6	13	8	3	10	5	12
6th Pos:	10	5	12	7	2	9	4	11	6	13	8	3

THE V CHORD:

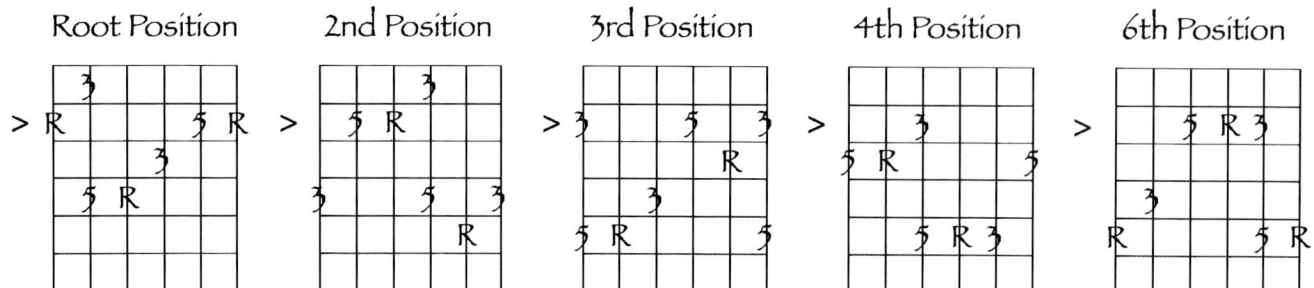

V CHORDS	G	D	A	E	B	F#	Db	Ab	Eb	Bb	F	C
Root Pos:	3	10	5	12	7	2	9	4	11	6	13	8
2nd Pos:	5	12	7	2	9	4	11	6	13	8	3	10
3rd Pos:	7	2	9	4	11	6	13	8	3	10	5	12
5th Pos:	10	5	12	7	2	9	4	11	6	13	8	3
6th Pos:	12	7	2	9	4	11	6	13	8	3	10	5

THE VI CHORD:

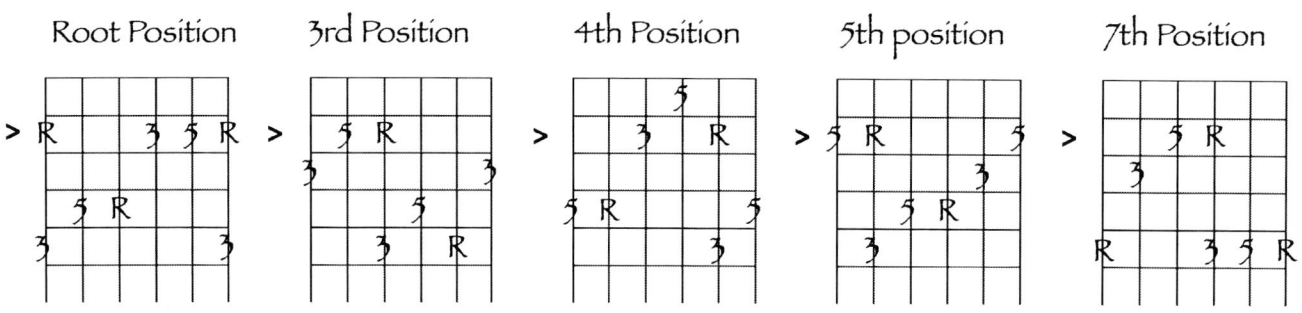

VI CHORDS	Am	Em	Bm	F#m	C#m	G#m	Ebm	Bbm	Fm	Cm	Gm	Dm
Root Pos:	5	12	7	2	9	4	11	6	13	8	3	10
3rd Pos:	8	3	10	5	12	7	2	9	4	11	6	13
4th Pos:	10	5	12	7	2	9	4	11	6	13	8	3
5th Pos:	12	7	2	9	4	11	6	13	8	3	10	5
7th Pos:	3	10	5	12	7	2	9	4	11	6	13	8

Major Scale Triad Pairs

Merely practicing these arpeggios up and down will familiarize you with them but won't necessarily give you a musical command over them. These runs below will get you a little closer to that. What we have here, are triad combinations made up of two opposing triads. By "opposing", I mean that there are no common tones between the two involved chords. Sometimes these figures are played over a perfectly corresponding chord vamp. The good news is that they can just as easily be applied over one static chord, and in some cases, the chord doesn't even have to be one of the two triads involved.

Here we have four runs for each chord combination. The first of which ascends the first chord, then connects to the nearest note above of the second chord, then it descends that chord and connects to the nearest note above of the first chord, which will, as a result, be the next available position. This process continues to the top of the position. The second run starts in the highest register of the position ascending the first chord, connecting to the closest note below in the opposing chord, descends that chord and connects to the closest note below in the original chord. The following two runs just flip the two smaller directions. The resulting effect is that the two opposing chords are almost always connected by a scale-step, which allows them to move in a smooth, flowing fashion.

These triad pairs can be used over either chord that each one is made up of. Each pair can be placed over certain chords that aren't involved in the pair. Below, I've included a table that provides a list of the triad pairs that I've included along with a guide indicating what chords that particular triad pair can be played over. The possibility furthest to the left is the closest related context, and as you progress to the right the context become more loosely related. As a result, the applications become more sneaky sounding. Feel free to experiment beyond these possibilities because these are the ones that I know work and I've never claimed to know everything..

Triad Pairs:	Can Be Applied Over These Static Chords: (In C major)
Am - G	Am, Am7, G, G7, F, Fmaj7, Dm, Dm7, C, Cmaj7
F - G	F, Fmaj7, G, G7, Dm, Dm7, C, Cmaj7
Dm - Em	Dm, Dm7, Em, Em7, F, Fmaj7, G, G7, C, Cmaj7
Em - F	Em, Em7, F, Fmaj7, Dm, Dm7, G, G7, C, Cmaj7

Since the shapes lay out on the fretboard differently, from position to position, I've included all positions for each pair of triads. Even though this takes up a good deal of space in the book, it barely scratches the surface of possibilities, since we could also work with other groupings of notes within the same concept. For instance, we could do the same thing with three-note or two-note groups. If you're daring, you could even try it with 5 note groups. On top of that, you could sequence any of these possibilities in different ways, rhythmically. For instance, you could take the four-note groups and sequence them against a triplet rhythm or any other rhythm. Musical application of these types of ideas simply boils down to judicious use. While practicing these patterns start to finish will do you some good, it's also important to get used to starting at different points throughout. This will give you a strong command over these patterns and allow you to use any chunk, starting and ending just about anywhere. Now get to work!

Am-G: C Major 5th Position, Ascend-Descend, Ascending

Am-G: C Major 5th Position, Ascend-Descend, Descending

Am-G: C Major, 5th Position, Descend-Ascend, Ascending

Am-G: C Major, 5th Position, Descend-Ascend, Descending

Am-G: C Major, 6th Position, Ascend-Descend, Ascending

Am-G: C Major, 6th Position, Ascend-Descend, Descending

Am-G: C Major, 6th Position, Descend-Ascend, Ascending

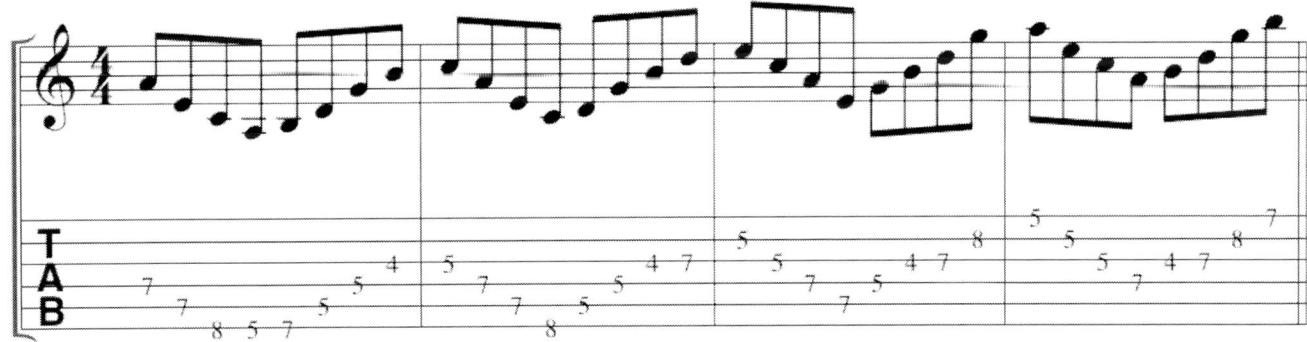

Am-G: C Major, 6th Position, Descend-Ascend, Descending

Am-G: C Major, Root Position, Ascend-Descend, Ascending

Am-G: C Major, Root Position, Ascend-Descend, Descending

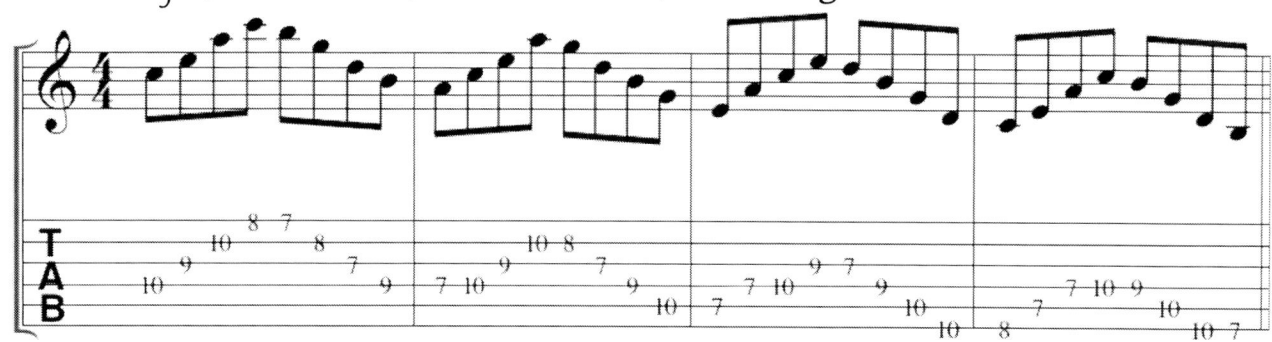

Am-G: C Major, Root Position, Descend-Ascend, Ascending

Am-G: C Major, Root Position, Descend-Ascend, Descending

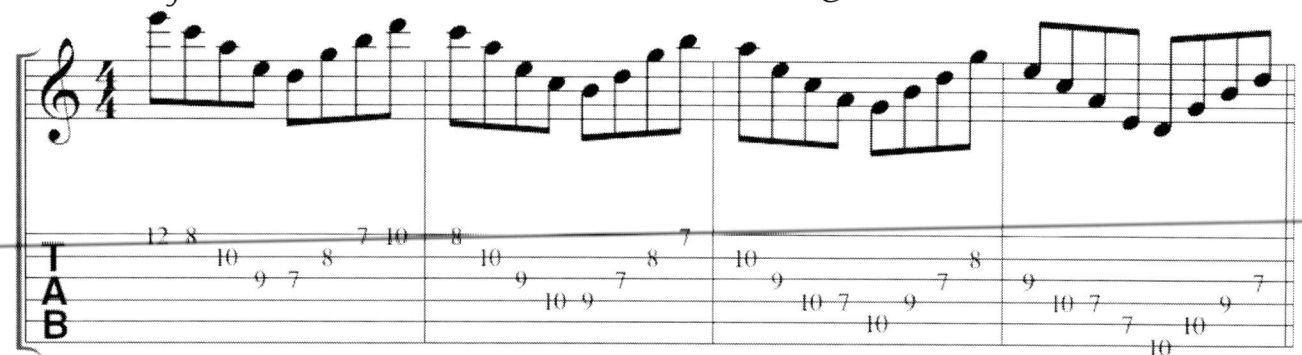

Am-G: C Major, 2nd Position, Ascend-Descend, Ascending

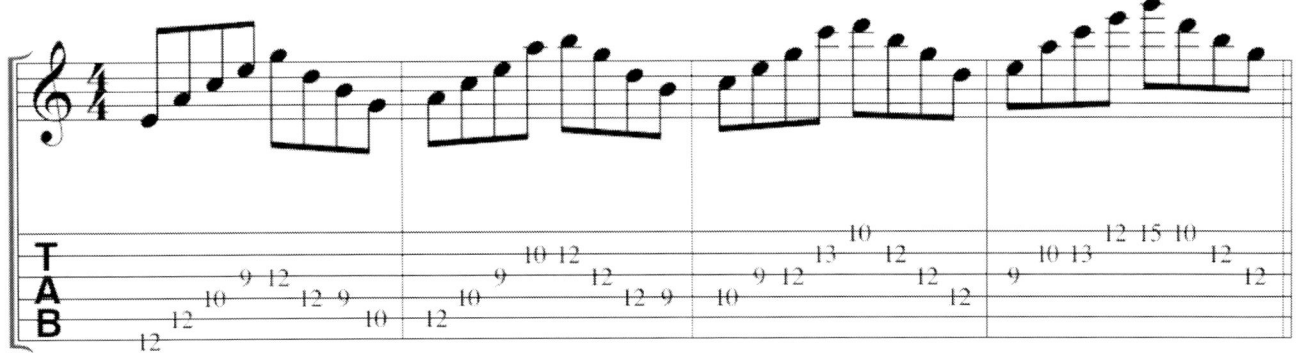

Am-G: C Major, 2nd Position, Ascend-Descend, Descending

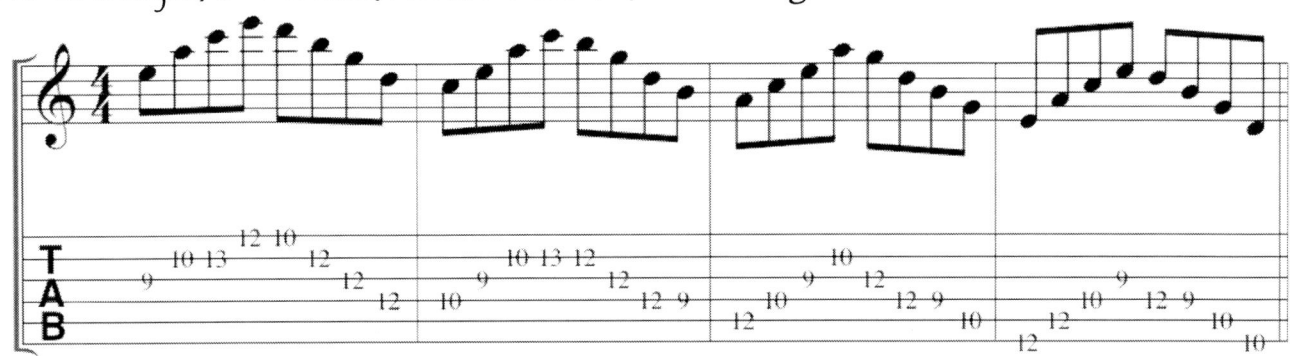

Am-G: C Major, 2nd Position, Descend-Ascend, Ascending

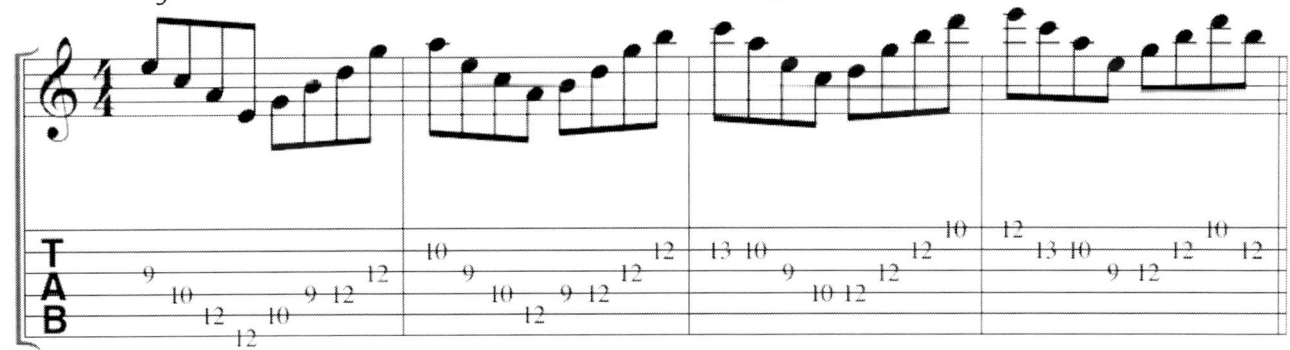

Am-G: C Major, 2nd Position, Descend-Ascend, Descending

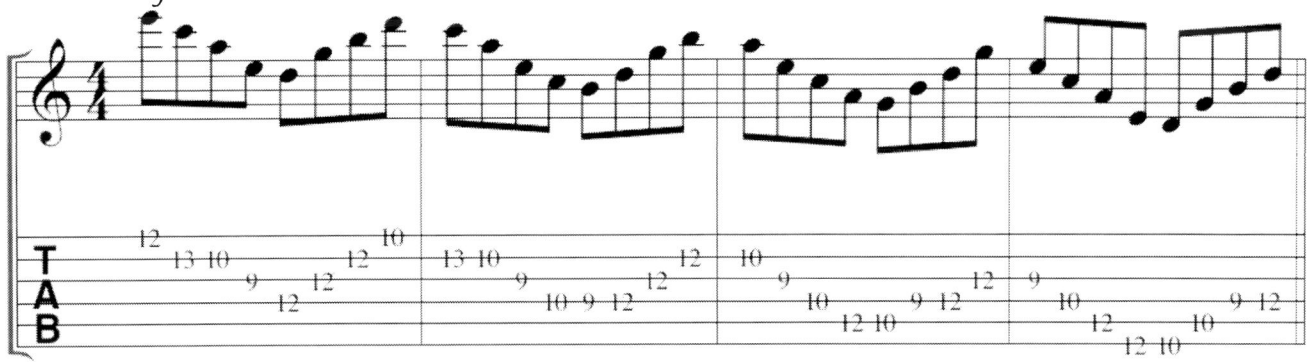

Am-G: C Major, 3rd Position, Ascend-Descend, Ascending

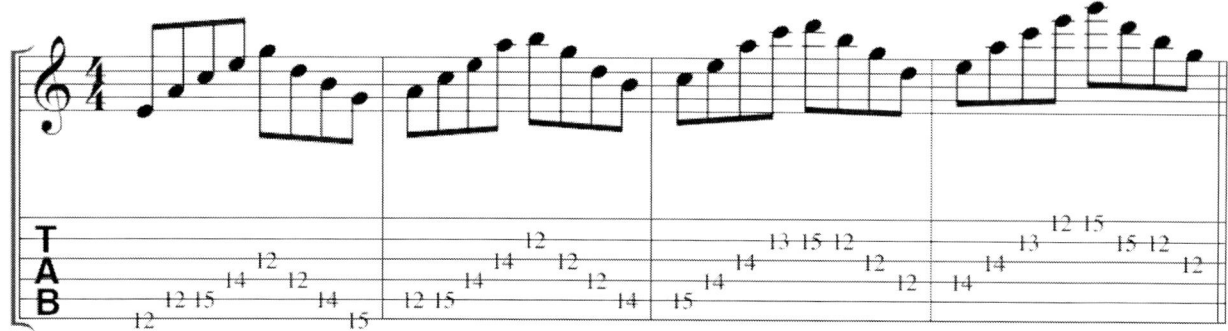

Am-G: C Major, 3rd Position, Ascend-Descend, Descending

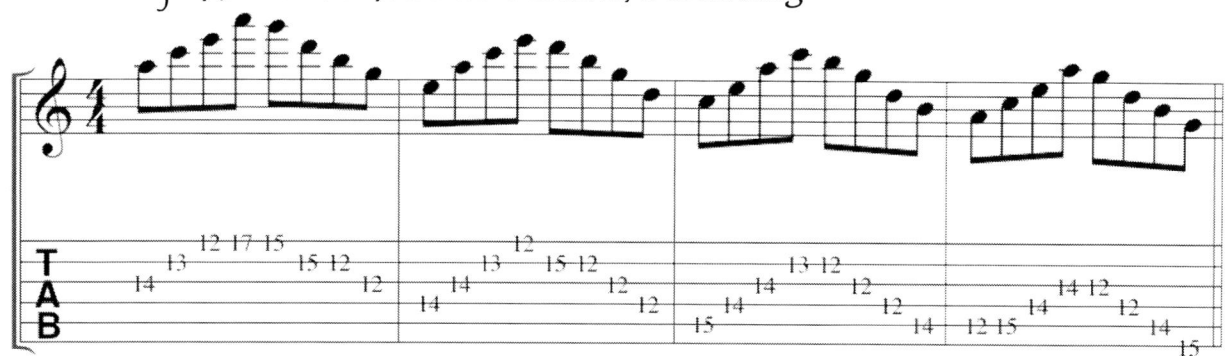

Am-G: C Major, 3rd Position, Descend-Ascend, Ascending

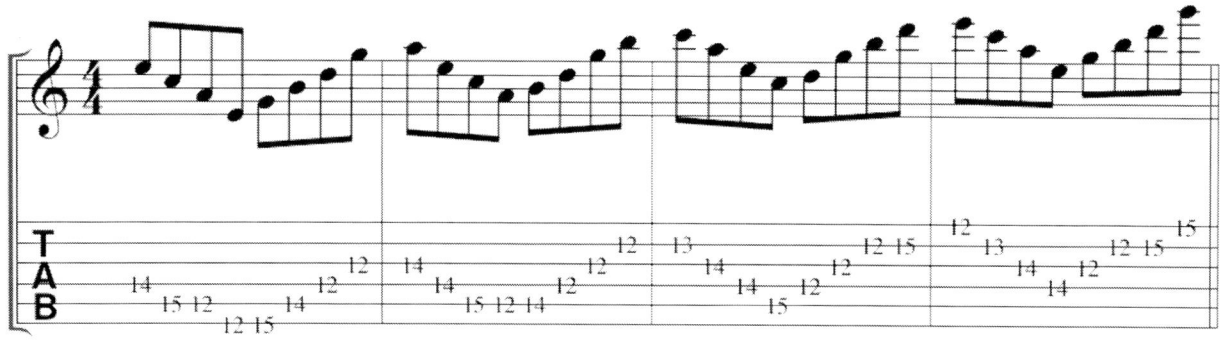

Am-G: C Major, 3rd Position, Descend-Ascend, Descending

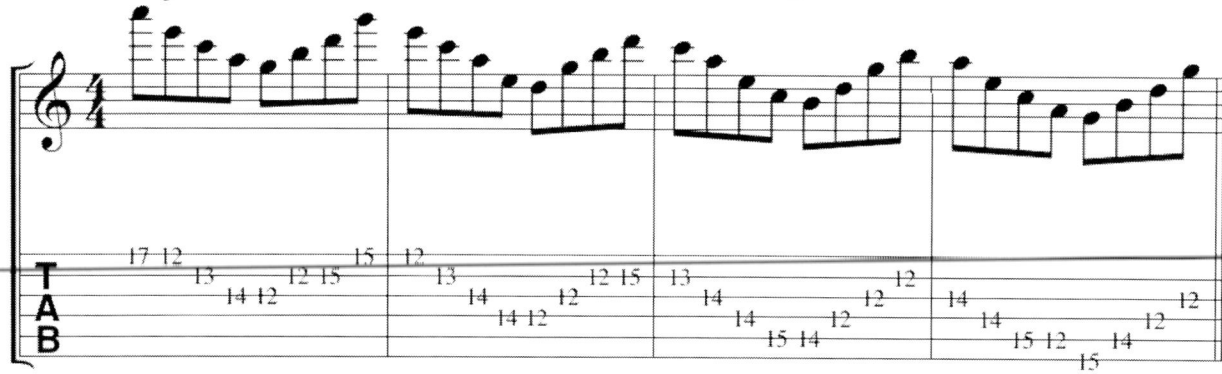

F-G: C Major, 5th Position, Ascend-Descend, Ascending

F-G: C Major, 5th Position, Ascend-Descend, Descending

F-G: C Major, 5th Position, Descend-Ascend, Ascending

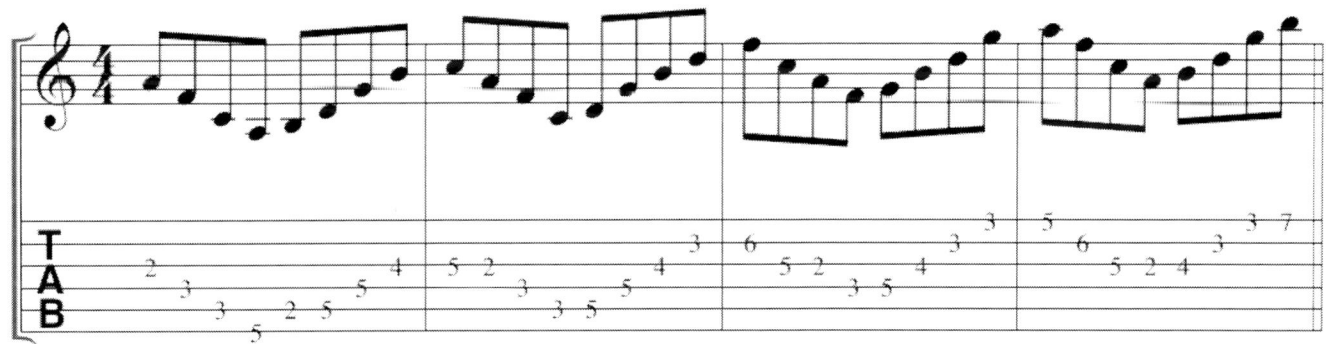

F-G: C Major, 5th Position, Descend-Ascend, Descending

F-G: C Major, 6th Position, Ascend-Descend, Ascending

F-G: C Major, 6th Position, Ascend-Descend, Descending

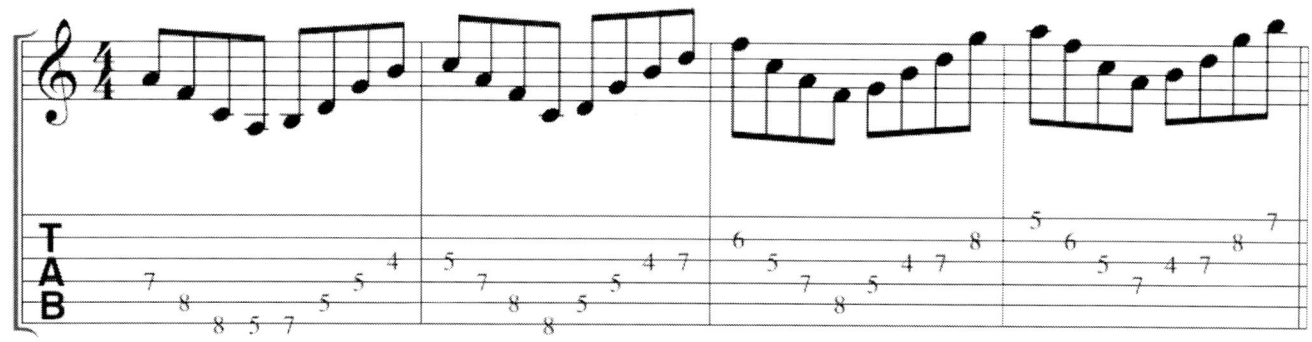

F-G: C Major, 6th Position, Descend-Ascend, Ascending

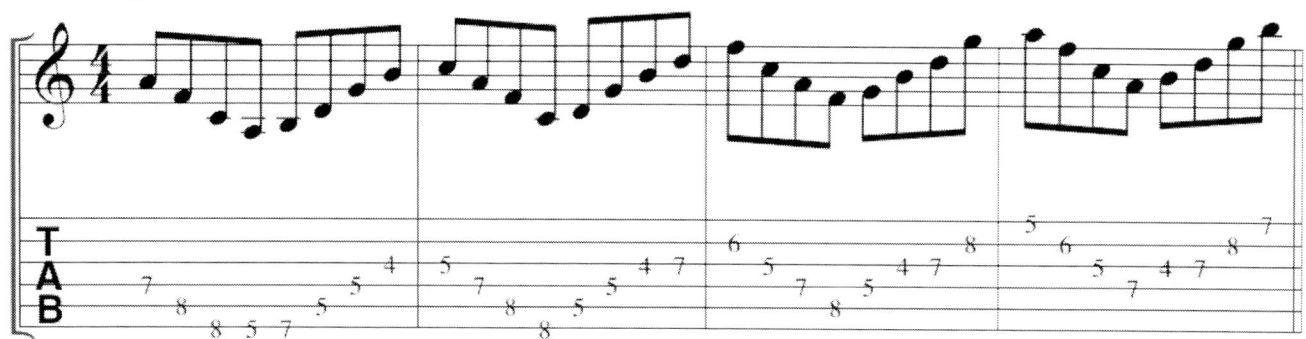

F-G: C Major, 6th Position, Descend-Ascend, Descending

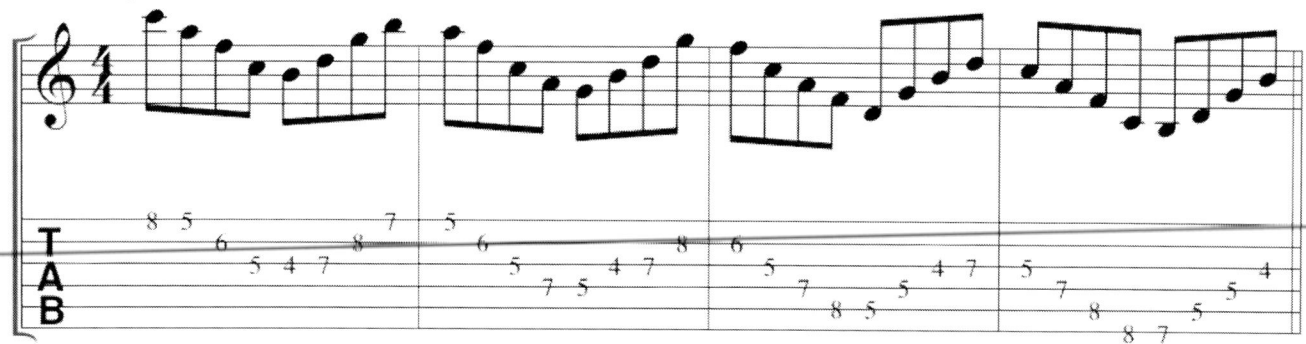

F-G: C Major, Root Position, Ascend-Descend, Ascending

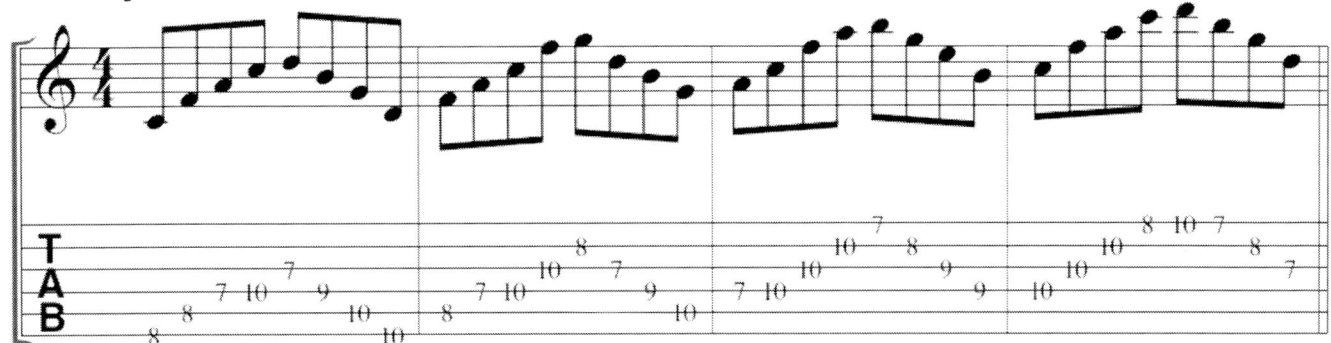

F-G: C Major, Root Position, Ascend-Descend, Descending

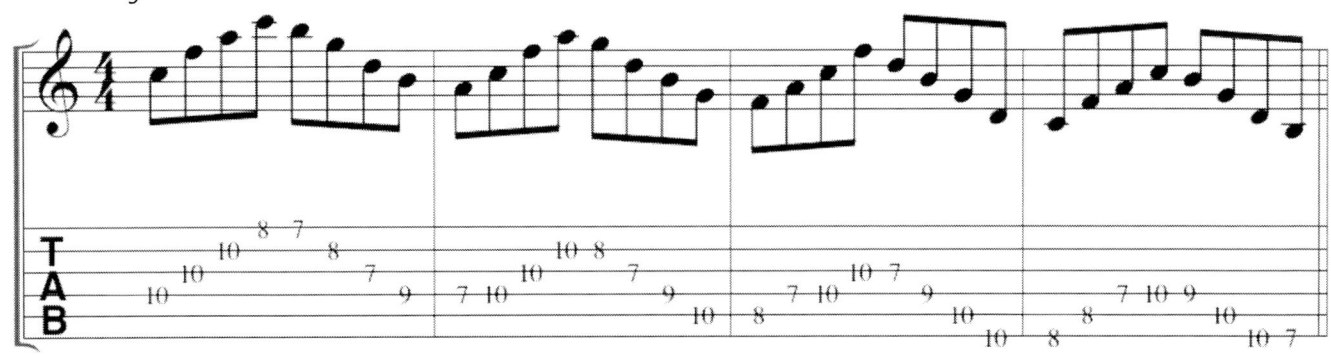

F-G: C Major, Root Position, Descend-Ascend, Ascending

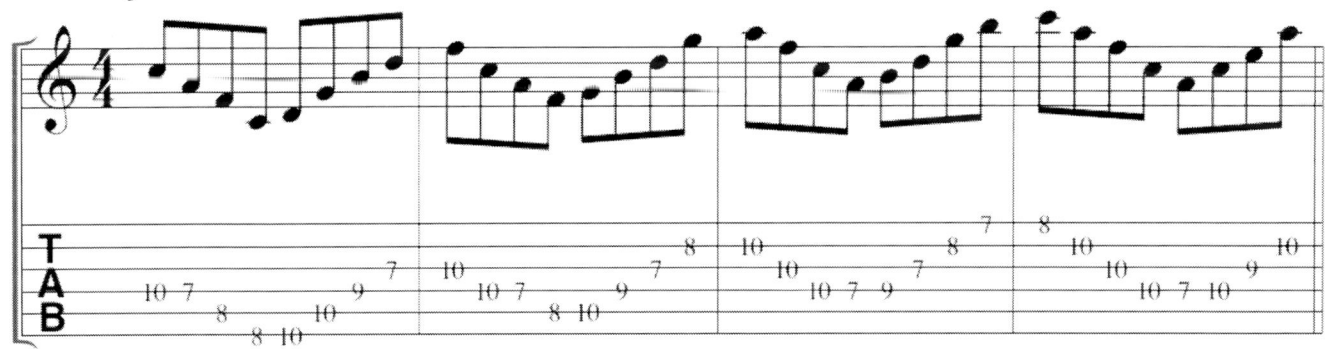

F-G: C Major, Root Position, Descend-Ascend, Descending

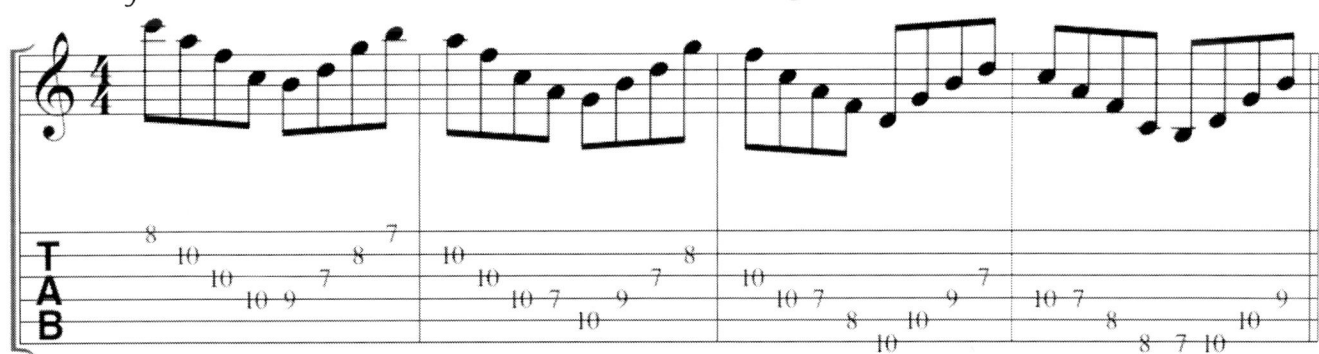

F-G: C Major, 2nd Position, Ascend-Descend, Ascending

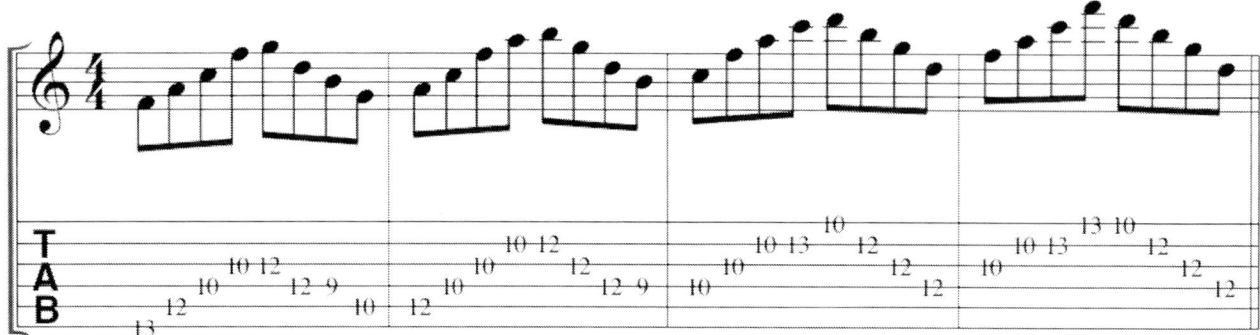

F-G: C Major, 2nd Position, Ascend-Descend, Descending

F-G: C Major, 2nd Position, Descend-Ascend, Ascending

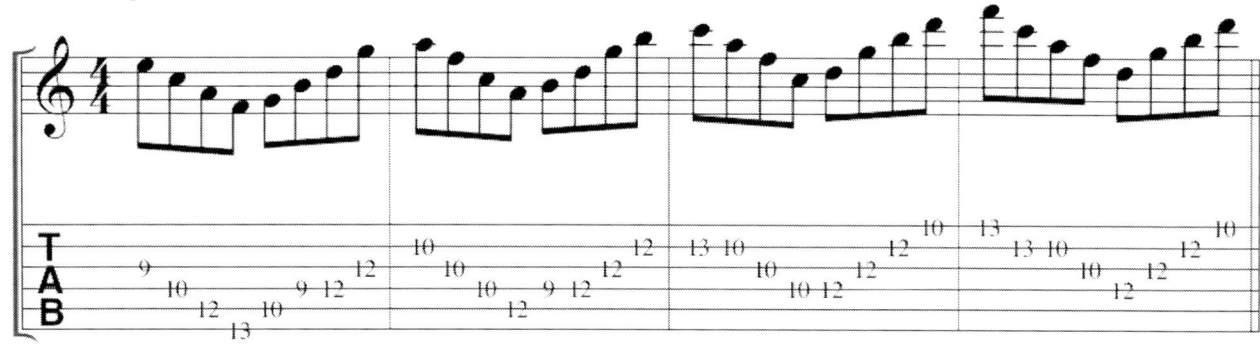

F-G: C Major, 2nd Position, Descend-Ascend, Descending

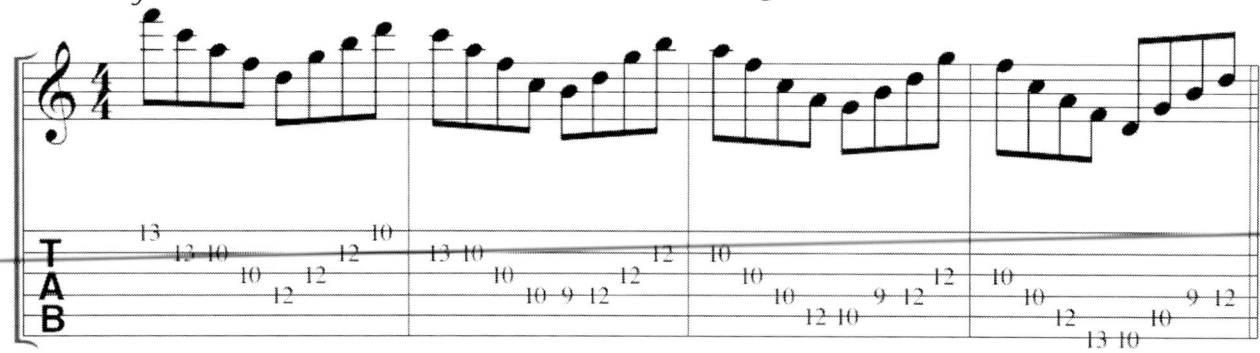

F-G: C Major, 3rd Position, Ascend-Descend, Ascending

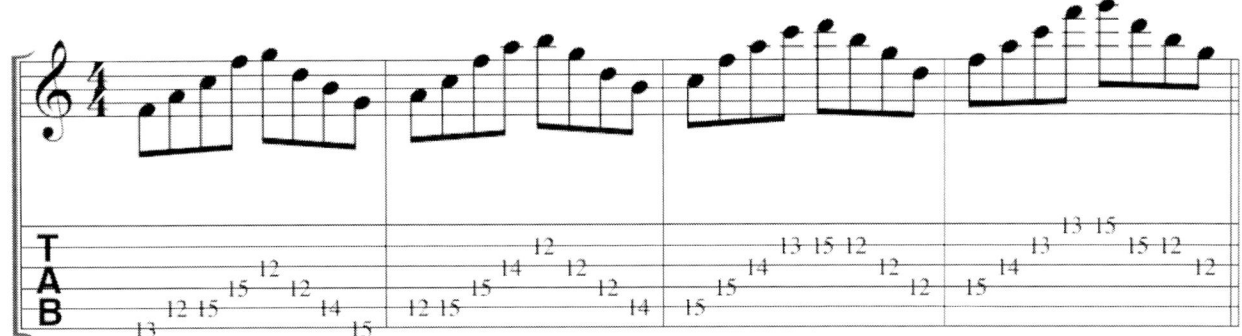

F-G: C Major, 3rd Position, Ascend-Descend, Ascending

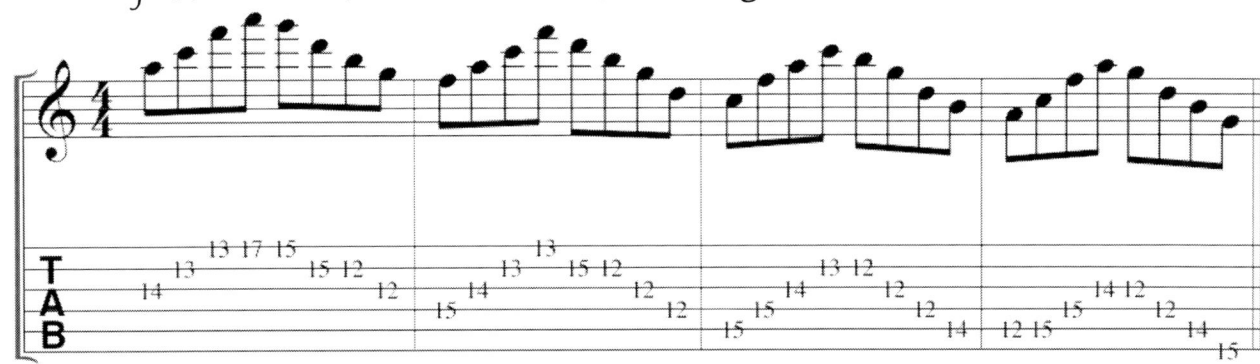

F-G: C Major, 3rd Position, Descend-Ascend, Ascending

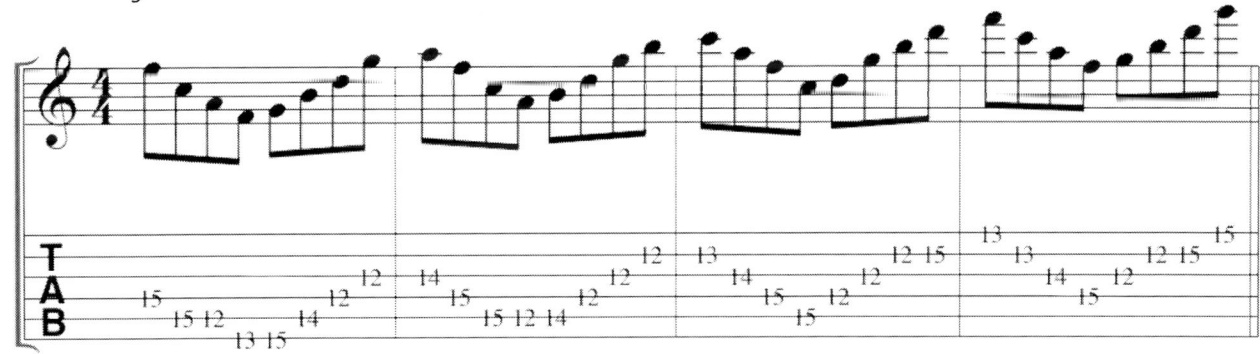

F-G: C Major, 3rd Position, Descend-Ascend, Descending

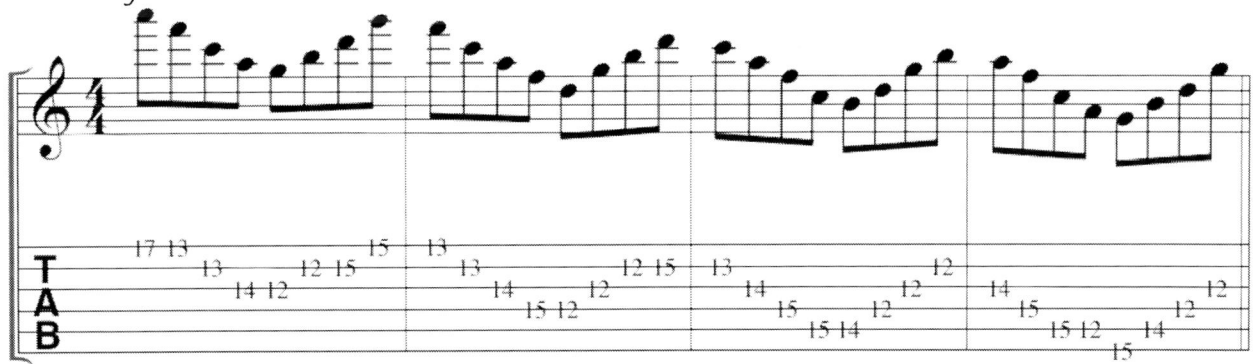

Dm-Em: C Major, 5th Position, Ascend-Descend, Ascending

Dm-Em: C Major, 5th Position, Ascend-Descend, Descending

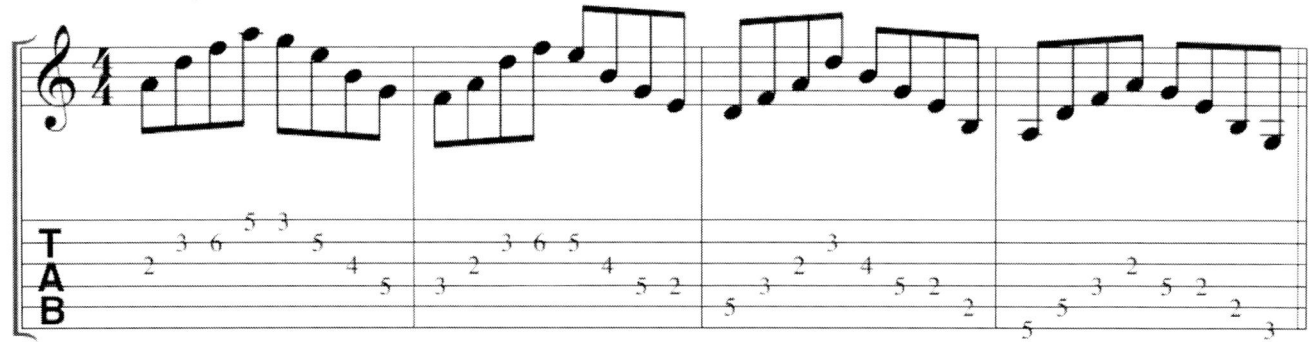

Dm-Em: C Major, 5th Position, Descend-Ascend, Ascending

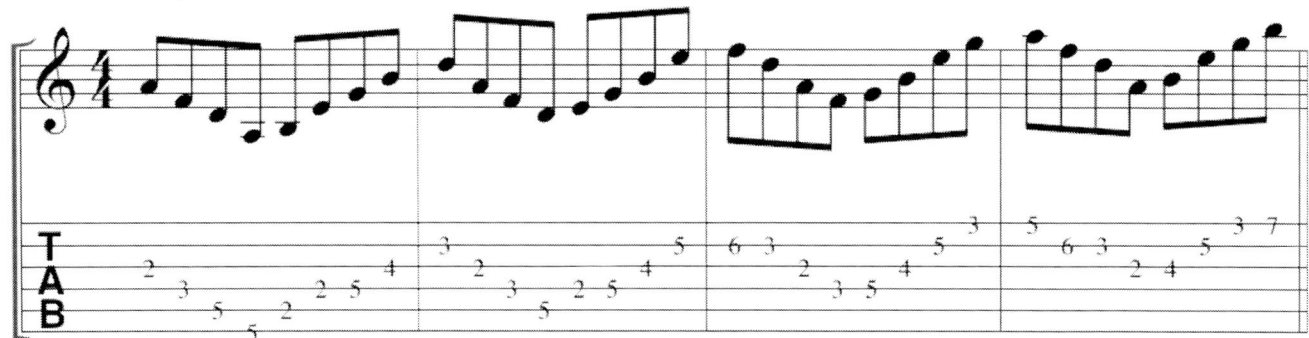

Dm-Em: C Major, 5th Position, Descend-Ascend, Descending

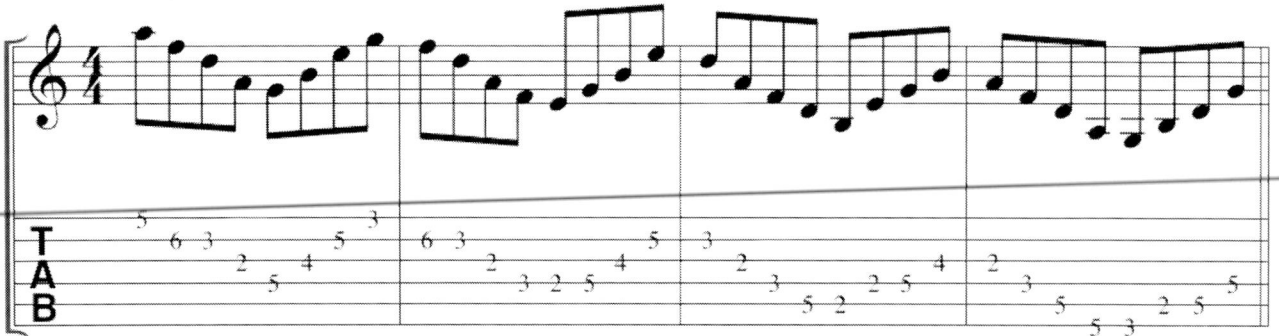

Dm-Em: C Major, 6th Position, Ascend-Descend, Ascending

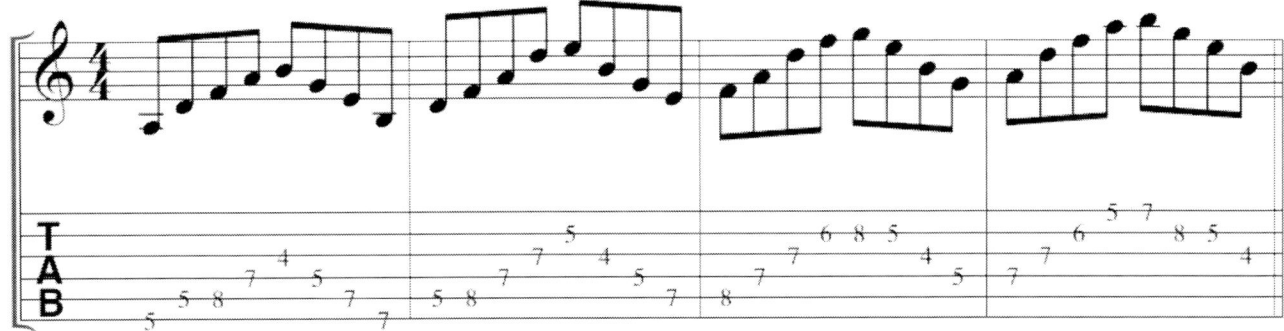

Dm-Em: C Major, 6th Position, Ascend-Descend, Descending

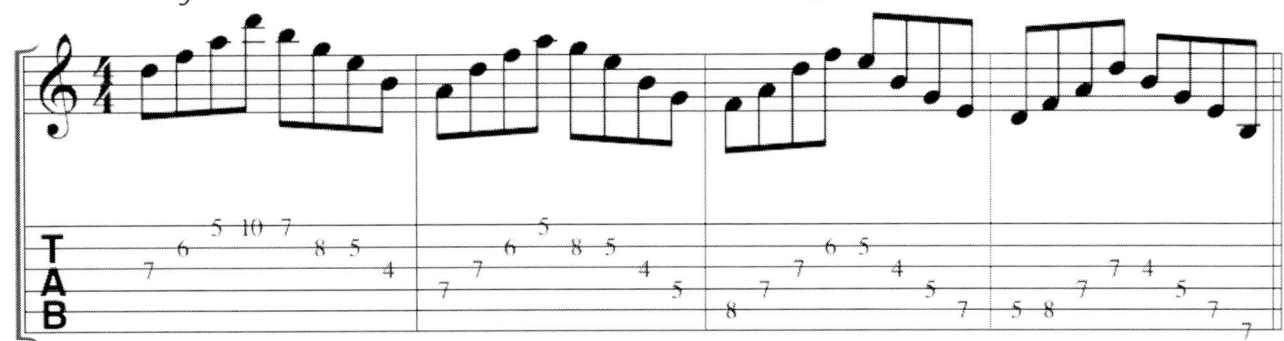

Dm-Em: C Major, 6th Position, Descend-Ascend, Ascending

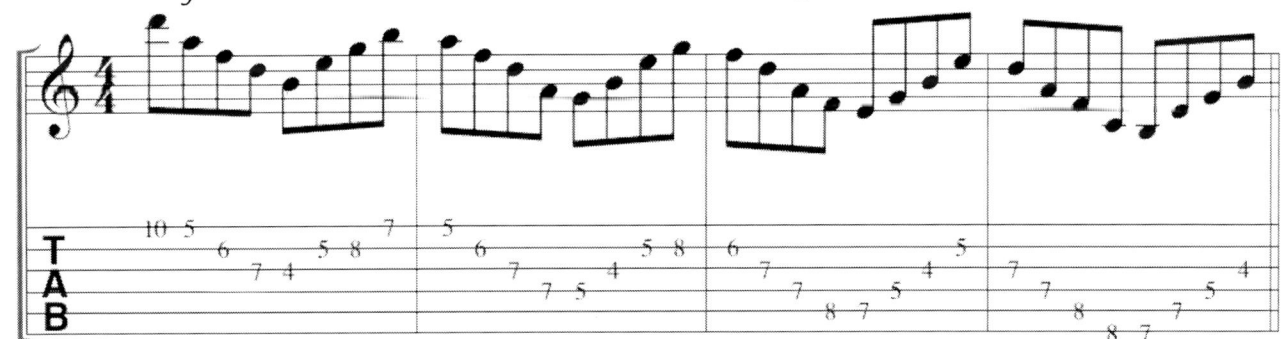

Dm-Em: C Major, 6th Position, Descend-Ascend, Descending

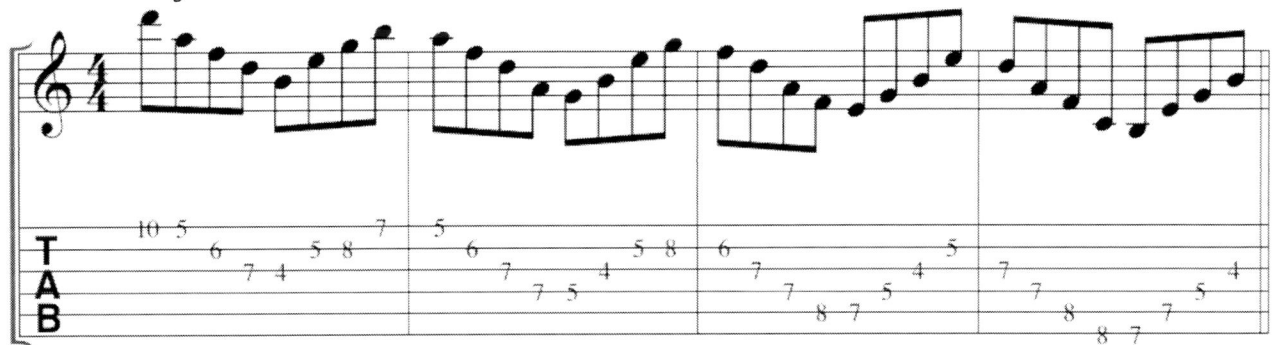

Dm-Em: C Major, Root Position, Ascend-Descend, Ascending

Dm-Em: C Major, Root Position, Ascend-Descend, Descending

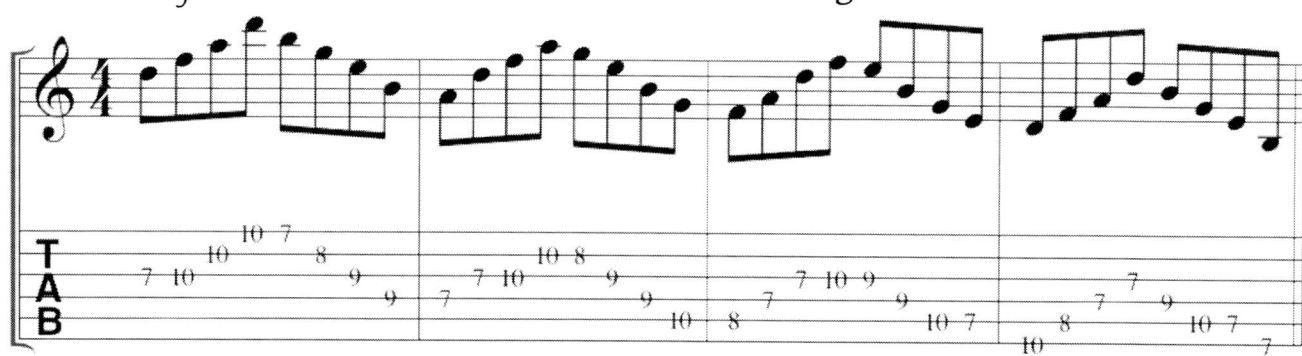

Dm-Em: C Major, Root Position, Descend-Ascend, Ascending

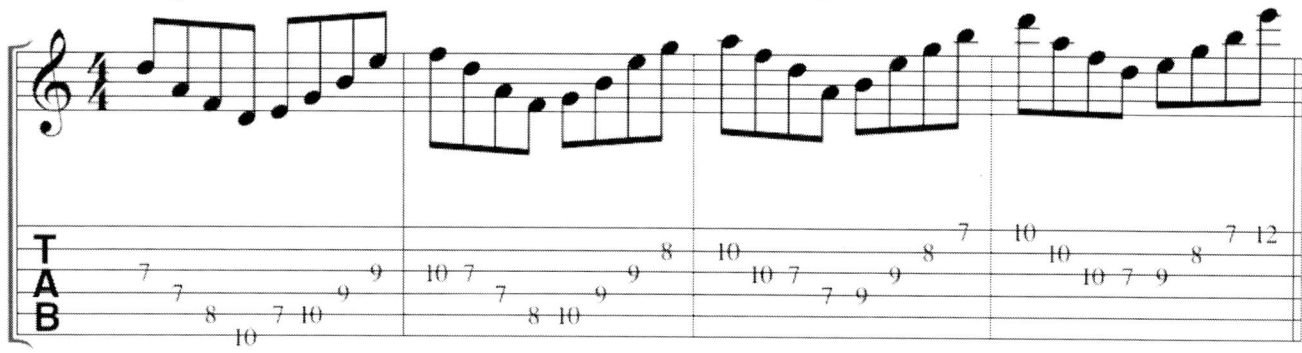

Dm-Em: C Major, Root Position, Descend-Ascend, Descending

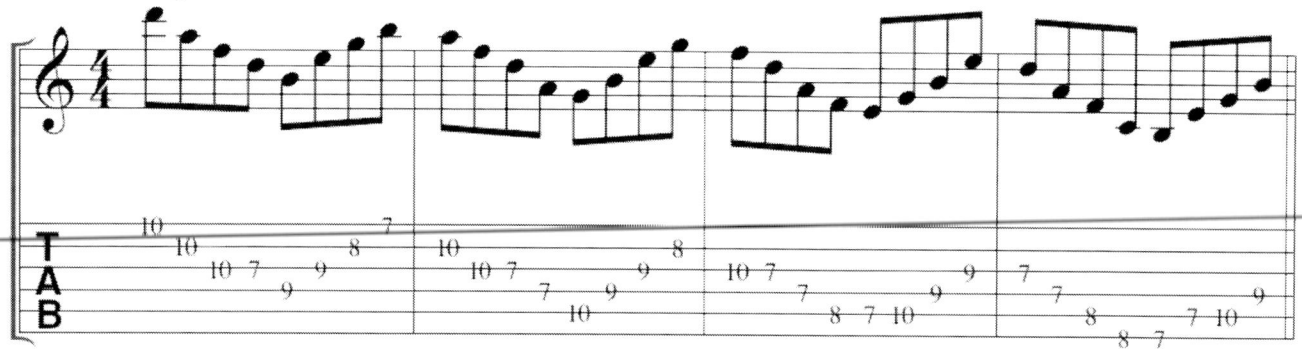

Dm-Em: C Major, 2nd Position, Ascend-Descend, Ascending

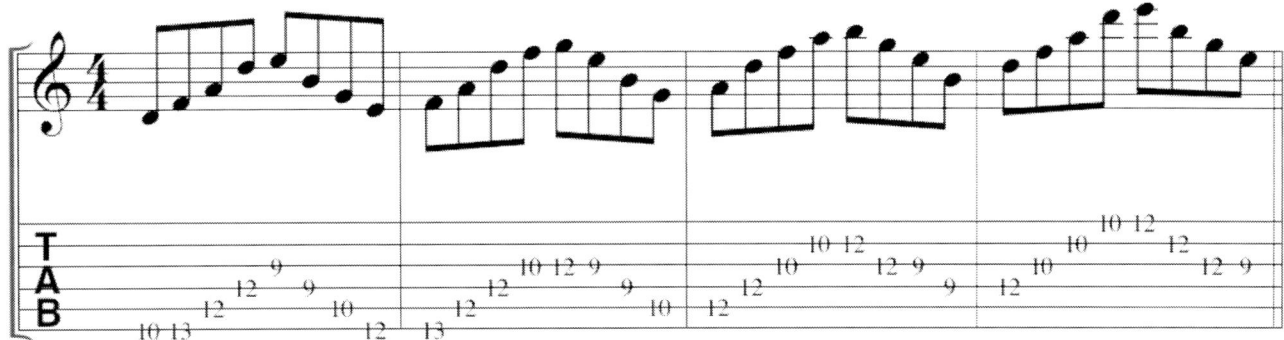

Dm-Em: C Major, 2nd Position, Ascend-Descend, Descending

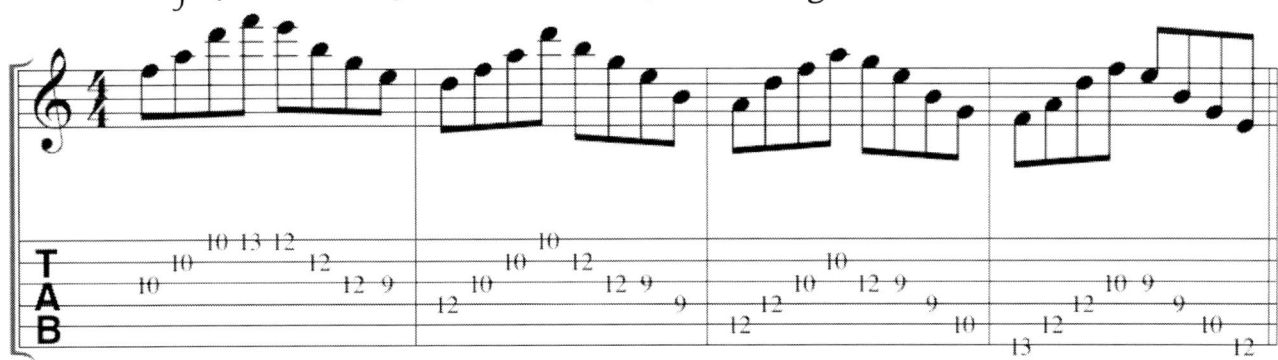

Dm-Em: C Major, 2nd Position, Descend-Ascend, Ascending

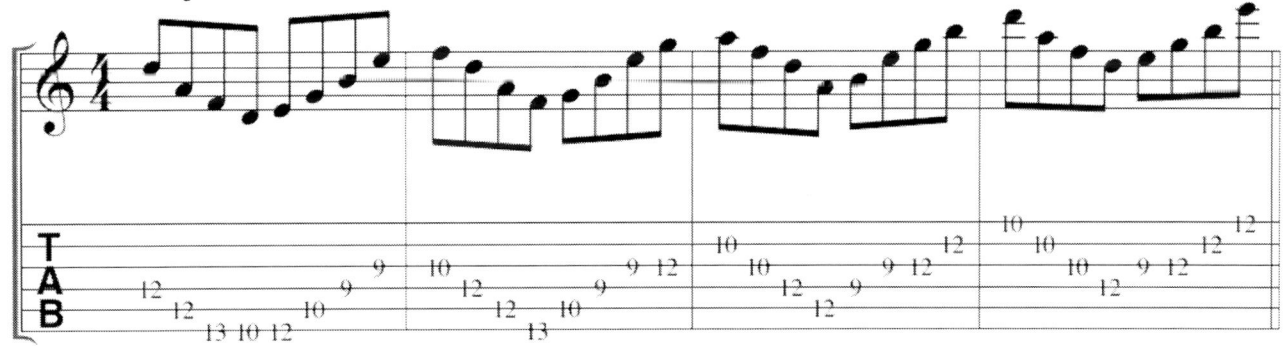

Dm-Em: C Major, 2nd Position, Descend-Ascend, Descending

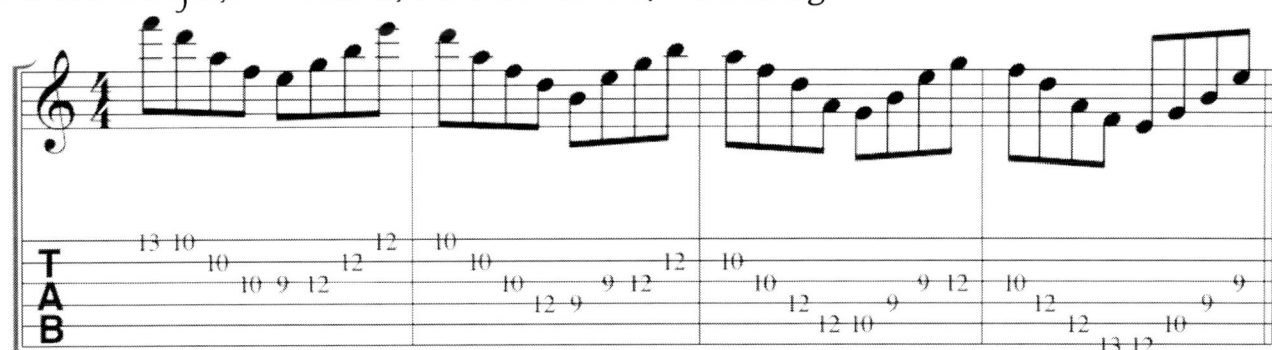

Dm-Em: C Major, 3rd Position, Ascend-Descend, Ascending

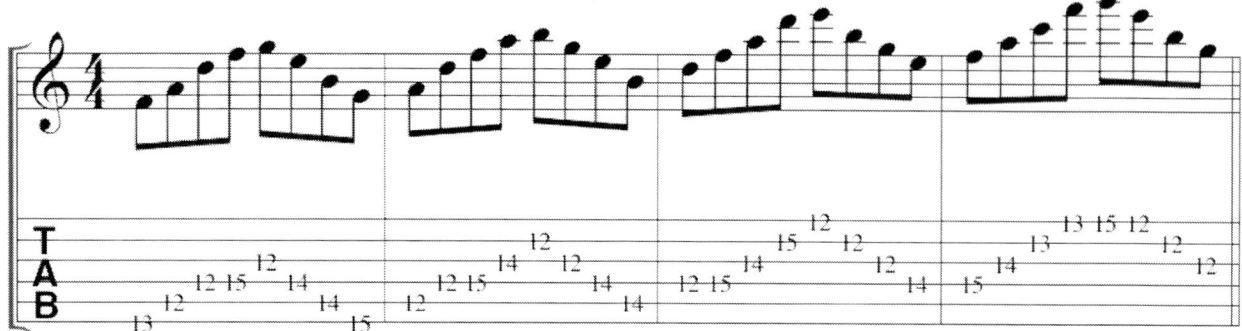

Dm-Em: C Major, 3rd Position, Ascend-Descend, Descending

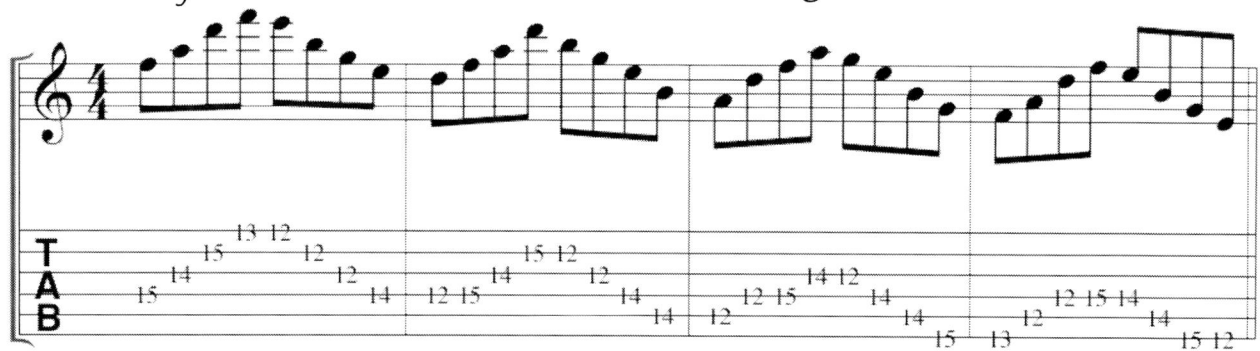

Dm-Em: C Major, 3rd Position, Descend-Ascend, Ascending

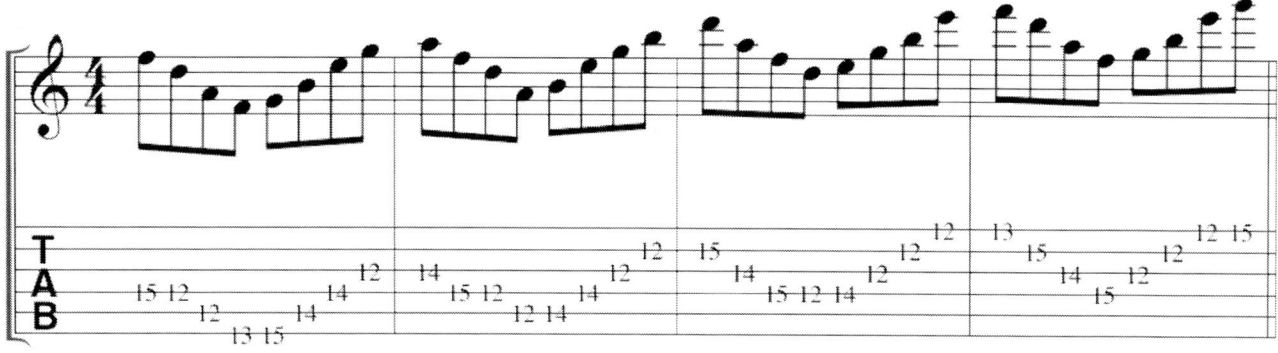

Dm-Em: C Major, 3rd Position, Descend-Ascend, Descending

Em-F: C Major, 5th Position, Ascend-Descend, Ascending

Em-F: C Major, 5th Position, Ascend-Descend, Ascending

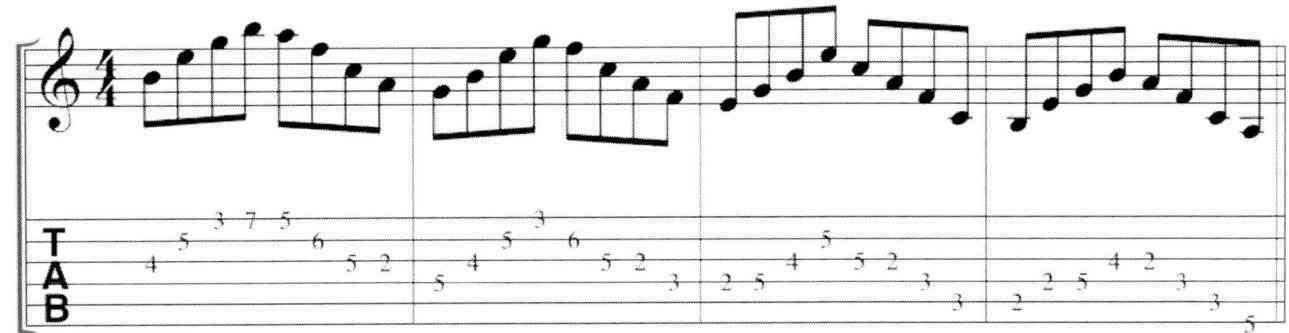

Em-F: C Major, 5th Position, Descend-Ascend, Ascending

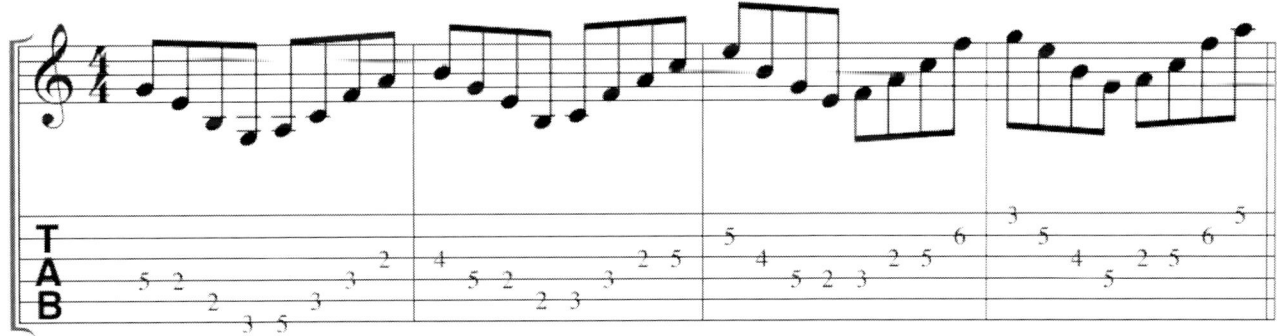

Em-F: C Major, 5th Position, Descend-Ascend, Descending

Em-F: C Major, 6th Position, Ascend-Descend, Ascending

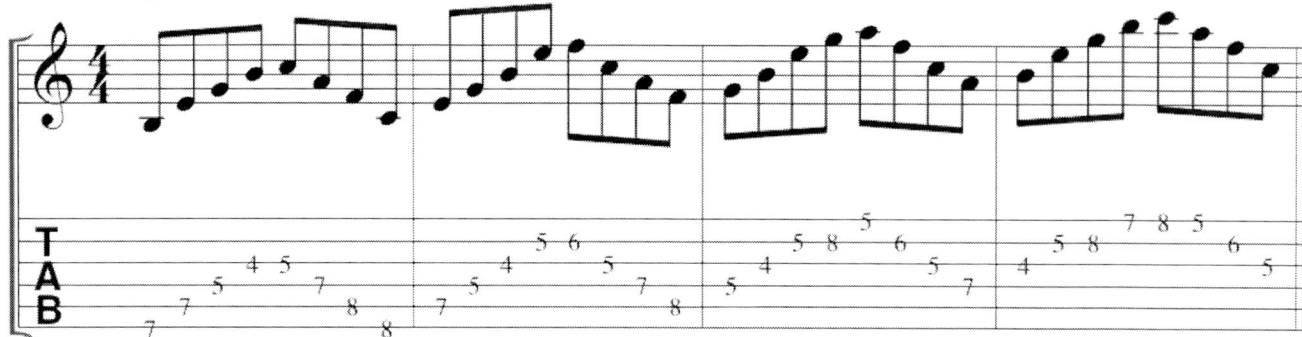

Em-F: C Major, 6th Position, Ascend-Descend, Descending

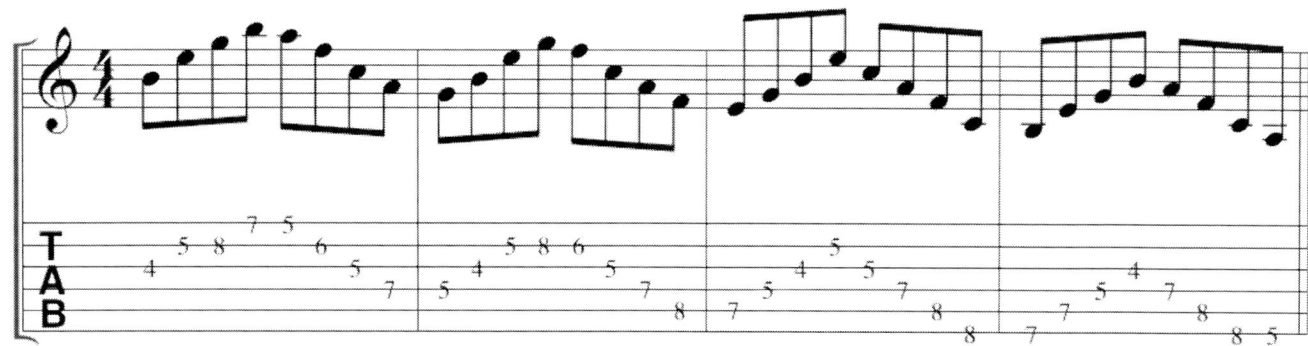

Em-F: C Major, 6th Position, Descend-Ascend, Ascending

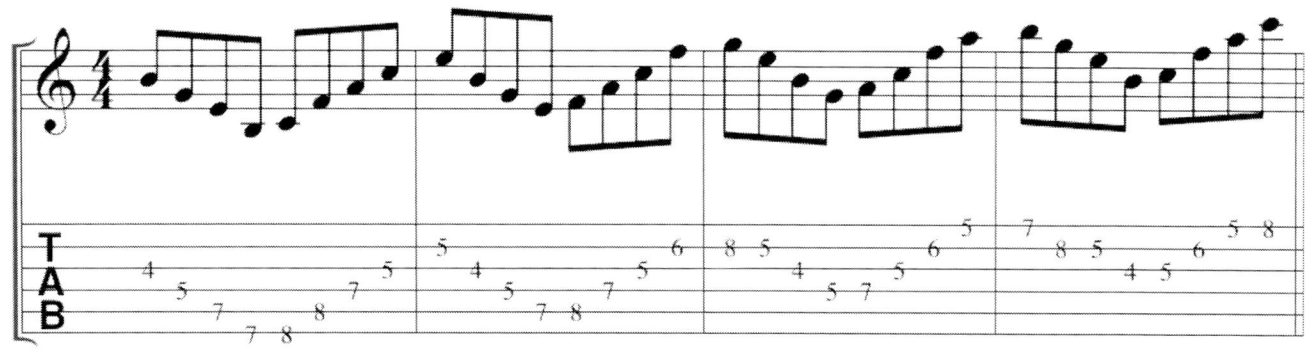

Em-F: C Major, 6th Position, Descend-Ascend, Descending

Em-F: C Major, Root Position, Ascend-Descend, Ascending

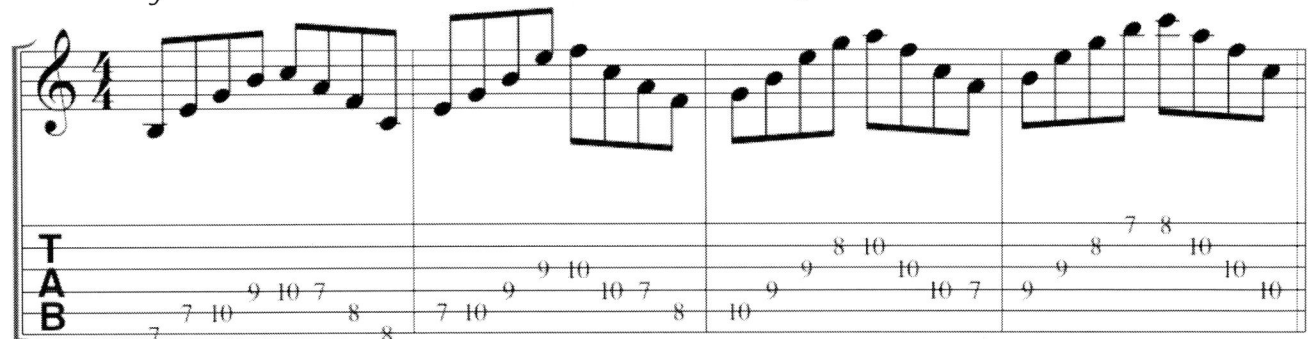

Em-F: C Major, Root Position, Ascend-Descend, Ascending

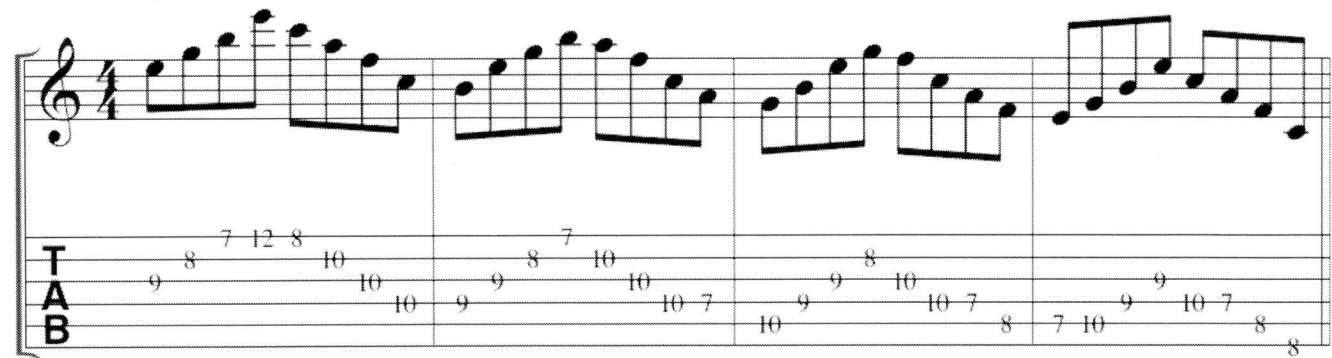

Em-F: C Major, Root Position, Descend-Ascend, Ascending

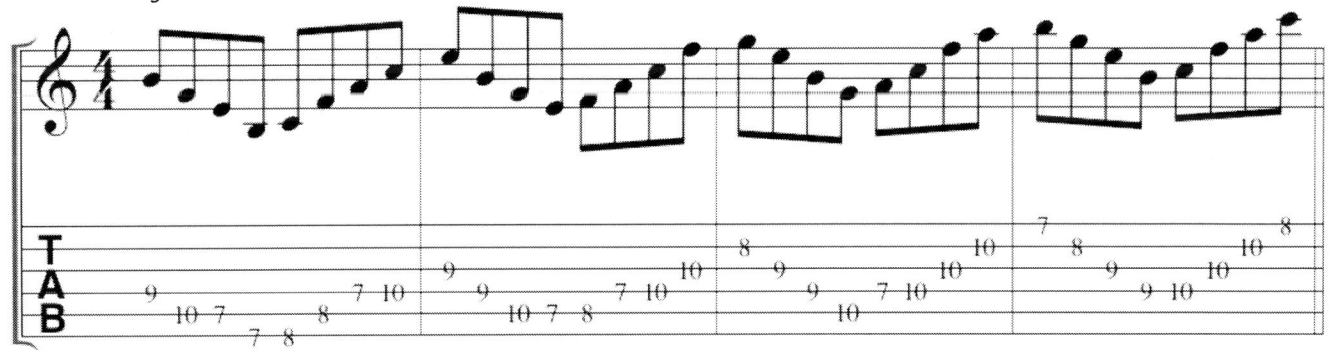

Em-F: C Major, Root Position, Descend-Ascend, Descending

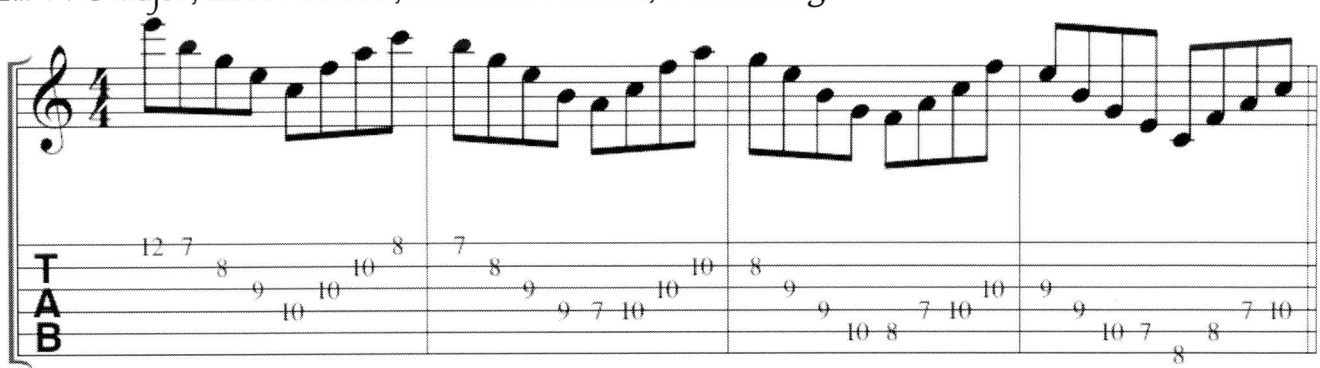

Em-F: C Major, 2nd Position, Ascend-Descend, Ascending

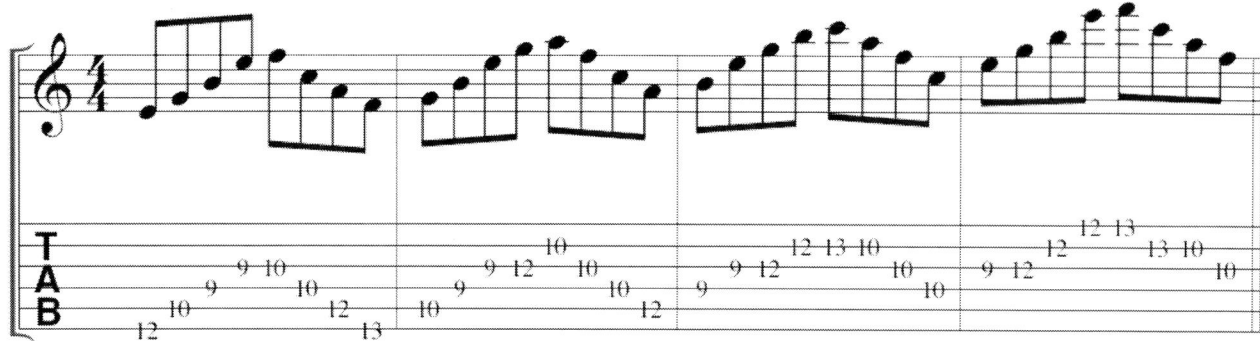

Em-F: C Major, 2nd Position, Ascend-Descend, Descending

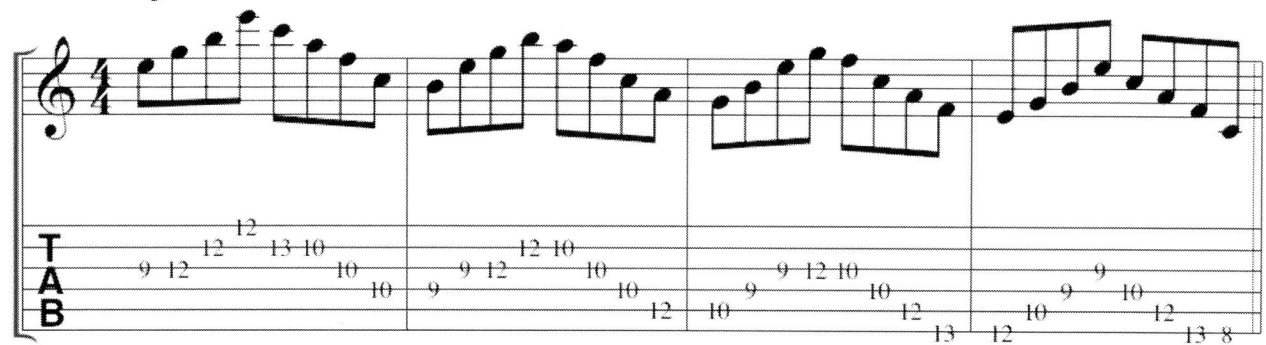

Em-F: C Major, 2nd Position, Descend-Ascend, Ascending

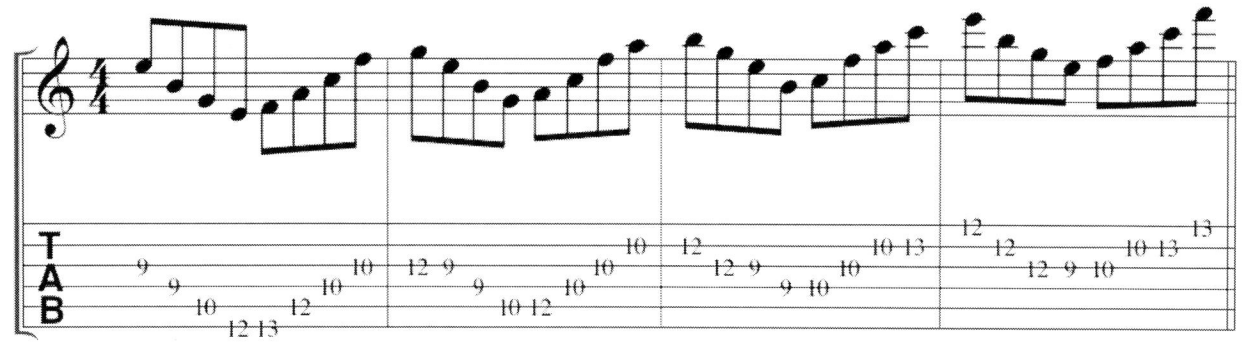

Em-F: C Major, 2nd Position, Descend-Ascend, Descending

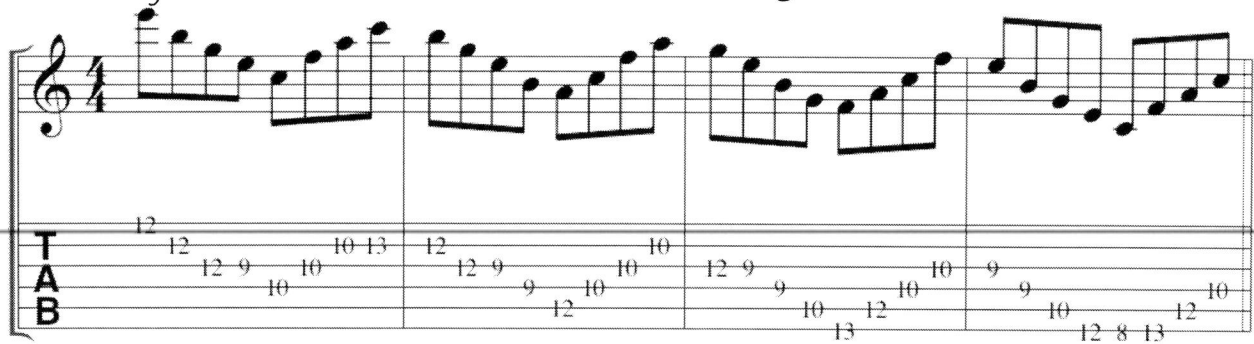

Em-F: C Major, 3rd Position, Ascend-Descend, Ascending

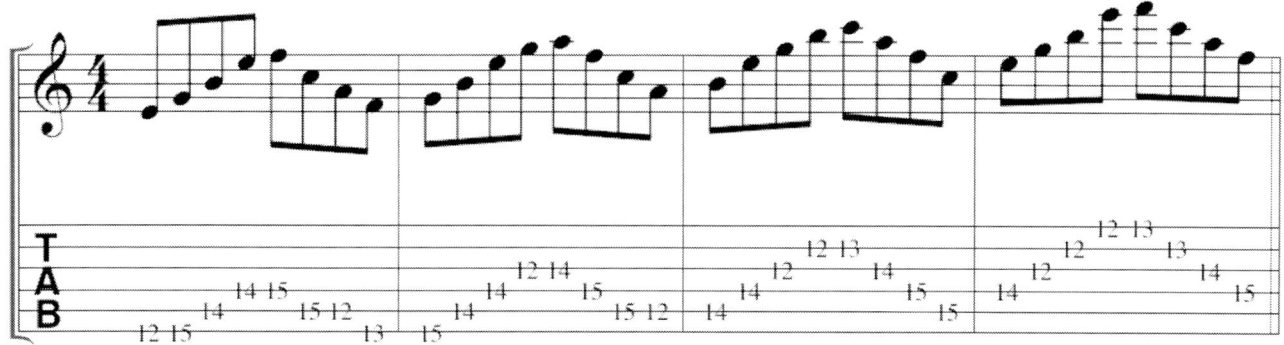

Em-F: C Major, 3rd Position, Ascend-Descend, Descending

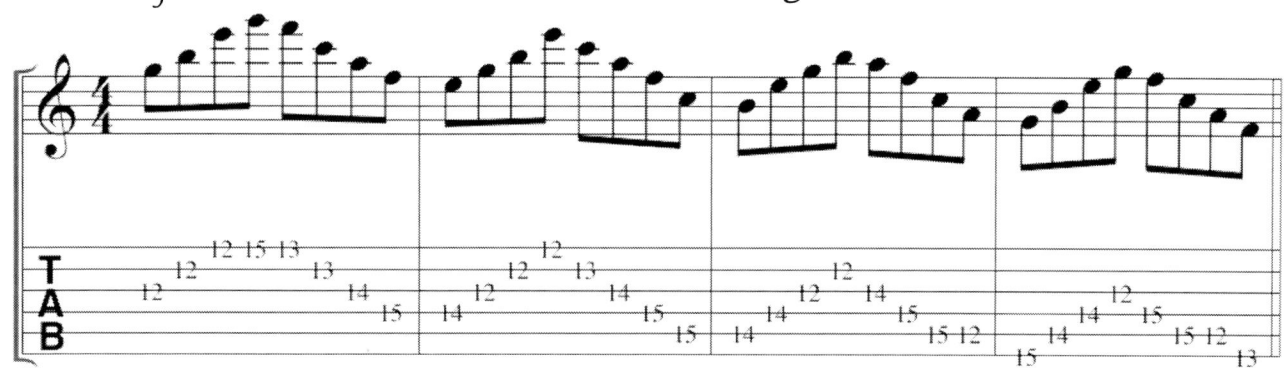

Em-F: C Major, 3rd Position, Descend-Ascend, Ascending

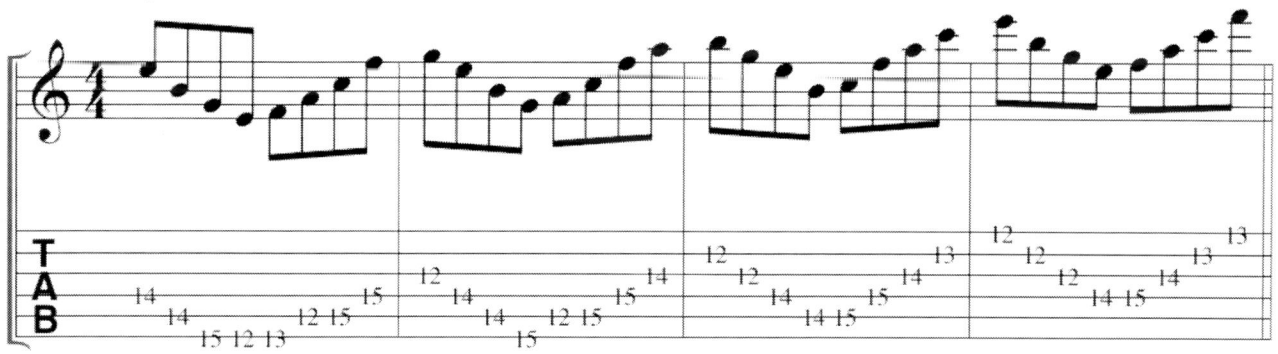

Em-F: C Major, 3rd Position, Descend-Ascend, Descending

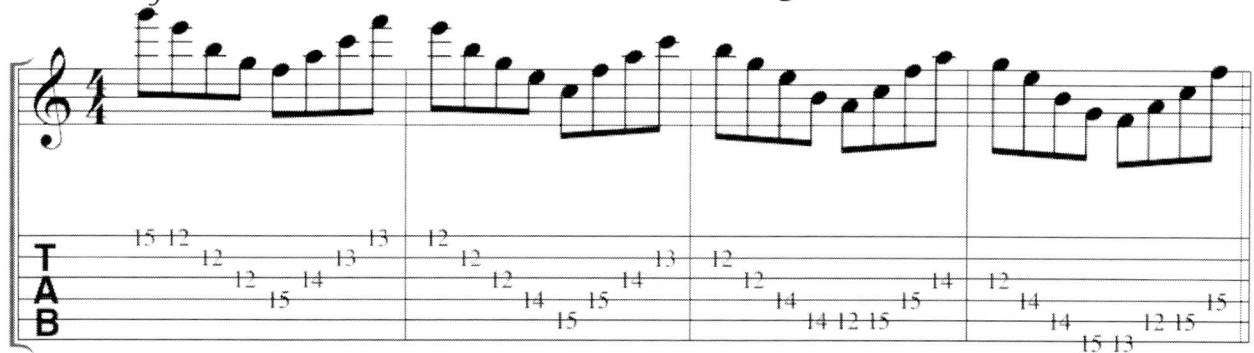

CHORD PROGRESSIONS – part 3: The 12-Bar Blues

The twelve bar blues form, while having originated from the blues, has made its way into most modern styles of music. Unless you're truly familiar with this form, it can go by without you having any notion of the blues influence in the music. The reason is that it's not necessarily the 'style' itself, its vocabulary or its nuances that are being expressed but merely it's *form*. How many measures of this chord, how many measures of that chord, etc.

Borrowing forms from various styles is a great way to expand your pallet as a songwriter, while remaining stylistically true to the sound you want to achieve. Forms aren't very recognizable to the average listener, or at least not easily associated with particular styles. The vocabulary and its inflections are the elements that are easily recognizable to most people as a particular style.

Standard forms help to give a song a certain degree of predictability, which, I know, is something that creative people love to say they hate. The fact is, music that has zero sense of predictability is totally lost on most people and they find it boring no matter how fast and crazy technical it is. If the form of the song is easily established, on the other hand, people are going to be able to more easily enjoy any less predictable twists and embellishments that you work into the form. The music that the average person seems to enjoy the most, in my own experience is something relatively standard that has a slight twist that gives it a unique identity.

A Few Words On My Creative Ethics

This is a good opportunity to offer my personal philosophy on the whole commercial/true-art issue. I think that making music that's purely for yourself, while being a decent learning process for a while, eventually leads you to an artistic dead end. Making music for no one but yourself is going to be an isolating experience. It's going to be self centered, self-absorbed and self-limited. What is art, but communication of feelings and concepts? And what point is there to communicating to nobody but yourself or people just like you? That's called preaching to the choir and there's not much point in it from what I could gather as a very 'selfy' pie in the sky, "true artist" in my early 20s. These days, I write, record and perform with a desire for people to enjoy it and to take something home from the experience. I make art to help unify us and to try and be one of "us" a little better.

Another great thing about standard forms, such as our 12-bar blues form, is that it gives musicians a way for random groups of them, who've maybe never even met, to get together and make good coherent music on a first try; granted the musicians are cool enough to know their standard forms. If you have a desire to be a truly competent, versatile player on any instrument, even drums, you really should have a good knowledge of common forms.

Without further ado, let's explore this form. We're going to start with the most basic traditional blues version of this form, then we'll move on to the common blues variations, followed by some pop and rock variations. Further into the book we'll be revisiting this form to learn some common jazz variations once we've covered the necessary harmonic material to understand them. Take plenty of time to explore these progressions in different rhythmic styles, tempos, chord voicings and keys. For the sake of simplicity, these progressions will be written out in whatever key is going to relate closest to the key of C, where everything is nice and natural.

Basic 12-Bar Blues in G:

G7			
C7		G7	
D7	C7	G7	D7

In the basic 12 bar blues form, we have three phrases, each one lasing for four measures. Each phrase has twice the amount of changes as the previous phrase. The first phrase is simply four solid measures of the I chord. The second phrase spends it's first half on the IV and returns back to the I for the latter half. The third phrase, known as the turnaround, is divided into four quarters, the first of which being the V chord, the second bar being the IV chord, the third bar resolving to the I and the fourth and final measure leading back to the V.

The effect of the changes doubling their rate with each passing phrase is one of momentum being built towards the release that occurs when the cycle starts over. This cycle can be repeated for as long as the song needs to be. At a typical jam session you can wind up with a whole lot of soloists lined up to take a crack at it. In order to end it, when it comes time to do so, the final V chord is replaced with a variety of melodic walks to a final I chord. Bear in mind that this can be in any time signature, although 4/4 is the most common, by a long shot; following in commonality would be 3/4 or 9/8. Anything else is pretty rare.

12-Bar Blues in G with a Fast IV:

G7	C7	G7	
C7		G7	
D7	C7	G7	D7

In this case we've made two slight alterations. The first of which is mentioned in our descriptive title, the fast IV. That's what we call it when the IV chord is placed in bar two with a resolve back to the I, in bar 3. This is done generally to break up the monotony of spending four measures on a static I chord. The slower the 12 bar, the more likely it's going to call for a fast IV. Before playing a 12 bar blues with a group of musicians, it's a good idea to clarify whether or not there's going to be a fast IV because if half of the players are hitting the IV, while the other half keep on playing the I, it can sound pretty stupid.

The second alteration was made, simply by moving the final V ahead, by two beats. If we're in 4/4, this means we have six beats of the final I, followed by only two beats worth of the final V. This is more common, and has been, at least since the 1950s. I'm assuming this developed as a way to make the final phrase a little less V-heavy. It helps provide an easier backdrop for melodic fills. Usually the last note of the final vocal phrase (of the cycle) lands somewhere around beat one of bar eleven. Bars eleven and twelve are typically used as a chance for a lead instrument to respond to the vocal line.

By spending 6 beats on one, we can hang on the A blues scale just a little longer and wrap it up around beat three of the final bar. Typically, the fill starts around beat 2, so you really only have six beats worth of time to operate comfortably. Good lead guitar players are stocked up with lots of basic 5 or 6 beat licks designed to serve this roll. It's also worth noting that good musicians don't pull these licks off in the same way. They're always looking for new ways to use the old material. Later on we'll be looking at ways to reapply old ideas.

12-Bar Blues In G w/ Fast IV & II-V Turnaround

G7	C7	G7	
C7		G7	
A7	D7	G7	D7

This variation takes us a little further in the jazz direction, but it's still pretty straightforward. Being slightly between a simpler variation and a more sophisticated variation, it's not a very common cycle. What we've done is deleted the IV chord from bar 10, moved the V from the previous bar to bar 10, and put an appropriate approaching chord to the V into bar 9. This is more common in up-tempo swings and shuffles. However, in most cases, a couple other variations are used elsewhere in the progression, along with these. That would be opening up a whole new can of theoretical worms right now and I'm already pushing 1 with some of these examples, so lets wait on it.

12-Bar Blues In G w/ Fast IV & V-bVI-V Turnaround:

G7	C7	G7	
C7		G7	
D7	Eb7 D7	G7	D7

This is a pretty common variation on the basic 12 bar blues, within the blues genre. We've replaced the IV chord in bar 10 with a half measure of the bVI chord and a following half measure of the V chord. This gives the turnaround a slightly more diabolical flavor in my opinion. The use of the bVI chord and its justification will have to be tackled a little further in. For the time being, be confident that for whatever reason the bVI 7 chord in there sounds pretty cool and is commonly used.

12-Bar Blues In G w/ Fast IV & II-IV Turnaround & bVI-V Tail:

G7	C7	G7	
C7		G7	
A7	C7	G7	Eb7 D7

This is a variation that I love soloing over because it has a wide variety of tonal possibilities. This is a result of the increased use of non-diatonic chords. In this case we've started out as if we were going to do a typical II-V-I type turnaround and instead of leading to the V chord, it skips the V and moves right on to the IV chord, which makes the turnaround section in this cycle much more smooth and relaxed. It has a casual feel to it. For the sake of at least having one V chord in there somewhere, I tagged the bVI – V onto the last measure. This also allows a couple more chromatic notes to apply.

As far as a traditional blues examples go, these cover a lot of ground. Other common examples can be discovered by combining elements of these same examples. Before moving onto to the pop and rock variations, I'd like us to observe the minor equivalents to these variations. These, while still being very easy to find in the blues, are also going to be more common in rock music.

Basic Minor 12-Bar Blues in A:

Am7			
Dm7		Am7	
Em7	Dm7	Am7	E7

Here it is, in it's elegant simplicity. The same thing as the standard 12 bar blues, to the tee, except that all the chords are minor. All of them except for the final V chord in bar 12. This progression can work in any style, from disco to reggae to metal.

Minor 12-Bar Blues in A w/ Fast IV:

Am7	Dm7	Am7	
Dm7		Am7	
Em7	Dm7	Am7	E7

This one is pretty self-explanatory. It's also a very diverse, solid sounding progression.

Minor 12-Bar Blues in A w/ Fast IV & II-V-I Turnaround:

Am7	Dm7	Am7	
Dm7		Am7	
Bm7b5	E7	Am7	E7

This on takes on a very classic jazzy characteristic for how relatively diatonic it remains. The minor II-V-I progression always has depth and class and using it as a turnaround on a minor blues is no exception.

Minor 12-Bar Blues in A w/ Fast IV & V-bVI-V Turnaround:

Am7	Dm7	Am7	
Dm7		Am7	
E7	F7 E7	Am7	E7

This variation has a certain emotional urgency to it that makes it a very popular type of minor blues cycle. The A minor blues scale fits nicely against the F7 (bVI) chord in bar 10. This is a good relationship to bear in mind even when you're playing a major blues with a bVI chord in there. The #4/b5 of the parent minor blues scale serves as the b7th of the related bVI chord. You may want to repeat that out loud until you're sure you follow the train of logic. An understanding of these types of relationships is invaluable to improvising.

Minor 12-Bar Blues in A w/ Fast IV & bVI-II-V Turnaround & bVI V Tail:

Am7	Dm7	Am7	
Dm7		Am7	
F7	Bm7b5 E7	Am7	F7 E7

The IIm7b5 in this variation adds a touch of class to the minor blues cycle. Notice that we have the bVI chord popping up in a couple measures, in this case. This is about as fancy as we can get before getting into the details of non-diatonic harmony. We'll be breaking this down further into the book and revisiting the 12-bar blues. At that point, we'll be discovering a lot more possibilities with the blues cycle.

For the time being, there are plenty more variations on the 12-bar blues that are easy to understand. These are more common to rock, pop and country songs. Keep in mind that chord progressions are public domain and you're free to write new songs based on these progressions. Below are some of my favorite variations:

12-Bar Blues in G w/ Fast bVII-IV & II-IV Turnaround:

G	F C	G	G7
C	F C	G	G7
A7	C7	G7	D7

This variation lends itself well to early rock & roll, classic and southern rock feels.

12-Bar Blues in G w/ Fast bIII-IVs & V-bIII-IV Turnaround & bVII-IV Tail:

G7	Bb C	G7	
C7	Bb C	G7	
D7	Bb C	G7	F C

The same would be true of this one.

12-Bar Triad Blues in G w/ Fast IV, Minor V & bVII-IV Tail:

G	C	G	G7
C		G	
Dm7	C	G	F C

This blues cycle is made from purely G Mixolydian chord relationships, whereas most classic blues progressions tend to slightly shift in tonality with each passing chord. Some would say this gives it a more modern sound but some would say it sounds more ancient. Both would be right

12-Bar Triad Blues in G w/ V-bVII-IV Turnaround & Fast Vm-IV Tail:

G F	G F	G F	G F
C Bb	C Bb	G F	G F
D	F C	G	Dm7 C

This variation is based on the idea of replacing dominant 7th chords with major triads alternating to related major triads, one whole step below. In other words G to F back and forth serves the same function as G7. This feature, along with the V-bVII-IV turnaround lends this cycle a classic hard rock feel.

12-Bar Dorian Blues in D w/ Fast IV & bVII-IV Tail:

Dm7	G7	Dm7	
G7		Dm7	
Am7	G7	Dm7	C G

Here we have another modal blues that fits diatonically, this time, in the D Dorian mode. Again, it has the effect of simultaneously sounding more ancient and modern, this time with a slightly darker vibe. This would sound great as a tight funk feel or loose psychedelic groove.

12-Bar Dorian Triad Blues in D:

Dm G	Dm G	Dm G	Dm
G F	G F	Dm G	Dm
Am Dm	G Am	Dm G	Dm Am

This one, another Dorian cycle, could work as a disco as easily as a rustic folk ballad. These are just examples. Feel free to try any of these in any style you can conjure.

12-Bar Minor Blues in A w/ bVI Subbing for IV & I-bVII-bVI-V Tail:

Am7	Fmaj7 G	Am7	C
Fmaj7	G	Am7	
Em7	Fmaj7 G	Am7 G	F Em7

In this example, we've really strayed quite a bit from the sound of the blues but the underlying form is still present and detectable. This cycle would be perfect for a pop song. Using the Fmaj7 in place of the Dm7, while being a fairly elementary substitution, really serves to disguise the blues element.

12-Bar Minor Blues in A w/ bVI Subbing for Final I & a IV-bVII Tail:

Am7		Am7	
Dm7		Am7	
Em7	Dm7	F	Dm7 G

In this variation, melodically, you can keep treating the bVI as if it were the Im.

Major 12-Bar in C w/ VI Subbing for IV & V-IV Tail:

C	Am	C	
Am		C	
G E7	Am F	C	G F

This one has a very folk and/or pop quality to it. For now, don't worry about why the E7 works.

Basic 12-Bar Blues Shuffle in A:

This 12-bar form, like all the others, can be played either in straight eighth notes or in an eighth note swing feel. In order to achieve this effect, you want to think of each pair of eighth notes as an eighth note triplet group with an eighth note rest in between the two notes. You could also think of the pair of notes as a quarter note followed by an eighth note together under a triplet bracket. If you're having any trouble following me, just think of the timing of "Pop Goes The Weasel".

Played as a straight (even) feel, this shuffle pattern will sound much like a 1950s style rock & roll tune. Played as a swing (lopsided) feel, it will sound like a typical blues tune.

Basic 12-Bar Blues Shuffle in G:

This 12-bar is a little more difficult, now that we're off of the open strings. Whereas normally you would play the power chord shape using your left-hand index and ring fingers, you may want to replace the ring finger with the middle finger. This will allow you to stretch your pinky up to the alternating notes with more ease, which is more or less necessary, depending on the size of your hands.

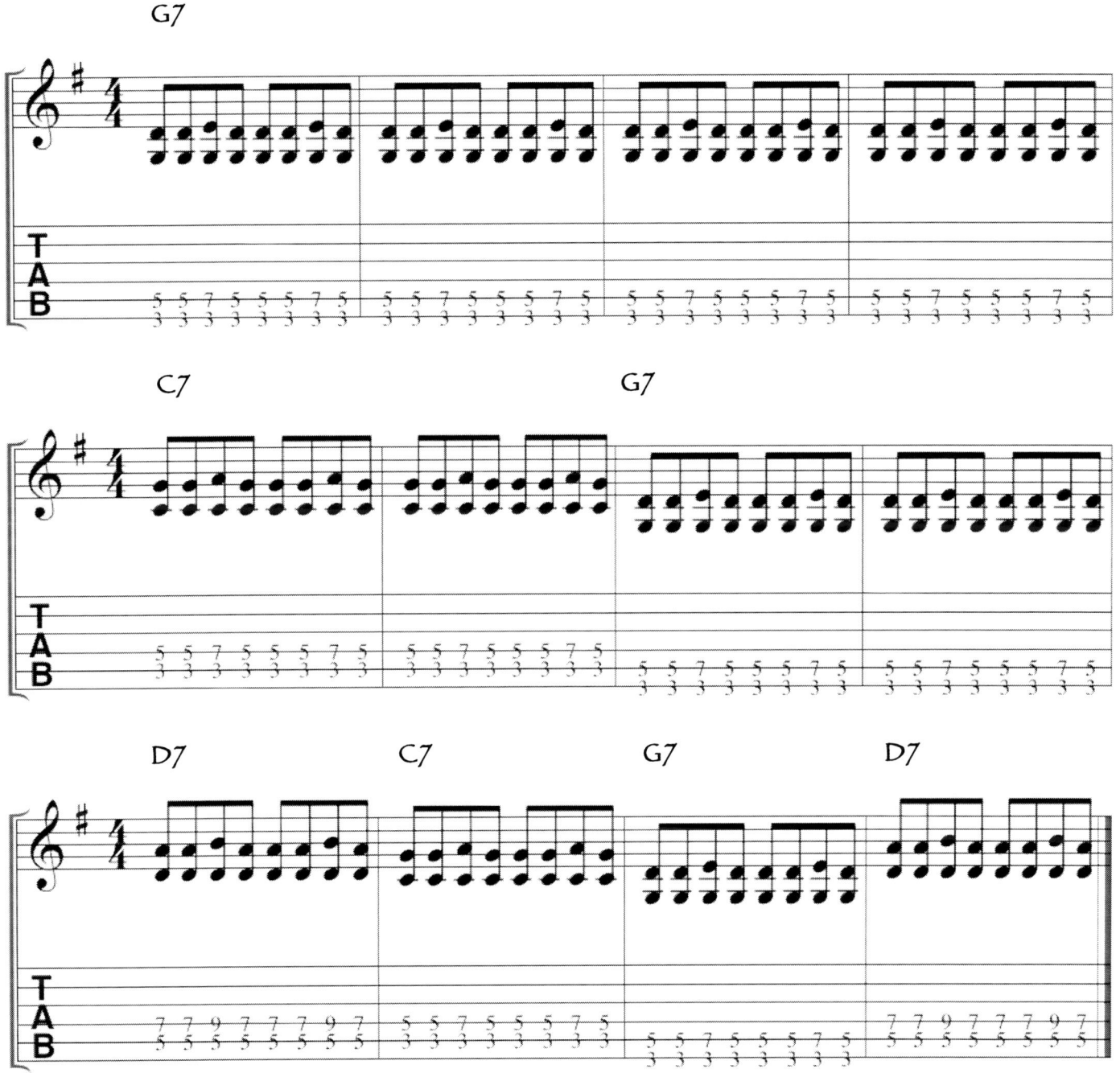

Basic 12-Bar Blues in G, with a Walking Bass-Line:

Aside from the shuffle pattern, another common rhythm guitar approach is employing a walking bass line. In the blues vein, you'll typically find yourself playing this in unison with a bass player. Notice that during the measures that fall right before a pivotal chord change, we're using chromatic motion towards the root note of the next chord. In walking bass-lines, this technique can be employed anywhere you might find a chord change. If the chord lasts for four beats, the first beat would be where you'd sound the root of the current chord. Beats 2, 3 and 4 will lead, in half-steps, either up or down into the following chord. Experiment with this concept on a variety of progressions so you can decide what approach scenarios you like and dislike.

Basic 12-Bar Blues in G, with a Classic '50s Walking Bass-Line:

This is another very common walking bass-line pattern. In scale-tone numbers the pattern is Root-3rd-5th-6th-b7th-6th-5th-3rd. It works over dominant chords, and the blues has plenty of those.

Boogie Patterns

In the last blues example, we ran into the classic 1950's style walking bassline pattern, AKA the basic boogie pattern. In terms of scale-tones, we can summarize the basic pattern as R-3-5-6-b7-6-5-3. This simple melodic progression lends itself nicely to variation. The basic pattern, while not all that impressive, can be developed into some pretty animated patterns that can be a whole lot of fun to apply in a rhythm or lead guitar roll. These variations are all rhythmically based on solid strings of 8th notes. From one to the next, the developments are rather subtle, but from the first example to the last you'll see a striking increase in melodic activity. These are all presented on an A7 chord. Use your developing mapping skills to figure these out in some movable positions! Figure them out in all keys. They work just as well on any dominant chord in the key, not just the I chord.

Variation 1:

Variation 2:

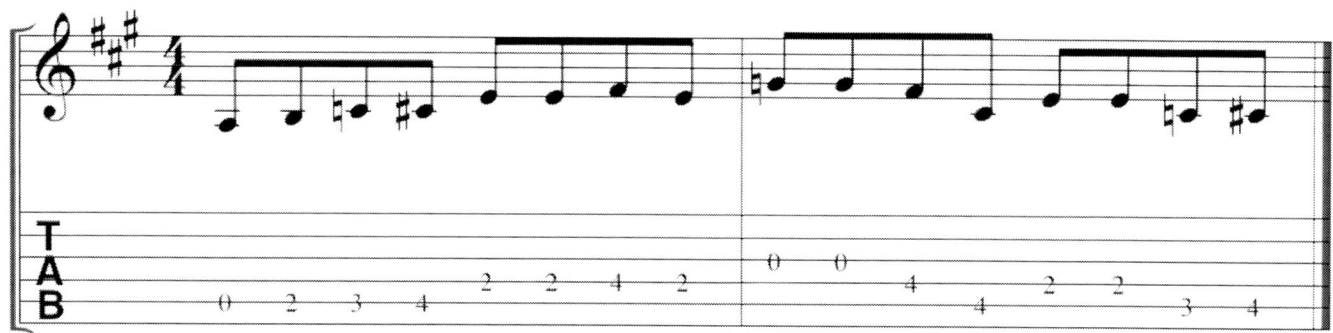

Variation 3:

Variation 4:

Variation 5:

Variation 6:

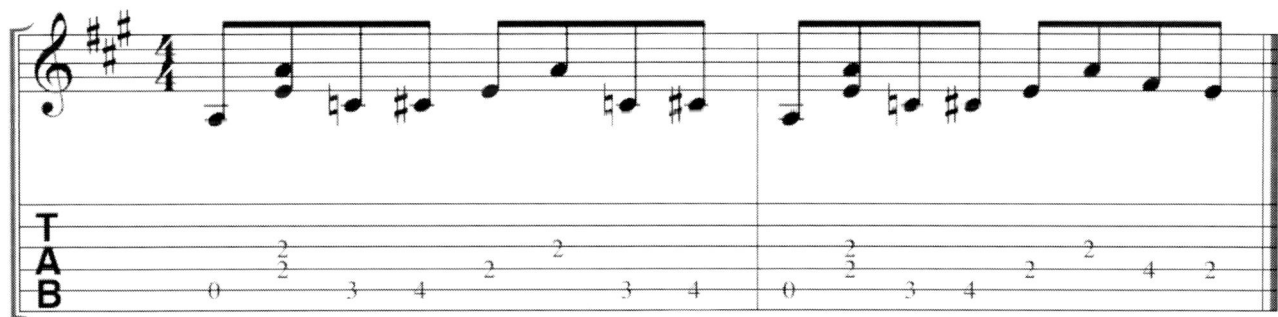

Variation 7:

Other Common Blues Rhythm Guitar Figures

There a quite a few ways for a guitar player to fill space in a blues scenario. These next couple pages represent the tip of a rather large iceberg. Hopefully these will get your mind open to some of the different modes of approach. Once this is accomplished, you won't have much trouble thinking up similar ideas. With all of this material it's a good idea to practice them with an even 8th-note feel, as well as a 8th-note triplet feel.

Figure 1:
It would be wise to note the use of the D major triad as a "passing" chord. Most good, musical rhythm guitar parts aren't based entirely on the notes of the given chord. There are usually some non-chord tones and contrasting chord voicings contained within.

Figure 2:

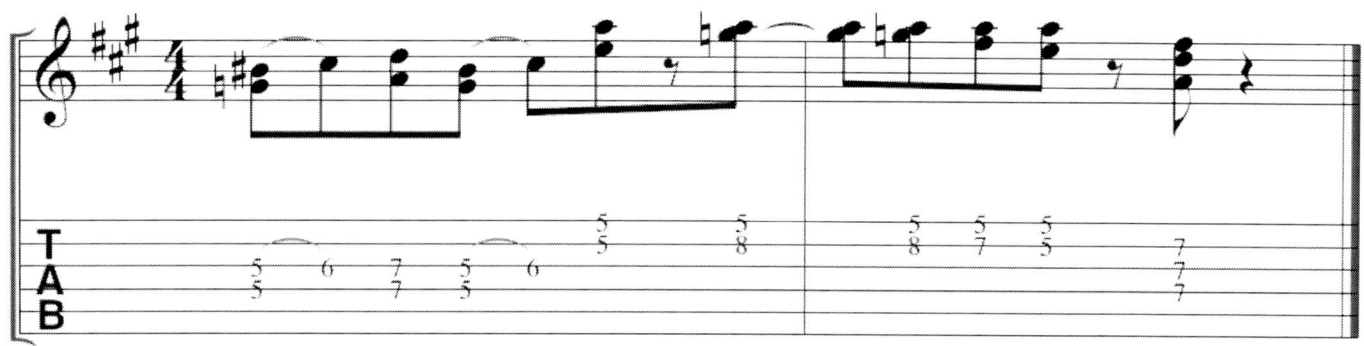

Figure 3:

*= slide entire chord up and back.

Figure 4:

On these types of figures, I like to use my pick on the bass notes and use my right-hand middle and ring fingers to simultaneously pluck the chord notes. It's a technique that can be used anywhere but is especially useful in cases where you have unused strings between your chord-tones. Another technique to tackle these kinds of figures is to allow a fretting finger to hang over onto the unused string. This is a little easier, but not as clean of a sound.

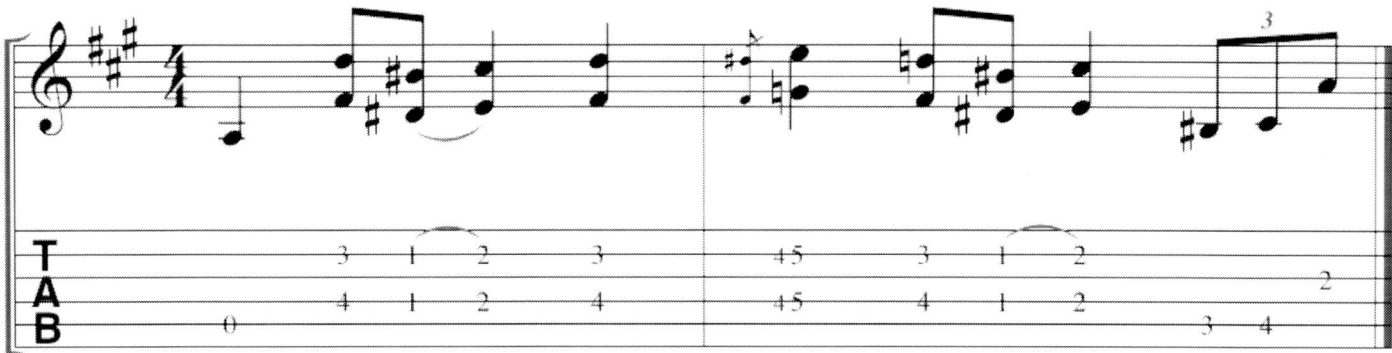

Figure 5:

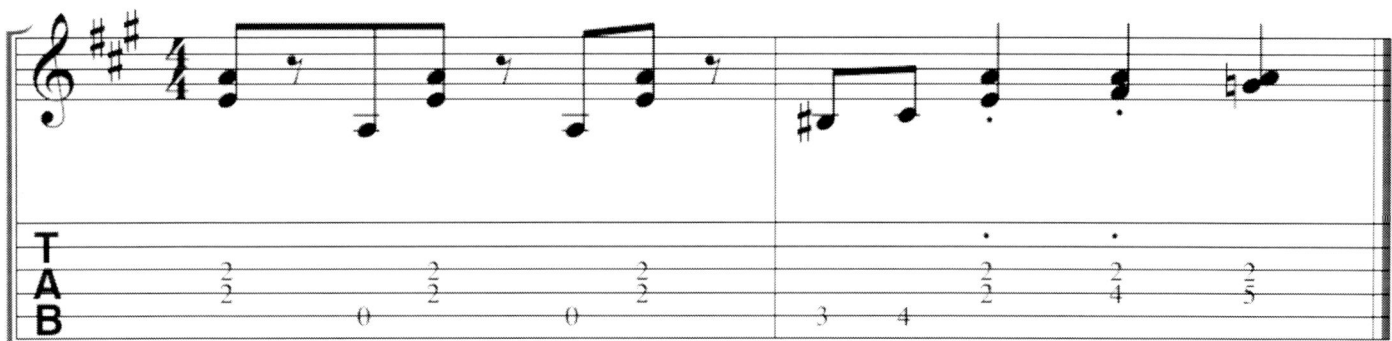

Figure 6:

This one probably could have also gone with the boogie patterns.

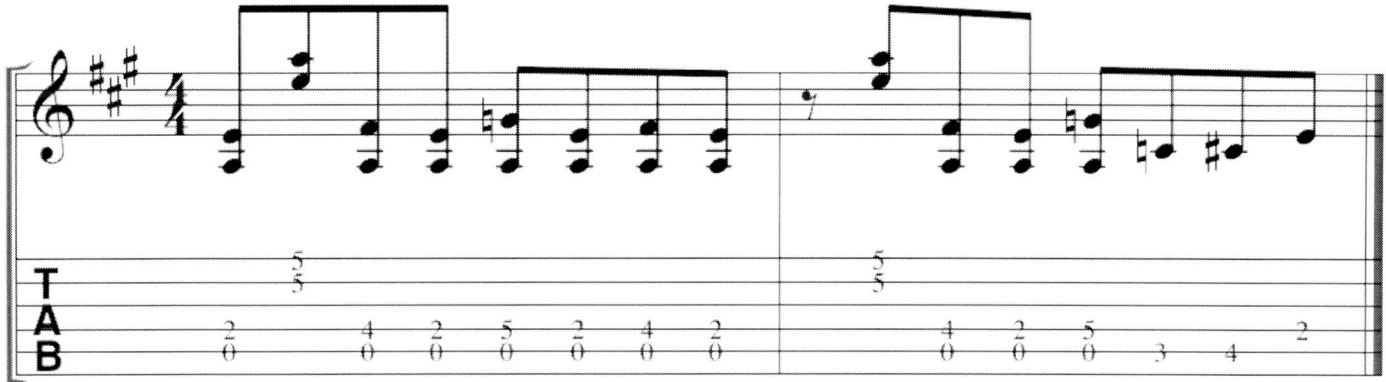

Common Blues Guitar Tails and Endings

Think of these following figures as classic ideas to fill the final two measures of a blues chorus. This area is called different things by different people. I tend to call it the Tale but I hear it called the Wind-Up in certain circles. Some people call it the Final Two as in "final two bars". If you want to use one of these tale-figures in the final chorus as an ending, simply swap out the bVI7 V7 (F7 E7) for bII7 I7 (Bb7 A7).

Figure 1:

Figure 2:

Figure 3:

Figure 4:

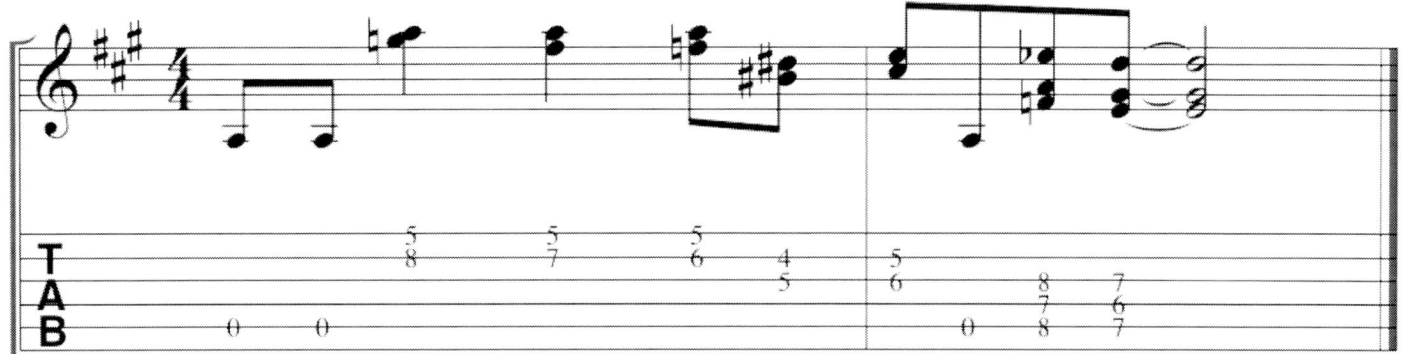

Figure 5:

A simple rhythmic variation on Figure 4

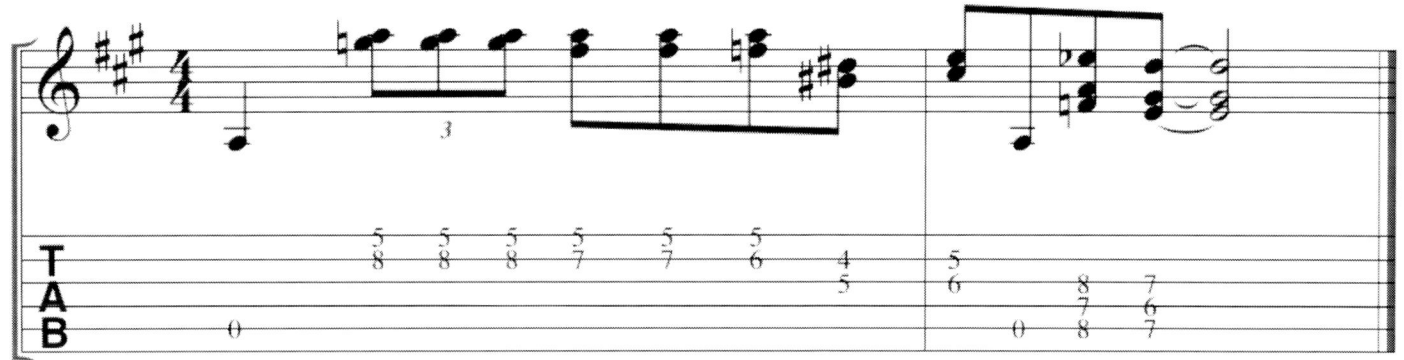

Figure 6:

This sort of phrasing lends itself really well to the hybrid picking technique, where the lower notes are picked and the upper notes are plucked using the middle finger.

Figure 7:
Another simple variation of the previous figure.

Figure 8:
Since this was the final example, I put the ending chords in the final bar.

In conclusion to the last few sections dealing with blues material, it's good to bear in mind that the blues has been developing for well over a century now; this is only an introduction to it's basic moving parts. If you want to develop an authentic approach to playing the blues, it's important to do a lot of watching and listening to the greats of the genre. Any reading you can do about playing the blues certainly won't hurt you either.

I don't personally hold a huge interest in the blues, but as a guitar player who enjoys jamming with complete strangers frequently, I consider it necessary for myself to have a solid working blues vocabulary and a good understanding of it's structure. Without this combination of skill and knowledge, my musical encounters would be frequently embarrassing, as the 12 bar blues structure is STILL the single most popular structure for group improvisation in our culture. If you attend a public jam session, chances are, you're going to be playing on that structure, so get to know it!

RHYTHM – part 4: Syncopation

Quite a lot of the modern music that we've grown up with is filled with syncopation. For those unfamiliar with the term, syncopation refers to rhythmic content that sets up a contrast to the underlying beat. A good example of a non-syncopated melody would be that old classic: Twinkle Twinkle Little Star. Awesome tune, right? (I know that sarcasm is best left out of a technical instructional book but sometimes I just can't help myself.)

Now let's take a tune just as readily associated with modern childhood but one that includes syncopation: the Super Mario Brothers Theme. Tap your foot in quarter notes and mentally go over that melody in your head. Notice that some of the most emphasized notes in the melody land between the beats. Furthermore, notice that many of the strong beats (1 & 3) are left entirely empty. This is a good example of syncopation. Now perform the same experiment with Twinkle Twinkle and you'll have a good idea of what the absence of syncopation sounds like.

Those are extreme examples of how the abundance and absence of syncopation can exist within a string of straight 8th notes. One simple way of doing this would be through the use of accented notes. Below is an example of a very non-syncopated accent pattern on a string of 8th notes:

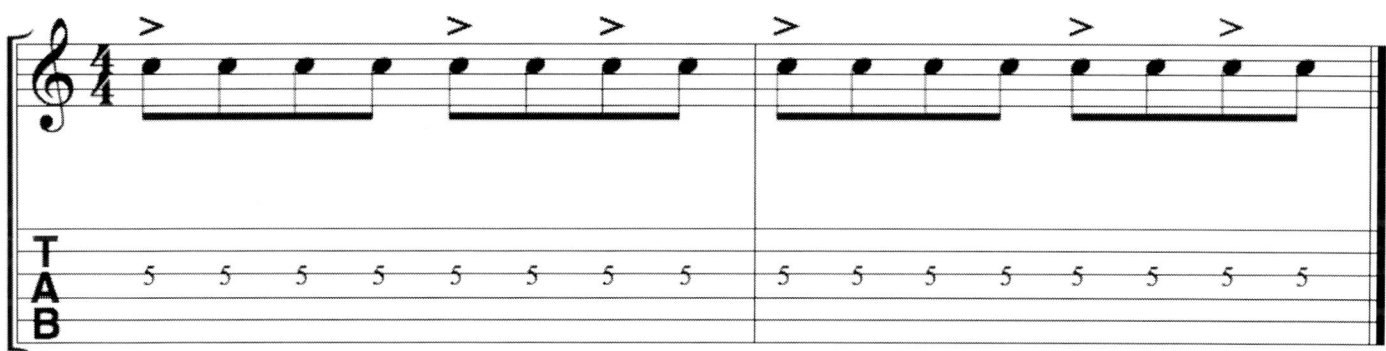

Now in the next example, we can see a syncopated accent pattern occurring. This adds quite a bit of musical interest even to a row of uniformly pitched and timed notes:

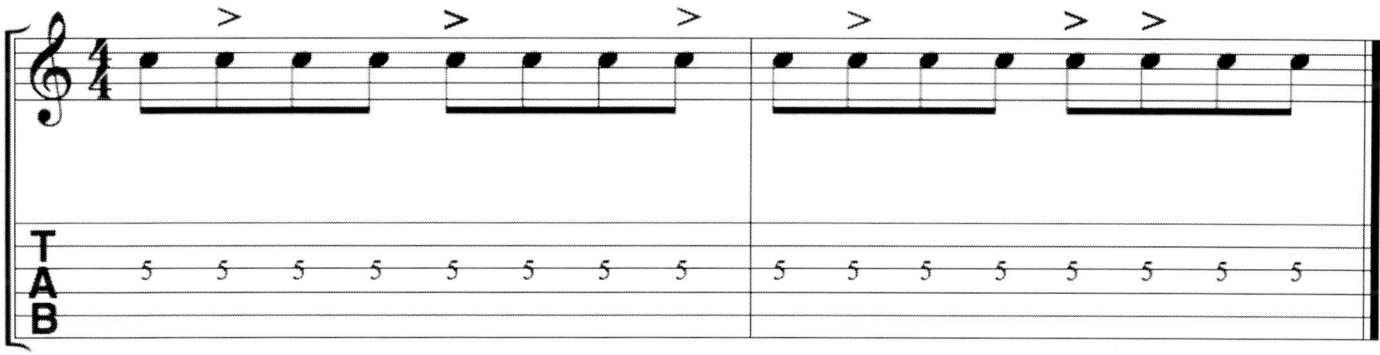

Another way syncopation can be achieved in a string of straight 8th notes is by the placement of contour shaping pitches. In this next example we have a very non-syncopated 8th note melody. Each upward melodic leap occurs on a beat. This has the effect of agreeing very closely with the beat:

In this following example we have inserted an extra 8th note at the beginning. This creates naturally occurring accents, which rhythmically off-set the line. It puts these same upward melodic leaps in between the beats and as a result, we get some added rhythmic interest to the line:

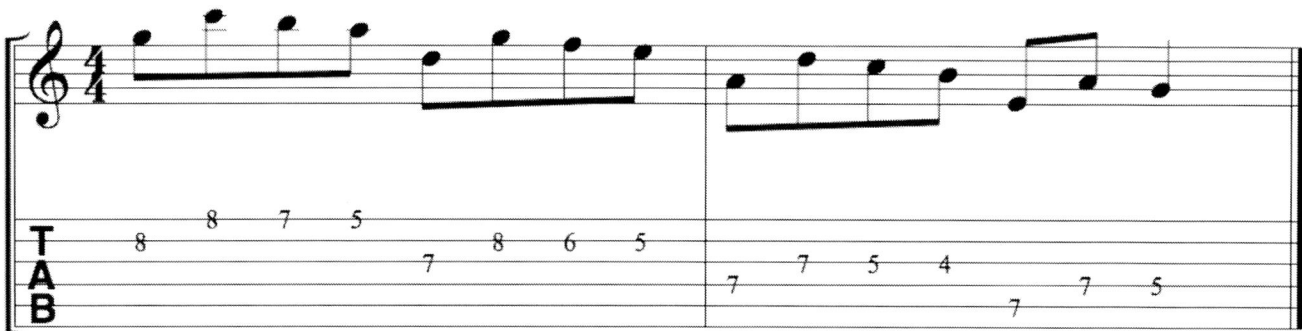

Another common way of achieving syncopation within strings of consecutive 8th notes, or 16th notes, is to run a melodic pattern contrary to the meter. For example, you could use a three-note pattern over a couple measures of 4/4. The result will be that certain natural accent points within the phrase will line up with the beats, whereas others will fall in between the beats. You can experiment with any odd numbered grouping against any even meter, or vice versa. This alone is a seriously big exploration of syncopation.

Most syncopation occurs as a result of rests and ties. Below is another variation of the previous line. This time, I've replaced certain notes with rests. When a note that's on the beat is replaced with a rest, the result is a very syncopated sounding rhythm:

In this following variation, I've let the notes before the rests hold over into the empty space where the rest was before. In most cases, the resulting notation will be two notes tied together. 8th notes that fit into a half measure of 4/4 don't need to be tied. The two tied 8th notes would instead be one quarter note. In the realm of 8th notes, ties are only needed for the barline and the half-way point of the measure. Once 16th notes are involved, ties are needed for any notes that hold over any beat.

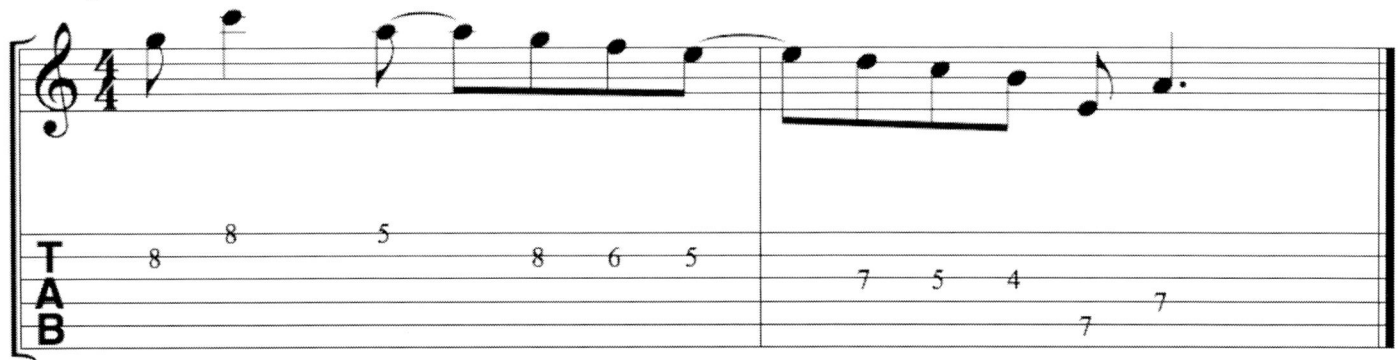

Below is a collection of syncopated rhythms made up of quarter notes and 8th notes. On the left side, you'll see the rhythm as it would be notated with rests for a more staccato effect. On the right, you'll see the same rhythm written out with ties which would be used to communicate a more legato effect.

One of the best ways to strengthen yourself rhythmically is to get yourself some transcriptions of recordings that have some heavy rhythm and train yourself to follow along on the page as you listen to the recording. Band-In-A-Box by PG Music was a HUGE help for me in my music reading skills. I would type in some chord changes and have it generate a solo and I would read along, watching the notes light up. Any activity like that will make a big difference if you do it enough.

CHORD PROGRESSIONS – part 4: Interval Patterns

In playing with chord progressions, you may have already figured out that some changes have a much stronger effect than others. I could hear that this was the case for years before I finally came to understand why. Once I finally did, it was a serious forehead-slapping moment for me. The factor that governs how strong a particular change is going to sound turns out to be rather simple. Before I impart this on you, I feel I should first tell you this, in the world of chord progressions, the terms 'strong' and 'weak' bear no negative/positive connotations.

When two chords share the majority of their tones in common, they create what we call a weak change. Try playing an Am7 leading to Cmaj7 and listen closely. Now let's think about the notes of the chords:

Am7:   A C E G
Cmaj7:   C E G B

It's easy now to see how this change (in either direction) is a weak change. Moving from Am7 to Cmaj7, however, is even weaker than moving from Cmaj7 to Am7. The reason for this is as follows: The primary note that the ear picks up within a chord is the bass note. When the bass note of the new chord is a note that was NOT a member of the previous chord it has a stronger effect than if the new bass note was just heard as chord tone of the previous chord. Any time you move from chord to chord, diatonically, by the interval of a third, you will see the same relationships between the chord tones of those two chords. This is clearly illustrated below:

Triads:
Dm: D F A
F: F A C
Am: A C E
C: C E G
Em: E G B
G: G B D
Bdim: B D F
Dm: D F A

7th Chords:
Dm7:   D F A C
Fmaj7:   F A C E
Am7:   A C E G
Cmaj7:   C E G B
Em7:   E G B D
G7:   G B D F
Bm7b5:   B D F A
Dm7:   D F A C

Now that we've taken a close look at the relationship of chords by the interval of a third, and established that it's the weakest possible change, let's take a broad look at intervalic chord relationships. The graph following this paragraph shows all of your different intervallic chord relationships, and organizes them from strongest (top row) to weakest (bottom row). The chord changes are organized horizontally in a manner intended to keep the VIIdim chord on the far right. This will allow you to play straight through the whole row of changes without running into our unstable little friend until the end of the sequence, right before it would start over.

If you spend some time playing through these intervalic chord progressions, conscious of the interval at hand, you will build up a recognition of the sounds and sights of them. This will give you a strong ability to hear, identify and reproduce chord changes from any music, as well as a strong command over composing chord progressions that make an identifiable statement.

Strong/Weak Changes by Interval:

2nds	Imaj7-IIm7	IIm7-IIIm7	IIIm7-IVmaj7	IVmaj7-V7	V7-VIm7	VIm7-VIIm7b5	VIIm7b5-Imaj7
7ths	VIm7-V7	V7-IVmaj7	IVmaj7-IIIm7	IIIm7-IIm7	IIm7-Imaj7	Imaj7-VIIm7b5	VIIm7b5-VIm7
4ths	IIIm7-VIm7	VIm7-IIm7	IIm7-V7	V7-Imaj7	Imaj7-IVmaj7	IVmaj7-VIIm7b5	VIIm7b5-IIIm7
5ths	IVmaj7-Imaj7	Imaj7-V7	V7-IIm7	IIm7-VIm7	VIm7-IIIm7	IIIm7-VIIm7b5	VIIm7b5-IVmaj7
6ths	V7-IIIm7	IIIm7-Imaj7	Imaj7-VIm7	VIm7-IVmaj7	IVmaj7-IIm7	IIm7-VIIm7b5	VIIm7b5-V7
3rds	IIm7-IVmaj7	IVmaj7-VIm7	VIm7-Imaj7	Imaj7-IIIm7	IIIm7-V7	V7-VIIm7b5	VIIm7b5-IIm7

The art of writing a good chord progression lies in the interplay of opposing elements. The main elements of opposition are that of tension/resolution, governed by the amount and degree of active/inactive tones within the chords themselves, as well as strong/weak changes. The idea is to create an interplay between the strong and weak changes that ultimately manifest some sense of balance.

You'll notice that it's easier to get away with long strings of 4th and 5th interval changes (as they are the moderate changes) than it is to get away with long strings of 2nd, 7th, 6th and 3rd interval changes. The more strong or weak the change, the less time you should spend moving by that interval. This is something that your ears would most likely teach you, but knowing it up front will allow you to consciously experiment with it.

Spend as much time as you can looking at and listening to chord progressions of popular songs, old and new. Think about the progressions and how they behave, not only in terms of tension and release, but also in terms of strong and weak changes. Another thing that tends to get overlooked by a lot of not-so-great songwriters is the element of *harmonic rhythm* which simply refers to the rhythmic length of each chord and the interplay that it produces. This is something worth studying closely with your favorite songwriter's songs.

Below are some simple pop progressions made up of triads and 7th chords, in the key of C that have a nice interplay of strong/weak changes. Write them down in numerals and try using any and all voicings you can think of. Use a variety of rhythms in different key and time signatures, different tempos and feels. Try arpeggiating these changes and combining approaches to come up with some realistic and lively guitar parts that clearly reflect the changes.

1:

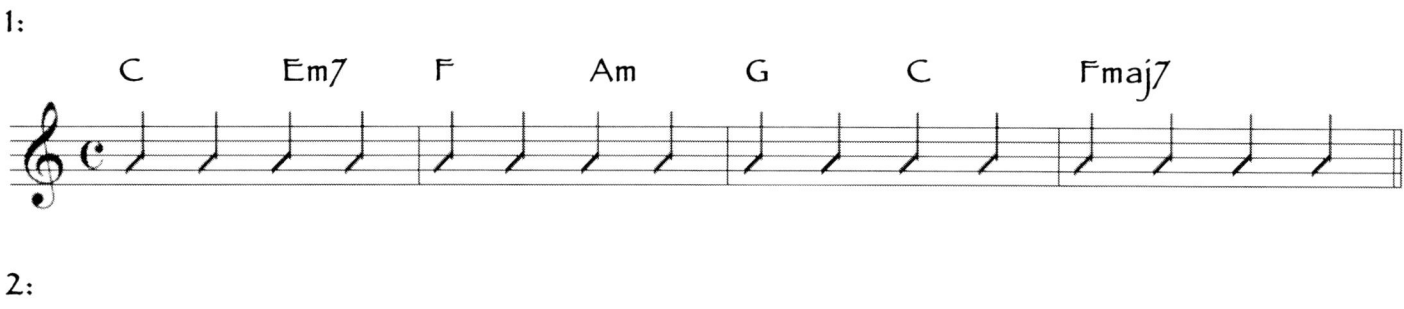

2:

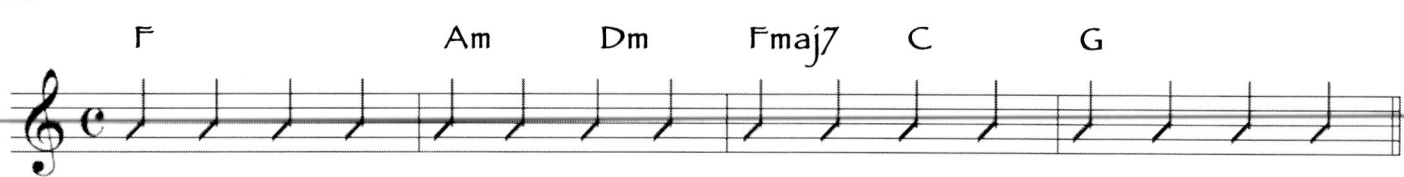

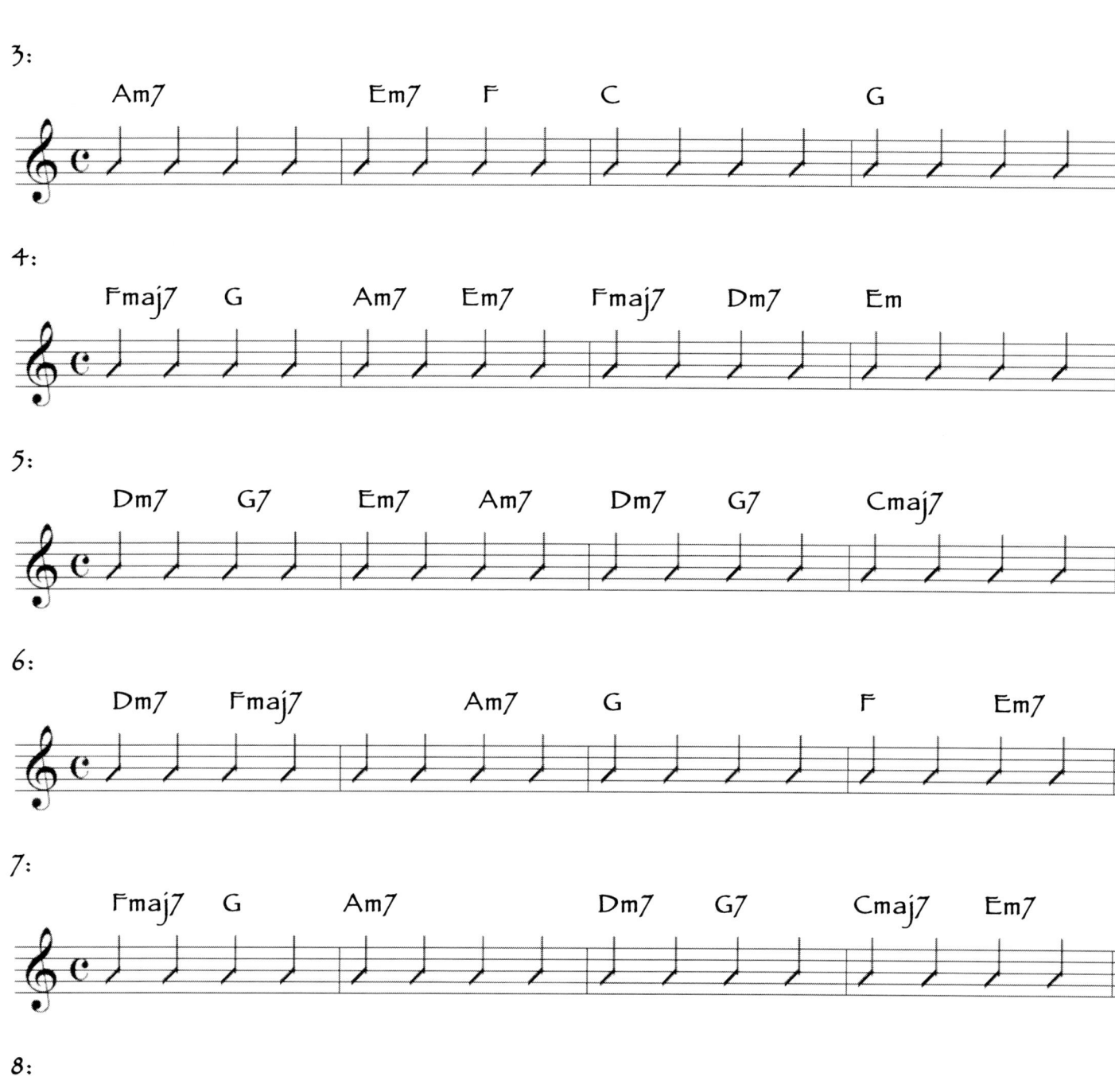

DIATONIC HARMONY - Part 5: Chords of the Harmonic Minor Scale

The harmonic minor scale was a discovery of sorts by the composers of the early classical era as a means of getting a certain trio of chords together on certain terms. What they wanted was a minor key that had a dominant 7th chord as its V. In effect they wanted these three primary chords: Im IVm V7. In order to make this happen, they simply had to alter one note of the pre-existing natural minor scale, AKA the Aeolian mode:

Instead of deriving their chords from R 2 b3 4 5 b6 b7, they derived them from R 2 b3 4 5 b6 7. They simply raised the flat 7th to a natural 7th.

In the key of Am:
A B C D E F G#

From there, they learned what they could do with the remaining chords and incorporated them judiciously. For the most part, they avoided using this new scale as a melodic platform because they weren't comfortable exposing what they considered a rather imperfect gap of 1½ steps between the b6th and major 7th. To compensate melodically, relating to the chords but avoiding the demon's gap as we'll call it, composers used a minor scale with an adjustable 6th and 7th degree.

Below, we can clearly see how our basic triads lay out in the key of A minor. You'll notice some new chord symbols in the right column. The "o" is a universal symbol to indicate a diminished chord. The "+" is used to indicate an augmented chord.

As we've already established, a diminished triad results from a stack of minor thirds or 1½ step intervals. An augmented chord is basically the opposite of a diminished chord. It is a stack of major thirds, or 2 whole-step intervals.
Both augmented and diminished chords are considerably more tense sounding than their major and minor counterparts. Because of the abundance of these chords in the harmonic minor scale, it's easy to come up with some rather haunting chord progressions. Another chordal feature worth noting that we don't find in the major scale or any of it's modes, is the occurrence of two major triads, one half step apart from each other. They occur at the 5th and b6th degrees of the scale.
This can clue you in to where the harmonic minor scale is an appropriate choice.

Harmonic Minor Scale-Based Triad Family

INTERVAL	Root	Distance	3rd	Distance	5th	CHORD
I	A	1½	C	2w	E	Am
II	B	1½	D	1½	F	Bo
bIII	C	2w	E	2w	G#	C+
IV	D	1½	F	2w	A	Dm
V	E	2w	G#	1½	B	E
bVI	F	2w	A	1½	C	F
VII:	G#	1½	B	1½	D	G#o

Harmonic Minor Scale-Based 7th Chord Family

INTERVAL	Root	Distance	3rd	Distance	5th	Distance	7th	CHORD
I	A	1½	C	2w	E	2w	G#	Am♮7
II	B	1½	D	1½	F	2w	A	Bø7
bIII	C	2w	E	2w	G#	1½	B	Cmaj7#5
IV	D	2w	F	1½	A	2w	C	Dm7
V	E	2w	G#	1½	B	1½	D	E7
bVI	F	2w	A	1½	C	2w	E	Fmaj7
VII:	G#	1½	B	1½	D	1½	F	G#o7

The chart below illustrates the make up of chords in the harmonic minor scale, in all twelve keys. Note that they are mostly presented as triads, with the exception of the V7 and VIIdim7. This conforms to general classical use of the scale, which is also basically the pop use of the scale. The one difference between a harmonic minor scale based classical piece, as compared to a pop tune based on the same scale, would typically be in the bIII chord. In pop music, songwriters normally use a normal major triad. Another way to put it is:

Im	W	IIdim	H	bIII+	W	IVm	W	V(7)	H	bVI	1½	VIIdim7	H
Am		Bdim		C+		Dm		E7		F		G#dim7	
Em		F#dim		G+		Am		B7		C		D#dim7	
Bm		C#dim		D+		Em		F#7		G		A#dim7	
F#m		G#dim		A+		Bm		C#7		D		E#dim7	
C#m		D#dim		E+		F#m		G#7		A		B#dim7	
G#m		A#dim		B+		C#m		D#7		E		Gdim7	
Ebm		Fdim		Gb+		Abm		Bb7		Cb		Ddim7	
Bbm		Cdim		Db+		Ebm		F7		Gb		Adim7	
Fm		Gdim		Ab+		Bbm		C7		Db		Edim7	
Cm		Ddim		Eb+		Fm		G7		Ab		Bdim7	
Gm		Adim		Bb+		Cm		D7		Eb		F#dim7	
Dm		Edim		F+		Gm		A7		Bb		C#dim7	

Harmonic Minor Scale Positions

Even though the harmonic minor scale has only one note in contrast to the Aeolian mode, the harmonic minor positions as they lay out on the guitar are strikingly different looking. As any new scale that you add to your arsenal of tools, it will take some getting used to but will be well worth it. Melodic use of this scale has a very exotic sound that is closely associated with old-world Gypsy culture of eastern Europe.

This makes for a scale that may or may not be really useful to you. I rarely find myself using this scale for melodic improvisation unless I'm jamming some 1980s guitar-nerd metal or Klezmer music with someone. Still, with as few opportunities I have to use this scale as a melodic device, I'm still glad that I put the time in to practicing it.

As with any scale, try spending less time running straight up and down the notes and more time playing through any and all melodic patterns that you know of, arpeggiating the chords of the scale and any other truly musical exercise involving the scale tones. These are MUCH better ways of spending your time. Being able to play really fast, up and down a scale will do very little to make you a better musician. Learning how to construct natural musical statements from raw harmonic and tonal material however, will help immeasurably.

Below are the 5 basic positions as well as a graph indicating the fret locations for each position in each key:

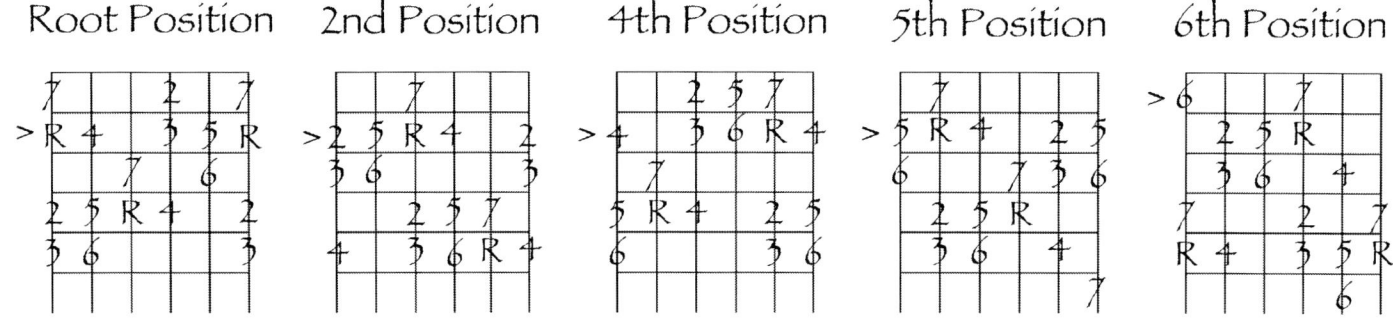

	A	E	B	F#	C#	G#	Eb	Bb	F	C	G	D
Root Pos:	5	12	7	2	9	4	11	6	13	8	3	10
2nd Pos:	7	2	9	4	11	6	13	8	3	10	5	12
4th Pos:	10	5	12	7	2	9	4	11	6	13	8	3
5th Pos:	12	7	2	9	4	11	6	13	8	3	10	5
6th Pos:	13	8	3	10	5	12	7	2	9	4	11	6

The Modes Of The Harmonic Minor Scale

When we learned the modes of the major scale we found that all but one of them are natural enough in their make-up to base entire songs from them. Our exploration of the harmonic minor scale modes won't be quite so fruitful. There are three modes of the harmonic minor scale that I've personally found to be useful. The other four modes, I just hate. I'm going to give you a run-down of all seven of them and then we'll go into some depth on the three commonly used modes.

Mode:	R		2		3		4		5		6		7
A Harm. Minor	A	w	B	h	C	w	D	w	E	h	F	1½	G#	h
B Locrian ♮6th	B	h	C	w	D	w	E	h	F	1½	G#	h	A	w
C Major #5th	C	w	D	w	E	h	F	1½	G#	h	A	w	B	h
D Dorian #4th	D	w	E	h	F	1½	G#	h	A	w	B	h	C	w
E Maj. Phryg.	E	h	F	1½	G#	h	A	w	B	h	C	w	D	w
F Lydian #2nd	F	1½	G#	h	A	w	B	h	C	w	D	w	E	h
B Locrian bb7	G#	h	A	w	B	h	C	w	D	w	E	w	F	1½

Mode I: Harmonic Minor – R 2 b3 4 5 b6 7 – can be used over minor triads or m♮7 chords and works well.

Mode II: Locrian ♮6th – R b2 b3 b4 b5 6 b7 – can be used over a min7b5 (half diminished) but sounds very watered down, due to the major 6th being very contrary to the dark quality of the half-diminished chord.

Mode III: Major #5th – R 2 3 4 #5 6 7 – can be used over an augmented triad if you want to sound like you aren't sure how to play over an augmented triad.

Mode IV: Dorian #4th – R 2 b3 #4 5 6 b7 – can be used on a minor triad or a m7 chord and works quite nicely.

Mode V: Major Phrygian – R b2 3 4 5 b6 b7 – can be used on dominant 7th chords resolving to minor chords a fourth up (2½ steps) or a 5th (3½ steps) down.

Mode VI: Lydian #2nd – R #2 3 #4 5 6 7 – theoretically, can be used on a maj7 chord, as it contains the Root, 3rd, 5th and 7th but sound very unnatural because of the lack of a rather balancing natural 2nd. In some styles, people will frequently add 2nds (aka 9ths, more on this further in) and the #2nd can really muck things up.

Mode VII: Locrian bb7 – R b2 b3 4 b5 b6 bb7 – could be used over a dim7 chord but there is a much better scale choice for dim7 chords that we will be learning about, pretty soon.

Harmonic Minor Mode I: Harmonic Minor

We already have the scale positions and key locations established for the harmonic minor scale so we'll jump straight into some licks that nicely convey the harmonic minor sound. These ten licks all relate directly to an Am or an Am♭7 chord, although you may identify a few Dm and E7 arpeggios within the licks. These are present in order to set up points of tension against the chord.

A Harmonic Minor Lick 1:

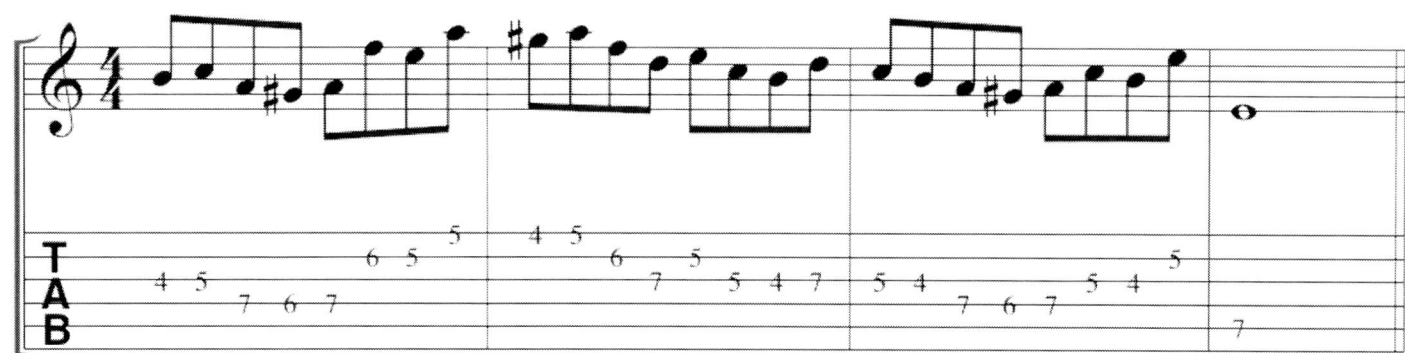

A Harmonic Minor Lick 2:

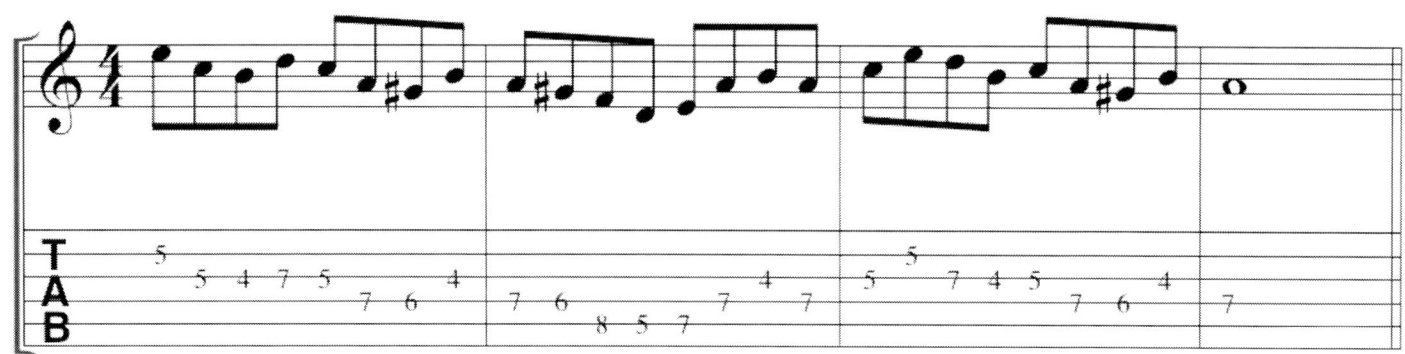

A Harmonic Minor Lick 3:

A Harmonic Minor Lick 4:

A Harmonic Minor Lick 5:

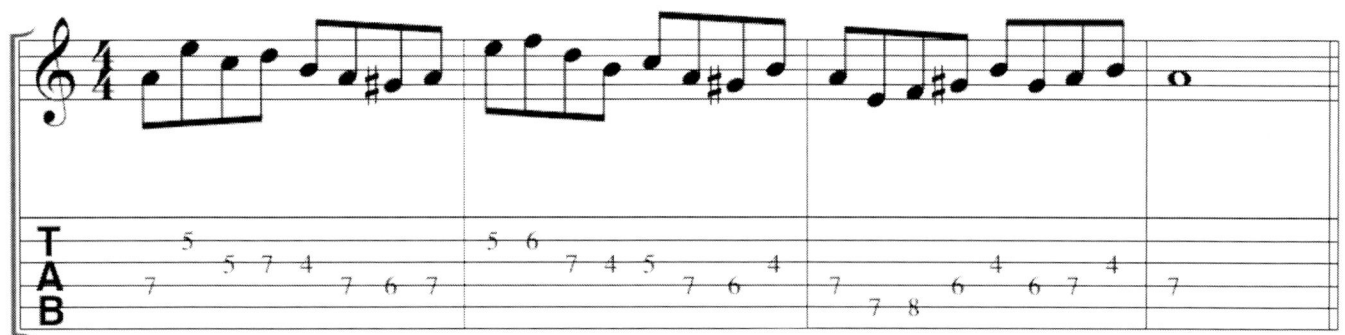

A Harmonic Minor Lick 6:

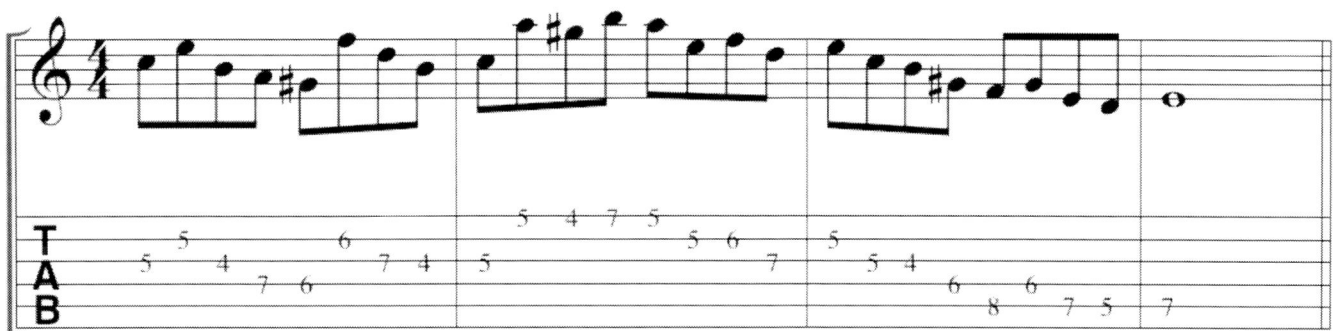

A Harmonic Minor Lick 7:

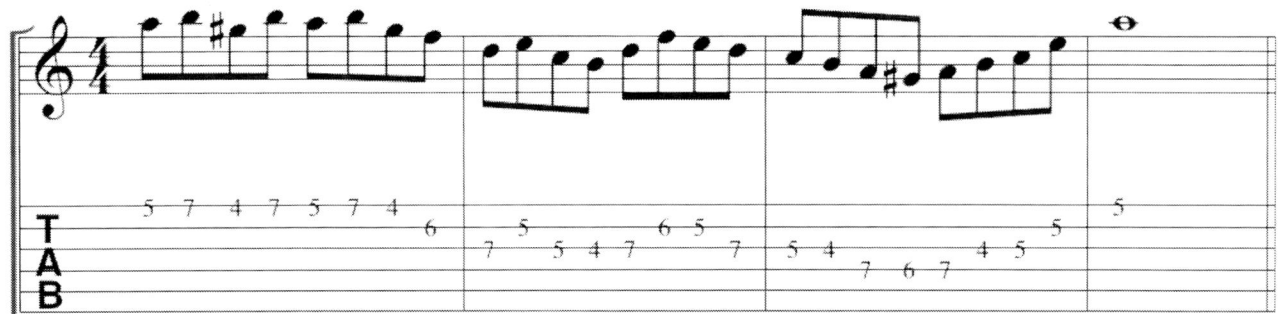

A Harmonic Minor Lick 8:

A Harmonic Minor Lick 9:

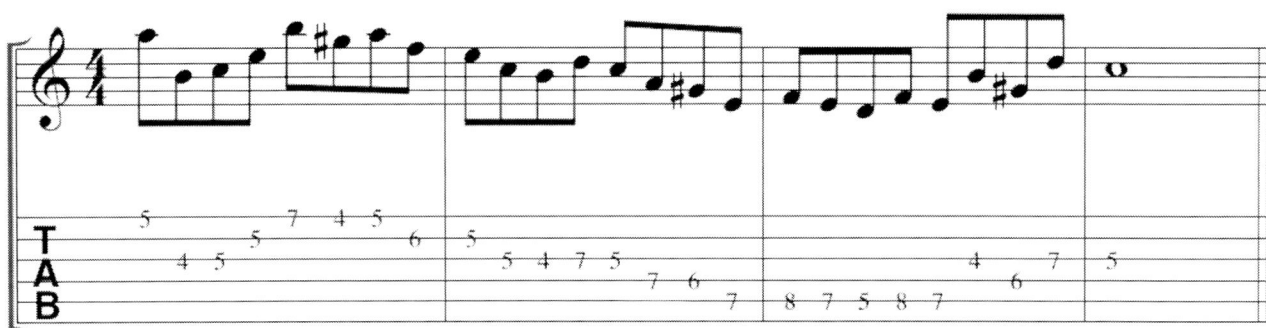

A Harmonic Minor Lick 10:

HARMONIC MINOR - MODE IV: DORIAN #4ᵀᴴ

This one might be my personal favorite harmonic minor mode. I like to play a lot of jazz, which is filled with IIm7 chords and if you want to add an exotic/ethnic flavor to a IIm7, this scale is one of your best options. In general, the Dorian mode is some really common territory in group jams of most styles. Raising the 4ᵗʰ doesn't interfere with a basic minor triad or most minor chords that someone might play in place of it. In short, D Dorian #4ᵗʰ will work over any Dm chord other than a Dm11. If the reason isn't clear yet, it'll become clear when we delve into extended harmony.

Below are the 5 basic positions as well as a graph indicating the fret locations for each position in each key:

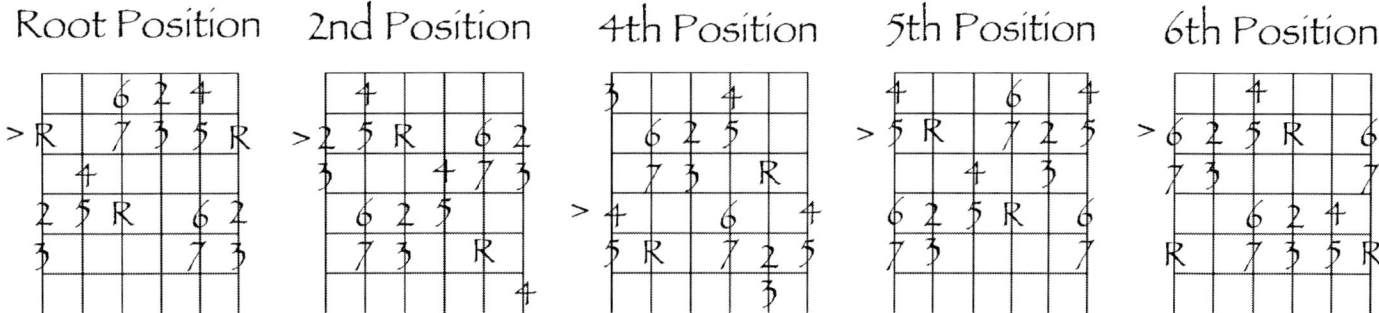

	D	A	E	B	F#	C#	Ab	Eb	Bb	F	C	G
Root Position:	10	5	12	7	2	9	4	11	6	13	8	3
2nd Position:	12	7	2	9	4	11	6	13	8	3	10	5
4th Position:	4	11	6	13	8	15	10	5	12	7	14	8
5th Position:	5	12	7	2	9	4	11	6	13	8	3	10
7th Position:	8	3	10	5	12	7	2	9	4	11	6	13

The next pages contain 10 licks based on the Dorian #4ᵗʰ mode. As was already stated, you can play these licks over any Dm chord other than a Dm11. You'll find some very unpredictable sounding strings of notes in these licks. You'll also be running into some counter-chord type ideas that we talked about in the A Harmonic Minor Licks a few pages back. In this case, it will be the very unlikely sounding E major triad. The E, G# and B notes of this triad have a really interesting sounding tension against the static Dm or Dm7 chord.

D Dorian #4th Lick 1:

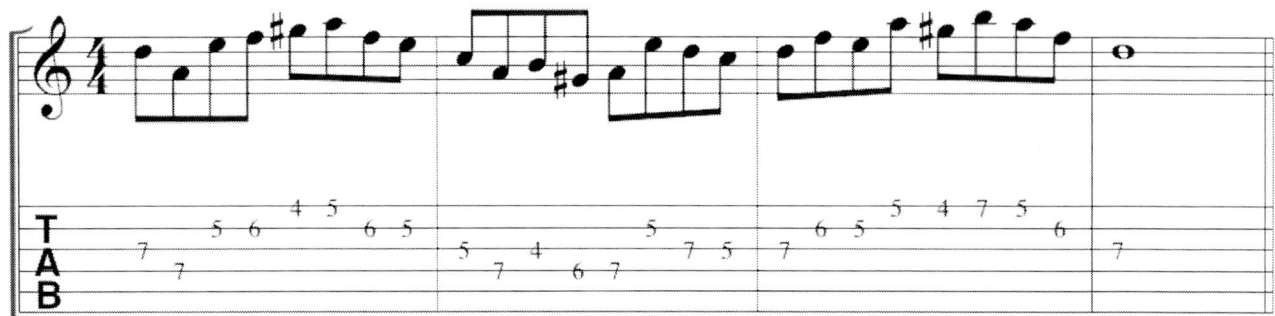

D Dorian #4th Lick 2:

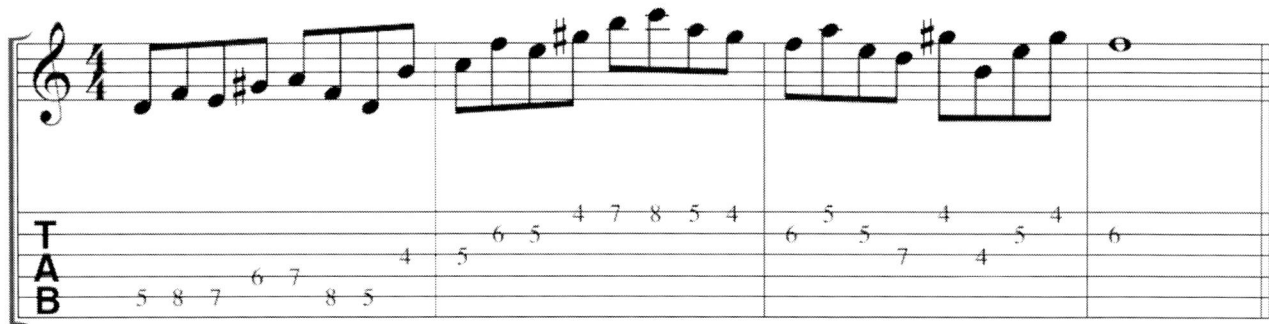

D Dorian #4th Lick 3:

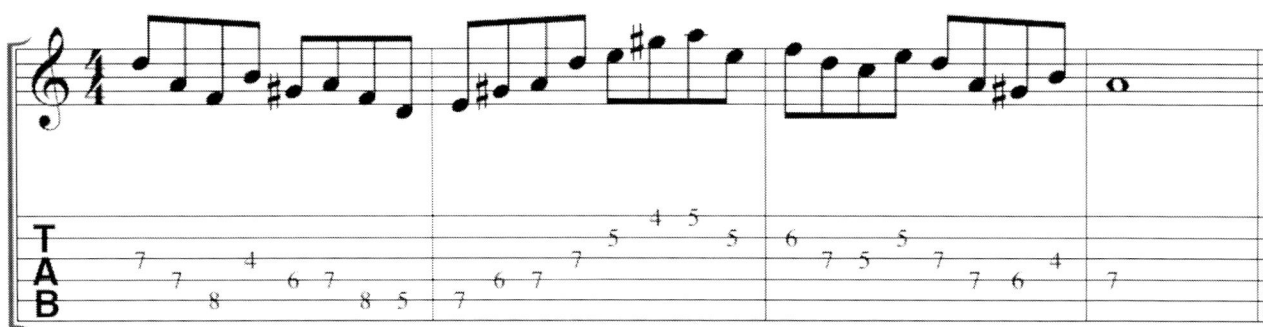

D Dorian #4th Lick 4:

D Dorian #4th Lick 5:

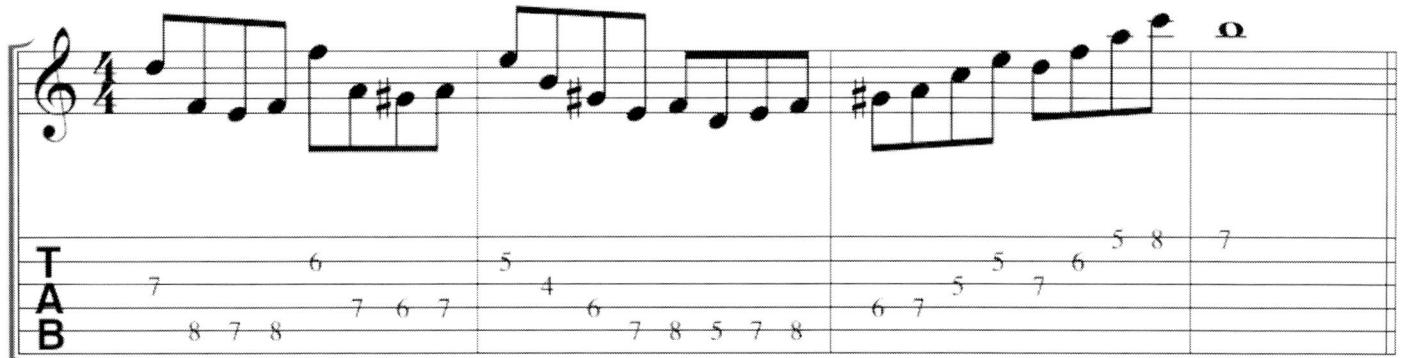

D Dorian #4th Lick 6:

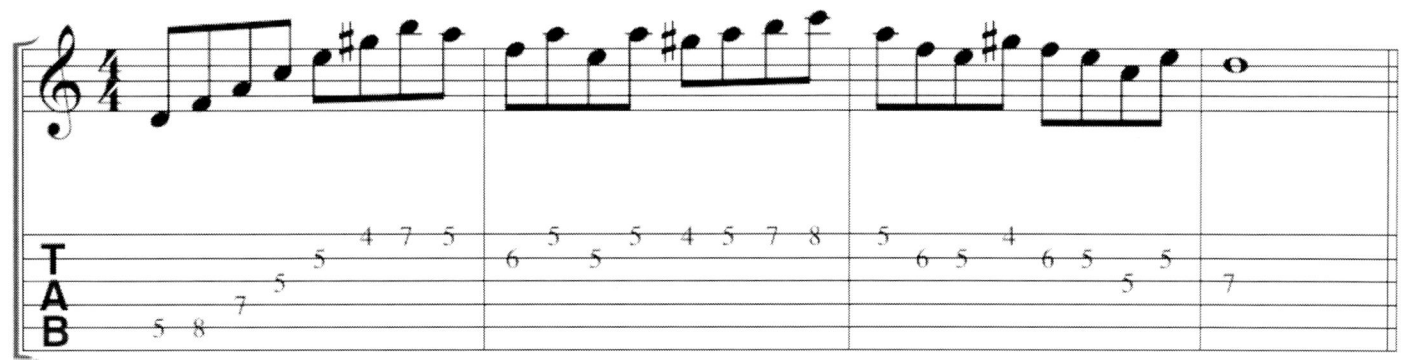

D Dorian #4th Lick 7:

D Dorian #4th Lick 8:

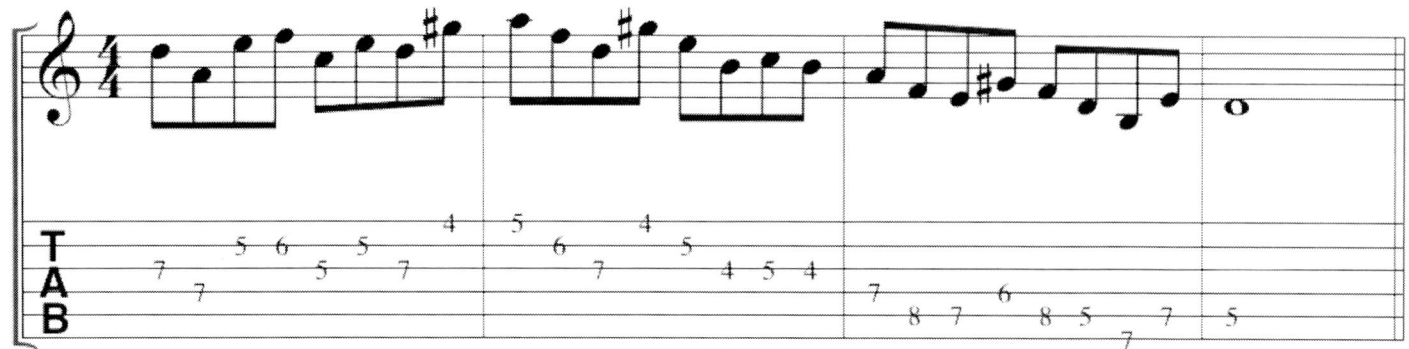

D Dorian #4th Lick 9:

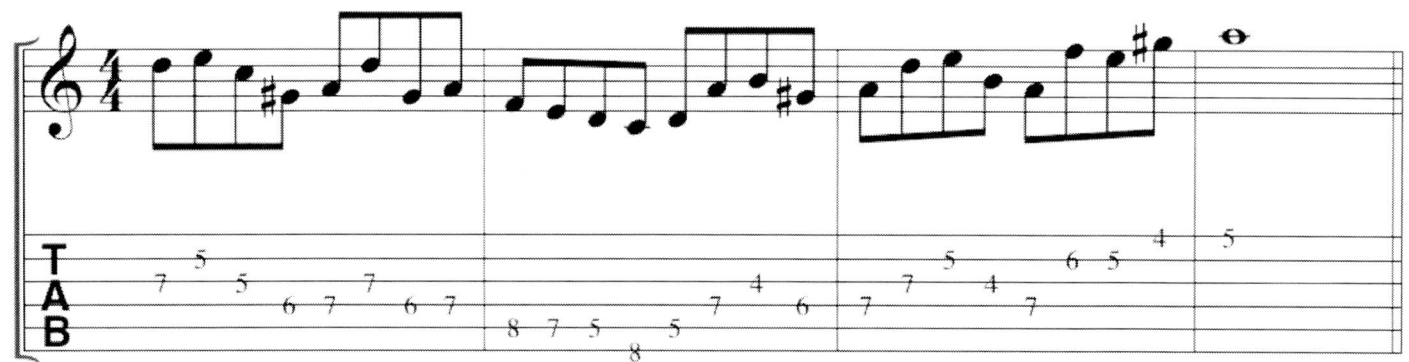

D Dorian #4th Lick 10:

Harmonic Minor - Mode V: Major Phrygian

Aside from mode I, this is certainly the most common harmonic minor mode. Anytime another guitar player around you starts strumming through E and F major chords in the classic mach-flamenco bullfighting style, this mode is the perfect vehicle to write or improvise a melody to fit it. This is one scale that it wouldn't hurt to do some old-fashion speed training, because the styles of music that most frequently use this mode are heavy on fast, scalewise runs. Flamenco, progressive rock, metal and fusion are the styles that come to mind, but I've even heard it used in a couple bluegrass tunes and it shows up frequently in Klezmer music.

Below are the 5 basic positions, as well as a graph indicating the fret locations for each position in each key:

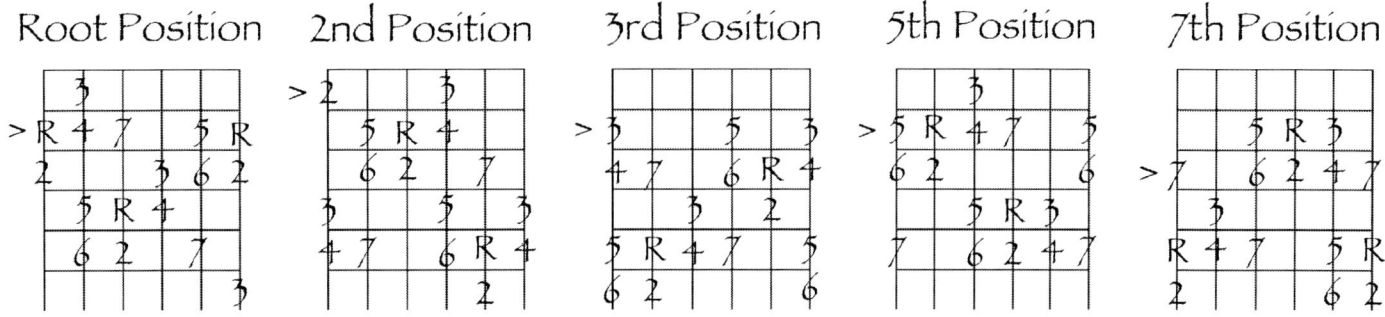

	E	B	F#	C#	G#	D#	Bb	F	C	G	D	A
Root Position:	12	7	2	9	4	11	6	13	8	3	10	5
2nd Position:	1	8	3	10	5	12	7	2	9	4	11	6
3rd Position:	4	11	6	13	8	3	11	5	12	7	2	9
5th Position:	7	2	9	4	11	6	13	8	3	10	5	12
7th Position:	10	5	12	7	2	9	4	11	6	13	8	3

As you may have expected, the next few pages hold some licks that will give you ideas of how you can really capitalize on the characteristic sound of this scale. Generally speaking, when it comes to building solid, musical licks, it's best to always be thinking in terms of setting up points of tension and release. I should point out that I've intentionally kept all these modal lick examples in the realm of straight 8th notes. My hope is that you will take all that you've been learning about rhythm and syncopation, and apply those concepts to any of the licks contained within this book and elsewhere.

E Major Phrygian Lick 1:

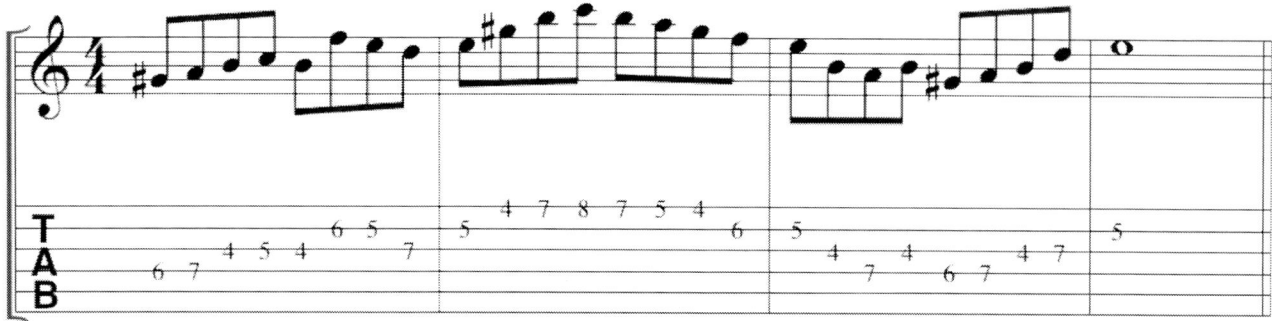

E Major Phrygian Lick 2:

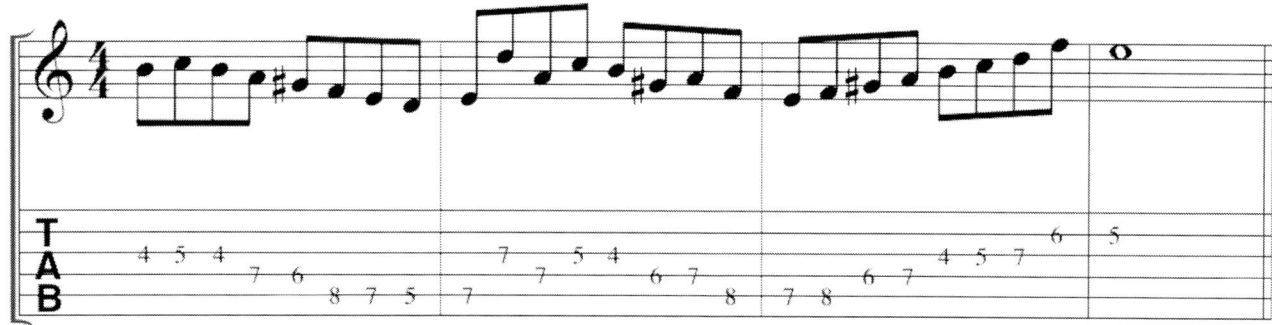

E Major Phrygian Lick 3:

E Major Phrygian Lick 4:

E Major Phrygian Lick 5:

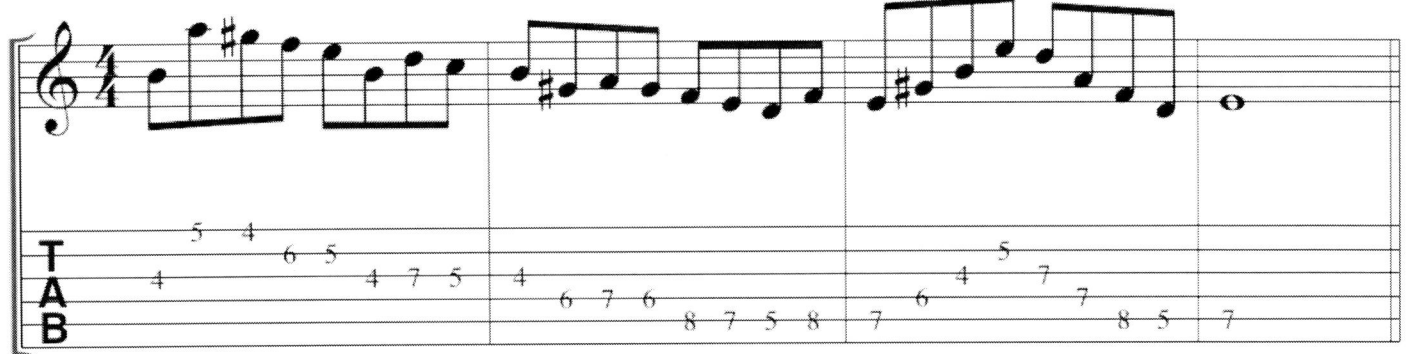

E Major Phrygian Lick 6:

E Major Phrygian Lick 7:

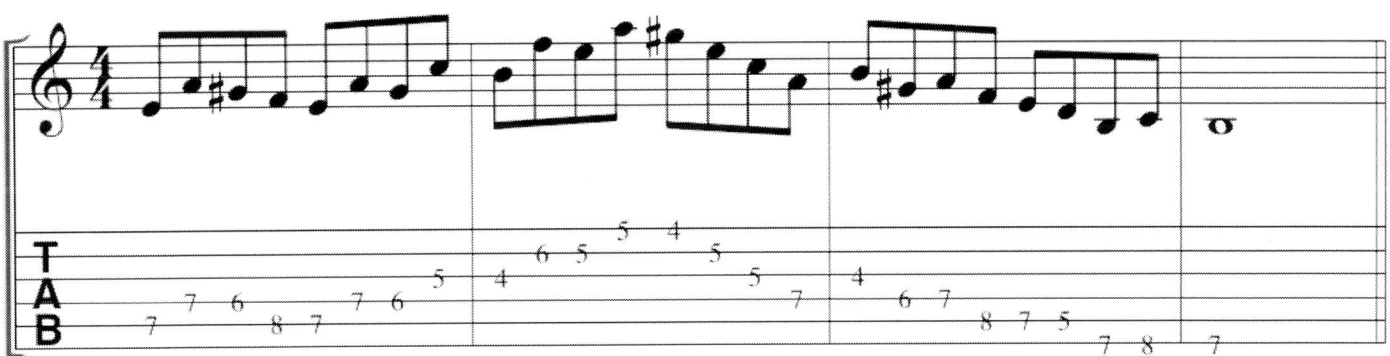

E Major Phrygian Lick 8:

E Major Phrygian Lick 9:

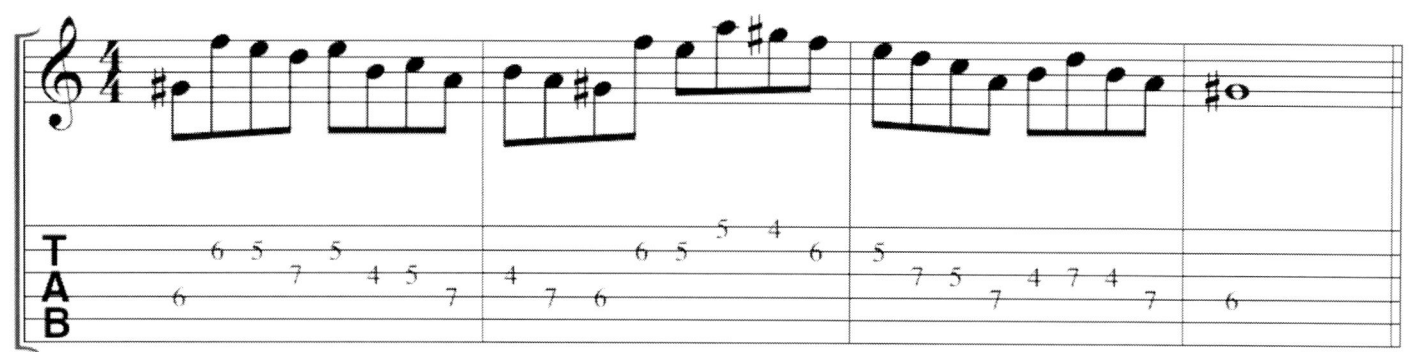

E Major Phrygian Lick 10:

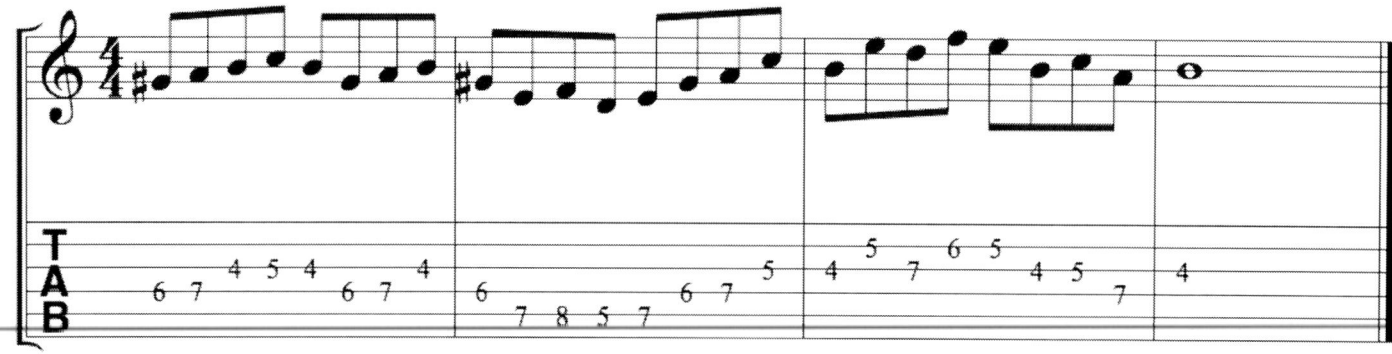

Harmonic Minor Chord Pairs

Considering that the initial purpose for the harmonic minor scale was for the sake of its harmonic possibilities, it would be a good idea to spend some time getting to know how these harmonies are laid out on the fretboard. In this section we are going to look closely at pairs of chords within the scale, much like the way that we explored triad pairs within the major scale. In the case of this section we won't be looking solely at triads, rather a combination of minor triads, dom7 chords and dim7 chords. Each of these written examples is intended to work over one of the three primary chords of the minor key; Im, IVm and V7.

Specifically, there are eight lines that correspond to the Am (Im) that use E7 and G#dim7 as counter-chords, for the sake of internal tension. There also eight lines that correspond to the Dm chord, using the same E7 and G#dim7 as counter chords. In the real world, in the key of A minor, you'll hear A7 being used as a counter chord to Dm even though the A7 chord has a C# as its major 3rd, even though C# is not a member of the scale. There is a very specific reason why this works and we will soon be looking at this.

Keep in mind though, that the relationship between Am and E7 is identical to that of Dm and A7. This means that once you've taken this material and transposed it to all keys, you'll already know how to handle that particular chord-pair in all keys regardless if it's being based off the Im or IVm. Also, when you are on the V7 in a minor key, you can use the Im or the IVm as a counter-chord. I should also point out that for reasons we will soon be covering, the VIIdim7 chord is very interchangeable with the V7. By the time you've internalized these exercises, you'll have the facility to cover the V7 as easily as the Im and IVm.

Am-E7 Chord-Pair Exercise #1:

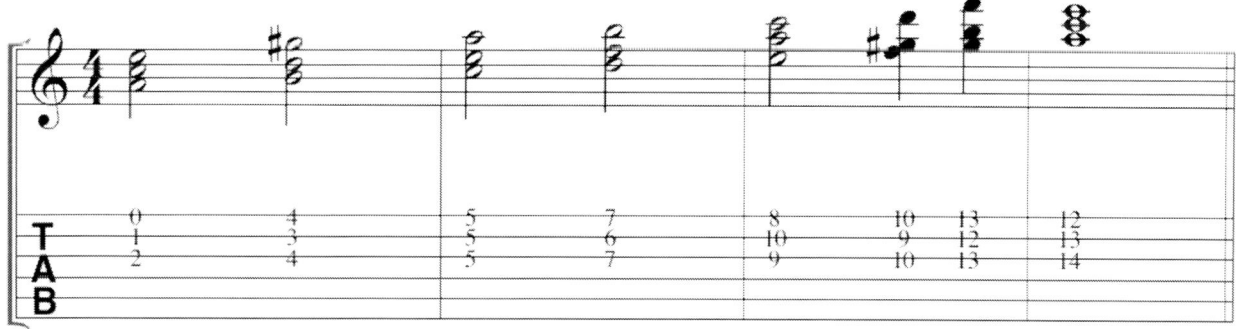

Am-E7 Chord-Pair Exercise #2:

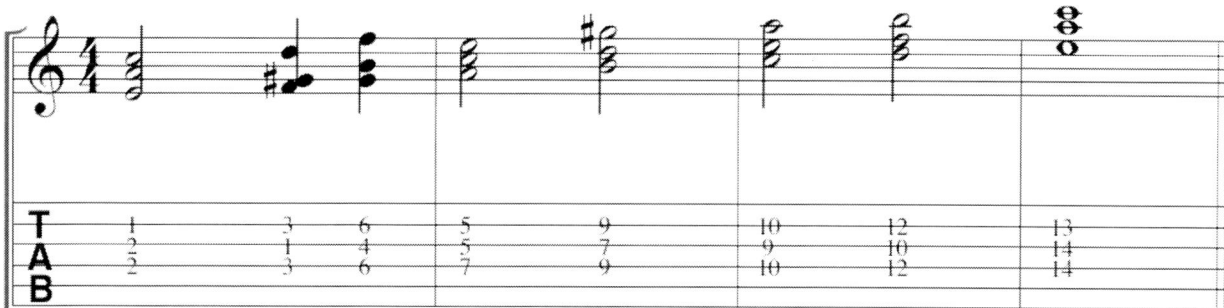

Am-E7 Chord-Pair Exercise #3:

Am-E7 Chord-Pair Exercise #4:

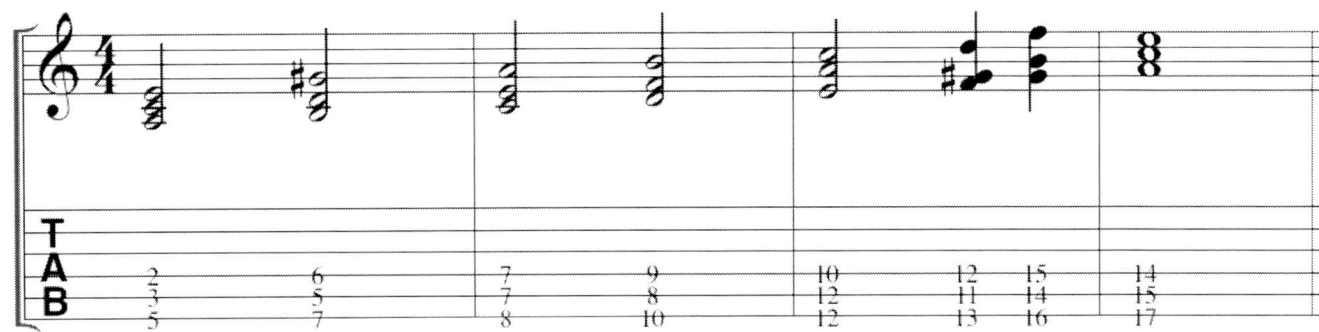

Am-E7 Chord-Pair Exercise #5:

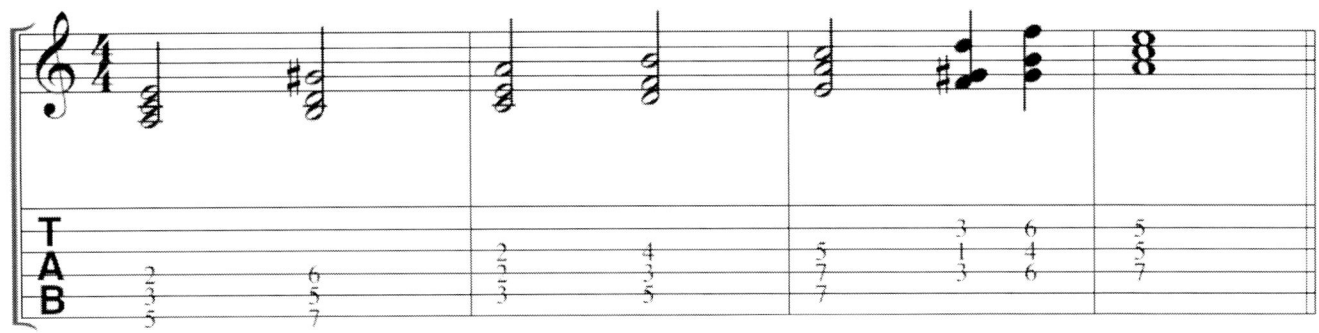

Dm-E7 Chord-Pair Exercise #1:

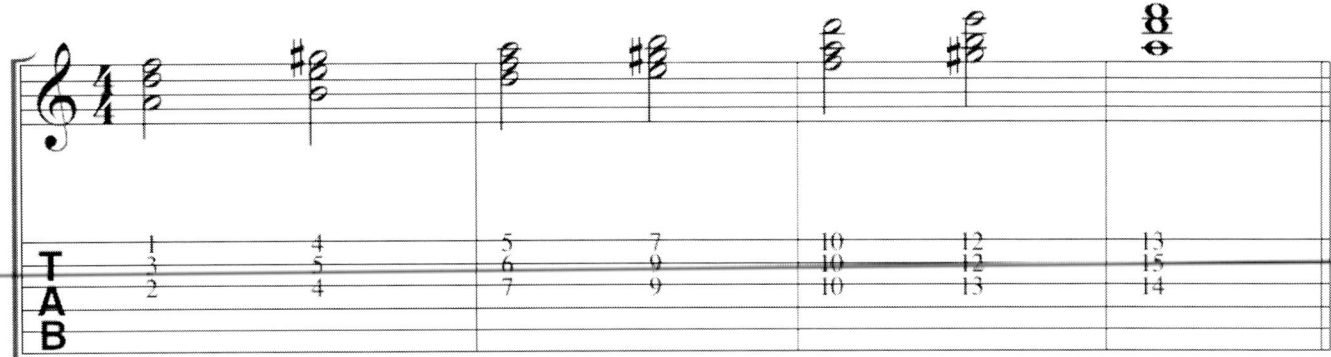

Dm-E7 Chord-Pair Exercise #2:

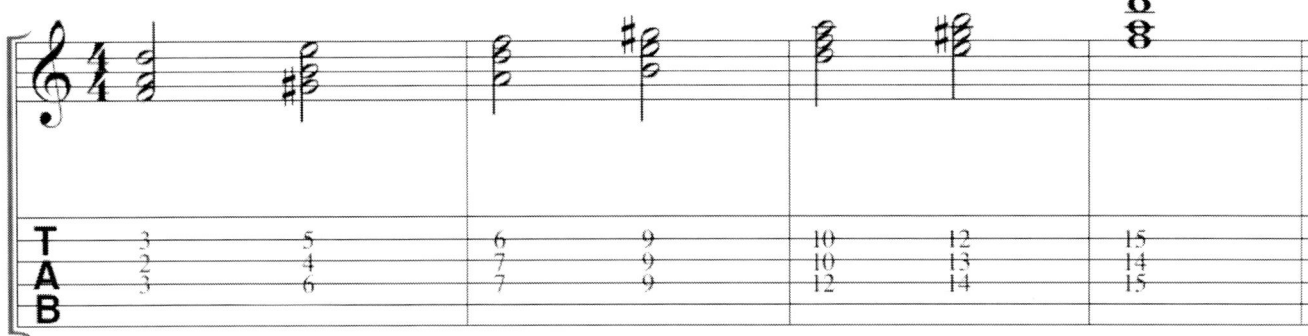

Dm-E7 Chord-Pair Exercise #3:

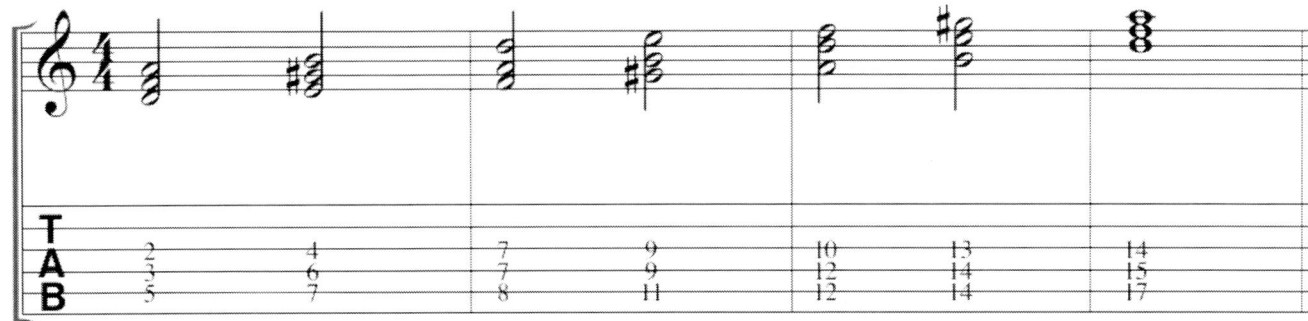

Dm-E7 Chord-Pair Exercise #4:

Dm-E7 Chord-Pair Exercise #5:

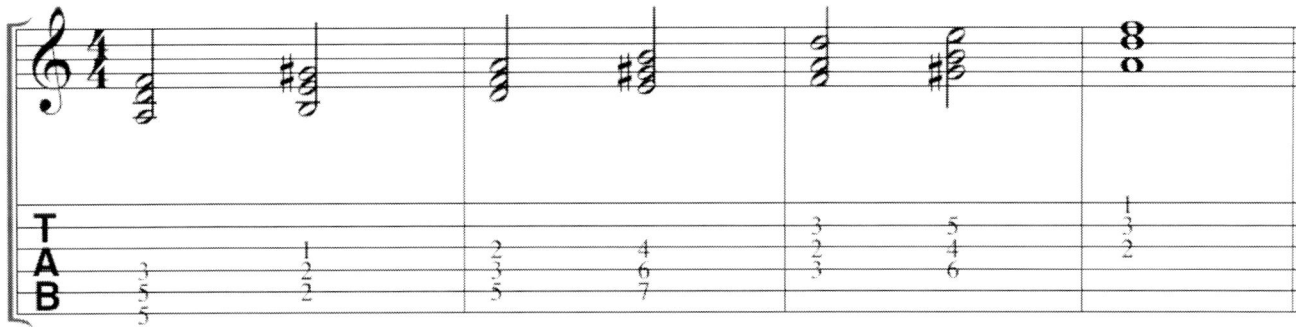

ARPEGGIOS – Part 2: Chords Of the Harmonic Minor Scale

As we learned within the major scale, we can build some very concise melodic runs from two contrasting arpeggios within that scale. The best choice of chords to use in this manner, within the harmonic minor scale, would be Am and G#o7 (G#dim7). The Am chord contains all of the inactive tones and the G#o7 contains all of the active tones of the scale. Needless to say, having a strong command over these arpeggios can really help you to set up points of tension and release within the minor key.

These exercises are very similar to the triad-combo arpeggios that we studied earlier. There is one major difference that effects the way these arpeggios will flow from one to another. One of these chords is a triad and the other is a four-note 7th chord. This means that at some point, in each line, we will need to compensate by way of melodic direction in order to get smooth, step-wise transitions from chord to counter-chord (or from counter-chord back to chord). Spend some time going very slowly, while being very conscious of your fingering choices. Make sure that you're using the best fingering strategy. This won't necessarily be what feels the easiest at first. It will be the fingering that allows for the least left hand movement. The fingering situation that will slow you down the most is when you use the same finger on two notes that are at least a string apart as well as at least a fret apart. In other words, avoid hopping around on one finger at all costs!

Am-G#o7 Arpeggio Run, 6th Position (Ascending):

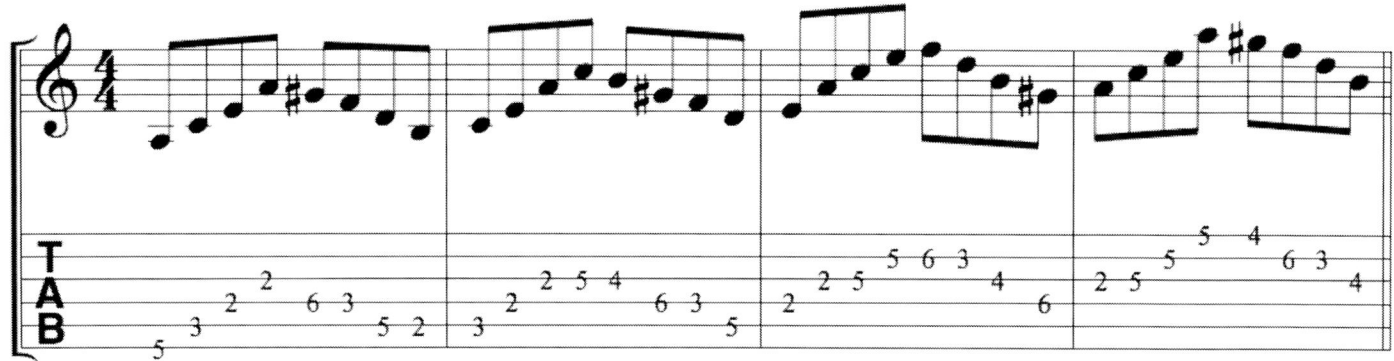

Am-G#o7 Arpeggio Run, 6th Position (Descending):

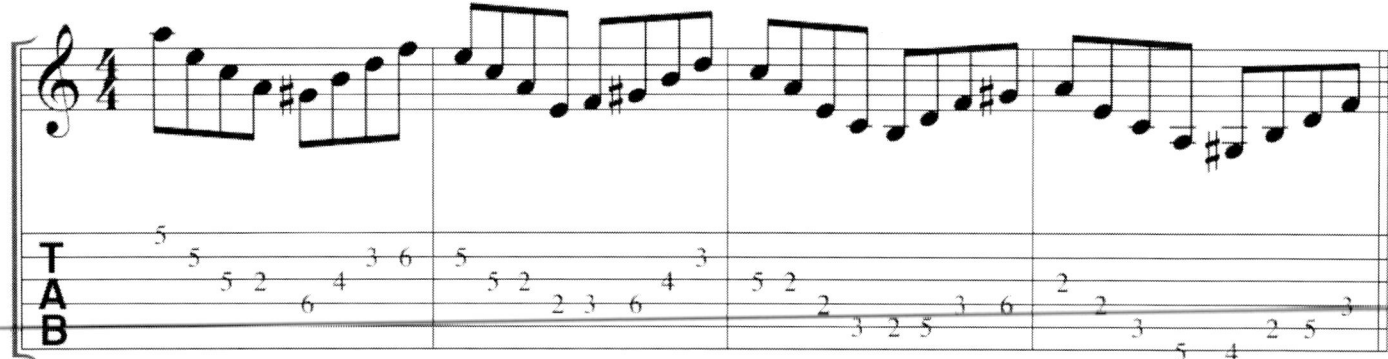

Am-G#o7 Arpeggio Run, Root Position (Ascending):

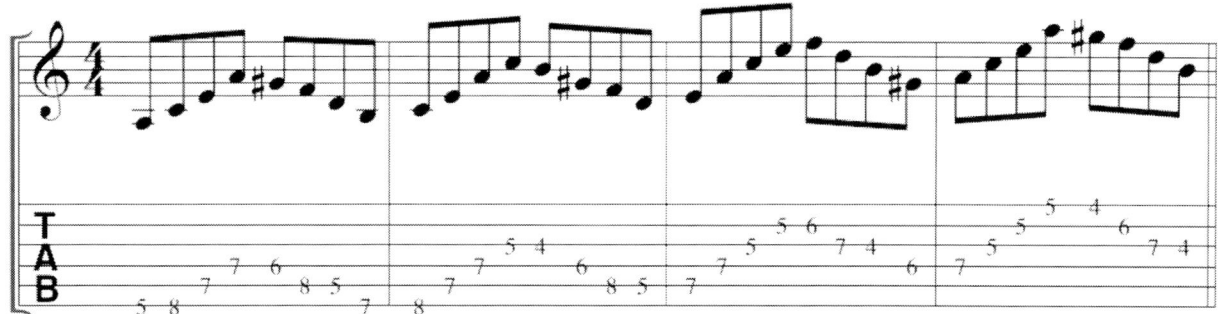

Am-G#o7 Arpeggio Run, Root Position (Descending):

Am-G#o7 Arpeggio, 2nd Position (Ascending):

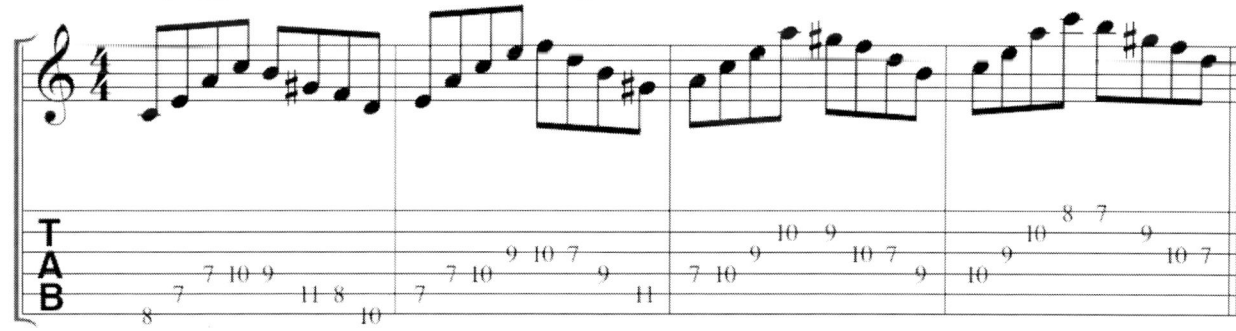

Am-G#o7 Arpeggio, 2nd Position (Descending):

Am-G#o7 Arpeggio, 4th Position (Ascending):

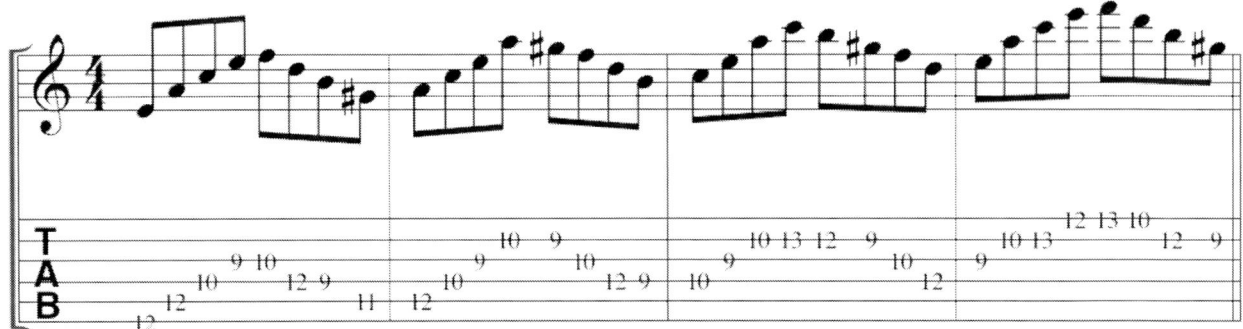

Am-G#o7 Arpeggio, 4th Position (Descending):

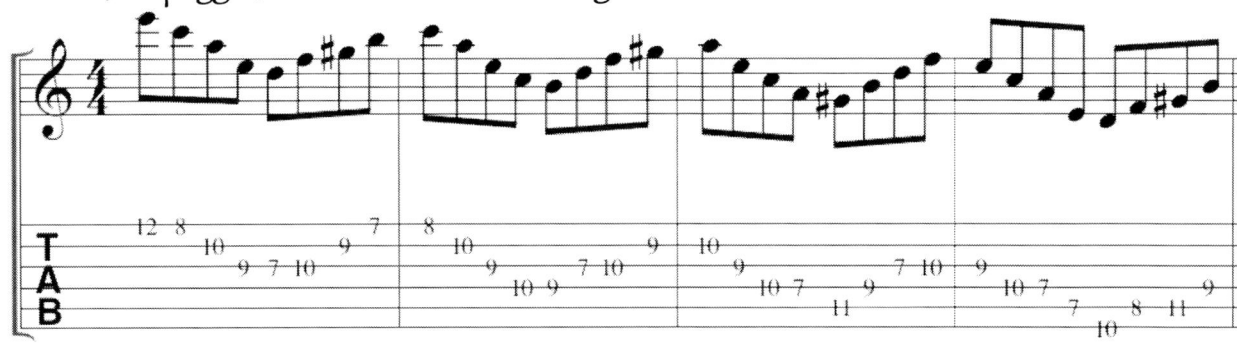

Am-G#o7 Arpeggio, 5th Position (Ascending):

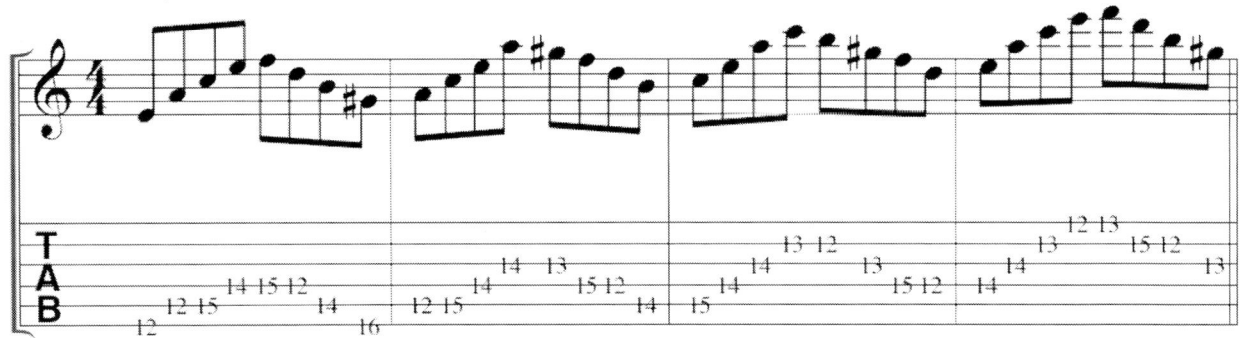

Am-G#o7 Arpeggio, 5th Position (Descending):

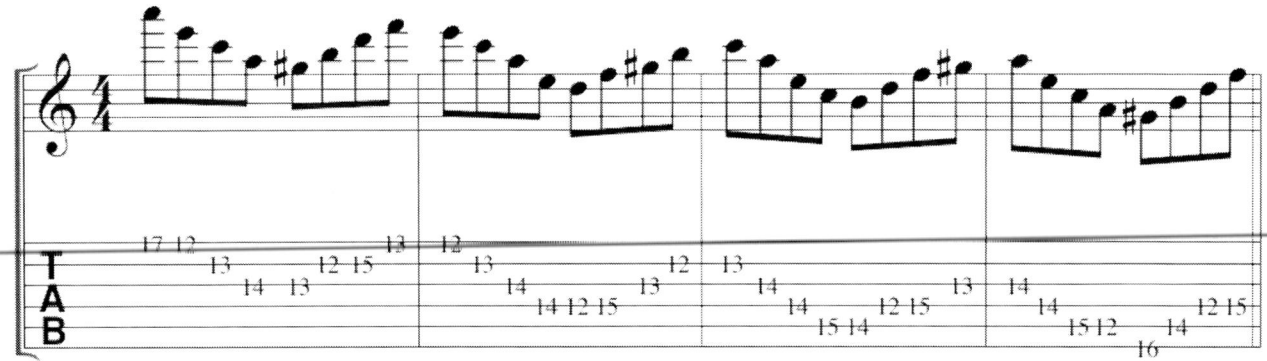

SYMMETRICAL HARMONY – part 1: Simple Math

Symmetrical harmony simply refers to chords that are constructed of tones that are equal intervals apart from one another. There are only two types of symmetrical chords, both of which we have already discovered within the harmonic minor scale. These two symmetrical chord types are the augmented (+) triad and the diminished 7th (o) chord. Though we've already been introduced to these chords within one of their natural habitats, there are some interesting things about these chords that you may not immediately recognize.

Let us examine the notes of a C+ triad:

Root   3rd   #5th
C 2w E 2w G# 2w

Now, let's look at the notes of an Ab+ triad:

Root   3rd   #5th
Ab 2w C 2w E 2w

And how about an E+ triad:

Root   3rd   #5th
E 2w G# 2w C (B#) 2w

You've probably noticed that these three augmented triads are all made up of the same three pitches. In other words, any note of an augmented chord could potentially be regarded as the root. C+ could also be considered an E+ or an Ab+. These three augmented are not distinct. They all share 100% of their notes with one another. Now that we've established this, we have a good question to ask. How many distinct augmented chords exist? The answer could be found by asking a simpler question: How many times does three go into twelve?

Below is a table that illustrates the relationship of our augmented triads to one another:

Augmented Triad #1:	Augmented Triad #2:	Augmented Triad #3:	Augmented Triad #4:
C 2W E 2W G# 2W	F 2W A 2W C# 2W	D 2W F# 2W A# 2W	G 2W B 2W D# 2W
E 2W G# 2W C 2W	A 2W C# 2W F 2W	Gb 2W Bb 2W D 2W	B 2W D# 2W G 2W
Ab 2W C 2W E 2W	Db 2W F 2W A 2W	Bb 2W D 2W F# 2W	Eb 2W G 2W B 2W

This knowledge has more applications than I will impart on you once we get a little deeper into it. For now, work on trying to reproduce the above table with pencil and paper, or on your computer/tablet without using this table as a visual. It's not important that you put the distinct triad columns in the same order as I put them. (I put them in what is essentially a chromatic, upward order: C, Db, D and Eb), but disguised it by putting the most natural root notes on the top row.) Work on this until you can do it very quickly without hesitation.

The dim7 chord has the same sort of internal relationship, except it's based on minor third intervals rather than the major third intervals from which we base the augmented chord. In the case of the dim7 chord we have a chord where any of the four chord-tones could be considered the root note. Just as three tones go into twelve tones four times, as we saw in augmented chord land, four tones go into twelve tones three times. Following, is a chart that shows the relationships between the three existing distinct dim7 chords and their twin siblings.

Diminished 7th Chord 1:	Diminished 7th Chord 2:	Diminished 7th Chord 3:
C 1½ Eb 1½ Gb 1½ A 1½	F 1½ Ab 1½ B 1½ D 1½	G 1½ Bb 1½ Db 1½ E 1½
Eb 1½ Gb 1½ A 1½ C 1½	Ab 1½ B 1½ D 1½ F 1½	Bb 1½ Db 1½ E 1½ G 1½
Gb 1½ A 1½ C 1½ Gb 1½	B 1½ D 1½ F 1½ Ab 1½	Db 1½ E 1½ G 1½ Bb 1½
A 1½ C 1½ Gb 1½ Gb 1½	D 1½ F 1½ Ab 1½ B 1½	E 1½ G 1½ Bb 1½ Db 1½

Below are some simple applications of symmetrical harmony, beginning with a pair of augmented triads, a half-step apart, followed by their inversions which are all identical augmented triad voicings:

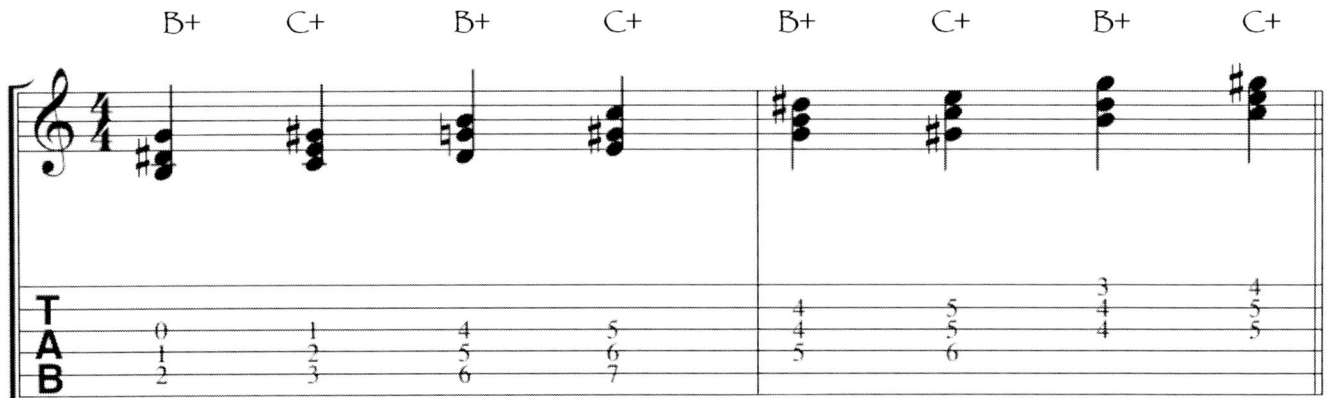

The chord run below is made up of two diminished chords, one half-step apart, followed by their inversions which are all identical dim7 chord voicings:

The musical applications of this sort of harmony will become more clear in following chapters. Until then, listen closely for the use of symmetrical harmony in recorded music. It's most commonly found in jazz and cinematic suspense music, but you can occasionally find it used in heavy metal, progressive rock and progressive electronic music.

RHYTHM – part 5: Odd Subdivisions

A beat is essentially a division of the measure. Typically, one beat equals one quarter note. When we play anything smaller than that quarter note, we are sub-dividing the beat. Regular subdivisions would be 8th notes (two per beat), 16th notes (four per beat), 32nd notes (eight per beat) and 64th notes (sixteen per beat - yikes). There are even such a thing as 128th notes, which would have five beams and fit 32 notes to the beat. I've never played any, but they exist.

When we divide the beat into an odd number of notes, or even an even number that can only be cut in half once, we are creating odd-subdivisions, known as tuplets. Below I've presented a list of beat subdivisions, even and odd, from simplest to most complex, showing a one-measure example of each one.

Eighth Notes – Two Per Beat:

There shouldn't be much that I need to tell you about these. Sometimes eighth notes work best as all downstrokes, especially at tempos slower than 150 BPM and when playing repeated notes. If you get much faster than 150 BPM, alternate picking becomes very handy. If you feel like you can't get your notes sounding even when you switch to alternate picking, go in the corner and practice all up-stokes for a total of six hours. That ought to take care of it.

Triplets – Three Per Beat:

Triplets are the most simple type of tuplets. I'll begin with what I consider the simplest triplet: the eighth note triplet. Traditionally, when you subdivide in odd numbers, your picking hand will continue in an alternating fashion so that beat 1 begins with a down stroke and beat 2 begins with an up stroke. The beats alternate in this fashion. Below is a simple example, with picking indications.

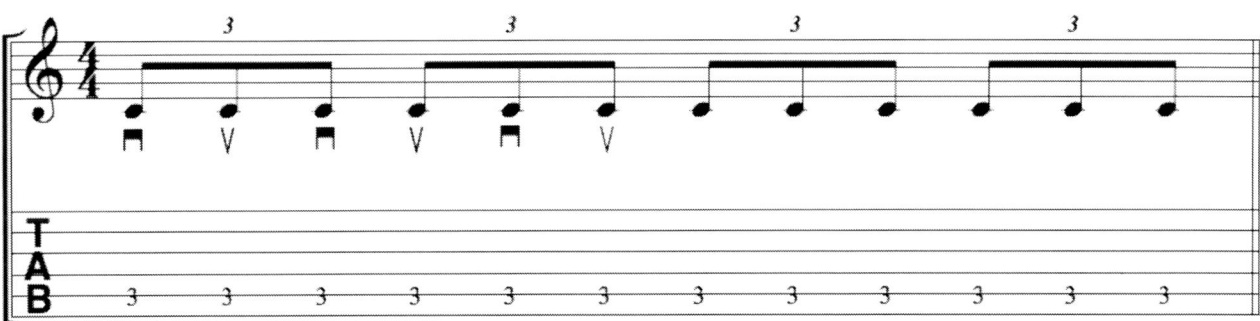

Now, we'll look at a more musical example in my favorite mode, D Dorian. I haven't bothered with picking indications here, because at least a few strategies will work and you'll have your own idea of what feels easier, depending on whether you're more inclined toward alternate picking or economy picking.

If we take a steady row of triplets on one pitch and tie each group of two notes together, we get the rhythm below. I left the upstroke indications in so you can clearly see why it's a good idea to use downstrokes when playing it. It helps you keep time. If you keep the 8th note triplet pulse in your head and line up your downstrokes and your silent upstrokes with it, you'll have it just right.

The tied eighth note triplet rhythm above is actually a quarter note triplet pulse. Here is how quarter note triplets are written:

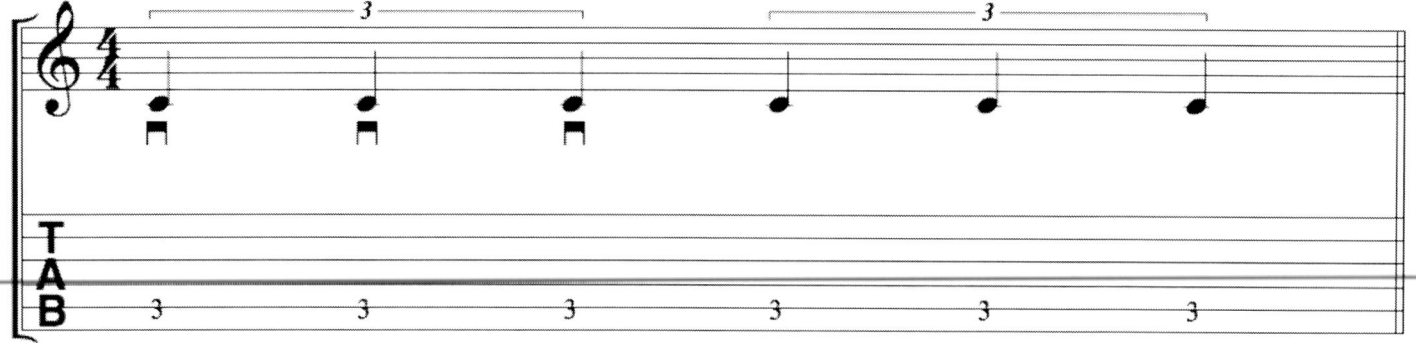

16th Notes – Four Per Beat:

We've been dealing with sixteenth notes for a good portion of this book. They are typically alternate picked.

Here is a musical example:

Quintuplets – Five Per Beat:

Quintuplets are quite a bit less common than triplets, but very musically interesting. They can add a special sense of fluidity to a rhythmic statement. People are often a bit intimidated by the idea of dividing the beat into five equal parts but as it has been with rhythm so far, language will prove to be a big help. Tap your foot in a steady quarter note pulse and repeat the word hippopotamus on each beat, taking care to get the syllables as evenly divided as possible. Now tap your hands on these syllables, alternating left and right. The first hippopotamus should begin with the right hand and the second hippopotamus should begin with the left hand. Now you can clearly hear the quintuplet pulse.

Here is a simple example with picking indications. Make sure to really accent the first note of each quintuplet group. In other words, bring out the hip in hippopotamus. Your beats will alternate beginning with downstrokes and upstrokes.

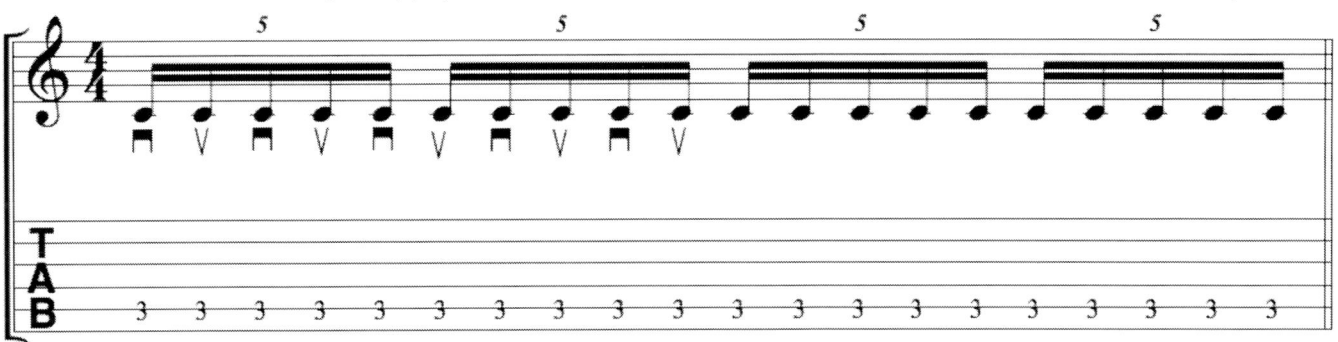

Here is a more musical example. Again, make sure that you really accent the first note of each beat and tap your foot to the quarter note pulse. Really make sure all your notes of equal rhythmic value. Experiment with picking direction, hammer-ons, pull-offs, etc.

The same way we were able to cut our 8th note triplets down to quarter note triplets by tying every group of two notes to one another, we can tie our quintuplets in the same fashion. This gives us five notes in the space of two beats. It's a peculiar sound and to the untrained ear, it can sound like somebody is playing with a complete disregard for the tempo.

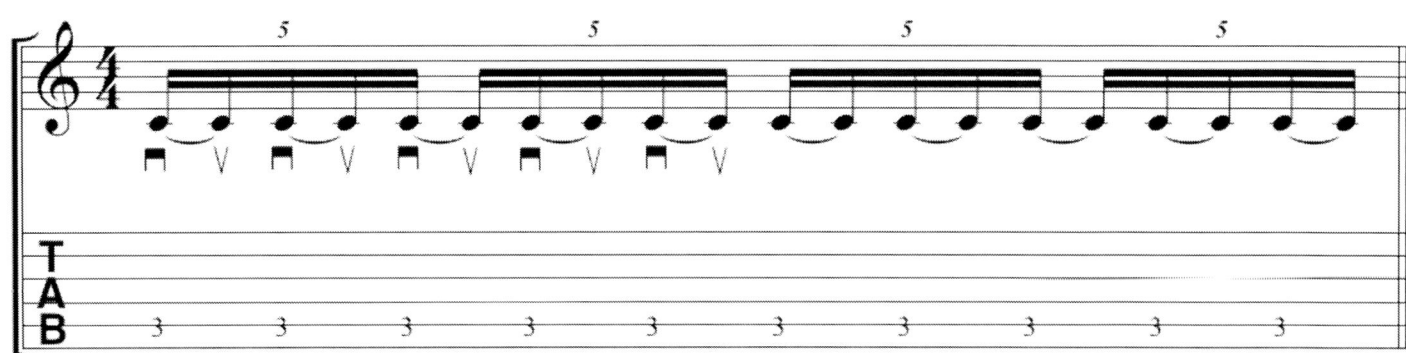

This pulse can be referred to as an 8th note quintuplet grouping. It could also be called a '5 over 2' grouping. It would typically be written out like this:

Sextuplets – Six Per Beat:

When you have three 16th notes fitting into the space allotted for two 16th notes, it's called a sixteenth note triplet. If you have two of those units in a row, within one beat, they are beamed together and called sextuplets. In other words, a sextuplet unit is made up of six 16th notes in the space of four 16th notes. They behave the same as triplets. Below is a simple example:

And a musical example:

Septuplets – Seven Per Beat:

Septuplets are about as far out as I like to take things. I'm not the slowest player but I'm certainly not the fastest and the beat has to be moving pretty slow for me to even be able to fit in septuplets. Beyond these we have 32nd notes, nontuplets (nine notes to a beat), then you're looking at 32nd note quintuplets and so on. In my 25 years of playing, I still haven't gone there and it honestly hasn't hurt me. Here's the alternate picking scheme for septuplets. As usual, accent the first note of each beat.

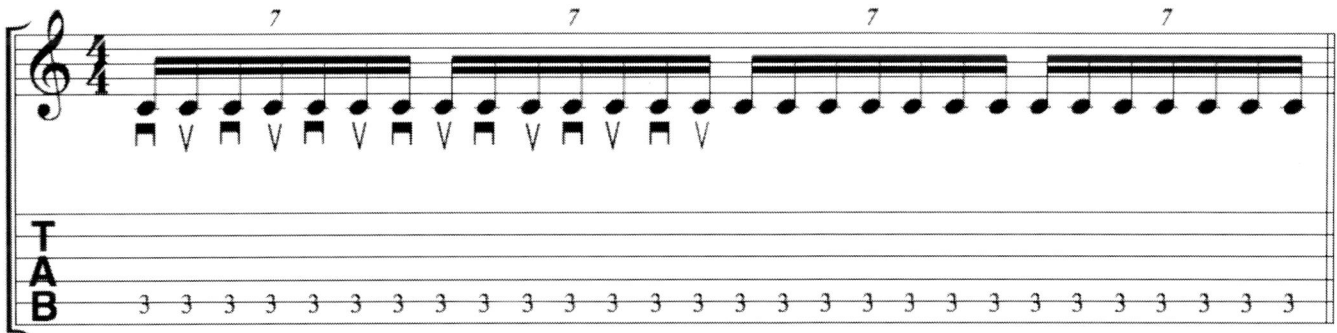

Here's a nice musical example:

As you may have guessed, we can tie each group of two notes in order to cut the speed in half and get seven notes evenly distributed among two beats. Neat!

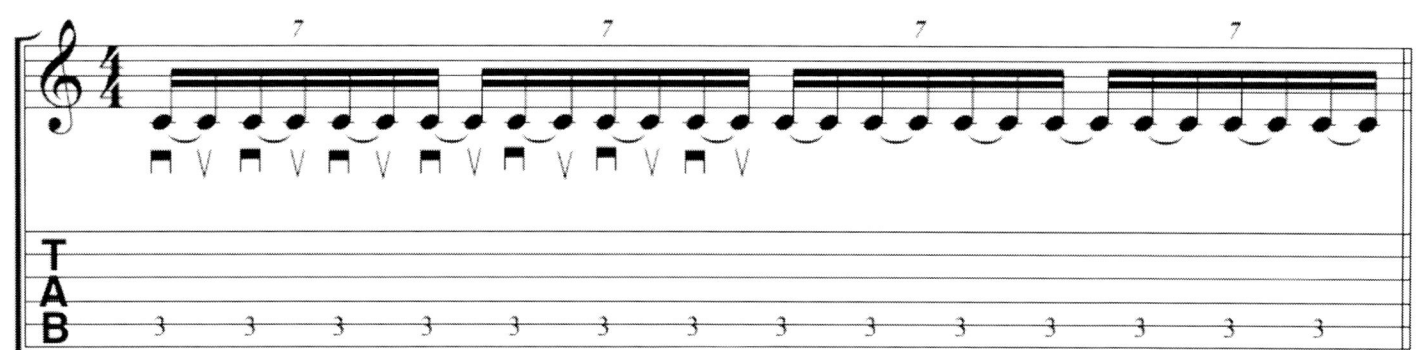

That would normally be notated like so:

In conclusion, if you want to be able to work this sort of rhythmically rich material into your music, you'll want to spend some serious time working out easy-to-play, tuplet figures that allow for a lot of speed without too much strain. As a guitarist, hammer-ons, pull-offs, sweep picking, economy picking, even tapping can all be your friends when you're trying to play really fast stuff. If you're a killer picker by nature, you may not need these devices but your sound is going to be a little more monotone than somebody who does take advantage of these "crutches".

Melodic Patterns – part 2: Musical Applications

By now, you probably have a decent arsenal of melodic patterns at your disposal. Before I go on teaching you more advanced diatonic and chromatic melodic patterns, I'd like to spend a section of this book teaching you some different ways in which you can use these patterns that you already know. It seems to me that the best way for me to do this is to present some licks that make use of these patterns while musically disguising them by various methods. I'll include a description/analysis of each lick.

Lick 1)

This lick begins with a permutation of a descending four-note coil pattern, yet it is sequenced in sextuplets. This creates an interesting rhythmic texture as the first grouping begins on beat 1, the next group begins two thirds of the way through beat 1 and the third group begins one third of the way through beat two. The fourth group fills up beat 3, but rather than doing so as a solid string of 16th notes, it's phrased as an 8th note, followed by a 16th note triplet group. At this point we lead down by one extra note to play a grouping from the original coil pattern. The first two beats of bar 2 are filled with the same permutated 4-note coil, sequenced in sextuplets. This is followed by a leap from the 2nd to the 5th of the underlying chord, which serves as a nice ending that offers variety.

Lick 2)

This lick begins with a three-note coil, sequenced in 16th notes. It sets up natural accent points on beat 1, the 'a' of beat one, the 'and' of beat 2, the "e" of beat 3 and directly on beat 4. Beat 1 of bar 2 begins a descending weaving 5ths pattern sequenced in sextuplets which creates another natural accent pattern similar to the beginning of Lick 1.

Lick 3)

This lick is the basic ascending R543 pattern, sequenced at first in a 'da diddila da diddila' rhythm, followed by a septuplet group and a couple 16th notes. The 'and' of beat 4 begins a descending four-note coil. The rhythmic phrasing lays out evenly but creates a rhythmic permutation as a result of the pattern being started halfway through the beat. Patterns can start on the 'ee' or 'a' of the beat.

Lick 4)

This one is a single statement. It is the ascending R5432R pattern, beginning on beat 1, on the 5th of D Dorian, sequenced in 16th notes, concluding on the b3rd of the Dm7 chord, on the 'and' of beat 4, bar 2. Group 1 begins on beat 1, group 2 begins on the 'and' of beat 2, group three begins on beat 4 and carries over into bar 2. Group 4 begins on the 'and' of beat 1, group 5 begins on beat 3 and closes out the bar.

Lick 5)

Here's a wild one. It starts with an ascending weaving pattern, sequenced in quintuplets. This creates a row of three quintuplet groups, each of which has an entirely different melodic contour. On beat four we cut the pattern short and tie over into beat 1 of bar 2. On the 'and' of beat 1, we begin a new pattern. It's a descending five-note coil pattern, sequenced in 16th note triplets, creating another couple of oddly contoured note groups.

This one is likely to take a little more practice time than most of the others. In order to get this up to tempos beyond 100bpm, you may want to practice using economy picking. This simply entails allowing the pick to move in the same direction as the string shifts as much as possible. Place some preferred picking indications above the notes and consistently practice the lick with the same picking strategy to a metronome. If you find something wrong with your strategy and you find a plausible alternative, go with that. Just be confident that I haven't provided you with something impossible to play.

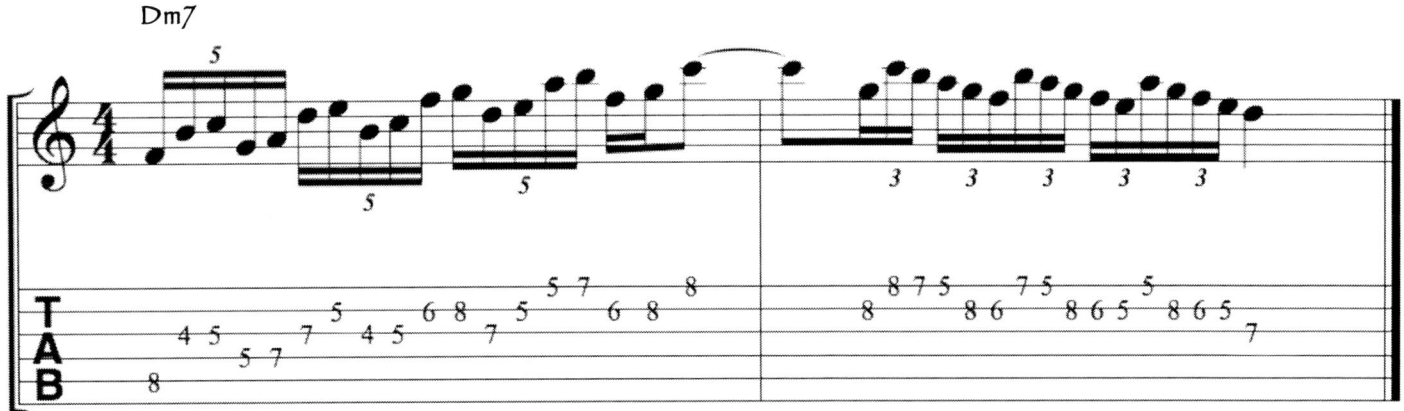

Lick 6)

Here's another quintuplet heavy lick that applies a couple four-note patterns. Bar 1 makes use of the descending, inverse weaving 3rds pattern and ties over to bar 2, which makes use of the descending weaving 6ths pattern. When you get these types of licks up to speed, you'll find that the rhythmic content sounds very rich and bubbly, especially when quintuplets are involved. As far as working this lick up to tempo goes, everything I stated above the previous lick holds true, and will hold true for almost anything you want to play.

Lick 7)

This one works a five against four scheme but does so by making use of a grouping made up of two 16th notes and a sixteenth note triplet group. We're running a simple three note pattern through this particular rhythmic gauntlet and get some very nice resulting contours to our beat groupings in bar 2. Bar 1 makes brief use of the descending R543 pattern, sequenced in sextuplets, with a couple notes added at the end.

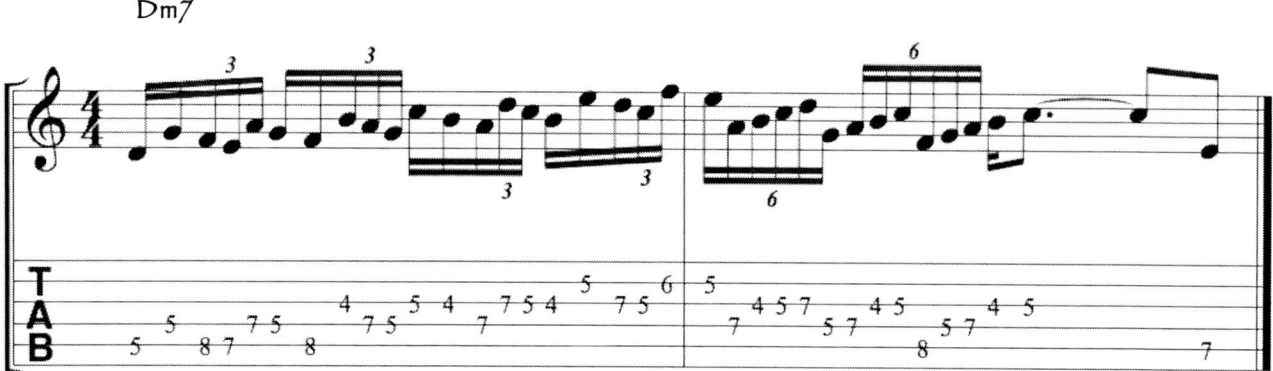

Lick 8)

OK, here's an easier one. We begin halfway through beat 1 with a three-note pattern of diatonically descending arpeggios sequenced in 16th notes, and follow it through to the 'e' of beat 3 in bar 2. We find the natural accents points of bar 1 on the 'and' of beat 1, the 'e' of beat 2, directly on beat 3, on the 'e' of beat 3 and on the 'and' of beat 4. In bar 2, they land on the 'e' of beat 1 and directly on beat 2.

Lick 9)

This lick reminds me of something Zappa might have written or improvised. He was a fan of this sort of rhythmically off-kilter phrasing. We begin on the 'a' of beat 1 in bar 1 with the descending weaving 6ths pattern, sequenced for a couple beats in sextuplets. In the final beat of bar 1, we continue the pattern for a beat in 16th notes before continuing in quintuplets for a beat in bar 2. We wrap it up with a simple statement.

Lick 10)

This lick is a wacky idea. It's the R5432R six-note pattern sequenced in Da Diddilas. All of the sudden it becomes far less apparent to the listener that we are using a pattern. It sounds a lot more random than it is and that has it's advantages. The only difference between music and noise is that music makes sense. On what levels it makes sense is up to the performer and their decision making in this area greatly influences the reaction of the listener.

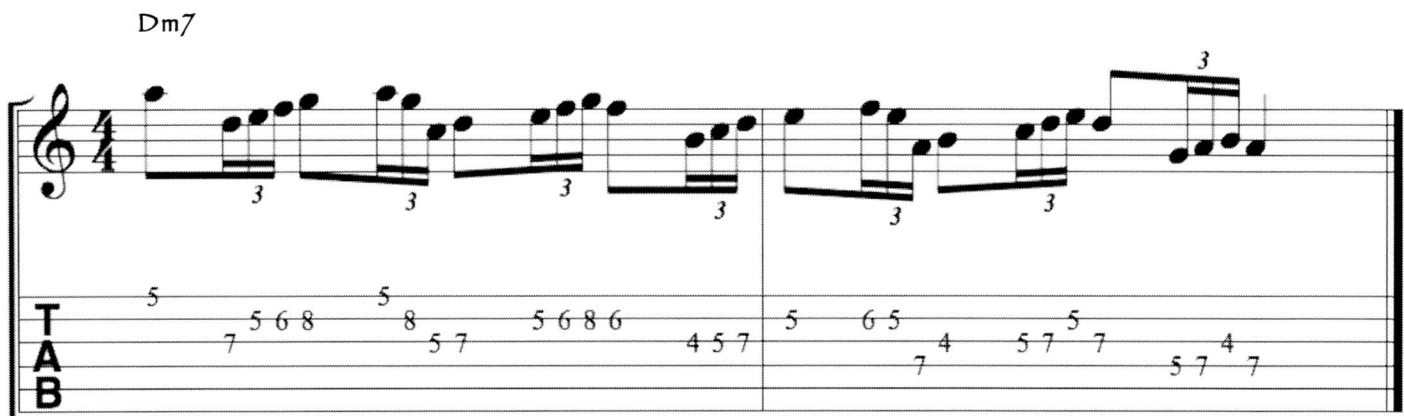

Note: I wrote these licks without the use of string bending, hammer ons, pull-off and slides. This will allow you to experiment, replacing normally articulated notes with anything you wish to use. Any tones that are a scale step apart are easily replaced with a string bend. Notes more than a scale step apart can be slid to and fro, which might mean that you'll have to move a note from one string to another. Hammer-ons and pull-offs can be used at will.

NON-DIATONIC HARMONY – Part 1: Secondary Dominant Chords

Upon looking at the harmonic minor scale, we learned that the original b7th of the natural minor was raised by a half step to become a major seventh and that the reason for doing this was in order to place a V7 chord on the 5th interval, rather than the usual Vm. Dominant chords create a very strong resolution when moving 2½ steps up or 3½ steps down. The reason for this is as follows:

The major third of the V7 chord leads a half step up to the root of the corresponding I (major or minor) while at the same time, the b7th of the V7 chord leads either a half-step down to the 3rd of the corresponding I (major), or a whole step down to the b3rd of the Im. To top it off, these two operative notes in the dominant chord are a tri-tone apart from one another, which happens to be the most dissonant interval available to us. So, when these arguing notes pull away from one another, naturally, there's a sense of relief.

This was well understood by composers going back even a little before J.S. Bach. They liked the effect so much that they invented a whole new scale to use, just to have access to the same effect. Before long, somebody started wondering why you couldn't approach any chord in the key by its own borrowed dominant chord. They ultimately found no reason why not to do so and the effect sounded great. This came to be known as the concept of secondary dominant chords. Below is a table that shows the complete secondary dominant chord relationships in all twelve major keys. These can be used the same way in relative minor and other relative modes.

	V7	V7 of IIm	V7 of IIIm	V7 of IV	V7 of V	V7 of VIm	bV7 of VIIm7b5
C Major	G7 – C	A7 – Dm	B7 – Em	C7 – F	D7 – G	E7 – Am	F7 – Bm7b5
G Major	D7 – G	E7 – Am	F#7 – Bm	G7 – C	A7 – D	B7 – Em	C7 – F#m7b5
D Major	A7 – D	B7 – Em	C#7 – F#m	D7 – G	E7 – A	F#7 – Bm	G7 – C#m7b5
A Major	E7 – A	F#7 – Bm	G#7 – C#m	A7 – D	B7 – E	C#7 – F#m	D7 – G#m7b5
E Major	B7 – E	C#7 – F#m	D#7 – G#m	E7 – A	F#7 – B	G#7 – C#m	A7 – D#m7b5
B Major	F#7 – B	G#7 – C#m	A#7 – D#m	B7 – E	C#7 – F#	D#7 – G#m	E7 – A#m7b5
Gb Major	Db7 – Gb	Eb7 – Abm	F7 – Bbm	Gb7 – Cb	Ab7 – Db	Bb7 – Ebm	B7 – Fm7b5
Db Major	Ab7 – Db	Bb7 – Ebm	C7 – Fm	Db7 – Gb	Eb7 – Ab	F7 – Bbm	Gb – Cm7b5
Ab Major	Eb7 – Ab	F7 – Bbm	G7 – Cm	Ab7 – Db	Bb7 – Eb	C7 – Fm	Db7 – Gm7b5
Eb Major	Bb7 – Eb	C7 – Fm	D7 – Gm	Eb7 – Ab	F7 – Bb	G7 – Cm	Ab7 – Dm7b5
Bb Major	F7 – Bb	G7 – Cm	A7 – Dm	Bb7 – Eb	C7 – F	D7 – Gm	Eb7 – Am7b5
F Major	C7 – F	D7 – Gm	E7 – Am	F7 – Bb	G7 – C	A7 – Dm	Bb7 – Em7b5

It should be noted that the first column, simply labeled V7, is made up of regular dominant chords as these fit entirely within the key and resolve directly to the I chord. They are NOT secondary dominant chords. However, the other six columns are all made up of secondary dominant chords. A good exercise to familiarize yourself with the sound and function of these chords is to play straight through each row. Aside from the VII chord column, I wrote the destination chords as triads, but in practice they can be 7th chords or anything else.

Each of these secondary dominant chords contains at least one note that is not a member of the key in which we're working. When we use all of our secondary dominant chords, we are making use of all 12 notes. The goal is to know which secondary dominant chords produce which chromatic tones. I can't emphasize just how useful it is to know this by heart.

For improvising musicians who don't know this really well, a secondary dominant chord within a progression can be like a thorn in their side, never being quite sure how to melodically treat it. For somebody who has a good grasp on which scale tone is altered in relation to any given secondary dominant chord, any appearance of one in a progression is an opportunity to shine, as they know exactly how to highlight what makes the chord unique to the key.

The table below illustrates which note(s) of each secondary dominant chord serve as a chromatic note and what that note is, in relation to the key center. Memorize this and make immediate use of it!

Secondary Dominant Chord	Operative Chord-Tone	Corresponding Scale-Tone
V7 of I	N/A	N/A
V7 of IIm	3rd	b2nd
V7 of IIIm	3rd & 5th	#2nd & #4th
V7 of IV	b7th	b7th
V7 of V	3rd	#4th
V7 of VIm	3rd	#5th
bV7 of VIIm7b5	b7th	b3rd

In some cases the idea of the secondary dominant approach is extended out to include the m7 or m7b5 chord (depending on whether you're approaching a major or a minor destination) leading to the V7 chord and ultimately to the scale-tone chord destination. In these cases, the secondary dominant approach becomes the secondary II-V approach. The table below illustrates these relationships in all twelve keys.

	IIm7 V7 of I	IIm7b5 V7 of IIm	IIm7b5 V7 of IIIm	IIm7 V7 of IV	IIm7 V7 of V	IIm7b5 V7 of VIm	bV7 of VIIm7b5
C Major	Dm7 G7 C	Em7b5 A7 Dm	F#m7b5 B7 Em	Gm7 C7 F	Am7 D7 G	Bm7b5 E7 Am	F7 – Bm7b5
G Major	Am7 D7 G	Bm7b5 E7 Am	C#m7b5 F#7 Bm	Dm7 G7 C	Em7 A7 D	F#m7b5 B7 Em	C7 – F#m7b5
D Major	Em7 A7 D	F#m7b5 B7 Em	G#m7b5 C#7 F#m	Am7 D7 G	Bm7 E7 A	C#m7b5 F#7 Bm	G7 – C#m7b5
A Major	Bm7 E7 A	C#m7b5 F#7 Bm	D#m7b5 G#7 C#m	Em7 A7 D	F#m7 B7 E	G#m7b5 C#7 F#m	D7 – G#m7b5
E Major	F#m7 B7 E	G#m7b5 C#7 F#m	A#m7b5 D#7 G#m	Bm7 E7 A	C#m7 F#7 B	D#m7b5 G#7 C#m	A7 – D#m7b5
B Major	C#m7 F#7 B	D#m7b5 G#7 C#m	E#m7b5 A#7 D#m	F#m7 B7 E	G#m7 C#7 F#	A#m7b5 D#7 G#m	E7 – A#m7b5
Gb Major	Abm7 Db7 Gb	Bbm7b5 Eb7 Abm	Cm7b5 F7 Bbm	Dbm7 Gb7 Cb	Ebm7 Ab7 Db	Fm7b5 Bb7 Ebm	B7 – Fm7b5
Db Major	Ebm7 Ab7 Db	Fm7b5 Bb7 Ebm	Gm7b5 C7 Fm	Abm7 Db7 Gb	Bbm7 Eb7 Ab	Cm7b5 F7 Bbm	Gb – Cm7b5
Ab Major	Bbm7 Eb7 Ab	Cm7b5 F7 Bbm	Dm7b5 G7 Cm	Ebm7 Ab7 Db	Fm7 Bb7 Eb	Gm7b5 C7 Fm	Db7 – Gm7b5
Eb Major	Fm7 Bb7 Eb	Gm7b5 C7 Fm	Am7b5 D7 Gm	Bbm7 Eb7 Ab	Cm7 F7 Bb	Dm7b5 G7 Cm	Ab7 – Dm7b5
Bb Major	Cm7 F7 Bb	Dm7b5 G7 Cm	Em7b5 A7 Dm	Fm7 Bb7 Eb	Gm7 C7 F	Am7b5 D7 Gm	Eb7 – Am7b5
F Major	Gm7 C7 F	Am7b5 D7 Gm	Bm7b5 E7 Am	Cm7 F7 Bb	Dm7 G7 C	Ebm7b5 A7 Dm	Bb7 – Em7b5

CHORD PROGRESSIONS – part 5: Using Secondary Approaches

Now that we've learned how and why these secondary V and II-V approaches work so well, let's start using them. I'll start by presenting a very common, very simple diatonic pop chord progression in a generic measure table. The measures can be however many beats you want as long as they are equal to one another.

	Measure 1:	Measure 2:	Measure 3:	Measure 4:
Original:	C	G	Am	F
Variation 1:	C D7	G E7	Am C7	F G7
Variation 2:	C Am7 D7	G Bm7b5 E7	Am Gm7 C7	F Dm7 G7
Variation 3:	C D7	G Bm7b5 E7	Am C7	F Dm7 G7
Variation 4:	C Am7 D7	G E7	Am Gm7 C7	F G7
Variation 5:	C	G E7	Am Gm7 C7	F
Variation 6:	C D7	G Bm7b5 E7	Am	F G7
Variation 7:	C Am7 D7	G	Am C7	F Dm7 G7
Variation 8:	C Am7 D7	G E7	Am	F Dm7 G7
Variation 9:	C D7	G Bm7b5 E7	Am Gm7 C7	F

Here's a very common diatonic jazz progression with some possible variations, making use of the secondary approach concept. Notice that I took some extra liberties in measures 3 and 4 in variations 5-8. In measure three, I replaced Dm7 to D7 with a whole bar of D7. In measure 4, I swapped a whole measure of G7 for Dm7 to G7. These are both common substitutions in old jazz and pop material.

	Measure 1:	Measure 2:	Measure 3:	Measure 4:
Original:	Cmaj7	Am7	Dm7	G7
Variation 1:	Cmaj7 E7	Am7 A7	Dm7 D7	G7
Variation 2:	C Bm7b5 E7	Am7 Em7b5 A7	Dm7 Am7 D7	G7 Dm7 G7
Variation 3:	Cmaj7 E7	Am7 Em7b5 A7	Dm7 D7	G7 Dm7 G7
Variation 4:	C Bm7b5 E7	Am7 A7	Dm7 D7	G7
Variation 5:	Cmaj7	Am7 Em7b5 A7	D7	Dm7 G7
Variation 6:	Cmaj7 Bm7b5 E7	Am7	D7	Dm7 G7
Variation 7:	Cmaj7 Bm7b5 E7	Am7 Em7b5 A7	D7	Dm7 G7
Variation 8:	Cmaj7 E7	A7	D7	Dm7 G7
Variation 9:	Cmaj7 E7	Am7 A7	Dm7 Am7 D7	G7 Dm7 G7

Now, let's look at how we might apply these secondary approaches to a basic 12-bar blues in Bb with a IIm7 V7 turnaround. Let's begin with the basic structure:

12 Bar Blues in Bb w/ IIm7-V7 Turnaround

Bb7	Eb7	Bb7	
Eb7		Bb7	
Cm7	F7	Bb7	Cm7 F7

Now we will add a couple of basic secondary dominant chords to the structure:

12 Bar Blues in Bb w/ V7 of IIm7 Approach and I-V of II-II-V Tail

Bb7	Eb7	Bb7	
Eb7		Bb7	G7
Cm7	F7	Bb7 G7	Cm7 F7

And now, if we add some secondary II-Vs, we arrive at a progression quite elusive to most guitar players: the jazzy 12-Bar Blues. I recommend transposing this progression to the eleven other available keys. It's a common one, especially in any of the flat keys.

12 Bar Blues in Bb w/ Secondary IIm7-V7s

Bb7	Eb7	Bb7	Fm7 Bb7
Eb7		Bb7	Dm7 G7
Cm7	F7	Bb7 G7	Cm7 F7

If you have a catalog of chord progressions that you hold dear, spend some time experimenting with these secondary approaches. They can breathe much life into an otherwise boring progression, but sometimes they can detract from the desired effect, with cooler sounding diatonic progressions. Use your ears and your sense of taste to decide where these might be useful in composing new material. If you are going for a really modern sound, chances are that you won't be using a lot of these but don't count me as 100% certain. You may decide that you're going to bring back the secondary approach concept and put it in a strikingly new sonic context, and voila! You have a sound all your own on which to capitalize!

The Melodic Minor Scale

The Melodic Minor scale is one of special interest to me because it's a widely misunderstood concept, even in college level education. There are a few out there who understand the governing principles and the only one I personally know of is Dr. Gerald Eskelin, an excellent educator and author whose material I recommend. He shed a lot of light on this in his book, "Lies My Music Teacher Told Me" and I recommend that you read his take on this as well as mine. He's a far more credible guy. I'd like to thank him and George Orwell, who I feel did a good job as authors, of making the point that consensus does not dictate reality. 2+2=4

The Widely Accepted Myth:

The melodic minor scale has different notes, depending on whether it is ascending or descending. Upon ascending the scale tones are R 2 b3 4 5 6 7 R. When descending, the scale tones are R b7 b6 5 4 3 2 R. In other words, only the 3rd is flat on the way up and the 3rd, 6th and 7th are all flat on the way down.

When I first heard this, I was pretty puzzled because from what I had gathered up to that point, a scale wasn't merely used as a series of notes. A scale, in terms of western music as a whole, is a family of notes that can be utilized in an astronomical amount of combinations and orders to create chords and melodic statements. Another reason this didn't make sense to me is that even in the relatively simple little Bach for guitar pieces that I'd learned, there were instances of the 'rule' not being followed.

Ten years later, I learned some basic history that opened my eyes in the aforementioned book.

A Brief History Of The Minor Scale In Classical Composition:

Way back in the day, when composers started using the harmonic minor scale (before it had it's current name) to compose minor key music, they took great issue with the sound of the 1½ step gap between the b6th and natural 7th. To them, it seemed to be a very awkward sound. They felt that things lost their melodic continuity, when leaping over said abyss. Before long they all started to agree that the harmonic minor scale me known and used as just that. They used it for chord structures.

When dealing melodically with the underlying harmonic implications of these harmonic minor-based chord progressions they had to make adjustments if they wanted to avoid the demon's gap, as we learned in the Harmonic Minor Scale section of this book. Here is a clear look at how these adjustments were made.

The Im

When writing a melody over a Im chord, they would use either a b6th and b7th or the major 6th and 7th. In most cases, in upward motion, they would use the major 6th and 7th because the major 7th serves as a leading tone to our root note. On the way down they usually used the b6th and b7th, since the b6th serves as a downward leading tone of sorts to the 5th of the key.

The IVm

At any point that they found themselves on the IVm chord, they used the b6th and b7th exclusively, regardless of melodic direction, because the IVm chord possesses the b6th of the key as its own b3rd. To use a natural 6th and 7th would cause a nasty clash, and to use a b6th and a natural 7th would be to leap over the demon's gap.

The V7

When composing melody over the V7 chord they typically used a natural 6th and 7th. The major 3rd of the V7 chord is the major 7th of the scale to which it belongs. The natural 6th ensured that no leaps would occur, but sometimes they would make use of the b6th for dramatic effect, but almost always with the absence of the 7th in the melodic passage.

So as I stated originally, in the Harmonic Minor Scale section, composers used a minor scale with an adjustable 6th and 7th degree. Harmonic context was the primary governing factor in their choice of 6th and 7th, with melodic direction being a secondary concern.

THE TRUTH ABOUT THE MELODIC MINOR SCALE:

Just like the other scales we've learned so far, it is a family of notes. The notes never change and if they do, it's because you're no longer using the melodic minor scale. Here is a table providing you with the step pattern for the scale as well as the notes for the scale in all twelve keys.

	R w	2 H	b3 w	4 w	5 w	6 w	7 H
C Melodic Minor	C	D	Eb	F	G	A	B
G Melodic Minor	G	A	Bb	C	D	E	F#
D Melodic Minor	D	E	F	G	A	B	C#
A Melodic Minor	A	B	C	D	E	F#	G#
E Melodic Minor	E	F#	G	A	B	C#	D#
B Melodic Minor	B	C#	D	E	F#	G#	A#
F# Melodic Minor	F#	G#	A	B	C#	D#	E# (F)
Db Melodic Minor	Db	Eb	Fb (E)	Gb	Ab	Bb	C
Ab Melodic Minor	Ab	Bb	Cb (B)	Db	Eb	F	G
Eb Melodic Minor	Eb	F	Gb	Ab	Bb	C	D
Bb Melodic Minor	Bb	C	Db	Eb	F	G	A
F Melodic Minor	F	G	Ab	Bb	C	D	E

Even though chord progressions aren't typically built from the melodic minor scale, it's still beneficial to look at the chords contained within the scale, given that this scale can be used as a melodic replacement of these chord types. We will be looking at the harmonic implications of this scale in more depth in the Extended Harmony section of this book. For now, here is a table of triads from the scale.

Melodic Minor Scale-Based Triad Family

INTERVAL	Root	Distance	3rd	Distance	5th	CHORD
I:	C	1½	Eb	2w	G	Cm
II:	D	1½	F	2w	A	Dm
bIII:	Eb	2w	G	2w	B	Eb+
IV:	F	2w	A	1½	C	F
V:	G	2w	B	1½	D	G
VI:	A	1½	C	1½	Eb	Ao
VII:	B	1½	D	1½	F	Bo

Melodic Minor Scale-Based 7th Chord Family

INTERVAL	Root	Distance	3rd	Distance	5th	Distance	7th	CHORD
I	C	1½	Eb	2w	G	2w	B	Cm♮7
II	D	1½	F	2w	A	1½	C	Dm7
bIII	Eb	2w	G	2w	B	1½	D	Ebmaj7#5
IV	F	2w	A	1½	C	2w	Eb	F7
V	G	2w	B	1½	D	1½	F	G7
VI	A	2w	C	1½	Eb	2w	G	Aø7
VII:	B	1½	D	1½	F	1½	A	Bø7

The following page contains a table illustrating the melodic minor scale seventh chord family. Before we look at it, I'd like to take a little space to clarify that there are multiple symbols used for certain chords. You'll notice in the following table that I have used a couple different symbols, between the numeric labels in the top row and those used in the subsequent key signature specific rows. I'm going to be totally honest and tell you that my half-diminished (aka m7b5) symbol (ø) as you can see, messes with the spacing of my rows and I'm trying to keep it clean, for the kids. This also happens with my natural symbol, so I only used these symbols in the top row.

Since the minor natural 7th chord (Im♮7), is the minor relative of the bIII+ chord, I like to use the + (aug) symbol to represent the augmented triad that's contained within the chord. I've gotten a few people wagging their finger at me about it but if they saw the symbol, they would probably play the right chord. When I say it out loud, I say "minor, natural seventh".

The point I'm making is that symbols are only symbols and you will find variation from one circle of musicians to another, so be prepared for that. Learn chord progressions from a wide range of styles and you will get to know all the common symbols and nomenclature.

Melodic Minor Scale-Based 7th Chord Family In All Twelve Keys

Im♮7	W	IIm7	H	bIIImaj7#5	W	IV7	W	V7	H	VIø7	1½	VIIø7	H
Cm+7		Dm7		Ebmaj7+		F7		G7		Am7b5		Bm7b5	
Gm+7		Am7		Bbmaj7+		C7		D7		Em7b5		F#m7b5	
Dm+7		Em7		Fmaj7+		G7		A7		Bm7b5		C#m7b5	
Am+7		Bm7		Cmaj7+		D7		E7		F#m7b5		G#m7b5	
Em+7		F#m7		Gmaj7+		A7		B7		C#m7b5		D#m7b5	
Bm+7		C#m7		Dmaj7+		E7		F#7		G#m7b5		A#m7b5	
F#m+7		G#m7		Amaj7#5		B7		C#7		D#m7b5		E#m7b5	
Dbm+7		Ebm7		Fbmaj7#5		Gb7		Ab7		Bbm7b5		Cm7b5	
Abm+7		Bbm7		Cbmaj7#5		Db7		Eb7		Fm7b5		Gm7b5	
Ebm+7		Fm7		Gbmaj7#5		Ab7		Bb7		Cm7b5		Dm7b5	
Bbm+7		Cm7		Dbmaj7#5		Eb7		F7		Gm7b5		Am7b5	
Fm+7		Gm7		Abmaj7#5		Bb7		C7		Dm7b5		Em7b5	

Improvisationally and compositionally speaking, the parent mode of the melodic minor scale can be used in correspondence with a basic minor chord, a m+7 or a m6 chord (R b3 5 6) of the same root note as the scale. To be clear, it can be used in either direction with its notes in any order.

As much work as it is, it would be a worthy endeavor to practice your entire repertoire of melodic patterns with the scale positions given on the following page. These patterns will ultimately be useful in any of the melodic minor scale modes that you will be learning further into the book. Even if this first mode of the scale doesn't sound like something that you are going to want to use, don't let that stop you from really digging into it with as much intensity as you have with the major scale and its modes. The modes of this scale bear some of the most mysterious sounds that western music has to offer.

On the following page, you will find the melodic minor scale positions along with a corresponding table of keys.

Melodic Minor Scale Positions

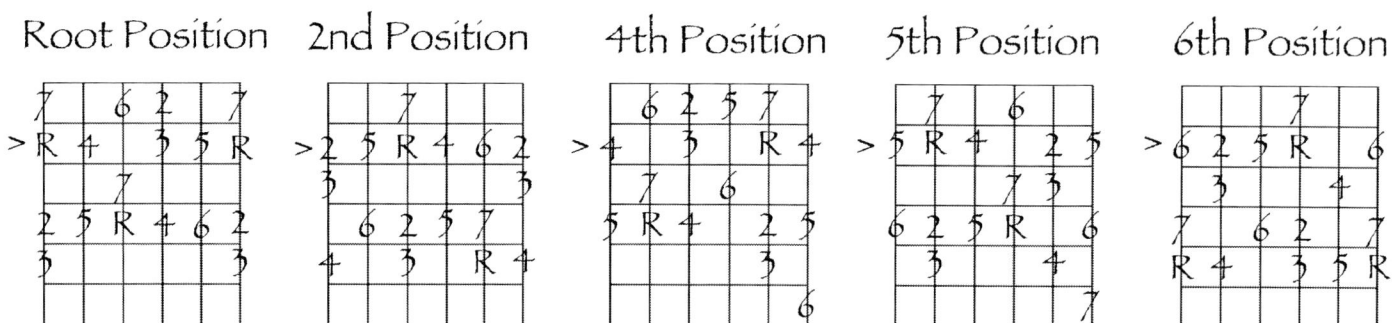

	A	E	B	F#	C#	G#	Eb	Bb	F	C	G	D
Root Pos:	5	12	7	2	9	4	11	6	13	8	3	10
2nd Pos:	7	2	9	4	11	6	13	8	3	10	5	12
4th Pos:	10	5	12	7	2	9	4	11	6	13	8	3
5th Pos:	12	7	2	9	4	11	6	13	8	3	10	5
6th Pos:	2	9	4	11	6	13	8	3	10	5	12	7

There are basically a couple types of seven-tone scales, those that build a sturdy family of chords and those that don't. The scales that build an odd or unstable family of chords (where not all of the scale tones extend outward to form an intelligible chord) are typically referred to as exotic scales. The scale tone pattern isn't particularly useful as a practice tool for exotic scales. However, it is very useful on scales like the major or melodic minor scale.

The following pages take us through the melodic minor scale-tone pattern in all positions. Play these until you can hold a conversation while playing them. This is always a good sign that you've achieved a second-nature-type inner awareness of the material.

The A Melodic Minor Scale-Tone Pattern, 6th Position, Ascending:

The A Melodic Minor Scale-Tone Pattern, 6th Position, Descending:

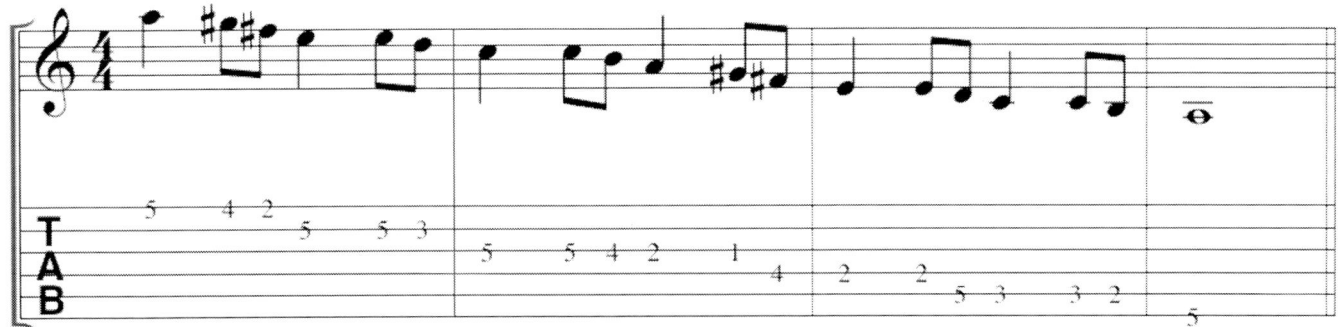

The A Melodic Minor Scale-Tone Pattern, Root Position, Ascending:

The A Melodic Minor Scale-Tone Pattern, Root Position, Descending:

The A Melodic Minor Scale-Tone Pattern, 2nd Position, Ascending:

The A Melodic Minor Scale-Tone Pattern, 2nd Position, Descending:

The A Melodic Minor Scale-Tone Pattern, 4th Position, Ascending:

The A Melodic Minor Scale-Tone Pattern, 4th Position, Descending:

The A Melodic Minor Scale-Tone Pattern, 5th Position, Ascending:

The A Melodic Minor Scale-Tone Pattern, 5th Position, Descending:

Melodic Minor Licks

The following ten licks are all based on the parent mode of the melodic minor scale and should give you a good idea of the basic melodic function and color of the melodic minor scale-tones. Be sure to analyze these licks in terms of scale tone numbers because learning a lick without this piece of the process is much like learning to quote something in a foreign language without being concerned with what it means. It won't help you have a conversation in that language and will only impress those who can't speak it at all.

Melodic Minor Scale Lick 1:

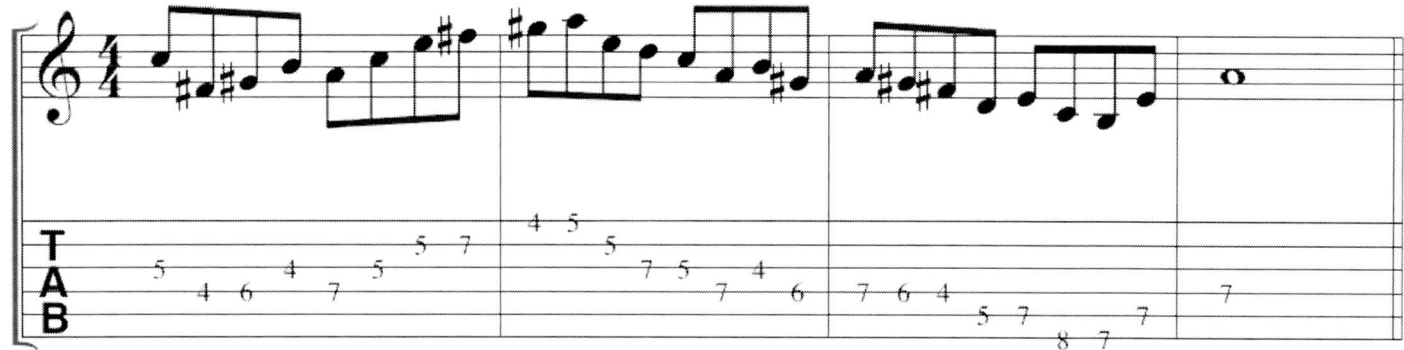

Melodic Minor Scale Lick 2:

Melodic Minor Scale Lick 3:

Melodic Minor Scale Lick 4:

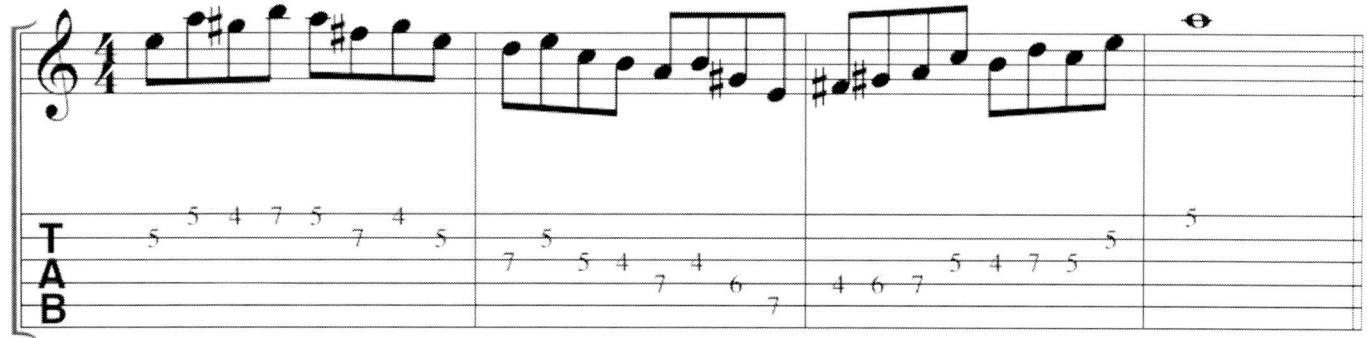

Melodic Minor Scale Lick 5:

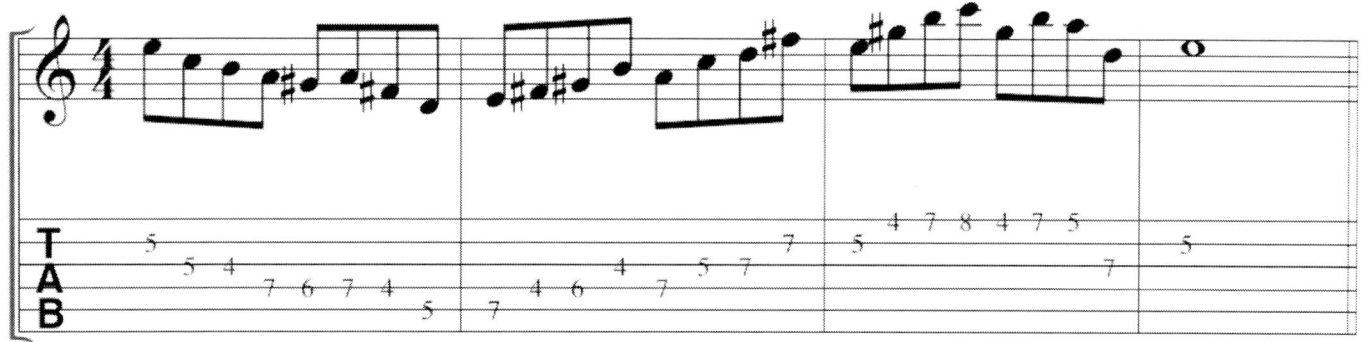

Melodic Minor Scale Lick 6:

Melodic Minor Scale Lick 7:

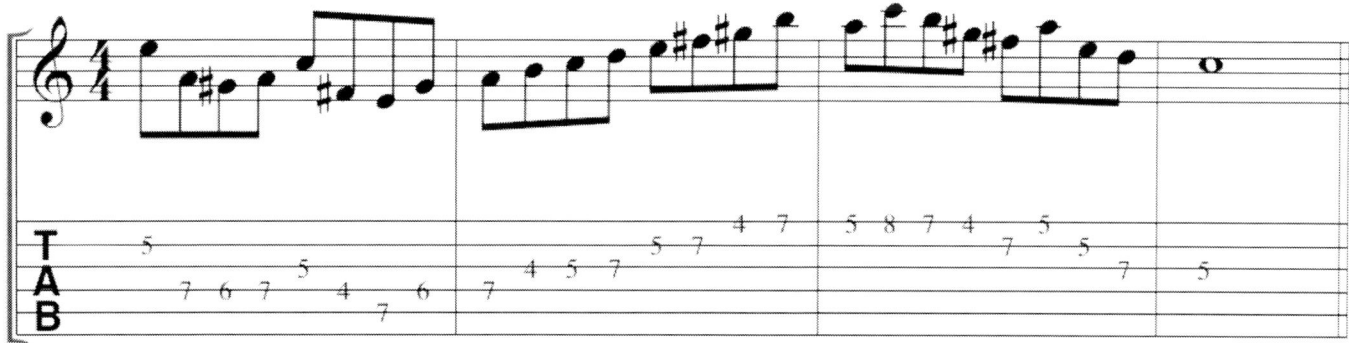

Melodic Minor Scale Lick 8:

Melodic Minor Scale Lick 9:

Melodic Minor Scale Lick 10:

The Modes of the Melodic Minor Scale

As we saw with the modes of the Harmonic Minor scale, not all of these modes are going to be especially useful. In the case of the Melodic Minor scale, we are looking at a slightly more useable group of modes. We have four modes of common use, two that get used occasionally, and one that has pretty much been deemed utterly useless. Below is a modal table so you can see the intervallic design of each mode, clearly.

Mode:	R		2		3		4		5		6		7	
C Melodic Minor	C	w	D	h	Eb	w	F	w	G	w	A	w	B	h
D Dorian b2nd	D	h	Eb	w	F	w	G	w	A	w	B	h	C	w
Eb Lydian #5th	Eb	w	F	w	G	w	A	w	B	h	C	w	D	h
F Lydian b7th	F	w	G	w	A	w	B	h	C	w	D	h	Eb	w
G Mixolydian b6th	G	w	A	w	B	h	C	w	D	h	Eb	w	F	w
A Aeolian b5th	A	w	B	h	C	w	D	h	Eb	w	F	w	G	w
B Super-Locrian	B	h	C	w	D	h	Eb	w	F	w	G	w	A	w

I'll start by getting the least useable modes out of the way before we get into descriptions, scale positions and example licks for the common-use melodic minor modes. In fact, I think I'll start at the very least useable of all melodic minor modes:

Mode II: Dorian b2nd

This mode is a complete piece of garbage. In my twenty some years of playing guitar, I've have never created, discovered or learned of any useable application for this mode. You can go ahead and try all you want to make this mode sound like anything but tedious confusion. The way the b2nd and the major 6th in this context seem to just absolutely hate each other is almost comical. I welcome the chance to be proven wrong, as I am all about having a larger arsenal of scales to apply and imply.

Mode VI: Aeolian b5th (Locrian ♮2nd)

This mode does actually have a viable chordal context application. It can be used over a m7b5 (half-diminished) chord. In other words, it can sometimes work in place of the Locrian mode. Sometimes you may run into a m7b5 chord whose ultimate destination is a *major* chord a whole-step down, as opposed to its traditional minor chord resolution. This is your best opportunity to take advantage of this particular mode. I haven't bothered with positions and example licks for this mode because it can be used by simple means of substitution. The rule goes as follows:

Use the parent mode of melodic minor based off of the b3rd of your corresponding m7b5 chord.

Examples: Dm7b5 = F Melodic Minor
F#m7b5 = A Melodic Minor
Bbm7b5 = Db (C#) Melodic Minor

Mode III: Lydian #5th

This one is also useable to some degree. It relates directly to the maj7#5 (maj7+) chord. If you don't play modern jazz, you are very unlikely to run into this chord type in the process of building your song repertoire and you'll be unlikely to find a musical use for it in your own tunes. However, if you are interested in jazz later than 1960, you'll certainly run into the occasional maj7+ chord. It's good to bear in mind that this chord is essentially a bass-note with a major triad, one major 3rd above it. When you do run into this chord type, follow this simple rule:

Use the parent mode of melodic minor based 1½ steps beneath your corresponding maj7+ chord

Examples: Fmaj7+ = D Melodic Minor
Amaj7+ = F# Melodic Minor
Dbmaj7+ = Bb Melodic Minor

That concludes what we could consider the outer modes of the melodic minor scale. The following pages are a rather lengthy section on the remaining three of the four inner modes of the scale. (We already covered mode I) Do NOT skim over it. These four modes are truly gems, loaded with musical potential most commonly found in jazz, but used in rock, soul, etc by some of the masters in very striking ways. If you want to create rock music that has really distinguishing qualities, harmonically (e.g. like Led Zeppelin) you want to get to know every scale and mode that you can. If you want to play jazz at all, these are absolutely necessary tools to understand.

MELODIC MINOR MODE IV - Lydian Dominant: R 2 3 #4 5 6 b7

This mode has a rather mysterious and other-worldly sound to it. When you first get accustomed to this scale, you may find it sounds really strange, especially on a straight descend. Don't worry about how odd it might sound to you. Just let your ears get to know the sound as it is a really commonly used mode. You'll find it in jazz, rock, soul, R&B and even the occasional country ballad. It has some really interesting features that we'll be learning how to use in the course of the example licks. To start, here are the scale positions and the corresponding table of keys. Following that, we will look at the scale-tone pattern in all five positions and ten example licks in the 5th position.

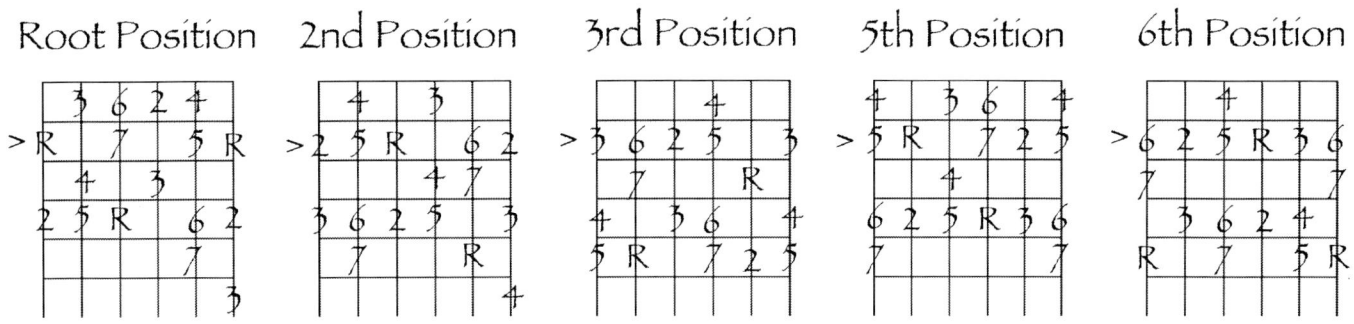

	D	A	E	B	Gb	Db	Ab	Eb	Bb	F	C	G
Root Position:	10	5	12	7	2	9	4	11	6	13	8	3
2nd Position:	12	7	2	9	4	11	6	13	8	3	10	5
3rd Position:	2	9	4	11	6	13	8	3	10	5	12	7
5th Position:	5	12	7	2	9	4	11	6	13	8	3	10
6th Position:	7	2	9	4	11	6	13	8	3	10	5	12

D Lydian Dominant, Scale-Tone Pattern, 3rd Position, Ascending:

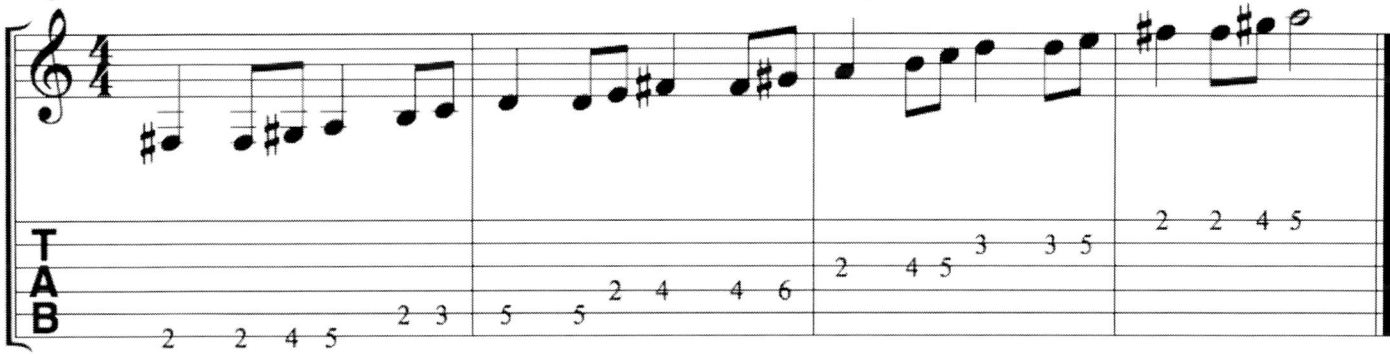

D Lydian Dominant, Scale-Tone Pattern, 3rd Position, Descending:

D Lydian Dominant, Scale-Tone Pattern, 5th Position, Ascending:

D Lydian Dominant, Scale-Tone Pattern, 5th Position, Descending:

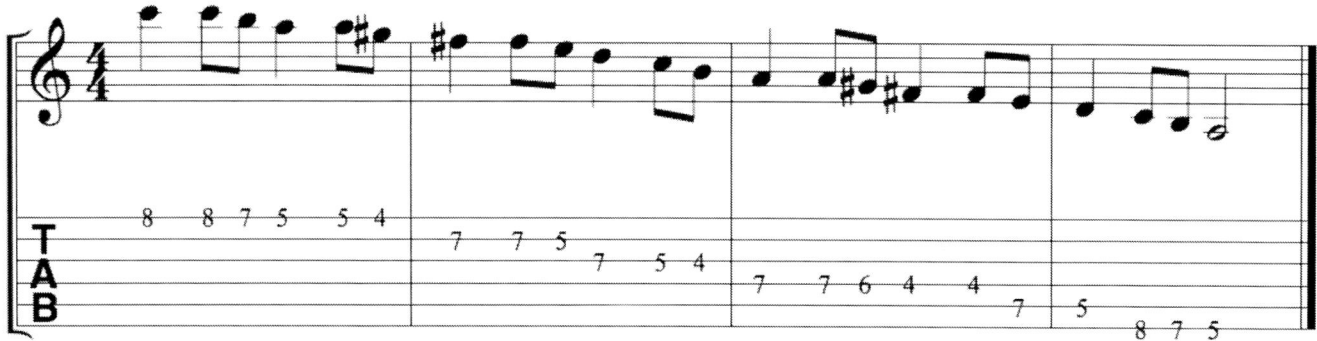

D Lydian Dominant, Scale-Tone Pattern, 6th Position, Ascending:

D Lydian Dominant, Scale-Tone Pattern, 6th Position, Descending:

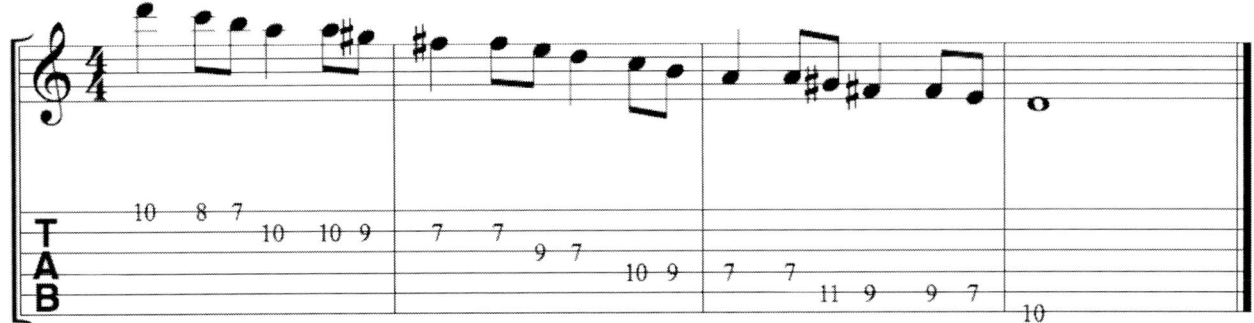

D Lydian Dominant, Scale-Tone Pattern, Root Position, Ascending:

D Lydian Dominant, Scale-Tone Pattern, Root Position, Descending:

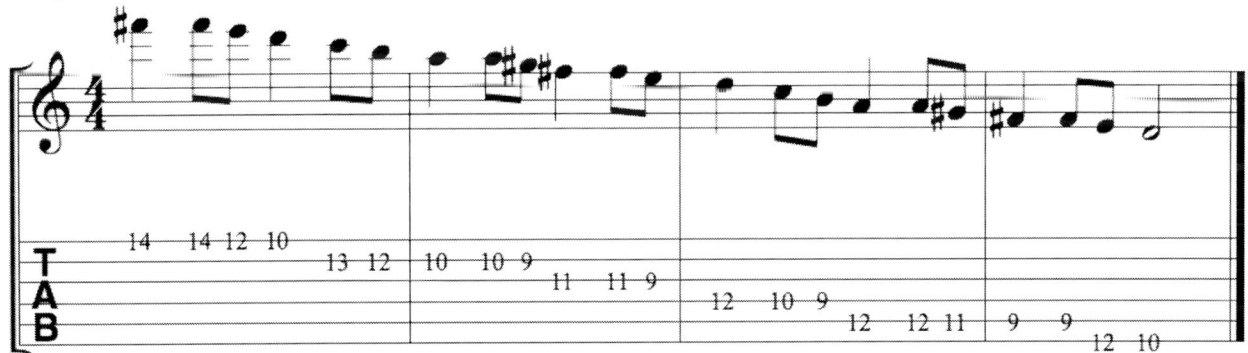

D Lydian Dominant, Scale-Tone Pattern, 2nd Position, Ascending:

D Lydian Dominant, Scale-Tone Pattern, 2nd Position, Descending:

D Lydian Dominant Lick 1:

D Lydian Dominant Lick 2:

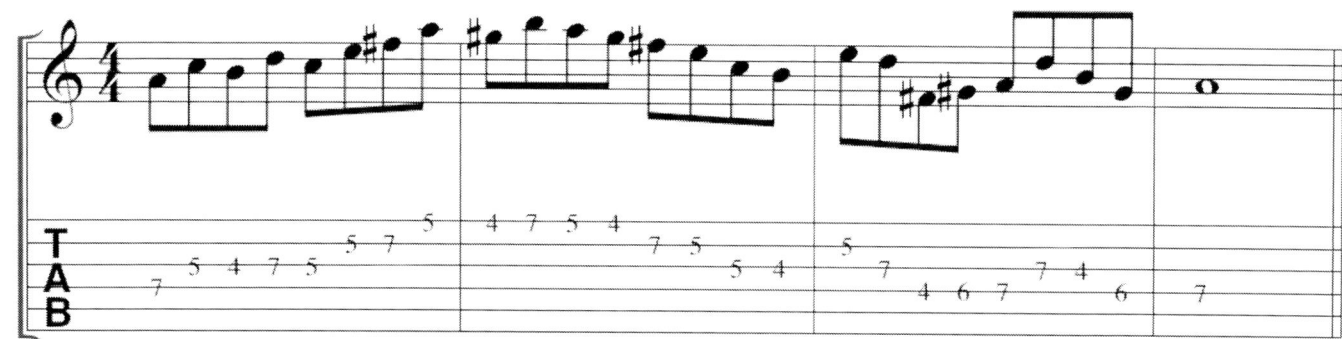

D Lydian Dominant Lick 3:

D Lydian Dominant Lick 4:

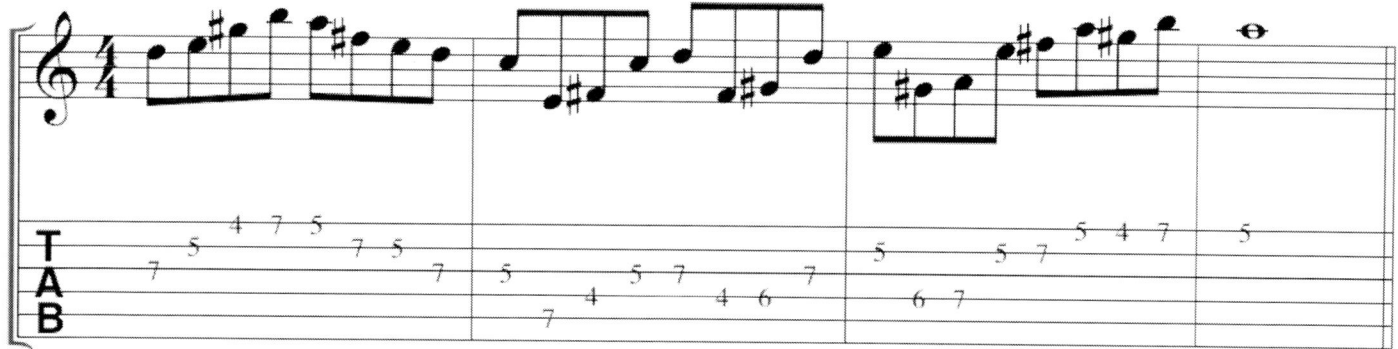

D Lydian Dominant Lick 5:

D Lydian Dominant Lick 6:

D Lydian Dominant Lick 7:

D Lydian Dominant Lick 8:

D Lydian Dominant Lick 9:

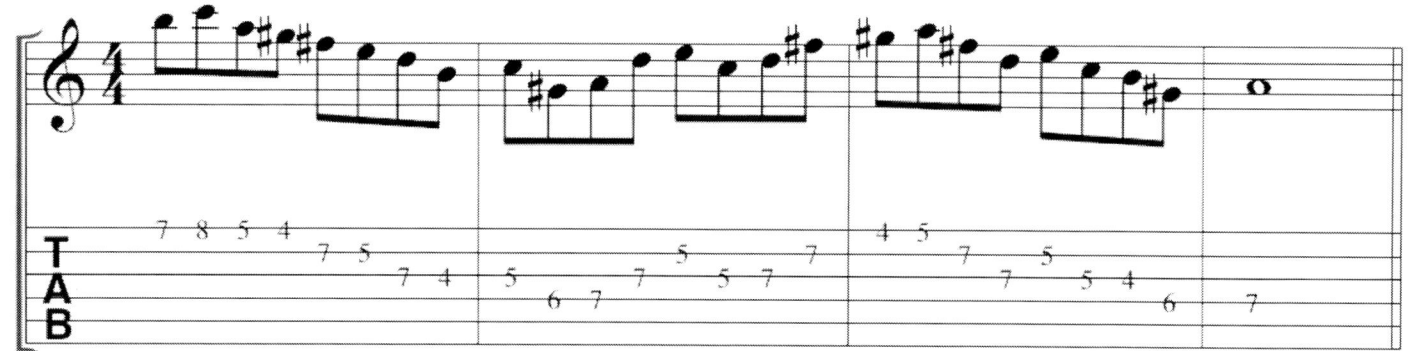

D Lydian Dominant Lick 10:

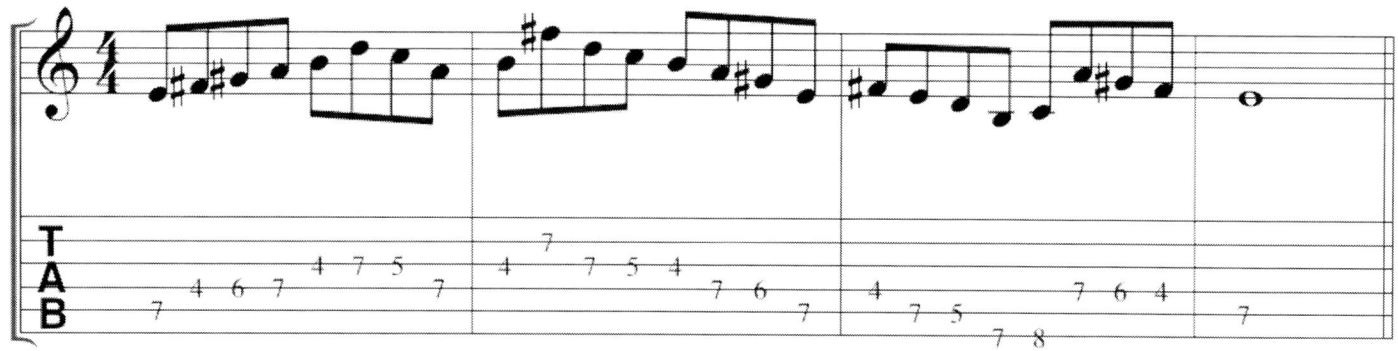

MELODIC MINOR MODE V – Mixolydian b6th: R 2 3 4 5 b6 b7

This mode has a very interesting effect, as the lower tetrachord (R 2 3 4 5) is major, but the upper tetrachord (5 b6 b7 R) is like that of natural minor scale. It can come across as sounding somber, romantic, epic and exotic. It has various applications, harmonically speaking, that we'll be getting into very soon. Until then, spend some time internalizing the sounds and shapes associated with it, by means of the material presented below and on the following few pages.

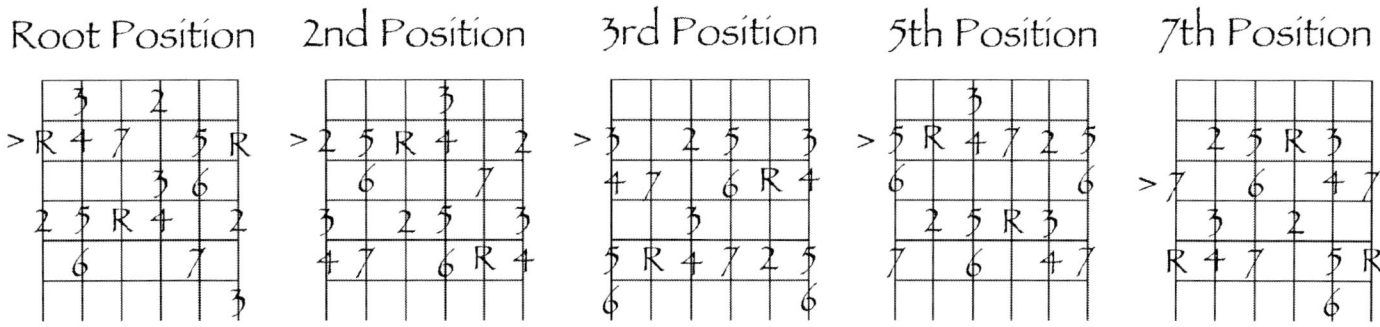

	E	B	F#	C#	Ab	Eb	Bb	F	C	G	D	A
Root Position:	12	7	2	9	4	11	6	13	8	3	10	5
2nd Position:	2	9	4	11	6	13	8	3	10	5	12	7
3rd Position:	4	11	6	13	8	3	10	5	12	7	2	9
5th Position:	7	2	9	4	11	6	13	8	3	10	5	12
7th Position:	10	5	12	7	2	9	4	11	6	13	8	3

E Mixolydian b6th, Scale-Tone Pattern, 2nd Position, Ascending:

E Mixolydian b6th, Scale-Tone Pattern, 2nd Position, Descending:

E Mixolydian b6th, Scale-Tone Pattern, 3rd Position, Ascending:

E Mixolydian b6th, Scale-Tone Pattern, 3rd Position, Descending:

E Mixolydian b6th, Scale-Tone Pattern, 5th Position, Ascending:

E Mixolydian b6th, Scale-Tone Pattern, 5th Position, Descending:

E Mixolydian b6th, Scale-Tone Pattern, 7th Position, Ascending:

E Mixolydian b6th, Scale-Tone Pattern, 7th Position, Descending:

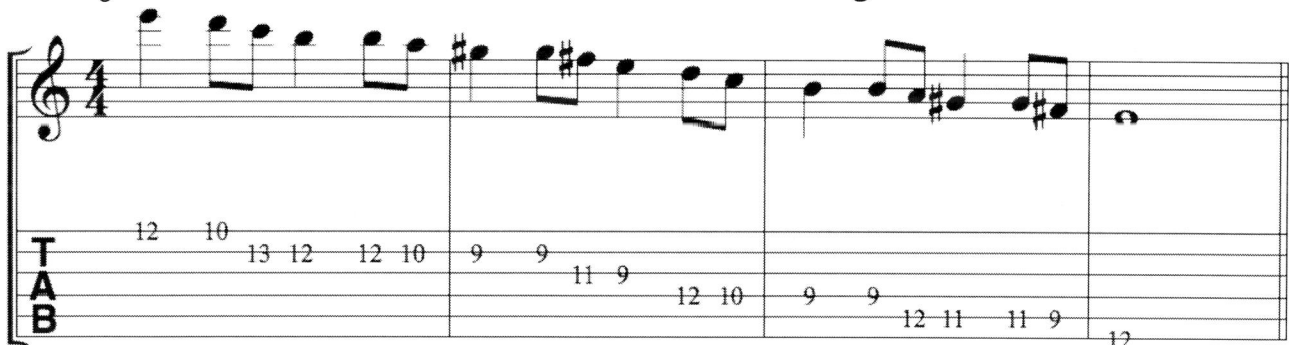

E Mixolydian b6th, Scale-Tone Pattern, Root Position, Ascending:

E Mixolydian b6th, Scale-Tone Pattern, Root Position, Descending:

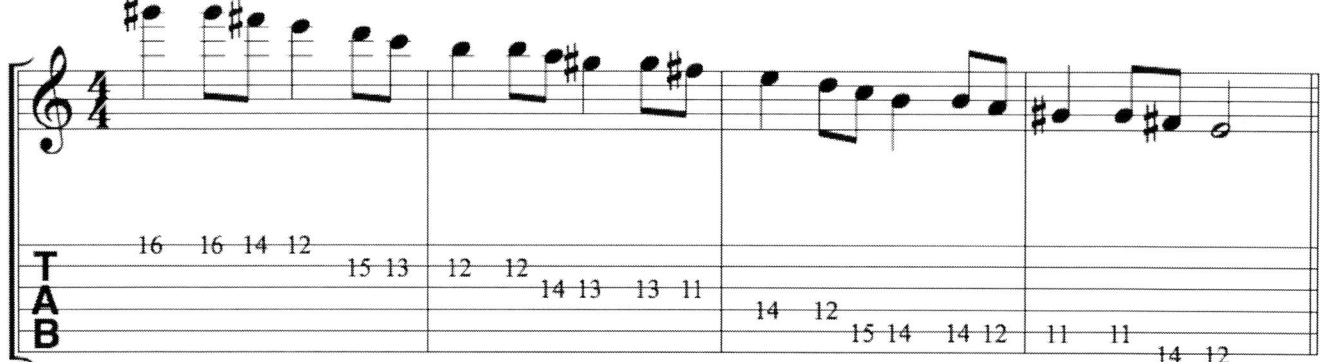

E Mixolydian b6th Lick 1:

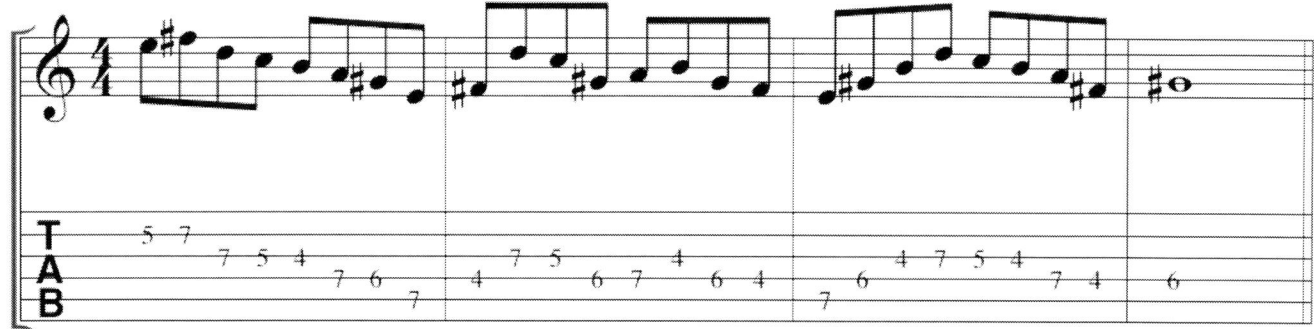

E Mixolydian b6th Lick 2:

E Mixolydian b6th Lick 3:

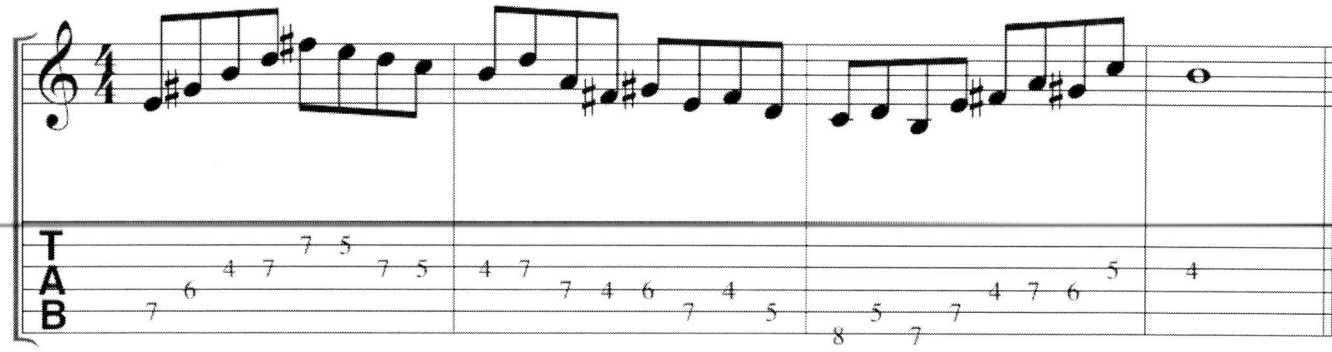

E Mixolydian b6th Lick 4:

E Mixolydian b6th Lick 5:

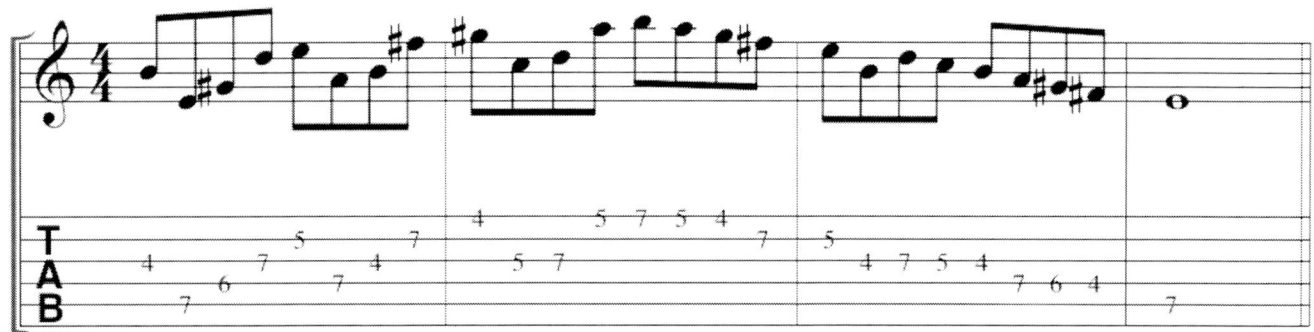

E Mixolydian b6th Lick 6:

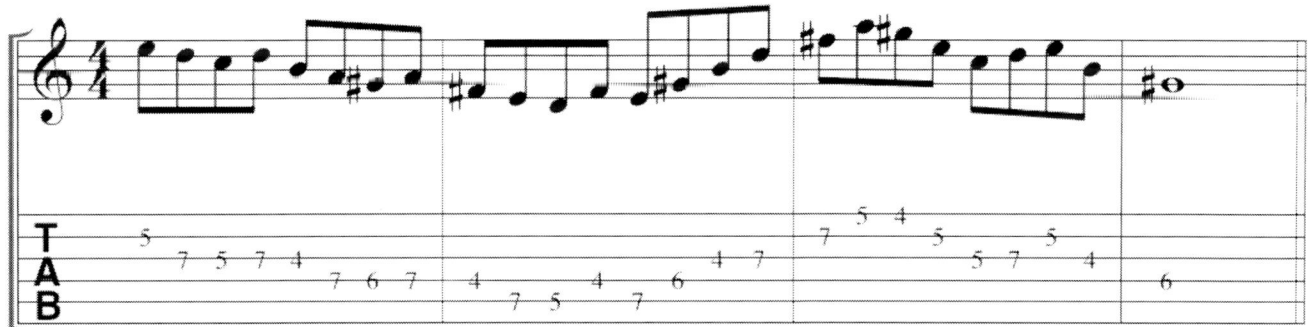

E Mixolydian b6th Lick 7:

E Mixolydian b6th Lick 8:

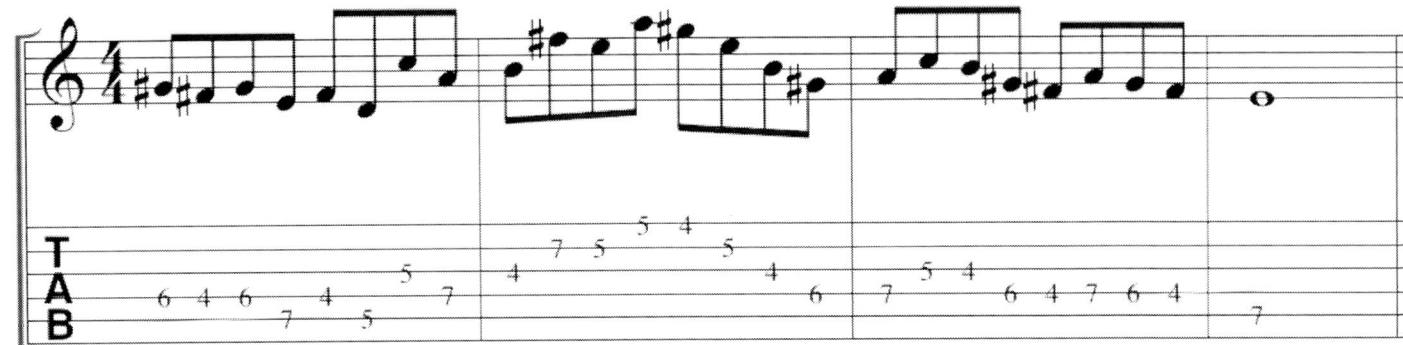

E Mixolydian b6th Lick 9:

E Mixolydian b6th Lick 10:

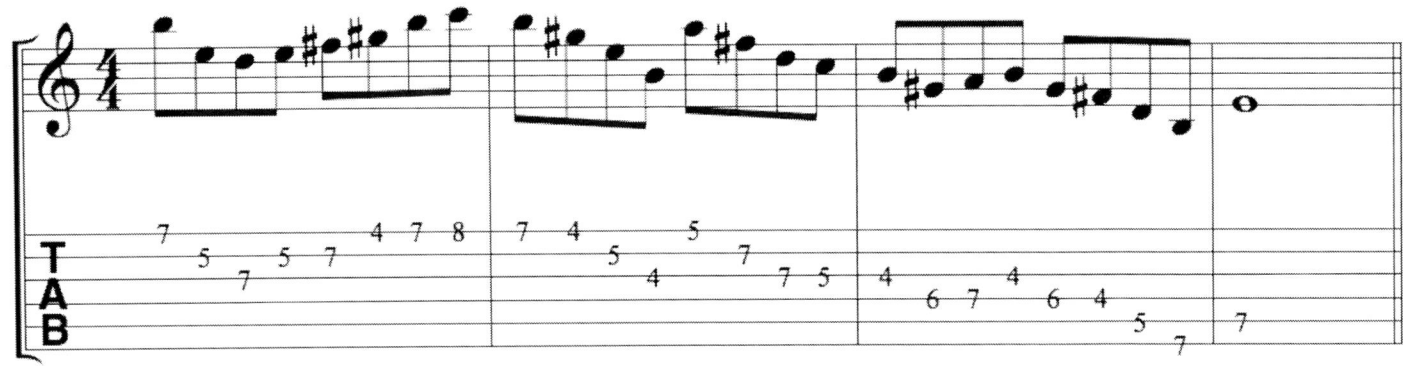

MELODIC MINOR MODE VII – Super-Locrian: R b2 #2 3 b5 b6 b7

Even though the Super-Locrian mode is the most dissonant of all the Melodic Minor scale modes, it's also one of the most useful. It's going to require a little more explanation than the others on my part and somewhat of a leap of faith on your part but the intense musical effect that you can achieve through the use of this mode makes it well worth digging into, sooner than later. First, we'll need to establish a few musical facts that we'll be learning more about, further into the book.

1) Chords can be extended beyond the 7th, into the next octave, where the 2nd becomes the 9th, the 4th becomes the 11th and the 6th becomes the 13th. This adds a certain degree of tension to the chord. Since the role of the dominant chord is to provide tension, they are the most likely chords to be extended.

2) To take the dominant chord tension heightening concept a step further, jazz improvisers commonly alter the extended tones (9th, 11th, 13th) and the 5ths of dominant chords. This is called an altered dominant chord.

3) Dominant chords that lead to any chord 2½ up or 3½ down (a V7 – I relationship) are considered functioning dominant chords, these can almost always be altered. Dominant chords that lead anywhere else are non-functioning dominant chords. They are built diatonically from the Lydian Dominant mode and remain natural aside from the #4 (#11).

4) The Super-Locrian mode is also known as the Altered scale because it has the three essential dominant chord tones (R, 3 and b7) plus all possible altered extended tones and 5ths. This makes it the ideal scale to use on a dominant chord that you want a sense of dramatic tension. This is especially true of dominant chords that logically lead us to a minor chord, but in jazz, they alter major key V7s almost as frequently.

5) The numbering of the scale-tones will seem very odd at first. There are two 2nds (9ths) between the root and 3rd. There is no 4th other than the b5th which is the same thing as #4th or #11th (at least on an equal tempered instrument) the b6th or b13th could also be regarded as a #5th.

Here are the G Super Locrian notes as they relate to a G7 chord:

G	Ab	A#	B	C#/Db	D#/Eb	F
Root	b9th	#9th	3rd	#11 / b5	#5th / b13th	b7th

My scale tone numbers for the Super-Locrian mode positions are a combination of the traditional scale tone names and the extended harmony numbers. Basically, I wanted to avoid any two-digit numbers in the diagrams, so the #11th/b5th is simply represented by a 5 and the #5th/b13th is represented by a 6. The corresponding table of keys starts at G Super-Locrian, which is note relative to A Melodic Minor as the other modes were. G# would be the relative Super-Locrian but G# Super-Locrian is enharmonically rather hairy. All of the following musical material on this mode will be in G Super-Locrian for the same reason.

Super-Locrian Mode

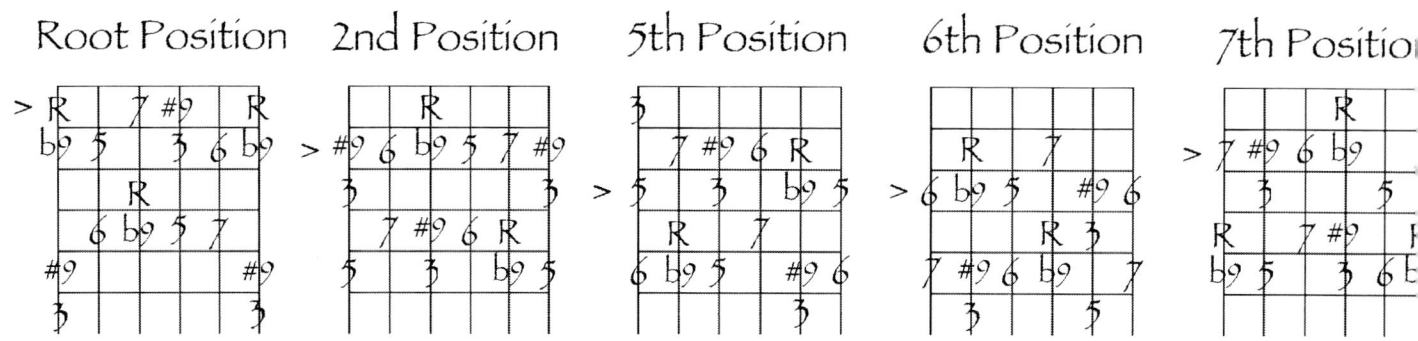

	G	D	A	E	B	F#	C#	Ab	Eb	Bb	F	C
Root Position:	3	10	5	12	7	2	9	4	11	6	13	8
2nd Position:	6	13	8	3	9	5	11	7	2	9	4	11
5th Position:	9	4	11	6	13	8	3	10	5	12	7	2
6th Position:	11	6	13	8	3	10	5	12	7	2	9	4
7th Position:	13	8	3	10	5	12	7	2	9	4	11	6

The scale tone pattern for this one is different from the others because of its two tones between root & 3rd, and its lack of two notes between altered 5th and the following root. Since the concept of heightened tension is at work with this mode, and every scale tone can be interpreted as a chord-tone, the scale-tone pattern isn't quite as relevant but if it generally helps you internalize your shapes, here it is.

G Super-Locrian, Scale-Tone Pattern, Root Position, Ascending:

G Super-Locrian, Scale-Tone Pattern, Root Position, Descending:

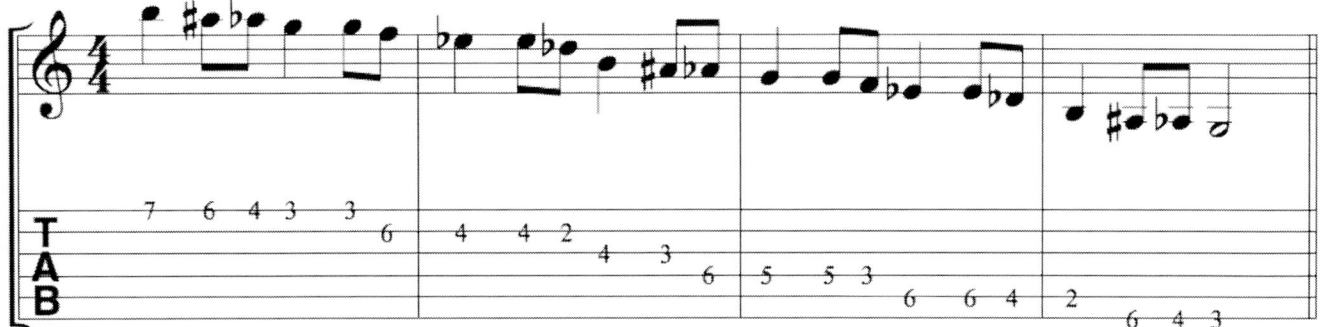

G Super-Locrian, Scale-Tone Pattern, 2nd Position, Ascending:

G Super-Locrian, Scale-Tone Pattern, 2nd Position, Descending:

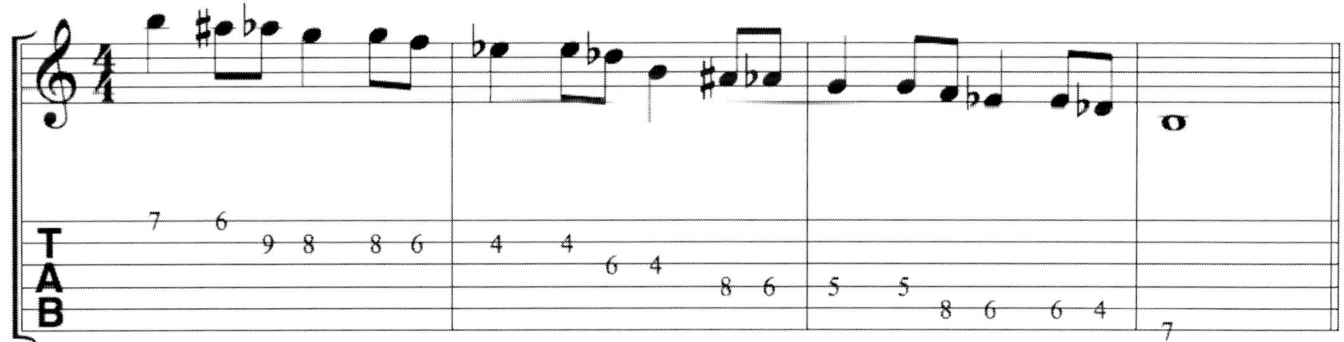

G Super-Locrian, Scale-Tone Pattern, 5th Position, Ascending:

G Super-Locrian, Scale-Tone Pattern, 5th Position, Descending:

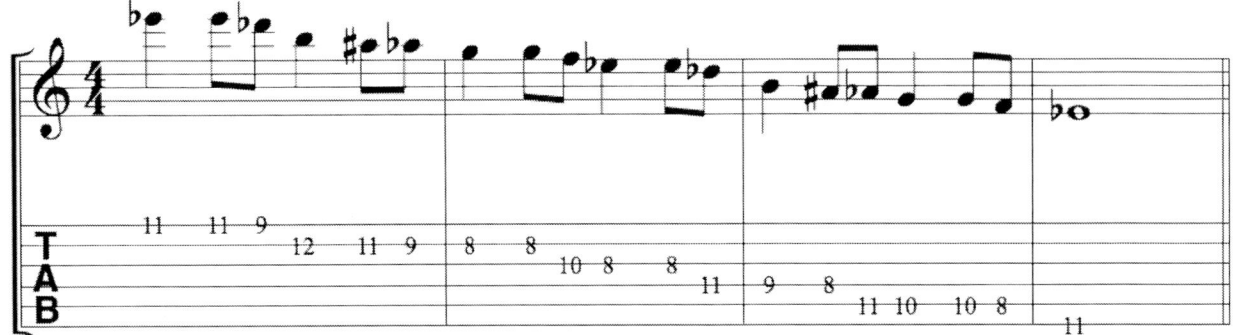

G Super-Locrian, Scale-Tone Pattern, 6th Position, Ascending:

G Super-Locrian, Scale-Tone Pattern, 6th Position, Descending:

G Super-Locrian, Scale-Tone Pattern, 7th Position, Ascending:

G Super-Locrian, Scale-Tone Pattern, 7th Position, Ascending:

G Super-Locrian Lick 1:

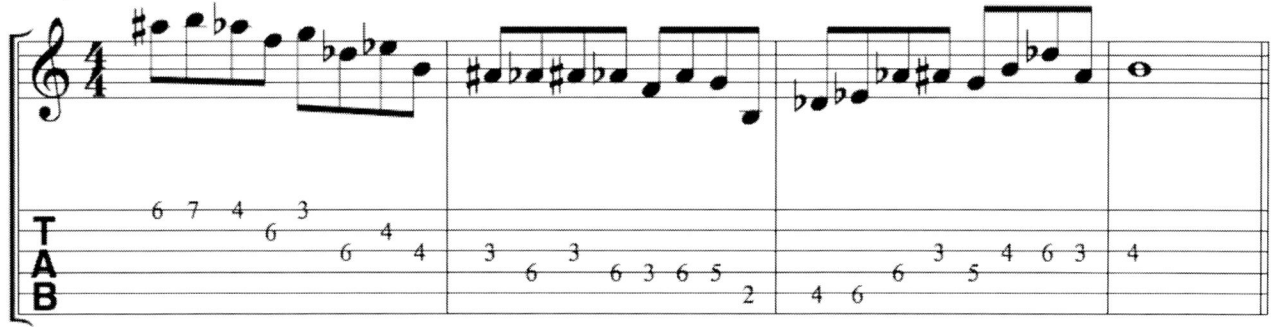

G Super-Locrian Lick 2:

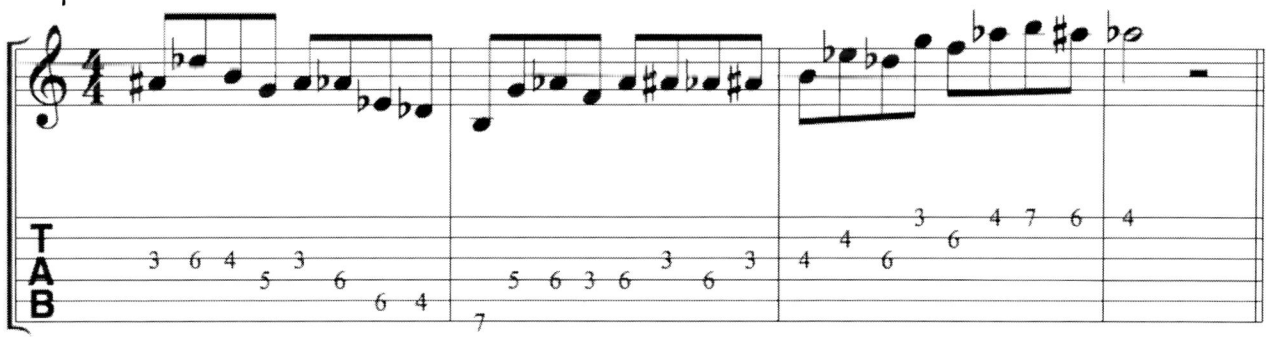

G Super-Locrian Lick 3:

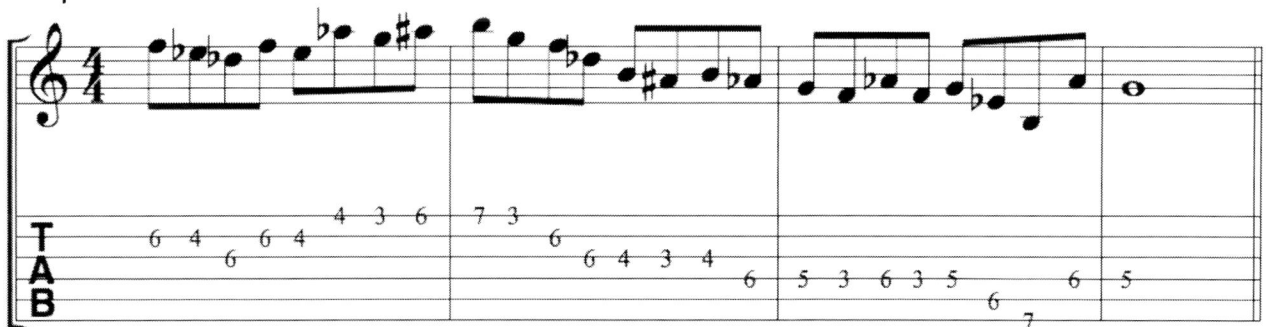

G Super-Locrian Lick 4:

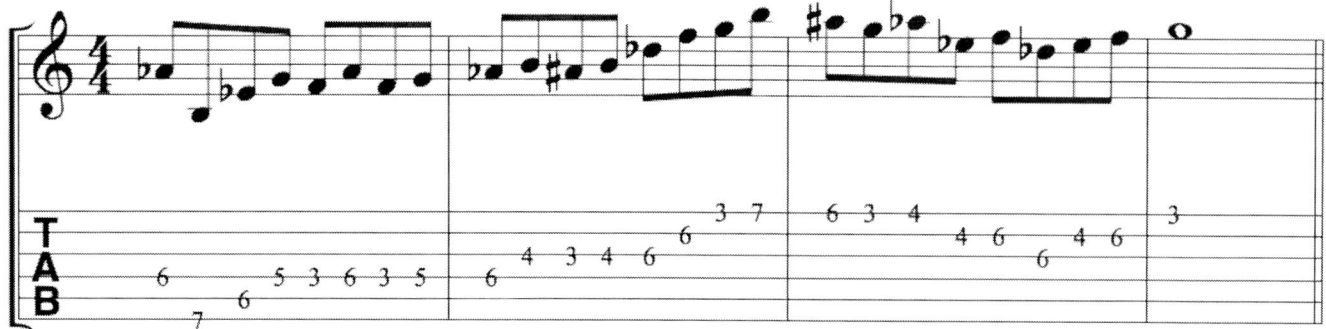

G Super-Locrian Lick 5:

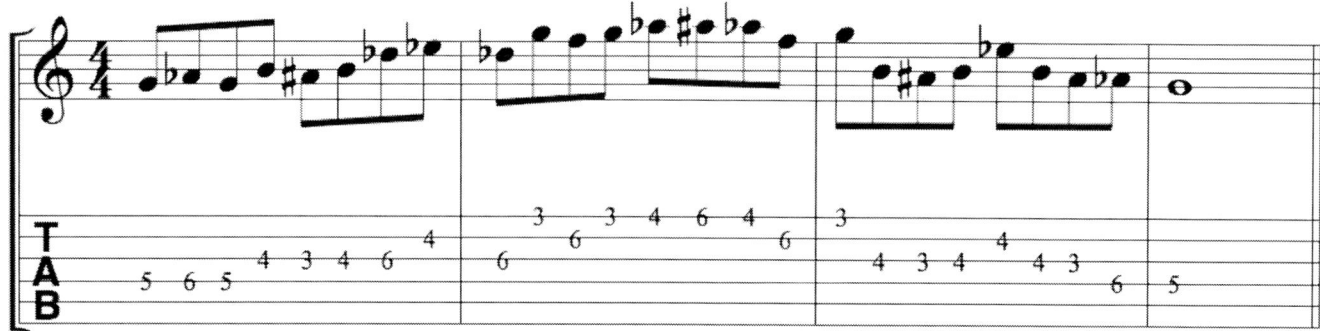

G Super-Locrian Lick 6:

G Super-Locrian Lick 7:

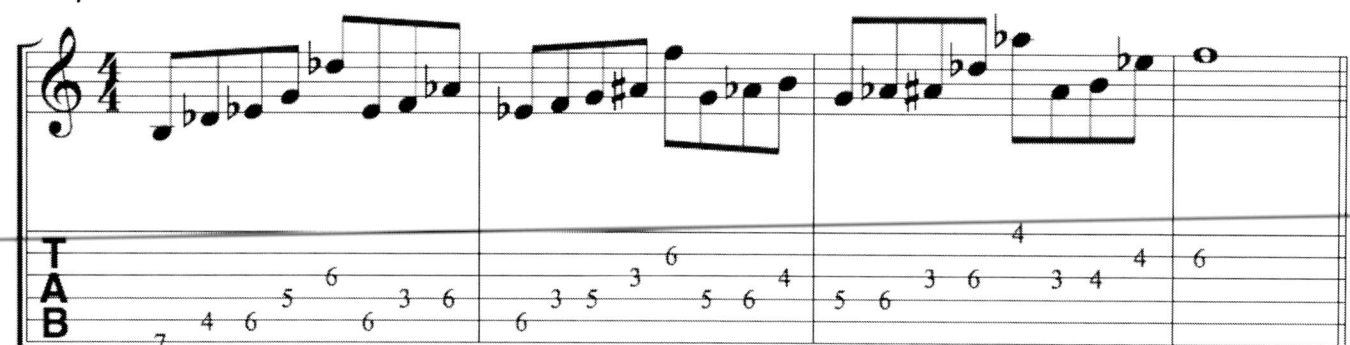

G Super-Locrian Lick 8:

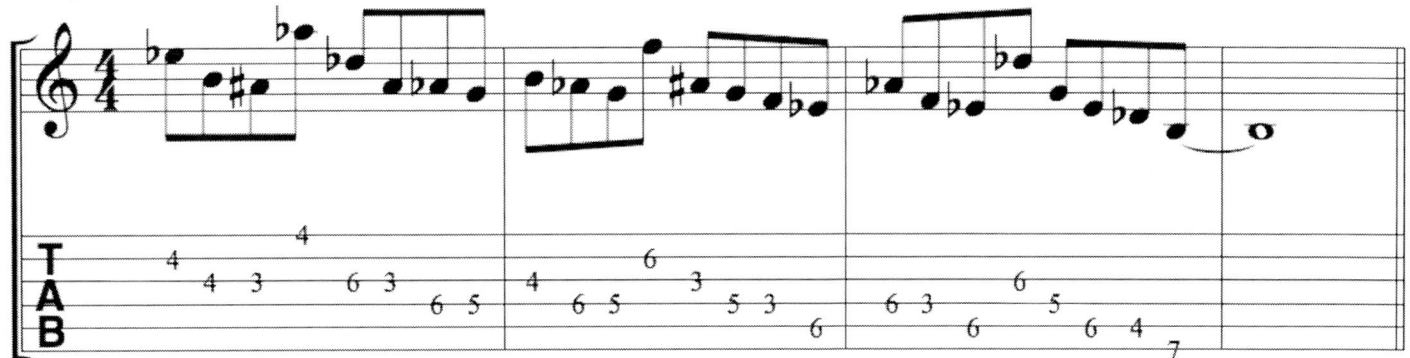

G Super-Locrian Lick 9:

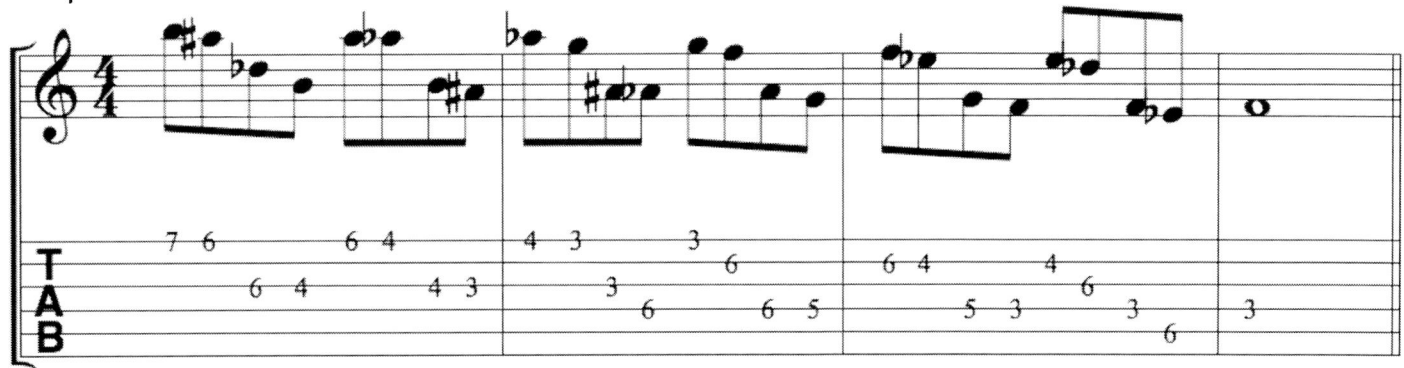

G Super-Locrian Lick 10:

THE MELODIC CRAFT – part 1: Properties Of Melody

In this section, we're going to learn about some of the basic techniques of melodic composition. By melodic composition, I mean the art of writing melodies. A melody can be defined as a meaningful succession of tones. We've learned a fair amount about harmony and rhythm. We've built up a vocabulary of licks and melodic patterns and that's a good start; now it's time to start learning how to put all of it together and gain a true artistic control of our music.

Learning the art of melodic composition will do many things for you. It'll help you to become a better songwriter, arranger, producer and most importantly, a better improviser. Improvisation is simply composition without the safety nets of time and privacy. Someone can have all the technique, speed, knowledge of scales and chords, and still lack as an improviser if they don't have an understanding of some fundamental composition concepts. Most people slowly gain these skills instinctually from hours of dedicated listening. When you sit down and look at these concepts dead-on, you gain a very clear concept of how to make an effective musical statement much more quickly.

The Basic Properties of Melody

1) Contour
2) Rhythm
3) Harmonic Background

These four elements all play off of one another to give you the combined grand total that is your melodic content. When these elements are combined in very obvious and trite ways, the result will be nursery-rhyme-like melodies, which can be useful in pop songwriting and production. When these elements combine in a way where each element seems to have no regard for the next, you'll wind up with very amateur sounding melodies. If you want to write melodies that could stand the test of time like Paul McCartney, Stevie Wonder or Kurt Cobain for instance, you want learn all you can about these four basic properties. Let's take a closer look.

Property 1: Contour
This simply refers to the direction of the pitches within the melodic statement. Contour has the greatest effect of any of these basic properties. It's the one thing a non-musician can describe to someone about a melody. It's hard to classify, right up front, what sorts of effects you will get with each choice of contour, as these effects depend greatly on the other three governing properties: rhythm, harmonic background and tone selection.

There are only a few general shapes a melody can take. On the following few pages, we'll look at these possible contours with some original melodic examples, complete with harmonic backgrounds. I wrote them all in a mostly diatonic pop style in the key of C major, 4/4 at 120 BPM. We will be looking at some of these again to analyze some other aspects of them. Before playing the contour examples, bear in mind that a contour can sound a million different ways, these are merely singular examples.

1) The Up-Hill:

The melody starts on a low pitch and makes its way (with the occasional downward motion, in most cases) up to its highest pitch at the end of the phrase.

2) The Down-Hill:

The melody starts on a high pitch and generally makes its way down to its lowest pitch at the end of the phrase.

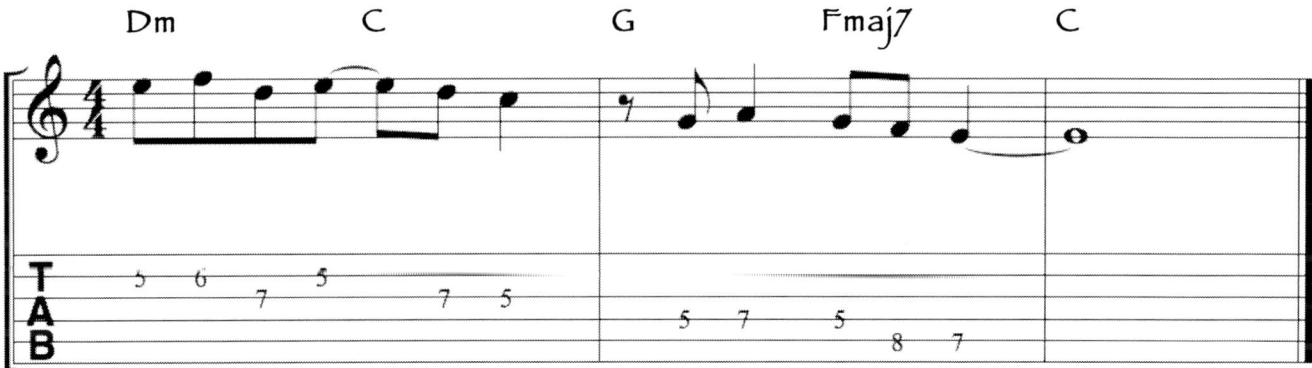

3) The St. Louis Arch:

The melody starts low, goes high and then returns to its home in the lowlands.

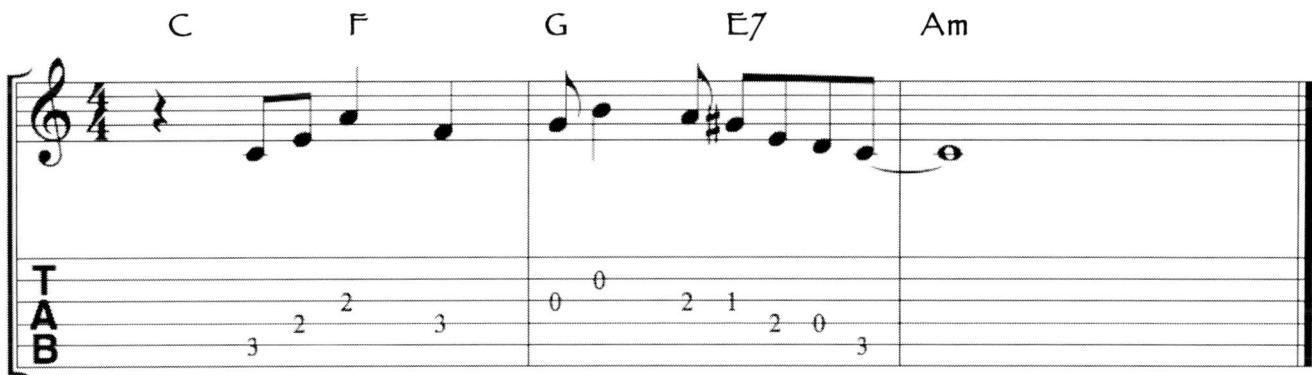

4) The Half-Pipe:

The melody starts high, goes low and returns to it's lofty abode. Note that it doesn't go straight down. The general direction is what we're looking at with melodic contour.

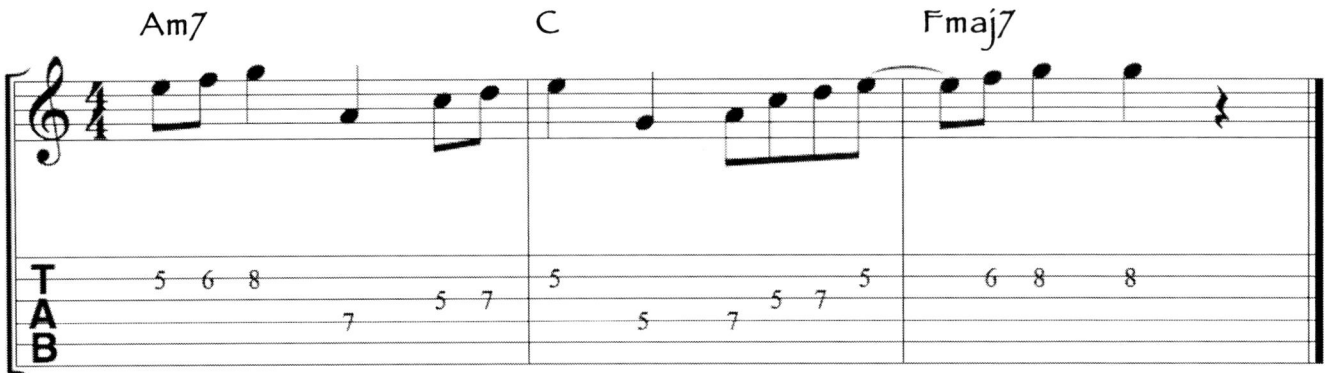

5) The Cola Wave:

The melody starts in the middle, goes low, goes high and then returns to the middle. (You can swap the low and high positions)

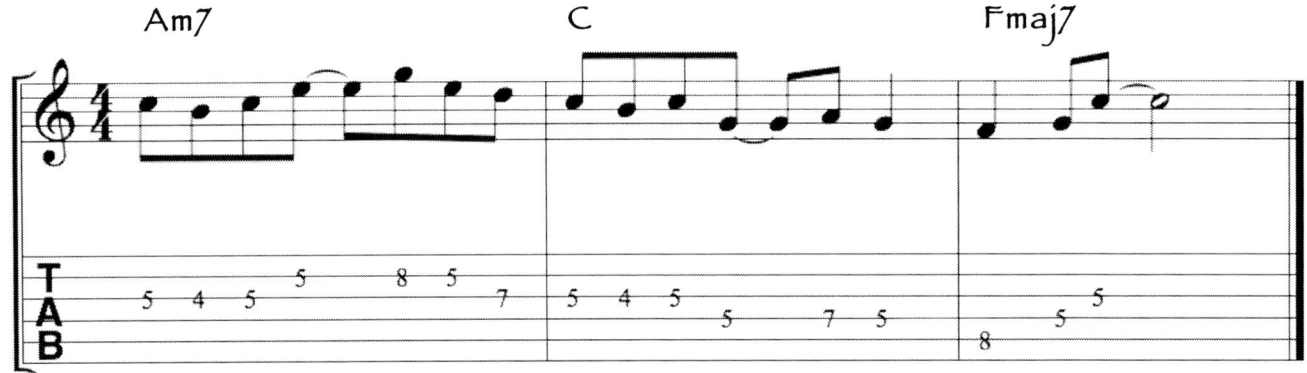

6) The Sneaker Swoosh

The melody starts in the middle, goes low and then ends high. (The direction of this one can also be switched.)

I'm not sure whether it was Mozart or Beethoven who came up with these names, but nonetheless, deciding on one of these contours is a good place to start when building a melody. Variations on these can be created by choosing how quickly or slowly you move from one point to the next. A leap in either direction greatly changes the effect of the contour. The other three properties of melody will bear some effect on the finer lines of your contour.

Property 2: Rhythm

We've already learned quite a bit about rhythm so I'm just going to summarize the main rhythmic considerations that we have when creating a melody. These considerations have an effect on everything the rhythm touches, including the exact shape of your contour, and the aspect of tension and resolution.

1) Chord-Tone Placement

What types of notes are landing directly on the beats? When we get notes that relate directly as chord tones of the underlying chord on the beats, especially the strong beats (1 and 3) we get a very direct and strong sounding melody. When we have non-chord tones on the beats, with our chord tones placed in between the beats, we get a melody of a more subtle, feminine nature.

Most memorable and appealing melodies make judicious use of both types of placement. Notice, in the following example, how we begin with a simple C major figure on the C chord but then repeat the same idea over Dm, where the notes relate as outer tones to the chord, but toward the end of the phrase we are landing on chord tones of the F and G chords.

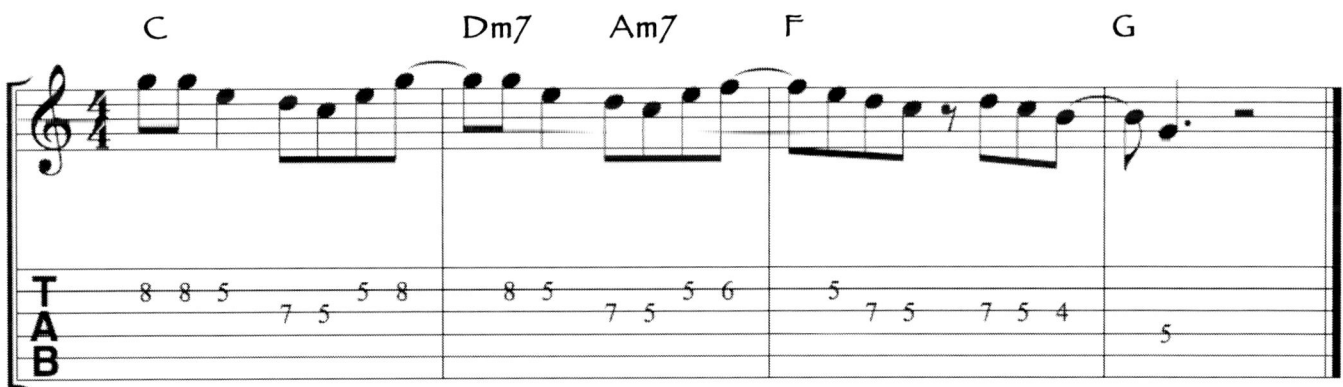

2) Rhythmic Phrasing

Where in the measure does the melody begin and end? Is the melody made of one uniform note value, or does it use a small variety of note values to create either an expanding or contracting effect? Really look at the rhythmic content of your all-time favorite melodies. Take this content and experiment with it, using your own choice of harmonic background and melody notes. This is one good way to become very conscious of what rhythmic phrasing does for a melodic statement.

The following example starts after a 1½ beat rest and mostly uses repeated 8th notes until it concludes on beat 2 of bar 4, with a quarter note, followed by a half note rest. The common tendency is to start on beat 1 of bar one and end on beat 1 of bar 4. This is fine occasionally, but too much of anything is never good.

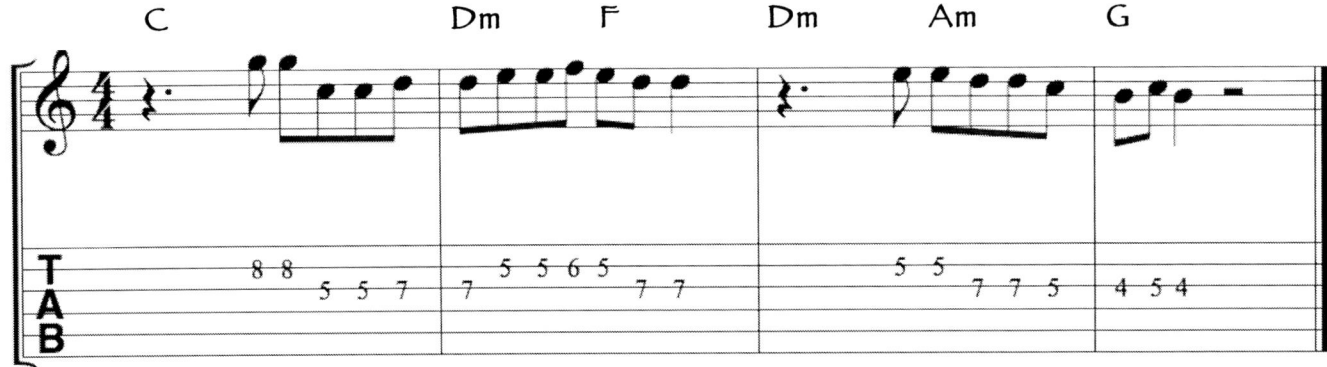

3) Syncopation

Is the syncopation based on rest, ties, accents or a combination these? Are the accents dynamic, or naturally occurring, from the use of long note placement on or between weak beats, tied notes or odd note sequences? These are all valid options, but an overuse of any one of them will become annoying to hear in a hurry. That's why you want to be very conscious of this rhythmic element. Look back on all the examples in this section and think about them in terms of the syncopation they use. Do the same with your all-time favorite melodies.

Property 3: Harmonic Background

The chords beneath your melody greatly effect how your melody will come across. For a simple example, try singing or playing Jingle Bells over a static IIm7 (in the key of the song: Jingle Bells in C, Dm7 chord). It's starts to sound like a 1980s R&B melody. Spend ample time in creating harmonic structures that have a good sense of direction and shape to them, because melody flourishes in that sort of environment. Also spend time learning how to write interesting melodies of static chords of all types.

Any time that you run into a nasty conflict between chord and melody, you really want to change one or the other until you find something that works. Below are a couple of simple considerations you can make, in order to have a clear idea about how you're melody interacts with the underlying chords, you've chosen.

1) Do the tension and release points of the melody correspond to each individual chord or directly to the parent I chord? Typically, a combination of both is ideal. In pop music, you can pretend that you're on the I chord when you aren't to a certain degree. Many of the forgotten pop songs of the past couple decades were songs that made overuse of this effect to the point where singing the melody without the chords sounded nothing like the song.

In the following example, the first two measures relate very vaguely to the underlying chords. I've used a melodic figure that seems to imply a Cmaj7 chord over the Dm and then repeated over an F, I use a variation of it over the Am7 where the tones fit more closely and I close out with a phrase that closely outlines the underlying G chord. This creates a nice balance.

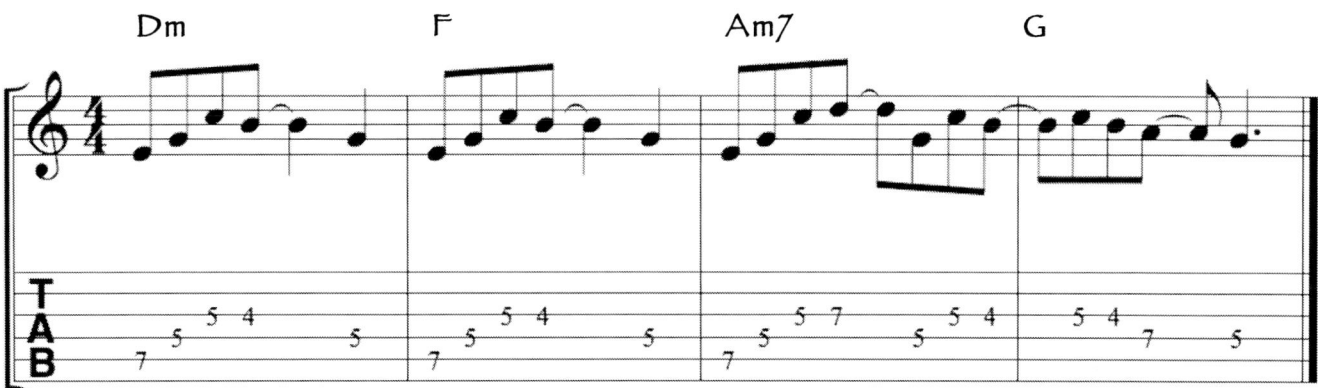

2) When you have an emphasized melody note that is not a member of the underlying chord, try holding the note out for a measure or two over the chord. Does it sound mysterious and interesting, or does it sound just plain bad? If it sounds bad, either rethink your melody note or your chord. When we dig into extended harmony, you'll learn exactly what the criteria is regarding which non-chord tones you can emphasize.

Most of the melodies in the previous examples make some use of emphasized non-chord tones. Look them over in this light and then look at the following example of a bad non-chord tone being used poorly. The motive works nicely on the F chord and then the C note immediately works very poorly on the Em. I go a step further in badness by repeating the same poor relationship with an emphasized F on the Am chord. Note the E note held out against the G chord seems to work just fine.

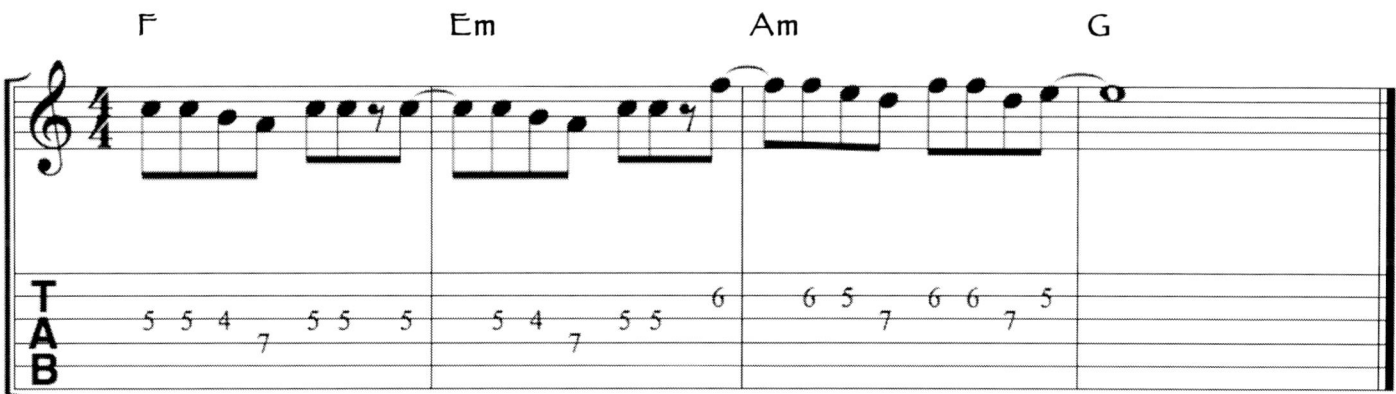

The more conscious of these basic properties of melody you become, the more effectively you will be able to compose and improvise good melodies. I should take a moment to let you know that when I first became aware in a clear way of these basic considerations, it initially had a somewhat paralyzing effect on my creative flow. It lasted a few months. In my case, but I could have pushed myself through it a lot quicker. I think the idea is to allow yourself some time to write melodies with these factors in mind, on a purely academic level. Don't worry about anything but learning to think comfortably in terms of these basic properties. If you happen to come up with a melody that you really love in the process, then by all means, use it in a song you write. Otherwise, just throw them out afterward. On the following pages I've laid out a step-by-step process to writing a pop melody. Make repeated use of this process and you will see a big boost in your ability to write good melodies.

Step-By-Step Melody Writing

There is no singular way to go about writing a melody. There are many approaches that will work. The following are a couple approaches that I use with a great deal of my students and I've been really pleased with the results. After you try these methods a few times, you can modify any step of any process to suit your tastes.

Method 1:

Step 1: Start with a chord progression. I chose I – IV – VIm – V7 of V – IV. Note that my secondary dominant chord is not leading to it's intended destination. This makes it a non-functioning dominant chord. When writing melody in the context of this chord, we will want it to correspond to D Lydian Dominant.

C   F   Am   D7   F

Step 2: Pick a note to showcase on each chord. For the many advantages it gives us later on, stay within an octave. In the case of my example below, I chose the roots of the I and IV chords, the 5th of my VIm chord, the b7th of my V7 of V.

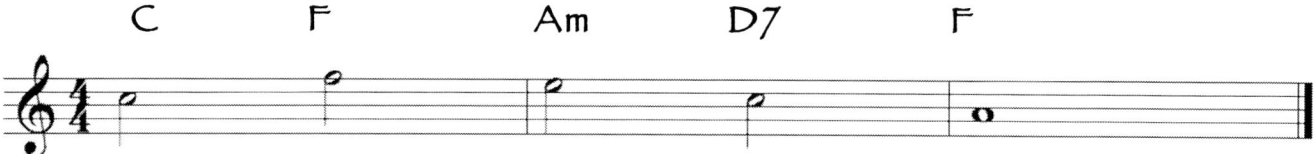

Step 3: Choose some notes to go between your target tones. Use between one and three notes per target note. For now, stay with notes that naturally correspond to the key unless there is a chromatic chord such as a secondary dominant chord. In the case of one, use the melodic minor mode that best corresponds to the chord.

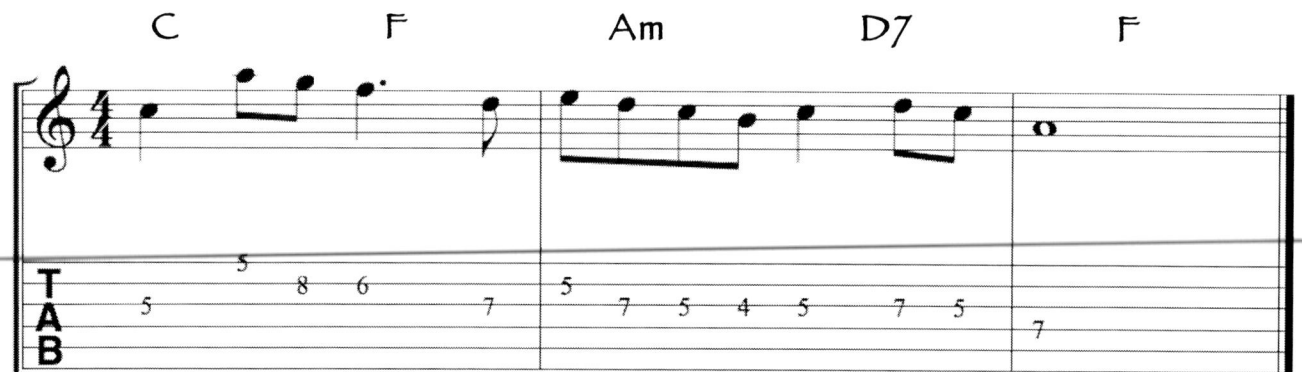

Step 4: Move these notes around rhythmically, making use of ties, rests, dots and repeated notes. Experiment until you arrive at a solid statement that you enjoy. If you have an idea that would require you to flip a couple notes, add a note, subtract a note, trade a note, etc, by all means, do it.

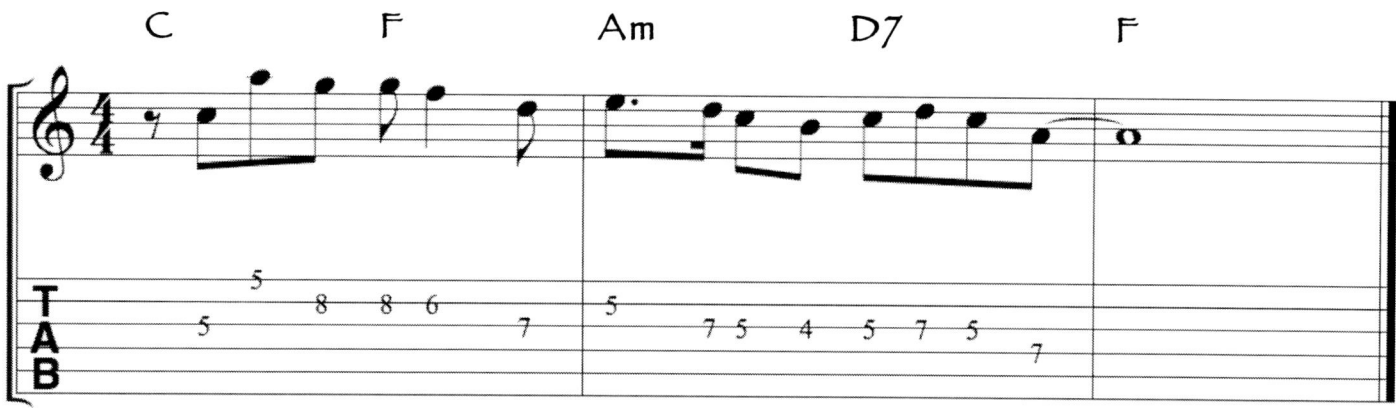

Step 5: Add pick up notes to the beginning and a couple notes on the end at will. If it detracts from your initial idea, don't feel obligated to add anything at this point. However, if you can find a pick-up and/or a tail that enhances your statement, this is the point at which to do so.

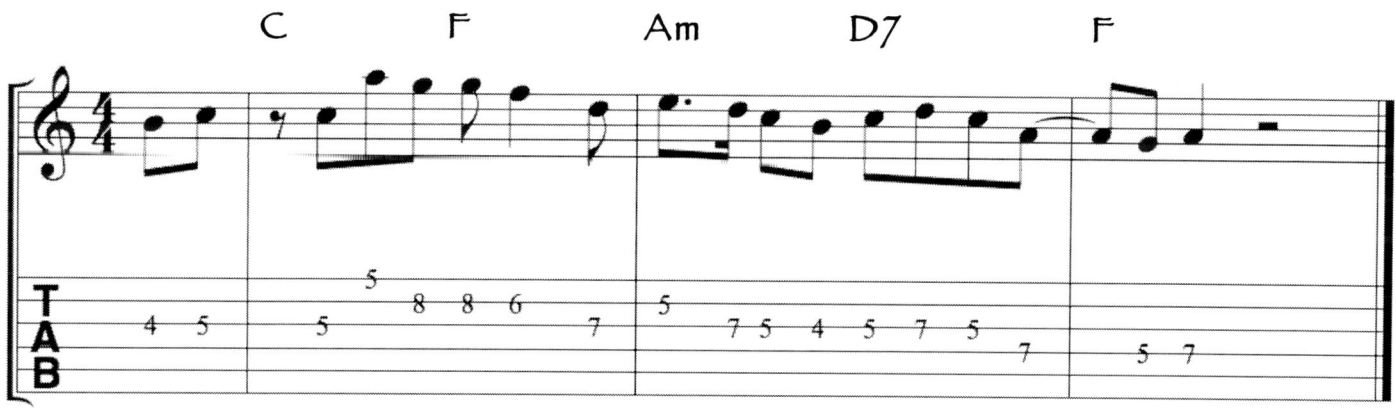

Step 6: Once you have completed steps 1 through 5, you should have a fairly complete sounding melody. If there's anything that sounds awkward about it, go through and isolate the problem and make any adjustments that are needed. If nothing is needed, the final step is to experiment with chord substitutions and melodic variations. Catalogue your melody along with its variations and treat yourself to an ice cream cone. Good job!

Method 2:

Step 1: Start with a row (specific order) of tones that sound good to you. The row should be anywhere from 4 to 8 notes long. Here's my row.

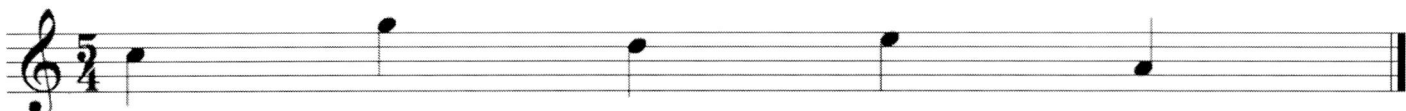

Step 2: Find a rhythmic phrasing for this row that flows well and allows you to fit the entire row into one measure in your chosen time signature. Make it something strong that bears repetition.

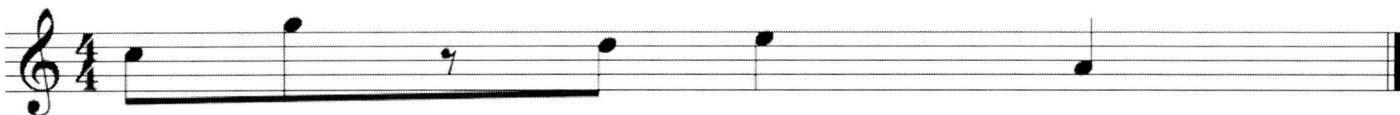

Step 3: Fill the first three measures of your four measure phrase with this motive that you've written.

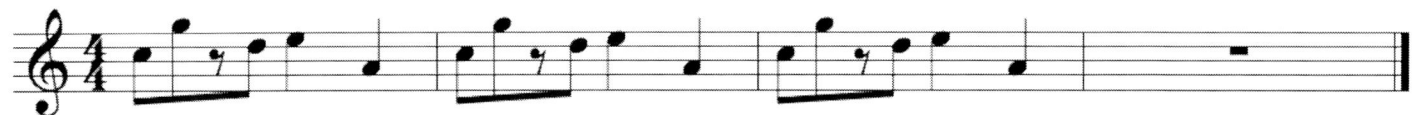

Step 4: Add any sort of rhythmic variation that you would like, within those first three measures. In this step, allow yourself the opportunity of changing the pitch of only one note within the first three measures. In the case of this example, I left the original pitches as is.

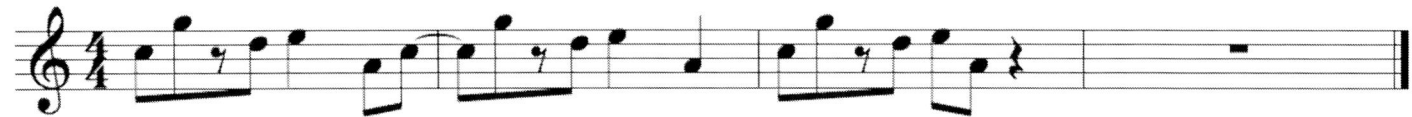

Step 5: Compose a tone row that contrasts and compliments our original statement. It can be four to eight notes long. Simple is usually better.

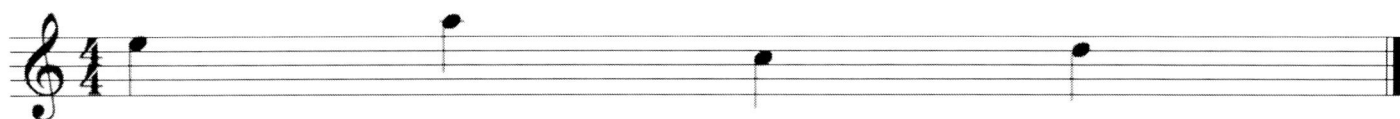

Step 6: Add this tone row to the original phrase where we left off.

Step 7: Assign some rhythmic value to the notes. Set them up so they provide some contrast against the phrasing of the previous motive. You could add pick-up notes at this point if you wanted to. In this case, I'm going to let the melody start on beat 1. Notice that I took advantage of the rest time that I had left at the end of measure 3 by tying the first note of the row from the "and" of beat 4.

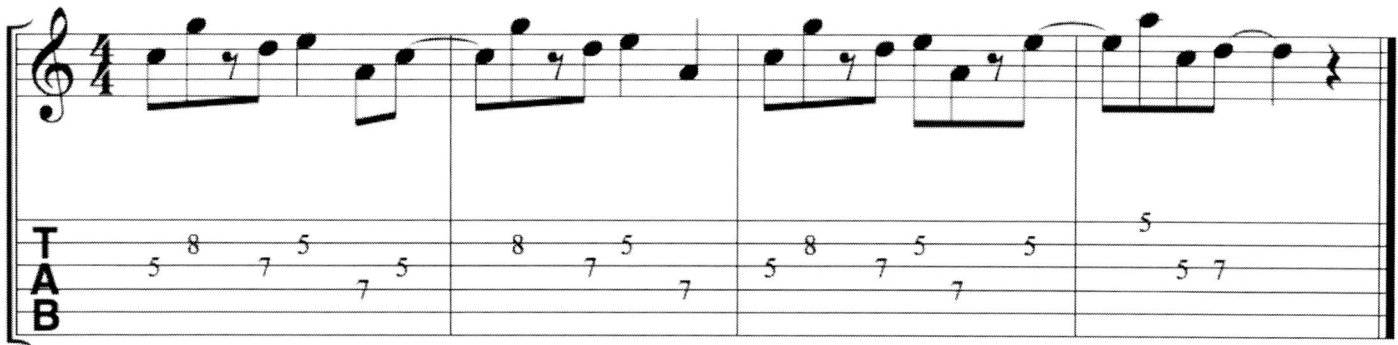

Step 8: Choose a chord scheme that brings life to the repeated motive. Remember that most non-chord tones are OK, just not the ones that sound bad. You'll learn the difference, very soon. Record the melody so you can experiment with different chord changes until you find something that brings out a unique quality or a strong emotional effect.

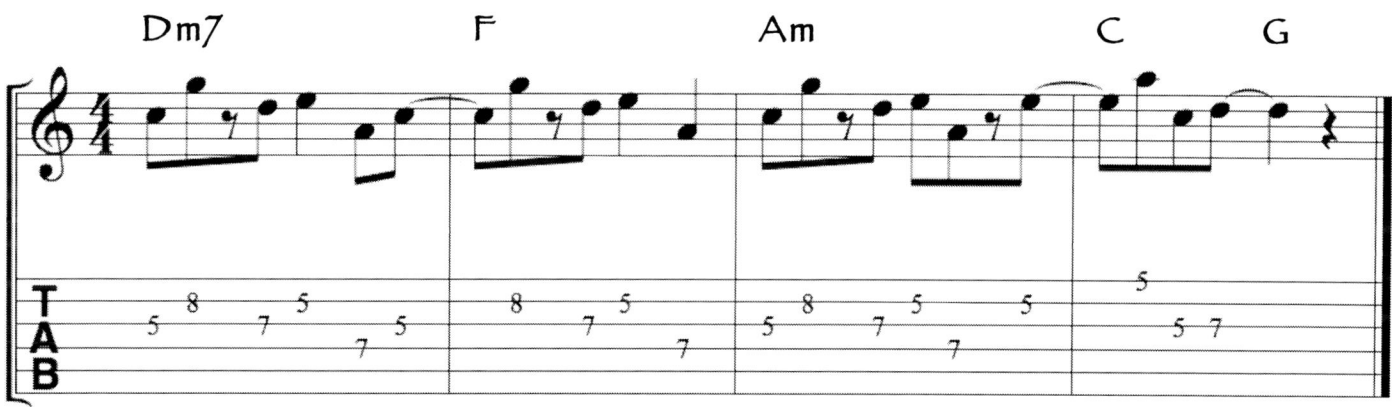

Now we have a solid, workable melodic phrase that could be used in any sort of modern pop or rock song. It takes up an octave, which means that any singer could find a good key in which to sing it and singable harmony parts could be written for it. It's like a little gold brick in the bank.

I've reached a stage where I see modern pop songwriting as a high-art that gets quickly dismissed because of all the bad music that's on the charts as a result of backroom deals and social/family favoritism. Good popular music stands the test of time. Bad popular music rarely does and when it does, it does so as little more than a cute joke. A lot of serious musicians and students of music turn up their nose at popular music as a whole. I urge you not to do this. It's a certain way to entirely cut yourself off from the majority of people.

RHYTHM – part 6: Compound Time Signatures

So far we've looked at all the simple time signatures which are all made of either groups of two, (duple meter) or groups of three (triple meter). Compound time signatures are made of measures that have groups of both two *and* three. Compound time signatures are far less common than simple times. Most songs are made up of 4/4, 3/4, 6/8, 12/8 and the occasional 9/8, which can all be regarded as simple time signatures.

However, jazz, rock and pop and modern classical music make the occasional allowance for compound times. Progressive rock typically makes heavy use of odd time signatures. Modern musicians have experimented with adapting traditional Latin, jazz, funk and reggae grooves to compound time signatures. Using compound time signatures will open you up to thinking in new ways melodically and rhythmically. Learning to improvise in odd times takes lots of practice and offers a special challenge in rhythmic focus that will ultimately strengthen your general musicality.

Practice improvising on simple chord vamps and progressions played in these time signatures. As of the date of publishing, the quickest way of doing this would be either playing over a recording yourself playing a rhythm guitar figure in each time signature, using the iReal (iReal b) app for smart phone or computer, or using Band-In-A-Box by PG Music for Windows or Mac. Band-In-A-Box is much more expensive but much more equipped to handle compound times and far more feature rich.

The more musically fulfilling, yet more slower process is to make your own tracks using midi. To date, my favorite software to program instrument parts for a backing track is GarageBand, which is only available for Mac computers, iPads and iPods . For final productions, I favor Abelton Live but the simplicity of GarageBand makes it ideal for simple backing tracks. It's easy to learn how to use it and will start you on a path to having some production skills. If you have a PC and don't have the budget, look into fruity loops. If you have a smart phone, look into Music Studio Pro. I have a book in the works for you to get you educated in confidently coming up with drum beats and fills, basslines, keyboard parts, etc. I believe Mozart would smack somebody in the face for not taking advantage of the musical technology that we have available to us in this exciting and frightening era.

Below are the most common compound time signatures represented with multiple musical examples.

5/4

5/4 time is made up of measures containing a group of 3 beats and a group of 2 beats. The group of three beats is typically phrased first, followed by the group of two beats. Here is the basic metrical division of the measure:

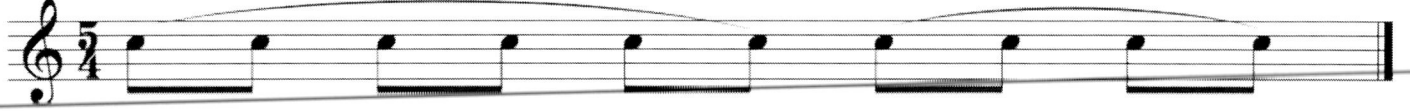

In most cases, both the 3 beat and 4 beat segments are divided in half to create this familiar accent pattern:

In stripping the unaccented notes away from the previous rhythm, we're left with this fundamental rhythm which happens the most common 5/4 rhythmic phrasing:

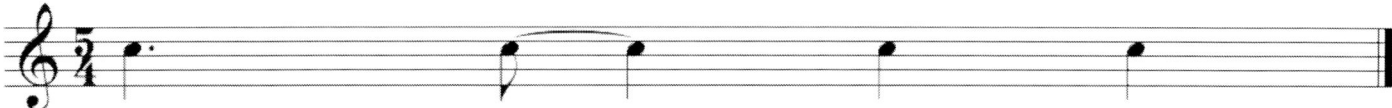

Here is how it would look in a more staccato, rest oriented notation:

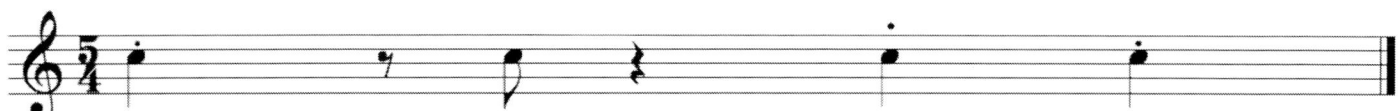

5/4 Variation 1:

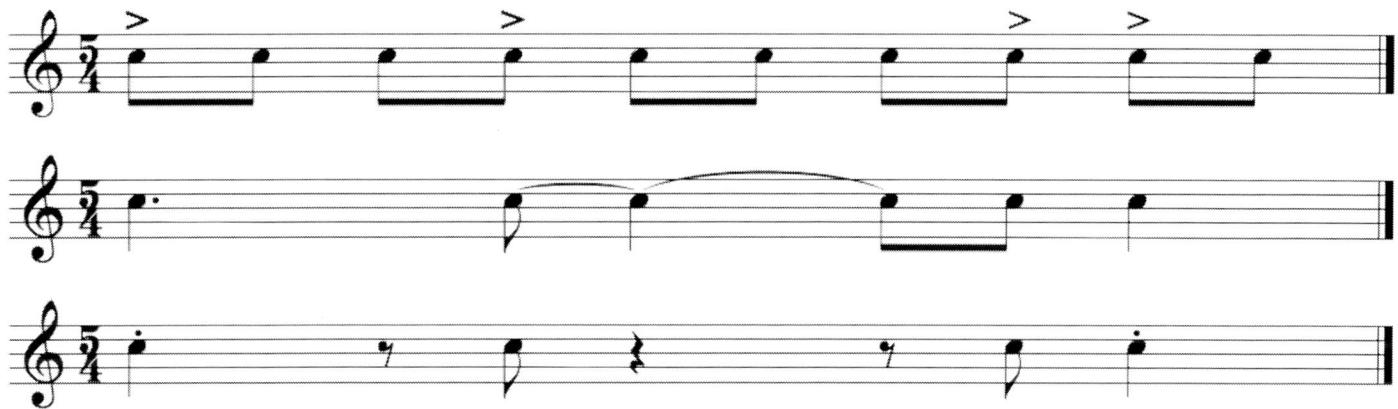

5/4 Variation 2:

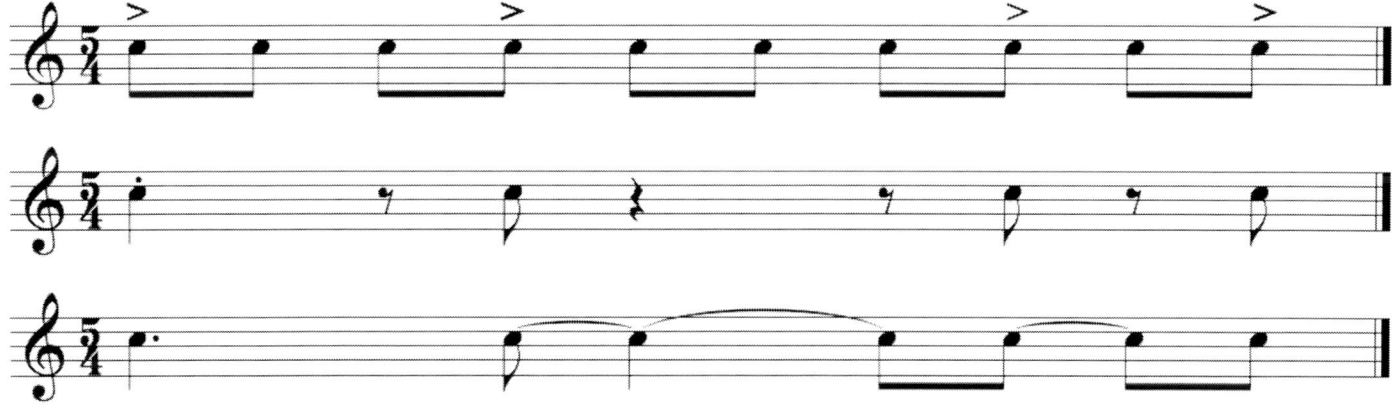

5/4 Variation 3:

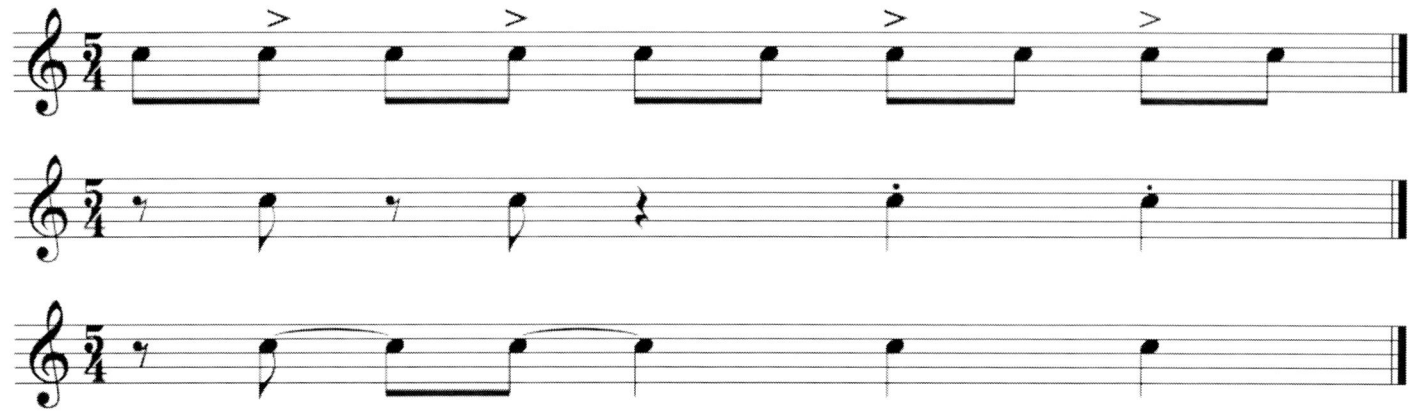

You can mix these rhythms up at will when writing or playing in 5/4 time. Furthermore, you can experiment with smaller sub-divisions (16ths, triplets, quintuplets, etc). These rhythms pretty much sum up popular contemporary use of the time signature. Whether it's the original *Mission Impossible theme* by Lalo Schifrin, *Take Five* by Dave Brubeck or *WTF?* by OK Go, these rhythms are at the heart of music in 5/4 time. Below are a few musical examples written in 5/4:

5/4 Example 1:

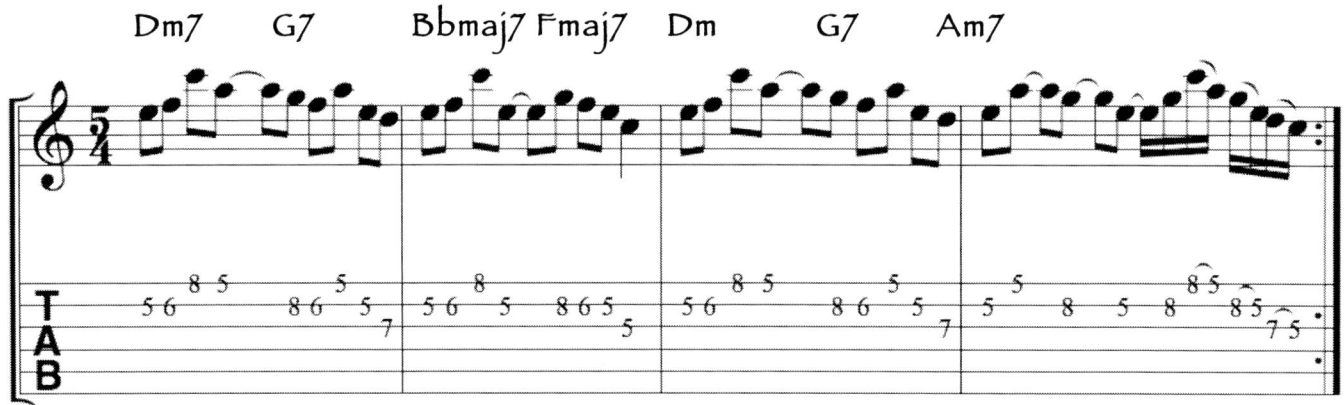

5/4 Example 2:

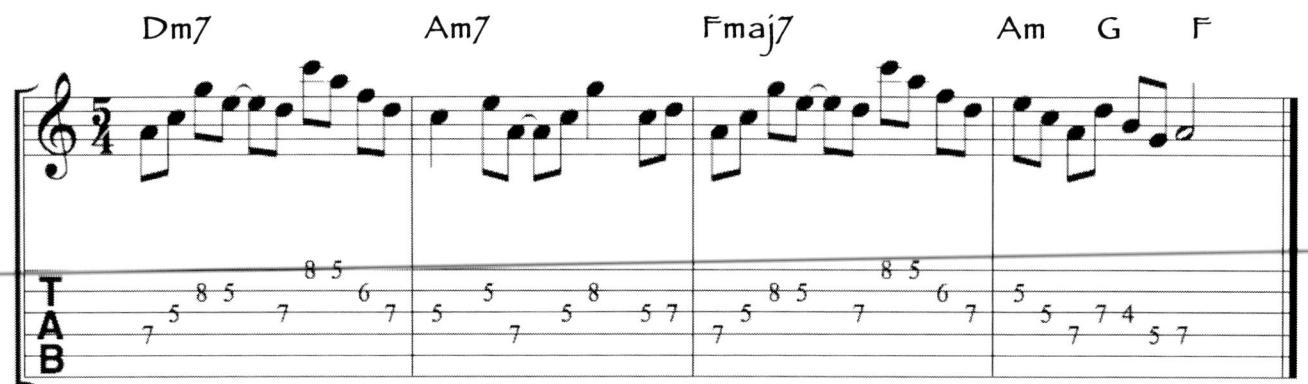

5/4 Example 3:

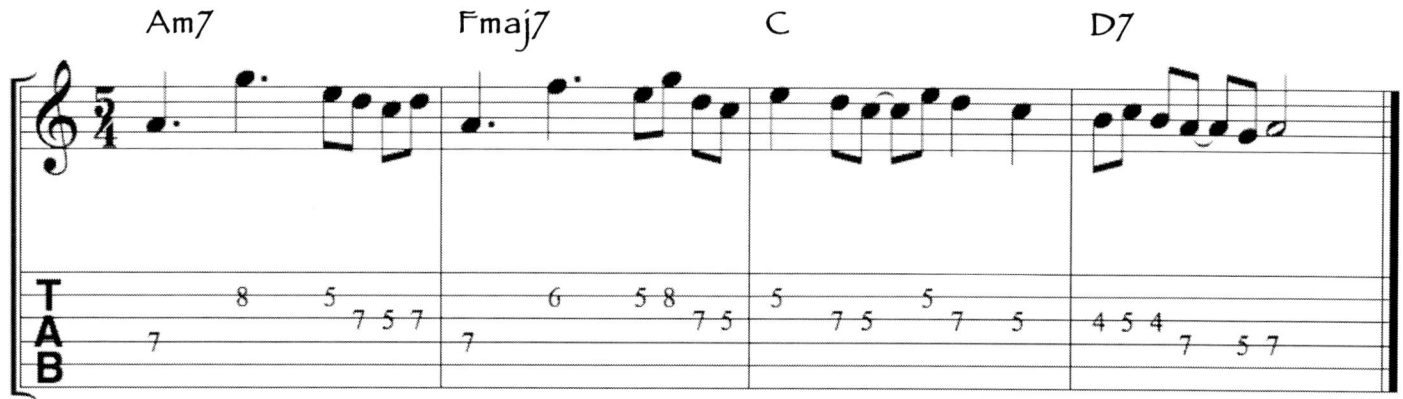

5/4 Example 4:

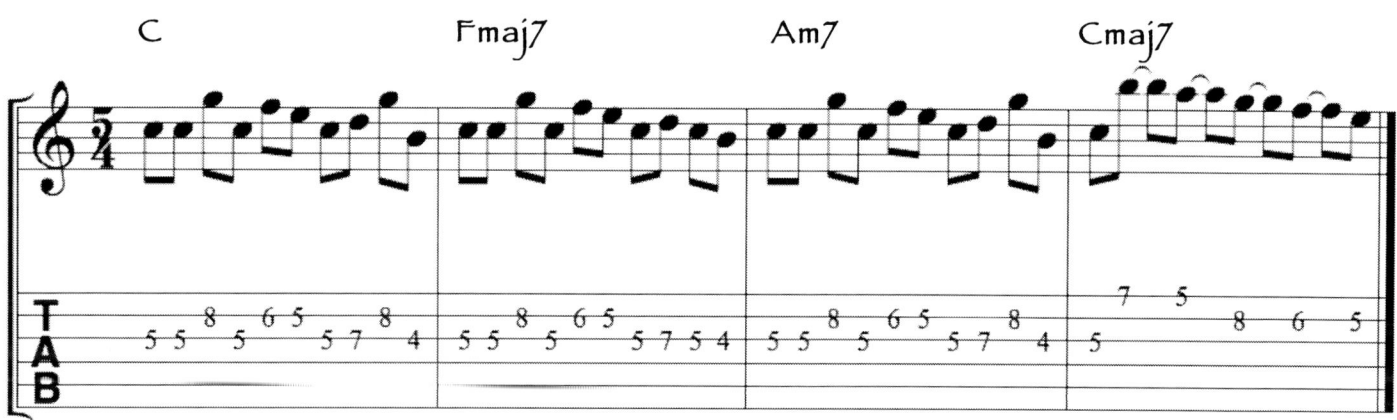

5/4 is one of my favorite time signatures. It works well in both straight and swing time and has a very natural flow to it, once you learn to feel it's pulse. The measures aren't too long or short and it works well at a lot of tempos. 5/4 is a very sturdy odd time signature. I would recommend spending ample time exploring it, compositionally and improvisationally.

It may seem very difficult at first but don't let this discourage you. Do some research on what songs there are in this time signature, listen and play along with those songs. Get used to applying these 5/4 rhythms as both chord voicings and melodies. Before long, your concept of the measures of 5/4 will be as clear as a mountain stream. I remember feeling a huge sense of accomplishment when all of a sudden, improvising in 5/4 felt every bit as natural as 4/4 or 3/4. This is possible with any time signature but 5/4 is an especially accessible time signature.

7/4

7/4 time is made up of measures containing a group of four beats and a group of three beats. The group of four beats is typically phrased first, followed by the group of three beats. Here is the basic metrical division of the measure:

We can apply the same sub-dividing to these groupings, cutting each group in half. Our result is this pattern of accents:

Subtracting the non-accented notes, we have this resulting rhythm:

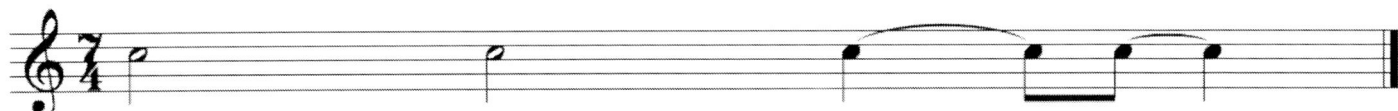

Since the first half of this rhythmic scheme is a mere pair of half notes, we can fill it in with any rhythm that we might fit into a measure of 4/4. Here's an example.

In this one I begin with an eighth-note rest which tends to be something that people are at first, scared to do. Also I alter the rhythm of what we'll call the 3-half.

In theory, you can build a measure of 7/4 by stringing any measure of 4/4 together with any measure of 3/4. The 4-half doesn't necessarily have to precede the 3-half. You can also take a two measure phrase in 4/4 and simply remove one quarter note worth of notes of rest time from anywhere within the phrase. This gives you quite a few possibilities, probably in the lower millions. Not all of these possibilities are going to sound like an easy to follow 7/4 rhythm.

In general compound time signatures require a little more repetition than simple time signatures in order to stick with the listener and keep them hanging in there with us. 7/4 also has the disadvantage of having very long measures. This makes it somewhat cumbersome but it has a close cousin that has advantages worth looking at.

7/8

7/8 time is made up of measures containing two groups of two eighth-notes and a group of three eighth-notes. The group of four eighth-notes is typically phrased first, followed by the group of three eighth-notes. Here is the basic metrical division of the measure:

When we trim away the fat, we have this basic rhythmic pulse.

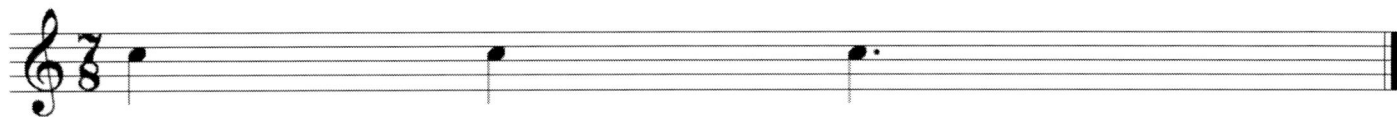

Practice tapping the pulse notated above with your right foot while either picking, strumming or clapping/tapping the following 7/8 rhythmic variations:

Variation 1:

Variation 2:

Variation 3:

Variation 4:

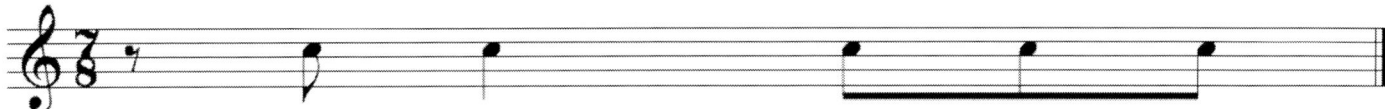

In the cases where the 3-half comes before the 4-half, the beaming will appear like this, though it is possible that you may see the a long beam, straight across the 4-half.

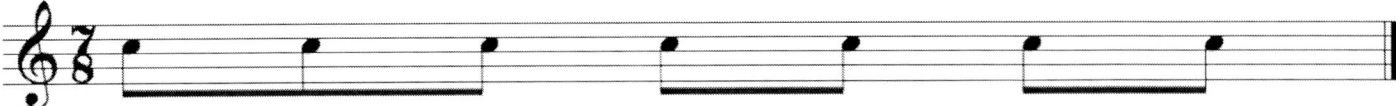

The general pulse of this brand of 7/8 goes a little something like this. Hit it.

You can practice the same 7/8 rhythmic variations over this pulse, as it is just the flipside of the original pulse. Make sure you mentally account for every eighth note place in the measure and whether it's the foot, the hand, the foot and hand, or a rest. Being able to hear and comprehend different rhythms simultaneously is a necessary skill in order to play in a real group improvisational setting without faking it

The two separate phrasings are interchangeable just as 7/8 is interchangeable with 7/4. You can have two people playing, with one playing a bass-line in 7/4 for instance, while the other person plays a melody in 7/8. Just as 3/4 and 6/8 can be simultaneously played by a group, so can 7/8 and 7/4. The one difference being that in a 7/8-7/4 situation, different players are counting measures at different speeds, but as long as that is accounted for, it can work quite nicely.

Here are a couple solid 8th note musical examples of 7/8 in action.

7/8 Example 1:

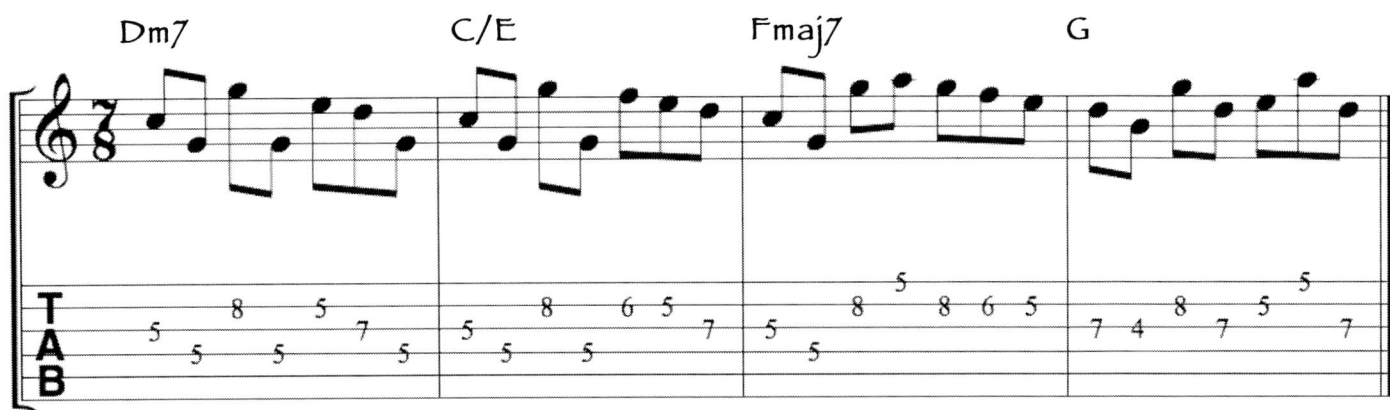

7/8 Example 2:

Here are a couple examples that make use of our four 7/8 rhythmic variations.

7/8 Example 3:

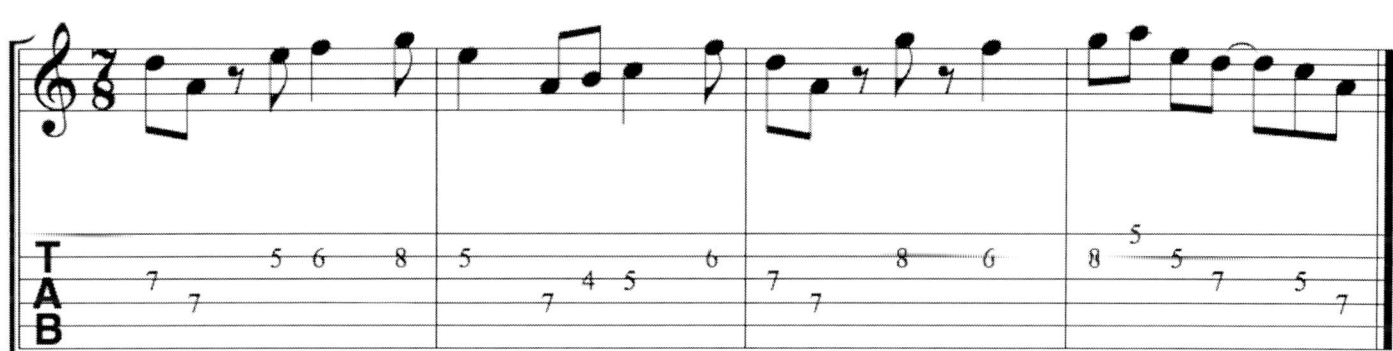

7/8 Example 4:

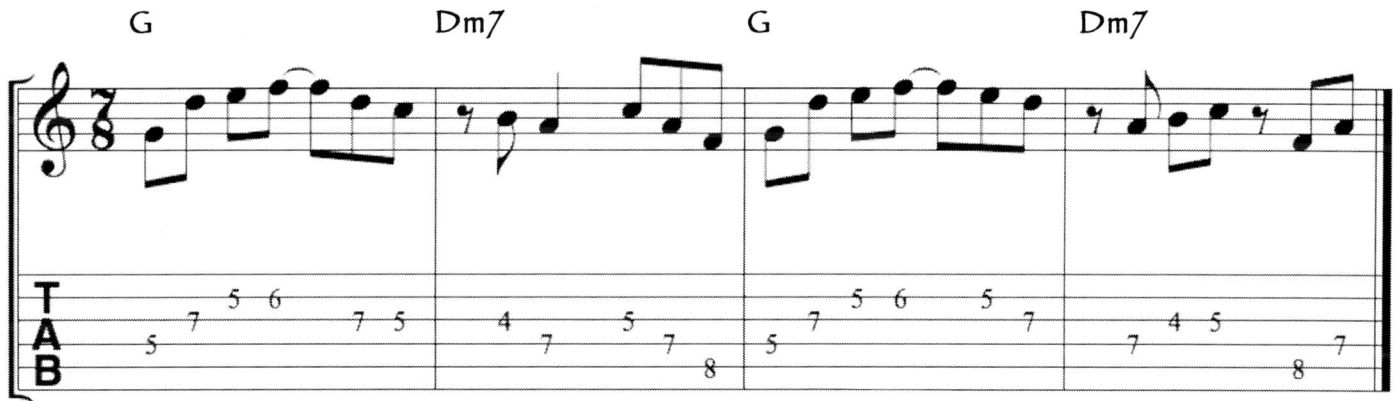

9/8

9/8 is an especially interesting time signature since it can serve as both a simple and a compound time signature. When the nine eighth-notes are grouped as a simple three groups of three, it's a simple time signature. If it is grouped as three groups of two and one group of three, it becomes a compound time. Here's the most common grouping for a compound 9/8 measure.

That leaves us this basic underlying pulse:

Although, in many cases, it gets phrased like this. In effect, what we've done is moved the long note from beat 4 to beat 2. Putting the fold, so to speak, in the middle of the measure makes it sound nice and natural upon arriving back at beat 1. (Listen to "I Hung My Head" by Sting for a nice example of the phrasing below.)

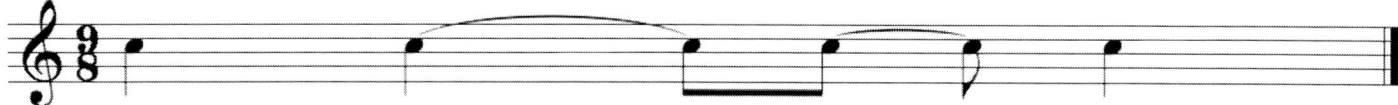

If you superimpose a measure of simple 9/8 (3 dotted quarters) within a compound 9/8 measure, the rhythm will look something like this:

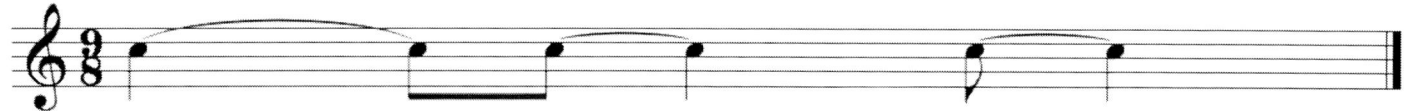

Here are some common 9/8 compound rhythmic variations:

Variation 1:

Variation 2:

Variation 3:

Variation 4:

Here are a few musical examples of a compound 9/8 meter.

9/8 Example 1:

9/8 Example 2:

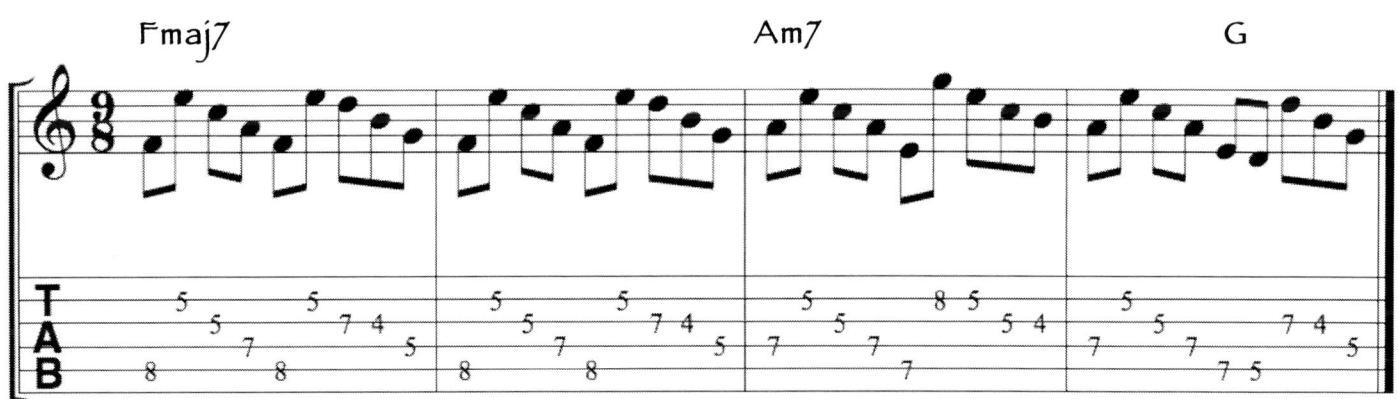

9/8 Example 3:

9/8 Example 4:

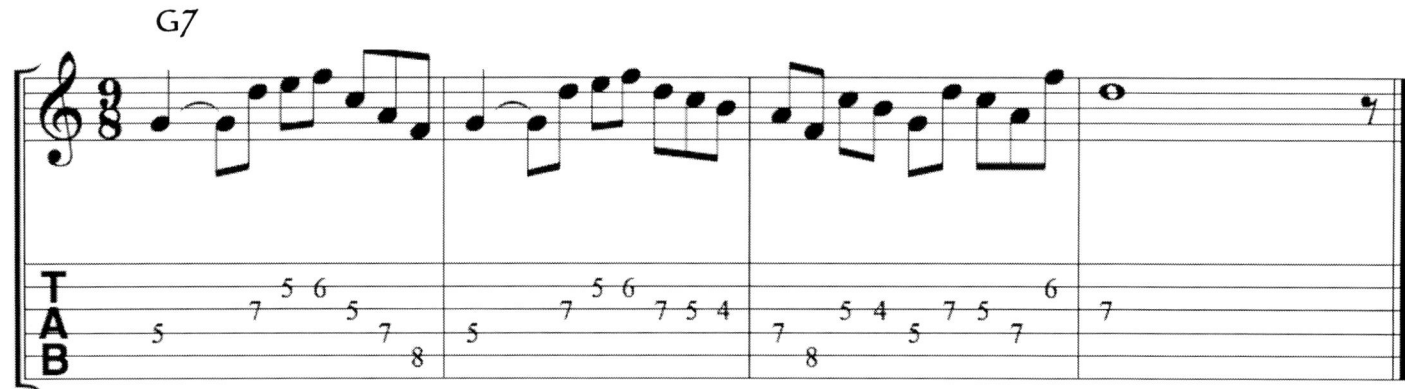

The compound meters we've gone over in this section are the most commonly used. If you get to where you feel comfortable composing and improvising within these compound times and you're feeling adventurous for more metrical challenges, there is more to explore. First off you can experiment with 11/8 and 13/8. If you still haven't had your fill, you can build compound times from a 16th note base. Some possibilities are 11/16, 13/16, 15/16 and 17/16. If you get comfortable with these and want to explore further yet, seek out mental help in the yellow pages.

But seriously, if you want to explore beyond that point you'll have to get imaginative and build composite meters out of alternating odd times and so forth. It can't hurt to take it as far as you can. Not permanently, at least. You may get a little hung up on it for a time but that won't last if you continue to learn, listen and practice.

DIATONIC HARMONY – Part 6: Extended Chords

Extended harmony can really blow things wide open as far as harmonic and melodic possibilities go. Upon learning this material, you're going to feel that you have far more in the way of options. You'll all of a sudden realize why certain seemingly "wrong" things work, things that you've probably been wondering about. You'll have more chord voicings and melodic choices. You'll see many chords as being any combination of notes within the scale that you desire at that instant and you'll see other chords as being almost as wide in possibility, with only one scale tone to avoid. This will be a serious growing period for you if you can keep an open mind to new sounds and ideas. Let us begin.

We have gone over building triads and seventh chords and we've built them from various scales. In theory a chord can be extended past the 7th into the next octave. This is where we get what we call our upper extensions, 9ths, 11ths and 13ths.

Here's how it looks on the IIm7 in the key of C major:

	1½		2W		1½		2W		1½		2W		1½	
Root		b3rd		5th		b7th		9th		11th		13th		
D		F		A		C		E		G		B		

9th = 2nd, 11th = 4th, 13th = 6th

What we're looking at here is the ideal situation for most extended harmony. Notice that when we start at the 2nd of the major scale, we get alternating major and minor 3rd intervals from one chord to the next. This creates a smooth harmony to which you could resolve. Any time you get either two major 3rds or two minor 3rds in a row, our result is a much more dissonant effect. On the following page, we have a table illustrating extended harmony as it applies to each cord within the major scale.

The far right columns are the labels for the chord functions (white box) and chord names (black box). The grey columns represent the chord-tone number (light grey box) and beneath it, the chord tone's note name (dark grey box). The white columns represent the distances between the chord-tones.

Notes found in parenthesis, in this case the F#, are points within the chord where in jazz, they will borrow from a key, a fifth away (G in our case) in order to extended out naturally, in alternating major and minor 3rds. If you try to use the F natural instead of the F#, you'll quickly hear why this adjustment is made. In most other styles of music, in the case of a repeated interval within an extended chord, the note in question is avoided altogether, with no 4th or #4th (of the key) on those particular chords (Imaj7, IIIm7, VIm7). You're going to want to read that over, after you've studied the table.

This occurs as the #11th of the Imaj7 chord. This allows us to extend smoothly all the way up to the 13th which gives us seven possible chord tones. We obviously can't use all seven at once on a conventional guitar but we can find a multitude of interesting chord voicings combining four, five or six of these notes at a time. More on that, soon.

The next place that it occurs is one the IIIm7, where we would borrow the F# to use as a 9th on the chord. Like I've said, this is how it's handled in jazz. In other styles, we simply avoid putting a 9th on our IIIm7 chord. In the same chord, we run into another situation where we would get two minor third intervals in a row. If we were to raise this C as we did with the F, we would in effect be raising the root note and taking yourself another key further away from shore. This gets too hairy and is typically avoided like the plague, so no 13th on the IIIm chord.

Our adjustable tone occurs once more as the 13th of our VIm chord. This gives the VIm chord an unexpected brightness just as the very same note effected the sound of the Imaj7 chord. It's worth noting that every time we ran into the double interval phenomenon, we always found ourselves landing on the 4th of the key. This is true with the exception of the b13th of the IIIm7, which happens to be the root note of our key.

The IIm7 lays out perfectly with alternating scale tones. This is what makes Dorian the easiest and most natural minor mode for improvisation. Absolutely any tone in the scale can be considered a chord tone. In jazz, the VIm chord gets modeled after the IIm7, causing us to borrow from the key a 5th away, where our current VIm7 would serve as the IIm7. The IVmaj7 lays out perfectly as well. This makes Lydian the most natural major mode for improvisation as any scale-tone can be a chord-tone. When we raise the 11th of the Imaj7, we are basically pretending that we are on the IVmaj7 of the key, a 5th away.

The V7 does not lay out in alternating intervals as we like to see with our major and minor chords. This is OK though as the V7 chord is kind of like that quirky wild card of an aunt that makes family holiday gatherings a little more interesting. We love her for her quirkiness. In fact, we like to make sure that she has plenty to drink. This is my analogy for altering the 5th and/or the 9th, 11th and 13th of the V7 chord. This heightens the tension and adds character and color to the chord. This is wonderful for us because the whole function of the V7 is TENSION! Now that this is clearly seen, revisit the Super-Locrian mode section of the book.

Imaj7	Root	2W	3rd	1½	5th	2W	7th	1½	9th	2W	#11th	1½	13th
Cmaj7	C	2W	E	1½	G	2W	B	1½	D	2W	(F#)	1½	A
IIm7	Root	1½	b3rd	2W	5th	1½	b7th	2W	9th	1½	11th	2W	13th
Dm7	D	1½	F	2W	A	1½	C	2W	E	1½	G	2W	B
IIIm7	Root	1½	b3rd	2W	5th	1½	b7th	2W	9th	1½	11th	1½	b13th
Em7	E	1½	G	2W	B	1½	D	2W	(F#)	1½	A	1½	C
IVmaj7	Root	2W	3rd	1½	5th	2W	7th	1½	9th	2W	#11th	1½	13th
Fmaj7	F	2W	A	1½	C	2W	E	1½	G	2W	B	1½	D
V7	Root	2W	3rd	1½	5th	1½	b7th	2W	9th	1½	11th	2W	13th
G7	G	2W	B	1½	D	1½	F	2W	A	1½	C	2W	E
VIm7	Root	1½	b3rd	2W	5th	1½	b7th	2W	9th	1½	11th	2W	13th
Am7	A	1½	C	2W	E	1½	G	2W	B	1½	D	2W	(F#)
VIIm7b5	Root	1½	b3rd	1½	b5th	2W	b7th	1½	b9th	2W	11th	1½	b13th
Bm7b5	B	1½	D	1½	F	2W	A	1½	C	2W	E	1½	G

Extended Chord Voicings for Guitar, E Form, Major:

These major voicings all have their bass notes on the low E string. The top row are all smaller voicings that will work better in most band situations and much more suitable for pop application. The bottom row will be more at home in a jazz style. It's worth mentioning that the bass notes become expendable when playing with a bass player and without the bass-notes, you'll obviously want to rethink your fingerings, so be sure to practice these with and without the bass notes, as they are a quite different physical experience from one another.

When building extended chords, the most expendable notes are first and foremost, any doubled notes and secondly, any 5ths as they don't provide any specific major, minor or dominant qualities. Pay special attention, not only to what notes are *not* present just as closely as which notes *are* present. Remember that both nomenclature and usage of extended harmony remains rather loose, being that the majority of it is very interchangeable.

Another thing to bear in mind is that if you are using these voicings in jazz, you can use any one of them for any maj7 chord function. If you are using these in a pop, or rock style, you probably want to avoid using any of the voicings that include the #11th when you are on the I chord. You will find the occasional #11th on a I chord in some musically daring rock songs but it is very rare.

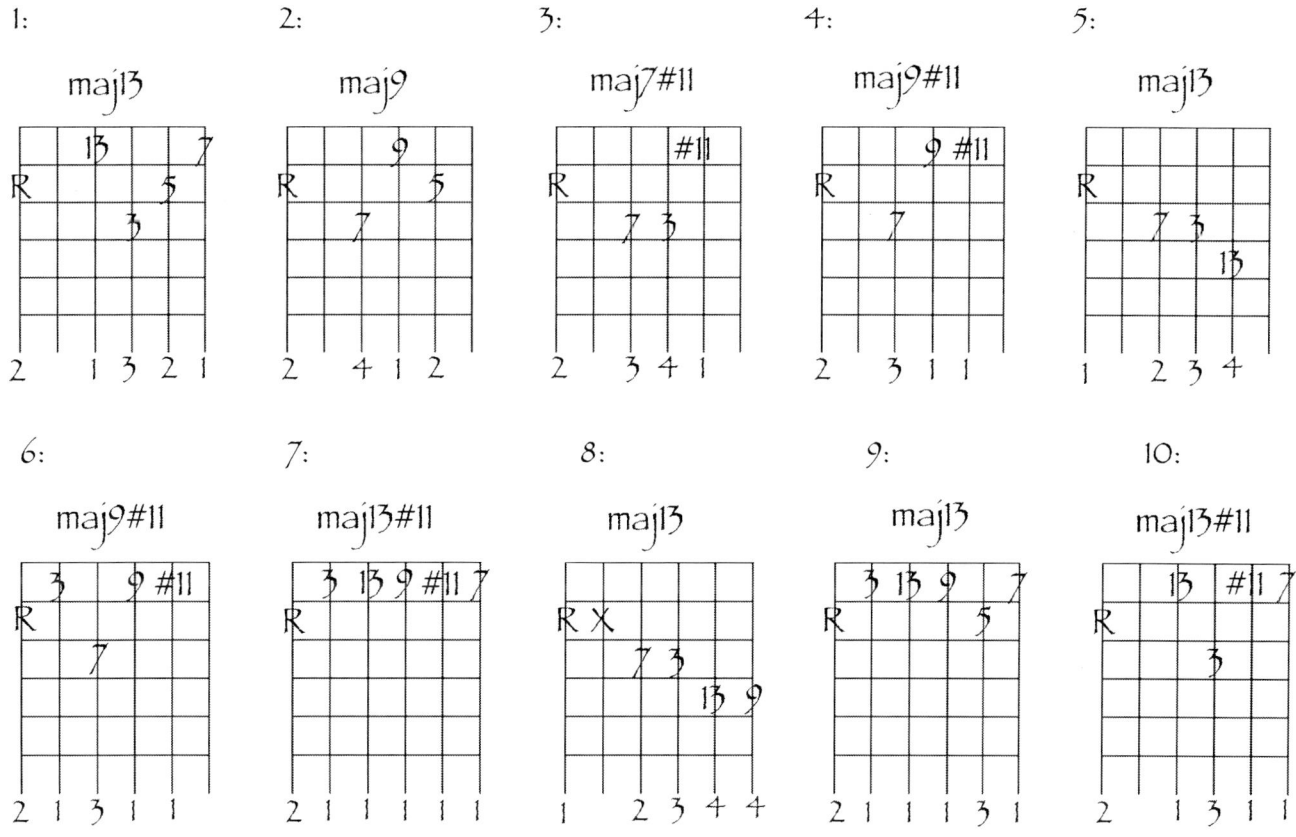

Extended Chord Voicings for Guitar, A Form, Major:

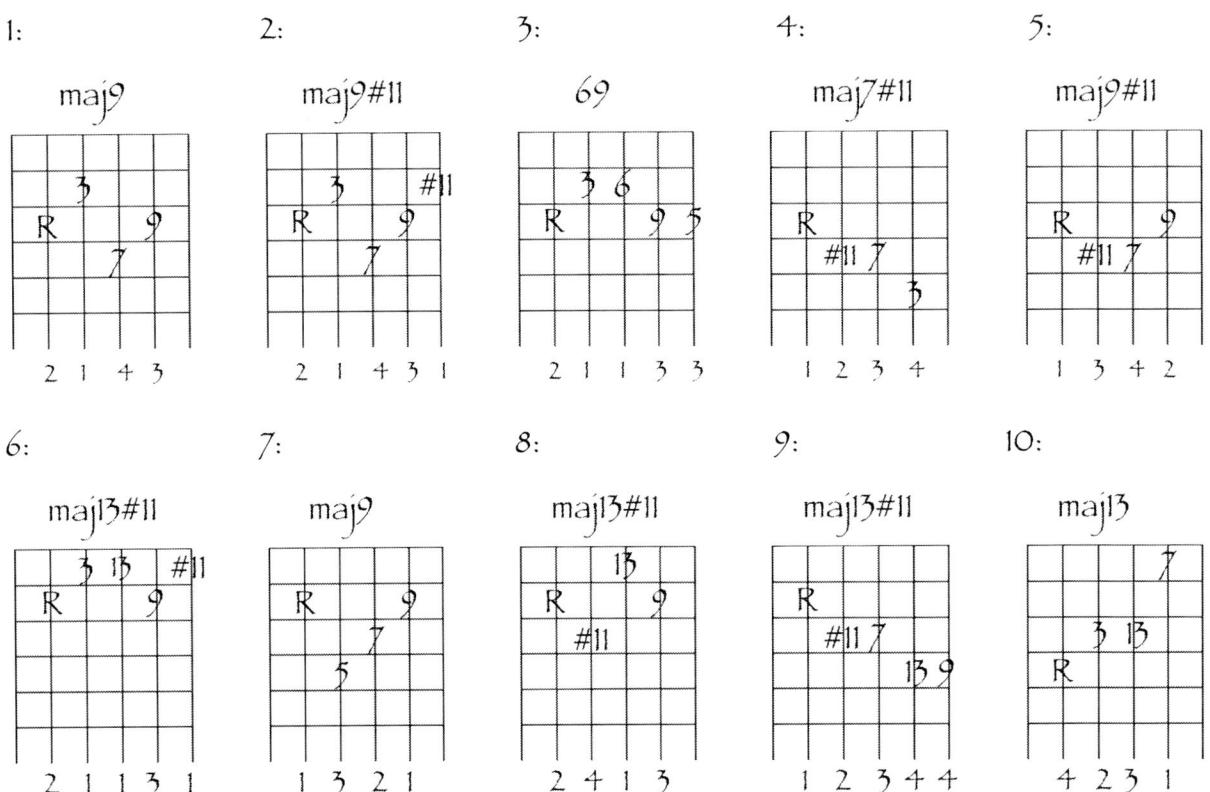

Extended Chord Voicings for Guitar, E Form, Minor:

In jazz, any of these voicing can be used for any minor chord function. In pop and rock however, the 13ths are typically avoided, especially on the VIm chord. I have notated use of the left hand thumb to fret the bass note of chord voicing number 8. Voicings 9 and 10 are voicings that only work in the context of playing with a bass player. This is why the bass notes are in parenthesis on these two chords. Just as I had written in relation to the major chords, you want to practice the rest with and without the bass notes.

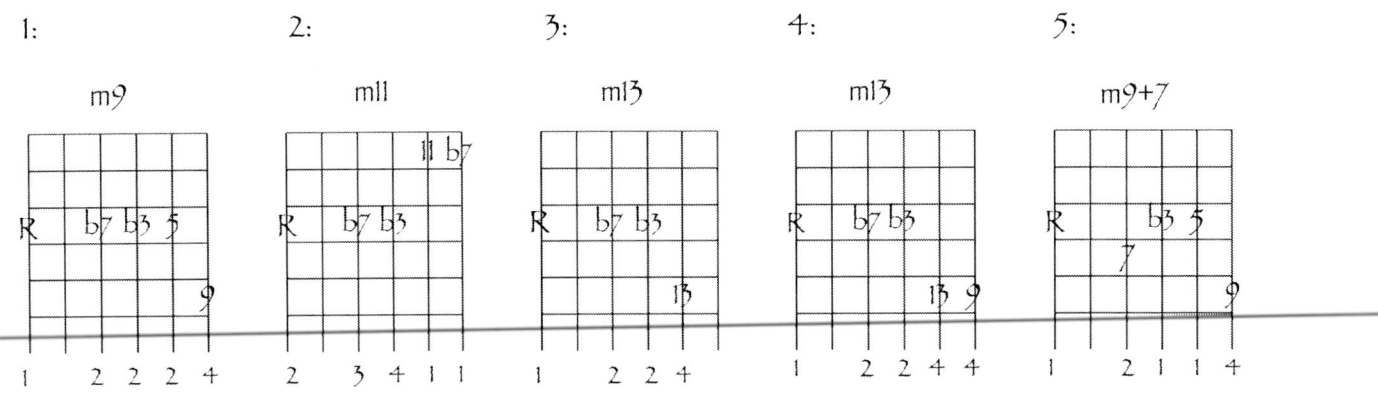

Extended Chord Voicings for Guitar, E Form, Minor, continued:

6: m9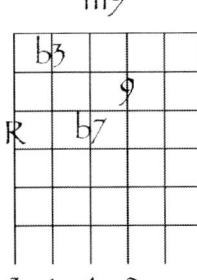

7: m11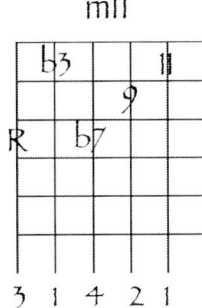

8: m11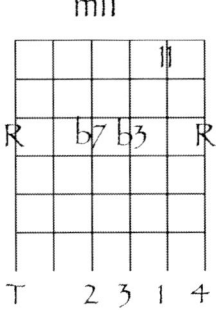

9: m11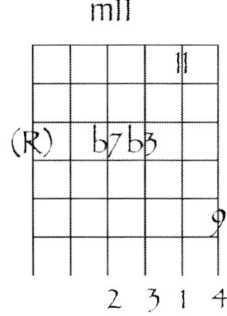

10: m13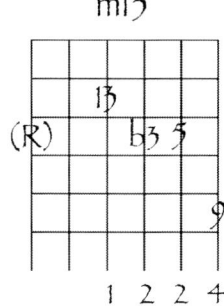

Extended Chord Voicings for Guitar, A Form, Minor:

1: m9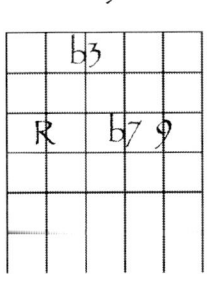

2: m9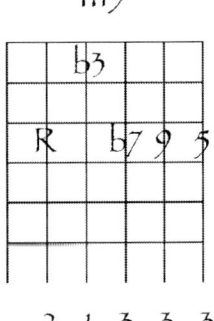

3: m11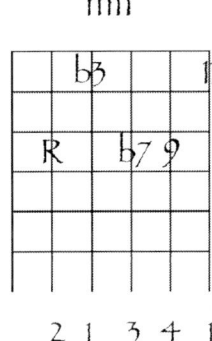

4: m11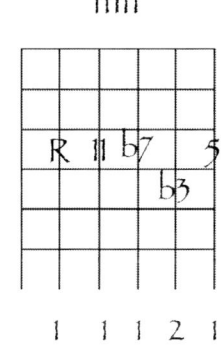

5: m11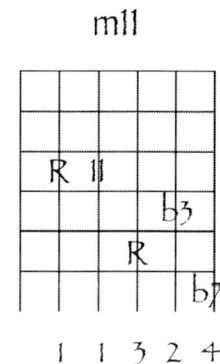

6: m13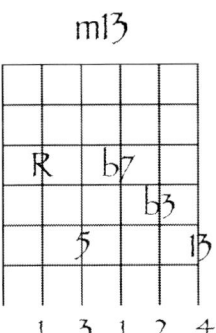

7: m13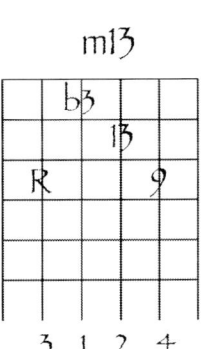

8: m9+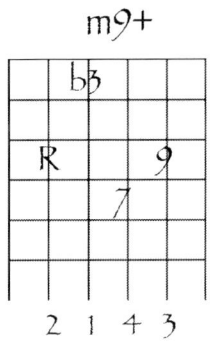

9: m9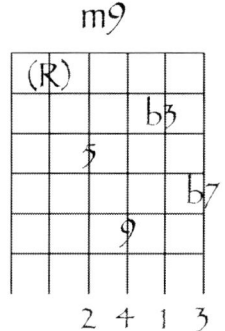

10: m13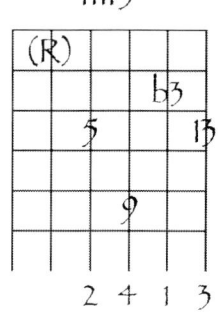

Extended Chord Voicings for Guitar, E Form, Dominant:

The top rows of both the E form and A form dominant are made up of what we consider natural dominant chord voicings. This is in spite of the fact that a couple of these voicings contain #11ths. 9#11 chords derive most naturally from the Lydian Dominant mode, and apply directly to what we call non-functioning dominant chords. The bottom row of both the E form and A form dominant chords are made up of altered dominant chord voicings, which derive from the Super-Locrian mode.

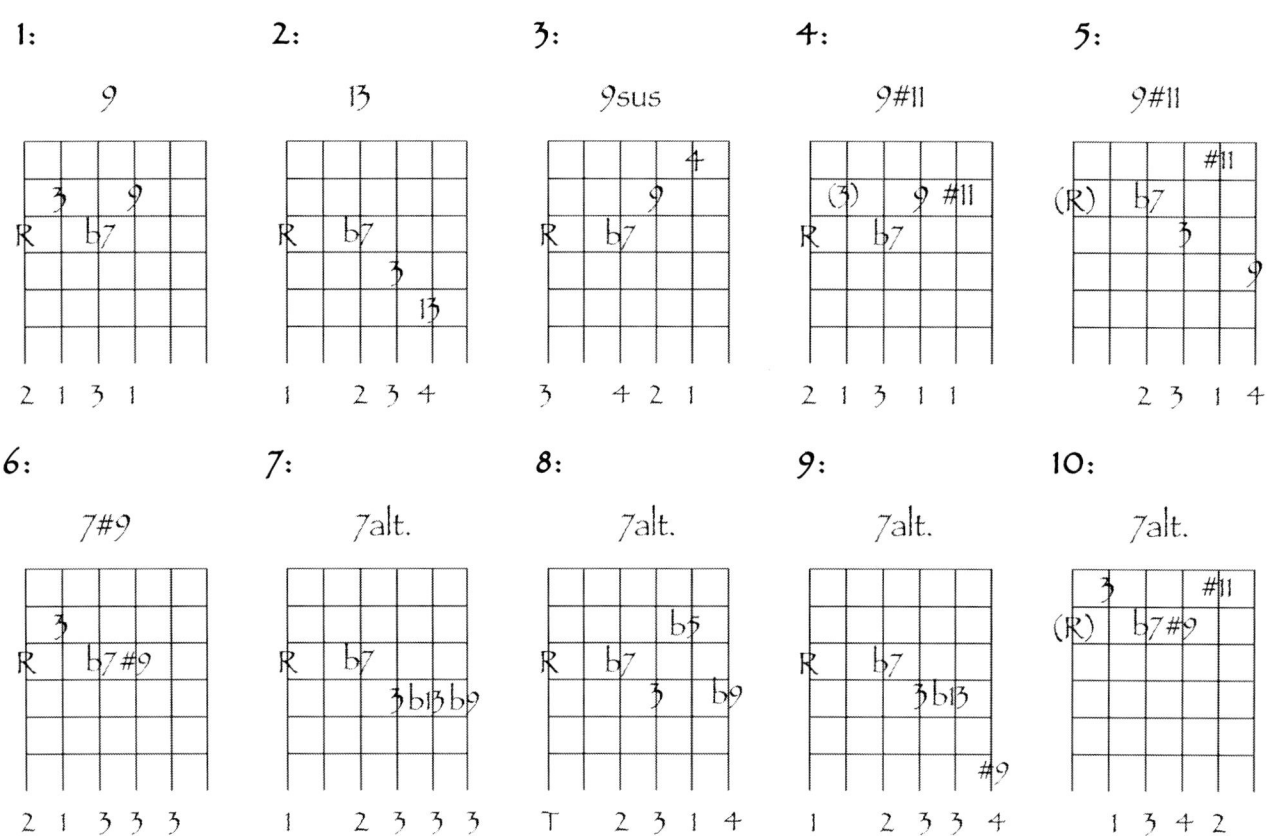

Extended Chord Voicings for Guitar, A Form, Dominant:

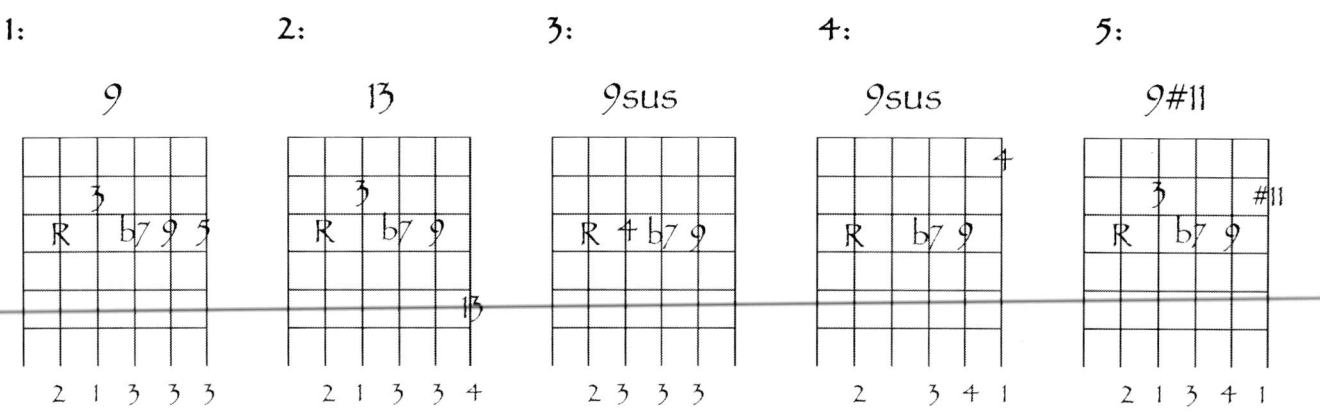

Extended Chord Voicings for Guitar, A Form, Dominant, continued:

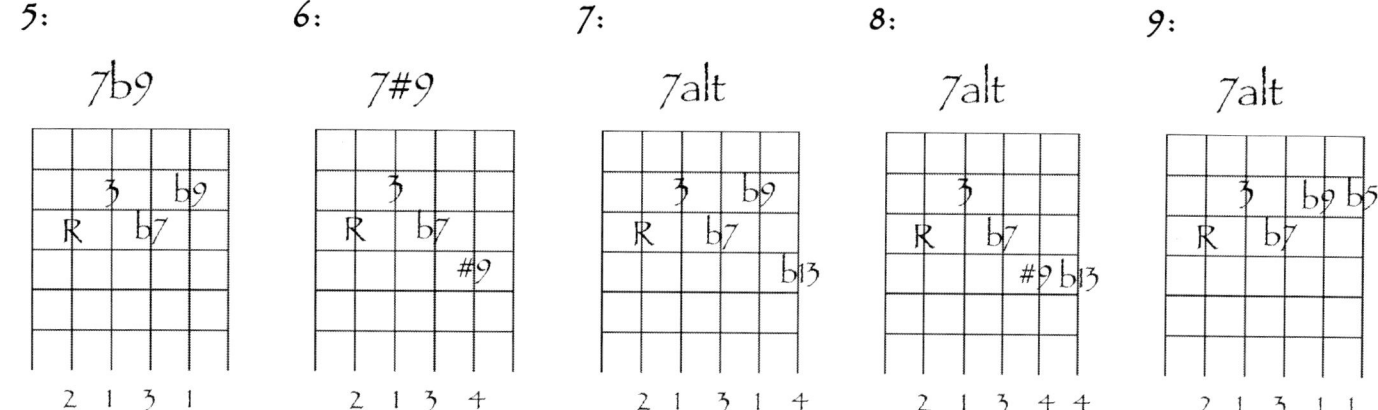

Triad Super-Imposition

When I'm playing in a full band situation or layering tracks in a recording, I rarely use voicings that I've listed above. I use them when I play in a trio, duo or solo context. In larger groups and multi-instrument recordings, I prefer implying extended chords by playing triads that contain the upper extensions of the actual underlying chords. It makes for physically easier parts to play that contain just as much color and musical depth. Here's how this works:

Each extended chord is a stack of overlapping triads. Just as we learned that we could imply a Cmaj7 by playing an Em triad over the C bass note, we can imply a Cmaj13#11 chord by playing a D major triad over the C bass note. The root of the D triad serves as the 9th of C, the 3rd of the D triad, F# serves as the #11th of the C and the 5th of the D triad, A serves as the 13th. Below is a table in the key of C major that should help you see the possibilities clearly.

	Triad Off Root	Triad Off 3rd	Triad Off 5th	Triad Off 7th	Triad Off 9th
Imaj7	C: C E G / R 3 5	Em: E G B / 3 5 7	G: G B D / 5 7 9	Bm: B D F# / 7 9 #11	D: D F# A / 9 #11 13
IIm7	Dm: D F A / R b3 5	F: F A C / b3 5 b7	Am: A C E / 5 b7 9	C: C E G / b7 9 11	Em: E G B / 9 11 13
IIIm7	Em: E G B / R b3 5	G: G B D / b3 5 b7	Bm: B D F# / 5 b7 9	D: D F# A / b7 9 11	☹
IVmaj7	F: F A C / R 3 5	Am: A C E / 3 5 7	C: C E G / 5 7 9	Em: E G B / 7 9 #11	G: G B D / 9 #11 13
V7	G: G B D / R 3 5	Bdim: B D F / 3 5 b7	Dm: D F A / 5 b7 9	F: F A C / b7 9 11	Am: A C E / 9 11 13
VIm7	Am: A C E / R b3 5	C: C E G / b3 5 b7	Em: E G B / 5 b7 9	G: G B D / b7 9 11	Bm: B D F# / 9 11 13
VIIm7b5	Bdim: B D F / R b3 b5	Dm: D F A / b3 b5 b7	F: F A C / b5 b7 b9	☹	☹

340

Upon doing this sort of analysis with this scale and others, I've arrived at these seven triad super-impositions that I find myself frequently using. The first three are relationships that we can clearly see in the previous table. Number 4 relates to the Lydian Dominant mode, number 5 relates to the Diminished scale, number 6 relates to both the Diminished scale and the Super Locrian mode and number seven relates to the Super Locrian mode.

1) maj13#11: Major triad played a whole-step up from the chord.

2) 9, 9sus, m9: Minor triad based on 5th of chord.

3) 9sus: Major triad played a whole-step down from the root of the chord.

4) 9#11: Augmented triad played a whole-step up or down from the root of the chord (or a tritone away).

5) 13b9: Major triad played a step and a half down from the root of the chord.

6) 7alt (b5, b9): Major triad played a tritone away from the root of the chord.

7) 7alt (b9, b13): Minor triad played a half-step up from the root of the chord.

When you use these super-impositions, especially in a rock or pop context, it's important that you aren't using them in the exactly the same register as somebody who's playing the foundational notes of the chord. Either invert upward or get them to invert downward until there's a clear sonic separation between the foundational tones and the upper extensions. When you abide by this around 95% of the time, with the occasional exception, you can get some really sophisticated sounds with two guitars (or a guitar and keyboard) each playing two or three notes.

A little food for thought:

It's good to know that nothing but the bass note and the superimposed triad is enough to get the quality of the chord across the to the listener, being that we as humans have an incredible ability to fill in the blanks. When someone creates music with this human ability in mind, it can result much more compelling music than you would otherwise hear from them.

ARPEGGIOS — Part 3: Triad Pairs of the Melodic Minor Scale

Previously, with arpeggios, we combined triads from the major scale in order to build nicely moving melodic patterns. We'll now go into how this can be done with certain triad pairs from the Melodic Minor scale. Some of the opposing (no notes in common) triad pairs in the Melodic Minor scale are the same as what we find in the major scale. We have two minor chords a whole-step apart from one another. We have two major chords one whole step apart from one another. Other pairs are different from what we find in the major scale. We have two diminished triads, a whole step apart from one another, which is fairly unique to the scale, but given the fact that diminished triads are not very useful in the first place, these are not really of any interest to us.

That leaves us with only two triad pairs that are unique to the scale. The first of which is a minor triad a half-step beneath an augmented triad (IIm, bIII+). The second of which is an augmented triad a whole-step beneath a major triad (bIII+, IV). Here's a guide to how these triad pairs can be applied to some static chords:

Triad Pairs:	Can Be Applied Over These Static Chords: (In C major)
Gm – Ab+	Bb9#11, E7alt, C9b13, Fm9+
Ab+ – Bb	Bb9#11, E7alt, C9b13, Fm9+

In this section, we're going take the two triad pairs and build the same melodic patterns from them. We'll start with the IIm bIII+ pair:

Gm – Ab+, Weaving Pattern at the 3rd Fret, Ascending:

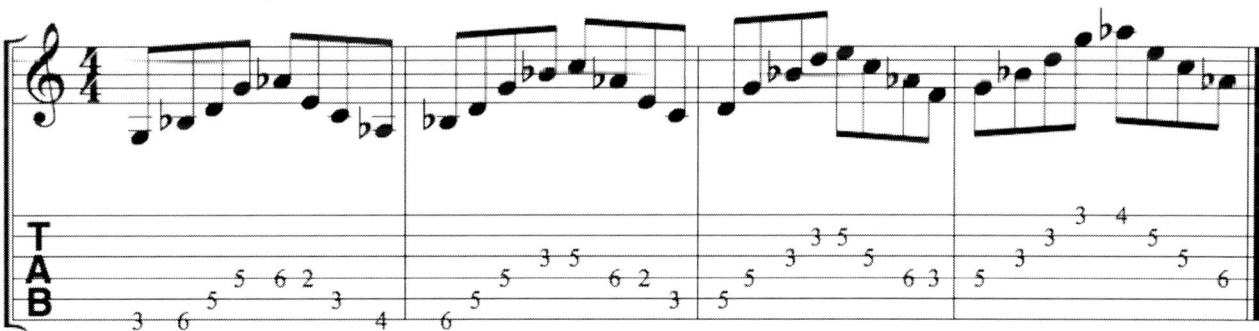

Gm – Ab+, Weaving Pattern at the 3rd Fret, Descending:

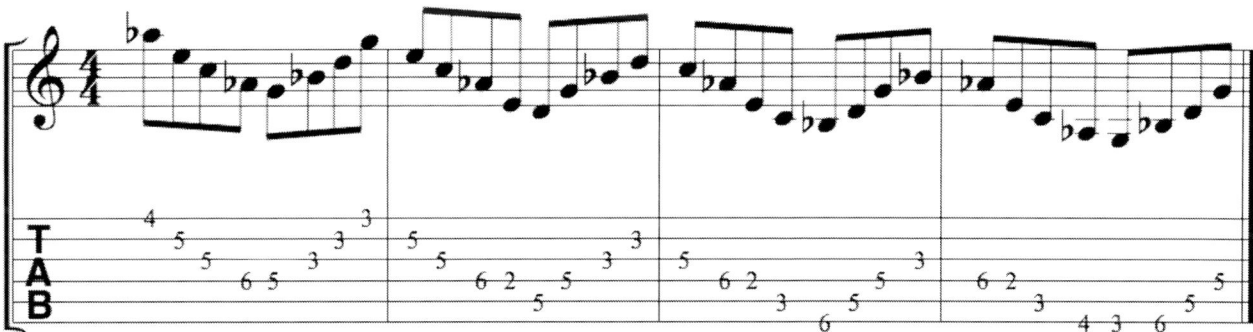

Gm – Ab+, Weaving Inverse Pattern at the 3rd Fret, Ascending:

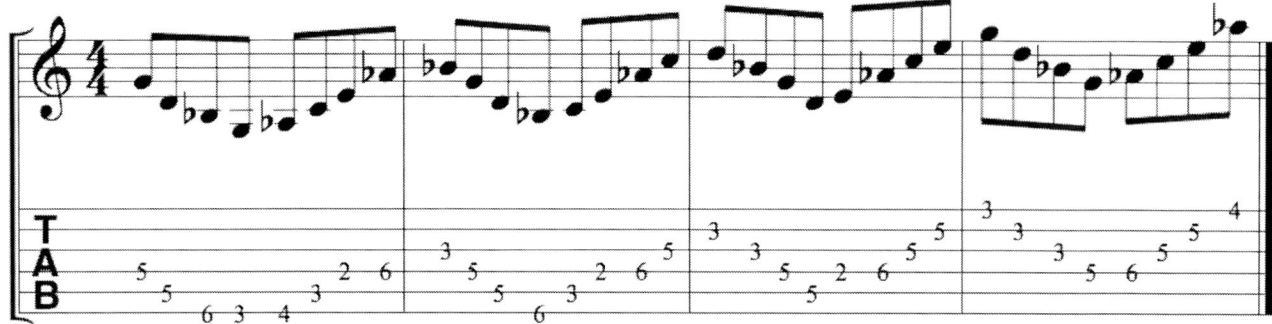

Gm – Ab+, Weaving Inverse Pattern at the 3rd Fret, Descending:

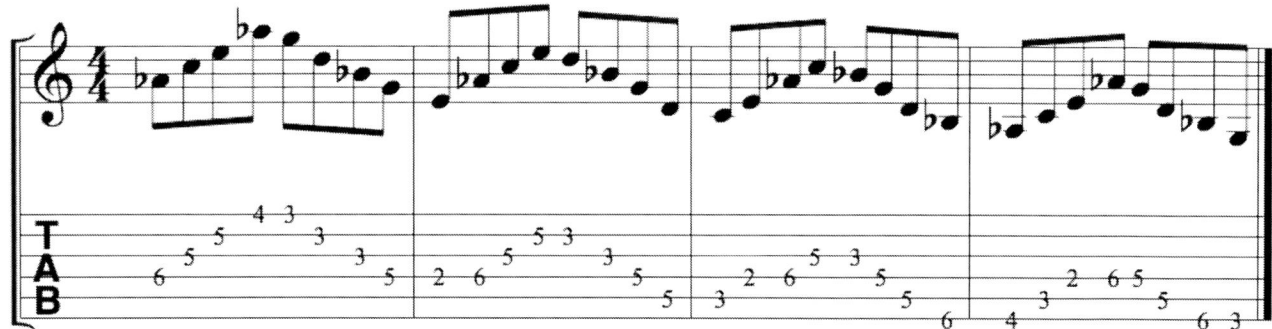

Gm – Ab+, Weaving Pattern at the 5th Fret, Ascending:

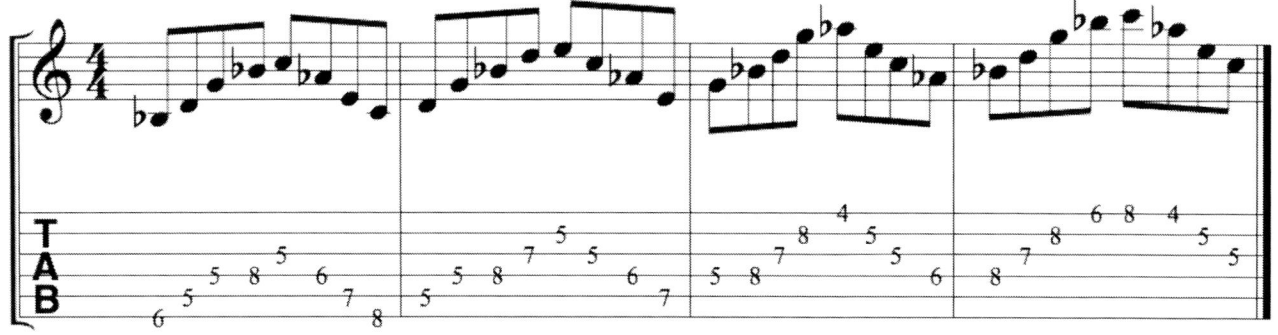

Gm – Ab+, Weaving Pattern at the 5th Fret, Descending:

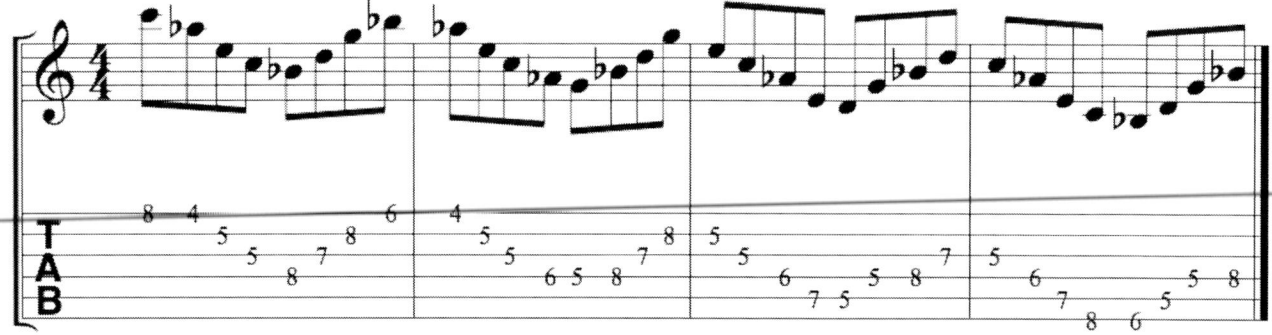

Gm – Ab+, Inverse Weaving Pattern at the 5th Fret, Ascending:

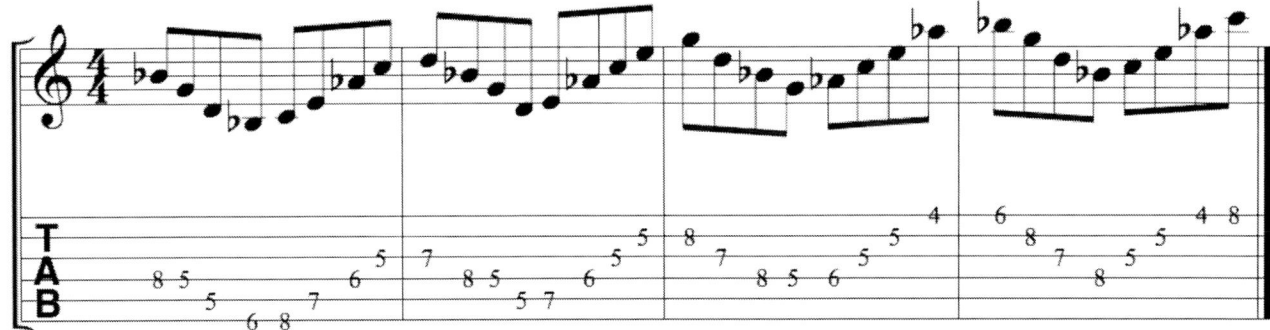

Gm – Ab+, Inverse Weaving Pattern at the 5th Fret, Descending:

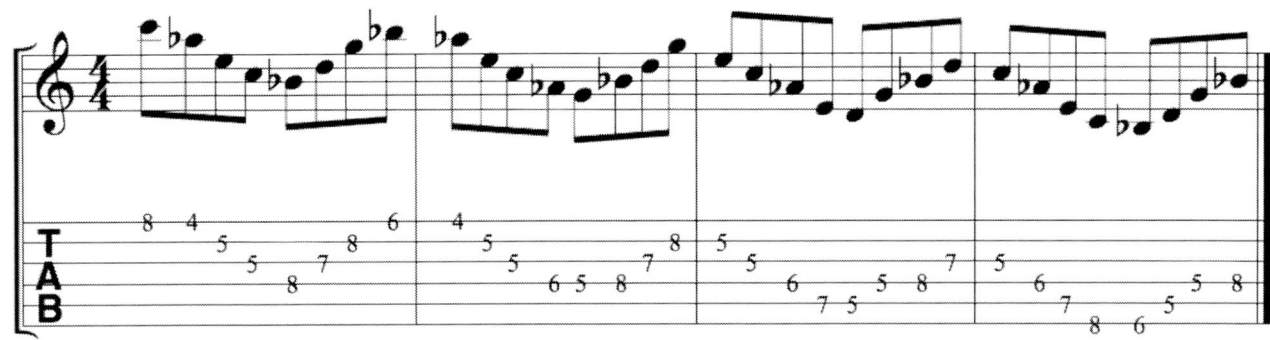

Gm – Ab+, Weaving Pattern at the 7th Fret, Ascending:

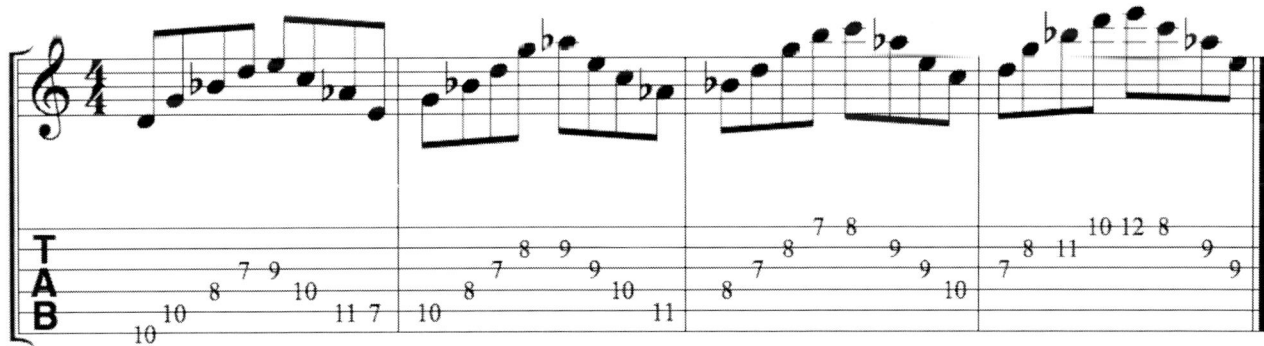

Gm – Ab+, Weaving Pattern at the 7th Fret, Descending:

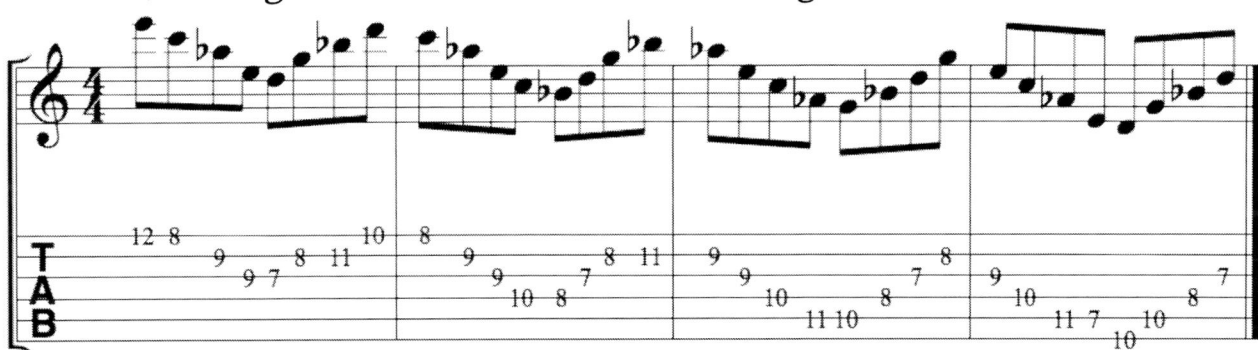

Gm – Ab+, Inverse Weaving Pattern at the 7th Fret, Ascending:

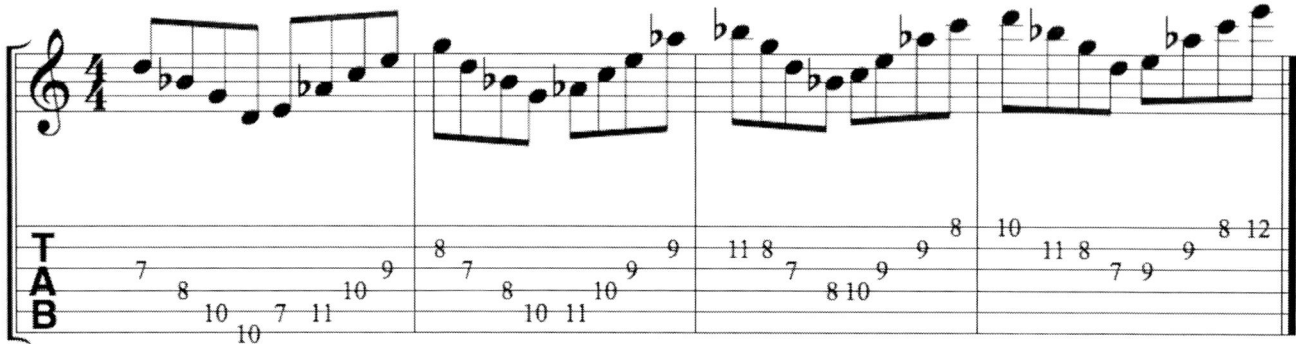

Gm – Ab+, Inverse Weaving Pattern at the 7th Fret, Descending:

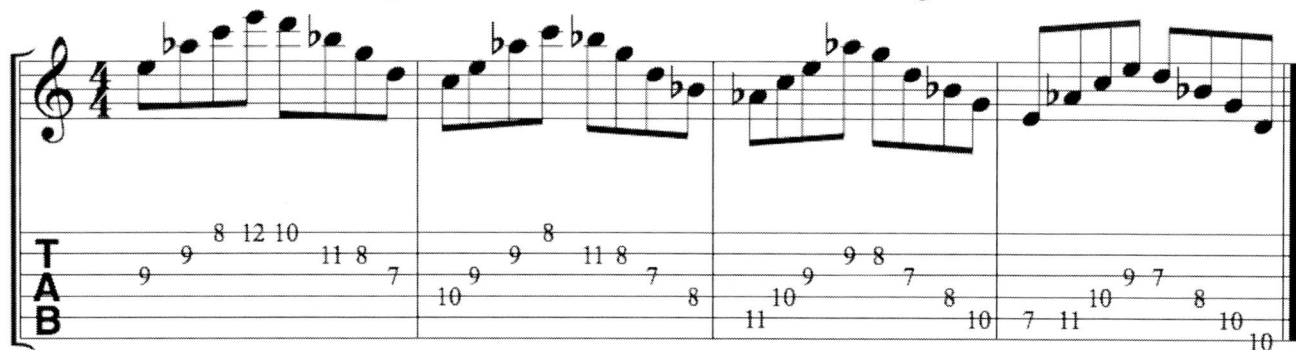

Gm – Ab+, Weaving Pattern at the 9th Fret, Ascending:

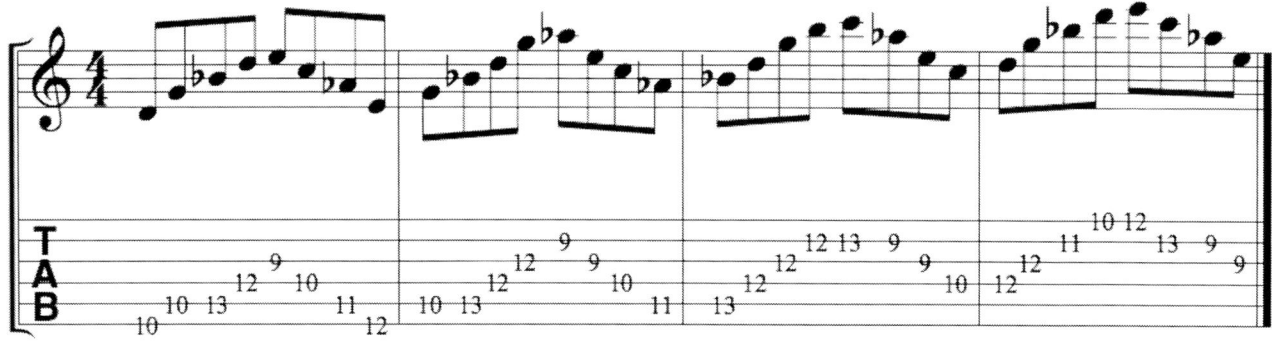

Gm – Ab+, Weaving Pattern at the 9th Fret, Descending:

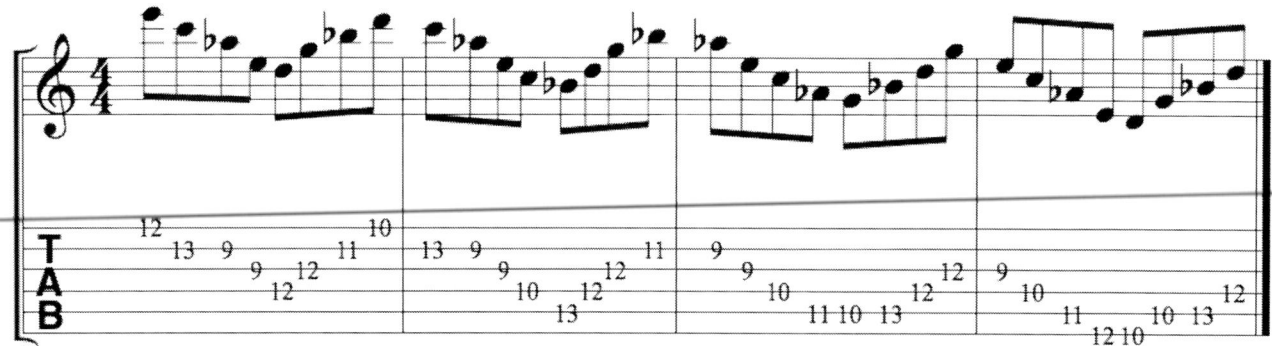

Gm – Ab+, Inverse Weaving Pattern at the 9th Fret, Ascending:

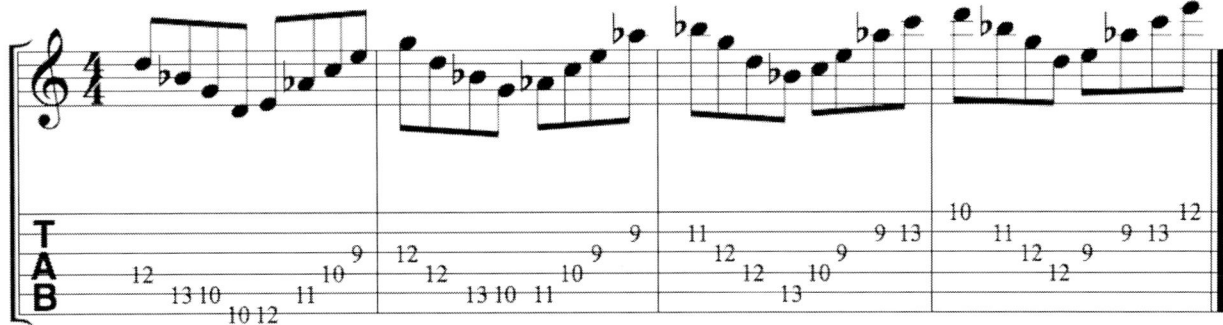

Gm – Ab+, Weaving Pattern at the 9th Fret, Descending:

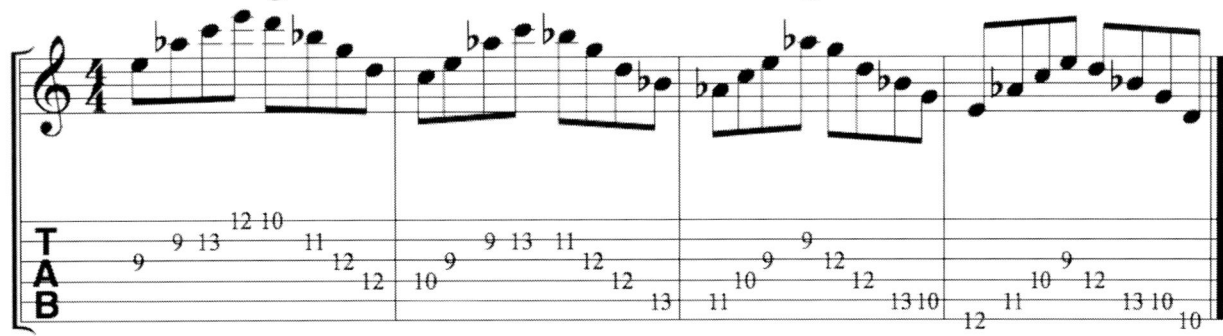

Gm – Ab+, Weaving Pattern at the 12th Fret, Ascending:

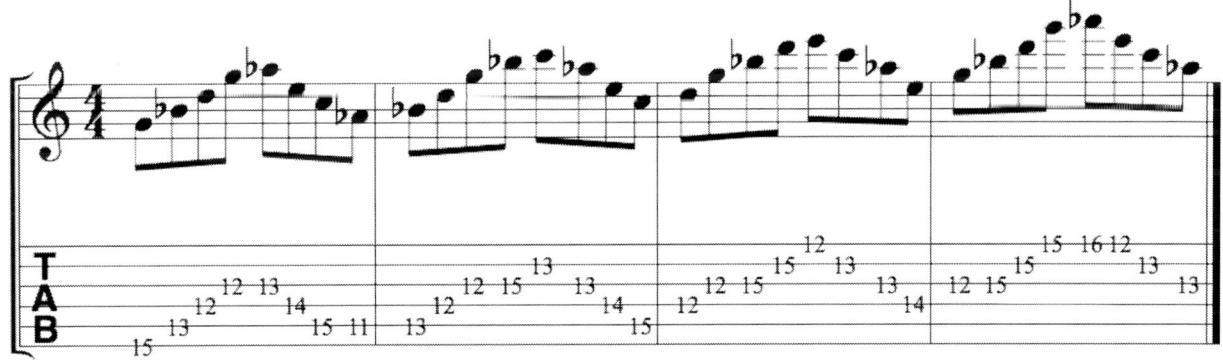

Gm – Ab+, Weaving Pattern at the 12th Fret, Descending:

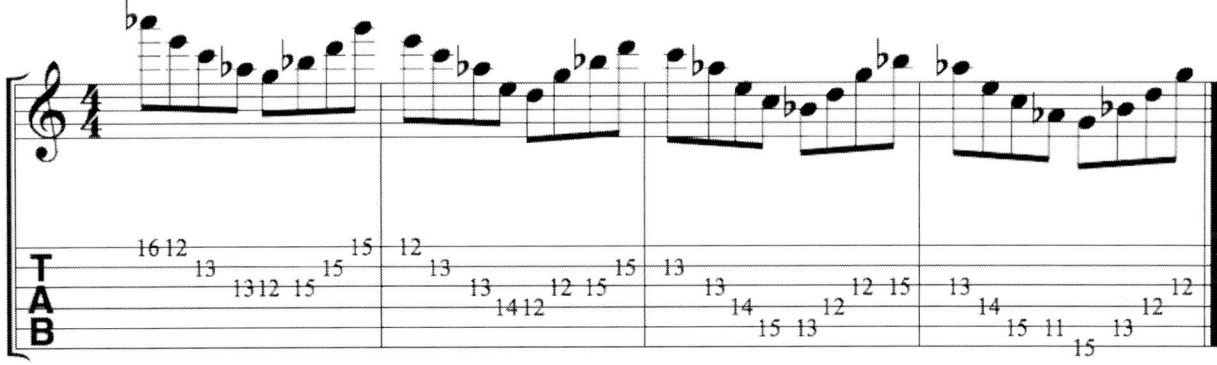

Gm – Ab+, Inverse Weaving Pattern at the 12th Fret, Ascending:

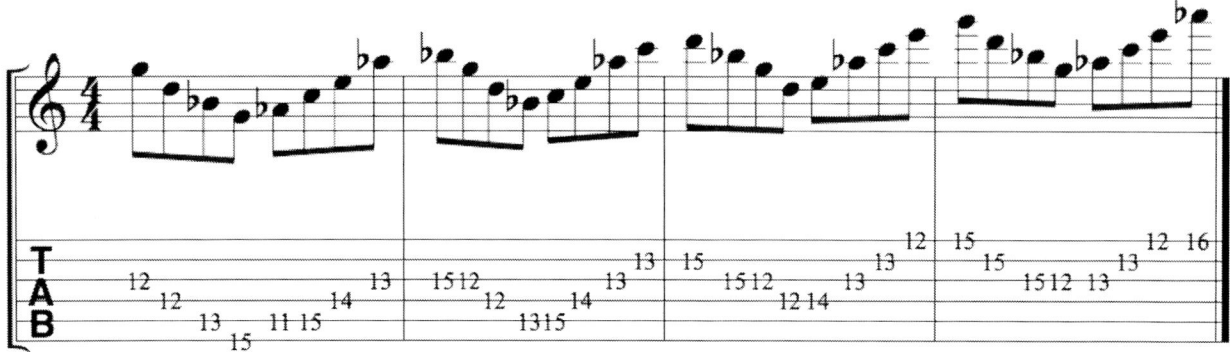

Gm – Ab+, Inverse Weaving Pattern at the 12th Fret, Descending:

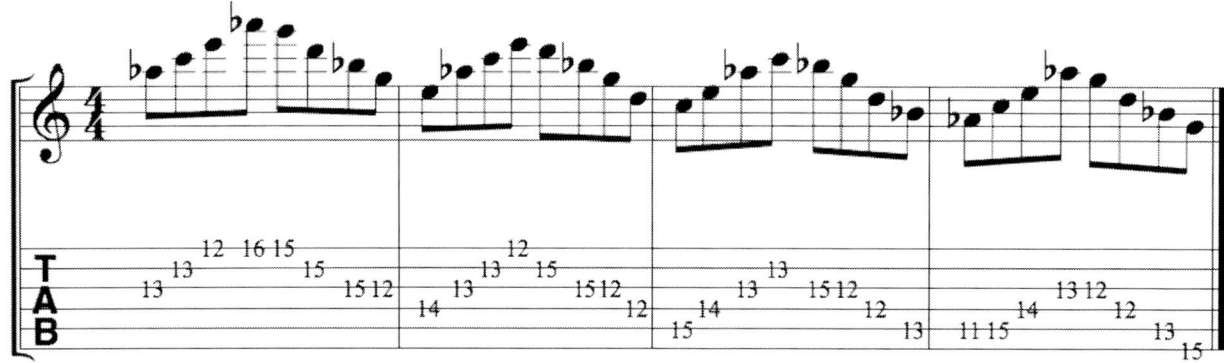

Ab+ – Bb, Weaving Pattern at the 3rd Fret, Ascending:

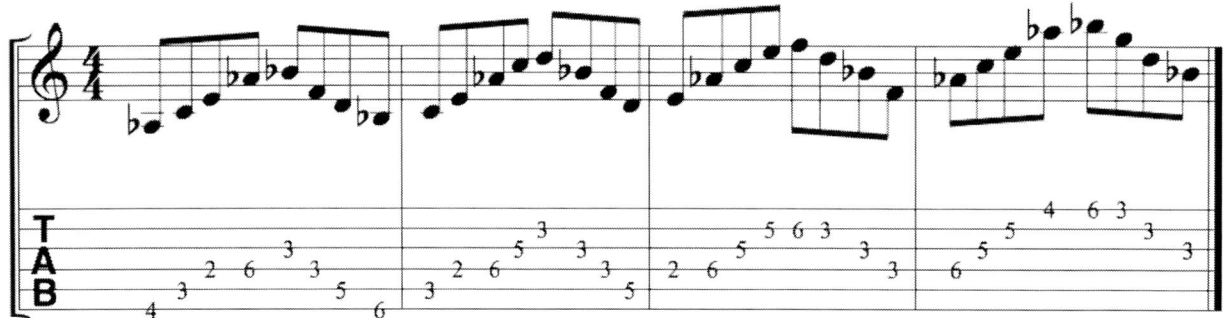

Ab+ – Bb, Weaving Pattern at the 3rd Fret, Descending:

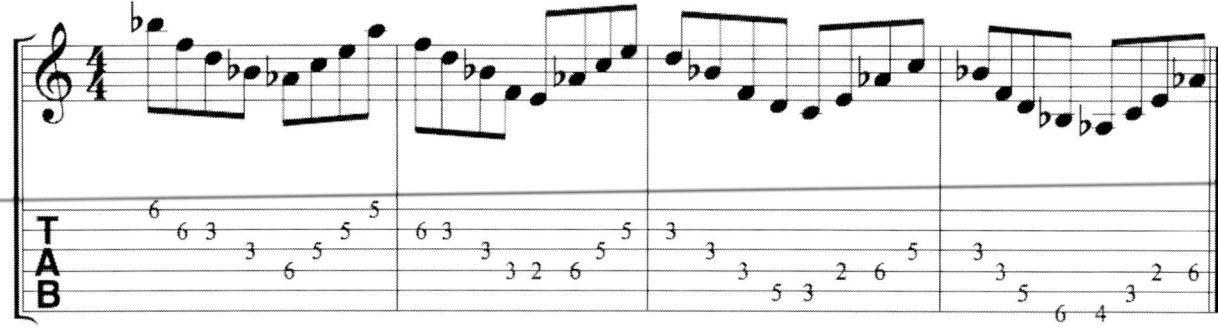

Ab+ – Bb, Inverse Weaving Pattern at the 3rd Fret, Ascending:

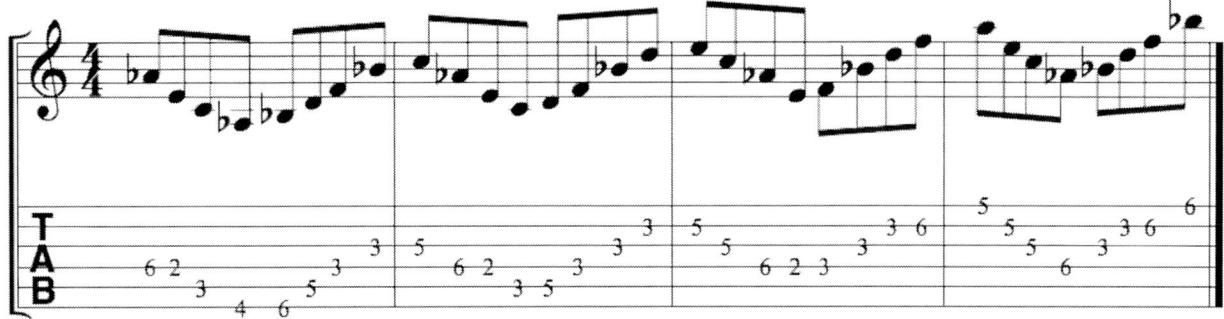

Ab+ – Bb, Inverse Weaving Pattern at the 3rd Fret, Descending:

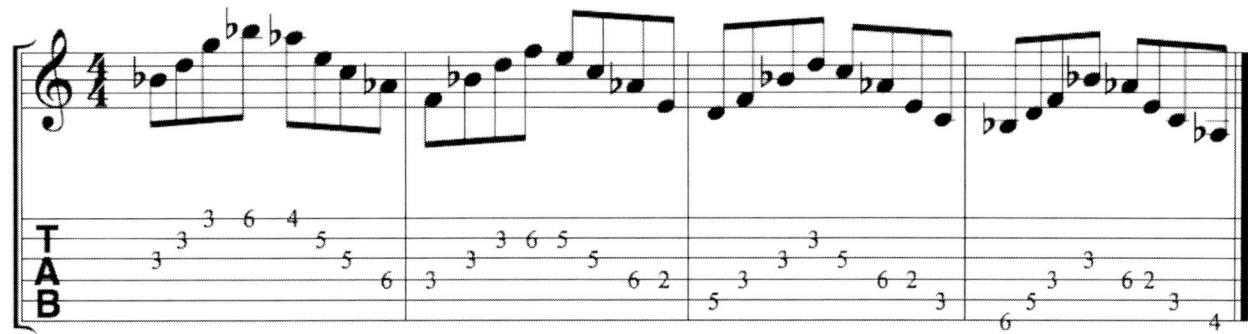

Ab+ – Bb, Weaving Pattern at the 5th Fret, Ascending:

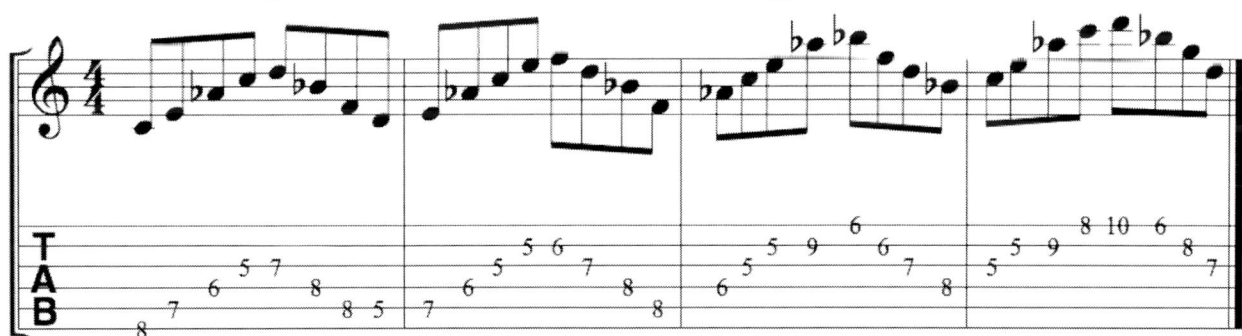

Ab+ – Bb, Weaving Pattern at the 5th Fret, Descending:

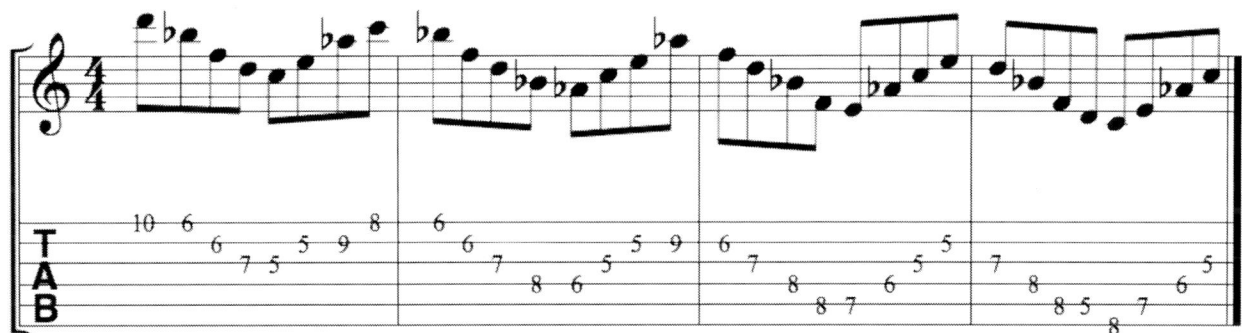

Ab+ - Bb, Inverse Weaving Pattern at the 5th Fret, Ascending:

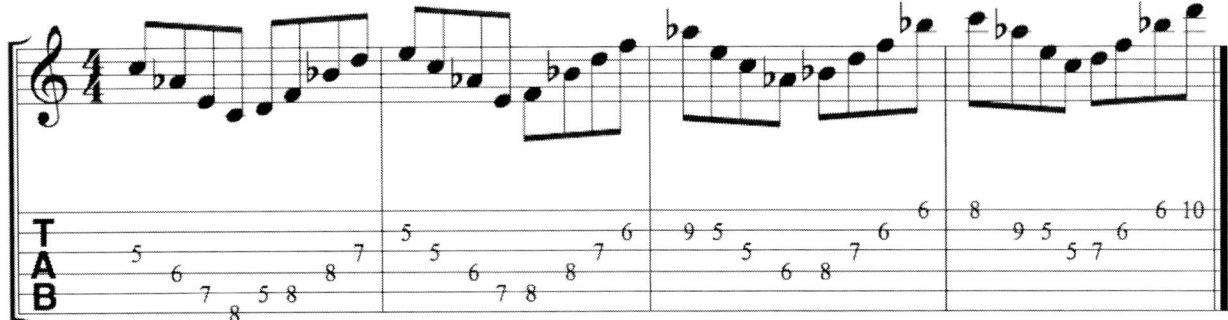

Ab+ - Bb, Inverse Weaving Pattern at the 5th Fret, Descending:

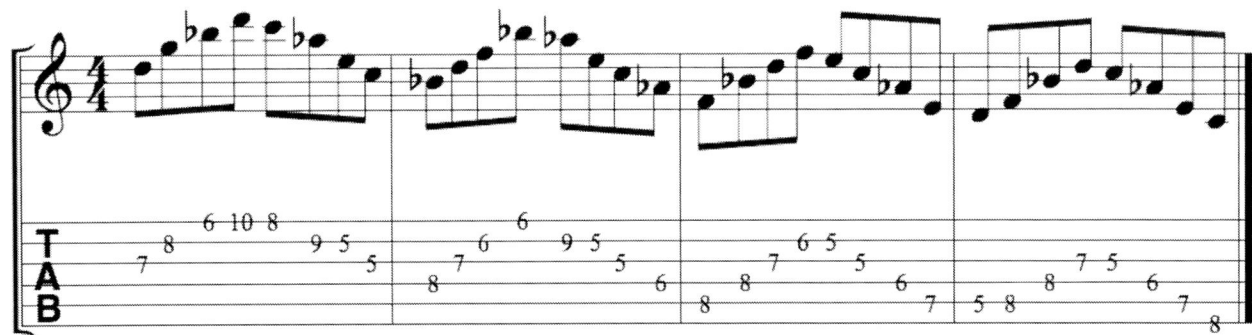

Ab+ - Bb, Weaving Pattern at the 7th Fret, Ascending:

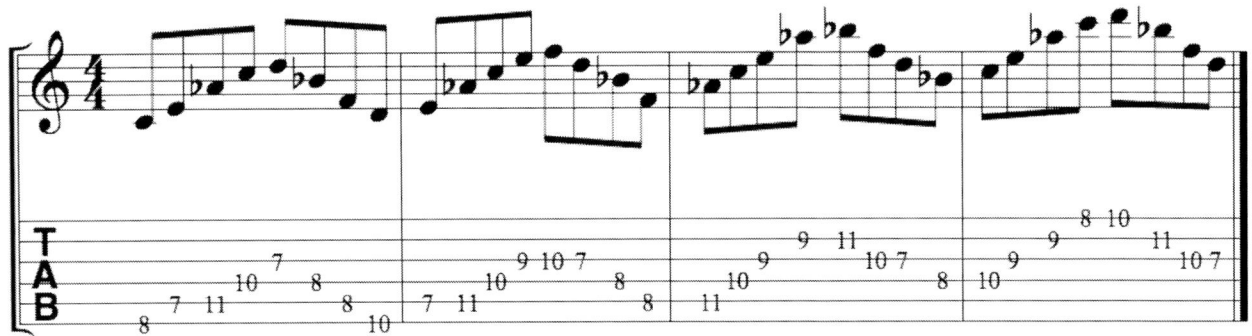

Ab+ - Bb, Weaving Pattern at the 7th Fret, Descending:

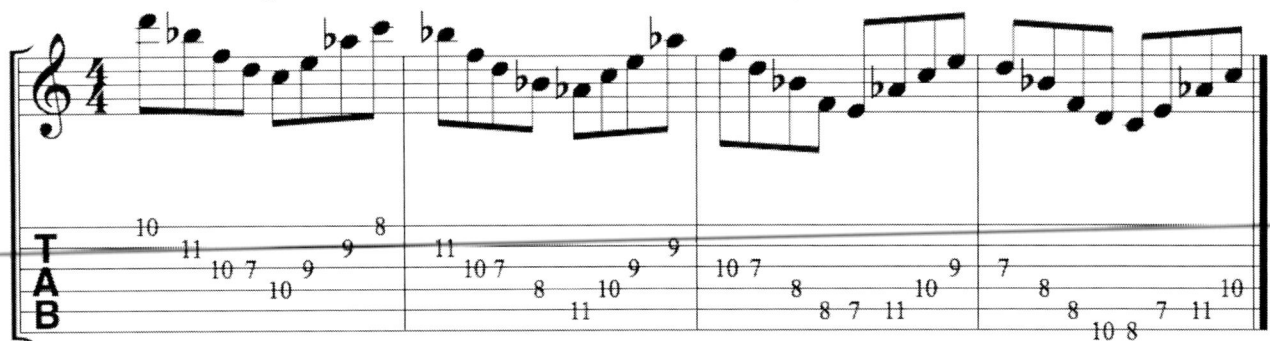

Ab+ – Bb, Inverse Weaving Pattern at the 7th Fret, Ascending:

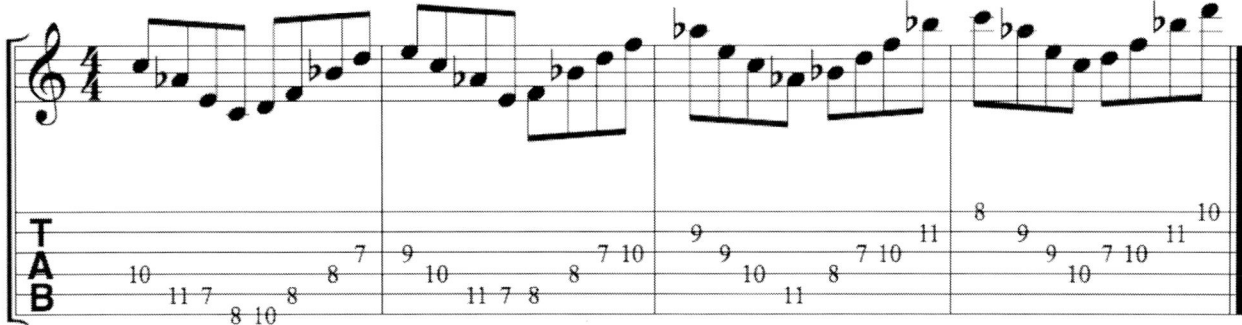

Ab+ – Bb, Inverse Weaving Pattern at the 7th Fret, Descending:

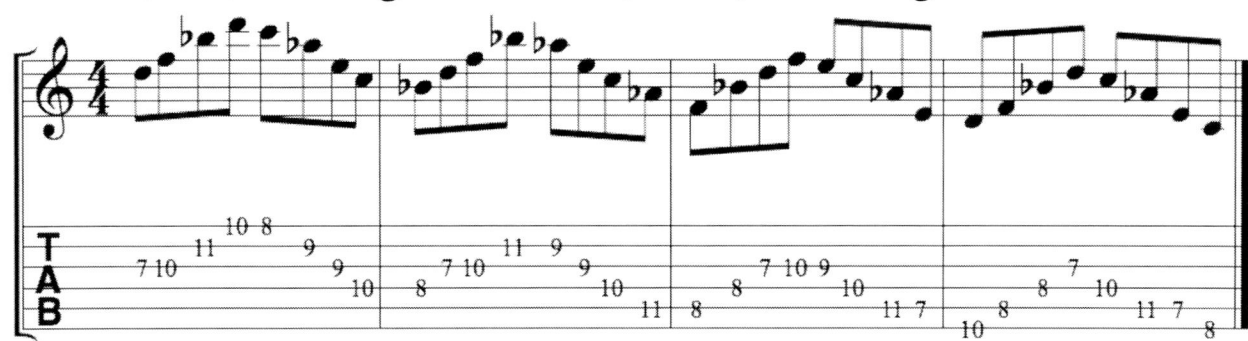

Ab+ – Bb, Weaving Pattern at the 9th Fret, Ascending:

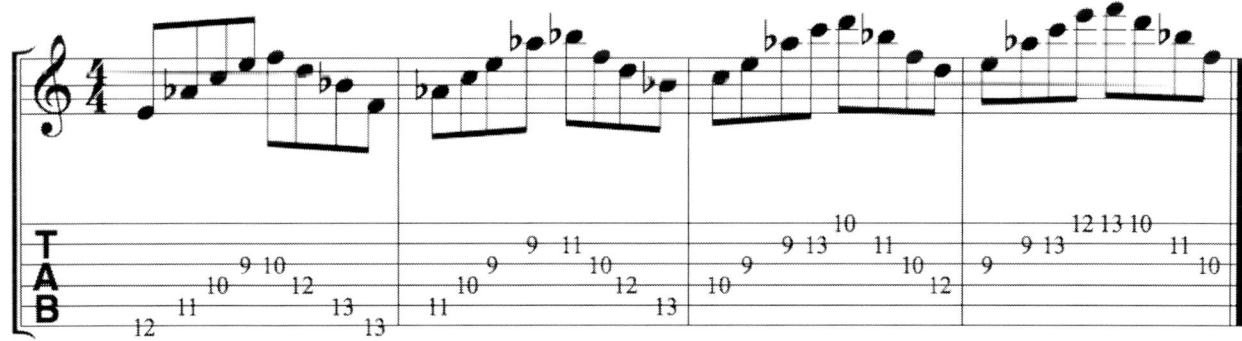

Ab+ – Bb, Weaving Pattern at the 9th Fret, Descending:

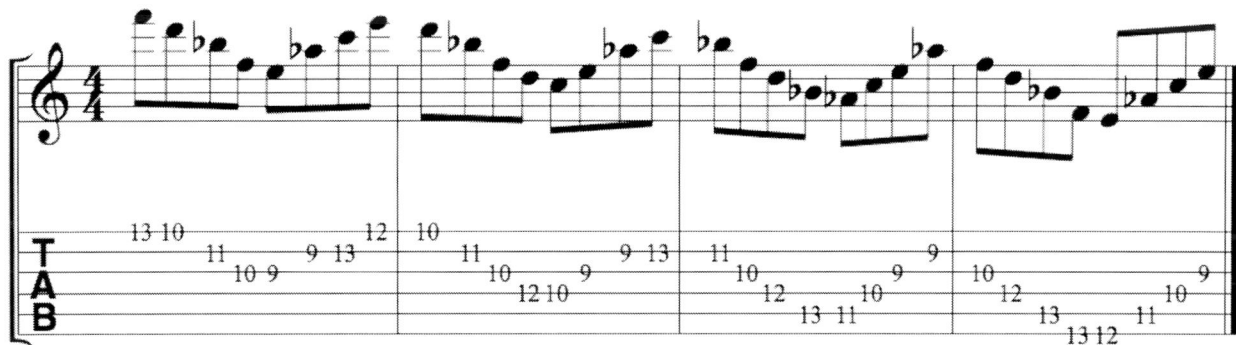

Ab+ - Bb, Inverse Weaving Pattern at the 9th Fret, Ascending:

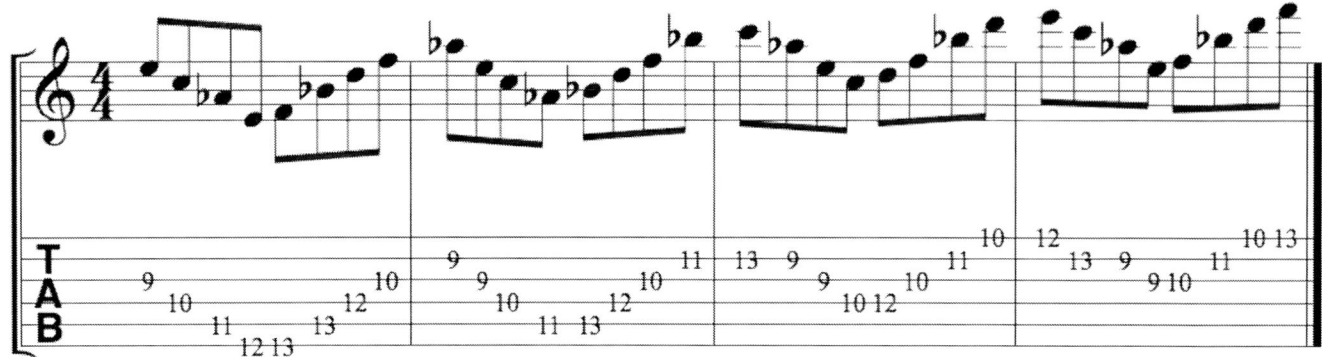

Ab+ - Bb, Inverse Weaving Pattern at the 9th Fret, Descending:

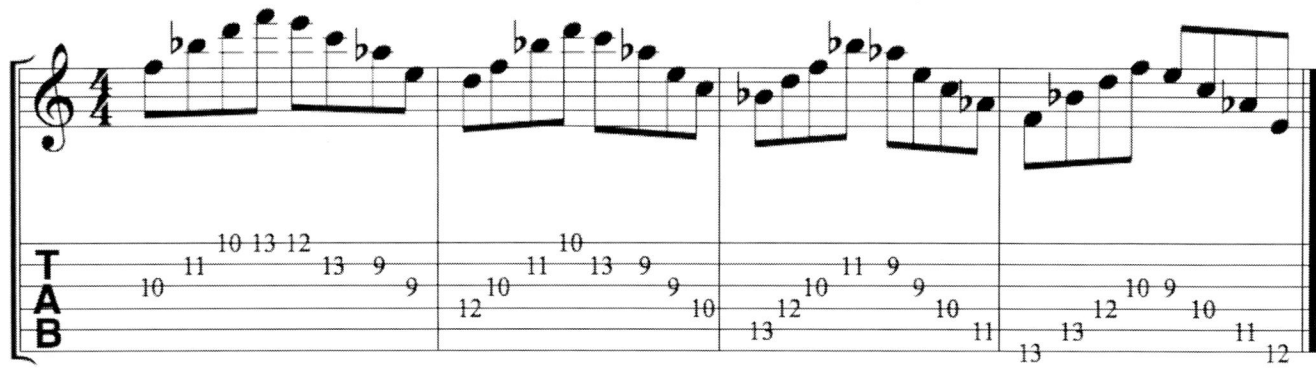

Ab+ - Bb, Weaving Pattern at the 12th Fret, Ascending:

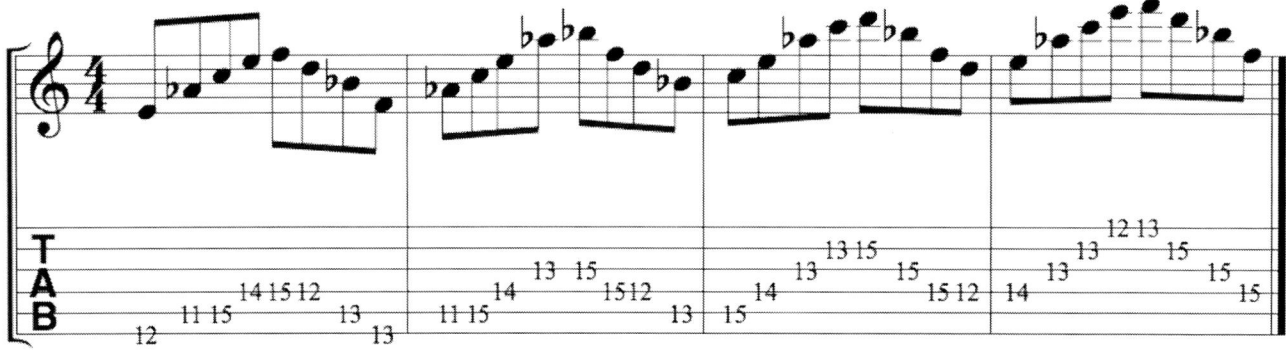

Ab+ ~ Bb, Weaving Pattern at the 12th Fret, Descending:

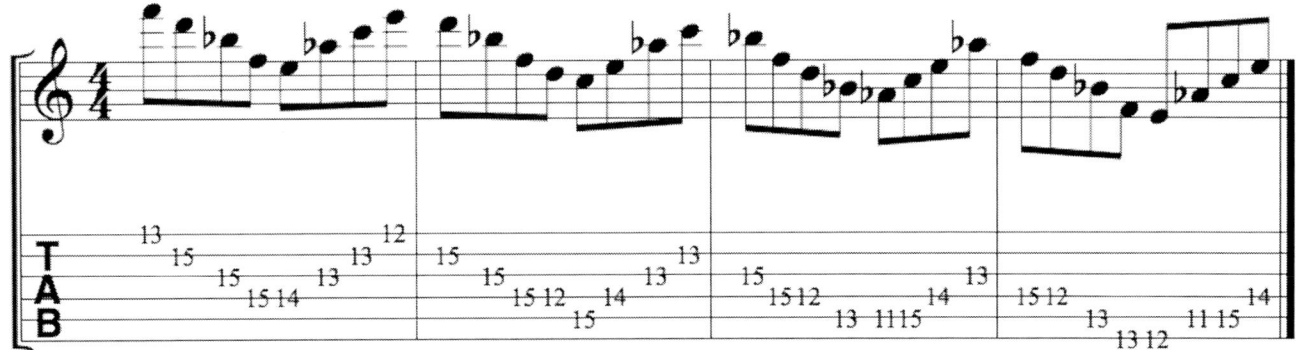

Ab+ ~ Bb, Inverse Weaving Pattern at the 12th Fret, Ascending:

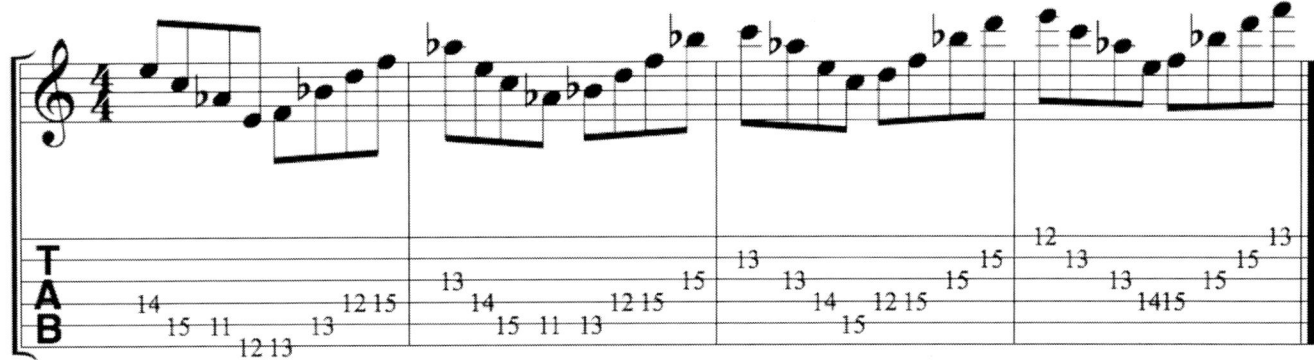

Ab+ ~ Bb, Inverse Weaving Pattern at the 12th Fret, Descending:

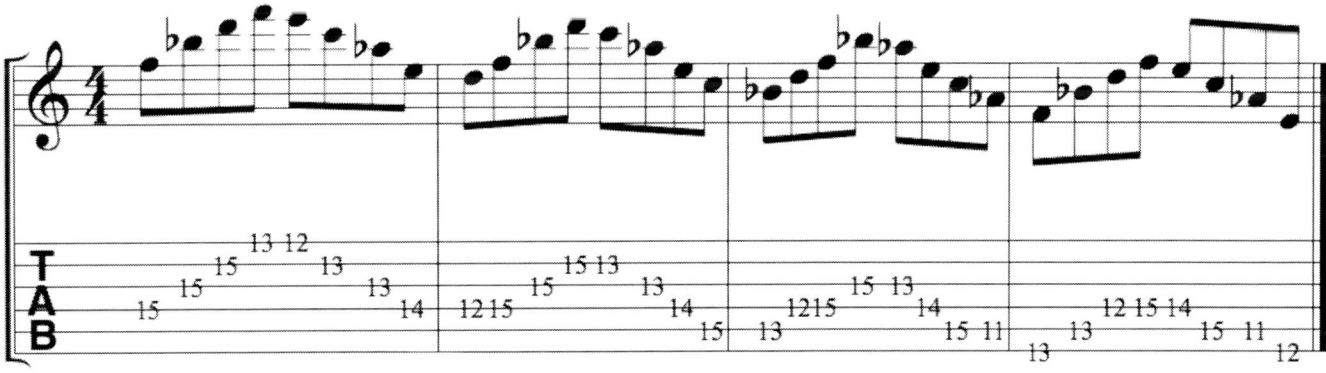

CHORD PROGRESSIONS – part 6: Key Modulation

By this point, you are probably aware of the basic concept key modulation, or key changes. You've probably learned at least a couple tunes where one section of the song is in one key and another section moves to a totally different key center. In this section of the book, we're going to take a close-up look at the basic considerations of key modulation. As with anything else, having a clear concept of a machine's moving parts is going to allow you a more intuitive experience while operating it.

First, I'm going to present each of the possible modulation types with some pertinent information about how the two keys involved relate to one-another. I'm going to present these in a very specific order; starting with the closest related modulations, first in the darker direction followed by the brighter direction and then working through, in the same fashion, to the most distantly related modulations.

Modulation In 4ths

Here, we can clearly see that when we modulate by the distance of a 4th, all but one note remain the same in the destination key. We can see that the 7th of the original key must be lowered to become the 4th of the destination key. We can also see that the root note of the original key goes on to be the 5th of the destination.

Original Key	Root	2nd	3rd	4th	5th	6th	7th
	C	D	E	F	G	A	B
Destination Key	C	D	E	F	G	A	Bb
	5th	6th	7th	Root	2nd	3rd	4th

Here, we can get a clear look at both the common and contrasting chords between these two keys. What we find is that even when there is only one tone in contrast between two keys, there are fewer chords in common than there are in contrast. In this case, we have three chords in common between the two keys and four chords in contrast. I've included the notes of each chord in order for you to have a clear view of what's happening within the contrasting chords.

Original Key	Imaj7	IIm7	IIIm7	IVmaj7	V7	VIm7	VIIm7b5
	Cmaj7 C E G B	Dm7 D F A C	Em7 E G B D	Fmaj7 F A C E	G7 G B D F	Am7 A C E G	Bm7b5 B D F A
Destination Key	C7 C E G Bb	Dm7 D F A C	Em7b5 E G Bb D	Fmaj7 F A C E	Gm7 G Bb D F	Am7 A C E G	Bbmaj7 Bb D F A
	V7	VIm7	VIIm7b5	Imaj7	IIm7	IIIm7	IVmaj7

Modulation In 5ths

This modulation is the same distance in the opposite direction from the previous interval by which we modulated. As before, there are six common tones and one contrasting tone between the two keys. There are also three common chords and four contrasting chords between the two keys.

Original Key	Root	2nd	3rd	4th	5th	6th	7th
	C	D	E	F	G	A	B
Destination Key	C	D	E	F#	G	A	B
	4th	5th	6th	7th	Root	2nd	3rd

Original Key	Imaj7	IIm7	IIIm7	IVmaj7	V7	VIm7	VIIm7b5
	Cmaj7	Dm7	Em7	Fmaj7	G7	Am7	Bm7b5
	C E G B	D F A C	E G B D	F A C E	G B D F	A C E G	B D F A
Destination Key	Cmaj7	D7	Em7	F#m7b5	Gmaj7	Am7	Bm7
	C E G B	D F# A C	E G B D	F# A C E	G B D F#	A C E G	B D F# A
	IVmaj7	V7	VIm7	VIIm7b5	Imaj7	IIm7	IIIm7

Modulation In b7ths

When modulating by the interval of a b7th, our two keys share five notes in common with each other and have two notes in contrast to one another. The root, 2nd, 4th, 5th and 6th of the original key become the 2nd, 3rd, 5th, 6th and 7th of the destination key. These two keys share one chord in common with each other. The IIm7 of the original key serves as the IIIm7 of the destination key.

Original Key	Root	2nd	3rd	4th	5th	6th	7th
	C	D	E	F	G	A	B
Destination Key	C	D	Eb	F	G	A	Bb
	2nd	3rd	4th	5th	6th	7th	Root

Original Key	Imaj7	IIm7	IIIm7	IVmaj7	V7	VIm7	VIIm7b5
	Cmaj7	Dm7	Em7	Fmaj7	G7	Am7	Bm7b5
	C E G B	D F A C	E G B D	F A C E	G B D F	A C E G	B D F A
Destination Key	Cm7	Dm7	Ebmaj7	F7	Gm7	Am7b5	Bbmaj7
	C Eb G Bb	D F A C	Eb G Bb D	F A C Eb	G Bb D F	A C Eb G	Bb D F A
	IIm7	IIIm7	IVmaj7	V7	VIm7	VIIm7b5	Imaj7

Modulation In 2nds

The major 2nd modulation is the mirror image to the b7th modulation. In this case, we move to a key two shades brighter, rather than a key two shades darker, as we saw with the b7th modulation. As with the previous relationship, we have five common tones and two contrasting tones. We also have one common chord and six contrasting chords.

Original Key	Root	2nd	3rd	4th	5th	6th	7th
	C	D	E	F	G	A	B
Destination Key	C#	D	E	F#	G	A	B
	7th	Root	2nd	3rd	4th	5th	6th

Original Key	Imaj7	IIm7	IIIm7	IVmaj7	V7	VIm7	VIIm7b5
	Cmaj7	Dm7	Em7	Fmaj7	G7	Am7	Bm7b5
	C E G B	D F A C	E G B D	F A C E	G B D F	A C E G	B D F A
Destination Key	C#m7b5	Dmaj7	Em7	F#m7	Gmaj7	A7	Bm7
	C# E G B	D F# A C#	E G B D	F# A C# E	G B D F#	A C# E G	B D F# A
	VIIm7b5	Imaj7	IIm7	IIIm7	IVmaj7	V7	VIm7

Modulation In b3rds:

The minor 3rd modulation gives us four common tones and three contrasting tones between keys. By the time we've sailed this far out from shore, we no longer have any common chords between our two keys. This doesn't mean that we can't modulate by this interval or even a more distantly related interval.

Original Key	Root	2nd	3rd	4th	5th	6th	7th
	C	D	E	F	G	A	B
Destination Key	C	D	Eb	F	G	Ab	Bb
	6th	7th	Root	2nd	3rd	4th	5th

Original Key	Imaj7	IIm7	IIIm7	IVmaj7	V7	VIm7	VIIm7b5
	Cmaj7	Dm7	Em7	Fmaj7	G7	Am7	Bm7b5
	C E G B	D F A C	E G B D	F A C E	G B D F	A C E G	B D F A
Destination Key	Cm7	Dm7b5	Ebmaj7	Fm7	Gm7	Abmaj7	Bb7
	C Eb G Bb	D F Ab C	Eb G Bb D	F Ab C Eb	G Bb D F	Ab C Eb G	Bb D F Ab
	VIm7	VIIm7b5	Imaj7	IIm7	IIIm7	IVmaj7	V7

Modulation In 6ths

The major 6th modulation is the mirror image to the b3rd modulation. In this case, we move to a key three shades brighter rather than a key three shades darker. As with the previous relationship, we have four common tones and three contrasting tones. Again, we have no common chords.

Original Key	Root	2nd	3rd	4th	5th	6th	7th
	C	D	E	F	G	A	B
Destination Key	C#	D	E	F#	G#	A	B
	3rd	4th	5th	6th	7th	Root	2nd

Original Key	Imaj7	IIm7	IIIm7	IVmaj7	V7	VIm7	VIIm7b5
	Cmaj7	Dm7	Em7	Fmaj7	G7	Am7	Bm7b5
	C E G B	D F A C	E G B D	F A C E	G B D F	A C E G	B D F A
Destination Key	C#m7	Dmaj7	E7	F#m7	G#m7b5	Amaj7	Bm7
	C# E G# B	D F# A C#	E G# B D	F# A C# E	G# B D F#	A C# E G#	B D F# A
	IIIm7	IVmaj7	V7	VIm7	VIIm7b5	Imaj7	IIm7

Modulation In b6ths

The minor 6th modulation gives us three common tones and four contrasting tones between keys. Because of this, b6th modulations and all of the following modulations are what we consider very distant.

Original Key	Root	2nd	3rd	4th	5th	6th	7th
	C	D	E	F	G	A	B
Destination Key	C	Db	Eb	F	G	Ab	Bb
	3rd	4th	5th	6th	7th	Root	2nd

Original Key	Imaj7	IIm7	IIIm7	IVmaj7	V7	VIm7	VIIm7b5
	Cmaj7	Dm7	Em7	Fmaj7	G7	Am7	Bm7b5
	C E G B	D F A C	E G B D	F A C E	G B D F	A C E G	B D F A
Destination Key	Cm7	Dm7b5	Ebmaj7	Fm7	Gm7	Abmaj7	Bb7
	C Eb G Bb	D F Ab C	Eb G Bb D	F Ab C Eb	G Bb D F	Ab C Eb G	Bb D F Ab
	IIIm7	IVmaj7	V7	VIm7	VIIm7b5	Imaj7	IIm7

Modulation In 3rds

The major 3rd modulation is the mirror image to the b6th modulation. In this case, we move to a key four shades brighter, whereas with b6th modulations, we move to a key four shades darker. As with the previous relationship, we have three common tones and four contrasting tones.

Original Key	Root	2nd	3rd	4th	5th	6th	7th
	C	D	E	F	G	A	B
Destination Key	C#	D#	E	F#	G#	A	B
	6th	7th	Root	2nd	3rd	4th	5th

Original Key	Imaj7	IIm7	IIIm7	IVmaj7	V7	VIm7	VIIm7b5
	Cmaj7 C E G B	Dm7 D F A C	Em7 E G B D	Fmaj7 F A C E	G7 G B D F	Am7 A C E G	Bm7b5 B D F A
Destination Key	C#m7 C# E G# B	D#m7b5 D# F# A C#	E7 E G# B D#	F#m7 F# A C# E	G#m7 G# B D# F#	Amaj7 A C# E G#	B7 B D# F# A
	VIm7	VIIm7b5	Imaj7	IIm7	IIIm7	IVmaj7	V7

Modulation In b2nds

The minor 2nd modulation gives us two common tones and five contrasting tones between keys. Even though a minor 2nd is of the two smallest intervals, it is one of the two second most distant modulations. Modulation by this interval has a very notable effect.

Original Key	Root	2nd	3rd	4th	5th	6th	7th
	C	D	E	F	G	A	B
Destination Key	C	Db	Eb	F	G	Ab	Bb
	7th	Root	2nd	3rd	4th	5th	6th

Original Key	Imaj7	IIm7	IIIm7	IVmaj7	V7	VIm7	VIIm7b5
	Cmaj7 C E G B	Dm7 D F A C	Em7 E G B D	Fmaj7 F A C E	G7 G B D F	Am7 A C E G	Bm7b5 B D F A
Destination Key	Cm7b5 C Eb Gb Bb	Dbmaj7 Db F Ab C	Ebm7 Eb Gb Bb Db	Fm7 F Ab C Eb	Gbmaj7 Gb Bb Db F	Ab7 Ab C Eb Gb	Bbm7 Bb Db F Ab
	VIIm7b5	Imaj7	IIm7	IIIm7	IVmaj7	V7	VIm7

Modulation In 7ths

The major 7th modulation is the mirror image to the b6th modulation. In this case, we move to a key four shades brighter, whereas with b6th modulations, we move to a key four shades darker. As with the previous relationship, we have three common tones and four contrasting tones.

Original Key	Root	2nd	3rd	4th	5th	6th	7th
	C	D	E	F	G	A	B
Destination Key	C#	D#	E	F#	G#	A#	B
	2nd	3rd	4th	5th	6th	7th	Root

Original Key	Imaj7	IIm7	IIIm7	IVmaj7	V7	VIm7	VIIm7b5
	Cmaj7	Dm7	Em7	Fmaj7	G7	Am7	Bm7b5
	C E G B	D F A C	E G B D	F A C E	G B D F	A C E G	B D F A
Destination Key	C#m7	D#m7	Emaj7	F#7	G#m7	A#m7b5	Bmaj7
	C# E G# B	D# F# A# C#	E G# B D#	F# A C# E	G# B D# F#	A# C# E G#	B D# F# A#
	VIm7	VIIm7b5	Imaj7	IIm7	IIIm7	IVmaj7	V7

Modulation In Tritone

The tritone modulation is the mirror image to itself. When we modulate by a tri-tone interval, we have only one actual common tone. Really, there are two common tones, but one of them falls in a new slot. In this case, we have a Cb, which is the same as B but since there is a Bb taking the place of B, the Cb takes the place of the C. This is the most distant key modulation.

Original Key	Root	2nd	3rd	4th	5th	6th	7th
	C	D	E	F	G	A	B
Destination Key	Cb	Db	Eb	F	Gb	Ab	Bb
	4th	5th	6th	7th	Root	2nd	3rd

Original Key	Imaj7	IIm7	IIIm7	IVmaj7	V7	VIm7	VIIm7b5
	Cmaj7	Dm7	Em7	Fmaj7	G7	Am7	Bm7b5
	C E G B	D F A C	E G B D	F A C E	G B D F	A C E G	B D F A
Destination Key	Cbmaj7	Db7	Ebm7	Fm7b5	Gbmaj7	Abm7	Bbm7
	Cb Eb Gb Bb	Db F Ab Cb	Eb Gb Bb Db	F Ab Cb Eb	Gb Bb Db F	Ab Cb Eb Gb	Bb Db F Ab
	VIm7	VIIm7b5	Imaj7	IIm7	IIIm7	IVmaj7	V7

You can obviously modulate from a major key to a minor key or vice versa. Let us use these major key modulations as a starting point and look at the major/minor possibilities of each. The table below serves as a decent summary to what we just covered and also gives you some major/minor equivalent modulations.

Original Modulation Type	Basic Effect of Change by Shade	Notes In Common/ /Notes In Contrast	Major->Minor Equivalent Modulation	Minor->Major Equivalent Modulation
4th Modulation	1 shade darker	6/1	2nd	b6th
5th Modulation	1 shade brighter	6/1	3rd	b7th
b7th Modulation	2 shades darker	5/2	5th	b2nd
2nd Modulation	2 shades brighter	5/2	7th	4th
b3rd Modulation	3 shades darker	4/3	Unison	b5th
6th Modulation	3 shades brighter	4/3	b5th	Unison
b6th Modulation	4 shades darker	3/4	4th	7th
3rd Modulation	4 shades brighter	3/4	b2nd	5th
b2nd Modulation	5 shades darker	2/5	b7th	3rd
7th Modulation	5 shades brighter	2/5	b6th	2nd
b5th Modulation	6 shades either/or	1/6	b3rd	6th

Key Modulation Devices

Now that we have a good idea of the harmonic and tonal ramifications of all our possible modulations, let's take a look at the different ways that we can set up for a modulation of any kind. There are only a few basic means by which we can set up for a key change:

1) The Straight-Away:

The Straight-Away is what I call any occurrence of a key modulation where there is no preparation chord to bridge us from one key to the next. They are most common in pop songwriting. Here's a simple example where we begin with a I-V-VIm-IV progression and continue with the same progression after a modulation a 5th away:

```
    C   G   Am  F   C   G   Am  F   G   D   Em  C   G   D   Em  C
C:  I   V   VIm IV  I   V   VIm IV G: I   V   VIm IV  I   V   VIm IV
```

Here the same idea, employing a major third modulation this time:

```
    C   G   Am  F   C   G   Am  F   E   B   C#m A   E   B   C#m B
C:  I   V   VIm IV  I   V   VIm IV E: I   V   VIm IV  I   V   VIm IV
```

Straight-Away modulations usually work best on distant modulations like this. The most commonly occurring straight-away is that of the half-step up key change found on the final chorus of countless pop songs.

2) The Pivot Chord:

The Pivot Chord is quite useful as a compositional device. A Pivot Chord is simply a chord that serves one function in one key, a different function in another key and is used as a bridge between the two keys. Pivot Chords are commonly found in classical music, theater music, rock music, classic pop music, but can occasionally be found in modern jazz and modern pop. Below are a couple examples of basic Pivot Chord usage. You can play these in whatever style you like, assign any harmonic rhythm to the chords, and extend them diatonically to whatever degree you choose.

	Dm	F	Am	G	Dm	F	Am	D	C	G	F	Am	Bb	F
C:	IIm	IV	VIm	V	IIm	IV	VIm			C: V	IV	VIm		
								G: IIm	V	IV	I		F: IIIm	IV	I

It would seem that Pivot Chords can only get you to the closely related keys, considering the fact that we need a common chord between these keys. Soon we'll be getting into some functioning non-diatonic chords that can be used with in the key. Once the concepts of the 1) the Pivot Chord and 2) the non-diatonic chord are combined, you can easily connect any key to any other key by means of a Pivot Chord. It'll just be a non-diatonic pivot. For the sake of offering you an example of this ahead of time, one common non-diatonic chord is a bVI major chord. I'll use it as a singular occurrence this first example:

	Dm	G	C	Am	Ab	C	G
C:	IIm	V	I	VIm	bVI	I	V

In this variation, the bVI is being used as a pivot to the key of Ab:

	Dm	G	C	Am	Ab	Eb	Db
C:	IIm	V	I	VIm	bVI		
					Ab: I	V	IV

Here's another example, making use of both diatonic and non-diatonic Pivot Chords. Notice that there are some spots where we can interpret the chords a couple different ways. This is common with less conventional types of chord changes.

	F	C	G	Dm	Eb	Bb	Ab	Cm	F	Gm	Gb	Ab	Db
C:	IV	I	V	IIm	Eb: I	V	IV	VIm			Db: IV	V	I
				Bb: IIIm	IV	I	bVII	IIm	V	VIm	bVI		

Pivot Chords are a great way to get quite a distance from where you started, while maintaining some sense of natural movement. In some cases, even concealing the fact that you have changed keys. They aren't the best choice for getting a dramatic effect in most cases but they can add a lot of depth to a progression and create much added interest for the listener.

3) The Dominant Approach:

All it really takes to make a rather natural sounding jump to any key is to approach the new key by its V7 chord and resolve to the Imaj7 of the new key. This is very common in jazz. Extending this idea, you can approach the new key by the V7 of any chord within the new key as long as it's eventually made clear where the new Imaj7 resides. Extending this idea a step further, we can approach by a IIm7 V7 or a IIm7b5 V7 to any chord of the new scale. Some jazz tunes make heavy use of key changes with V7 and IIm7 V7 approaches. A classic example would be "Giant Steps" by John Coltrane, a tune that took me at least a hundred hours to learn to navigate.

Below, I've written some examples in a jazz style. I've set the harmonic rhythm in the case of these examples but try them in different tempos and rhythmic feels.

Example 1:

This one modulates through a cycle of keys a minor 3rd apart from one another, using the IIm7 and V7 of the new key as approaching chords.

```
    Cmaj7        Fm7  Bb7    Ebmaj7     Abm7 Db7
||: / / / / | / / / / | / / / / | / / / / |

    Gbmaj7      Bm7  A7     Dmaj7      Gm7  C7
 | / / / / | / / / / | / / / / | / / / / :||
```

Example 2:

This one modulates through a cycle of keys a minor 6th apart from one another, using the IIm7 and V7 of the new key as approaching chords.

```
    Cmaj7       F#m7 B7     Emaj7      Bbm7 Eb7
||: / / / / | / / / / | / / / / | / / / / |

    Abmaj7     Dm7  G7    Cmaj7 A7    Dm7  G7
 | / / / / | / / / / | / / / / | / / / / :||
```

Example 3:

This one modulates through the minor 3rd cycle and back through the cycle in 6ths, using only the V7 of the each destination key to get there.

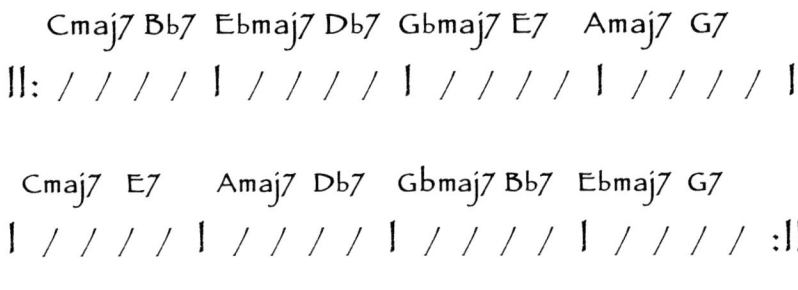

Example 4:

This progression serves as sort of a 3rd/b6th equivalent to Example 3.

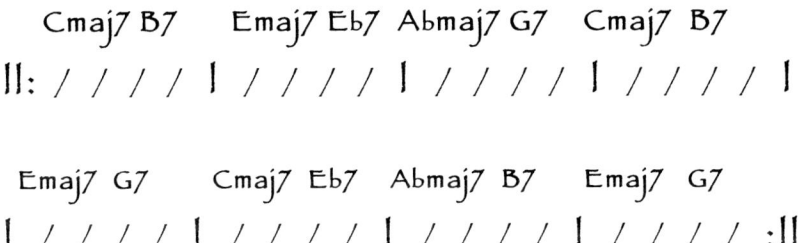

Example 5:

This next progression is from a jazz tune that I wrote, called "Everywhere You Want To Go". It uses every single possible type of major to major modulation and does so in a pattern similar to how I presented these modulations in the first part of this section. If you were to practice this starting from all twelve keys, you would play every type of modulation in every possible key. That makes this progression an excellent improvisational work-out to keep your growth well-rounded.

The pattern moves as follows:
Modulation 1: One shade darker
Modulation 2: Two shades darker
Modulation 3: Three shades darker
Modulation 4: Four shades darker
Modulation 5: Five shades darker
Modulation 6: Six shades darker/brighter
This is just past the halfway point. From here, we begin our journey home.

Modulation 7: Five shades brighter
Modulation 8: Four shades brighter
Modulation 9: Three shades brighter
Modulation 10: Two shades brighter
Modulation 11: One shade brighter
Modulation 12: Six shades brighter/darker

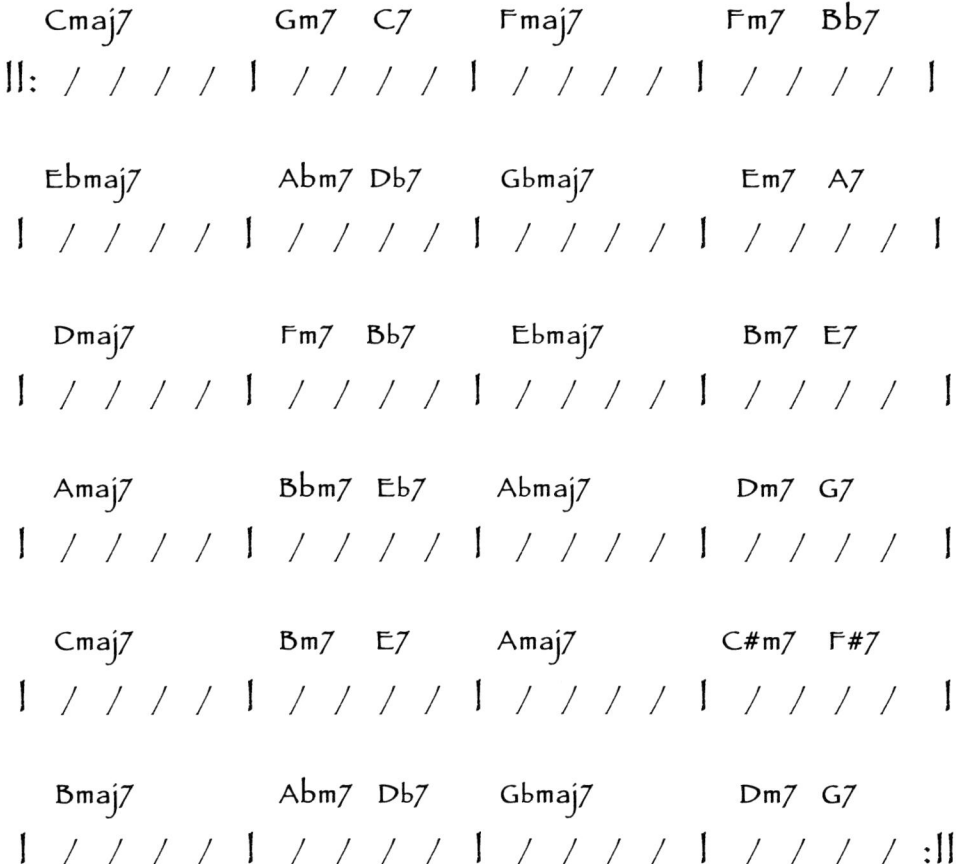

Upon first getting to know this progression and others like it, you'll probably feel a bit intimidated by the prospect of navigating these kinds of changes in the course of an improvisation. I certainly did. I spent a couple years sounding absolutely awful in these situations because I didn't have a system to learning to navigate changes. I kept forcing myself to try improvising on changes that required me to change scale from chord to chord and eventually I developed a basic positional approach to it and got to where it became my greatest strength. I immediately saw how as a side effect, it improved the way I improvised on diatonic changes just much as non-diatonic changes and key modulations. The following section is walk-through of the system I used for myself.

Navigating Modulations and Non-Diatonic Chords

Like I previously stated, this is an area that is intimidating when you first begin to immerse yourself in it, but this self-immersion is what's necessary in order to achieve a natural ability to do this. The way I got myself confident with playing over non-diatonic changes and key modulations was to look at the scales and arpeggios that I needed to cover a particular progression in one specific area of the fretboard. As an example, I'll present the scales and arpeggios that I would normally use over a Imaj7 – V7alt of IIm7 – IIm7 – V7alt, which is a very common jazz progression. Here are my first choice of tools for the progression in the key of C, at the third fret:

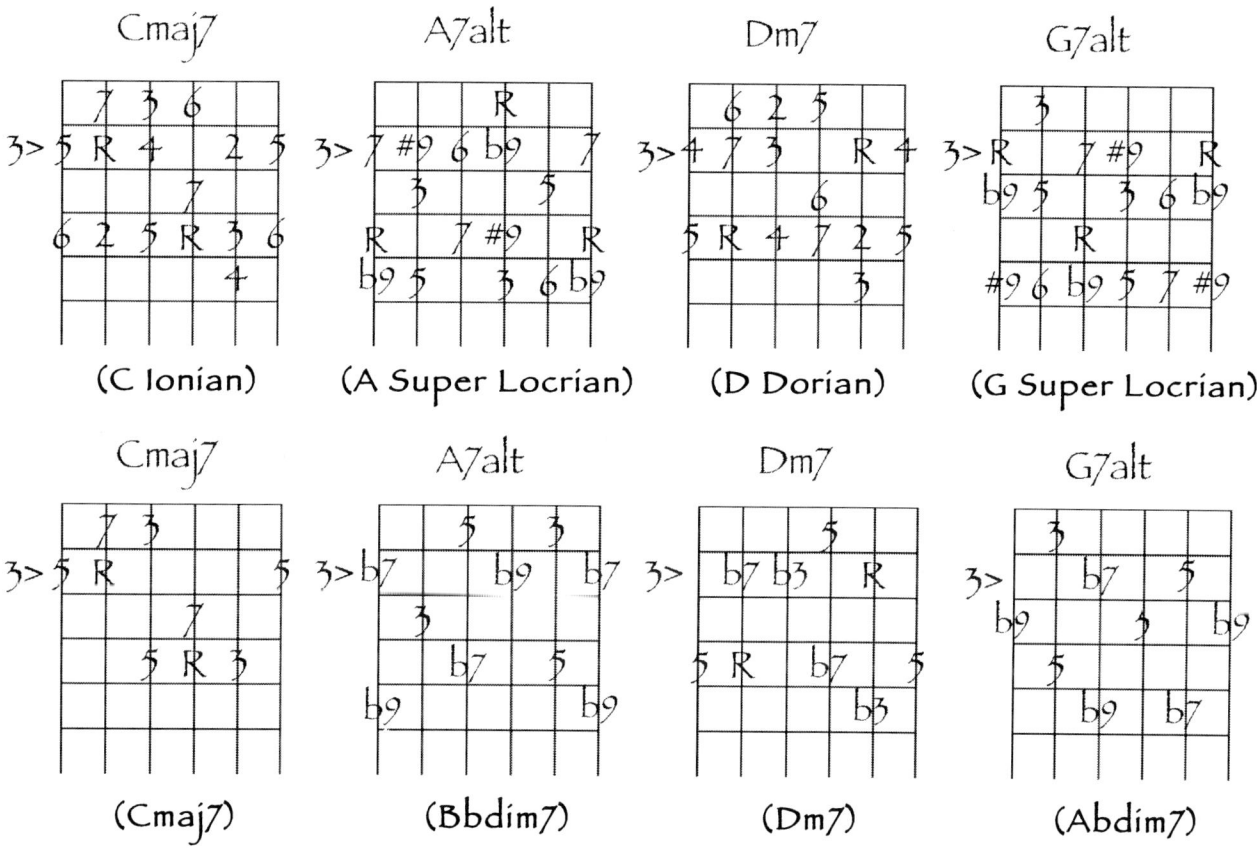

This gives us a nice way to look clearly at what notes we have available to us on each chord in the progression. We could do this with any scales or arpeggios that we want to relate to the chords. The triad super-imposition information in the extended harmony section will certainly come in handy in this regard.

After having mapped out the same material at the 5th, 7th, 9th and 12th frets, I spend time improvising on the first set of shapes over a slow recording of the changes, at first only on strings 1 and 2, then only on strings 3 and 4 and so on. I repeat the process on sets of three strings (strings 1, 2 & 3 followed by 2, 3 & 4, etc). Following that, I personally like to work with broken sets for a bit (strings 1 & 3 followed by 2 & 4, etc. I repeat this entire process in all positions. After this, I take away the string boundaries and increase my tempo by 5BPM every 30 minutes worth of practice time until I can play it fast.

The following row will work over any progression that modulates in 4ths, starting at any mode of C major. Note that only one note per octave changes from one shape to another.

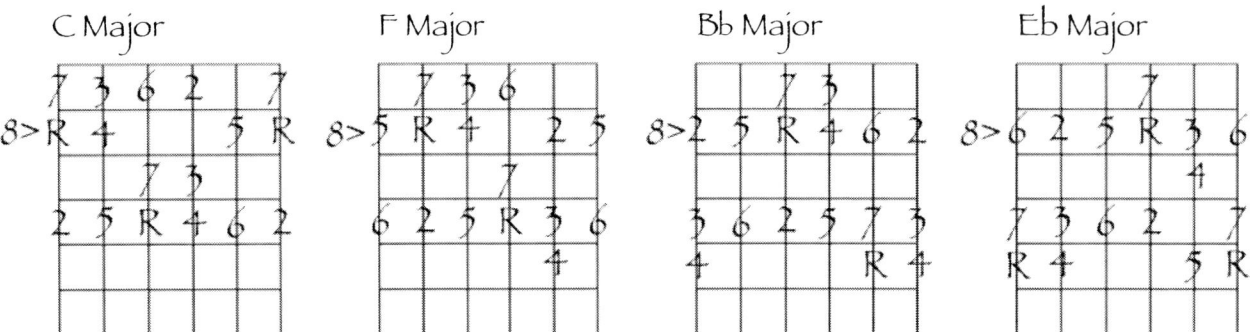

This next two rows present three major keys, related equally to one another by major 3rd intervals; a necessary navigation to play over the classic "Giant Steps" progression by John Coltrane. I've displayed the relationship in two separate positions.

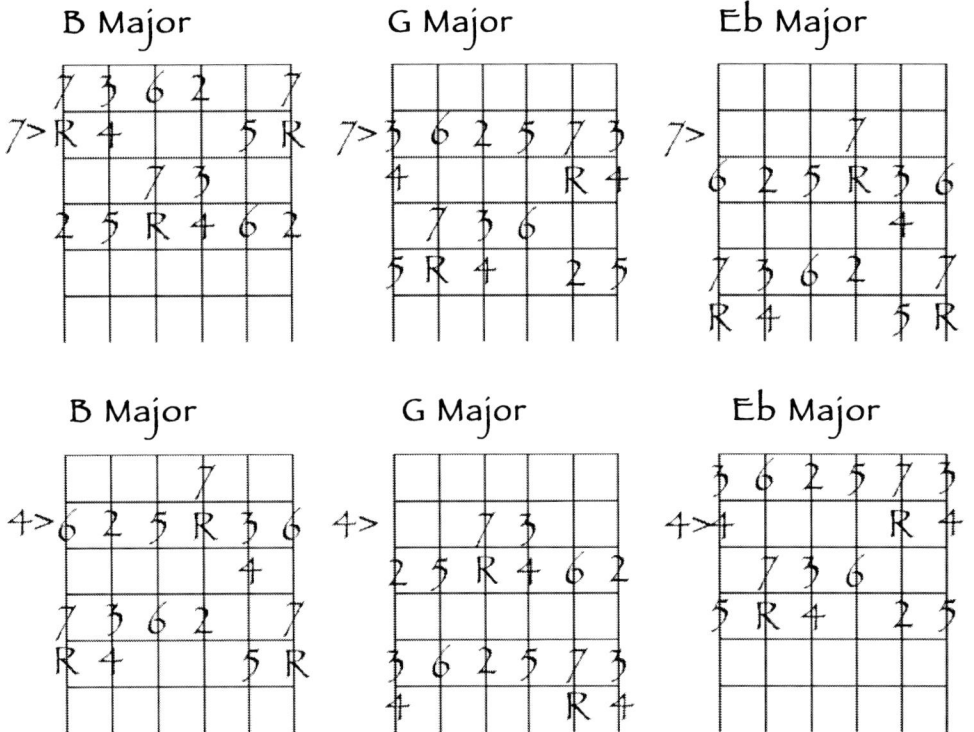

The idea is to do this in all positions with countless chord progressions. You'll develop the ability to navigate any sort of modulation comfortably. I've put a blank chord/scale diagram page in the back of this book for you to run off a hundred copies and work out the tonal motion of your favorite chord non-diatonic/modulating progressions all over the fretboard.

MELODIC PATTERNS – part 3: Advanced Diatonic Motion

In this section, we're going to look at some patterns that can breath some very interesting life into any scale you employ. Most of them will seem strikingly different from the patterns that we've learned up to this point. These patterns will find themselves right at home in progressive rock, modern jazz and fusion but that's not to say that a clever pop/rock writer couldn't make use of them in instrumental melodies. We'll be looking at these patterns in the C major scale but I highly encourage you to work these patterns out with any scale that you feel comfortable.

The first melodic pattern we're going to look at in this section is honestly not really an advanced melodic pattern. In fact, it's one that I mentioned in the list at the end of Melodic Patterns pt. 1. I felt that this was one essential enough to look at in depth. I decided to put it at the beginning of this section as a warm up of sorts, partly because of that and partly because of the absurd length of the first Melodic Patterns section.

R543 Pattern, In C major, 5th Position, Ascending:

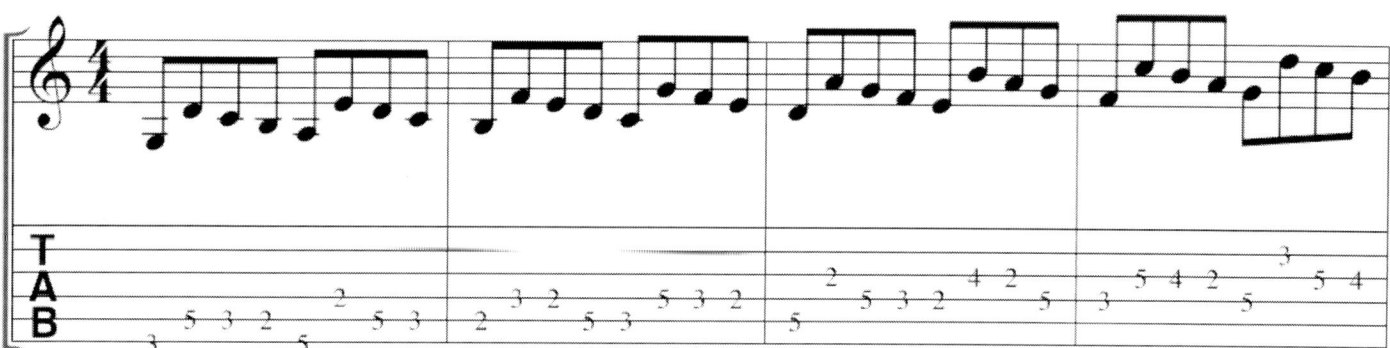

R543 Pattern, In C major, 5th Position, Descending:

R543 Pattern, In C major, 6th Position, Ascending:

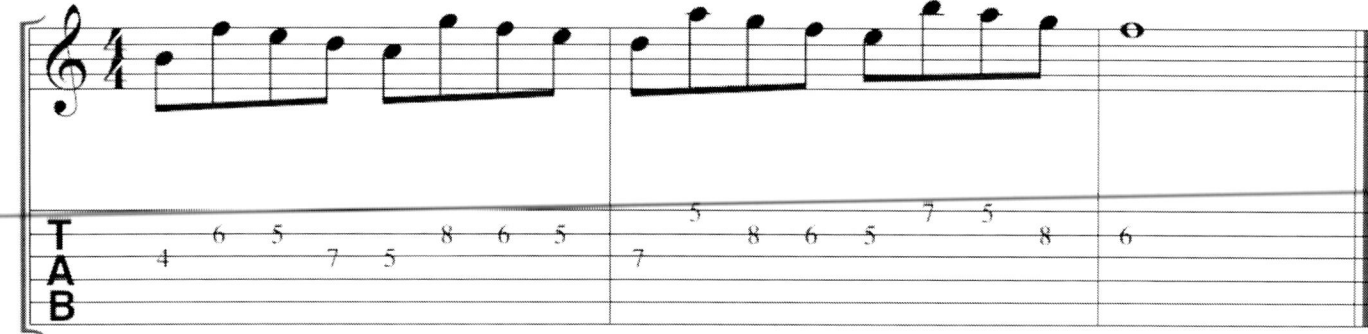

R543 Pattern, In C major, 6th Position, Descending:

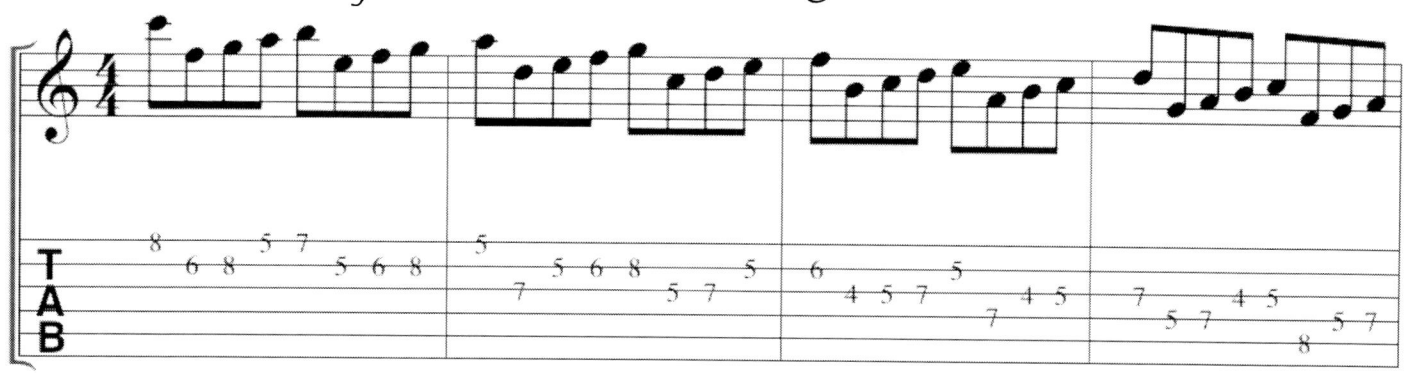

R543 Pattern, In C major, Root Position, Ascending:

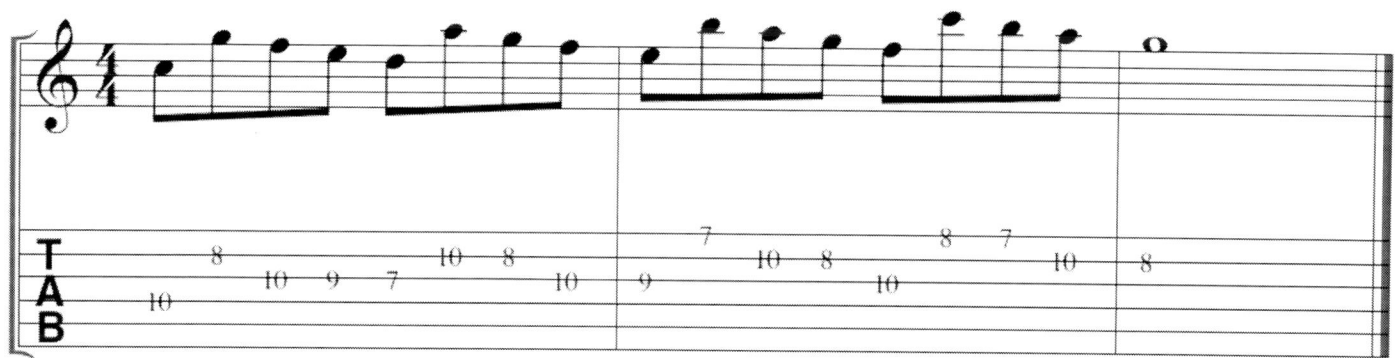

R543 Pattern, In C major, Root Position, Descending:

R543 Pattern, In C major, 2nd Position, Ascending:

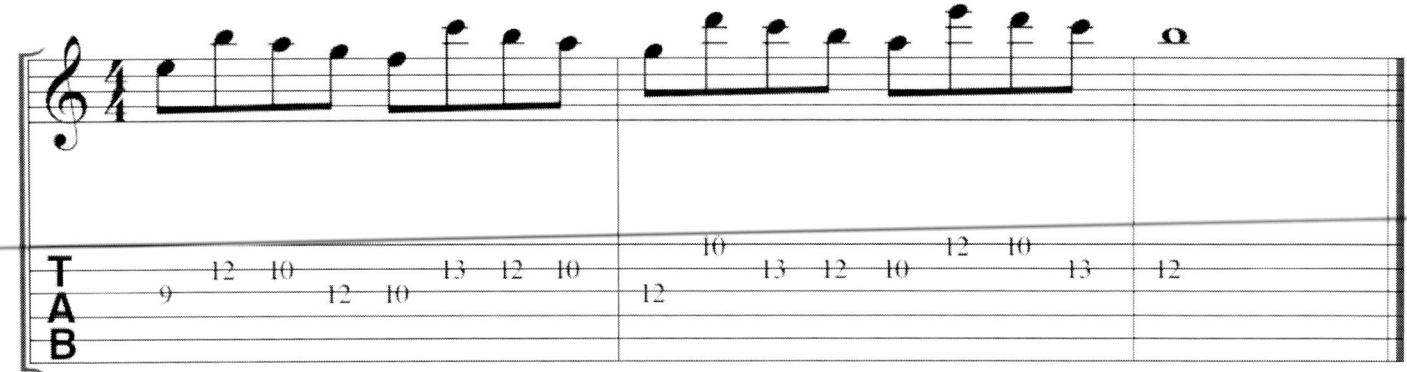

R543 Pattern, In C major, 2nd Position, Descending:

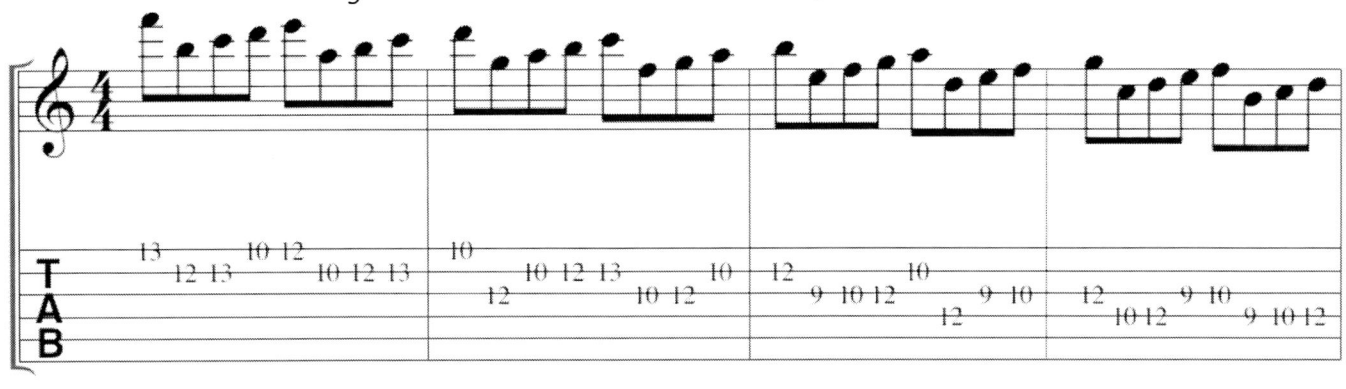

R543 Pattern, In C major, 3rd Position, Ascending:

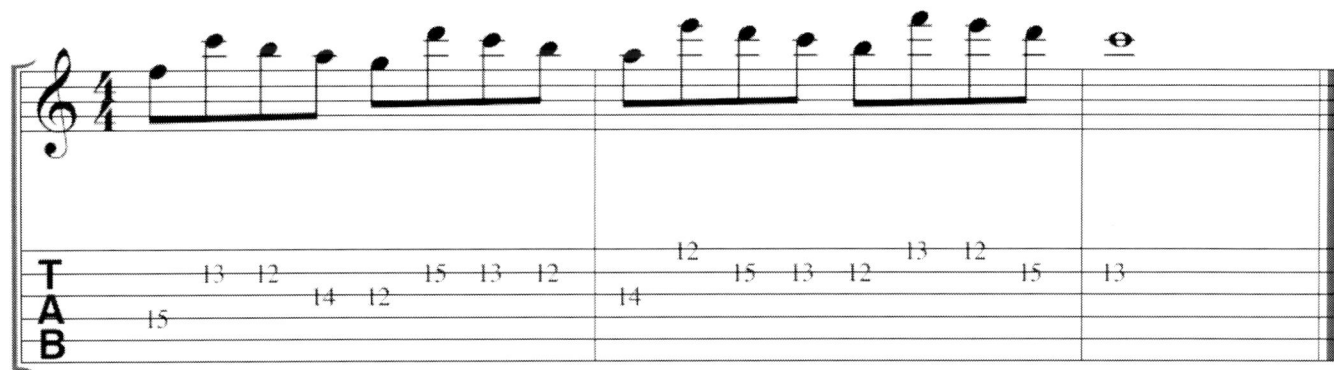

R543 Pattern, In C major, 3rd Position, Descending:

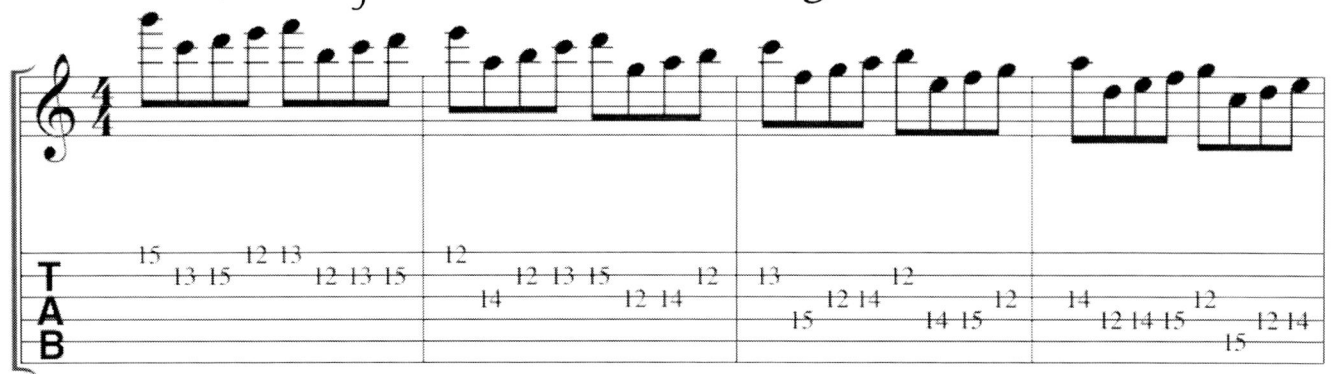

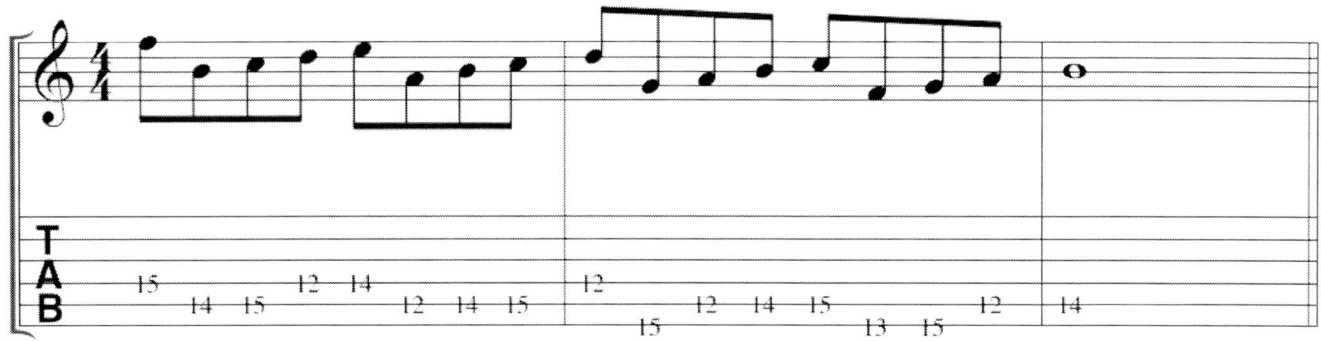

R534 Pattern, In C Major, 5th Position, Ascending

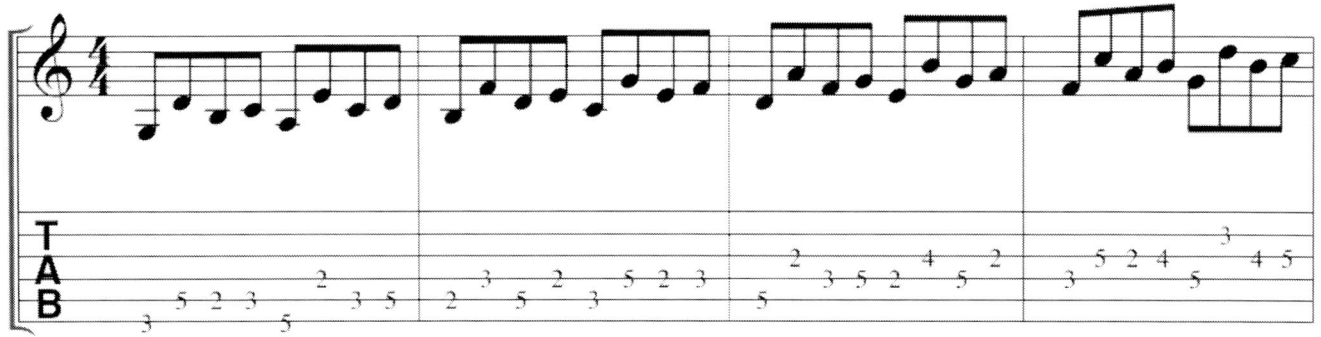

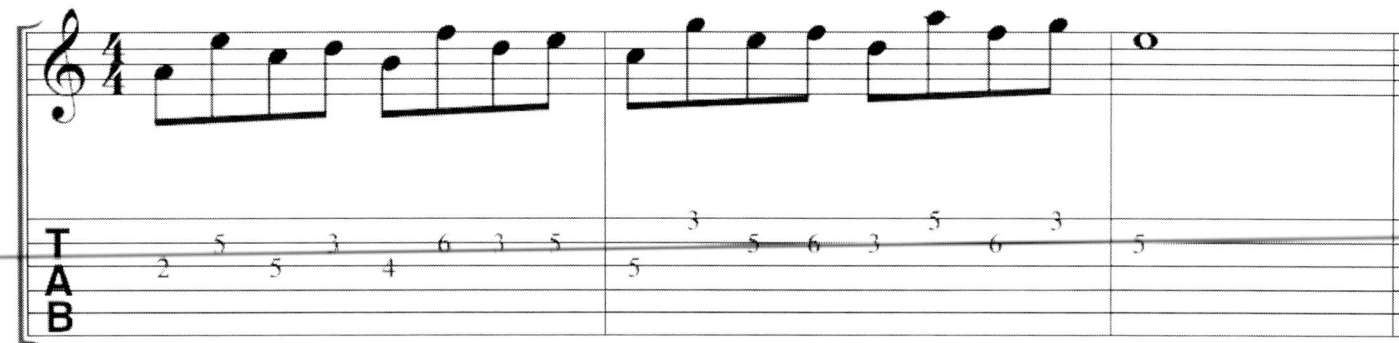

R534 Pattern, In C Major, 5th Position, Descending

R534 Pattern, In C Major, 6th Position, Ascending

R534 Pattern, In C Major, 6th Position, Descending

R534 Pattern, In C Major, Root Position, Ascending

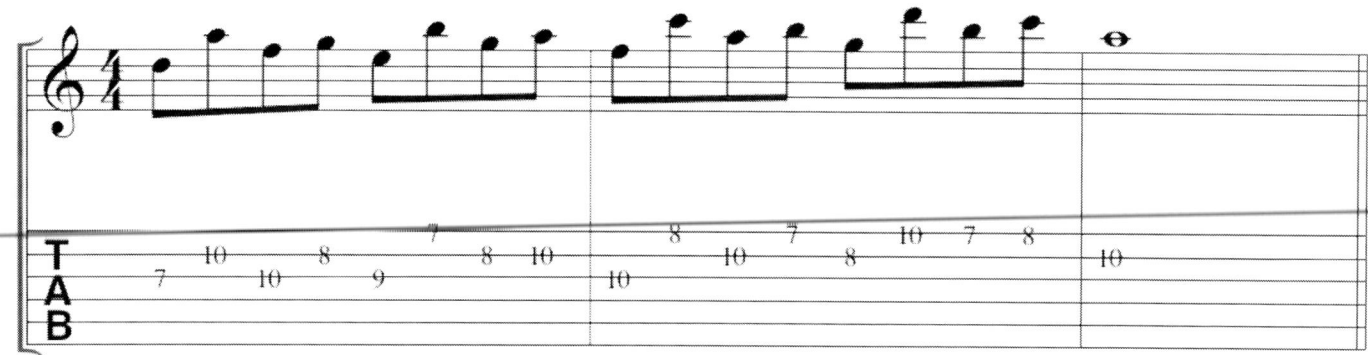

R534 Pattern, In C Major, Root Position, Descending

R534 Pattern, In C Major, 2nd Position, Ascending

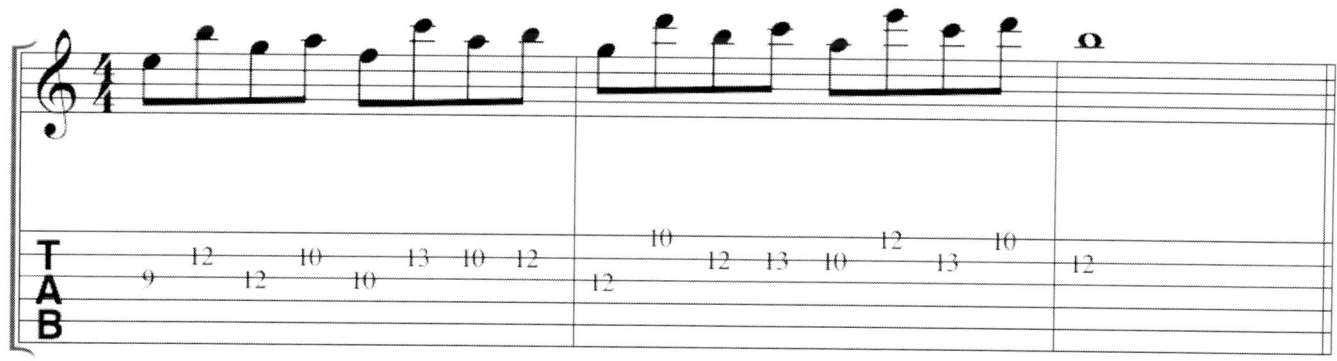

R534 Pattern, In C Major, 2nd Position, Descending

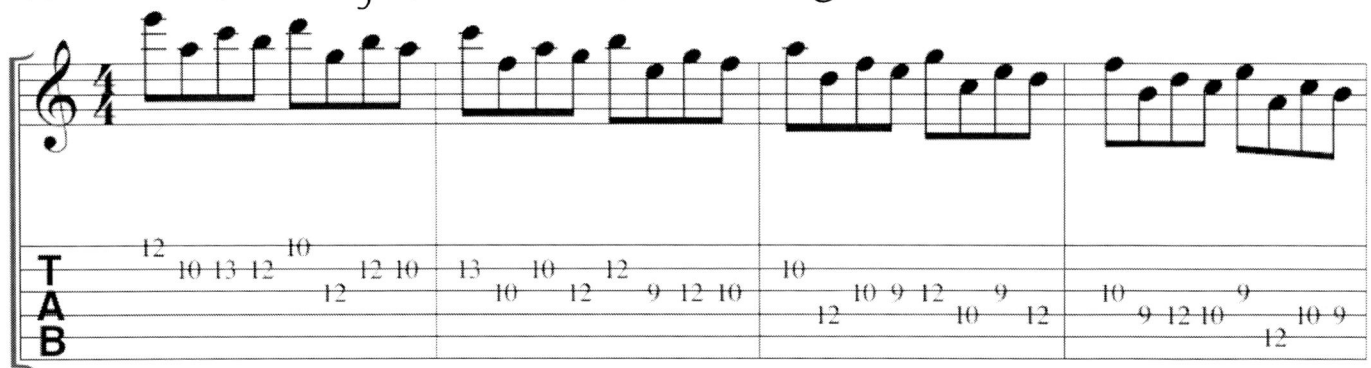

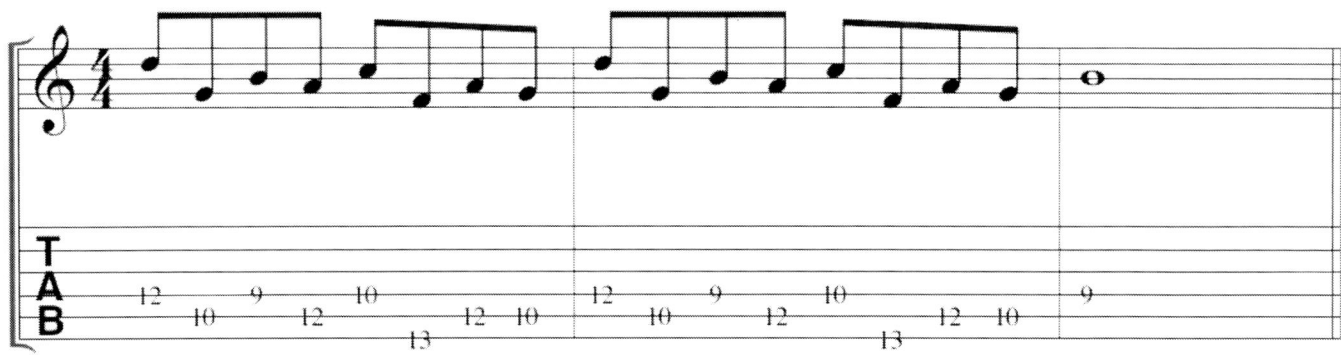

R534 Pattern, In C Major, 3rd Position, Ascending

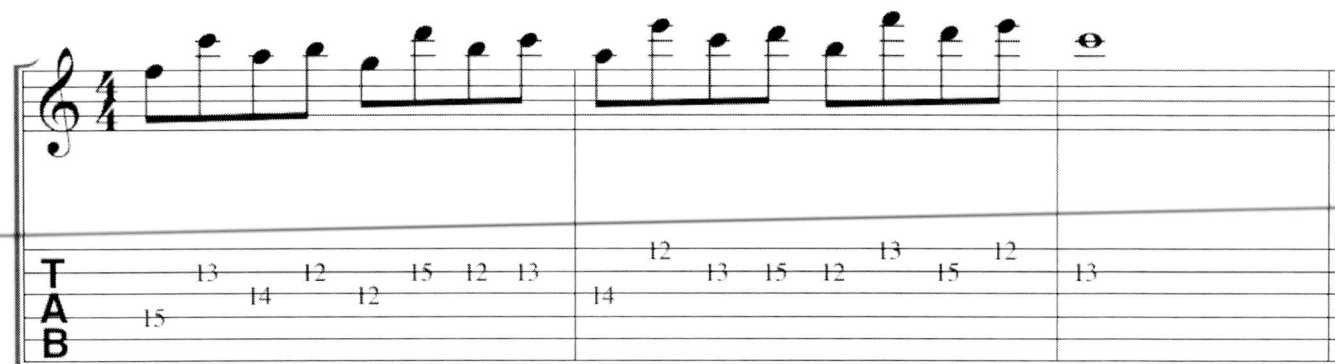

R534 Pattern, In C Major, 3rd Position, Descending

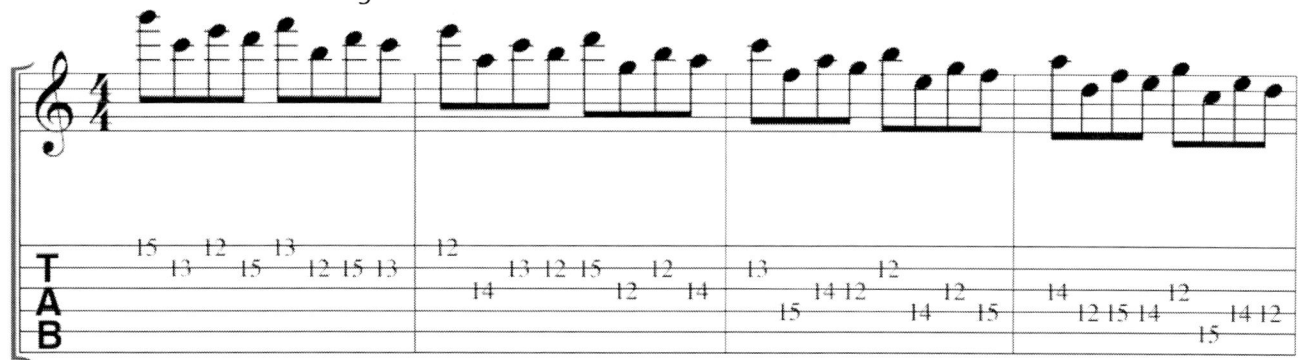

Adjoined 4ths Pattern, In C major, 5th Position, Ascending:

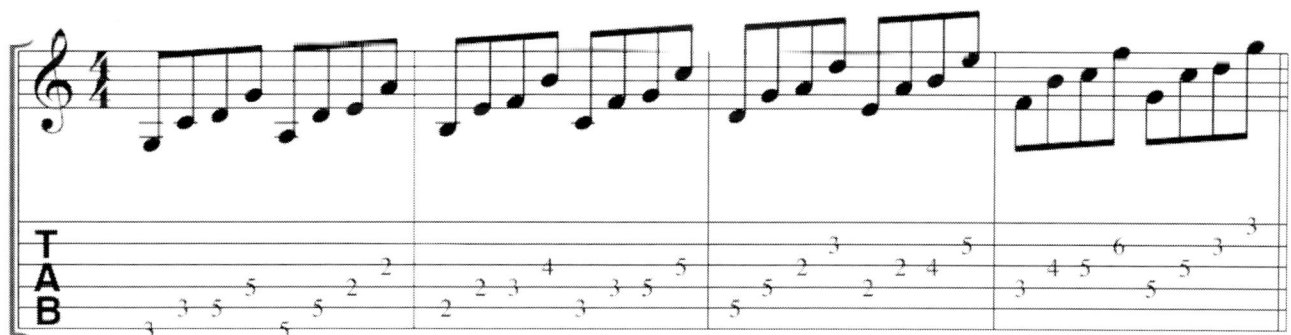

Adjoined 4ths Pattern, In C major, 5th Position, Descending:

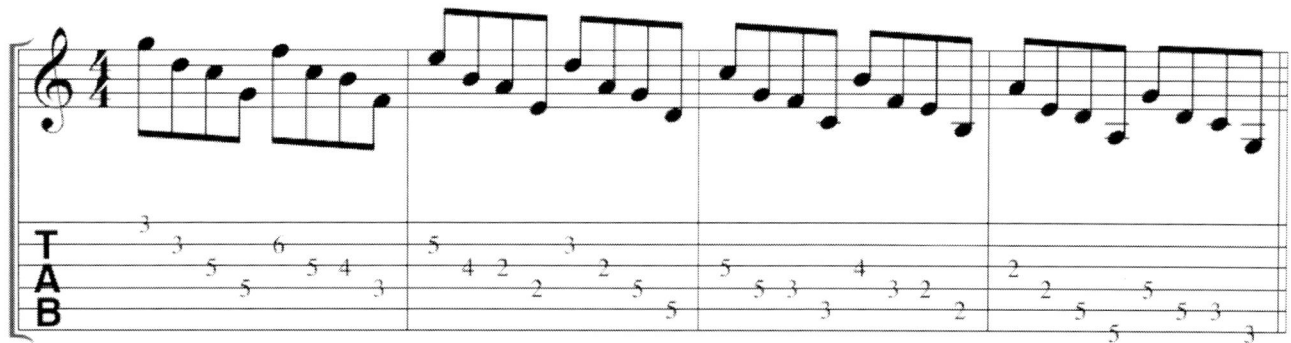

Adjoined 4ths Pattern, In C major, 6th Position, Ascending:

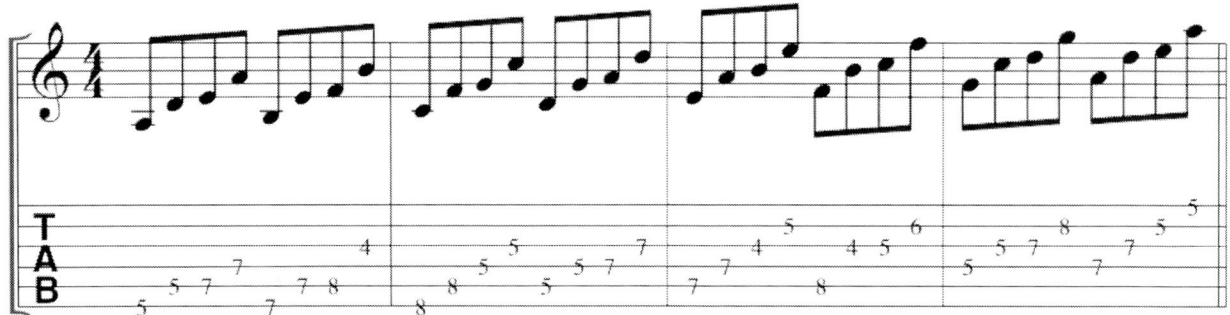

Adjoined 4ths Pattern, In C major, 6th Position, Descending:

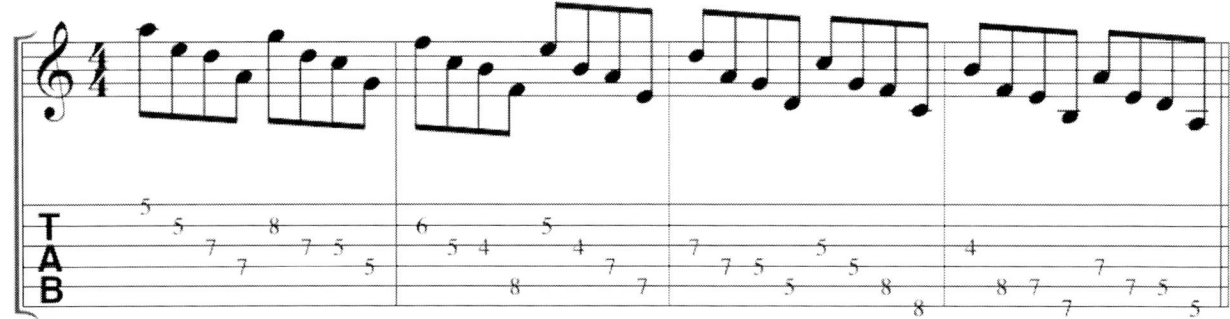

Adjoined 4ths Pattern, In C major, Root Position, Ascending:

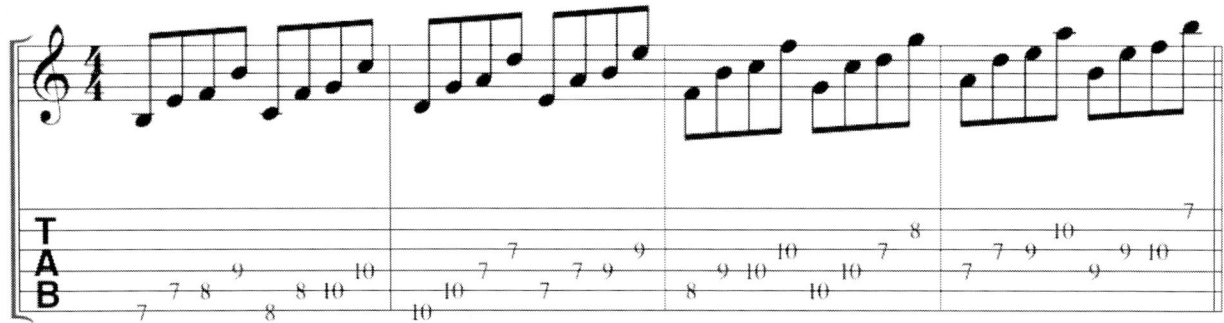

Adjoined 4ths Pattern, In C major, Root Position, Descending:

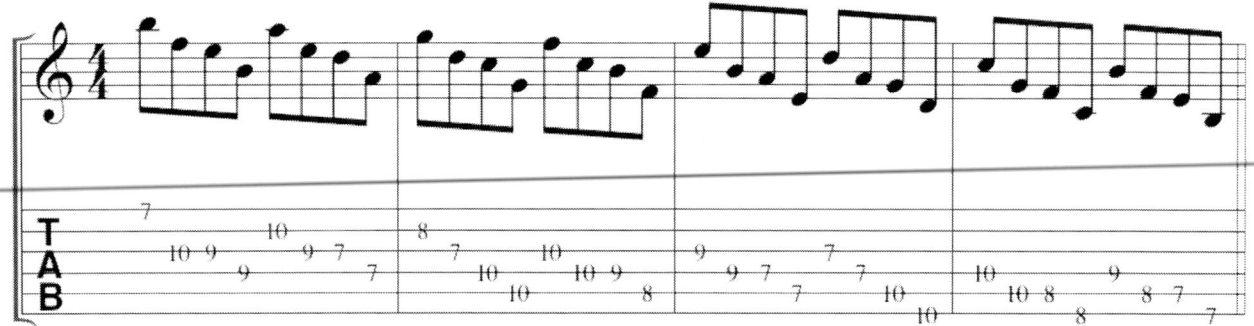

Adjoined 4ths Pattern, In C major, 2nd Position, Ascending:

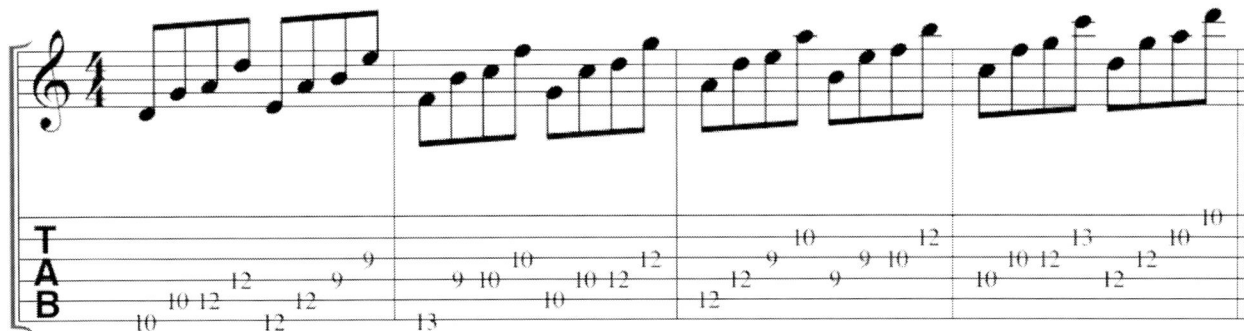

Adjoined 4ths Pattern, In C major, 2nd Position, Descending:

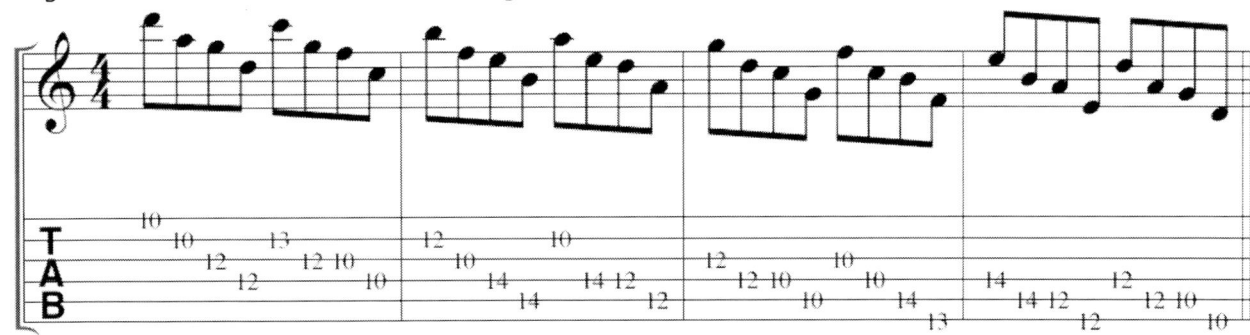

Adjoined 4ths Pattern, In C major, 3rd Position, Ascending:

Adjoined 4ths Pattern, In C major, 3rd Position, Descending:

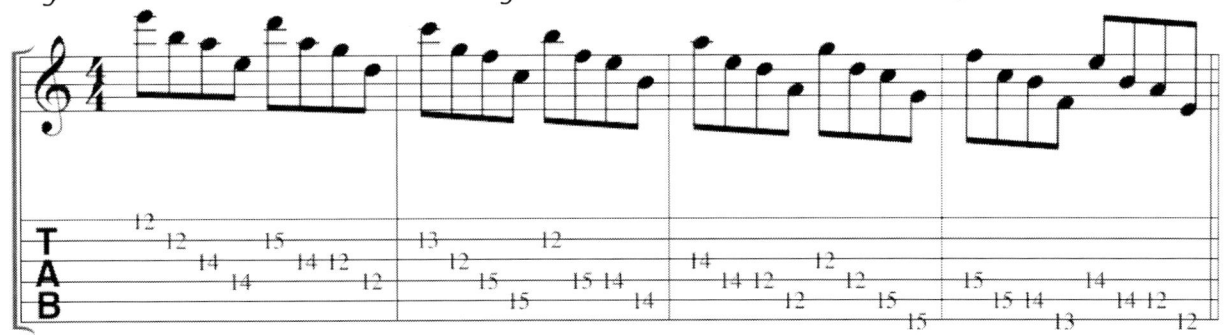

In this following pattern, we move from one scale tone another, always a 5th away (3½ up or 2½ down) from the previous tone. This creates a very modern and somewhat neutral sort of sound. Working with 4ths and 5ths, melodically or harmonically usually tends to lend a sense of ambiguity to the music which can be very useful.

Exclusive 5ths Pattern, In C major, 5th Position:

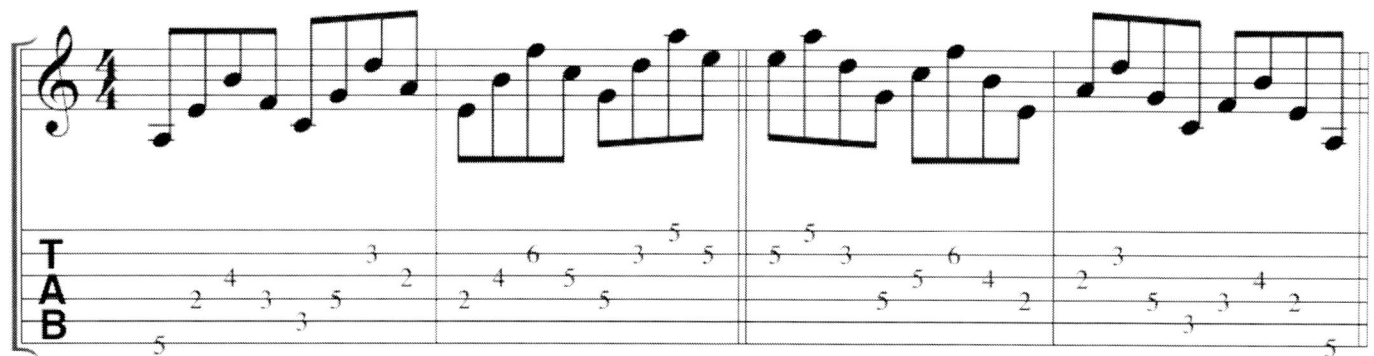

Exclusive 5ths Pattern, In C major, 6th Position:

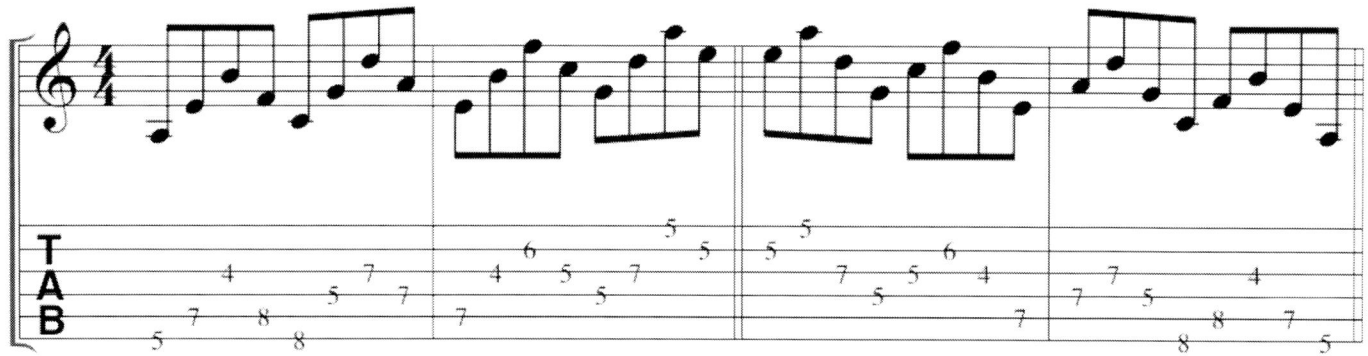

Exclusive 5ths Pattern, In C major, Root Position:

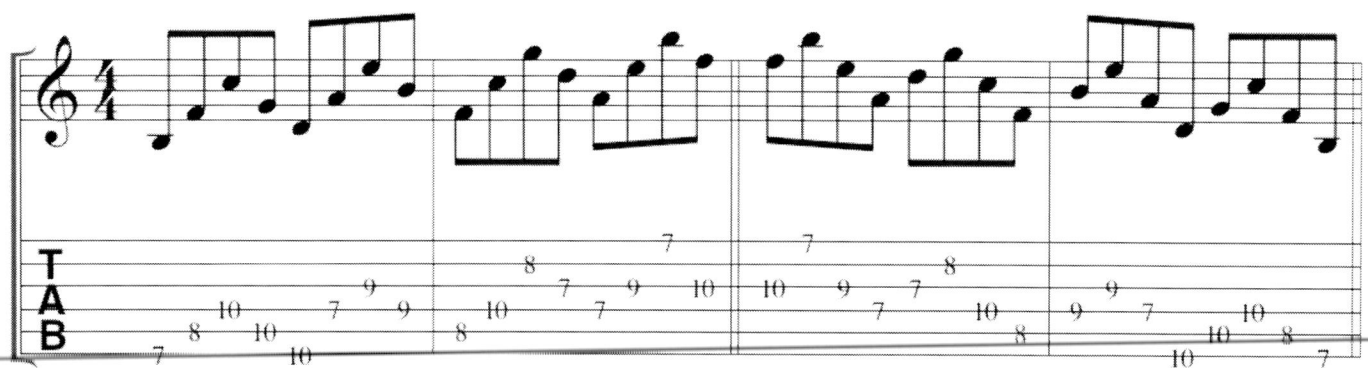

Exclusive 5ths Pattern, In C major, 2nd Position:

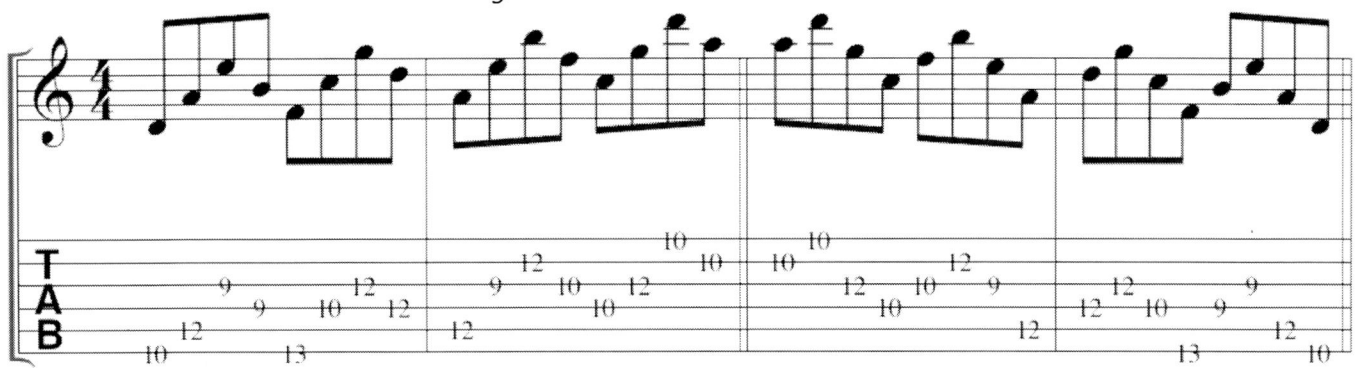

Exclusive 5ths Pattern, In C major, 3rd Position:

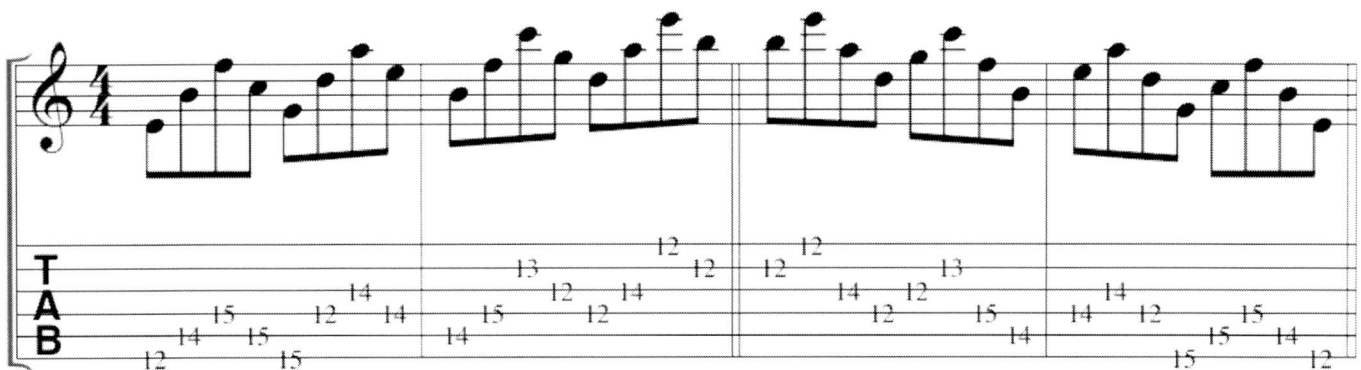

In this next pattern, we are working with a similar motion, this time in 4ths. The contour of this pattern repeats every five notes. When played in 8th notes or 16th notes we get a nice rhythmic overlapping effect that creates an interesting syncopation. This pattern would, of course, lay out neatly on the beats if it were played in quintuplets or any derivative thereof.

Exclusive 4ths Pattern, In C major, 5th Position, Ascending:

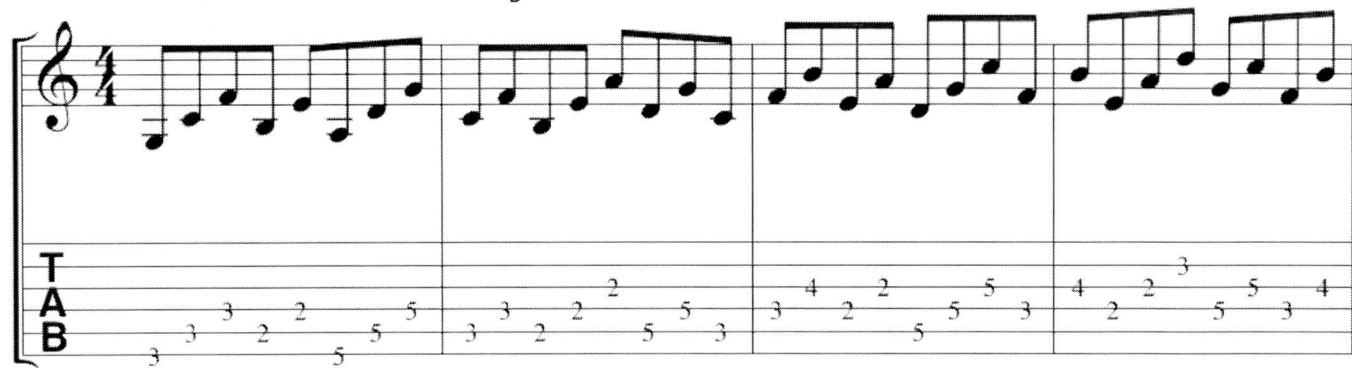

Exclusive 4ths Pattern, In C major, 5th Position, Descending:

Exclusive 4ths Pattern, In C major, 6th Position, Ascending:

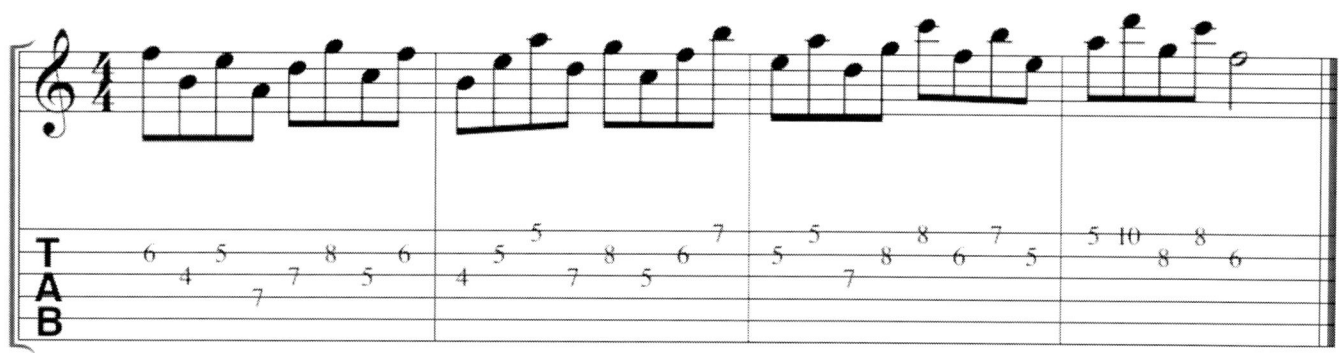

Exclusive 4ths Pattern, In C major, 6th Position, Descending:

Exclusive 4ths Pattern, In C major, Root Position, Ascending:

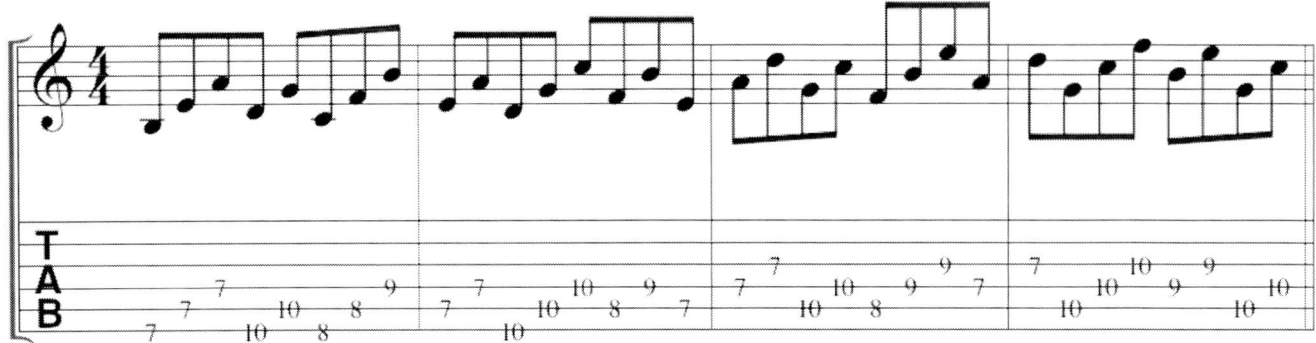

Exclusive 4ths Pattern, In C major, Root Position, Descending:

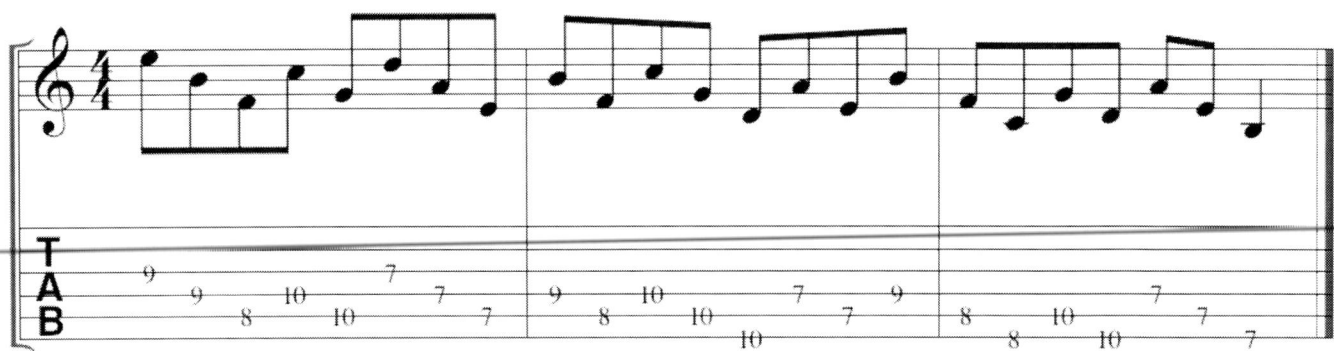

Exclusive 4ths Pattern, In C major, 2nd Position, Ascending:

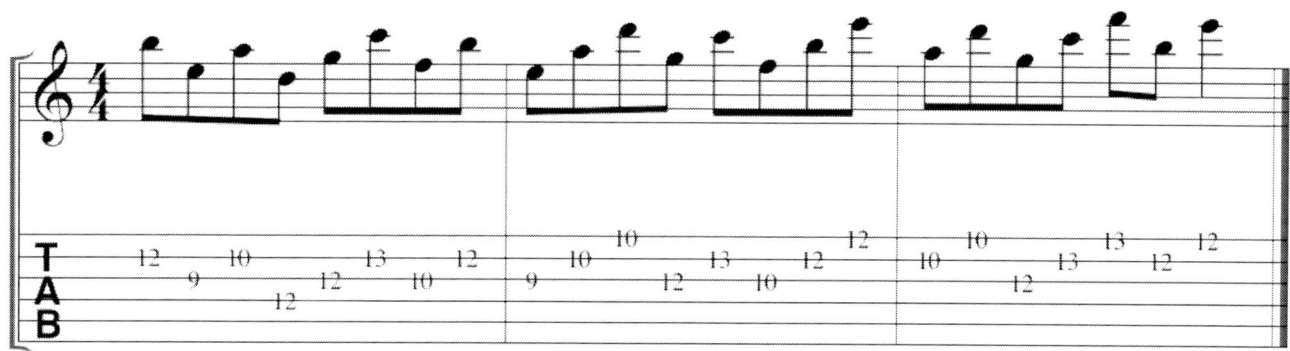

Exclusive 4ths Pattern, In C major, 2nd Position, Descending:

Exclusive 4ths Pattern, In C major, 3rd Position, Ascending:

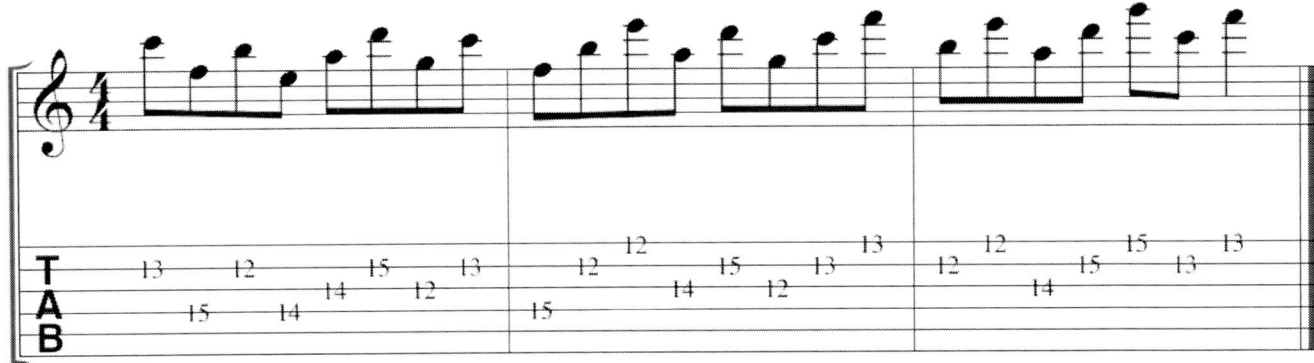

Exclusive 4ths Pattern, In C major, 3rd Position, Descending:

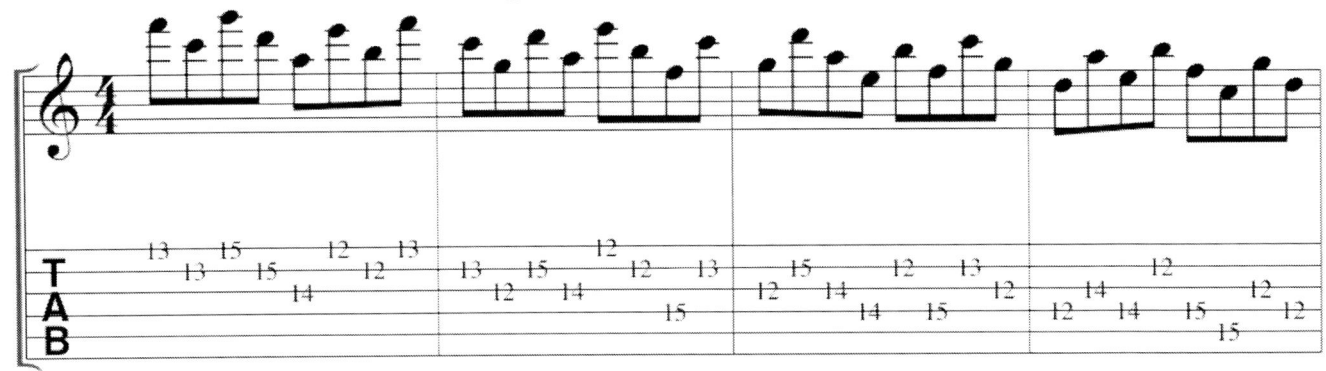

NON-DIATONIC HARMONY – part 2: Tritone Substitution

The feature that is unique to the dominant 7th chord is the tritone interval that occurs between the major 3rd and b7th of the chord. A dominant 7th chord located a tritone away from your original dominant 7th chord is going to share the same 3rd and b7th, only their roles will be reversed. Here is an example:

E7:   E   G#   B   D
          Root   3rd   5th   b7th

Bb7:   Bb   D   F   Ab
           Root   3rd   5th   b7th

This Bb7 chord can be used as a substitute for the E7 and vice versa. This is true for any two dominant chords, a tritone apart from one another. Tritone substitutions can breath life into progressions that you might find boring or basic. They can be played as chords by a whole band, or implied by a melodic part or soloist over the original chord.

If the dominant chord that you're substituting contains extensions and/or alterations, these same notes can be carried over into the substituted chord. If these tones are Super-Locrian related tones in the original chord, the same tones will serve as Lydian Dominant related tones in the substitution and vice versa. Below is an example:

E7alt: E   G#   Bb   D   F   G   C
             Root   3rd   b5th   b7th   b9   #9   b13

Bb13#11:   Bb   D   F   Ab   C   E   G
               Root   3rd   5th   b7th   9   #11   13

Here's a simple table of tritone substitutes:

Lydian Dominant	Super-Locrian
C9#11	Gb7alt
G9#11	Db7alt
D9#11	Ab7alt
A9#11	Eb7alt
E9#11	Bb7alt
B9#11	F7alt
Gb9#11	C7alt
Db9#11	G7alt
Ab9#11	D7alt
Eb9#11	A7alt
Bb9#11	E7alt
F9#11	B7alt

Here is a major IIm7-V7-Imaj7 progression with a tritone substitute:

```
    Dm7         Db7         Cmaj7
||: / / / / | / / / / | / / / / | / / / / :||
```

Here's a minor IIm7b5-V7-Im7 progression with a tritone substitute:

```
    Bm7b5       Bb7         Am7
||: / / / / | / / / / | / / / / | / / / / :||
```

This next example is made up of the first nine bars from the final example in the Modulations section, now with tritone substitutes on the dominant chords.

```
    Cmaj7         Gm7  Gb7    Fmaj7        Fm7  E7
||: / / / / | / / / / | / / / / | / / / / |
    Ebmaj7        Abm7 G7     Gbmaj7       Em7  Eb7     Dmaj7
    / / / / | / / / / | / / / / | / / / / | / / / / :||
```

In this final example, I mix up some major and minor II-V-I progressions, all using tritone substitutes.

```
    Ebmaj7        Dm7b5 Db7   Cm7          Bbm7 A7
||: / / / / | / / / / | / / / / | / / / / |
    Abmaj7        Dm7  Db7    Cmaj7        Bm7b5 Bb7
    / / / / | / / / / | / / / / | / / / / |
    Am7           Cm7  B7     Bbmaj7       Fm7  E7
    / / / / | / / / / | / / / / | / / / / :||
```

THE MELODIC CRAFT – part 2: Chromaticism

There is one particularly wonderful little golden musical rule. It goes as follows: No matter what key you are in, there are no wrong notes. There are only wrong ways to use notes. To elaborate, there are very few wrong ways to use scale tones but there are plenty of wrong-ways to use non-scale (chromatic) tones. However, there are a couple right ways to use chromatic tones. The two basic functioning roles that chromatic notes serve as, within melodies are that of the neighboring tone and the approaching tone.

A neighboring tone sits rhythmically and tonally between any two scale tones that are a whole step apart and is always rhythmically deemphasized. Chances are that you've used these to some degree already, just from seeing others use them.

Below are a couple musical examples of neighboring tones being used in any mode of C major. Notice how the scale tones are always on the beat and the chromatic tones fall between the beats. Also notice that the chromatic notes never go to or come from anywhere but a scale-tone a half-step away. These are the earmarks of neighboring tones.

Neighboring Tones, Example 1:

Neighboring Tones, Example 2:

The following is an exercise taking you through most of the C major 6th position (A minor root position) making use of neighboring tones. Transcribe this in all twelve keys in both the major/natural minor scale and the melodic minor scale.

Neighboring Tone Exercise:

Approaching tones are simply notes that come right before a chord-tone or scale-tone, approaching from a half-step beneath. The easiest device to quickly build some very musical approaching tone phrases is the enclosure. An enclosure is a two-note approach that begins with a note one scale-tone above our target note, continues to the note a half-step down from the target note and then resolves to the target note.

Your target notes can be whatever you like. A simple example would be an arpeggio. Here's a Dm arpeggio with enclosures:

Enclosures can be rhythmically phrased in various ways. In this next example, I'm phrasing in triplets, but I begin with an un-enclosed note in order to get my target notes on the beats.

We can always apply the three over four phrasing in order to get a mix of chromatic tones and scale tones on the beats. The beats will remain more populated with scale-tones since the chromatic only makes up one third of an enclosure.

If we want to use enclosures in 8th notes with a more *even* sort of contour, we simply revisit the target note in the process. This gives us a really sturdy phrasing.

When the enclosing notes are on the strong beats, the enclosure suggests what we call a feminine cadence.

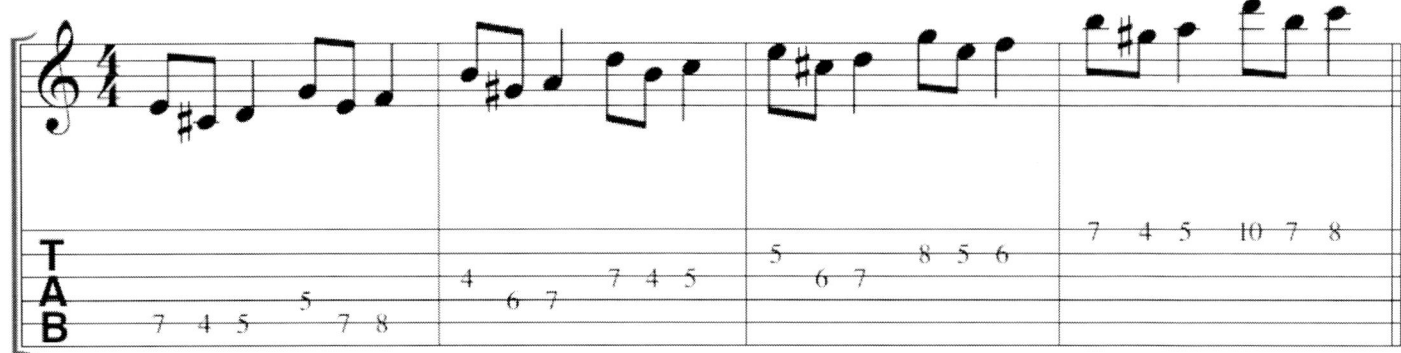

When the target notes are on the strong beats, the enclosure suggests what we call a masculine cadence. Both approaches are useful and depend upon one another for contrast. Make sure you don't wind up picking one over the other.

One great exercise is to practice your scale positions, employing enclosures on every note.

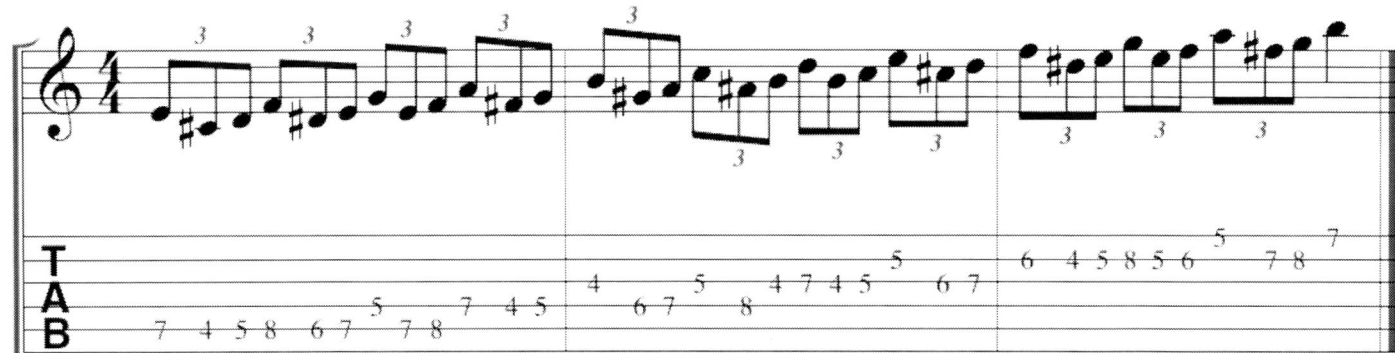

We can phrase it rhythmically, however we choose, granted we take the time to practice it in all the different ways we can think up.

Below, I'm enclosing the entire scale in a three-over-four phrasing:

In even fours:

Chromatic Licks in the Seven Major Scale Modes:

These licks should help give you a frame of reference concerning how Chromaticism is used in every-day musical conversation. Any of these licks can be altered to fit any mode to which you would like to relate them. In cases of neighboring tones, when reworking a lick for a new scale or mode, you may in some cases, have to replace one with an enclosure. This works the other way around, too.

C Ionian Chromatic Lick 1:

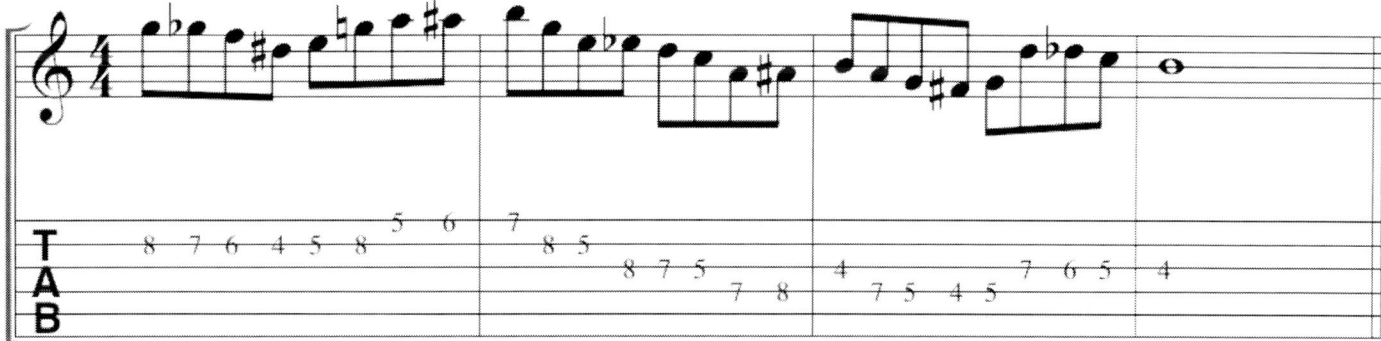

C Ionian Chromatic Lick 2:

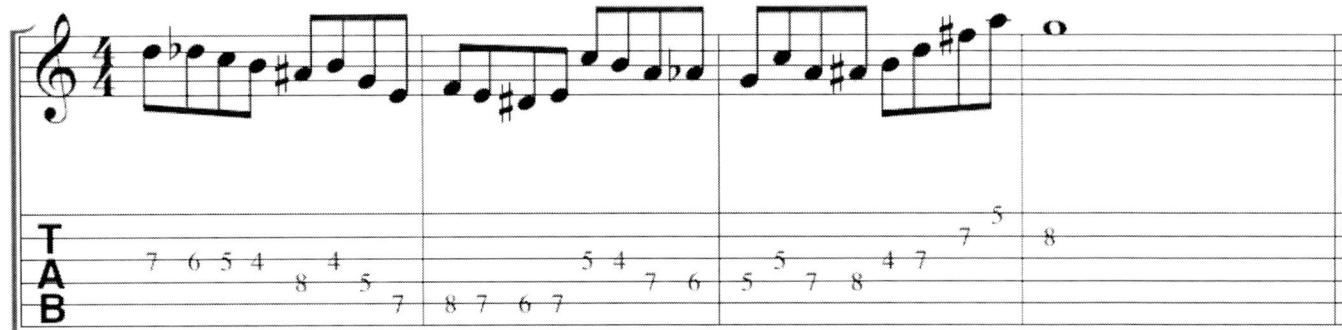

C Ionian Chromatic Lick 3:

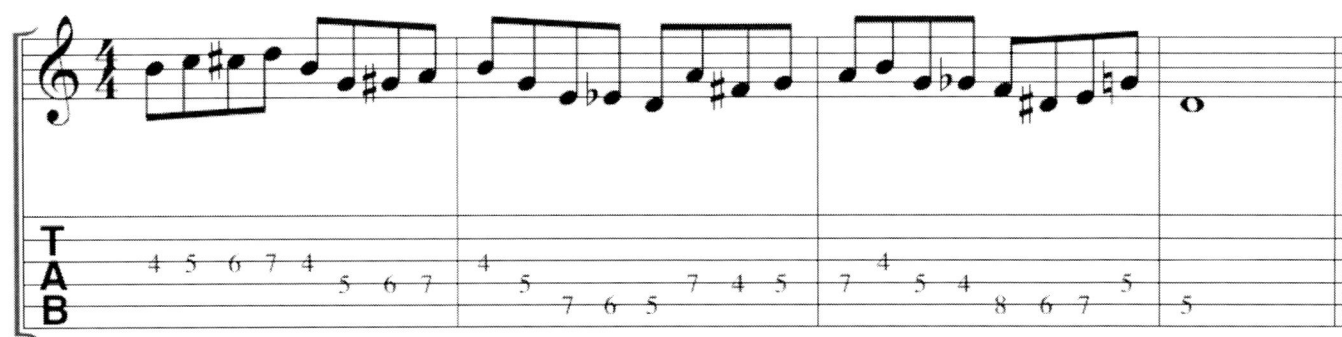

C Ionian Chromatic Lick 4:

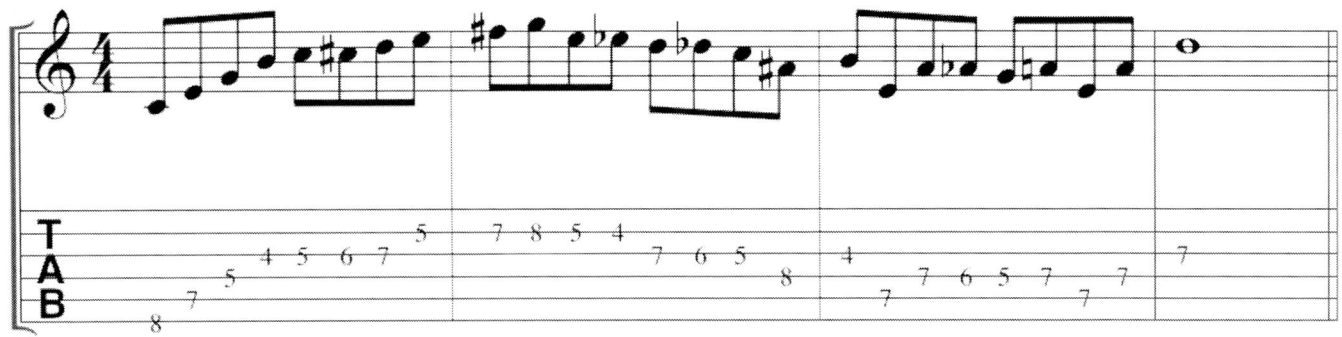

C Ionian Chromatic Lick 5:

D Dorian Chromatic Lick 1:

D Dorian Chromatic Lick 2:

D Dorian Chromatic Lick 3:

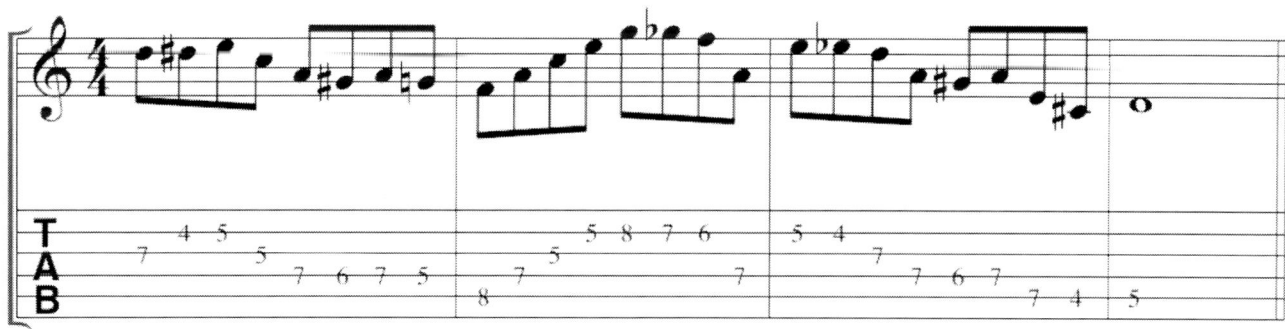

D Dorian Chromatic Lick 4:

D Dorian Chromatic Lick 5:

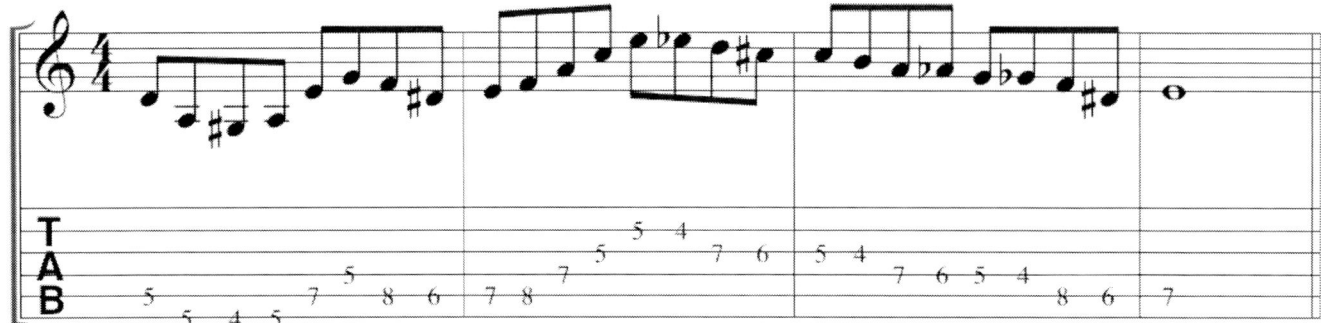

E Phrygian Chromatic Lick 1:

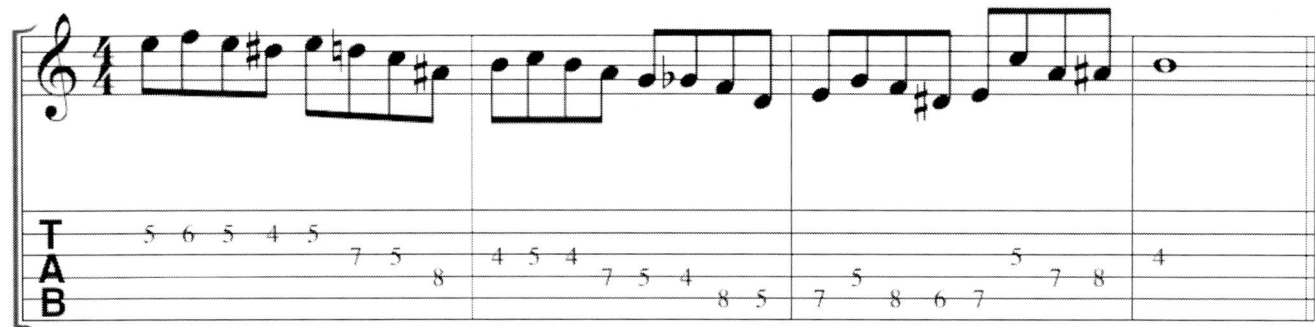

E Phrygian Chromatic Lick 2:

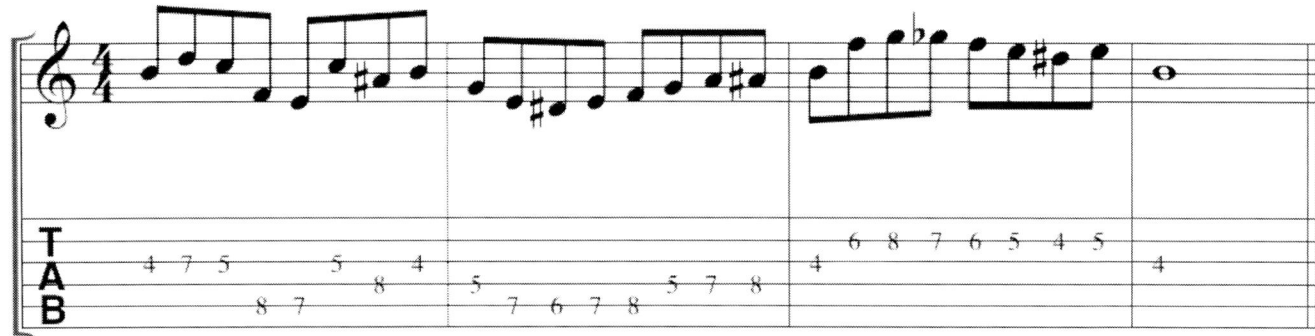

E Phrygian Chromatic Lick 3:

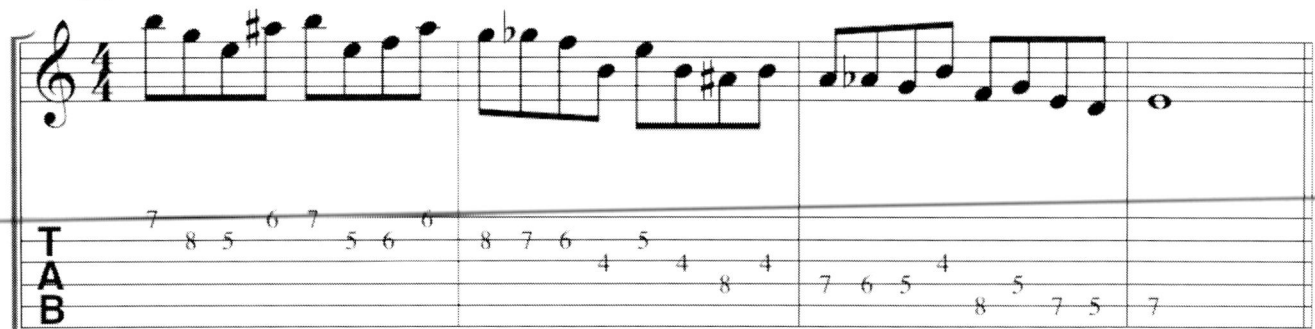

E Phrygian Chromatic Lick 4:

E Phrygian Chromatic Lick 5:

F Lydian Chromatic Lick 1:

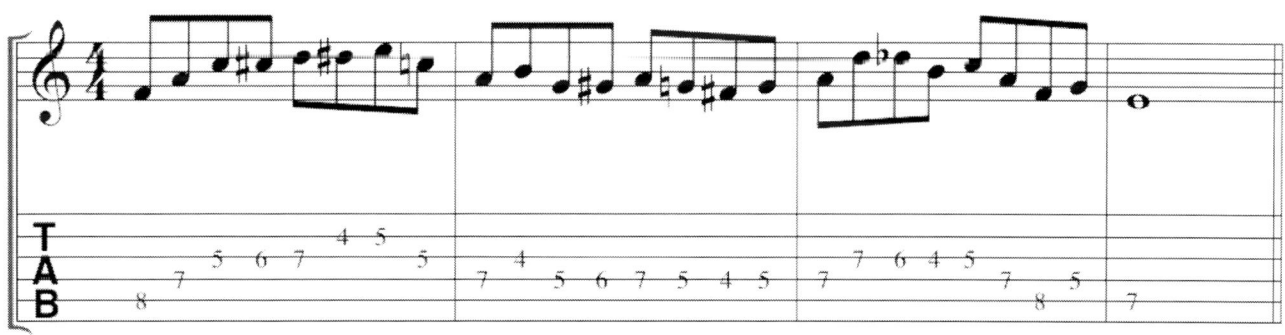

F Lydian Chromatic Lick 2:

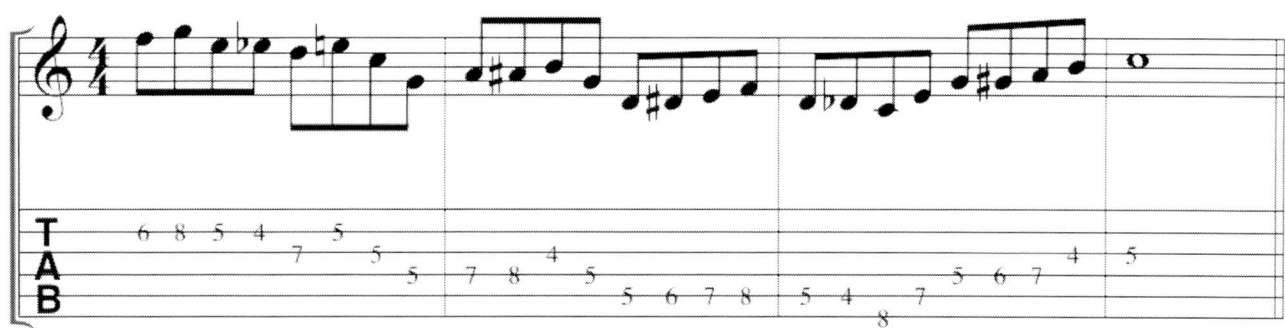

F Lydian Chromatic Lick 3:

F Lydian Chromatic Lick 4:

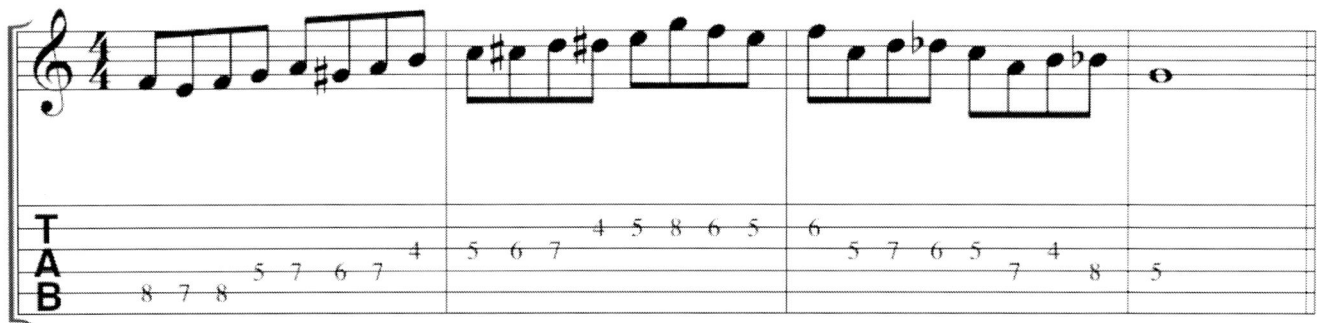

F Lydian Chromatic Lick 5:

G Mixolydian Chromatic Lick 1:

G Mixolydian Chromatic Lick 2:

G Mixolydian Chromatic Lick 3:

G Mixolydian Chromatic Lick 4:

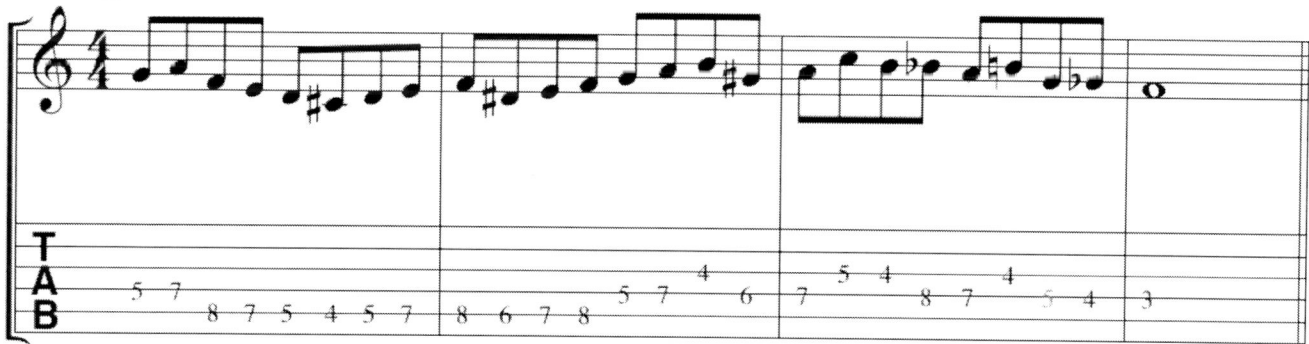

G Mixolydian Chromatic Lick 5:

A Aeolian Chromatic Lick 1:

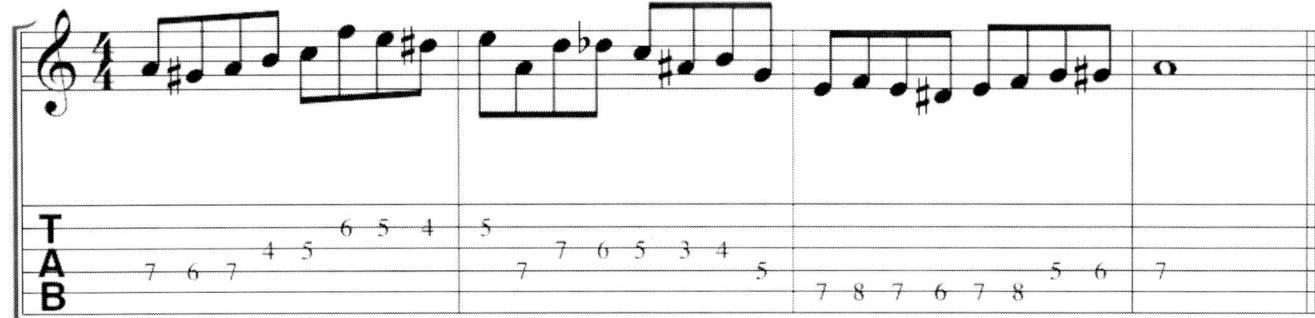

A Aeolian Chromatic Lick 2:

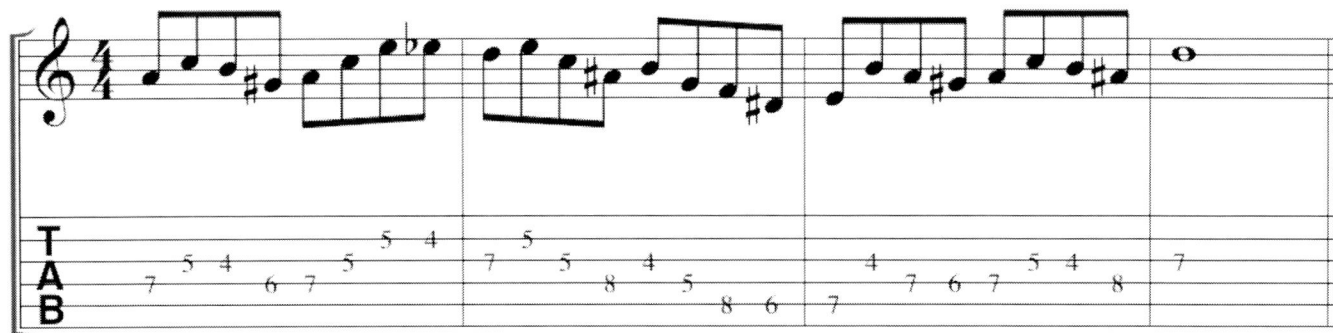

A Aeolian Chromatic Lick 3:

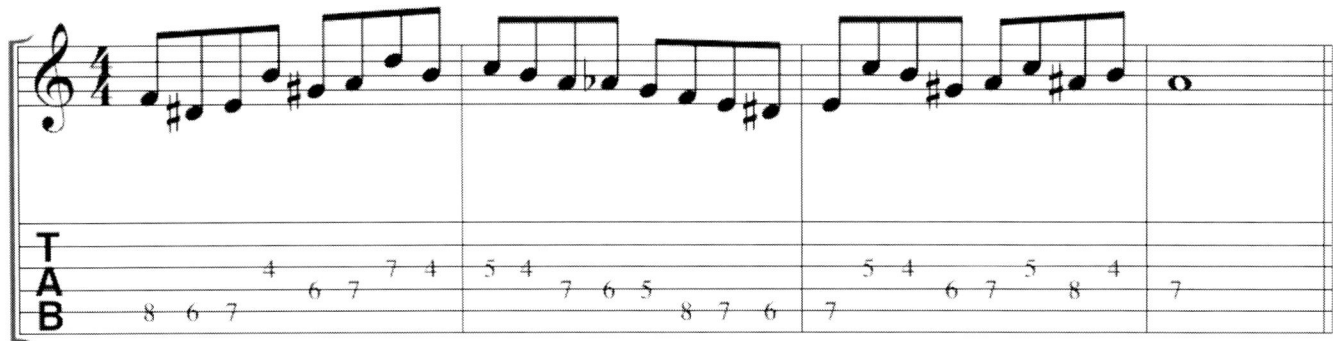

A Aeolian Chromatic Lick 4:

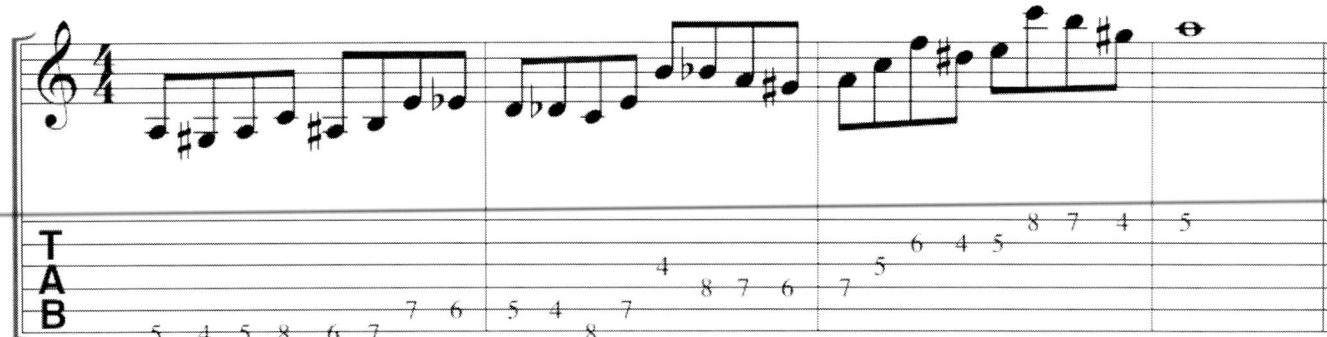

A Aeolian Chromatic Lick 5:

B Locrian Chromatic Lick 1:

B Locrian Chromatic Lick 2:

B Locrian Chromatic Lick 3:

B Locrian Chromatic Lick 4:

B Locrian Chromatic Lick 5:

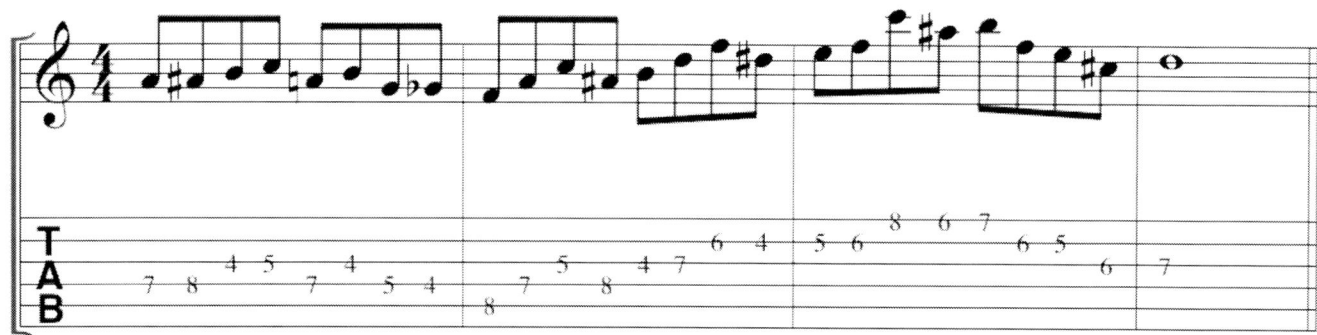

Pentatonic Chromatic Lick 1:

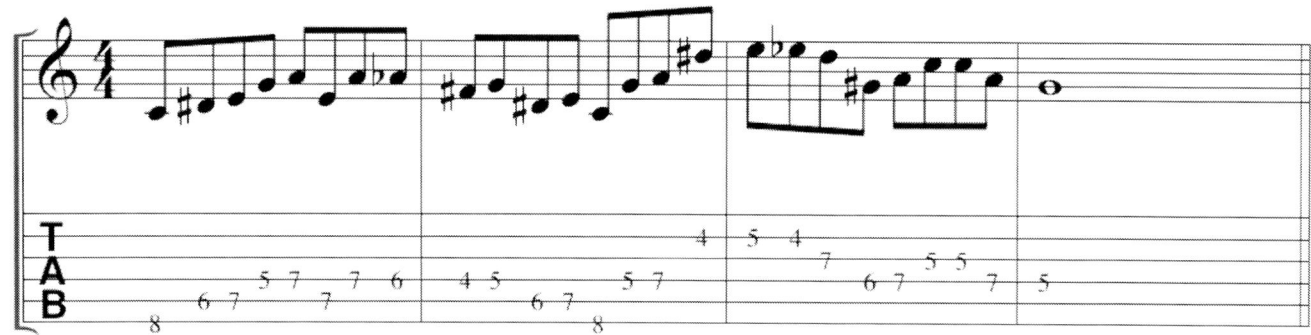

Pentatonic Chromatic Lick 2:

Pentatonic Chromatic Lick 3:

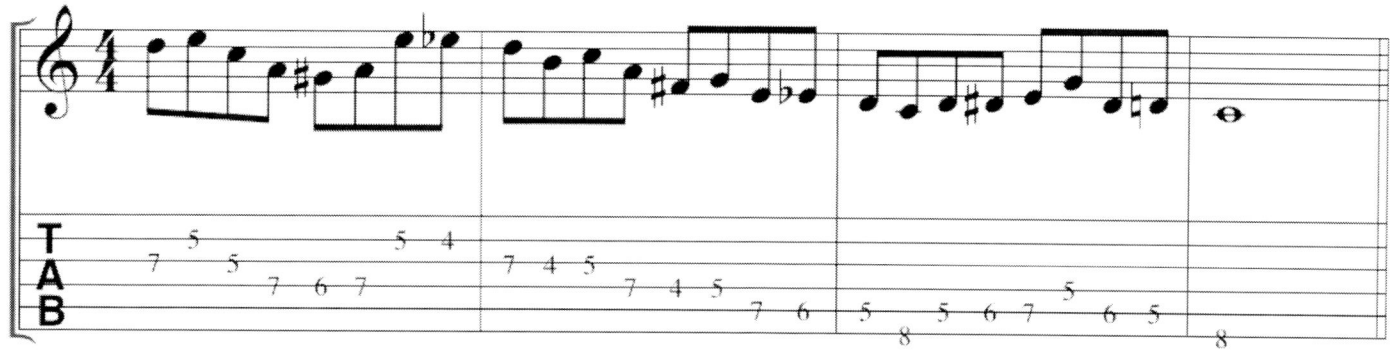

Pentatonic Chromatic Lick 4:

Pentatonic Chromatic Lick 5:

Outside Playing:

A common effect in jazz, outside playing refers to extended streams of notes that seem to relate to something other than the tonality of the music. It ultimately resolves back inside the tonality in order to let the listener know that you aren't just crazy. A couple ways that you can experiment with outside playing on any given chord are playing a half-step up or down from the chord or implying the altered dominant of the chord you're on. We'll be looking at other outside devices soon. Outside playing works best on weak beats (2 and 4) but can work on strong beats and even carry over multiple beats, as long as it makes a graceful return home to the tonality of the chord over which you're playing.

NON-DIATONIC HARMONY – Part 3: More Chromatic Chords

We've learned how to diatonically substitute our major and minor chords. We've learned how to chromatically substitute our dominant chords. Now we are going to look at chromatically substituting our major and minor chords. It should first be pointed out that these types of substitutions are a little more drastic and aren't the type that people can imply while others are playing the original changes. Substitutions like the ones that we're about to look at are the type that must be written into a song or a particular arrangement of a song. These will offer you some excellent new options with song writing and song re-harmonization.

Reversed Polarity Triads:

These are a little trick used by a lot of pop and rock songwriters. If the melody avoids the 3rd of the current major or minor chord, the chord can be replaced with its opposite. F could be replaced with Fm. Am could be replaced with A. This holds true of any triad other than the I or VIIdim of the major key, and the Im and IIdim of the minor key. We avoid reversing the polarity of the I because it winds up being misinterpreted as a failed key change. We avoid reversing the polarity of the diminished triads because they have no polarity to begin with, as a result of their b5ths.

One general rule to keep in mind is that it's usually not going to work well to go from one reversed polarity chord straight to another. The one exception I can find to this rule is the IImaj – IVm – I progression. It seems to work well, but in most cases, two of these in a row will make things tonally very awkward and vague for the listener. Below is an illustration of the reversed polarity triads as they relate to the key of C major.

I	IIm	IIIm	IV	V	VIm	VIIb
C	Dm	Em	F	G	Am	Bo
X	D	E	Fm	Gm	A	X
X	IImaj	IIImaj	IVm	Vm	VImaj	X

When improvising over a progression that uses reversed polarity chords, make sure to never lose sight of the thirds of these chords, as they are the notes that are chromatic to the key and as a result, give these chords their unique color. When you can manage to highlight these notes in the course of a melodic part, written or improvised, you'll add a nice layer of depth to your line(s).

Here are some examples of progressions using reversed polarity chords in the key of C major.

Example 1:
```
     C    E    F    C    D         F    Fm
||: / / / / | / / / / | / / / / | / / / / :||
```

Example 2:
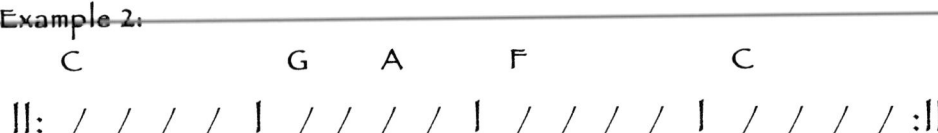

```
     C    G    A    F         C
||: / / / / | / / / / | / / / / | / / / / :||
```

403

Example 3:
```
     C    Fm      C    Am     D    F       C    G
||:  /  /  /  /  |  /  /  /  /  |  /  /  /  /  |  /  /  /  / :||
```

Example 4:
```
     C            D    F       C           Gm    F
||:  /  /  /  /  |  /  /  /  /  |  /  /  /  /  |  /  /  /  / :||
```

Example 5:
```
     G    C       Fm   C       E    F       C
||:  /  /  /  /  |  /  /  /  /  |  /  /  /  /  |  /  /  /  / :||
```

Example 6:
```
     F    G       Am   D       F    D       F    D
||:  /  /  /  /  |  /  /  /  /  |  /  /  /  /  |  /  /  /  / :||
```

Example 7:
```
     Am   F       G    D       F    D       F    G
||:  /  /  /  /  |  /  /  /  /  |  /  /  /  /  |  /  /  /  / :||
```

Example 8:
```
     D            F    C       E            F
||:  /  /  /  /  |  /  /  /  /  |  /  /  /  /  |  /  /  /  / :||
```

Example 9:
```
     C    E       F            Fm   C       D
||:  /  /  /  /  |  /  /  /  /  |  /  /  /  /  |  /  /  /  / :||
```

Example 10:
```
     Am   D       Am   F       C    F       C    E
||:  /  /  /  /  |  /  /  /  /  |  /  /  /  /  |  /  /  /  / :||
```

Flat Scale-Tone Chords:

These are used by pop, rock and jazz writers alike. On minor chords, if the melody is situated on the b3rd of the current chord and doesn't use the chord's root or 5th, we can lower the root and 5th of the chord to apply what we call a flat scale-tone chord. Am becomes Ab. Am7 becomes Abmaj7. This brings a somewhat more exotic quality to the overall music. This only works with minor triads, m7 chords and the diminished triad or m7b5 chord. Whether you're altering a triad or a 7th chord, you only flat the root and the 5th. In the case of the diminished triad or m7b5 chord, the 5th is already lowered so you only need to lower the root note.

Here are the flat scale-tone triads as they relate to the key of C major:

I	IIm	IIIm	IV	V	VIm	VIIo
C	Dm	Em	F	G	Am	Bo
X	Db	Eb	X	X	Ab	Bb
X	bII	bIII	X	X	bVI	bVII

Here are the flat scale-tone 7th chords as they relate to the key of C major:

Imaj7	IIm7	IIIm7	IVmaj7	V7	VIm7	VIIm7b5
Cmaj7	Dm7	Em7	Fmaj7	G7	Am7	Bm7b5
X	Dbmaj7	Ebmaj7	X	X	Abmaj7	Bbmaj7
X	bIImaj7	bIIImaj7	X	X	bVImaj7	bVIImaj7

When improvising or composing a melody over a flat scale-tone chord, use a Lydian mode based off of the root note of the given flat scale-tone chord. This always works. I should mention that these chords can be extended just as readily as the diatonic chords. They would extend outward through the Lydian mode, ultimately to wind up as maj13#11 chords.

Below are some examples of flat scale-tone chords in use:

Example 1:

```
   C    Bb   F              Dm           G7
||: / / / / | / / / / | / / / / | / / / / :||
```

Example 2:

```
   Am7          Abmaj7        Dm7   G7    Cmaj7  E7
||: / / / / | / / / / | / / / / | / / / / :||
```

Example 3:

```
   Em7  Ebmaj7 Dm7  G7    Cmaj7  Ebmaj7  Abmaj7
||: / / / / | / / / / | / / / / | / / / / :||
```

Example 4:
```
  C     Dm7    Ebmaj7 Dm7    C     Bb      Am    F
||: / / / / | / / / / | / / / / | / / / / :||
```

Example 5:
```
  Cmaj7 Abmaj7   Fmaj7 Dbmaj7  Cmaj7 Abmaj7   Bbmaj7 Fmaj7
||: / / / / | / / / / | / / / / | / / / / :||
```

Example 6:
```
  Fmaj7         Abmaj7         C              G
||: / / / / | / / / / | / / / / | / / / / :||
```

Example 7:
```
  Cmaj7 Abmaj7 Dbmaj7 G7    Ebmaj7 Abmaj7  Dbmaj7 G7
||: / / / / | / / / / | / / / / | / / / / :||
```

Example 8:
```
  Dm7  Dbmaj7  Cmaj7 Bbmaj7  Am7  Abmaj7   G7
||: / / / / | / / / / | / / / / | / / / / :||
```

Example 9:
```
  Am7          Bbmaj7 F    Ab           C    G
||: / / / / | / / / / | / / / / | / / / / :||
```

This last example combines approaches and makes use of a reversed polarity chord, the IImaj. It also happens to be an unbroken string of 5ths until the final change where it moves by a minor 3rd, followed by another minor 3rd change when it starts over:

Example 10:
```
  Ab    Eb    Bb   F     C     G     D    F
||: / / / / | / / / / | / / / / | / / / / :||
```

The table below will give you a birds-eye view of your entire family of chord possibilities in the key of C, both diatonic and non-diatonic. It doesn't account for extensions, 6th and 6/9 chords or suspended chords since these are simple alterations that can be made. These are just basic chord functions that can be colored however you choose.

The first row displays the notes of each chord, along with their chord tone labels. The following diatonic 7th chord row displays only the added 7th of each chord since the rest of the notes can be found in the box on the previous page. The following rows only display the chromatic notes that occur within each chord.

Note that I gave each dim7 chord two names. Each one really has four possible names but space did not permit. My strategy for the primary dim7 name was to take the 3rd of the dominant 7th chord for which it's being used as a substitute. This works out to being a half-step beneath the destination chord. The strategy for the secondary names was to boil them all down to Cdim7, Fdim7 and Gdim7, so you can clearly see which chords use the same diminished approach.

C Major	I	II	III	IV	V	VI	VII
Diatonic Triad	C: C E G R 3 5	Dm: D F A R b3 5	Em: E G B R b3 5	F: F A C R 3 5	G: G B D R 3 5	Am: A C E R b3 5	Bo: B D F R b3 b5
Diatonic 7th Chord	Cmaj7: B 7	Dm7: C b7	Em7: D b7	Fmaj7: E 7	G7: F b7	Am7: G b7	Bm7b5: A b7
Secondary Dominant	G7	A7: C#	B7: D#, F#	C7: Bb	D7: F#	E7: G#	F7: Eb
Secondary Tritone	Db7: Db Ab	Eb7: Eb Bb Db	F7: Eb	Gb7: Gb Bb Db	Ab7: Ab Eb Gb	Bb7: Bb Ab	B7: D#, F#
Secondary Diminished	Bdim7 Fdim7 Ab	C#dim7 Gdim7 C# Bb	D#dim7 Cdim7 D# F#	Edim7 Gdim7 C# Bb	F#dim7 Cdim7 D# F#	G#dim7 Fdim7 G#	Adim7 Cdim7 D# F#
Secondary Super-Tonic	Dm7	Em7b5: Bb	F#m7b5: F#	Gm7: Bb	Am7	Bm7b5	X
Reverse Polarity	X	D: F#	E: G#	Fm: Ab	Gm: Bb	A: C#	X
Flat Scale-Tone	X	Db: Db Ab	Eb: Eb Bb	X	X	Ab: Ab Eb	Bb: Bb
Flat Scale-Tone 7ths	X	Dbmaj7: Db Ab	Ebmaj7: Eb Bb	X	X	Abmaj7: Ab Eb	Bbmaj7: Bb

In the back of this book, you will find a blank version of this chart. Your mission, should you choose to accept it, is to make copies of this, (blow it up if you need to) and fill one out for each of your eleven other major keys. It's not that I'm being lazy. I actually took the other eleven out after spending the time on them. Going through the whole process was enriching enough that I didn't want to rob you of the experience points.

Relating this info to the minor key is as simple as considering the VI column to be the I column and making appropriate minor scale adjustments to suit your intended style.

Symmetrical Scales

We've come to understand the symmetrical nature of diminished and augmented chords; what we will now explore are the scales that can be built from these structures. I hate to sound like I'm hyping things but this section is going to open you up to a whole new variety of mysterious and otherworldly sounds. When you start implying this material in your playing, other musicians start calling you things like the dark wizard.

We'll start by defining what a symmetrical scale is. It is a scale where the step pattern starts over before reaching the octave. By this definition, the chromatic scale is a symmetrical scale since it has a singular step pattern of h (half-step) that repeats, every note. The chromatic scale contains every possible chord so beginning our study of symmetrical scales here would be a bit frivolous.

A better place to begin our study of what symmetrical scales can offer us would be the diminished scale. It has an alternating step pattern of whole-step and half-step, which repeats in minor 3rds. In effect, we've divided the octave into four equal and identical parts. Another way to construct the diminished scale is to take a dim7 chord and approach each tone by a half-step below. Just as the dim7 chord has four possible names, so does the diminished scale.

Whether it is the whole-step or half-step following the note you consider the root note is what determines which of the two modes of the scale you are using. Each of these two modes has a very practical function. Here are the two modes in parallel terms. I made the primary chord tones larger note names. It's good to know that in the case of mode 1, these larger letters also happen to be other possible root notes for the diminished scale of the same mode.

The C Diminished Scale, Mode 1, (Whole-Half Diminished) as related to Cdim7:

	W		H		W		H		W		H		W		H
Root		2nd		b3rd		4th		b5th		b6th		bb7th		7th	
C		**D**		**Eb**		**F**		**Gb**		**Ab**		**A**		**B**	

C Whole-Half Diminished could be used over Cdim7, Ebdim7, Gbdim7 or Adim7, being that they are all made up of the same four notes. It can also be said the C, Eb, Gb and A whole-half diminished scale could be used over the Cdim7 chord, being that they are all made up of the same eight notes.

The C Diminished Scale, Mode 2, (Half-Whole Diminished) as related to C7:

	H		W		H		W		H		W		H		W
Root		b9th		#9th		3rd		#11th		5th		13th		b7th	
C		**Db**		**D#**		**E**		**F#**		**G**		**A**		**Bb**	

C half-whole diminished could be used over C7, Eb7, Gb7 or A7, being that these four chords are all found within the scale. The C half-whole diminished scale is also the Eb, Gb and A half-whole diminished scale.

In the table below, I've shaded the rows to give you a clear visual concept of how the diminished scale repeats itself throughout the cycle of 5ths. Basically speaking, there are only three distinct diminished scales; the white one (C, Eb, Gb, A) the light grey one (G, Bb, Db, E) and the dark grey one (F, Ab, B, D). You will find enharmonic note spellings but as long as you account for these, you'll see the relationship clearly. Keep in mind that the half-whole diminished scale is simply the alternate mode of this one and therefore has the same relationship with itself.

C Diminished Mode 1:	C	D	Eb	F	Gb	Ab	A	B
G Diminished Mode 1:	G	A	Bb	C	Db	Eb	E	F#
D Diminished Mode 1:	D	E	F	G	Ab	Bb	B	C#
A Diminished Mode 1:	A	B	C	D	Eb	F	Gb	G#
E Diminished Mode 1:	E	F#	G	A	Bb	C	Db	D#
B Diminished Mode 1:	B	C#	D	E	F	G	Ab	A#
Gb Diminished Mode 1:	Gb	Ab	A	B	C	D	Eb	F
Db Diminished Mode 1:	Db	Eb	F	Gb	G	A	Bb	C
Ab Diminished Mode 1:	Ab	Bb	B	Db	D	E	F	G
Eb Diminished Mode 1:	Eb	F	Gb	Ab	A	B	C	D
Bb Diminished Mode 1:	Bb	C	Db	Eb	E	F#	G	A
F Diminished Mode 1:	F	G	Ab	Bb	B	C#	D	E

One thing that's really nice about symmetrical scales is the fact that each one only has a couple basic scale positions at most. Either of these two diminished scale positions can be moved up and down the neck in increments of three frets. Another nice fact is that scale tone labels are not needed. In the diagrams below, the black dots are possible roots, b3rds, b5ths and bb7ths of mode 1 (whole-half) and the grey dots are the same for mode 2. In other words, if you are playing on a dim7 chord, align any black dot with the root of the chord and if you're playing over a dominant chord, align any grey dot with the root of the chord.

I would like to offer some honesty here and tell you that I never use position 2, but it's available to you in case you hate it any less than I do.

Diminished Scale Position 1:   Diminished Scale Position 2:

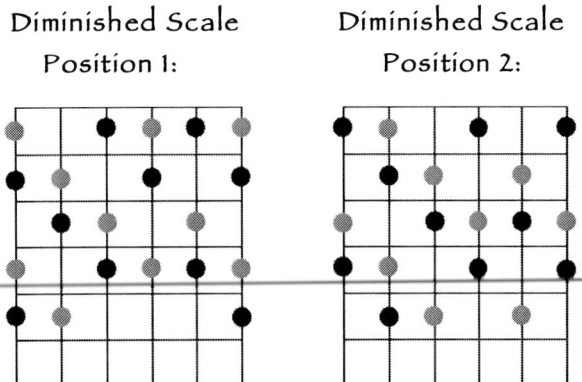

409

I should warn you that upon first practicing this scale, it's going to be tough to get a sense of how these notes sound together. You won't be as readily able to recognize wrong notes and for that reason I urge you to practice these at a snail's pace for a good couple hours before you start increasing speed. Spend less time running straight up and down the scale and more time applying melodic patterns to the scale. Make copies of the transcription paper of your choice from the back of the book. Pick out your favorite melodic patterns and start transcribing and practicing.

There's also a common diagonal position that's fun to use but I'll illustrate that one in guitar tab, in order to more easily indicate fingerings. This diagonal position is simply made of a four-note shape, modulating by tritone, from string to string.

F Diminished Mode 1, G Diminished Mode 2, Diagonal Position, Ascending:

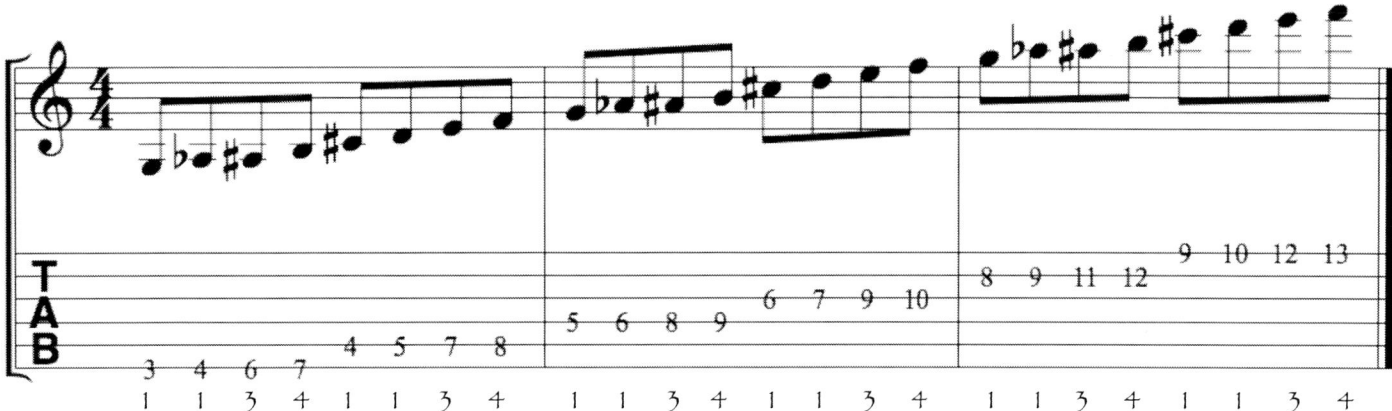

F Diminished Mode 1, G Diminished Mode 2, Diagonal Position, Ascending:

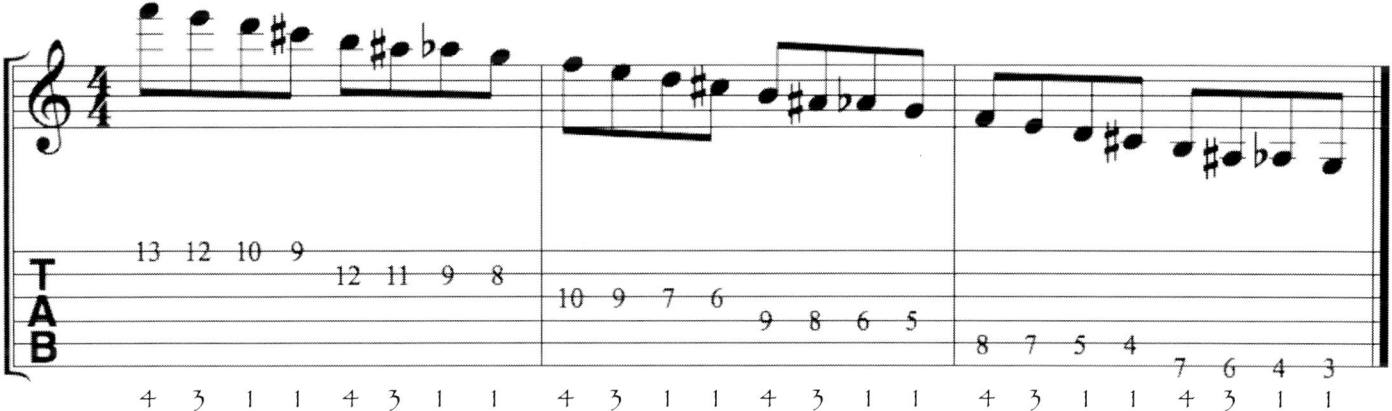

The following couple of pages contain some examples of basic diminished scale licks. We're going to be looking at other types of diminished scale licks in a later section. These are based on basic melodic pattern fragments, for the most part. I wrote them with G7 in mind but they will work over any of these eight chords: G7, Bb7, Db7, E7, Fdim7, Abdim7, Bdim7 and Ddim7. These licks, just like the position they came from, can be moved up the fretboard, three frets at a time, and remain in the same key.

Diminished Scale Lick 1:

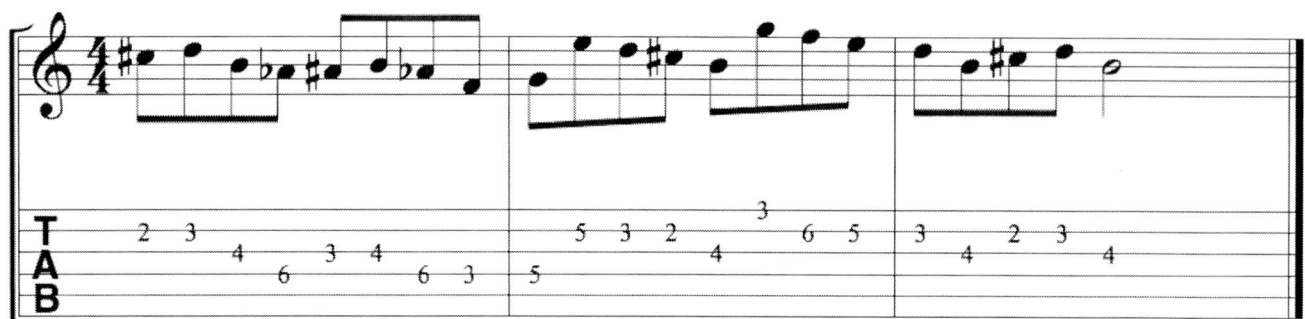

Diminished Scale Lick 2:

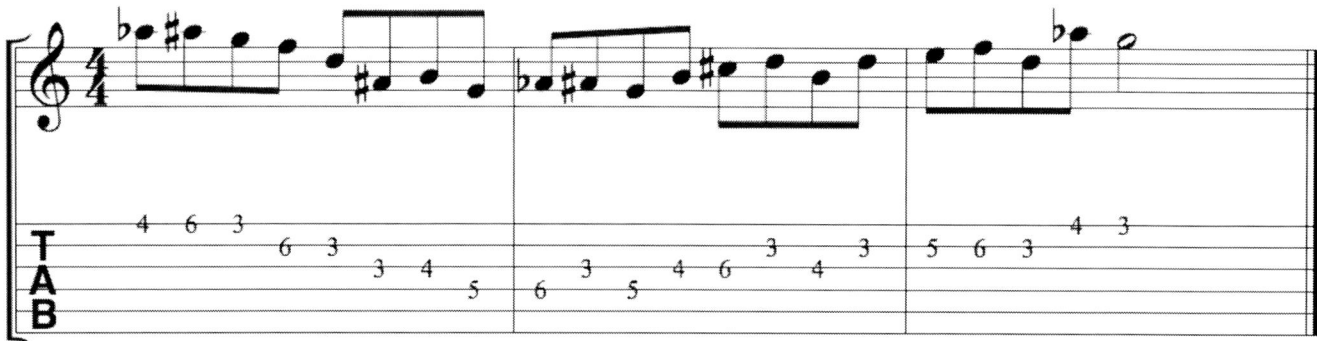

Diminished Scale Lick 3:

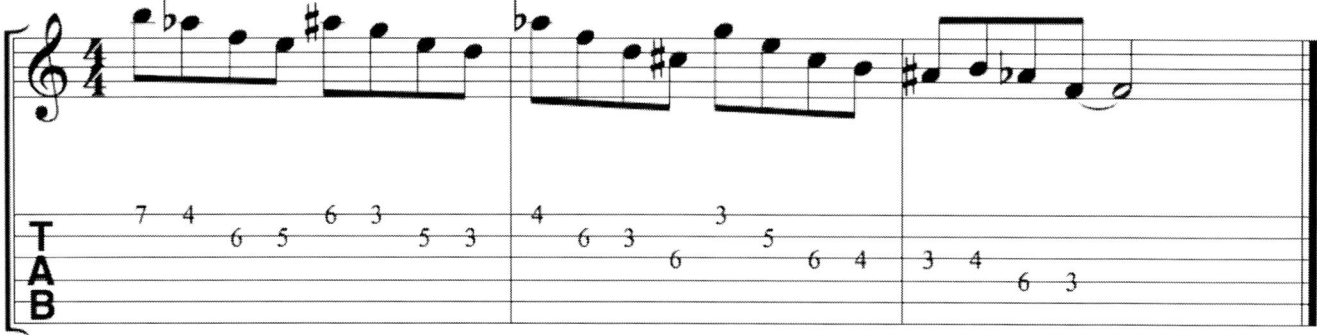

Diminished Scale Lick 4:

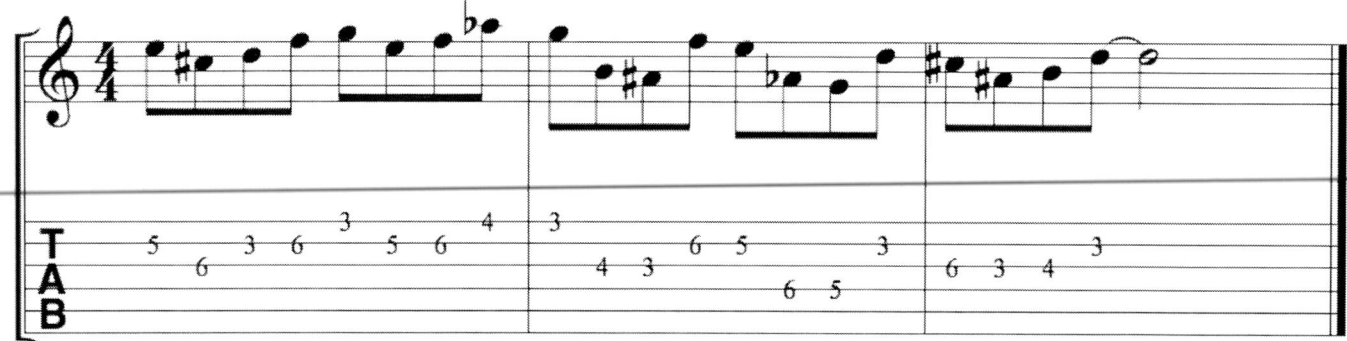

Diminished Scale Lick 5:

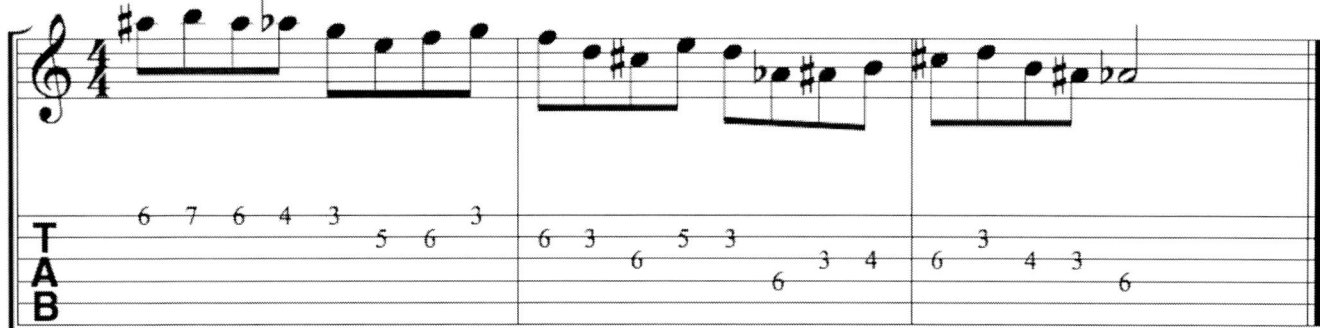

Diminished Scale Lick 6:

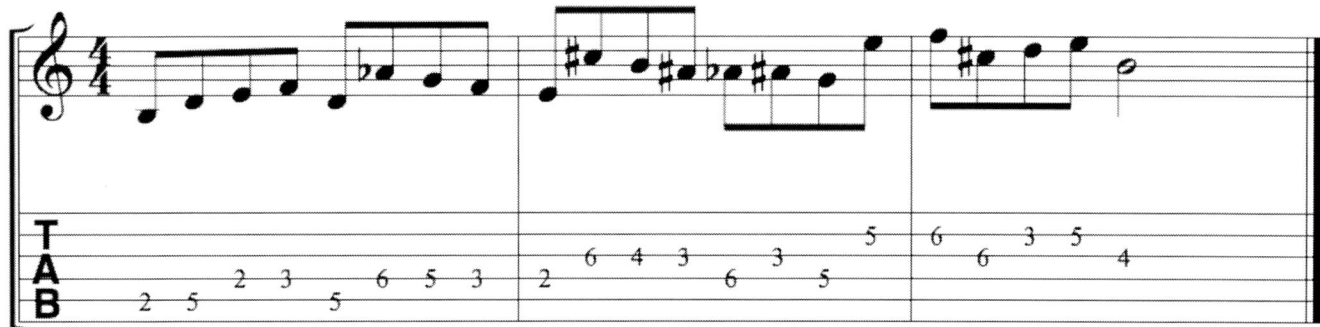

Diminished Scale Lick 7:

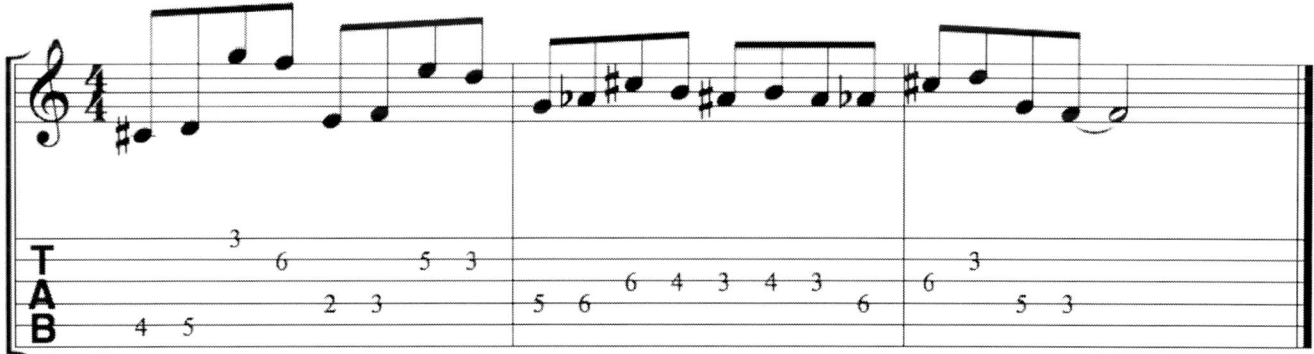

Diminished Scale Lick 8:

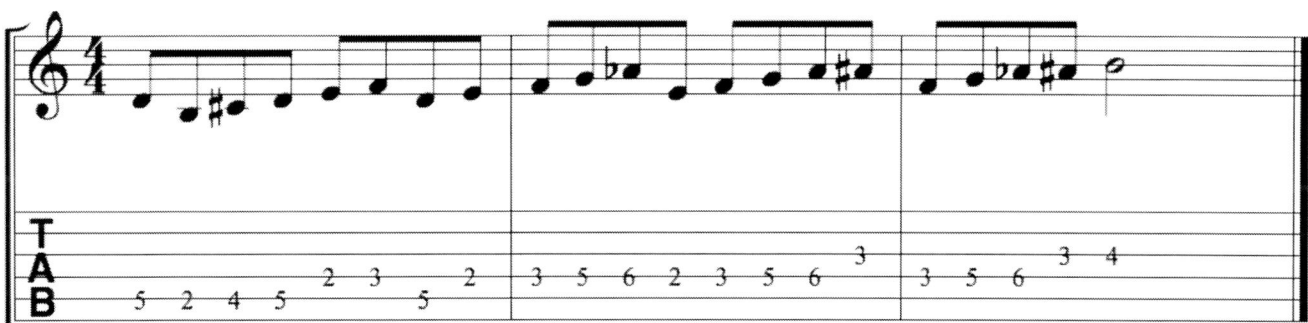

Below is a short list of specifically colored dominant 7th chords that relate directly to the diminished scale. Get to know the sound of each of these chords, because anytime you hear any of these in use, you're hearing a prime opportunity to use the half-whole diminished scale.

7#9
7b9
7#11
7b5
13#9
13b9
13#9#11
13b9#11

As we now understand it, the diminished scale is simply a dim7 chord with approaching tones a half-step below each of the chord tones. We know that because of the symmetrical nature of this scale, there are only three distinct diminished scales and the other nine are simply permutations of the original three. We also know that for the same reason, there are only two modes of the scale. These are the basics in understanding the diminished scale. Practice these licks in all possible contexts and in all keys. Following that, try to come up with some of your own lick ideas, possibly using fragments of the eight that you've learned. Acquaint yourself with this scale for at least 20 hours before moving ahead.

The Augmented Scale

This is a very useful but seldom known scale. Most of the time when I mention it, people ask me if I'm talking about the whole-tone scale. I'm not. The augmented scale has more in common with the diminished scale than the whole-tone scale does. The whole-tone scale is the result of two augmented chords, a whole step apart. Compare that to the augmented scale, where just as the diminished scale is the result of two dim7 chords a half-step apart, the augmented scale is two augmented triads, a half-step apart.

C Augmented Scale

	1½	H	1½	H	1½	H
Root	#2nd	3rd	5th	b6th	7th	
C	D#	E	G	Ab	B	

The augmented scale has a step pattern of a step and a half, followed by a half-step (H 1½), which repeats every two whole-steps (every major 3rd). This means that the notes of the C augmented scale are going to be the same as that of the E augmented scale and the Ab augmented scale. With the diminished scale, we had four scales in one and as a result, only three distinct diminished scales, as four goes into twelve only three times. With the augmented scale, we have three scales in one. Three goes into twelve an even four times. This means there are only four distinct augmented scale. The following table will provide a clear illustration of the relationships that these augmented chords have to one another.

C Augmented	C	D#	E	G	Ab	B
G Augmented	G	A#	B	D	Eb	F#
D Augmented	D	E#	F#	A	Bb	C#
A Augmented	A	B#	C#	E	F	G#
E Augmented	E	G	G#	B	C	D#
B Augmented	B	D	D#	F#	G	A#
Gb Augmented	Gb	A	Bb	Db	D	F
Db Augmented	Db	E	F	Ab	A	C
Ab Augmented	Ab	B	C	Eb	Fb	G
Eb Augmented	Eb	F#	G	Bb	Cb	D
Bb Augmented	Bb	C#	D	F	Gb	A
F Augmented	F	G#	A	C	Db	E

The augmented scale theoretically has two modes, but the second mode doesn't really have any musical application to speak of. However, its first mode has both a major and a minor application. Since the scale does in fact have a natural 5th in it, it doesn't need to be reserved for augmented chords. It can be used on major, minor and even dominant chords.

Here's how the C augmented scale relates to a **Cmaj7** chord (chord tones are in larger type):

Root   #2nd   3rd   5th   b6th   7th
C   D#   **E**   **G**   Ab   **B**

Here's how it relates to a **Am7** chord:

b3rd   #4th   5th   b7th   7th   9th
C   D#   **E**   **G**   G#   B

Here's how it just barely relates to a **D7** chord:

b7th   b9th   9th   11th   #11th   13th
C   Eb   E   G   G#   B

Using the augmented scale in the context of these normal chord-types will make it sound like you just tapped into the dark mirror underworld of the changes. It's a really cool effect when used sparingly. This scale really doesn't have a melody-friendly structure but there are some amazing things that we can do with the arpeggios found within it. We will be covering these in the next section. For the time being, you can get an ear for this scale with the following C augmented scale example licks. Play them over C, E or Ab major chords, Am7, C#m7, Fm7 and even D7, F#7 and Bb7. The chord will change the effect but the melody will always fit in a very bizarre way.

Augmented Scale Lick 1:

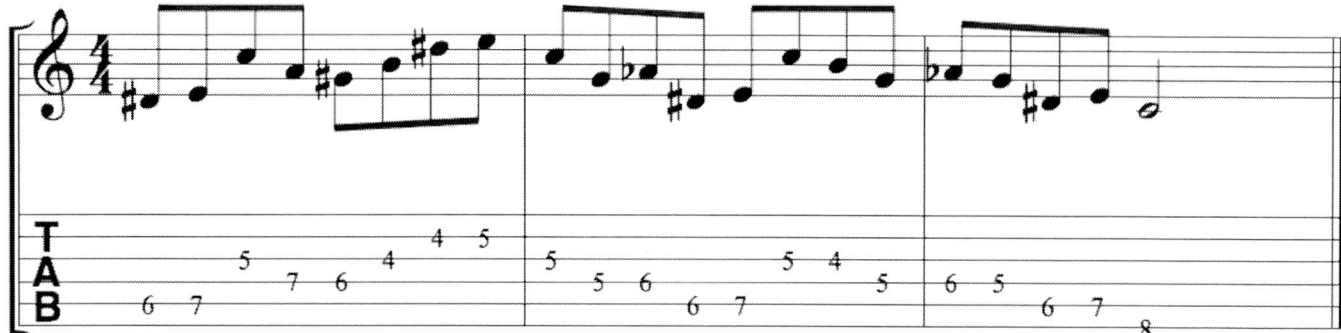

Augmented Scale Lick 2:

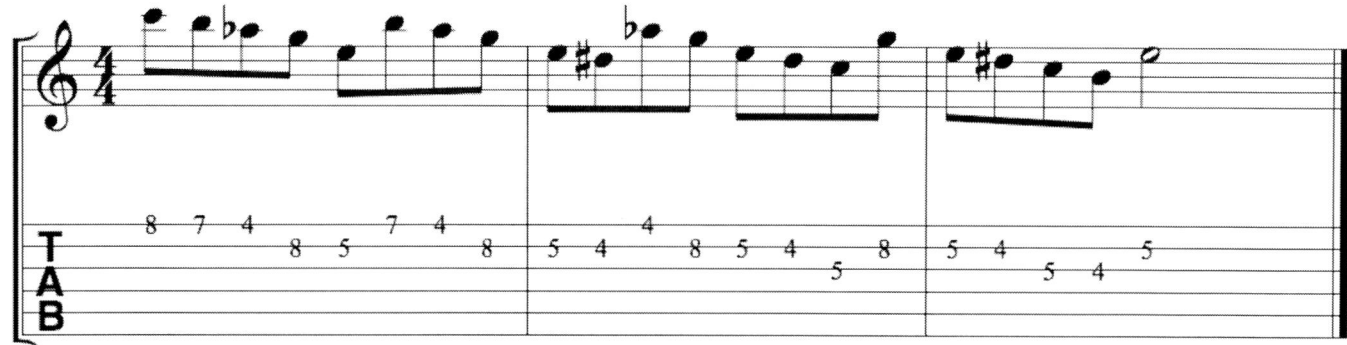

Augmented Scale Lick 3:

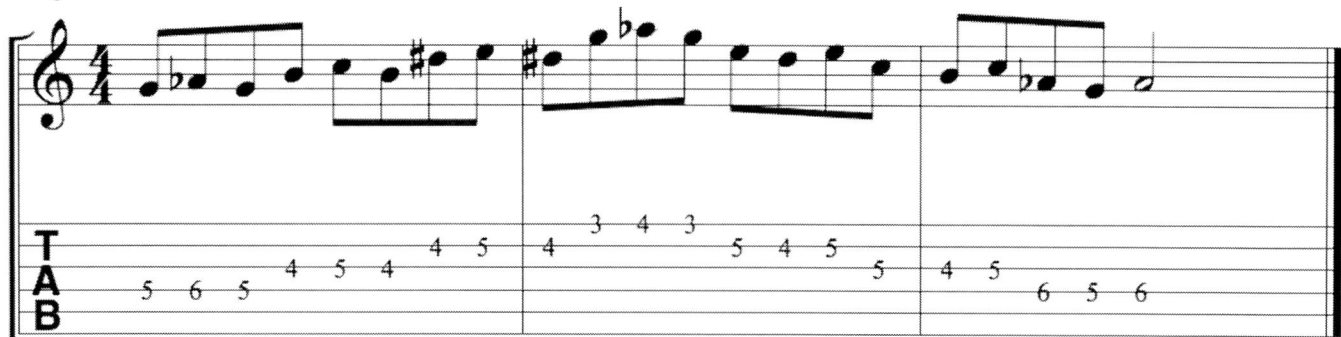

Augmented Scale Lick 4:

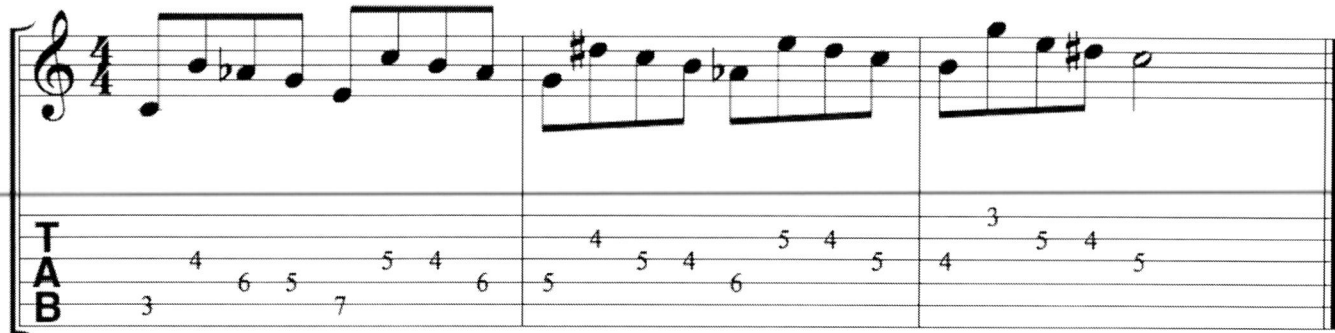

Augmented Scale Lick 5:

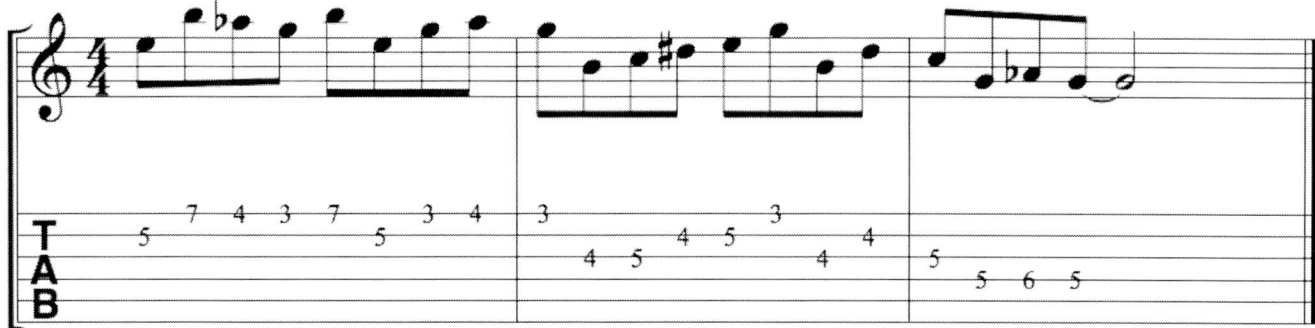

Augmented Scale Lick 6:

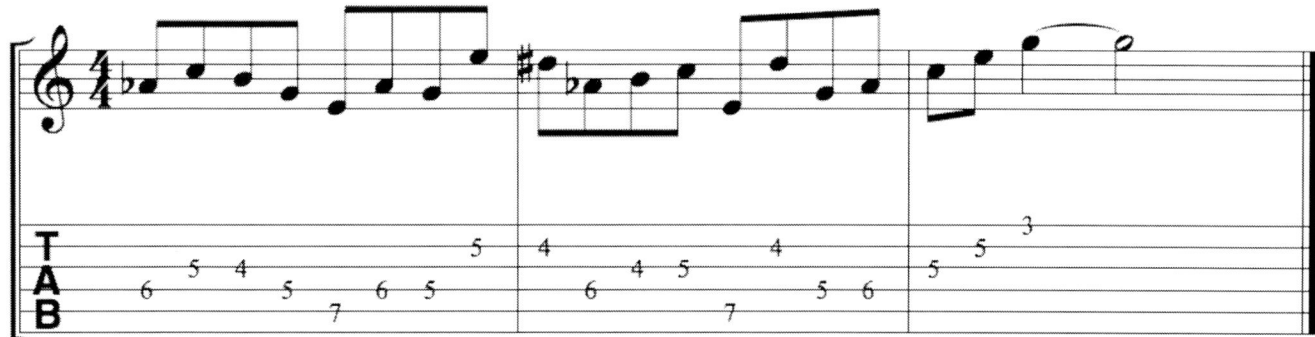

Augmented Scale Lick 7:

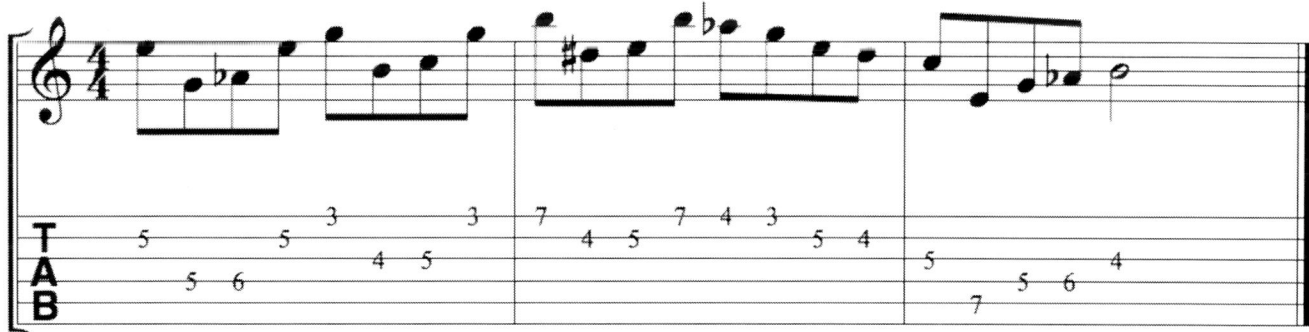

Augmented Scale Lick 8:

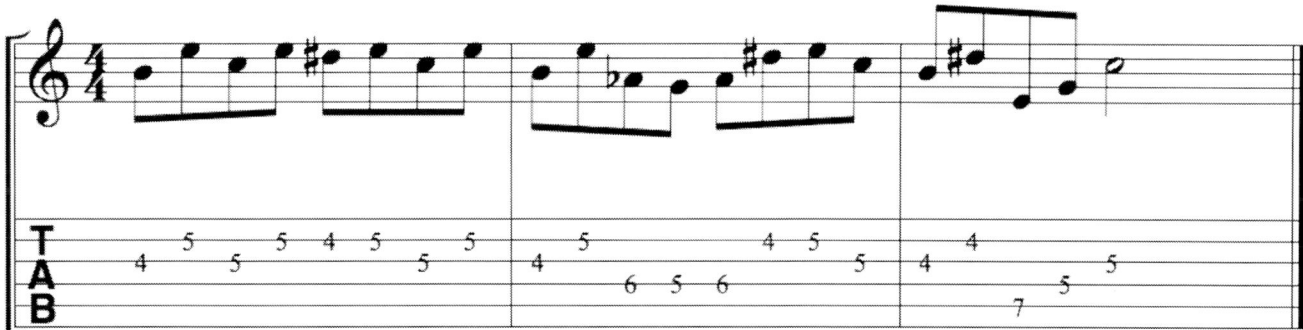

The Whole-Tone Scale:

The whole-tone scale, like the diminished scale, relates to dominant chords, though it relates in a much different way. As we learned a few pages back, the whole-tone scale is the result of two augmented chords, a whole-step apart. The resulting step pattern is that of W which repeats itself six times per octave. Six only goes into twelve twice, meaning that there are only two distinct whole-tone scales. This certainly has some advantages. You'll commonly find dominant chords moving in 4ths. One simple way of playing over this, achieving a more outside sound, is to alternate these to whole-tone scales.

Here is the C Whole-Tone scale as it relates to C7:

	W		W		W		W		W		W
Root		2nd		3rd		b5th/#11th		b13th		b7th	
C		D		E		Gb		Ab		Bb	

Keep in mind that this exact same scale will relate identically to the D7, E7, F#7, Ab7 and Bb7 chords.

Here is the F Whole-Tone scale as it relates to F7:

	W		W		W		W		W		W
Root		2nd		3rd		b5th/#11th		b13th		b7th	
F		G		A		B		Db		Eb	

This same scale will relate identically to the G7, A7, B7, Db7 and Eb7 chords.

Below is a table that shows how the twelve whole-tone scales work out to really being two distinct scales. The white rows are the essentially all C whole-tone scales and the grey rows are all essentially all F whole-tone scales.

C Whole-Tone	C	D	E	Gb	Ab	Bb
G Whole-Tone	G	A	B	Db	Eb	F
D Whole-Tone	D	E	F#	Ab	Bb	C
A Whole-Tone	A	B	C#	Eb	F	G
E Whole-Tone	E	F#	G#	Bb	C	D
B Whole-Tone	B	C#	D#	F	G	A
Gb Whole-Tone	Gb	Ab	Bb	C	D	E
Db Whole-Tone	Db	Eb	F	G	A	B
Ab Whole-Tone	Ab	Bb	C	D	E	Gb
Eb Whole-Tone	Eb	F	G	A	B	Db
Bb Whole-Tone	Bb	C	D	E	Gb	Ab
F Whole-Tone	F	G	A	B	Db	Eb

It's because of scales like this one and the Super-Locrian that jazz players generally avoid voicing any 5ths in their dominant chords. If the 5th is not present in the chord voicing, any 5th can be implied by the soloist. This obviously gives the soloist a much broader palette. Dominant chords are the chords that hold the most possibilities for melodic choices so it's a good idea to keep those options unhindered, since all it takes is excluding the most neutral of chord-tones.

The whole-tone scale, like any other symmetrical scale is going to take some getting used to, regarding the sound that it possesses. Be sure to practice the scale slowly, until your ears begin to guide you. When you feel like a wrong note becomes very obvious to your ear, pick up the tempo. Spend plenty of time practicing melodic patterns within the confines of this scale. This will help both your hands and ears to get acquainted with it to a point where you will feel capable of thinking creatively within the scale.

Here is a list of dominant chords that relate directly to the whole-tone scale. Consider it a given that natural 5ths are not present with any of these chords.

7	9b5
9	9#5
9#11	9b13

There are only two guitar positions for the whole-tone scale, both of which are quite usable shapes. In order to switch from one whole-tone scale to the other, simply slide the shape that you're using by one fret in either direction. Below are the two whole-tone scale positions:

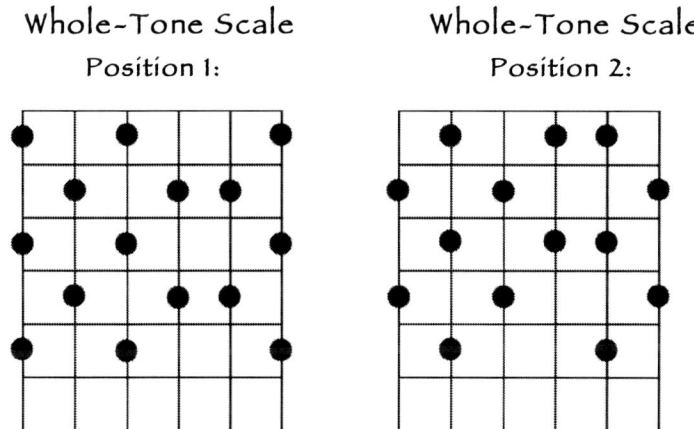

The following couple pages offer you some whole-tone scale example licks. Try each of these licks against all six possible dominant chords. Each lick will play out differently from chord to chord, but they will all work.

Whole-Tone Scale Lick 1:

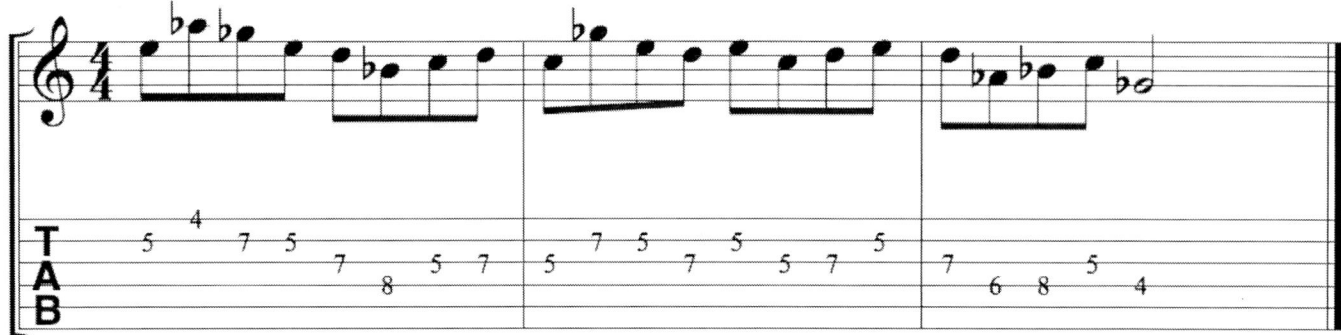

Whole-Tone Scale Lick 2:

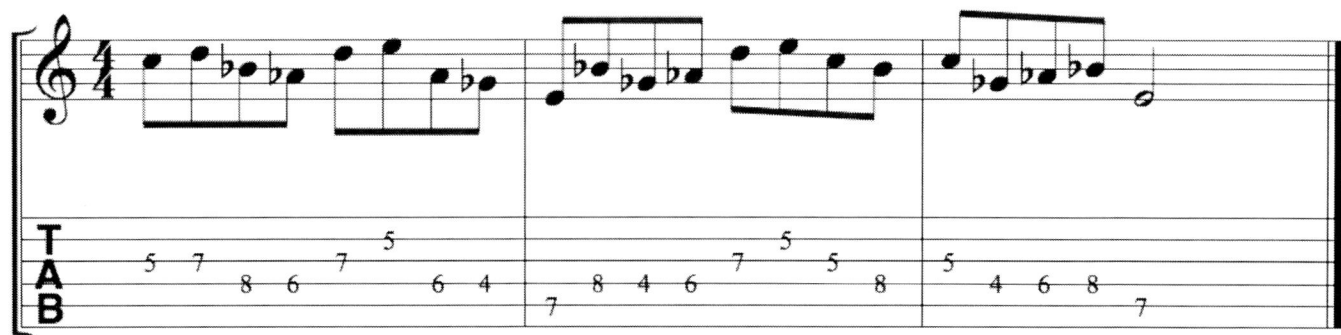

Whole-Tone Scale Lick 3:

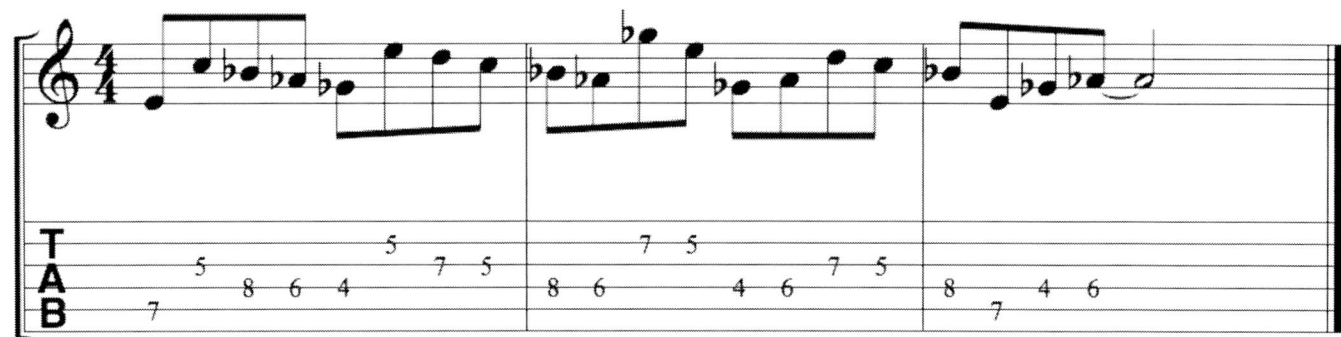

Whole-Tone Scale Lick 4:

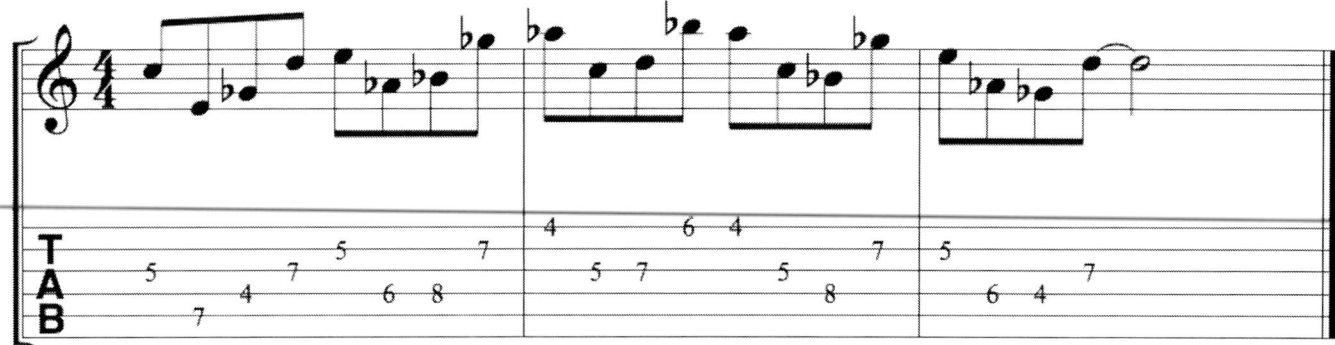

Whole-Tone Scale Lick 5:

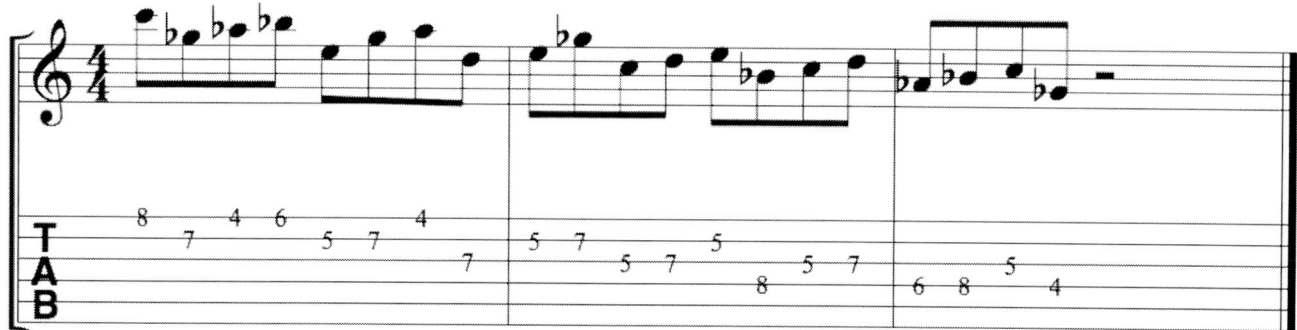

Whole-Tone Scale Lick 6:

Whole-Tone Scale Lick 7:

Whole-Tone Scale Lick 8:

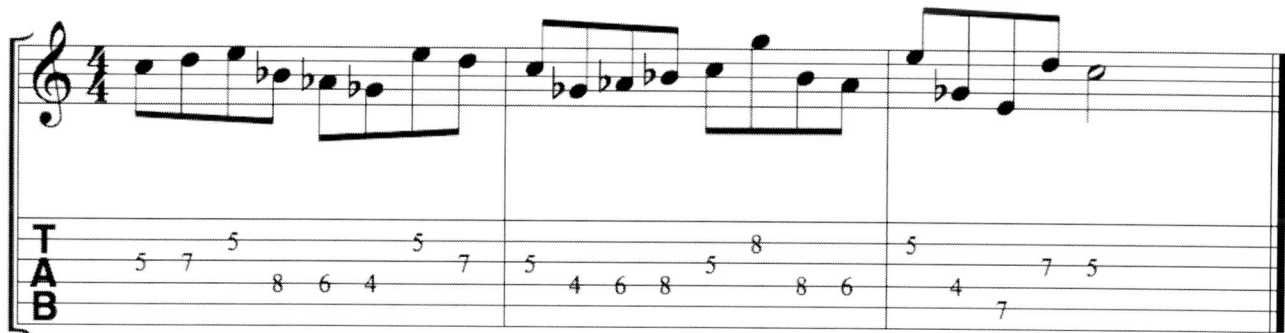

SYMMETRICAL HARMONY – part 2: Hidden Triad Families

What we are about to get into in this section is one of my favorite methods for playing outside the basic harmony. The basic idea is that within the diminished and augmented scales there are families of symmetrically related major and minor triads that can be used in combination with one another as a harmonic or melodic substitute for any major, minor or dominant chord. I consider these triad families to be hidden universes of sorts that one can slip into at any point. I'm kind of nerdy like that.

Here's how it lays out in the diminished scale. It makes the most sense to present these triads as they relate to the half-whole diminished, the reasons for which will become clear upon looking at it. We have four major triads and four minor triads, all of them minor 3rds apart from one another. The G half-whole diminished scale triad family can be applied to anything where you could use the G half-whole and F whole-half diminished scales.

G Half-Whole Diminished Scale:

	H	W	H	W	H	W	H	W
Root	b9th	#9th	3rd	#11th	5th	13th	b7th	
G	Ab	A#	B	C#	D	E	F	

G: G B D   Gm: G Bb D
Bb: Bb D F   Bbm: Bb Db F
Db: Db F Ab   C#m: C# E G#
E: E G# B   Em: E G B

In the augmented scale, we have three major and three minor triads that we find located in intervals of major 3rds from one another. This family can be applied to any chord where you could use the C Augmented scale.

C Augmented Scale:

	1½	H	1½	H	1½	H
Root	#2nd	3rd	5th	b6th	7th	
C	D#	E	G	Ab	B	

C: C E G   Cm: C Eb G
E: E G# B   Em: E G B
Ab: Ab C Eb   G#m: G# B D#

The following six pages are made up of example licks based on these triad families. Experiment with these on different chords, in different keys and in different positions. You'll quickly get an ear for the sound of these families.

Diminished Scale, Major Triad Combo Lick 1:

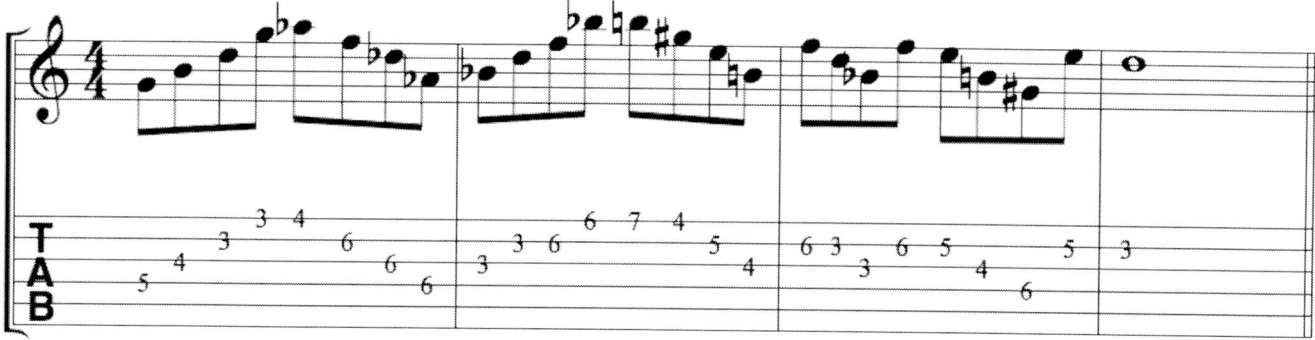

Diminished Scale, Major Triad Combo Lick 2:

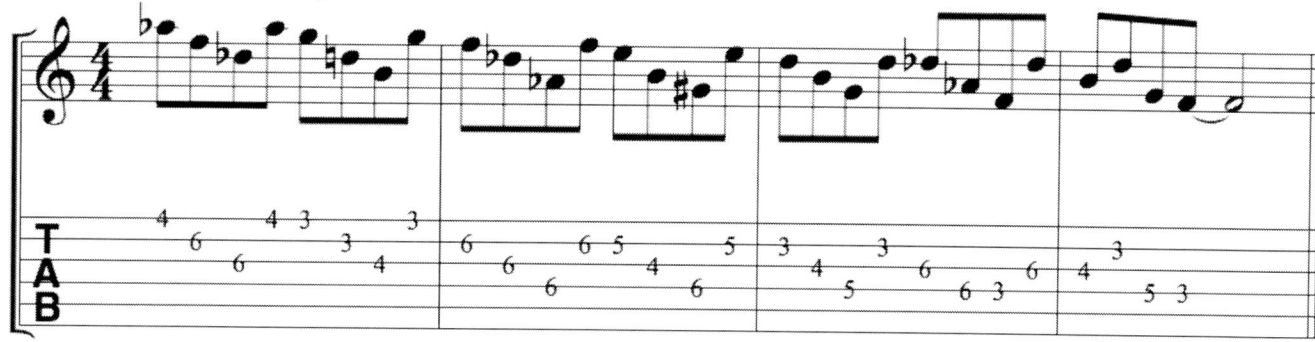

Diminished Scale, Major Triad Combo Lick 3:

Diminished Scale, Major Triad Combo Lick 4:

Diminished Scale, Minor Triad Combo Lick 1:

Diminished Scale, Minor Triad Combo Lick 2:

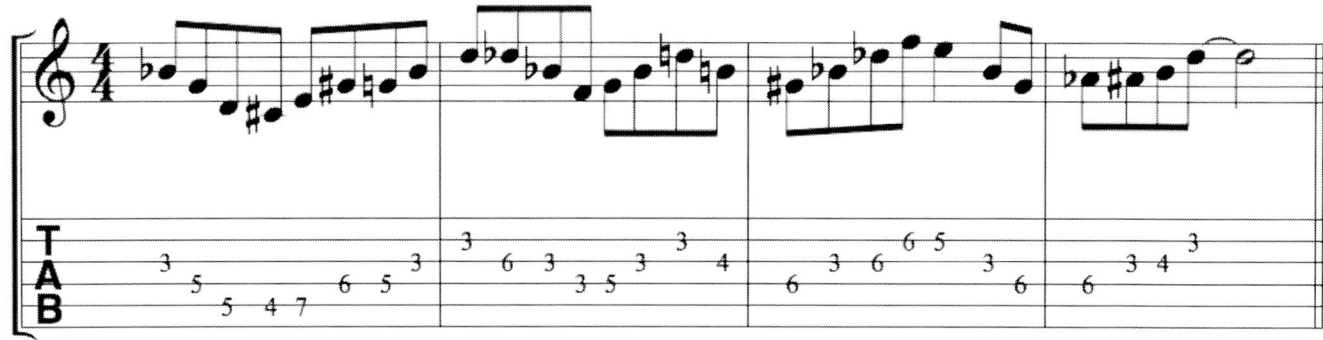

Diminished Scale, Minor Triad Combo Lick 3:

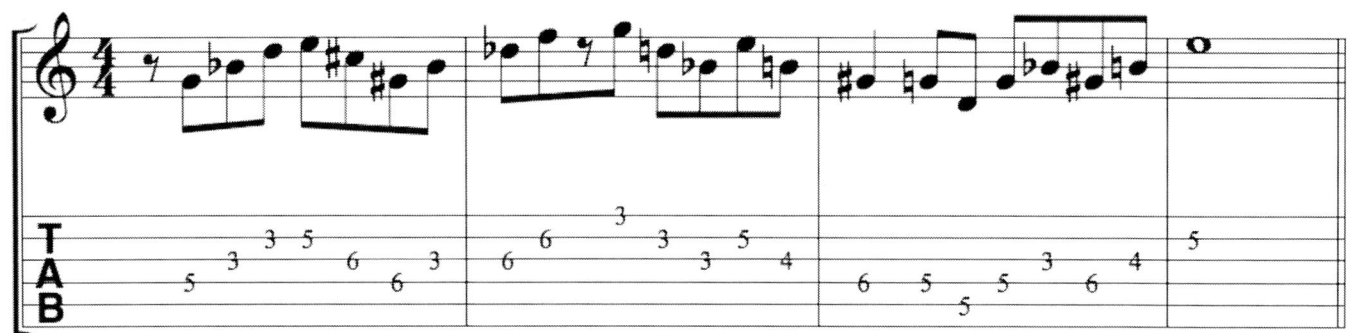

Diminished Scale, Minor Triad Combo Lick 4:

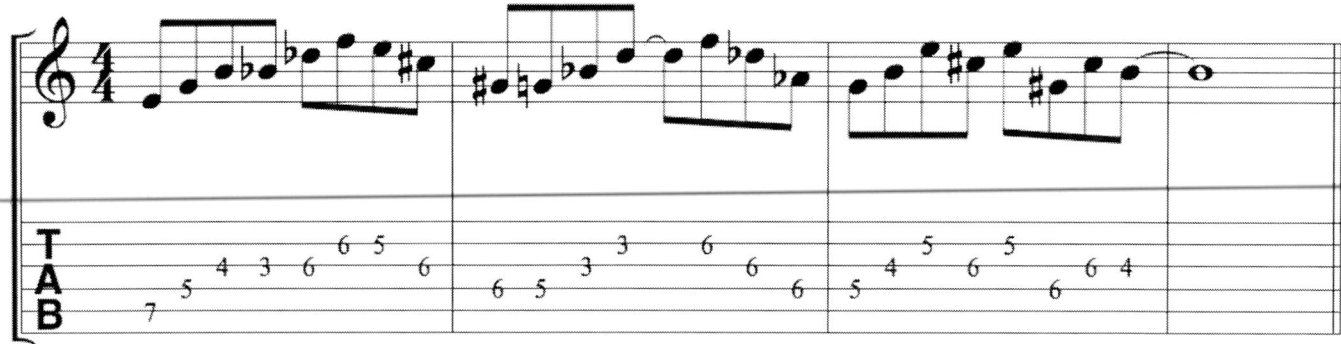

Diminished Scale, Mixed Triad Combo Lick 1:

Diminished Scale, Mixed Triad Combo Lick 2:

Diminished Scale, Mixed Triad Combo Lick 3:

Diminished Scale, Mixed Triad Combo Lick 4:

Augmented Scale, Major Triad Combo Lick 1:

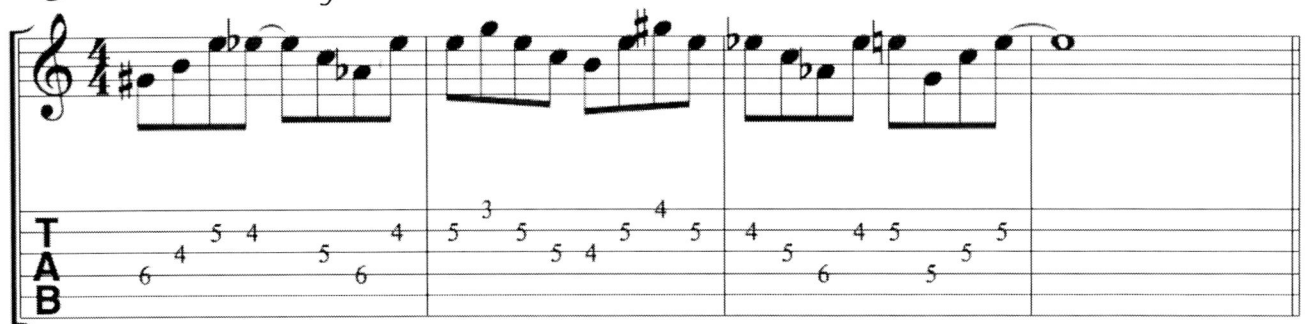

Augmented Scale, Major Triad Combo Lick 2:

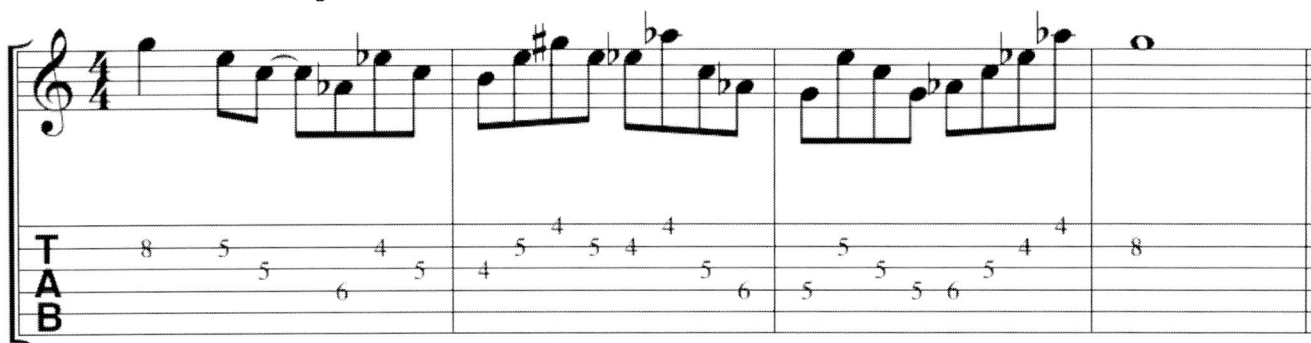

Augmented Scale, Major Triad Combo Lick 3:

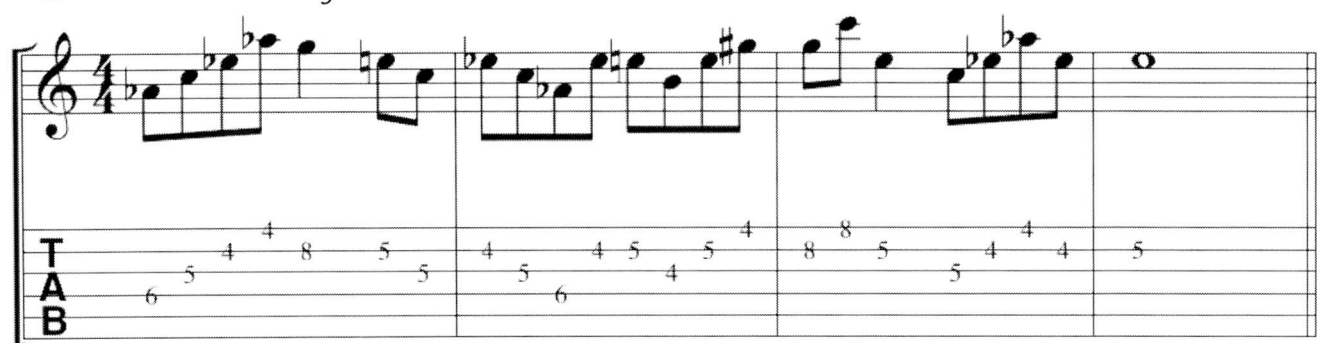

Augmented Scale, Major Triad Combo Lick 4:

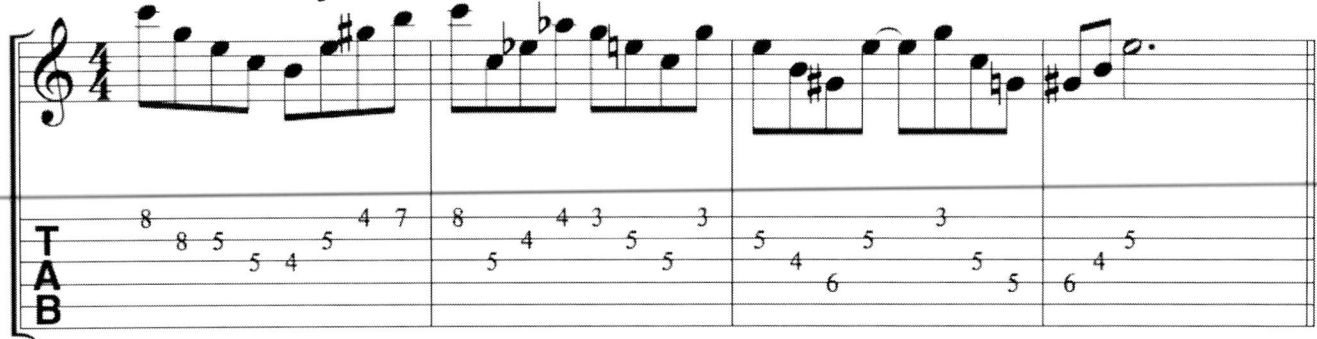

Augmented Scale, Minor Triad Combo Lick 1:

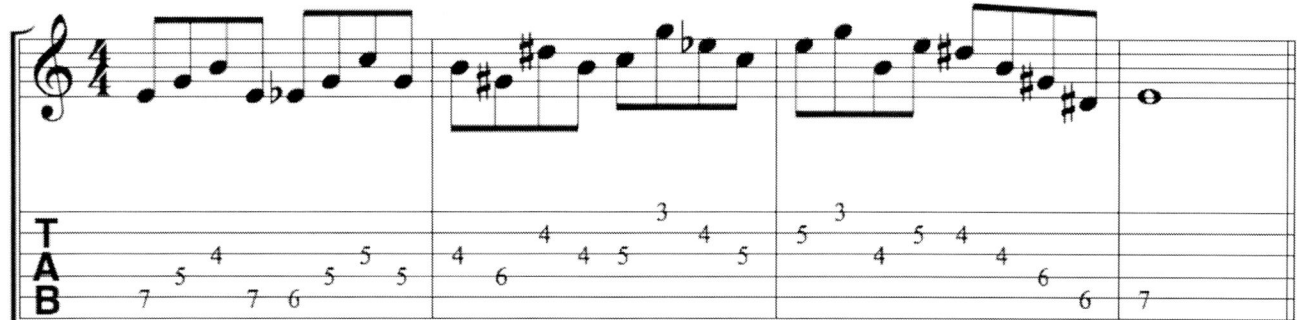

Augmented Scale, Minor Triad Combo Lick 2:

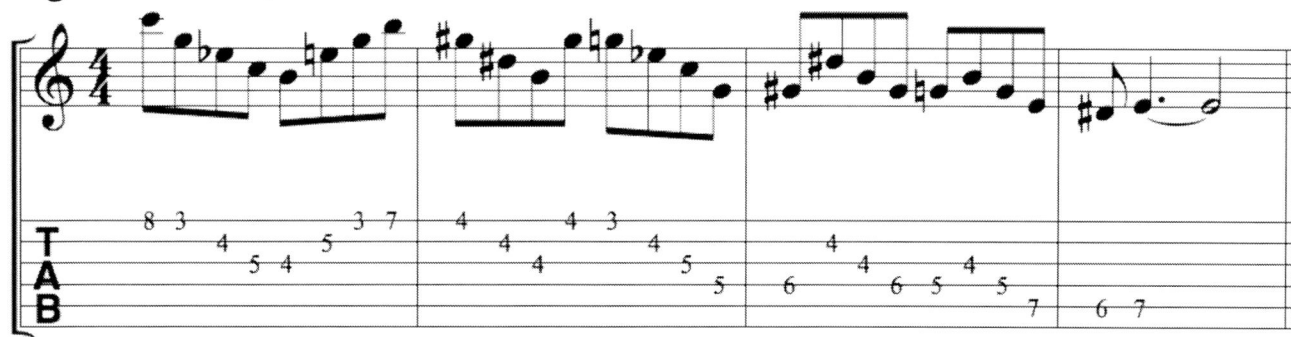

Augmented Scale, Minor Triad Combo Lick 3:

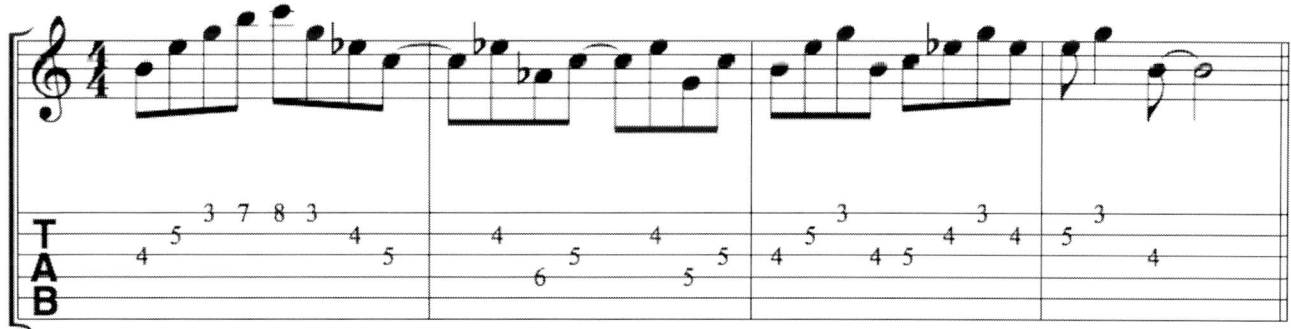

Augmented Scale, Minor Triad Combo Lick 4:

Augmented Scale, Mixed Triad Combo Lick 1:

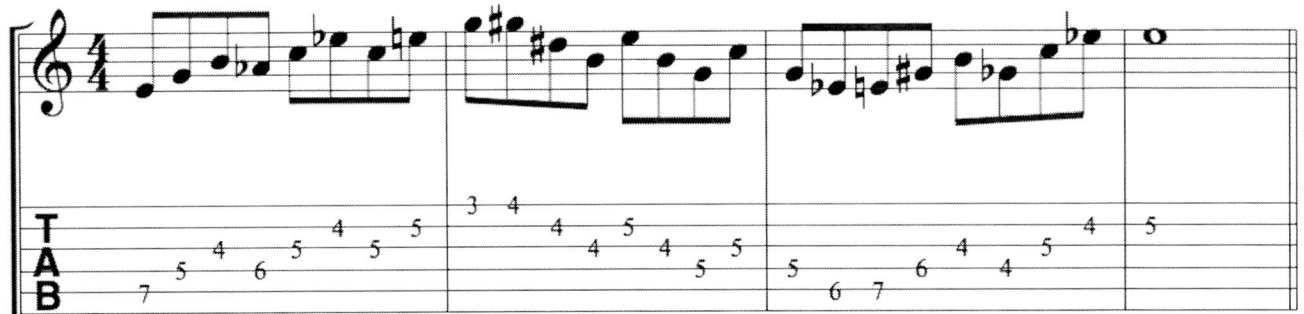

Augmented Scale, Mixed Triad Combo Lick 2:

Augmented Scale, Mixed Triad Combo Lick 3:

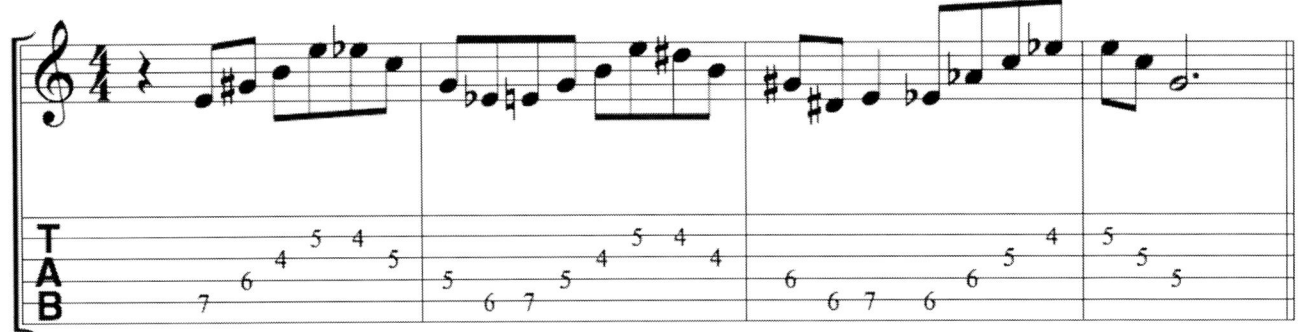

Augmented Scale, Mixed Triad Combo Lick 4:

MELODIC PATTERNS – Part 4: Non-Harmonic Patterns

A non-harmonic pattern is any chromatic sequence whose logical order is clear enough to supercede the harmonic context of the rhythm section. As long as there is a pattern that the ear can follow, one that's entirely non-biased to any particular key, it matters none at all what the underlying chord happens to be. This is something that can offer the improviser and composer much melodic freedom, as there are at least a million non-harmonic patterns that one can pluck from the tree of possibility. In this section, I'll be sharing my personal favorites that I've discovered over the years.

Most people would consider this device more of a seasoning rather than a main ingredient. Too much of this becomes unbearable for most people. But throwing a non-harmonic pattern in towards the end of a eight or sixteen bar section will heighten the intensity. Then comes the hard part, summed up by the following metaphoric truth. Learning how to land is at least twice as important learning how to fly. In other words, once you've become comfortable with some non-harmonic material you'll also need to develop the ability to think ahead about how you'll resolve into the harmony.

Non-Harmonic Pattern 1:

This first one is a weaving chromatic made up of major second and perfect fourth intervals. This pattern is especially chromatic because it's what we call a twelve-tone pattern, meaning that it makes its ways through all twelve notes before repeating a note. That's the point at which the pattern repeats. There are quite a few twelve tone patterns and are worth looking into further.

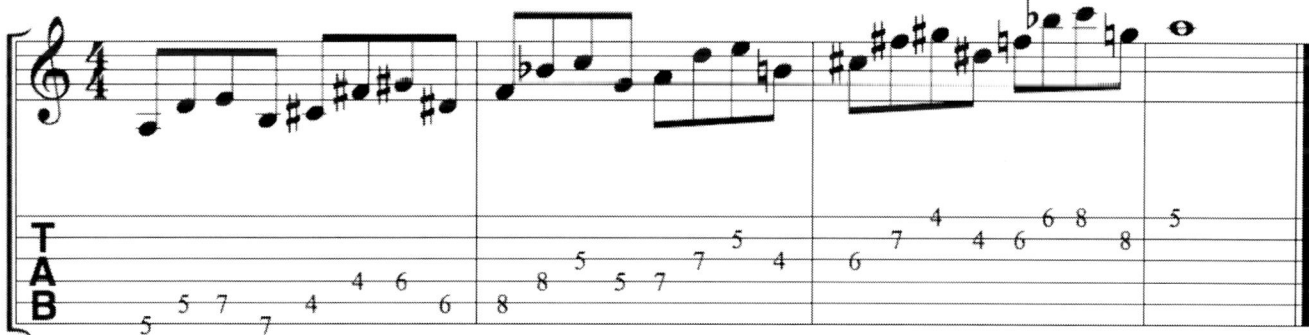

Non-Harmonic Pattern 2:

In this pattern, I took the first eight notes from one of my favorite twelve-tone patterns and sequenced it up in 4ths.

The following ten pages were all derived from the first measure of the first line. The methods by which this was achieved will be covered in reasonable detail in the Motive Development section. The original one is a rather gnarly chromatic idea that we sequence upward in minor 3rds.

Non-Harmonic Pattern 3:

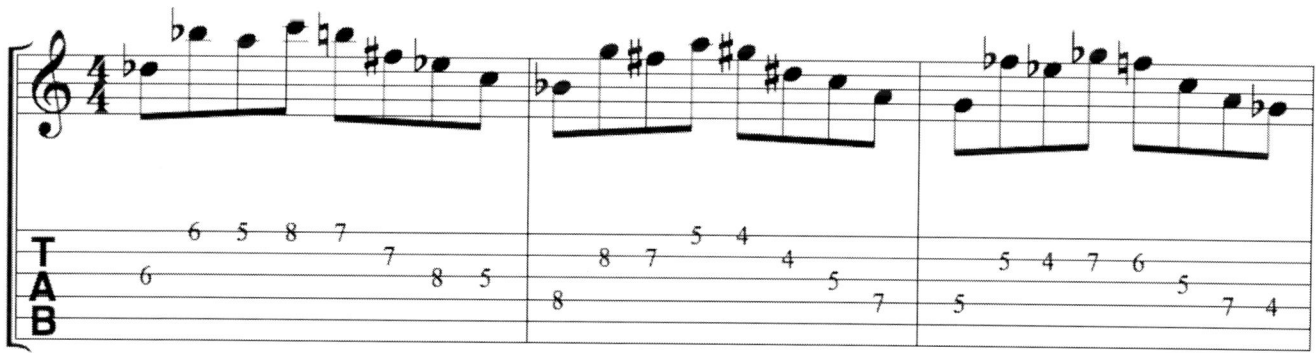

Non-Harmonic Pattern 3, Variation 1:

431

Non-Harmonic Pattern 3, Variation 2:

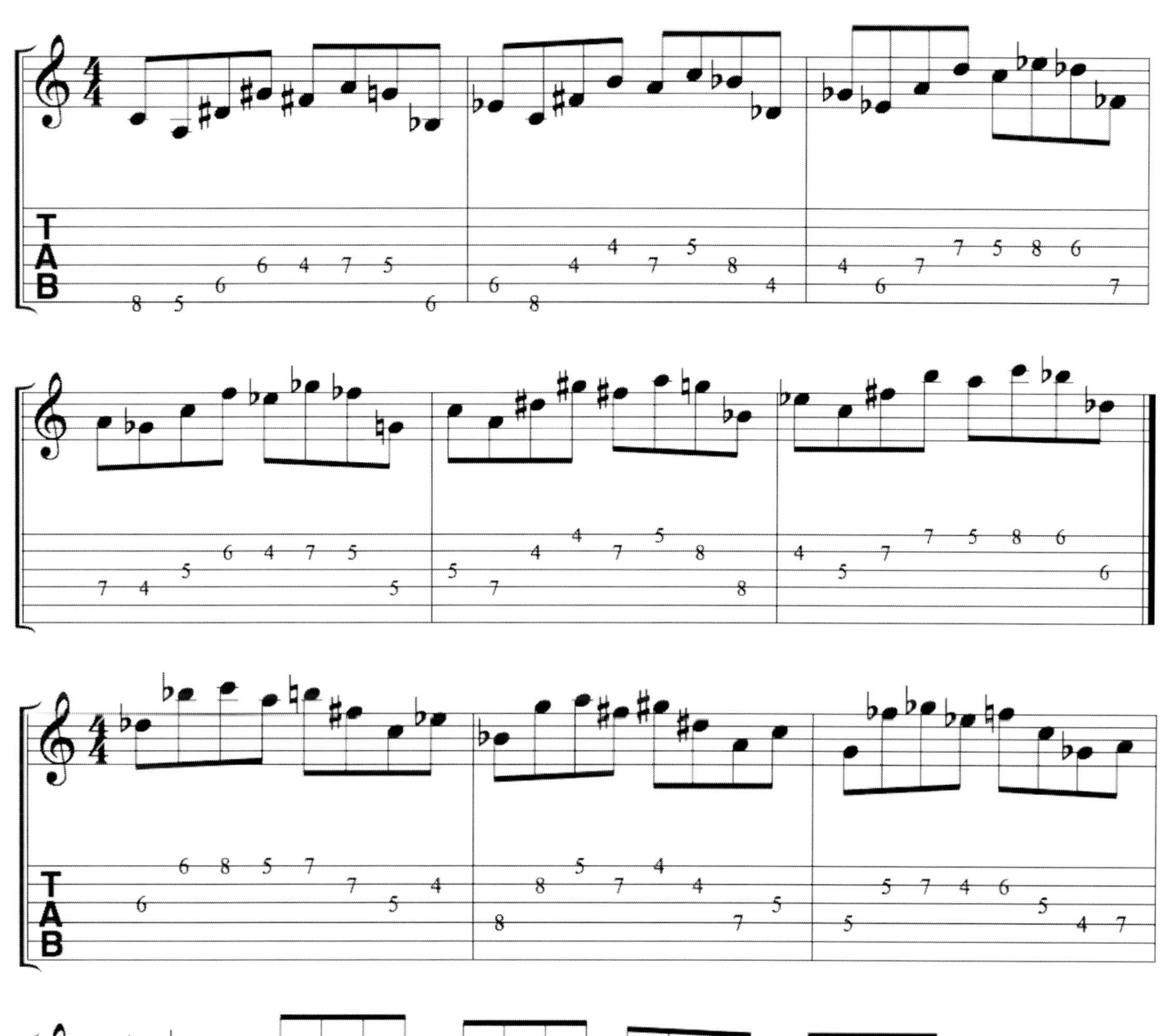

Non-Harmonic Pattern 3, Variation 3:

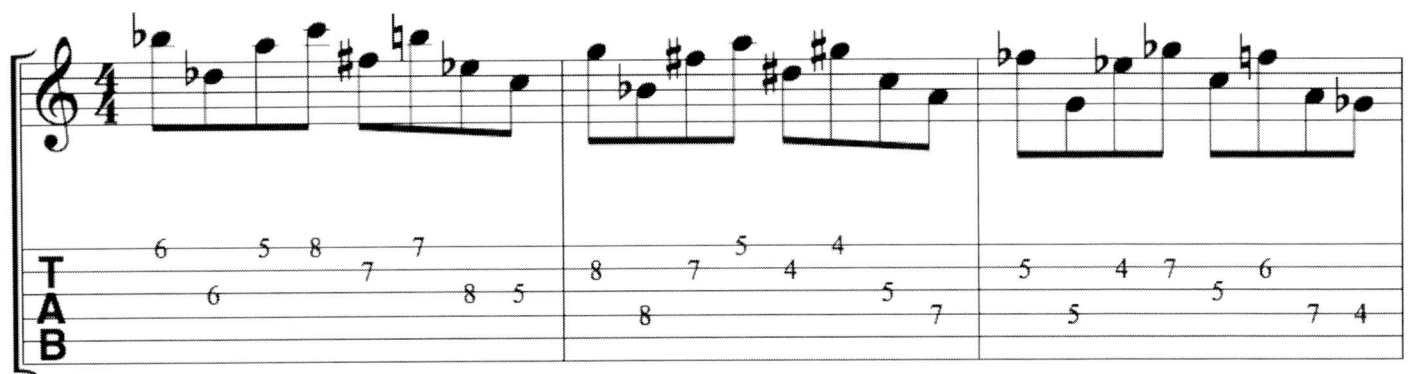

Non-Harmonic Pattern 3, Variation 4:

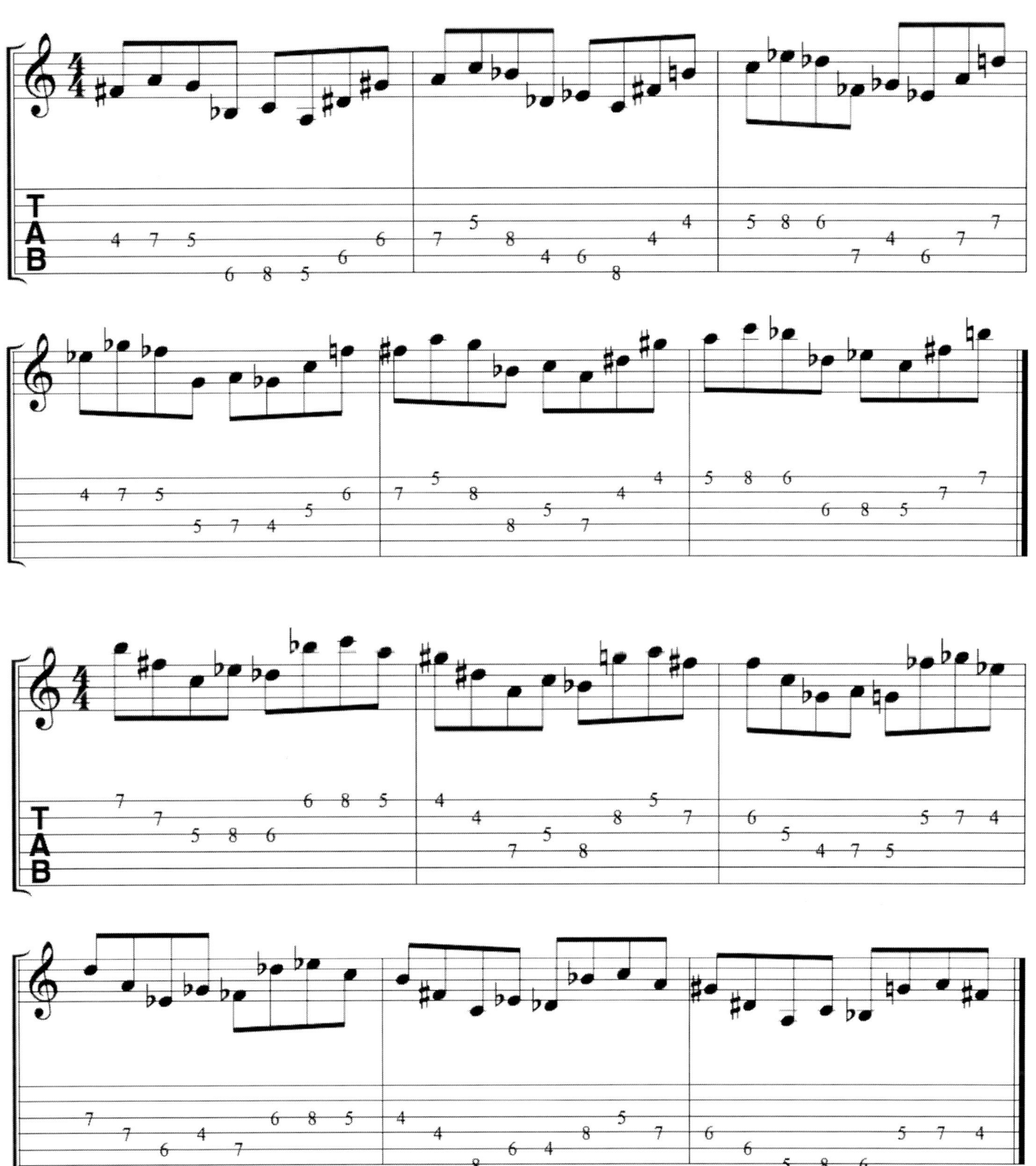

Non-Harmonic Pattern 3, Variation 5:

Non-Harmonic Pattern 3, Variation 6:

Non-Harmonic Pattern 3, Variation 7:

Non-Harmonic Pattern 3, Variation 8:

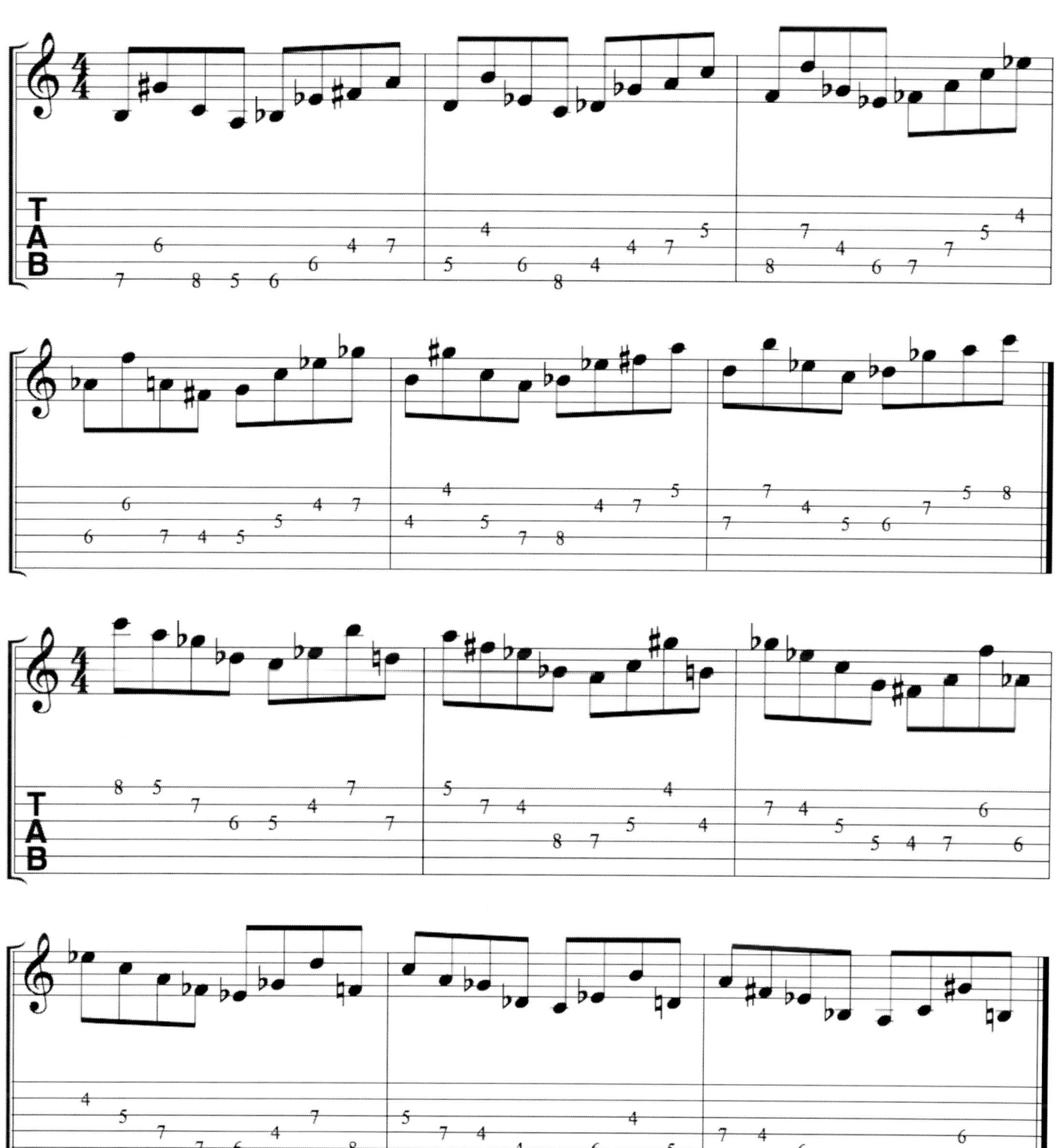

Non-Harmonic Pattern 3, Variation 9:

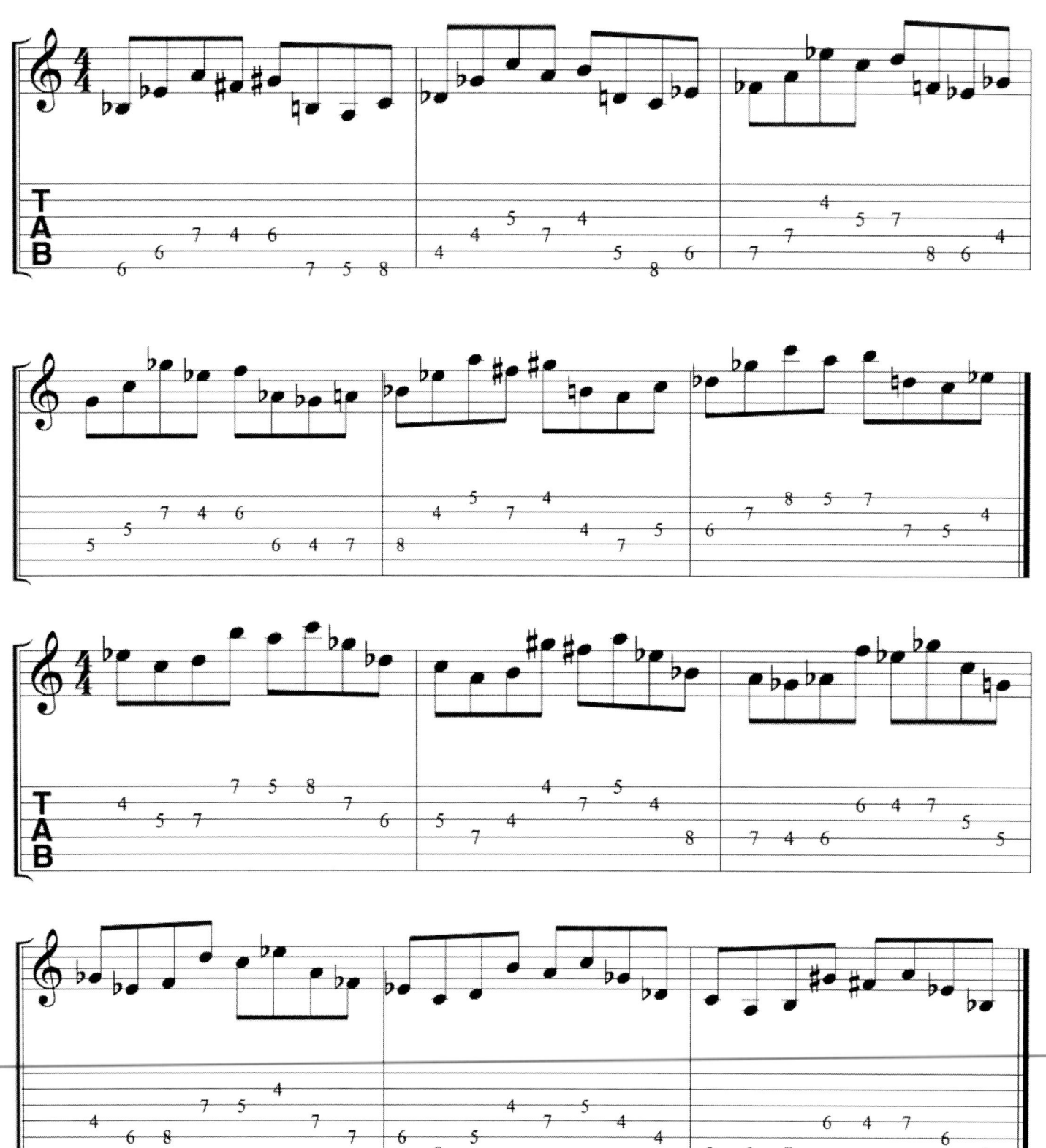

JAZZ LICKS — Over a IIm7 V7 Imaj7 Context

This collection of licks represents some of the common melodic jazz vocabulary. This first half of the licks relate to a long IIm7-V7-Imaj7 progression. The second half were written over a IIm7-V7-Imaj7-V7 of IIm7- IIm7-V7-Imaj7 progression where the chords are moving at twice the rate. These licks make musical use of many concepts from throughout the book, including syncopation, chromaticism, various scales and modes, substitution, etc. Learning these licks and doing some serious analysis of them should help you grow more comfortable in recognizing and utilizing these various devices.

Long Cadence Lick 1:

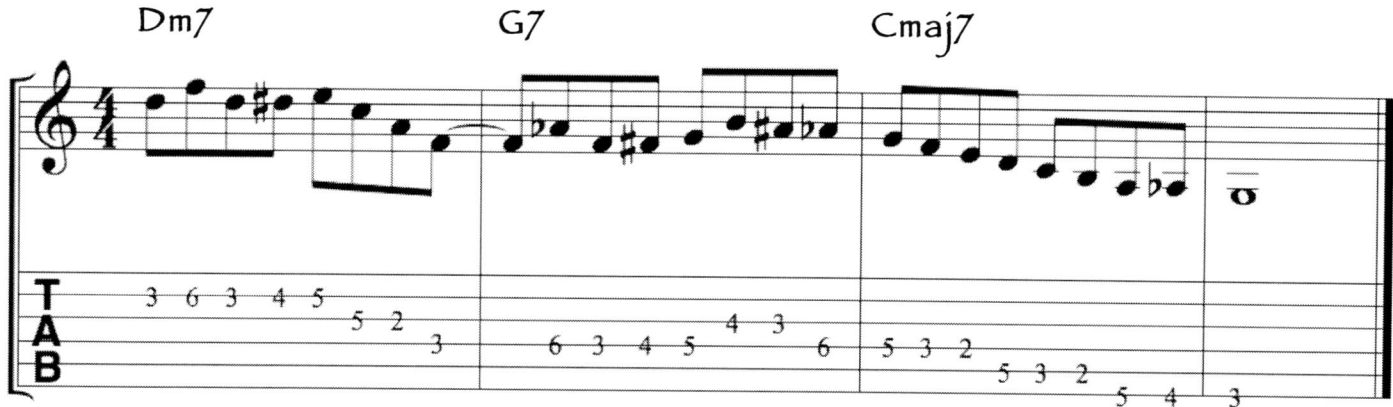

Long Cadence Lick 2:

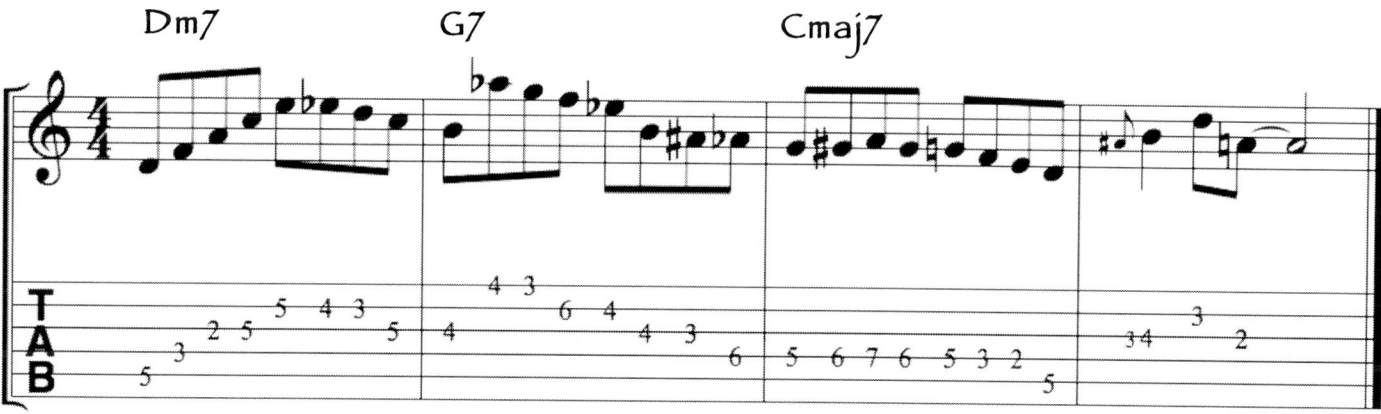

Long Cadence Lick 3:

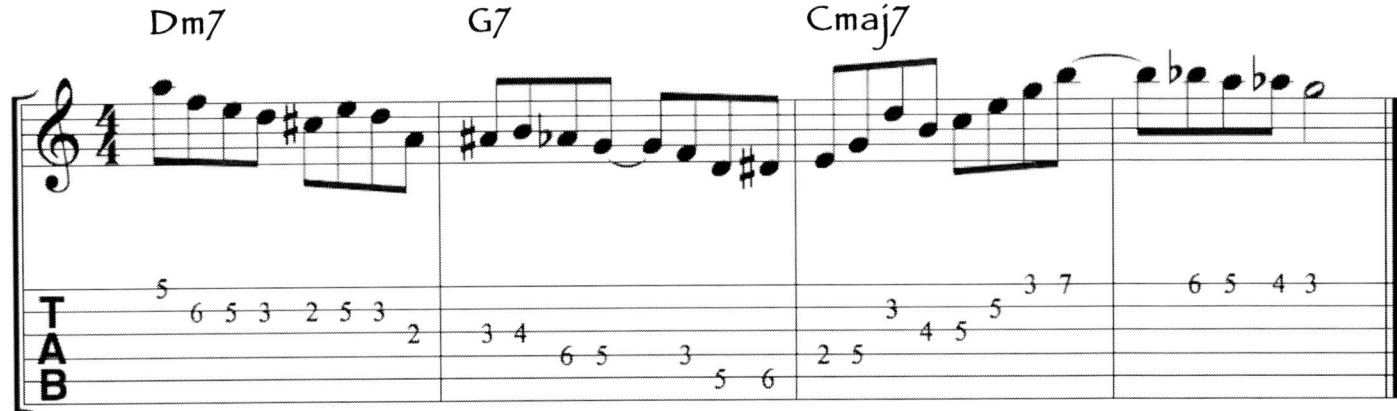

Long Cadence Lick 4:

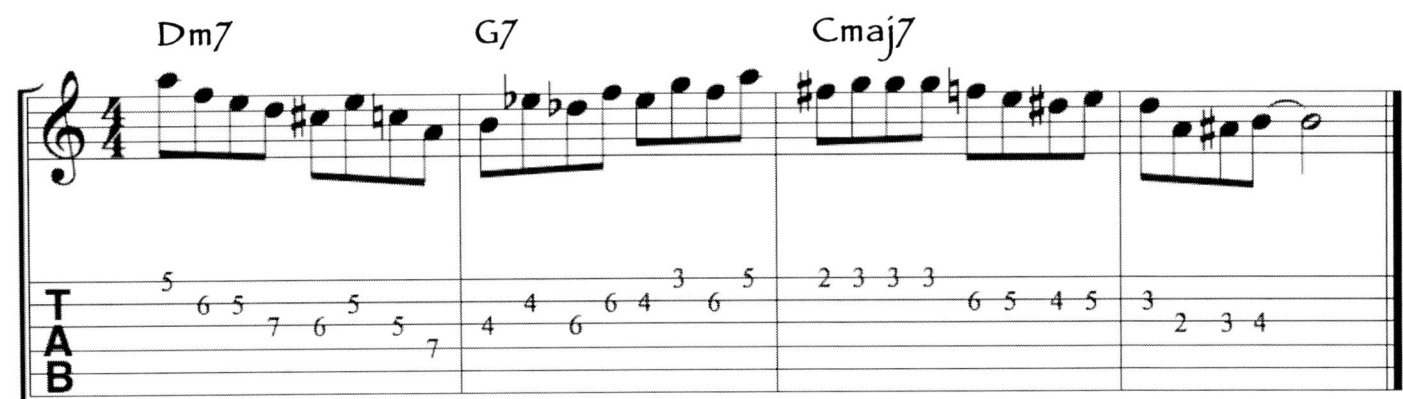

Long Cadence Lick 5:

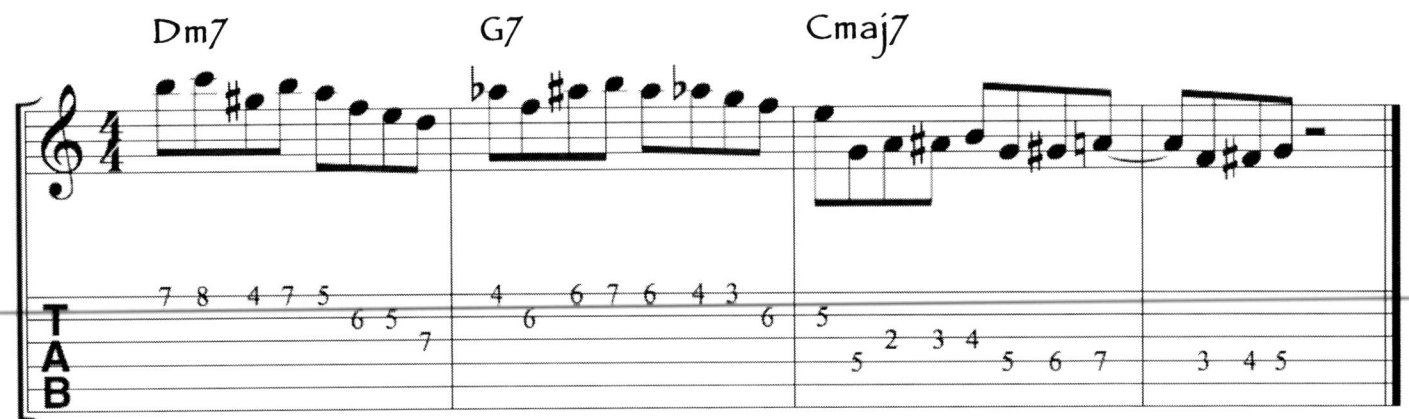

Long Cadence Lick 6:

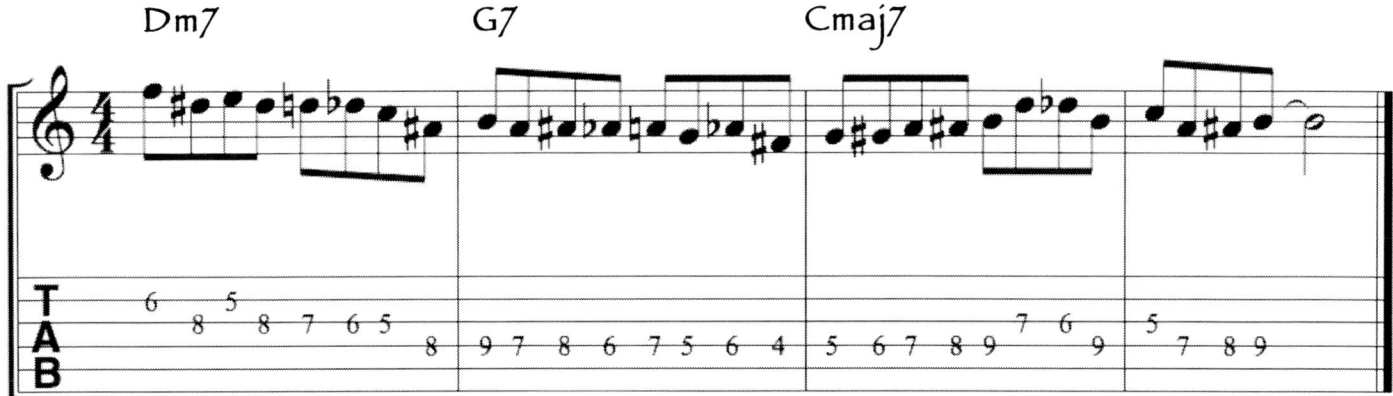

Long Cadence Lick 7:

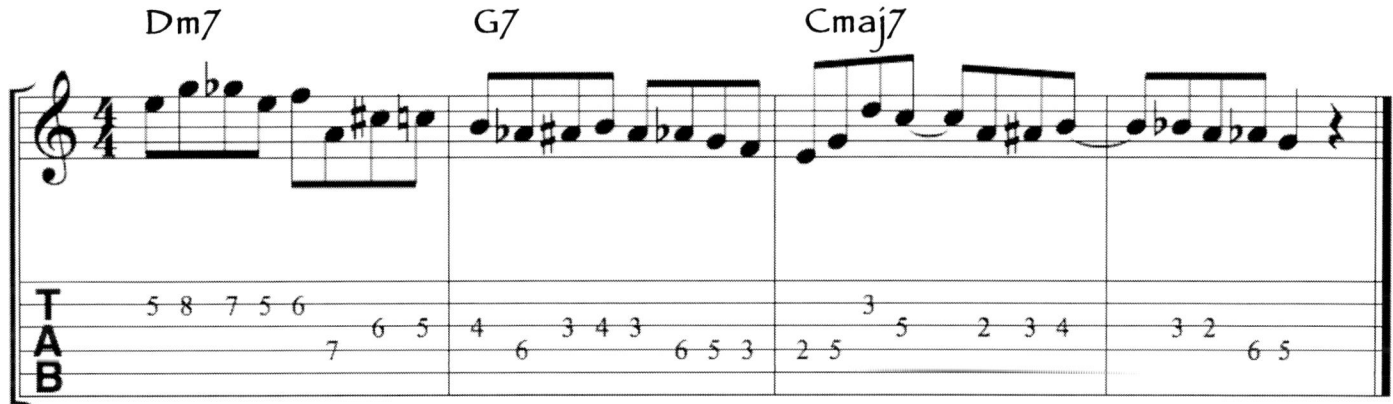

Long Cadence Lick 8:

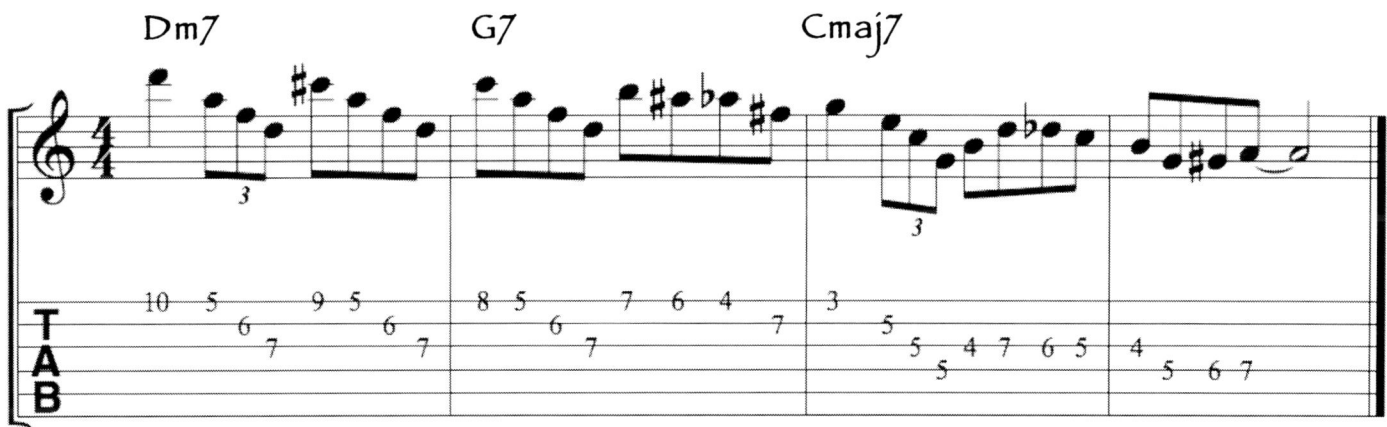

Long Cadence Lick 9:

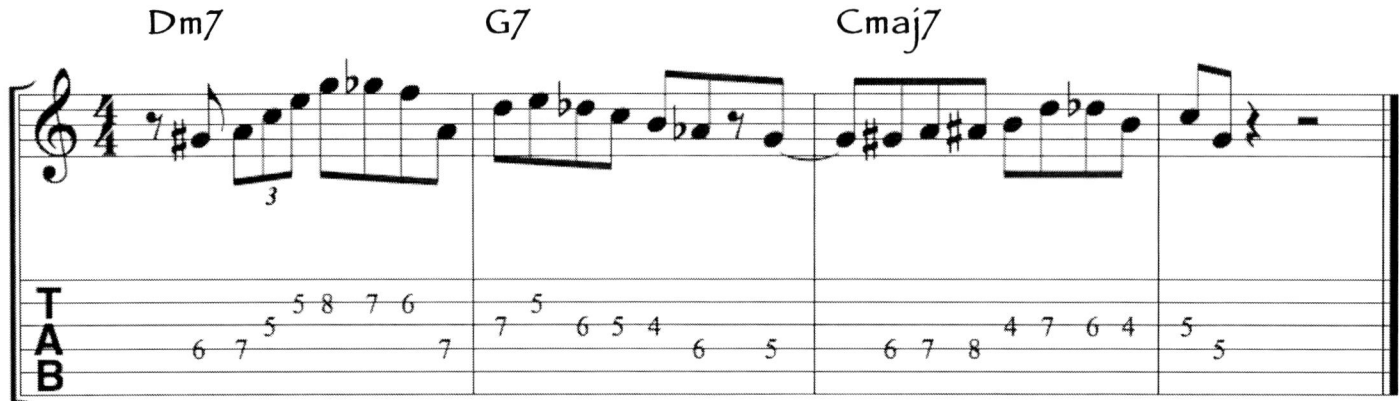

Long Cadence Lick 10:

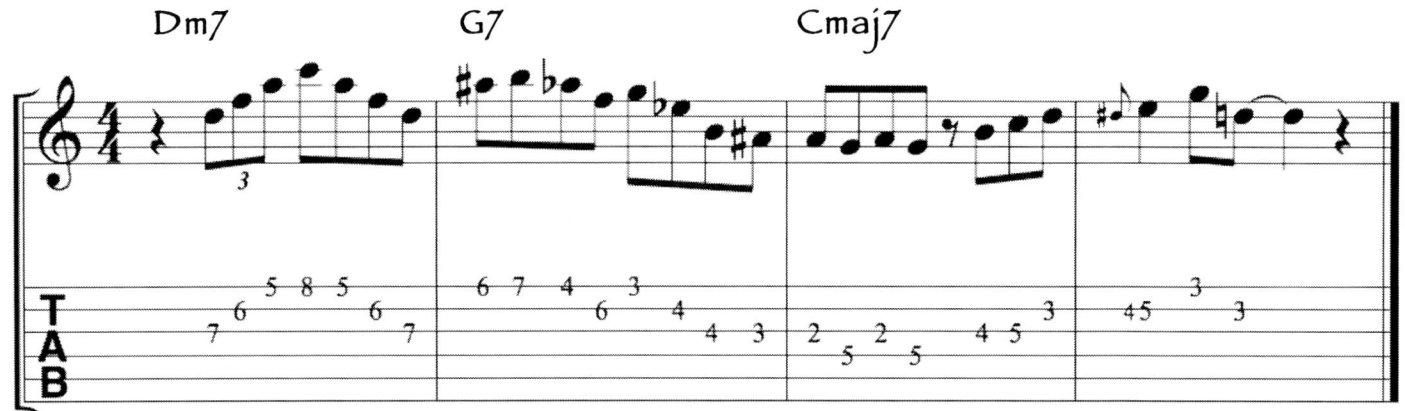

Long Cadence Lick 11:

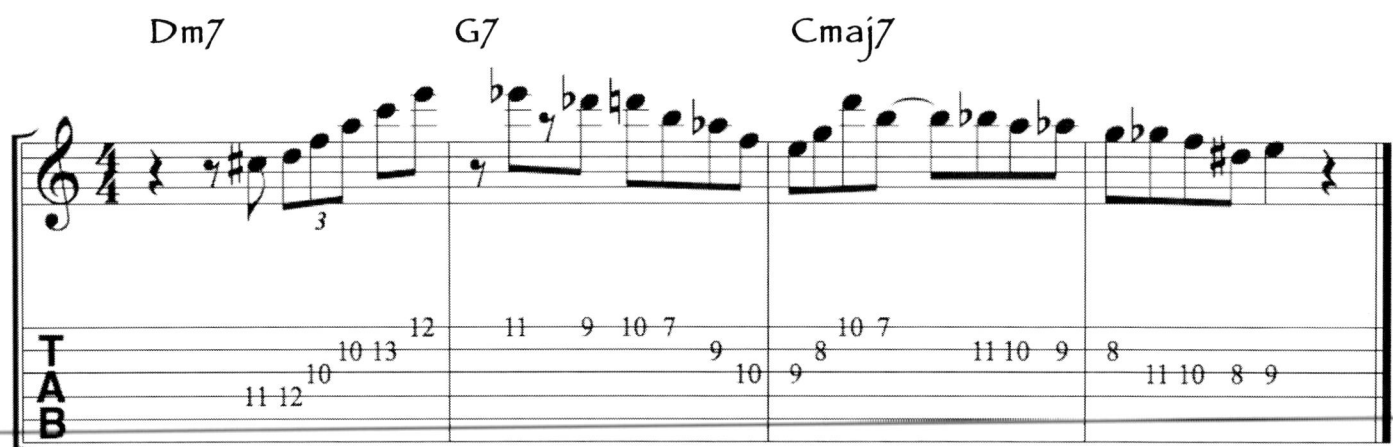

Long Cadence Lick 12:

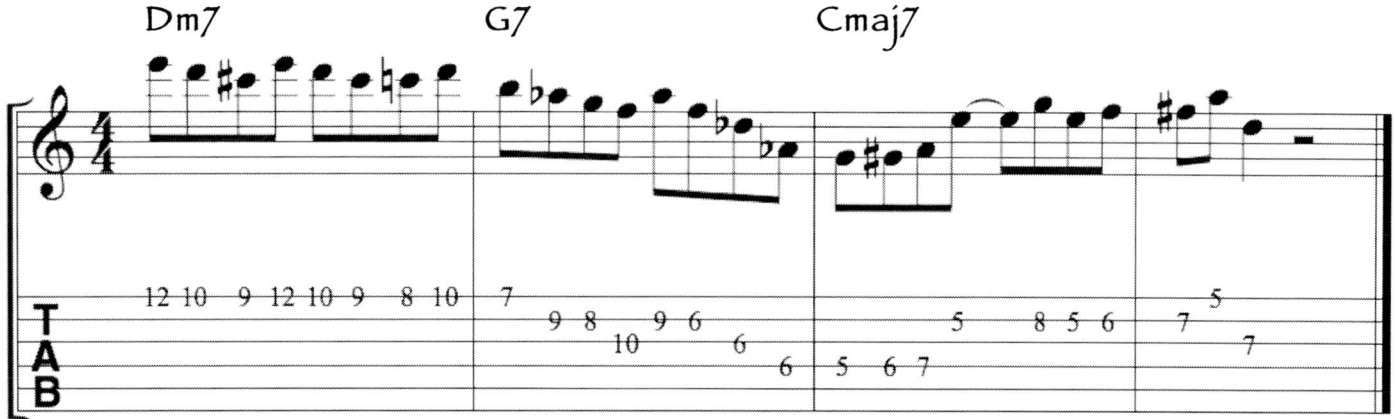

Long Cadence Lick 13:

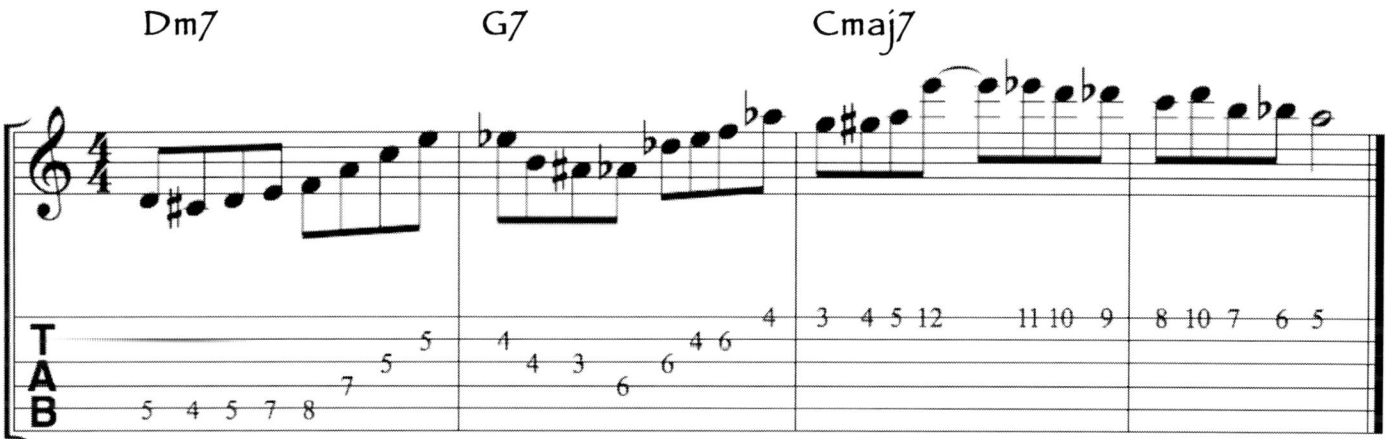

Long Cadence Lick 14:

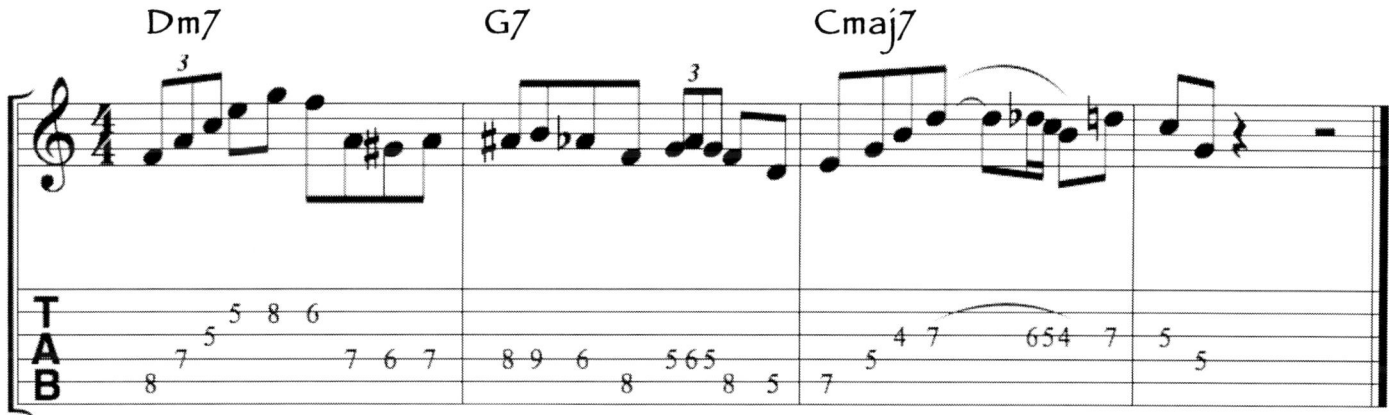

Long Cadence Lick 15:

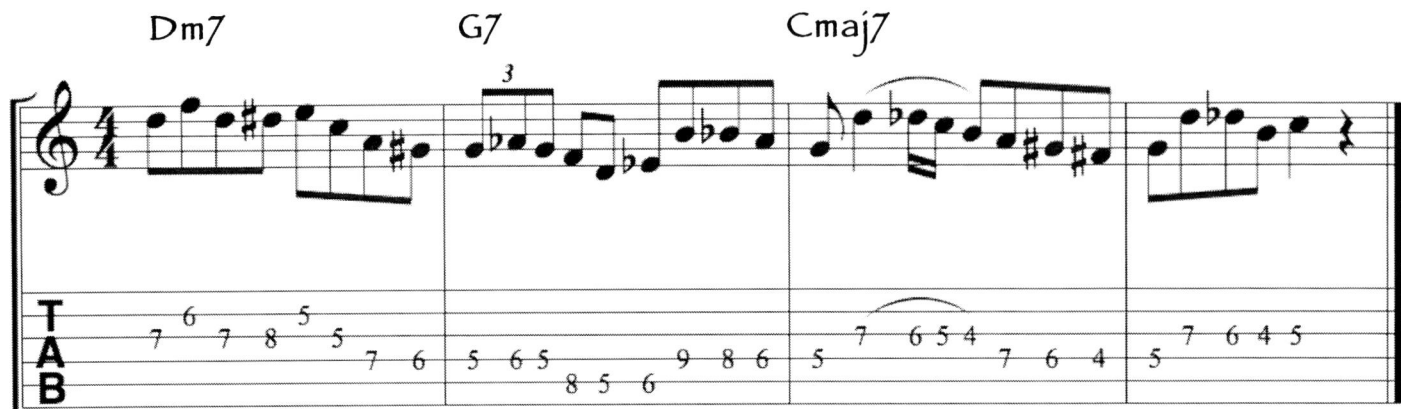

Long Cadence Lick 16:

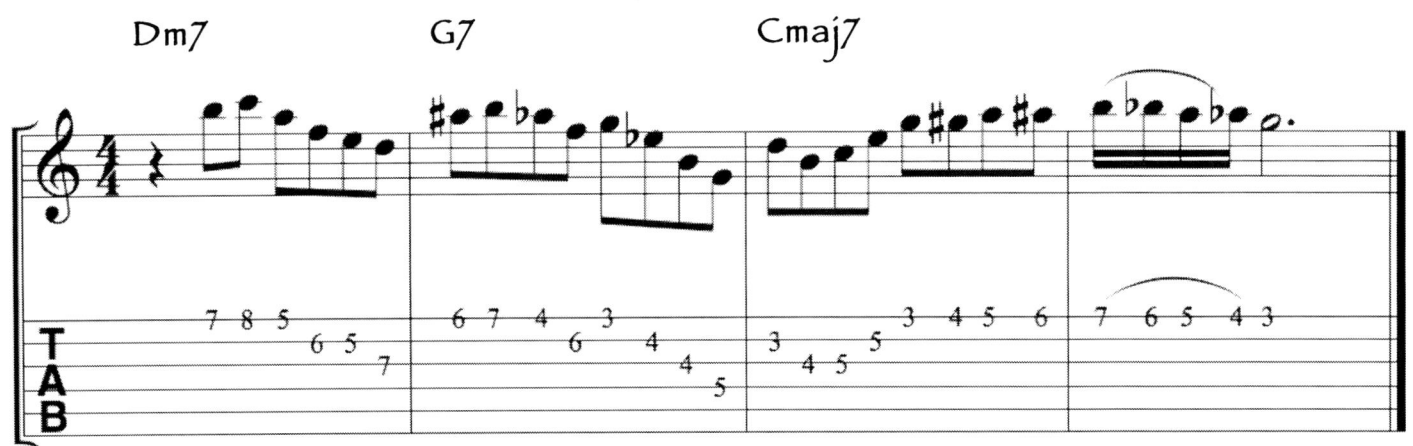

Short Cadence Lick 1:

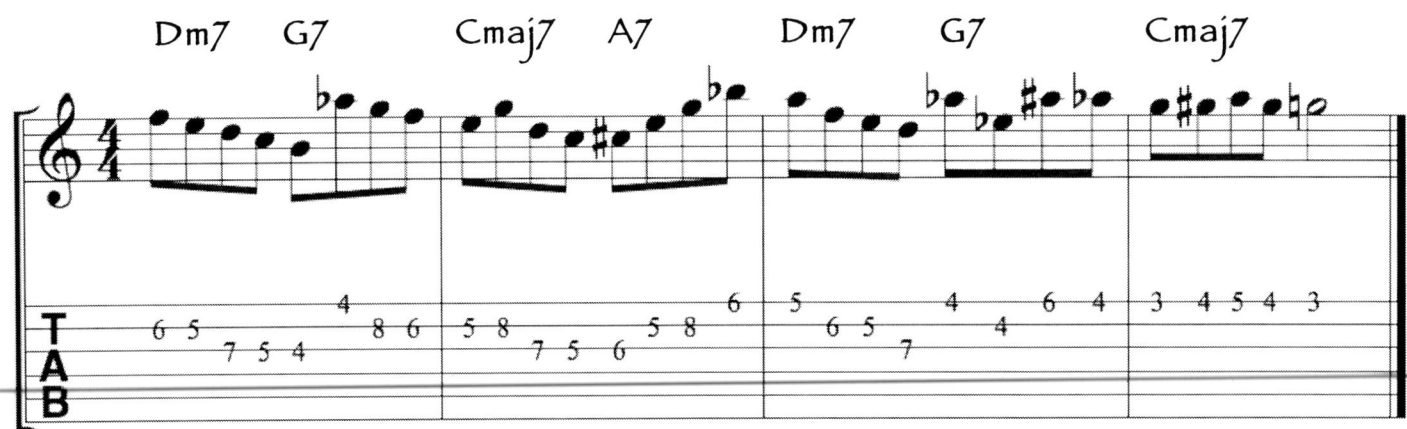

Short Cadence Lick 2:

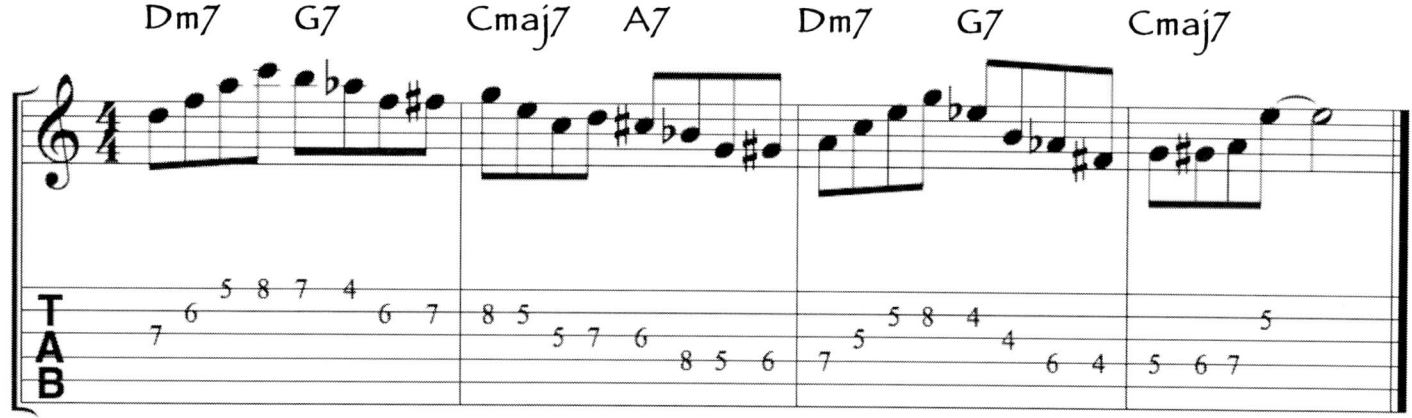

Short Cadence Lick 3:

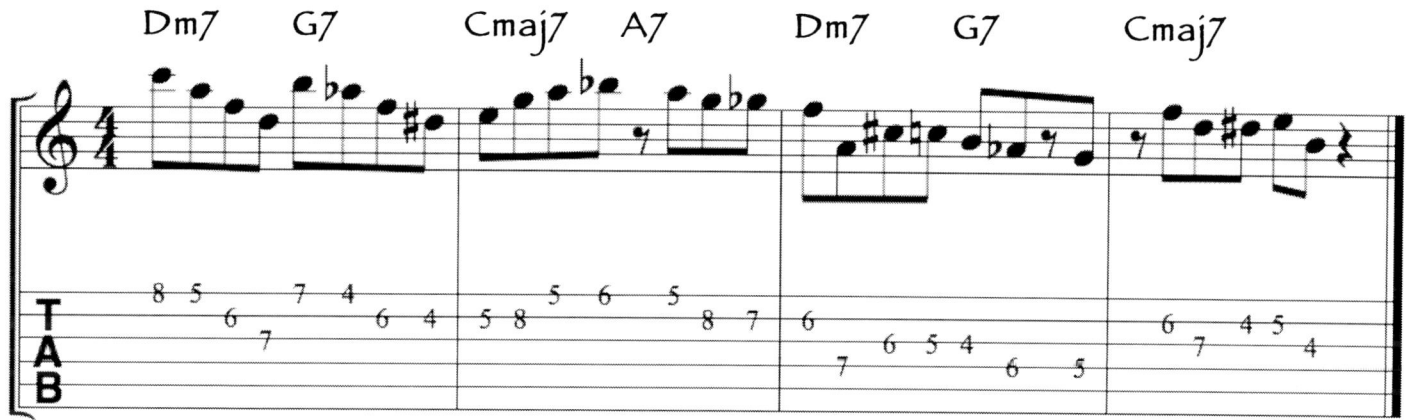

Short Cadence Lick 4:

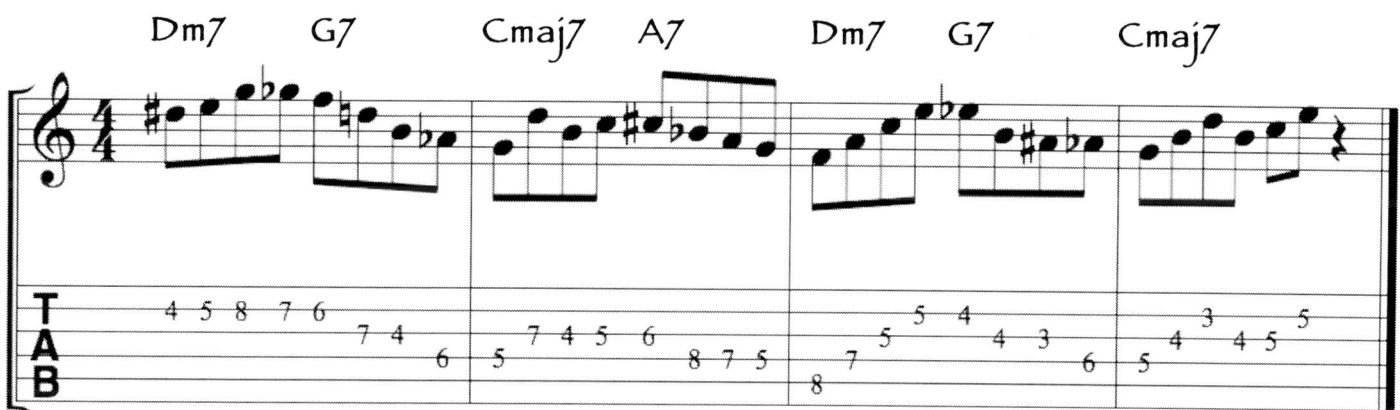

Short Cadence Lick 5:

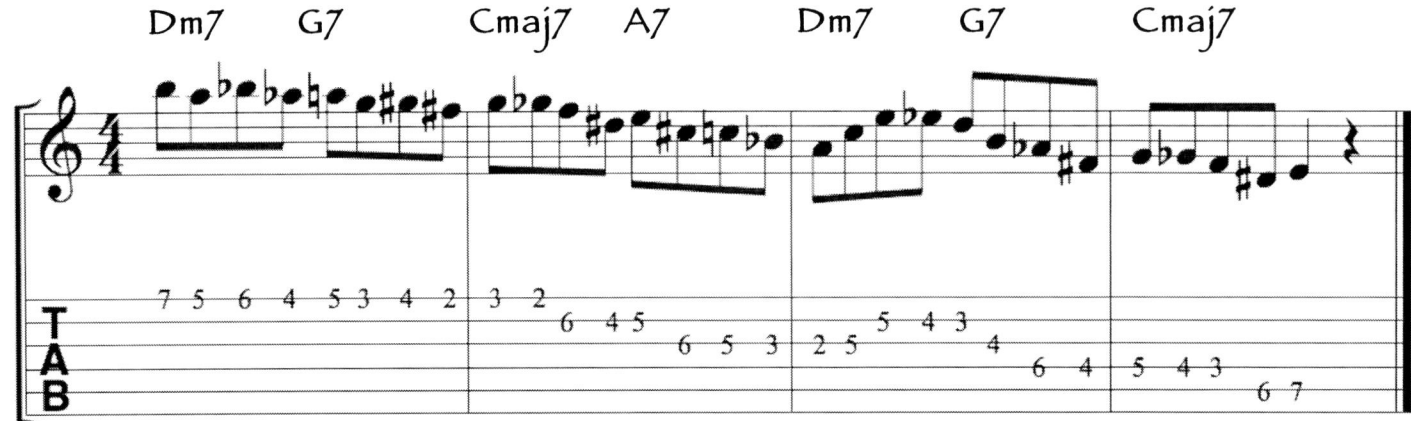

Short Cadence Lick 6:

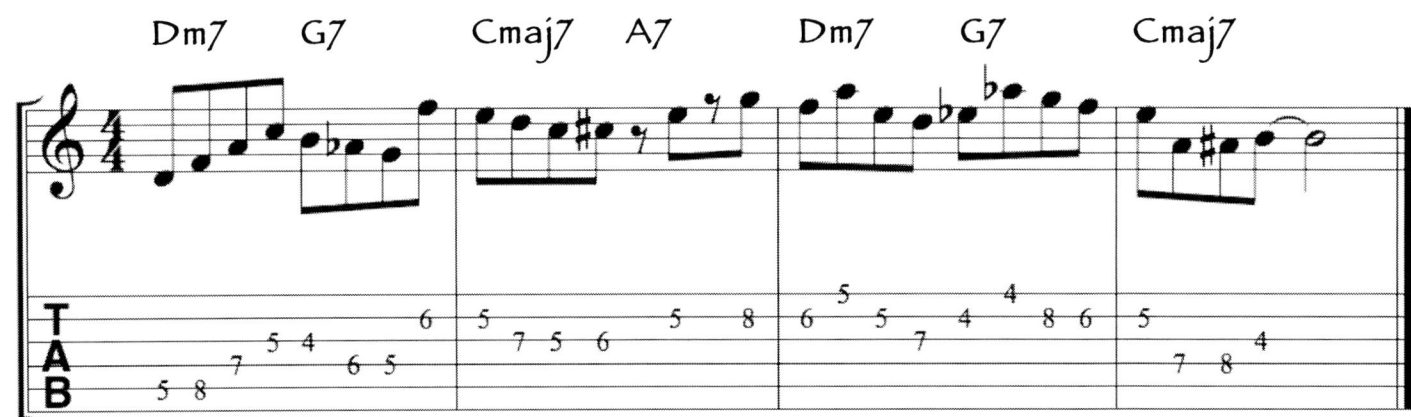

Short Cadence Lick 7:

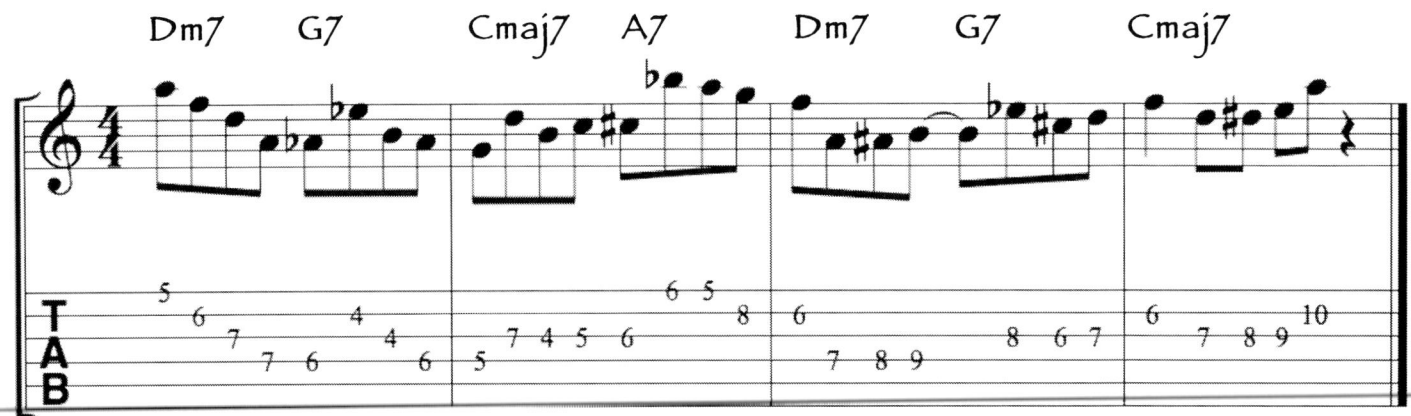

Short Cadence Lick 8:

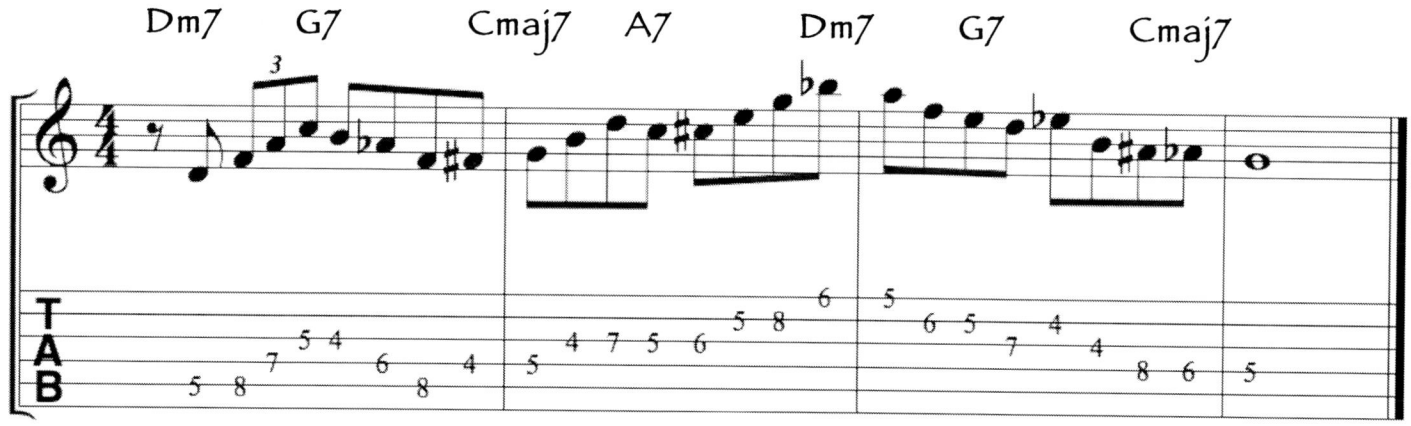

Short Cadence Lick 9:

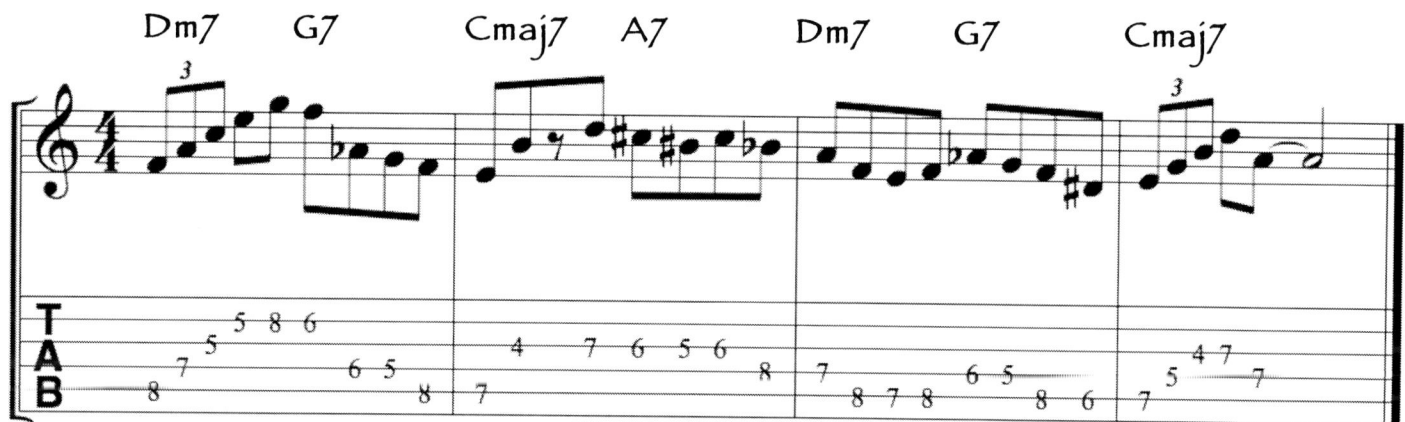

Short Cadence Lick 10:

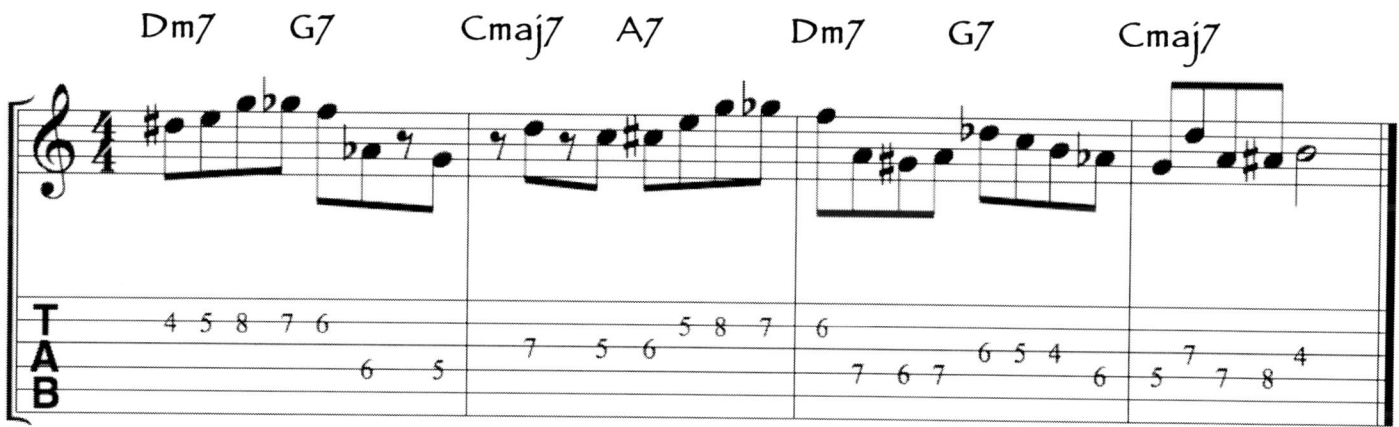

Short Cadence Lick 11:

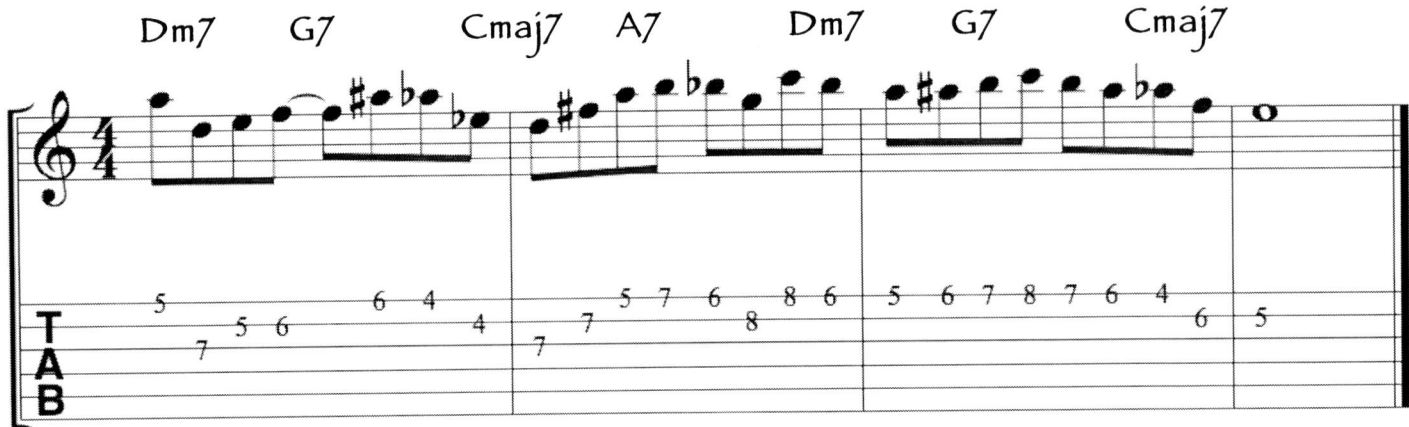

Short Cadence Lick 12:

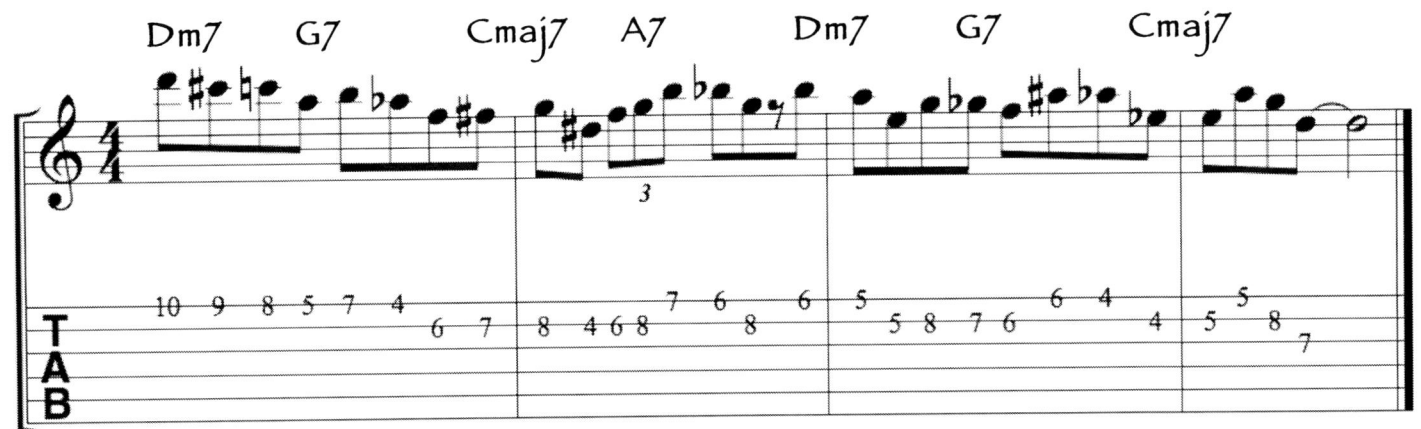

Short Cadence Lick 13:

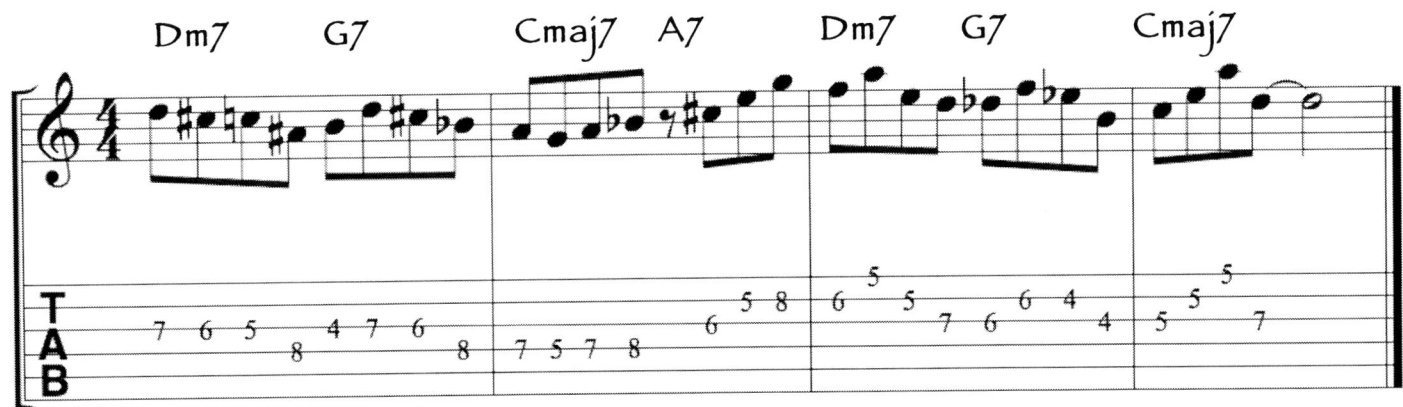

Short Cadence Lick 14:

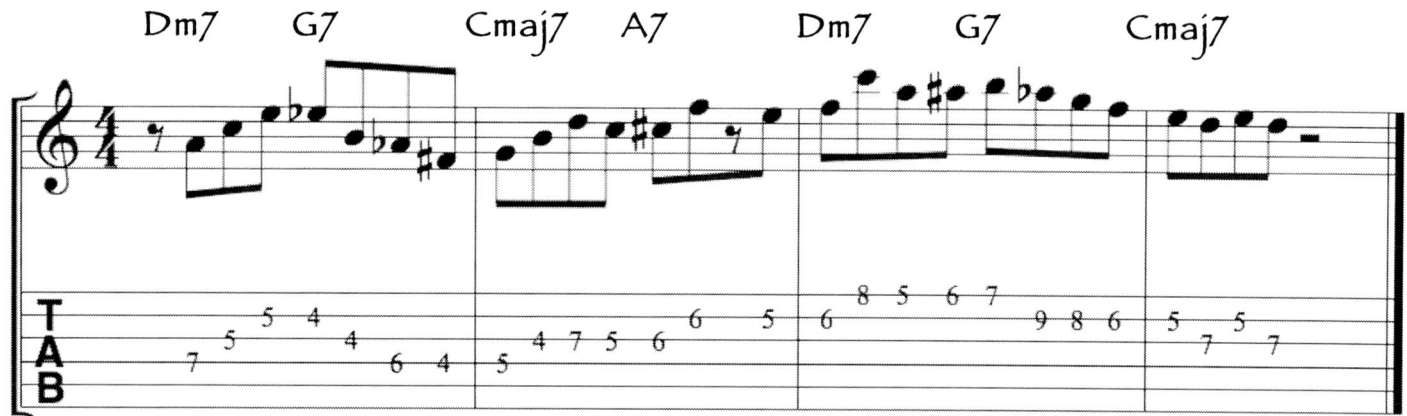

Short Cadence Lick 15:

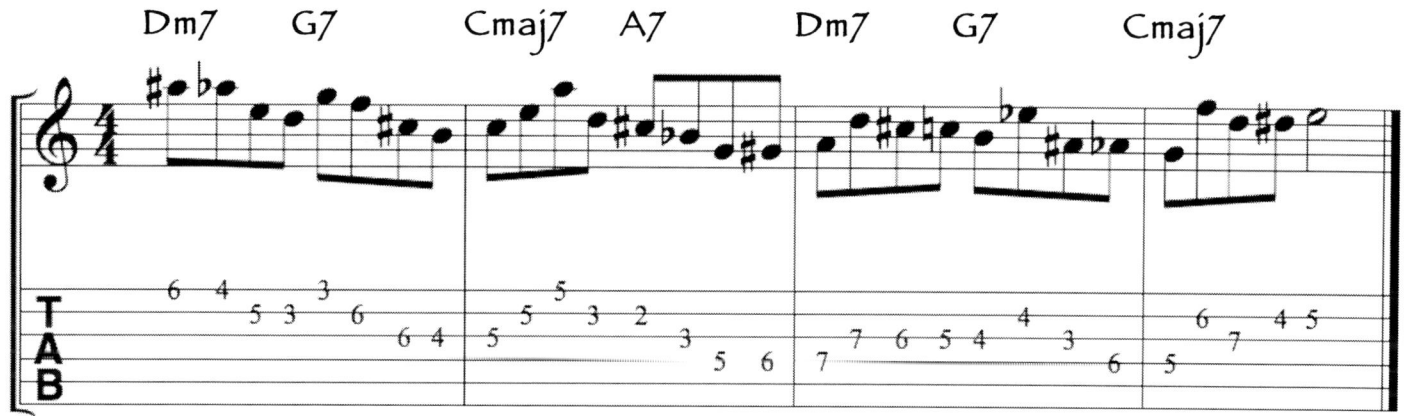

Short Cadence Lick 16:

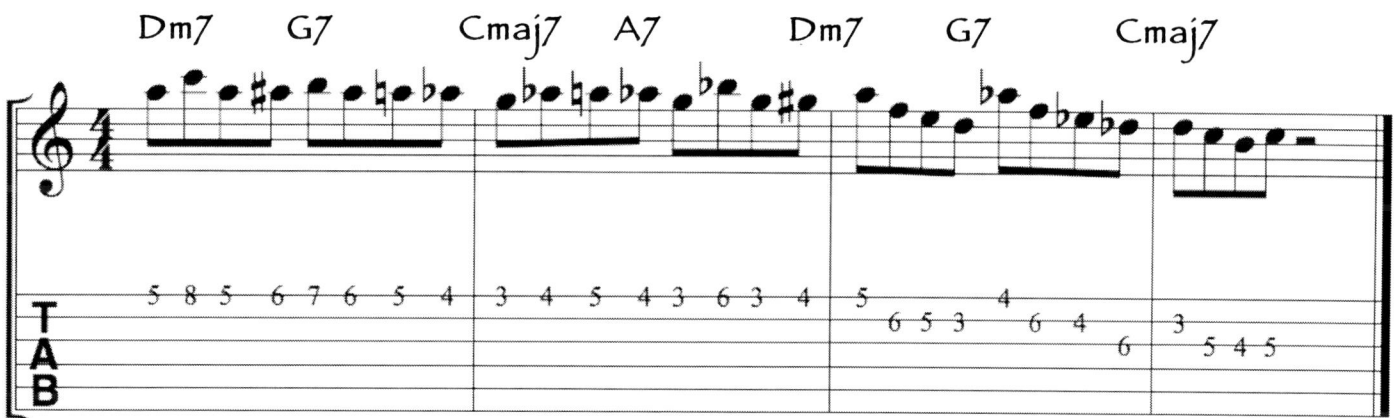

DIATONIC HARMONY – Part 7: Quartal Harmony

Quartal Harmony refers to the practice of building chords from notes stacked in 4ths rather than 3rds. The resulting chords relate in conveniently vague ways to whatever our underlying chords happen to be. They aren't typically written into chord progressions, but used on pre-existing chords as a coloring since any one of these Quartal triads can relate to a number of chords. Below, we'll look at an A Quartal triad as it relates to various chords:

A Quartal Triad:	A	D	G
Cmaj7:	6th	9th	5th
Dm7:	5th	Root	11th
Em7:	11th	b7th	b3rd
Fmaj7:	3rd	6th	9th
G7:	9th	5th	Root
Am7:	Root	11th	b7th
Bbmaj7:	7th	3rd	13th
Ebmaj7:	#11th	7th	3rd

Below, we have a table that shows us the quartal triads that can be derived from the C major scale:

	Root		4th		5th	
I:	C	2½	F	3W	B	H
II:	D	2½	G	2½	C	W
III:	E	2½	A	2½	D	W
IV:	F	3W	B	2½	E	H
V:	G	2½	C	2½	F	W
VI:	A	2½	D	2½	G	W
VII:	B	2½	E	2½	A	W

If you spent adequate time with the Extended Harmony section of this book, you're well aware that there are certain chords in the key that can be extended all the way out to include every scale tone, namely the IIm, IV and V7. This means that when you're on these chords, you could use these quartal harmony triads indiscriminately. If you want to use quartal triads indiscriminately on the I, IIIm or VIm chords, you will want to borrow them from the key a 5th away. For example, if you were in the key of C major and you were on the I, IIIm or VI minor chord, you would use the quartal triads that relate to the key of G major. This is the same way that we extend these very same chords when dealing with traditional extended harmony.

The following few pages illustrate the quartal triads in the key of C major, up and down the fretboard. Practice these against all possible chord contexts. When you feel comfortable walking up and down each string set, work on combining strings sets in order to work your away across the fretboard in a more horizontal fashion. In an attempt to keep this book under 500 pages, I'm going to leave it up to you to map out the quartal triads in the eleven remaining keys. Make use of either the chord diagram paper or the tab paper in the back of the book.

Quartal triads can be built from the melodic minor scale or any other seven-tone scale. The more exotic of a structure the scale has, the fewer actual perfect 4th intervals you will find between the notes of the chords. Even with the melodic minor scale, you'll find a couple major 3rds. This won't stop these triads from being useful, but it will take your ear some getting used to, in order to really clearly hear the logical order.

C Major Quartal Triads, Root Position, Set 1:

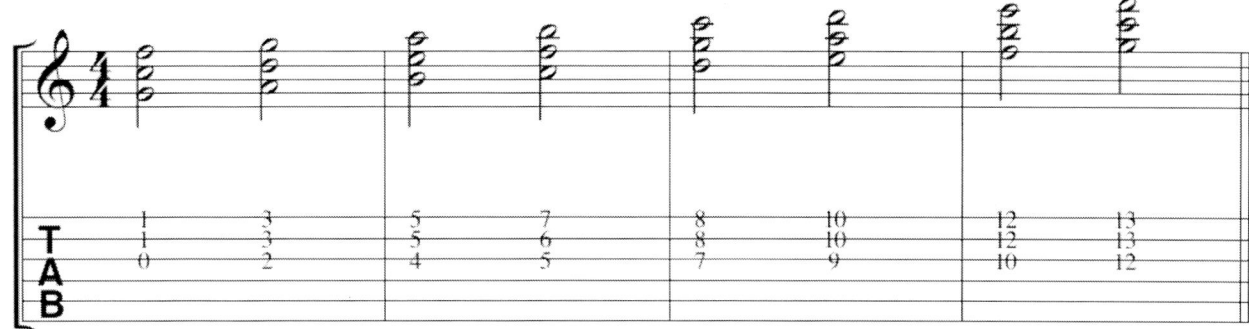

C Major Quartal Triads, Root Position, Set 2:

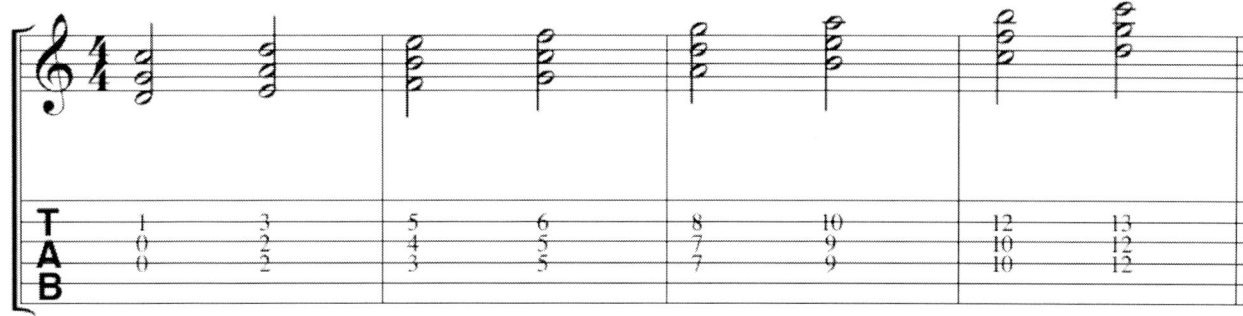

C Major Quartal Triads, Root Position, Set 3:

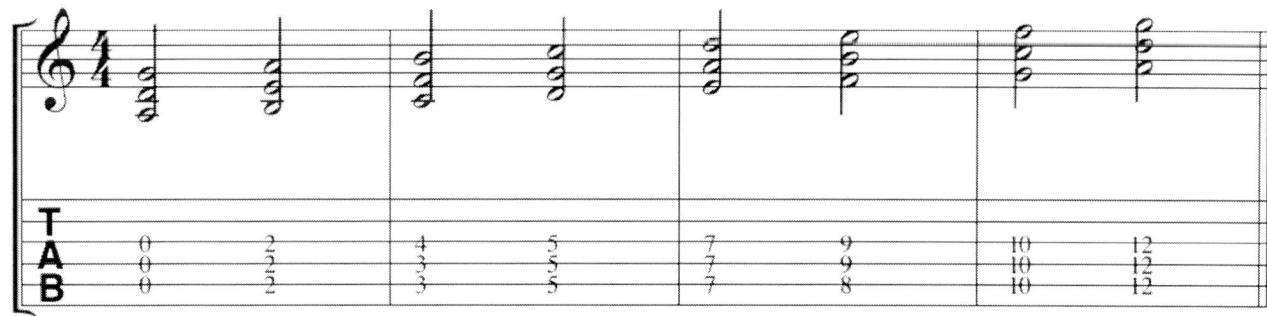

C Major Quartal Triads, Root Position, Set 4:

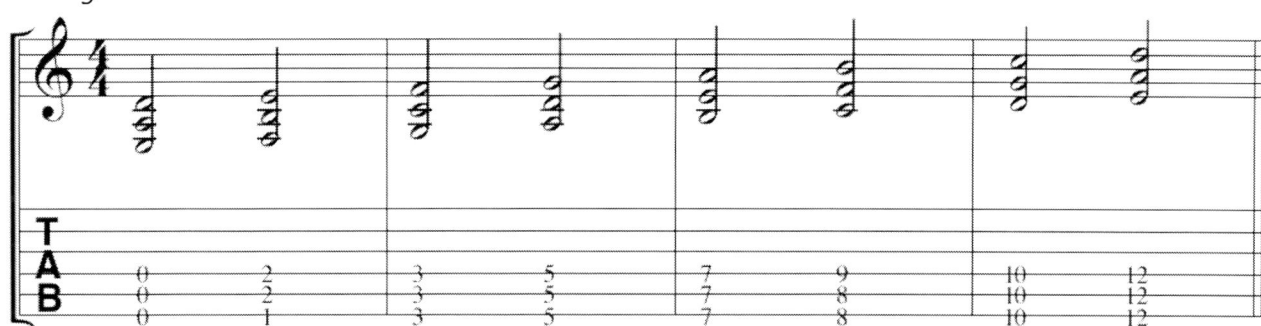

C Major Quartal Triads, First Inversion, Set 1:

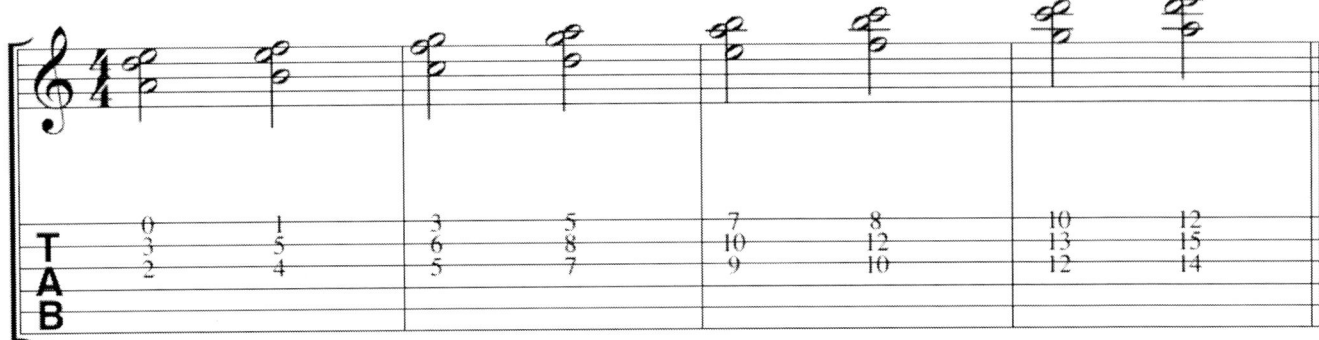

C Major Quartal Triads, First Inversion, Set 2:

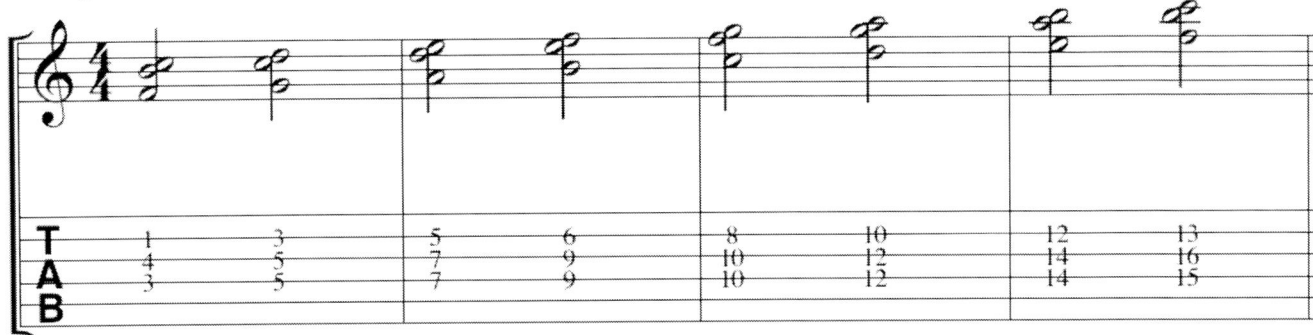

C Major Quartal Triads, First Inversion, Set 4:

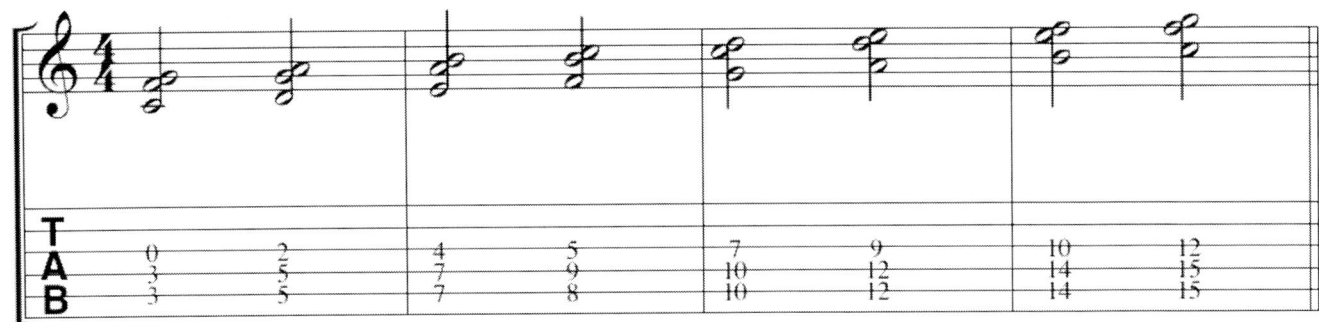

C Major Quartal Triads, First Inversion, Set 4:

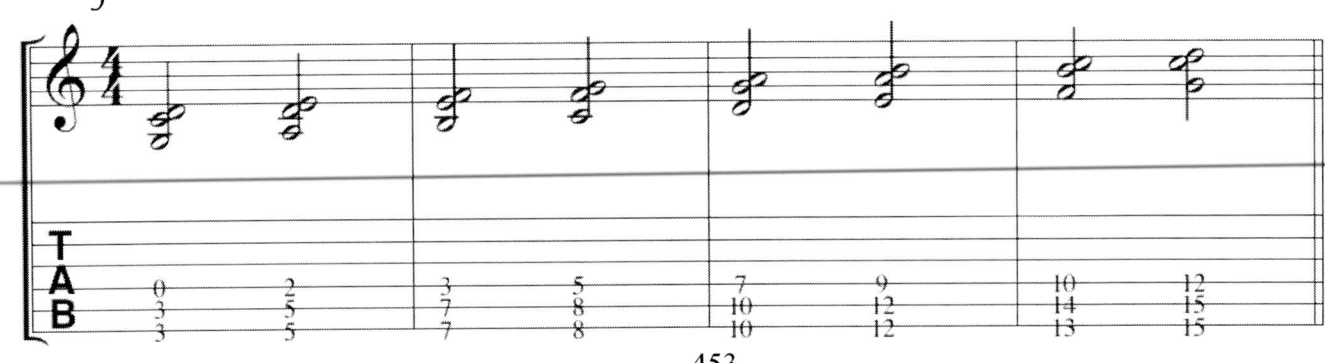

C Major Quartal Triads, Second Inversion, Set 1:

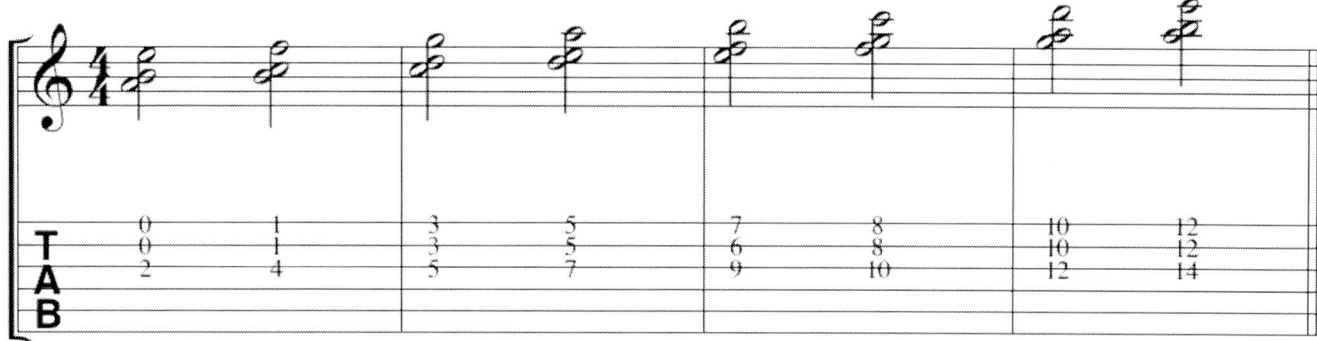

C Major Quartal Triads, Second Inversion, Set 2:

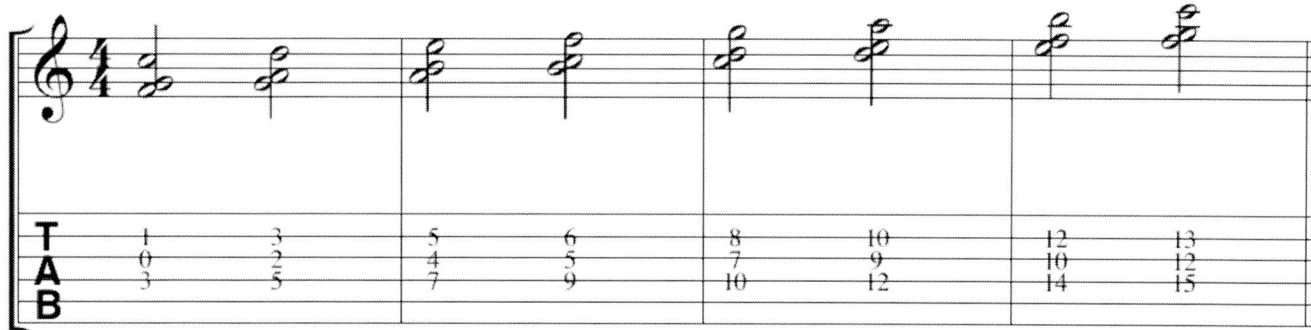

C Major Quartal Triads, Second Inversion, Set 3:

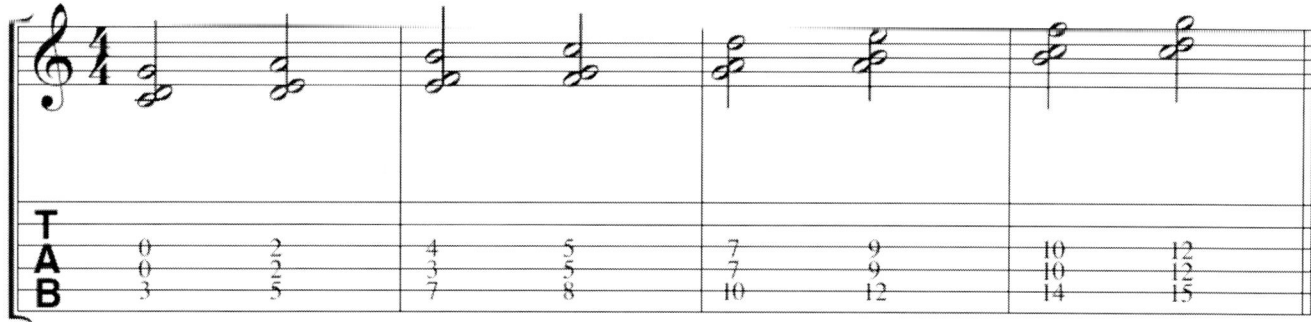

C Major Quartal Triads, Second Inversion, Set 4:

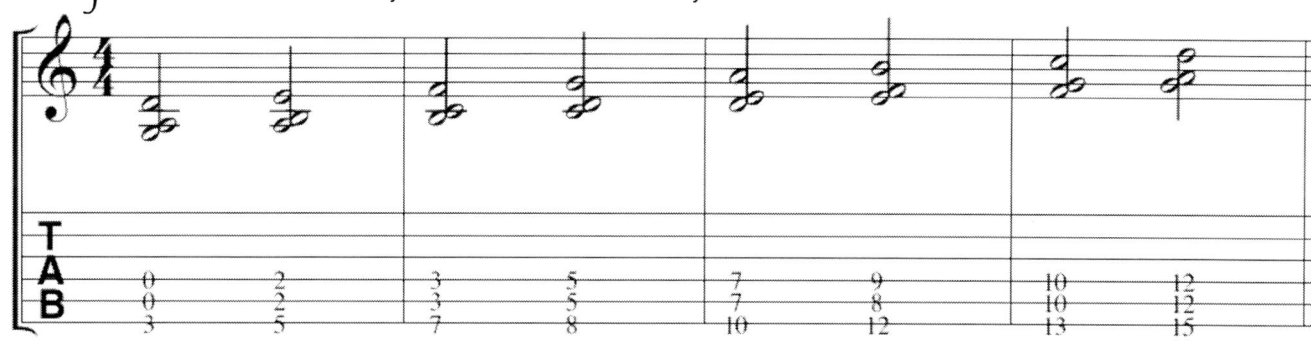

THE MELODIC CRAFT – part 3: Motive Development

There are a lot of so called "serious musicians" out there who've never developed the skill to improvise well. Many of these people have learned how to appreciate what makes a melody a good melody but have not realized that the same "compositional" techniques that make a written melody a success can be applied to creating an improvised melody. When you become truly comfortable with some basic compositional tools, improvising a worthwhile and memorable melody line becomes a natural thing to do. Improvisation and composition in their ideal form are the very same activity, performed at different speeds.

Motive development constitutes a very useful set of tools for the improviser/composer. The idea is simple; it starts with a short melodic statement, maybe a half a measure to two measures long. This is your motive. Developing it means that you're altering it in different ways in order to create relatable melodic material to use with your original motive. There are a few ways that we can develop the motive. Let's look at each technique.

Melodic Inversion:

Melodic inversion is simply the act of flipping the melody upside. Where the original melody moves up by a 3rd for instance, the inverted melody will move down by a 3rd and vice versa. There are two types of melodic inversion. The first and most commonly applied type is that of the tonal inversion. In the tonal inversion, we adjust the major and minor intervals of the inversion in order to keep the notes within the original key. The other type is the real inversion, which is where the original major and minor intervals are maintained upon inversion, resulting in a new tonality.

The other big consideration when inverting a melodic idea is what we call the pivot note. The pivot note is the note that will remain the same between the original and inverted version of the motive. The obvious choice is the first note of the melody but this isn't always the most musically useful option. It's best to choose your pivot note in relation to scale tone rather than sequential order. I personally find the most readily usable inversions to be the ones where chord tones remain chord tones. I'd like to show you how I figured out what my ideal choice was in order to achieve this effect.

First, I compared the original notes to the inverted notes with the root note being the pivot point. This was as simple as writing out the scale tones in ascending order and lining up the descending scale-tone directly beneath them, the root notes lined up with one another.

Melodic Inversion at the Root:

Root	2nd	3rd	4th	5th	6th	7th	Root
Root	7th	6th	5th	4th	3rd	2nd	Root

As you can see with the melodic inversion at the root, our roots remain roots, our 3rds become 6ths and our 5ths become 4ths. That means the when we invert at the root, we're probably going to want the inversion to relate to a different chord than that of the original idea. Most likely, the best choice would be the chord that serves as a IV to whatever chord to which your original motive related.

Here's a simple motive with a tonal inversion at the root with suggested chords. Notice that I began the inversion on the root note an octave higher than the original motive. This was done to keep the inversion within the same register as the original and is common practice.

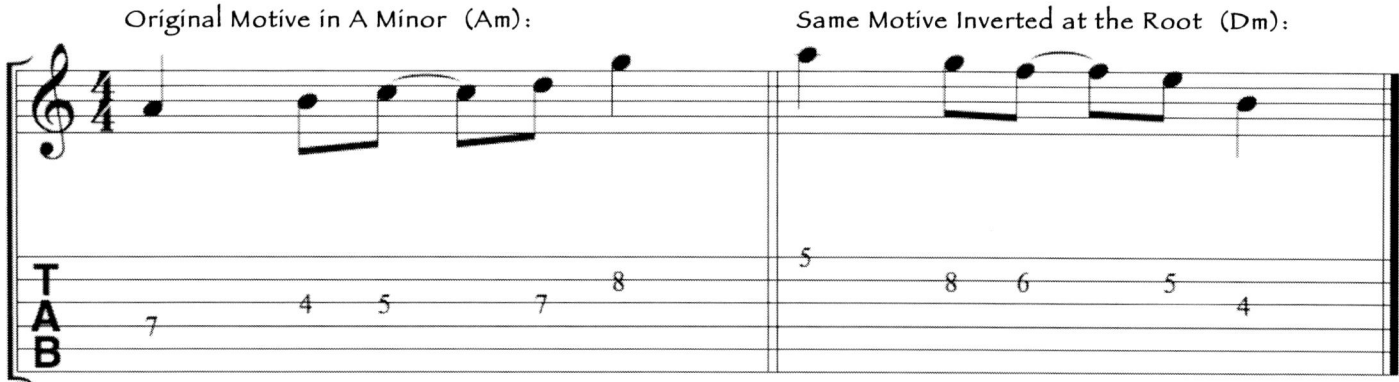

Melodic Inversion at the 5th:

5th	6th	7th	Root	2nd	3rd	4th	5th
5th	4th	3rd	2nd	Root	7th	6th	5th

When we use the 5th as the pivot note, our 5ths remain 5ths, our 3rds become 7ths and our root notes become 2nds, which can of course serve as 9ths. This type of inversion will work pretty well in jazzier contexts within the original harmony and if done tastefully, jazzier elements can be a part of pop and rock music as well.

Here's the same original motive, now inverted at the 5th:

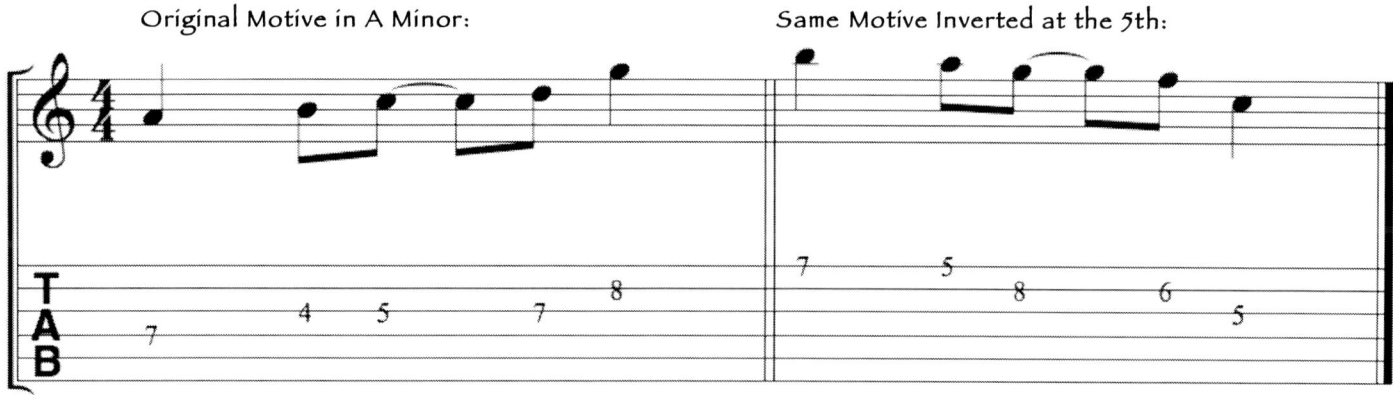

Melodic Inversion at the 3rd:

| 3rd | 4th | 5th | 6th | 7th | Root | 2nd | 3rd |
| 3rd | 2nd | Root | 7th | 6th | 5th | 4th | 3rd |

As we can see, melodically inverting at the 3rd allows our primary chord-tones to remain primary chord-tones. The 3rd remains as the 3rd, while the root becomes the 5th and the 5th becomes the root. This is definitely the most easily applicable melodic inversion but it won't always be the right one for the motive you've chosen to use. In the case of the following example, we'll hear that the inversion at the 3rd isn't quite as natural in relation to the chord as the original was.

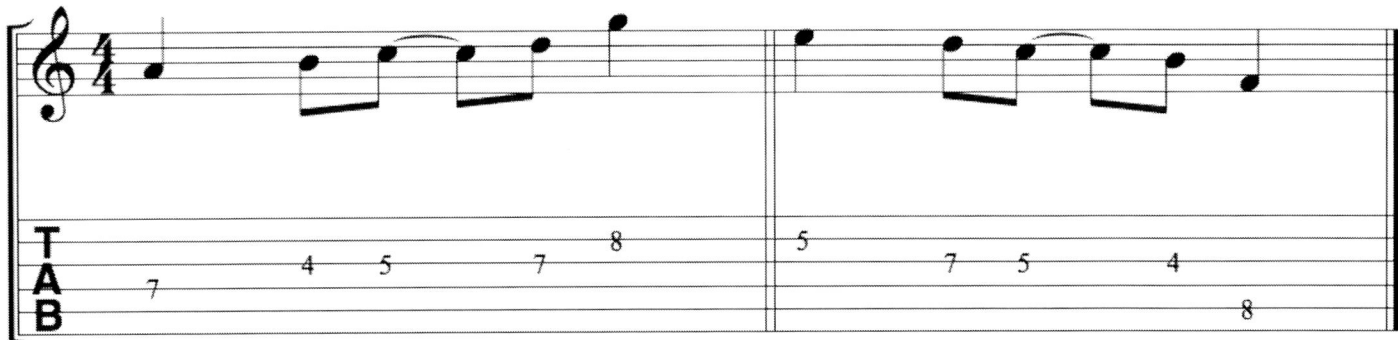

It's always worth experimenting with all of your options. This same process can be repeated with your non-chord tones being used as pivot notes for melodic inversions.

Melodic Inversion at the Root (Real):

Real (or chromatic) inversions almost always lead you towards a different key. As a result, there's typically not as much room for them. They are usually executed with the root note being the pivot note, but just as the case with the tonal inversions, you can invert them at any interval you desire. Below is our same motive, this time with a real melodic inversion at the root. In the inversion we see the presence of an F# note which is the result of maintaining our original intervals in the opposite direction.

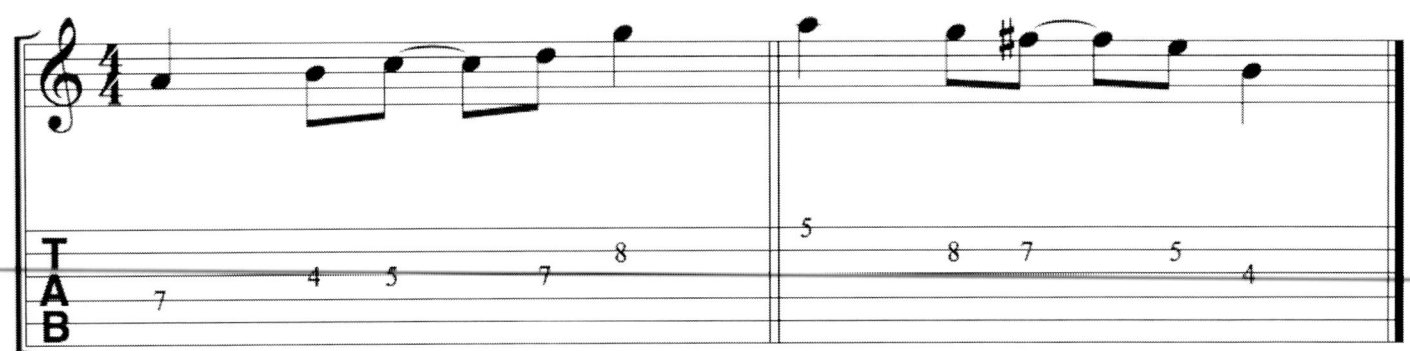

Retrograde:

Whereas with melodic inversion, we flip a melody upside down, with a retrograde we simply flip the melody backwards. If the contour of the melody in that of an arch, the retrograde will only sound vaguely different from the original motive unless their considerably more notes in either the first or second half of it. Motives with upward or downward contours are the most useful for a retrograde.

Below is our original motive followed by it's own retrograde:

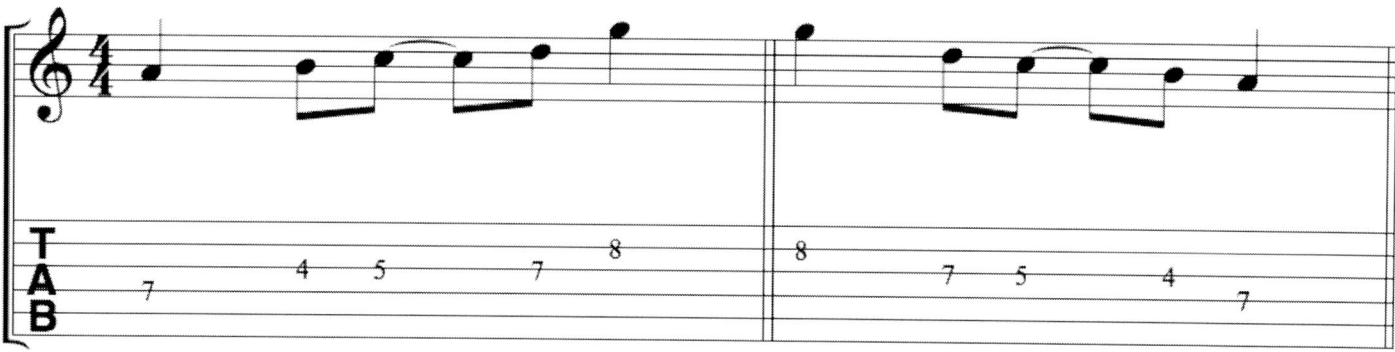

In the case of the example above, we have a motive whose rhythm is symmetrical. That of course means that when we flip the motive backwards, the rhythm remains the same. This won't always be the case. The more asymmetrical the rhythm, the more rhythmically noticeable a retrograde will be.

Transposition:

In melody writing, we have two different types of transposition. We have tonal (diatonic) transposition, which occurs when the intervals of the melody are adjusted to fit in the original key and we have real (chromatic) transposition, where the original intervals are preserved, which puts the transposition in a new key. Repeating a motive transposed at different intervals is known as creating a sequence. When we create melodic patterns, this is what we are doing. We're taking a motive and diatonically transposing it to each scale degree within the key.

On the following couple pages, we are going to take a new motive and look at all of it's possible tonal transpositions, along with the inversion, the retrograde and the inverted retrograde of each transpositions. This gives us quite a large cross-section of melodic material that directly relates to the new original motive. For the inversions, I used diatonic inversion at the 3rd, which I find to be the most readily usable type of inversion. This is also the case for the inverted retrogrades. This material could be used to build a full arsenal of melodic material that can be used to write a simple pop melody or a 20 minute prog-rock opus.

Following this sub-section, you will find a melody that I composed using this material with labels above the music indicating from where each particular note-group was derived, using simple abbreviations. You can study this and try writing some of your own melodic ideas from the very same material.

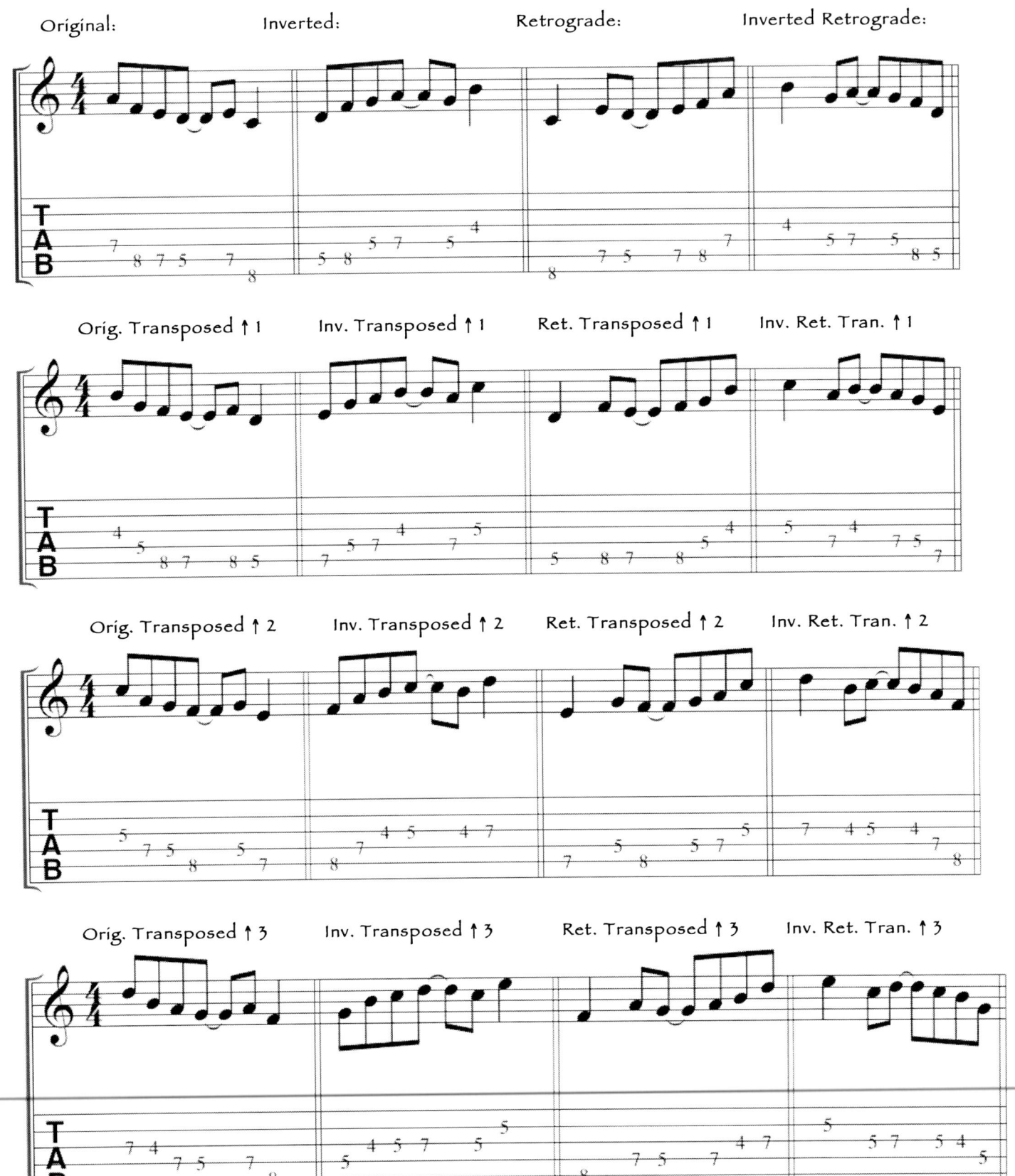

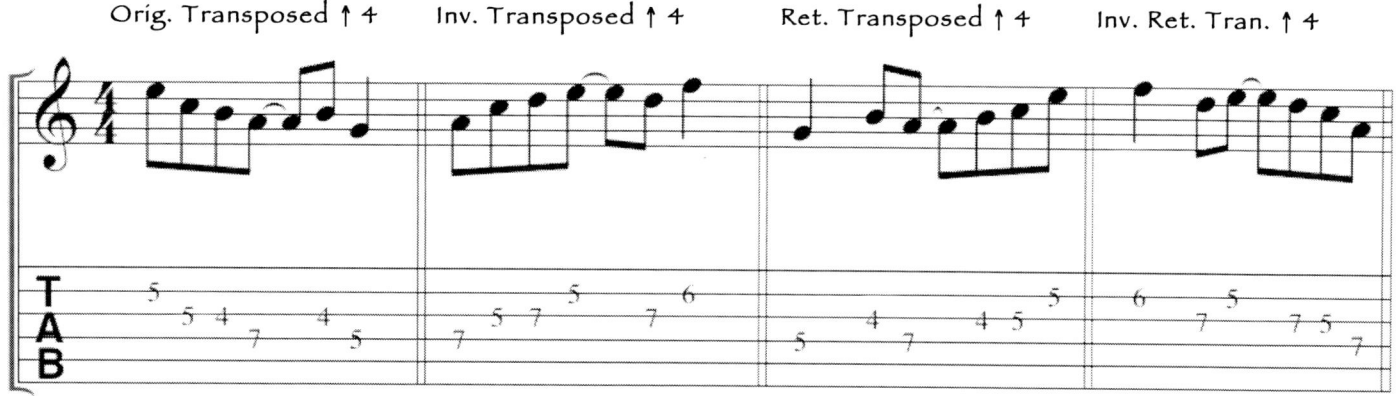

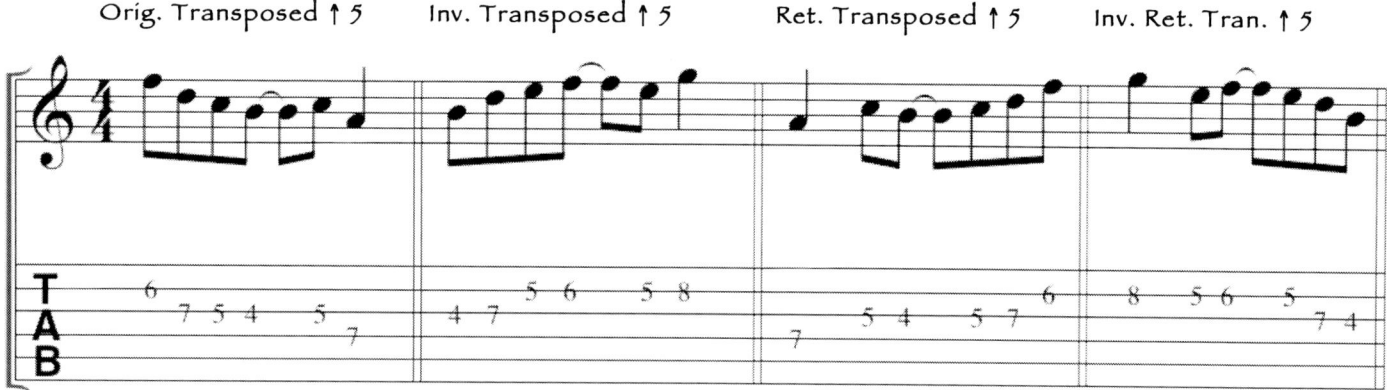

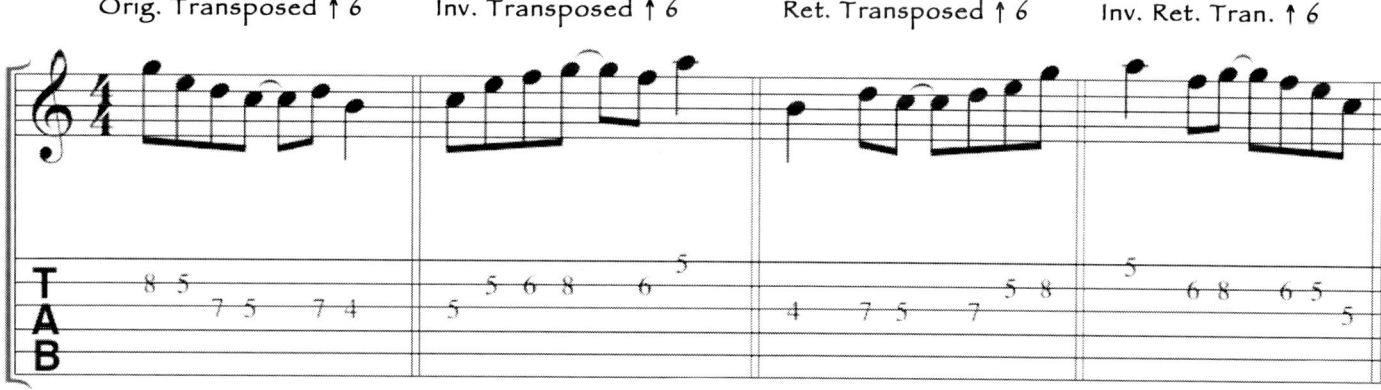

There are a few other simple means by which we can develop the motive. We can rhythmically diminish the motive, which is to squeeze the notes into half of the space, using smaller note values. We can also rhythmically augment the motive which would be the opposite of diminishing it. We can add notes between the existing notes of the motive, or we can subtract notes from it, in both cases, creating a different rhythmic content from the original motive. These processes can be applied to any transformation of the motive as well, including inversions, transpositions and retrogrades. We can also borrow the original contour and rhythm of the motive and repitch the notes to fit any harmonic context we may want to use.

Another thing that we can do is to break the motive into smaller sections called sub-motives and apply any motive development technique to them. This further expands the range of compositional possibilities.

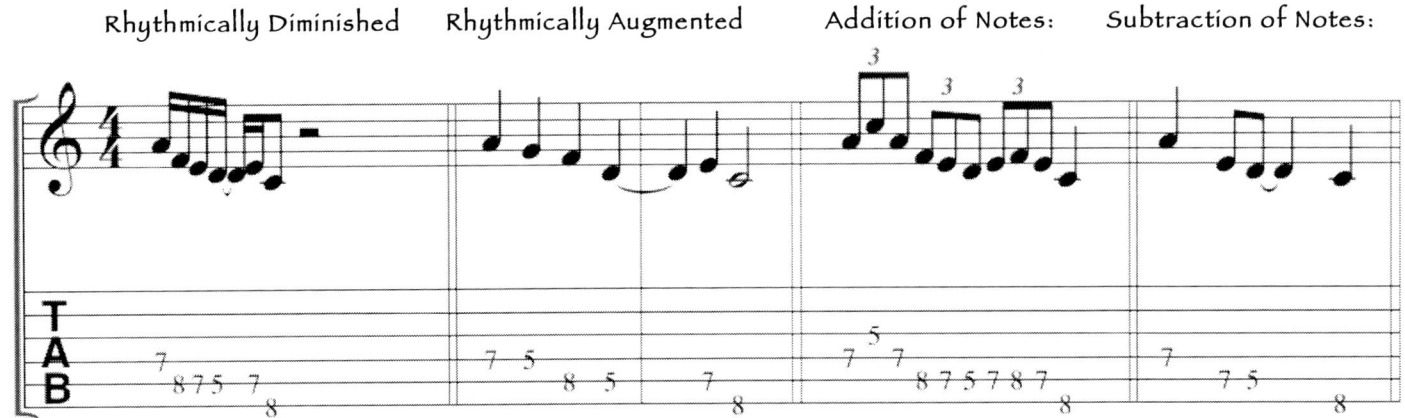

Division of Motive Into Submotives

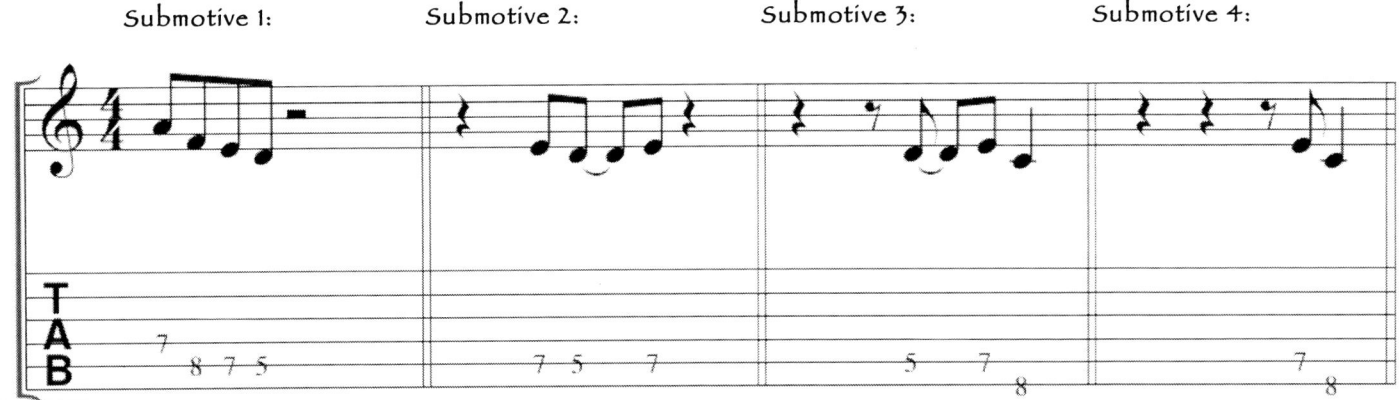

The following example shows us how we can take these sub-motives and place them rhythmically in different parts of the measure in order to create some rich rhythmic content. This example was made from transpositions of sub-motives 1 and 3.

Odd Rhythmic Sequencing of Sub-Motives:

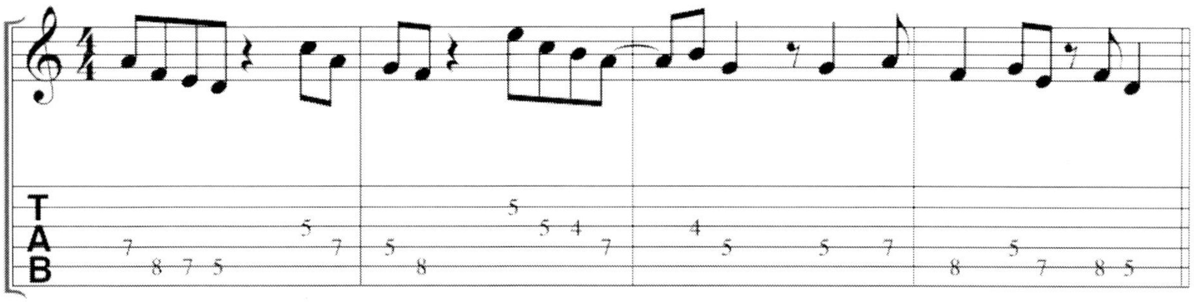

T = Transposed   R = Retrograde   I = Inversion   S = Sub-Motive

Don't Feel Much Like Dyin' - Geoff Stockton

Harmonization

Harmonizing a melody can add a lot of thickness, color and dimension to it. My first conscious exposure to harmonized melodies came when I was 12 years old, listening to Metallica albums, namely "Master Of Puppets" and "…And Justice For All". Many of the lead guitar parts were harmonized. When I learned of this and how it sounded, I soon discovered that harmonized melodies could be found in almost every style of music. My path to learning harmonization was a slow and rocky one. The following pages represent the lessons I wish I would have received 20 years ago.

Before we get into the different ways in which we can harmonize a melody, it's important to establish a few things. First off, we want to be able to identify the different types of notes that function within a melody as the more musical method of harmonizing requires that we treat these different types of melody notes differently from one another.

The Four Basic Types of Melody Note Functions:

1) Chord Tones (Notes that are members of the underlying chord)
2) Non-Chord/Non-Passing Tones (Same as extended tones, they are emphasized notes on the strong beats, lasting for one beat or longer)
3) Scale-Wise Passing Tones (Diatonic non-chord-tones situated rhythmically and tonally between chord-tones.)
4) Chromatic-Passing Tones (Non-diatonic non-chord-tones situated rhythmically and tonally between scale-tones.)

The Four Types of Harmonic Motion

1) Parallel Motion (Both voices move in the same direction by the same interval)
2) Similar Motion (Both voices move in the same direction but by two different intervals)
3) Oblique Motion (One voice moves while the other voice stays at it's previous pitch)
4) Contrary Motion (Both move in opposite directions, either away from, or towards one another)

Over the next few pages, we're going to go over the most common means by which a melody is harmonized. The first two are variations of one another just as is the case with the third and fourth methods.

The Three Common Types of Harmonization:

1) Parallel Harmonization
2) Adjusted Parallel Harmonization
3) Modern Block Harmonization

The easiest place to start is with parallel harmonization. The way it works is simple. The second voice (the harmonizing voice) begins at any particular interval from the first voice (the melody) and continues to relate by that same interval for every note in the melody. For instance if the first and second voice are a 3rd apart on the first note, the two voices will remain a 3rd apart for the duration of the melody. With a couple distorted guitars and some judicious palm-muting, this generates the classic Iron Maiden/Metallica sound.

Below is an example of a melody in A minor (bottom guitar) being harmonized diatonically in thirds (top guitar).

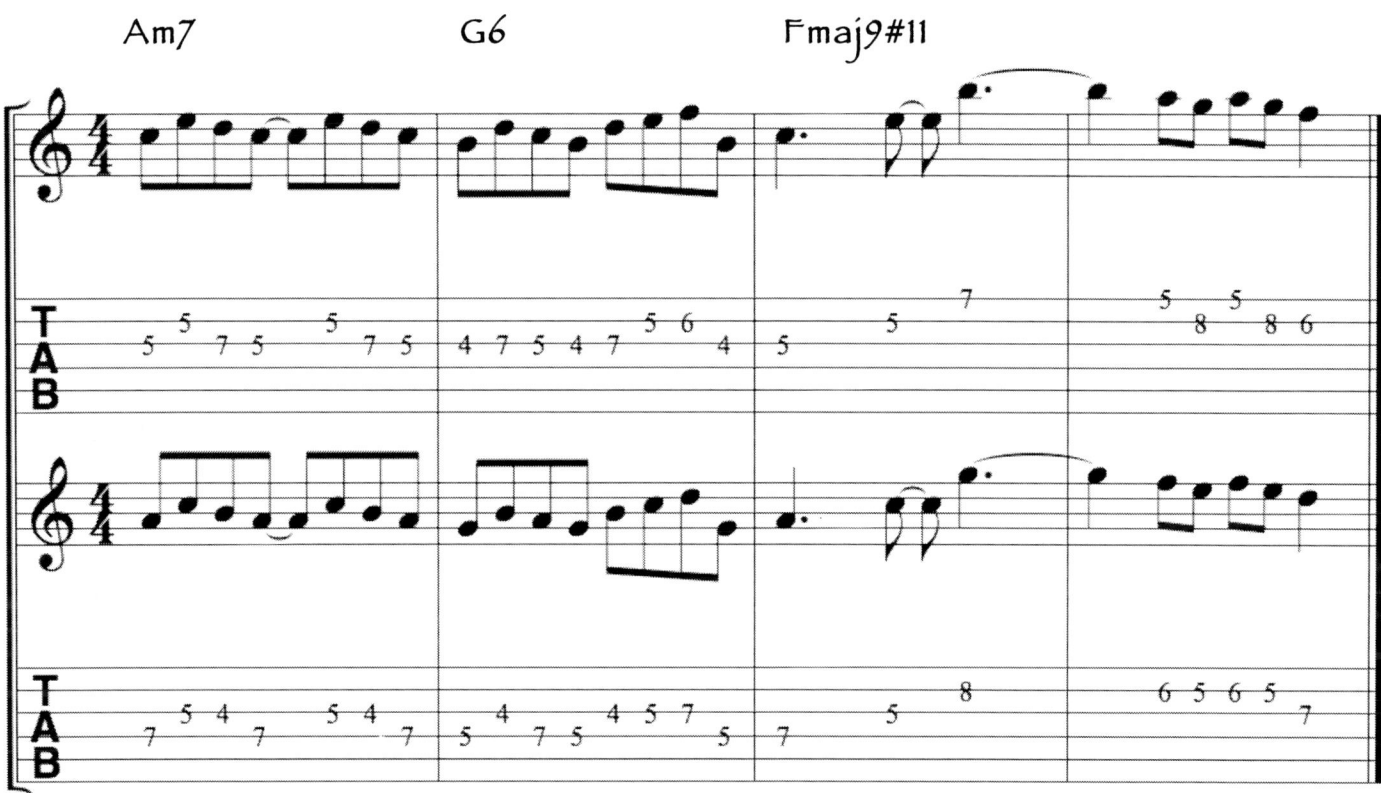

In the previous case, the notes produced by the harmony part worked well with the chords but in some cases, you won't be so lucky. The following example demonstrates the sort of problem that can occur with parallel harmony. The melody employs sustained use of the 2nd in relation to the underlying C chord. The upper harmony part winds up making sustained use of the 4th in relation to C, which when combined with the 2nd, takes us pretty far from the underlying harmony. Matters continue in a similar way when the same basic idea is related to an underlying Am chord. The D in the melody serves as a relatively acceptable 11th in relation to the Am but the F in the melody registers as a definite non-chord-tone.

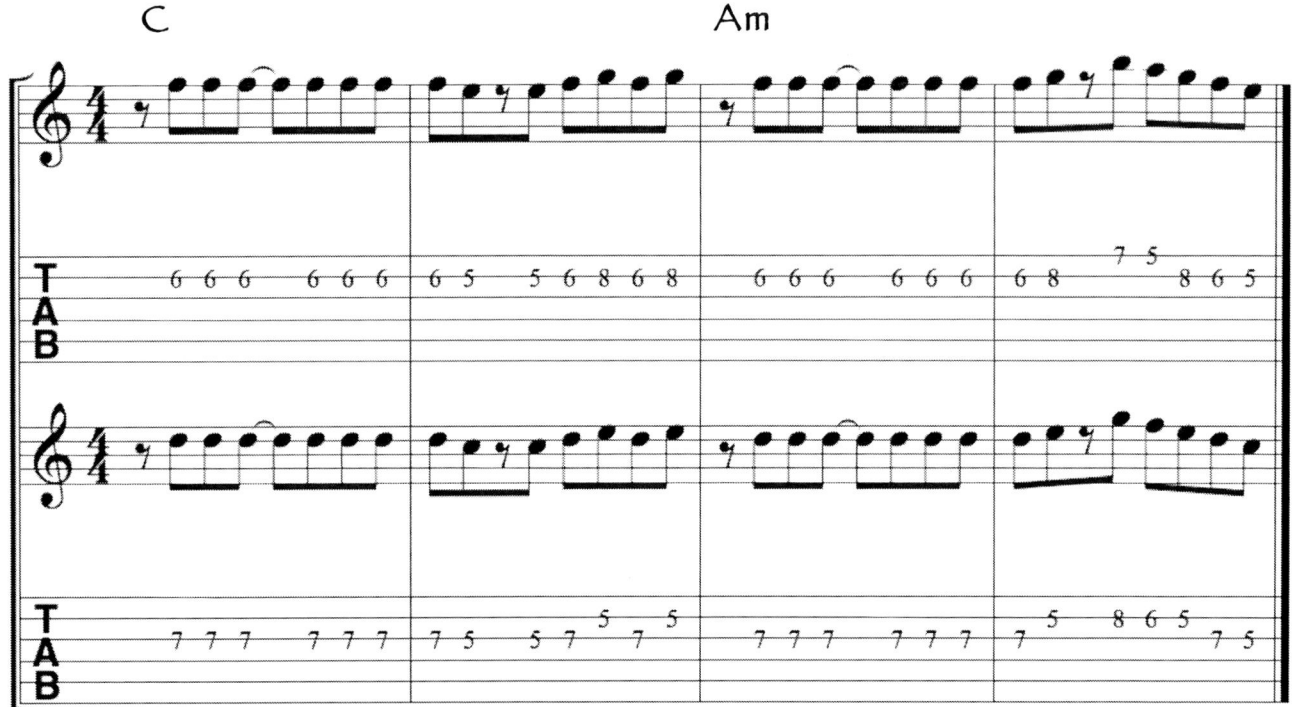

Below is an alternative harmonization where we've changed most of the F notes to G which relates as a 5th to the C chord and as a b7th to the Am chord. The F note at the beginning of bars 2 and 4 were maintained. This offers us some oblique motion between the two voices.

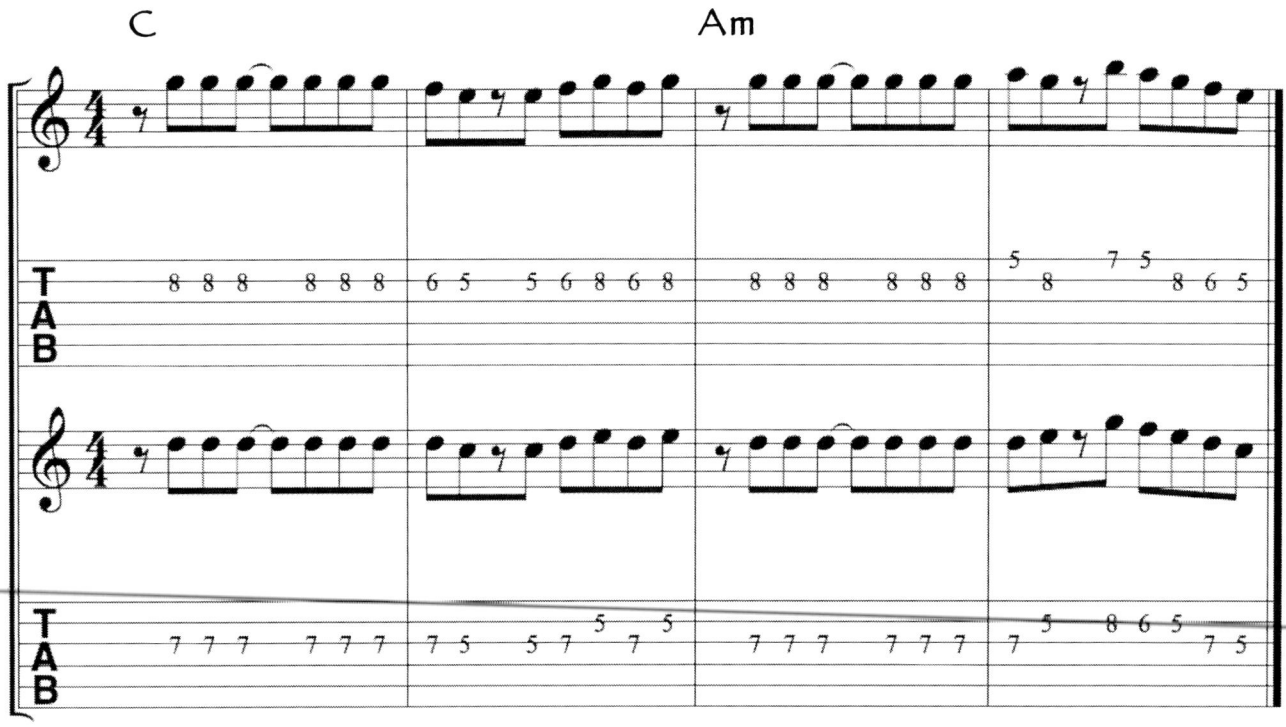

This method of adjusting crucial non-chord tones, while otherwise remaining with a parallel harmony, is what we call "adjusted parallel". It is very common in popular music. Parallel two-part harmony works best in imperfect consonances (major/minor 3rds and 6ths). Parallel perfect interval two-part harmonies (octaves, 4ths, 5ths) will sound thin and colorless in comparison but they sometimes get used as a special effect of sorts.

In three-part and four-part harmony, parallel 3rds and 6ths can overpower the underlying chord progression because each melody note will have an entire triad or 7th chord built off of it, and in many cases, these incidental chords will clash with your actual chords. Parallel 4ths and 5ths become more usable with an added voice or two. The result will sound very dense and colorful, though the combinations of notes will be ambiguous enough to rarely create a clash between harmonized melody and underlying chords. This has an unmistakably suspenseful modern jazz sounding effect and has limited application in pop music.

Here's a basic melody idea over a IIm7 V7 vamp:

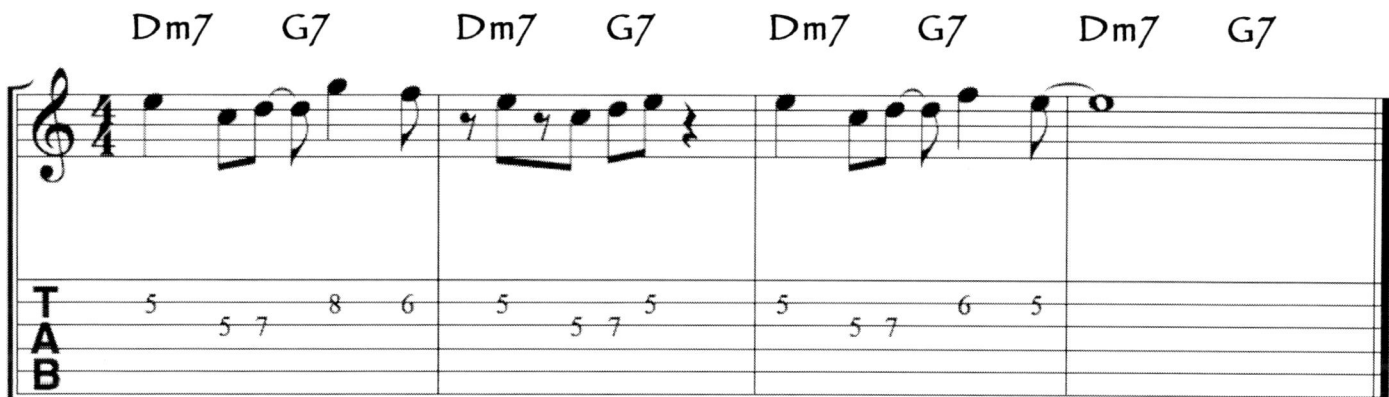

And here it is, transposed an octave higher, harmonized in four-part parallel 4ths:

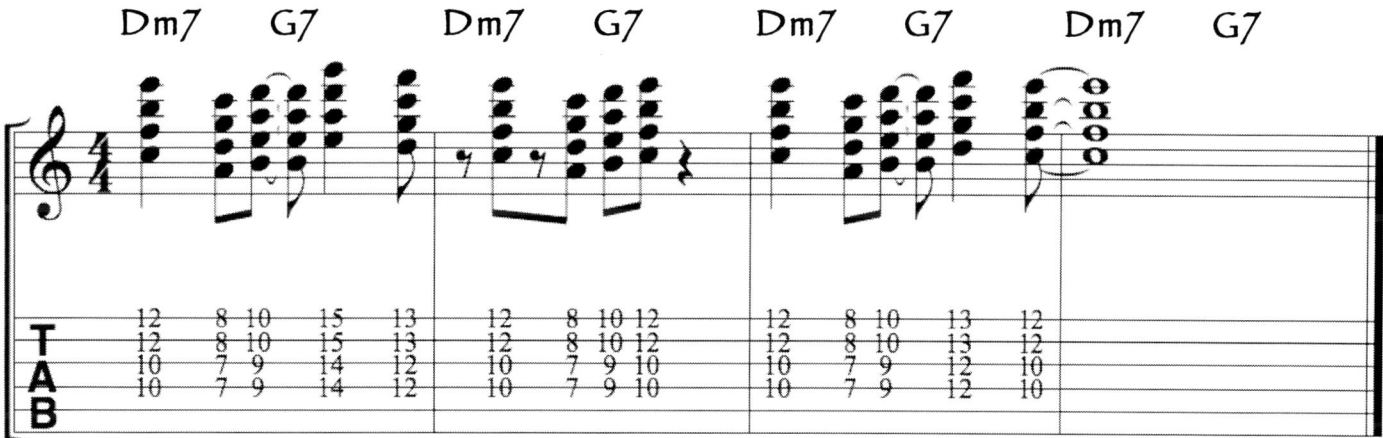

(Note: These harmony parts could also be distributed to three other guitars and multitracked. In this case, I arranged the harmony for one guitar in order to save some space.)

Modern block harmonization is a more intensive process. It requires that you fully understand the function of each note in your melody. It's also typically a much more rewarding process as the results are more musical. Let's look at a melody that makes use of all four types of melody notes and identify them. This is the first step in the modern block harmonization process.

Legend:
- O = Chord Tones
- X = Non-Chord/Non-Approach, Extended Tones
- S = Scale-Wise Passing Tones
- C = Chromatic Passing Tones
- » = In relation to following chord as an anticipation

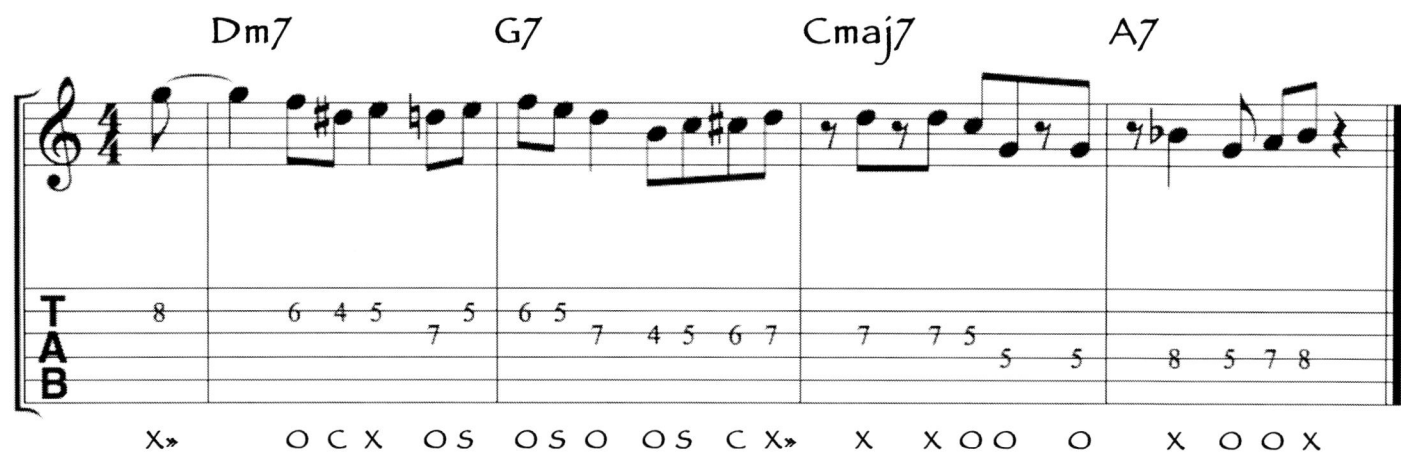

Now that we know which notes serve which roles, we need to know what the appropriate treatment is for each of these types of melody notes. These are the principles of modern block harmonization. These principles will help you to achieve some very solid and musically functional harmonizations. These guidelines can be altered to suit your own stylistic needs, but to have these principles as a core guide will help you immeasurably.

Before we can cover these, we need to know the principles of voice-leading. These principles are guides to help you achieve harmonies that allow the listener to clearly hear the independent melody lines that comprise them. When choices are made in conflict with these basic principles, we tend to run into clunky and confusing sounding material. Don't get me wrong, rules get broken, even and especially by the greatest of composers but never without a clear musical, artistic reason for doing so. A firm knowledge of these principles can only serve to musically strengthen not only your harmonization abilities, but also your melodic composition and improvisation abilities.

Principles of Voice-Leading:

1) When chords change, the voices playing/singing the notes that are common to both chords will remain static, upon the change. This will ensure that you employ a healthy amount of oblique motion and minimize the amount of motion required to follow the chords. This principle is also very useful as a melodic improvisation/composition concept.

2) Avoid the use of parallel perfect intervals (4ths, 5ths and octaves). You wind up with something that sounds more like one big, wide melody rather than a group of interdependent melodic lines. This is because the voices are all moving at exactly the same interval, and not only that, but these are the most consonant intervals. Sometimes we want the effect of one big, fat melody. In these cases, we obviously don't follow this guideline.

3) Avoid the crossing of voices within the harmony. In other words, a lower voice shouldn't arrive at a pitch higher than that of the upper voice's previous pitch. An upper voice should also not arrive at a pitch lower than the pitch just sounded by the voice beneath. Crossing voices confuses the ear with which notes comprise which voice and then each overlapping melodic line is lost on the listener. Though crossing voices causes a problem, overlapping voices doesn't and is sometimes necessary. A voice can arrive at a pitch that was just sounded by the voice above or below it.

4) In the top voice, avoid melodic leaps (anything more than a scale tone in either direction) to or from notes that harmonize as a perfect interval with the voice beneath. In instances where these upper leaps to or from consonant notes, it typically gets perceived by the ear to be a reduction in parts.

5) When working with triads in four-part writing, double the notes of the triads that serve as the root, 4th or 5th of the key. These are considered the tonal notes and when they are the doubled notes, we get a strong, tonally reinforced harmonization.

6) When moving from one perfect consonance (4th, 5th or octave) to another, proceed in contrary or oblique motion.

7) When moving from a perfect consonance to an imperfect consonance (3rd or 6th), use similar, oblique or contrary motion.

8) When moving from an imperfect consonance to a perfect consonance, proceed in oblique or contrary motion.

9) When moving from one imperfect consonance to another, proceed in any type of harmonic motion.

10) Avoid the tri-tone cross relationship. This occurs when the pitch of uppermost voice is a tritone away from the previous pitch of the lowest voice. Of all the voice-leading principles, this is the one that I find to be the least important.

Principles of Modern Block Harmonization

1) Make use of voice-leading principles. You won't find yourself abiding by every rule, every time, but a general adherence to these guidelines will allow you to avoid many pitfalls.

2) Any chord-tone within the melody can be harmonized with other chord tones. This simply reinforces the sense of the underlying chord and adds strength to the tonality.

3) Non-chord/non-passing/extended tones are harmonized with chord tones, omitting the nearest chord tone to it. This helps you avoid harsh dissonances within the harmony. Sometimes, these clustered notes can have quite a nice effect. In these cases, if we want to take advantage of that sound, we can omit the next note down in the chord instead. Approaching tones that are on strong-beats and last for at least a beat, fall into this category.

4) Harmonize any scale-wise passing-tone to it's very own dim7 chord. For instance, if we were on a C chord and the melody used an F note as a passing tone between the 3rd and 5th, we can harmonize it to an Fdim7 chord. This has a classic sort of effect that can be heard anywhere from Duke Ellington to Queen and beyond. A somewhat more common approach, these days, is to harmonize scale-wise passing-tones to another chord diatonic to the key but sharing no more than one common tone with the underlying chord. We can call these diatonic counter-chords.

5) A chromatic passing tone is harmonized as a member of a chromatic passing chord of the same direction. For instance, if we we're on a C chord and we used F# as a chromatic passing tone to G as the 5th of our chord, we would harmonize the F# note to a B chord and all the notes would lead up by a half-step to become members of the C chord. This is a good example of a situation where the guidelines concerning the avoidance of parallel motion don't really apply.

6) On any note that serves as an anticipation note to the following chord, harmonize the anticipation note to the following chord rather than the current chord. This gives the harmony parts the same amount of forward motion that is perceived in the melody.

Now that we've gone over the guidelines of voice-leading and block-harmonization, we're ready to put them to work. We'll take the previous melodic example and harmonize it according to these guidelines, attempting to maintain judicious balance between our block-harmonization principles and our voice leading principles.

I've presented it on four staves in standard notation, followed by the same thing on four staves in tablature. Multitrack these parts to a click track and you won't even need chords behind it in order to hear the richness of the harmony.

It gets a little muddy at the bottom, towards the end of the harmony. The next thing we might try is moving the whole melody and harmonization up by an octave:

These examples are made up of what we call closed voicings, which means that these voices are as close together as they can get. When we take it an octave higher, things sound a little thin. We can expand this harmony into what we call open voicings by the simple act of taking the second voice from the top and moving it down by an octave. This is also known as a drop-2 harmony. This can be applied to any sort of three or four-part harmony. It'll give our melody a bright, yet wide quality.

This particular example that we're working with is a rather jazzy example but this is less because of the block harmonization and more because of the fact that we started with a jazzy melody over a jazzy chord progression. If we had started with a pop oriented melody and changes, there would be less chromaticism happening in the harmony parts. Modern block harmonization will conform to whatever the style of the melody and changes are, in most cases.

There are four simple measures that you can take when writing to ensure that your melodies will be naturally playable on most instruments and singable for the average singer, not to mention easy to harmonize and add background parts beneath:

Four Tips on Writing Workable Melodies

1) Keep the melody within an octave, ideally but no more than an octave plus a 3rd. This will ensure that every singer will find an ideal key in which to sing it and will also ensure sonic space for a four-part harmony beneath it.

2) Use a minimal amount of melodic leaps within the melody. You certainly want one or two but too many leaps make for a very hairy harmonization situation and they're rough on the human voice and most brass instruments.

3) Make judicious use of rests and longer notes since these elements leave space for voices, winds and brass to breath. These spaces also come in handy when it comes time to write a background part.

4) Use motives with strongly identifiable rhythmic features, as these will be much more useful in developing related material for a background.

Now that you're familiar with the basic concepts of harmonization, be sure to spend lots of time harmonizing melodies, in order for you to grow totally comfortable with the process. Start with very simple melodies and work your way onto more complex melodies. Any single melody can be harmonized a number of different ways. Experiment as much as possible, as there are worlds yet unknown to be discovered. These techniques can be applied to horn-sections, string-sections, background vocals and choirs, guitars, synths, etc. A person with a strong and confident ability to compose harmony parts and orchestrate them is a valuable member to any band.

BACKGROUND WRITING – The Art of the Counter-Melody

Background writing is the process of writing a melody that works simultaneously with the original melody in both contrasting and complimentary ways. This is known as counterpoint. A relatively simple musical context can be fleshed out to become a rather elaborate soundscape simply by adding some harmonization and counterpoint. We can also add harmonization to our countermelody once it's in place. We're going to look at a few simple guidelines that will allow you to avoid many of the common pitfalls associated with background writing.

1) When the melody employs shorter notes and busier rhythms, employ long, sustained notes in the counter-melody. When the melody makes use of long, sustained notes, employ shorter notes and busier rhythms in the counter-melody. This will ensure a balance between both melodic lines.

2) When changing from chord to chord, use step wise motion just as you would in writing a harmony part. While you're on a chord, leaps may occur, but avoid them upon changing chords, especially if the change is non-diatonic. This just helps with creating a sense of connection between harmony and counter-melody.

3) In places where a melody-note and counter-melody note sound simultaneously, keep the two notes at least a 3rd apart from one another but no more than an octave apart. This helps prevent a sense of crowdedness or sparseness between the melody and counter-melody. If crowdedness or sparseness are a desired artistic effect for a particular passage, this guideline can be disregarded, but you typically won't want to do this for an extended period, as it will in fact anger the listener.

4) In places where the melody and counter-melody notes don't attack simultaneously, the two parts may cross above or below each other. In all other cases, much care should be taken to prevent the two parts from crossing. A background part can bob and weave above and below the melody as long as you take advantages of the melody's long notes and rests as opportunities to cross.

5) Apply the four tips on writing workable melodies from the previous section to your counter-melodies. This will ensure that you will have an easy time harmonizing your background.

On the following pages are a couple examples of counterpoint between melodies and backgrounds. The melodies are written on the top staff and the backgrounds are written beneath.

Counter-Melody Example 1:

Counter-Melody Example 2:

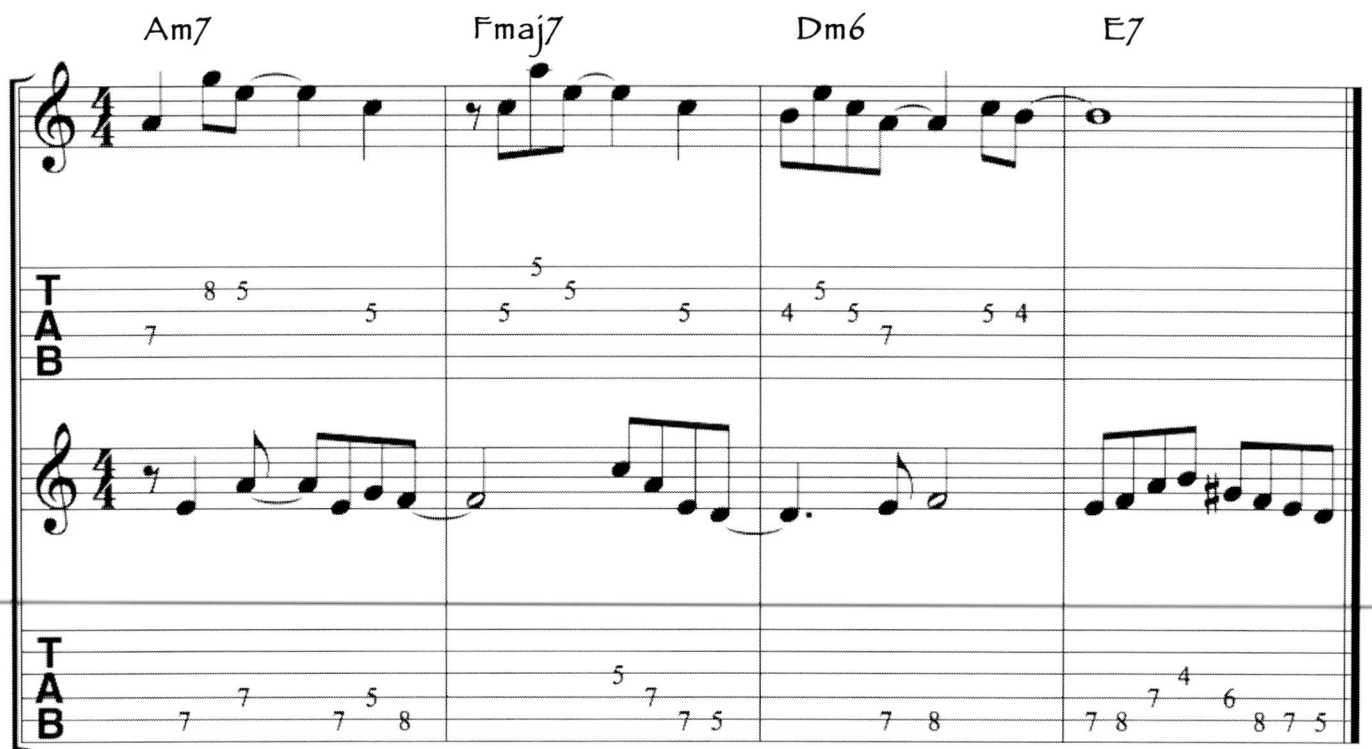

Counter-Melody Example 3: (Note the opposing rhythms employed in this one.)

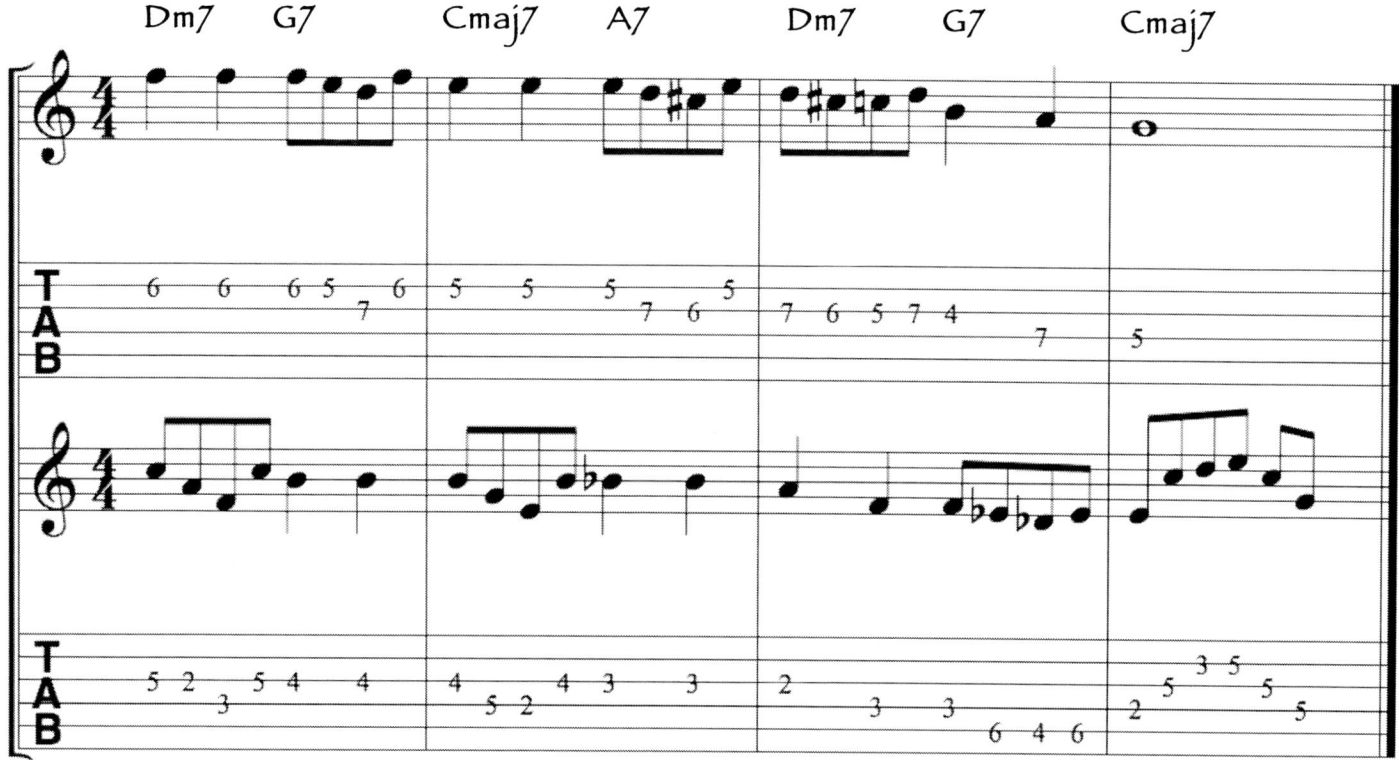

And now with a harmonized background. It's a little tricky but playable with a little practice:

About the Author

Geoff Stockton was born in Ann Arbor, MI, October 15th of 1977. At age 11, he picked up the guitar with the help of his father, uncles and family friends. He has led and played with many talented local bands throughout southern Michigan and remained a devoted student of music throughout. For the past ten years, Geoff Stockton has lived in Kalamazoo, MI, supporting his family as a local musician and educator. "I love Kalamazoo. There's a lot of music history in this little town and it's home to all kinds of people." A prolific writer of original music in many styles, Geoff continues to grow as a self-sufficient home-producer and plans to start releasing albums of his material, independently as soon as his recordings are meeting his own standards.

Positional Sight-Reading Reference

C major/A minor, Open Position:

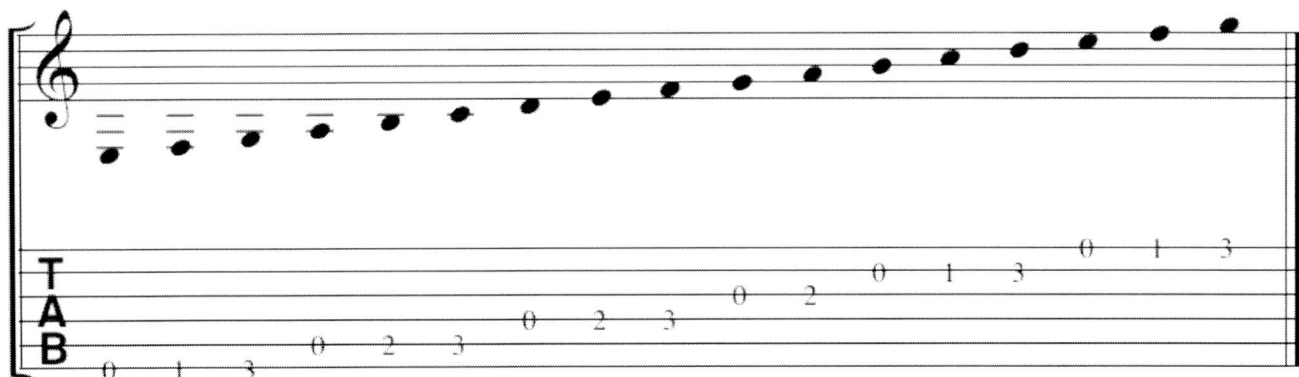

G major/E minor, Open Position:

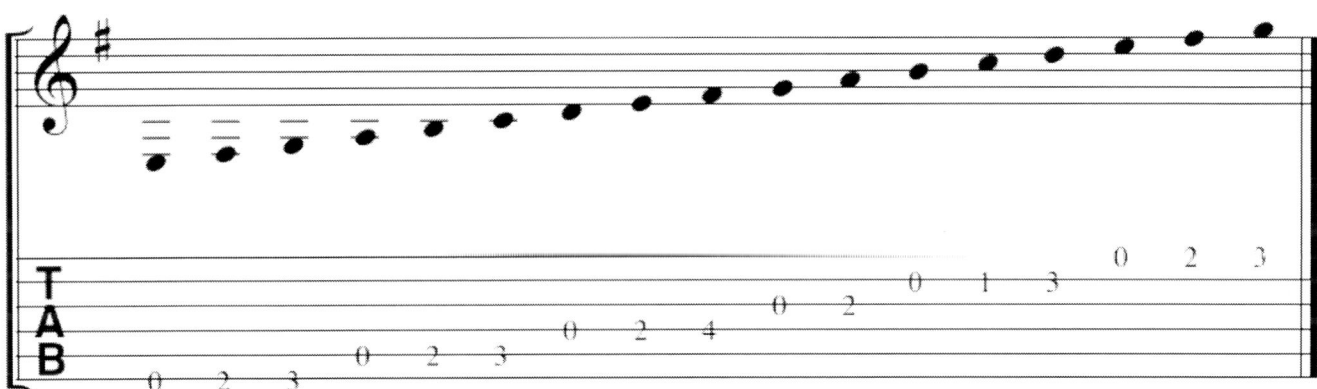

D major/B minor, Open Position:

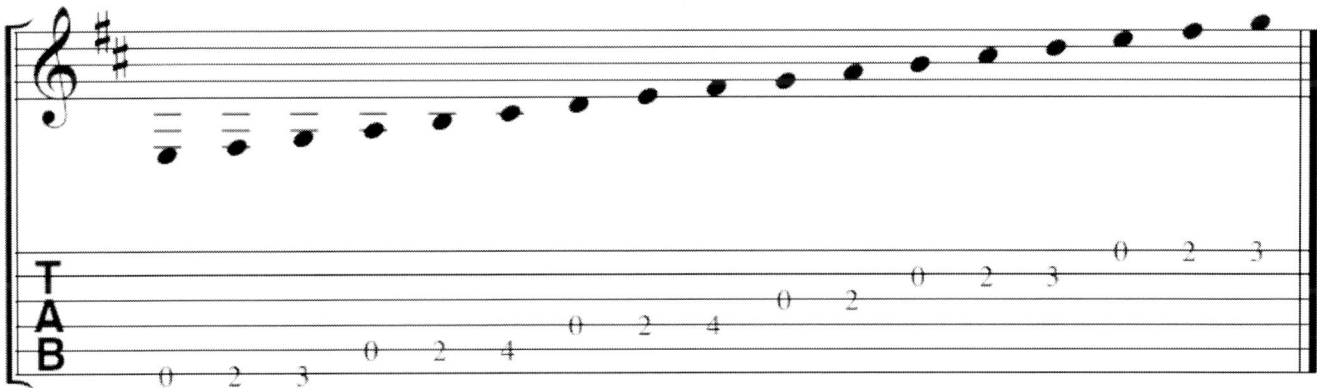

A major/F# minor, Open Position:

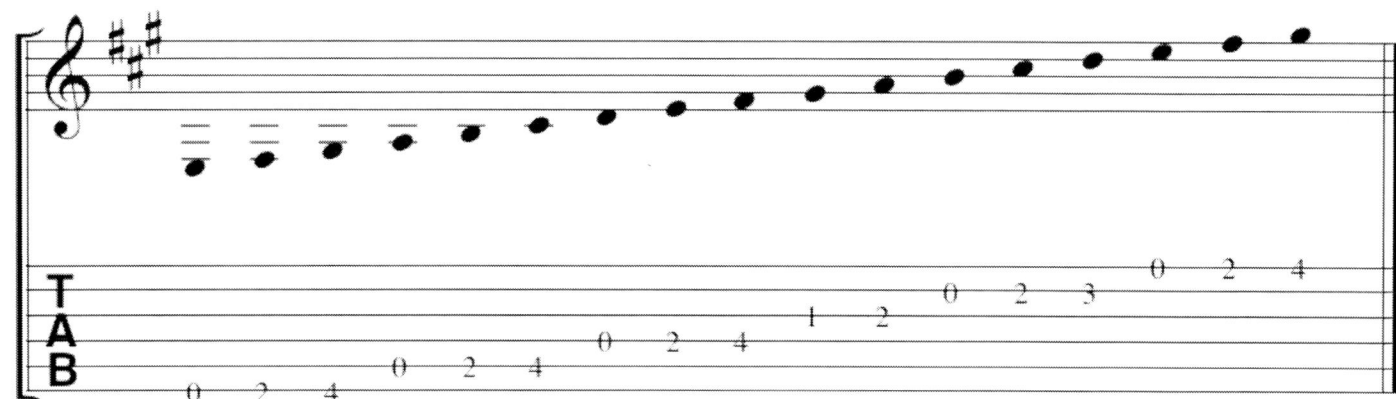

E major/C# minor, Open Position:

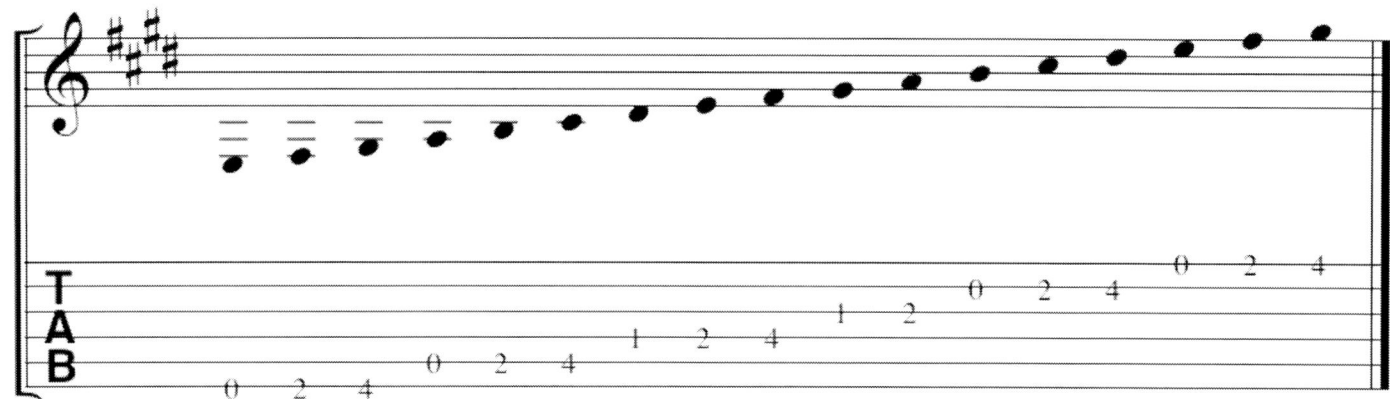

B major/G# minor, Open Position:

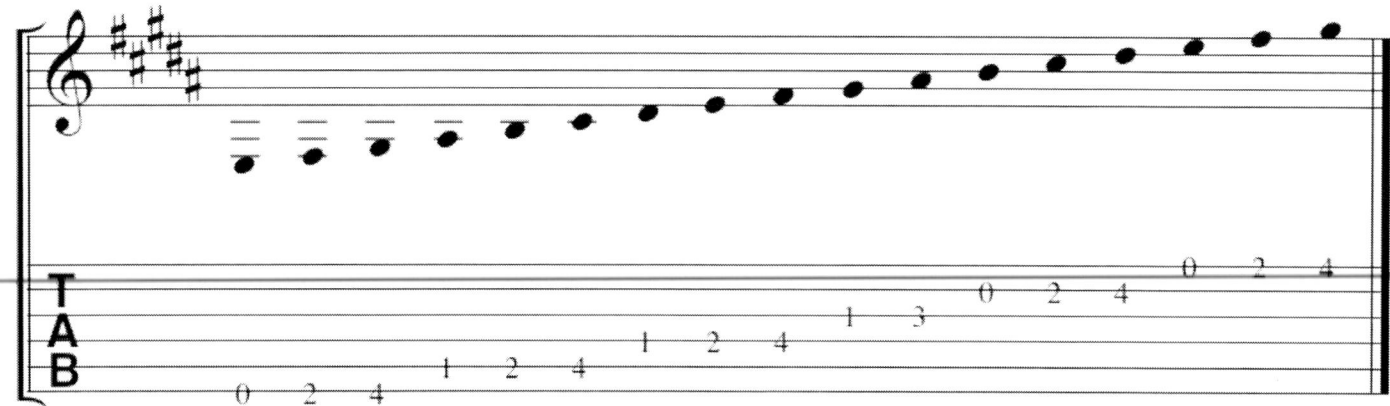

Gb major/Eb minor, Open Position:

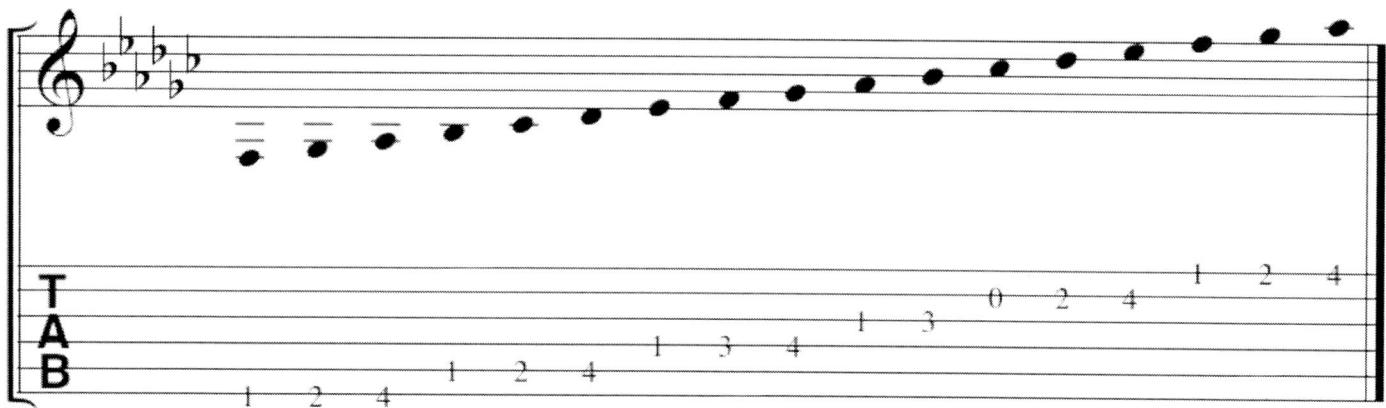

Db major/Bb minor, Open Position:

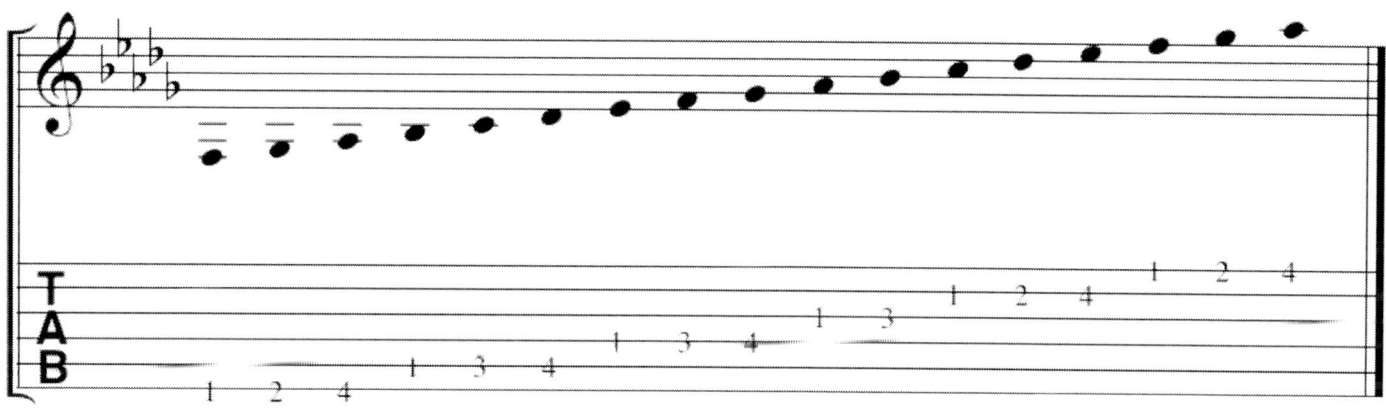

Ab major/F minor, Open Position:

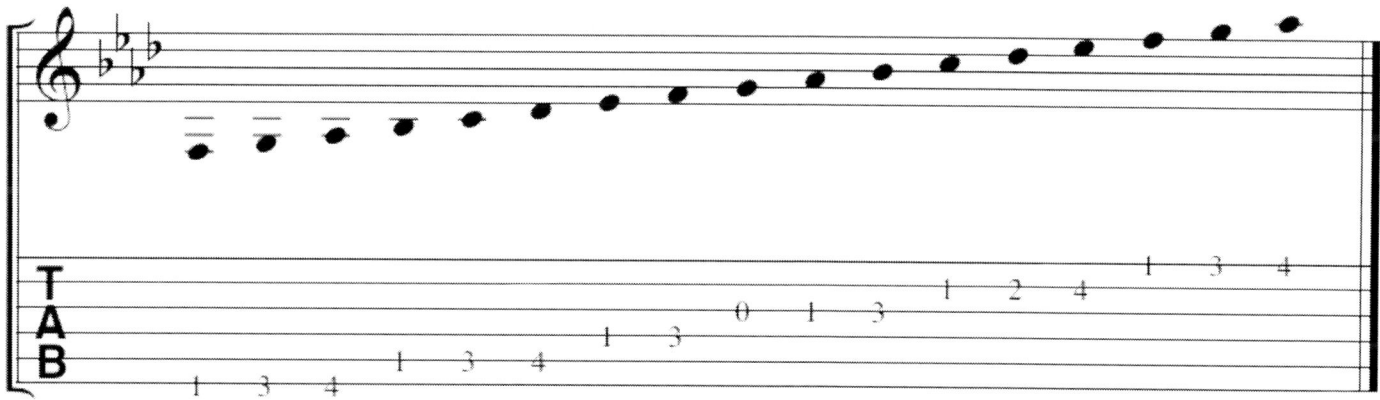

Eb major/C minor, Open Position:

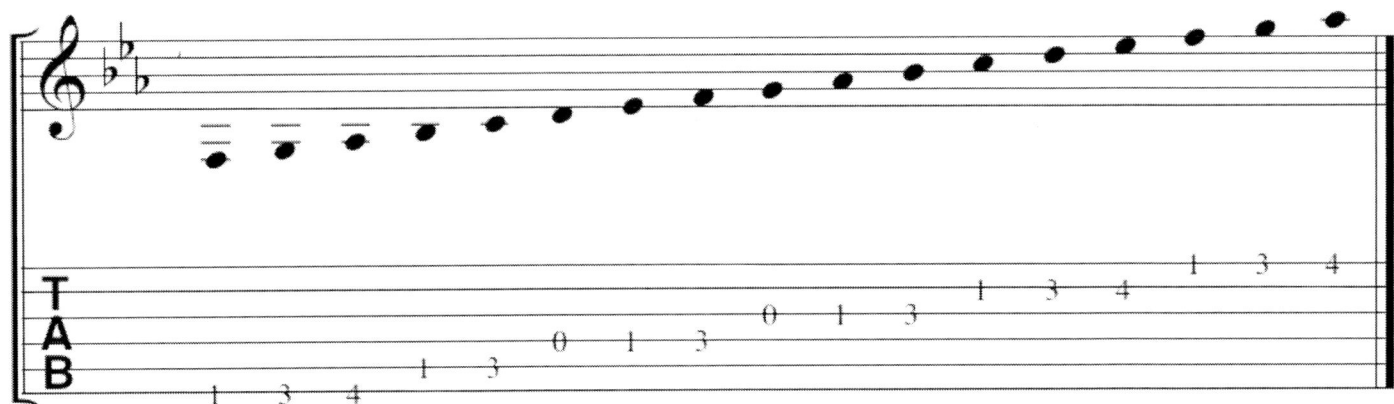

Bb major/G minor, Open Position:

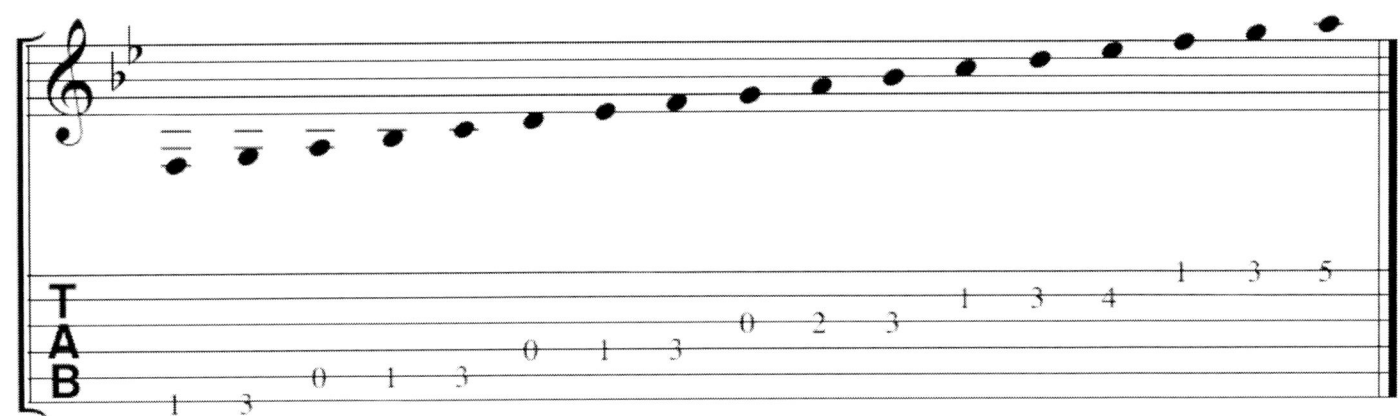

F major/D minor, Open Position:

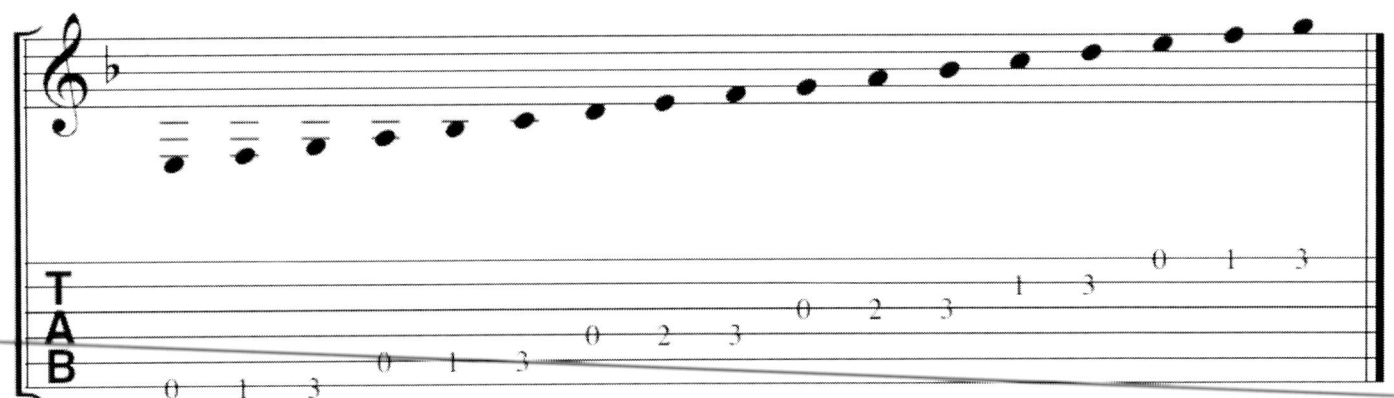

C major/A minor at the 3rd fret:

G major/E minor at the 3rd fret:

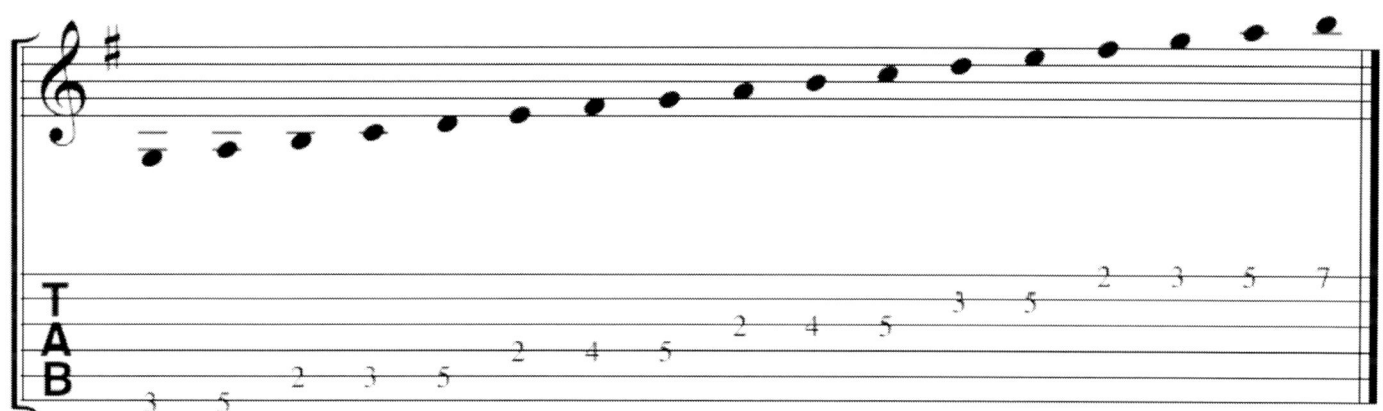

D major/B minor at the 3rd fret:

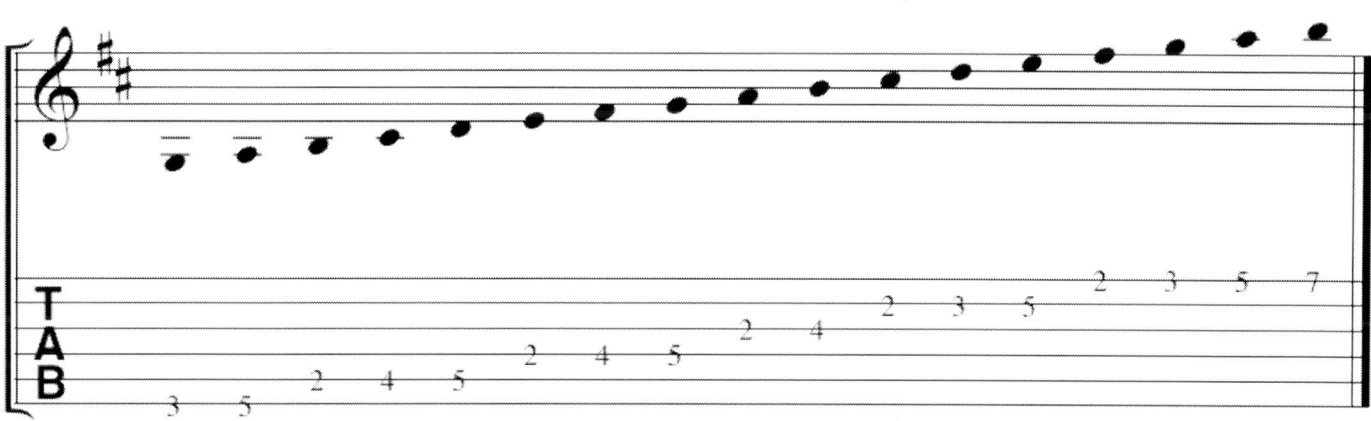

A major/F# minor at the 3rd fret:

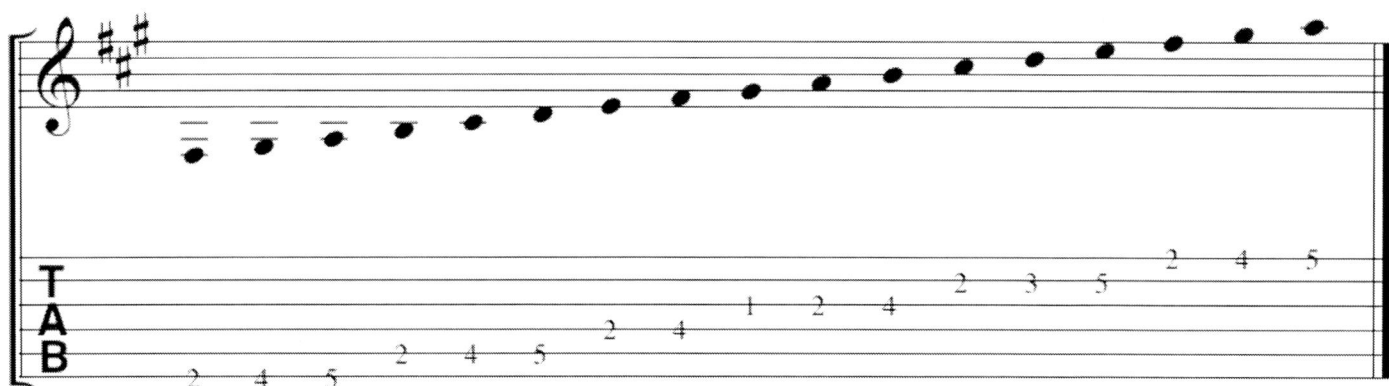

E major/C# minor at the 3rd fret:

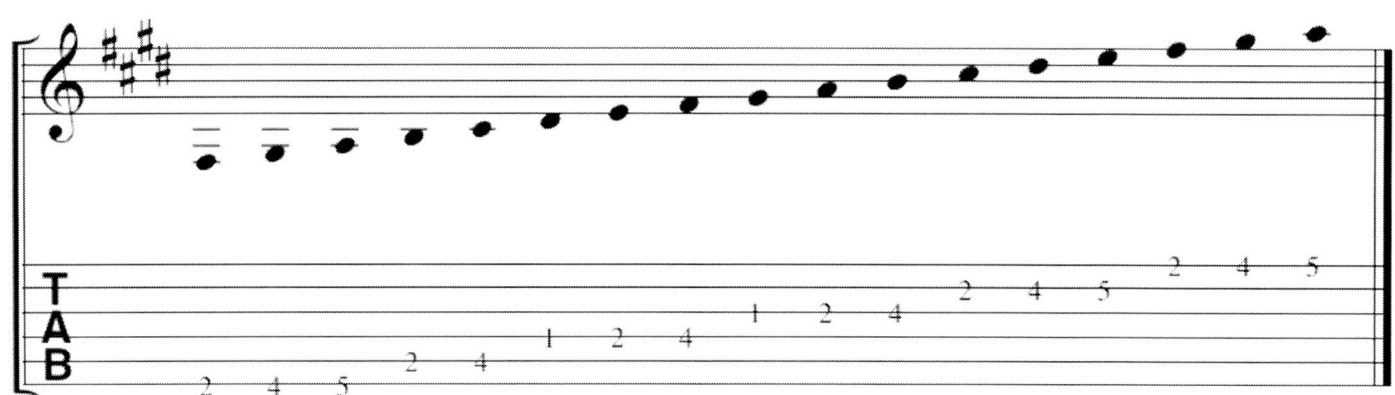

B major/G# minor at the 3rd fret:

Gb major/Eb minor at the 3rd fret:

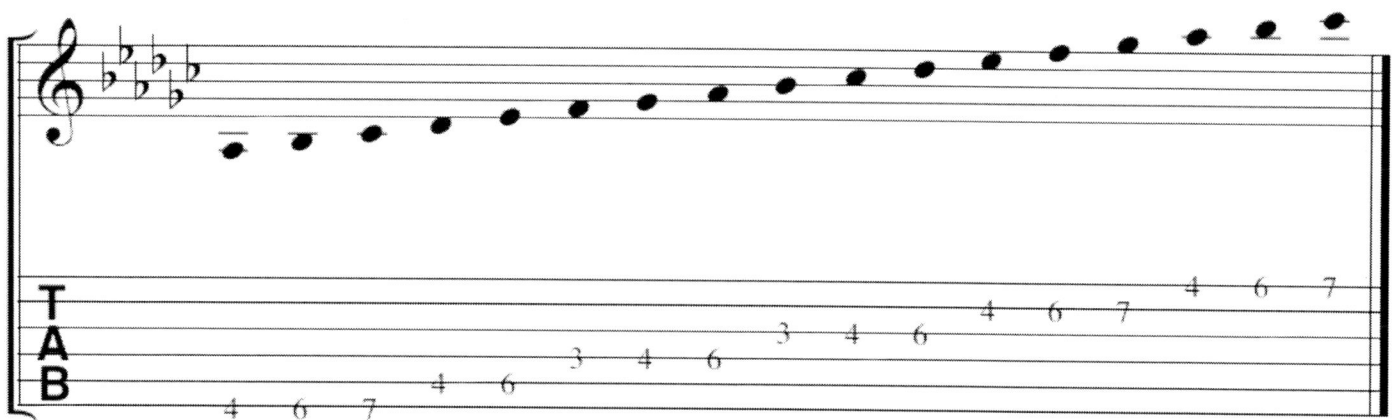

Db major/Bb minor at the 3rd fret:

Ab major/F minor at the 3rd fret:

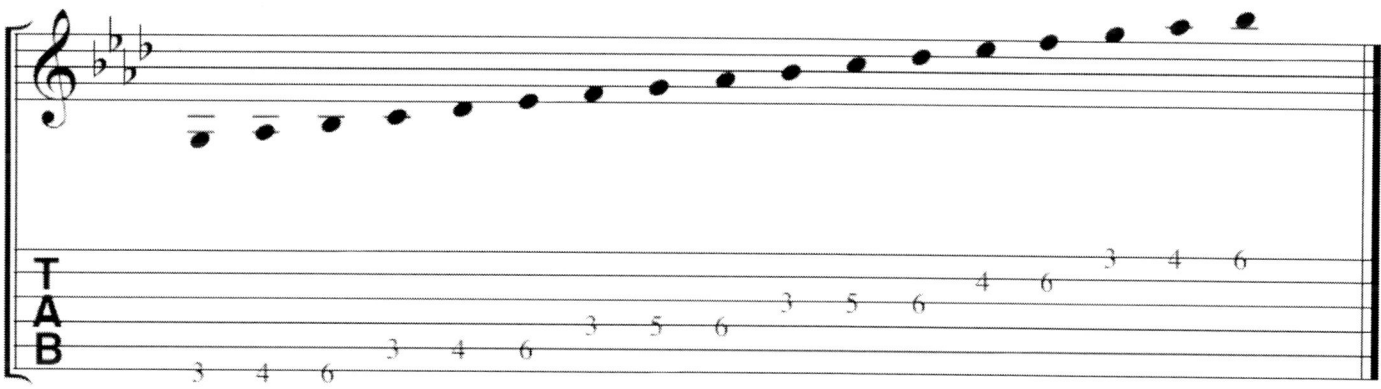

Eb major/C minor at the 3rd fret:

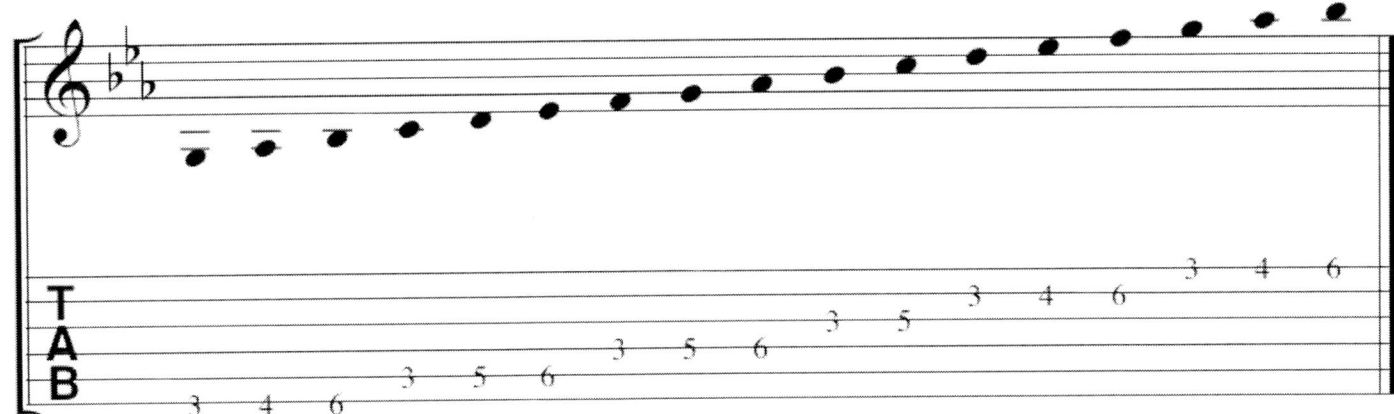

Bb major/G minor at the 3rd fret:

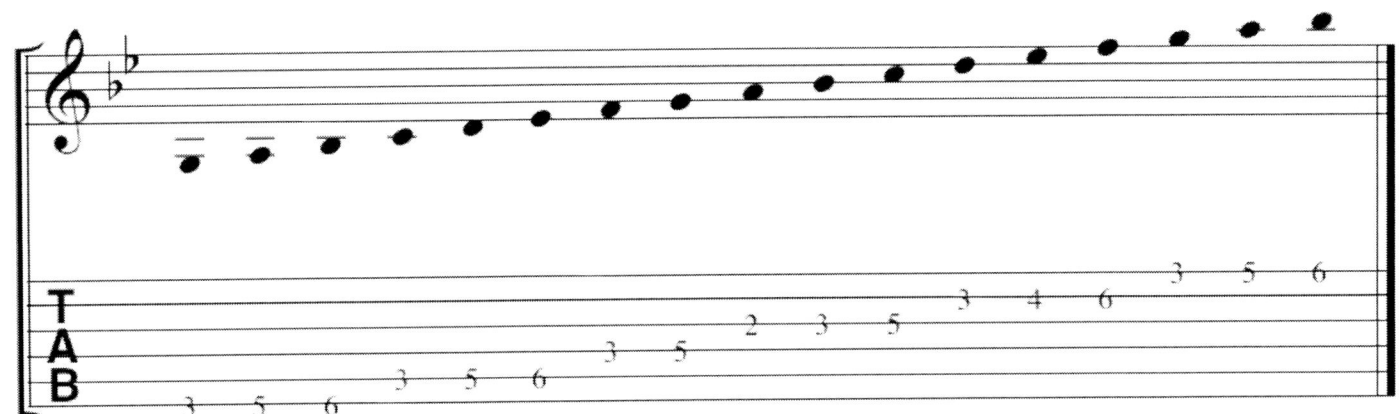

F major/D minor at the 3rd fret:

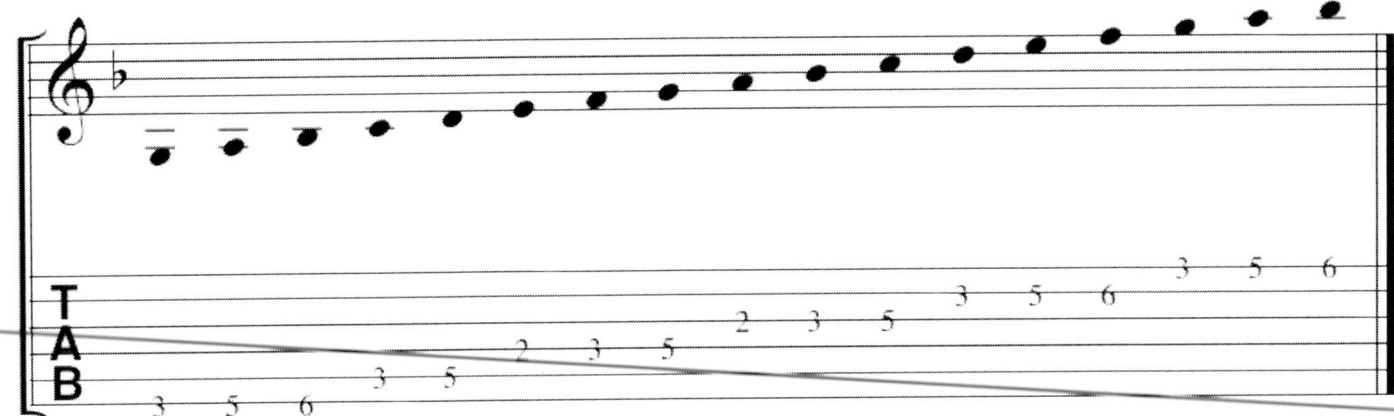

C major/A minor at the 5th fret:

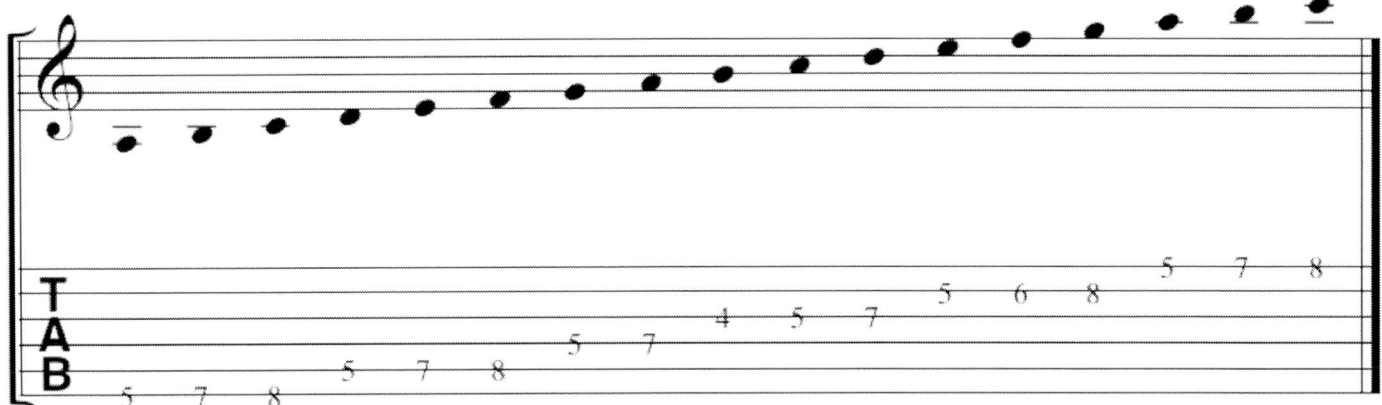

G major/E minor at the 5th fret:

D major/B minor at the 5th fret:

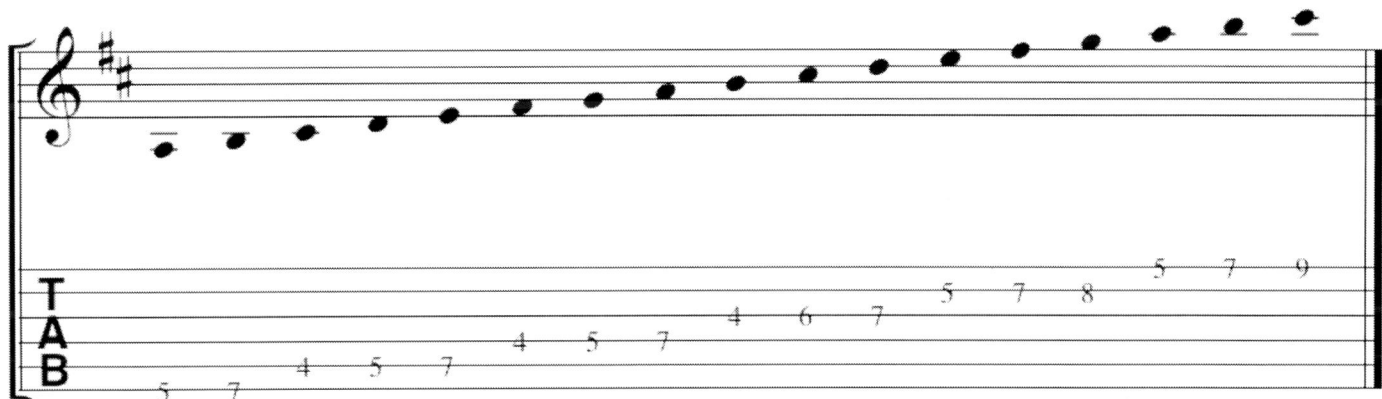

A major/F# minor at the 5th fret:

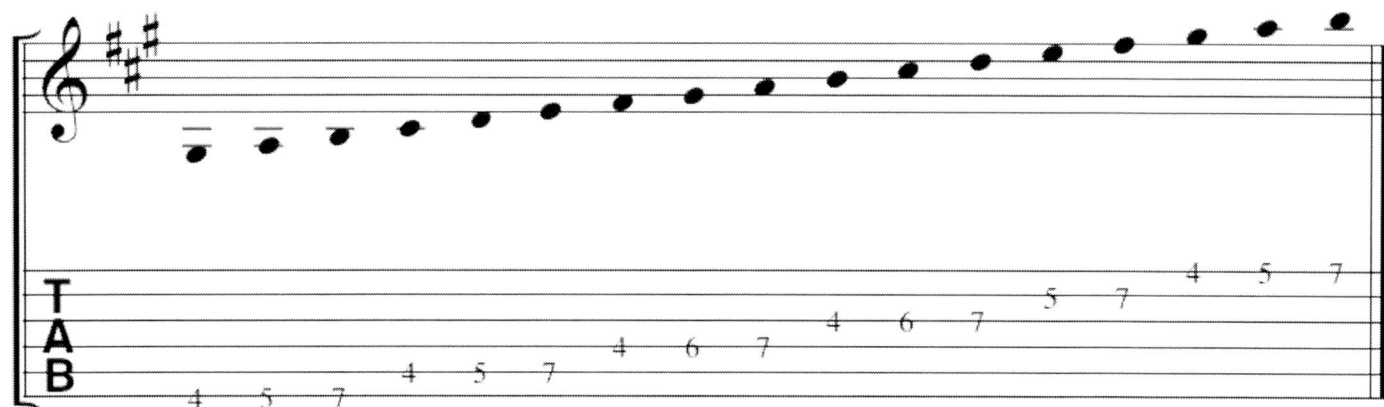

E major/C# minor at the 5th fret:

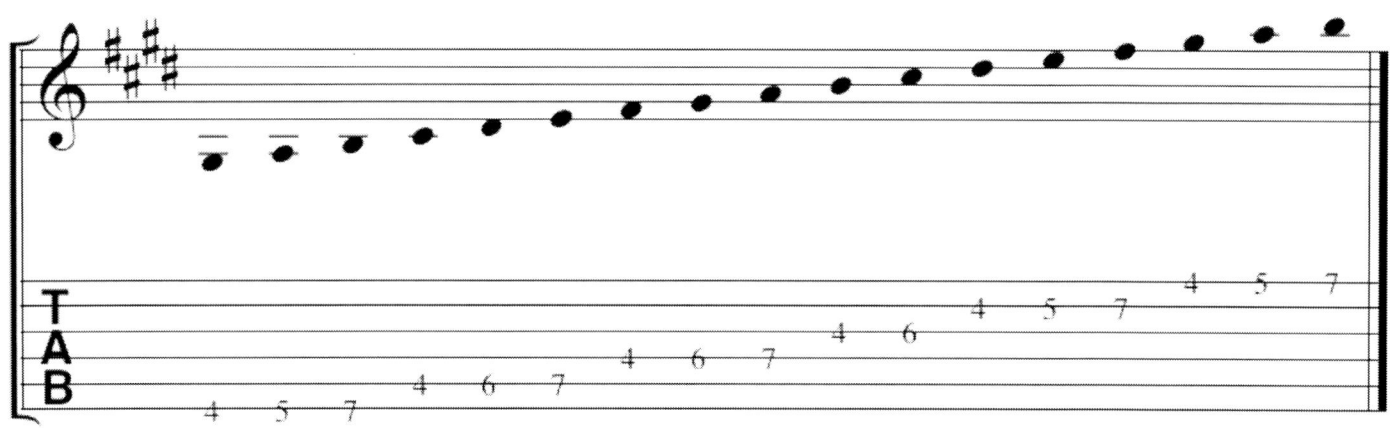

B major/G# minor at the 5th fret:

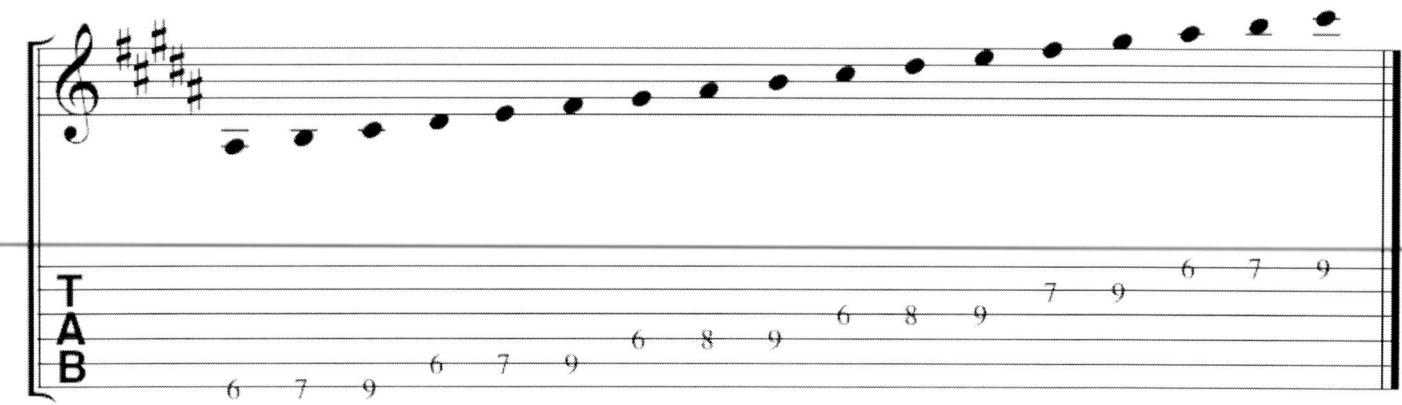

Gb major/Eb minor at the 5th fret:

Db major/Bb minor at the 5th fret:

Ab major/F minor at the 5th fret:

Eb major/C minor at the 5th fret:

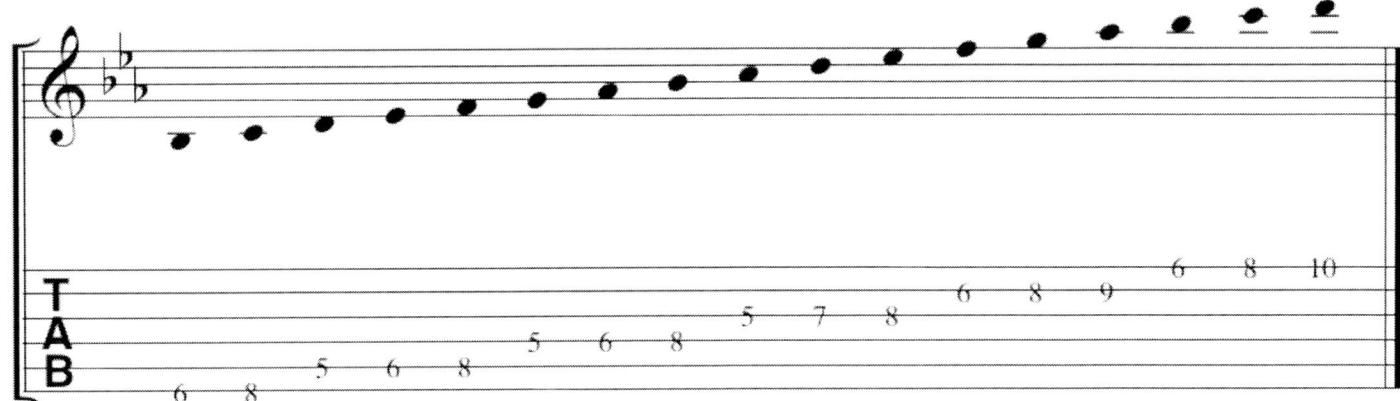

Bb major/G minor at the 5th fret:

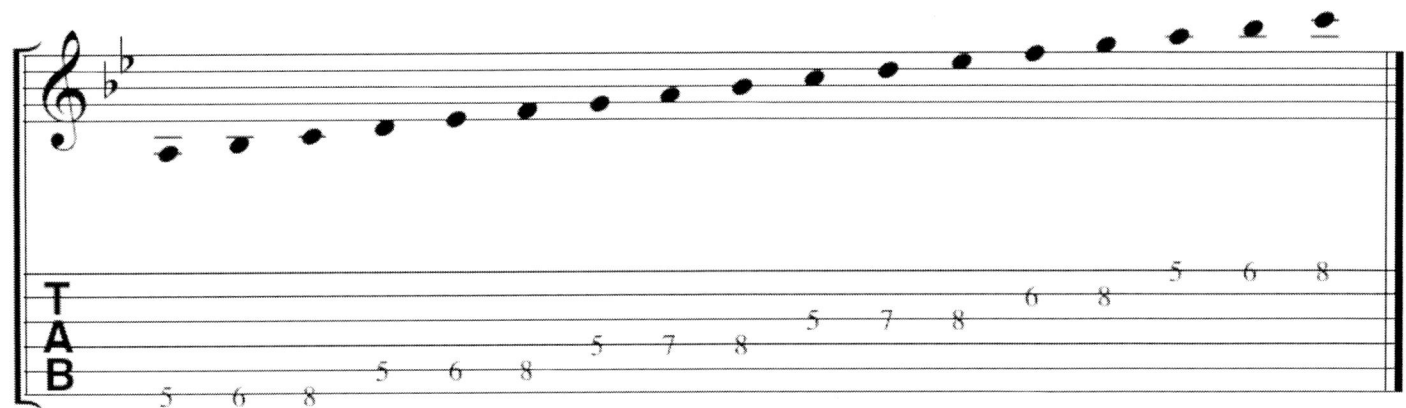

F major/D minor at the 5th fret:

C major/A minor at the 7th fret:

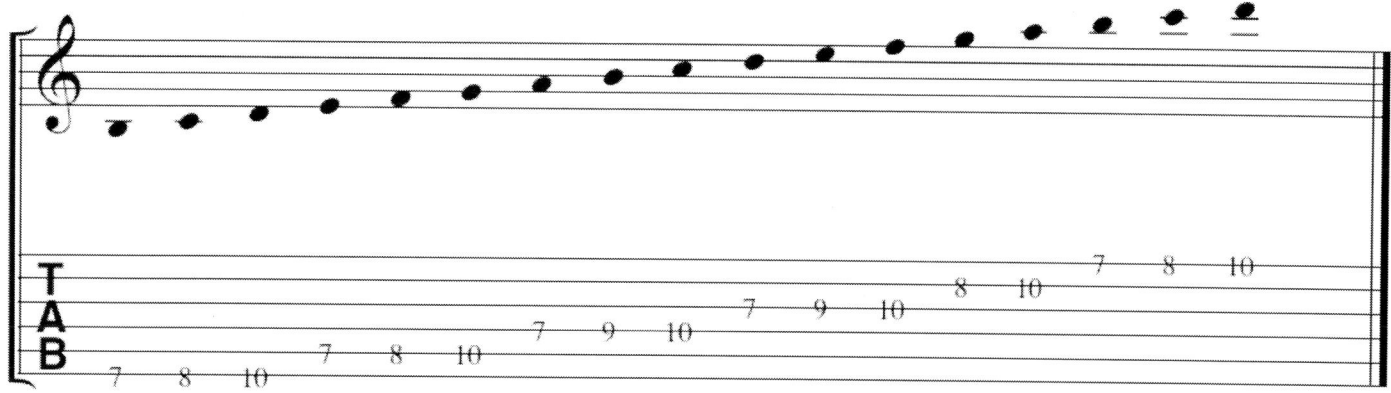

G major/E minor at the 7th fret:

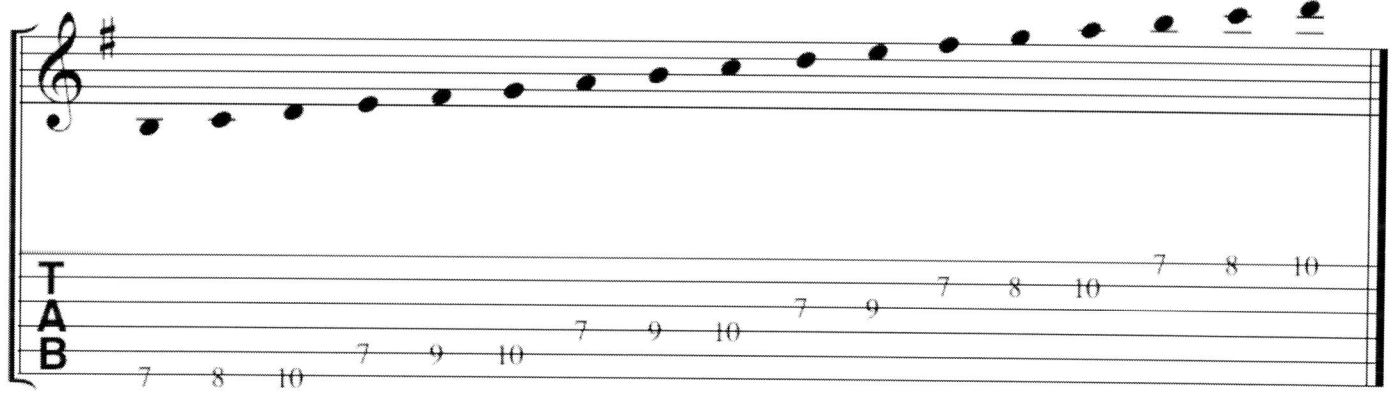

D major/B minor at the 7th fret:

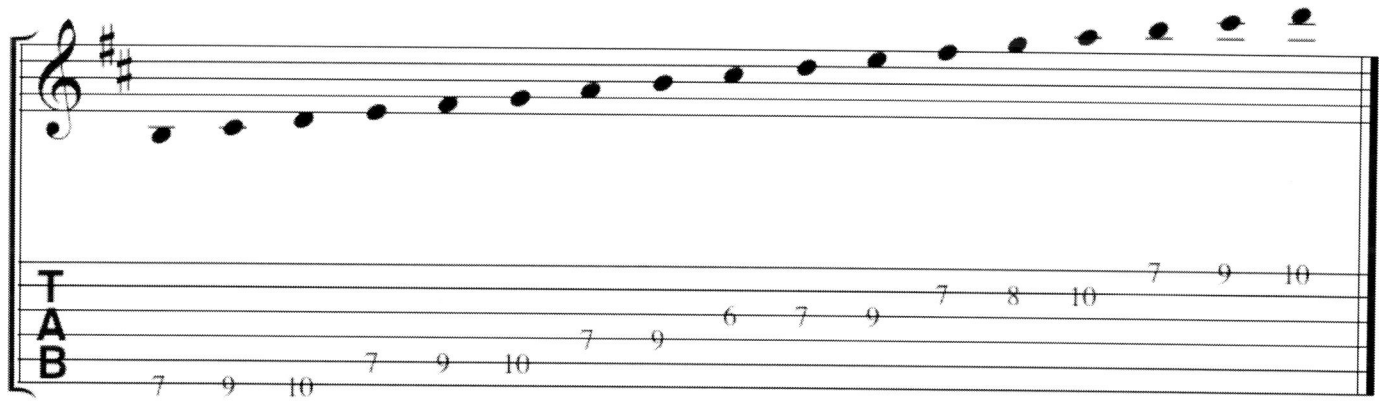

A major/F# minor at the 7th fret:

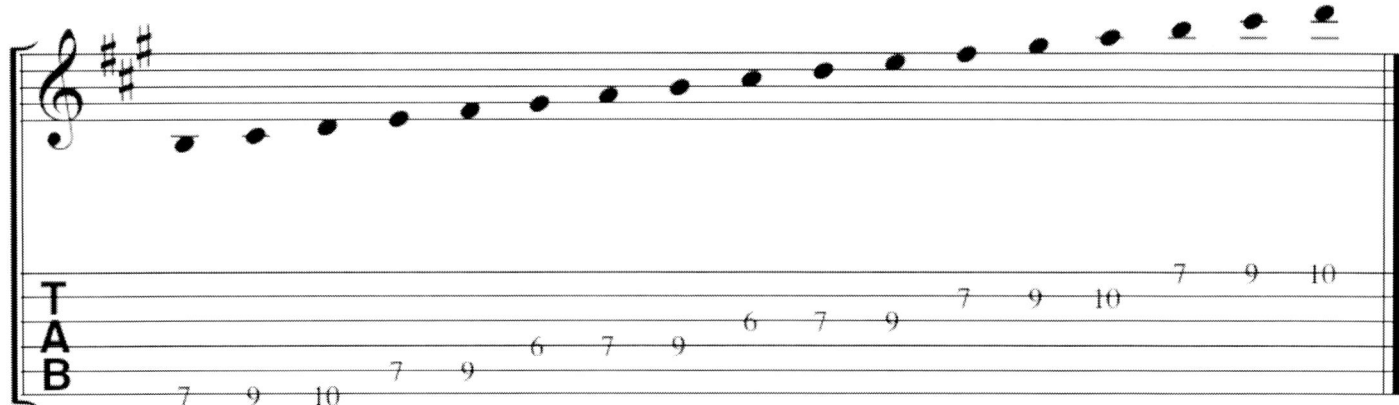

E major/C# minor at the 7th fret:

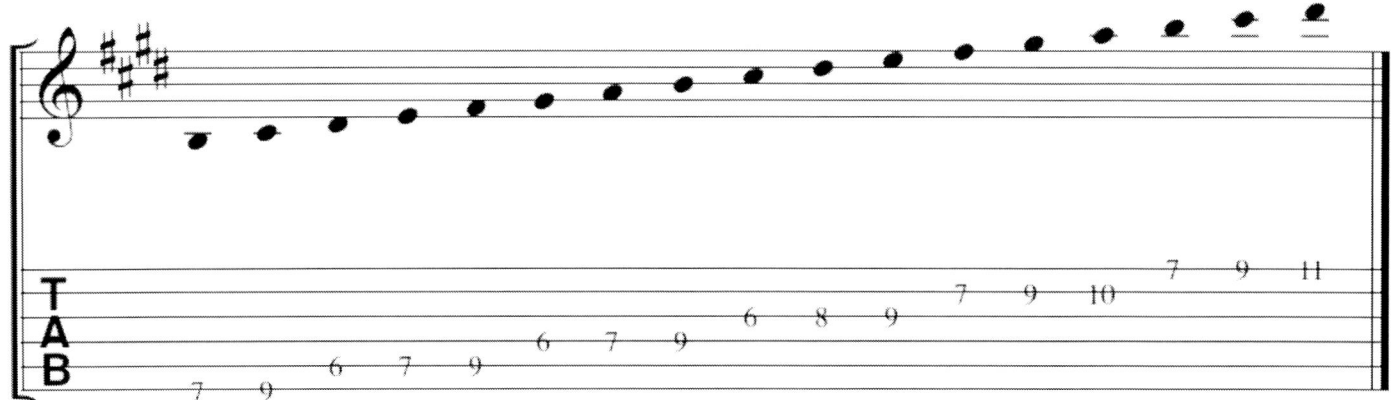

B major/G# minor at the 7th fret:

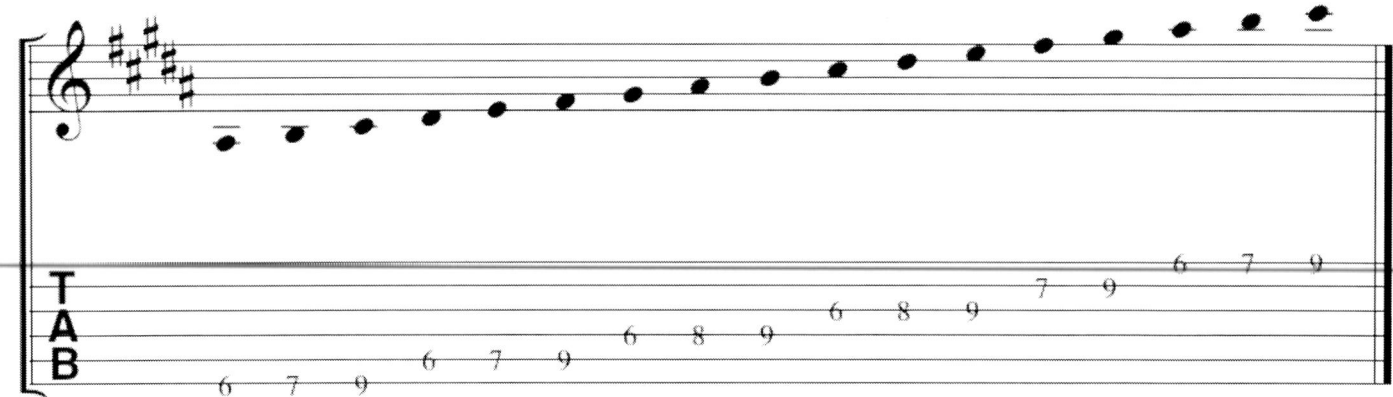

Gb major/Eb minor at the 7th fret:

Db major/Bb minor at the 7th fret:

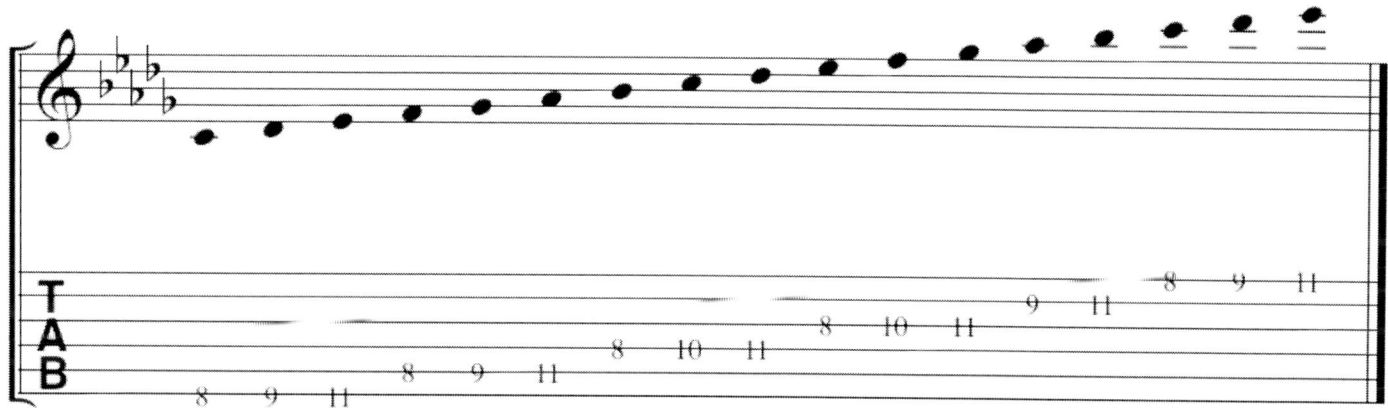

Ab major/F minor at the 7th fret:

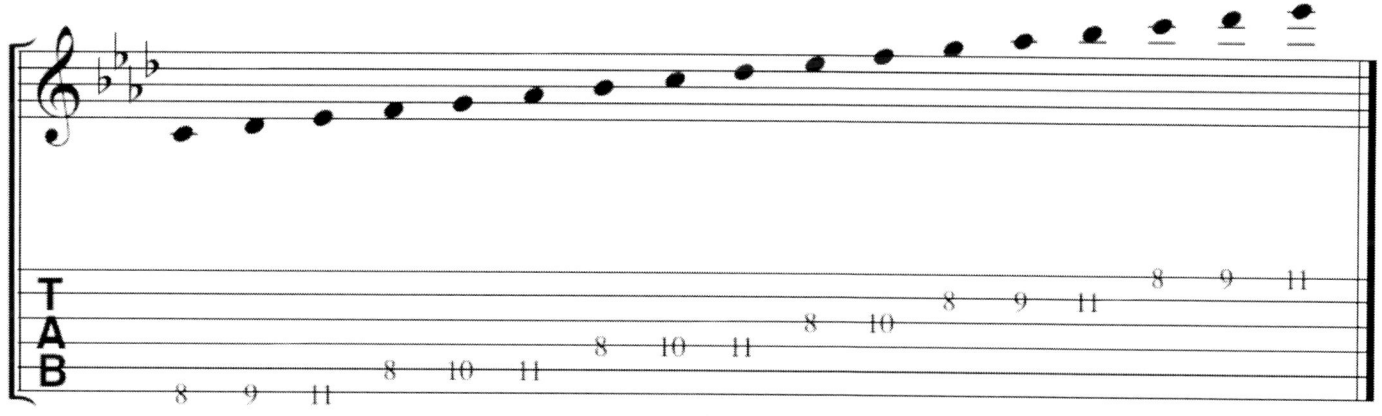

Eb major/C minor at the 7th fret:

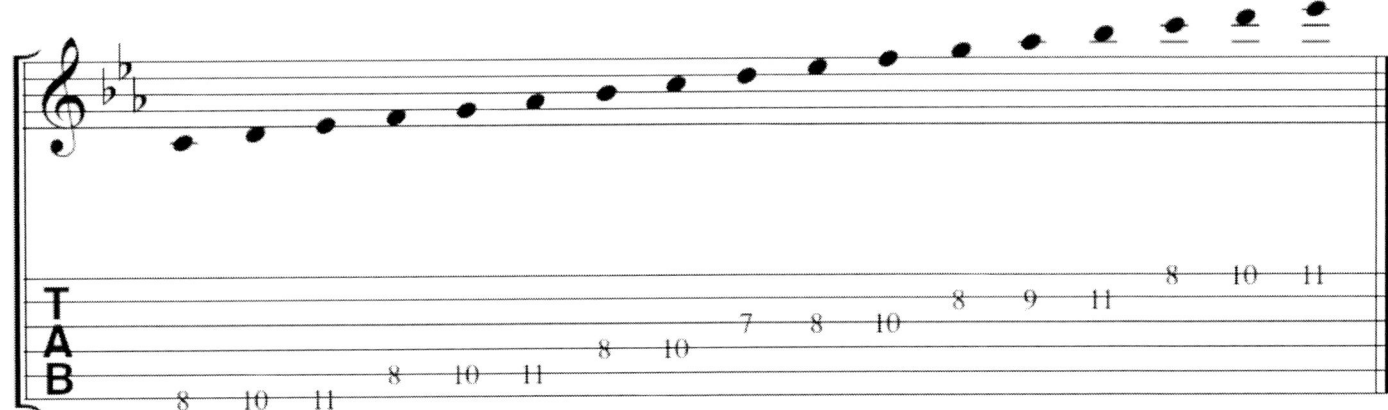

Bb major/G minor at the 7th fret:

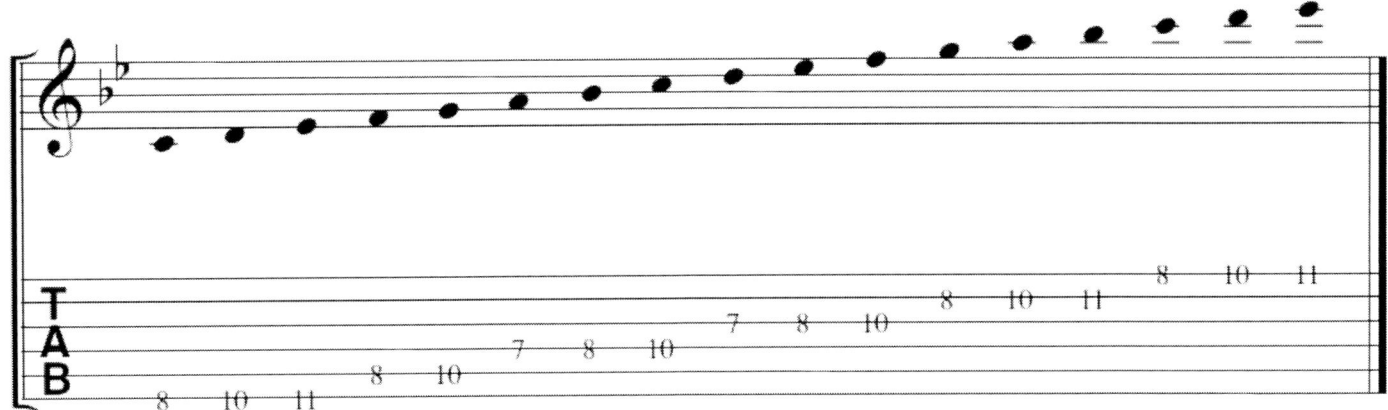

F major/D minor at the 7th fret:

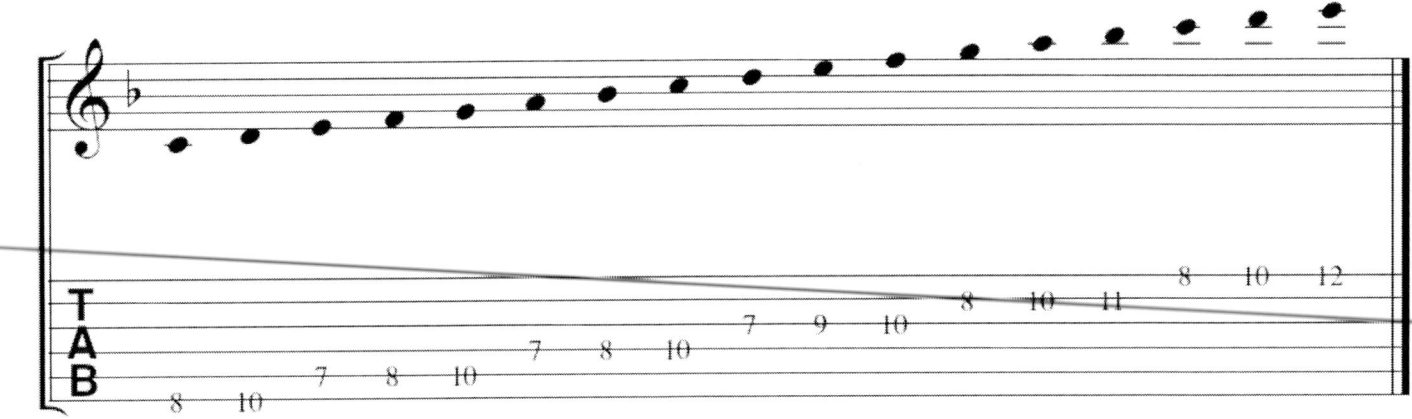

C major/A minor at the 9th fret:

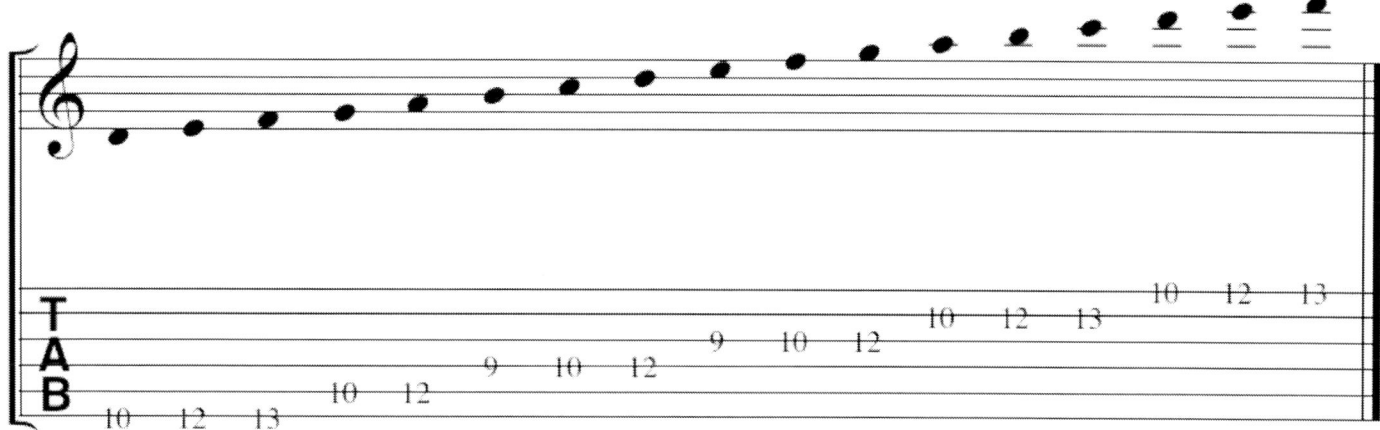

G major/E minor at the 9th fret:

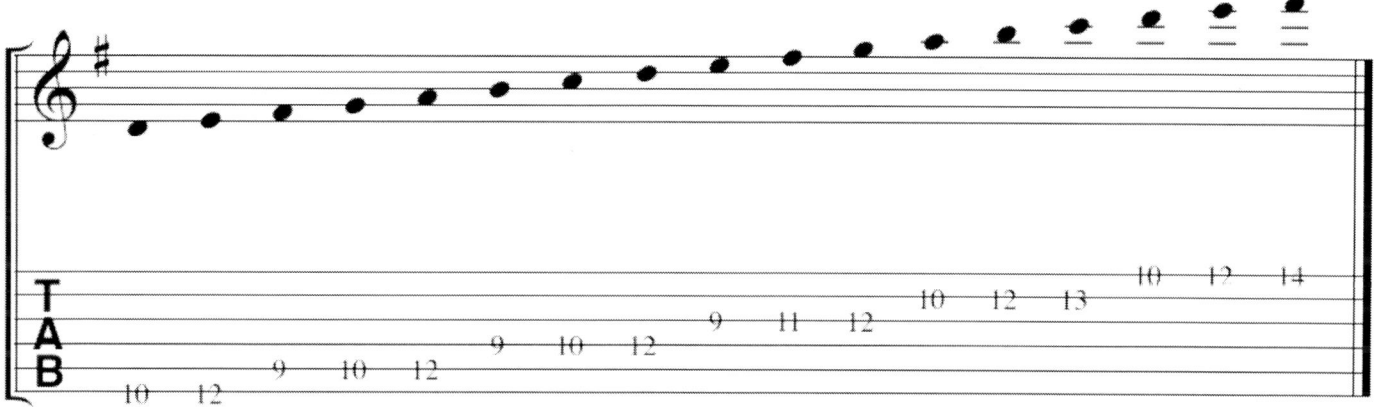

D major/B minor at the 9th fret:

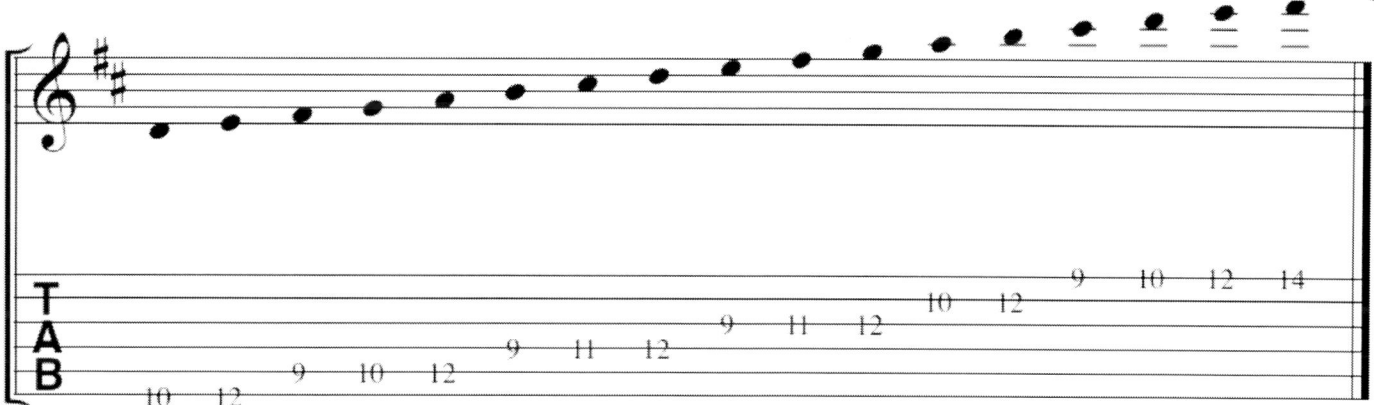

A major/F# minor at the 9th fret:

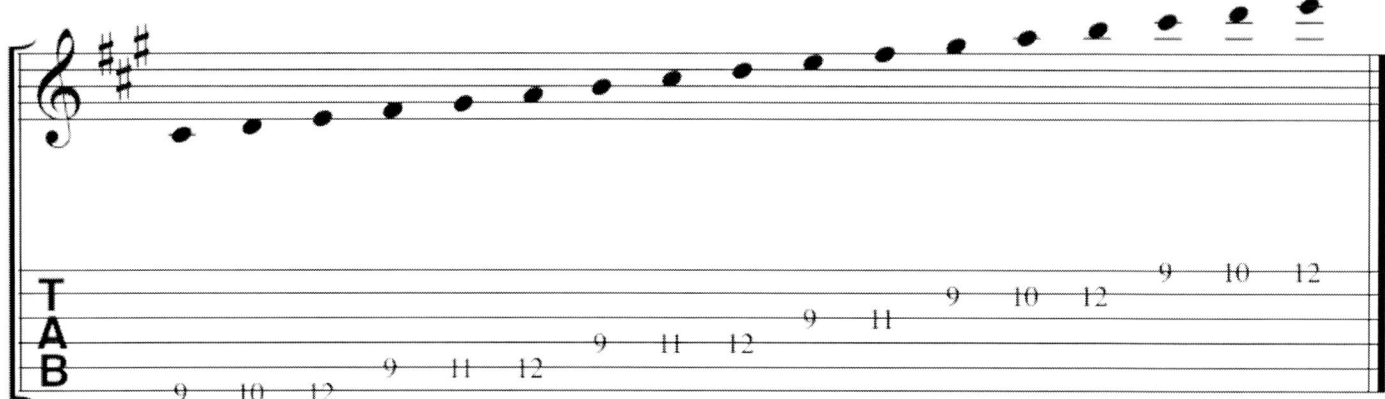

E major/C# minor at the 9th fret:

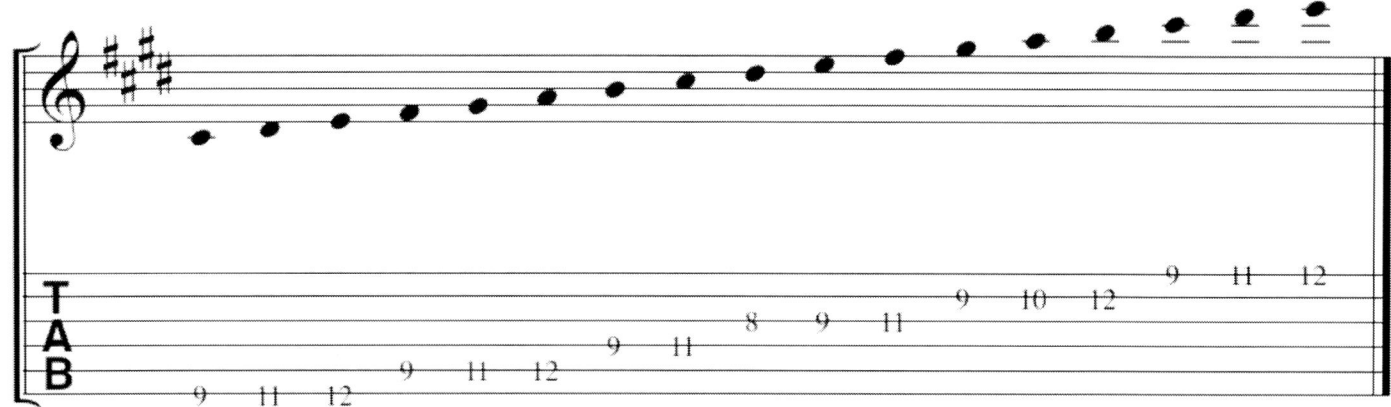

B major/G# minor at the 9th fret:

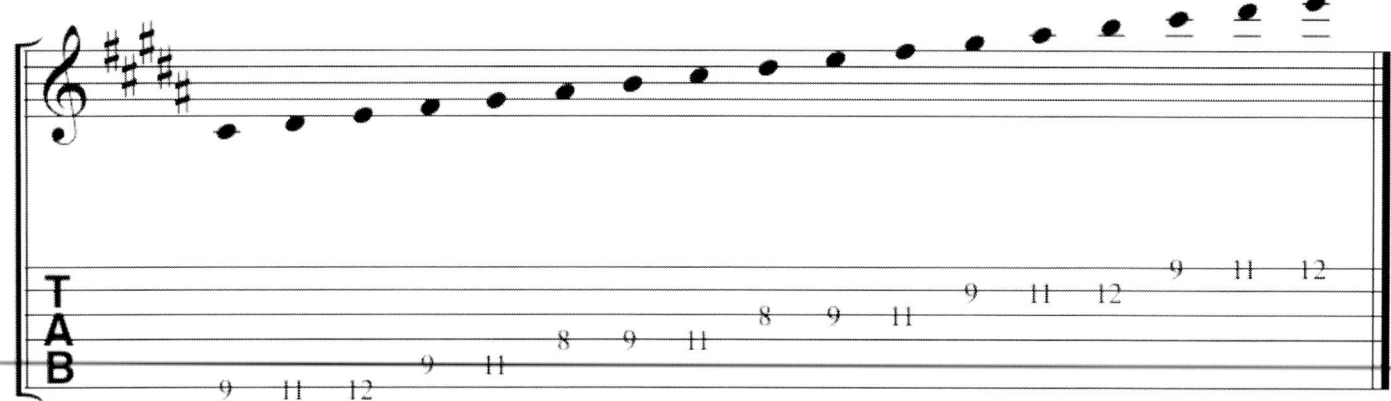

Gb major/Eb minor at the 9th fret:

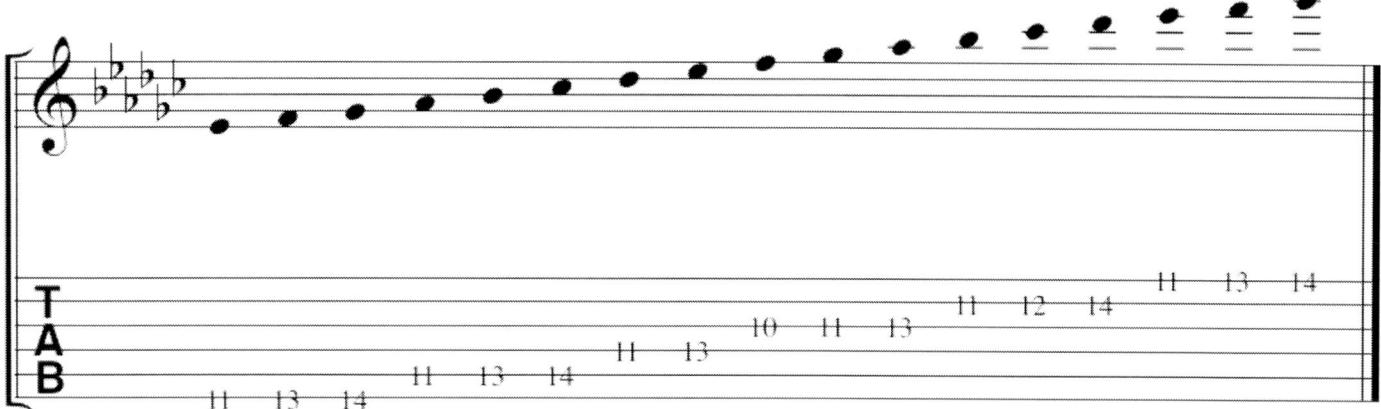

Db major/Bb minor at the 9th fret:

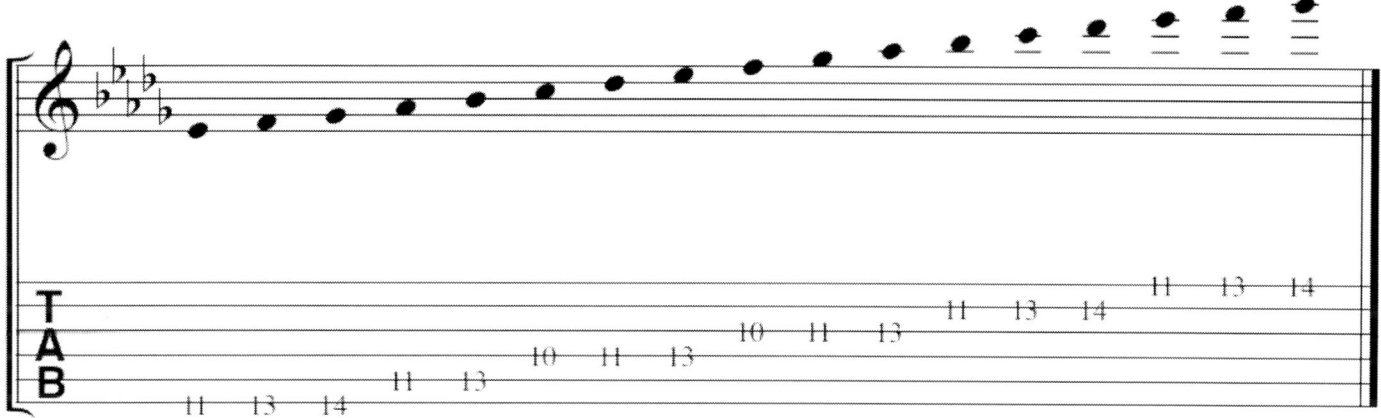

Ab major/F minor at the 9th fret:

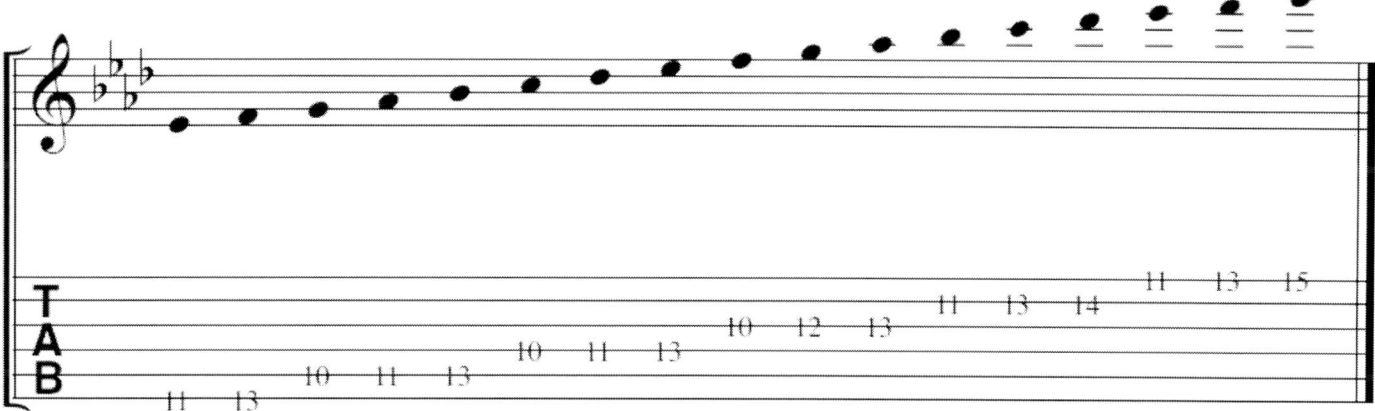

Eb major/C minor at the 9th fret:

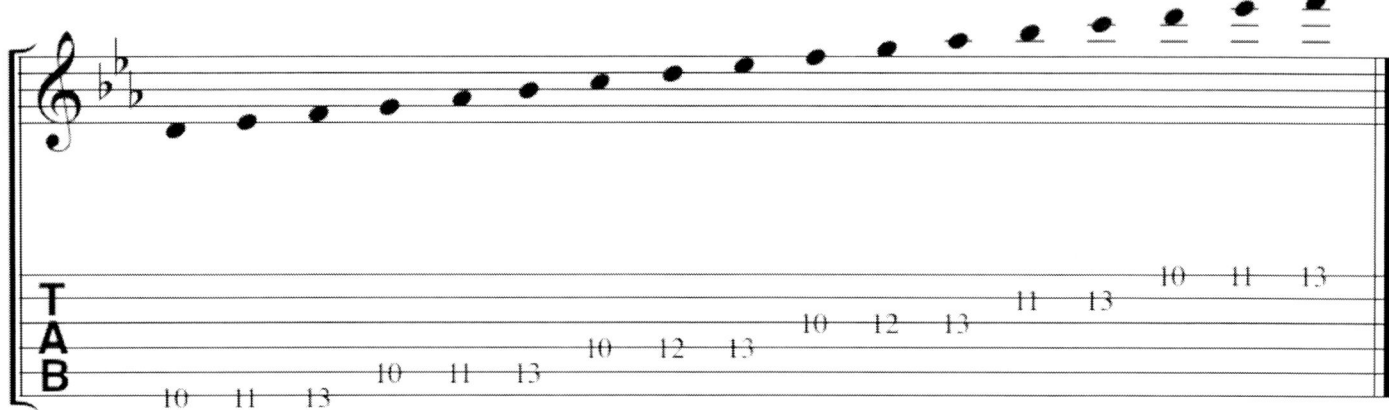

Bb major/G minor at the 9th fret:

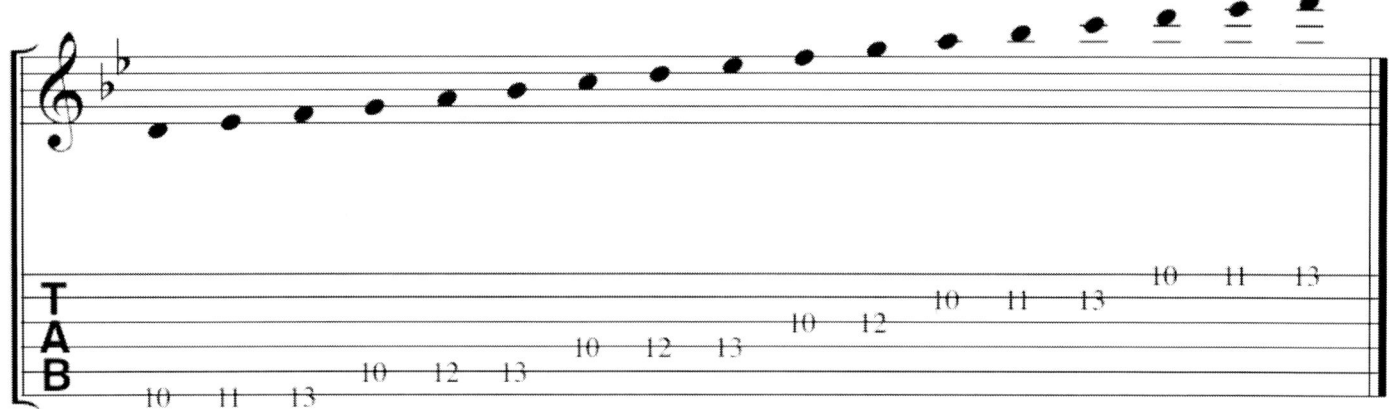

F major/D minor at the 9th fret:

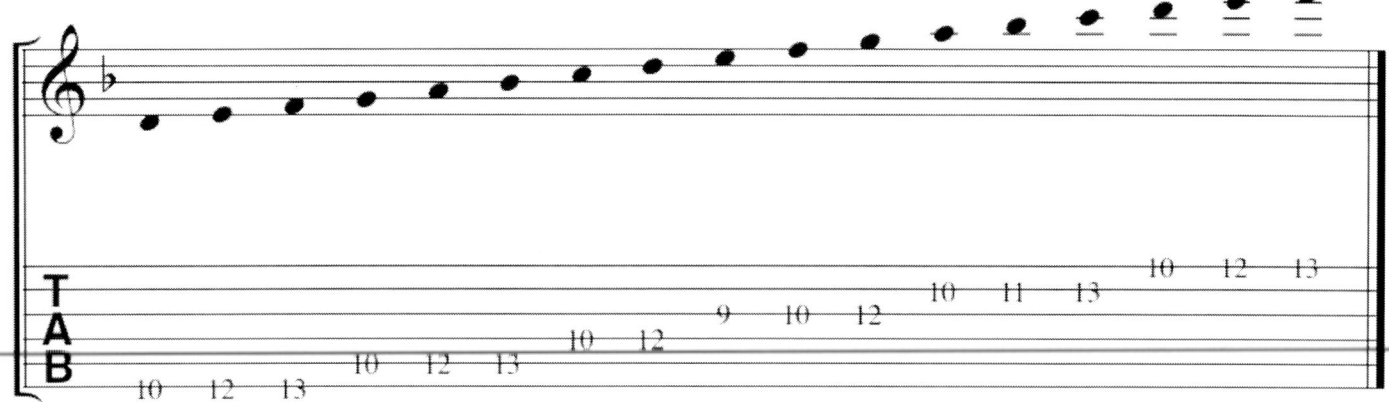

C major/A minor at the 12th fret:

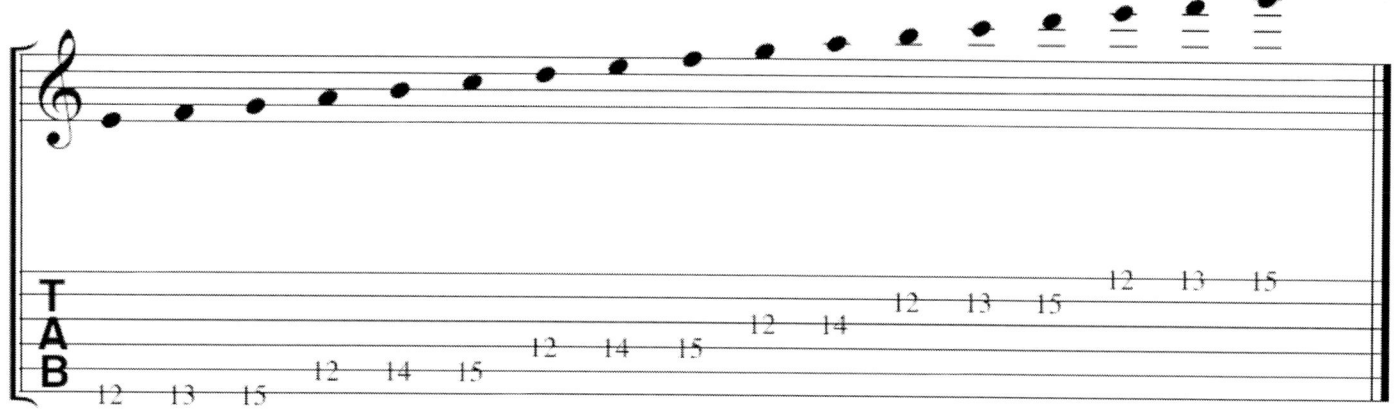

G major/E minor at the 12th fret:

D major/B minor at the 12th fret:

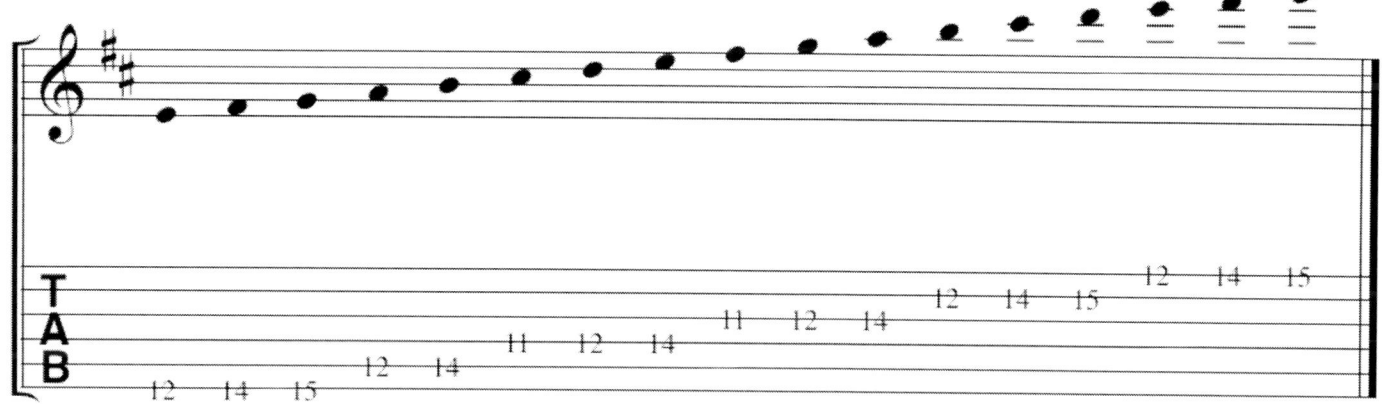

A major/F# minor at the 12th fret:

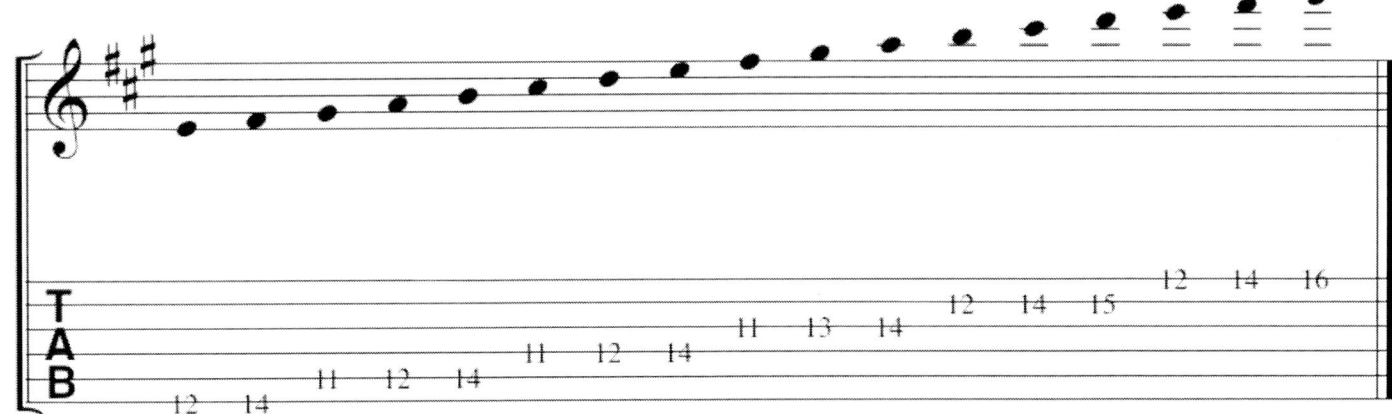

E major/C# minor at the 12th fret:

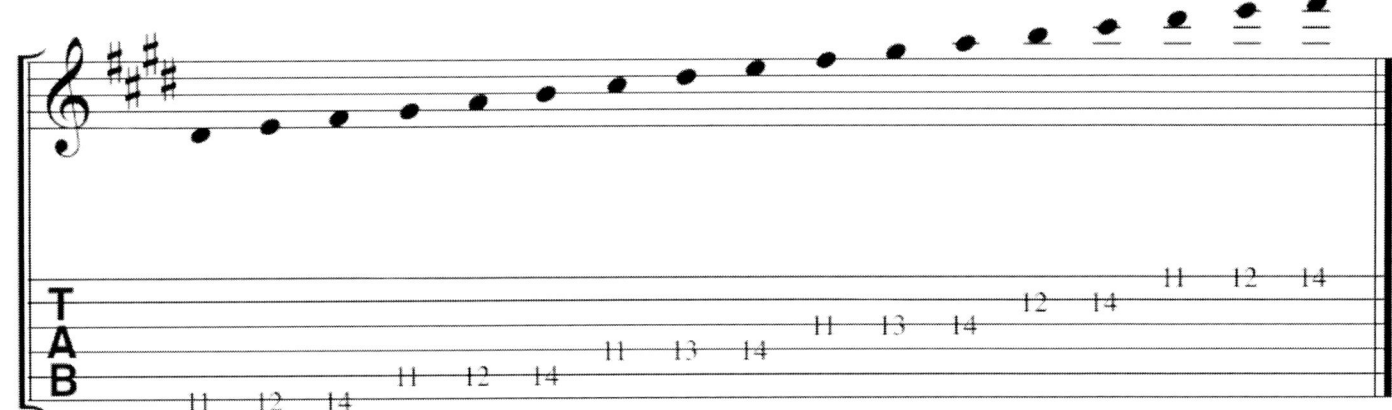

B major/G# minor at the 12th fret:

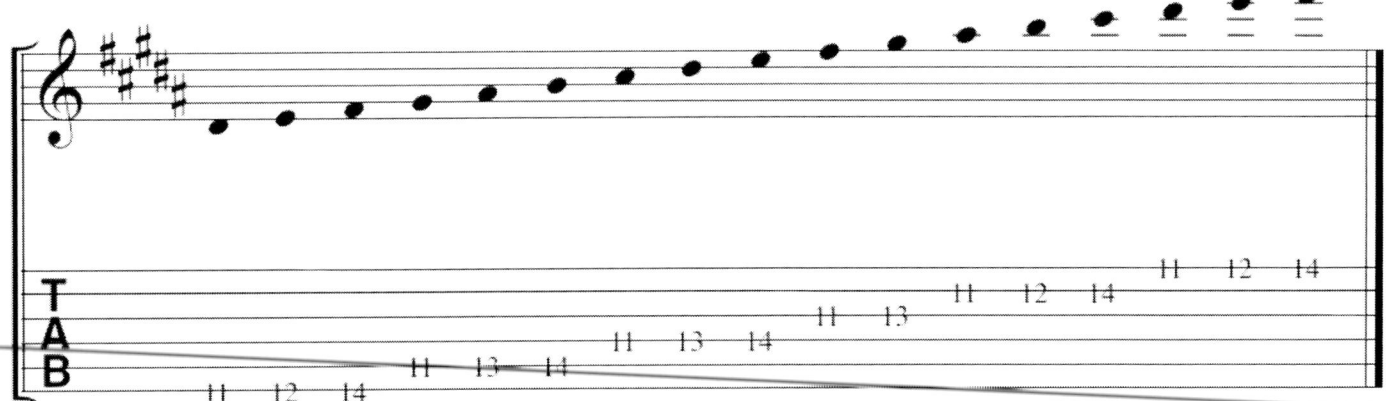

Gb major/Eb minor at the 12th fret:

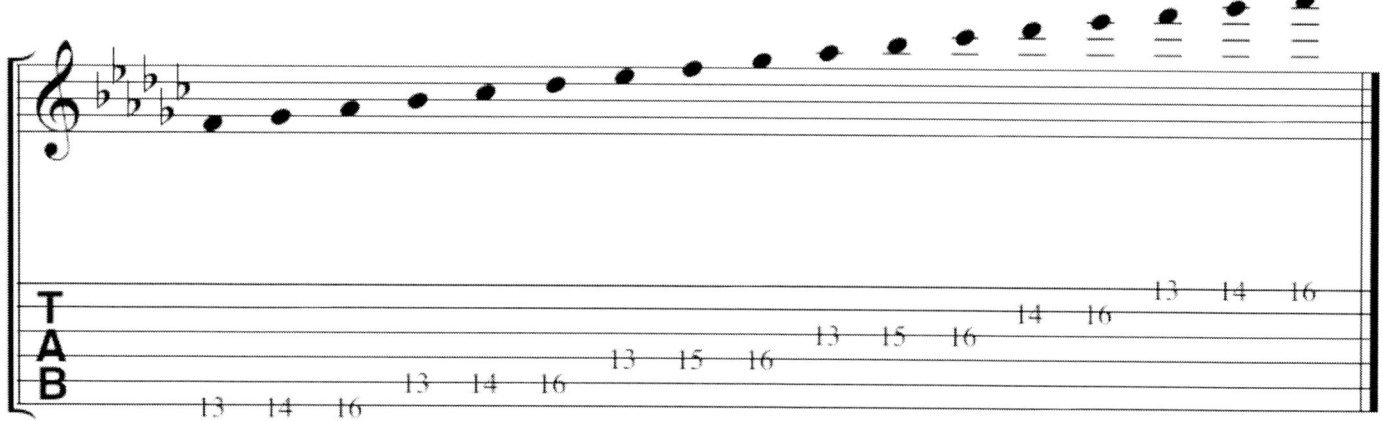

Db major/Bb minor at the 12th fret:

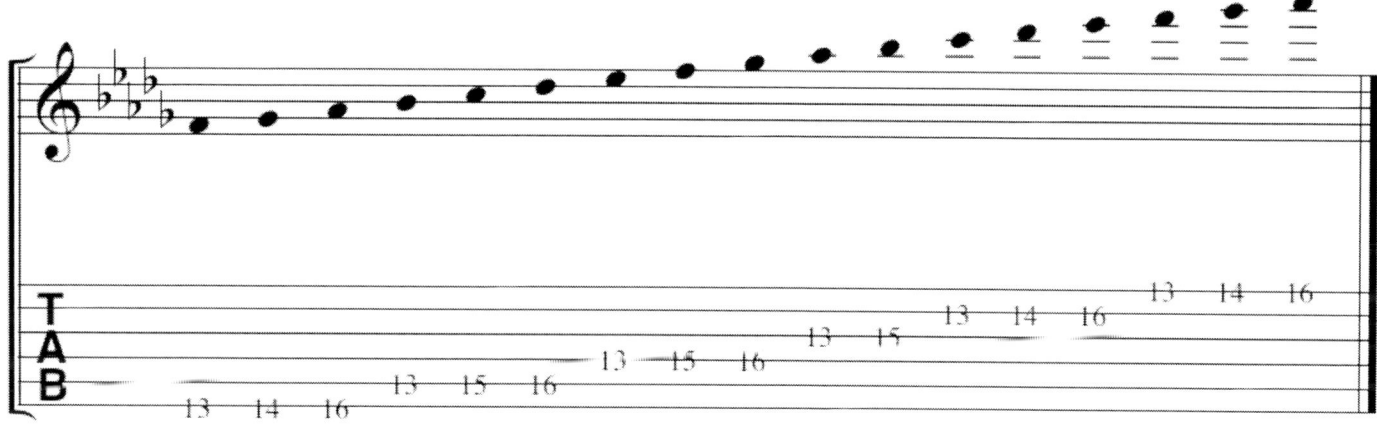

Ab major/F minor at the 12th fret:

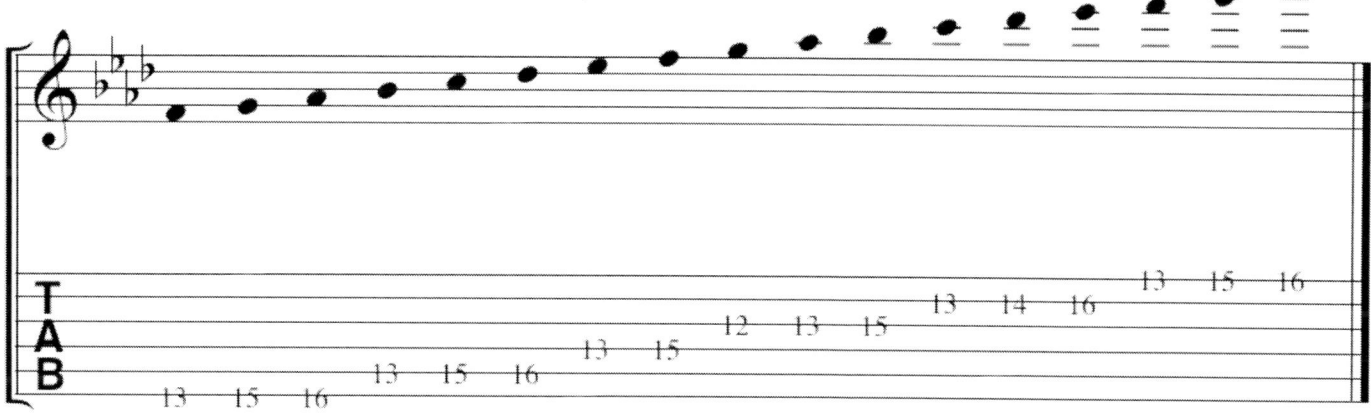

Eb major/C minor at the 12th fret:

Bb major/G minor at the 12th fret:

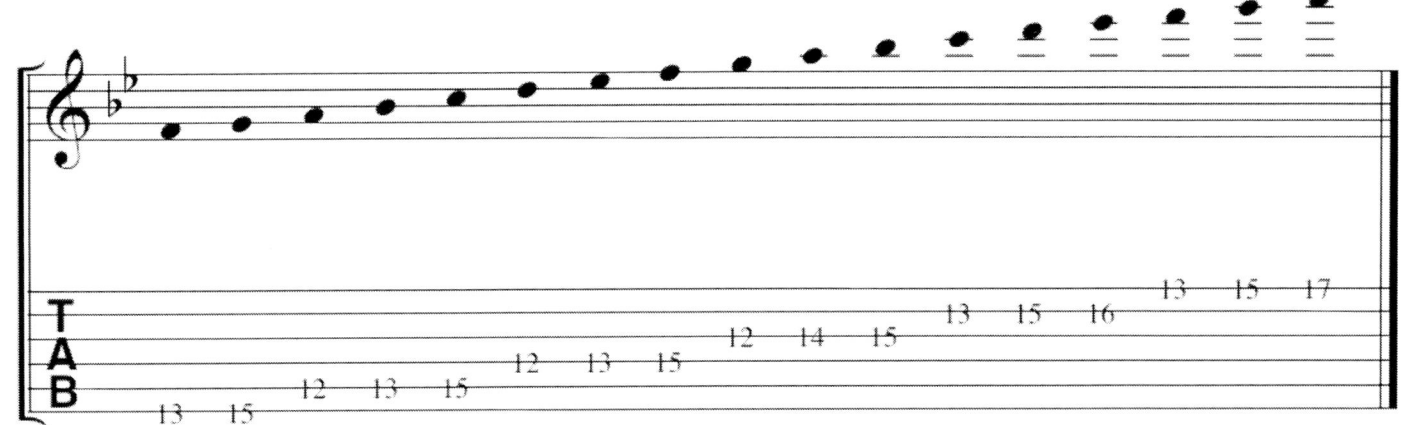

F major/D minor at the 12th fret:

C major/A minor at the 15th fret:

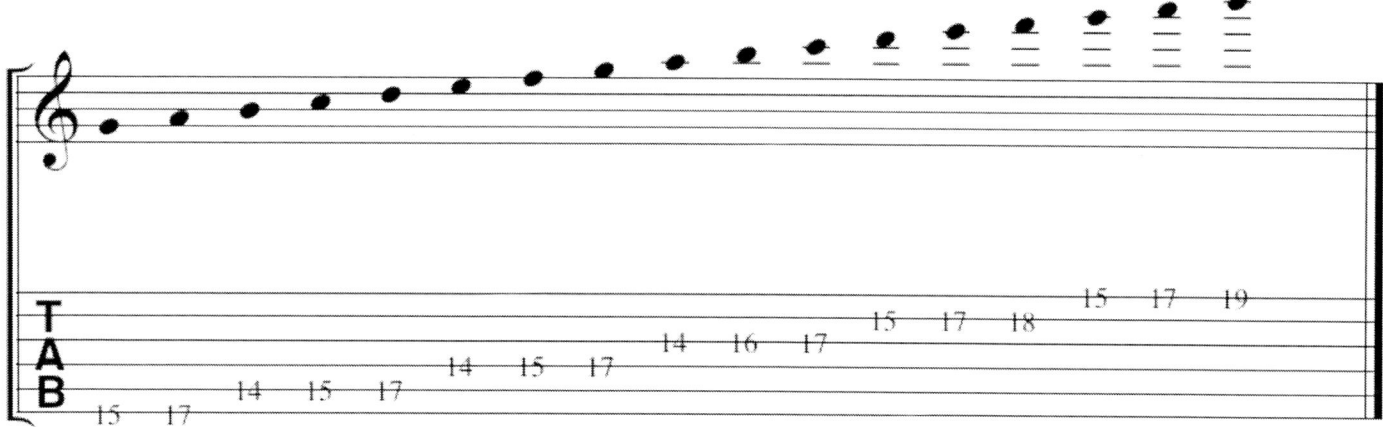

G major/E minor at the 15th fret:

D major/B minor at the 15th fret:

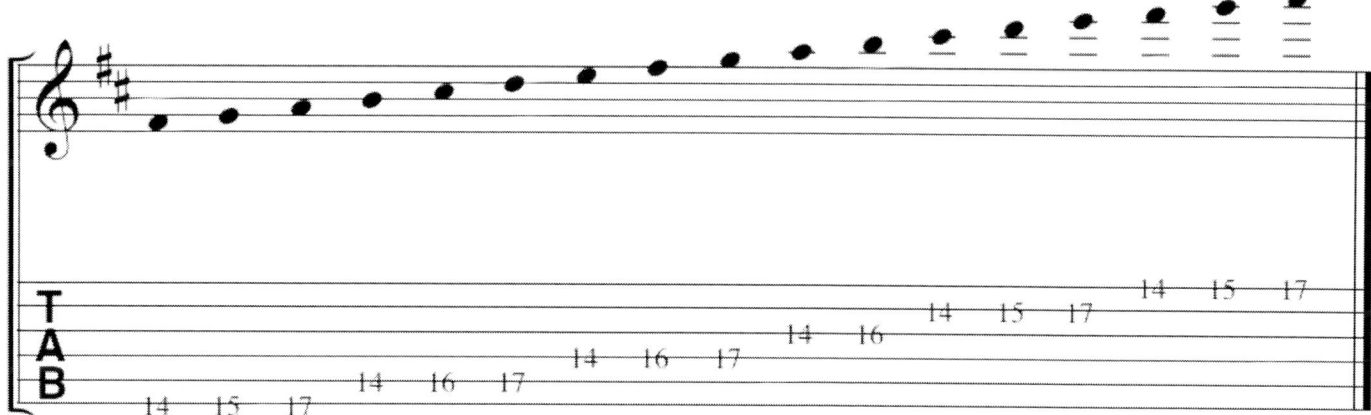

A major/F# minor at the 15th fret:

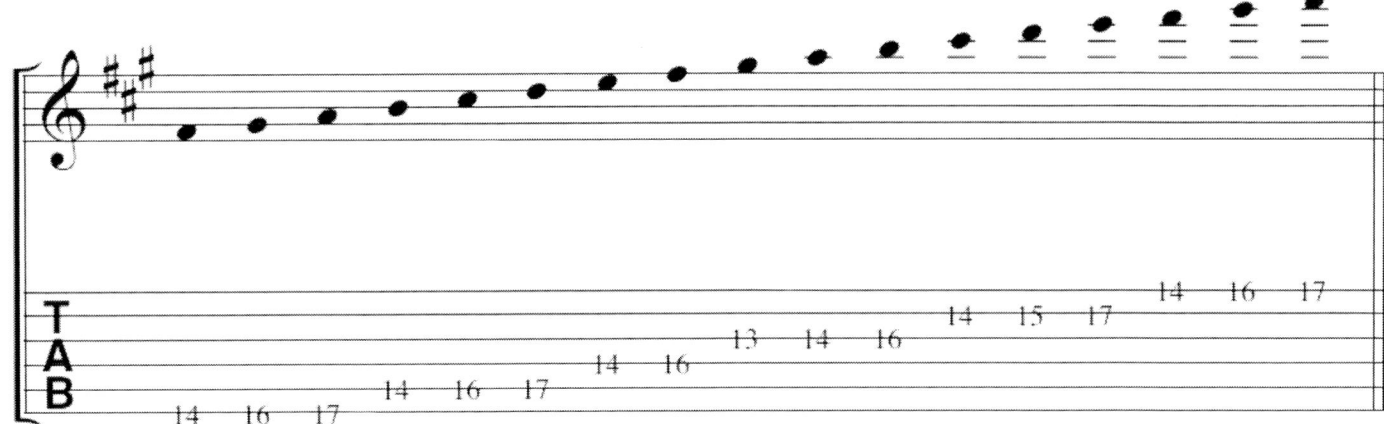

E major/C# minor at the 15th fret:

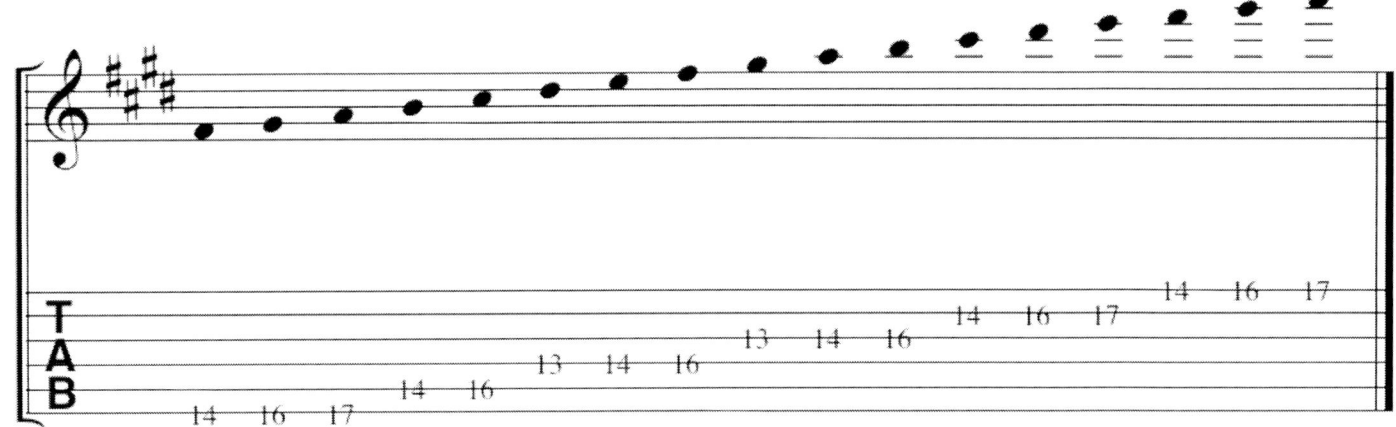

B major/G# minor at the 15th fret:

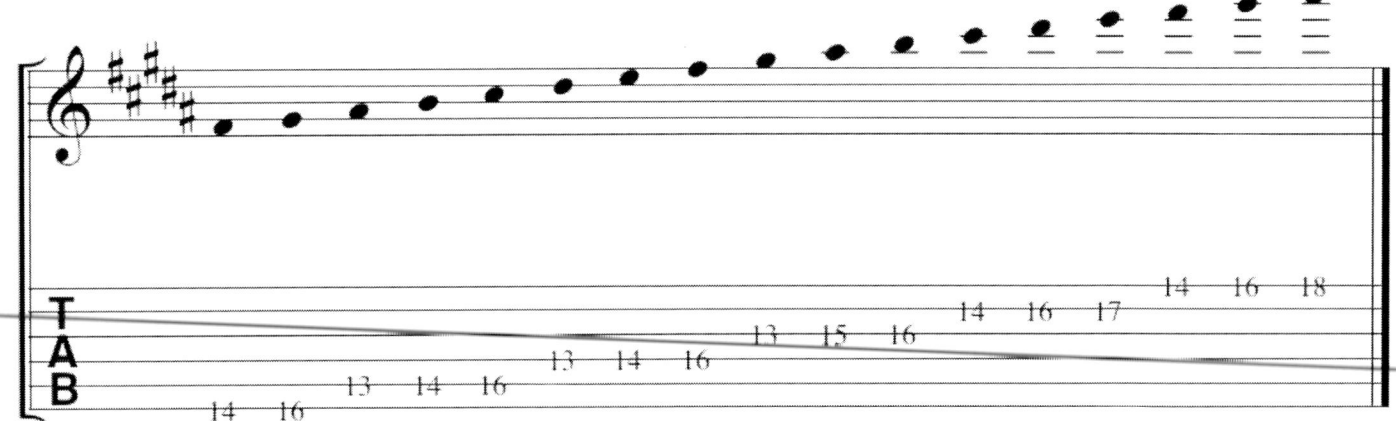

Gb major/Eb minor at the 15th fret:

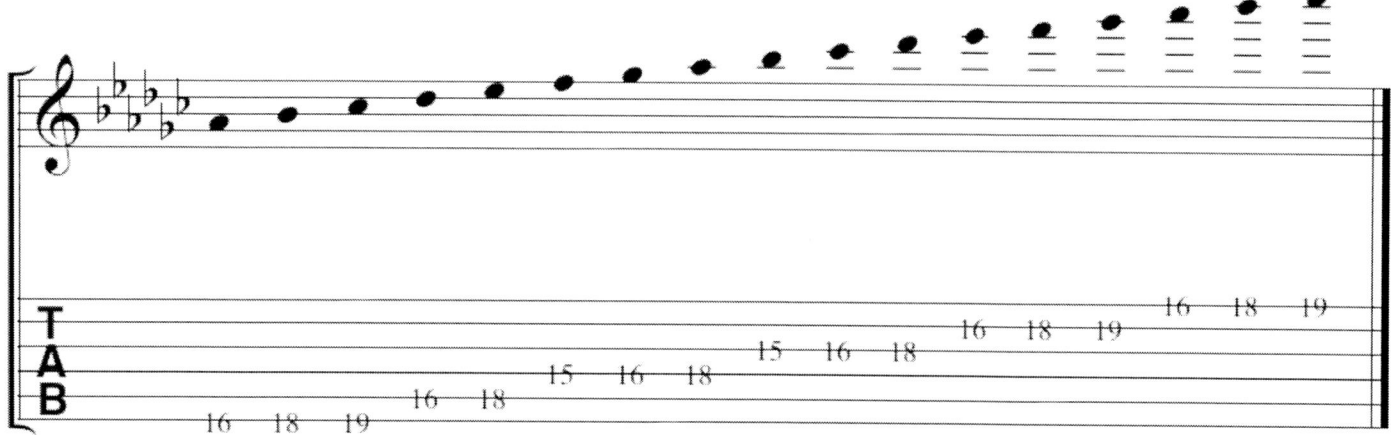

Db major/Bb minor at the 15th fret:

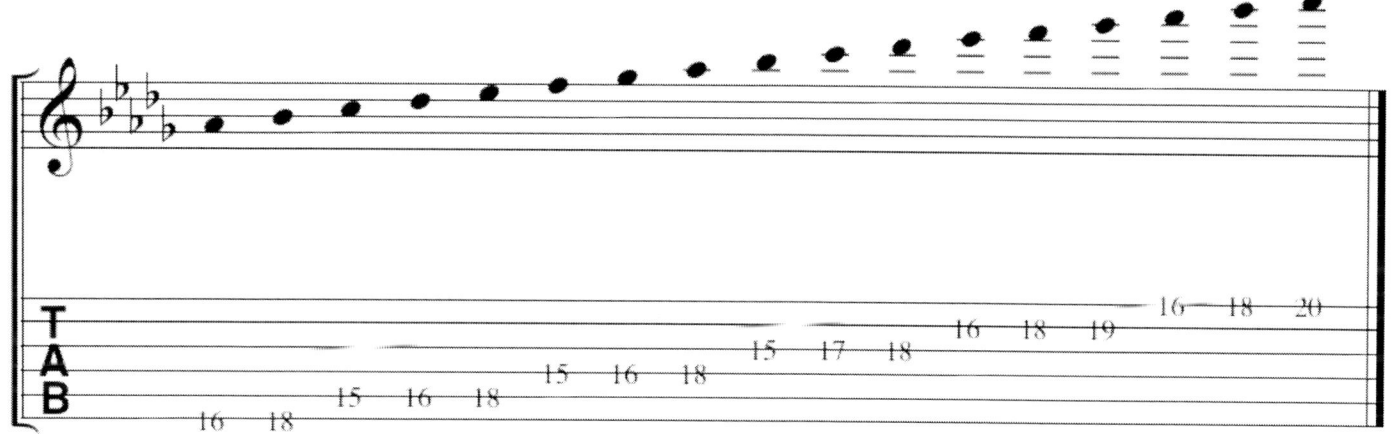

Ab major/F minor at the 15th fret:

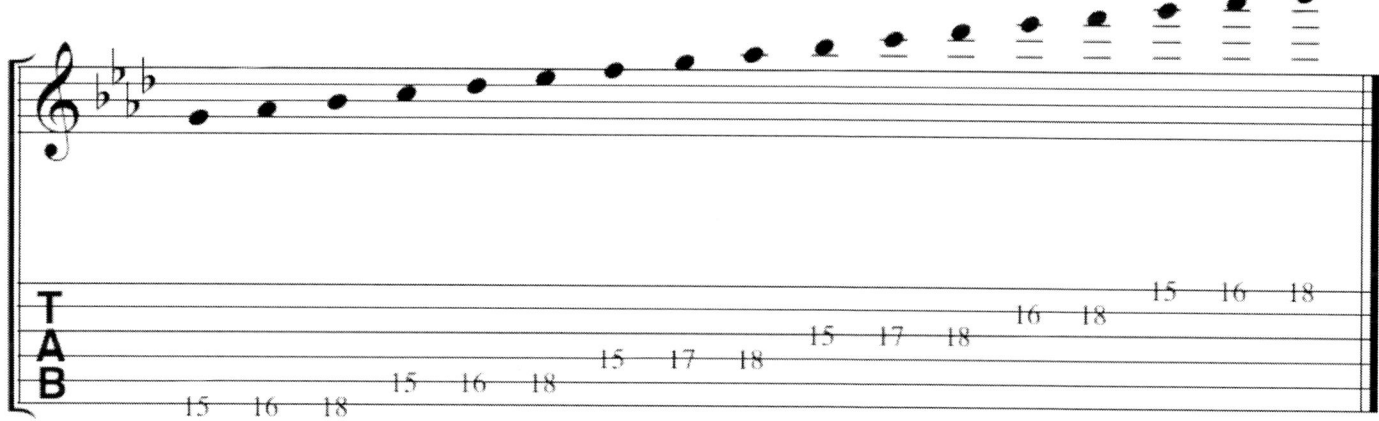

Eb major/C minor at the 15th fret:

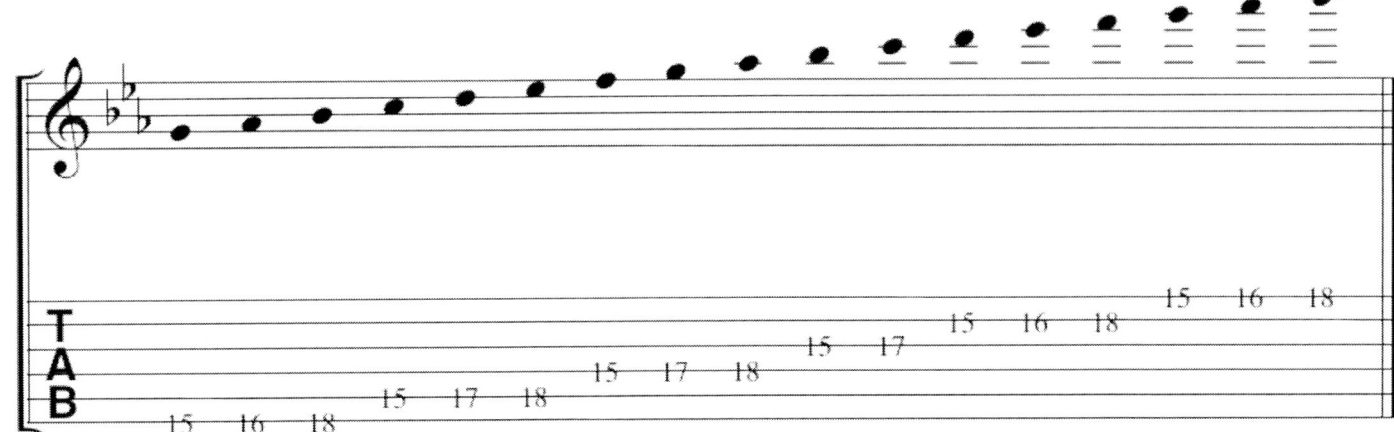

Bb major/G minor at the 15th fret:

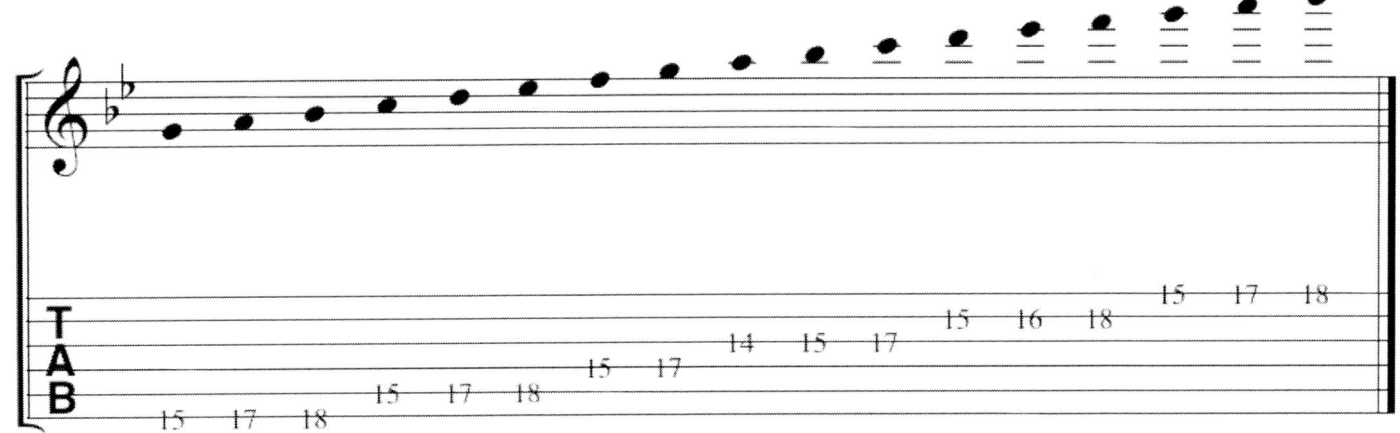

F major/D minor at the 15th fret:

C major/A minor at the 17th fret:

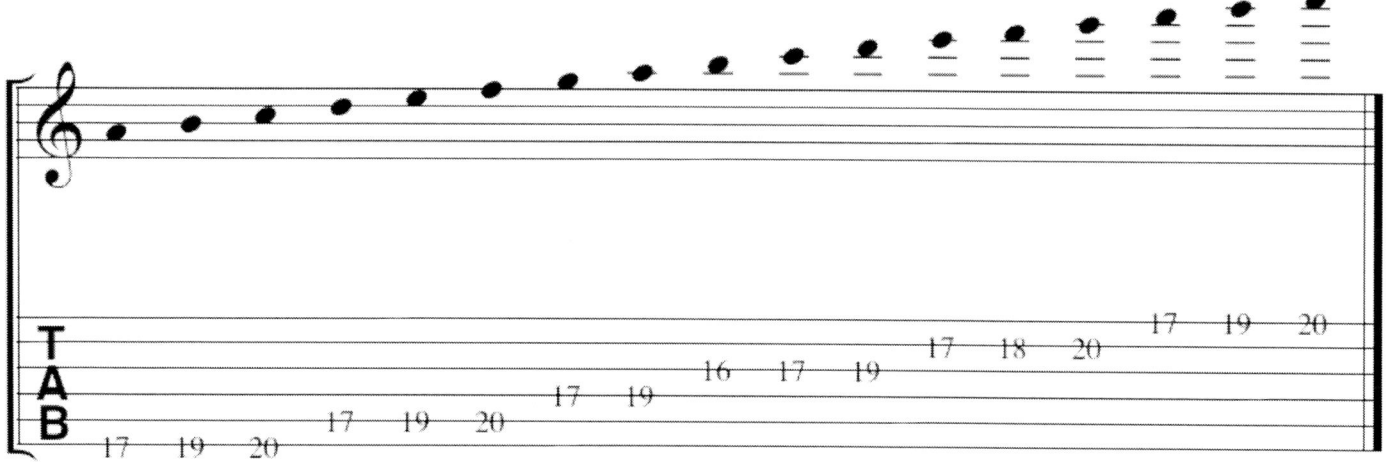

G major/E minor at the 17th fret:

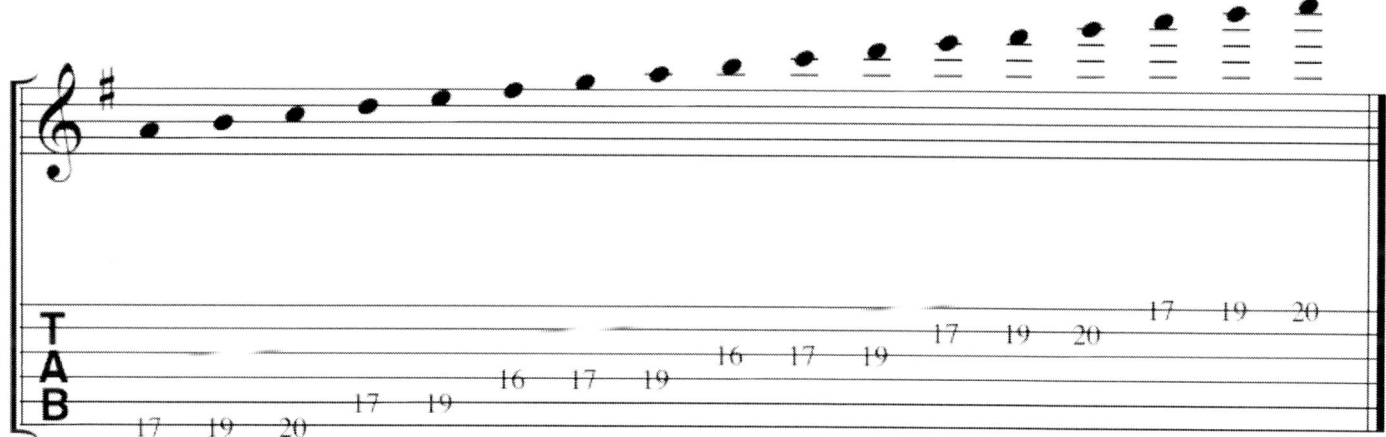

D major/B minor at the 17th fret:

A major/F# minor at the 17th fret:

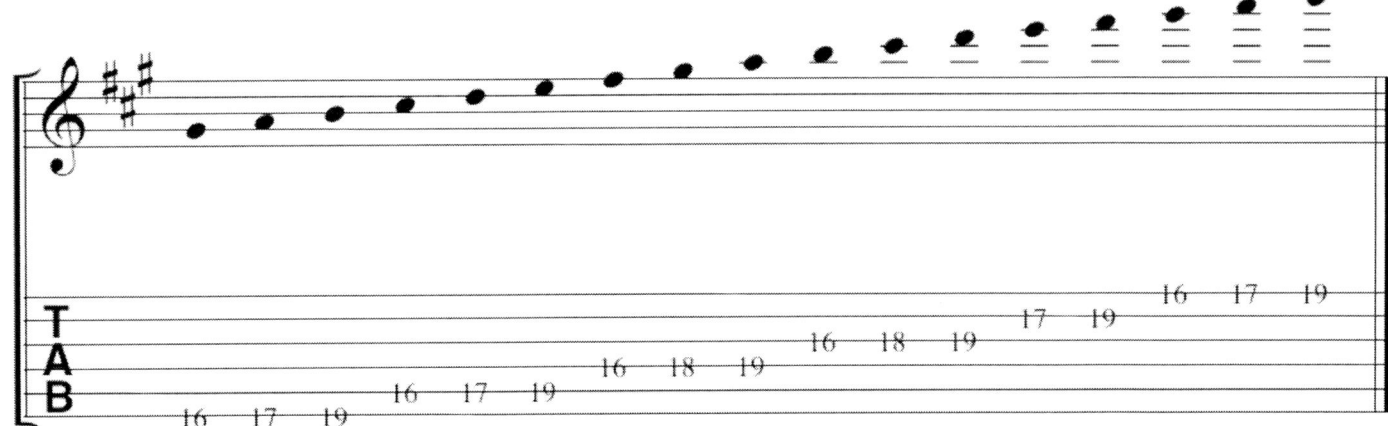

E major/C# minor at the 17th fret:

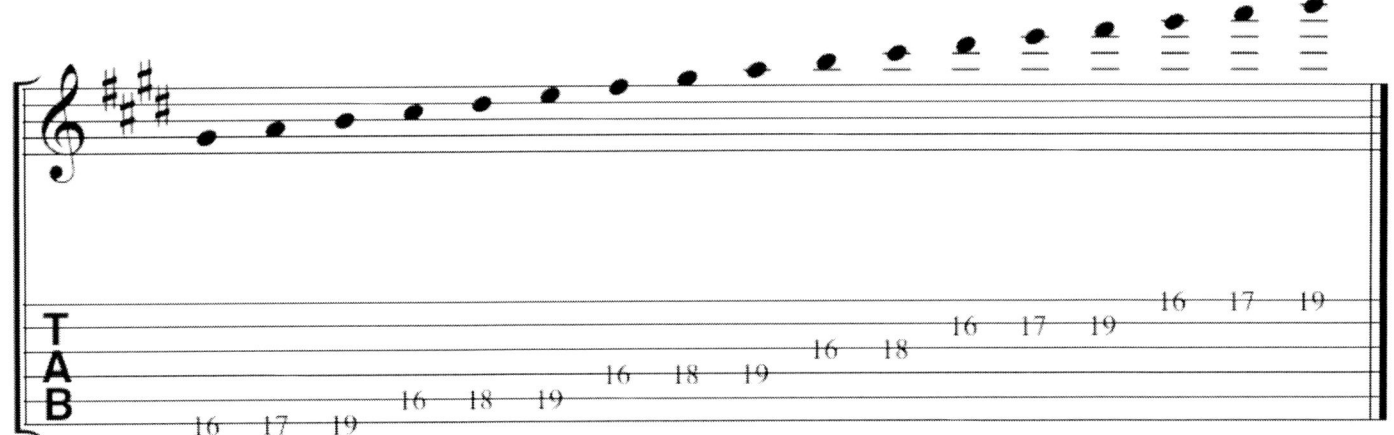

B major/G# minor at the 17th fret:

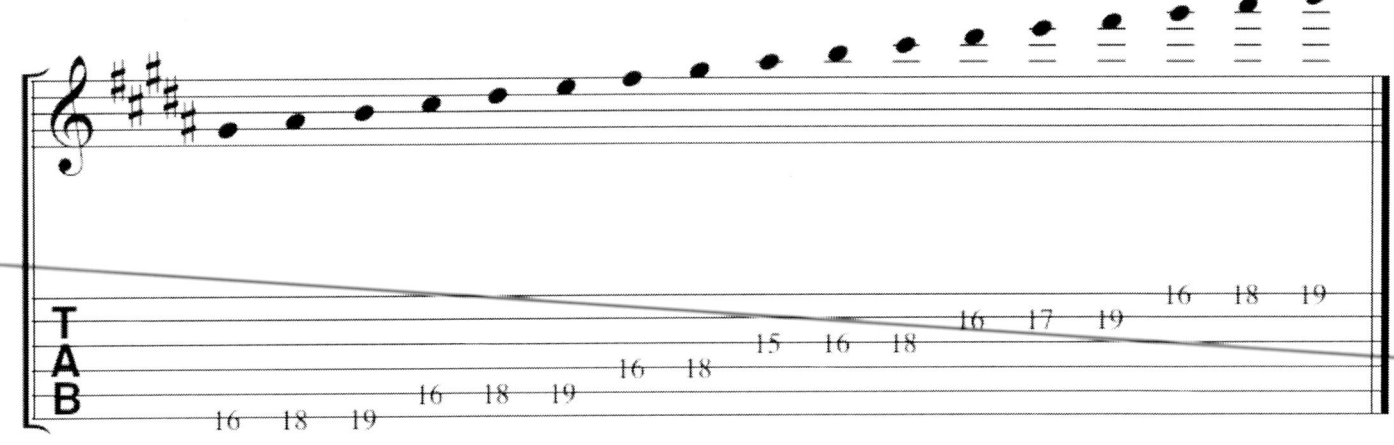

Gb major/Eb minor at the 17th fret:

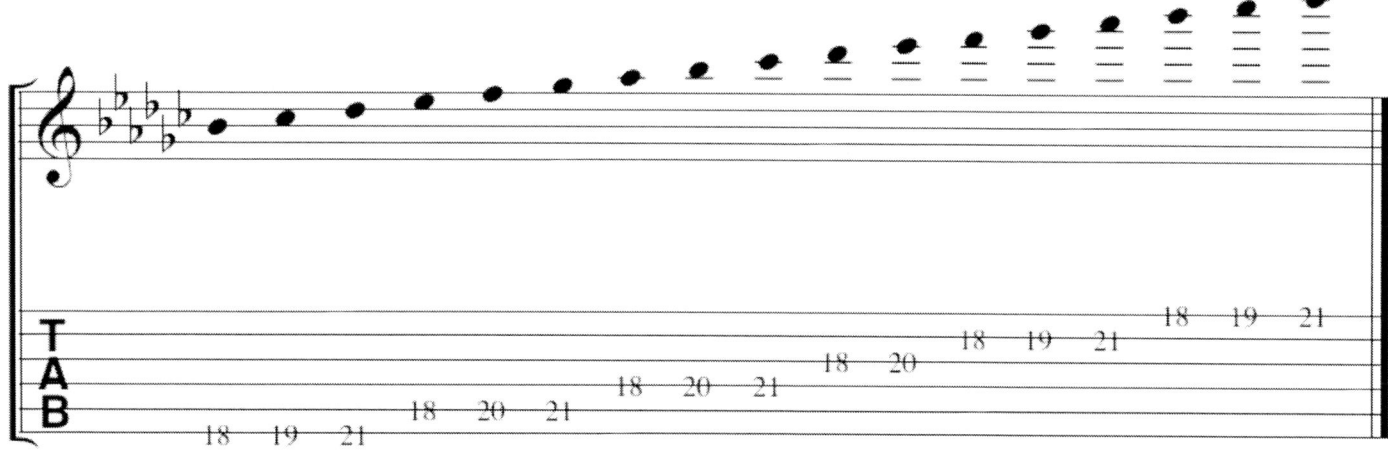

Db major/Bb minor at the 17th fret:

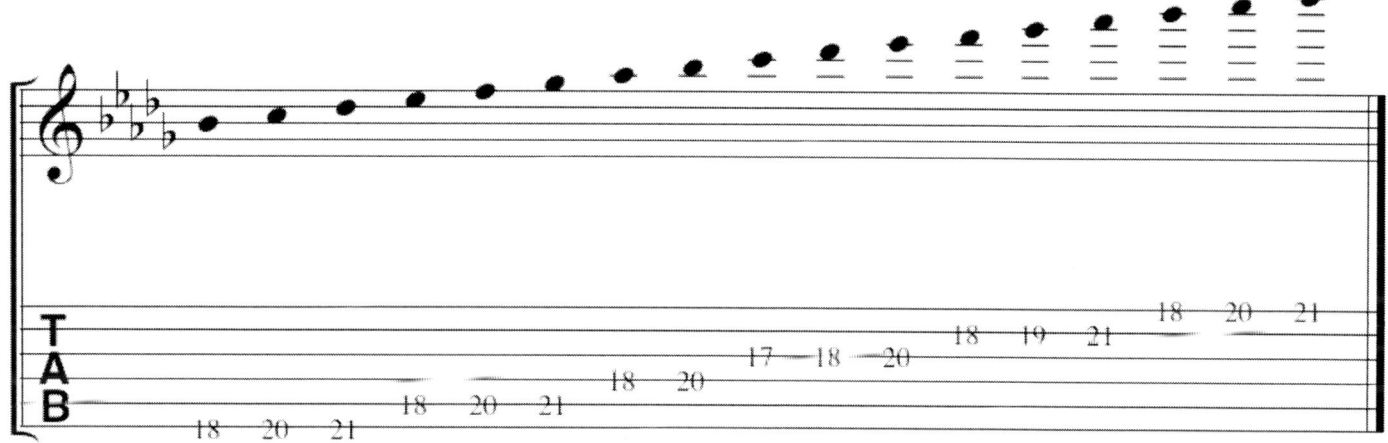

Ab major/F minor at the 17th fret:

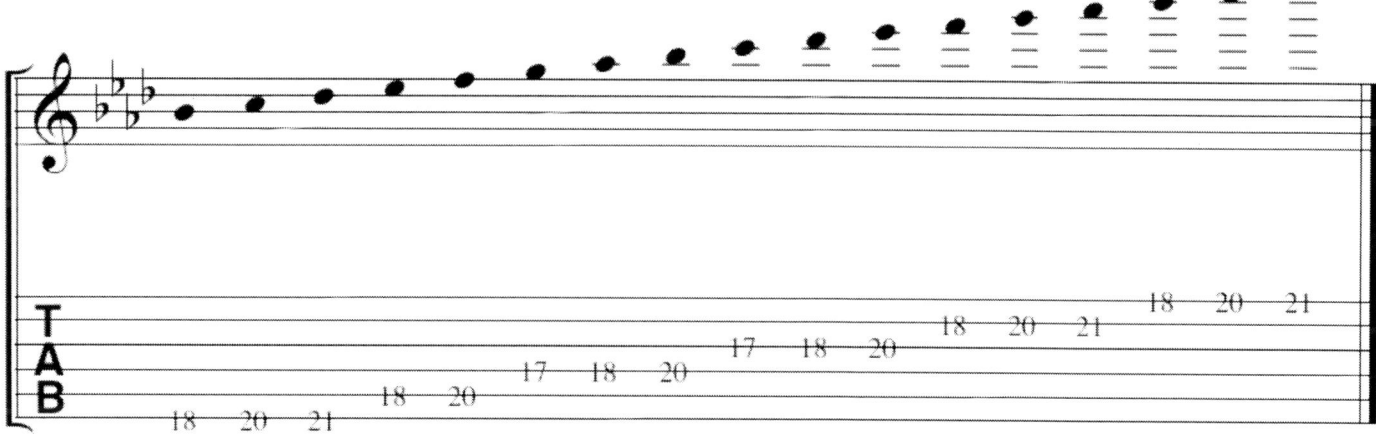

Eb major/C minor at the 17th fret:

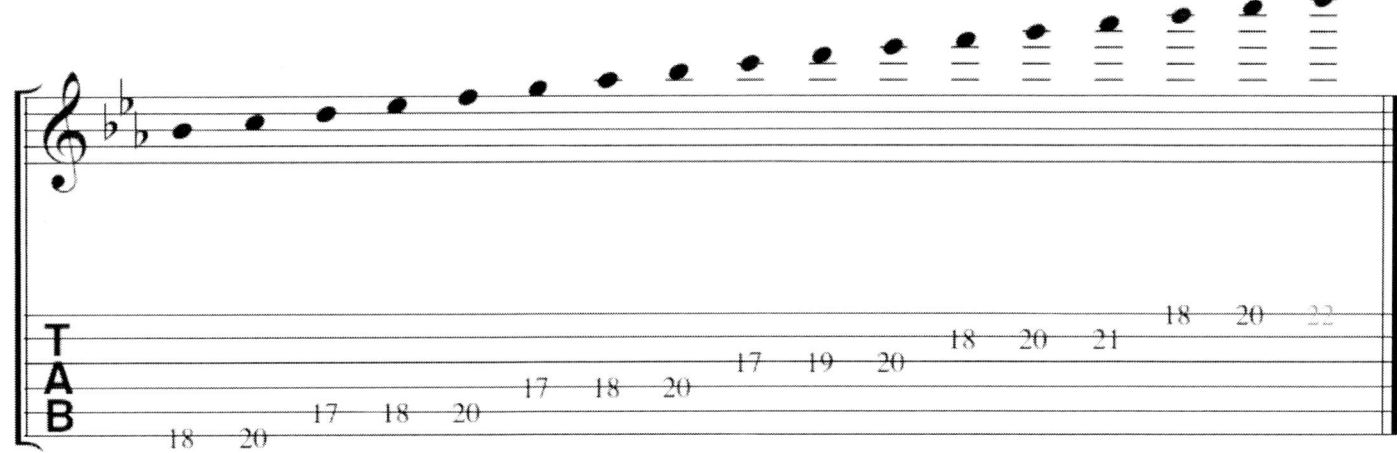

Bb major/G minor at the 17th fret:

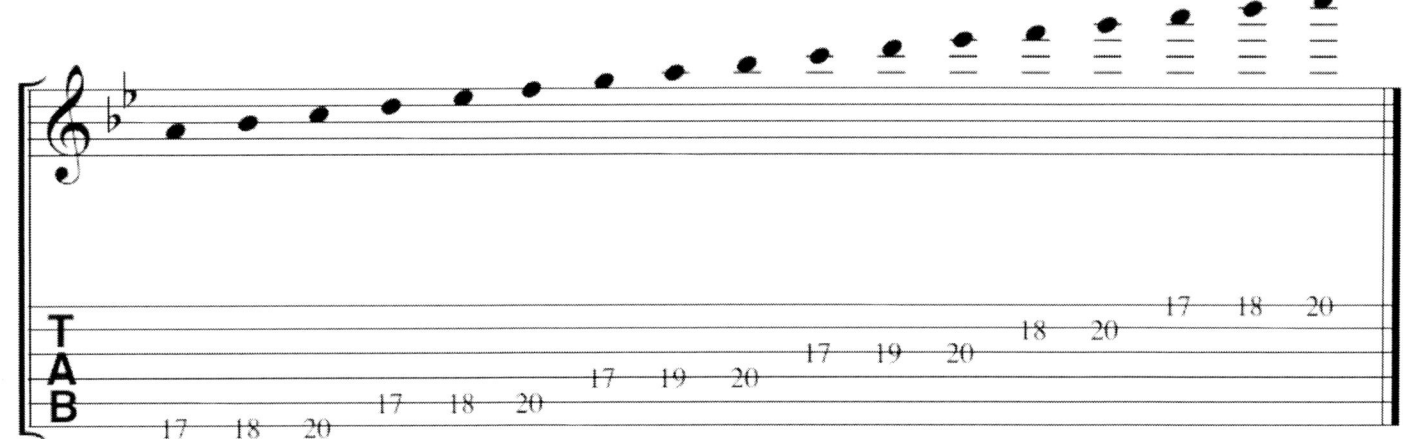

F major/D minor at the 17th fret:

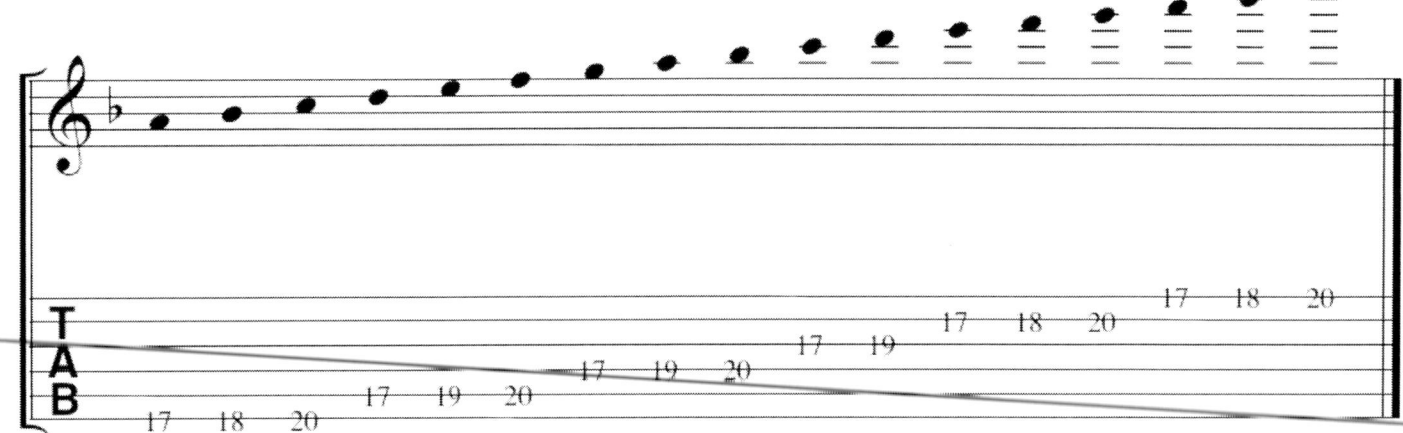

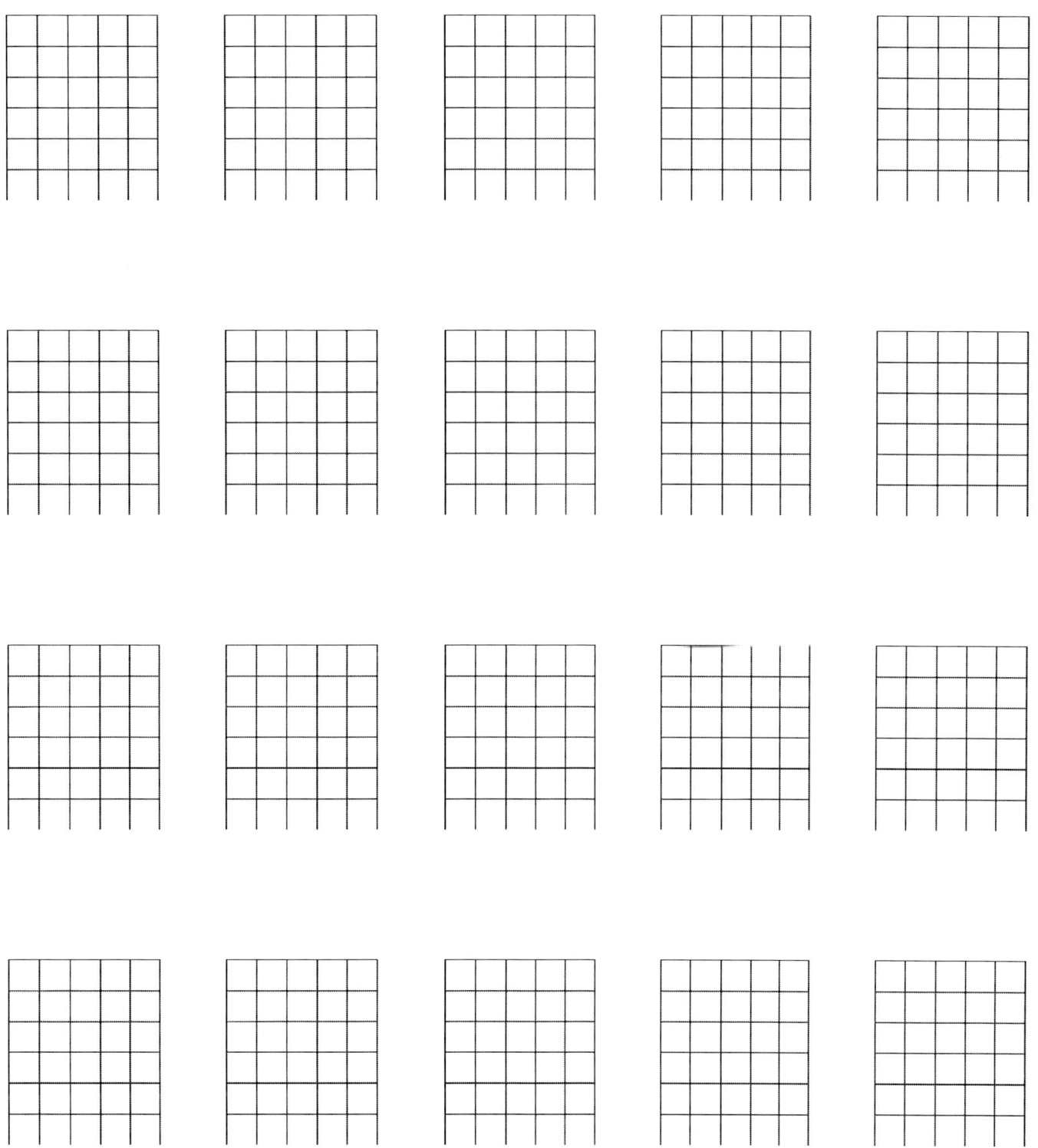

	I	II	III	IV	V	VI	VII
Diatonic Triad							
Diatonic 7th Chord							
Secondary Dominant							
Secondary Tritone							
Secondary Diminished							
Secondary Super-Tonic							
Reverse Polarity							
Flat Scale-Tone							
Flat Scale-Tone 7ths							

	I	II	III	IV	V	VI	VII
Diatonic Triad							
Diatonic 7th Chord							
Secondary Dominant							
Secondary Tritone							
Secondary Diminished							
Secondary Super-Tonic							
Reverse Polarity							
Flat Scale-Tone							
Flat Scale-Tone 7ths							

MAN IN THE ARENA
NEVER SAY QUIT

AN AUTOBIOGRAPHY BY
DAVID MICHAEL SEMAS

 FriesenPress

One Printers Way
Altona, MB R0G 0B0
Canada

www.friesenpress.com

Copyright © 2022 by David Michael Semas
First Edition — 2022

All rights reserved.

No part of this publication may be reproduced in any form, or by any means, electronic or mechanical, including photocopying, recording, or any information browsing, storage, or retrieval system, without permission in writing from FriesenPress.

Edited by William Greenleaf

ISBN
978-1-03-913276-4 (Hardcover)
978-1-03-913275-7 (Paperback)
978-1-03-913277-1 (eBook)

1. BIOGRAPHY & AUTOBIOGRAPHY, BUSINESS

Distributed to the trade by The Ingram Book Company

CITIZENSHIP IN A REPUBLIC

"THE POOREST WAY TO FACE LIFE IS TO FACE IT WITH A SNEER. THERE ARE MANY MEN WHO FEEL A KIND OF TWISTED PRIDE IN CYNICISM . . . THERE IS NO MORE UNHEALTHY BEING, NO MAN LESS WORTHY OF RESPECT, THAN HE WHO EITHER REALLY HOLDS, OR FEIGNS TO HOLD, AN ATTITUDE OF SNEERING DISBELIEF TOWARD ALL THAT IS GREAT AND LOFTY . . . A CYNICAL HABIT OF THOUGHT AND SPEECH, A READINESS TO CRITICIZE . . . ALL THESE ARE MARKS, NOT . . . OF SUPERIORITY BUT OF WEAKNESS. THEY MARK THE MEN . . . WHO SEEK, IN THE AFFECTION OF CONTEMPT FOR THE ACHIEVEMENTS OF OTHERS, TO HIDE FROM OTHERS AND FROM THEMSELVES IN THEIR OWN WEAKNESS. THE ROLE IS EASY; THERE IS NONE EASIER."

—THEODORE ROOSEVELT, 1910

TABLE OF CONTENTS

PREFACE VII

INTRODUCTION 1

PART I 5
CHAPTER 1 – A BUDDING ENTREPRENEUR 7
CHAPTER 2 – SOWING WILD OATS 43
CHAPTER 3 – A CAREER IN CONSTRUCTION 59
CHAPTER 4 – WHERE THERE'S A WILL, THERE'S A WAY 87
CHAPTER 5 – CENTURY PAST: VISIONARY IDEA OR NEMESIS? "THE PHILIPPINE CONNECTION" 115
CHAPTER 6 – ONE, TWO, THREE STRIKES AND YOU'RE OUT 155
CHAPTER 7 – A NEW BEGINNING 179
CHAPTER 8 – BANANAS AND BOONDOGGLES 209

PART II 223
CHAPTER 9 – WHAT IS ANODIZING, ANYWAY? 225
CHAPTER 10 – METALAST®—THE BUSINESS 231
CHAPTER 11 – CONSPIRATORS EMERGE 243
CHAPTER 12 – RUDE AWAKENING TO AN IRS NIGHTMARE 263

CHAPTER 13 – THE BREAKTHROUGH MOMENT 275
CHAPTER 14 – BEING A BOSS ISN'T EASY 283
CHAPTER 15 – ONE STEP FORWARD, TWO STEPS BACK ... 293
CHAPTER 16 – FINALLY, A MAJOR INVESTOR? 301
CHAPTER 17 – T-REX: GO BIG OR GO HOME! 311
CHAPTER 18 – ANCHORS AWEIGH WITH THE NAVY 327
CHAPTER 19 – METALAST APPEARS TO BE
COMING OF AGE 341
CHAPTER 20 – HERE WE GO AGAIN 349
CHAPTER 21 – THE WHISTLEBLOWERS SHOW
THEIR HAND 375
CHAPTER 22 – UNDER THE MICROSCOPE 381
CHAPTER 23 – THE PERFECT STORM 391
CHAPTER 24 – STAYIN' ALIVE—TRYIN' TO SURVIVE 399
CHAPTER 25 – METALAST—DECEIVED BY
A FAIR-WEATHER FRIEND 407
CHAPTER 26 – AN UNEXPECTED CALL
AND MEETING A POLITICAL ICON 419
CHAPTER 27 – LITIGATION IN FULL SWING—
BACK IN THE SADDLE AGAIN! 443
CHAPTER 28 – THE MAN IN THE ARENA 465

EPILOGUE 471
ACKNOWLEDGMENTS 477
DEDICATIONS 485

PREFACE

I began writing this book in the winter of 2008 as snowflakes drifted in the gentle breeze and slowly blanketed our vineyard and orchards. Our home sat beneath the Sierra Nevada, which, draped with snow-covered ponderosa and Jeffrey pines, made for a beautiful winter wonderland. I wanted to share my story with family and friends. As the words of each chapter came to life on paper, it became more apparent to my editor and publisher that my autobiography had broad commercial value and that a much wider audience could benefit from its contents.

Usually, readers don't learn about the difficulties encountered over a lifetime or the financial challenges that most small startup companies face. Either the young, struggling business simply fails, or the entrepreneur doesn't wish to disclose his or her setbacks and failures. In my story, however, I want to be upfront about what it takes to put together a business so I can share the numerous life lessons I've absorbed throughout my career. Ultimately, you must be willing to accept financial risks if your business is to succeed and your dream realized. With every failure, you can't become jaded. The tenth time a door closes might be the time when another opens. A successful entrepreneur is part visionary, strategic thinker, and inspirational motivator. A leader is an intense listener, a consummate dealmaker, and a perpetual problem-solver. I can't honestly say that I embody all those virtues, but over my lifetime, I have certainly tried to do so.

As a leader, you will realize your job is about recognizing and defining problems and implementing solutions effectively. Rarely do things in life go as planned. It's not about passing the buck, finding blame, or giving excuses for why something didn't work as anticipated. In the end, it's about taking personal responsibility, creative thinking, and grabbing the bull by the horn so you can make things happen.

Circumstances change for a person with an entrepreneurial spirit on a weekly, if not daily, basis. Someone on a fixed career path might find his or her life to be fairly consistent from day to day, while others choose the direction I have taken. It's exciting and quite invigorating but has its drawbacks. Every decision I've made, nearly every person I've met, had an impact on my life, for better or worse.

Not everyone has the desire to become the boss. Indeed, the world runs on the manpower of dedicated employees who are ready, willing, and able to deliver goods or services to people all over the globe. Businesses succeed through a team effort, not just due to the leadership atop a corporate hierarchy.

For the young person entering the business arena today, once you begin to experience the reality of adult life, you'll likely be in for a rude awakening. News flash: society doesn't revolve around you, no matter who you are. As M. J. Croan once said, "Maturity is when your world opens up and you finally realize you're not the center of it." In order to appreciate the sweet taste of success, you must first experience failure and other life-altering events that will change your outlook forever—hopefully for the better.

Accept that life usually isn't fair for the majority of the people around the world. It's not fair that those in third-world countries are born into poverty and will never have the opportunity you've been given, so don't squander it. Appreciate the fact that you have

> **LIFE LESSON #1:**
>
> "IF I HAD SIXTY MINUTES TO SOLVE A PROBLEM, I'D SPEND FIFTY-FIVE MINUTES DEFINING IT AND FIVE MINUTES SOLVING IT."
>
> —ALBERT EINSTEIN
> (THEORETICAL PHYSICIST, 1879–1955)

a chance at the American Dream—that is, if you work hard and smart to achieve it. Be aware that the employer will nearly always hire the best qualified and pass on the least. He or she will retain and reward the most competent and fire the incompetent. Life is about knowing how you deal with the curveballs thrown at you and how you react. To savor success is terrific, but the real question is this: How do you handle defeat or rejection? There are no guarantees in life, so simply accept reality and enjoy the ride. When the going gets tough, learn to cowboy up!

You need to be comfortable in your own skin and to be a good person to others. Don't worry about who you strive to be; just be the very best you can be in whatever profession or career you choose for yourself. Don't lose sleep over not being the greatest. Learn from your mistakes, always try to do the right thing, and be a loving son or daughter and a kind and considerate spouse. As a parent, teach your children the virtues of honesty, integrity, respect, personal responsibility, and faith in God, the Father Almighty. The rest will take care of itself.

If you evolve into a Renaissance person with talents in a wide variety of fields, great! Now that I've been given the opportunity to look back at my life, I must admit that I was never really great at any single thing, but I'm pretty good at a number of things. Humility is to be embraced. Never take yourself too seriously. One of the most valuable assets of a person's character is honesty and integrity. Simply stated, keep your word, be truthful, take responsibility for your actions, be timely, and treat people the way you want to be treated. Be respectful to others, especially those less fortunate and those who could use a helping hand. Have a grounded moral compass, and always strive to do the right thing. When reasonable, don't take no for an answer, and when possible, never give up and never say quit.

The substance of President Theodore Roosevelt's "The Man in the Arena" passage from his "Citizenship in a Republic" speech in 1910 is not about race, religion, class, or ideology. His eloquent writings are meant to pay tribute to those individuals who have the tenacity to fight every day for what they believe in. Whether they fail or succeed, the credit goes to those who have the courage to jump into the arena in the first place.

"The Man in the Arena" has played a crucial part in my perspective for my entire adult life. I have identified with it since that early morning in October 1965, when, as a sophomore, I gave my first speech before Mr. Cargile's public speaking class at Santa Clara High School. I spent weeks preparing for my elocution debut in front of my classmates by studying at the city library in the heart of downtown Santa Clara. Even at that age, I enjoyed reading about US and world history and was fascinated by great leaders of the past and present.

While conducting research for my speech, I was drawn to charismatic Teddy Roosevelt's autobiography, which told the captivating story of a sickly, underweight boy burdened with poor vision, who suffered from asthma. This physically challenged young man possessed incredible determination and persistence to rise above adversity. He lifted weights, took boxing lessons, and became a voracious reader and outdoor enthusiast.

Teddy Roosevelt's love of forests, mountains, lakes, streams, and hunting and fishing—and his eventual Rough Rider persona—inspired me. I felt that his commitment to do the right thing and his relentless desire to achieve greatness were to be admired, while his sense of integrity was to be embraced and adopted.

Over a century ago, on April 23, 1910, one year after his presidency, Theodore Roosevelt delivered what is considered one of his most memorable and inspirational speeches before an impressive audience of French dignitaries and the faculty and student body of Sorbonne University in Paris. In my research in 1965, I read every word of text but was drawn in particular to the notable "The Man in the Arena" passage from his "Citizenship in a Republic" speech, which reads as follows:

LIFE LESSON #2:

"CHOOSE A JOB YOU LOVE, AND YOU WILL NEVER HAVE TO WORK A DAY IN YOUR LIFE."

—CONFUCIUS (CHINESE PHILOSOPHER, 551–479 BC)

It is not the critic who counts—not the man who

MAN IN THE ARENA – NEVER SAY QUIT

points out how the strong man stumbles, or where the doer of deeds could have done them better. The credit belongs to the man who is actually in the arena; whose face is marred by dust and sweat and blood; who strives valiantly; who errs and comes short again and again; because there is no effort without error or shortcoming; but who does actually strive to do the deeds, who knows the great enthusiasms, great devotions; who spends himself in a worthy cause; who—at the best—knows in the end the triumph of high achievement, and who—at the worst—if he fails, at least fails while daring greatly, so that his place shall never be with those cold and timid souls who know neither victory nor defeat.

At age forty-two, Teddy Roosevelt was the youngest person to serve as president of the United States. I have spent much of my life trying to emulate his love of America, his never-ending zest for life, his "bully for you" tenacity, and his steadfast determination.

It's understandable to want the winning hand, my father often told me, but when you've been dealt a pair of twos and not a full house, play the hand you're dealt. Don't make excuses or blame others for your predicament, setback, defeat, or failure. Legendary Olympic swimming coach George Haines embodied that tenacious attitude and forever embedded in my mind the following: no matter how many times you may fail, stumble, or fall, never give in, never give up, and never say quit.

After more than seventy years on planet Earth, I believe my destiny was to spend a lifetime reaching for the brass ring and living life to the fullest so that one day I could share my stories with you.

LIFE LESSON #3:

"THE WHOLE SECRET OF A SUCCESSFUL LIFE IS TO FIND OUT WHAT IS ONE'S DESTINY TO DO, AND THEN DO IT."

—HENRY FORD (FOUNDER OF FORD MOTOR COMPANY, 1863-1947)

INTRODUCTION

For fifty years, even with all its ups and downs, I've enjoyed nearly every day of my adventurous life. Unlike those less fortunate, I've been blessed with good health and surrounded by family and close friends. Although at times stressful, my lifetime journey has been about never giving up. Rarely have I wavered from that mantra. If I failed, I chalked it up to another learning experience, dusted myself off, and waited for sunrise, mindful that life is about the journey and not the destination. That wasn't because I was fearless, but like many before me, *I didn't know what I didn't know*.

Today I am back at the helm as a real estate developer (sierradorado.com). Together with my longtime friends we are in the process of selling a 155-acre parcel of land for an industrial park project in Reno, Nevada. Additionally, we are in the planning phase for a luxury hotel, golf resort, and residential community in Nayarit, Mexico. The 1,200-acre proposed Las Islitas Resort project, with four miles of beachfront on the Pacific Ocean is eighty-five miles north of Puerto Vallarta in the historic fishing village of San Blas (lasislitasresort.com). We also recently put under contact and entered into an escrow to acquire a 3,000 acre property located in the Shasta Cascade region of Northern California. The land is zoned and entitled for 3,700 homes and a championship golf course, with an impressive 1,400 acre Open Space preserve.

However, it wasn't that long ago that I fell into a litigious abyss, mired in judicial chaos. These writings are of a mere mortal—an American-born man of proud Azorean Portuguese descent, a baby boomer who had the privilege of growing up in a typical 1950s American household before toiling for years to build several business careers. This book is not about great achievements but rather about perseverance and lessons learned. While at times I've had success and made millions along the way, I've also lost millions many times over. I've come to realize that failures are nothing more than learning experiences—sometimes merely blips in the road and other times life-altering. Remember: don't let life pass you by. Stop and look around once in a while.

This autobiography provides a detailed road map of trials, challenges, and pitfalls that might await you, the reader, in your personal life and business career. These writings and observations, together with various quotes from famous people and occasionally myself, are meant to give advice and counsel. The anecdotes and stories contained herein might one day provide you with the knowledge needed to face a formidable problem, challenge, or awkward situation—and even to anticipate one before it occurs in the first place.

They say that early childhood shapes our social skills and behavior in adulthood. This book is an honest account of my personal and business life. The chapters are sprinkled with many interesting characters, places, and events, including those from my hilarious, rambunctious teenage years in the Valley of Heart's Delight.

Shortly after the launching of my business career, my story unfolds with an incident that took place a lifetime ago halfway around the world. It involved international intrigue and corruption at the highest levels of government. Looking to finance a $50 million real estate project ($288 million in 2022 dollars), I became involved with some rather unsavory characters and the political and military hierarchy of the Philippine government shortly after the end of the Vietnam War during the mid-1970s.

From the beginning of my early childhood in 1951, in the agricultural town of Santa Clara, California, located in the heart of Silicon Valley, I had no inkling of where my life journey would lead. Throughout my career, I've experienced the thrill of victory and the agony of defeat. During thirty years in construction, real estate development, and finance, I've endured incredible hardships, but founding and nurturing a non-real-estate business dwarfed every other difficulty I faced before or after.

Almost from the beginning of that adventure, I was subjected to vindictive retaliation by a few disgruntled employees. On top of this, we were working to change an old-fashioned, multi-billion-dollar industry that had been around for hundreds of years. In our bid to bring more efficient processes and "green" specialty chemicals to the metal-finishing and corrosion-control industry, we went up against many deeply entrenched competitors.

After raising more than $100 million in investment and after two decades of R&D and extensive marketing, the company I founded was hurt by a devastating global financial collapse. Vengeful employees subjected us to three retaliatory lawsuits and caused two unwarranted criminal investigations. One was by the criminal division of the IRS and the other, a decade later, by the powerful Securities and Exchange Commission (SEC). Considering that whistleblower investigations typically result in hefty fines, criminal prosecution, or both, I was relieved when the baseless and intrusive investigations were concluded without fines or penalties of any kind. However, the damage to our trademark brand and my professional reputation was considerable and the financial loss to our shareholders and my family quite devastating.

To exacerbate matters further, a person I believed to be a friend and an investor in our company betrayed my trust and acted in bad faith when he spearheaded a deceptive hostile takeover of the business. Based on carefully crafted self-serving lies and gross misrepresentations, I was removed as president of the company that I had founded twenty years earlier and built from the ground up. Prior to my removal, and in an effort to save the business and protect the investment of our shareholders, my wife and I had invested $10 million in the business. We lost another $6 million in real estate equity, not including my 20 percent ownership of the company itself. Thankfully, good fortune comes when you least expect it—and usually from the sheer will to persevere.

Ultimately, determination and a commitment to integrity prevailed. With the grace of God, a great deal of hard work, and creative financing, we managed to right the ship. Thanks to help from a few other loyal friends, some good old-fashioned luck, and what must have been divine intervention, I was able to stay the course and follow the guiding principles outlined by President Teddy Roosevelt in the "The Man in the Arena." Somehow, I managed to pull through and redirect my career to the real estate development industry, where it all began a half century earlier.

Many years ago, I promised my father, Leonard "the Colonel" Semas, and my mentor, Benjamin "Ben" Harrison Swig, the founder of the world-famous Fairmont Hotel chain, that I would one day share their words of wisdom. This book passes along their business savvy and good, old-fashioned horse sense, along with my own personal observations, to family, friends, and future generations.

With these writings, I am fulfilling commitments made to my supportive teachers, motivational mentors, influential friends, and loved ones that guided me along my exciting journey. The spirit of our forefathers lives inside each of us. Our ancestors traveled far and wide and dared to dream and conquer the endless obstacles and challenges of everyday life in what has been called the Great American Experiment. To all those, without gender distinction, who have chosen the risky but rewarding entrepreneurial path, you, too, represent the heart and soul of "The Man in the Arena."

LIFE LESSON #4:

"THE TWO MOST IMPORTANT DAYS IN YOUR LIFE ARE THE DAY YOU ARE BORN AND THE DAY YOU DISCOVER WHY."

—MARK TWAIN (AMERICAN WRITER, 1835-1910)

PART I

CHAPTER 1

A BUDDING ENTREPRENEUR

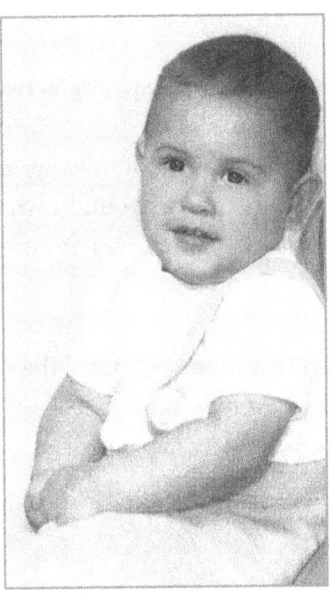

A young David Semas at the age of two

I have often teased my parents about their lack of creativity in naming me. I imagine them standing at the front window of our house in Pacific Grove, California, just two blocks up from the ocean and the beach at Monterey Bay. It's a brisk evening, and logs are burning in the fireplace, keeping the cold ocean air at bay. The homes on our street are meticulously maintained, most of them owned by first- or second-generation Americans with ancestry from the old European countries. Many completed their tour of duty and military service after World War II and decided to relocate to this quaint beachside community. Our yellow, three-bedroom home, built in the 1930s, has white trim and horizontal wood lap siding. It features a front porch, a small front yard, a beautiful palm tree in our side yard, and a white picket fence.

In my imagined scene, my mother, Mary, six months pregnant, has already had a long day corralling my three gregarious older siblings: Judy, Joan, and Lenny. Meanwhile, my father, Leonard, has spent the last twelve hours as a field superintendent supervising his construction crew. Too busy to pick a suitable name for their fourth-born, my father looks out the front window of the house and notices the dimly lit sign for David Avenue, the street we live on, right there at the corner of the yard.

"Look, why don't we make it simple?" he says, placing an arm around my mother's growing waistline. "If it's a boy, we'll be creative and call him David."

"Oh, Leonard," Mom says, exasperated, "what's the matter with you?" I will hear this line countless times during my childhood years.

Dad shrugs and gives her a dashing smile. "What's the difference? It's a great biblical name, isn't it?"

It is indeed and means "beloved" in Hebrew.

Charmed as always by the sparkle in his eyes, Mom relents. "Well, all right."

Satisfied with their effort, Mom turns toward Dad as they wrap their arms around each other and wonder what new grievances another boy will bring them.

My mother, still smiling at ninety-seven, denied the David Avenue story until the day of her passing on November 20, 2020, but I still suspect that's how it really happened.

Leonard and Mary Semas on their wedding day in 1941

At 3:31 a.m. on June 17, 1949, David Michael Semas was born to Leonard Furtado Semas and Mary Christine Lopes Semas at the thirty-bed Peninsula Community Hospital, formerly Grace Deere Velie Harris Carmel Clinic, founded in 1929 by one of the four heirs to the John Deere tractor fortune. Weighing in at nine pounds, I was quite the little beefcake. At two years old, my feet were so pudgy that Mom had to split my shoes to get them to fit.

Me with my mother, Mary, in 1950   Me, my brother, Lenny, and my father, Leonard, in 1950

My family history stretches across the Atlantic to the Azores Islands, located almost one thousand miles west of Portugal's mainland. Colonized by the Portuguese in the fifteenth century, the Azores are comprised of nine islands, volcanic in origin. It has been said that for more than ten generations, my heritage can be traced back to the Azores and before then to the Iberian Peninsula and Spain. Based on recent DNA testing, it looks like our ancestral roots also go back to the United Kingdom and the surname Sims. This might explain why my brother Len and sister Judy have fair skin, whereas my sisters Elizabeth (Joan) and Marie and I have a darker olive Portuguese complexion. The actual DNA test shows my ancestral roots can be traced to the Portuguese colony of the Azores (94 percent), Spain (2 percent), England and Ireland (3 percent), and the Republic of Mali in northwest Africa (1 percent).

On my father's side of the family, my grandpa (*Vo-Vô* in Portuguese), John Furtado Braga Semas, was born in 1890. My grandma, Roselina Pereira "Perry" Semas (*Avó*, pronounced "A-Vah"), was born in 1890. Vo-Vô came from the Vila Franca do Campo and Avó from the Povoação and Ponta Delgada area, which is the largest municipality and capital city of the autonomous region of São Miguel, Azores of Portugal. In America, we pronounce this island as "San" Miguel. Vo-Vô and Avó came to America in 1906. Like most immigrants at the time, they arrived in New York harbor and were processed at the Ellis Island port of entry.

Vo-Vô and Avó Semas, circa 1916

On my mother's side of the family, my grandma was Mary A. Mello Lopes, and my grandpa was Manuel Costa Lopes. Both were born in 1895. I've been able to trace the last two hundred years of our extensive family tree. Surnames related to our family include Semas, Simas, Furtado, Perry, Pereira, Lopes, Mello, Abilla, Almeida, Amaral, Braga, Carreiro, Costa, Fernandes, Ferreira, Figueires, de Gloria, de Jesus, Leite, Medeiros, Motta, Paul, Pacheco, Quarta, Raposa, Rosa, Salvatores, Silva, Silvia, Sims, Sousa, DeSouza, Torres, and Vieira.

The Lopes family, circa 1900

Grandma and Grandpa Lopes in 1959

For ten generations, the Semas, Furtado, Lopes, and Mello clans were born and raised in the Azores. Some came from the islands of Pico and Faial, but most came from São Miguel, known as the Green Island, which is the largest and most populated of the Azores. The island is about thirty-nine miles long and ten miles wide and boasts a population of about 140,000.

My father, Leonard Furtado Semas, was born on April 15, 1922, in Taunton, Massachusetts, which is fifty miles south of Boston and twenty miles east of Providence, Rhode Island.

Dad was one of sixteen. From the oldest to the youngest were Beatrice, Bella, Lena, Margaret, Edward, Evylen, Leonard (Dad, the seventh child born), Helen, Lorraine and Lorreta (twins), Louise, Anthony, Elva, Rosie, and Johnny (twins), and Charlie, who was affected by Down syndrome. Although it was said Uncle Charlie wouldn't make it past seventeen, he lived to the age of sixty-seven.

From L-R, Grandpa John, Grandma Rosalina, and Uncle Charlie in 1940

Each pair of grandparents emigrated to the United States between 1906 and 1912 and, in European immigrant tradition, promptly started a business. In the town of Taunton, Massachusetts, my paternal grandparents, Vo-Vô and Avó, financially supported their rather substantial family of eleven girls and five boys with cash flow generated by the Semas Dairy and the lucrative ash and trash disposal contracts they held with the town and Bristol County. As Vo-Vô always reminded us, "It's ash and trash, not garbage." Supporting the family during and after the Great Depression was no small feat, yet all sixteen children lived to adulthood.

Grandma Mary Mello Lopes, my maternal grandmother, was born on São Miguel, Azores. Like Vo-Vô, Grandpa Manuel Costa Lopes came from the town of Vila Franca do Campo and the civil parish of Furnas. Mom, also from Taunton, was born on May 18, 1923. Grandpa and Grandma Lopes raised their family of five in Fall River, Massachusetts. From oldest to the youngest were Manny, Noah (Noel), Mary (Mom), Margaret, Estelle, and Emily.

Grandma Avó, Roselina Semas, baking bread

In 1951, the Lopes family, except for Uncle Manny, moved from Fall River, Massachusetts, out to the West Coast. After working for many years in the clothing industry and then later in the shoe factories in New Bedford, Grandma Lopes bought a roadside diner in Redondo Beach, California. Mary's Hilltop Café became a favorite among locals and truckers. Only 4'10" tall, she was a real go-getter.

Beginning in 1955, we would all sit around in our living room and watch *Father Knows Best* on our new black-and-white television set. It was about then that I recall visiting my sweet Grandma Lopes. We would pile into Dad's eight-passenger Mercury station wagon and make the seven-hour drive to Southern California to spend a few days with her. Our next treat was to

> LIFE LESSON #5:
>
> "A PEOPLE WITHOUT THE KNOWLEDGE OF THEIR HERITAGE, ORIGIN, CULTURE, AND TRADITIONS WOULD BE LIKE A GIANT OAK TREE WITHOUT ITS ROOTS."
>
> —DAVID SEMAS

visit the fantastic, brand-new theme park called Disneyland, built in the sprawling orange grove orchards of Orange County, California.

The highlight of the Southern California trip for Lenny and myself was going to Grandma's Hilltop Café to chow down on as many delicious, greasy, thick, and juicy hamburgers and French fries as we wanted. We topped off our epicurean feast with root beer floats and apple pie. For a special dessert, Grandma Lopes would sometimes bring out a large navy-blue-and-white-speckled covered roaster pot. Under the heavy lid was a brown paper bag filled with her homemade pastry delights called malasadas. These heart-attack-in-a-bag eatables were a type of Portuguese confection made of small apple-sized and fritter-shaped balls of dough deep-fried in oil, tossed into a paper bag, and coated with granulated sugar.

We would also visit other relatives on my mom's side of the family: Aunt Margaret and her son, Eddie; Aunt Estelle and her two pretty daughters, Susie, and Debbie; and my Aunt Emilie. Aunt Margaret relocated to the small San Joaquin Valley town of Exeter, near Visalia and eighty miles north of Bakersfield. Aunt Estelle moved to Santa Clara and passed away in 2018, but her daughters and grandchildren still live in the San Francisco Bay Area.

Aunt Emilie, the youngest of the Lopes family, also moved to Santa Clara, where she met, fell in love with, and married my uncle, Joe Lascala. In 1971, Aunt Emilie and Uncle Joe returned to his family roots in Buffalo, New York, where they raised their three daughters, Lisa, Gina, and Gia, and a whole troop of grandchildren. Mom's brother, Uncle Manny, lived in Massachusetts with his wife, Theresa Marie Lopes, and his two very pretty daughters, Valerie, and Kathy. Kathy was tragically killed in an automobile accident when she was only seventeen years old. Uncle Manuel Alfred Lopes passed away in 1997.

Grandpa Vo-Vô Semas had sixty head of Holstein-Friesian and Guernsey milking cows and was a rough, tough, old Portuguese guy with hands the size of baseball mitts and a two-pack-a-day Camel cigarette habit. He didn't smile much. My father was the exact opposite. He could be tough but always had a grin on his face and relished telling jokes. Known as Big Leonard by his construction buddies and Twinkle Toes by their dinner club and dancing partners, he was quite the ballroom dancer and very light on his feet, despite his hefty 275-pound build and height of nearly six feet. He was a typical survivor of the Great Depression, who knew the value of hard work and making a buck.

As a young man, Dad was always up for seeing the world, so when the Japanese attacked Pearl Harbor on December 7, 1941, and World War II broke out, he, along with just about every other able-bodied man in America, signed up for the armed services. He was nineteen. Already a good carpenter, he joined the Navy Construction Battalions (CBs), a branch better known as the Seabees, whose motto is "We Build, We Fight." He was attached to Unit 585 and received the World War II Victory Medal, Seabee Insignia, American Theatre Medal, Asiatic Pacific Medal, and the Philippine Liberation Medal. Stationed in the South Pacific on the Marshall Islands, he spent a great deal of time on a fifty-ton D9 Caterpillar bulldozer, building landing fields, runways, command buildings, barracks, bridges, and roads for the rest of the Allied forces.

His unit typically landed as part of the second wave of soldiers on the beachhead right behind where the Marines' first strike force had landed. As Big Leonard put it, with the encampment protected by the Marines, whom he most respected, the perimeter trees were "usually thick with Japanese snipers," who did their best to shoot him off the dozer time and time again. But he simply put up the gigantic front blade of the D9—twelve feet wide and six feet tall—and kept that big old diesel engine chugging along. Besides giving him a great appreciation for teamwork, organization, scheduling, and personal discipline and responsibility, his military career taught him how to operate and maintain heavy equipment and build bridges and roads—skills he would put to good use in his lifelong career in the construction industry.

After the war ended in 1945, Big Leonard was temporarily stationed at Fort Ord, Monterey, California. He received his honorable discharge papers, and his separation date from the US Navy was December 9, 1945, nearly four years to the day after Pearl Harbor was attacked. He and my mother knew that one day they would come back to Monterey and the warm, sunny California coastline. Three years later, they

Big Leonard Semas in the Navy Seabees, 1941

left their childhood memories and hometown of Taunton, Massachusetts. They returned with my three siblings (Judy, Joan, and Lenny) to the quaint seacoast town of Pacific Grove, which sits between Carmel and Monterey. My official birthplace was Carmel, only a few miles from our home.

Upon recognizing greater business opportunities "over the hill," our family relocated a few years later to the lush, agricultural Santa Clara Valley. The city of Santa Clara was an hour south of San Francisco and a thirty-minute drive from the Pacific Ocean and small community of Santa Cruz, where us kids could enjoy the surf and sand. Throughout the summer, my family would head for the beach nearly every weekend. We would drive on Highway 17, past Los Gatos, and over the Santa Cruz Mountains, and just before Santa Cruz, we would stop and spend the morning at Santa's Village theme park and ride the Magic Train, visit the Gingerbread House, and of course see Santa, his elves, and reindeer. My childhood memories were formed here.

Santa Clara County, now known as Silicon Valley, boasts a population of about two million people today. But back in 1950, the Santa Clara Valley only had about 290,000. The quaint city of Santa Clara was home to just under 12,000. This sleepy, blue-collar town was one of the great farming and ranching jewels of California. Agricultural products like apples, prunes, walnuts, apricots, cherries, pears, and peaches with the "Grown in Santa Clara Valley" label were well known throughout the western United States. Vast stretches of farmland dotted the landscape from one end of the fifty-mile-long valley to the other. Lush orchards and abundant fruit trees, rolling-hill vineyards, dairy farms, sprawling cattle and horse pastureland could be seen from Palo Alto at the north end of the valley to Gilroy at the southern end, where the Santa Clara County and San Benito County lines meet.

Santa Clara is home to one of the original twenty-one Franciscan missions, nine of which were founded in the eighteenth century by the legendary Roman Catholic Spanish Franciscan priest (now a saint), Father Junípero Serra. Considered the "Apostle of California" and known as "The Father of the California Missions," he built Mission Santa Clara de Asis in 1777, now the magnificent architectural centerpiece of Santa Clara

University, which was founded in 1851. SCU is a widely regarded private Jesuit university with an enrollment of about 9,200 students.

In more recent years, SCU has established an outstanding reputation for its graduate degree programs, such as the Leavey School of Business, School of Law, and School of Engineering. It gained national prominence when Babe Ruth, the Sultan of Swat, visited the university in 1931. It received further acclaim in 1937 when, during that year's football season, the relatively unknown SCU Broncos stunned the collegiate sports world by defeating Louisiana State University in the Sugar Bowl. In 1938, the Sugar Bowl defending champions once again beat LSU.

Father Serra headed Mission San Carlos Borromeo del Carmelo (Carmel), the headquarters of the Alta California Missions, from 1770 until his death in 1784 and was buried there. In 1776, he also built Mission San Francisco de Asis, the oldest structure in San Francisco to survive the 1906 earthquake, and the sixth religious settlement in California.

Founded in 1885 by railroad magnate and former California Governor, Leland Stanford the expansive 8,180 acre Stanford University is located in the city of Palo Alto at the north end of Santa Clara County. One of the world's leading research and teaching institutions, Leland Stanford built the university as a fitting memorial to his son, Leland Stanford Jr., who tragically passed away from typhoid fever at the age of fifteen. The Leland Stanford connection would one day intersect with the crossroads of my life.

I have wonderful memories of my early childhood in Santa Clara. As a toddler, my daily routine was sometimes rudely interrupted by my older brother, Lenny, who found it quite amusing to fill my diapers with golf-ball-sized rocks. Assuming I'd had an accident, I would go running to my mother in bewilderment about the added weight in my trunk.

Me with Lenny, Joan (Elizabeth), and Judy in 1951

On warm summer days, the powerlines from pole to pole would emit a slight high-pitched ringing tone. When I was about five years old, I often sat on the curb in front of our modest home on Los Padres Boulevard, wearing my Davy Crockett coonskin cap and singing "Home on the Range" while the powerlines sang above me.

Our neighbor from across the street, Mrs. Nonie Quilici, would often come to the door in her apron and wave to me. "Davey, stay on the curb and don't cross the street," she would warn. Los Padres was only a two-lane street at that time and dead-ended in an orchard a couple of houses down, so I was in little danger.

Nonie was married to Aldo Quilici, and their family of six children—Cathy, Chris, Cindi, Cory, Mary, and Joey—became my second family in high school. Cathy and I were so close that when Noni couldn't find Cathy, she would send me out looking for her.

As a youngster, every afternoon I sang my songs and watched the occasional car go by as I patiently waited for the donut truck to appear with its sweet smell of freshly baked pastries. Through the double doors in the back, handmade wooden trays slid out to display delectable sugar-coated and chocolate-covered goodies. While munching down my flour dough treats, I enjoyed watching the activity in the neighborhood: men coming home from work and mowing their lawns, women unloading bags of groceries from the trunks of their cars.

One incident gave a good indication of where I was headed in life. At the ripe young age of four, I found a $100 bill sticking out of the bottom right-hand corner of my father's freestanding safe. Believe it or not, a $100 bill then would be a $1,000 bill today. As far as I was concerned, I could use this paper currency to buy a bag of potato chips, peanut butter filled candy bars, and chocolate milk at the local P&X Market grocery store, located just around the corner from our house near the corner of Los Padres Boulevard and the El Camino Real (Spanish for The King's Highway). Without another thought, I walked to the store all by myself and confidently approached the checkout counter. The grocery store clerk probably assumed my mother must be around somewhere, so he cashed the $100 bill and put the change in the paper bag with my delectable goodies. When I returned home, my parents realized that I had made a shopping trip all by myself, and after seeing the ninety-six dollars and change, they were flabbergasted, angry, and bewildered.

My father held up the cash. "Where did you get all this money, Davey?"

"The man behind the counter at the store gave it to me."

At first puzzled, Dad thought about it for a while. Then he left another $100 bill sticking out of the corner of the closed safe and called me into the room.

When I saw the money, I yelled, "Daddy, there's another one!"

He claimed for the rest of his life that this was a defining moment for me—one that foreshadowed my enthusiastic interest in the monetary system and American capitalism.

From L-R Judy, Joan, Lenny, and Marie with our mom and dad in 1957

By the end of the 1950s, Big Leonard had become a successful Bay Area school and commercial builder through Leonard Semas & Company, which had a bonding capacity of about $10 million, or about $100 million today. Four hundred men were on the payroll, and the company construction yard overflowed with millions of dollars' worth of equipment, like Caterpillar bulldozers, earth movers, scrapers, motor graders, backhoes, excavators, loaders, cranes, forklifts, trenchers, paving equipment, and dump trucks.

Dad told us many times about the building boom of the 1950s and how the Caterpillar corporation gave him a free six-month trial to persuade him to ultimately purchase the equipment. He signed up for the program and then leased the equipment out to other commercial contractors and highway builders. By the end of the first six months, he had enough for a sizable down payment toward the purchase of the equipment. Already Big Leonard was teaching me something about equipment financing leverage.

In 1953, my father built Mariani's Motel and Restaurant on the El Camino Real for Lou and Jack Mariani, the founding patriarchs of the well-known Mariani fruit brand. They were good friends of our family—a fact Mrs. Mariani made certain to remind me of this twenty years later.

By 1954, Dad's business was doing great, so he built a spacious 4,500-square-foot home for our family, complete with a sprawling office, family room, and recreation room basement. The home had a large backyard and covered patio, with a barbeque area and an 18x36-foot swimming pool, where, water-logged like a fish, I could be found swimming laps at least four hours a day, seven days a week.

In 1956, Dad was appointed to the Santa Clara City Planning Commission, and a year later he became its chairman. He became involved in local politics and served as a civic leader. As the chairman of the Santa Clara County Red Cross, Mom was likewise involved in the community. For many years, she was an active member of the Santa Clara City Women's Auxiliary League and the PTA, and in 1956, she was honored with Santa Clara County's Mother of the Year Award.

Leonard and Mary Semas in 1955

The award was well deserved. Mom was a model mother, kind and affectionate, but also a disciplinarian who instilled responsibility and accountability in her children. With their attractive dark features and fair skin, she and Dad made a handsome couple when they went out for dancing at dinner clubs like the Hawaiian Gardens, where, after an invitation by the local MC host and singing celebrity Jerry Paul, I made my onstage singing debut at the ripe old age of nine before a crowd of five hundred patrons.

When Juan (João) Rodrigues Cabrillo sailed into San Diego Bay on September 18, 1542, the earliest history of the Portuguese migration to California began. My dad and mom were both extremely proud of their heritage and belonged to the Santa Clara *Sociedade do Espirito Santo* (Society of the Holy Ghost) Portuguese Hall, which was established in 1942. Anytime they met someone that came from the Azores or was of Portuguese descent, they would invite them over for coffee and Portuguese pastries or for dinner, as was the custom in the Azores. Like most Portuguese people, they were also always inviting familiar faces in off the street for dinner. Over the years, we met Uncle Jonny and Aunt Rosie Silvia, Uncle Oscar and Aunt Eva Rodrigues, Gilbert and Evelyn Simmons, Guillermo "Bill" and Adele Maldonado, Al Vierra, Frank Barcells, Danny and Laura Texera, Johnny and Sue Costa, Jimmy and Vincee Amaral Viso, and a host of others. Dad was also quite the pool shark and was highly proficient at the game of billiards.

Like my parents, when I meet someone for the first time, I'm always inquisitive of their ancestral background. I believe people should be proud of their family's heritage, religion, and culture. Every now and again, I'll meet someone with a Spanish surname like Fernandez, Gonzalez, Hernandez, Rodriguez, or Lopez, but if that same name ends with a letter *s* instead of a *z*, they might be Portuguese, not Spanish or Mexican. On numerous occasions, I have passed this information along to people who thought they were Spanish, and after conferring with their family, they have come to the realization that they are in fact Portuguese. My wife, Susan, jokingly calls me the Portuguese Whisperer.

In 1956, Mom and Dad were constantly traveling the country to visit family and friends. They decided the time had come to hire a full-time live-in nanny to watch their young family—in particular their toddler, Marie "Weeds," and their two mischievous boys, Lenny and Davey. Marie June, born June 14, 1954, received her nickname after I called her "Marie-zee" when I was a little boy. We changed it to "Weedzie" before finally settling on "Weeds."

Mammie Rodriquez was from Guadalajara, Mexico, and twenty years old at the time. She was full-figured and one of the sweetest and most jovial people we had ever met. She was always in a good mood, almost always smiling, and even when she tried to discipline Lenny and me, she couldn't help but break into a grin. Her laugh was infectious and her positive attitude contagious. As youngsters, we always told her she had a beautiful face and reminded us of Aunt Jemima from our favorite pancake syrup brand—even though our sweet Mammie was Hispanic, not African American.

If you were to look up "little angels" in the dictionary, you wouldn't find a picture of Lenny and me. On the other hand, if you looked up "mischievous little rascals," we fit the bill to a T. We were always looking for creative ways to scare the bejesus out of Mammie. On one Friday evening in early October 1957, our parents went out for dinner and dancing at the Hawaiian Gardens dinner club with all their friends. Our older sisters, Judy, and Joan, were at slumber parties, and baby Weeds, who was three years old, was asleep. As was our custom, we went into Mom and Dad's bedroom, sprawled atop their gigantic bed, and watched a scary movie on their black-and-white television (we didn't get our first color television set until 1962). Although Mammie loved watching horror movies, if she heard an unusual sound or even the house creaking, she would practically jump out of her skin.

This was just too darn tempting for eight-year-old and ten-year-old brothers to let pass. As the better storyteller of the duo, I spun a tall tale about a gorilla breaking loose from the Barnum & Bailey Circus train on its way to San Francisco. Mammie's eyes grew wider and wider as I spoke. We were watching the 1951 sci-fi motion-picture thriller *The Thing from Another World*, starring James Arness. Toward the end of the movie, the gigantic creature walked down a wooden plank hallway that had been wired to electrify it. When it suddenly stepped off the planks, Mammie let out a scream.

"Mammie, I'm not kidding," I said, taking advantage of her agitated state. "A gorilla really escaped from a circus train. I heard the man on the radio say the police are looking for him in Santa Clara."

"Davey, are you serious," Mammie asked, "or is this another one of your stories?"

"Cross my heart and hope to die. It's the truth." Of course, my fingers were crossed behind my back.

I knew Mammie didn't believe me, but that was A-okay, because Lenny and I already had a scheme in the works. During the TV commercial, Mammie jumped up from the bed to go to the kitchen to make us peanut-butter-and-jelly sandwiches. She turned on the lights in our 1950s modern kitchen, set the bread on the ceramic tile counter, went to the walk-in pantry for peanut butter, and retrieved the jelly out of the refrigerator. As she began to spread gobs of Skippy peanut butter on Wonder Bread, our favorite, she heard a strange grunting sound outside. At first, she thought she was hearing things. Then, right before her eyes, a huge furry creature, hunched over and walking on two legs, scurried in front of the kitchen window. Still in Mom and Dad's bedroom, I could hear Mammie's scream all the way down the hall. So could our neighbors on each side of us up and down Lexington Street.

Being the hero, I rushed to her rescue.

"*Ay, Dios mío* (Oh my God)!" she blurted out. "Davey, call the police! There's a gorilla in our backyard! He's here! He's here! I'm not kidding!"

I couldn't contain myself and fell to the floor in hysterics just as Lenny entered through the back door wearing Mom's full-length mink coat. For the next ten minutes, she yelled unfamiliar Spanish words at us as she chased us around the house with a broom. Afterward, we all laughed and grabbed our peanut-butter-and-jelly sandwiches to watch the rest of *The Thing from Another World*.

I did my best to keep up in elementary school at C. W. Haman, which was located at the corner of Los Padres Boulevard and Homestead Road, less than one mile from our home. I loved school, but unlike my siblings, I didn't earn the best grades. I was always weak in reading and usually ended up with a C or maybe a B-, if I was lucky. For some reason, I found it difficult to read and interpret the written word. My skills lay in the spoken word. It wasn't until many years later that I discovered I had a moderate form of dyslexia. In those days, little attention was paid to learning disabilities, and having been raised to be relatively self-reliant, I just thought I wasn't as bright as my siblings. I really didn't mind because I had figured

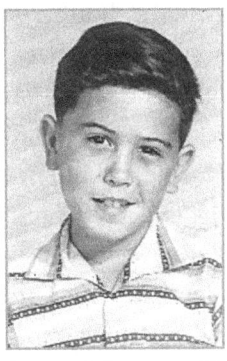

Me at eight years old in Mrs. Black's third-grade class

LIFE LESSON #6:

"A PESSIMIST SEES THE DIFFICULTY IN EVERY OPPORTUNITY; AN OPTIMIST SEES THE OPPORTUNITY IN EVERY DIFFICULTY."

—SIR WINSTON CHURCHILL
(PRIME MINISTER OF UNITED KINGDOM, 1874-1965)

out how to work around it. My optimistic attitude and vivid imagination made up for it.

To me, school was mostly a place to meet friends, play sports, and flirt with girls. I was quite the social butterfly. My first-grade teacher, Mrs. Battle, recorded in my report card: *David is doing average work, and I feel he could do a little better.* At the end of the year, she wrote: *David has done a little better. It has been a pleasure having him in my class.* In second grade, Mrs. Evans wrote: *What a pleasure David is!* In third grade, Mrs. Black hit it right on the nose: *David needs to be encouraged to do more reading.*

In the fourth grade, I had my first real romance with Pat "Patsy" Morrell. One day, while trying to show off my athletic talent, I took a full swing with a baseball bat and unaware that she was standing so close, I accidentally grazed her head with the bat. Needless to say, that was the end of our brief courtship.

By 1959, our favorite TV show at home was *Bonanza*, with Ben, Adam, Hoss, and Little Joe Cartwright. I guess my love of cowboys, horses, and the Old West came from watching television shows like *Gene Autry*, *Roy Rogers*, *Davy Crockett*, *Cheyenne*, *Gunsmoke*, *Rawhide*, *Lawman*, *Maverick*, *Have Gun Will Travel*, and of course, *Wyatt Earp*. In those days, it was still acceptable for my buddies and me to play what we called "cowboys and Indians."

In the fifth grade, I had for the first time a male teacher, Mr. Tholl, who served as a great role model. He helped me with my homework, taught me how to focus, and constantly told me that I could do anything if I prepared, worked hard, and put my mind to it. A fantastic teacher, he was extremely dedicated to his students. Despite their young age, he was committed to preparing them to enter the adult world one day.

After my fiasco with Patsy Morrell, I came to realize that I had a crush on Kit Holmes, another beautiful girl in my class. Kit lived around the corner from our house on De La Pena Avenue, but I was afraid to talk to her.

One day, after much planning and preparation, I walked up to her and said, "Hello." We sat next to each other for lunch that day, and within a matter of weeks, she became my girlfriend. This puppy-love romance must have been fairly serious, because my mother sometimes gave me some of her extra costume jewelry, which I in turn gift-wrapped as a surprise for my new girlfriend.

Eventually, I realized that Kit had grown too accustomed to my generosity. Week after week, I could see that she was starting to expect a gift, and this went on for most of the school year. So, one day I came home and told Mom, "That's it. I've had it. No more jewelry, and no more gifts. I think she's a gold digger! But it's okay. I have a new girlfriend."

"Oh, really?" Mom said. "And who might that be?"

"Chris Holmes, Kit's twin sister!"

Except for the lack of a dead teenager down by the railroad tracks, our small town resembled the backdrop for the classic 1986 Rob Reiner coming-of-age movie *Stand by Me*. Santa Clara was pretty much a blue-collar community and modest suburban town. Our household was something like the *Ozzie and Harriet* television show. My mother and three sisters played the piano, and all five of us

Our home at 1872 Lexington Street in Santa Clara

children sang, although at the time, I was the big ham and the lead singer of the group, mainly because I couldn't play an instrument or harmonize nearly as well as the others. We were also referred to as the Cleaver family, from the hit television show, *Leave It to Beaver*, which aired on CBS from 1957 to 1958, then on ABC until 1963. Brother Lenny was Wally, and I was the troublemaking Theodore "Beaver" Cleaver. One of Lenny's close friends, who shall remain nameless, reminded me of the outwardly polite but inwardly conniving next-door neighbor, Eddie Haskell.

By the age of seven, I was an ambitious entrepreneur. When my buddies and other neighborhood kids opened their lemonade stands or sold apple cider, I noticed that just about everyone was constantly falling off wagons, bikes, or skateboards, the latter of which were constructed in those days by nailing rolling skates to the bottom of a 2x4-foot piece of lumber. If they didn't get hurt while wandering the neighborhood, they inevitably scraped or cut some extremity while climbing trees and fences, playing on the basketball court or baseball diamond, or swimming at the community pool.

Seeing an obvious market in the making, I took my red wagon, had my dad build a wooden cabinet box with dividers, loaded it up with medical supplies from Mom's kitchen and bathroom, and attached a red light and a hand-crank siren. My Triple R Ranch ambulance, named after the 1950s television series featuring Spin and Marty, not only provided my neighborhood with a great service but turned out to be profitable as well—especially considering that I got my supplies for free. Charging a flat rate of a quarter per patient, I used tweezers to pull out Steve Ferreira's splinter and came to the rescue with my small bottle of mercurochrome antiseptic when Mark Stefani tore his leg on a barbed wire fence. My patients were happy because they didn't have to go home to their mothers, which would have dashed all hope of playing outdoors for the rest of the day.

Though my ambulance service lasted only one summer, it was just the beginning of my entrepreneurial pursuits.

One Saturday morning when I was about eight years old, Big Leonard came to me and said, "I'm going out for the day to visit some of my construction projects. I'll pay you a whole two dollars if you'll take care of mowing the lawn and trimming the shrubs. You think you can do that?"

I smiled with delight. "Sure!"

Within minutes after Dad left, my buddies, Mark Stefani, Steve Ferreira, Steve Lay, and Danny Rotter, stopped by and invited me to join them for a bike ride to the recreation center.

I told them I had some yard work to do, so I couldn't go and hang out, but if they were to offer to help, we could get the job done four times as fast. "I'll pay you twenty-five cents each."

They eagerly agreed. So, I gave the lawnmower to Mark, the trimmer to Steve Ferreira, the hoe

---

LIFE LESSON #7:

"LIFE IS A SUCCESSION OF LESSONS, WHICH MUST BE LIVED TO BE UNDERSTOOD."

—RALPH WALDO EMERSON (AMERICAN LECTURER, PHILOSOPHER, AND POET, 1803–1882)

and rake to Steve Lay, and the lawn edger to Danny. While they got to work, I supervised the crew.

Having forgotten something at home, Dad returned within the hour to find me sitting on the porch while my four friends did the work. After stepping out of his car, he looked at me and then at Mark, Danny, and the two Steves sweating in the yard. "Davey, I thought I told you to mow the lawn, trim the shrubs, and pull the weeds from the garden," he said sternly.

"No, Dad, what you said was for me to take care of mowing the lawn and trimming the shrubs and pulling the weeds, and that's exactly what I'm doing."

He folded his arms as he mulled over my response. "Do I dare ask if you're paying them?"

"What kind of a boss do you think I am?" I said. "I'm paying them a fair wage of twenty-five cents each, and I keep the one dollar because I'm their boss and the landscaping superintendent and the one with the work contract."

Laughing and shaking his head, he returned to his car and then drove off, leaving me to my supervising.

I was about eight years old when Dad took me to Santa Clara Lumber Company one Saturday afternoon. The store, on the corner of El Camino Real and Lincoln Street, was owned by Dad's good friend, Eugene Enos, and Eugene's son, Bob. While Dad walked the aisles in search of a few hardware items, I spotted a small bottle of Elmer's Glue. I had a school project that needed white glue, so I took it off the shelf and put it in my pocket. Distracted by looking at the cool Schwinn Corvette bicycle that Mr. Enos had in the store window, I forgot to tell my father about the glue when he went to the counter to check out.

A school portrait of me in 1957

When I got home, Dad saw that I had, as he put it "shoplifted" the item and raised his glasses to his forehead. "Davey, where did you get that glue?"

"I got it off the shelf from Santa Clara Lumber," I replied. "I'm sorry I forgot to tell you because I was all excited about the Schwinn bicycle Mr. Enos had in his window that was just like the bike I saw advertised on TV." This was during a commercial for one of my favorite TV shows, *Cheyenne*, starring my hero, Clint Walker.

"No, you *stole* it off the shelf from Santa Clara Lumber and my friend Mr. Enos's store. Now we're going to go back there, and you're going to return the Elmer's Glue and tell Mr. Enos how sorry you are for being a little thief. You will then ask for his forgiveness and ask him how you can make things right and pray he doesn't call the police and have you put in jail."

By this time, my eyes had welled up with tears and I was shaking in my shoes, knowing the last thing in the world I wanted to do was return to the store and tell Mr. Enos I was a crook. Before I could dwell on my predicament, Dad grabbed me by the scruff of the neck, and the next thing I remember was standing before Mr. Enos.

I struggled to speak and could only whimper. "Mr. Enos," I finally blurted out, "I stole some glue from your store, and here it is." I gave him the bottle of Elmer's Glue. "I'm so sorry. I will never do it again. Please, please, don't have me put in jail. I'll do anything you ask of me to make up for what I did."

Mr. Enos looked over at Dad. "Leonard, what do you think? Do you think Davey is really sorry for what he did and learned a valuable lesson?"

"Maybe Davey got the message," Dad said, "but just to make certain he'll never forget this painful experience, I have a suggestion. I happened to notice earlier this morning some dust on the counters and a lot of empty boxes lying around. The floors look like they need to be swept, and the parking lot has some weeds. What if Davey were to come here early Saturday morning and work all day to take care of these items for you?"

"Great idea." Mr. Enos looked down at me. "Davey, is that okay with you? If you come and work off your bad behavior, I'll forgive you and chalk up the entire incident to a lesson learned. Okay?"

Relieved I wasn't going to jail, I showed up the following morning at seven-thirty and worked until my mom came to pick me up at five o'clock in the evening. I swore I would never steal or shoplift anything again and would always abide by the rules.

As anyone who knows me can attest, I never stole anything for the rest of my life. If a store cashier gives me too much change, I always return the money. If a restaurant waiter or waitress forgets to add something to my check, I bring it to his or her attention. When I see a sign that says *No Trespassing*, I don't enter. Other than my rebellious teenage years and maybe a little speeding now and then, I obey the law, abide by established rules, and always try to extend courtesy and respect to others, especially law-enforcement officers.

Me saddling up and sitting on a pony in 1959

On Saturday mornings during the summer of 1957, Dad would take my brother and me in his gray 1956 Cadillac Coupe de Ville to go for our weekly grocery shopping adventure, usually at the big Safeway supermarket on El Camino Real. But on one particular morning, we went to the local Emo Biagini's Sunnyway Market, located at the corner of Lexington Street and Gould Avenue (now Scott Boulevard). Dad loved to take us boys shopping with him because it was the only time, he could buy the volume of groceries and the types of food that Mom would never allow if she was there. Dad had been just seven years old when the stock market crashed in 1929 and remembered the hard times and food shortages of the 1930s. Now, as a successful businessman, Big Leonard didn't buy the small or medium size of anything. He always bought the jumbo size—usually in quantities of a half dozen each (pre-Costco).

We looked forward to the weekly trip because we could get Dad to buy all our favorite kids' foods, like Marshmallow Crème with Skippy Peanut Butter, Welch's Grape Jelly, Oscar Mayer Hot Dogs, Kraft Macaroni & Cheese, Wheaties, and deli bologna rounds and salami sticks. As we roamed the aisles, Dad routinely stopped to chat with old friends or the Biagini brothers. By the time we were through with our hour-long shopping spree, he needed Lenny and me to help push several loaded shopping carts.

On this particular trip, Lenny and I saw Dad talking to someone at the end of the aisle and watched him give the man some money.

When we asked Dad who the person was, he just said, "He's a new friend."

We didn't know what had happened until sometime later, when we overheard Dad tell Mom the story. Apparently, while we were walking up and down the aisles, Big Leonard had noticed a young, handsome Hispanic-looking man with his beautiful blonde-haired wife and three well-groomed and meticulously dressed children checking prices against their food budget on a piece of paper.

Dad waited until the man was alone, approached him, and introduced himself. "Hello. My name's Leonard Semas. I'm a local general contractor here in town. I couldn't help but notice that you appear to be very carefully choosing food for your family. Do you mind if I ask if you're looking for work? Because if you are, we have a position available with good pay and benefits for a hardworking construction laborer."

The man smiled. "My name's Bill Maldonado, and that's my wife, Adele, and my three children. You're very gracious to ask. I'm attending school at San Jose State University, studying to be an electrical engineer, and I *am* looking for work."

"Great. Here's my business card. How about I advance you a hundred dollars for now, and I'll see you Monday morning?"

Bill, being a proud man, said, "Thank you, but I'm not looking for a handout."

"Hell," Dad replied, "this isn't a handout. It's merely a loan against my new employee's future wages. I've always taken pride in knowing a good man when I see one, and I'm looking at one now! You'll be at work on Monday, won't you?"

"I sure will," Bill assured him.

I asked Dad why he'd offered the man a job and gave him an advance of a hundred dollars when he didn't even know him.

He stopped what he was doing to answer my question. "Davey, honest, hardworking, and loyal employees don't grow on trees. Sometimes they're far and few between. Every employee in a company is important, just like spokes in a wheel of a wagon. If one or two spokes break, the wheel becomes less safe, and if a few more spokes break, the wheel collapses. If you're in the middle of nowhere and you lose a wheel, you're in real trouble. Let me give you an example. You know Stan Cabral, my chief mechanic, don't you?"

"Sure," I said. "Stan's the greatest. On Saturdays, when you're working in the office, I go out back to the construction yard to help him work on your trucks and tractors, and he always gives me Tootsie Rolls as a reward."

"Yes, Stan is the greatest, but in terms of his position in the company, I have many more people that I pay a higher salary because they have more responsibilities. So, on the surface, you'd think maybe he wasn't as important as everyone else in the company, but if you thought that, you'd be dead wrong. Stan may not be an executive vice president, my chief estimator, a construction manager, or one of my superintendents, but as my chief mechanic, he's just as important as everyone—and sometimes maybe even more important than I am. I have millions of dollars invested in construction equipment, and if Stan isn't there to maintain it and fix it when it breaks down, I'm out of business. Stan is a valuable part of the whole Leonard Semas & Company team. Remember: you're always in the people business. Without good employees or coworkers, you're just one spoke in the wheel, and you can't move a loaded wagon on one spoke or on three wheels."

Bill Maldonado showed up, as promised, that Monday morning.

LIFE LESSON #8:

"WHEN YOU ARE ASKED IF YOU CAN DO A JOB, TELL 'EM, 'CERTAINLY I CAN!' THEN GET BUSY AND FIND OUT HOW TO DO IT."

—THEODORE ROOSEVELT (TWENTY-SIXTH PRESIDENT OF THE UNITED STATES, 1858-1919)

He not only became one of my dad's best employees, but he rose from construction laborer to foreman and then to superintendent. He and his family bought a house near ours and became our good friends. Bill graduated from San Jose State with engineering and business degrees. About six years later, he approached Dad and told him that he had an opportunity to work for a company that was building microwave towers in Mexico. Dad asked Bill what he knew about building microwave towers, and Bill told him, "Not a thing." They both laughed, and Dad told Bill that he understood and that he should do whatever was best for him and his family.

Bill, Adele, and their family moved to Mexico, but the Maldonados remained close to us. Adele called my mother at least once a month for many years. Dad stayed in touch with Bill as Bill was promoted up the ladder at the microwave company, ultimately becoming vice president of South American operations. Unfortunately, his marriage to Adele ended. Years later, she became a state senator in Mexico.

Guillermo "Bill" Maldonado married Minerva and went on to become chairman and CEO of Square D International, which in 1991 became the flagship brand of Schneider Electric. With a market cap of $90 billion, Schneider is the world's largest manufacturer of electrical equipment and provides energy management and automation solutions.

Although my father never told anyone outside our family about that story, it taught me an important lesson that has stayed with me to this day: whenever possible, give somebody else a helping hand, even if you've never met the person before. Dad approached Bill in a delicate way, so he didn't embarrass him. He saw somebody beginning his life journey and gave him a job, and they became lifelong friends. Yet Dad was humble and never made a big deal about his gesture to help a young family get a start in life, and I have no doubt that Bill Maldonado paid forward that gesture many times over.

Recently, when I researched what had become of Bill, I learned he had retired and was living in Mexico City with Minerva, his wife of twenty-five years. He returned my call in December of 2016, and we reminisced about Dad, Mom, and our families in the 1950s and 1960s. Bill was as gracious and dignified as I had remembered. They say you can't turn back the clock. Well, sometimes you can, even if it's just for an hour over the phone!

Big Leonard was a rough-and-tumble 275-pound construction boss who got his start on the back of a D9 Cat bulldozer in World War II, but he had a big heart that many people never saw. Dad taught us important lessons about extending a helping hand and giving somebody a break. He believed that was the way the world should work. He said, "You get out as much of life as you put into it."

During our early teenage years, we enjoyed extended weekend hunting trips in late fall, during which Dad also taught my brother and me lessons about survival, hardship, teamwork, and commitment to excellence. Using his experiences as a Navy Seabee in the jungles of the South Pacific, he showed us how to properly select a suitable location near a stream and in the trees for protection from wind, rain, and the elements. He showed us how to prepare our temporary quarters, set up tents, and establish a first-rate campsite.

We would go deer hunting and then have a great time sitting around the campfire telling stories, laughing, and enjoying camaraderie amongst the hunting party, which was comprised of then brother-in-law Chester "Chet" Campbell (Joan's first husband and my nephew Bill Campbell's father), Gilbert Simmons (Dad's hilarious cousin), and Lenny and me. In the early morning hours, usually about four o'clock, we climbed out of our warm sleeping bags, made breakfast, and cleaned up the campsite. We were assigned a hunting partner for the day and learned about hunting and firearms safety.

For several years, starting when I was about ten years old, we hunted near the coastline in Mendocino County, about five hours north of

> **LIFE LESSON #9:**
>
> "THERE IS A DESTINY WHICH MAKES US BROTHERS; NONE GOES HIS WAY ALONE. ALL THAT WE SEND INTO THE LIVES OF OTHERS COMES BACK INTO OUR OWN."
>
> —EDWIN MARKHAM (AMERICAN POET, 1852-1940)

San Francisco, in and around the towns of Garberville, Whitethorn, and Shelter Cove. Then, beginning in 1962, about the same time our favorite TV show was *The Beverly Hillbillies*, Dad started taking us mule deer hunting in the eastern high desert just over the Sierra Nevada, near the Nevada border. Coincidently, forty years later, I became friends with Max Bear Jr., who graduated from Santa Clara University in 1937 and played Jethro Bodine on *The Beverly Hillbillies*.

I was thirteen years old, and my brother was fifteen, when Dad decided one day to head for the high desert. We were traveling on a two-lane asphalt road north of Reno, Nevada. On this stretch of Highway 395, which curves back into California, the wind routinely gusts up to eighty miles per hour. Dad had just bought a brand-new Aristocrat red-and-white travel trailer to tow behind his stylish 1960 Lincoln Continental Mark V. He had loaded the inside of the car to the roof, which effectively covered the back window of the car. I had pushed some of the clothes aside so I could see out the back window, since I was becoming bored with the long, monotonous drive. For a while, I gazed out the window at the travel trailer as it swayed from side to side with the crosswinds.

Dad was going about sixty-five miles per hour down the highway with the radio on and having a great old time when all of a sudden, I saw the trailer lurch from one side to the other. I hadn't seen it do that before. I kept watching as the little red-and-white trailer swerved, dipped, and swerved again. The trailer tongue dipped down some more, and I heard the sound of the safety chain breaking. Without warning, the trailer flew upward and did a 360-degree turn in midair before crashing down. It bounced once, rolled over, slammed into the shoulder of the road, and broke into pieces.

Shocked, I turned and said, "Dad, didn't you feel that?"

"No. Feel what?"

Being a typical thirteen-year-old smart aleck, I said, "Well, let me put it to you this way: remember the trailer we used to have behind us?"

"Davey, shut up and quit clowning around."

"I'm not clowning around. Our trailer is now in a million pieces on the side of the road about a mile back."

Dad slammed on his brakes, pulled onto the shoulder of the road, and climbed out of the Lincoln. He looked behind the car as though the trailer was still there, turned to me and my brother, looked down the road behind us, shook his head, and threw his hands in the air. "Oh, crap!"

We drove back to find the trailer shredded into pieces and scattered along the side of the road. We gathered up a few belongings and were amazed to find that our rifles and much of our gear were still intact.

We headed up the road about ten miles and came to the thriving metropolis of Doyle, California, which boasted a population of one hundred people and the famous Buck Inn Tavern and Doyle General Store and Hotel. Inside the general store, established in the early 1900s, we met an old-timer in his eighties smoking a pipe, his feet propped up on a small table next to a potbelly stove. The hotel was located directly above the store. Each of the sixteen rooms had a porcelain washbasin with a distorted mirror above it, a tall wooden dresser, and two twin beds with brass headboards and what must have been fifty-year-old mattresses. The wallpaper was peeling off at the edges, but the lace curtains were a nice touch. The occasional mouse was included in the price. The men's and women's bathrooms were located at the end of the long hallway. Like the Leland Stanford connection, the small town of Doyle, California and the famous Buck Inn Tavern and Doyle General Store and Hotel would intersect with the crossroads of my life nearly a half century later.

That year, we hunted within a twenty-mile radius of the town, and the store and hotel served as home base. Year after year, we returned to hunt deer near Doyle and would always stop in to say hello to local rancher Dominic Azevedo and our friends at the Buck Inn and the Doyle General Store and Hotel.

Starting in 1969, the year Apollo 11 landed on the moon, until 1979, I hunted for mule deer near Doyle with my buddies and notorious hunting partners, the Ky-Dogs. The group grew over the years and included Mike

Doyle, CA General Store and Hotel in 2012

Carey, Ed Quintal, Frank Cano, Paul Kerper, Dan Gallagher, Gary Plaza, brother Len, Phil Lebowski, Steve Ferreira, and brother-in-law Bob Golden.

By today's standards, we would be considered strict conservationists and staunch animal rights activists, because in ten years, the only thing the Ky-Dogs ever killed were mosquitoes. When the Ky-Dogs pulled into our hunting designated area, most of the wildlife around could be heard chuckling. This collection of hapless hunters was all about enjoying the outdoors, camping, and cooking over an open campfire. During a seven-day hunt, the guns were unloaded and stowed away each night, and our band of urban cowboy outdoorsmen would sit around the campfire under moonlit skies, imbibe alcoholic libations, and smoke cigars while telling tall tales, laughing, and thoroughly enjoying some good, old-fashioned camaraderie.

Ky-Dog Doyle hunting camp in 1978

Ky-Dog hunting club patch

One year, while driving for hours on winding dirt roads until the middle of the night with only a full moon guiding our way, we found our best campsite ever. It was the ideal base camp, nestled beneath magnificent ponderosa pines against a steep hillside sheltered from the wind and elements, with a beautiful running stream and an abundance of rainbow and brook trout. We looked at each other and almost in unison said, "We're in heaven." After getting up at 4:00 a.m., eating breakfast, and stationing ourselves at our designated hunting sites before the break of dawn, we didn't spy a single big mule deer buck in our rifle sights. Eventually, we got hungry and met up again, piled into the Jeeps, and headed to Doyle for a nice lunch. We couldn't understand why other hunters were nowhere to be found. We stopped by the ranger station to pick up some maps. I glanced over and started looking carefully at the large topographical map on the wall and was shocked when I realized we were not only camped in a national forest but a game refuge where hunting was illegal. *Well*, I thought, *there goes our Shangri-La campsite.*

As a ten-year-old who loved baseball, I tried out for and was selected to play for the Santa Clara Lions Little League team. Mr. Rankin, Kent's father, was our head coach, followed later by Mr. Rogers (Kenny Rogers's father).

I initially played centerfield but soon moved to first base on the roster. I was pretty good, but many of my teammates and others in the league were far more talented, like Dave Bauer, Dennis Grist, Joey and Ricky Cardenas, Kent Rankin, Pat Galos, Jim Rice, Kenny Rogers, and Chris Serrano. After games, we ate gigantic, delectable cinnamon rolls and glazed donuts at Stan's Donut Shop on Homestead Road. The newly opened shop belonged to our teammate's father, Stan Wittmayer.

As I moved through intermediate school, I appreciated having three smart older siblings pave the way for me. By the time I started a class, the teachers would say, "Are you related to Judy, Joan, and Lenny Semas?" and then go on to comment about their smarts and what great young people they were. While at William A. Wilson Intermediate School, located right across the street from our house on 1872 Lexington Street, I was elected president of Block W (Lettermen's Club) and played on the football, basketball, baseball, and wrestling teams and enjoyed swimming in the summers.

Like myself, many at Wilson School were raised Catholic, so after school, we attended catechism classes next door at the Carmelite Monastery. Following our afternoon religious teachings, we would hang out with our buddy, "Cowboy" Jim Donovan, who at only five feet tall, was still a big man around town and a living legend at the Santa Clara City Council meetings. He lived on Benton Street right across the street from the side entrance of the Carmelite Monastery. Cowboy Jim was the only resident who could keep farm animals at his home. His family property had been grandfathered in before Santa Clara was incorporated in 1850 and passed city ordinances prohibiting the keeping of livestock within the city limits in 1948.

My family's spacious home, which included a large backyard equipped with a basketball court, barbecue, and swimming pool, became the perfect spot for me and my gang of friends to hang out every summer. We had barbecues and swim parties all the time, and my friends loved being there, not just because of the obvious frills but also because of my sisters' hot girlfriends, who were frequently around. This was a fabulous time, but our world was shattered when, on February 3, 1959, the day after my brother Lenny's twelfth birthday party, Buddy Holly, Ritchie Valens, and the Big Bopper were killed in an airplane crash. It was indeed "the day the music died."

In the summers of 1962 and 1963, my friends, along with just about every one of Santa Clara County's 650,000 residents, would partake in the activities at the Santa Clara County Fair, located on Tully Road, now in the middle of Silicon Valley. Back then, it was in the boondocks. The carnival featured games, fun zone, rides, and, most importantly, food, including my favorite Neto Sausage linguica sandwiches. It also showcased exhibits, 4-H Club competitions, and concerts by country western acts like Willie Nelson, Merle Haggard, Conway Twitty, Johnny Cash, and teenage idols like Ricky Nelson, Frankie Avalon, and Fabian. We saw the Beach Boys, Sonny & Cher, and We Five. In 1968, the Santa Clara County Fairgrounds hosted the Northern California Folk-Rock Festival with Jimi Hendrix, Janis Joplin, the Doors, Jefferson Airplane, and a host of others.

During this time, I competed locally as a 50-meter and 100-meter freestyle swimmer for the Santa Clara Swim Club (not Swim Team). I briefly had the privilege of being taught by one of history's greatest swimming coaches, All-American Coach of the Year George Haines, also known as "Maestro." He was about forty years old, physically fit, and handsome, with a California tan, and could usually be found wearing his safari hat and sunglasses.

I was a pretty good swimmer and thought I could become a great one. While Coach Haines encouraged me and did his utmost to motivate me to rise to a higher level, after two years spent swimming for him, I realized I wasn't in the same league with his other gifted swim students. There were quite a few that were already US Olympians and many others of Olympic caliber. These swimmers were better than I could ever hope to be, and instead of trying to improve and putting my nose to the grindstone, I took the easy way out.

I had just finished dead last in a 100-meter freestyle race. Hanging on to the side of the pool, I looked up at Coach Haines and said, "Coach, I don't think this is for me. I'm seriously outclassed. I have no business competing with these truly great athletes."

He looked down at me. "Semas, you can be anything you want to be, but you have to be willing to pay the price. You have the talent to be a world-class swimmer, but you lack the willingness, commitment, and discipline it takes to achieve greatness."

I pulled myself out of the water and grabbed my towel. "I don't want to let you down, but I just don't have what it takes. I guess I'm not willing to put in the hours of practice and make the commitment you're talking about to be a great swimmer."

Coach Haines shook his head. "Semas, Semas, Semas. You're not letting me down; you're letting *yourself* down, because you could have been a great swimmer. I can see that your heart just isn't in it, and if you're going to be a part of the Santa Clara Swim Club, I need your body, heart, mind, and soul to be one-hundred-and-ten percent committed. In the future, I want you to promise yourself that whatever you do in life, you will do your best to never give in, never give up, and never say quit. Reach down inside yourself and find that special place that will give you the strength to succeed."

That day, I went home feeling awful for quitting the swim club, but I gave serious thought to what Coach Haines had told me.

Throughout my high-school years, at least once a week I'd pass Coach Haines in the hallways, in the locker room, or at the Santa Clara War Memorial Swimming Pool.

Most times, he would stop and put his hands on my shoulders, give me a Cheshire Cat smile, and say, "Semas, Semas, Semas. You could have been a great swimmer!"

Every so often, I would stop by his office and ask the coach for advice. He was always willing to lend an ear, but even after his words of encouragement, he would perform the same "Semas, Semas, Semas" routine the next time I saw him.

As it turned out, for a brief time I swam in the shadow of a true Olympic dynasty that included Donna de Varona, Don Schollander, Terry Stickles, Pokey Watson, Mitch Ivy, and many others. They were the greatest swimmers of our generation, and the most famous among them was Mark Spitz, who was in my Spanish class with Miss Mendia. He won seven gold medals and set seven world records at the 1972 Munich Olympic Games. George Haines coached swimmers seven times in the Olympics and was a three-time head coach of the US Olympic Swim Team.

Many years later, in 1999, as a fifty-year-old business executive, I called Coach Haines at his Carmichael, California home, near Sacramento and told him what an inspiration he had been to me over the years. I felt privileged for the opportunity to thank such a remarkable man before he suffered a stroke a few years later and passed away in 2006.

Rarely does a day go by that I don't recall Coach Haines's never-say-quit attitude. He knew that, like everyone else, I would face adversity in the future and wouldn't always be able to turn and run. Sometimes I would have to stand my ground, look inside myself, and in his words, "Never give in, never give up, and never say quit." Those were the right words to tell a teenage boy about what it takes to be great. It takes more than talent. It takes determination, persistence, and willpower. I have carried that advice and can-do spirit with me ever since.

LIFE LESSON #10:

"OUR GREATEST WEAKNESS LIES IN GIVING UP. THE MOST CERTAIN WAY TO SUCCEED IS ALWAYS TO TRY JUST ONE MORE TIME."

—THOMAS EDISON (AMERICAN INVENTOR, 1847-1931)

CHAPTER 2
SOWING WILD OATS

Monday morning, September 2, 1963, dawned under clear blue skies and with a brisk chill in the air. As I walked onto campus on the first day of my freshman year at Santa Clara High School, I felt as if I had stepped back in time. The high school was founded in 1872, shortly after the conclusion of the American Civil War and thirteen years before Stanford University was established in 1885, and many of its buildings had been constructed at the turn of the century. The elegant, traditional red-brick structures were covered with lush green ivy that climbed toward the Spanish clay tile roofs. Unfortunately, just a few months into my freshman year, the school district began to demolish some of the classic older buildings, including the administration building, because they had been erected with unreinforced masonry and didn't meet the new California earthquake standards. Considering the San Andreas Fault is only fifteen miles to the west, running along the western edge of Santa Clara Valley and at the base of the Santa Cruz Mountains, the Santa Clara School Board's decision at the time was most prudent.

Growing up in Santa Clara Valley could be a little unnerving. Because we lived next to the San Andreas Fault and smaller tributaries like the Loma Prieta, Hayward, Calaveras, and San Benito, the possibility of an earthquake was always in the back of our minds. On countless occasions, the apprehensive residents of Santa Clara Valley awoke in the middle of the night to the ground shaking and their homes swaying. When a noticeable earthquake hit—we endured several moderate quakes and hundreds of minor tremors each year—everyone paused and asked themselves, "Is this the Big One?" After a few minutes or so, as long as the house was still standing, we shrugged it off and went about our daily lives.

Me in my freshman year at Santa Clara High School in 1963

On November 22, 1963, at 10:30 a.m., Mrs. Yerman, my third-period English teacher, rushed into the classroom in tears to announce the horrific news that the thirty-sixth President of the United States, John F. Kennedy, had been assassinated. We were all in shock when Principal Philip Dougherty's voice came over the loudspeaker and dismissed classes for the rest of the day.

During my high school years, I began putting into practice the work ethic my dad had instilled in me from a young age. I worked two times a week at Don Lombardi's Shell gas station on El Camino Real. On the weekends, I could be found stocking shelves and bagging groceries at Hob Nob grocery store behind our home at the corner of Donovan Avenue and Wade Avenue near the intersection of El Camino Real and Bowers Avenue in Santa Clara. On Wednesdays after school, I drove a van truck and delivered floral arrangements around the Bay Area to funeral homes for Mission City Florists on Franklin Street in old town Santa Clara, a block from A&W Root Beer and nearly next door to owner Pete Talia and manager Al Viera's Santa Clara Sports Shop.

Work was nothing new to me. Throughout my childhood, Dad was constantly remodeling our home, building fences, adding a garage, pouring concrete, or doing some other type of construction around the house and yard. Dad had purchased the Donovan Avenue home in 1963 after selling our custom home on Lexington Street across from William A. Wilson School because of a financial downturn in the economy.

Several years prior, when I was ten years old and Dad had his successful general contracting business, he assigned me one of my first jobs: to sweep the floors, empty the trash, wash the windows, and wander around the construction yard with a magnet to pick up nails. Every hour or so, I entered the office to get a drink of water and tell Dad what I had accomplished, interrupting him during a hectic workday. After three days of this, and on what happened to be bid day, with the telephones ringing off the hook as subcontractors called in the bid proposals, he fired me and didn't hire me again until I graduated from high school.

A couple of years later, I started my first summer job as a laborer, hauling lumber and digging ditches for friends of my father, the Bevilacqua brothers in San Leandro. As I grew older, I often worked on the weekends as Dad's carpenter apprentice while he remodeled our home. I learned how to read blueprints, hammer a nail, Skilsaw lumber, frame a room, cut stairs, hang sheetrock, apply stucco, shingle a roof, and even lay bricks. When I was old enough, Dad began dropping me off on his way to work at my next summer job with Eichrome Lumber Co. in Redwood City, where I laid out wall sections, built prefab framed walls and roof trusses, and drove a huge lumber carrier forklift.

At least twice a week during the school year, while on our off-campus one-hour lunch break, my buddies and I would drive over to McDonald's on El Camino. Each of us would scarf down three cheeseburgers, two bags of French fries, and a Coca-Cola, all for less than a buck. I thoroughly enjoyed my after-school jobs, summer employment, and the freedom to go out. I was earning my own money and saving to buy a car. It gave me a sense of pride and independence because I could go on dates with a pocket full of the money I had earned. I didn't have to ask my parents for an allowance, although I never refused to accept an Andrew Jackson twenty-dollar bill when it was offered. I opened a bank account and received a Social Security card at fourteen. The jobs also taught me personal responsibility. If I made a commitment to be somewhere for a job, I had to be there, no matter what. There were many a Friday night when we partied until the wee hours, but I still showed up ready to work at Hob Nob bright and early the next morning, often but a few hours after my head had hit the pillow.

McDonald's advertisement, 1965

McDonald's on El Camino Real, Santa Clara, CA, 1965

Like most teenagers, I sometimes forgot about my responsibilities, such as when my friends and I got the harebrained idea to cut football practice and "borrow" my father's car. It was a cool, canary-yellow 1963 Ford Galaxy 500 XL fastback hardtop, with bucket seats, floor-mounted auto drive, mag wheels, and a 289 high-performance engine. To add to the drama of the incident, we borrowed the car without permission while Dad and Mom were out of town. And while I knew how to drive a car, I was fifteen years old and didn't have a California driver's license or even a learner's permit.

Santa Clara High School, 1964

It happened on August 24, 1964, right after my summer construction job had ended. As part of our annual pre-season training, that Saturday morning our football teammates were preparing to run up and down the field wearing heavy metal cleats and twenty-five pounds of pads, helmets, and other gear in the sweltering hot summer sun. We decided it would be hilarious to drive by the football stadium and practice field, wave at our buddies, and then head over to Mel's Drive-in or Kirk's Steakburgers for lunch.

As we cruised down Bellomy Street from Scott Boulevard, past the Bellomy Market and then the cemetery, we spotted a motorcycle cop parked off to the side of the road. He seemed to pay particular attention to us as we passed him, although I was driving only slightly over the twenty-five-miles-per-hour speed limit. I turned right onto Jackson Street, with Townsend Field on our left and War Memorial Swimming Pool straight ahead, and when I glanced up at the rearview mirror, I saw the cop turn on his red light and siren.

Mel's Drive-In, our favorite hangout

I yelled out some choice words, which mostly amounted to, "What in the hell do I do now?"

In Three Stooges fashion, my friends Mark, Steve, and Greg shouted in unison, "Stop!" "Go!" "Pull over!" "Step on it!" "Run!" "Get the hell out of here!"

Without much thought, I put the pedal to the metal, and the race—or I should say the Gumball Rally—was on, and our football teammates watched from the field in disbelief. I ran the first stop sign and turned right, racing toward Monroe Street. After running the next stop sign, I turned left, traveling south on Monroe at maybe sixty-five miles per hour. About a mile later, we reached Newhall Street, with a red signal light, which I proceeded to run as I made another right-hand turn, swerving through two lanes of westbound traffic. With his siren blaring, the motorcycle cop stayed hot on our heels.

Everything was happening so fast. Adrenaline rushed through my veins, and my heart raced. Survival instinct had taken over my physical motor functions as we sped toward another red light. Just before the intersection of Newhall Street and Winchester, I saw three police cars racing toward us from the west and a city bus approaching from the south. Once again, I ran the red light and skidded around the corner. We all gasped when we saw three more police cars, two motorcycle cops, and a police paddy wagon heading right for us. The vehicles then proceeded to block off our escape route.

"What the hell do we do now?" my sidekicks blurted out.

"No problem," I said and turned toward the gates of the Catholic cemetery.

Unfortunately, the gates were closed and locked. Police officers surrounded the car, and our escapade came to an abrupt end.

The motorcycle officer who had been chasing us for several miles leapt off his monster Harley-Davidson motorcycle looking more than a little miffed. He approached my window and, after making a visible effort to remain composed, asked for my license.

"Sir, I don't have one," I said.

"Then let me have your learner's permit."

"Uh, sir, I don't have one."

The officer lost his patience. "What in the hell are you doing driving?"

By then, we could see his fellow officers, a group of about twelve men strong, all in their SCPD blue, chuckling and shaking their heads.

The motorcycle cop asked for the vehicle registration. When I handed it to him, he glanced at it and then surveyed the law enforcement contingent that had gathered around. "Let me take a wild guess," he said. "Are you Leonard and Mary Semas's son?"

"Yes, sir," I said sheepishly.

He asked for the IDs of Mark, Steve, and Greg and fixed his gaze on Mark in the front passenger seat. "Mark, you're Harry and Miriam's son, right?"

Mark nodded.

He turned to Steve in the back seat. "Sam Ferreira's son, right?"

Steve nodded.

As he was writing down the names in his ticket book, he moved on to Greg. "Well, what do you know. I don't know your parents, do I?"

"Sir, I sure hope not."

The police officers became rather jovial as they realized that the car hadn't been stolen and that we had only been out joyriding with Big Leonard's car, albeit recklessly. Unfortunately, the Santa Clara chief of police, Frank Sapena, was my father's golf buddy and, as is the case in a lot of small towns, was a good friend of the family—all of which would further my parents' embarrassment.

"I initially tried to stop you because you didn't have a current-year sticker on the vehicle license plate," the motorcycle officer explained. "But now I see that your father mistakenly put it on the front plate instead of the rear plate. Why didn't you stop when you saw the red light and heard my siren?"

Like a teenage idiot, I said, "I didn't know you were chasing us."

The officer's eyes widened in disbelief. "Are you nuts? Are you saying you always drive like that? The little fat guy in the front seat saw me the entire time and watched me chase you as you failed to stop for a police officer, ran stop signs and red lights, drove recklessly, and broke just about every traffic law known to mankind."

Mark glanced at me and then at the police officer with a bewildered look on his face and said, "Hey, man," no doubt offended by the fat comment. By now, the rest of the officers were slapping their knees, shaking their heads, and nearly falling on the ground in hysterics.

The motorcycle officer handed me a ticket with citations for driving without a license, failure to stop, reckless driving, excessive speed, running a red light, and endangering the life of a police officer. One of the other police officers said he would return Dad's car to our home, while another loaded us into the paddy wagon so he could drive us home.

From the back seat, I asked one of the officers, "You mean you're not going to take us to jail or juvenile hall?"

He gave me a big grin. "Oh, no. I think once your parents are told, knowing Leonard, you won't be able to sit for quite a while. You'll wish you were in jail."

First, they dropped off Steve at his house on Benton Street and went up to the front door. After the officer spoke briefly, I saw Steve's dad, Sam, grab him by the ear and yank him inside, and before we pulled away, we could hear loud voices and banging on walls emanating from the house. Mark and I exchanged looks, wondering how Miriam was going to react.

Next, the officers drove us around the corner to Mark's home on Kay Drive, just off Las Padres Boulevard, because I was staying with Mark while my mother and father were on vacation. Mark told the officers it would be better to knock on the back door, since he figured his mother was in the kitchen making lunch at this time of day.

The officer knocked on the back door, and Mark's mother appeared. Her puzzled look turned stern. "What did the boys do now?"

"Miriam, it's nothing to be too worried about," the officer assured her. "David took his father's car, and the boys went for a wild joyride. No one was hurt."

To my surprise—and no doubt Mark's too—Miriam took the news well. "Thank you, Officer," she said with a sweet smile. "You know, boys will be boys."

The police officer left to take Greg Moffitt home, and I was first to enter the house, followed by Mark. I stepped into the kitchen and turned around in time to see Miriam hit Mark on the back of the head with her open hand repeatedly.

After grabbing him by the scruff of the neck, she dragged him down the hallway, yelling, "You're on restriction! And wait until your father gets home!"

I was expecting a similar treatment, but she just gave me a smile.

"Miriam, I'm really sorry," I said. "It was my fault, not Mark's, so you have every right to give me the same punishment."

"Oh no, Davey, I'll leave that up to Leonard," she said. "Because

> **LIFE LESSON #11:**
>
> "IT WAS THE BEST OF TIMES, IT WAS THE WORST OF TIMES, IT WAS THE AGE OF WISDOM, IT WAS THE AGE OF FOOLISHNESS . . ."
>
> —CHARLES DICKENS

when Leonard comes to pick you up in the morning, you may not even make it to the car in one piece."

My mouth went dry.

Sure enough, Dad showed up bright and early at eight o'clock Sunday morning and knocked on the glass panes of the front door.

"Mrs. Stefani," I said as Miriam walked to the door, "my life is in your hands. Please don't open the door."

Unfortunately, she did.

Big Leonard's giant hand appeared through the opening, and his finger curled back and forth, signaling me to come. The temper that I had seldom seen was in full bloom as he proceeded to kick me in the butt all the way to the car and tell me I was grounded for life. I thought he meant it!

By the mid-1960s, the streets of San Francisco teemed with hippies and flower children. Haight-Ashbury—or simply, the Haight—was the epicenter for the Summer of Love and the gathering place for psychedelic happenings. The Vietnam War was just beginning to escalate, and the mantra of my generation was: "Make love, not war." We witnessed the 1962 Cuban Missile Crisis, followed by the horrific assassinations of President John F. Kennedy, Martin Luther King Jr., and Bobby Kennedy, although we also saw the Civil Rights Act of 1964 become a reality. The Beatles' Paul McCartney, The Rolling Stones' Mick Jagger, and The Doors' Jim Morrison were the rage amongst teenage girls. The Beach Boys and Dick Dale were hot, and surfing at Santa Cruz hit the spot. The space race was on, and by the end of the 1960s, Neil Armstrong had walked on the moon.

My friends and I celebrated the fun and excitement of high school. We went to Friday night football and basketball games, attended nonstop parties, and always sought the cutest, most popular girls to date. We joined thousands of high-school kids from all over the Santa Clara Valley and cruised First Street in San Jose in our hot rods and muscle cars, looking for female talent and flexing our teenage testosterone.

Toward the end of my senior year, I drove a coral-colored 1964 Pontiac GTO and later a burgundy 1966 GTO with mag wheels, Hurst linkage, bucket seats, a 389 engine, three deuces (three two-barrel carburetors), and four-on-the-floor, better known as a four-speed transmission. At the time, I was known by my friends as the Organizer, in part because I was the planner of once-a-month outdoor events, including our semi-annual bash at the Spot. Situated four miles up a winding mountain road, atop a beautiful high meadow way above Stevens Creek Reservoir and Dam, the Spot looked out over twinkling Santa Clara Valley.

During the spring of my senior year in 1967, we held our last open-air party at the Spot, which was private property. While we removed the chain from the locked gate, a mile-long parade of muscle cars rumbled up the dusty gravel road. There were Pontiac GTOs (like mine), and my good buddy, Sub Bosco, arrived in his cool, red 1962 Corvette. Pontiac Firebirds, Ford Mustangs, Chevy Camaros, Dodge Chargers, and a whole host of vintage street rods and 1956 and 1957 Chevy Impalas pulled in through the open gates. Within an hour, the Spot was crammed with at least a hundred cars and about four hundred teenagers, music blaring. Olympia beer and Colt 45 malt liquor was flowing, and a few of the guys and gals were smoking a little weed.

By 10:30 p.m., the hillside bash was in full swing when suddenly we spotted four Santa Clara County Sheriff patrol cars coming up the road with their red and blue lights flashing but no sirens blaring.

Kids started heading for the hills, but most of us stood our ground. We were just having a little fun, and as high-school seniors ages seventeen and eighteen, we figured at worst they would confiscate our beer and make us leave the property. There were just too many of us to arrest or issue citations to.

The officers seemed to be in a pretty good mood as they approached a group of kids gathered by Mark Ardizzone's 1932 Ford three-window-coupe roadster.

As far back as the seventh grade, Frank Cano and I had made a habit of stopping by Mark's house on the way home from school to watch him and his father painstakingly transform an old, dilapidated piece of automotive scrap into the coolest, most spectacular hot rod that Santa Clara Valley had ever seen. Now, six years later, Mark's pristine, yellow street rod with cocoa-brown fenders was the talk of the Bay Area.

When the deputy sheriffs asked the partygoers who was in charge, everyone pointed at me. The ten officers walked over to me with smiles on their faces.

"So," a sergeant among them said, "you're the man."

"Yes, sir," I responded. "We're all seniors from Santa Clara, Buchser, and Wilcox High Schools, and next month we graduate, so we're just unwinding and having a little party to celebrate our scholastic achievement. Isn't the view from here spectacular? Boy, what a beautiful evening it is! Isn't it? Everyone is on their best behavior and enjoying the camaraderie of our buddies and girlfriends. I hope we weren't too loud and didn't cause any problem for the neighbors. We figured we were quite a distance from the nearest house, which appears to be at least a mile away."

"I can see why you're the head honcho and the spokesman for the group," the sergeant said. He went on to explain he had been on a routine patrol around Stevens Creek Dam when he spotted all the lights and activity on the hillside and called for backup. "Do you know you're on private property?"

"Yes, I do," I said. "The land belongs to my father."

No doubt those standing close enough to hear my reply were stunned to learn that my family owned the property we were partying on.

The officers exchanged looks, and the sergeant took out his pencil to write down the information in his notebook. "And your father's name?"

"Why, his name is Steven," I said, pausing for effect. "Steven Creek."

Everyone, including the deputy sheriffs, most of whom were in their early-to-mid-twenties, burst into laughter.

"Okay," the sergeant said. "Very clever. Your quickness on your feet will bode well for you in the future, but for now, before I change my mind, get in your cars, and hightail it out of here. And don't come back to this place again. You'll need to find another location for your future parties."

LIFE LESSON #12:

"A SENSE OF HUMOR IS PART OF THE ART OF LEADERSHIP, OF GETTING ALONG WITH PEOPLE, OF GETTING THINGS DONE."

—DWIGHT D. EISENHOWER (THIRTY-FOURTH PRESIDENT OF THE UNITED STATES, 1890-1969)

"What about our beer?"

The deputy sheriffs guffawed again.

"Are you kidding?" the sergeant said. "Get the hell out of here, or all of you will spend an uncomfortable night in a ten-by-ten jail cell as the guests of the Santa Clara County Sheriff's Office."

We scurried to our cars, and as we drove off, we saw the cops loading at least twenty cases of beer into the backs of their squad cars. We knew that beer would never find its way to the evidence locker at the station.

During Easter week each year, all of Santa Clara High School, along with many other high schools in the area, converged on the small, sleepy beach town of Santa Cruz. My involvement with the tradition began during my sophomore year, coming swiftly on the heels of my joyride just a few months earlier. With the help of some older friends, I arranged for three awesome motel rooms on the second story of the Terrace Court Motel, which was located right on Beach Street, just two blocks from the boardwalk overlooking Santa Cruz Beach, with its roller coaster, arcades, roller-skating arena, and dance ballroom.

The ten guys in our group were blown away when they found out I had landed the Terrace Court as our home base. Located at 125 Beach Street, the forty-room motel was one of the premiere locations in Santa Cruz. The guys wore their baggy surfer swim trunks, and girls basked in the sun by the hundreds in their smokin' hot bikinis.

We arrived on a Friday afternoon, got started at dusk, and partied well into the early morning hours. Beach Street in Santa Cruz was our version of the 1973 film *American Graffiti*. The classic cars and street rods would circle the block, hour after hour, past girls standing on the sidewalk and sitting in parked cars, not to mention all of us hanging over the motel balconies. We stayed up Friday night and slept on the beach while we caught some rays on Saturday. We saw some of our girlfriends and, after meeting other girls from different high schools, invited them to Rick Strini's beach bash that night. It was held at his grandmother's house, just around the corner from the Terrace Court Motel. Most of the surfers and a good portion of the student bodies from Santa Clara, Buchser, Wilcox, and Lincoln High Schools would be there in Santa Cruz all Easter week.

We started drinking a few beers late in the afternoon and dressed for Rick's party. We went over at six o'clock and met the girls as the Rolling Stones' song "Satisfaction" blasted on the stereo. There must have been at least two hundred people in and around the two-story 1930s Craftsman-style house. A group of my friends sat outside on the front porch with a bunch of girls.

The sun had gone down when we heard some guys running down the hill from Pacific Avenue. We couldn't hear what they were yelling about, so we walked over to the sidewalk to see what was going on. In the distance, it looked as though a small group of teenagers was running toward us and being chased by a much larger mob.

We exchanged glances with each other and said, "It looks like they're in trouble. Let's go help 'em out."

We ran up the street and met the advancing group, who slowed down long enough to hand us their beers before continuing past us. We exchanged glances, thinking that was a pretty nice thing to do. Then we glanced back up the street to see a street gang, probably fifteen to twenty strong, closing in on us. We decided to stand our ground, hold on to our beers, and clench our fists, ready for a street brawl.

The menacing gang of thugs came closer and closer, and by the time we realized who they were, it was too late. The vicious gang carrying flashlights turned out to be Santa Cruz's finest: police officers from the Santa Cruz City Police and Santa Cruz County Sheriff's Office.

Those smart enough to hightail it in the other direction didn't suffer the same fate as the rest of us. Since we were all minors—I, for one, had yet to turn sixteen—we were arrested and taken to the county jail. I was separated from my friends because I was a juvenile and was placed in a holding cell at "juvie hall." It was bad enough to be so stupid as to hold an open container of beer on a city sidewalk and then get arrested, but to be treated like a little kid and told they were going to call my parents was even more humiliating.

I was locked in my cell at about 9:30 p.m. and, hour after hour, I waited for Big Leonard to show up on the other side of the bars. I knew that when I got home, he was going to kick my butt and likely restrict me for the next three months. After two hours, I called out through the bars of my cell to the officer and asked him if he had spoken with my parents.

He looked over at me with an ear-to-ear grin. "As a matter of fact, I did speak with your mother and then your father. While your mother said they would be here within the hour, your father countermanded that statement and said to let you, as he put it, 'rot in jail' overnight. He said he might come and get you tomorrow afternoon or maybe Monday morning—if he felt like it and if his schedule permitted."

I sat down on my narrow bunk in shock. The more I thought about it, though, the more I realized that Big Leonard was trying to teach me a lesson. The ten-by-twelve-foot cell where I spent the next two days was dark and dingy.

Dad finally showed up Monday morning with a little smirk on his face. "Well, did you learn something from that experience?" he asked.

I hung my head in shame.

Although I had just gotten off probation after my summer joyride fiasco, I found myself once again grounded and on probation until summer. I didn't return to Santa Cruz during Easter week until my senior year of high school.

Surrounded by hippies, wild parties, booze, and a little marijuana, a small contingent of us went to school and studied just enough to get by. We could hang with the jocks, drop out with the hippies, crash with the surfers, mingle with the tough guys, and party with the gang—Jerry Moffitt, Bob Ahern, Frank Cano, Frank D'Ambrosio, Paul Seago, Skip Lazarus, Randy Bezore, Bobby Huber, Steve Garrity, Vince Texera, Danny Baldwin, and Mark Ardizzone—at Jim Sotelo's backyard hangout, otherwise known as "the Place." On occasion, we held stimulating conversations with the intellectually gifted. Needless to say, many of us weren't the best students. Jim's family ended up buying the home our family had owned back in 1953. This was before Dad had moved the family from this house on Las Padres Boulevard into our new home at 1872 Lexington Street, directly across the street from William A. Wilson Intermediate School, now the Wilson Adult Community Educational Center.

We cut classes, hung out with the wrong crowd, got in a few fights and minor scrapes, smoked a little weed, and messed up a bit.

One morning around two o'clock, about ten of my high-school buddies and I kidnapped—or let's say *borrowed*—the twenty-foot-tall Babe the Muffler Man statue to deliver it to the front steps of the high-school administration building. We had to abandon the task when we realized we couldn't complete the final few blocks of our escapade because of low power lines crossing the street.

Then came the day when Vice Principal Don Bordenave, the school disciplinarian, with my parents in his office, told me to take a break—a politically correct way of saying I had been expelled. I was to spend the second half of my junior year getting back on track at Buchser High School, located across town (ironically, it became Santa Clara High School many years later). We called Mr. Bordenave the Tasmanian Devil, although obviously not to his face. With his military flattop haircut and solid build, he looked like he could have been one hell of a tough college football player. He made it clear to me that I had to change my ways and get back on track. I had started hanging around with some guys who were cutting classes and getting into trouble. I realized that if I continued down this path, I might get into serious trouble.

While at Buchser High School, I made many new friends, like Kathy Azzarello, Dave Becker, Robert "Fatty" Bowen, Elodie McKee, Barbara Moniz, Ken Mucha, Paul Ponce, George Schrader, Jim Wilhite, and teacher Richard Candelaria and principal Don Callejon. After a six-month sabbatical and being on my best behavior, I got my act together and returned to Santa Clara High School and graduated with my friends and longtime classmates in 1967. I hung out one last time with my buddies during our graduation party at the Frontier Village theme park on old Monterey Highway 101 at the southern end of San Jose.

I could have gone down a very bad path if Mr. Bordenave hadn't intervened. I credit him, Mr. Cargile, Mr. Holthouse, Mr. Meyers, Mr. "Buck" Polk, Mr. Webb, Mr. Gates, Dean of Students Eugene Unger, Coach Lee Volta, Coach Fiore, and of course, Coach George Haines with helping me turn my life around. Had these teachers not taken the time to notice or care enough to get involved, who knows where I would have ended up.

There are many times in our lives when we come to a fork in the road, and often it's one particular person or event that causes a life-altering change. In my case, getting kicked out of school for two semesters was one of those events that led to a favorable outcome.

My high school graduation photo, 1967

After graduation in June 1967, I was champing at the bit to get started in the real world. In the back of my mind were the lessons I had learned from my father and all my teachers. Then there was Mr. Cargile's class and "The Man in the Arena" speech I had presented to my fellow students. The speech had a lingering effect on me. For the first time, I had read something that deeply impacted my life. Every word resonated with me, and as I stepped out into the world as a young man, I finally started taking a serious look at my life and my destiny.

The following quote is from a famous motivational speaker and author of seventeen different works, from books to videos. Jim Rohn was a dear friend to my sister Elizabeth. My wife, Susan, and I had the pleasure of spending a quiet New Year's Eve with them at her home in Indian Wells, California, before his passing. Jim's skills had been honed and influenced by James Earl Shoaff, a famous entrepreneur. Jim, in turn, had mentored Mark R. Hughes, the founder of Herbalife International and the mentor and life coach to Tony Robbins, the internationally known fire-walking guru.

> **LIFE LESSON #13:**
>
> "IF SOMEONE IS GOING DOWN THE WRONG ROAD, HE DOESN'T NEED MOTIVATION TO SPEED UP. WHAT HE NEEDS IS EDUCATION TO TURN HIM AROUND."
>
> —JIM ROHN (MOTIVATIONAL SPEAKER AND AUTHOR, 1930-2009)

CHAPTER 3

A CAREER IN CONSTRUCTION

After graduating from high school, I couldn't wait to go to work. I knew I wasn't destined to attend college. I wanted to learn through hands-on realty and practical experience from business leaders and not theoretical observations from educators.

In retrospect, do I regret not getting a four-year college degree? At my age, it's a little late for that, but I would be the first to say that, had I attended college, it would have positively impacted my early business career. But who can say for certain?

As my friend and mentor Ben Swig once said, "If there aren't guys around like me, who'd be here to hire the ones with a college degree?" Those words helped build my confidence as a young businessman. But if you

> **LIFE LESSON #14:**
>
> "THE FUNCTION OF EDUCATION IS TO TEACH ONE TO THINK INTENSIVELY AND TO THINK CRITICALLY. INTELLIGENCE PLUS CHARACTER—THAT IS THE GOAL OF TRUE EDUCATION."
>
> —MARTIN LUTHER KING JR. (AMERICAN BAPTIST MINISTER AND CIVIL RIGHTS LEADER, 1929-1968)

aren't going into a trade and aren't quite certain where you're headed, I would encourage you to attend a community college and earn a two-year degree—at the very least. Unless you're serious about liberal arts, humanities, mathematics, hard science, education, nursing, or criminal justice, roll up your sleeves and major in business, finance, accounting, engineering, communications, sales, marketing, human resources, computer science, or cyber security. These areas of study will help you no matter which profession or industry you end up selecting.

On the other hand, college isn't for everyone. A person might have a host of reasons for not pursuing an undergraduate or graduate degree. Obtaining a college education gives you a significant leg up, but accumulating $100,000 or more in tuition debt can be fiscally irresponsible, especially if your area of study is a professional dead end. Meanwhile, opportunities in the trades or vocations are abound. The pay is most times excellent, and the rewards of accomplishment are always fulfilling. For example, the oil and gas industry is booming. Welders, mechanics, truck drivers, carpenters, plumbers, electricians, and solar engineer technicians are needed by the tens of thousands around the country.

Ultimately, the real-life experiences, hands-on training, and friendships that you build in or out of college will last you a lifetime. I've given the same advice to our five children, all of whom graduated from college—two with undergraduate degrees and three with master's degrees. As I've learned, life is about dealing with real-world problems and taking responsibility for your actions. It's also about enjoying your career path, listening, reading, and learning. In the end, preparation, organization, discipline, communication, and life lessons will produce the most fulfilling reward.

Not long after graduation, I tried to join the local San Jose United Brotherhood of Carpenters Union but was told I would have to

---

LIFE LESSON #15:

"WHILE FORMAL SCHOOLING IS AN IMPORTANT ADVANTAGE, IT IS NOT A GUARANTEE OF SUCCESS NOR IS ITS ABSENCE A FATAL HANDICAP."

—RAY KROC (FOUNDER OF MCDONALD'S, 1902–1984)

wait until September. I wasn't about to let any grass grow under my feet. I wanted to get my own apartment, buy some furniture, and start my career. I had people to see, places to go, and things to do.

I called a high-school friend, Rick Squires, whose father worked at FMC Corporation near the San Jose Airport. Rick passed me on to his dad.

"It's going to take me several months before I can get accepted into the local carpenters union," I told Mr. Squires. "I was wondering if there might be any positions available at FMC."

"Well, son, with the Vietnam War in full swing, we're working on a twenty-four/seven basis. Can you start immediately? Are you willing to work the graveyard shift?"

"No problem. I'm your man."

"How soon can you start?"

"How about tonight?"

And with that, I was gainfully employed at FMC Corporation (originally Food Machinery Corporation). FMC was located at the corner of Brokaw Road and Colemen Avenue in Santa Clara, directly across the street from the backside of the San Jose Airport, and a block away from the Coleman Still Restaurant. During the graveyard shift, I made sixty-millimeter mortar shell casings at a starting wage of an impressive $5.40 per hour. For a forty-eight-hour week, that added up to $1,100 per month or $13,200 annually. Wow! Not a bad start.

That very first night, I was excited to go to work and arrived at ten-thirty, a half hour before my shift. Early the next morning, after my shift, I walked out to a bright, sunny June day. A few of my new work friends and I had breakfast at Sambo's Coffee Shop on Alameda in San Jose, and afterward I drove around looking for another job to increase my income. Over breakfast, I'd figured if I worked the graveyard at FMC, I could be home at 9:00 a.m. and sleep until 2:00 p.m., which meant I could get a part-time job working from 4:00 to 9:00 p.m., go back home, get a quick bite to eat, change into my FMC work clothes, and then go to my graveyard job six days a week.

I decided to drive down West San Carlos Street, starting in downtown San Jose, and then heading toward the city of Santa Clara. I drove past Mel Cotton's Sporting Goods, Sears, Lou's Village Restaurant, Race Street Fish

& Poultry, Mel's Drive-In (our favorite high-school hangout), a bowling alley, and many more restaurants, appliance stores, grocery stores, liquor stores, and giftshops. As I crossed over the top of Highway 17, the route to Santa Cruz Beach, the sprawling Valley Fair Shopping Center came into view on one side of the street. Town & Country Village, now the Santana Row mixed-use complex, stood on the other, with the enormous Courtesy Chevrolet occupying the corner of Winchester and Stevens Creek Boulevard across from another of our favorite hamburger joints, Bob's Big Boy, right on the border between Santa Clara and San Jose. This was also just down the street from the world-famous Winchester Mystery House.

There were so many possibilities for employment, I didn't know where to start. *Department store, grocery store, gas station, liquor store*, I thought to myself. *No. Been there, done that. I could try a fast-food restaurant or a clothing store, like Lenny did when he worked for Eli Thomas in the Town & Country Shopping Center. Or maybe sell appliances, furniture, cars, stereo equipment, or electronics. No, I don't think so.*

The ten-story Bekins Van Lines building caught my attention. Then, while looking next door, I noticed the Grand Auto sign. *Now there's an idea!* Thinking ahead like a good chess player, I figured I could get a discount on auto parts for my 1966 GTO while working in a nice, air-conditioned store and selling automotive parts—something I knew quite a bit about.

I pulled into the Grand Auto parking lot, went up to the door, and realized that they didn't open for another forty-five minutes. I took a chance and knocked on the door.

A tall, clean-cut man in his forties, dressed in a green Grand Auto jacket, opened the door. "Sorry, we're not open for business yet," he said. "But can I help you?"

"Yes, sir, you can. My name is David Semas. I just graduated from Santa Clara High School, and I'm waiting to join the local carpenters union. Until then, I've taken a graveyard position at FMC Corporation, and I'd also like to work part-time to supplement my income. Maybe something from four to nine or so."

The blond-haired man introduced himself as Roger Johnson, general manager. "David, thank you for being direct. That's the clearest, most succinct thirty-second interview I've ever had the pleasure of receiving. How many hours a week would you like to work? I can guarantee you at least thirty hours a week."

"That sounds great, sir."

"Would four to nine, Monday through Friday, with the occasional Saturday, be okay? I can pay you four-fifty per hour, and you'll get twenty-five percent off auto parts. Are you interested?"

"I sure am."

"When can you start?"

"How about tomorrow?"

He crossed his arms and took a good look at me. "Are you sure you want to jump in with both feet that fast?"

"Absolutely, sir!"

I got back into my car, ecstatic about my new jobs. After running the calculations in my head, I knew I'd make $550 a month at Grand Auto, plus $1,100 a month from FMC. The day before, I had talked to the property manager at the brand-new El Matador Apartments on Homestead Road, a block from San Thomas Expressway in Santa Clara. I figured if I rented a one-bedroom apartment there, I'd have my own place and would be in hog heaven while waiting to join the San Jose carpenters union. Rent was only $150 a month.

I moved into my new apartment building the very next Sunday while two gorgeous twenty-year-old Santa Clara University co-eds were moving in at the same time. They were both athletic types. Sharon was a petite blonde, and Jennifer was a tall brunette. That evening, we had dinner together and talked about how great it was going to be living on our own. Over the next week, my two jobs went well, but I was eager to join the carpenters union so I could begin my career in the construction industry.

Shortly after I moved in, Sharon came over and asked if I could install shelves in her pantry. By this time, I was a pretty good carpenter. I had been helping my father remodel our family home for years and had installed many a shelf. I told her I could.

LIFE LESSON #16:

"NEVER PUT OFF FOR TOMORROW WHAT YOU CAN DO TODAY."

—THOMAS JEFFERSON

I already had plenty of tools in preparation for my upcoming carpenter job, so that weekend, between my two jobs, I set up sawhorses outside on Sharon's front balcony and went to work. I installed five shelves with trim, set and puttied the nail holes so the girls could paint the shelves, and finished the project in about four hours. The wood and materials cost around twenty dollars, so I knocked on Sharon's door to ask if she would reimburse me for my out-of-pocket expenses. Her father opened the door.

"Is Sharon home?" I asked.

"Daddy, it's okay!" she yelled from her bedroom. "That's our next-door neighbor—the young man who did such a beautiful carpentry job on our pantry."

"You did do a great job," her father said. "How can I repay you?"

I showed him the receipts for the materials.

He pulled out a twenty-dollar bill and then a fifty-dollar bill and said, "Thank you."

"Sir, I don't have change."

He smiled. "No, the twenty is for your building materials, and the fifty dollars is for your labor and a nice profit."

I returned to my apartment and realized that I had netted fifty dollars, or about twelve dollars per hour for four hours of work, which was more than double my FMC wage. Plus, it was cash. (Let's hope the IRS doesn't read my book.)

Minutes after I returned home, another neighbor came over and asked if I would do the same thing for him.

"Sure. Is seventy-five dollars for labor and materials okay?"

He agreed, and I installed his shelves. Over the next few months, other neighbors came over and asked if I would install *their* shelves. Some wanted to make them a little more complex, so my prices ranged from seventy-five to one hundred dollars.

During the summer of 1967, it seemed like I was working around the clock for FMC, Grand Auto, and my apartment complex neighbors, most of whom ended up asking me to build them shelves. But over the weekends I still had plenty of time to party and rest up for the following week's adventure.

MAN IN THE ARENA - NEVER SAY QUIT

Just before I went to the San Jose Carpenters local, I told my FMC boss that I thought I would be leaving soon.

"Is there any way you would consider staying with FMC?" he asked. "Maybe on the swing shift after you become an apprentice carpenter?"

"Thank you, but I don't think I can. I have to sleep sometime, and it might affect my performance on the job. It could even be dangerous."

He nodded. "I understand, son. I want you to know how much I've appreciated your hard work, and I'd be happy to give you the highest possible job reference. You have a job waiting anytime if you want to return to FMC."

The same thing happened when I told Roger Johnson, manager at Grand Auto, that I would be leaving.

He patted my shoulder and said, "David, we think the world of you. You're one of the hardest workers I have in my store. Every time I've asked you to do a task, you jump right on it with a smile on your face and do it better and faster than I expected. I've already spoken to my district manager about you, and I want to tell you that you have a full-time opportunity at Grand Auto in management. So if things don't work out for you as a carpenter or in the construction business, you have a home here."

I thanked Roger for the kind words of encouragement. I understood that anything might happen in the future, but I hoped to move up in the construction ranks as my father had done thirty years before me. I would start as a carpenter apprentice and then graduate to journeyman. From there, the possibilities of advancement went as follows: foreman, project superintendent, project manager, general superintendent, construction manager, vice president, and finally, company president. I wanted to prove to my family that I could do this and that I was as smart as my brother and sisters were. In fact, at the time, it was probably more important for me to prove it to them than to myself. I wasn't afraid to try and fail. The courage to go out and give it my best had been bred into me as a youngster. If I failed, I would get up, keep my nose to the grindstone, and go make it happen.

I went back to the San Jose Carpenters Union in September 1967, and while in the process of signing up to join the union, I let them know that I had worked in construction and for a lumber company during the summers ever since I was twelve years old. I told the union business agent that I'd like to be able to challenge in advance my annual apprenticeship tests so that I could perhaps accelerate the four-year apprenticeship process required for becoming a journeyman carpenter. The agent said that they didn't offer that flexibility at his local, but that Carpenters Local 1622 in Hayward did. It was on the other side of the San Francisco Bay, just thirty miles north of San Jose.

Armed with that knowledge, I drove to Hayward and walked into the modern office building that housed Hayward Carpenters Local 1622. Elmer Borg, the primary union business agent for the local, happened to be sitting behind the reception counter, shuffling papers. He was a stocky and no-nonsense kind of guy like you'd expect at the carpenters union. After he introduced himself, I asked if I could challenge my four-year apprenticeship tests and become a journeyman. I could see the wheels turning in his mind as he listened intently. At only eighteen years old, I was a little surprised that the top dog in the carpenters union would even give me the time of day.

"By any chance, are you any relation to the builder Leonard Semas of Santa Clara?" Mr. Borg asked.

"Yes, sir. He's my father."

There was an uncomfortable pause until he finished his train of thought. "Now I understand why you're so knowledgeable about construction at your age. I'll tell you what. You join Local 1622 now, go to work, and show me that you're serious and that you have the skills of a real journeyman carpenter, and I'll let you challenge each year of the four-year program, one at a time. I'll require that you attend a construction management night class offered at San Jose City College. I want to make it clear the only caveat is that if you fail to pass any of the four year-end final tests—the

> **LIFE LESSON #17:**
>
> **"FEW THINGS HELP AN INDIVIDUAL MORE THAN TO PLACE RESPONSIBILITY UPON HIM AND LET HIM KNOW THAT YOU TRUST HIM."**
>
> —BOOKER T. WASHINGTON (AMERICAN EDUCATOR, AUTHOR, AND ADVISOR TO US PRESIDENTS, 1856-1915)

written and before the apprenticeship committee—you can't retake the test until the following year."

"Yes, sir, I agree and will prove I haven't wasted your time!"

I filled out application forms to join the union and gave him my personal check for seventy-five dollars. He then issued my temporary first-year apprentice card for Hayward Carpenters Local 1622. I told him I would start studying for the exams immediately and would be ready within a few weeks.

I returned to my El Matador Apartment and told my buddies, Sharon, and Jennifer, what had happened. We all jumped for joy and popped open a bottle of champagne in celebration of my new career in construction. Then I called a few friends, and we hung out that night at their favorite hangout, the Bronco Burger Pit near Santa Clara University.

Later that day, I called my father and said, "Dad, do you know Elmer Borg?"

"Sure, what about that son of a bitch?"

Surprised by his reply, I told Dad how Elmer had treated me very respectfully and what he had done for me. "Why don't you like him?" I asked.

"He and I have had a few run-ins over the years." When I pressed the subject, he explained. "I was building a large apartment complex in Hayward, and Elmer came on the job as the local business agent. Elmer told me he was going to shut the job down if I didn't comply with his demands, so I grabbed him by the shirt, walked him over, and threw him into the clubhouse swimming pool. Elmer started screaming that he couldn't swim, so I said, 'Well, you should have thought about that before you pissed me off!' I walked away, and if the carpenters on the job hadn't jumped in to save him, he would have been toast."

This kind of encounter wasn't new to me. While my dad was well liked and admired by nearly all his men and most of his subcontractors, he had quite the short temper—a Portuguese fuse.

In the summer of 1960, when I was about eleven years old, I traveled with him on a Friday afternoon from one of his school construction projects to another one. He pulled up to the project and saw many of the carpenters standing around. The superintendent was nowhere to be found.

While I waited in the car, Big Leonard got out of his gray 1960 Lincoln Continental Mark V and, after looking around, finally found the superintendent sitting behind a building, shooting the bull. Apparently, the job was already behind schedule, and Dad had previously warned this man on many occasions about his lack of work ethic.

I heard Big Leonard screaming for a while, and like Donald Trump on *The Apprentice*, he yelled, "You're fired!" Then, as he walked around the jobsite, he fired both of the foremen and everyone else who came within earshot. I heard him try to fire three men who were standing nearby and watching all the excitement.

"Leonard, we're electricians," one of them said. "We don't work for you."

Dad was irate, and it took a good thirty minutes before he calmed down.

Once back in the car, he looked over at me and said, "Davey, it's not a good thing to lose your temper, but sometimes you just have no choice. If you're getting a paycheck for an honest day's work and you're not working, you're cheating your employer and stealing money, and considering that many others on the job put in the hours and the team effort for the company, that's just not right for those few to take advantage."

Boy, I took those words to heart and thought that I would never want to have him that mad at me.

Now that he had regained his composure, he told me, "Find one of the foremen and help them shut down the generators, wrap up the electrical cords, pick up the Skilsaws, and put the other pieces of equipment away."

Not wanting to upset him further, and knowing that no one was left, I timidly replied, "Dad, you fired the foremen."

"Well then, find one of the carpenters."

"You fired them too."

Big Leonard groaned. "Well, just have one of the laborers do it."

Not wanting to set him off again, I slowly got out of the car, walked about twenty feet away, and declared, "Dad, you fired everyone—the superintendent, the foremen, and the carpenters and laborers. There's no one left on the job to help me roll up the cords."

"Goddammit, Davey! Come over here, and I'll give you twenty bucks to go find some people off the street to help."

I took the money and found two college students who jumped at the chance to make ten dollars each, and we got the job done.

"There's a solution to every problem," Dad said afterward. "You just have to be creative enough to find it." Then he gave me a ten-dollar tip!

In the construction and real estate industries during the 1950s and 1960s, as well as in political circles in Northern California, the name Leonard Semas was well known. Some people loved him, and others did not. One of his favorite sayings was, "David, a third of the people you meet in life will love you, a third will hate you, and a third won't really give a damn." He taught me that it's not about the people who don't know you and what they think about you. What really matters is your love for family and friends, the lives you touch, and the legacy you leave for future generations.

When I joined Hayward Local 1622, Big Leonard was the general superintendent for a longtime Bay Area building and real estate development company called Oliver Rousseau Homes. Rousseau was a trained architect whose father had built traditional Craftsman, English, and colonial-style homes throughout San Francisco in the 1920s, 1930s, and 1940s. Dad arranged for me to get my first full-time construction job on a large Oliver Rousseau five-hundred-home subdivision in Pleasanton called Pleasanton Meadows. Big Leonard's superintendent on the Pleasanton Meadows tract was one of his longtime friends and former employees, Bill Bennett.

Like many of Dad's construction friends of Irish heritage, Bill had reddish-blond hair and a fair complexion. Stocky and built low to the ground, Bill was about forty-two years old and full of life and vigor. He could scream with the

LIFE LESSON #18:

"PROBLEM-SOLVING BECOMES A VERY IMPORTANT PART OF OUR MAKEUP AS WE GROW INTO MATURITY OR MOVE UP THE CORPORATE LADDER."

—ZIG ZIGLAR (MOTIVATIONAL SPEAKER, 1926-2012)

best of them but also knew how to motivate his men and had great people skills. A natural-born leader, he spoke with authority but always made certain to treat people with respect. What he lacked in height he made up for with his go-make-it-happen attitude. Looking back on it now, I'd have to say that Bill Bennett was one of my first real building-industry mentors.

Bill Bennett in 1968

During the sweltering summer months in Pleasanton, it wasn't uncommon for daytime temperatures to climb into the low 100s and occasionally as high as 110 degrees. As I worked in the hot sun, baking, Dad would drive by once or twice a day in his green 1967 Chevrolet Impala with his air-conditioning going full blast. He'd give me a slight wave of the hand, a smile, and a nod as he passed by. It was at this time that I changed his nickname from Big Leonard to the Colonel, reminiscent of a Kentucky colonel overseeing the workers on his vast tobacco plantation. The nickname stuck, and for the rest of his days, he was affectionately known as the Colonel.

I started to work for Bill on the last Monday of October in 1967 as a first-year carpenter's apprentice, which meant I was entitled to 60 percent of a journeyman's wages, or about $4.80 per hour. Dad's early teachings on how to read blueprints, which had begun when I was about ten years old in the basement office of our Lexington Street home, would soon pay off. On many occasions, I had sat on a stool next to him at his plan desk while he "took off" (calculated and estimated) a set of blueprints. In those days, the plans were blue with white ink images and writing, in contrast to today's plans, which feature blue-ink images on a white background. I not only learned how to read blueprints but also how to calculate lumber, sheetrock, and concrete quantities and began to learn the basics behind estimating labor and materials.

Within a matter of days, Bill Bennett took notice that I was doing the work of a journeyman carpenter, and without my knowledge, he went to the Colonel to ask if he could give me a raise to the wages of a full journeyman carpenter. After all, I was doing the same work as all the other journeymen. Dad told him no.

The tract foreman for the job was Bill Edwards, who supervised all the carpenters and reported directly to Bill Bennett. Meanwhile, Bennett, as superintendent, ran the entire project, including the coordination and scheduling of all subs. Edwards was about thirty-five and had been a job foreman since he was twenty-six. Built like a football linebacker, he had big, strong carpenter's hands. He drove a 1964 Ford Bronco and was a nationally ranked Western single-action pistol-style fast-draw professional.

Edwards was surprised when he learned I was only eighteen years old. He immediately saw that I had an eye for detail and was proficient at reading blueprints, so he moved me from being a rough-frame carpenter into the job of layout man. The layout man is the person responsible for reading blueprints and snapping chalk lines on the floor of the structure to identify wall locations for the rough-frame carpenters. He cuts the 2x4-foot Douglas fir lumber top and bottom plates for the walls and puts markings on the plates to identify locations for the main, corner, and partition studs, window and door openings, and so on. Basically, the layout man makes certain that the walls are square and are located correctly in accordance with the plans. He's more or less the field architect who makes certain that the building plans are followed, so the position of layout man carries a great deal of responsibility and respect.

Pleasanton Meadows had five different model home styles with a total of twelve different floor plans. I took the plans home and studied them night and day, and within a week I had committed them to memory. There were about two hundred carpenters and laborers on the job, plus four framing crews, comprised of four framers and one

> **LIFE LESSON #19:**
>
> "I'M A GREAT BELIEVER IN LUCK, AND I FIND THE HARDER I WORK, THE MORE I HAVE OF IT."
>
> —THOMAS JEFFERSON

laborer. Each crew could frame and stand a house in one day. This meant that the four-carpenter layout crew, consisting of two two-man teams, would have to do at least two houses per day (one in the morning and one in the afternoon) per team to keep up with the framers.

With the help of my high-school classmate and good buddy Frank Cano, whom I had hired as an assistant a few weeks earlier and was teaching the trade, we were able to keep up with the pace, partially due to the fact that I had memorized the plans and didn't need to go back and forth looking at them every five minutes. It also helped that Frank and I made a good team. We were able to lay out, cut, place, and mark top plates at the rate of two houses per day—twice as fast as our predecessors.

Edwards was also impressed and told Bennett that I should be paid full journeyman wages. So once again, Bennett, knowing what the answer would be, went to my father and asked that I at least be paid that of a second-year apprentice—70 percent of a journeyman's wages. Dad once again told him no.

"Why are you being so hard on him?" Bennett asked.

"I don't want it to appear that there's any type of nepotism on the job," he said. "If Dave wants a raise, he'll only get it by passing the apprenticeship tests, and if the carpenters union says he's entitled to a higher wage, then he'll get it."

Edwards called me into the construction shack and told me what they had tried to do and what my father had said.

I waited until that weekend before going over to my parents' house on Saturday morning to politely confront Dad. I found him at the dining table by the bay window eating his customary breakfast of eggs, toast, and Portuguese linguica sausage. The sausage was made by our friends, the Costa family, owners of the locally well-known Neto Sausage Company of Santa Clara, established in 1949, the year I was born. Decades later, I still buy my linguica from Ed Costa, the grandson. He and his wife, Mary, are longtime friends.

I sat down and let Dad know that Bennett and Edwards had told me what had happened. "Dad, you've always taught me that a man should be paid a fair wage for a fair day's work. What you're doing isn't fair, because in reality, it's a form of reverse nepotism."

Dad wiped his mouth with his napkin and gave me a little smile. "I figured you'd come by and ask about this. First of all, who ever told you life was fair? Because it's not." Naturally, I'd heard this before. "You're my son, and I work for Oliver Rousseau as well. I can't have my boss thinking that I'm favoring my son. Until you pass the tests and the carpenters union and Elmer Borg require that your wages be increased, I have to hold firm and deny their request just to show there is no favoritism here."

As much as I hated to admit it, I understood where he was coming from. "Well, I disagree, but I guess if I were in your shoes, I'd do the same."

Mom, always happy when I stopped by on a weekend, put a serving of eggs, toast, and sausage onto a plate for me, and I dug in.

The following Monday, I called Elmer Borg, my carpenters union agent, and told him what my father had said.

"That's exactly what I would expect from that tough old bird," he replied. "How about you come in tonight and take the first-year examination? Are you ready?"

"Absolutely."

I took the test and passed with a score of 95 percent.

Bennett was notified by Borg the following day, and my next paycheck reflected that I was now a second-year apprentice, earning 70 percent of journeyman wages.

Within thirty days, I challenged and passed the second-year test with a score of 90 percent, and within six months, I had passed all four years of my California State apprenticeship examinations, both written and oral, and became a journeyman carpenter three months before my nineteenth birthday in June 1968.

Then Bennett accepted a new position with another large real estate development company, and Edwards was promoted to tract superintendent. Edwards told Dad he would accept the position only under the condition that I became his tract foreman. According to him, Dad gave in and reluctantly agreed, although he did have a smile on his face.

Being a nineteen-year-old construction foreman was a little tricky. As the boss, I was trying to supervise experienced men who were five to twenty-five years older than me—men who had likely forgotten more about the construction business than I knew.

"Dave, you don't demand respect," Bill Bennett said. He had always taught me this. "You have to earn it. If you know what you're talking about and you're a true leader, your men will follow, and you'll gain their respect. Just remember to lead by example, and don't ask them to do something that you're not willing to do yourself."

Edwards enjoyed working with the subcontractors but wasn't keen on dealing with the public or the new home buyers, so he turned over to me the responsibility of handling buyer walk-throughs of completed homes. Once the tract home was ready for occupancy, I would walk through the finished home with the new homeowners to identify any incomplete, damaged, missing, or improperly installed items; create a punch list; and schedule our service department to correct them. I was also put in charge of dealing with the subdivision architects, building designers, and interior decorators, which helped to further expand my knowledge of architecture, design, staging models, marketing, and merchandising.

In August 1968, less than eighteen months after we had started dating, I married the very pretty and sweet Kathy Carey, who was one year behind me in high school and the daughter of Stan Carey, captain of detectives at the Santa Clara Police Department. My young career was just starting, and although unaware of it at the time, I stood at the beginning of a lifelong journey, destined to go places and do things that I never imagined in my wildest dreams.

LIFE LESSON #20:

"LEADERSHIP IS THE ART OF GETTING SOMEONE ELSE TO DO SOMETHING YOU WANT DONE BECAUSE HE WANTS TO DO IT."

—DWIGHT D. EISENHOWER

Me, Kathy, and our wedding party in 1968

From L-R, Stan and Carol Carey, me and Kathy, and my parents

Within just a few months after my promotion to foreman at Pleasanton Meadows, I got a telephone call from Bill Bennett, who wanted to know if I would like to work closer to home and become his tract foreman. I thought this would be a great opportunity for me to get out on my own and no longer be under my dad's wing. I also recalled how Bennett had taught me a lot about managing people and honing my leadership skills, so I jumped at the chance.

In September of 1968, I went to work for Superintendent Bill Bennett and McKeon Construction, a large Sacramento-based builder and developer of fourplex condominium projects throughout California. The 460-unit project, located in San Jose, was called Cherry Plaza. Not only was my work now much closer to my home, but as it turned out, Kathy and I purchased our first brand-new condominium, still under construction, at Cherry Plaza. Located off Branham Lane and down the street from the Pizza Hut on Capay Drive, our condo cost a whopping $14,750 and required a $500 down payment. We were elated! Every morning I walked out the front door to go to work. A few months later, our first beautiful child, Wendi Christine, was born.

Baby Wendi with her favorite blanket

When Bennett left the company for a better opportunity, I became acting superintendent of the project at age nineteen. But after several months, McKeon Divisional President Bob Quinn brought in another superintendent named Hank Godwin. Bob said that, although I had done a great job, he believed I was still too young and inexperienced and could learn a great deal from his longtime friend, whom he had brought out of retirement. I was somewhat disappointed but realized that Bob was right, so I welcomed Hank, albeit skeptically, when he showed up the following week. I would soon learn the true meaning of the adage that you should never judge a book by its cover.

Hank Godwin pulled into the Cherry Plaza development the following Monday morning at about six o'clock. I was the only one on the job and was going over plans in the construction trailer. The door opened, and the trailer shifted eight inches to one side as Hank stepped inside. He was about six feet tall and five feet wide and must have weighed in at four hundred pounds. The lenses of his black-rimmed glasses were so thick that they looked like they were made from Coca-Cola bottles. His thinning gray hair looked like it hadn't been combed. He wore 1950s-style khaki pants, a Hawaiian shirt, a horrible purple cotton vest, a floppy golf hat, and shoes that must have come from an army surplus store. He had a slight speech impediment and a short attention span. To say I was caught off-guard by this portly character, who appeared to be straight out of a comic book, is putting it mildly. I wondered what on earth the brilliant and talented Bob Quinn saw in this rather obese and completely unassuming man.

Hank held out his hand. "Good morning. I'm Hank Godwin, whom you will have the great pleasure of working for, learning from, and assisting in our relentless pursuit of excellence. Young man, I have heard a great number of accolades bestowed upon you by many I deeply respect, and it is with that reverence that I address you here this morning. Let us embark in my four-wheel-drive form of vehicular transportation and tour the project for the next hour, so you can brief me on the physical layout, phasing status, existing problems or challenges, our crew, subcontractors, city officials, and others with whom you have professionally associated on our project."

Wow! I had never heard someone speak so articulately before. I wondered if this guy was for real or if he was just a well-educated bag of wind. In the next six months, on a nearly twenty-four/seven basis, Hank Godwin

LIFE LESSON #21:

"THE DELICATE BALANCE OF MENTORING SOMEONE IS NOT CREATING THEM IN YOUR OWN IMAGE BUT GIVING THEM THE OPPORTUNITY TO CREATE THEMSELVES."

—STEVEN SPIELBERG (AMERICAN FILMMAKER, PRODUCER, AND DIRECTOR, 1946-)

demonstrated to me that he was one of the toughest, smartest, and most observant, hands-on construction managers I would ever meet.

Hank held advanced degrees in structural engineering and mathematics and had minored in time-management studies and advanced scheduling. He also held undergraduate degrees in environmental and soils engineering. He was a brilliant leader and construction management strategist, a tremendous motivator, and an honest-to-goodness genius, with an IQ that had to be at least 140. In spite of his tough talk, occasionally colorful vocabulary, tenacious style, and propensity to assign people unflattering names like Dipshit (my nickname), he was a kind and gentle soul.

Just six months after first showing up on the job—and after becoming my construction life coach—Hank became terminally ill. Unbeknownst to me, he was battling stage 4 cancer. I visited Hank at least twice a week until his passing. If God reserves a special place in heaven for the finest people, Hank Godwin is there now.

I continued as a superintendent with McKeon Construction until October 1970 when, at the age of twenty-one, I became a little too cocky and mistakenly concluded that I couldn't be replaced.

Every time I went over to our sister project, Blossom Hill Estates, I couldn't find Billy Baker, the tract superintendent. Time and time again, I stopped by the jobsite, and he never seemed to be there.

I approached Bob Quinn in his office and suggested that instead of having two superintendents for the two San Jose projects, he could eliminate one—Billy Baker—and I would be willing to run both. I thought he might turn me down but figured it couldn't hurt to ask. Unfortunately, I had made a serious miscalculation. As I would later learn, Billy Baker was Bob Quinn's brother-in-law.

Bob sat back in his chair and gazed at me for a moment, his expression unreadable. "David," he finally said, "it sounds to me like you're not happy here. With that in mind, I think we'll just get you your paycheck."

My mouth dropped open in shock. I tried to interrupt and assure him I was fine right where I was, but to no avail. I had let the proverbial horse out of the barn, and it was too late to lead it back inside.

MAN IN THE ARENA – NEVER SAY QUIT

After his secretary cut me a check, Bob handed it to me. "David, I appreciate the work you've done here, but I don't want people working for me who don't have one hundred percent loyalty and support for the company."

Although I truly thought I was looking out for the best interest of the company, I stood up and said, "Yes, sir, I'm very sorry."

"That's all right, David. You're a talented and hardworking superintendent but still need to mature a bit. I wish you the very best."

We shook hands, and I walked out with my tail between my legs, wishing I could take back every word that had come out of my mouth. I needed to grow up and understand that anybody doing a job could be replaced at any time—even me.

That was the last time I was ever fired as an employee, and I never forgot that valuable lesson. But for the moment, I had other things to worry about: I had a wife and new baby to support and was out of work, with winter just around the corner.

After a brief move to Massachusetts, where my parents had relocated in 1968 in order to be closer to Vo-Vô, Big Leonard offered me a position as assistant project manager on a massive 400,000-square foot concrete tilt-up building (almost ten acres under roof). The project was located in Mansfield, forty miles south of Boston and about twenty-five miles from his home in Middleboro, right off the old Cape Cod Highway. Hoerner Waldorf Corporation, with roots dating back to 1886, was a successful St. Paul, Minnesota company producing more than 500,000 tons of recycled paperboard annually while supplying printed boxes to large consumer products companies like General Mills and Procter & Gamble.

> **LIFE LESSON #22:**
>
> "NEVER GIVE AN ULTIMATUM TO YOUR BOSS UNLESS YOU'RE PREPARED TO ACCEPT THE OUTCOME, WHICH MIGHT NOT BE WHAT YOU ANTICIPATED."
>
> —DAVID SEMAS

I was responsible for all onsite construction and took hands-on control over site engineering and the land surveying of a twenty-two-acre parking lot, complete with a railroad spur that went right through the middle of the massive manufacturing plant. My survey crew consisted of a civil engineer, lead surveyor, soils engineer, transit operator, two stake men, and four laborers. The large parking area featured some steep grades and twists and turns, and it required the installation of hundreds of massive precast concrete curbs. The winter snow was about to arrive, and I had to oversee the grading and paving project and have it wrapped up, come hell or high water, before the following spring.

The real challenge was to make certain that, once completed, the expansive parking area had the correct pitch and slope, so it would drain correctly, and no pooling of water would occur. Somehow, with the grace of God and a little luck, we got the grading, cuts and fills, and finish elevation right on the money, and during the first heavy rain of spring, the parking lot drained like a charm.

"David," Big Leonard said, "great job. You're a real land and construction surveyor, which is quite an accomplishment for a guy without formal training in civil engineering!"

I, on the other hand, was relieved that my calculations had been correct. Had they not been, I would have faced Dad's wrath. The last thing I wanted was to disappoint him and make him look bad in the eyes of his boss.

In the spring of 1970, I returned to California with Kathy and Wendi, our baby daughter. I was hired as an onsite construction superintendent and began building a five-model-home complex as a part of a 120-lot residential single-family home subdivision in Newark, California, for a well-established Santa Clara-based real estate development company Duc (pronounced "Duke") & Elliott. The first objective was to complete the model home complex in under fifty working days. I boldly committed to a thirty-seven-day production-and-finish schedule, though Freddie Boitano, my boss and general superintendent, along with most of my carpenter crew and the subcontractors believed that it was a real stretch in such a short timeframe and that I was putting my ass on the line.

On the same day we started grading the building pads for the five model homes, Duc & Elliot co-owner Jules Duc stopped by with Executive Vice President Jack Aiello, his longtime trusted employee, to say hello.

After the usual pleasantries, Jules took me aside and said, "Young man, you'd best be able to deliver on your thirty-seven-day completion date, because I'm about to spend thousands of dollars on advertising, promotion, goodwill, and an expensive public relations campaign. Needless to say, I won't be pleased if for any reason the models aren't open. So, you understand, I'm not accustomed to failure or excuses. Now do you comprehend the responsibility that you've taken on?"

"Yes, sir, I do," I replied. "Come hell or high water, the model homes will be open for business with fencing, walkways, and landscaping in place. By the way, out of curiosity, what would happen if I didn't meet the deadline?"

Jules gave a big grin and pointed at a pile of dirt. "That's easy. You'll be back digging ditches before sunrise the following day."

I turned and asked Jack, "Is he kidding?"

Jack Aiello, a tall man with Sicilian ancestry, had gotten his start at Leonard Semas & Company twenty years earlier. "I think not. David, you gave your word. Now honor it. You set the timeframe, and you have a deadline to meet, so go out and make it happen."

I took the bull by the horns and relished the task at hand and was able to get the subcontractors, or "subs," to rise to the occasion. I wisely contacted the Newark Building Department in advance and invited the chief building inspector to lunch. I explained to him what I was up against and asked for his full cooperation. A day later, he called and told me that he, the mayor, and members of the Newark City Council loved the idea of a race to build a model home complex. During the early 1970s, people were actually standing in line to buy new homes, so this would be a great public relations opportunity and help further promote Newark to Bay Area residents.

From the first day of trenching the foundations, the subs worked like a well-oiled machine. While the electricians were drilling holes and pulling Romex electrical wire through the studs, the plumbers were soldering copper water pipe, and the sheet metal workers were hanging heating ducts in the rafters. The building inspector stood by to approve each process, and right behind him the wall insulation was going in and the sheetrock was being unloaded in the center of each room. By the thirty-second day, the sod grass had been laid, sprinklers had been installed, pathways were in, white picket fences had been installed, and mature olive trees, colorful flowers, and hundreds of fifteen-to twenty-five-gallon shrubs had been planted. I walked the five-unit model home complex with a punch list in hand to check for any minor items that might need repair or correction.

As promised, on the thirty-seventh working day, the completed and fully furnished model homes were ready to showcase. The grand opening was held on time, on budget, and on schedule.

At ten o'clock that morning, moments before the widely publicized event was to begin, I told Jules and Jack and my immediate boss, General Superintendent Freddie Boitano, "Everything is ready to go, except for one minor thing."

Jules raised an eyebrow and gave me this stern "oh no" look.

"The models are carpeted and fully furnished and decorated," I explained, "but the walls are freshly painted. They're still wet, so try not to touch them."

They all broke out in laughter.

Jules patted me on the back. "Dave, you are to be congratulated. You've beaten a long-held record. It's been more than ten years since anyone built a model home complex from scratch in less than forty working days."

"Really? Whose record did I beat?"

Jules looked left to Freddie and then over at Jack before turning back to me. "Why, it was done in thirty-nine working days by none other than Jack Aiello."

I looked over at Jack and grimaced.

Jack grinned. "That's quite all right, Dave. I couldn't have asked to be beaten by a more talented young man. Great job! You did it!"

With the first phase of the project completed, I accepted the position of Northern California

---

LIFE LESSON #23:

"OBSTACLES ARE THOSE FRIGHTENING THINGS YOU SEE WHEN YOU TAKE YOUR EYES OFF YOUR GOAL."

—HENRY FORD

---

construction manager for American Housing Guild, a national real estate development firm. I was responsible for overseeing and managing construction operations on a total of 4,000 homes and apartments. This included direct supervision over none other than Bill Bennett, who was the general superintendent; Thad Corbett, my friend and licensed civic engineer, who was the offsite improvement superintendent; fourteen project superintendents, who handled day-to-day construction activities for twelve different subdivisions located in San Jose, Sunnyvale, Cupertino, Mountain View, Redwood City, Burlingame, Half Moon Bay, Fremont, Hayward, Fairfield, and Vacaville; and two large apartment complexes: Sunburst in Santa Cruz and Park Victoria Apartments in Milpitas.

AHG president Barry Berman, an assistant producer to the Walter Cronkite CBS Evening News broadcast from 1962 to 1968, enjoyed helping young people get a start. He always rooted for the underdog and certainly took a chance hiring a twenty-two-year-old construction manager. I made the decision easier for him by telling him I was twenty-seven. That well-intentioned white lie came back to bite me in the ass many years later when I accepted the position of executive vice president for a Fortune 500 company. In the end, though, my bosses found it humorous that someone would be untruthful about their age in reverse. They were used to job candidates pretending to be much younger than they were.

I began to ponder whether I should stay at American Housing Guild or start my own business. A few years earlier, I had stopped by the offices of Jack Copple Construction after my untimely and abrupt departure from McKeon Construction. Mr. Copple's offices were located on North First Street in San Jose, just down from the Caravan Inn (later to be known as the Hyatt House Motor Lodge). I had dropped in just before lunch—without an appointment—to see if they might have an opportunity for someone with my construction expertise and onsite construction management skill set.

I was talking to the secretary at the front desk when an elderly gentleman shuffled by on crutches that wrapped around his forearms. I could plainly see his limp was not from a broken leg or minor surgery but rather from a serious physical condition. I tried not to look in his direction, which I thought might make him feel uncomfortable.

To my surprise, he turned toward me and addressed me. "Young man, I overheard you mention your name. I'd like to speak to you if you have a moment."

I was puzzled and wondered why this meticulously dressed gentlemen, who looked like a US senator or local politician, would want to talk to me.

He reached out to shake my hand and then introduced himself as non-other than Jack Copple. "Step into my office", he said.

Over the next six hours, I heard the life story of this gregarious and affable businessman, who was a highly accomplished California Class A and Class B-1 general contractor and commercial builder.

Jack was deeply rooted in the San Jose business community and was a generous benefactor to many local charities. Following our lengthy afternoon meeting, he invited me to his home on Cherry Avenue in Willow Glen, an affluent San Jose suburb, for dinner that evening, where I met his lovely wife, Barbara. Dinner lasted until ten o'clock. I was fascinated with this articulate, courageous, and determined man.

In 1964, Jack survived a horrific airplane crash on a snow-covered 11,000-foot peak in the Sierra Nevada near Mono Lake and became a lifetime paraplegic. A down-to-earth person with a booming laugh, Jack had made and lost several fortunes during his career. He was active in the Republican Party and an original member of the San Jose Redevelopment Agency.

Over the years, Jack built houses, shopping centers, and gas stations throughout Northern California. He was the father of seven children and enjoyed telling them how he'd made certain that the San Jose Airport was designed so that airplanes wouldn't fly over the family's Cherry Avenue house. To this day, I'm convinced the story was true, not a boastful tale. The airport was later renamed the Norman Y. Mineta Airport after his good friend, the former mayor of San Jose, who also served as the secretary of transportation under George W. Bush during 9/11.

"Come on into my study," Jack said after dinner. "I want to show you something."

We retired to Jack's gorgeous mahogany-walled study, and he reached behind his bookcase and grasped a complete set of blueprints.

As he started to unroll the architectural drawings, he stopped, looked up at me from his seated position at his desk, and said, "David, I haven't been entirely open with you. I know who you are, and I've known and watched your dad with admiration for twenty years, even back before he started his own construction company, when he was a project manager for Barrett & Hilp in Palo Alto. Leonard was one of the first general contractors in the country to ever use tilt-up construction on a large-scale project when he built San Jose City College. I read all about it in *Engineering News* and marveled at his engineering prowess, willingness to take a risk, and sheer tenacity. If you're a chip off the old block like I think you are, you'll want to see and will undoubtedly appreciate what I'm about to show you." He unrolled the blueprints all the way. "Go ahead and study them and take a good, long look."

After turning past the cover page and index section, I ran my hand back and forth over the third page with a great deal of interest. I studied each word, specification, and visual detail in the drawing. After a few minutes, I turned to page four and did the same thing for at least ten minutes, continuing on to the last floor plan and interior layout and the exterior building elevations.

I skimmed through the detailed cross-sections on the back pages and then sat down in a chair in front of Jack's desk, so we were at eye level. I gave a nod and smiled. "Jack, this is fantastic! These plans appear to be the design and construction drawings for an eighty-thousand-square-foot modular home factory." I proudly told him that I had built prefab walls with Eichrome Lumber Company in Redwood City and had been a laborer digging ditches and operating a jackhammer for Bevilacqua Brothers Construction in Hayward during the summer months in high school. I also described how, as a young journeyman carpenter a few years earlier, I had been the head

> LIFE LESSON #24:
>
> "THERE ARE NO STRANGERS HERE; ONLY FRIENDS YOU HAVEN'T YET MET."
>
> —WILLIAM BUTLER YEATS (IRISH POET, 1865-1939)

layout man for Oliver Rousseau Homes on a large five-hundred-home tract with prefab walls in Pleasanton. I told him that in my youth I had traveled with my father to his construction sites on the weekends. "I've always been fascinated by modular construction methods."

"After spending the day with you," Jack said, "that's exactly what I suspected. No need to discuss it further, because I'm pretty tired now and will retire for the evening. David, it's been a real pleasure spending the day with you. Drive home carefully, and thank you for listening to my story and taking such an interest. I don't have all my financing in place yet but soon will have. You'll be hearing from me real soon."

Afterward, I considered it an honor to have spent so much time with such a kind and talented man, a legendary San Jose business leader and creative visionary.

Me shortly after Jack Couple meeting, 1971

CHAPTER 4

WHERE THERE'S A WILL, THERE'S A WAY

In early 1972, while I was still working as a construction manager for the Northern California division of American Housing Guild (AHG), I set out to complete the first project I could truly call my own. My goal was to design, finance, and build with my two hands a 2,500-square-foot custom home on a modest but ideally located lot at 778 Frederick Avenue, just two blocks from the Lexington Street home that my father had built for our family in 1953. Wendi Christine, my first born, was nearly two years old, and my son was on the way. I had little cash but good credit and a secure job and felt it shouldn't be too difficult to get a bank loan—which proved to be a little more challenging than I had initially believed.

When I told my father about my plans, he said it was a waste of time. "Even with good credit, the bank will never give you a construction home loan unless you own the land with clear lien-free title."

He's still stuck in the old days, I thought. *Things are different now.*

I opened escrow to buy the parcel for $9,500 and put a $500 deposit on the lot with a six-month close of escrow. I designed the 2,500-square-foot single-story Mission-style home and drew the building plans, complete with material specifications, as I had learned to do in architectural drawing classes with Mr. Holthouse in high school.

I collected bids from subcontractors and assembled a loan package that contained construction drawing blueprints, building permits, financial statements, subcontractor bid proposals, photographs, renderings of the home landscaped, an appraisal of the improved lot, and an appraisal value of what the completed home would be worth. Fully prepared, I waltzed into our local Crocker National Bank at the corner of Stevens Creek Boulevard and Saratoga Avenue and sat down with the bank manager, Mr. Bob Canote.

Mr. Canote looked like a typical middle-aged banker, with thick, black-framed glasses, a receding hairline, and gray hair at his temples. He was dressed conservatively in a dark blue suit, white shirt, and red tie. "How can I help you?" he asked.

After explaining what I wanted to do, I showed him that I had an appraisal of $55,000 for the completed home, and cost estimates for $21,000 from my subcontractors, plus another $9,000 for the land. I was only requesting a loan for $30,000—a very reasonable 54 percent loan to value (75 percent was customary at that time). I explained that I was a licensed B-1 general contractor—one of the youngest to receive a contractor's license in California—so I could build the home for far less than the average layperson. I wouldn't take profit and would do most of the carpentry, plumbing, and electrical work on the weekends.

"David, while I'm impressed with your initiative and knowledge, I can't make a loan to you for thirty thousand dollars to build your home unless you own lien-free title to the land."

Dad's warning had come back to haunt me. Still, I figured there must be some way I could do this.

I thought for a moment. "If I owned the land, would you then loan me the thirty thousand?"

He nodded. "Yes, I certainly would."

I then asked him if he would issue me a $30,000 loan commitment letter for a modest fee of $300, and to my surprise, he agreed.

I felt if I could show another bank a source of repayment, they might make me an unsecured loan for $10,000 to buy the land. I drove to Palo Alto and asked my oldest sister, Judy, if she would introduce me to her boss, since she was the executive assistant to Kirk Jeffrey, president of the Stanford Bank of Palo Alto.

"I want to know if the bank might consider a personal unsecured loan of ten thousand dollars," I explained, "if I can show a source of repayment from a portion of my home loan proceeds. I actually have a loan commitment from Crocker Bank for thirty thousand dollars."

Judy knew that I was honest, paid my bills on time, and had good credit and a secure job, so she thought a loan officer might approve my request. "Mr. Jeffries is gone for the day, but I'll introduce you to a friend and one of our senior loan officers."

When I met with the banker, he asked me a long list of questions. "If your credit report checks out and I can verify your employment," he said, "I'll go ahead and make you an unsecured loan for ten thousand dollars."

Everything went as planned. I received the $10,000 loan from Stanford Bank, paid off the $9,000 balance on the lot so that I owned it free and clear, and then went back to Mr. Canote of Crocker Bank.

He was a little surprised to see me so quickly, just three days later. "Okay, so far you've proven to me that you are a responsible young man. I'll make the construction loan at two points over prime or an annual interest rate of 7.75 percent. Upon completion of the construction loan, your home loan will convert to a permanent thirty-year mortgage for thirty thousand dollars, with a 7.15 percent annual interest rate. Okay?"

"Yes!" I jumped for joy.

After shaking his hand enthusiastically, I drove to my parents' home and told Big Leonard, now the Colonel, who was both dumbfounded and delighted.

"David, you just don't take no for an answer, do you?"

"Dad, you taught me over the years that where there's a will, there's a way."

I started construction of my home in the summer of 1972, and while we were in the process of installing the floor girders, our son, Gregory David, was born. I worked Monday through Thursday evenings and

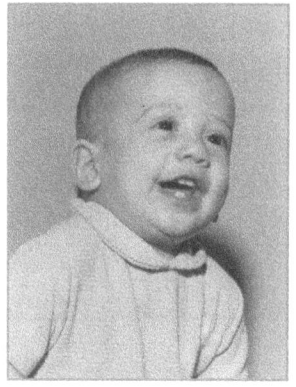

Gregory "Greg" David Semas, 1972

Me with Greg in 1974

LIFE LESSON #25:

"IF SOMEONE TELLS YOU THAT YOU CAN'T DO SOMETHING, THAT DOESN'T NECESSARILY MAKE IT SO!"

—DAVID SEMAS

---

all-day Saturday and Sunday pouring concrete, framing, doing finish carpentry, installing electrical and sheetrock, plumbing, roofing, and painting. I completed our beautiful Spanish-style home less than six months later, right before Christmas.

With the proceeds from my last construction loan draw from Crocker Bank that I had set aside during construction, I went back to see the loan officer at the Stanford Bank and paid off my $10,000 personal loan.

"If you ever need another unsecured loan," he said, "come see me anytime."

After that, I called Bob at Crocker Bank and asked him to lunch. I wanted to come clean with what I had done.

When I told him the story, he laughed. "David, you're pretty darn creative. All I told you was that you had to own the land free and clear. Whether you got the money from your parents, a friend, or another bank wasn't my concern, as long as there were no liens against the property. You did it. The home looks beautiful, and you're to be congratulated on a job well done!"

It was then that I realized I had actually built my first custom home for $500 in cash, which was the money for the deposit on my lot in the first place. At this point, I began to fully appreciate the real estate development term known as leverage, meaning a greater combination of debt (bank or otherwise) than hard cash equity.

After all that effort, less than one year later, a local businessman approached me to ask if I would sell my new home. Kathy's response? "No way."

I figured the house was worth maybe $55,000 to $60,000, so I told him he could buy the house for $65,000, thinking he would refuse. Instead, he agreed and placed a substantial deposit into escrow! We entered a sixty-day escrow, he bought my home, and I turned a $35,000 profit. I promised Kathy I would use the profit to build her a larger, even more beautiful home for our growing young family.

778 Frederick Avenue

During the escrow period, I found an even larger lot in an area comprised of custom homes in a gorgeous part of Santa Clara about three miles from our home, near Kathy's grandparents, and right next door to a lot owned by Lee Volta, my high-school football coach. I put up a $5,000 deposit with a purchase price of $15,000 on the 7,800-square-foot parcel located at 2136 Denise Drive.

Once again, I personally designed and drew the plans, this time for a 3,500-square-foot home. I again collected bids from subcontractors and put together a loan package. I called Bob at Crocker Bank, and over lunch I showed him my new loan package, which contained a supporting finished home appraisal of $145,000 and a conservative loan request of 52 percent loan to value, or $75,000. This allowed $10,000 for the balance on

LIFE LESSON #26:

"TRUST TAKES
YEARS TO BUILD,
SECONDS TO BREAK,
AND FOREVER
TO REPAIR."

—ANONYMOUS

the lot with sidewalks and underground utilities in place and $65,000 for home construction.

"Are you going to ask me to give you a loan commitment again so you can go over to the Stanford Bank to borrow the money for the lot?" Bob asked.

"I would have, but thanks to the thirty-five-thousand-dollar profit, I already have the cash from the sale of my Frederick Avenue home," I replied.

Bob laughed. "I thought so. Why don't you forget using your cash or any other unsecured loan maneuvering, and I'll make you a construction loan for seventy-five thousand dollars with a fifteen-thousand-dollar land draw."

I was a little surprised. "Great! But I thought you couldn't do that."

"David, you can always change the rules for the right borrower."

In the winter of 1973, I started construction on my second Mission-style home, but this time, as promised, it was a much larger two-story structure totaling 3,538 square feet. I subcontracted much more of the carpentry and tradesman work on the construction of this new home because I was busy and still figuring out whether to launch my own construction and real estate development company. By the late summer, our beautiful home was finished, with its carved wooden front doors, expansive Spanish tile entry, interior balconies overlooking the main foyer, sunken living room, and spacious family room with a massive stone fireplace and corner wet bar. In 2002 Zillow put the home value at $2,472,600.

In December of the following year, Aimee Michele, my youngest daughter, was born. At the age of twenty-five, I had a nice young family of three, with two daughters and one son, and a blossoming career. It felt like I had come a long way in a short period of time and had accomplished a lot for a young businessman.

Grandma Lopes with
Aimee, 1974

Wendi, Greg, and Aimee, 1974

Wendi and Greg in 1974

Wendi, Greg, and Aimee, 1975

One hot summer day in 1972, just after lunch, my mobile telephone rang, and on the other end was Jack Copple, the community leader who had invited me to dinner at his home.

"Hi, David," he said. "I called your office, and your secretary gave me your mobile number. Wow! What will they think of next? A mobile telephone in a car? She told me you're on the road traveling between subdivisions you're building throughout Northern California, from Santa Cruz to Milpitas and all the way up to Vacaville. Sounds like you're pretty busy, but that's no surprise to me."

In those days, my black Motorola rotary-dial radio-mobile telephone looked like a princess-style home telephone, but a heavy twenty-five-pound transmitter about the size of a small suitcase sat in the trunk of my car. In 1972, there were only three-party line channels on the west side of the Bay Area. I shared the telephone with a few hundred other customers that also had radio-mobile telephones. If I wanted to make a call and someone else was on one of the three mobile telephone channels, I would just have to wait my turn, which could be rather frustrating. This was ten years before cellular technology and a year before Steve Jobs of Apple fame graduated from Homestead High School. (I would eventually become acquainted with him as a Santa Clara County planning commissioner.)

"David," Jack said, "are you ready to come on board and become my vice president of operations? I really need you right now to work side-by-side with Chuck Dougherty, my vice president of engineering, to help design, lay out, and build the modular home factory. Chuck has done a great job on the engineering and conceptual assembly line design, but you bring to the table a B-1 general contractor's license. Your knowledge of residential and commercial construction, prefab assembly, and full-scale production would provide the hands-on experience we need. I know you have a great job now and are considering starting your own business, but if you'll give me at least a one-year commitment, and if you'll start next month, I'm willing to give you a two-thousand-dollar signing bonus and increase your annual salary by ten thousand to fifty thousand a year." He paused a moment to let me think about the numbers, which were huge at the time. "Do we have a deal?"

Like any sane person, I said yes.

About the same time, we broke ground on the construction of our new home in Santa Clara, then I got into my new canary-yellow 1973 Oldsmobile Cutlass Supreme and left the Frederick Avenue house to make the easy twenty-minute drive to Jack's empty 80,000-square-foot warehouse, located east of Highway 101 in San Jose.

In front of the large concrete tilt-up box building was 10,000 square feet of two-story office space. The office portion had been nicely partitioned into eight large executive offices, six smaller offices, two conference rooms, and several large bullpen areas for sales and accounting. From the rear of the offices on the first floor, I entered an expansive, open warehouse about two hundred feet deep by four hundred feet long. The warehouse ceiling was thirty-six feet high—the height required to operate overhead cranes and lift roof sub-assemblies.

After examining every nook and cranny of the building with Chuck for more than four hours, I could tell the warehouse was ideal for a fully automated modular home production manufacturing line. We had a lot of work to do, but Chuck had done a nice job on his floor plan and assembly line layout. Now it was up to me to hire a crew to get the facilities fully operational within ninety days.

I recruited my close friend since high school, Jerry Moffitt as our chief electrician and another good buddy, Gary Pitts, a highly skill residential and commercial plumber. They showed up in a few days, and within a week, we had assembled a team of twenty more tradesmen to help build the production line. About thirty more joined a little later and would eventually evolve into our fifty-five-man full-time assembly and production crew.

Jerry Moffitt, me, and Gary Pitts at Heritage Homes in 1972

We assembled and installed two massive overhead cranes, which were used to lift specially designed Kaiser K Beam steel girders, panelized walls, assembled roof structures, and other heavy objects. In less than three months, we converted an empty warehouse into a full-blown assembly-line production factory that could turn out two homes per day, helping Jack Copple realize his dream of delivering about five hundred homes a year to general contractor customers, who would deliver freight on board to our San Jose facilities.

The Jack Copple Heritage Homes Modular Home Factory, 1972

Heritage Homes assembly line

In effect, a modular home section would roll off the production assembly line every two hours, and each modular home was completed over a two-day period. The half-homes rolled out on steel girders that were hydraulically lowered onto flatbed truck/trailers. The two sections were then delivered onsite anywhere in the Western United States. If memory serves, each finished Heritage Home sold for an average price of $25,000, representing annual sales in the neighborhood of $12 million ($81 million in 2022). Not bad in 1972.

Heritage Homes first home off the assembly line with L-R, Jack Copple, and San Jose Mayor Norman Mineta in the window

When the day came, San Jose mayor, Norman Mineta, other local politicians and dignitaries, and members of the news media showed up to watch the first modular home roll off the assembly line and then get loaded onto two flatbed trucks.

At the end of my year-long contract, I had a tough decision to make but with his best wishes and full support parted company with Jack under the best of circumstances and remained in close contact with him throughout the 1970s. Jack Copple passed away in 1994. Barbara, his wife, followed more recently in 2014.

Having served as the vice president of operations at Heritage Homes and construction manager for American Housing Guild, I could see that I wasn't going to become president of any company without many more years under my belt. With the completion of our second home, I felt I was ready to move on to bigger and better things in the business world. I had some lengthy discussions with Kathy, her parents, my parents, and sister Judy to get their opinions, although I had already made my career change decision.

Even though they discouraged me from starting my own business and felt I should gain more experience and have more capital behind me, I was champing at the bit. Now that I had learned how to finance and build my own home, I started thinking, *I can do this. I can build projects. Why not?* I didn't want to wait any longer. I wanted to create my own destiny. Moreover, it had become apparent as I climbed the professional ladder that future employers would start looking more closely at my lack of a formal education. I figured if I owned my own business, I wouldn't have to worry about that.

In retrospect I probably should have listened to everyone's advice, which was sound. Unfortunately, I failed to remember one of my father's favorite sayings: "God gave you two ears and one mouth for a reason."

I wasn't afraid of failure. I figured if I went for it and failed, I would go back to being a construction manager and wait for another day. The time to do it was now, not when I was forty, which seemed like a lifetime away.

Ever since turning fifteen, I'd heard the same advice from my family: I wouldn't enjoy any long-term success unless I graduated with a master's degree in business, marketing, or finance. While I appreciated their good intentions and have since emphasized a college education to our children, I believe that when all is said and done, you must follow your own instincts and be the architect of your own destiny.

Soon I was president of my own real estate development firm called SEM Developers, Inc. SEM stood for Semas, Estes (Bud), and Miller (Bob). After buying out my partners early on, the SEM name remained (abbreviation for Semas) and I would later change the name to SEM Development Company.

My first office was a small corner office that was a part of a much larger executive suite business that occupied the fourth floor of the prestigious eighteen-story Pruneyard Towers in Campbell. During the first several months of business, I spent nearly everyday meeting with Santa Clara Valley's ranchers and farmers, many of whom were longtime friends of my family or the parents of kids with whom I had gone to school. I assumed all these contacts could help me find some unimproved land to buy and develop, but most of the properties for sale were large land parcels in the range of one hundred acres or more, which was far beyond my limited pocketbook and access to capital. I decided to start looking at smaller, infill-improved land parcels in Santa Clara, San Jose, and Sunnyvale.

I soon began to see the drawbacks of working for myself. I had nobody to assist me in putting these projects together, and because of my limited finances, I didn't have the money to hire anyone. The good news? I was forced to learn every aspect of the development process, from land acquisition, zoning and entitlements, master planning, finance, estimating, bidding, and construction to sales, marketing, leasing, asset management, property management, and the sale of the project. Nevertheless, I missed having the camaraderie of friends and associates around and began questioning whether I should have launched my business in the first place.

One day, while working at my office in the Pruneyard, I received a call from Danny Texera, the father of Vincent, a childhood friend who had been tragically killed in an automobile accident when he was in high school. I hadn't seen Danny or his sweet wife, Laura, since the funeral many years earlier. He wanted to meet for lunch at the Townhouse Restaurant (later to be known as JR Chops), a popular local spot for lunch and dinner located just a few blocks from my Denise Drive home in the Mervyn's Plaza shopping center near Scott Boulevard and the El Camino.

Danny walked in with his sidekick, Johnny Costa, a local painting contractor and longtime friend of my father's. Danny hadn't changed a bit. His family had come from the Portuguese island of Madeira off the African coast, and it showed in his black hair, dark eyes, and olive skin. He was a true gentleman who always wore a smile on his face.

As we sat down for lunch, Nick and Dino Tsamis, owners of the Townhouse Restaurant, came over to say hello. It was like the good old days all over again.

Finally, Danny said to me, "I guess you're wondering what this meeting is all about. I heard you were looking for land, and I want to help—but under one condition."

"What's the condition?"

"If you're successful in putting the land project together, you'll hire me as your construction superintendent and right-hand project manager sometime in the future."

I agreed to the proposal in concept, and Danny went on to tell me about a pocket listing (not on the open market) that was a perfect two-acre, fully improved parcel, zoned office-commercial, that could be bought for $1.15 per square foot, or about $100,000. It was a fair price for a fully improved and zoned property, which usually fetched at least $1.50 per square foot or about $65,000 per acre.

"What's the catch?" I asked.

"Simple. The land is owned by Santa Clara University. SCU would like to approve the ultimate buyer and be certain that the property will be developed using Mission-style architecture and that the project meets Jesuit Catholic standards. First, David, you're a good Catholic, and your father is well liked by the university. They never forgot that he donated hundreds of thousands of dollars to help build their local youth center."

Built in the 1950s, the youth center was officially called the Father Walter E. Schmidt Santa Clara Valley Youth Village, but no one could remember its name. People often asked, "What's the name of the club?" Thus, it became known as the "What's It Club" abbreviated to the "Wutzit". Father Walter E. Schmidt was the founder and patriarch of the Wutzit and mentor to Santa Clara County youth. The Wutzit had originally been envisioned as a response to a rise in juvenile delinquency during wartime. Father Schmidt had been appointed director in December 1944, and one of his first major donations was from his old friend, Frank Sinatra. Many decades later, "Old Blue Eyes" supported the Wutzit and other programs benefitting SCU, like the Louie B. Mayer Theater and SCU's annual fundraising gala, the Golden Circle Theater Party.

"The fact is," Danny continued, "your family has been involved in Santa Clara politics for many years, made sizeable contributions to the Santa Clara University, and has a great deal of respect from many people in the community. You're a shoo-in to be approved by the Jesuits and the university."

He reminded me that my oldest sister, Judy, had attended SCU, my father-in-law Stan Carey was highly respected as the captain of the Santa Clara Police Department, and my mother-in-law, Carol Carey, worked as the executive assistant to SCU President Father Thomas Terry and the SCU Alumni Office and was also a secretary for the influential A. P. "Dutch" Hamann, the former city manager, often called "the father of San Jose," who later became an advisor to my SEM board.

"Wow, I never thought about it that way," I said.

"I know, and that's why we're here today having lunch."

Afterward, I called the Colonel and told him about this great opportunity.

"Leave it to my son David to start off with a multimillion-dollar office building complex rather than a custom home," my dad replied. "Why can't you be like most startup builders and begin with a spec home? Do you have to launch your development career with a million-dollar office complex?"

"I don't care what other people do or say, Dad. In reality, it takes as much effort to build a small project as it does a larger one."

I took Danny's advice and called Father Walter Schmidt, who was still very involved with the college and served as vice president for university relations. Father Schmidt was an old family friend, one of the great civic leaders of our community, a dedicated advocate for helping teenagers learn Christian ethics, and a real character. Along with his many other duties, he served as the chairman for SCU's annual $100-per-person Golden Circle Theater Party concert, which benefitted the Louis B. Mayer Theatre, and each year featured a star-studded cast, including such figures as Milton Berle, Bob Newhart, Don Rickles, Red Skelton, Ed McMahon, and Jonathan Winters. The headliner was usually Father Schmidt's longtime friend, Old Blue Eyes himself, Frank Sinatra. Over the years, I was fortunate to befriend Frank, Don Rickles, and other celebrities backstage as a member of a private security detail that worked alongside a detachment of plainclothes San Jose and Santa Clara police officers.

Every time I stopped by to say hello to Father Schmidt in his cozy apartment in the back of the Wutzit Club, I found him sitting in his smoke-filled living room in his favorite recliner, wearing his favorite Hawaiian shirt. After listening to his golf stories and his fabulous corny jokes, I had to remind myself that he was a Jesuit Catholic priest. Father Schmidt was short and slight in stature, with gray hair and a reddish complexion, and on occasion, he loved his imported scotch whiskey.

When I called Father Schmidt this time, he invited me to come see him, and when I arrived, I found him waiting in front of his apartment. He opened my car door, sat down, and said, "David, drive on." Although he had a great gift

> **LIFE LESSON #27:**
>
> "IT TAKES AS MUCH TIME AND EFFORT TO UNDERTAKE A SMALL DEAL AS IT DOES A BIG ONE—THAT IS, PROVIDING THAT YOU'RE UP FOR THE TASK."
>
> —DAVID SEMAS

Golden Circle Theater Party and Frank Sinatra in in the Mercury News, 1973

for gab and loved people, on this occasion he was a man of few words and got right to the point.

Father Schmidt took me to the SCU administrative offices, where I said hello to my mother-in-law, Carol Carey, at her desk. I followed him past her to the office of the president of the university, Father Thomas D. Terry, who would serve from 1968 to 1976. Father Schmidt explained to Father Terry that I was interested in the Homestead Road property and was the son of Leonard Semas. Father Patrick Donohoe, the former university president, stepped in and joined the conversation.

"Do you have the one-hundred-thousand-dollar purchase price?" Father Terry asked.

"No, sir, but I'm confident I can get the money to buy the property once we sign a purchase agreement, I design the project, receive necessary zoning and architectural approvals from the city, and arrange for bank financing."

"First, I appreciate your honesty," he said, "and you seem like a well-organized and hardworking young man. Next, I think highly of your mother-in-law. Lastly, Father Schmidt tells me that he has known your parents and your family for years and tells me you're quite determined and a can-do-anything type of businessman. With those references, that's good enough for me."

Surprised by the quick endorsement, I took Father Schmidt back to his apartment. Before I left, he asked if I would agree to be a board member of his Santa Clara Valley Youth Village. I agreed and proudly served on his board of directors until 1980.

That afternoon, SCU's real estate broker drew up a purchase-and-sale agreement, and I put up a $10,000 deposit, opened escrow, and went to work designing a suitable old Mission-style garden office project. The finished master plan showed four separate single-story Mission-style 5,000-square-foot buildings faced with real adobe brick. The 20,000-square-foot complex would feature carved wooden entry doors, Mexican floor tiles, and six-foot-wide circular water fountains located in the center foyer of each building. The project was to be richly landscaped with lush green lawns, garden lighting, and mature olive trees.

Within thirty days, I presented the renderings and master plan of the Las Fuentes (The Fountains) garden office complex to Father Terry and Father Donohoe for approval. They were delighted with the attention to detail I had paid to the project design and invited me to join them in enjoying a glass of red wine and some delicious cheese from our hometown favorite, Crystal Creamery.

I submitted Las Fuentes for zoning approvals from the City of Santa Clara Planning Department, started collecting bids for the projects, and began to assemble a loan package for financing. As a part of my financing efforts, I felt that it would be beneficial and would add credibility to form a board of directors consisting of respected businessmen and local civic leaders, including my father-in-law, real estate investor Oscar Donian, landscape architect Ken Schmidt, my CFO and good friend Bud Estes, and the jovial and large-statured Irish press agent Jackson George Faulkner.

Just as I was assembling our board of directors, Danny Texera, whom I had hired as SEM construction manager and who was also a Santa Clara city planning commissioner, asked if I would consider becoming his campaign manager for his run for the Santa Clara City Council. I agreed, and Danny; his beautiful daughter and co-campaign manager, Sue; her husband and my old high school friend, Jim Davis; and other members of his family, together with our volunteer staff of fifty, ran a great campaign. He was elected city councilman in 1973. He also became the newest member of the SEM board of directors.

Now with an impressive board of directors in place, I felt like everything was coming together quite nicely—with one exception: the financing.

I approached my first bank, the Santa Clara main branch of Bank of America, and met with branch manager and Vice President Bob Finocchio, a family friend, to see if I could borrow $2.1 million to build Las Fuentes.

Bob was courteous as he listened to my presentation. Then he turned me down.

"Can you tell me why?" I asked.

He leaned back in his chair and shrugged. "Well, there are many reasons."

I pressed further. "Such as? How can I expect to learn about how to get my project financed if I don't know the reasons for your denial?"

He thought for a moment. "Fair enough," he said and proceeded to tear my Las Fuentes loan package apart, piece by piece.

I went back to the drawing board, incorporated all of Bob's recommendations, and resubmitted my new loan package to the Construction Lending Group at Crocker National Bank. I was summarily denied again. As before with Bob Finocchio, I asked the loan officers if they would tell me why, and they gladly did so. They tore my loan package apart even more thoroughly than Bob had. I went to a third bank, the United California Bank, followed the same process, and was once again rejected.

Giving up or quitting was just not an option. I continued to ask questions, listened to the answers, and learned every time I did another presentation. On each occasion, my loan package and presentation became better and more sophisticated. But most of the bankers fell back on the claim that I was too young and inexperienced and didn't have a personal track record of designing, constructing, leasing, and selling office building complexes. Never mind that I had been the vice president and construction manager for a nationally recognized development company.

Each time, I asked the banker, "How can I get a track record unless someone loans me the money to build my first project?"

One by one, they all shrugged and said, "Sorry, that's just the way it is."

With each rejection, I became more committed to the project. I met with Santa Clara Savings & Loan, American Savings & Loan, First National Bank of San Jose, Union Bank, and Security Pacific Bank, all of whom said no. I pushed on to other financial institutions like World Savings & Loan, Eureka Federal, and Downey Savings, only to receive more rejections.

After a few days of self-pity, I became even more determined. I recalled the words of George Haines, my high school swimming coach, when he said, "David, never give in, never give up, and never say quit. Reach down and find that special place in your physical being that will give you the strength to succeed."

Finally, in March 1973, I walked into the Oakland offices of my twenty-third lender prospect, Home Savings & Loan. I sat down in front of Mr. Burton Sharpe, vice president, and handed him my rather impressive loan package that had been modified, amended, refined, and greatly improved, thanks to the input from twenty-two other bankers and construction real estate loan officers. After I shook his hand and introduced myself, he sat down, opened the loan package, and began to read.

The room was dead silent for at least ten minutes as he studied the loan package. With his head still down, Mr. Sharpe looked over his glasses at me and said, "Well, David, how can I help you?"

Over the last several months, I had tried many different approaches with other lenders, and obviously nothing had worked. This time I decided to put my cards on the table. "Sir, I've been turned down by twenty-two other banks. I'm a licensed California State B-1 general contractor. I was born and raised in the building business, and I've climbed the construction ranks from carpenter to foreman, superintendent, project manager, general superintendent, construction manager, vice president of operations, and now president of a young startup development company. I don't have a commercial building track record of accomplishment yet because no bank believes that I've proven myself worthy of their trust. Obviously, I can't prove myself worthy until the first lending institution gives me

---

LIFE LESSON #28:

"CRITICISM IS SOMETHING WE CAN AVOID EASILY BY SAYING NOTHING, DOING NOTHING, AND BEING NOTHING."

—ARISTOTLE (GREEK PHILOSOPHER, 384-322 BC)

---

a break and offers me my first construction loan. I have the Las Fuentes proposed office building complex thirty percent pre-leased, and most of my subcontractors are smaller local subs, since the larger subcontractors appear to be too preoccupied. I have very little working capital and just a small office staff. I can tell you that I am determined to get this project financed, even if I'm forced to go to the ends of the earth to do it. Now if you consider any of this troublesome, I would prefer not to waste your time, or mine. If you're not interested, I'll just be on my way. Thank you very much for your consideration."

Mr. Sharpe leaned back in his chair, folded his hands on his desk, and smiled. "Is this supposed to be your best sales pitch for a $2.1 million loan request?"

"No, sir. I'm sorry for being so abrupt, and I apologize for my outward frustration. I guess all the rejections are finally taking their toll. I'll show myself to the door and won't take up any more of your valuable time."

"First, you can call me Burt," he said. "Secondly, the good news is that your loan is hereby approved. The bad news is that I will issue you a loan commitment, but I expect you to pay Home Savings and Loan a one percent upfront fee for the issuance of the commitment. Can you have a check here tomorrow for twenty-one thousand dollars?"

I almost fell out of my chair. "Don't you have to take this to a loan committee?"

"Son, in Northern California for loans up to three million dollars, I *am* the loan committee."

I told him that I would never forget his trust and promised I wouldn't let him down. I asked him if he could give me until the following week to pay the $21,000 fee.

"You don't have the money, do you?" he asked.

"No, sir, but I can get it."

He chuckled. "Are you always so frank? I'll see you next week."

Groundbreaking of Las Fuentas Office Complex, 1973

From L-R, at the Las Fuentas groundbreaking: Santa Clara Mayor Gary Gillmor, Miss Santa Clara, me, my sister Marie as 1972 Miss Massachusetts, and a Grubb & Ellis agent

We broke ground on the Las Fuentes complex and completed the first phase in the spring of 1974. About one hundred people attended the ground-breaking ceremonies, including Santa Clara Mayor Gary Gillmor, my sister Marie in her official capacity as Miss Massachusetts, our local Miss Santa Clara, our real estate agent with the brokerage firm of Grubb & Ellis, board member Oscar Donian, PR and press agent Jackson George Faulkner, father-in-law Stan Carey, board member Ken Schmidt, CFO Bud Estes, and Danny Texera.

Just after ground-breaking of the Las Fuentas office complex, Danny Texera, our new Santa Clara city councilman and SEM board member, asked me if I would accept an appointment to the Santa Clara County Planning Commission. I told Danny I would be honored, and within a few days I received a telephone call, followed by a personal visit from Ralph Merkins, the county board's distinguished supervisor. Accompanying him was A. P. "Dutch" Hamann, our mutual friend and San Jose's legendary city manager. Dutch had served during its early explosive growth years of 1950 to 1969.

"David," Ralph said, "we could really use someone with your construction and land development expertise on the county commission. The seven-member board is one of the most powerful advisory bodies and influential government land use and general planning authorities for the Santa Clara County Board of Supervisors."

"This is quite an honor," I replied, "and at the same time a huge responsibility for all the members of the planning commission."

"Yes," Ralph said, "the district runs from Saratoga to the south; Palo Alto and Stanford University to the north; then from the western border of Santa Clara County along the ridge of the Santa Cruz Mountains on Skyline Boulevard; and finally to the eastern edge of Milpitas at the base of the East Foothills. Do you understand the huge responsibility I'm about to bestow on you, and are you ready to accept the appointment?"

"Absolutely," I replied.

"Good luck," Ralph said. "And buckle up. You're in for a real ride in one of the fastest-growing counties in America. Santa Clara County is destined to become the semiconductor and computer capital of the world, which is why the Venture Capitalists call this Silicon Valley."

A few weeks later, I took the oath of office as one of seven Santa Clara County planning commissioners serving the five-member Santa Clara County board of supervisors. At the age of twenty-four, I was one of the youngest county commissioners to ever have been appointed in the state.

In tandem with six other appointed members of the planning commission, I approved many public infrastructure projects, including the Highway 85 bypass that connected Sunnyvale through Cupertino and Monte Sereno to South San Jose at Highway 101. We recommended approval to the SCC board of supervisors for many large-scale residential, industrial, and commercial real estate developments. This included the expansion of the Eastridge Shopping Center and the controversial annexation of the Dorcich, Jamison, and Rodriquez fruit orchards along Coffin Road to the City of Santa Clara. This annexation and rezoning resulted in final approval of actor Fess Parker's Frontier Land, which became Marriott's Great America Theme Park and the eight-hundred-acre Marriott Industrial Park.

Public hearings were often held before we made our final decisions. One such hearing, held on a Thursday afternoon, involved the well-respected Mariani family, which ran one of the largest ranching, farming, food processing, and packing operations in Santa Clara County and hoped to receive a zoning approval for their home parcel, an eighty-acre orchard near the intersection of Homestead Road and Lawrence Expressway at the border between the City of Santa Clara and Sunnyvale.

As the hearing progressed, a few neighbors in attendance voiced their opposition. They wanted to see the orchard remain as open space and thus opposed its transformation into a residential subdivision with 285 homes.

The Mariani's attorney stood up to speak but was cut off by Mrs. Mariani, who marched to the podium and gently nudged him aside. Short in stature but tall in the saddle and the owner of a quick temper, Mrs. Mariani appeared unfazed by the full house of about nine hundred citizens in attendance. As an agricultural pioneer, she wasn't about to take any guff from Johnny-come-lately agitators that had moved into the valley from big cities. She lowered the microphone to match her 5'2" frame, and my fellow commissioners and I waited with bated breath to hear what she was going to say.

"Davey," she said, turning to look at me, "do you remember when you cut 'cots for the Mariani family?"

I nodded. In my youth I worked for the Marianis during my summer school break and had "cut cots" or sliced open apricots, removed the pits and placed them on drying trays.

"Davey, as I recall, I told you I would pay you fifty cents per tray, which had to be filled with apricots sliced open in halves. You were excited and buzzed away like a busy bumblebee, anxious to make money to add to your weekly allowance. Do you recall that day?"

I assured her that I did.

She glanced at the other six commissioners and then at our fifteen-member staff situated between us, grabbed the microphone out of the stand so she could hold it in her hand, and turned to address the audience. "Well, Davey thought he could leave large spaces between each piece of fruit, thereby filling up two trays in an hour. I slid my arm across the two trays, raking his work into one tray of fruit. Davey's eyes got as big as saucers when he saw his hourly pay had been cut in half as quick as a flash."

Those in attendance were nearly falling out of their chairs in laughter as I shrank in my seat. Besides being embarrassed, I couldn't help wondering where she was going with her story.

Mrs. Mariani turned back to the commissioners. "Now, Commissioner Semas, I've known you and your family for a long time. I know you've been raised by your mother and father to always do the right and honorable thing. The right thing now is to vote in support of our request to allow development to occur on our family homestead, which, as you know, is bordered by two large subdivisions to the west and north." She placed the microphone back

---

LIFE LESSON #29:

"IF YOU CAN LAUGH AT YOURSELF, YOU'RE WELL-GROUNDED. IF YOU CAN LAUGH WITH OTHERS, YOU'RE POLITE. BUT, WHEN YOU CAN LAUGH WITH OTHERS LAUGHING AT YOU, YOU'VE MATURED."

—DAVID SEMAS

into the stand, looked over at me with a smile, and winked at me as she returned to her seat.

Over the next thirty minutes, her attorney and engineer finished their detailed presentation with maps and architectural drawings.

When they were finished, I turned to the chairman and asked for a point of order.

The chairman acknowledged my request. "Yes, Vice Chairman Semas, you have the floor."

I waited a moment before responding. "I would respectfully request the chair rule on whether I should abstain from voting on this matter."

Chairman Ray Benich, a well-respected fruit rancher in his own right, suppressed a laugh. "I don't think it will be necessary for you to abstain just because you incurred a financial loss of fifty cents fifteen years ago. You probably lost much more in pride and self-esteem just now."

The chambers once again burst into laughter, and with levity filling the air, we unanimously approved the Mariani proposed development. The commission continued into the wee hours of the night, ruling on many other important matters while carrying out the county's planning and zoning business.

We sold the Las Fuentes office complex in 1974 for a nice profit. Despite some hiccups in financing the project, we finished in about nine months. Danny Texera was promoted to construction manager, Bud Estes was our CFO, and Mike Carey, my brother-in-law, became our construction superintendent. We all felt proud of the work we had done, and I felt I had proven myself in my new position as CEO.

At our first annual Christmas party in 1973, I announced we had just arranged $4 million in financing for a 40,000-square-foot, two-story garden office complex called Old Mission Center, located directly across the street from Santa Clara City Hall. Unlike Las Fuentes, this time I engaged the services of Sonneblick-Goldman, a highly respected commercial mortgage brokerage group. Coldwell Banker, a construction disbursement agent for Aetna Life & Casualty, financed Old Mission Center, providing the construction loan and a thirty-year permanent loan, which was quite unusual at the time. The beautiful, traditional Mission-style building with a clay tile roof, balconies on each side, and lush landscaping with mature olive trees still stands today, nearly a half-century later.

Old Mission Center in 1975

Old Mission Center in 2020

While completing both projects, I realized that starting a company involved much more than a single real estate project. I had to worry about payroll, utilities, rent, marketing, hiring leasing agents, and on and on. This was quite a bit for a twenty-five-year-old to take on, and I hadn't really thought it all through. Nevertheless, the success of two major real estate projects had helped rebuild my confidence. Regardless of the challenges I faced, I felt confident I could plunge ahead.

Unfortunately, I bought a beautiful, but gas guzzling 1973 Corvette just as the oil crisis hit Americans in October of that year. Lines of cars and pickup trucks at gas stations, sometimes one or two blocks long, could be seen in most US cities. The period brought considerable inflation and economic instability.

Despite forming my company on a shoestring budget, I weathered the economic downturn. Meanwhile, I continued to promote the idea of Century Past, the multi-themed restaurant, shopping center, and dinner-theatre entertainment complex I had conceived in 1972, just prior to the formation of SEM. It proved to be an exciting but formidable challenge and ultimately one of my first life-altering business defeats. However, it was a terrific educational experience that greatly broadened my horizons. The venture introduced me to many titans in the business, entertainment, and political worlds, but in the end, it became just a memory of what could have been.

Pruneridge Mission Center, 1979

CHAPTER 5

CENTURY PAST: VISIONARY IDEA OR NEMESIS? "THE PHILIPPINE CONNECTION"

In the latter part of 1972, as a twenty-three-year-old upstart real estate developer in the San Francisco Bay area, I was inspired by Walt Disney's Pirates of the Caribbean amusement ride at Disneyland to create my Century Past project. A dinner-theater and broadcast television complex, my proposed 120,000-square-foot entertainment development was way ahead of its time. Today, Las Vegas-themed hotel casinos mirror much of what I envisioned nearly fifty years ago, but while those well-financed developers succeeded, I, still a young man at the time, was looking at an unattainable pipe dream.

Century Past brochure, 1974

In the spring of 1973, my design concept ballooned from a $7 million real estate project into a $50 million entertainment-oriented development  ($317 million in today's dollars). The initial budget for the first phase of the mixed-use complex consisted of seven themed restaurants and matching retail shopping arcades and a 4,500-seat dinner theater.

Aerial photo of Century Past model

A rendering of the Century Past interior and center stage

The adjoining proposed office buildings, 400-room hotel, apartments, and condominiums would eventually add another $200 million to the cost of the project. The development was highlighted by beautiful flowering gardens with park benches, meandering pathways, towering specimen trees, waterfalls, streams, and bridges. Inside, the centerpiece of the dinner theater was a sixty-foot, semi-circular, artificial tropical island, lushly landscaped, that would slowly sink below the waterline of the Century Past lagoon. The massive wooden main platform would slowly appear as hydraulic pumps below ground level magically lifted the proscenium center-stage in preparation for the featured performance of headline entertainers. Behind, its thirty-foot-high waterfall would shut off, and the backstage drawbridge would drop down and connect to the island stage, which was surrounded by a lagoon and the River Boat Raft floating restaurant.

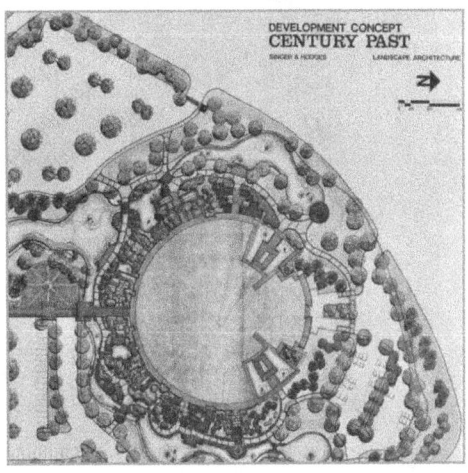

Development concept master plan for Century Past

This allowed dinner patrons to watch headliners and star-studded acts perform. Or the audience could delight in participating in the occasional broadcast television special or daily televised game show while comfortably seated at their dining tables on the docked rafts at the water's edge.

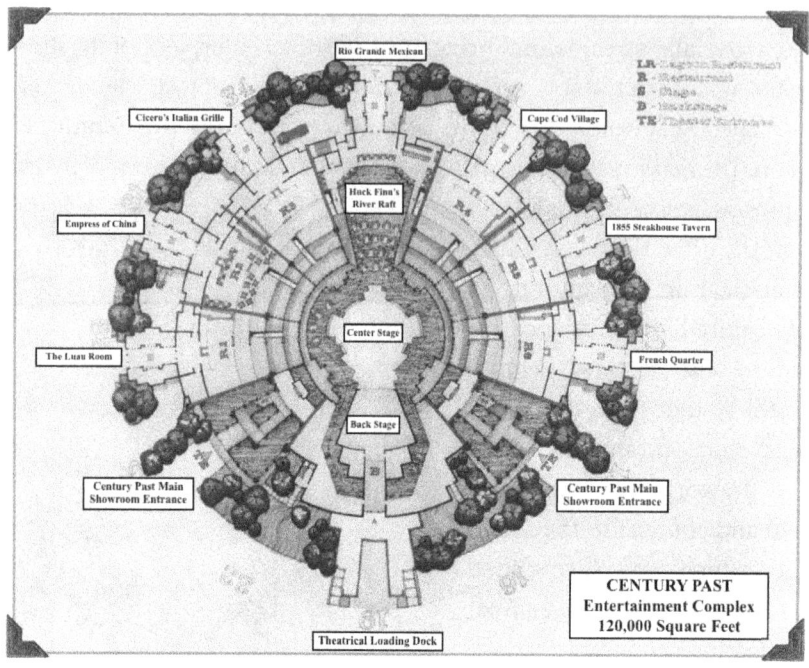

A detailed floor plan of Century Past

Each of the seven restaurants seated three hundred diners. With the addition of the 2,400-seat balcony, this gave Century Past an impressive seating capacity of 4,500 patrons. The San Jose Civic Auditorium, in comparison, could seat 2,850. During daytime operation, the balcony was concealed behind dim backlighting, and the massive Century Past domed ceiling projected nighttime images of the moon, stars, an occasional rain shower, and once an hour, the Aurora Borealis, better known as the Northern Lights.

LIFE LESSON #30:
"FIRST THINK.
SECOND, DREAM.
THIRD, BELIEVE.
AND FINALLY, DARE."

—WALT DISNEY (AMERICAN ANIMATOR, FILM PRODUCER, FOUNDER OF DISNEYLAND, 1901–1966)

Rendering of Century Past New Orleans entrance

Rendering of New England Fishing village entrance

Rendering of Mexican village plaza entrance

Rendering of park bench and meandering walkway

Rendering of stone bridge and waterfall

Rendering of Century Past parking area riverboat ferry

DAVID MICHAEL SEMAS

Me and Gary Plaza in 1975

Early on, I brought in my show-business friend, Gary Plaza, who was an original band member of the Del Rays, the opening act for Louie Prima in Las Vegas. With Gary at my side from 1973 to 1976, we met with hundreds of investors. Typically, I traveled alone around the country and internationally, so that Gary could hold down the fort while I met with senior-level executives at banks and other financial institutions. I also met with private equity investors, gatekeepers for family offices, and as many people as I could find, because it was impossible to predict where a connection might lead. As I had already learned, a meeting or conversation that seemed minor could turn out to be significant.

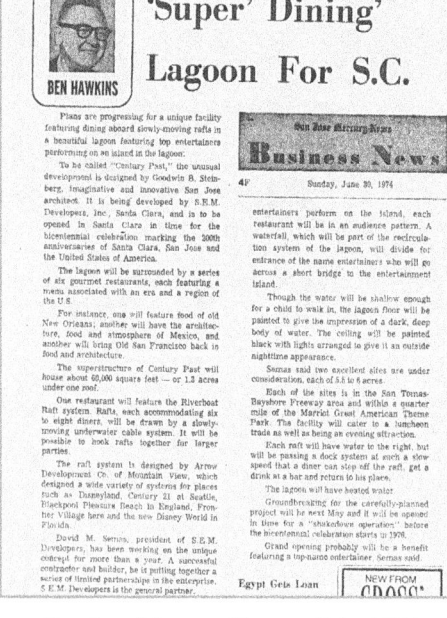

San Jose Mercury News article, 1974

On June 30, 1974, Ben Hawkins, business writer for *The San Jose Mercury News*, gave us front-page coverage in the business section with a nice article entitled, "Super Dining Lagoon for S.C." While my young children, Wendi, Greg, and baby Aimee, were growing like weeds, I kept busy by meeting with financiers, wealthy businessmen, political leaders, Wall Street investment bankers, and famous show-business personalities like Frank Sinatra and Merv Griffin. Even the former governor of Nevada,

Grant Sawyer, who was well connected in the gaming industry, listened to my story. But while many were intrigued and thought the concept was fascinating, none showed real investment interest.

In my relentless pursuit of financing, I approached other private investors and real estate moguls, including shopping-mall developer Edward J. DeBartolo Sr., hotelier Harry Helmsley of New York, and restaurateur Kee Joon Lee, owner of the Empress of China restaurant in San Francisco's Chinatown, among others. I traveled around the globe to meet with wealthy international businessmen, the rich and the powerful.

At one point in June of 1974, my friend Hubert Walsh, general manager of the famous Luau Restaurant on Rodeo Drive, and owner Steve Crane, twice married to Hollywood starlet Lana Turner, introduced me to a wealthy Beverly Hills heiress, Paula Verdier "Parvaneh" Hargrove. Her husband, Dean Hargrove, had written and/or produced the hit television shows *Man From U.N.C.L.E., It Takes a Thief, Columbo, Perry Mason, McCloud,* and *Matlock*. She was the first cousin of a two-star general in the Islamic Republic of Iran's military.

As a result of that introduction, I made two trips to Iran for meetings with Bijan Esfandiary-Bakhtiari and a group of his business associates. Bijian was the brother of Queen Soraya, the Shah of Iran's second wife. During my first visit to Tehran, I also had the honor of meeting His Majesty Mohammad Reza Shah Pahlavi, the Shah of Iran.

I was in my mid-twenties, with no real-world experience in restaurants, dinner theaters, or the entertainment industry. It would be an understatement to say that obtaining the funding for my $50 million single-purpose dinner theatre and entertainment complex was a long shot, but no one ever said I lacked chutzpah. At the time, I had no idea of the monumental challenge that lay before me.

Me at the San Francisco Airport for Iran trip in 1974

After a year of traveling from coast to coast, over the pond, and to the far reaches of the Middle East and the Pacific Rim, I was running out of options. I spoke with my old family friend Father Walter Schmidt, the Jesuit priest from Santa Clara University, who introduced me to the much-admired San Francisco hotel magnate and billionaire Benjamin Harrison Swig. Ben was the founder of the Fairmont Hotel chain, a beloved philanthropist, and chairman of the board of trustees for Santa Clara University. He was a visionary in his own right. After buying the tired, run-down, and neglected Fairmont Hotel in 1945, he'd had the foresight to turn the white elephant into a world-class luxury hotel, which from its location atop world-famous Nob Hill became the internationally recognized crown jewel of San Francisco.

In the late summer of 1974, I met Ben for lunch at his penthouse suite apartment located at his landmark Fairmont Hotel. A no-nonsense hotelier and financier with a brilliant entrepreneurial spirit, Ben was sharp as a tack, despite being about eighty years old at the time. He had been born in 1893 and had grown up in Taunton, Massachusetts, coincidentally my parents' hometown. Like my father, Ben was the seventh born of a large family—eleven in his case, as compared to sixteen for my father. Ben and I took an instant liking to each other. It certainly didn't hurt that Father Schmidt and Father Terry, president of Santa Clara University, had introduced us. Ben was a major real estate investor, and I was a young and energetic business entrepreneur, but we each had roots in the construction business, which helps explain why we hit it off so well from the start. I assumed he had graduated from an Ivy League college like Harvard or Princeton, since he was from the Boston area.

Ben was affable and always had a smile, but when the situation required it, he could appear a bit gruff. Everyone who knew him considered him a shrewd negotiator. As thousands of friends, recipients of his generosity, and nonprofit organizations around the world can attest, Ben Swig had a kind heart and was the stuff of legend. He was a close friend to former California Governor Pat Brown (Governor Jerry Brown's father) and palled around with US Supreme Court Chief Justice Earl Warren.

After our first several meetings, he offered guidance. We spoke over the telephone often and met every few months so I could learn from this business icon. His encouragement usually came in a single soundbite or a rhetorical question. Having lived through the Wall Street crash of 1929 and the Great Depression and having watched his father's Tremont Trust Company of Boston suffer the fate of most other financial institutions, Ben didn't mince words. He was nearly always on point, and his advice hit home. He could take the most complex business problem or intricate financial structure and break it down so the common man could understand it.

Initially, I was a little disappointed when he said he wouldn't invest directly in my projects and instead offered to mentor me. Yet I came to appreciate his willingness to make introductions, cultivate my knowledge, educate me on deal-making and business negotiations, and guide me toward my stated goals. He introduced me to many other successful businessmen, including A. N. Pritzker, chairman of Hyatt Hotels, and J. Willard Marriott, founder and chairman/CEO of the Marriott Corporation. He also introduced me to Frank Sinatra and future California Governor and US President Ronald Reagan, among others.

After I had met with Ben on four or five occasions, he asked me, "David, by the way, what school did you go to? Was it Santa Clara?"

Too embarrassed to further clarify, I merely answered, "Yes."

No doubt sensing a slight hesitation in my answer, Ben said, "You mean Santa Clara University, right? What was your major?"

I wasn't about to be untruthful. "I graduated from Santa Clara *High School*, not Santa Clara University. Other than a few night classes over a year-long period at San Jose City College, I never attended a university or received an advanced degree."

Ben paused for a moment, gave me a hard look, and then threw his arms into the air. "I knew I liked you when we first met. Your honesty is refreshing. I'm constantly surrounded by cock-and-bull stories! Hell, don't even think about it, David. I didn't have time for college as a young man. I started my career as a shoe salesman in Albany, New York before I went into banking and then the real estate business in Boston in the 1920s. If there weren't guys around like me, who'd be here to hire the ones with the college degrees?"

I never forgot his enlightening and uplifting words to a young, up-and-coming businessman.

On one occasion in the summer of 1977, Ben invited me to a luncheon at the prestigious San Francisco's Banker Club. "David," he said, "I have a meeting with two of my friendly hotel competitors whom I would like to introduce you to."

Delighted, I said yes without hesitation and drove to San Francisco the following day. When I arrived about fifteen minutes early, the maître d' escorted me to Mr. Swig's table. Ben arrived first but didn't hint at the identity of the surprise luncheon guests. A few minutes later, two dapperly dressed gentlemen arrived—one with a shorter and thicker stature and the other, whom I recognized, taller and trimmer.

They sat at our table, and Ben introduced me to the first businessman. "David, I would like you to meet hotelier and accomplished entrepreneur Mr. A. N. Pritzker, founder and chairman of Hyatt Hotels." He then turned toward the other businessman. "And this longtime friend and hospitality industry giant is Mr. J. Willard Marriott, founder and chairman/CEO of the Marriott Corporation."

I stood up and shook their hands. "It's an honor."

I wasn't certain if Mr. Marriott would remember me, but I had met him, his son Bill, and David Brown, vice president of theme park operations, in 1973 and on several occasions while consulting with Fess Parker regarding the controversial zoning and approval process for a eight-hundred-acre parcel of land that became the Marriott Industrial Park and Marriott's Great America in Santa Clara. Only a year had passed since the grand opening of the theme park (now California's Great America), where Mr. Marriott and I had sat on a park bench together and talked for thirty minutes. I had been fascinated to learn about Mr. Marriott's humble origins as a franchise owner of a nine-stool A&W Root Beer stand in 1927, which became The Hot Shoppe. Having come up with the bright idea of box lunches for airline passengers in 1942, Marriott had established an 80 percent market share by the late 1950s to become the world's largest airline catering company. His visionary son, Bill, recognizing the handwriting on the wall after Pan American, Trans World Airlines (TWA), American Airlines, United Airlines, Delta Airlines, and Eastern Airlines began building their own in-flight service kitchens in 1957, steered the family business toward the hotel industry. They opened their first hotel in Arlington County, Virginia, and the rest was history.

To my surprise and before I could say another word, Mr. Marriott looked at me and then over to Ben. "I remember David very well. We met several times with our partner, Fess Parker, and then just a few years ago during our land planning phase and again at the grand opening of our Marriott's Great America theme park. David and I sat on a park bench in front of our beautiful Columbia Carousel and reflection pond near the main entrance and had a nice conversation for quite a while." At the age of seventy-five, which seems pretty young now, this brilliant and revered Mormon businessman was 100 percent on his game.

We made small talk over lunch at first, but then Ben, Mr. Pritzker, and Mr. Marriott talked for an hour about the ins and outs of the hotel business, how to deal with customer complaints, and the hospitality industry. I listened to every word as though I was a fly on the wall and thought, *What an unbelievable opportunity it is to sit over lunch with three of the most famous and respected hotel operators and hospitality financiers in the world.*

Toward the end of the conversation, Mr. Pritzker spent at least ten minutes sharing the virtues of training the Hyatt's front-desk staff at their education facility, which he called Hyatt University. He spoke about the importance of customer service, courtesy, politeness, proper vocabulary, neatness, timeliness,

> **LIFE LESSON #33:**
>
> **"WE CAN'T HELP EVERYONE, BUT EVERYONE CAN HELP SOMEONE."**
>
> —RONALD REAGAN (FORTIETH PRESIDENT OF THE UNITED STATES, 1911–2004)

> **LIFE LESSON #31:**
>
> **"I LIKE TO LISTEN. I HAVE LEARNED A GREAT DEAL FROM LISTENING CAREFULLY. MOST PEOPLE NEVER LISTEN."**
>
> —ERNEST HEMMINGWAY (JOURNALIST AND NOVELIST, 1899–1961)

and treating all guests as though they were VIPs. He then turned to Mr. Marriott. "Bill, how do you train, educate, and motivate your hotel staff?"

Mr. Marriott paused, glanced around the table at each of us, and then wiped his mouth with his napkin. "Why, A. N., we just hire nice people." He wasn't being curt or disingenuous but rather plainspoken and frank.

Century Past Hospitality Magazine article, 1975

I suddenly appreciated the fact that sometimes a short answer will suffice. I would never forget the lesson.

Because I could call on Ben anytime, he was instrumental in helping me get moving in business. During one such meeting, he said, "David, you can never repay me, but I would ask that one day you do the same thing for others deserving. Once you make it big—and I know you will—don't wait for your last will and testament to help those in need."

Grateful for all the attention he had bestowed on me, I took his words to heart. Ben Swig passed away in October of 1980, shortly after I moved to Southern California.

LIFE LESSON #32:

"THE MOST VALUABLE OF ALL TALENTS IS THAT OF NEVER USING TWO WORDS WHEN ONE WILL DO."

—THOMAS JEFFERSON (THIRD PRESIDENT OF THE UNITED STATES, 1743-1801)

I continued to meet with prospective investors and promoted Century Past in various trade publications. I left no stone unturned and was relentless in my pursuit of funding. Now that the 1973–1975 recession was behind us, I felt that my timing couldn't be better. In June 1975, though Century Past still existed only on paper, *Hospitality Magazine,* with its impressive circulation of 125,000 subscribers, published a six-page, full-color feature story entitled "Century Past: A Bold Look Forward."

The following month, on the front page of *Business World* in the *San Francisco Chronicle*, another feature story, entitled "Unique Entertainment Complex—A Young Tycoon's Vision," included a photograph of me standing behind the scale model of Century Past.

Then, in December 1975, in my search for financing, I started down a path that would lead me on an incredible and intriguing adventure.

I was in a meeting with Doc Cannis, a well-respected East Bay (Oakland and Fremont area) real estate leasing agent, about his commercial real estate project in Hayward, California. Doc, a small man who wore thick-lensed glasses and walked with a shuffle, was in his mid-seventies. His name was well known in real estate leasing circles, because he had been responsible for much of the commercial leasing with Safeway grocery stores throughout Northern California for many years. Doc was a friend of my father when he worked for the Bevilacqua twin brothers in the 1960s while building several Safeway shopping centers.

During a meeting with Doc, he noticed my Century Past model and renderings and was fascinated. He asked about the project, and I spent a good hour explaining the concept behind the massive

San Francisco Chronicle "A Young Tycoon's Vision" article in 1975

LIFE LESSON #34:

"NEVER FALL IN LOVE WITH A DEAL. STAY FOCUSED, WELL GROUNDED, AND OBJECTIVE, AND CHECK YOUR EGO AT THE DOOR."

—DAVID SEMAS

---

dinner-theater complex. When I was done, he asked for a copy of my loan package and photographs that he wanted to share with someone.

After years of financing projects and learning how to prepare a proper investment presentation, I felt that I knew what I was doing. I showed him a two-inch-thick, leather-bound book and loan package, along with separate appraisals, market studies, general construction costs, and preliminary drawings prepared by the famed Stanford University graduate and my good friend Goodwin "Goody" B. Steinberg. Goody's wife, Geraldine "Gerry" Steinberg, and I served on the Santa Clara County planning commission, and in 1976, she was elected to the Santa Clara County board of supervisors.

"How much of this would you like?" I asked him.

"As much of it as you'll let me have, because I know some people who may just be able to arrange for the money you're looking for."

I had heard this many times before from others, but what did I have to lose? I gave him all the documentation and went about my business working on Century Past and other real estate developments in San Jose, Milpitas, Santa Clara, and Los Altos Hills.

About a month later, Doc called and asked if I could come to San Francisco on Thursday of that week to meet with him and a few of his business friends who were flying in from Chicago. I agreed and drove to the city, checking into the luxurious Hyatt Regency Hotel in the financial district of downtown San Francisco.

Over a four-hour-long dinner that evening with Doc and his friends, Jack Amato and Abe Chapman (pronounced "Abe-Bee"), I listened to a story right out of the pages of a modern-day *French Connection* novel. It involved detailed disclosures of high finance, corruption, counterfeit currency, greed, money laundering, and power wielded by the highest-ranking officials of the Central States Pension Teamsters Fund and others affiliated with, let's just say, organized crime. The latter included names like Jimmy Hoffa, Roy Lee Williams, and Allen Dorfman, the teamsters' senior loan advisor behind the financing of many Las Vegas casinos. Abe died in 2001, so I feel free to use his real name. On the other hand, Jack Amato, like many others in this book, is a fictional name.

After patiently listening to these unbelievable stories of conspiracy and intrigue, I asked, "What, if anything, does this have to do with me?"

Jack Amato, acting as the main spokesman, replied in his Chicago accent, "Plenty. Do you want to get your project financed? If so, we can make that happen in a heartbeat—if you help us accomplish our objective."

"Yes, I'm looking for fifty million dollars of funding for my project, but how can I help you? I'm just a young real estate developer looking to finance his project."

Jack, Abe, and Doc exchanged smiles.

"No, you're much more than that," Jack said. "You're exactly what we need to transact some high-level financial business, someone to serve as a liaison between our group and the Philippine government. We need someone like you—a successful West Coast businessman, well respected. And being a Santa Clara County planning commissioner certainly doesn't hurt. We also need someone without baggage, and most importantly, someone who doesn't speak with a Chicago or New York accent."

I was befuddled. At the same time, I was fully aware that the Central States Pension Fund had provided much of the funding for Las Vegas casinos and appeared to be a logical potential lender for Century Past. While I found most of what I heard that evening to be right out of a movie script, I knew Doc had been around a long time, and if he was willing to vouch for these people, there must be something to this.

When the evening was over, I asked Jack, "Where do we go from here?"

"We'll be in touch, and Abe will be my local contact with you."

I went home, and that weekend, during our usual Sunday afternoon dinner at my father-in-law's house, I asked him if he knew the names Jack Amato or Abe Chapman. An FBI Academy graduate in his twentieth year as captain of detectives for the Santa Clara Police Department, Stan was well connected in law-enforcement circles. Most importantly, Stan was also a highly respected member of the Association of Law Enforcement Intelligence Units (LEIU), an organization comprised of leading law-enforcement

---

LIFE LESSON #35:

"BEWARE OF GREEKS BEARING GIFTS."

—VIRGIL'S AENEID, BOOK 2, 19 BC

---

agencies around the country that monitored and tracked the movements of organized-crime figures. I thought if Stan could validate the names of these two men, maybe there was something to the remarkable and somewhat unbelievable story I had heard in San Francisco.

When I asked Stan during a televised, sold-out football game between the San Francisco 49ers and the Los Angeles Rams if he knew the names Jack Amato or Abe Chapman, he nearly choked on his potato chip. He took a gulp of his Jack Daniels on the rocks and said, "Are you kidding? Did you just say Abe Chapman?"

"Yes, Abe Chapman, who lives south of Oakland in the Hayward area and has something to do with the Central States Teamsters."

Stan turned white as a ghost. "Dave, you're asking me about one of the most infamous gangsters and the last surviving member of Murder, Inc. Abe Chapman—or maybe I should call him by his real name, Abraham Chalupowitz—is better known as Trigger Abe and was a go-to hitman for the mob in the San Francisco Bay Area. You know that Murder, Inc. was the notorious organized-crime group that started the term 'putting a contract' on a person's life? Murder, Inc. is believed to be responsible for at least one thousand unsolved murders and contract killings, and Trigger Abe about a hundred of them. This sweetheart spent nine years in the federal penitentiary on Alcatraz Island and served with James 'Whitey' Bulger and the Birdman of Alcatraz. His buddies were Meyer Lansky, Mario Balistreri, Waxey Gordon, and Bugsy Siegel. Abe is a mobster. How on earth do you know him?"

I explained that I'd had dinner with some Central States Pension Fund officials the other night, and a short, seventy-year-old Jewish man by the name of Abe Chapman was there.

"Be very—I mean *very*—careful," Stan warned me.

I assured him I would and thought, *Well, I guess these people are on the level!*

I should have been frightened, but instead I was relieved. These were not conmen who had fooled Doc and only claimed they were connected to the Teamsters. They were the real deal.

MAN IN THE ARENA - NEVER SAY QUIT

Several weeks later I received a call from Abe, who said he was only thirty minutes away from my offices in Santa Clara and asked to stop by. As I escorted my wife, Kathy, and my baby daughter, Aimee, out to the reception area, Abe swaggered in with two muscular "businessmen" dressed in blue pinstriped suits. Abe commented on how beautiful baby Aimee was, and then he and his bodyguards, both of whom remained silent, walked back to my private office.

"Everything has been arranged for your trip to the Philippines," Abe said. "You'll be receiving a telegram sometime today or tonight from Jack Amato. He's traveling in Europe, but within the next few days, he'll be calling you personally."

Within about thirty minutes, Abe and his companions had left.

The next day I received a telegram from Jack telling me to arrange my trip to the Philippines via Los Angeles International Airport (LAX) on Saturday, December 6, 1975. This was before the widespread commercial use of fax machines, let alone FedEx or email. The telegram confirmed that he would be calling me to discuss other details of the trip. I was still suspicious about whether any of this was really on the level, but I thought I would just wait for Jack's call to see how everything unfolded.

Sure enough, Jack Amato called my office a few days later. As I peppered him with questions, he said, "All in good time. I must keep this brief, so just listen." He explained that I would be departing sometime Saturday morning from LAX on the daily Philippine Airlines flight to Manila. I was to make my reservations, and the airline was expecting my call.

Expecting my call? This sounds a little strange, I thought, *but okay*.

He told me to book a five-day stay at the Manila Hilton. I was also

> **LIFE LESSON #36:**
>
> "THE ONLY ORGANIZED GROUPS MORE DANGEROUS THAN THE TEAMSTERS AND THEIR MAFIA CONNECTIONS ARE THE IRS AND SEC!"
>
> —DAVID SEMAS

to reserve a suite at the Hyatt near LAX the night before my flight so I could meet with Lieutenant Colonel David J. Willis, United States Marine Corps. I was told by Jack that Lieutenant Colonel Willis would brief me on the trip and provide me with answers to my questions.

"The people I represent are prepared to make a loan to the Philippine government for one and a half billion dollars," Jack explained. "Let's say there are a few issues that prevent the Philippine government from securing the loan from the IMF (International Monetary Fund) directly. The terms and conditions can't be negotiated over the phone; the process must be initially conducted face-to-face with an emissary such as yourself. You'll be meeting with some very high-ranking government officials, including President Ferdinand Marcos and his longtime friend, General Marking, governor of the Veterans Bank. Lieutenant Colonel Willis will tell you the whole story when you meet him in Los Angeles."

My mind swirled with questions, but two in particular seemed most important. "If I'm successful in assisting you and your group in consummating this transaction, will I be paid a fee? And will the Central State Teamsters loan fifty million dollars for Century Past?"

Jack merely replied, "Both."

Well, here we go!

I booked my flights and hotel reservations, flew down on PSA Airlines from the San Jose Airport to LAX, and checked into the Hyatt Hotel on Friday afternoon. Late that night, Lieutenant Colonel David Willis called my room and asked me to join him in the cocktail lounge for a hot toddy or cup of coffee.

As I stepped into the lobby bar, a man approached me and introduced himself. "Good evening, Dave. I'm Lieutenant Colonel David J. Willis. It's a pleasure to meet you." He was a muscular marine in his mid-forties, with a square jaw, light-brown hair cut in a flattop, and deep-set blue eyes.

I wondered how he could have known who I was, but he beat me to the punch.

"Jack Amato gave me a good description," he said with a polite smile.

We sat down at a table in the far corner of the lounge, and Willis explained that he had been a marine sniper and later a chief intelligence officer and had been in the service for about twenty-five years, serving in South Korea and Vietnam before moving to the Pentagon.

I realized that his length of service equaled my age.

"The real story begins after I arrived back in Washington, DC," he said. "I suggest we go up to your hotel room, where we can talk freely."

I was on pins and needles to hear what this was all about. We ordered cocktails to go and went up to my room, settling into plush armchairs in the sitting area.

"What I'm about to tell you might sound impossible to believe," he stated bluntly. "But it's absolutely true, and soon you'll receive further confirmation. When you arrive in Manila, you may not have access to all the puzzle pieces or a full understanding of all the people involved, and I believe it's safer that way. But you'll come away convinced of my story. Once you experience how you'll be officially received by high-ranking government officials in a country under martial law like the Philippines, you'll come to realize there's no other logical explanation but the one I'm about to give you."

As the lieutenant colonel explained, upon his return to the Pentagon in 1972, he had received orders from the highest levels of the Nixon administration and the Pentagon to depart immediately for Manila and report to President Ferdinand Marcos of the Philippines on assignment from the US government. His orders were to assist Philippine President Marcos and his senior military staff and other Philippine banking and financial regulatory advisors in an investigation into allegations of corruption, money laundering, and illegal drugs that were allegedly being shipped to and from the Philippines and Vietnam via military transport. The drug trafficking was suspected at two US military bases, then located in the Philippines.

Within days of his orders, Lieutenant Colonel Willis was in the Philippines meeting with high-ranking military officials and having many one-on-one meetings with President Marcos himself. The president, a former military officer during World War II, assured him he was committed to getting to the bottom of the scandal and finding out why so many young American and Filipino soldiers were returning home as drug addicts.

President Marcos gave Willis carte blanche on behalf of the Philippine government to travel freely from Clark Air Force Base on Luzon Island to and from Vietnam and Cambodia with all the resources of the Philippine military at his disposal. Willis had standing authority, as granted to him by the Pentagon, to conduct his nearly thirty-six-month-long investigation into these criminal allegations.

By February 1974, he had accumulated enough testimony and hard evidence to, as he put it, "bring down a house of cards" that would stretch from Vietnam, Cambodia, the Philippines and its US military bases, all the way to the Pentagon, Congress, the Washington political elite, the CIA, and many captains of industry. He wouldn't divulge any specific names. He would only say, "It's best if you don't know. I can only tell you that the individuals behind this highly sophisticated multi-billion-dollar criminal drug ring and money laundering scheme includes some of the most powerful and well-recognized names in America and in political circles."

At this point, I was in a state of disbelief. I couldn't entirely grasp what the lieutenant colonel was saying. My mind raced. *Is this man a conspiracy theorist?* I wondered. *Is he delusional? What possible motivation could be behind his claims? Should I still get on a plane for the Philippines in a few hours? If this is for real, is my life in danger? Is my family safe? How did I get in the middle of all this?*

I realized I didn't know much, and I had no access to name names or places. I regained my composure and asked Willis to continue.

"I know it's hard to believe," he said, "but it's the truth. Just imagine for a moment that a group of unnamed conspirators made up of government officials, politicians, businessmen, and a criminal element joined forces to mastermind one of the greatest financial scams in world history. We're talking about billions upon billions of uncirculated US dollars used to buy drugs, starting back as far as the Cuban Missile Crisis and continuing until the fall of Saigon."

Willis detailed the elaborate plan, claiming that actual US Mint monetary printing plates in $20, $50, and $100 denominations had been smuggled into Vietnam via military transport through one of the two US military bases, along with huge rolls of monetary linen paper stock and the specialized ink to complete the printing process. In a secret location in Saigon, this operation printed millions of dollars on a twenty-four/seven basis.

"While the money is actual US paper currency," Willis said, "it's unauthorized by the US Treasury. I believe it to be one of the main reasons why the US government went off the gold standard in 1971."

Willis also alleged that this clever and highly sophisticated operation was the main culprit behind runaway inflation in the 1970s, because billions of unauthorized US dollars were flooding the world economic markets. He believed that the 1973–1975 oil crisis was directly tied to this criminal conspiracy as well.

"Now let me explain further," he said. "Each month, or more often, if necessary, the money launderers—let's just call them the Vietnam drug cartel—would purchase hundreds of tons of marijuana, heroin, opium, LSD, or whatever drugs they were selling at the time to the local population and troops from countries all over the world. The heroin and opium came from the interior countryside of Southeast Asia, and most of the other drugs were imported using military transport planes routed through the Philippines. The cartel merely printed money to buy the illegal drugs, which in turn they sold to hundreds of thousands of soldiers and civilians every day, basically representing a near one hundred percent net profit margin.

"When you consider that in 1968 the US military reached a peak of nearly 550,000 in Vietnam, and then add Australia, Canada, the Montagnards, New Zealand, Philippines, South Korea, and the South Vietnamese themselves, well, the dollars involved, and the monthly cash flow had to be staggering as the unauthorized currency was circulated worldwide. As the illegitimate currency was laundered, the 'clean' money was in turn collected and assembled at predetermined distribution points all over Southeast Asia. I have proof of who was collecting, where they were collecting it from, and how they were transporting it to one central location near Saigon for transport to the Philippines and back to the US for distribution amongst the cartel leaders."

In a nutshell, the cartel was printing its own US currency to buy illegal drugs to cut, package, and sell to hundreds of thousands of servicemen to make billions of dollars. Not only had they destroyed the lives of countless young men, but they had also wreaked havoc on world economies and created an inflationary cycle in the US, which Willis said we might not fully recover from for decades.

"Who do you think benefits from high interest rates? The same people who have all the cash."

Willis brought the entire conspiracy into focus for me when he said, "Now you know the truth, so it's time to give you the last missing piece of the puzzle and the reason for your involvement. As the world knows, this occurred only a few months back, in April. At the time, everyone in 'Nam knew that the end was in sight, because the North Vietnamese were encircling Saigon about a month before the collapse of the city. My sources told me that the cartel began to dismantle their currency printing and smuggling operations about three weeks prior to the collapse of Saigon in preparation. Printing presses, engraving plates, linen paper, ink, and some remaining currency were wrapped, boxed, then sealed and marked in about twenty shipping crates, which were then ground-shipped to Saigon for air transport to one of the two US military bases in the Philippines: the naval base at Subic Bay and Clark Air Force Base. The bills of lading and customs documents were marked with a special military 'Pentagon—Top Priority' seal. Only a few people were privy to the exact location of the containers, the specific bills of lading numbers, and the designated security code name required for retrieval of the illegal contraband.

"I was one of those few people who were part of the inner circle that possessed the bills of lading numbers and the designated security code names. When the containers were shipped to the Philippines, I arranged to divert the sealed shipping containers to a different location, which has been exclusively under my control since then. President Marcos is aware that only I know the exact location and have the newly issued security codes. I understand that he has already been in touch with the members of the cartel and with the highest levels of the Ford administration about his knowledge and the whereabouts of these highly sensitive items. I can also tell you that President Marcos is committed to the removal of the US military presence in the Philippines. He intends to use the currency plates as leverage to accomplish the withdrawal of all US military personnel and the closure of the two military bases sometime in the future."

My mind was reeling. I looked over at the clock. It was now nearly three o'clock in the morning, and my flight to Manila was scheduled to depart in eight hours. "Okay, I guess I understand the basics of the story and probably know all I want to know about it," I said. "First, are you asking me to do anything illegal? Second, what is it you want me to do, and who am I meeting with in Manila? Third, if this is successful, how do I know that I'll ever receive my funding for Century Past?"

"Fair enough," he said, nodding. "You're not doing anything that's illegal or even unethical in any way. You're merely acting as an emissary, a go-between for several motivated parties that wish to consummate a financial business transaction. The circumstances are this: I have control over the location of the items in question, and I can't return to the Philippines for obvious reasons and must keep a low profile. President Marcos would like to use this information for his political advantage and, knowing him, also for his financial gain. The cartel desperately wants these items back in their possession to protect their identities and to make certain that the truth behind this money-laundering scheme and drug ring is never publicly disclosed. I can't say for certain, but I expect that the US government and the Ford administration would like to make certain that this scandal is sealed forever, and they probably have many ideas about how to use this information to their benefit. Jack Amato and his Central State Teamsters group have their own reasons for making the billion-dollar loan to the Philippine government. I have no knowledge of that, other than to say they have assisted in identifying you and arranging to have you act as our designated emissary to high-ranking officials within the Philippine government.

"Lastly, regarding the financing of your entertainment complex in Santa Clara, I believe that it's a win-win for all involved. All you have to do is meet with certain government officials and personally hand letters to the individuals to whom they are addressed. No, I can't guarantee one hundred percent that the Central State Teamsters or Jack Amato will do what they say, but I don't see any reason why they wouldn't. I can tell you their insider group includes the moneyman to the Teamsters. Allen Dorfman and his Amalgamated Insurance arranged financing for Caesar's Palace, Circus Circus, the Desert Inn, and the Dunes Hotel and Casino. Generally, he receives ten percent off the top of the loans for Teamster-funded real estate deals. He usually pays a finder's fee of one percent to someone like Abe Chapman. Because this involves a huge favor for the Teamsters Union, he'll probably pay you two percent and take seven percent for himself on a fifty-five-million-dollar loan, so you'd still net fifty million dollars to build the Century Past project."

He paused to give me time to absorb this, then continued.

"Quite frankly, Dave, you've come this far, and in the big scheme of things, considering you've been traveling all over the world to try to finance your project for several years, what do you have to lose?"

I thought about it and realized he was absolutely right. Heck, it would be the adventure of a lifetime. Over the next six days, I would be meeting some very interesting and influential people in Manila.

"All right," I finally said. "I'm tired and need some sleep to prepare for my fifteen-hour flight. What are my marching orders? What else do I need to know?"

"When you arrive in Manila, you'll probably be met by one of General Marking's administrative aides, who will take you to the Manila Hilton."

"General Marking?"

"Yes. To be accurate, his name is Marcos Villa Agustin Marking. Before World War II, he was a former taxicab driver and boxer from Manila. During the war, the general led the most feared home-grown fighting force the Japanese ever faced, and he remains the most highly regarded—many would say the most revered—former Filipino military officer of all time. It has already been arranged for you to meet with him on Monday morning. Please send him my best wishes and hand him his sealed envelope. The general and his aide-de-camp, Colonel Francisco Quesada, will be your point men the entire time you're there. Remember: the country is under martial law, so there will be armed soldiers on every street corner. Stay close to the general. As I said, he's a true national treasure and World War II hero who led the famous Marking's Guerillas, the Filipino resistance group that

---

LIFE LESSON #37:

"GO OUT ON A LIMB. THAT'S WHERE THE FRUIT IS."

—JIMMY CARTER (THIRTY-NINTH PRESIDENT OF THE UNITED STATES, 1923-)

fought the Japanese during their occupation of the islands. Make certain to give the marked envelopes to the corresponding individuals. Just handle yourself professionally, answer questions when asked, be courteous, and enjoy your visit. I'll try to call you each night at about midnight Philippine time to brief you further. I think you're as ready as you'll ever be."

With that, our meeting came to an end, and I fell into bed with anticipation about what the next day would hold.

At about ten-thirty Saturday morning, I boarded a full flight on a Philippine Airlines Boeing 747 jumbo jet, Flight No. 1. The captain kept the cockpit door open, allowing the first-class upper-deck passengers to see the aircraft controls and listen to his radio communication with the traffic controller. The enormous plane vibrated as the four powerful Pratt & Whitney engines spooled up and pushed us down the runway. After taking off on schedule, we rose through the clouds into the endless blue skies. We soared across the Pacific Ocean, stopped on the island of Guam for refueling, and continued our journey halfway around the world to the Manila International Airport.

The plane landed in the dark around 9:00 p.m. and pulled up a hundred yards away from the lighted terminal. In those days, there was no jetway, so the ground crew rolled up a staircase for the passengers to disembark. It was a warm, humid summer night.

As I reached the bottom of the stairs, a short, well-dressed Filipino gentleman approached me and asked, "Are you David Semas?"

Knowing there were at least ten tall Americans with olive complexions and dark hair, I was somewhat surprised he knew who I was. "Yes, I am."

"Hello. My name is Colonel Francisco B. Quesada. I'm an aide

LIFE LESSON #38:

"WHEN YOU EXPECT THINGS TO HAPPEN—STRANGELY ENOUGH—THEY DO HAPPEN."

—J. P. MORGAN (AMERICAN FINANCIER AND BANKER, 1837–1913)

to the general. Welcome to Manila and our beautiful country. You may feel free to call me Kits, as General Marking does."

In his mid-fifties, Colonel Quesada was very personable, and I felt comfortable from the first moment we met. That was a good thing, because as he led me away from the plane, two military jeeps filled with armed soldiers in camouflage garb, sitting behind mounted fifty-caliber machine guns, came into view. The jeeps bookended a black stretch limousine with the Philippine flag on the right front fender and a flag with a government seal on the left fender. Two uniformed officers stood next to the limo.

Kits introduced the men to me as federal customs officials, and they asked to see my passport. They asked me a few questions, looked me up and down, and glanced at my passport before stamping it.

"You are in good hands," one official said. "You are free to go."

"Don't I have to clear customs?" I asked Quesada as he ushered me into the limo.

"You just did. There is no need to wait in line. Give me your baggage claim tickets, and I will have one of my men pick up your luggage. It will be waiting for you in your room when you check into the Hilton."

Even before I got into the limo with Kits, I felt like I was traveling as a VIP under a diplomatic passport. Although I had been on Philippine soil for less than thirty minutes, it was apparent that David Willis was in fact who he said he was.

During the short ride to downtown Manila, I said to Kits, "When I came off the plane, you approached me immediately. How did you know who I was with three hundred passengers on board, including about ten who were tall, dark-haired Americans?"

Kits smiled. "That was easy. That's why we call it Philippine Airlines. I radioed the captain, gave him your name from the passenger manifest, and asked him to have a stewardess get a description of you. Considering you're tall, with long dark hair and a mustache—and look like the singer Tony Orlando, as the stewardess put it—it was easy."

This was my first of several "Big Brother is watching" experiences.

Manila was bustling even at ten o'clock in the evening. Military personnel, jeeps, and machine guns were everywhere. It was obvious the city was under martial law, but I was told curfew ran from midnight to 4:00 a.m.

We drove down a treelined four-lane highway with the pitch-black Manila bay on the left and the brightly lit city on our right.

Soon, our three-vehicle caravan pulled under the Hilton's porte-cochere, and Kits ushered me inside. I felt like some dignitary arriving at the hotel. The general manager, who obviously knew Kits, approached me and asked how he could be of assistance.

"David," Kits said, "this is my friend Mr. Joaquin Ramirez Santos. Joaquin, David is our special guest, a personal friend of General Marking and President Marcos. He's registered under David Semas. He just arrived from America, and I believe you have a complimentary bay view suite for him, checking out this Friday. Is that correct?"

Me as the so-called "Tony Orlando" look-alike in 1975

"Yes, sir, all the arrangements have been made. Why don't you and Mr. Semas enjoy a few hors d'oeuvres and cocktails in our lounge while I get his suite prepared?"

Kits and I retreated to the lounge, flanked by the armed soldiers, who stood by the entrance while we sat at a corner table. Kits told me a bit about his and General Marking's exploits during World War II. As it turned out, not only was General Marking a highly decorated war hero, but Colonel Francisco Quesada was a World War II hero in his own right as well. He remained modest as he told me that he had been involved in a highly successful Allied rescue operation in nearby Los Baños.

Many years later, I researched and confirmed that the Raid at Los Baños, as it's known, occurred in the Philippines on February 23, 1945, and was a joint US Army Airborne and Filipino guerrilla operation that resulted in the liberation of more than 2,100 Allied civilian and military prisoners from a Japanese internment camp. Although Colonel Quesada was only twenty-four years old at the time, he commanded a group of former ROTC cadets and college students directly involved in the rescue. According to military historians and General Colin Powell, the Raid at

Los Baños is regarded as the most successful rescue operation in modern military history.

After Kits and I said goodnight, I took the elevator to my suite on the twentieth floor. Upon opening the carved wooden double doors, I entered Shangri-La, complete with palm trees, fountains, and a garden. The sprawling and beautifully appointed presidential suite must have been at least 2,000 square feet. The Hilton was one of the tallest buildings in the city, and my balconies overlooked downtown and the bay. I paused to take in the twinkling lights of the ships in the harbor and the streetlamps that cast a golden light on the streets.

Just minutes after entering my room, I fell into the king-sized bed, knowing that 8:00 a.m. would come too soon.

The next morning, I took a minute to enjoy the sunlit view of the glittering bay from my balcony and then hurried down to the coffee shop, eager to meet General Marking. At eight o'clock sharp, Kits entered with three armed soldiers, followed by a man who was a little shorter than Kits—at most 5'4" tall and maybe 130 pounds.

Is this small figure the famous decorated war hero of the Filipino people? I wondered.

As General Marking entered the room, I realized that indeed he was. Like most other men I had seen in Manila so far, he wore an elegant hand-embroidered white silk shirt over dark slacks. Not only did the general have a certain presence and mystique about him, but Filipino men and women applauded as he passed them. Some walked over to shake his hand, while others bent down to kiss it. The reverence given him was unlike anything I had witnessed before.

> **LIFE LESSON #39:**
>
> "SINCE THERE IS NOTHING SO WELL WORTH HAVING AS FRIENDS, NEVER LOSE A CHANCE TO MAKE THEM."
>
> —FRANCESCO GUICCIARDINI (ITALIAN HISTORIAN AND STATESMAN, 1483–1540)

General Marking approached my table, and I stood up to shake his hand.

"You must be David," he said, pronouncing it *Day-bid*. "There is no one else in this coffee shop who stands so tall and looks like Tony Orlando. I am General Agustin Marking, and it is indeed a pleasure to make your acquaintance. Let us sit for a while and get to know each other better, and then we can order some breakfast."

We talked for an hour before ordering breakfast. General Marking told Kits to take me sightseeing and shopping later so he could buy me three traditional Barong Tagalog dress shirts like the ones they wore. I was dressed in a light-weight sport coat and a short-sleeve silk shirt in the 95-degree weather with 98 percent humidity. A Barong Tagalog shirt no doubt provided a more comfortable alternative.

I reached inside my coat pocket and handed General Marking the letter from Lieutenant Colonel Willis. "General," I said, "I would like to very respectfully extend to you the best wishes of Lieutenant Colonel David Willis and personally hand you this confidential letter he asked me to deliver."

It was apparent that he was expecting the letter. He showed no sign of surprise and was very gracious. "How is my old friend Lieutenant Colonel Willis? We have been great friends for many years. Now you and I will become great friends as well."

I was taken aback by his comment but honored and pleasantly surprised.

General Marking, Kits, and I leisurely enjoyed each other's company while we ate our American-style breakfast. He spoke of the modern-day Philippines, the workings of the government, his involvement as the governor for the Veterans Bank, and his longtime friendship with President Marcos, and eventually even shared some of his World War II stories. He asked if my father had served in the military, and I told him Dad had been a Seabee in the South Pacific. His eyes lit up as though I were speaking about one of his best friends.

Finally, announcing that he had other appointments, the general stood up to leave. "Kits will take you shopping and return you to the hotel in a few hours. Make certain that you rest, shower, and wear one of your new dress shirts for the activities this evening, which will begin promptly at five-thirty." The general left two of his soldiers to escort Kits and me down the streets of Manila.

When I walked outside for the first-time during daylight hours, I was amazed to see the armed soldiers up close. They were stationed on every street corner. Kits bought me the shirts as gifts from the general and returned me to the hotel. At five-thirty, he showed up again, this time in his military dress uniform, and we ducked into the limousine.

I was taken to an ornate structure called the Malacañang Palace, the palace of the president, located in Manila on the banks of the Pasig River. With its marble floors, marble columns trimmed with gold leaf, and elaborate chandeliers, it matched what I had imagined a presidential palace would look like. I was taken to a formal banquet room with high ceilings and ornate wall carvings and moldings and noticed that fine china and silver had been set out on long tables.

As I walked down the reception line, General Marking personally introduced me to President Marcos and First Lady Imelda Marcos; General Fabian Ver, who served as the commanding officer of the armed forces; and Gregorio Licaros, governor of the Central Bank. We enjoyed cocktails and dinner with the president and first lady, along with about sixty or so other dignitaries. At our table sat Ricardo Salazar, a famous Filipino investigative journalist, who told fabulous stories of intrigue and criminal activities by the Philippine government. At one point in the evening, he lifted his shirt and showed me three large scars on his chest—the result of being shot three separate times during the 1960s.

Toward the end of the festivities, Imelda Marcos got up from her place next to the president and joined the sixteen-piece orchestra to sing several classic American songs, including Bobby Darin's version of "Mack the Knife." She finished with a traditional Filipino song, which she sang in Spanish and partly in her native Tagalog language. She had heard that I was an excellent singer, so she invited me on stage to sing the Elvis Presley song "It's Now or Never," which was received with delight by the audience.

When Kits returned me to the hotel around midnight, he asked, "Do you have the letter for President Marcos?"

"The remaining letters are in a safe deposit box in the hotel."

"Fine, but make certain that you bring the letter for the president tomorrow."

The next day, Kits and General Marking took me in the limousine to a presidential luncheon honoring the investigative reporter we had met the prior evening. Over the first portion of the luncheon and after roasting our host, the distinguished journalist was called to the podium and began to tell stories of corruption, Mafia-like criminal activities, and unbelievable bravery. Many of his friends from the audience would cheer and shout out his name in support.

We take much for granted in America, like our safety, security, police protection, and largely law-abiding population. Several years prior to my arrival in the Philippines, after a huge spike in burglaries, kidnapping, armed robbery, rapes, murders, and criminal mayhem on the streets of Manila, the third-world country had come to resemble the Wild West. In September of 1972, President Marcos declared martial law to restore law and order. From that day until January 1981, military jeeps with machine guns mounted on the back, armored tanks, and military trucks traveled up and down the highways and in the Manila city center. Heavily armed soldiers could be seen on every street corner, along the highways, and at the airport, hotels, government buildings, schools, churches, hospitals, and even in shopping centers. Nightly curfews starting at midnight became an everyday part of Filipino life.

After the luncheon, Kits escorted me toward the back of the building and down a long hallway to another room, where we met President Marcos, General Marking, and ten heavily armed soldiers. The general once again introduced me to President Marcos.

I gave a slight bow and said, "Good afternoon, Your Majesty. My name is David Semas, and I

> LIFE LESSON #40:
>
> "FOR TO BE FREE IS NOT MERELY TO CAST OFF ONE'S CHAINS, BUT TO LIVE IN A WAY THAT RESPECTS AND ENHANCES THE FREEDOM OF OTHERS."
>
> —NELSON MANDELA (SOUTH AFRICAN ANTI-APARTHEID REVOLUTIONARY AND POLITICAL LEADER, 1918-2013)

most humbly thank you for graciously extending an invitation to me to attend your dinner last evening and the luncheon today."

"Young man, you are very welcome," President Marcos replied. "Yes, I do remember you from last evening. You are very tall amongst our smaller Philippine people, so it's easy to pick you out of the crowd. Tell me: how is my old friend, Lieutenant Colonel David Willis? General Marking tells me you have a letter for me."

"Yes, sir, I have the letter right here." I handed it to President Marcos.

He took the letter and paused. "David, I know you are American, but are you of Spanish descent? You are a very handsome young man, and you should consider spending a little more time in Manila, as we have some very beautiful women here."

I smiled, somewhat embarrassed. "Thank you, Mr. President, but I'm married with three small children."

He and his entourage laughed and looked at Kits and General Marking. "So? That doesn't stop you from admiring beauty, does it?"

"No, Your Excellency, not at all."

Back in the limousine, as we returned to the Hilton, the general said to me, "Lieutenant Willis would be proud of you. You did a great job and handled yourself very diplomatically in front of President Marcos. I think he was very impressed and taken with you. You made a very good impression."

The next morning, General Marking, Colonel Quesada, and I took a hovercraft to Corregidor Island, about fifty miles on the other side of Manila Bay. The general wanted me to see Corregidor because of its historical significance during the war. General Douglas MacArthur had used the island as Allied headquarters until 1942. General Marking also knew that my father would be pleased to learn that I had visited there, because he had served as a Seabee in the Marshall Islands during World War II and admired the Filipino military and civilian population very much. Many locals had served with him in the South Pacific in various capacities, including as translators.

In the afternoon, the general's armed security entourage took us to my last meeting, with Central Bank governor Licaros. He chatted with me for a few moments before asking if I had a letter from Lieutenant Colonel Willis.

I handed the letter to him.

"Thank you," he said. "It was a pleasure meeting you."

After I returned to the hotel, General Marking told me to enjoy the next day on my own. Tomorrow evening, he informed me, he would have a surprise for me. He advised me to pack my luggage and be prepared to check out of the hotel late tomorrow afternoon. I thought perhaps I was going to spend my last night at General Marking's home estate.

I spoke with Lieutenant Colonel Willis that night and gave him a summary of all that had occurred.

"Great work," he said. "I've already got a briefing from General Marking. Take care. We'll speak after your return home."

Feeling great, I decided to do a little sightseeing and shopping. I walked up and down the streets of Manila and in and out of gift shops and jewelry stores, always aware of the armed soldiers on every street corner, though I felt fairly safe during the daytime hours. Around two o'clock Thursday afternoon, I was in the back of a small retail shop when someone tapped me on the shoulder. I nearly jumped sky-high.

It was Kits.

"How on earth did you find me?" I asked.

He laughed. "David, haven't you learned by now that we are the eyes and ears of Manila? We know everything that is going on. For your personal safety, when you make a move, our soldiers are watching and telling my surveillance team of your location. I have the limo waiting outside. Let's go back to the Hilton and pick up your things."

After retrieving my luggage, we spent the next few hours at a health spa with a masseuse, steam room, and individual sleeping rooms where we could take a nap after our experience. That evening, we met up with General Marking, Kits, and a group of his friends at a local restaurant for an eight-course dinner around a traditional circular table.

After dinner, the general said, "David, we are now going to take you back to Malacañang Palace for a nightcap with ourselves and a brief farewell with President Marcos, who would like to see you one last time before you depart for the US. You will spend the night in the palace, and the presidential limousine will take you to the airport in the morning."

Once again, I was pleasantly surprised.

We arrived, sat down in an exquisitely decorated sitting room, and enjoyed an after-dinner cocktail with President Marcos, who briefly joined us. A Malacañang Palace guard and butler then escorted me through the lobby to my ornately appointed eighteenth-century room, which was more like a Spanish king's master bedroom suite and featured a view of the Pasig River. I was so tired I fell asleep when my head hit the pillow.

I awoke to a knock on my door. Breakfast was ready downstairs. I had a quick bite to eat and left for the airport, where I found General Marking and Kits talking with customs officials. My new friends said goodbye, and we promised to stay in touch. I cleared customs nearly the same way I had arrived. With a simple wave of the arm from Kits and General Marking, the customs official placed a stamp on my US passport.

All the way home on my return flight, I kept thinking that my wife and close friends would never believe me when I told them of the last several days. Hell, *I* didn't even believe it, and I had been there.

For weeks afterward, I wondered what had really happened. What did the letters say in the four envelopes that I had delivered? Were the Central State Teamsters and Jack Amato going to follow through on their promise? Was I ever going to hear from Lieutenant Colonel Willis again? How would I know if the currency plates were ever returned? Who could I tell this unbelievable story to without sounding like I had lost my mind? I came back with many more questions than I'd had when I left. All I could do was continue with other financing prospects, fulfill my responsibilities as county planning commissioner, and work on my various real estate development projects.

I told the story to Kathy and a few close friends and, for safekeeping, gave my entire hard-copy file of original notes, letters, airline tickets, hotel receipts, and telegrams from Jack Amato to my close friend and golf and hunting partner, Bob Lynch, owner of the Ford dealership in Gilroy, California. Bob passed away long ago without betraying my secrets. Before moving to Gilroy, he was the general manager of an auto dealership in Cleveland and was a good friend to James T. "Jackie White" Lacavoli and his associates.

When the letter from the Central States Pension Fund finally arrived at my office, I was in the middle of a three-week vacation at the 160-acre ranch I had just purchased in northwestern Montana. The ranch, which I named Stonewood Ranch Outfitters & Company, was located in the tiny town of Swan Lake, about sixty miles from the Canadian border and just fifteen miles from Flathead Lake. I had been a North American big-game hunter since I was a teenager and thought the place would be a great getaway for my family and friends.

Stonewood Ranch, MT arial, 1975

Swan Lake entrance road to Stonewood Ranch, 1975

Sandy Calhoun, my secretary, called and told me the letter had arrived in my absence, and of course I was ecstatic. After seven months that had seemed like an eternity, the Central States Teamsters Pension Fund had issued a $50 million letter of commitment for the construction of the Century Past project to SEM Development Company. It was unbelievable. *My God*, I thought. *I've actually pulled off the impossible.* I celebrated with my family when I returned to California, and a few days later flew down to Las Vegas to party with friends. The *San Jose Mercury News* published a full-color, eight-page layout on Century Past in its Sunday supplement with the headline: "A Setting for Stars."

Unfortunately, within a matter of weeks after receipt of the commitment letter, my house of cards came tumbling down. I'd heard some scuttlebutt about Congress trying to pass some legislation that would limit pension funds but hadn't imagined that it would have any impact on my financing. Then I got a call from Jack Amato informing me the Teamsters had been forced to withdraw their commitment and back out of funding for Century Past.

> **LIFE LESSON #41:**
>
> **"WHEN THE GOING GETS TOUGH, THE TOUGH GET GOING."**
>
> —JOSEPH P. KENNEDY SR. (AMERICAN BUSINESS TYCOON AND FATHER OF JOHN F. KENNEDY, 1888-1969)

Starting in 1974, with the adoption of ERISA (Employee Retirement Income Security Act), Congress had begun looking seriously at what were considered improprieties on the part of pension funds and in particular the Central State Teamsters. Shortly after my Century Past financing was approved, Congress passed the ERISA Fiduciary Duty/Tax Reform Act, which stated, "Any fiduciary who breaches any obligation or duty imposed by the fiduciary responsibility requirements of ERISA is personally liable to make good on any losses incurred by the plan resulting from the breach." With individual pension fund board members' financial estates on the line after the passing of ERISA legislation, we witnessed the beginning of pension fund advisory firms and the end of pension funds making direct investments in real estate projects like Las Vegas casinos and speculative real estate ventures like Century Past.

As a result, within a year, the Teamsters withdrew from all speculative real estate financing projects around the country and pulled their $50 million loan commitment to SEM. Four years of blood, sweat, and tears went out the window. I forfeited my land option deposits, and hundreds of thousands of pre-development dollars were lost. Century Past was reduced to renderings, scale models, marketing studies, appraisals, and piles of paper and became nothing more than a memory.

I was devastated. My dream had gone up in smoke. I knew that no one else was ever going to finance my project. Only then did I admit to myself that perhaps I shouldn't have tackled something as unattainable as financing Century Past in the first place. I also learned not

> **LIFE LESSON #42:**
>
> **"LIFE IS WHAT HAPPENS WHILE YOU ARE BUSY MAKING OTHER PLANS."**
>
> —JOHN F. KENNEDY (THIRTY-FIFTH PRESIDENT OF THE UNITED STATES, 1917-1963)

to celebrate until the money was in the bank.

Strangely, about two years later, while recovering from knee surgery at O'Connor Hospital in San Jose, I awoke from a medically induced sleep to see Lieutenant Colonel David Willis standing at the foot of my bed. At first, I thought I was dreaming. But then he started speaking and told me he was still trying to make the deal happen. He explained that, for personal safety reasons, he had relocated to Bangkok, Thailand. Moreover, he said he had written a book about some of his experiences. Toward the end of his visit, he reassured me that I would be hearing from him in the near future. After the thirty-minute visit, he turned to leave when Kathy and Aimee happened to enter my room. To make certain I wasn't dreaming, I told Kathy who had just visited and asked her to remind me later so I would know that it had really happened. I still don't have any idea how he found out I was in the hospital. Months and then years went by, but I never heard from him again. In the immortal words of Forest Gump: "That's all I have to say about that."

I received Christmas cards every year from General Marking until his death in 1984. Colonel Francisco Quesada, my companion during my days in Manila, stayed in touch with me after he relocated to America to serve as an administrative aide to then San Francisco mayor Dianne Feinstein. Kits,

> LIFE LESSON #44:
>
> "LET SLEEPING DOGS LIE."
>
> —CHARLES DICKENS (ENGLISH WRITER, NOVELIST, AND SOCIAL CRITIC, 1812-1870)

> LIFE LESSON #43:
>
> "TWENTY YEARS FROM NOW YOU WILL BE MORE DISAPPOINTED BY THE THINGS YOU DIDN'T DO THAN BY THE ONES YOU DID. SO, THROW OFF THE BOWLINES, SAIL AWAY FROM THE SAFE HARBOR, CATCH THE TRADE WINDS IN YOUR SAILS. EXPLORE. DREAM. DISCOVER."
>
> —MARK TWAIN

known to his family as Paquito, passed away in 2008 in Las Vegas, Nevada. May his soul rest in peace.

Later, from 1988 to 1992, the George H. W. Bush administration tried to renegotiate the terms of a lease extension of the military bases at Subic and Clark. But negotiations deteriorated with the Philippine government. On December 27, 1991, Philippine President Corazon Aquino issued a formal notice for the United States to vacate both bases. The Subic Bay Naval Station was the largest US overseas defense facility after Clark Air Base, and both ceased US operations in 1992. Why would the United States government give up its most strategic military bases in the South China Sea?

Was what I was told in 1975 actually true? I can only guess that, in the interest of national security and considering the controversy around the Vietnam War, decisions were made at the highest level of the United States government to conceal these historical facts. I will never know what really happened behind the scenes during my whirlwind adventure a half century ago. Over the years, I've tried to contact David Willis, but to no avail. My guess is today he would be in his late eighties.

CHAPTER 6

ONE, TWO, THREE STRIKES AND YOU'RE OUT

After the Century Past financial fiasco, I marched forward once again, remaining optimistic as I looked to the future. Given the life lessons I had already learned to date, I was beginning to appreciate my dad's early advice: "Don't try to be a pioneer, because most of the time, pioneers end up face-down in the mud with arrows in their back." So, I picked myself up, dusted myself off, and focused on more conservative land holdings for the development of conventional projects, like garden office buildings, townhouses, and two proposed residential hillside development projects.

By 1977, the prime lending rate was at 7.50%, and things were finally looking up. Wendi, Greg, and Aimee were attending the same elementary school I had attended: C. W. Haman, located at the corner of Los Padres Boulevard and Homestead Road, only a block away from my Las Fuentes office building project and within a short walking distance of our home on Denise Drive. I had many projects under construction and others in the midst of the zoning and entitlement process throughout Santa Clara County. As was the case with larger scale projects and hillside developments, it could easily take two years or more to receive all the necessary governmental approvals.

In the summer of 1977, Bud Estes left SEM Development to join his wife's cosmetic marketing company. While hiring a new CFO, I recalled more of the Colonel's thought-provoking insights. During my youth, he had told me more than once to never make fun of or disrespect other people because of their nationality, race, religion, personal appearance, or lifestyle. As he put it, "We're all different and speak with an accent in one form or fashion. It just depends on what part of the earth you're occupying. So never disrespect someone because they're different. One day that 'different' person might be you."

I recalled this advice while interviewing a young man by the name of Harry Smith. Harry had his advanced degree in accounting from San Jose State and appeared to be the most qualified. He was professional, articulate, and well-groomed. He seemed like a good guy with a great sense of humor. When I offered him the job, he appeared surprised.

"Is there something wrong?" I asked.

He hesitated for a moment. "David, I have to be completely honest with you. I must tell you something."

"Okay. Go ahead."

"Well, I'll just come out with it. I'm gay."

I paused. "Will that affect your ability to do your job?"

"Absolutely not!"

"Well then, as long as you excel at your job, have a good work ethic, are loyal to the company, are a good person, and don't hit on me, we should do just fine."

We shared a laugh, and Harry became one of the most loyal, hardworking, and conscientious employees I ever had.

Shortly after I hired Harry, he introduced me to his friend, Sandy Calhoun. Sandy was an administrative assistant to the president of a large public company based in San Francisco but was tired of commuting fifty miles a day. Tall, impeccably dressed, attractive, and highly intelligent, she spoke Spanish and French, took shorthand, and typed 120 words a minute. She had grown up on Hilton Head Island in South Carolina. Her father was a golf professional, and because of growing up around the sport, she was a scratch golfer. Harry gave me a heads up that she was a lesbian and assumed that wouldn't be an issue with me.

"Great!" I said. "That means I don't have to worry about you having an office romance, do I?"

Harry laughed. "David, you're unbelievable. You have no idea how refreshing and welcome your attitude is to those of us that have lived in the closet all these years. I'm no longer even welcome at my family home."

"That's your family's loss," I said. "You and Sandy are now a part of the Semas family, and you, Sandy, and your significant others are always welcome in our home and certainly in our lives."

A few years later, I experienced two tragic and potentially life-threatening events that taught me how fragile life can be. One moment you're here, and the next you're in the midst of heavenly angels.

The first event occurred in the winter of 1978 during a hunting trip to British Columbia with my brother-in-law, Mike Carey. Because I was busy with land-use zoning hearings on several projects, I had Sandy book our airplane reservations. Mike and I were set to fly over the Canadian Rockies to Calgary, Alberta for the night and then land the following day at the unmanned airport tower in Cranbrook, British Columbia. This was near the Canadian border, only 250 miles north of my ranch in Swan Lake, Montana. After buying Stonewood Ranch in Montana in my mid-twenties, I started hunting grizzly bear, bighorn sheep, timber wolf, mountain goat, mountain lion, moose, caribou, elk, and other big game animals. At least once a year, I arranged a ten-day hunting trip to Stonewood with friends. I had already hunted many times for big game in Alaska and Canada. My friend Jack Atcheson, a world-renowned taxidermist and hunting

> **LIFE LESSON #45:**
>
> "PREJUDICE CANNOT SEE THINGS THAT ARE BECAUSE IT IS ALWAYS LOOKING FOR THINGS THAT AREN'T."
>
> —MARK TWAIN

consultant, arranged the seven-day cougar hunt in British Columbia for Mike and me.

Stonewood Ranch Ky-Dogs annual hunting trip gathering, 1977

Several days before our scheduled departure from San Francisco, I noticed that Sandy had booked us to fly from San Francisco to Calgary on Friday, with a one-night stay before departing the next morning for Cranbrook. Without telling Sandy, who had taken a few days off, I changed our reservations to take us to Vancouver, British Columbia, instead of Calgary, so we could enjoy the sights and nightlife for a few days before flying on to Cranbrook for our hunting expedition that Saturday morning.

Our flight to Vancouver went as planned, and several days later, on Saturday, February 11, 1978, we boarded a Pacific Western Airlines plane, a Boeing 737, bound for Cranbrook Canadian Rockies International Airport. We left on schedule, and as the plane began its final approach from the vast, wide-open blue skies at 22,000 feet, we slowly descended into the clouds for what seemed like an eternity.

When there were no signs of land for thirty minutes, I began feeling anxious. I glanced at Mike and said, "Where the hell is the ground? I can't see a thing." Though I had never had much fear of flying, my sense of dread only worsened the longer we lingered in the clouds.

Me and Mike Carey in route to Cranbrook, BC, 1978

Suddenly, trees appeared right below us. We were only about five hundred feet above the ground. I breathed a deep sigh of relief. Snow was falling heavily by the time the wheels touched the runway and the captain hit the thrust reversers. The aircraft came to a stop, and as we deplaned down the ramp stairs, I was thrilled to be on solid ground. I kissed the ground, turned, and took a photo of our Boeing 737.

Our Pacific Western Airlines (PWA) Boeing 737 in Cranbrook, BC, 1978

Mike and I stowed our gear away in an airport locker and decided to grab a cab and find a local diner for breakfast. Heinz Leuenberger, our guide, hadn't expected to pick us up at the airport until about noon. About an hour later, as we gazed out the window of the '50s diner, we saw fire trucks, police cars, and ambulances racing with sirens blaring toward the airport. We soon learned that a commercial jet had crashed, resulting in a significant number of fatalities. PWA Flight 314—the very flight that Sandy had originally booked for us—had departed Calgary shortly after we had left Vancouver and had crashed right there at the Cranbrook airport.

Apparently, the estimated time of arrival given by Calgary traffic controllers had been in error by fifteen minutes, and the flight crew hadn't reported to airport ground personnel that the plane was arriving earlier than scheduled. Just as the Boeing 737-200 aircraft was about to touch down in the near whiteout, the pilots noticed a snowplow on the runway. A touch-and-go was initiated, but the thrust reversers hadn't stowed away properly, and hydraulic power had been automatically cut off at liftoff in Calgary. During the final approach maneuver, the pilot reacted by pushing the thrust lever full forward to spool up the twin Pratt & Whitney JT8D-1 jet engines with their 14,000 pounds of thrust. The plane pulled up, barely avoiding the snowplow as the pilot attempted to climb above the trees. The captain banked the plane to the southeast, but tragically, both engines stalled, and the aircraft side-slipped into the ground and crashed, killing forty-two of the forty-nine passengers.

My heart sank. After Mike and I called home to make sure that our families didn't think we had been on the ill-fated flight, I felt an acute sense of my own vulnerability and how close death could be at any given moment. Like many other young people, I had been under the mistaken impression that I controlled my own destiny and that a long life and many opportunities still lay ahead of me. But as I sat in our front booth in the '50s diner, I knew for the first time that this was in no way guaranteed; live for today, for tomorrow may never come.

Mike and I remained in a state of shock during our seven-day hunting trip. Although we felt horrible for the families of all those precious souls that had perished that horrific morning, we realized that there was nothing we could do. Life would go on for us but not for the victims.

Later that week, we departed Cranbrook on a PWA flight bound for Vancouver. As the plane climbed and banked just above the airport, we saw the burnt wreckage

---

LIFE LESSON #46:

"FOR GOD SO LOVED THE WORLD THAT HE GAVE HIS ONE AND ONLY SON, THAT WHOEVER BELIEVES IN HIM SHALL NOT PERISH BUT HAVE ETERNAL LIFE."

—JOHN 3:16

of Flight 314 below off the east end of the runway. Feeling sick, I sat back in my seat, grateful for the extra time Mike and I had been granted by the good Lord.

The second potentially near-death event came only a year later, in the spring of 1979, while on a big game hunt for black bear, grizzly bear, and timber wolf in northern British Columbia with Mike and my friend Jim "Bugs" Haney, a Canadian outfitter and guide. On that cold, foggy, drizzly morning, I had a life-altering, nearly life-ending encounter with one of North America's most unpredictable and ferocious big game animals. Over the years, I've successfully tracked and hunted *Ursus arctos horribilis*, better known as the grizzly bear. No doubt a few tracked and stalked me more than I hunted them. My ten-day hunting adventure with Mike started forty miles up the Stikine River in British Columbia, outside of Wrangell, Alaska, when we came across a rather cantankerous 700-pound bruin.

Me on Big Horn Dahl Sheep hunt in Yukon Territory, 1978

While traveling upriver, we spotted the big grizzly lying atop an old moose kill on a small sandy beach across the river inlet. We tied up our sixteen-foot aluminum classic dinghy fishing boat on the far side of the little island separating the main Stikine River from the left fork of the stream fork inlet, where the bear appeared to be busily feasting. As we cautiously crept over the brush-covered strip of ground, navigating past fallen trees and large chunks of driftwood, the grizzly came into view. We crouched lower than the tall grasses. We were downwind, about a hundred yards away, and took shelter behind a large, downed tree. I patiently raised my .375 H&H Colt Sauer rifle and looked through the crosshair sites of my Weatherby 6x power scope. After lining up the shot, and over the span of about ten seconds, I squeezed off one shot at a time and landed three direct shoulder and body hits. The powerful grizzly swatted at the air as though he had only been struck by nonlethal bean-bag rounds and then scurried up the riverbank into a dense willow thicket.

Mike and Bugs turned to each other in amazement and said in unison, "Wow! That was impressive!"

"Not really," I replied. "My shots were only one hundred yards away."

"No, you idiot," Bugs said as he and Mike laughed. "I was talking about the bear."

We peered through our binoculars to see if we could locate the grizzly across the stream, but the scrubby bush was as impenetrable as a ten-foot-tall hedge.

A few minutes after my adrenaline rush subsided and my heart rate slowed, Bugs raised an eyebrow and said, "Well, Dave, you know what comes next."

Me reloading for third shoot at Grizzly running into dense thicket, 1979

Once a grizzly was wounded, it could be extremely dangerous, and for the sake of the animal, it had to be taken down quickly so as not to suffer further. Knowing I was going into thick brush, I reloaded the four-shot rifle and handed Mike my .375 H&H Colt Sauer scoped rifle, which was firing a 260-grain bullet. In exchange, Mike gave me my powerful backup, a safari-grade .378 Weatherby Magnum without a scope. It featured a shorter barrel length for maneuverability in the thick brush and fired a 300-grain bullet. In 1953, while on safari with a .378 Weatherby Magnum, famed rifle-maker Roy Weatherby killed an African elephant with one shot.

Mike prudently acted as my backup and stayed put on the opposite side of the stream, while Bugs and I took his small aluminum boat around the Stikine River to the narrow island inlet. We cut the engine, and the current carried us onto the shoreline where moose carcass lay. After dragging the lightweight boat onto the beach, we walked up the twenty-five-foot riverbank. Our feet slipped backward with every step and sank into the sandy soil. We stopped at the top and at the edge of the dense thicket. The terrain was relatively flat with some tall grass but mostly thick brush shrublands. As we trampled and hacked our way through the impenetrable willow and alder stand, it took us a good fifteen minutes to go ten yards. This was nothing less than a bushwhacker's nightmare.

I was shaking in my boots, for I understood the perilous danger that Bugs and I were facing. We could see the furious bear less than fifty feet in front of us. We were a handful of yards from an extremely unpredictable wounded animal that had ten times the strength of a man. We were so close I could see his squinting eyes and smell his foul odor. I was trembling in my boots at the sight of his scowl and the sound of his deep, guttural growl. A North American grizzly bear, cousin to an Alaskan brown bear, can sever a man's head from his shoulders with a single swipe.

We cautiously approached the wounded grizzly, knowing if it charged, it could mow down the willow and alder brush and even three-inch-diameter trees as though they were toothpicks. Mosquitos attacked from all sides, the sun glaring between the branches, partially obstructing my vision. I wiped the sweat from my brow yet still managed to keep a watchful eye on the wounded bear. Over the next treacherous thirty feet, we tripped, stumbled, and fell, and although it took only a few minutes, it felt like an eternity. Haney was finally in position to circle to the backside of the animal, while I remained facing the downed bear from the front.

Finally close enough to deliver the kill shot, I placed my fourth shot at its neck and shoulder to immobilize the beast. A bear's power is located in its upper body, so the shot was meant to prevent any further forward movement. We stopped and waited five minutes, which in hindsight should have been more like fifteen minutes. Bugs came within a few feet of the bear's hindquarters and poked it with the end of his rifle barrel. This method is always used to make certain the animal is in fact dead.

Me in dense thicket of willows and alder brush with a downed Grizzly

To our surprise, the bear was indeed alive. With its last ounce of strength, it rose on all fours, let out a hellacious roar, and lunged directly at me. I jumped back, stumbled, and fell in the brush while simultaneously firing my fifth shot and the last bullet in my rifle. It was a direct hit to the head, and the bear dropped a mere eight feet in front of me. Still in shock, I continued to try to reload by pulling back the rifle bolt, locking it in place, and dry-firing repeatedly. I had forgotten that I had exchanged rifles with Mike. The .378 Weatherby Magnum only held two rounds, not four like

the .375 H&H Colt Sauer, and unfortunately, the only cartridges in my hunting vest were for the .375 H&H.

Lower left, Ed Quintal and me during Alaskan brown bear hunting trip 1977

Throughout my North American hunting adventures, I would never come closer to facing my own death. In the end, the last of my five shots hit home. Had it not, I'd be with our Heavenly Father above.

Shortly after that harrowing experience, Bugs told me the tragic story of Bob Hahn, his fellow Alaskan native and Canadian outfitter and good friend. I had met Bob once while shooting pool when the boys were in town, and he had told many fascinating tales about his outdoor adventures.

He was a fearless hunter and guide who had a great love and respect for the Canadian wilderness, big timber, and all of its thriving wildlife.

Being a larger-than-life character himself, Bugs told the story of Bob crossing the frigid and muddy waters of the Stikine River in his small aluminum boat. Bob spotted a large grizzly leisurely swimming in the river directly ahead of him and heading upriver not too far from his hunting camp near the historic town of Telegraph Creek, British Columbia, about fifty miles east of Wrangell, Alaska.

Bob thought it would be a real hoot to lasso this big ol' "grizz" so the bear could him toward Wrangell. Several hunters on the opposite shoreline, which was about two hundred yards away, witnessed Bob's harebrained scheme and the ensuing encounter with a big grizzly bear that was merely minding its own business. After three attempts, Bob's rope landed around its intended target, and as Bob had planned, the bear's powerful swimming stroke carried his boat downstream—until the grizzly grew tired of the game. The bear abruptly turned and grabbed the rope and pulled Bob and his boat toward it, eventually overturning the boat. Bob was thrust into the near-freezing glacier-melt waters of the unforgiving Stikine River. Between the bone-chilling Alaskan water and the muddy silt filling Bob's pockets and pants, he never made it to the river's edge. His remains were recovered a few days later, washed ashore downstream.

The story doesn't end there. Only a year earlier, Bob had written a poem that, as I recall, was published in *Field and Stream*. The provocative poem appeared to lack its final stanzas, which I've added in honor of Bob. His adapted poem follows.

"I'm Not a Killer, Oh No, No, Siree"

In the fall of the year the hunters go forth
They climb over the hills from the south to the north
To experience the challenge, excitement and thrill,
of a stalk and a chase and perhaps even a kill
"What's that you say, a kill, a kill. Never, oh never,
oh never I will"

DAVID MICHAEL SEMAS

*You jeer from your pedestal way up high, looking down
at the hunters as they're crawling by
"I'm too far above that, I'm human, you see. No destroyer
of wildlife, no murderer me"
Yet isn't that coat you so proudly wear made of smooth
leather, devoid of all hair?
And what of the dinner you're planning to make, potatoes
and peas, but best of all, steak?
"But I'm no killer, oh no, no, siree, you see, someone else
does the killing for me!"
In the fall of the year comes Veterans Day, to honor the
men and women who fought far away
They picked up their rifles and took careful aim, with every
intention to kill and to maim
But this is an honorable thing that they did. To make the
world safer for me and my kid
War is much different from hunting, you see, for man
shooting man and is necessary?
The creatures all live in complete harmony, with only
hunters to fear, don't you see?
To end all this killing, that's what I'm wishing. Oh, pardon
me, but I have to go fishing
"But I'm not a killer, oh no, no, siree, you see, someone else
does the killing for me!"
As most of us know, a license and a gun don't make a
hunter, though he may look like one
For within all races, all colors, and all creeds, we have some
bad apples from some bad apple seeds
Some hunters are sportsmen, some hunters are not. The
poacher causes problems, making others hot
But don't condemn all for the actions of a few, unless you
condemn mankind for what felons do
But then tell me, brethren, how do we draw the line? What
of the little mouse in your house so fine?
Look at the spider that had woven her web, and what of*

the flies buzzing over your head?
It's a jungle out there in the wilderness. God's creatures are subject to tension and stress
The rabbit, the mouse, the wolf, the deer, the bear, or the fly. Who will go next, who will soon die?

Man, the hunter, becomes part of this scene. For he is a predator, deep down in each gene
Not so grand as a wolf or a soaring eagle, with his ragged clothes he's far from regal
But he's taking the part of what nature intended, not merely to see that some lives are ended
It's plain to him in the scheme of all things that death must occur for the life that it brings!
Where would this land of America be without our forefathers who hunted frequently?
"That's immaterial, it's not necessary now. We live in no danger, our meat's from a cow"
Your arguments are fair, but listen to me, of a chase in the mountains, unfettered and free
No cars and no phones, no muggers to fear. Only me and animals and the silence to hear
A climb after a goat where the air may grow thin, and the ledge suddenly ends and no other begins
What a feeling! What a life! The goat gets away, so what, who cares! 'Twas a glorious day!
So climb off your pedestal way up high, come down to the real world where all things must die
Be it bear, deer, weasel, or a plethora of fleas, trout or ants or even the germs of disease
All is according to the Creator's great plan, but did he consider the stupidity of man?
Dam all the rivers, that's really neat, and cover the farmlands with miles of concrete
Clear-cut the forests, pollute the streams, only to satisfy

> *man's greedy dreams*
> *Progress is the villain, destroyer of life, don't blame the lawful hunter for all of the strife*
> *"But I'm not a killer, oh no, no, siree, you see, someone else does the killing for me!"*
> *Many's the hours I've spent in the wood. And I'd spend many more if I reasonably could*
> *If these wild creatures would someday be gone, my heart would be heavy with the break of each dawn*
> *Yet I stalk these wild ones, without worry or care, I've paid all my dues and don't even take my share*
> *So don't curse the man who pulls the trigger, sit down and consider, reason and figure*
> *All of us are killers to a certain degree. Your mother, your brother, your sister, and me*
> *Don't be too quick to judge or to sway unless you know in your heart that you can honestly say*
> *"I'm not a killer, oh no, no, siree, there's no one who does any killing for me!"*

Bob Hahn's words, at the very least, give the reader the opportunity to see through the eyes of an honorable hunter. This man, like most true hunters and sportsmen, loved the outdoors, life, and all of God's creatures. Unfortunately, many of those city dwellers and tree huggers misunderstand. The vast majority of Americans today have never set foot in the great outdoors or experienced firsthand the thrill of the hunt with a gun, bow and arrow, or even a camera. To many non-hunters and those opposed to what Bob Hahn's word represent, his message may ring hollow, but maybe, just maybe, a few who read this poem will come away with a different understanding of the "fair-chase" big game hunter.

Various hunting trips, 1975-1980

During 1976 and 1978, SEM Development completed a number of townhouse developments, including Tudor Village and Madison Gardens in Santa Clara and several custom homes. The company also designed two beautiful multi-use complexes, incorporating English Tudor, and Mission-style Spanish architecture. Additionally, we were negotiating to acquire four-ten-acre office-building-zoned parcels in Walnut Creek, Fresno, Palm Springs, and San Diego. At the same time, I was working on an 810-acre project in Los Altos Hills called Stonebrook Estates. A large-scale 142-lot hillside development, it involved more than $28 million in financing. The project encompassed nearly four years in designing, engineering, and zoning and required an Environmental Impact Report (EIR) and public hearings.

Rendering of Kensington Gardens, 1978

Rendering of Tudor Village, 1979

Tudor Village townhomes sales ad, 1979

Tudor Village townhome development, 2020

Due to its location in Los Altos Hills, with its rolling pastures and majestic live oak trees, Stonebrook Estates was politically controversial. It took three years to negotiate with the surrounding property owners to reach a reasonable compromise on lot sizes, density, traffic, noise abatement, and other sensitive entitlement issues. We ended up dedicating four hundred acres of permanent open space by donating nearly half the property to the newly formed Midpeninsula Regional Open Space District, now comprised of 60,000 acres.

Meanwhile, I went about my other developments. We completed the construction of a few more residential projects and made a handsome profit by

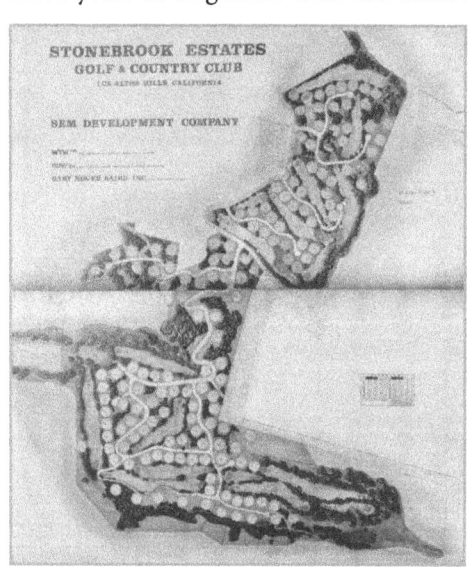

Stonebrook Estates Master Plan, Los Altos Hills, CA in 1979

selling off other large land parcels for which I had obtained zoning approvals for homes and apartments.

In January of 1979, a few of my fellow Ky-Dogs hunt-club members came up with the idea of holding a charity football game benefitting the Santa Clara High School Athletic Program and the Santa Clara Police Athletic League. I had been the announcer and color commentator for Santa Clara Police Athletic League (PAL) youth boxing matches for several years, so I thought this would also provide a good opportunity for community outreach. We received huge community support, including support from Santa Clara High School, Buchser High School, and Wilcox High School. The city council joined with civic leaders and local businesses, and Marriott's Great America Theme Park contributed to the cause financially and allowed the promotional and marketing use of their Bugs Bunny cartoon character.

Santa Clara Super Bowl program, 1979

The football game featured alumni from the local schools against the Santa Clara Police Department, San Jose Police Department, and Santa Clara County Sheriff Department. The grueling gridiron game was initially called the Santa Clara Pig Bowl, but we opted to change the name to the Santa Clara Super Bowl I, pitting the Santa Clara Ky-Dogs against the mighty Santa Clara Police Porkers. I don't recall the final score or the winner, but I do remember the Santa Clara Police Porkers were called for a personal foul ten seconds before halftime. Thanks to our local farmer friend who provided us with one of his prized family possessions, a young piglet scurried across the field, disrupting play. The frustrated referee threw his yellow flag, blew his whistle, and announced the Porkers were being penalized fifteen yards for too many pigs on the field. The event was a great success, and we raised more than $20,000 for Santa Clara High School and PAL.

By 1979, several years after the Century Past loss, I assumed that rocky financial times were behind me. The odds of something like it happening again were small. In fact, I had nearly forgotten all about it. The human brain, perhaps in an effort to protect itself, has a way of shutting out unpleasant thoughts and erasing certain events from memory. But sometimes lightning does strike in the same place twice.

Santa Clara Super Bowl team, 1979

We were finally making headway on our zoning approvals and tentative map for Stonebrook Estates when, in August, the bank prime-lending rate rose significantly from 7.50% to 12.50%. By December, it had jumped to 15.25%. My construction loans, like most, floated at 1% over the prime lending rate, meaning my interest rate had just doubled almost overnight. Inflation had once again reared its ugly head. Paul Volcker, chairman of the Federal Reserve Board, and President Jimmy Carter were determined to break the back of inflation. All of a sudden, interest rates began to climb to 17%, then 18%, then 19%, until they finally skyrocketed to 21.50% by December 1980. This was the highest prime rate ever recorded in US history—and remains so today. As a result, the interest rate on my various construction loans was an astonishing 23% annually—or three times more than I had anticipated.

With $28 million of construction and land development loans outstanding at 1% over prime, I was screwed. Instead of making interest-only monthly payments during development, I eventually found myself paying the equivalent of $1.9 million annually. As I withdrew funds from my interest reserve accounts within each construction loan, my annual interest payments exploded more than three-fold to the equivalent of $6.5 million, or $26 million today.

As a result, my construction loan interest reserve accounts were depleted in less than a year, but I had budgeted to allow four years of construction before generating revenue from townhouses, office building condos, and lot sales. I used up all my other cash reserves and did my best to stay afloat, but to no avail. I tried to work with my bankers and real estate lenders, but as they put it, I didn't owe them enough money for them to bail me out. Had I been a high-rise developer with $100 million in delinquent loans with the banks, insurance companies, or pension funds, they would have tried to work with me. Once again, I felt like David facing Goliath, and my slingshot was broken. I was busted, out of money, and found myself flat broke.

I couldn't have foreseen such an economic downturn. Indeed, no one had ever before witnessed 21.50% interest rates. The fact is, no matter how experienced or smart you are, many factors remain beyond your control. Zoning approvals and land-use entitlements can be granted one day and denied the next because of negative public opinion or political pressure. If you have the misfortune to discover an Indigenous burial ground during construction, your project could be put on hold indefinitely. This assumes that you get the project financed in the first place. Then there are cost overruns and unforeseen events. The unpredictable circumstances that affect someone's ability to succeed in the real estate development business—and in life, for that matter—can vary widely.

This was the first time I couldn't fix the problem, delay creditors, or work out some type of repayment plan. I wasn't in debt for a few hundred thousand dollars, as I'd been during the 1973–1974 recession. I owed multimillions, and like many builders and developers around the country, I had little choice but to face the music. When

> **LIFE LESSON #47:**
>
> "DON'T THINK IT CAN'T HAPPEN AGAIN, BECAUSE IT CAN."
>
> —DAVID SEMAS

> **LIFE LESSON #48:**
>
> **"IT'S NOT WHETHER YOU GET KNOCKED DOWN; IT'S WHETHER YOU GET UP."**
>
> **—VINCE LOMBARDI (NFL COACH, 1913-1970)**

the dust settled, I filed for Chapter 7 bankruptcy for $28 million ($112 million in 2022 dollars).

I found myself broke and embarrassed by my failure. To make matters worse, I wasn't an unknown that had moved to California from Chicago; I was a well-known native son. Seven years earlier, on the front page of the business section of the *San Jose Mercury News*, columnist Ben Hawkins had written a full-page article entitled, "Old Hand of 24 Heads New Firm." Later that same year, the *Mercury News*, *San Francisco Chronicle*, and other Bay Area publications ran front-page stories with titles like, "Young Builder Nominated as County Planner," touting me as "the up-and-coming young builder tycoon." Throughout the 1970s, I had received a great deal of favorable publicity associated with zoning approvals and public hearings on twelve separate projects, a few of which were quite controversial.

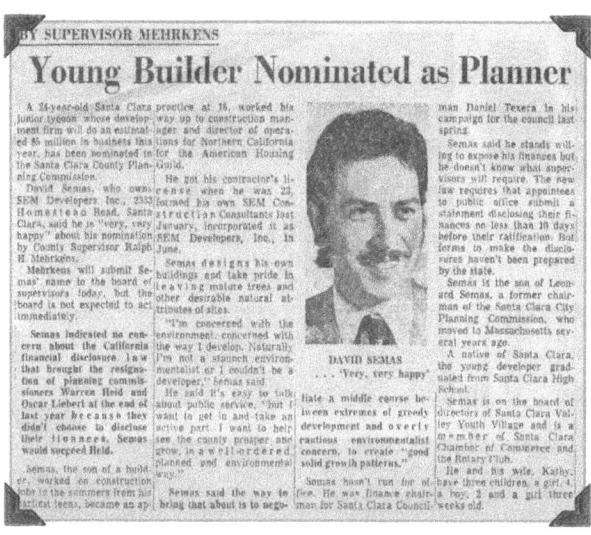

San Jose Mercury News, "Young Builder" article in 1973

MAN IN THE ARENA - NEVER SAY QUIT

After filing for bankruptcy for $28 million, if I'd had enough money in my pocket for taxicab fare, speaking metaphorically, I would have jumped off the Golden Gate Bridge. Instead, I had to settle for a few months of mild depression. I withdrew from everyone, even my family. I spent my time at the local Denny's, sipping coffee or a cocktail and paying no attention to the world around me. I just wanted to melt into the crowd.

> **LIFE LESSON #49:**
>
> "SUCCESS IS WALKING FROM FAILURE TO FAILURE WITH NO LOSS OF ENTHUSIASM."
>
> —SIR WINSTON CHURCHIL

I'd never experienced this kind of failure before. To make matters worse, Kathy and I ended up filing for divorce. I didn't know what I was going to do or how I was going to do it. I didn't blame Paul Volcker, Jimmy Carter, or the economy for my situation. However, I believed then, as I do now, that you create your own destiny by what you do or fail to do. True, no one could have foreseen a 21.50% interest rate, but neither had anyone forced me to borrow millions of dollars on real estate projects. Bottom line: if you're going to take credit for your success, you have to take responsibility for your failure.

Since that time, I've come to believe that setbacks or so-called failures are not failures but rather learning experiences. Like most people, I've spent time wallowing in self-pity on occasion, only to wake up and tell myself, "Stop your whining and complaining. Grow up and deal with it. Many people are far worse off."

Determined to start over again, I made a life-altering decision to relocate to Orange County. I'd been traveling back and forth to SoCal throughout the 1970s, always landing at the Santa Ana Orange

> **LIFE LESSON #50:**
>
> "A BEND IN THE ROAD IS NOT THE END OF THE ROAD—THAT IS UNLESS YOU FAIL TO MAKE THE TURN."
>
> —HELEN KELLER (AMERICAN AUTHOR, POLITICAL ACTIVIST, AND LECTURER, 1880-1968)

County Airport (renamed the John Wayne Airport in 1979). The time had come to search for new career opportunities and to identify an organization that could benefit from my considerable experience in the ups and downs of the construction industry and the real estate development business.

John Wayne Airport logo, Orange County, CA

CHAPTER 7
A NEW BEGINNING

After experiencing strike one and losing a few million dollars during the 1973–1974 recession, strike two after the enormous disappointment of Century Past, and strike three with bankruptcy, I realized that I had learned a great deal about myself and hoped my most difficult times were finally behind me. I was ready to move on. Yet I was still waiting for strike four, because when you experience one failure after another, it's natural to lose some confidence in your abilities.

By the fall of 1980, I had picked myself up by my bootstraps and relocated to Irvine, California. Employment opportunities were scarce, but I felt good about my prospects because I was working with a well-connected executive recruiter. He soon arranged for an interview with a mortgage banking firm called Western Pacific Financial (WesPac), based in Newport Beach. They were looking for a seasoned executive with a solid real estate

> **LIFE LESSON #51:**
>
> "THE BEST THING ABOUT THE FUTURE IS THAT IT COMES ONLY ONE DAY AT A TIME."
>
> —ABRAHAM LINCOLN (SIXTEENTH PRESIDENT OF THE UNITED STATES, 1809–1865)

development and construction background and who had hands-on experience in the residential and commercial building industry—ideally someone with expertise and knowledge of project management, construction lending, finance, and the land-use entitlement process as well. Few people possessed all those attributes, but I knew the WesPac job description was a perfect match for my diverse and extensive background in residential, commercial and land development.

The economy was still in turmoil, with inflation out of control and a sky-high prime lending rate forcing developers to file for bankruptcy throughout all fifty states. As a result, WesPac had some forty projects in distress and being carried on the books as REO (real estate owned) that needed to be either built out, turned around, or liquidated.

After an initial interview with President Roger W. Luby that seemed to go well, I was called in for a second interview. I was acutely aware that not having an MBA or even a four-year college education hurt my prospects, but my secret weapon was Carol Blakeslee, Roger's trusted advisor and longtime administrative assistant. She and I had become fast friends when Roger was running about an hour late for our first meeting.

"David! Come in, come in," Roger said, shaking my hand vigorously as I entered his office. Roger was a larger-than-life character of full-blooded Irish ancestry, six-foot-tall mortgage banking professional with dark curly hair and a firm handshake. Always dressed in beautiful suits, he had the gift of gab and made me feel totally at ease. He was the past president of the Mortgage Bankers Association. "Sit down. I'm glad you agreed to come back in and see me. How've you been?"

After we exchanged pleasantries, he cut to the chase.

"I was wondering if you could provide me with a little more detail about your background—in particular, your general contracting experience in the commercial and residential sectors. I'll also need your California State General Contractors license number. And lastly, I'd like to know more about your bankruptcy, which I must admit I appreciate you disclosing up front."

I gave him a detailed explanation of my business career and the circumstances that had led to my substantial financial loss. He listened quietly to my life story. After describing my quick rise through the ranks, I asked how anyone could have predicted that interest rates would skyrocket from 7% to 21% in less than eighteen months, and Roger nodded in agreement with my rhetorical question. Toward the end of the interview, I could see he was still pondering his decision.

> LIFE LESSON #52:
>
> "IF YOU TELL THE TRUTH, YOU DON'T HAVE TO REMEMBER ANYTHING."
>
> —MARK TWAIN

"It still bothers me a little that you filed for bankruptcy for twenty million dollars," he said, glancing down at some papers on his desk. "We're a public company and under scrutiny of Wall Street analysts and of course our shareholders, not to mention the US Securities and Exchange Commission."

"Actually, Roger, that's not quite true." I paused for effect. "I filed for bankruptcy for twenty-*eight* million dollars."

He looked up at me and grinned. "Good answer."

Within the hour, Roger accepted the fact that I had lost $28 million due to the economic downturn. He appeared relieved that I hadn't filed for bankruptcy over $50,000 of credit card debt.

"So, in other words, you're basically a self-made young man who started as a carpenter and went on to earn and lose twenty-eight million dollars before you were thirty years of age?"

"Yes, sir."

"I guess there are those that would consider that quite an accomplishment, and I must admit that really is remarkable." He nodded thoughtfully. "However, I have several other candidates with advanced degrees, one in particular whose father is a very successful and prominent Southern California real estate developer and a very close friend of my boss, partner,

> LIFE LESSON #53:
>
> "LOYALTY MEANS NOTHING UNLESS IT HAS AT ITS HEART THE ABSOLUTE PRINCIPLE OF SELF-SACRIFICE."
>
> —WOODROW T. WILSON (TWENTY-EIGHTH PRESIDENT OF THE UNITED STATES, 1856–1924)

and chairman of the company, Frank O'Bryan. In 1946, Frank's grandfather, Frank Whitelock, founded what was called then Southern California Mortgage, which became Western Pacific Financial and is now WesPac."

I accepted my inevitable fate and assumed I wasn't going to get the job.

As I prepared to stand up and leave, Roger spoke again. "Unlike the other candidates I've interviewed, you're a seasoned veteran of construction, development, syndication, finance, land use, zoning, sales, and marketing. You have exactly the type of practical experience we need and are the type of pull-yourself-up-by-your-bootstraps person and hands-on manager I want. Oh, what the hell! You're hired." He stuck out his hand once again.

Roger W. Luby, 1981

As we shook hands, I was surprised, if not dumbfounded, that this man would go out on a limb for someone he didn't know. I swore to myself that I would do everything possible to be a loyal employee and a great senior executive for Roger.

Within a few weeks, Roger asked if I would consider hiring a young man by the name of Clay Stuard. He had been among my competitors during Roger's candidate search and was the son of the prominent real estate developer friend of Chairman Frank O'Bryan that Roger had mentioned during my last interview.

"If he's that talented to make a lasting impression on you—and hopefully smarter than me—sure," I said, "I'll hire him!"

A few months later, WesPac was acquired by Shearson Loeb Rhoades, a securities firm whose celebrated CEO was Sanford I. "Sandy" Weill of Wall Street fame. In 1998, Sandy had put the largest financial merger together at the time when Travelers Insurance merged with Citi Corp for $76 billion to become Citigroup. Sandy served as its chairman/CEO until 2003.

Shortly after the Shearson Loeb Rhoades merger, our name was changed to Shearson/WesPac, but within a few more months, we were acquired by American Express. By the end of 1980, our official name was Shearson/

American Express Mortgage (SAEMC) and Shearson/American Express Development Corporation (SAEDC).

We relocated our offices to the top four floors of the 19000 MacArthur Boulevard office building in Irvine, directly across the street from the John Wayne Airport and next door to the Chanteclair Restaurant, owned by my friend Larry Cano, a prominent restaurateur. Larry had founded the El Torito Restaurant in 1954, building it into a nationwide chain with annual sales of nearly $500 million in 1987. *Time* magazine called him one of the "Enchilada Millionaires" during the Mexican dining trend that boomed throughout the 1970s and 1980s. Larry is credited with making "Taco Tuesday" part of everyday lingo. Larry and I became friends during my time in Southern California and remained so until his passing in 2014.

Me at the SAE corporate offices, 1982

I held the position of vice president of SAEMC and executive vice president of SAEDC and was responsible for construction lending and the real estate joint-venture department, managing hundreds of millions of dollars of joint ventures and corporate REO properties. Our joint venture lending department was charged with managing more than forty troubled assets across the country and, when possible, liquidating and recovering as much of our investment capital as possible. With projects in Washington, Oregon, California, Arizona, Colorado, Utah, Texas, Florida, Georgia, South Carolina, and Virginia, we faced quite a challenge. Yet my considerable experience served me well.

After nine months, interest rates began to drop. By the summer of 1983, they were hovering around 10%. Through restructuring partnerships, renegotiating with our short- and long-term lenders, working with bankruptcy courts, selling off projects, and syndicating through our

5,000-strong NASD securities rep network, we were able to dispose of a large portion of the REO portfolio in about twenty-four months.

We had two large subdivision projects outside of Phoenix, Arizona, with Bill Krim, Roger's brother-in-law, who was a great guy and an honest, highly competent developer. The Marguerite Place and Grass Valley shopping centers were syndicated through the Shearson system. I traded fifty improved residential lots in a land development we owned in Myrtle Beach, South Carolina for a $2 million estate in Rancho Santa Fe, which we sold a few months later for $2.3 million.

In another example of liquidating REO assets, I terminated our partnership with a dishonest joint-venture partner on a residential housing project in Boca Raton, Florida. I convinced corporate executives to invest another $2 million in the development and hired a new project management team, sales manager, architect, general contractor, and site engineer. We changed the name of the project, took it off the market for six months, invested another $1 million in landscaping, and sold the project within eighteen months at a tidy profit.

Next, I began to assist P. Russell "Russ" Frerer, Roger's right-hand man, in his efforts to expand the SAEDC syndication department. Soon I was overseeing seventy-two separate real estate developments and properties. Russ, meanwhile, was put in charge of fifteen real estate projects in the Pacific Northwest, part of our acquisition of the securities firm Foster & Marshall of Seattle, Washington. Russ and I would become good buddies and mentors to each other over the ensuing years.

Michael Foster, president of our sister company Foster & Marshall, called one day and asked if I could assist the owners of the Red Lion Hotel chain in refinancing several of their properties. When it acquired the eighty-nine-room Thunderbird Motor Inn near Portland's Memorial Coliseum, Red Lion had fifty-seven hotels with 16,000 rooms located in nine western states. In August of 1983, under my signature as EVP, I issued a loan commitment for $164 million for five Red Lion Hotel properties. The company became the largest privately held hotel chain west of the Mississippi and sold the chain a year later to KKR (Kohlberg Kravis Roberts) for a reported $600 million.

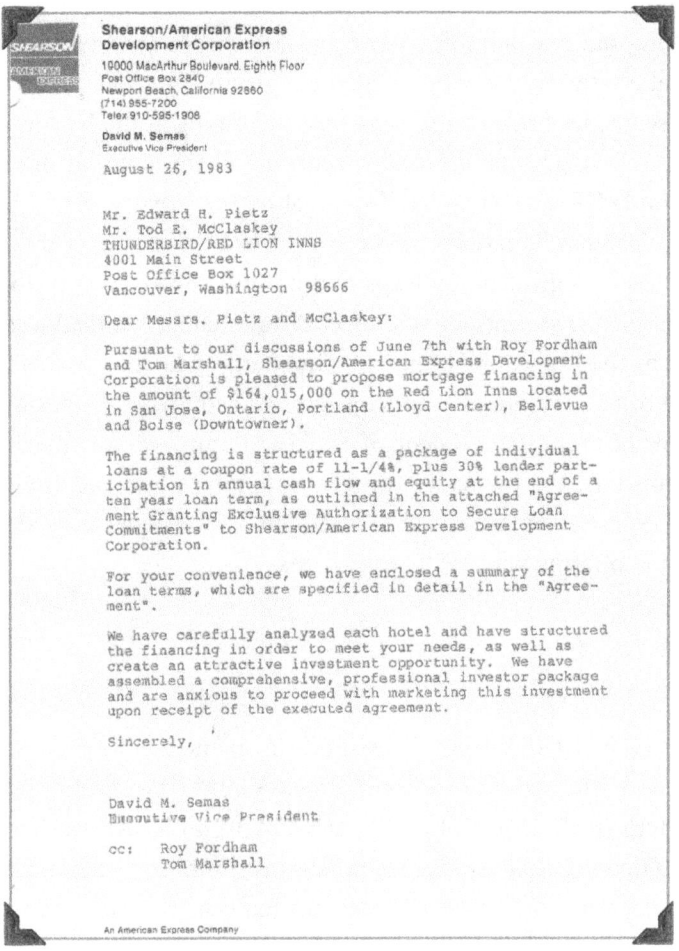

Red Lion Hotels $164 million financing commitment in 1983

At SAEDC by mid-1983, most of the REO assets in my department were either sold or in the process of being liquidated. Russ and his syndication department had acquired several large apartment complexes that were syndicated throughout our NASD securities network. In one case, the equity capital raise for a 250-unit Southern California private placement syndication was set at $9 million. Our SAEDC syndication group was establishing quite a name for itself and a well-deserved reputation as a savvy real estate investment management group. The Shearson/American Express securities brokers and reps were champing at the bit for our next offering. At 9:00 a.m. on a Monday morning in the summer of 1983, the Regulation D ("Reg D") private placement hit the street, and within fifteen minutes, the $9 million offering was over-subscribed.

SAE was also growing by leaps and bounds through acquisitions like that of the NASD securities firm Foster & Marshall of Seattle, Washington, followed by the Robinson Humphrey Company of Atlanta. In 1982, for the tidy sum of $103 million, American Express acquired the nation's largest syndicator of real estate, Balcor of Skokie, Illinois, whose chairman was Jerry Reinsdorf, the owner of the Chicago White Sox and the Chicago Bulls. In 1982, Balcor had raised $1 billion in private equity capital through syndication offering with Wall Street firms.

By early 1984, I had effectively wound down most of our construction lending and REO operations, and Russ's SAEDC syndication unit had merged into the Balcor group. My current role with SAE was coming to an end. Knowing Russ, it was his persuasive prompting that encouraged a senior executive of Shearson/American Express in New York to ask if I would be interested in a position with them as a real estate liaison between the various integrated divisions, like SAEMC, SAEDC, Balcor, American Express, Fireman's Fund, Foster & Marshall, and Robinson Humphrey.

However, having three young children in Northern California, and deep down not being a big-city type of person, I respectfully declined the offer. I had also recently married Paulette Suzanne Cloutier, expanding my family to include her two beautiful daughters: fourteen-year-old Raquel and eleven-year-old Rae Lynn. I didn't want to move them to New York City just as we were beginning a new life together. As it turned out, the marriage was short-lived, and we divorced only a few years later but remained friendly. The bottom line: I was staying in California for the time being.

In terms of my career, it was time to move on. Nonetheless, I had thoroughly enjoyed the work. Thanks to Roger, Frank, and Russ, I had matured as a businessman and learned a considerable amount about the workings of Wall Street while structuring complex transactions, monetizing financial instruments, underwriting loans, and much more. I had further honed my skills as a senior executive, manager, contract negotiator, and financier. Learning became my life's work. Roger would sit on my METALAST® International, Inc. board of directors from 1998 until 2013, and my dear friend Russ passed away in 2005.

But even as a real estate lender and investment banker with the financial giant Shearson/American Express, I had once again found that my earnings and bonus compensation were tied to the success of a single project or transaction. Either through salary, bonuses, commissions earned, or fees paid on the sale of an asset like an office building or apartment complex, my financial future always seemed to depend on one transaction or another, which troubled me.

Having overseen the sale of hundreds of millions of dollars of unwanted REO assets with Shearson/American Express, I decided to form American Realty Advisors (ARA), a real estate property origination, syndication, and investment company, with Larry Vinti, former senior vice president of syndications for Russ and SAEDC.

Just before the Christmas holiday of 1983, I gave SAEDC a sixty-day notice so they would have adequate time to either promote from within or find a suitable replacement. Roxwell "Rocky" Hafdahl, an old friend, called and asked if he could bring an associate by my office for a brief meeting. Rocky introduced me to John Kennington, who laid out a plan to arrange for a partner to provide a $20 million credit line and all the working capital required for ARA,

> LIFE LESSON #54:
>
> "ANYONE WHO STOPS LEARNING IS OLD, WHETHER AT TWENTY OR EIGHTY. ANYONE WHO KEEPS LEARNING STAYS YOUNG. THE GREATEST THING IN LIFE IS TO KEEP YOUR MIND YOUNG."
>
> —HENRY FORD

our new company. John said his friend, Ed McBirney, was CEO of Sunbelt Savings of Texas and wanted to have a sit-down to see if we could come to terms.

Ed and his attractive administrative assistant arrived in his Falcon 20 jet at the private terminal of John Wayne Airport. I picked them up and drove them to The Ritz Restaurant at Fashion Island in Newport Beach for a luncheon meeting. Present were Rocky, John, Ed, and his assistant, Larry Vinti, my future partner at ARA. Larry's primary responsibility as partner would be to arrange all syndication and real estate acquisition-related financing. Everyone sat down and, over a two-hour lunch, discussed a joint venture structure in which Ed and Sunbelt Savings would provide $2 million of equity capital and a $20 million credit line. This would provide cash to acquire each property so we wouldn't be forced to arrange a bridge loan or flip a property before close of escrow.

Although a great offer, the proposal began to unravel when Ed said he wanted 60 percent of ARA, which in and of itself wasn't unreasonable. The Golden Rule: he who has the gold makes the rules. Rocky then spoke up and said he wanted 10 percent ownership for his introduction to John, leaving 30 percent for Larry and me. This meant I would receive 15 percent ownership over a company I had founded and for which I was going to be the primary business development driver and the person who would originate nearly all the future real estate acquisition opportunities. I was the one with the national contacts and relationships with property owners, property managers, asset managers, builders, developers, private equity groups, and pension fund advisors.

Unwisely, I expressed my concern and Ed replied, "Why is Rocky getting ten percent ownership merely for an introduction to John? He's not entitled to equity ownership for a simple introduction. Let's just pay him a reasonable finder's fee."

Rocky stood up and was about to leave the meeting, and

LIFE LESSON #55:

"BUSINESS OPPOR-
TUNITIES ARE LIKE
BUSES: THERE'S
ALWAYS ANOTHER
ONE COMING."

—SIR RICHARD BRANSON
(BRITISH BUSINESS MAGNATE,
VIRGIN GROUP, 1950–PRESENT)

unfortunately, I allowed our friendship to get in the way of making a great deal. However, I didn't blame Rocky for the desire to have equity; I probably would have asked for the same thing if I'd been in his shoes.

Thinking I could get Rocky to agree to an equitable 5 percent ownership position, with Larry and I each receiving 22 percent, I asked Ed if he would consider a 51 percent ownership position in ARA, but he withdrew his offer, and the meeting ended abruptly.

A month later, feeling a little guilty about the McBirney fiasco, Rocky brought two investors to the table: Reggie Del Ponte and Bill Wall. But they could only invest $500,000, which, while a sizable amount of money, wasn't nearly enough to fund the capital requirements of the business. I was somewhat concerned but had hoped maybe we could arrange some credit line financing from one of my other sources. As it turned out, both Reggie and Bill were great partners and good guys.

After only one year of operation, despite being under-capitalized in 1985, ARA boasted gross sales of $16 million generated from the sale of institutional-grade real estate projects like apartments and commercial and industrial buildings. Under the business model, ARA would acquire real estate for a set price, conduct due diligence, underwrite the investment, and arrange to either syndicate (raise capital through private investors) or sell the project to other syndication firms, pension funds, or high-net-worth investors. ARA put under contract the property at one price and sold its position at a higher price, in most cases making a 4 to 10 percent fee on the sale price of the real estate.

The very next year, ARA made an offer of $12.5 million to CNA Financial of Chicago to purchase Kimberly Place Apartments, a mature, beautifully landscaped 203-unit complex located in Monterey. Five other bidders made offers ranging from $10,250,000 to $11,750,000, so my competitors were all of the opinion that, at $61,500 per unit, ARA was overpaying for the property. (As point of reference, today

> **LIFE LESSON #56:**
>
> "YOU CAN BID ALL YOU WANT, BUT IF YOU DON'T CONTROL THE ASSET, YOU'LL NEVER MAKE A DEAL."
>
> —DAVID SEMAS

in 2022, California apartments can easily range between $300,000 to as high as $420,000 per unit or up to seven times the amount in 1985.)

A $500,000 deposit was required with only a thirty-day due diligence period and a ninety-day close of escrow. I scrambled but came up with the deposit and then worried how I would come up with the $12 million. Within a few days, Duncan Matteson, a Northern California investor and major apartment owner, called and offered to buy our position directly out of escrow. We made a deal and sold the complex for a $1 million profit.

Don Zellner, a good friend of mine, a Southern California home and apartment developer, and president of Zellner Communities, called a month later and asked if ARA would be interested in buying an apartment complex, he was about to break ground on. Don asked if I would be willing to issue a forward equity commitment for $6,750,000, or $53,500 per unit, to purchase his yet-to-to-be built 146-unit garden apartment complex located in Buena Park. He needed a takeout commitment from a bona fide buyer for Sanwa Bank, his construction lender, to go forward with the project.

I sent out the ARA due diligence team, which was led by Jeff Mackinen, my senior underwriter and analyst. Jeff liked the price and the complex itself but wasn't keen on the location—rightfully so, because it sat right in the flight path of Fullerton Airport, a small private airport. His concerns were well founded, and normally I would have declined to buy the complex. But with apartment occupancy rates in the Buena Park area at 98 percent, I wasn't going to be dissuaded by a private small-craft airport. I decided to issue the forward equity commitment, but even before I could put up the required $500,000 deposit, Phil McNamee and Mark Dorian of Village Investment, two other friends and business associates from my SAE days, put up the

> LIFE LESSON #57:
>
> "BE SMART AND NEGOTIATE FROM STRENGTH, BUT DON'T GET GREEDY, AND ALWAYS LEAVE ROOM ON THE TABLE FOR THE OTHER GUY TO MAKE A PROFIT."
>
> —BEN SWIG (FOUNDER OF THE FAIRMONT HOTEL CHAIN, REAL ESTATE DEVELOPER, AND PHILANTHROPIST, 1893–1980)

$500,000 deposit. They paid ARA a profit of $1 million to flip our position to them.

Before the Zellner Village Manor apartment complex was completed, Village Investments sold their position for a $1 million profit, and their buyer syndicated the apartment complex for another $2.5 million profit. Needless to say, had we been able to fund the entire purchase of the apartment complex and syndicate the project ourselves, we would have made more than four times the profit.

After returning from a trip to Northern California to attend my daughter Wendi's father-daughter dance at Archbishop Mitty High School in San Jose in the spring of 1985, I found myself researching the oil industry. Crude oil prices, which had been in the thirty-five-dollars-per-barrel range in 1980, had plummeted to less than twelve dollars per barrel by 1986. I had a few friends in the oil business who felt confident that eventually we would see an upsurge in crude oil prices. One of those friends recommended that I contact Bruno Hanson, a savvy Texas oilman. Bruno ran Hanson Oil Company in Midland, Texas and was looking for $100 million in backing to acquire stripper wells from the big oil companies in West Texas.

Father-daughter dance with Wendi, 1985

Bruno and his son, Eric, flew to California to meet with my staff and me to discuss the opportunity. They arrived bright and early on a Monday morning at the ARA corporate offices in Costa Mesa. Bruno had been a geologist for Humble Oil Company (now Exxon-Mobile) in the 1950s and later served as president of the West Texas Geological Society and president of the Permian Basin Petroleum Society. He became president of Hanson Oil in 1960 and was a well-respected Midland-based oilman, wildcat driller, and cattle rancher. Bruno was in his fifties, a kind soul, and a big man who wore tinted, wire-rimmed glasses. Many that knew him well called him a "tough old buzzard" because of his sheer tenacity and zest for life.

In the ARA conference room, Bruno and Eric explained their objectives to me and several members of my due diligence team, including Jeff Mackinen and Merrill Butler III, whose father, Merrill Butler II, had been a joint venture partner of mine during my days with Shearson/American Express. Also in attendance were Larry Vinti and Rob Henderson, our analyst and number cruncher. Bruno had several agreements in place with large oil and gas companies, including Exxon, Texaco, and Arco, to buy producing stripper well production at twelve dollars per barrel in established oil fields with verified reserves.

"Bruno, before we go much further," I said, "I would really like to have you and Eric educate my team and myself on all aspects of the oil and gas business, from soup to nuts. Would that be okay?"

"Sure, David," Bruno replied with his Texas drawl. "Where would you like for me to start?"

"Why . . . at the beginning."

Bruno chuckled. After looking over at his son, who appeared to be in his late twenties, he said, "Hell, that would be the dinosaurs."

"Great," I replied. "Let's start there."

He gave a deep, guttural laugh, and the others at the conference table joined him. Then he studied me more closely. "You aren't kidding, are you?"

I smiled. "Actually, no, I'm not."

Bruno obliged, launching into a discussion of dinosaurs, jungles, organic matter, and the oil exploration theories of petroleum geologists. He went on to explain that quite a few geologic elements, including sedimentary rock, sand, and matter of organic origin, are required for oil and gas to accumulate in sufficient quantities to create a pool large enough to be worth drilling. These elements include an organic-rich source rock to generate the oil or gas, a porous reservoir rock to store the petroleum, and some sort of a trap to prevent the oil and gas from leaking away. Traps generally exist in predictable places, such as at next to seismic faults or in sandstone beds.

Over the next several days, it was 90 percent listening and 10 percent questions. My team and I learned a lot about the prehistoric origins of crude oil and the ins and outs of the oil business. If you really want to understand a subject, surround yourself with the most knowledgeable people you can, and most importantly, focus, take notes, and *listen!*

Unfortunately, my financial partners didn't share my enthusiasm for the oil business. I couldn't convince them to invest, even with a twenty-four-month payback at an eleven-dollars-per-barrel assumption. A few years later, as anticipated, oil prices exploded when crude more than doubled to twenty-three dollars per barrel. This would have been a twelve-month payback, not a twenty-four-month one, producing an IRR (internal rate of return) of 64 percent or more. Crude oil shattered the ceiling in July 2008, when it reached $145 per barrel. Bruno passed away in 2000, and sadly his son, Eric, died less than a decade later in 2009.

By 1986, it looked as though all the stars were aligning for ARA. Bobby Roberts, my show-business friend and associate that I had previously assisted in resolving a $500,000 loan dispute with a prominent Southern California bank, invested heavily in ARA and came on board as its chairman. Over the prior twelve-month period, we had successfully put nearly $300 million of prime real-estate projects under contract to purchase and another $100 million in finance underwriting, and we were well-positioned to turn a profit of about $50 million.

Then the House and Senate passed—and President Reagan signed into law—more devastating legislation: the Tax Reform Act of 1986. This legislation was meant to simplify the tax code, but in reality, it eliminated nearly all real estate tax shelters. As a result, the tax-shelter syndication business, which had generated tens of billions of dollars annually for real estate, solar energy, and wind-farm investment from 1980 to 1986, came to a screeching halt. Our business, poised for its

> LIFE LESSON #58:
>
> "YOU WERE BORN WITH TWO EARS AND ONE MOUTH FOR A REASON."
>
> —THE COLONEL

biggest payday ever, was preparing to sell and provide financing for $300 million worth of tax-shelter real estate investments, but the new legislation abruptly shut down our company and hundreds of others like ours around the country.

I wasn't forced to file for bankruptcy, but I knew we had to downsize ARA and let our staff go. This meant I had to simplify my operation into a one-man real estate consulting and advisory business. It took a few years, but I paid off ARA's outstanding debt and moved on. I kept the ARA name and formed another company called Institutional Capital Marketing, Inc. (ICM) as my own private real estate advisory and project consulting businesses.

No matter how many times I got knocked down, I remained determined to get back up. As a result, I had internalized a fundamental lesson: success takes hard work, talent, a commitment to excellence, and just plain tenacity. As Calvin Coolidge, the thirtieth President of the United States, is reported to have said, "Nothing in the world can take the place of persistence. Talent will not; nothing is more common than unsuccessful men with talent. Genius will not; unrewarded genius is almost a proverb. Education will not; the world is full of educated derelicts. Persistence and determination alone are omnipotent."

As I looked for other real-estate-related business opportunities, my telephone rang with calls from old friends wanting my expertise, seasoned experience, and private equity contacts. The collapse of the tax-shelter syndication business brought me back to the hotel and hospitality business and real estate consulting and advisory services. Over the next five years, I acted as a project originator and analyst on a fee basis and sometimes a principal on various real estate projects, including several hotels.

I approached my friend Bob Bicek and his attorney, Bob Keck with the idea of acquiring undervalued hotel resort properties. I had helped Bob, a Chicago developer, with the $168 million financing of his One Financial Place, a forty-two-story high-rise at the base of LaSalle above the Chicago

Train Station. Bobby Roberts, my ARA partner, and I formed a partnership with Bob called First Wellington Group, and he capitalized the company with $15 million in cash for the purpose of acquiring several hotels.

In January 1986, prior to the tax-reform legislation becoming law, Bobby called and told me we had been invited by Wayne Newton, an old show-business friend of his, to have dinner with him the following week. Bobby and Wayne had known each other since Bobby's discovery of Ann-Margret Olsson, whom he introduced to his good friend, George Burns, when Wayne was just beginning his career. Wayne told Bobby he'd be staying at casino magnate Bill Harrah's Lake Tahoe guesthouse while headlining nightly performances at the 750-seat South Shore Room at the beautiful Harrah's Lake Tahoe Hotel & Casino. Wayne told him he wanted to meet me to discuss the possible syndication of twenty-five of his beautiful Arabian horses.

Me with ARA business partner Bobby Roberts, 1985

While this wasn't something I was really interested in, I knew Bobby's wife, Lynne, and my wife at the time, Paulette, were excited about going to Lake Tahoe and meeting Wayne Newton.

"Oh, by the way," Bobby added, "Wayne would also like to introduce us to Paul Lowden, the owner of the Hacienda Hotel and Casino at the west end of the Las Vegas Strip. He also owns the Sahara Hotel and Casino at the opposite end. Paul wants to sell the Hacienda."

Now this was something that piqued my interest. "Great. When do we leave?"

Bobby said on Friday we were to meet at the private jet terminal at

LIFE LESSON #59:

"EVERYONE FALLS DOWN. GETTING BACK UP IS HOW YOU LEARN TO WALK."

—WALT DISNEY

LAX at 10:00 a.m. Wayne's Lockheed L-133 JetStar would be standing by, fueled and ready for its return trip to Tahoe.

That Friday we all met and boarded Wayne's private aircraft, with wheels up promptly at ten-thirty on a cool and slightly overcast morning. The airplane took off over the Pacific Ocean, heading due west, and made a gradual turn to the right, heading north along the California coastline until just south of Santa Barbara. The pilot altered his heading in a northeasterly direction, putting us directly over the horse country of San Ynez Valley, where Fess Parker and I had met on several occasions to discuss the Santa Clara Marriott's Great America Theme Park project a decade earlier. The flight went as smooth as silk over the majestic snowcapped Sierra Nevada, and soon we were nearing the approach at the north end of Lake Tahoe, west of Incline Village. The pilot continued his descent at one thousand feet per minute and touched down under beautiful clear blue skies on time at exactly noon.

Mona, Wayne Newton's longtime Filipino administrative assistant, had arranged to have the Harrah's limousine pick us up at the airport. After disembarking from the private jet at the Lake Tahoe Regional Airport, we walked across the expansive black tarmac and saw a large, muscular Samoan gentleman approaching us with his hand extended. He was dressed in a Hawaiian shirt and slacks.

"Good afternoon," he said with a warm smile. "My name is Bear, and on behalf of Mr. Newton, welcome to Lake Tahoe."

We were driven to Harrah's Lake Tahoe Hotel & Casino, where we checked into our luxurious individual tower suites on the sixteenth floor. The limo driver would meet us downstairs outside the main lobby at five-thirty that evening to take us to meet Wayne Newton at Bill Harrah's guesthouse. There we would enjoy cocktails, followed by dinner, and then return to Harrah's Hotel & Casino as guests of Mr. Newton for his nine-thirty performance.

After we arrived at Harrah's multimillion-dollar lakeside guesthouse, Wayne Newton himself opened the front door. He welcomed us with open arms and gave Bobby a warm smile, followed by a big bear hug. "Bobby, my old friend, it's been too long since we've seen each other and reminisced about days gone by."

During the conversation over cocktails, I learned that Bobby and Wayne had first met when Wayne was invited to attend one of Ann-Margret's shows in Las Vegas at the Dunes Hotel & Casino. I was surprised to learn that Paul Lowden, the Hacienda and Sahara casino owner had been Ann-Margret's music conductor and arranger in Las Vegas. Bobby had served as her business manager until Roger Smith, her husband, took control of her career in 1967.

Bobby and Wayne reminisced about the good ol' days over dinner, and they laughed about the time Bobby repeatedly tried to get Wayne to record a song to which Bobby owned the music and publishing rights.

Before disclosing the name of the song, Wayne recalled, "I told Bobby that there was no way I would ever record that song, because it was too much of a bad cliché. It would appear to my fans as egotistical and boastful."

Wayne believed the Hal David and Albert Hammond song had a nice melody and good rhythm, but the lyrics were too bold and brash, and he thought the song was destined to be consigned to the dark and dusty archives of rejected sheet music. He thought it was doubtful the song, if ever recorded, would even make the bottom of the Billboard Hot 100 Chart.

"Never was I so mistaken," Wayne admitted. "Every time I hear that song, which is quite often, this story is the first thing that comes to mind." He turned to me. "If you're wondering, the song was 'To All the Girls I've Loved Before.'"

After Julio Iglesias and Willie Nelson recorded it in 1984, it reached number five on the Billboard Hot 100 Chart. The song became Julio Iglesias's biggest hit in the United States and Canada, and in 1984, the Country Music Association named Willie and Julio Duo of the Year. It was the best single of the year by the Academy of Country Music.

"This was undoubtedly a one-in-a-million career maker," Wayne told everyone at the table. "Well, so much for my crystal ball."

Toward the end of the evening, Wayne talked about his passion for Arabian horses and asked if I would be interested in syndicating them. I told Wayne I didn't have any experience in syndicating horses but had a friend in the business to whom I would introduce him. In appreciation, he changed the topic to his very close friend, Paul Lowden, the chairman, owner, and operator of the nine-hundred-room Hacienda Hotel & Casino in Las Vegas. Paul was hoping to sell the property. Wayne explained that he and Paul had been friends for a good number of years and said he had never performed at the Hacienda but had performed at the Sahara at least twenty weeks since 1983, after Paul had bought the hotel from Del Webb.

"Yes," Bobby said, "I remember when Paul was Ann-Margret's music conductor. He's the owner of two Las Vegas casinos on the Strip? Wow, he's really stepped up in the world."

The possibility of buying a hotel casino on the Strip intrigued me. I asked Wayne if he knew the price and terms of the deal, and he said he didn't but would call Paul Lowden the next day and make the introduction.

I received a telephone call on the following Monday morning from Paul Lowden, who invited me to Las Vegas to tour the Hacienda as his guest. A few days later, I flew to Vegas and met Paul for lunch and later for dinner with his accomplished wife, Sue, who many years later became a Nevada state senator and chairman of the Nevada Republican Party.

After lunch, I was treated to a VIP tour of the nine-hundred-room property, the facilities, landscaped grounds, and mobile-home park. While the casino was strictly a cash-and-carry joint with modest mom-and-pop table play, it was a well-run slot machine gaming operation that sat on a fifty-acre parcel with tremendous potential. The offering price was $65 million. The thirty-year mortgage was for $55 million, featured a fixed 9.75% interest rate, and still had a full twenty-six years remaining on it. The Hacienda produced a handsome 13 percent positive cash flow on a $10 million investment based on ten-year Arthur Andersen-audited financial statements. This was an excellent opportunity to move into the gaming business.

While Bobby and I wanted to buy the Hacienda, Bob Bicek, our Chicago financial partner and the check writer, wasn't so enthusiastic about owning a lower-end gambling casino, particularly one that lacked curb appeal. Bob was a Caesar's Palace kind of guy. My idea was to turn the property into the Yellow Rose of Texas, with live bull-riding, saloon gals, covered wagons, and an authentic 1880s cowboy flair, but it simply wasn't meant to be. I did my very best to convince Bob, but based on advice from his attorney, he was focused on acquiring the Canyon Hotel and Golf Resort in Palm Springs, which I had put under contract a month earlier.

I was overruled in the end, so I informed Paul Lowden we had to take a pass. The Hacienda property was eventually sold to CEO Bill Bennett of Circus Circus Enterprises in 1995 for $80 million and then demolished. Its formal demise and demolition occurred when it was imploded on national television during the Fox Network's New Year's Eve 1996 telecast. Built at a cost of $950 million, the Hacienda property is now the forty-three-story, 3,300-room Mandalay Bay Resort & Casino, which boasts a 135,000-square-foot gaming area.

Canyon Hotel and Golf Resort aerial in Palm Springs, 1986

First Wellington Group's first acquisition was a $22 million purchase of the famous five-hundred-room Canyon Hotel Golf Resort in Palm Springs, California, which we bought from Sid Bass of Bass Brothers fame. I personally negotiated the deal over a four-hour conference call with Bob Kolba, Sid's representative. The second acquisition was the small Las Casitas Resort property located on Catalina Island at Avalon Harbor adjacent to the golf course we had bought from Jay Feinberg of Long Beach. We entered a purchase contract on the Balboa Inn in Newport Beach but opted out of the deal because we were unable to get political support from the California Coastal Commission.

Canyon Hotel main entrance, 1986

Canyon Hotel lobby, 1986

Canyon Hotel Tournament Tennis Center, 1986

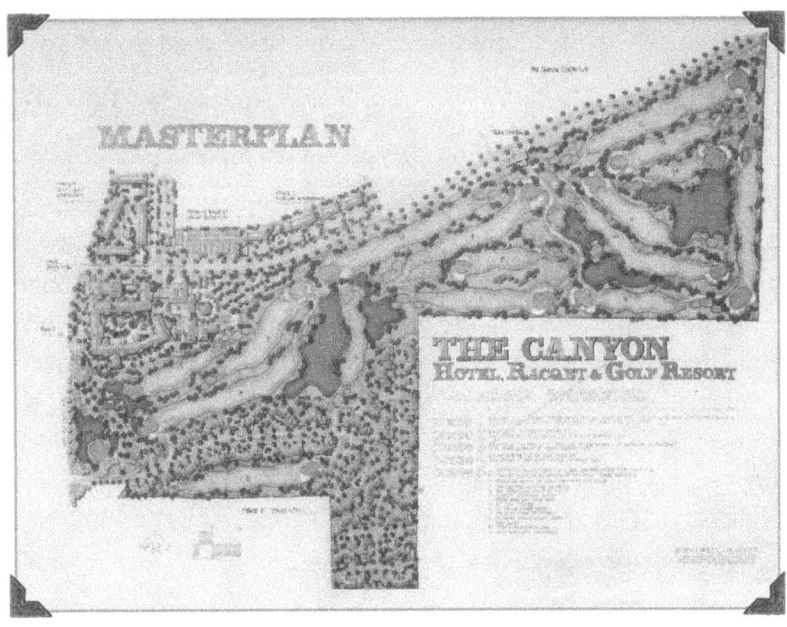

Canyon Hotel masterplan, 1988

At that time, the Canyon Hotel was being used as a boxing training camp for Top Rank Sports. Middleweight Rockin' Robbie Simms and Roberto Duran trained with us. World Middleweight Champion Marvelous Marvin Hagler, Robbie Simms's half-brother, trained with us for his fight against Tommy Hearns. He also trained at the Canyon Hotel for six weeks for his biggest payday fight ever—estimated at $35 million—against Sugar Ray Leonard in April 1987. The bout ended in a controversial split decision. During that training period, on any given day, fight fans like Sylvester Stallone, Chuck Norris, and Bo Derek arrived at the Canyon to watch Marvin's daily workout and sparring session. One of Marvin's favorite boxers was Rocky Marciano, a close family friend of my uncle, Johnny Silvia. Both had grown up in Brockton, Massachusetts. Marvin became a good friend during that time.

Sadly, my old friend, boxing legend and undisputed middleweight champion of the world from 1980 until 1987, Marvelous Marvin Hagler, passed away in March of 2021.

Meanwhile, I teamed with Bob Bicek, my dear friend Bobby Roberts, and record executive Marshall Blonstein to found Dunhill Compact Classics, one of the recording industry's first independent compact disc labels. Marshall was the brains behind the operation and the one who ran the business and made it a success.

Bobby became chairman of Dunhill Compact Classics, which was later renamed DCC Compact Classics. He was a show-business icon and had been a member of Dunhill Productions, a legendary tap-dancing group from the 1950s. The famous tap-dancing trio opened for Danny Kaye around the world and were frequent guest performers on *The Ed Sullivan Show*. In the early 1960s, Bobby, Al Bennett, and Pierre Cossette formed Dunhill Records with famous record producer Lou Adler, the recording genius behind the Mamas & the Papas, Johnny Rivers, Carole King, and others. DCC Compact Classics went on to acquire recording rights to Ray Charles, Jim Croce, Sam Cooke, Judy Garland, Lionel Hampton, and others. DCC also released audiophile editions of best-selling record albums by Elvis Presley, Frank Sinatra, the Doors, the Eagles, and the Grateful Dead.

While Bobby was known by many in the entertainment industry as a savvy business manager, record and movie producer, and dealmaker with the Midas touch, those that knew him best, including George Burns and Milton Berle, thought he was one of the greatest tap dancers that ever lived.

Once a month, usually on a Wednesday night, Bobby and I would have dinner at Matteo's Restaurant on Westwood Boulevard in Los Angeles. Even though Bobby was a respected entertainment executive, his show business buddies would egg him on to stand up and perform a little soft-shoe routine right in the middle of the restaurant, and he always acquiesced.

Bobby passed away in 2004, and Lynn, his sweet and beautiful wife, joined the love of her life in 2018. I figure Bobby's in heaven signing God's chosen angels to lucrative business representation agreements. When he's not doing business, he's tap dancing and entertaining all with his soft-shoe routine on the tips of the clouds at the request of admiring celestial bodies.

Father-daughter dance with Aimee, 1988

After returning from a weekend in San Jose to attend my youngest daughter Aimee's high-school father-daughter dance in the spring of 1988, I received a telephone call from Stan Castleton, previously introduced to me by Rocky Hafdahl. I was dumfounded to learn from Stan that he and John Kennington had arranged to acquire out of bankruptcy a large portfolio of properties from C-D Investment Company, a Los Angeles construction and development firm led by principals Alexander "Al" Coler and Naftali Deutsch. The assets had been acquired at a deep discount for a price of $800 million. The properties included the Los Angeles Hilton and Anaheim Hilton Hotels; the

LIFE LESSON #60:

"RATHER FAIL WITH HONOR THAN SUCCEED BY FRAUD."

—SOPHOCLES (GREEK PLAYWRIGHT, 497-406 BC)

twenty-nine-story, one-million-square-foot Beaudry Center office building; the Pacific Stock Exchange Building; and the fifteen-story, 156-unit partially completed Park Wilshire high-rise residential condominium complex located on Wilshire Boulevard in Westwood.

Stan told me that John and Ed had turned over day-to-day operations of the entire portfolio of projects to him, and he had formed his own company called Stanwill Properties. The real shocker came when Stan told me that Ed McBirney's Sunbelt Savings, one of the biggest financial disasters in the savings and loan industry, had required a $6 billion bailout by the Federal Savings and Loan Insurance Corporation (FSLIC).

As it turned out, criminal charges for bank fraud were filed against Ed McBirney, and as a result, FSLIC was going to allow Stan and his company to take charge of all assets and agreed to fund the necessary capital to make the projects profitable in an effort to return as much of the original investments as possible back to the Sunbelt Savings depositors and shareholders. Stan was now in the catbird seat and asked if I would be interested in consulting with him in overseeing some of the assets, to which I agreed. For the next two years, I worked with Stan and helped manage some of the assets, along with selling a few office buildings and working on some new ventures for him.

My career path was constantly evolving. I took one fork in the road after another, moving down new pathways in search of my life's work. The hospitality and music industries were interesting and a fresh change of pace, and the knowledge I gained, especially about merchandizing and marketing, was tremendous. But deep down, I knew this wasn't the direction I wanted to go.

By 1988, I had sold my positions in the two hotels and the compact disc company and had begun looking for something I could sink my teeth into. I wanted to keep my real estate consulting business but eventually wanted to build an operating business that would generate ongoing cash flow.

In the summer of 1988 my dear friend Aissa Wayne (John Wayne's daughter) called and asked if I would escort her to the John Wayne Cancer Institute annual charity event held in Beverly Hills. Aissa and her mom Pilar had been good friends ever since 1980 after being introduced to them by my boss Roger Luby. Roger and Aissa dated for a while, and later when he married Pam, they continued to be close friends. The black-tie affair was a smashing success raising over $1 million for the fundraising gala benefitting cancer research.

It was during this time, and being a bachelor once again, that I hit the hot dining spots around Newport Beach with my good friends Jeff Mackinen, Jim McWalters, Russ Frerer, and Vic Boyd. Our two or three times a week quasi-business lunch gatherings were held at Muldoon's Irish Pub, Dove Street, Bob Burn's, La Cave, El Torito, 94th Aero Squadron, The Quiet Woman, or Benningan's located at the South Coast Plaza Shopping Mall.

Friday was always a special late-lunch day at Hans Prager's, The Ritz restaurant in Fashion Island, Newport Beach. Dressed-to-impress twenty- and thirty-something female talent throughout Orange County arrived in twos, threes, and fours. All afternoon future trophy wives put on what can best be described as a fashion show while they flaunted their voluptuous feminine attributes looking for a seventy-year-old rich guy with a bad heart.

The Ritz Restaurant, Newport Beach, 1988

For early evening dining, we'd venture over to 21 Oceanfront, Oyster's, Cano's, Tutto Mare, or Chanteclair. The Arches on the Pacific Coast

Highway (PCH) down the road from the Balboa Bay Club was always a great spot and John Wayne's favorite dinner hangout in his day. By eight o'clock we were off to the nightclub on the top floor of the Marriott Hotel across from "The Ritz." If the action at the Marriott was slow, we'd head over to Rex Chandler's The Rex Restaurant and Nightclub (now the Cheesecake Factory) or maybe the Devil's Triangle and Blackbeard's. Many times we'd go to Bistango in Irvine on Von Karman Avenue located at ground level of the Atrium office building, or another favorite was the Red Lion Hotel on Bristol Street in Costa Mesa (now the Hilton).

Playing the piano and singing classic 1960s and 1970s hits on the weekends was good friend Donnie Singer. During the week, jazz piano playing vocalist Caesar provided the perfect musical venue for our late-night cocktails at Trees of Corona del Mar. This was nearly always followed by a final-final at midnight until two o'clock in the morning at Villa Nova located on the PCH at the end of the Newport Entrance Channel. Most would have called it a night, but not our wooden-leg wanderers as we scarfed down breakfast at twenty-four-hour Norm's Coffee Shop on Harbor Boulevard, which remains open to this day.

On Tuesday, lady's night, and Thursday, talent night, Vic Boyd and I could be found at the Crazy Horse Saloon in Santa Ana. To this day, Vic is fond of reminiscing about how I was always in cowboy attire, and he, as a successful Orange County real estate developer, was usually dressed to the nines in a three-piece suit and tie. Ladies would comment on my cowboy boots, hat, or Scully hand-laced fringe and leather-trimmed beaded jacket. They would ask if I was a real cowboy, assuming Vic was just some local businessman dude. My response always caught them off-guard. I would say, "I sit a pretty good saddle, but Vic is the real cowboy and champion team roper." Vic loved to see the look on the face of the Orange County fashionable cowgirls, and I believe it was the reason he always wore a suit.

While pondering my next move, I received a telephone call from Mom saying that she and Dad wanted to drive down and spend a week visiting in

Southern California. During their trip, we went out to dinner almost every night and had a terrific time. I nearly forgot about my upcoming musical debut later in the week. I had won several singing contests at the Crazy Horse Saloon over the previous year and the finalists, including myself were to preform that Thursday night.

Mom and Dad were excited about going, so I invited several people to attend: Jeff Mackinen, Russ Frerer, Jim McWalters, Roger and Pam Luby, my daughter Wendi, and family friend Delaine Quintal. I would be competing against seven talented singers in the final performance. The Crazy Horse Saloon, a cozy 250-seat showroom, had been voted the number-one country-western nightclub in America ten years in a row and was Orange County's top country music venue. It hosted virtually every big name in the genre, including Merle Haggard, Johnny Cash, Buck Owens, Conway Twitty, Ray Charles, Jerry Lee Lewis, Charlie Daniels, Willie Nelson, Clint Black, Billy Ray Cyrus, and Tammy Wynette. Before Garth Brooks hit it big, he serenaded dinner crowds in front of Crazy Horse's neon bucking-bronco logo outdoor sign right off the 55 Freeway.

A few years prior, the Crazy Horse started a weekly singing contest in which any patron brave enough could come on stage with sheet music in hand and become the lead singer of a live country-western band, which usually consisted of seven musicians: drummer, lead guitar, bass guitar, steel guitar, fiddle, piano or keyboard, and sometimes banjo. Typically, about ten to twelve contestants would perform. One was selected as the week's winner, and later, a winner was chosen for the month. The first- and second-place quarterly winners would compete at the finals, with the grand finalist earning a recording contract. I won the first night, the next month, and the next quarter and found myself

---

LIFE LESSON #61:

"MANY PEOPLE DIE WITH THEIR MUSIC STILL IN THEM. WHY IS THIS SO? TOO OFTEN IT IS BECAUSE THEY ARE ALWAYS GETTING READY TO LIVE. BEFORE THEY KNOW IT, TIME RUNS OUT."

—OLIVER WENDELL HOLMES (US SUPREME COURT JUSTICE, 1841–1935)

in the finals. I hoped a young, up-and-coming talent deserving a break in the music business would win. Fortunately, I came in second place. Thank God!

Once I finished my consulting assignment with Stanwill, I teamed up with my good friend Don Saunders. After years of tedious legal work and getting approvals from various governmental agencies in Florida, Don introduced the very first timeshare in the country. Since the early 1970s he has been known as the grandfather of resort timesharing. He is credited with introducing the timesharing concept to what became the vacation club industry around the world. Don and I worked together for several years on a wide variety of real estate projects, including a large land and residential lakeside development in east Texas, a golf resort in Southern California, an office building in downtown Los Angeles, and a restaurant in Orange County.

I helped him underwrite an acquisition of an insurance company and several apartment projects and provided him with insight into various creative and complex credit-enhanced financing methods. Don even had me spend several months conducting extensive due diligence on a purchase of a Falcon 20 jet aircraft. My dear friend Don passed away in 2007. I still remain in contact with Bonnie, his adoring and beautiful widow, and their children.

LIFE LESSON #62:

"YOU CAN'T MAKE OLD FRIENDS. YOU EITHER HAVE THEM OR YOU DON'T."

—KENNY ROGERS (AMERICAN SINGER, SONGWRITER, AND ENTERTAINER, 1938-2020)

CHAPTER 8
BANANAS AND BOONDOGGLES

At the age of forty-one, I was in the prime of my life and business career. Yet I still felt that I had little control over my destiny. Over the years, it had often been feast or famine. Though I was proud of my accomplishments, I had little to show for my efforts, other than some hands-on business experience, new friends, a considerable number of battle scars, and a few fleeting memories. Looking ahead, not knowing what my future might hold, I thought, *What should I do now?*

Just prior to a scheduled business trip to Tokyo, I jumped on an American Airlines flight bound for San Jose to celebrate my parents' fiftieth wedding anniversary and met up with all my siblings at our sister Judy's home in Willow Glen, a quaint district of San Jose.

The Leonard and Mary Semas family, at Judy's house in 1992
L-R Judy, Mary, me, Leonard, Len, Marie, and Elizabeth in front row

After returning from my San Jose trip on a foggy and misty Saturday morning in August of 1992, I boarded an American Airlines flight bound for Tokyo. Traveling with me was James G. "Jim" McWalters, my friend and the managing director of PMRealty Advisors (PMRA), a wholly owned subsidiary of Pacific Mutual Life (now Pacific Life). I had just formed a joint venture partnership with PMRA to market their real estate financial advisory services to Japanese financial institutions.

After stowing our bags in the overhead bin, we settled down in our business-class seats and prepared ourselves for the eleven-hour flight while the remaining passengers filed past our seats to the back of the jumbo jet. This was Jim's first business trip to Japan, but for me, international flights to Japan, Hong Kong, and Taiwan had become just another part of my routine in the last several years. I had made more than twenty trips to the Far East.

In 1989, certain that the financial bubble was about to burst in Tokyo, I had contacted PMRA to discuss working together on Japanese-owned American real estate assets and properties. Over the years, the Japanese had overpaid for a lot of American real estate holdings. To make matters worse, Japanese interest rates had exploded. The Bank of Japan's discount rate had tripled, going from 2.25% to 6.5% annually. Considering most Japanese investors borrowed money from their banks, they were about to have their American real estate assets foreclosed on by their Japanese bankers. The Japanese financial institutions would need qualified US asset managers to help in the properties' disposition. With more than $4 billion of institutional-grade real estate already under management, PMRA was looking to grow the business and was interested in my Japanese and Asian contacts and my knowledge of real estate construction, development, REO management, and finance. Jim and I had become fast friends and soon formed a partnership between PMRA and my Institutional Capital Marketing, Inc. (ICM), which I incorporated for this purpose.

My other company ARA, meanwhile, continued to provide real estate advisory and acquisition underwriting services for other clients, like McDonnell Douglas Realty, Stanwill Properties, private equity investor Don Saunders, Fairmont Hotels, and First Wellington Group. I was pleased with the lucrative 75 percent PMRA and 25 percent ICM profit split agreement.

The ICM partnership brought me business opportunities in the Asian market while also aligning me with Pacific Life, a 150-year-old company and the parent company of PMRA. I knew that the Japanese tend to be leery of newcomers and young companies. By partnering with a $100 billion company founded in 1868, I gained credibility in the Japanese institutional financial marketplace—something that is vital in any business endeavor in Japan. The partnership also gave me the chance to hone my skills and expand my knowledge base. I would learn a great deal about Japanese business culture and gain experience negotiating with foreign investors from Asia.

I told Takanori "Ted" Ozaki, a longtime associate of mine based in Tokyo, about my newest venture and recruited him to become part of the team. Ted was a senior executive at Sumitomo Corporation, one of the oldest and largest trading companies in the world. Formerly the executive vice president of Sumitomo Metals and Mining, he had excellent contacts in Japan's banking community and was confident he could arrange meetings

LIFE LESSON #63:

"CONDUCTING BUSINESS IN DIFFERENT COUNTRIES AND CULTURES PRESENTS ITS OWN UNIQUE SET OF CHALLENGES."

—DAVID SEMAS

for us. I made many trips with Ted between Los Angeles and Japan, laying the groundwork for PMRA.

From L-R, Ted Ozaki, me, Ted's female companion, and Jim McWalters in the Roppongi nightclub district of Tokyo, 1992

Now, as I stared at the water droplets condensing on the plane's window, I couldn't help but mull over the mounting problems of our venture. Although I enjoyed a friendly relationship with Jim and others at PMRA, the venture had already proved costly, time-consuming, and somewhat cumbersome to manage due to the difficulties of trying to forge business relationships between companies separated by the Pacific Ocean. PMRA and its partners were some 5,500 miles apart, and there was a sixteen-hour time difference between Los Angeles and Tokyo.

It was becoming apparent that while the idea of trying to open real estate asset management markets for PMRA was sound, it involved cultivating business alliances on a different continent with people who spoke a different language and belonged to a 2,800-year-old culture that was distrustful of non-Japanese and Americans in general. The Japanese banking community tended to move cautiously and at a snail's pace into any new business venture. Worse, we had to delicately inform Japanese bankers that they had not made the most prudent of business decisions in the past and that their American real estate assets were about to plummet in value—something no one likes to hear. To top it off, it was American real estate firms and asset managers that had likely sold them the over-priced properties in the first place.

Nevertheless, the trip with Jim went well.

When we first landed, I took Jim down to the Tokyo subway station that was located right next to the Tokyo Narita International Airport.

Jim stopped, his eyes wide in amazement. "Oh my God! Are you kidding?" He began to read the sign just above the nearby entrance turnstiles. The large hanging display showed a map of all the subway train routes in different colors. "How in the hell are we going to figure out where we're going? First, I see the Ginza Line, then the Marunouchi Line, the Hibiya Line, and on and on. Holy smokes!"

"Jim, don't worry about it. I've been to Tokyo tons of times. Just follow my lead and pay attention to the colors and letters. For example, we're staying at the Grand Prince Hotel in the Akasaka District near the nightclub Roppongi district. Look at the map, and you'll notice the lighter mint-green Shinjuku Line begins right here at the airport. Now look at all the stops. Once we arrive in downtown Tokyo, just past the red Marunouchi Line at the Awajicho Station, you'll see the Ogawamachi Station with the letter C."

"Okay," Jim said, appearing to relax. "Gotcha."

"The darker or forest-green line with the letter C represents the Chiyoda Line, where we transfer, and the subway train takes us right to the Akasaka District and within walking distance of our hotel."

Jim sighed in relief. "Okay, I'll just follow you."

Ted and I took Jim out to an authentic Korean barbeque restaurant close to our hotel on the first night. The restaurant was beautifully appointed in Japanese décor, complete with koi fishponds, waterfalls, and massive carved-wood ceiling beams about sixteen feet high. The high ceiling made room for three enormous mahogany- and copper-countered U-shaped tables. We had a fabulous dinner and a great time.

At about ten o'clock that night, we walked down the street and crossed the large intersection under an overpass. Suddenly, we arrived at the world-famous Roppongi district, where English, French, and German are spoken. We traveled from one karaoke bar to the next, enjoying cocktails and singing songs from the 1960s and 1970s until two in the morning. One of the pretty Japanese hostesses joined us, and we all had a terrific evening. We were ready to begin meetings with executives from Sumitomo Bank the next morning at 8:20.

For five days, we had formal meetings with Tokyo-based banking executives, drinking tea with them and going out for more relaxing dinners in the evenings. We drank sake and ate Korean barbecue most nights but also sampled exotic foods like shark's fin soup. As we did the first night, and as is the custom while doing business in Tokyo, we always ended the evenings at a karaoke bar in crowded Roppongi, the nightclub district, drinking brandy and Rémy Martin with the banking executives until one o'clock in the morning. Then we'd be back in meetings at nine o'clock the next morning. All in all, Jim was impressed with the groundwork I had laid over the months with these executives on behalf of his company.

During the trip, we formed a relationship with Dai-Ichi Kangyo Bank. At the time, it was the largest bank in the world. In our second meeting, the Dai-Ichi Kangyo Bank executives introduced us to twelve properties and land-development projects they owned in the US. There were six different properties in Hawaii, four in Seattle, and two in Portland.

"How do we move forward from here to engage your services?" one of the Japanese bankers asked.

"First," I explained, "we will need to conduct a comprehensive on-site inspection of each property and conduct a detailed due diligence investigation of the books, records, and physical condition of the property or project itself. We'll also need to compile market data, historical trends, and competition. We'll need to gather local and statewide statistical data and address applicable governmental requirements, rules, regulations, restrictions, land-use entitlement issues, zoning, and other related matters. Our staff will visit and speak with the various city and county engineering, building, planning, fire, public safety, and law enforcement officials. Once finished, we will prepare a comprehensive Property Analysis Report or PAR."

The bankers were pleased with my answer and hired our team to prepare PARs for all twelve properties.

After arriving back in California on Friday, however, I still felt preoccupied as I unpacked my bag in my Newport Beach apartment. I knew I needed to keep looking for something I could call my own. This was just another short-term business opportunity that might last only four or five years.

Twenty years had passed since I'd begun my journey in construction and in the business world as a senior executive and entrepreneur. I was a partner of PMRA and was working with global Japanese banking giants. Nonetheless, I was still only providing a service, essentially acting as a paid consultant whose job was to deliver business to PMRA from Japanese banks. Real estate was a transactional kind of business; I had to go out and find an opportunity and then make some money from it. Once that opportunity was gone and that asset was sold, I had to go out and find another asset or build another relationship. It was time to go out and build a business outside of real estate.

During Ted's twenty-five-year tenure at Sumitomo Corporation and Sumitomo Metals & Mining, business opportunities came across his desk all the time. With his high-level Japanese contacts, I thought he might be able to identify a Japanese-based technology that could be built into an ongoing business. While I continued my work with PMRA, I evaluated Ted's proposals, hoping to find a gem. Naturally, this was easier said than done.

From 1992 through 1993, Ted inundated me with proposals and executive summaries—sometimes four or five per month. Most of them sent us on a wild goose chase. They would appear interesting on the surface, but after we had asked a few questions and conducted some due diligence, it would become apparent that the product, technology, or enterprise was ill-conceived or overvalued. The prospective investments came from a wide range of industries, including oil and gas, mining, Chinese silk apparel products, Columbian cigarettes, limited edition celebrity photographs, low-density polyethylene coating resins, an inorganic chemical liquid hardener, and a video on demand investment proposal. Most of the individuals involved in the businesses were fairly naïve and lacked hands-on experience in their chosen field or endeavor. We conducted due diligence and gained knowledge and valuable experience in where not to invest our money.

Ted was a loyal friend with good marketing skills and good intentions, but his strengths lay outside prognostication and the intricate details of due diligence.

Ted presented one of his funniest boondoggles to me in March 1992. It involved, of all things, the Indonesian banana business. He sent me a fax stating that he had come across a terrific business opportunity with Nanko Group Company, which was looking to partner with an American produce company interested in importing Indonesian bananas to the United States.

According to Ted, Nanko could deliver 8,000 tons per month at $650 per ton of Cavendish banana varieties, which represented more than $5 million per month.

Hank Matil, a good friend from my days at Shearson/American Express, had a business relationship with John Penny, who just happened to be the president and CEO of Cal Fruit Company, one of the largest produce companies on the West Coast. With Hank's assistance, I contacted John, who was based in Los Angeles, and John expressed interest in further investigating the project. As he explained, the money to be made in importing bananas didn't come from the sale of the fruit but from the money that could be made in "back-hauling" the container ship from the US back to the Asian markets. The idea was that we could turn this into a trading company and move into something far bigger than just bananas.

Month after month, I participated in conference calls between John, Ted, executives from Sumitomo Fruit Company, and the Indonesian businessmen, which included Nanko Group Company and the agricultural production company Bakrie & Brothers. We were told Bakrie & Brothers owned a banana plantation of nearly 10,000 acres. At the time bananas were selling for about twenty-eight to thirty-five cents per pound. There are thirty-six different types of bananas, with Cavendish being the primary variety of choice among American consumers. John discussed issues with me like commissions, production schedules, final contract terms, and the proposed brand name.

According to Ted's contact in Indonesia, the plantation had been in operation for five years. This was good, according to John, because it took three years or longer before banana production even reached maturity and an annual harvest could begin. Time and time again, John asked me if I was certain that the Indonesian plantation was in operation, and time and time again, I confirmed this with Ted, who

> **LIFE LESSON #64:**
>
> "IT TAKES LESS TIME TO DO A THING RIGHT THAN TO EXPLAIN WHY YOU DID IT WRONG."
>
> —HENRY WADSWORTH LONGFELLOW (AMERICAN POET AND EDUCATOR, 1807–1882)

told me he had further confirmed it with the Indonesian group including Bakrie & Brothers.

In September 1992, Ted said we were about to finalize the deal and that it was necessary for John, Ted, and me to meet with representatives from Nanko Group Company and Bakrie & Brothers in Jakarta, Indonesia, within the next sixty days to inspect the 92,665 acres of planted banana production. We had conducted a tremendous amount of due diligence, reviewing studies, reports, and statistics and talking to two leading fruit companies, and everybody seemed enthusiastic about the opportunity. So, we moved ahead.

After months of planning and many rounds of negotiations, a letter of intent between the parties was executed. Ted and I, along with John and his partner, boarded a Singapore Airlines Boeing 747 for our twenty-three-hour-long trip from LAX to Jakarta, via Hong Kong and Singapore. Upon our arrival, we met with the Indonesian businessmen and were wined and dined that evening. In the humid ninety-degree air, our clothes stuck to us like fly paper. The Indonesian businessmen, no strangers to the heat, wore short-sleeved, embroidered silk shirts loosely over slacks.

The next day, we caravanned in five four-wheel-drive vehicles from our hotel through the Jakarta streets, which were crowded with motor scooters and bicycles, and past the city limits. We continued for three hours and ventured about seventy-five miles into the vast jungles of Indonesia on paved, then gravel, and finally dirt roads, passing small villages, huts, and massive rubber tree and banana plantations. We arrived at what can best be described as hundreds of acres of open forestland, a dense jungle, a few banana trees, and a large one-hundred-acre terraced and open rice paddy.

I got out of the car and said, "Where the hell are the bananas?"

The Indonesian businessmen politely replied that they had not been planted yet but soon would be.

After months of due diligence, faxes, and conference calls with Ted, the Nanko Group Company, and Bakrie & Brothers, not to mention tens of thousands of dollars, I might as well have been talking to Forrest Gump and Benjamin Buford Blue about launching the Bubba Gump Shrimp Company.

On the drive back, I suggested that we might as well stop in one of the villages and have lunch. Though the dignitaries in our entourage were reluctant, I wanted to get something out of this excursion, and I was curious to see the people and how they lived. While we ate under a covered ramada, clouds moved in quickly, giving way to a downpour. After a half hour, the hot sun returned just in time to bake us as we loaded back into our vehicles. It continued like this for the rest of the trip, alternating between unpredictable storms and withering heat. The weather seemed to have taken a cue from my sour mood, although the next morning the sun was shining, and I was feeling much better.

From here on out, I would never jump on an airplane and travel halfway around the world without first reviewing verifiable documents and photographs. And I would always insist on speaking directly with industry experts, governmental officials, and competitors involved in the specific industry in question. To build a successful business, I would need to conduct the due diligence myself.

No matter how much due diligence you conduct, things can still go wrong.

Bobby Roberts, a former partner in Dunhill Compact Classics, knew an artist named Brett Livingstone-Strong, the grandson of the renown African explorer David Livingstone from the famous phrase ("Dr. Livingstone, I presume"). Brett was a close friend of Michael Jackson and was known for having carved John Wayne's face in a 116-ton rock that fell onto the Pacific Coast Highway in Malibu. The sculpture reportedly sold for $1 million in 1979. Among other things, he had also painted a portrait of Michael Jackson entitled *The Book*, which had sold to a Japanese businessman a few years

> **LIFE LESSON #65:**
>
> **"BELIEVE IN HALF OF WHAT YOU HEAR, VERIFY WITH QUALIFIED THIRD-PARTY EXPERTS, AND TRUST YOUR OWN INSTINCTS."**
>
> —THE COLONEL

earlier for the incredible sum of $2.1 million. Bobby knew I had many business contacts throughout Asia and thought we could work together to help Brett sell serigraph prints of *The Stream*, his newest, unreleased painting of Michael Jackson. Considering the Japanese people's infatuation with Michael Jackson and his music—and the fact that he was about to resume his Dangerous World tour—I felt that with Ted's assistance we could easily identify a qualified buyer in Japan.

In November 1992, ICM entered a contract with Brett and Michael Jackson in a joint venture called the Jackson Strong Alliance (JSA) to buy 1,000 serigraph prints of *The Stream* for $2,500 each. We provided him with a $100,000 deposit. The only other condition of the transaction was that I could show the prospective buyer only a Polaroid photograph of the painting, and I was not under any circumstances to let it out of my possession. Not even Michael had seen the painting—nor would he until Brett held a public unveiling, which was to happen sometime before the launch of Michael's world tour.

Brett was pleased and even spoke with Michael to obtain his approval and support. Michael was enthusiastic and told him to inform me that anyone who purchased the print would receive free tickets to his concert. The first hundred buyers would get to meet him backstage for photographs and signed autographs.

Ted found a Japanese art dealer who stepped up to the plate and signed a contract to purchase the 1,000 prints for $5,000 each, for a total of $5 million. In December of 1992, Mr. Akito Abiko, the buyer of the serigraph prints, wire-transferred a $500,000 deposit into my Security Pacific National Bank account with a close of title to occur within thirty days.

This time, everything seemed to be in order. We were working directly with the seller of the artwork, an established artist located in Southern California. I had seen the nearly finished painting of *The Stream*. Michael Jackson and his business agent were on board, and the buyer was a Tokyo art dealer who had already put up a sizable deposit. The only thing left was for Brett and JSA to physically deliver the prints and for ICM to transfer the total sum of $2.4 million to JSA from the $5 million purchase price we were to receive from Mr. Abiko.

Meanwhile, I had flown to Jakarta to complete the, "then pending" Indonesian banana deal. At 7:00 a.m. on Tuesday, the day after our excursion to the nonexistent banana plantation, I received a telephone call in my hotel room from an irate Billy Brown, Michael Jackson's business manager. When I finally got Billy to calm down, he informed me that someone named Mr. Abiko and the TAM Connection Group had placed an advertisement in the *Tokyo Times* claiming to be JSA's liaison office in Tokyo.

Apparently, as collectors called to acquire the prints, they had been told that if they bought a print of *The Stream* for $6,000, they would also receive front-row seats at one of Jackson's upcoming concerts, and the first hundred to buy the artwork would get to meet him backstage. The catastrophic icing on the cake was that Mr. Abiko had also provided the newspapers with the never-before-seen photograph of *The Stream*, which they unwisely published on the front page of their newspapers. For reference, *Asahi Shimbun* is one of the world's largest newspapers, with a daily circulation of twelve million.

My heart dropped to my stomach. Although I had warned Ted and told him under no circumstances to give the Polaroid photograph to anyone, especially Mr. Abiko, he had failed to heed my warnings. Suddenly the transaction was spiraling out of control, and Billy demanded a face-to-face meeting with Bobby and me, together with Brett and Michael in his office in Los Angeles.

"Brett is upset," he said, "and Michael is more than displeased and wants to speak with you personally—first to hear an apology and then to discuss how you plan to correct the wrongdoing and retract the newspaper article."

To say that I was in hot water with Michael, his manager, and his attorneys would be an understatement.

"I'm in Indonesia now, Billy," I explained. "I knew nothing about this. Let me investigate it and get back to you."

Frantic, I called Ted in his room and told him I needed to meet him immediately in the lobby downstairs, where I explained the situation as calmly as I could. Ted's jaw dropped in disbelief. Apparently, Mr. Abiko had promised he would keep the photograph to himself and had been sworn to secrecy. Regardless of what Ted had done, however, I understood that I was still the responsible party and accountable for what had happened, like it or not.

I returned from Indonesia a few days later and met with Billy and Michael Jackson's legal counsel in their Los Angeles offices. Michael was on the speakerphone. Once I had finally calmed everyone done, I was able to convince Michael and his advisors that this unfortunate incident had not been intentional. I had a retraction printed in the *Tokyo Times*, Mr. Abiko's deposit for $500,000 was returned, and ICM never realized its $2.5 million in profit. For extra measure, we lost our $100,000 deposit, which was a small price to pay compared to what could have been a multimillion-dollar lawsuit. Coming right on the heels of the failed banana deal, this latest fiasco proved a major disappointment.

Somehow, I survived 1992. I was looking forward to the upcoming Christmas holiday and hoping I could put all this nonsense behind me when I received an email from Ted about another business opportunity. This time he stated that he had been working on a patented aluminum anodizing technology that he referred to as Metal Coat and that a Dr. Asano, an associate of the inventor, Minoru Mitani, owner of Soken Kako Company, Ltd., had given him the right to handle the project in the United States. Ted would be coming to the US right after the first of the year and wanted to meet with me to discuss it.

On January 4, 1993, Ted arrived from Tokyo and visited my home. We discussed the opportunity over breakfast on my balcony overlooking the Back Bay, an idyllic natural habitat. We talked all morning about the Metal Coat process and looked at samples and literature he had brought. Ted shared what he

LIFE LESSON #66:

"THE SUCCESSFUL MAN WILL PROFIT FROM HIS MISTAKES AND TRY AGAIN IN A DIFFERENT WAY."

—DALE CARNEGIE (AMERICAN WRITER, LECTURER, AND MOTIVATIONAL SPEAKER, 1888-1955)

knew about the technology, which involved the use of proprietary chemicals applied during the aluminum anodizing process. Having grown up in the building industry, I was familiar with the anodizing process, which was the primary surface treatment used to protect aluminum products such as window frames, sliding doors, and hardware. Still, what I knew about it could fit in a thimble.

Ted's information about this seemed more complete than that of his previous potential investments. He didn't know much about bananas, but he had a background in the metals and mining business. He brought sample aluminum coupons (four-by-four-inch test panels) that had been finished with conventional processing and samples that had been finished with Mr. Mitani's Metal Coat process. The latter were shinier, smoother, and more attractive, with a richer color. The improvement in the process was visible to the naked eye. That didn't mean that it would necessarily demonstrate an improvement in laboratory testing, but the new process appeared to be far superior to conventional anodizing methods.

If Mr. Mitani had companies like Toyota, Sony, and Nissan interested in this technology, I thought that maybe there really was something to it.

PART II

CHAPTER 9
WHAT IS ANODIZING, ANYWAY?

Simply stated, anodizing is the ability to reproduce a naturally occurring process by artificially creating an environment for aluminum to grow its own skin. If steel is left exposed to weather, it will rust. In the case of aluminum, it will turn white in color or oxidize. It's this aluminum-oxidized surface that protects the underlying substrate from corrosion and provides an efficient wear-resistant surface.

Three different types of anodizing provide different levels of thickness and protection. Type I, boric sulfuric anodizing, is a very thin coating, less than seven microns (the human hair is about one hundred microns), and is mainly used for aircraft paint adhesion. Type II, architectural anodizing, is used for decorative or architectural products that are typically colored, like a flashlight, cell phone, computer, or window frame, and produces a coating of about twelve to eighteen microns (one half to three quarters of a millimeter) as thin as tissue paper. This type represents about 65 percent of the market. Type III, hardcoat anodizing, is the most durable anti-corrosive of all the anodizing processes and is used for cookware (like Calphalon), engine pistons, water pumps, and products that require optimum protection from the elements. This coating, representing about 33 percent of the market, is thicker, typically at least fifty microns, or about half the thickness of business card stock (two millimeters).

Pleased by what I had learned, I registered the name Metal Coat USA about a month after my meeting with Ted. Then I started contacting friends and associates who might be able to steer me in the right direction so that I could get a handle on the technology's benefits and viability in the market. In January 1993, I moved ICM and ARA into the Omni Executive Suites, now called Regus Suites, located on the tenth floor of a prestigious eleven-story building. We officially opened the Metal Coat USA offices at 5000 Birch Street in Newport Beach, near the John Wayne Airport.

Since the beginning of my career, I have always enjoyed using acronyms for the naming of my projects, businesses, or products. I felt that it was necessary to establish a completely different brand name for this Japanese technology that would be owned and controlled by my company, ICM. After several weeks, I came up with what I felt was a great name and announced the name of the company during my daily lunch break with friends at our usual hangout, Muldoon's Irish Pub in Newport Beach.

The whole gang was there, including Roger Luby, Russ Frerer, Hank Matil, Jeffrey Mackinen, John Block, and Marcel the bartender, and they were eager to hear what name I had come up with. I told them that the new name would be METALAST International, and they agreed that it was a great name.

"Actually," I said with a smile, "the name is an acronym."

"You're kidding!" they replied.

"No, I'm not. METALAST stands for Metal Engineering Technology Aluminum Anodic Surface Treatment and will soon be a registered trademark with the United States Patent and Trademark Office (USPTO)."

They all broke into laughter but agreed that it was a great acronym.

Over the next few months, I continued to test parts treated with the METALAST® anodizing process at General Motors, Ford Motors, Chrysler, Toyota, and many of their top-tier suppliers, and the test results came back positive each time. The process produced superior performance characteristics over conventional anodizing, especially in the areas of wear resistance, corrosion, lubricity, and smoothness.

Premiere Metal Finishing (PMF) became interested in learning more about METALAST and began conducting their own due diligence about the process. In September 1993, we were invited to PMF's anodizing facility in Green Bay, Wisconsin to further explore the METALAST process with their technical staff, including Byron Estes, Keith Johnson, and the PMF chairman. The METALAST team included my son Greg, Ted Ozaki, the inventor Minoru Mitani, and his three-man team.

Minoru Mitani and Ted Ozaki, 1995

Byron welcomed us into the plant to watch the anodizing process in action. Most job shops tend to be small, between 4,000 and 8,000 square feet, with twenty to thirty employees. PMF's facility was one of the largest in the country, probably 40,000 to 50,000 square feet, with 1,500- to 2,000-gallon baths for processing large parts. PMF's annual revenues were in the neighborhood of $30 million at the time. In the world of anodizing, this was a large, well-respected job shop operator. The anodizing process, meanwhile, appeared to be done at extremely high temperatures and in a somewhat dangerous environment. Fumes were coming off the line, exhaust fans running, overhead cranes clanking, and baths bubbling with agitation to keep parts cool. Nevertheless, we learned that anodizing is one of the more environmentally friendly metal-finishing processes, because unlike some plating processes, it doesn't use cyanide or dangerous carcinogens.

One of the benefits of the METALAST process is the Mitani-Lyte chemical. This "secret sauce" lets the finisher process parts faster, provides a better and more uniform coating by making the electrolyte bath operate more efficiently, and greatly reduces the odds of burning or crazing (surface cracking). In a nutshell, the METALAST process produces a superior product, can greatly increase productivity (as much as twice as fast), and can deliver a smoother and more lubricious finish that is harder, denser, and more corrosion-resistant than conventional anodizing.

Though they had seen some of these results in the lab, senior executives and technical staff at PMF were still not fully convinced of the METALAST process, so they asked if I would consider conducting further testing and validation at the corporate offices and testing lab of PMF's chemical company, Sandoz Chemicals, in North Carolina.

About a month later, the METALAST and Soken Kako team arrived in Charlotte, North Carolina to meet with PMF's R&D group. Sandoz had assembled their technical group as well. After an initial meeting over lunch, we planned to meet at the Sandoz offices the next morning to begin two-week-long METALAST test trials.

Around eight o'clock the next morning, I drove to the hotel where Ted Ozaki and the Soken Kako team were staying. Mr. Mitani, his son Yoshi Mitani, Mr. Ueda, and Dr. Asano, it turned out, were degreed chemical engineers and highly accomplished anodizers. In fact, Dr. Asano had a PhD in metallurgy from prestigious Tokyo University. However, none of them spoke English. Along with Ted Ozaki, who was fluent in English, they made for a quirky little group. Many who met them during the days of Sandoz testing thought they were a tad eccentric, and they were, but also extremely talented.

As I waited in front of the hotel, the Japanese businessmen exited the lobby. I wasn't paying much attention, but upon closer inspection I noticed they were wearing heavy rubber yellow raincoats. It was a mild, sunny day without a cloud in the sky. All three scientists carried buckets and one-gallon bottles filled with some type of liquid. Mr. Ueda carried automotive jumper cables. Ted, with his customary cigarette hanging from his mouth, held some type of electronic oscilloscope. To top it all off, they wore cumbersome construction-worker-style black boots with large buckles down the sides.

I wasn't certain if we were going to pour a concrete patio in the rain or if they were expecting some type of nuclear fallout. I got out of the car and started laughing, nearly falling on the pavement as I opened the trunk so they could put away their wares.

Ted sat in the front seat, while the other four squeezed into the back seat. With their matching yellow raincoats, they looked like they were about to make an appearance on a television sitcom or *Saturday Night Live*.

We drove over to the Sandoz lab and, after clearing their security office, were brought upstairs to the lab. Mr. Mitani had had equipment delivered, including a small, refrigerated bath with its own power supply. We spent the day getting everything ready so we could commence work the next day and begin testing METALAST technology.

Sandoz, being a large chemical company, had a sizable campus with huge warehouses and stainless-steel tanks for mixing chemicals. Depending on the chemical, some of the tanks were refrigerated and some were heated. All had large mixing devices for stirring. They also had a research lab to support the manufacturing operation and customers, but the lab was much smaller, about 2,000 square feet, with thirty-gallon baths. No overhead cranes were required, just an operator who hung a rack, manually immersed the parts in one bath, set the timer, and moved them to the next bath.

With Byron Estes and Keith Johnson from PMF at his side, Mr. Mitani started running parts and anodizing the very next morning. He was showing the other scientists, engineers, and anodizers how he could greatly accelerate the anodizing process and still produce optimum results. He conducted experiments on many different types of aluminum alloys at different bath temperatures, using different current densities (amps per square foot), even up to 100 ASF. This meant he could anodize a coupon five times faster—in twelve minutes instead of an hour. This was huge for production anodizers because it meant they could double their output, or process parts twice as fast.

Everyone was impressed with Mr. Mitani's knowledge and the ability of METALAST to perform in several different environments. The testing continued for two straight weeks, and I gained a considerable amount of knowledge about the anodizing process and about the application of the METALAST technology.

Despite the others' enthusiasm, inwardly I was becoming more and more discouraged. It wasn't that METALAST was not performing as advertised, because it was. It was the fact that every time Mr. Mitani processed a different set of coupons, and different alloys he slowly ramped up the electrical current over one minute, two minutes, three minutes, or more. Then he would adjust the electrical current three, four, five, or as many as eight times per thirty-minute process run. As I sat there day after day, I began to realize that an operator would have to be a rocket scientist to figure out which of Mitani's hundreds of production formulas or recipes to use while processing as many as fifty different types of aluminum alloys.

In the real world of anodizing, such a feat would be much too complicated for any technician to replicate properly and consistently. Changing electrical current, ramping voltage, varying process times as many as ten times in a thirty-minute run and using a variety of different alloys and temperatures would be quite a challenge for anyone. How could we possibly license this technology and simplify and standardize the METALAST process?

LIFE LESSON #67:

"IF YOU CAN'T EXPLAIN IT SIMPLY, YOU DON'T UNDERSTAND IT WELL ENOUGH."

—ALBERT EINSTEIN

CHAPTER 10

METALAST®—THE BUSINESS

A few months passed, and Byron Estes and Keith Johnson of PMF called to tell me that the test results from Sandoz were so impressive that they wanted to know if the METALAST team would be willing to once again travel to Sandoz Labs in Charlotte to continue testing and validation.

METALAST International, Inc. logo

PMF had been sending out test coupons processed at Sandoz to certified labs for corrosion and salt-spray testing. While most adhesion, bonding, and electrical conductivity tests can be completed in a one- or two-week period, corrosion and salt-spray testing can take considerably longer. In a salt-spray or salt-fog test, parts are placed into an airtight chamber for extended periods of time and exposed to 99 percent salt spray at 99 percent humidity in order to accelerate the corrosion process. Some test standards require one week in the chamber, sometimes two weeks, but often the manufacturer will want to see optimum performance of 3,000 hours or over four months. Other tests can last for 8,500 hours or one year. The Department of Defense (DoD) often field tests in a real-world environment exposed to saltwater and inclement weather on a beach. This was why the test results for the METALAST process were so long in coming.

In February 1994, I flew back to Charlotte with the R&D team from PMF and the Soken Kako group, and they immediately went to work at the Sandoz facilities. While the processes were underway, I was still trying to figure out how to simplify, standardize, and replicate the METALAST anodizing process. There had to be a way to make the technology scalable so that it could be licensed.

At the end of the first week of testing, I watched and learned as Mr. Mitani anodized parts, Byron made notes, and Keith moved parts from bath to bath. I even racked parts, prepped, and anodized firsthand a few times so I could understand the entire process.

While glancing around the room, I happened to notice an unusual piece of equipment on top of a cabinet. The device had what looked like an oscilloscope on the front of it, with gauges, switches, knobs, and colored lights. I used a step stool to get a closer look at the compact object and saw that it had been manufactured by an Italian company called Italtecno. Something told me it must have something to do with processing.

Pinakin Patel, director of technical support for Sandoz, saw me and came over to see what I was doing.

"What does this piece of equipment do?" I asked him.

"It's used to control a process. It's called a process controller."

"Do you mean that in theory you could program the voltage and electrical current changes, ramp the current, start, stop, pause, and do just about everything during a typical formulated anodizing process run?"

"Absolutely. And if you designed and manufactured your own process controller, you could have it do just about anything, like controlling the amps and volts, retrieving valuable data, and formulating recipes and process runs. You could design it so that you could set an operator ID, establish repeatable process runs by programming a set part or product number, print out reports, sound alarms, and send out signals. You could probably even control it remotely over telephone lines."

The proverbial lightbulb went on inside my head. A process controller could be programmed with Mr. Mitani's hundreds of process recipes to standardize the METALAST anodizing process! All I had to do now was identify a process-control engineer capable of designing such a system. Coming from Silicon Valley, I figured it shouldn't be that difficult to find a qualified professional who could design, build, and manufacture a process-control unit.

Now I had a solution to the problem of how to make METALAST a viable and scalable technology that could be internationally licensed. As I had learned earlier, most every problem has a solution; you just have to figure out what it is.

I arrived back in Los Angeles on Wednesday, champing at the bit to find a process engineer who could design and build the process controller, which I dubbed the METALAST Process Control System, or MPCS. I phoned my brother, Len, in San Jose to see if he had any contacts that could help me, and before long, he introduced me to Rod Friedline, a rather quirky but brilliant software programmer/engineer.

The gauntlet had been thrown, and now I had to get busy figuring out how to raise the tens of millions of dollars it was going to take to build METALAST into a full-fledged business. I had first put the name METALAST into commerce in January of 1993 while operating under a DBA (doing business as) of METALAST USA. My next step was to register the name METALAST and incorporate METALAST International, Inc. as

LIFE LESSON #68:

"TELL ME AND I FORGET. TEACH ME AND I REMEMBER. INVOLVE ME AND I LEARN."

—BENJAMIN FRANKLIN (AMERICAN STATESMAN, INVENTOR, AND FOUNDING FATHER, 1706–1790)

a Nevada subchapter S corporation, which would make me the manager of a limited liability company and owner of the METALAST trademark. Under IRS code, S corporations don't pay any income taxes. Instead, the corporation's income or losses are divided among and passed through to its individual shareholders. The shareholders must report the income or loss on their own tax returns.

Next, I looked around for a home for METALAST and a personal residence. After forty-five years in California, the time had come for me to look for a less crowded place to live, a place with wide-open spaces reminiscent of the Santa Clara Valley in the 1950s. Northern Nevada seemed like the perfect choice.

I was engaged to be married, and my fiancée, Susan, and I wanted a setting with wide open space, natural beauty, abundant wildlife, horses, farming, ranching, and a quality of life that we could embrace while enjoying the four seasons.

Carson Valley, fifteen miles east of Lake Tahoe and forty-five miles south of Reno, was just such a place. Douglas County, with its quaint towns of Minden, Gardnerville, and Genoa, had a population of 40,000—just one-tenth the size of Santa Clara County in 1950. Orange County, where I currently lived, was about eighty times more densely populated.

Me and Susan—Hawaiian theme party at Irvine Sports Club, 1994

Carson Valley sits at an elevation of 4,700 feet and is nestled below the majestic snow-covered peaks of the Sierra Nevada, whose 8,000- to 10,000-foot-tall mountains are home to numerous alpine and cross-country ski areas. While the Sierra Nevada might receive the occasional six-foot dump of snow from a big storm, Carson Valley sees maybe six to eight inches—just enough to cover the ground and create a winter wonderland. In addition to golfing at beautiful Genoa Lakes Golf and Country Club, outdoor activities include skiing, hiking, biking, parasailing, ballooning, horseback riding, scuba diving, hunting, and fishing. We also considered that both of our families were a mere four- to six-hour drive away.

From a business perspective, the Meridian Business Park location was a perfect selection in Northern Nevada as the new home for the METALAST Tech Center (MTC). Nevada collects no personal income taxes, and the political climate was friendly to growing businesses wishing to relocate.

Meridian Business Park, Minden, NV

The building permit and entitlement process in Northern Nevada would produce the necessary government agency approvals within several months, whereas in California, it would have likely taken several years. The easily accessible Reno/Tahoe Airport would provide excellent access for our business partners and customers. Meanwhile, Northern California's twelve million people would provide the company access to skilled professionals from Silicon Valley, the Bay Area, and Sacramento. I suspected that many California residents would like to improve their quality of life by seeking employment opportunities near the breathtakingly beautiful Lake Tahoe and Carson Valley.

Lastly, we thought it would be easier to convince a senior business executive, scientist, or chief engineer from Boeing, Lockheed Martin, Ford Motors, GE, or other Fortune 500 companies to visit METALAST headquarters if they were located next door to one of the world's great ski and hotel casino resort areas.

Now that I had found a home for METALAST and had given Rod Friedline the go-ahead to start work on the MPCS design, it was imperative that I bring in investment capital. Together with my own capital and investment from some business associates and friends, Martin Burke and Rob Deutschman, I was able to bring over another $1 million in first-round equity. My friend Marc Harris, a Southern California financial advisor and real estate broker, introduced me to a Riverside-based CPA firm that brought in a group of private investors ready to commit another $750,000. On the capital-raising front, we were making some real headway.

However, it was also becoming apparent to me that we were going to need a heck of a lot more money if we were going to develop our own process-control system technology and proprietary algorithms, build a complete technology center, and buy 100 percent of the Metal Coat process rights and chemical formulations, and the anodizing recipes from Mr. Mitani for about $2.5 million. As I began to establish a budget for the building, tenant improvements, laboratory equipment, automated process line, staff of scientists, administrative personnel, and a sales force, I realized we were going to need a first round of funding of at least $12 million.

I began to meet with business associates and friends who I hoped might be interested in investing. One of my most memorable turndowns occurred when my sister Elizabeth introduced me to a man she was dating. He and I spoke over the telephone at great length. He had an engineering degree and an extensive background in the automotive industry and was thus quite familiar with anodizing. He reviewed my business plan and asked me several questions about the business model, financial projections, competition, market, and barriers to entry. Needless to say, he was extremely sophisticated and knowledgeable.

Finally, he said, "David, this is just not my type of investment. Why would you want to go into such a dirty, grimy, mom-and-pop type of business like anodizing? It's fragmented, antiquated, and riddled with potentially hazardous waste problems."

"I understand and appreciate what you're saying," I replied. "But if the industry was well organized, not antiquated or fragmented, and was already green and environmentally friendly, why would they need a guy like me?"

I thanked my sister's boyfriend for taking the time to review my business plan and for giving me his opinion on the industry. On a side note, his name was Lido Anthony "Lee" Iacocca. I didn't realize it at the time, but Lee, the former chairman of Chrysler, was in the process of mounting a hostile takeover of

> LIFE LESSON #69:
>
> "YOU CAN HAVE BRILLIANT IDEAS, BUT IF YOU CAN'T GET THEM ACROSS, YOUR IDEAS WON'T GET YOU ANYWHERE."
>
> —LEE IACOCCA (AMERICAN AUTOMOTIVE EXECUTIVE, 1924–2019)

Chrysler with the help of billionaire Kirk Kerkorian. In the end, I should have read his book more carefully.

Earlier, in 1993, an acquaintance named James Bradock (not his real name) had approached me at Muldoon's Irish Pub and said that he had overheard many of my recent discussions there with friends about METALAST and wanted to know if I had an executive summary that he could review. Seizing on an opportunity to possibly raise funds, I gave him a concise document that provided information about the METALAST process, anodizing in general, testing results, the industry, the market, my background, and so on. I thought that Bradock's background as a NASD (National Association of Securities Dealers) securities rep might come in handy one day as we began raising capital.

Almost a year later, my colleagues and I were sitting in our usual places at the end of the bar in Muldoon's when Bradock appeared again and asked if the two of us could have lunch and talk. He and I settled into one of the private booths in the dining room, which featured a fireplace, dark wood, and upholstered walls. Over lunch, he said he had reviewed the METALAST executive summary and was certain that he could raise the money we needed. He described some of his work with Trans Western Securities (TWS), a large regional NASD broker-dealer firm, and mentioned that he and his partner had successfully raised money for other private equity ventures. He agreed to take a 10 percent commission if he directly raised capital for us or a 2 percent fee if he acted as a wholesaler dealing with independent reps.

When I asked about his background, he said that he had been an undercover agent for the DEA and prior to that had been with the Palm Springs Police Department. I wasn't surprised. To tell the truth, he had shifty eyes and looked a little shady with his amber-tinted glasses, quiet demeanor, and wiry build. He talked under his breath and rarely looked anyone in the eye. He didn't give me a warm, fuzzy feeling, but I chalked it up to his being undercover for five years. In years past, my gut instincts had usually been correct when I didn't get a warm and fuzzy feeling about a person. When I got that uneasy feeling, the person nearly always turned out to be a snake.

He further explained that after two failed business attempts, he had learned about the tax-shelter securities business, where he had spent his last five years.

"Why are you so willing to help me now?" I asked.

"I'd like to eventually become your NASD broker-dealer wholesaler," he said.

A broker-dealer wholesaler coordinates with other securities broker-dealer firms and registers representatives in closing investment sales, usually receiving a 2 percent override commission on capital raised from the broker-dealer firms.

What do I have to lose? I thought. *We'll keep an eye on him. If he can raise the kind of capital we need, why not?*

When lunch was over, we shook hands.

"Okay, Jim, you've got a deal," I told him. "We'll bring you on board."

He wasn't going to work directly for the company, but as a consultant, he would be paid commission on the money he raised.

A month later, Bradock and I met with a team of lawyers from a corporate law firm that specialized in private placement offerings. Bradock was convinced that if I hired a prestigious Los Angeles law firm like Nossaman Gunther Knox & Elliott to prepare our offering, he could get TWS, his broker-dealer, to sell the investment product to their client base with their impressive 450 NASD registered reps. I engaged the firm to prepare a private placement offering memorandum (PPM) for $11,250,000, and they said that we could probably have it ready by the end of the year.

About the same time, the chairman of Premiere Metal Finishing (PMF) and I, on behalf of METALAST, executed a letter of intent for PMF to become the first licensee for the METALAST technology. It was an exciting first step. We started preparing for the installation and field beta testing at PMF's Minneapolis facility, which meant that potential users could start testing the process and provide feedback.

In October, I headed to Minneapolis to meet with Ted Ozaki and the Soken Kako team, and engineer Rod Friedline began the setup for beta testing. Monday morning, the Japanese team and I showed up at the PMF Minneapolis facility and were given a tour of the impressive 100,000-square-foot building. The team spent most of the day discussing the basic ideas behind the beta trial and installed Mitani-Lyte in the 1,500-gallon Type III hardcoat bath. Mr. Mitani said it would take at least twenty-four hours before the additive would stabilize and be ready for initial processing.

The next morning, Friedline called to say that he would arrive in Minneapolis the following day and asked if I could pick him up at the airport. He described himself as a fifty-year-old white guy, six feet tall, with a moustache. When I picked him up, I discovered that Friedline somewhat resembled the nutty professor in the movie *Back to the Future*. With his long hair, baggy shorts, and Birkenstock sandals—it was a below-freezing thirty degrees outside—he looked like a throwback from the 1960s. When I found out that he lived in the sleepy town of Big Basin near the hippie haven of Santa Cruz, it all made sense.

In a small office trailer behind the PMF building, I asked Rod how far along the software development was and if he thought the system was at least operational enough to begin some basic beta testing. He dropped a bombshell in response: he didn't understand the most basic operational concepts or even the functional purpose of the MPCS. The hardware he had brought with him looked fine—it was a piece of equipment resembling a computer—but very little had been done with the software.

Nevertheless, I had to put that behind me for the moment and focused on the real question: *What the hell do we do now?*

Friedline began providing me with a laundry list of questions, all of which I had previously answered over the last six months while spending $225,000. He then began directing his questions to Mr. Mitani, with Ted Ozaki translating. It would have been comical, had it not been so infuriating. The icing on the cake was when Friedline asked Mr. Mitani if his technology provided for the DC electrical current to pulse. After Mr. Mitani replied that it did, Friedline asked questions like, "What type of electrical pulse is it? How often does it occur? How many times during a process run do I have to program the system? What is the length of wave forms? Does it repeat or remain constant?"

Here I was, having spent nearly two years and millions of dollars to help modernize a one-hundred-year-old industry, watching a non-English-speaking Japanese scientist attempt to communicate with a hippie straight out of the 1960s using hand gestures and knocking sounds reminiscent of the Stone Age.

I told them to continue their discussion while I went to the local Kinko's, where I spent the rest of the day preparing a detailed memorandum that defined the functions, features, and operating parameters of the proposed MPCS. After reviewing the report, Friedline worked around the clock over the next few days to get the MPCS to work, writing code and designing features I thought had already been completed.

There are a vast number of aluminum alloys, and there are countless variables in anodizing based on what the manufacturer wants. The software had to let the operator program all these variations. Once it was fully operational, the finished MPCS would automate the complex adjustments Mr. Mitani normally made manually to the voltage, current, and other settings throughout the process run. A recipe for a particular method of anodizing could be entered into the computer, and four different job shops around the country could put that same recipe into the MPCS and get identical results, as opposed to varying results not only from shop to shop but very likely shift to shift.

Thanks to Friedline's dedication and impressive programming skills, the MPCS began to perform its many complex functions flawlessly. The engineers and anodizing line staff at PMF were impressed with the consistency and uniformity it delivered. Most importantly, with METALAST and the Mitani-Lyte chemical additive in the anodizing bath, we could operate at higher current densities with more amps per square foot, meaning the part could be anodized faster and the anodizing layer would be denser and harder, creating a more

> LIFE LESSON #70:
>
> "NEVER TELL PEOPLE HOW TO DO THINGS. TELL THEM WHAT TO DO, AND THEY WILL SURPRISE YOU WITH THEIR INGENUITY."
>
> —GEORGE S. PATTON (AMERICAN FOUR-STAR GENERAL, 1885-1945)

durable finish. The ability to anodize faster also saved money and increased profits considerably.

We had managed to pull off our visit to Minneapolis. PMF became the first beta-testing licensee of our technology, and the process controller, called the MPCS, was coming together.

CHAPTER 11

CONSPIRATORS EMERGE

Other than the hiccup with the MPCS, things continued progressing smoothly for METALAST. That winter, I flew up to Reno and identified an ideal site for offices and research and development (R&D) laboratory: an attractive tilt-up construction office building situated in the middle of Carson Valley. The Pine Nut Mountains loomed in the east, and we enjoyed a majestic view of Jobs Peak and the Sierra Nevada to the west.

The area boasted several four- and five-star restaurants, many coffee shops, golf courses, and the charming, recently built Carson Valley Inn and Casino, just a five-minute drive away. The METALAST Tech Center (MTC) would be conveniently located only two short blocks from Minden-Tahoe Airport, a converted Air Force base with an 8,000-foot-long runway that could accommodate private prop and luxury jets. Several of the METALAST board members had private aircraft.

I designed the floor plan for the MTC and began working with a Southern California architectural firm to complete working drawings

---

LIFE LESSON #71:

"PLANS ARE NOTHING; PLANNING IS EVERYTHING."

—DWIGHT D. EISENHOWER

---

for tenant improvements. While design work was ongoing, Hixson Metal Finishing (HMF) agreed to let us establish a temporary lab within their facilities in Newport Beach, just a few miles from the Pacific Ocean. I also hired a vice president of technology—Carl Grunwald (not his real name) from Sandoz Chemicals—who would be running sample parts, helping develop formulas, working with Friedline, and testing the patented anodizing process. The temporary Hixson lab in Southern California proved extremely beneficial over the following months until construction of the METALAST Tech Center was completed and the MTC laboratory and wet process line became operational.

From July through December, Jim Bradock had been able to help us raise an additional $800,000 of equity investment prior to bringing our $11.2 million PPM to the street. He and I had agreed that he would be paid a 10 percent commission and 2 percent override on broker-dealer sales.

Then, in mid-December, he came to my office and appeared frantic. He said that he needed to get out of the securities business and leave TWS. He was anxious to go to work and raise money for us and asked if he could start working out of our offices in Newport Beach. He wanted to make the move before the PPM hit the street so he could start preparing to contact other NASD broker-dealer firms as our wholesaler, while also working with Arthur Hickman, the due diligence officer of TWS.

"Okay, Jim," I said, somewhat confused by his urgency, "we'll get you some office space down the hall. You can share an office with my daughter, Wendi, and work out of here for now and go ahead and prepare for the PPM offering."

I was still a little wary of Bradock, but he did have clients. He had worked for Arthur Hickman (not his real name) and Jonathan McBride (not his real name) of TWS for five years and knew them well. He had the ability to help raise the $11 million and maybe one day the $50 million we would eventually need to successfully build the business.

In February 1995, Susan and I were invited to attend the TWS Top Producer Conference, an annual four-day gathering of the top fifty producing securities reps within TWS. The conference was held at the beautiful Alisal Guest Ranch and Golf Resort in the quaint Danish town of Solvang, California, just northwest of Santa Barbara.

Since our $11.2 million PPM was officially on the street, I made several presentations to the group and generated considerable interest from many of the TWS reps, all of whom knew Jim Bradock. To give the NASD broker-dealers a degree of comfort for their clients, we established a minimum funding floor requirement of $2.5 million with the PPM. This meant that until the minimum amount was reached, the funds would be held in trust by First Interstate Bank of Nevada (FIB). This way, investors were assured that we would have to raise at least enough money to build the tech center and launch basic operations. The conference raised $1.5 million initially, and Ron Melanson, a securities broker, single-handedly raised more than $6 million over an eighteen-month period.

In anticipation of breaking the $2.5 million floor, we began work on designing and building our automated wet-process anodizing line, to be installed in our new laboratory at the MTC for R&D purposes. I relocated to Minden and leased a nice home that was less than I would have paid for an apartment in Southern California. I rented some temporary office space in the quaint town of Genoa for METALAST until the MTC was scheduled to be completed later in the year.

By now, Jeffrey M. "Jeff" Mackinen, my longtime friend and former vice president at American Realty Advisors, was also on board full-time as the vice president of administration. My brother Len, daughter Wendi, and son Greg had also joined METALAST. Wendi, now twenty-five years old and a highly competent manager of a Southern California escrow company, had agreed to join METALAST as our office manager and bookkeeper. Greg had just graduated from Northern Arizona University with a bachelor's degree in international marketing and business. He had approached me right after graduation to see if he could come work for us. At that point, the budget had been pretty tight, so I suggested that instead I make a few telephone calls to see if I could find him a position in another company. But he was quite persistent that he wanted to work for me.

From L-R: Aimee, Greg, me, and Wendi at Greg's NAU graduation, 1993

After nearly a month of debating the point, I said, "Okay, Greg, I'll give you room and board, pay you $500 per month, and you'll go to work on an anodizing line at Hixson Metal Finishing in Newport Beach with five non-English-speaking Hispanics." Having been raised by Big Leonard, I refused to allow even the *appearance* of nepotism at METALAST.

"No problem," he said, and with that, he was hired.

Everything seemed to be going well until Wendi came to me with some concerns about Jim Bradock, who shared her office. She suspected that he had been looking into her files on her computer. She noticed that things were being moved around on her desk; she would turn her computer off and later find it turned back on. We would return from lunch and find him already working in her office. We immediately set up a more sophisticated password structure to prevent this from happening in the future. Within weeks, I also noticed that some confidential files in my desk had been rearranged and things were misplaced on my desk. I made a point of paying more attention. Thinking that Bradock might be the culprit, I began locking my desk drawers, and Jeff Mackinen and I also began locking our shared office that was down the hall from him.

It was unfortunate that I had to deal with this type of employee distraction, but we couldn't afford to lose Bradock at this critical time; we needed him to assist in raising the balance of the capital. He was constantly reminding me that the owners of TWS were his close golfing buddies, and if he wasn't the METALAST NASD broker-dealer wholesaler, TWS would pull out and stop raising money for our company. Basically, he had me over a barrel, so for the moment, I was forced to put up with him.

Then came the kicker. On Monday, July 24, 1995, I was at my Genoa office, located in an old Victorian-style building about five miles from the

MTC, when the phone rang. I picked up the phone and heard my daughter's frantic voice on the other end of the line.

"We just reached the two and a half million floor and now have access to the funds held in the FIB trust account, only to have money stolen!" she exclaimed. "He's a thief and a liar. I can't believe it, but he stole one hundred and eighteen thousand dollars from our bank account. He should be put in jail!"

I had a pretty good idea who she was referring to but asked, "Who are you talking about?"

"Dad, it was Bradock!"

"How could he steal bank trust account funds when only Jeff and I have signing authority on the FIB trust account?"

"Apparently, he called the bank every day last week to find out how close we were to reaching the minimum. On Friday, when he heard that we reached it, he called the FIB trust officer and pretended to be Jeff Mackinen. When that didn't work, he threatened and bullied her into wire-transferring the money into the escrow account he had set up to buy his new house in Gardnerville. This guy is a crook."

Being a former escrow officer and manager of an escrow office, Wendi was a detail-oriented person who did things by the book. I knew she wouldn't be making such accusations unless they were true. Bradock indeed had no authorization to sign on the bank accounts.

Now I had a major problem: Should I call the authorities and have him arrested? I was pretty sure that such a course of action would shut down our company. At this point, millions of dollars of hard-earned money from shareholders had been entrusted to me. I began to calculate how much Bradock was actually entitled to as a part of his wholesaler's fee of 2 percent of the amount raised. No matter how I looked at it, though, of the $2.5 million raised to date, he had earned only $50,000, meaning at the very least, he had embezzled $68,000 in cash. *Should I have him arrested and thrown in jail? Should I have the FIB trust officer fired? Should I file a lawsuit against FIB? Or should I try to somehow work around this?* I felt I had little choice but to choose the latter.

I called Bradock and confronted him over the telephone. "What the hell do you think you're doing? How dare you put the company and me in this position? Who gave you the authority to embezzle one hundred and eighteen thousand dollars from the trust account?"

"The company was going to eventually have to pay me anyway, so I went ahead and took it," Bradock replied in an arrogant tone. "The FIB trust officer let me have the money and wired the funds directly into my escrow account, so you should talk to her, not me. I did what I had to do to close escrow on my house. I would have lost my deposit had I not put the money into escrow on Friday. As far as me being a thief, well, I guess you'll just have to prove it, won't you?"

My failure to listen to my gut was coming back to haunt me. Though I was ticked off, I felt I had no choice but to bite the bullet and swallow my pride. At least I had the records to prove he had taken the $118,000 and had it wired to his own account. There would come a time to settle the score, but it had to be on my terms so it wouldn't hurt the company or our shareholders.

After hanging up on Bradock, I called Wendi and Jeff and told them of my decision. While they weren't happy, I explained my position. "If we're to remain in good stead with TWS and finish raising our capital on behalf of investors and members, I have little choice."

From that day forward, we had to be cautious in how we dealt with Bradock, and we had to make certain that he had no access to confidential written materials, computer files, books, or records. This would prove to be nearly impossible, but I had to do everything within my power to control the manipulative crook. Eventually, when we'd raised most, if not all the money for the initial round of funding, we could get rid of him.

> LIFE LESSON #72:
>
> "I SAVED YOU," CRIED THE WOMAN, "AND YOU'VE BIT ME EVEN WHY? YOU KNOW YOUR BITE IS POISONOUS, AND NOW I'M GOING TO DIE." "OH SHUT UP, SILLY WOMAN," SAID THE REPTILE WITH A GRIN. "YOU KNEW DAMN WELL I WAS A SNAKE BEFORE YOU TOOK ME IN."
>
> —LYRICS BY AL WILSON (AMERICAN SOUL SINGER, 1939-2008)

Having the documentation of his actions, I could show TWS and others what he had done and explain that I'd had little choice but to work around him until I could terminate him.

Unfortunately, this was only the beginning of our troubles related to Bradock, who would later swear a vendetta to destroy the Semas family.

In August, I received an odd telephone call from Arthur Hickman, due diligence officer for TWS. They were getting a little concerned that I didn't have more oversight in place. He strongly suggested—or should I say, *demanded*—that if they were going to continue to raise money for us, I needed to hire a CFO immediately. Arthur wanted to fly up to meet with me and look over our books as part of his ongoing due diligence, and they were going to temporarily suspend raising capital for METALAST until he satisfied himself that everything was copasetic.

It seemed coincidental that Arthur was suddenly concerned about this issue. I was highly suspicious that Jim Bradock, Arthur's golf buddy, was behind it.

Arthur came up later that week and spent most of the day going over documents and bank records with a fine-toothed comb. Because he was more concerned about how we were spending money from our bank account, he didn't uncover the $118,000 that Bradock had fraudulently wire-transferred; we'd had little choice but to book his theft in our accounting records as commissions advanced.

Arthur told me that everything seemed to be in order and that he would lift the suspension, although he said that as the company grew, we needed to have tighter controls on expenditures and needed to run the business by the book. He then told me to give him a call when I found a suitable candidate for the CFO position.

We placed an employment ad in the *Reno Gazette Journal*, and I started asking friends and business

---

LIFE LESSON #73:

"PICK AND CHOOSE YOUR BATTLES. DON'T RUSH INTO A FIGHT BUT IMPLEMENT YOUR BATTLE PLAN AT THE RIGHT TIME."

—THE COLONEL

---

associates if they knew of anyone with an advanced accounting degree who might be looking for a job.

Michael Ornelas, a realtor friend of mine, stopped by my Genoa offices a few days later. "I have the perfect candidate," he said. "His name is Dwight Morris (not his real name). I met him while I was selling two custom homes he recently built just down the road in Genoa."

"Can you arrange a meeting?"

"I don't have to, because he's standing outside." Michael opened the door and waved to Morris to come inside.

After Michael left, Morris and I started to talk. Though he was thirty-three years old, with his slight build, Ivy League-style haircut, dental braces, plaid button-down shirt, and penny loafers, he looked like a college student who had just stepped out of Harvard GQ. As it turned out, he'd earned his MBA from Northeastern University and spoke in what I would refer to as a "Kennedy Bostonian" accent. He had worked as an audit clerk and staff public accountant for Price Waterhouse and Deloitte & Touche out of Boston. He was an intellectual type that tried to impress everyone with his highbrow academic vocabulary.

While a little inexperienced, he seemed like a nice young man, and I felt I could help him grow into the position of CFO. We entered into a consulting agreement with him that would convert into full-time employment at the option of the company. Morris seemed like a person that wanted to climb the corporate ladder for the benefit of his wife, Angela, and young daughter, which was admirable.

Within the next few months, I had Morris assist me in tightening up financial controls in the company, particularly with Bradock. I told Morris to be careful around him and explained how he had embezzled more than $100,000 from METALAST and used the money to buy his house. Even after that warning, however, I noticed that he and Bradock were becoming rather chummy. I would have expected

> LIFE LESSON #74:
>
> "AN INTELLECTUAL IS A MAN WHO TAKES MORE WORDS THAN NECESSARY TO TELL MORE THAN HE KNOWS."
>
> —DWIGHT D. EISENHOWER

him to be appalled by Bradock's thievery, but they shared close quarters in our temporary offices.

I'd learned through firsthand experience that Bradock, thanks to his undercover background, was highly skilled in the methods he employed to befriend, put at ease, and manipulate his subordinates, coworkers, and peers. Eventually, Bradock, Morris, and Carl Grunwald began going out to lunch together. A few months later, I would learn they were hatching a plan to take over the company by discrediting me in the eyes of Bradock's friends at TWS. A good friend who just happened to have been sitting in a booth behind the trio at a local restaurant during the lunch hour overheard them gossiping about nearly everyone at the company and boasting amongst themselves how I was clueless about their takeover plans.

Meanwhile, I was busy raising capital, building the MTC, working with Friedline on the MPCS design, and trying to satisfy the concerns of TWS, our biggest NASD broker-dealer. While I was disappointed and somewhat concerned about the disloyal employees plot to mutiny and gain control of the company, I also knew it was the blind leading the blind. A marginal securities broker, upstart bean counter, and a chemist who didn't have a clue on how to run a business as complex as METALAST, nor did they have the support of my board of directors or even shareholders, for that matter. I didn't give the burgeoning relationship too much thought.

By mid-November, we had completed construction of the MTC and moved into the building. The following week, we flew to Newport Beach and held a conference with the key technical and sales members of the company to brainstorm the future goals, priorities, and objectives of METALAST.

LIFE LESSON #75:

"GREAT MINDS DISCUSS IDEAS; AVERAGE MINDS DISCUSS EVENTS; SMALL MINDS DISCUSS PEOPLE."

—ELEANOR ROOSEVELT (FIRST LADY, 1884-1962)

MTC Tech Center

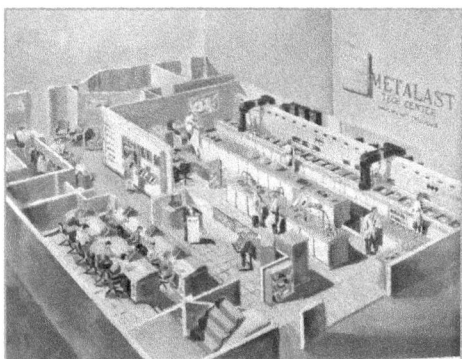

MTC lab rendering

MTC lobby

Upon my return that Monday, Morris told me that Hickman had called while I was away and had said he was shutting down funding for the second time until he could come back for another review of the books and records.

"Don't worry about it," Morris said after I asked him what was going on. "There won't be any problems. I'll handle Arthur when he arrives."

I was apprehensive and suspected they would use this opportunity to sow the seeds of discontent, but I needed for them to make their move. I knew everything was in order, especially since we had implemented better accounting controls. The only way to eventually expose and terminate the takeover conspirators was for them to unwittingly fall into my trap and show their hand to TWS, METALAST board members, and our largest shareholders.

This time when Hickman showed up, he brought along Jonathan McBride, president and CEO of TWS. To my surprise, Morris had scheduled the onsite audit and financial review when I was tied up in meetings all day in Reno. Upon my return late that night, I found out that Morris, Bradock,

Hickman, and McBride had all gone out to dinner. I just assumed I would see Arthur and Jonathan the next morning at the office, but not only did I not see them, I learned later that morning that the four of them had all played golf together. I had been neither informed in advance nor invited.

Late that afternoon, I entered Morris's office. "Where are Arthur and Jonathan?"

Morris looked up from his work and shrugged. "They left."

Again, I was quite surprised. "So how did it go?"

"Not really well." Morris had an odd look on his face—almost a scowl. "I'm sorry, David, but I had to show them how the funds in the early days were misappropriated. I told them that I felt there were very few financial controls in place on how the money was being spent until I came on board. They were very upset and told me to tell you that until I'm given complete signing authority over the bank accounts, with Bradock as a second signatory, all funding will be officially halted."

MTC board room

Here we go. My mouth dropped as I realized I had been set up a little quicker than anticipated. Morris was trying to paint a picture that I had done something wrong even though he knew it was untrue. Before any of the METALAST business entities had been formalized, I had owned all the shares of my predecessor company, Institutional Capital Marketing, Inc. The company had bought the METALAST rights from ICM, and this had been completely disclosed in the private placement offering memorandum. My personal ICM bank records had nothing whatsoever to do with the METALAST company or its shareholders. He and Bradock were using them to falsely claim that I had misappropriated funds from my own company.

Once again, I found myself in a precarious position. If I were to fire Morris and Bradock on the spot, it might look as if I were retaliating, which might give the appearance to Arthur and Jonathan of TWS that I was guilty and had done something wrong.

I began to implement the first phase of my plan in which Morris would soon entrap himself. Then I would take care of Bradock and Grunwald at the appropriate time.

I called Jim Kieckhafer, our METALAST CPA and founder and partner of Kieckhafer & Schiffer, LLP to explain what had happened. I was actually stunned to learn that Morris had the chutzpah to have flown down to Orange County to meet with Jim the week prior and had given him the same story about the ICM bank records, trying to win his support to oust me from the company. Morris was unaware that Jim also oversaw the accounting records for me personally as well as ICM and METALAST and knew that the two companies were separate businesses with different bank accounts and shareholders and no comingling of any kind ever occurred.

That afternoon, I stopped by Morris's office again. "Everything's been straightened out with Arthur Hickman, Jonathan McBride, and TWS, and they've resumed funding," I told him. I played dumb and didn't reveal to him or Bradock that I knew about their scheme to turn my board members and CPA against me.

Within several weeks, Morris came to me and said that with all the liability and responsibility involved in being the CFO, he felt he was entitled to a raise.

"Well, Dwight," I said, "you're the CFO and have every right to give yourself a raise." This was a setup on my part that I would soon use against him. I would only provide the rope by which he would metaphorically hang himself.

He promptly did so by increasing his salary by a whopping 50 percent. Thus emboldened, he began signing checks for more than $10,000 without my approval and without a second signature, which was against company policy. I knew once Arthur and Jonathan heard the truth that I personally owned 100 percent of ICM, and that our CPA could confirm that Morris had flown to Orange County to meet him to attempt to gain control of the company, I was ready to make my next move.

It was snowing on Monday, February 5, 1996, at the MTC when I called Morris into my office. I informed him that I knew about the sneaky, unethical actions he had taken to try to gain control of the company. He was in shock, thinking there was no way I would fire him in the middle of fundraising. Though he denied every accusation, I found his Academy Award-winning performance unconvincing. After administering a thirty-minute ass-chewing, I fired him on the spot and had him escorted from the building carrying his personal belongings with him in a bankers box with his tale between his legs.

Later that day, Bradock, hearing the scuttlebutt that Morris had been escorted out, and seeing his world quickly collapsing around him, apologized to me for his bad behavior and dishonesty, swearing that he would turn over a new leaf if I would give him one more chance.

I didn't believe a word that came out of his mouth, but I shook his hand and said, "All is forgiven." Unfortunately, Bradock still had a good relationship with the TWS executives, our primary broker/dealer. TWS had raised all investment capital from our private placement offering, so I was forced to tread lightly until the time was right. Then I patiently waited for what I guessed would only be a few months for the real Bradock to show his face again.

In the summer of 1996, about six months after I'd fired Morris, Bradock boldly challenged me during one of our Tuesday-morning staff meetings. "Has anyone ever gone to Mr. Mitani's plant in Tokyo to witness the METALAST process?" he demanded. "Here we've spent millions of dollars, and no one has cared enough to conduct due diligence on the technology in Japan."

I shook my head at his idiotic statement. "We didn't buy his factory in Japan. We acquired the rights to his anodizing process. This is not about Mr. Mitani and his anodizing factory or whether it works in his operation in Japan, which it obviously did. It's about the viability of a process that works in America and that we can one day license around the world."

This was the last straw. I had heard rumblings that Bradock and Morris had not only contacted

> **LIFE LESSON #76:**
>
> **"KEEP YOUR FRIENDS CLOSE; KEEP YOUR ENEMIES CLOSER."**
>
> —SUN TZU (CHINESE STRATEGIST, GENERAL, AND PHILOSOPHER, 544–496 BC)

NASD broker-dealers, shareholders, and potential investors, they had gone to the Securities and Exchange Commission (SEC), the office for the secretary of the state of Nevada, and the criminal division of the IRS. They were certainly leaving no stone unturned in their efforts to smear me, have me removed as manager, and bring all the progress we were making as a company to a screeching halt.

Just a few days after the staff meeting, on Friday, July 26, 1996, my brother Len, METALAST's executive vice president, strongly encouraged Bradock to "voluntarily" resign. At this point, Bradock had little choice because of his earlier embezzlement. In his letter of resignation, he stated, *I find I am unable to continue to meet the requirements of my position.* I gazed out the window of my upper-story office and watched with satisfaction as he was escorted to his car carrying his banker box of belongings.

Len Semas, 2000

Within hours of his forced resignation, I turned over all documents relating to his $118,000 embezzlement to the Douglas County Sheriff's Office for arrest and the district attorney's office for prosecution. Unfortunately, because I had waited so long to file charges, and he had continued to be employed by METALAST for a year beyond the incident, the district attorney elected not to prosecute—but not before the Douglas County Sheriff's Office came knocking at his door. From that day forward, Bradock and I became mortal enemies.

By the time Bradock left the company in July 1996, Friedline had completed the development of the MPCS '95, our process control computer, and it was now fully operational. My solely owned company, METALAST International, Inc. filed for a USPTO registration on the METALAST® trademark. We debuted the METALAST technology with our first-generation MPCS in our impressive trade show booth at the annual Surface

Finishing Conference held in Cleveland, Ohio. The conference, produced by the American Electroplaters and Surface Finishers Society, serves as the metal-finishing industry's premiere convention, with attendance of about 20,000.

During the four-day extravaganza, metal-finishing job shops, manufacturers, chemical company executives, equipment suppliers, and engineers attended seminars and technical presentations held in breakout sessions. Others walked the floor of the convention hall, viewing the latest and greatest products and technologies. The word had spread about our anodizing technical center in Nevada, and as a result, there was quite a buzz about METALAST. The trade show would pave the way for us to license several companies, including Universal Metal Finishing of Chicago. My brother and I became fast friends with Charlie Roberts, UMF's founder. Charlie was a great guy with a terrific sense of humor and a go-make-it-happen work ethic.

We had fine-tuned our automated process line and began processing parts and conducting R&D at the MTC rather than our Hixson/METALAST lab. Our R&D team was making progress in expanding our technology and developing new MPCS recipes for many aluminum alloys. We began R&D work with Ford Motors and Applied Materials, and the technical staff was working closely with three licensees. By this time, we had purchased 75 percent of the worldwide rights to the METALAST® technology, including all anodizing recipes and chemical formulations. We asked for the chemical formulations, Mr. Mitani handed them over, and soon we began to manufacture our own version, called the METALAST® AA-100 additive. A few years later, we created a more stable and improved version: METALAST® AA-200. I renegotiated our contract with Mr. Mitani and his company, Soken Kako, four separate times until the fall of 1996, when we acquired 100 percent of the worldwide rights to METALAST and the goodwill that came with it.

LIFE LESSON #77:

"YOU HAVE ENEMIES? GOOD. THAT MEANS YOU'VE STOOD UP FOR SOMETHING SOMETIME IN YOUR LIFE."

—SIR WINSTON CHURCHILL

Finally, the employee distractions and hostile elements in the company seemed to have been corrected. Susan and I hadn't taken a real vacation in three years, so I surprised her when I booked a ten-day cruise aboard the luxury Royal Caribbean cruise ship *Legends of the Seas*. Unveiled to much fanfare in 1995, the 1,800-passenger, 720-crew, 867-foot-long, 70,000-ton luxury liner was the first of six ships in Royal Caribbean's successful Vision Class series.

It was a beautiful late-summer afternoon in Reno when we departed on Friday, September 13, 1996, from McCarran International Airport for Vancouver, British Columbia. As we were on our final approach, we could see the golden lights of Vancouver's downtown historic Gastown District glowing against the backdrop of the city streets. Upon our arrival, we checked in to the magnificently restored St. Regis Hotel, which was located only a few blocks away from the Gastown District and the cruise ship terminal where we would be departing that Sunday.

For the next two days, we enjoyed the sights and sounds of downtown Vancouver and were eager to board *Legends of the Seas*. We set sail Sunday morning, September 15, slowly departing from English Bay, through the Strait of Georgia, then on to the Strait of Juan de Fuca, and finally out to the open waters of the Pacific Ocean. The romantic ocean voyage covered 2,600 nautical miles, and with a cruising speed of 25 knots, or 29 miles per hour, it took four days to reach the Hawaiian Islands. We anchored in the ports of Honolulu, Lahaina, and finally Hilo and even had time to play a round of golf. Throughout our cruise ship adventure, the food was a sheer epicurean delight. We enjoyed the sun and made a few friends, and I even ended up winning $8,000—nearly enough to pay for the trip—playing blackjack.

Legends of the Sea, 1996

Susan and I with the captain of Legends of the Sea, 1996

> **LIFE LESSON #78:**
>
> "IN TIMES OF STRESS OR ADVERSITY, IT'S ALWAYS BEST TO KEEP BUSY, TO PLOW YOUR ANGER AND YOUR ENERGY INTO SOMETHING POSITIVE."
>
> —LEE IACOCCA

While on vacation, I began to feel concerned that although we were making progress proving the METALAST process and exposing our technology to more OEMs, such as Chrysler, General Motors, NASA, and Westinghouse, we had only added two more licensees to our network. We had increased the size of our technical staff, hired two more distinguished scientists—Dr. Sjon Westre and his wife, Dr. Tami Westre—and added six salesmen to represent METALAST in strategically located regions around the country. We also recruited my friend, Byron Estes, the former PMF executive and a thirty-year veteran of anodizing. With the added staffing and growing operational expenses, we were going to need to raise a lot more money than expected. Indeed, our payroll was now approaching $2 million annually.

We brought another private placement offering (PPO) to the market for $21 million, and Arthur Hickman of TWS agreed to sell the PPO, even introducing me to the thirteen NASD broker-dealers' firms of the Nationwide Financial Network (NFN). The group of broker-dealers had 2,000 registered representatives who would likely raise all the money for us. The one caveat to signing up with such an impressive network of money-raisers was that METALAST would be required to engage the services of Marshall E. Talbot & Co. to conduct a due diligence review of our company, technology, and management.

> **LIFE LESSON #80:**
>
> "RUMOR TRAVELS FASTER, BUT IT DOESN'T STAY PUT AS LONG AS TRUTH."
>
> —WILL ROGERS (AMERICAN ACTOR, HUMORIST, COWBOY, AND POET, 1879-1935)

As it turned out, Mr. Talbot's fifty-page report stated, "Metaphorically speaking, this is truly a classic example of 'build it and they will come.' President and CEO Semas is to be congratulated on the fine job he has done in creating a first-class research and development facility and assembling an impressive staff of employees."

"David," Hickman said, "I've known Marshall for twenty years, and that's one of the most complimentary due diligence reports I've ever read by him. Now that you have most of the lies and false rumors behind you, I'd like to recommend a gentleman by the name of Nic Pilger. You should interview him to become your NASD broker-dealer wholesaler because you will need one."

By the end of the year, we received formal approval by the United States Patent and Trademark Office (USPTO), and METALAST® International, Inc. (MII) was awarded a registered trademark. My personal company MII owned the trademark, so without charging royalties of any kind, I licensed the trademark to the operating company METALAST International, LLC (MILLC). I only required MILLC to pay the minimal legal costs and filing fees of about $2,000 per year to maintain the trademark with the USPTO.

At the recommendation of Hickman, we hired the highly experienced and well-respected broker/dealer wholesale professional, Nic Pilger, and he started making calls to his broker-dealer friends around the country. It helped that we were armed with the Marshall Talbot report, but in nearly every instance, as Nic spoke with prospective securities firms to assist in raising the $21 million PPO, he was met with resistance because they had heard Bradock's false rumors of corporate misappropriation, malfeasance, and fraud.

For the next six weeks, I was either in joint meetings with Nic or on the telephone defending the company and my innocence. Time and time again, I had to explain what had actually happened. We ultimately raised about $12 million. To this day, I still don't know how many broker-dealers chose not to offer our securities just because of the hassle and controversy, but that was just something we had to overcome.

LIFE LESSON #79:

"THE TRUTH IS INCONTROVERTIBLE. MALICE MAY ATTACK IT, AND IGNORANCE MAY DERIDE IT, BUT IN THE END, THERE IT IS."

—SIR WINSTON CHURCHILL

CHAPTER 12

RUDE AWAKENING TO AN IRS NIGHTMARE

METALAST was making headway, our staff seemed to be getting along well, there was enthusiasm and excitement in the air, and all seemed calm when, early on a Wednesday morning in February 1998, I woke to hear the coyotes howling as if they had some poor, unsuspecting critter in their grasp. I jumped out of bed and looked out the window to see what was happening, but in the darkness, I saw only the shadows of my Jeffrey pine trees swaying in the cold, brisk Lake Tahoe-fed winds. It seemed like a typical morning. I had no way of knowing that what awaited me would be anything but typical.

IRS Criminal Investigation Special Agent badge

I turned on the light and pulled on my sweatpants and slippers. After throwing cold water on my face, I shuffled into the kitchen to brew a pot of coffee. Then I strolled across the fieldstone entry hall to the front door and turned on the porch light to see if my *Reno Gazette Journal* had been delivered. As I peered through the door's etched-glass window and down the length of my driveway, I took a long, hard look to make certain that the

LIFE LESSON #81:

"IT'S A GOOD IDEA TO MAKE CERTAIN A PESKY MOUNTAIN LION ISN'T LURKING ABOUT WHEN YOU GO OUT TO GET THE PAPER."

—DAVID SEMAS

pesky mountain lion that sometimes strolled past my home before dawn wasn't lurking nearby.

All appeared to be clear, so I stepped outside, walked down my driveway about fifty feet, and picked up the newspaper. Turning my gaze to the sky, I took in the millions of stars that glistened above the snowcapped mountains. The glowing moon looked like it had come straight out of an Ansel Adams photograph.

I had purchased our rustic stone and cedar-shingled Lake Tahoe-style custom home from my good friend, Raleigh Finkelstein. At 4,200 square feet, it was located just off the seventh fairway of the Genoa Lakes Golf Course, about a mile north of the sleepy little town of Genoa (population 939). Up here at 4,800 feet, directly beneath the 10,000-foot-high peaks of the Sierra Nevada mountains, the air was clean and the constellations bright in the dark sky. I no longer missed Southern California, with its crowds, smog, and glaring city lights that obscured the stars.

Our home on Aspen Drive in Genoa, Nevada, 1998

Genoa Lakes Golf Course in the Carson Valley

A few years earlier, I had moved my company to the nearby town of Minden, just a few miles away from Genoa. I'd relocated to the area from Newport Beach so that Susan and I could enjoy a better quality of life in the high desert, with its wide-open spaces and breathtaking views, while at the same time being able to leave the hustle and bustle of our home state of California. Susan was still living in the master-planned community of Irvine, about forty-five miles south of Los Angeles, with her two young sons, Jordan and Derek, and commuting to Minden about once a month, so I spent many of my mornings in quiet solitude.

Susan and her sons, L-R, Jordan and Derek, 1994

Me and Susan at the Nevada Governor's Ball, 1996

After retrieving the newspaper, I began my typical morning routine. I made toast, spread on a little apple butter, and sat down with the newspaper. Around five-thirty, I turned on the television to Reno ABC-KOLO Channel 8 News and watched my favorite morning anchor, Karen Reuter—wife of Lars Perry, one of our corporate attorneys—to catch up on the news, weather, and local happenings. A little after six o'clock, I made my first telephone call to Ted Ozaki in Tokyo, sixteen hours ahead. After wrapping up my business calls, I headed for the gym I had set up in the garage to begin my daily workout.

After lifting some light weights for about a half hour, I had just stepped onto the treadmill when the telephone rang. I picked up the handset and heard the voice of Melinda, my highly competent secretary, on the other end of the line.

At first, she sounded calm. "David, good morning. When are you coming in?"

I glanced at the clock. "I'll probably be at the office around nine-thirty."

"That's not quite good enough," she replied, her voice suddenly sounding tense. "I need you to come in now."

"Relax, Melinda. I'll be there in about an hour or so."

"I really need you to come in immediately."

By this time, I knew that something was seriously wrong. "Is everything all right?"

"Not really." Melinda, normally cool and calm, sounded like she was almost in tears.

It's amazing how fast our minds can switch into fast-forward and begin imagining the worst. I thought that maybe the building was on fire, or an armed gunman was holding her hostage, or an employee had thrown a temper tantrum and quit the company—something that wouldn't have been too unusual. As I had learned the hard way we'd had several bad apples that worked for us, self-important—real prima donnas and troublemakers.

Realizing that I probably wouldn't be finishing my workout, I grabbed a towel and wrapped it around my neck. "Okay, Melinda, calm down and tell me what the problem is."

She paused before blurting out, "There are eleven armed federal agents standing in front of me with the Criminal Investigation Division of the Internal Revenue Service confiscating files, books, and computers. They're taking employees into separate rooms to interrogate them privately. Special Agent John Heeran is standing right next to me and told me to tell you that he wants to see you here at the building immediately."

I suddenly felt a little lightheaded and sat down on the weight bench. Although caught off-guard by the news, I was well aware that Bradock and Morris had been running amuck. Apparently, they had carried out one of their threats, which had been to go to the IRS.

Shortly after their terminations a few years earlier, Bradock and Morris had begun to hatch a plan under the auspices of the IRS Whistleblower Law, which was originally meant to protect a person who is truthfully alleging misconduct, corruption, failure to pay taxes, or some other violation of federal tax law. I was fairly certain they were the ones behind the

IRS raid, because they had been bragging around town that it was just a matter of time before the IRS came calling.

I thanked Melinda for the heads-up and returned to my office. Not being prone to panic, I first called Lars Perry, our corporate counsel, and told him what had happened.

"Go to the office to meet with the IRS agent," he advised. "I'll stop by the federal courthouse to see if I can get a copy of the affidavit and search warrant filed with the magistrate judge. Once the affidavit is filed with the court, it can sometimes remain unsealed for a short period of time."

Next, I called my brother, Len. At first, he sounded dumbfounded by the news, but he was well aware of the vindictive nature of Bradock and didn't seem too surprised.

"Can you pick me up and drive me to the office?" I asked.

"What's wrong?" His voice rose a notch. "How come you're not going yourself?"

"Len, it's okay. Calm down. There's nothing to be alarmed about. I don't want to drive in case they arrest me on the spot."

"But I thought you didn't do anything wrong."

"I didn't, Len, but we don't know what the people responsible for this might have told the IRS. Who knows what could happen?" By this time in my career, I had seen a lot of things, so nothing much surprised me. I knew I hadn't done anything wrong, and our financial records and bank accounts were impeccably maintained, so I was able to keep my head. "I'm sure the two culprits behind this charade are Bradock and Morris. If Lars is successful in getting the affidavit, we'll know if my suspicions are correct."

When Len and I pulled up to the two-story METALAST Tech Center a half hour later, I saw a large number of unfamiliar vehicles

---

LIFE LESSON #82:

"TRY TO STAY CALM, COOL, AND COL-LECTED IN THE HEAT OF BATTLE. WORRYING DOESN'T SOLVE ANYTHING, NOR DOES IT MAKE A PROBLEM GO AWAY."

—BEN SWIG

parked out front and people carrying boxes from the front door to a large white van.

As Len and I approached the office entrance, an armed federal agent opened the door and said, "Can I help you?"

"My name is David Semas," I said. "I'm the chairman and CEO of METALAST, International, Inc., and manager of METALAST International, LLC."

I was whisked through the empty reception area toward the second-floor conference room while another agent escorted Len downstairs.

"Special Agent Heeran is waiting for you," my escort informed me. "Please don't talk to any of your employees. We're interviewing them as well."

As we took the stairs, I saw unfamiliar individuals walking the hallways, sitting at computers, and packing boxes. I wondered where all my employees were.

Inside the conference room, a small, slight, gray-haired gentleman around sixty years old stood at the head of the table, studying some files. His briefcase lay on the table before him. He looked up as we entered. "Come on in and sit down. I'm Special Agent Heeran." His badge was prominently displayed and hung from the pocket of his sports coat, and his firearm hung at his side. "Mr. Semas, we have a court order here to interview you and confiscate books and records at this facility. We have eleven agents here on site interviewing your employees separately. We're not making any specific allegations at this point. Your employees know that the IRS is conducting a criminal federal tax evasion investigation."

"My legal counsel is on the way," I informed him.

While I waited for my attorney to arrive, Heeran and the other agent left me alone for an agonizing forty-five minutes. When Lars showed up, he was smartly dressed in a suit and his hair was neatly combed, as usual. He was smiling from ear to ear, which, given the circumstances and considering my predicament, I found a little odd.

"I got it," he said. "I was able to get a faxed copy of the Application and Affidavit for Search Warrant. And yes, you were one hundred percent right. Page after page, you can read references to IRS whistleblowers Jim Bradock and Dwight Morris. By the way, you should take notice that this warrant also gives the IRS the right to search and seize records, files, and the computer hard drive from your personal office in Genoa and from your home, which they've probably already done."

Lars handed me my copy of the IRS affidavit and search warrant, and I began to read the eleven-page document from front to back. At first, I was flabbergasted. However, I knew that Jim Bradock, in particular, was a manipulative, backstabbing individual who had honed his deceitful talents for seven years as a former undercover DEA agent. After all, according to my former father-in-law, who had served as the captain of detectives for the Santa Clara Police Department for twenty-eight years, if you're an undercover agent and not a good liar, you're likely a dead agent. The affidavit even referenced Bradock's past affiliation as an undercover agent, which he had no doubt used to establish credibility with Special Agent Heeran.

In the past few years, I had gotten to know Bradock for who he really was: a man who would do anything, including cheat, lie, and steal, to accomplish his objectives. Sometimes he didn't even care if you knew. His attitude was always, "Prove it!" From what I had seen, I wouldn't have been surprised to learn that many an unsuspecting drug dealer had served jail time as a result of Bradock's planting of evidence.

As I finished reading the affidavit, I felt my temperature rise. I looked up at Lars and said, "This is the most unbelievable pack of lies I've ever read. There isn't a shred of truth to anything in this document. After what appears to have been months of investigation, how could Special Agent Heeran be so gullible as to believe these lies without one piece of corroborating evidence? Where is the smoking gun?"

The affidavit alleged that of the initial $2.5 million of investment capital we had raised for METALAST in July 1995, "most of the funds appeared to have been spent on personal expenses for Semas." The document claimed that I had illegally stolen and sold hundreds of thousands of dollars of the company's treasury stock to buy my Genoa Lakes home. It claimed that I had millions stashed away in offshore bank accounts, that I had misappropriated millions of dollars, and that I lived a "very high and lavish lifestyle." The report made the ridiculous claim that the METALAST® technology was a farce and a scam, that our anodizing and computer control process systems didn't work, and that we had lied about licensing metal finishers.

From front to back, this so-called sworn affidavit was nothing more than innuendo, misrepresentations, and lies, which had been used to cause a federal magistrate to issue an unsubstantiated search-and-seizure warrant.

I shook my head in disgust. "The only thing missing from the affidavit is that I was the lone gunman on the grassy knoll at JFK's assassination."

Moments later, Agent Heeran opened the door and stepped into the conference room. When he saw that I held a copy of the complaint, he asked, "What are you looking at there? Did you go into my briefcase? How dare you!" He pointed to the briefcase still sitting on the table.

Lars quickly responded, "Calm down, Agent Heeran. I obtained a copy of the affidavit from the court prior to the document being sealed."

Heeran relaxed when he realized he had jumped to conclusions. He sat down at the conference table and asked, "Did you have time to read it? Do you have any comments?"

By that time, I was furious at the way I had been humiliated, especially in front of my employees. "Agent Heeran," I replied in a harsh tone, "the only thing that's accurate about this pile of garbage is likely your name and title. How does it feel to know that you've been duped into providing a federal judge with false testimony based on the outright lies of two former dishonest METALAST employees? Without the slightest bit of evidence or documented support, you have potentially destroyed a man's reputation and business career. You can take these documents and shove them where the sun doesn't shine."

Agent Heeran jumped to his feet and rested his hand on top of his gun. "I am a federal agent of the Criminal Investigation Division of the IRS." He turned to Lars. "You'd better get control of your client. I will not be spoken to in this manner."

Once Agent Heeran and I had both calmed down, we started going over the allegations contained in the affidavit, one by one.

"Did you misappropriate $2.5 million of METALAST corporate funds?" Heeran asked.

"No."

LIFE LESSON #83:

"NEVER LOSE YOUR TEMPER WITH AN IRS AGENT, ESPECIALLY AN ARMED ONE!"

—DAVID SEMAS

"Did you instruct Morris not to deduct federal taxes from your paycheck?"

"No."

"Did you sell corporate stock to buy your home in Genoa in 1995?"

"No."

"Did you use METALAST corporate funds to pay off your debts?"

"No."

"Did you pay your federal taxes on money you earned or received in any way?"

"Yes."

During the questioning, Agent Heeran proceeded to make what I thought was an unusual statement. "Mr. Semas, I don't care if you misappropriated, stole, or embezzled millions of dollars. I only care if you paid taxes on the money you misappropriated, stole, or embezzled."

I looked up at him and said, "The only one who has misappropriated, stolen, or embezzled money from METALAST is Jim Bradock, and the only ones who have lied to you are Bradock and Morris. I guarantee you, at the end of all this, I will be vindicated and owed an apology, which I doubt I'll receive."

For several hours, Agent Heeran went on to ask innumerable and highly intrusive questions about my background, education, family, bank accounts, investments, cash on hand, vehicles, homes, and other assets. Lars made it clear that the agent had every right to ask the questions and that I needed to be cooperative and not antagonistic. Once I settled down, I realized that this guy had been lied to and duped just like I had. I'm certain that in his mind, I was a liar and a crook. He was sure that he had himself a real culprit here—a thief and embezzler who had stolen funds, shirked his taxes, and lived a lavish lifestyle. As the hours passed, I wondered if he was going to arrest me.

Finally, after thoroughly ransacking the METALAST offices, the IRS agents had gathered up everything they wanted, and IRS Special Agent Heeran had asked all his questions. He turned to me and said, "Mr. Semas, we'll be back in touch with you." Then he and his fellow agents hurried back out the door to the vans, Crown Victorias, and black Chevrolet Suburbans clustered in the front parking lot.

Realizing that I wasn't being arrested, I stood up from the conference table and moved to the window to watch the vehicles pull away. I was amazed by the amount of planning, preparation, and coordination that must have gone into what I considered a witch hunt. I was certain that Bradock, Morris, and others were relishing the thought that, like the notorious Al Capone, I might be arrested for criminal tax evasion. That would put them in the ideal position to rejoin METALAST and take over the business—something they had tried to do in the past. I still found it hard to believe that I was being subjected to what most American citizens would deem Gestapo tactics.

I'm innocent and have done nothing wrong, I thought. *I can't believe this is happening to me.* We ran our company in an ethical and professional manner, with every dime accounted for. Yet in the eyes of the IRS, I was guilty until proven innocent.

How did this happen? I wondered. *What do I do now? If I could only turn back the clock.* I began to recall my gratifying successes and numerous failures as a young businessman in Santa Clara County.

Over the next few months, Special Agent Heeran was in constant contact with Lars, asking more questions and demanding more answers from me. It was becoming painfully obvious that Bradock and Morris were liars, and I had been telling the truth all along. Indeed, they hadn't found a shred of evidence to support a single allegation contained in the affidavit. Eight months later, the IRS returned our files and records, and a year later, I received a letter stating, "You are no longer the subject of a criminal investigation of the Internal Revenue Service. However, the agency reserves its right to reinvestigate this matter at a future date."

When all was said and done, this costly exercise, which had harmed not only my professional and personal reputation, but also the METALAST name brand as well, was nothing more than a witch hunt—a colossal waste of time, effort, and money. According to the sworn affidavit and search warrant

---

LIFE LESSON #84:

"TRUTH IS GENER-
ALLY THE BEST
VINDICATION
AGAINST SLANDER."

—ABRAHAM LINCOLN

---

requested by IRS Special Agent Heeran, issued by US District Magistrate Judge Phyllis Halsey Akins on February 13, 1998, Special Agent Heeran in his career "had conducted, assisted, and coordinated over seventy-five criminal tax investigations." Of the seventy-five, only two had resulted in no fines, penalties, or actions being taken against the target company. The investigation into me and METALAST was one of those two.

I never received a formal apology and was told by Lars that the IRS does not give them. The letter from Special Agent Heeran concluding their intrusive investigation into my personal and business affairs merely stated, "You are no longer the subject of an investigation." That was the closest I would come to ever receiving an apology.

LIFE LESSON #85:

"IF YOU CAN'T STAND THE HEAT, GET OUT OF THE KITCHEN."

—HARRY S. TRUMAN (THIRTY-THIRD PRESIDENT OF THE UNITED STATES, 1884-1972)

CHAPTER 13

THE BREAKTHROUGH MOMENT

Finally, it appeared I could focus on the company again. Many issues with our business model had to be resolved. The METALAST technology and the MPCS process controller were working as advertised, and manufacturers were impressed by the technology's ability to reduce rejects and improve quality and consistency. But the job shops and metal finishers themselves were not coming on board as we had hoped they would. We were generating modest revenue because a great deal of the R&D and sample processing that we provided to OEMs and manufacturers was free of charge. Until METALAST was further established in the eyes of the manufacturing community, Fortune 500 companies were not going to purchase our products or services in large numbers.

Meanwhile, as is the case with most young R&D companies, the need for more capital continued to grow. With all the new hires in the lab and technical, engineering, and sales departments, the cash necessary to operate the business had increased to $2.75 million in 1996, then $3.5 million in 1997, and was now running about $4 million annually. This was in addition to the $3 million used to purchase the technology in the first place, the $2 million needed to build the METALAST Tech Center, and the brokerage commissions and various legal, accounting, and marketing fees.

By the first quarter of 1999, we decided the time had come to increase our technical capabilities by hiring a team of research scientists skilled in the area of inorganic chemistry. After months of interviewing, we selected two husband-and-wife teams from China and helped them get their work visas through Canada.

To say that Dr. Shi Hua Zhang and his wife, Lynn, and Dr. Ling Hao and his wife, Dr. Rachael Chang, were brilliant scientists would be a gross understatement. Not only were these research scientists extremely talented in their field of chemistry and chemical engineering, but they were dedicated, loyal, hardworking, and creative. Over the course of six years, the team, as a group and individually, authored thirty technical papers and helped us submit for six research grants. They were major contributing factors in developing breakthrough chemistries for METALAST and became valuable personnel assets during our early growth years. Dr. Shi Hua Zhang eventually left METALAST when he was offered a senior technical position at Apple. Dr. Ling Hao became a senior scientist at Lacks Enterprises, an advanced automotive component manufacturer in Grand Rapids, Michigan.

We had already invested about $30 million in the venture, and it didn't appear we were anywhere near the halfway mark. This meant that our efforts to become the technology provider to the metal-finishing industry would cost $75 million or more. We desperately needed something greater than a handful of customers to make this a success.

To help me determine how to gain more acceptance of the METALAST brand in the market, I decided it was time to go on the road with our six regional sales managers (RSMs) to spend a few days with each of them calling on existing accounts and meeting with prospective customers. The idea was for me to hear firsthand what our RSMs were up against and see how I might be able to develop ideas and implement solutions, even if it meant that we needed to expand our product line and reinvent our business model.

One by one, over a five-week period, I met with anodizers from around the country. I asked questions and listened to responses. We ended up licensing four more job shops, but more importantly, we learned something very valuable from the job shop owners we met.

ElectroCal Plating in Cleveland, Ohio was one such job shop. President Harry Crowell was an articulate, well-dressed young man in his late thirties whose father had run the shop before him. He kindly gave us a tour of his facility—something most job shop owners will not do because of confidentiality concerns—and then brought us into his executive office decorated with golf memorabilia. ElectroCal was a successful $10 million plater, meaning Harry probably made $2million in profit each year.

Eric Tocco, my RSM for the Cleveland territory, and I spoke with Harry about his view on transitioning to METALAST technologies. Eric was an electrical engineer by trade and was a talented sales professional. He was quite affable, and our customers found him to be highly knowledgeable, supportive, and a team player.

"We've been doing this for a long time," Harry said. "The bottom line is, you may have a great system, but we don't want to invest the capital in these kinds of changes unless our customers tell us to do it."

Once again, the proverbial lightbulb went on. He was telling me what every other job shop manager had been telling me over that five-week period. They were doing things the same way their fathers and grandfathers had done them. They did well, and their customers were happy. They were in no rush to modernize or do things differently. This was a breakthrough moment. I finally understood.

It had become painfully clear that just because our product improved quality, reduced rejects, accelerated the anodizing process, provided process verification, and was cheaper, better, faster, and more efficient, it didn't mean the masses were going to buy it or sign up for a licensing model. Until the manufacturers themselves demanded the use of METALAST

LIFE LESSON #86:

"OUTSTANDING LEADERS GO OUT OF THEIR WAY TO BOOST THE SELF-ESTEEM OF THEIR PERSONNEL. IF PEOPLE BELIEVE IN THEMSELVES, IT'S AMAZING WHAT THEY CAN ACCOMPLISH."

—SAM WALTON (AMERICAN BUSINESSMAN AND FOUNDER OF WALMART STORES, 1918-1992)

products and services, the job shops were going to conduct business the same way they had for many years.

During my flight back from Cleveland, I realized I had to do something about the challenging problem facing my company. It was easier said than done to convince thousands of manufacturers around the country that they needed to tell their metal finishers to modernize and incorporate METALAST technology.

I did have a few ideas. For instance, we could hold seminars at the MTC—maybe even go on the road and hold small metal-finishing forums, where we could invite manufacturers close to their own corporate offices to learn about the benefits. But who to contact in these huge companies? What incentive was there to drive five miles to sit for a one-hour seminar, which they would likely view as a self-serving METALAST infomercial? I mulled this over on the plane while I sipped my drink and stared at the expansive farmland far below.

It wasn't enough to identify the roadblocks to our success. After making a $30 million investment, we had to figure out a way to make it work. Having learned a considerable amount in the field with our RSMs, I returned home to begin work on a new game plan that would address some of the inherent problems I saw with our business model.

Over the next few weeks, I formed the opinion that if we were to be taken seriously by manufacturers, job shops, and captive facilities (those that anodize their own products), we would have to offer more than just a licensing model, a process control computer, and a chemical additive that served only the domestic aluminum anodizing business. Anodizing represented less than 10 percent of the much larger $10 billion global and $1 billion domestic electrochemical processing and metal-finishing business, which included all types of plating, such as gold, silver, brass, nickel, cadmium, tin and chrome.

My senior staff and I agreed that if we were to succeed, we had to broaden our target market and vertically integrate into other disciplines involved in metal-finishing. To gain the attention of the large OEMs, we had to offer a broad range of products and services designed to help improve the quality, consistency, and reliability of their products. We had to move METALAST into a different direction, making it into more than a metal anodizing company. It was a process that would take time.

I believed the first step was to further broaden our manufacturing capabilities and move into the metal-finishing equipment business by forming a strategic alliance with an equipment manufacturer of automated wet process lines for the metal-finishing industry. We had discussed this idea previously at the annual conventions with Tom Phelps (not his real name), president and majority owner of Automated Process Lines, Inc. (APS), a well-respected and regarded precision equipment manufacturer of wet process lines.

LIFE LESSON #87:

"BEWARE OF THOSE THAT TELL YOU HOW HONEST THEY ARE, BECAUSE THERE IS NO NEED TO STATE WHAT IS FACT, ONLY FICTION."

—THE COLONEL

Tom was a degreed mechanical engineer, hands-on manager, and kind man whose word was his bond. Joe Conack (not his real name), Tom's junior partner, was a chemical engineer who had spent his last fifteen years in metal-finishing and equipment. While Joe appeared knowledgeable and technically savvy, his selling style was more along the lines of a used car salesman. He would always start off by telling a few jokes, touting how honest he was, and then lay on the charm. He said everything we wanted to hear, but we worried about his ability to deliver later.

Bill Campbell

We officially formed the METALAST-APS partnership in the summer of 1999 and trained APS personnel about our line of products. Joe Conack, meanwhile, began meeting with the METALAST regional sales managers, including my nephew, Bill Campbell, our newest and talented RSM. Bill had been involved in the auto-dealership business as a customer-support manager and service manager and had great people skills. He jumped into the role as a West Coast RSM

Jordan Woods

with both feet and for the first year invested countless hours learning about our products and services. Over the years, Bill matured into one of the top, if not *the* top, RSMs for METALAST.

Eventually, Bill and my stepson, Jordan Woods, became RSMs for the Western United States. Jordan actually spent one year in the lab working with Dr. Alp Manavbasi, vice president of technology. Jordan also worked closely with Keith Johnson, a senior anodizing specialist, to learn all aspects of chemistry, anodizing, and corrosion-control products. Jordan had natural sales and marketing abilities; people were immediately drawn to his cordial and courteous manner. After one year in the lab, he became one of the most technically savvy RSMs for METALAST. Bill and Jordan had come into their own and were maturing into top notch sales professionals.

Wendi Semas

I was very proud of the outstanding job my daughter Wendi was doing as vice president of accounting and investor relations. In addition to her accounting responsibilities, she did a fabulous job of keeping our METALAST LLC members fully informed. Wendi and her assistant Allison Young were greatly admired and respected by all.

Greg Semas

As I had done twenty-five years earlier in the construction business, Greg moved his way from working on an anodizing line, to a laboratory technician, to field salesman, to regional sales manager to national sales manager. In 2004, he became vice president of sales and marketing and the department head responsible for the tremendous success of the award-winning T-REX mobile marketing campaign. Eventually he became senior vice president of operations. He matured into a sales and marketing professional and inspirational team leader and business executive

To identify a suitable business opportunity at the right time is much like finding a needle in a haystack—even if you're willing to change directions, modify your business model, and adapt to setbacks and delays. You might have to start down fifty different pathways with twenty separate forks in the road before you ever find your way through. There really is no shortcut. It takes hard work, diligence, vision, commitment, and being at the right place at the right time. I've always believed that you make your own luck by what you do or fail to do, but there is also much to be said about old-fashioned good fortune and timing.

Building a business can be a tedious process, so you must surround yourself with competent and motivated employees that want to be part of a team that strives for excellence. You can buy buildings, lease office space, develop new and exciting products, and advertise and promote your products in the marketplace. At the end of the day, the number-one asset in any company is its work force and how you, as its leader, motivate and inspire confidence in all your employees.

Though 1999 proved to be an ongoing struggle for METALAST, I enjoyed many positive and life-altering changes at home. On August 28, Susan and I were married on a magnificent thirty-four-acre hillside parcel of land we had purchased in the high desert of Gardnerville, Nevada. Two year-round creeks flowed right through the property, joining in a beautiful grove of 2,000 aspen trees surrounded by pine trees, boulders, and sagebrush. We planned to turn the land into a small agricultural ranch and our new home, which we named Buffalo Creek Ranch.

There, on a redwood deck I had built beneath the aspens, we held a small private ceremony, celebrating our new life together with just our children and immediate family in attendance. After the brief but memorable wedding ceremony, we gathered on the top floor of the recently remodeled Harvey's Hotel & Casino to enjoy a fantastic dinner at Llewellyn's Dinner House. Through the windows we could see Lake Tahoe glowing in the moonlight. The majestic Sierra Nevada loomed in the distance.

L-R, Derek, Jordan, Susan, me, Greg, Wendi, and Aimee at our Buffalo Creek Ranch Wedding in 1999

L-R, Wendi, Derek, Aimee, Greg, Jordan, Susan, and me at Llewellyn's Dinner House top floor of Harvey's Hotel & Casino, Lake Tahoe, Nevada, 1999

CHAPTER 14
BEING A BOSS ISN'T EASY

As we explored ways to expand our business model, a milestone project arrived in the summer of 2000. Earlier that year, we had attracted the attention of Visteon, an automotive components manufacturer for Ford, after successfully developing an MPCS anodizing recipe for a seat belt buckle that had failed and resulted in the recall of about 350,000 cars. Our automated process had consistently delivered an anodized finish that would prevent the buckle from accidentally opening. This success had opened the door at Ford and Visteon, and many had become aware of our technical capabilities. Now they were looking for similar results on a more complicated project.

Establishing a relationship with a Fortune 500 company like Ford is no easy task. You can't simply call them up and ask to speak with somebody; you have to know someone. John Dempsey, our vice president of marketing, knew someone on the inside. John, a friend of mine, was a big Irishman who was a double-degreed engineer in electrical engineering and nuclear science. He had graduated at the top of his class from the US Naval Academy with our old friend, Jim McWalters, of PMRealty Advisors.

After college, John was handpicked by Admiral Hyman Rickover, the father of the US Nuclear Navy, and served two tours of duty on the nuclear submarine USS *Seawolf* during the

John Dempsey

Vietnam War. John had a photographic memory and twenty-five years of experience in the engineering and construction industry with Bechtel, one of the world's largest and most respected construction companies. He convinced his good friend, Joe Zuba, senior vice president of engineering at Ford, to let METALAST work on this new project for them. Now we finally had the opportunity to serve as a solutions provider for a large company and establish major credibility in the industry.

In July, Harish Bhatt, Visteon's senior technical specialist and vice president of metal-finishing processing, arrived at MTC to discuss this highly sensitive, top-priority project. My technical team, my brother Len, and I met him and his colleagues in the conference room, where they showed us renderings of the project, called the SIT (Slip-In-Tube) Propshaft. As Harish explained, the SIT Propshaft was a two-piece telescoping aluminum drive shaft initially designed for the Ford Bronco and other automotive companies' product lines. The six-foot-long and five-inch-wide cylindrical component was designed to reduce the weight of a conventional drive shaft by about ten pounds, improving fuel efficiency and providing safer operating conditions. The two drive shaft tubes locked into each other in a telescoping fashion, so that in the event of a rear collision, the drive train component would collapse into itself rather than buckle upward into the passenger compartment and potentially cause loss of life. This was the first time anyone had tried to manufacture and mass produce an aluminum drive shaft that telescoped into itself in a collision.

The challenge was to surface-finish the two components where they interlocked with an anodizing process that would provide maximum wear resistance, surface hardness, durability, and anti-corrosion protection. The drive shaft was able to withstand the rigors of the outdoor and highway road elements, but due to the requirements of precision machining, the process also had to deliver tight tolerances in a production environment. While the Visteon design team had been able to process and hardcoat anodize test samples of the SIT Propshaft, they knew that anodizing one or two parts at a time in a lab was far different than processing 40,000 drive shafts per month. Every anodizer's coating they had tried to date had failed to produce the consistent and uniform results they required.

I realized that this SIT Propshaft project could be a breakthrough event for us, an important project to showcase our technology. Instead of doing pizza pans and flashlights, we needed to be challenged by a project that would prove the durability, hardness, and corrosion resistance of METALAST anodizing. Anodizing a pizza pan didn't really prove anything. Anodizing a drive shaft that turned 3,000 revolutions per minute and would one day have 100,000 miles on it was an entirely different story. A drive shaft was subjected to a great deal of torque and sand-pitting from the road. In addition, because it came in two parts, the parts had to be extremely consistent, and tolerances had to be right on the money; otherwise the two pieces wouldn't go together. It was an exciting opportunity.

I took Harish and his colleagues downstairs to the training classroom and presented a slideshow on our technology. Then we moved to the MTC laboratory so that Byron Estes and Len could process some samples that Harish had brought, including a small prototype of the two-component drive shaft that had already been Type-III finished (also known as hard anodizing or a hard-coat anodizing, which results in the dark-gray Calphalon cookware aluminum finish that most consumers recognize). We were able to hard-anodize several coupons at a two-millimeter thickness in about forty-five minutes. Then we put them in the Taber abrasion machine, a piece of military specification equipment that turns 10,000 revolutions over several hours. The sample is weighed, machine grinded, and then reweighed. This indicates the wear resistance and surface hardness based on the weight loss of the coupon.

From L-R, Len Semas, Harish Bhatt, and Byron Estes in the lab, 2000

METALAST passed all the tests with flying colors. We showed Harish the MPCS, which satisfied him that we could develop recipe formulations that could be replicated in field production environments. Overall, they were impressed.

The real challenge would be to subject the driveshaft to far more rigorous testing. Over the next twelve months, we processed various SIT Propshaft component samples, which were then subjected to extensive independent testing and validation, first by Visteon engineers and then by their outside testing laboratories. In test after test, the METALAST process proved itself in corrosion resistance (salt spray), surface hardness, wear, durability, tolerances, target thicknesses, and finally in harsh sand-wash destruction testing. The Visteon team was thrilled with the performance of our process and the technical support we provided and ended up adding the registered METALAST brand name to the patent itself.

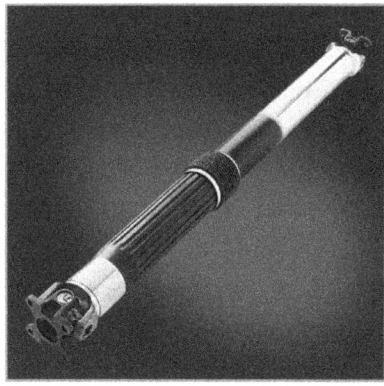

SIT Propshaft unit for JEEP Grand Cherokee, Liberty, and Commander

Like so many of the projects we became involved in, however, it took many years before the SIT Propshaft was fully implemented in a production environment. Ultimately, METALAST Type III anodizing was applied as the specified surface-treatment process for approximately two million SIT Propshaft units for the 2005–2010 model years of the Jeep Grand Cherokee, Jeep Liberty, and Jeep Commander without one anodizing-related reject. It stands as one of our most successful automotive R&D-to-real-world production projects to date. As I had hoped, the SIT Propshaft helped prove the METALAST process and establish our credibility in the industry, opening many doors for us in the years to come.

About the same time, METALAST was making a big impression with the US Navy. A couple of years earlier, John Dempsey had contacted another

friend of his, retired Rear Admiral Joseph Sansone Jr., to see if he could help open doors for us at the Department of Defense. Prior to his retirement, Admiral Sansone had been the highest-ranking admiral in the Naval Procurement Department, in effect serving as the Navy's top businessman in uniform. Working as our consultant, he coordinated our marketing efforts with governmental agencies.

In 2000, John's connections paid off in a big way when representatives from the Naval Aviation Depot (NADEP) in Jacksonville, Florida visited the MTC to discuss their F-16 and F-18 fighter jets. This was a big deal for us. A relationship with the Navy would help grow the business in many ways and prove our brand with a governmental agency.

NADEP was interested to learn how our technology could be used to help improve the quality, consistency, and repeatability of anodizing used at their facility on the fighter jets and other projects. After a preliminary investigation, the processing of sample parts, and two years of technical discussions, we were overjoyed when NADEP became a METALAST licensee and one of the most proactive supporters of our technology. NADEP became fully operational by the spring of 2003, using several MPCSs, our AA-200 anodizing additive, and many of our other specialty chemical products.

After twelve months of operation, NADEP became convinced of the enormous benefits of the METALAST process, and I received an exciting email from Ruben Prado, a NADEP anodizing process specialist. The email contained a six-page feature story he had written about METALAST for *Currents*, the Navy's award-winning environmental magazine. The glowing article provided independent validation of the METALAST technology. "I have always been an advocate for process control and cutting-edge technology," Prado wrote. "I believe the MPCS is a step in the right direction."

The *Currents* story validated every performance claim we had ever made, concluding that the METALAST system improved accuracy and repeatability of the process, lowered labor and energy costs, provided an affordable and user-friendly technology with minimal training required. The MPCS used less energy, extended the bath life and consumption of chemicals, and reduced the amount of aluminum buildup and other contaminants in the anodizing bath due to the use of the METALAST® AA-200 additive. The additive required much less replenishing, thus extending the bath life and reducing waste disposal. Prado's article presented technical findings and validated the performance benefits of the METALAST process unlike any other independent report or test study ever made available to us.

As impressive as the *Currents* feature story was, its observations were overshadowed by another comprehensive study conducted by Naval Air Systems Command (NAVAIR). NAVAIR is the department responsible for testing and approving the performance of new chemical products submitted for Qualified Product List (QPL) certification, providing unbiased confirmation of manufacturer performance claims. NAVAIR and the QPL certification are recognized globally by the industry as meeting the highest possible standards of testing guidelines and professional conduct.

The NAVAIR report, also prepared by Ruben Prado, was presented in front of two hundred attendees several years later at the Department of Defense Metal Finishing Workshop at Hill Air Force Base in Utah. Delivered as part of a detailed PowerPoint presentation, the report gave a succinct overview of METALAST's performance and production benefits. It concluded by calling for the implementation of our technology across Navy depots and making us the new standard for anodizing across the entire Department of Defense.

Within a year of the *Currents* story publication, NADEP notified us that they intended to make METALAST a sole-source provider for their metal-finishing needs. This meant the Navy would negotiate a contract with us without competitive bids, because they considered our company to be uniquely positioned to provide patented or proprietary technologies that were only available through METALAST. Following that, the Navy began using our METALAST AA-200 anodizing additive prior to installation of our complete technology. The project had been

> LIFE LESSON #88:
>
> "IF YOU'RE TO GAIN THE TRUST AND CONFIDENCE OF INVESTORS, KEEP OPEN AND HONEST LINES OF COMMUNICATION."
>
> —DAVID SEMAS

approved by the Department of Defense, and installation was projected to begin in 2003.

Yet another achievement in 2000 was our license agreement with Trico Products, the largest manufacturer of automotive windshield wipers in the world. Being able to refer to our successes with Ford and the Navy was extremely helpful in our discussions with Trico Products. We originated a $1.7 million contract for APS to manufacture an automated wet-process anodizing line for Trico and began training their technical staff and line operators in April. The APS wet process line was delivered and installed in October on budget and on time. By the end of the year, Trico had seen a dramatic reduction in their rejection rate, from about 5 percent down to less than one part per million (0.001 percent) of piece parts processed—commonly referred to as Six Sigma. This was another coup for METALAST with an internationally well-known and established automotive components manufacturer.

These success stories opened doors for us to do more R&D for other big companies, and we processed sample parts for many leading companies, including Applied Materials, Boeing, Bombardier, Chrysler, Ford Motors, General Motors, General Dynamics, Honeywell, Lockheed Martin, Motorola, Raytheon, and Sikorsky. The METALAST brand was beginning to make some headway, albeit at a much slower pace than I had ever imagined.

Although we continued to bring in investor capital to meet our ongoing costs of running the business, I could tell by the frequency and tone of the phone calls I was receiving from shareholders that they were becoming concerned about our future financial viability, which I totally understood. Instead of getting a few calls a week, I was getting about one per day. And I must admit, I couldn't offer a lot of answers.

I had implemented a policy since the inception of our company to provide shareholders with quarterly reports, annual financial statements, an annual manager's report, and of course our annual members meeting, generally held each year in October. I have long believed that the best way to maintain investor trust and confidence is to always maintain open lines of communication, consistently provide written quarterly reports, and be willing to return every telephone call in a timely manner, whether the call offers praise or criticism. It might not always be pleasant, but honesty truly is the best policy.

This management style isn't always enjoyable, but it's crucial if a company is going to have the support of its board of directors and shareholders (and ongoing creditors, if applicable). The only reason we hadn't experienced a shareholder revolt was because I had provided a consistent flow of communication and accurate information. I had done my best to make certain that shareholder capital was spent in accordance with sound and ethical business practices, making certain that corporate capital was invested prudently and honestly.

Several times during the 1970s, Ben Swig had provided me with valuable insight about running a business and being a CEO.

"Being the boss isn't easy," he'd said. "The bottom line is that if everything fails, you must be willing to stand before your shareholders, partners, or investors, take responsibility, and openly acknowledge, 'I failed!' On the other hand, if everything goes as planned and you hit a grand slam, you must also embrace the idea of standing before the same group and gracefully sharing the moment, giving praise to your employees. You must say, 'We succeeded,' and acknowledge all those who have made the company or project a success. A great leader stands tall in battle and takes responsibility for the actions of all and with humility and dignity shares the glory with those around him. When you can do these things, win or lose, you will become a winner and a true leader of men and women."

After years of experience, I had come to believe firmly in his wisdom and guidance.

> **LIFE LESSON #89:**
>
> "GENERALLY SPEAKING, BUSINESS STARTUPS COST TWICE AS MUCH AND TAKE TWICE AS LONG TO BECOME PROFITABLE."
>
> —DAVID SEMAS

Being the CEO of a metal-finishing and specialty chemical company was not the same as being the CEO of a real estate development company or running a chain of hotels. Some of the disciplines were similar, especially those that involved working with people, but now I also had to understand aluminum anodizing, specialty chemicals, the process-control computer technology, and how to engage huge companies like Ford Motors. One thing I hadn't counted on was the time, effort, and enormous capital investment required to change such a massive industry. We needed to convince hundreds of other large companies, like Boeing, Ford Motors, General Motors, General Dynamics, Honeywell, Lockheed Martin, Northrop Grumman, Pratt & Whitney, and Raytheon, if we were to inspire the industry to make a wholesale change.

CHAPTER 15

ONE STEP FORWARD, TWO STEPS BACK

At the beginning of 2001, we had been making good headway with APS, putting together projects and getting contracts awarded, like the Trico project the year before. We had also been awarded a contract for a $2.5 million APS process line at Modern Industries, a supplier to Applied Materials (AMAT), which provided nano-manufacturing technology for the fabrication of semiconductor chips and flat panel displays. The challenge of developing formulations for Modern Industries was daunting but proved successful. This was a major step forward in establishing the METALAST brand in the semiconductor industry, and it never would have happened if we had remained merely an anodizing technology. By aligning with APS, we were able to provide more solutions to manufacturers like Applied Materials.

The AMAT process line had been built, delivered, and partially installed by APS when Tom Phelps, the owner, called and told me that APS was experiencing financial difficulties. The capital equipment market had taken a turn for the worse, and it didn't look like they were going to weather the storm. This was unfortunate because Tom was a true gentleman, an outstanding partner, and a CEO who would go without pay so his employees didn't have to. I also knew firsthand the pressure he was under and the hardship this must have caused for his family. The loss of APS as a partner would be another setback. There had to be a way to help Tom weather the storm.

Over the next few days, he and I put our heads together and came up with a plan for METALAST to buy APS. This strategy would put us into the manufacturing business, broaden our product lines, and help us expand the chemical business we were preparing to launch, while at the same time greatly increasing our profit margins. All these changes would help to further reinvent the METALAST business model.

Considering that the financial markets were tightening up again, the question became this: Could we raise the money through another NASD private placement offering (PPO)? This time we brought a $21.5 million PPO to market and began to generate real interest. We were running short of capital ourselves, so the first priority was to use proceeds to build our cash reserves. Month after month, cash flow support money came in but not nearly at the rate we had hoped. To our disappointment, we ultimately had to delay the APS acquisition until we had enough funding to consummate the deal.

The good news was that we were just about ready to launch a complete line of anodizing pre-treatment chemicals (cleaners, deoxidizers, etchants) and post-treatment chemicals (sealants and dyes) with Southern Industrial Chemicals of Atlanta, our new manufacturing partner. Nevada governor Kenny Guinn honored METALAST by speaking at the public relations and Northern Nevada Development Authority (NNDA) event at our MTC announcing METALAST's entry into the specialty chemical business.

Me with Nevada Governor Kenny Guinn in 2003

Until now, METALAST had only one chemical on the market: our METALAST® AA-200 additive. If we were truly going to provide solutions to the industry, we couldn't provide only equipment and one chemical; we had to provide everything involved in the process. As a result, it was necessary to create our own private label line of chemicals. The alliance with Southern Industrial Chemicals (SIC Technologies) was our first real move into the specialty chemical business.

At the same time, I knew this was not the end-all solution. Breaking into a one-hundred-year-old chemical industry with metal finishers who had been purchasing their chemicals from the same company and the same salesman for the last twenty years was not going to be an easy task. We had a long haul ahead of us before we could make much headway selling generic chemicals that had been on the market for years. What we needed was a breakthrough specialty chemical that no one else had—a so-called Trojan horse product that could get us into customers' facilities. Nonetheless, we had to start somewhere.

DAVID MICHAEL SEMAS

On Monday, September 10, 2001, I flew to Philadelphia to make a formal presentation at an exclusive country club before an investment group called LORE Associates, a group of thirty retired CEOs. Jim and Jack Bradt, shareholders and friends of mine, had arranged for my introduction to this impressive gathering of prospective investors. I was optimistic that I would be able to raise millions of dollars of capital from this group as a part of our $21.5 million private placement offering, also known as a PPO.

During the flight, I reflected on our current situation. We were continuing to generate interest in METALAST from many leaders in the industry. Just five days earlier, CNBC had aired a fifteen-minute television special called *The Champions of Industry*, which we had produced as part of our continuing effort to bring awareness to METALAST. We were conducting R&D work for internationally recognized names like Apple, Boeing, Cessna, General Dynamics, IBM, Mitsubishi, Motorola, NASA, and even Robert Yates' NASCAR racing team. I believed that if we could continue to offer no-cost R&D and technical support to manufacturers, assisting them in improving the quality and performance of their products while bringing global awareness to our lines of environmentally friendly chemicals, eventually the METALAST brand would take hold.

On that beautiful clear day, I arrived in Conshohocken, Pennsylvania in the afternoon and checked into the Marriott Hotel. In the hotel restaurant that evening, I ordered a nice New York steak and savored a glass of Ferrari-Carano 1998 merlot produced and bottled by the Carano family, owners of the El Dorado Hotel & Casino and 50 percent partners in the Silver Legacy Hotel & Casino in Reno. Over dinner, I thought about the prospect of making my formal PowerPoint investment presentation the next morning at a nearby country club—after which I was looking forward to catching the train the following day, arriving mid-morning at Grand Central Station in New York. I would be staying the balance of the week with my friend Martin Burke, who remains one of my real estate development partners today.

At 8:45 the next morning, I was called into the conference room before the impressive group of retired CEO's to begin my investment slide show.

As I moved to only the third slide and began explaining our technology to the audience, a restaurant waiter barged through the doors into the room and yelled, "Oh my God! An airplane has crashed into the World Trade Center!" Then he bolted back out of the room.

For a moment, we all froze, stunned by the announcement. After gathering my wits, I stopped the presentation and turned on the lights, and the investors and I looked at each other in bewilderment, thinking that some poor, unsuspecting private aircraft pilot had crashed into one of the World Trade Center towers in fog or low clouds.

The waiter returned to the room a few moments later, saying that the news media was beginning to report rumors that it was a large American Airlines commercial jetliner. The former CEOs and investors sitting before me jumped to their feet and scrambled to the lounge, where a group of country club employees was gathered in front of a large-screen television.

The LORE group and I watched the television in horror as the second aircraft, United Airlines Flight No. 175, crashed into the South Tower of the World Trade Center at 9:03 a.m.

Within thirty minutes, the group had dispersed and left the building in different directions. I jumped in my rental car and hastily retreated to the Marriott, knowing that I would not be taking the Amtrak train to New York City the next day.

When I called Martin, he seemed as shocked as everyone else and told me that he had heard that the secretary of transportation, Norman Mineta, had halted virtually all air traffic throughout the United States. Norm was the former mayor of San Jose and a close friend to Jack Copple, my former boss at Heritage Homes. I turned on CNN and briefly watched the live broadcast.

With the airways shut down coast to coast, I attempted to get through to Amtrak, but it was impossible. I called my travel agent and asked if she could book me on a train to Reno.

"If you can make it to Chicago tomorrow," she said, "you can board the Amtrak there."

Within an hour after my return to the hotel I checked out and commandeered my rental car. Then, while downtown traffic was sparse and nearly everyone in Philadelphia remained glued to their televisions, I jumped on I-76, took I-476 north, and then headed west on I-80 all the way to Chicago.

Like all Americans, I was in disbelief and found it a bizarre time to be traveling on the highways alone. I drove in a daze while listening to every word coming over the airwaves. Within a few miles, I noticed something I had never seen before: there was not one plane, helicopter, or manmade object of any kind in the sky. Only birds. The eerie feeling was accentuated by Irish singer-songwriter Enya's angelic song "Only Time" playing on the radio. Her ethereal voice gave the whole experience a surreal quality.

I drove nonstop for about eight hours and then checked into a motel just past Cleveland. In the morning, I awoke hoping it had all been a bad dream. Of course, I knew better.

I was on the road by seven o'clock but soon realized that I was not going to make it to Chicago in time. I called my travel agent, and she changed my reservations to board a different Amtrak in Omaha, Nebraska, with a midnight departure the next day. I drove the eight hundred miles in twelve hours, made it to Omaha in time for dinner, and caught the Amtrak-California Zephyr train for Reno at 11:45 p.m.

> **LIFE LESSON #90:**
>
> "TERRORIST ATTACKS CAN SHAKE THE FOUNDATIONS OF OUR BIGGEST BUILDINGS, BUT THEY CANNOT TOUCH THE FOUNDATION OF AMERICA. THESE ACTS SHATTER STEEL, BUT THEY CANNOT DENT THE STEEL OF AMERICAN RESOLVE."
>
> —GEORGE W. BUSH (FORTY-THIRD PRESIDENT OF THE UNITED STATES, 1946-)

The next morning, I called my travel agent to let her know I was on the train.

"David, the original Amtrak you were supposed to board in Chicago crashed into an oncoming freight train early this morning in Wendover, Utah," she said. "It derailed and caught fire. I don't know about casualties yet."

I felt sick to my stomach. How much more bizarre could things get?

By the time we pulled into the station in Reno early Saturday morning, I was exhausted but relieved to see my wife Susan's beautiful, smiling face.

That single week was an unbelievable period of my life, as it was for most Americans. As a result of 9/11, everyone's focus became much more introspective for the next few years, and the last thing on the minds of the retired CEO group in Philadelphia was an investment in a metal-finishing technology company. If we were to continue to bring in capital, METALAST would have to look elsewhere for funding.

The year 2002 began with Bradock and Morris crawling out from under the rock they'd been hiding under for the last several years. This time they had convinced George McNally and Larry Winking, two unsuspecting but honorable attorneys, to file a phony class-action lawsuit on behalf of METALAST's shareholders, they were only able to muster three people—two of whom lived together—out of six hundred MILLC Members.

After speaking with our legal counsel and the attorneys for TWS, we learned that the lawsuit was about greed and had been directed at the insurance carriers for TWS, under what is referred to as investor suitability. Under the securities laws of California, the lawsuit contended, the NASD securities firm of TWS should have been more diligent in recommending a speculative investment like METALAST to their clients.

Ultimately, we reached a modest settlement by buying back the stock of the three shareholders, but the litigation itself was once again costly, time-consuming, and a major distraction and ended up dragging on for three more years. As anticipated, the insurance carrier for TWS settled the case and paid out several hundred thousand dollars to the plaintiffs. I'd never thought building

LIFE LESSON #91:

"ANYBODY CAN FILE A LAWSUIT AGAINST ANYONE. AT ANY TIME. FOR ANYTHING. UNFORTUNATELY, HE WITH THE MOST MONEY USUALLY WINS!"

—DAVID SEMAS

METALAST would be easy but also hadn't anticipated so many unforeseen challenges.

La Ferme Owner, Gilles Lagourgue, seated, and Chef Yves Gigot at La Ferme fine dining restaurant in Genoa, Nevada, 2008

Many years later, I ran across Larry Winking at our friend Gilles Lagourgue's five-star La Ferme Restaurant in Genoa. Gilles, a proud French Basque restaurateur, and his business partner and chef, Yves Gigot, have delighted their patrons with world-class country French dining for more than thirty years. Although the town of Genoa has a population of less than one thousand residents, dining patrons throughout northern Nevada, and especially Incline Village, would travel in their limousines to spend an evening with Gilles and Yves.

A few months later, Larry's former law partner, George McNally, invited me to lunch at Red's 395 Bar & Grill in Carson City, where he apologized on his and Larry's behalf for believing their dishonest client Bradock. I very much appreciated his sincere gesture.

CHAPTER 16

FINALLY, A MAJOR INVESTOR?

Despite the setbacks and the constant, time-consuming effort to raise capital, an idea was formulating in my mind of how we could influence metal finishers and coax them into switching to our technology. I knew we would need a lot of money to reach the thousands of specifying engineers, quality-control officers, and environmental compliance officers of the Fortune 500. I kept thinking that if I could just find a major investor that would invest $25 million, we could pursue this strategy and really accelerate our growth.

Then a well-positioned potential investor appeared, and I thought, *I wonder if it's someone that inherited great wealth?*

In July 2002, I spoke with good friend, Marty Cohen, a broker-dealer based in Dallas, and Marty introduced me to Allen Campbell, a Dallas-based investment banker. Allen was convinced he

---

LIFE LESSON #92:

"I MADE MY MONEY THE OLD-FASHIONED WAY. I WAS NICE TO A WEALTHY RELATIVE RIGHT BEFORE HE DIED."

—MALCOLM FORBES (FOUNDER OF FORBES MAGAZINE, 1919-1990)

could raise the $25 million needed to fully implement our strategic business plan.

"Does the name Paul Allred mean anything to you?" Allen asked.

It didn't.

Allen explained that Paul was the longtime friend of a prominent Boulder, Colorado family. Apparently, Paul had been roommates in college with the family's son, Raymond French. Allen told me more about Paul's background and why he felt that both Raymond and Paul would find the METALAST investment opportunity of interest.

"Twenty-five million dollars is a large amount of money, even for a wealthy family," I said. "What exactly does Raymond's father do?" I was thinking he must be an heir to one of the famous Colorado mining, oil, or natural gas families.

"Let's just say the extended family has substantial holdings," Allen replied. "If it's something that Raymond really wants to do, it shouldn't be too much of a problem."

I decided to just sit tight and see what would happen.

On September 25, 2002, Allen, Paul, and Raymond flew into Reno, and we met for dinner at Adele's, a five-star restaurant in Carson City owned by friends of ours. Courteous and soft-spoken, Raymond appeared to be in his mid-thirties and had a medium build and light-brown hair. He reminded me a little of John Denver.

For the first hour, we got to know each other and talked about our respective upbringings, families, kids, and then businesses.

At that point, I felt it would be appropriate to politely ask Raymond about his family and his interest in investing so much money in METALAST. Raymond had mentioned his father, so that gave me the perfect opening. "Paul and Allen tell me your father was an aeronautical engineer."

"That's right," Raymond said and went on to tell me more about his father, sister, and family. "David, hasn't Paul disclosed to you who my extended family is?"

"No, he hasn't. He believed it would be more appropriate for you to do so."

Raymond smiled. "I'm sure you're wondering about my ability to fund a twenty-five-million-dollar investment. I own a modest but successful niche

E-learning and learning-solutions company. Our E-learning products combine instructional design, practical interactivity, and adult-learning theory. We offer a wide variety of E-learning solutions to large companies around the country. I'm fascinated and intrigued with your 'solutions provider' concept, and in particular would like to hear more about how you intend to reach your market. Now to the point. As I mentioned earlier, I grew up and went to school in Dallas and now live in Boulder. My sister, Melinda, also grew up in Dallas and in 1986 received her bachelor's and MBA degree in computer science from Duke. Shortly after joining the Microsoft organization, she began dating her boss, and they married a few years later. Her name is Melinda French Gates, and Bill Gates is her husband and my brother-in-law."

Raymond talked for a while about Bill and Melinda in a discreet manner. He said it was a good sign that we were having dinner at Adele's Restaurant, because Melinda had just given birth a few weeks earlier to their third child, a daughter named Phoebe Adele Gates.

"So, David," Raymond said at last, "how do you intend to get your story out to the vast market? No offense, but to me it doesn't look as though you've made much traction in getting a large number of metal finishers to sign up. With the research we've conducted thus far, it would appear that you have a very long road in front of you to identify and then individually convince thousands of mom-and-pop job shop owners that they should become METALAST licensees and be willing to pay you monthly royalties. From a business-to-business selling perspective, just how do you propose to convince engineering and scientific professionals of the superiority of your products and technical services?"

"Over the years," I responded, "we've probably presented the complete METALAST story to hundreds of owners of metal finishing companies who might have heard the ten-minute elevator pitch that our RSMs were able to make to conference attendees as they passed by the METALAST exhibit booth during the Surface Finishing Convention or industry trade shows. I've come up with a solution, although it will cost five million dollars to implement. I've already plugged this amount into the twenty-five-million-dollar budget. Do you want to hear the idea?"

I had piqued the interest of my audience. They exchanged glances and then looked at me.

"Go on," Raymond said.

"Well, if you can't bring Mohammed to the mountain," I said, "then you have to bring the mountain to Mohammed. I propose that we design, build, and launch a mobile marketing campaign targeting the big Fortune 500 companies. The idea is to have a large tractor and semitrailer rig travel the country, going from manufacturer to manufacturer, conducting several educational seminars a day on the benefits of process control and process automation. The audience will include specifying design engineers, quality-assurance personnel, purchasing agents, environmental compliance officers, and senior management.

"Several months ago, I was invited to attend a NASCAR extravaganza in Phoenix by the racing team owner and engine builder, Robert Yates. Along with four hundred thousand other spectators, I saw impressive tractor and semitrailer rigs that had been essentially turned into retail shopping arcades, selling memorabilia for the celebrity NASCAR drivers. Many of the forty-eight-foot-long trailers were double expandable with about one thousand square feet of space, which is certainly large enough to hold at least a thirty-six-seat classroom.

"What I have in mind is to manufacture a small-scale wet process line that would be equipped with an overhead crane to give the audience the illusion of being in a job shop environment. This would replicate the same movements of a full-scale metal-finishing line. The state-of-the-art portable classroom would have two big screen televisions in the middle capable of presenting a one-hour-long video synchronized with the overhead crane so that, as the presentation unfolds, the crane moves up and down the line, showing the audience how parts are metal-finished. A satellite uplink would be tied to the MTC, and the live feed would be shown on twin big screens for a Q and A session after the initial program. The mobile classroom would have computers at one end of the trailer for the registration of each seminar attendee, a small bathroom, and even a kitchenette at the other end to serve coffee, soft drinks, water, and snacks.

"The mobile trailer would be decorated with wall-mounted photographs and graphics and fully furnished with classroom tables and chairs, and METALAST-processed samples would be wall-mounted in glass display cases. The mobile unit would be completely self-contained, with a ten-kilowatt generator, water supply, septic system, and entry staircase. We would develop a one-hour-long video presentation and provide each attendee with a METALAST notebook, pen, and some other type of collectible—maybe a mouse pad with our logo on it. Trained METALAST program moderators would rotate in and out every two weeks, following the mobile unit from city to city in a four-wheel-drive Jeep Grand Cherokee with our METALAST-processed SIT driveshaft. There are many other logistical issues that would have to be worked out, not the least of which would be identifying, contacting, and then convincing the Ford Motors, Boeings, and Lockheed Martins to allow us to bring a huge tractor and semitrailer to their secure facilities, which since nine-eleven would not be an easy task."

Raymond pushed himself back from the table. "I think that's the most ingenious marketing idea I've ever heard of in terms of reaching a business-to-business audience. I must admit, your approach sounds fascinating and appealing to the manufacturer. But how are you going to actually pull this off, assuming you have the money to do so?"

I knew what Raymond was driving at: there were a lot of moving parts to the concept. Did we have the experience, knowledge, and capabilities to implement a coast-to-coast mobile marketing campaign with all of its potential pitfalls?

For example, could we convince manufacturers to allow open access to their highly sensitive and secure facilities and employees? How would we go about doing this? How would we identify, out of 60,000 employees at Boeing, the right person to contact and the person responsible for signing up engineering professionals to attend our seminars? Who was going to drive this huge tractor and semitrailer around the country for fifty weeks a year? How could we locate and then design the trailer, manufacture a small-scale process line, and figure out ways to secure the high-tech equipment to withstand the constant jarring and shaking of highway travel? Who would develop the curriculum, produce the video, and prepare technical literature and marketing brochures?

Then there were other issues, like attendee pre-registration, security, insurance, lodging, moderator air travel, seminar site directions, DOT taxes, and the sheer hassle of setting up and tearing down each day without conflicting with the manufacturers' work shift changes. No doubt Raymond thought it would be a logistical nightmare.

I had given a great deal of thought to this plan, and now I had to somehow convey that confidence to Raymond while also convincing him of our ability to develop and fully implement such a challenging national campaign. I realized the best way to sell him on it was to simply show him our capabilities.

"As envisioned by me and spearheaded and implemented by my brother, Len, we've spent many years developing our highly sophisticated database systems, controls, procedures, and nearly paperless office. You will see tomorrow that for a young company, we have an administrative, sales, and marketing infrastructure second to none, which should give you a much better idea as to our capabilities.

"When the funding of twenty-five million dollars is in place, I will establish a mobile marketing department headed up by my son, Greg, that will be staffed with five full-time people. This department will consist of an advanced research assistant to identify and make initial contact with target companies and a liaison officer who will run the department and convince the manufacturers to hold onsite seminars. The mobile marketing coordinator's job will be to handle pre-registration, scheduling, technical literature, marketing materials, air travel, hotel reservations, general transportation, and all other logistical operating-related issues. We will also hire two training moderators and presenters that will rotate in two-week intervals. They will travel with the mobile marketing trailer, telling the METALAST story and introducing our products and services up to one hundred engineering professionals each day at many of the largest manufacturing corporations in the country.

"I can assure you, I have thought out this plan in intricate detail, from the design and manufacturing of the mobile unit to contacting manufacturers and its ultimate operation. You might consider me a big-picture visionary, but I believe after we have the opportunity to spend more time together and you've visited the Tech Center, you'll come to appreciate that I am a detailed, hands-on person. During my business career, which includes the construction, real estate, investment banking, and hotel businesses, I have always felt that God is in the details."

Raymond, Allen, and Paul seemed pleased with my answer. Over dinner, my guests continued to grill me with tough and insightful questions about our technologies, chemicals, market demand, competition, and exit strategy. When the evening wrapped up around eleven o'clock, we agreed to meet at the MTC the next morning.

After my three guests had grabbed cups of coffee and set their briefcases in our training classroom, I gave them a one-hour tour of the facility, introducing them to METALAST staff as we walked around the two-story, 17,000-square-foot Tech Center. I took them through our high-tech laboratory, our twenty-seat university-style training room, and the downstairs conference center. We moved on to the software and industrial-process-control research and assembly area, the warehouse, the chemical storage area, and our various offices, upstairs board room, the IT department, human resources, sales, marketing, and administration before finishing in my office.

"The METALAST laboratory brings together design, automation, computer science, chemical and metallurgical engineering, research and development, and testing," I explained as I showed them our research-scale anodizing chromate conversion wet process line, with its twenty-two tanks and computer-automated control and hoist system. Our other laboratory equipment included an analytical balance system, an atomic absorption spectrophotometer used to measure trace metals in bath samples, a UV/VIS spectrophotometer to measure organic components of the baths, a Taber abrasion testing device to specifically calculate wear resistance, the METALAST JobPro process control computer, and a salt-spray chamber that tested for corrosion protection.

At the end of the tour, the group told me they were impressed with the layout of the facility and visitor friendliness that had been incorporated into its design. This included a set of glass observation windows that looked down from the second floor, a set of windows looking into the laboratory from the training classroom, and still another large window from the main hallway near the reception area.

We finished the tour in my office on the second floor, with its breathtaking view of the snowcapped Sierra Nevada. We spent the remainder of the time on the audio/visual slide presentation, which included a tour of our website and sophisticated database administration system and an investor PowerPoint presentation. I showed Raymond, Allen, and Paul exactly how we ran the day-to-day business with our internally developed database administration.

My three guests were impressed with demonstrations of METALAST processing in the lab as the parts continued through the various stations. Raymond was impressed that a young company had the level of sophistication to set up systems and organize a corporate infrastructure that would allow it to grow into a big company. He appeared to be 100 percent convinced of the financial potential for the company, and by the end of the evening, he told me he was fairly certain his family would support him in becoming a major partner in METALAST. It would take a month or so for him to gain the support of the family, so he asked that I be patient.

The evening finished on a high note, and I felt good about the prospect of Raymond becoming our largest single investor. Everyone seemed to believe that it was not *if* but *when* Raymond would arrange for his capital.

After thirty days had passed, however, the mood seemed to shift. Paul's comments to me suggested that Raymond was becoming concerned that this wasn't the type of investment his family wanted him to pursue. As the discussions continued, my confidence level dropped. I didn't want to worry my senior staff and employees, who already knew we were struggling to stay afloat, so I kept my concerns to myself. Once again, a project seemed to be unraveling before my eyes, and there was little I could do to stop the downward spiral.

Finally, Raymond called.

"Is there really a shot that this could happen," I asked, "or should I move on?"

To his credit, he was frank and courteous. "David, I am impressed with you and your company. I think you have some great ideas, especially the mobile marketing campaign, and it appears that you're about to break out as a real business. While I would like to become involved, Bill, Melinda, and their financial advisors have asked that I withdraw. This is more about public perception and keeping family business investments private. I'm sorry."

I thanked him for his honesty and hung up the phone, feeling that all-too-familiar sense of disappointment. After a six-month process, it was over.

When do we actually catch a break? I wondered. It was just weeks before Christmas. We had worked so hard to put these kinds of deals together, only to have them derailed at the last moment. For a few short weeks, it had appeared that we had our $25 million to launch the mobile marketing campaign and buy APS, but it had completely unraveled. Working with Paul and Raymond had been a tremendous learning experience, and I had enjoyed meeting Raymond, but this was still a huge blow.

By the end of 2002, I was once again looking for additional METALAST financing and had no choice but to start the process all over again.

LIFE LESSON #93:

"STRENGTH DOES NOT COME FROM PHYSICAL CAPACITY. IT COMES FROM INDOMITABLE WILL!"

—MAHATMA GANDHI
(EAST-INDIAN LAWYER AND PEACE ACTIVIST, 1869-1948)

CHAPTER 17

T-REX: GO BIG OR GO HOME!

Over the years, I had learned how to bounce back, and this time was no exception. The idea for my mobile marketing campaign remained in the back of my mind as we moved forward with other projects.

T-Rex Is Coming Logo

Despite the disappointment with Raymond French, good things had been happening. Raytheon, Ford Motors, Northrop Grumman, Parker Hannifin, and Visteon Automotive had each informed us that they were seriously looking at adopting METALAST as their anodizing best practice. First-production runs of the SIT Propshaft were to begin the following summer. NADEP (Naval Aviation Depot) had decided to install two METALAST® JobPro computers at their facility in Jacksonville, along with the METALAST® AA-200 additive and specialty chemicals. Within days of installation, NADEP line operators were processing F-16 and F-18 fighter jet parts more efficiently, producing better quality and consistency, and experiencing a twenty-minute decrease in process time—about a 40 percent improvement in productivity and what is known as "throughput." Their entire engineering and production group was ecstatic.

An F-18 Fighter Jet being top-coated after a Navy TCP application

Navy TCP application on an F-18 Fighter Jet

I became convinced that we had to be bold and aggressive if we were going to turn the corner. Maintaining the status quo and calling on job shops one at a time or presenting METALForums once a month before a few engineers, as we had been doing, would only delay the inevitable: our financial demise. We had to do something that would rock the industry and our target market. We had to reach thousands of engineers and the vast manufacturing audience by whatever means necessary, no matter the cost. If we stayed the course, one day we would simply run out of money.

In August, the night before our quarterly board of directors meeting in Newport Beach, Susan and I had dinner with her son and my stepson Jordan, who was now twenty-two and studying business and marketing at California State University at Fullerton. We met at the Balboa Bay Club, a four-star restaurant and resort we'd been members of since the 1980s. Over steaks and a nice bottle of Duckhorn merlot, I explained to Jordan my concept behind the METALAST mobile marketing campaign that I had previously outlined to Raymond French. I described the large tractor and semitrailer that would travel the country, going from manufacturer to manufacturer and conducting daily educational seminars before engineering professionals. When I told Jordan that the forty-eight-foot-long trailer would be double-expandable, include a thirty-six-seat classroom, and feature a wet process line, two plasma televisions, and a satellite uplink tied to the METALAST Tech Center, he was blown away.

"It sounds awesome," he said. "So, what's the problem?"

"First, I have to give the marketing program a clever name and create a marketing image, and then I have to convince my board to help me figure out a way to fund it. I need to come up with a statement and an image that delivers a real message and a visual impact while being unique and special. It has to be eye-catching and something that engineers or scientists might relate to—maybe like a spaceship, satellite, or jet airplane. Maybe it would be an image of planet Earth, with streams, lakes, and mountains, or a wild animal, like a mustang, tiger, or lion. I want a theme that embraces a single object or a living thing."

We started jotting down ideas on a dinner napkin.

"What about something that roamed the earth millions of years ago, like a dinosaur?" Jordan asked. "Maybe a T-Rex?"

I jumped up. "That's it, Jordan! You've got it! That's the name of the campaign. We'll call it the T-REX Tour. Now let's figure out an acronym."

In less than thirty minutes, we came up with Touring Research and Educational Exhibit. And the rest, as they say, is history.

At the board of directors meeting the next day, I presented the T-REX mobile marketing campaign to my four directors and estimated the cost of the campaign to be about $5 million ($1 million to build, plus $1.3 million per year for a three-year tour). Roger Luby and Frank O'Bryan, my former bosses at Shearson/American Express, had known me for twenty-five years and were familiar with my propensity toward grandiose marketing concepts, but I believe I still caught them off-guard. Charlie Delle Donne, a former member of the Fidelity Investments board of directors, was a savvy marketing executive in his own right and loved the concept. Jerry Hollander, a thirty-year veteran of the metal-finishing business, always enjoyed playing the devil's advocate. Although he understood my logic, he wasn't keen on the idea.

Board member Arnie Gittelson, a successful business owner, was somewhat on board but needed convincing. "David, is this really going to work? You know you've tried things in the past that didn't. Moving a huge tractor and semitrailer around the country is a monumental task, and holding two-hour-long seminars and moving them from one manufacturing site to another on a daily basis has to be a logistical nightmare."

"Look, guys," I said, "here's the deal. Either we're going to do this, or we're going to fail, because the Fortune 500 are not going to spend millions of dollars testing chemicals from an unknown chemical company located in Minden, Nevada."

Though at first they thought I had lost my mind, they realized that I was serious and became convinced that without a directed marketing campaign toward the manufacturers and end-users of our products we were coming to the end of the road. They were justifiably skeptical about my ability to pull off such an ambitious and challenging plan. It was apparent to me that my ass was on the line. If the T-REX Tour failed, the blame would fall squarely on my shoulders—as well it should.

I still believed then, as I do now, that we had little choice. We needed something big, bold, and grandiose that would make a real statement and, more importantly, cause engineering professionals of the Fortune 500 to listen to our story. At the same time, we had to be careful in designing the mobile marketing concept. If the program was viewed as self-serving and thus perceived by the large manufacturers as an infomercial, they wouldn't participate. We had to design a seminar program that would wow the participants while also educating them. It would have to be seen as an advanced course in wet process control, automation, and metal-finishing production, providing consistency, traceability, quality assurance, and environmental compliance. The T-REX mobile seminar had to have the credibility of a university.

> **LIFE LESSON #94:**
>
> **SOMETIMES IN LIFE YOU MUST, "GO BIG OR GO HOME."**
>
> —PAUL WALKER (AMERICAN ACTOR, BEST KNOWN FOR THE FAST AND THE FURIOUS FRANCHISE, 1973–2013)

While a real estate developer in my mid-twenties, I had worked as part of the weekend security detail for Frank Sinatra during the Santa Clara University Golden Circle Theater Party Benefit for the Louis B. Mayer Theatre.

"David, it doesn't matter whether they talk good or bad about you," Mr. Sinatra had told me. "It only matters that they talk about you. Your brand must be something special."

I never forgot his advice. If you are to be remembered, you must be memorable. In my mind, T-REX was the most efficient and cost-effective way to present our comprehensive seminars to a targeted, captive audience and geographically diverse group of thousands of engineering professionals. Our message could not be told and comprehended in a five-minute sound bite at a trade show.

I was convinced the T-REX campaign would one day represent the pivotal turning point for our company. At the same time, I accepted that only time would tell whether my theory was correct—or the wishful thinking of an overly optimistic CEO.

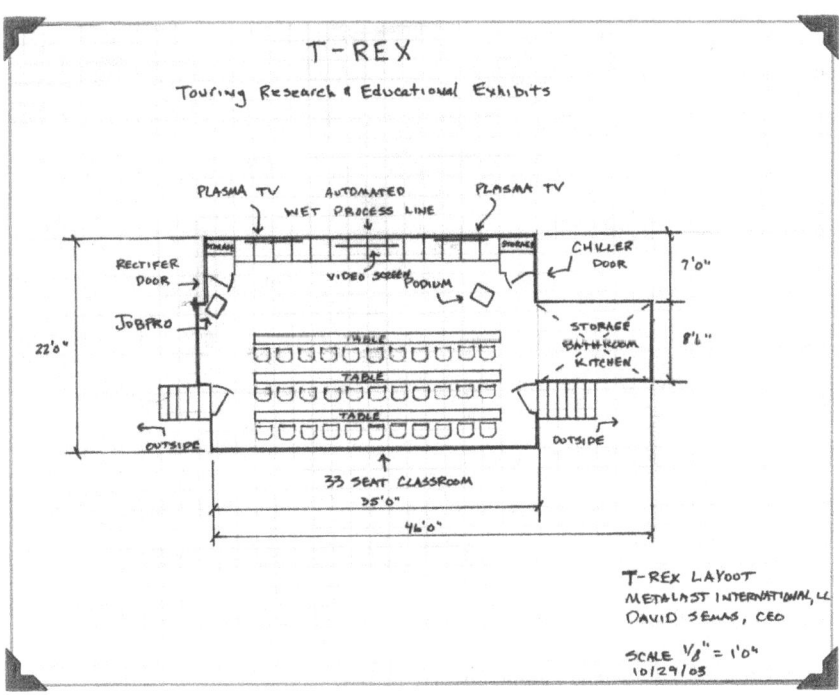

My hand-drawn floor plans for T-REX Semi-Trailer

For the startup of T-REX, I knew I would need someone from the metal-finishing industry to help me manage METALAST, someone who had the qualifications to take care of the technical side of the business. I hired Joe Conack, the former junior partner of APS and a chemical engineer with years of experience in the metal-finishing industry. He seemed like the technical person I needed to help manage our scientists, engineers, and technical sales group.

We found Harry Kurtz, president and CEO of Mobility Resource Associates, Inc. (MRA), a premier supplier of mobile event marketing exhibits and the pioneers in mobile marketing since 1989. They were truly a one-stop shop that provided vehicle design, modifications engineering, fabrication, outfitting, experienced big-rig tractor drivers, and even individual event design. Their main services and engineering center were located just ten minutes from Detroit Metropolitan Airport, ideally situated right in the middle of the US automotive industry. Their customers amounted to a who's who of recognizable brands: Boeing, Ford Motors, GlaxoSmithKline, Kodak, Mazda, Motorola, the Smithsonian Institution, and Swissair. Harry was a terrific CEO, and we became fast friends. While of relatively modest means, he became an investor in METALAST.

Throughout much of 2004, we worked around the clock with Harry Kurtz and his team, which was headed up by Dana Lee. Dana supervised the T-REX design, engineering, and installation of the interior classroom improvements to a forty-eight-foot-long semitrailer.

A rendering of the T-REX vehicle, front view

A rendering of the T-REX vehicle, rear view

My son Greg created, staffed, and managed the T-REX department, from soup to nuts. He hired and trained all personnel and established operating systems and procedures. With help from my friends Jerry McDonald and David "DT" Telling, we wrote and produced a sixty-minute T-REX training video that was synchronized with the mini wet process line and its overhead crane. Finding suitable companies as tour stops, identifying each company's go-to decision-maker, and scheduling and coordinating seminar dates was a monumental undertaking. The daily task of registering attendees and the complicated logistics of moving the drive team and moderators from city to city would have been a nightmare for most, but Greg and his team handled it like the professionals they were.

Most business-to-business marketing campaigns, including retail mobile marketing programs, move the massive tractor trailers from one site to the next once a month, every few weeks, or in some cases once a week. It would have been demanding enough to relocate and move the impressive T-REX tractor trailer on a weekly basis from one manufacturing facility to another, but to drive from one location to another on a daily basis was something else. Upon arrival at a given site, most of which were secured locations with gate-guarded entrances, the T-REX team would set up the trailer and then hold one, two, or sometimes three seminars in a single day. Then they would tear down and set up again at another location. Over the weekends, the team would wash the tractor and trailer and enjoy the local sights, sounds, and activities of the area and prepare to re-launch at 6:00 a.m. the following Monday morning.

By August of that year, everything was coming together nicely. I stopped by the new T-REX department, and for the next thirty days, the phones remained silent. None of the companies were signing up for the program. With a little help from Harish Bhatt, we got Ford Motors, General Motors, Motorola, and then Visteon Automotive to agree. The flood gates opened when Greg announced his team had also landed automotive companies like

> **LIFE LESSON #95:**
>
> **"WE WOULD ACCOMPLISH MANY MORE THINGS IF WE DID NOT THINK OF THEM AS IMPOSSIBLE."**
>
> —VINCE LOMBARDI

Daimler Chrysler, Delphi, Tenneco, and Walbro Engine. Next came aerospace and aircraft manufacturers like Boeing, Bell Helicopter, Cessna, General Dynamics, Honeywell, Lockheed Martin, Pratt & Whitney, and Raytheon. T-REX was invited to present its seminars before an audience at Lawrence Livermore National Laboratory, NASA, Warner Robins Air Force Base, Naval Air Systems Command, the United States Marine Corps, and the Universities of Michigan, Massachusetts, and Ohio.

> **LIFE LESSON #96:**
>
> "THINGS MAY COME TO THOSE WHO WAIT, BUT ONLY THE THINGS LEFT BY THOSE WHO HUSTLE."
>
> —ABRAHAM LINCOLN

Meanwhile, we had raised nearly all the $5 million needed to build T-REX and operate it for three years. During our mobile marketing campaign, we would use a northern route during the summer, visiting New York, Cleveland, Chicago, Denver, Salt Lake City, Reno, and the San Francisco Bay Area. The winter route would include Los Angeles, Phoenix, Dallas, Fort Worth, Atlanta, Jacksonville, and Miami. T-REX was scheduled to travel coast to coast at least three times over the three-year marketing campaign.

Everybody was excited, and we were running full steam ahead. I never admitted it to the T-REX team at the time, but I endured my share of sleepless nights praying and hoping that the campaign would be the success I had envisioned. Early results confirmed that T-REX was working like a charm as engineering departments from many of the largest corporations in the world opened their doors. Most importantly, the engineering professionals were convincing their labs and scientists to begin the tedious and costly

> **LIFE LESSON #97:**
>
> "FLAMING ENTHUSIASM, BACKED UP BY HORSE SENSE AND PERSISTENCE, IS THE QUALITY THAT MOST FREQUENTLY MAKES FOR SUCCESS."
>
> —DALE CARNEGIE

process of testing our chemicals, which was the first step to approval and eventually to manufacturer specifications.

On Sunday, October 31, 2004, Susan and I were in the process of moving into our new home, which I had just finished building at Buffalo Creek Ranch. Since buying the land in 1999, we had been going out to the ranch every weekend and staying in the log cabin while I worked on our ranch house and the fences, bridges, and outbuildings on the property. Snow was falling as we moved in.

Hand-hewn log cabin at Buffalo Creek Ranch

The upper pond and bridge

Susan and I at Buffalo Creek Ranch, 1999

Buffalo Creek Logo

I jumped on a plane for Detroit the very next day for the grand opening and unveiling of T-REX at MRA.

I had seen photographs of the gleaming eighty-one-foot-long tractor and semitrailer, but when I saw it in person, I was in awe and extremely proud. The sleek, polished black Volvo tractor pulled a semitrailer with an eight-foot-tall T-REX on all four sides. Members of the media, and metal finishers from the area were in attendance. Champagne and hors d'oeuvres were served. My friend, Mike Ornelas, flew out for the unveiling, and Raleigh Finkelstein, my friend and METALAST investor, drove down from Grand Rapids to join in the celebration. The following day, the T-REX Tour launched with our first presentation at Visteon Automotive.

The T-REX tractor-trailer

T-REX from the back view

I stayed with T-REX for its first week on the road and conducted seven seminars as moderator so that Byron Estes, our first T-REX moderator, could see how I handled the audience and video presentation. The seminar began with a forty-five-minute video presentation. Then the moderator explored the history of METALAST and the industry. The moderator delivered the "Solutions Provider" message while also introducing the wide range of products and services offered by METALAST and our sponsors. Finally, we finished with a Q&A. Our audience included product

> LIFE LESSON #98:
> "THERE IS NO SUBSTITUTE FOR PLANNING, ORGANIZATION, AND EXECUTION."
>
> —DAVID SEMAS

engineers, environmental compliance engineers, purchasing agents, departmental managers, engineering college students, and even a few executives. Sometimes there was standing room only. The attendees were extremely impressed by T-REX and our professionalism.

T-REX interior thirty-six-seat classroom. L-R, Me, Raleigh, and Mike

T-REX classroom marketing and promotional wall

T-REX made its way around the state for the next ten days, finishing in front of the eighteen-story General Motors Tech Center on November 11. The big rig was an impressive sight to see as it traveled down the interstate highways, drawing attention from young and old. Visitors and seminar attendees were speechless when they saw the interior of the T-REX, complete with its state-of-the-art AV equipment and automated wet process line replica.

Several months into the T-REX Tour, Harry Kurtz of MRA called me. "David, we've been in this business a long time. It's one thing to move an eighty-one-foot-long mobile unit like T-REX from one shopping mall to the next each weekend or from one company location to another every few weeks. But to move T-REX daily from site to site requires a level of sophistication and organization that most of our clients don't possess. I wanted you to know that your son, Greg, and his amazing T-REX department represents one of the most well-organized and coordinated efforts we've ever seen. Is it okay with you if we use your T-REX campaign as the model for success in mobile marketing?"

I agreed. I was flattered by Harry's praise of Greg and the T-REX department.

Harry also asked if he could submit the T-REX campaign for the following year's EX Awards, which recognized the best retail and business-to-business mobile marketing campaigns nationally. I was honored by the offer, and Harry submitted our T-REX Solutions Provider Tour program for consideration.

In 2005, thanks to the support of Harry and the MRA team, T-REX won the third-place Silver Ex Award in the Business-to-Business Mobile Marketing category from *Event Marketer* magazine, a prestigious industry trade publication. All told, thirty-seven campaigns had been entered. First place went to Shell Oil and second place to Kodak. We were honored to be recognized by several Fortune 500 companies and by so many professionals in the mobile marketing industry.

At the EX Awards in Detroit, with my son, Greg, far right, 2005

By September 2007, the T-REX Tour had come to a successful conclusion. Throughout its impressive three-year tour, T-REX presented a whopping 1,200 seminars in thirty-six states to about 400 companies, including many of the Fortune 500, at 450 different facilities and in front of 10,000 attendees. T-REX traveled the length of the country three times during its tour, covering nearly 100,000 miles.

CHAPTER 18

ANCHORS AWEIGH WITH THE NAVY

While the T-REX program was coming together, an opportunity arose to license an exciting new patented chemical. In early 2004, before the launch of T-REX, I received a phone call from Kurt Rued at the Montana State University Tech Link Center. Tech Link worked with the US Naval Air Systems Command to find potential partners to commercialize products they had patented and to bring them to the public market. It appeared we were a candidate to partner with the Navy, which had developed among other products a unique, environmentally friendly chemical for use in the anodizing process and corrosion control industry.

Kurt explained that the chemical was a green replacement for the known carcinogen hexavalent chromium, also known as Chrome 6 or Hex, an anti-corrosive chemical used in thousands of products. Hex, made infamous by the movie *Erin Brockovich*, was in the process of being banned worldwide. The Navy's replacement chemical, called Navy TCP, contained trivalent chromium, or Chrome 3, a green cousin to Chrome 6. The Navy was looking to license four companies to manufacture, sell, and distribute their own branded versions of the chemical, and it wanted two of its licensees to be small businesses.

Hex was not some obscure chemical used in only a small industry; it was one of the most widely used anti-corrosive chemical primers in the world and was used in aircraft, ships, military and defense applications, laptops, cell phones and 7,000 different automotive parts. If the replacement chemical really did what the Navy said it did, it was definitely something we should pursue.

For many years, I had been on the lookout for a breakthrough chemical that could become our showcase product while making METALAST a serious contender in the chemical business. I felt that this was the one. The contract with the Navy seemed like a reasonable deal and wouldn't cost a lot of money up front. Navy TCP, with our own brand name on it, could also serve as a showcase product for the T-REX campaign.

We assumed that the two big companies that the Navy had licensed already had so many chemicals on the market that they probably wouldn't bother trying to improve the formulation of this chemical; instead, they would just bring to the market the same chemical that the Navy had formulated. As it turned out, that's exactly what they did.

One of these licensees was Henkel, a powerful $30 billion German conglomerate known for its Duct Tape, Loctite, and Soft Scrub brands. Henkel was the world market leader in hexavalent chromium with its dominant anti-corrosive Alodine brand product. Logically, Henkel named the Navy's replacement chemical after their well-established brand, calling it Henkel Alodine T 5900. The only way we could hope to gain a sizable market share against two industry leaders would be to reformulate Navy TCP into a superior-performing chemical that could be specified by large manufacturers.

We worked around the clock in our labs to develop a formula that we submitted for the prestigious Qualified Product List (QPL) approval from NAVAIR. QPL, an extensive process that tests a manufacturer's claims of a product's performance, is extremely difficult to obtain and is a prestigious certification. After nearly twenty months of testing, we were granted QPL for our METALAST TCP-HF (Hex-free).

In the summer of 2006, we introduced our reformulated TCP-HF version. To handle the manufacturing and sales, we formed a partnership with a chemical company called Chemetall Oakite. They began promoting the chemical on their website, in trade publications, and on their corporate voicemail. Chemetall was a subsidiary of Chemetall Germany, which in 2016 was acquired by the $50 billion chemical giant BASF.

Jim White (not his real name), the senior vice president of Chemetall, contacted me and asked if we would be interested in forming a strategic alliance partnership with them. Mr. White and two other Chemetall executives flew out to the MTC in September 2005 to negotiate a license or joint venture agreement. Jeff Mackinen, my son Greg, and I met the group for dinner, and we gathered the following day at MTC in our upstairs board room.

The meeting began cordially enough, but after the first fifteen minutes, we got down to brass tacks.

Jim started the negotiation. "David, as you know, we're one of the largest suppliers of corrosion-control chemicals and metal-finishing products in the world. We're willing to offer your company a ten percent royalty on gross sales to license METALAST TCP-HF. We came here to make a deal and not to argue price, so we wanted you to know how serious we are and therefore didn't start the negotiations with a three percent royalty. Quite frankly, this partnership and the distribution and sale of METALAST TCP-HF will make your company a lot of money."

Over the years, I had read about and learned *The Art of The Deal* and had become a fairly savvy negotiator. As Jim spoke, I recalled the time in 1994 in the early days of METALAST when I had reached an agreement with a prominent Newport Beach family to invest $2.5 million into the company for 10 percent equity ownership. The oldest son, Brandon (not his real name), and I had sealed the deal with a handshake, but once the docs had been prepared and the time had come to execute the agreement and fund, the deal had changed.

Brandon called and said his father had changed his mind but was willing to invest $250,000 for 2 percent or double the equity ownership we'd agreed on. To make the offer even more tempting, Brandon said he had a $250,000 check in hand and was prepared to close the deal. I was under the gun because I had run out of capital, was one month behind in office rent, and hadn't taken a paycheck in several months.

"Thank you for the offer," I said, "but we made a deal at one percent per two hundred and fifty thousand dollars. If I were to accept two percent equity for two hundred and fifty thousand dollars, that would effectively mean my stated business valuation of twenty-five million dollars was double what METALAST was actually worth. If I were you, I'd be very nervous about going into business with someone of questionable integrity. Under the circumstances, I'll have to take a pass."

Jeff Mackinen, who was sitting only a few feet away and had been listening to the conversation, nearly fell out of his chair.

The telephone went silent for a good ten seconds, although it felt like an eternity.

"Wow!" Brandon finally replied. "You're willing to walk away from two hundred and fifty thousand dollars? You're either crazy, one hell of a negotiator, or an honorable man. I choose to think the latter, so come over and pick up your check and we have a deal for one percent of the business."

Back to the Chemetall negotiations.

Now that Jim had showed his cards, I responded without hesitation. "Thank you, Jim. I very much appreciate your candor. We're just a small Nevada-based specialty chemical company, but we're the one with the Navy master license. And there were only four issued—three of which were to your direct competitors. With no disrespect intended, we have the green alternative to your Chrome 6 product, and out of thirty-two known replacements for Chrome 6 in the world market, only two have ever received QPL approval, one of which is ours. We'd like to partner with Chemetall but not for a ten percent royalty. We'd like to partner on an equal, fifty-fifty basis."

"You can't be serious!" Jim replied.

"Yes," I replied, "I am. We're not a lone scientist that invented a chemical formulation that needs someone to manufacture, package, sell, distribute, and invoice. We

> LIFE LESSON #100:
>
> "IF YOU WISH TO HAVE YOUR PRODUCT WIDELY ACCEPTED, ALIGN WITH A WELL-RECOGNIZED BRAND TO ESTABLISH MARKET CREDIBILITY."
>
> —DAVID SEMAS

have our own chemical toll blender and are fully capable of continuing to sell our chemicals in North America and soon worldwide. I have an idea that might meet both our corporate objectives, making it a win-win for our respective companies."

An inquisitive look appeared on the face of each Chemetall executive.

"What do you have in mind?" Jim asked.

I wrote down the following on a notepad: *10 percent royalty to METALAST, then cost plus 20 percent to Chemetall for manufacturing, selling and distributing the chemical, and then a 50 percent-50 percent.* Then I slid the notepad across the table to Jim.

He glanced down and read what I had written. "What does this mean?"

"Simple," I answered. "We get a ten percent royalty off the top of all sales. Then Chemetall can charge the partnership actual manufacturing costs and add a twenty percent profit. Then we split the remaining profit *pari-passu,* or on a fifty-fifty percent basis."

Jim looked at his associates, and to my surprise, they nodded in approval, and we made the deal right then and there.

Before we finished the meeting, I clarified that we would provide the license, ongoing technical support, and the chemical formulation of METALAST TCP-HF to Chemetall. They in turn would manufacture, blend, package, sell, ship, invoice, collect, and pay METALAST net thirty days after invoicing and not collecting, since we had no way of approving credit extended to their customers. Once again, the group agreed, and we shook hands and executed the formal agreement over the next several weeks.

With Chemetall as our partner, companies like Apple, Boeing, Ford Motors, Honeywell, Lockheed Martin, Pratt &Whitney, Raytheon, and Sikorsky didn't have to wonder about METALAST's credentials or worry about specifying a chemical from a small Nevada-based company. Although they approached us, the bottom line was we'd had to align with a global company like Chemetall to be taken seriously.

LIFE LESSON #99:

"IN NEGOTIATIONS, HE WHO SPEAKS FIRST LOSES!"

—THE COLONEL

Meanwhile, T-REX was still traveling the country and opening doors at hundreds of facilities. With METALAST TCP-HF now added to our line of products and featured in our seminars, the T-REX Tour evolved. Now it was no longer just a solutions provider tour; it was introducing an environmentally friendly breakthrough in the multibillion-dollar world of anti-corrosives. The removal of Hex from supply chains was becoming a top priority to some of the biggest names in the industry.

With the official launch of METALAST TCP-HF, sample processing requests began pouring in to MTC and to Chemetall's New Jersey offices. Thanks in part to the T-REX mobile marketing campaign, we received many Hex replacement specifications from industry giants, including BAE Systems, Delphi, General Dynamics, GE Healthcare, Honeywell, Lockheed Martin, Northrop Grumman, Raytheon, Sikorski, and Weber Aircraft. With METALAST TCP-HF in our arsenal of proprietary environmentally friendly products, the Navy-licensed chemical was indeed one of the silver bullets I had long been waiting for.

Manufacturers sent in samples for processing, testing, and validation as we pursued more specifications for our branded chemical over those of our competitors. About 75 percent of the time that we competed head-to-head with similar products, our METALAST TCP-HF continued to outperform them, as independently validated by several industry giants. In 2007, leading companies went on record to say that METALAST TCP-HF was the best available Hex replacement in the world market. At a major aluminum extruder facility, tests conducted using TCP-HF as an anodizing seal showed production costs were cut by 25 percent—and with safer processing, with processing tanks operating at room temperature instead of the standard hot DI baths at 220 degrees.

Once again, we were reinventing our business model by redirecting our efforts toward the specialty chemical business. Under agreement with our Atlanta-based manufacturer, we had already developed a complete line of anodizing chemistries, including cleaners, deoxidizers, etchants, sealants, additives, and dyes, consisting of about eighty chemical products. With our showcased METALAST TCP-HF as an eco-friendly chromate conversion coating, we could build a new, successful business model that also represented a green approach to metal-finishing.

Although sample processing was moving along nicely, METALAST TCP-HF sales through our partner, Chemetall, were growing much slower than we had hoped. I thought I knew why, but I wanted to discuss it with our regional sales managers. In the summer of 2007, I held our annual sales conference at Buffalo Creek Ranch, bringing our RSMs in from all over the country for a picnic barbecue. Also joining us were Joe Conack, Jeff Mackinen, and my son, Greg.

Buffalo Creek Ranch picnic grounds

As we relaxed next to a creek beneath the swaying aspens and our ninety-foot-long railroad flatcar bridge, we discussed the issue of Chemetall sales while cooking hamburgers, steaks, and my Portuguese linguica sausage. The sales managers all expressed concern that the Chemetall salesmen were not aggressively selling TCP-HF. The problem seemed obvious: a Chemetall salesman probably made only half as much commission selling our chemical as he did selling their version containing hexavalent chromium.

Flatcar bridge to picnic grounds, log cabin, and Buffalo Creek Village

Ninety-foot flatcar bridge over picnic grounds and Sheridan Creek

I knew when we'd formed the partnership with Chemetall that they had a competing product containing Chrome 6 or Hex. I assumed government regulators would start forcing compliance with OSHA's new rules about Hex, causing metal finishers to switch over to non-Hex products and thus forcing Chemetall salesmen to sell our products. But that wasn't happening because the government was giving companies variances and extensions on the date of compliance. Until OSHA and the EPA forced compliance with the new governmental regulations, Chemetall would likely continue to advise their customers to use their less costly but more harmful Hex-based chemical.

The time had come to align with another chemical blender who would be capable of manufacturing our own private label brands. A provision in our contract with Chemetall allowed METALAST to start manufacturing the chemical ourselves after two years. In the meantime, Chemetall was still generating revenue for us, and as a globally recognized chemical company, they gave us top credentials in the world market.

Finding a new chemical blender would be a challenge since many were blending for competing companies. By spring of 2008, we would be able to look for independent distributors to start selling the chemical for METALAST under our sales program with our own regional sales managers, thus making us even more profit of at least 60 percent on gross sales. By then, if Chemetall had not converted one of their accounts to our product, we would have the right to convert that particular customer.

While discussing these issues, my sales managers and I moved from the picnic grounds to the conference room at our BCR train station for a meeting. The train station was a beautifully appointed meeting room next to a 1923 caboose that Susan and I had acquired and turned into a poker parlor. There, I gave Conack marching orders to identify a chemical blender for manufacturing TCP-HF and to start looking for potential distributors. At the same time, I instructed him to begin discussions with the Navy to expand our license rights from North America to worldwide.

Train station, caboose, waterfall, and pond beneath the aspens

The picnic area, fire pit, rock walls, and flatcar bridge

Train station meeting and conference room interior and bar

Interior of the caboose with hand-crafted oak wood trim

> LIFE LESSON #101:
> "SOMETIMES THE SHORTEST DISTANCE BETWEEN TWO POINTS ISN'T NECESSARILY A STRAIGHT LINE."
> —BEN SWIG

The T-REX campaign, though popular, wasn't a sales program. Thus, it wouldn't produce immediate results. The goals were to brand the name METALAST, demonstrate the superiority of our company and the prowess of our technical support, and embed in engineers' minds that we were the go-to company that could help them solve problems. We wanted to educate engineers and get technical personnel at these large corporations to start testing our products.

Manufacturer testing is also a long, drawn-out process, typically taking anywhere from three to as much as seven years. Adhesion salt-spray testing, for instance, requires 10,000 hours. The more alloys and parts involved, the longer the process. Three or four years might pass before a large company like GE or Ford actually specified our product. It would take an additional year for them to notify their supply chains and implement that specification. The finisher then had to deplete his inventories of the previous chemicals before he started using the new ones. Delivering the real-world application could take at least five years.

I was nevertheless exuberant as T-REX continued to travel around the country, holding seminars before thousands of manufacturers—our customer's customer. We had listened to the owners of job shops. After all, they had been metal-finishing products the same way for decades, and there was no need to change anything until their customers demanded it. The only way to get the metal-finisher's customers on board was to bring our message directly to them—at no cost and with no hassle. After the end of our three-year tour, we had successfully branded METALAST. By this time, few manufacturers were unaware of us.

Most of the puzzle pieces seemed to be falling into place—with one exception. Joe Conack, whom I had hired to oversee the technical side of METALAST, was becoming a major distraction. Although we'd had some work-related conflicts over the years, I had hoped he would be part of the team and prove himself professionally. No such luck.

His work ethic deteriorated after he opened his own eBay store. Eventually he was putting in a twenty-four-hour workweek at the MTC—at best. The last thing I wanted was to be left without a technical manager. It was becoming clear that Joe wasn't worth his sizable salary and generous stock options. After making numerous efforts to reel him in, I realized the time had come for us to part company, but the situation required that it be handled delicately. He had ingratiated himself with our broker-dealers, board members, and key customers.

After his departure, I spent weeks doing damage control. I rose at 4:30 a.m. to make phone calls to the East Coast, speaking to the Navy and assuring them that we had everything under control. I also had to calm the troops, which required that I institute immediate corrective measures to restore confidence in leadership.

LIFE LESSON #102:

"RUNNING AWAY FROM YOUR PROBLEMS IS A RACE YOU'LL NEVER WIN."

—TAYLOR COUNSELING GROUP

CHAPTER 19

METALAST APPEARS TO BE COMING OF AGE

We held our fourteenth annual members meeting in October 2008 at the Carson Valley Inn in front of a standing-room-only audience of about 150 shareholders. This looked like it would be the most challenging meeting of my career. Even though perhaps only ten of our shareholders were displeased with our progress over the last year, I still felt the pressure mounting as I prepared to stand before the group and disclose that we had yet to turn a profit. Each year it had gotten more tenuous, which I could appreciate, considering the fourteen years of red ink. Now there was additional concern about Conack's departure and upheaval in the company. To make matters worse, ominous signs suggested that the economy was in serious trouble. Nevertheless, with specifications mounting, I thought we would start to land some big accounts and was optimistic 2009 would finally be our breakout year.

After everyone enjoyed a buffet lunch, I stood before the crowd to present a slideshow, walking the shareholders through our accomplishments of the past year. Although a little nervous, I still felt proud of what we had achieved.

Our technical team had developed METALAST® TCP-HF EPA (Extended Protection Additive) to enhance the performance and general ease of use of TCP-HF. The METALAST AA-200 anodizing additive was also coming of age, with over twelve years of field validation. We had published many technical papers on AA-200's ability to increase throughput, enhance the surface finish, provide better corrosion protection, reduce crazing (surface cracking), and improve efficiency and had received independent validation from NADEP.

We were seeing increased interest in TCP-HF and AA-200 and now our TCP-HF EPA from job shops and manufacturers alike. We had been granted one of our most influential specifications from the aerospace technology giant Pratt & Whitney, which had begun requiring the use of TCP-HF as an anodizing seal. Pratt & Whitney had some 750 metal-finishing vendors of choice, and if they started using our chemicals that year, I felt confident we would start seeing significant revenue growth.

Lockheed Martin in Dallas had announced that METALAST TCP-HF had demonstrated the most impressive results they had ever seen, producing more than 1,560 hours (65 days) of salt spray on highly corrosive alloys. (Most non-Hex alternatives fail in less than one hundred hours.) There was a buzz around the aerospace community as Lockheed began disclosing to Boeing, Northrop Grumman, and others their impressive achievement with TCP-HF, which meant soon Lockheed might approve its use throughout their supply chain.

Finally, thanks to Greg's hard work and his methodical attention to detail, the tremendous success of the T-REX campaign, and fifteen years of perseverance by the entire METALAST staff, our 2008 revenues had surpassed the fiscal year of 2007 by nearly four times. If the economy didn't set us back, we felt confident that we would see some dramatic growth in 2009.

When I wrapped up my presentation, I invited questions from the audience. The vast majority of shareholders were supportive and recognized that we were working hard to achieve results despite facing some pretty formidable obstacles.

However, one shareholder stood up and said, "If we're still not profitable by the end of next year, are you willing to resign from the company?"

"I'm not going to resign," I said flatly. "But if you're not happy with me or management, you have every right to vote the manager out with a simple majority of fifty-one percent of the shareholders."

Overall, the reaction from the shareholders was positive. We had identified a new METALAST TCP-HF chemical manufacturer, were starting to sign up distributors, and had found a solution to the Chemetall sales problem. All these signs of progress gave our shareholders a feeling that we were moving in the right direction. We ended the annual members meeting on a high note.

Considering our struggle to penetrate a one-hundred-year-old industry, I appreciated the loyal support I had received from the vast number of our shareholders over the years. I knew that one of the main reasons for their support was my policy of maintaining open lines of communication and offering honest and direct answers. Burying my head in the sand and keeping shareholders and employees in the dark during difficult times would have only exacerbated whatever problems we faced.

Meanwhile, a recession on the scale of the Great Depression had set in and appeared to be growing worse by the day. All industrial sectors were being affected, and Fortune 500 companies announced mass layoffs to the tune of more than 650,000 workers in the fourth quarter of 2008. The unemployment rate was climbing higher than 10 percent in many parts of the country, and financial disaster loomed for many manufacturing companies. Yet despite the economic downturn, our brand was coming of age.

The MTC lab was running full-tilt, working with current and prospective accounts, conducting R&D, processing sample parts, and testing the performance of

LIFE LESSON #103:

"EFFECTIVE COMMUNICATION IS 20% WHAT YOU KNOW AND 80% HOW YOU FEEL ABOUT WHAT YOU KNOW."

—JIM ROHN

TCP-HF for existing and future specifying manufacturers. Greg, now our senior vice president of operations, was coordinating training sessions with the RSMs and our new distributor while spending days in the field holding welcome-aboard meetings with our one-hundred-man-strong and growing national distributor network. We were receiving favorable test reports and specifications requiring the use of TCP-HF and were continuing to reach agreements with chemical distribution companies. Forty companies now required that TCP-HF be adopted as their hexavalent chromium replacement.

One exciting project was the possibility of a Small Business Innovation Research (SBIR) grant from the US Air Force. Our distributors were opening doors for us at major job shops like Valmont/George Industries, a Southern California precision anodizer we had spent twelve years attempting to land. Companies like Raytheon and BAE Systems began specifying our chemical companywide. This meant that their vendors would be required to use TCP-HF, with no substitutes allowed.

In 2009, the Navy issued its NESDI (Navy Environmental Sustainability Development to Integration) Program Report for their 2008 fiscal year, and the report provided validation of METALAST. The Navy intended to have the METALAST technology specified throughout the entire Department of Defense worldwide, including the members of the DoD's 55,000 global suppliers involved in metal-finishing. One day, our technology and products would be found in metal-finishing facilities, government facilities, and the private sector globally.

Then in April, US Senator John Ensign (R-Nevada), serving as the ranking member of the Science, Technology, and Innovation Committee, presented a US Senate Proclamation in recognition of METALAST for "their world-changing technologies and commitment to science in the field of the elimination of hex chrome, while providing an excellent working environment and high-paying jobs in Nevada." Since 1995, with little fanfare, METALAST had effectively served as an ambassador of goodwill for the Silver State around the globe.

During an awards program, similar proclamations were made by Nevada's Lieutenant Governor Brian Krolicki, Nevada State Senator James Settlemeyer, the Douglas County Board of County Commissioners,

Northern Nevada Development Authority, and the Business Council of Douglas County. We felt truly honored.

Back in 1994, when I'd first started the company, I had believed our anodizing technology, process control computers, and METALAST AA-200 would serve as the backbone of our business. I had been incorrect. Since the beginning, we had been forced to adapt, reinvent ourselves, and change our business model repeatedly. By moving toward a solutions-provider approach and becoming a specialty chemical company, we had gained recognition for our brand, accumulated intellectual property, and grown revenues. We were also developing a recurring income stream through the sale of consumable products. Our website was receiving more than 2,000 inquiries monthly, with approximately 150 companies downloading technical literature each week.

We had weathered one catastrophic event after another, from a process control computer that didn't perform as advertised to disinterested customers, products that failed to perform, and disloyal employees bent on my personal destruction. I had experienced the shock of being wrongly accused and had been the recipient of an unwarranted raid by the IRS. We had seen economic booms, but each time we ramped up, we were always a day late and a dollar short. Rarely had I enjoyed a decent night's sleep. The thought that I had been entrusted with tens of millions of dollars of investment from family, friends, and shareholders, not to mention the livelihood of all METALAST employees, kept me up at night. Like it or not, I knew that if I was going to be the leader and CEO of a company, I had to be willing to accept the enormous responsibility, pressure, and stress that came with the title.

At about this time, as had been the case during the previous four years, we were in the midst of planning and organizing Carson Valley's fifth-annual

FEAT flyer, 2008

Families for Effective Autism Treatment (FEAT) Dinner Concert and Buffalo Creek Invitational Golf Tournament. In previous years, the weekend-long event had been a resounding success and had raised over $300,000 to date.

We were blessed the day Wendi gave birth to our grandson in 2002. Before his first birthday, David John Fauria was diagnosed with ASD (Autism Spectrum Disorder), but he continues to make positive strides every day and recently graduated from high school with honors. At the time, ASD affected one out of one hundred and twenty children born in America. Sadly, today that number is one in forty-four. ASD includes a range of developmental disorders characterized by unusual brain development. The cause of autism is still unknown, but many speculate that it is caused by a genetic susceptibility with an environment trigger. People with ASDs tend to have problems with social and communication skills.

In 2004, Wendi, her husband at the time Garritt Fauria, and their friends Tara and Ed Addeo and Toni and Allen Gumm formed FEAT to help Northern Nevada families whose children were impacted by ASD. Friends, family, and complete strangers rallied around the cause and graciously supported our event each year.

The annual FEAT dinner concert under the stars was always a sold-out event. Garritt greeted arriving guests at the security gate, and sixteen parking attendants directed each automobile to our eight-acre vineyard. A forty-passenger trolley car, tractor-drawn hay wagon, and old-fashioned carriage transported the five hundred dinner guests to a registration table beneath a grapevine-covered gazebo. Those in the receiving line, including Nevada governor Jim Gibbons, were greeted by 1880s-attired ladies and gents who escorted them over a bridge and creek to the beautiful outdoor concert site located among the aspens. Entertainment was provided by our buddies, David John and the Comstock Cowboys.

Sixty ten-person tables were decorated with cowboy boots and floral arrangements, which were surrounded by twelve VIP tents, two large silent-auction tents, and a professional stage with rigging and a canopy. Although we had originally acquired CoCo, a beautiful four-month-old Australian shepherd, to auction off and raise money for the charity, Susan had bonded with the puppy during its two-week stay with us, and there was no way she was going to let me be outbid. The only answer was to be the highest bidder and buy CoCo again. Our guests knew this, so a few of my friends kept bidding to drive up the price for CoCo and thus make more money for the charity. A few months later, we bought CoCo a companion: Black Jack ("Jack"), another Aussie and an ASCA and American Kennel Club sheep-herding champion. The inquisitive and always alert Aussie duo became the watchful proprietors of BCR and official greeters of all invited guests.

CoCo and Jack at Buffalo Creek Ranch house

Thanks to the generosity of Chip and Susan Hanly, Marsha & Bill Tomerlin, Tom and Judy Clydesdale many other Northern Nevada friends in 2009, the final year of the BCR Golf Tournament and the evening of the Comstock Dinner Concert, FEAT received nearly $150,000 in net proceeds.

I wondered what would have happened had we not been able to finance and launch the T-REX mobile marketing campaign. I knew that without reaching the manufacturers and educating engineers on the benefits of process control and eco-friendly chemical solutions, our business would have failed. At this point, we had raised more than $75 million of investment capital—an accomplishment that nearly every NASD broker-dealer, institutional investor, and private equity advisor had said was impossible. Against all odds, although nearly running out of operating capital, we were somehow still standing.

Even with all the good news on the horizon, however, we were still in the red, our cash reserves were rapidly depleting, and I was becoming more concerned about our ability to sustain operations as the recession worsened.

By now, nearly every industrial sector had been significantly impacted by the Great Recession. Many leading American financial and industrial icons had failed. Lehman Brothers Holdings had filed for Chapter 11 bankruptcy protection for a whopping $691 billion. The $690 billion bankruptcy of General Motors was the fourth largest in US history. In April, Chrysler filed bankruptcy for the tidy sum of $39 billion. Many of the largest corporations in America announced layoffs. We began feeling the impact as it became far more difficult to raise capital during the economic downturn.

Then, in the early morning hours of April 30, 2009, the same day Chrysler filed for bankruptcy, I received a disturbing telephone call from my administrative assistant, Jill Niichel. A few years later, Jill married my long-time friend, hunting partner, and Reno Rodeo cattle drive Buckaroo, Ed Quintal. She informed me that we had been served notice and demand for "Production of Documents" from the Enforcement Division of the Los Angeles Regional Office of the Securities and Exchange Commission (SEC).

LIFE LESSON #104:

"THE ULTIMATE MEASURE OF A MAN IS NOT WHERE HE STANDS IN MOMENTS OF COMFORT AND CONVENIENCE, BUT WHERE HE STANDS AT TIMES OF CHALLENGE AND CONTROVERSY."

—MARTIN LUTHER KING JR.

CHAPTER 20
HERE WE GO AGAIN

"Oh my God," I muttered. "Here we go again."

"It's an informal notice. They're asking you to voluntarily comply." Jill scanned the faxed document and emailed it to me.

My laptop sounded its familiar "ping," informing me that I had just received an email. I opened the PDF file, and there it was: a fax cover page from the US Securities and Exchange Commission, Pacific Regional Office in Los Angeles. Across the top of the page, in large bold print, were the words FOR IMMEDIATE DELIVERY.

US Securities and Exchange Commission logo

As I began to read the document, my eyes were drawn to one sentence in particular: "The staff of the Los Angeles SEC, as a part of its enforcement and regulatory responsibilities under federal securities laws, is conducting an informal inquiry regarding METALAST International, LLC." The ominous communication requested that we provide the SEC with all "offering documents used by METALAST; promotional and marketing materials; use of investor funds or proceeds; and a complete list of all METALAST investors from January 1, 1995, through the present." Although the letter stated that our cooperation was voluntary, it also contained language that threatened the use of subpoena powers by the SEC if we refused to cooperate.

Things were looking pretty bad. The economy was in a tailspin, and now this? The $65 billion Bernie Madoff scandal had caused a vehement public uproar still reverberating up and down Wall Street. The sheer mention of an SEC investigation sent shivers up the spine of Wall Street broker-dealers and investors alike. *The Washington Post* had reported that the SEC filed nearly as many formal investigations in 2009 as it had in any of the previous five years. The high-profile embarrassment over the Madoff scandal was prompting the SEC to launch widespread investigations. Many well-known public companies were being targeted by the SEC, persuaded by some well-meaning and not so well-meaning whistleblowers influenced by the rash of scandals.

Regardless of what was fueling this fishing expedition, I felt it was best to fully cooperate with the SEC and offer complete transparency. A cover-up is often worse than simply disclosing the truth about bad news. I immediately contacted Jeff Mackinen, Greg, Wendi, and our board members and investment brokers.

Then we set out to provide the SEC with all the documents they requested. In May, we delivered a box of marketing materials, corporate literature, source and use of investor funds, and a complete listing of the names and addresses of our nearly 1,000 shareholders. I was under the naïve impression that if we had nothing to hide and fully cooperated, the SEC would realize that we were an honest and reputable business. As a limited liability company that was not publicly traded, we should have never been on their radar screen in the first place. But a few disgruntled employees with an obvious grudge against management were out to get even.

Within days of receiving the documents from us, the SEC sent letters and a seven-page confidential questionnaire to most of our shareholders, informing them

> **LIFE LESSON #105:**
>
> **"FOR EVERY GOOD REASON THERE IS TO LIE, THERE IS A BETTER REASON TO TELL THE TRUTH."**
>
> —BO BENNETT
> (AMERICAN AUTHOR, 1972–)

of the METALAST investigation. Our telephones began to ring off the hook, emails inundated our servers, and letters demanding the return of individual investments in METALAST started pouring in. Between the troublemakers, the SEC's intrusive investigation, and the deplorable state of the faltering economy, the investing public was in a near-panic not seen since the Great Depression, and I had a bad feeling the company was going to suffer serious repercussions.

I always looked forward to participating in and being the primary sponsor of the annual five-day Reno Rodeo Cattle Drive. It helped me unwind. In June 2009, I decided to maintain that tradition and join the drive once again. There appeared to be a lull in the SEC activity, and I had been able to calm most of our shareholders by explaining that we had done nothing wrong and were fully cooperating with the SEC.

I had been involved in the cattle drive, which kicked off "The Wildest and Richest Rodeo in the West," since 1995 and had taken over as the main sponsor in 2007. Each year, I would invite a small group of business associates, company executives, family, and friends to join me. Most years, the group included my brother Len, my son Greg, my stepson Jordan Woods, Greg's college football sidekick Frank Romano, my son-in-law Larry Day, my nephew Bill Campbell, and my old high school sidekicks and hunting buddies Ed Quintal and Steve Ferreira. A few times METALAST CPA, business partner and good friend Jim Kieckhafer would join in on the cowboy adventure. Longtime friend and business partner Marc Harris and his two sons, Danny and Matt, joined us sometimes as well. Then there was friend Mark Meckler, co-founder of the Tea Party Patriots and President of the Convention of States Project; and good friend Mark Wyman, local Northern Nevada builder and craftsman. All signed up for the old west experience, which provided an opportunity to take a break from work and unwind. There were no cell phones on the dusty trail of the Nevada high desert.

DAVID MICHAEL SEMAS

ALL PHOTOGRAPHS AND IMAGES OF THE RENO RODEO AND RENO RODEO CATTLE DRIVE PROVIDED BY AND COURTESY OF RENO RODEO ASSOCIATION, KEVIN BELL AND MARI CLARK

Enjoying the rodeo in Reno in 2005

At the RRCD with trail boss Butch Van Leuven, 2012

The cattle drive always started the second Friday of each year. Just like the elephants coming to town promoting the arrival of the circus it was the advance public relations event announcing the beginning of the ten-day-long Reno Rodeo, which would begin the following Friday night. Guests would arrive from all over the country and sometimes from all over the world. Early Saturday morning, a beautiful washed and polished sixty-passenger deluxe motor coach would take cattle drive guests on a two-hour shopping spree to pick up last-minute items at my friend Jack Bassett's D Bar M Western Store. Later in the day, the motor coach would take the whole gang to the Bucket of Blood Saloon in Virginia City (VC) for an afternoon performance by Nevada's own David John and the Comstock Cowboys. The Comstock Cowboys and many of their guests always dressed in 1880s cowboy attire, complete with holsters and six-guns and even the occasional US Army Seventh Cavalry officer uniform. Guests would also spend the afternoon strolling Virginia City's main street with its gift shops, saloons, casinos, restaurants, museums, and tourist stops.

David John and the Comstock Cowboys at Bucket of Blood Saloon in VC

Me joining David John and the boys for a song, 2011

The motor coach would depart VC at five o'clock and head back to Reno for an authentic Basque dinner, after which the guests would retire for the evening. A safety briefing the next morning at the Reno Rodeo grounds would include a welcome by my first trail boss and future Reno Rodeo President, Brad Sidener. Beginning in 2012 trail boss duties were turned over to retired Reno Fire Department Battalion Chief and Lieutenant Colonel in the Nevada Air National Guard, Butch Van Leuven. Many other local luminaries and dignitaries were present for the opening ceremony, which sometimes included U.S. Senator Dean Heller. After formalities and before leaving the rodeo grounds for cattle camp, US Marshal J. D. Cahill (aka me) would give a five-minute speech in Old West cowboy lingo cautioning the guests to be on the lookout for Bad Man José and his dangerous band of Comanchero outlaws.

My first Trail Boss and future me as US Marshal J. D. Cahill, 2014

The official launch of the cattle drive began mid-Sunday morning, with participants departing from the Reno rodeo grounds around nine-thirty. The cattle drive contingent would head up Highway 395 about thirty-five miles and would include a staged kidnapping of the cattle drive's guests on Red Rock Road. Logically, the kidnapped dudes were rescued after a mock Old West gunfight between good guys Marshal Cahill and General Nelson Miles (aka my son Greg) and the bad guys. Participating in the event were Captain Richard Lee and his reenacting members of the Seventh Cavalry. Wes Farnham, Stan Lennon, Doug Dike, Herb Shrum and Andy Hughes with their "Sierra Six Guns" reenacting troop, which featured Wyatt, Virgil and Morgan Earp and of course Doc Holiday partook in the dude liberation. The good guys rescued the cattle drive guests from Bad Man José and his "Guns N Gals" ruthless band of Comancheros, portrayed by friend Randy Gomez and his wife Patty."

I salute all my cowboy guys and gals of the Reno Rodeo Cattle Drive Committee that put on this world-class wild west Buckaroo extravaganza. From the original brainchild of the Reno Rodeo Cattle Drive Trail Boss and Head Honcho, "Doc" Steve Milstein, to all my good friends thank you so much for letting me be a part of your lives. Because of you thousands of children and parents delight each year when horseback mounted Miss Reno Rodeo past and present, US Cavalry, Cowboys, covered wagons, Flying U Rodeo and Cotton Rosser's corriente roping steers and the entire cattle drive contingent makes its way through the streets of Reno to the fairgrounds.

A VERY SPECIAL THANK YOU TO, INCLUDING BUT NOT LIMITED TO; Randy, Terry & Jeremiah Bell, Kevin Bell, Alex Benna, Bill Bertelson, Regina Brush, Bruce Bye, Vicki Bowman, Joe Capurro, Mari Clark, Don Cose, Kari Cordisco, Gordie & Melinda Cowan, Dave Depoali, Dave Dohnel, George Dorsa, Steve Edgar, Mikey Efstratis, Mark Elston, Joe Enzenberger, Larry Fenkell, Jim Foster, Kurt Gale, Dave & Kat Grashuis, Greg Gross, Dan Hale, John Harp, Andrew Layman, Jenny Lesieutre, Kevin Linderman, Wayne Lund, Rich Massa, Mike Marusak, Mike McCreary, Jason McGraw, Tom Pagnano, Pam Peeks, Linda Potter, Bill Price, John Semas, Jim "Doc" Rappaport, John Schwartzler, Brad, Logan & Chelsea Sidener, Rod & Sharon Smith, Dan Snow, Doc Spogan, John Solari, Lisa

& Danny Stewart, Chris Stewart, Peggy Stromer, Matt Tobler, Red & Doug Taliaferro, Mike, Greg & Katie Torvinen, Butch Van Leuven, Clint Wells, Terry Vanzant and last, but not least our dearly departed friend and Reno Rodeo Cattle Drive Sponsor for ten years, Howard Weiss.

Marshal Cahill (aka me) and General Nelson Miles (aka Greg), 2014

From L-R, Bad Man Jose, trail boss Brad Sidener, and me in 2007

Gunfight in Doyle with "Marshal Cahill", Earps, and Doc Holiday, 2011

Son-in-law San Jose PD Sgt. (retired) Larry Day and Greg 2014

After a two-hour stop at the Buck Inn Saloon for alcoholic libations—or sarsaparillas for those wanting to wet their whistle with non-stimulating spirits—we drove to cattle camp in our symbolic stagecoach (motor coach) in preparation for our world-famous five-day cattle drive. The first base campsite was located at Stix Corrals, forty-five miles north of Reno and

US Army Lieutenant General Nelson Applegate Miles (aka Greg) 2014

about five miles south of the small outpost town of Doyle, California, with its general store and the Buck Inn. Everyone was preparing to ride their horses fifteen to twenty miles a day while sitting in a saddle and pushing three hundred head of roping steers for six hours a day—much like it was done 150 years ago along the Chisholm Trail.

We had cozy personal digs (two-man tents) and a main gathering tent. I built the portable customer-built Buffalo Creek Saloon bar trailer, re-named Sierra Dorado Saloon. In charge of the saloon thirst parlor were my "buckaroo buddies": Dan Hale, Terry Vanzant, Rod Smith, and my brother Len, resident joke-teller. I also had built a separate shower trailer with six enclosed hot water shower compartments, and of course men's and women's porta-potties.

Each early morning hour at four-thirty, we awoke to the sights and sounds of the Nevada high desert and the fresh aroma of Randy Bell's sweet and pretty wife Terry Bell's hot coffee brewing and crispy bacon cooking on the open grill. While the stars were still shining, the air was still chilly, and dew covered the ground, all sixty "city slickers," twenty cowboy buckaroos, and fifteen camp crew members were scurrying about.

At the cattle drive in front of the Buffalo Creek Ranch Saloon trailer. L-R, Steve Ferreira, Ed Quintal, me, Greg, Frank "the Italian" Romano, nephew Bill Campbell, and in front, Deb Perse and Cowboy Cory in 2008

L-R, RRCD bartender Rod Smith, Terry Vanzant, and brother Len 2014

The RRCD wagon train, 2015

Entertainment bosses Tom Pagnano and Mike Torvinen, camp boss John Harp, and wagonmaster John Schwartzler, along with his twenty-five covered wagon teamsters, swampers, and outriders and their ten teams of Percheron, Clydesdale, and Belgium draft horses and mules were preparing to hitch up their equestrian teams' Old West covered wagons. Eight "Biscuit Rollers", or Cookies (camp cooks) were busy preparing an out-of-this-world cowboy feast overseen by the multitalented, widely acclaimed, and fantastic Dutch Oven Diva, Terry Bell. Accomplished buckaroo and photographer Mari Clark and barkeep and mixologist Kari Cordisco awoke from their tents and chowed down with us on a break-of-dawn breakfast.

Each morning, before time was a wastin', the camp was torn down and tents and camp gear were loaded into the covered wagons, trucks, and trailers. Draft horses and mules were hitched to covered wagons, and the entire one-hundred-strong cattle drive contingent, with at least half the cowboy guests consisting of self-reliant Western equestrian women, saddled up for the day's adventure. Dave Dohnel, a great guy who pretended to be a cantankerous and crotchety old cowboy, was the proud owner of Frontier Pack Train out of June Lake and Bishop, California, and our jigger boss (third in command behind the trail boss and cattle boss). Dave and his team of six talented young cowboys were responsible for guest safety and the string of one hundred head of Western saddle horses.

Circling wagons and setting cattle camp outside of Doyle, California, 2015

Driving Corriente roping steers over a rocky cliff, 2013

Cattle on the move, eating grass along the high mountain trail

Cattle on grass land moving through valley toward Marshall Flats

Each day, after pushing cattle over a dusty fifteen-mile trail and after swallowing a pound of dirt, we arrived with dusty faces at the next cattle camp, which had been assembled by the camp crew and wagon teamsters only a few hours earlier. After cleaning up at the water trough, we would retreat to the Sierra Dorado Saloon for a few libations and a rehash of the day's events along the trail. Dinner followed. Then we would sit around the campfire inside the protected circle of covered wagons and over the years enjoyed gifted cowboy entertainers and cowboy poets, Michael Martin Murphey, Dave Stamey, Larry Maurice,

> **LIFE LESSON #106:**
>
> **"COURAGE IS BEING SCARED TO DEATH AND SADDLING UP ANYWAY."**
>
> —JOHN WAYNE (AMERICAN ACTOR, DIRECTOR, AND PRO-DUCER, THE DUKE, 1907–1979)

Richard Elloyan, Joe Cannon, Baxter Black, Waddie Mitchel, and Don Edwards organized by our dedicated and flamboyant friend, Tom Pagnano, who sadly passed away in 2012.

A cowboy and the full moon

Cowboy playing his guitar and singing around the fire, 2013

The cattle drive could be quite dangerous, as we rode horses weighing 1,000 pounds or more. Many a time, we had to helicopter out an injured cowboy (almost never a guest) that had been thrown from his horse, causing a broken collarbone or leg or fractured ribs. But usually, we just enjoyed the scenery, the comradery, and the experience, riding over the high desert and through beautiful valleys.

At the end of five grueling days, which included baking in hot and dry high-desert temperatures, being battered by howling Nevada winds, and often riding in rain and even snow, we arrived near our final destination: the Reno Rodeo Fairgrounds. Upon hitting the streets near the Dandini Research Park at the north end of Reno, we were met by covered wagons and the past and current Miss Reno Rodeo on horseback.

Cattle strung out preparing for arrival on the streets of Reno

We were also met by my brother Len, who was driving my sleek black 2012 Dodge Ram Limo (cowboy slang for a dually pickup truck). *The Magnificent Seven* theme song and "Garryowen," the Irish drinking song with a marching cadence made famous by George Armstrong Custer's Seventh Cavalry, emanated from the front grill. Also joining the parade were Reno's finest, the Reno police, on motorcycles, plus mounted deputies from the Washoe County Sheriff's Office. The cattle, horse, and covered-wagon parade traveling down the busy city streets of Reno was a sight to behold.

US Marshall J. D. Cahill (me) stopping traffic with the assistance of Reno's finest, the City of Reno Police officers in cars and motorcycles and the mounted Washoe County Sheriff's Department

Cowboys on horseback, nose to tail, keeping cattle in lockstep and protecting the onlooking crowds of 30,000 men, women, young cowboys and cowgirls, and moms with baby carriages

Under the protection of our law-enforcement escorts, we slowly and quietly moved the herd so as not to spook the cattle and start a stampede, which had happened on a few occasions. We cautiously advanced the herd under the noisy Highway 395 overpass and onto McCarron Boulevard. As we traveled down McCarron from Highway 395 and turned left (south) on Sutro Street, we could hear cheering from the 10,000 people that lined the streets, patiently waiting for the three hundred Corriente steers and one hundred cowboys to ride past.

The Cavalry in front of the cattle drive on the streets of Reno

Nearing the end of the cattle drive outside the Reno Rodeo grounds

I've ridden alongside and gotten to know cattle drive guests from every walk of life in at least twenty-five states. Others came from countries as far away as Japan, Australia, Portugal, and Israel, including a female member of the security detail for Queen Elizabeth's sister. Sharon was a member of the Royal Protection Group (SO14), a component of the Metropolitan Police Service (MPS) Protection Command. In appreciation for what she said was an experience of a lifetime, she presented me with an SO XIV lapel pin, which I still cherish to this day.

My Reno Rodeo Cattle Drive Nevada Buckaroo Code of Honor was presented to cattle drive guests and was signed by Governor Brian Sandoval and Senator Dean Heller and is proudly mounted on the wall of the Reno Rodeo offices.

RENO RODEO CATTLE DRIVE
NEVADA BUCKAROO CODE OF HONOR©

How do ya recite a Cowboy Code of Honor whilst
standing next to a Buckaroo brother?
Well, let me tell ya—canen't be done without the rhyming
of one set of words with another
Startin' at the rodeo grounds with Trail Boss Butch
and Marshal Cahill swearin' us Rangers in
One by one we all tooka' oath to be law abiden', honest,
above-board when givin' our tin

Next things I knowed we'd been kidnapped and robbed
by Bad Man José and his outlaw gang
'Twere Mexican Bandidos who'd kill ya 'cause
they didn't give a gosh-dang
The ol' stagecoach took us Dudes and Wranglers
to the Doyle Hotel & General Store
Then a gunfight broke out with J. D. Cahill, the Earps,
and Doc Holiday—need I say more?
The good guys won, a hangin' took place—we all had a

few shots of libations at the Buck Inn
Boarded the stagecoach again, headed for Stix Corrals
for this Old West adventure to begin
I recollect next mornin' wakin' to the aroma of hot coffee
when I wanted to sleep in late
'Twas well-done scrambled eggs a'steamin', crispy bacon
still fryin' when they hit my plate

Then ridin' a horseback, pushin' them there Corriente
steers in the Nevada hot desert sun
A heap of hard work for most Dudes & Dudettes,
but to Buckaroos it's nothin' but fun
On the high desert we pass Pinyon pine and sagebrush,
when purple lupine catches the eye
After twelve miles on the long, desolate trail, away off
yonder cattle camp silhouettes the Big Sky

Inta Campbell Springs, our faces covered in dirt
when we gave a big hoot and holler
It's hard to believe that Buckaroos of the Old West
did this for less than a silver dollar
Everyone fills their bellies with delectable grub,
then a Jack Daniels or maybe a few
All gathered 'round the campfire singing songs, tellin'
stories—maybe a poem or two

Nighttime Nevada high-desert skies turn from red,
orange, yellow to the color blue
Soon we hit the sack—Dudes, Buckaroos, Teamsters,
and even the gnarly Camp Crew
The sounds of crickets and frogs as the gentle wind
serenades us into a deep sleep
No roosters a crowin'—pitch black too—as all awake
without so much as a peep

MAN IN THE ARENA - NEVER SAY QUIT

This time breakfast comes quick—the camp is dis-
mantled, and all have their job to do
You can see people scurrin' about, pullin' up stakes,
and folding tables and chairs too
We saddle up again and push the cattle from one lonely
mountain over Rattlesnake Ridge,
Then down a nasty ravine, up a rocky draw, and over
Winnemucca Ranch Road Bridge
Wild mustangs roaming over them there rollin' hills—
what an awesome sight to see
Away off in the yonder a lone coyote, a soaring eagle,
and five-point mule deer bucks run free
I was feelin' like 'twas the ol' Chisholm Trail when
Marshall Flats was a sight for sore eyes
Cattle camp lay beneath rocky cliffs—with the sandy
ground a'strewn with cow pies

We awaken to mornin' dew and desert fog—our horses
champin' at the bit and all of us feelin' alive
Every single Dude is a little saddle sore, but roarin' and
ready for the longest day of the cattle drive
Twenty-one miles as wagons, chink-clad riders, and the
herd head south to the last cattle camp site
Dusty and dirty we arrive in Lemmon Valley, ready to
party, go to sleep and then ride at first light

This mornin' is special cause we're all dressed in pink,
preparin' for a first-class parade show
Cowboys, Wranglers, Cooks, horses, and cattle
and of course Buckaroos, don't you know
Our adventure nears the end—across the last mountain
range with Cattle Town Reno below
Yeah, a weather-beaten face—but unlike the drive of '95,
we made it thru in June, without snow

DAVID MICHAEL SEMAS

It's 10:30 a.m. when the covered wagons, horses,
and bovines hit the asphalt-covered ground
We're off the shale mountains, past the creeks—finally
the dust and dirt is nowhere to be found
Mindful of the stampede-inclined steers, we head down
Clear Acre to Wedekind and Sutro Street
With the grace of our Lord, we safely arrive at rodeo
grounds with family and friends to greet

Through the wide-open gates and into the outdoor arena
for the traditional group photo shot
Cowboys, Wranglers, Camp Crew are still the same—but
the used-to-be Dudes certainly are not
In a five-day span—with a'drinkin' and eatin', story-tellin'
and a'ridin' with new Pards at their side
What was considered an outsider and a Dude stranger
is now a real Buckaroo, ready to ride

Now that this years' Old West high-desert adventure
and cattle drive has come to a close
We don't need no applause, salute, or celebration,
although I guess I'll shed a tear, I suppose
The open trail and the sight of Nevada's alluring evening
skies will not be forgotten soon
I'll always cherish the smell of the mesquite campfire
and the sight of the glowing full moon

By and by—whilst I'd been a'jawin', a'readin', and a'rhymin'
abouts us stayin' alive
Nearly plumb forgot to tell y'all this took place whilst on
the Reno Rodeo Cattle Drive
Very few professions bring so much joy and inner peace
yet have a great deal of strife
Until the day I meet my maker, I'll always honor
and promote the Cowboy Way of Life

MAN IN THE ARENA - NEVER SAY QUIT

As soon as I left the high desert of the cattle drive and hit the streets of downtown Reno on Friday, I learned that we were now under full-blown investigation by the SEC. Thoughts of the trail left my mind when I read the formal subpoena for production of documents, which included a demand for an extensive amount of accounting records and customer files. The subpoena stated that if we did not fully comply, I would have to personally appear before the commission in ten days.

Several days later, I received another bombshell when I was personally served with an SEC subpoena, along with Wells Fargo Bank, for all of Susan's and my personal bank records dating back to 1995. Wow! We had nothing to hide, but nonetheless, this was not only damaging to employee morale but humiliating as well.

I had little choice but to fully cooperate. The SEC staff person assigned to our case was Dao Nguyen (not her real name), enforcement attorney. I called and told her that we would fully comply with the subpoena but asked for a little more than seven days to produce tens of thousands of pages of documents, files, and records.

We responded to the SEC subpoena by sending boxes of documents and a letter that stated, among other things, "The request for documents and information is quite overwhelming and quite voluminous. While many of the items can be provided within the eight working days you have allowed for, the balance will likely require a staff of people several months to comply. We are a small company and do not possess the personnel resources to timely respond and respectfully request a reasonable extension."

Fortunately, Ms Nguyen agreed. The first set of documents, contained in twenty boxes, included corporate records and files. We

---

LIFE LESSON #107:

"FACE REALITY AS IT IS, NOT AS IT WAS OR AS YOU WISH IT TO BE."

—JACK WELCH (AMERICAN BUSINESS EXECUTIVE AND FORMER CHAIRMAN OF GENERAL ELECTRIC, 1935-)

---

requested more time to provide the SEC with investor files that represented an estimated 50,000 pages of additional information.

The subpoena also required that I provide an explanation as to how the manager established salaries and set prices for products and services. I responded by informing them that METALAST was a privately held company and would not normally be subject to legitimate challenge by members (other than election of a new manager by 51 percent of common members at the annual meeting) or governmental agencies. "The Basis for Payments," as the SEC put it, was in fact at the full discretion of the manager—myself—but I believed it would be considered reasonable by any standard.

By the end of July, we had provided the SEC with the details for all payments made for interest, principal, or otherwise, to or from investors or members. We were also required to give the SEC signed copies of fifteen years of METALAST federal tax returns, including the individual K-1 forms for each of our nearly 1,000 LLC members, even though providing these documents was extremely time-consuming and a tedious task that placed a great deal of burden on the company's limited personnel resources.

The intrusive investigation was taking its toll on the company, and with the economic downturn, we were nearly out of operating capital again. Without an infusion of cash, we would be forced to cease operations. In addition to the negative impact the SEC investigation had on potential investors, it made it impossible to raise capital the way we had—via a private placement offering. While we were under investigation, there was virtually no way that the SEC would approve another offering from investors. In reality, the very people the SEC was sworn to protect—the investing public and private investors—were the same people that this investigation was harming.

I was able to arrange a $1.3 million bridge loan to shore up the business until I could figure out some other means of

> LIFE LESSON #108:
>
> "THE WAY I SEE IT, IF YOU WANT THE RAINBOW, YOU GOTTA PUT UP WITH THE RAIN."
>
> —DOLLY PARTON (AMERICAN SINGER, SONGWRITER, AND COUNTRY MUSIC LEGEND, 1946-)

permanent capitalization, although I knew that these funds would probably be depleted within a six-month timeframe. I began to author a proposal for $20 million of financing targeting institutional investors, a registered investment company, or perhaps a large, accredited investor that would be exempt from SEC regulations. Other than asking for our own shareholders to reinvest via a capital call from the manager, we had little choice if we were to survive the economic downturn that most experts agreed would probably represent a thirty-six-month-long recession, if not longer.

Throughout July and August, we heard scuttlebutt from some of our customers and alliance partners wondering whether METALAST was under some type of investigation by federal authorities. The potentially devastating rumors grew as our sales managers continued to field telephone inquiries questioning the integrity of senior management. At the same time, some of our customers were becoming distant and wouldn't even return phone calls.

Finally, someone had let the cat out of the bag. I was able to obtain confirmation that the SEC was secretly contacting all of our customers, partners, clients, and shareholders; many told me they had received an intrusive questionnaire from the SEC. It wasn't long before we started receiving similar confirmations of SEC inquiries from our partners, Chemetall and Pratt & Whitney, Applied Materials, Bell Helicopter, Boeing, General Dynamics, and Lockheed Martin. The SEC had even contacted the Navy, our METALAST TCP-HF licensing partner.

As furious as we were that an innocent company with fiscally responsible and honest management was being put through the ringer, I reluctantly acknowledged that Ms. Nguyen and the SEC were merely doing their job. They had apparently been told that I had engaged in fraud, misappropriation of funds, and luring new investors into METALAST by providing false statements about the names of our customers and specifying manufacturers. All we could do was continue to cooperate and hope that we would get through the process unscathed. We would also encourage the SEC to file criminal charges of whistleblower abuse against those self-serving individuals behind the lies that had prompted the painful investigative charade.

In the July 2009 METALAST quarterly publication, I reported, "Fueled by the sixty-billion-dollar Bernie Madoff scandal, 'Madoffism' is running amuck with investors. A few disgruntled former employees made false allegations of wrongdoing by management and have caused an investigation by the SEC of Los Angeles. They are in the process of confirming that investor funds have been properly used and no misappropriation has occurred. Our books and records are in order, and we have always acted as a proper fiduciary on behalf of our LLC members. We are fully cooperating with the SEC and are hopeful we will receive a quick resolution to this fact-finding inquiry. We will continue to work on your behalf to build METALAST into a successful business. Thank you for your continued support."

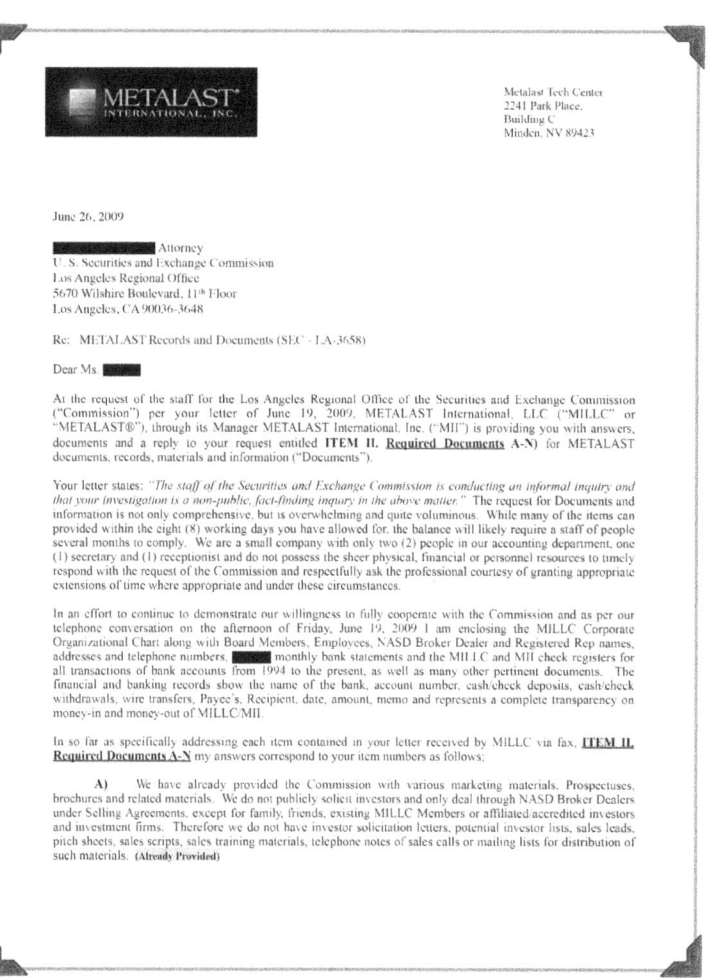

My response letter to SEC inquiry, June 2009

CHAPTER 21

THE WHISTLEBLOWERS SHOW THEIR HAND

The SEC dropped another bombshell when it sent us another subpoena on October 1, this time demanding that I produce what turned out to be eight hundred pages of documents. I was required to produce them on or before October 9—the day before the annual members' meeting. The missive, in my opinion, was meant to harass and intimidate. If I failed to comply, I would be required to testify and "show cause" before the SEC in Los Angeles on October 9 at 10:00 a.m. The SEC demanded proof that BAE Systems, Boeing, Lockheed Martin, Pratt & Whitney, the US Army, Department of Defense, and others were METALAST "clients," "customers," or "partners," or that the manufacturer had specified METALAST TCP-HF or another product or service.

Because the SEC could find no evidence of financial improprieties, the seemingly never-ending fishing expedition continued. It was becoming apparent that the SEC was being spoon-fed misleading and untrue information suggesting that we had misrepresented material facts to our investors and shareholders.

The night before the annual members meeting, I sat down to an enjoyable dinner with Susan and several board members in a private room of the Bimini Steakhouse at the Peppermill Hotel

Casino. We had a relaxing evening, which helped take my mind off what I anticipated would be a disruptive gathering orchestrated the following day by Clyde Burger (not his real name), a NASD broker/dealer who had raised capital for METALAST, and was also a minor shareholder.

The next morning, I arrived at the Peppermill banquet room at 9:30 a.m. to prepare for my board meeting at 10:00, which had been scheduled before the main meeting luncheon at 11:45. I stepped outside to make certain that the hotel had placed directional signs in strategic locations so that our guests would know where the members' meeting was being held.

Unbeknownst to Burger, I had already formed a plan, printed the agenda in advance, and was fully prepared for what I believed would prove an unsuccessful attempt to outsmart and embarrass the manager. During past member meetings, I had allowed shareholders to ask questions from their seats while a cordless microphone was passed around the room. They could ask virtually any question they wanted, since I placed no restrictions on the Q&A format.

I welcomed the hundred or so members to the meeting and introduced the board of directors, the METALAST employees present, and a few of our advisors.

A few shareholders addressed the group, some in support of management and some against but in a respectful manner. I could see that Nathan Silvester, one of Burger's cohorts, was champing at the bit to be called upon. I was curious to see how he would come across and to what lengths he would go to make his point that I should be ousted as the manager.

He shuffled through a few papers before choosing one and saying, "Your proxy says vote A for the manager or vote B against the manager, which doesn't provide us with a viable option. We need a complete list of the names, addresses, and telephone numbers of the shareholders so we can contact them to receive their input on what they think of the manager, and if they're dissatisfied, then we can decide who to replace you with. Are you willing to provide us with this information?"

"No, absolutely not," I replied. "As per the operating agreement, this shareholder listing is confidential. You can either vote A for the manager or vote B against the manager. Quite frankly, if the majority chooses to replace the manager, that's fine, as that's what the operating agreement provides for."

We went back and forth for nearly thirty minutes, and the other shareholders were becoming annoyed.

Finally, I stopped and said, "The names and addresses of our members are confidential, and considering that your group represents less than three percent of the company, I am not going to allow you to hijack this meeting with the other ninety-seven percent of members being in overwhelming support of management. If you want to vote against the manager, you're within your rights, but until you have more than fifty percent, I will run the business, as LLC members are prohibited from doing so."

Silvester looked sheepish as he sat down, and his wife came forward with similar nonsensical questions.

The final person I called on was Clyde Burger, who was sitting in the back of the room with his other supporters. With his gray hair, black Levi's, silver belt buckle, and signature red cowboy boots that he had worn at every annual meeting for the previous decade, he was hard to miss. He declined to come to the podium and instead blurted out, "How much shareholder money is spent paying for the security guard in the corner of the room?"

Yes, I thought, *let's not talk about the millions of dollars in damages you and your group are causing with the SEC investigation.*

Burger fashioned himself as a sales and marketing guru, but he had mysteriously turned in his broker-dealer license to the SEC in July. I suspected that the SEC had granted him immunity in exchange for his records, so-called insider information on METALAST, and his sworn testimony. Unfortunately, Ms Nguyen and the commission had been duped. If it had not been so devastating, their unsuccessful attempt at a takeover of

> **LIFE LESSON #109:**
>
> "COCKROACHES THRIVE IN THE DARK. THUS, THE BEST WAY TO GET RID OF THEM IS TO TURN ON THE LIGHTS."
>
> —THE COLONEL

METALAST would have been downright laughable.

I learned some specifics of the lies Burger was spreading when Kevin Monroe, a friend and broker for METALAST, contacted me to describe the four, long, ear-bending hours he had spent sitting next to Burger on his return flight home to Southern California after the annual members' meeting. I was shocked by what I heard but appreciative that Kevin had the courage to tell me the despicable things being said about myself and my family. According to Burger, I had committed fraud and embezzled tens of millions of dollars, had never filed or paid my taxes, had built a $30 million ranch, owned "a lot of expensive vehicles," and "lived an extravagant lifestyle." Burger also claimed that I had never bought the original METALAST patent from a Japanese scientist in the first place.

Burger knew all of this was false and was intentionally providing misinformation. His most earth-shattering observation was my so-called lack of qualifications to run the business because I was a carpenter and had nothing more than a high-school education. I thought this to be a statement of the obvious since my background had been well publicized. It appeared Burger had finally snapped.

Burger had even mentioned that he and Joe Conack had been feeding this information to "an Asian lady," whom he later admitted was the SEC investigator. Kevin had concluded that Burger was a bit deranged and that I deserved to know the harm being done by him and Joe. It was somewhat vindicating to hear. Over the previous year, other shareholders, broker-dealers, reps, and even a few board members had told me similar stories. Burger had

> **LIFE LESSON #110:**
>
> "A LIE CAN TRAVEL HALFWAY AROUND THE WORLD AS THE TRUTH IS PUTTING ON ITS SHOES."
>
> —MARK TWAIN

gone as far as writing to the board of directors on several different occasions, alleging just about everything in the book and ultimately calling for my removal as manager of the company.

We could only respond to the ever-growing false allegations of wrongdoing, cooperate with the SEC, and hope that eventually the nightmare would end. We were depleting the $1.3 million loan and cash reserves we had received earlier in the summer. Thus, my primary challenge was to focus on operations and the business at hand so that we could get back on track, hopefully close our proposed $20 million financial transaction, survive the economic downturn, build revenues, and finally become a profitable enterprise.

> LIFE LESSON #111:
>
> "NO MAN HAS A GOOD ENOUGH MEMORY TO MAKE A SUCCESSFUL LIAR."
>
> —ABRAHAM LINCOLN

CHAPTER 22

UNDER THE MICROSCOPE

On a Tuesday evening at the end of October 2009, I sat with Susan in a restaurant on Fisherman's Wharf. As I gazed out at San Francisco Bay and Alcatraz, I pondered the place I found myself. My two-day deposition—the SEC called it an "interview"—was scheduled to begin the next morning at their San Francisco regional office, right before the ghosts and goblins of Halloween hit the streets of the Golden Gate City. Though I loved Fisherman's Wharf, I couldn't enjoy the view or glass of Pinot Noir and Filet Mignon steak before me. I was too busy thinking about the upcoming deposition and wondering whether we were going to make it through this. I felt I would probably have to loan the company more money.

Susan and I had made the four-hour drive to San Francisco from Minden the previous Thursday so that I could sit in on the SEC preparation meeting with our attorney, Bruce Kelson, who worked for the prominent California-based national law firm of Manatt & Phelps. Wendi and Greg had undergone separate all-day interviews with Ms Nguyen the day before.

On the morning of my deposition, I had a brief preparation meeting with Bruce in a conference room at our hotel.

"Wendi did an excellent job," he told me with a reassuring smile. "She was cooperative, informative, and articulate. She provided the SEC with considerable detail concerning METALAST's financial, accounting, banking, and shareholder-related information. The lead investigator appeared impressed and comfortable with the testimony."

I had expected nothing less from my daughter.

According to Bruce, Greg had also handled himself like a true professional. Nguyen had fired the tough questions one by one, and after about five hours, she could see that he was a knowledgeable, hands-on departmental manager and well acquainted with every aspect of the METALAST sales and marketing department. Oddly, Nguyen repeatedly asked Greg his definition of a "customer," harping on this issue with him for several hours.

"He explained that, in his opinion, a customer was a person or company who used METALAST's products or services," Bruce told me. "She rephrased the question again and again, trying to solicit a conflicting response, but Greg's answer was always the same."

I knew as much because the answer happened to be the truth.

Greg was savvy enough to know exactly what she was trying to do. Nguyen was attempting to make his testimony appear as though he somehow knew that if a company didn't purchase our products or services directly from METALAST, they must not have been a customer. The point being if METALAST investor reports touted a Fortune 500 company as a customer, and according to the self-serving SEC definition they weren't, David Semas could be charged with misrepresenting a material fact, or fraud. Nguyen was trying to justify the time, money, and extensive resources being expended on this investigation by cleverly making a mountain out of a molehill.

In her six months of investigating and speaking with shareholders, customers, and alliance partners—after hundreds of thousands of taxpayer dollars and countless man-hours had likely been spent—all Nguyen could apparently come up with was to focus on the definition of a "customer." I knew what she was up to: she was attempting to build a shaky case around investor misrepresentations concerning our alleged partners, customers, and professional relationships.

Most would probably agree that, after months of scrutinizing our corporate books and records and my personal bank accounts and finding no misuse of funds, Nguyen was engaged in a witch hunt that showed government bureaucracy at its worst. It was an abuse of power.

The SEC was virtually destroying the reputation of our company while at the same time causing a small number of our shareholders to demand a return of their investments. Many were under the mistaken impression that there had been corporate malfeasance, though none existed. I was eager to tell my side of the story in a forthright manner and to answer Ms Nguyen's questions honestly and accurately. I assumed that many of the same questions given to Greg would be asked of me, but I also expected to testify under oath to my knowledge of investor origination, solicitation, stock sales, corporate procedures, and day-to-day management-related issues as the chairman/CEO for METALAST International, Inc. and manager for the company.

The SEC offices were located off Market Street, just a block from the world-famous cable cars running up and down California Street. The interview was conducted under oath with a court stenographer present, along with Nguyen and her immediate superior, Ms Linda Miller (not her real name), and our lawyer, Bruce Kelson. Ms Janet Simpson (not her real name), another SEC investigator from their LA office, participated via teleconference. Ms Nguyen was a slender, petite woman of Vietnamese descent in her early forties and wore her dark hair in a neat bob.

The interview began cordially enough, with Nguyen asking questions about my educational background, work experience, and the early history of METALAST. As the morning progressed, she began to move into our private placement offering and how we had raised our equity capital from our investors during the period of 1995 through 2004. At one point, just before we took a lunch break, she bluntly asked, "How did you establish the valuation of the business, and

> LIFE LESSON #112:
>
> "REPUTATION IS WHAT MEN AND WOMEN THINK OF US; CHARACTER IS WHAT GOD AND ANGELS KNOW OF US."
>
> —THOMAS PAINE (ENGLISH-BORN AMERICAN REVOLUTIONARY, ACTIVIST, AND FOUNDING FATHER, 1737-1809)

in particular, how did you arrive at a share price in 1995 of twenty-five dollars, which increased to thirty dollars in 1998, thirty-six dollars in 2000, and beginning in 2005 until the present time, at forty dollars per share?"

The question was certainly a logical one, I thought. "As a private limited liability company," I replied, "the manager of METALAST International, Inc., with myself as its chairman/CEO, arbitrarily set the price based on our opinion of a reasonable value. If my memory serves me correctly, sometime back in 2006, I prepared a comprehensive fourteen-page analysis of the business, its future potential, the market, and our industry in order to present logical findings, supportable data, and reasonable assumptions to our board and to the METALAST auditors, Grant Thornton, LLP, Reno."

I tried to set the stage and to educate her on the process involved in evaluating a company such as METALAST.

"The valuation of almost anything is based on what a qualified buyer is willing to pay and the price at which an agreeable seller is willing to sell. A company's earnings and price earnings multiple, or P/E, play a key role in determining the value of a publicly traded stock. However, it's still the perception of the worth of a business, meaning the perceived overall value of the enterprise as accepted by the buyer, that determines the real price of the sale or purchase of a privately held company. For example, a chemical company with generic products in the market, with a good brand name but few barriers to entry for another competitor to step in and capture a significant market share, would be worth much less than a chemical company whose branded products commanded specifications that required use by vendors worldwide."

Nguyen sat there looking perplexed. "Why do you feel that the process for valuating a private company should be any different from a public one?"

"Well, in the case of publicly traded companies on Wall Street, it's the investment banking firm that establishes the value of a business and sets the IPO (initial public offering) stock selling price. With a privately held business, such investment bankers aren't generally interested in helping establish a value for the business unless the company is positioned to go public in the immediate future, which we were not."

"What credentials do you have to value a business?" she asked in a harsh and condescending tone.

"You mean other than being a CEO or COO for thirty-five years while financing, constructing, acquiring, valuating, appraising, and managing billions of dollars of real estate assets and hotels; providing financial consulting services with a one-hundred-billion-dollar life insurance partner; and operating and evaluating various businesses, including this one?" I didn't mean to come across as pompous, but under the circumstances, I was pissed.

Nguyen shook her head in disbelief. "I completely disagree with your methods and your opinion that you are somehow qualified to valuate a company. I have seen thousands of companies valued by investment banking firms that have a long and well-established track record of performance, and you should have engaged a professional, as opposed to thinking that you were qualified for such a complex undertaking."

"How's that been working for Wall Street and the SEC?" I asked. "No offense, but considering the record plunge in the Dow 30, a near virtual collapse of Wall Street, the Bernie Madoff scandal, the demise of AIG and Lehman Brothers, the Chapter 11 bankruptcy filings by General Motors and Chrysler, and the overall dismal state of the automotive and financial services industries, I guess the Wharton and Harvard geniuses might have to sharpen their prognostication skills and rethink their valuation methods."

She looked at me with mild disgust, which didn't bother me in the least, and then we broke for lunch.

When we resumed the interview, Nguyen went from one topic to the next, none of which had anything to do with financial issues, misuse of funds, embezzlement, or misappropriations, since none existed. I kept waiting to see where she was heading.

Finally, toward the end of the afternoon, she blurted out, "How would you define a METALAST customer?"

Oh, here it is, I thought. This was the same angle she had tried to use on Greg the previous day.

LIFE LESSON #113:

"IF YOU'RE GOING THROUGH HELL, KEEP GOING."

—SIR WINSTON CHURCHILL

My answer was straightforward and to the point. "A customer is a company that either purchases, uses, or utilizes METALAST products, services, or technologies."

"You mean to tell me that although Chrysler has never paid METALAST a dime, you think they are your customer merely because they have a Visteon drive shaft that was processed using METALAST? Do you honestly think—and do you expect us to believe—that Chrysler is a METALAST customer? Do you take us for fools?"

You pompous, arrogant bureaucrat.

"No, not at all. I'm not asking you to think that I believe the fact that Chrysler is our customer. With two million of the METALAST-processed SIT drive shafts now in most Grand Jeep Cherokee, Jeep Commander, and Jeep Liberty four-wheel-drive vehicles since 2005, I am telling you that in fact Chrysler *is our custome*r. Who wrote the check is irrelevant, as is the case in any subcontractor relationship. Ms Nguyen, Chrysler and Visteon are our customers."

"Well, isn't that double-dipping?"

I chuckled. "I guess in that case, considering that we have a license and royalty agreement with Visteon Automotive, who pays us monthly, and their metal-finishing vendor, Nicro/Croni, who purchases our METALAST chemicals and uses our process control computers daily, you could say that we are triple-dipping, because all three companies—Chrysler, Visteon, and Nicro/Croni—are our customers."

Nguyen appeared frustrated as she moved on with her questioning. "If Chrysler, Visteon, and Nicro/Croni are your customers, then how would you define a client?"

Once again, I thought, *Is this her best shot?*

"A METALAST client would be a company like Boeing, Honeywell, Parker Hannifin, Raytheon, and, until recently, Pratt & Whitney, because we have conducted many years and hundreds of man-hours of R&D working on several projects together to improve the performance of our various chemical products."

"Why do you use the words 'until recently' when referring to Pratt & Whitney?"

"Because no thanks to the SEC's disruptive efforts to contact Pratt & Whitney and cause them to cease all communication with METALAST for nearly a month, last week we entered into a partnership agreement with them to globally commercialize a new patented chemical replacement for hexavalent chromium."

That finished the afternoon's interview, and we broke until the next morning.

At ten o'clock on Thursday morning, we began our second day of the interview. I was a little surprised when Ms Nguyen started a new line of questioning on private stock sales, since I thought she would have continued to harp on what did or what did not constitute a customer or client. Regardless, I was happy to talk about something else.

She asked about the modest stock sales by Wendi, Greg, my brother Len, and Jeff Mackinen from 2004 to 2008. "Who was the first person to ever sell private shares?"

"Why, that would have been your whistleblower buddy James Bradock back in 1996, who, as I recall, sold about four hundred thousand dollars' worth of METALAST shares."

She grimaced and then held up another piece of paper entitled *Private Share Exchange* and asked, "Do you know who authored this document?"

> **LIFE LESSON #114:**
>
> "NEVER BE BULLIED INTO SILENCE. NEVER ALLOW YOURSELF TO BE MADE A VICTIM. ACCEPT NO ONE'S DEFINITION OF YOUR LIFE BUT DEFINE YOURSELF."
>
> —HARVEY S. FIRESTONE (AMERICAN BUSINESSMAN AND FOUNDER OF THE FIRESTONE TIRE AND RUBBER COMPANY, 1868-1938)

> **LIFE LESSON #115:**
>
> "THERE'S A NATURAL LAW OF KARMA THAT VINDICTIVE PEOPLE, WHO GO OUT OF THEIR WAY TO HURT OTHERS, WILL END UP BROKE AND ALONE."
>
> —SYLVESTER "SLY" STALLONE (AMERICAN ACTOR, DIRECTOR, SCREENWRITER, AND PRODUCER, 1946-)

"Bradock or his broker-dealer who worked for Trans Western Securities."

We went back and forth on this line of questioning for nearly an hour before she abruptly said, "Mr. Semas, do you think that it was appropriate, responsible, or even ethical for you to have dumped millions of dollars of your stock without informing your shareholders that you were doing so?"

I tried not to react with anger as I said, "This is the same type of irresponsible, gross misrepresentation and innuendo that your whistleblowers are telling our shareholders. First of all, you are correct that it is *my stock*, and as such, it is my personal business and not that of our shareholders. However, I take offense at your allegation that I have 'dumped millions of dollars of stock.' My personal shares were issued to me in 1994, and it wasn't until 1999, five years later, that I sold one single share of stock. I sold my personal shares over a ten-year period and did not, as you have alleged, 'dump' them. I have guaranteed and lent millions of dollars in loans to the company so that we could make payroll on countless occasions, never taken a cash bonus, and am owed more than four years in back salary. Lastly, the term 'dumping shares' is an exaggeration that would indicate the METALAST manager was knowingly in direct conflict with our other shareholders. In reality, today I remain the largest single shareholder in METALAST, and if you consider my employee stock options, I am the largest shareholder by five times. Under these circumstances, I hardly think the term 'dumping shares' is appropriate or an accurate representation of the facts."

Ms Nguyen was caught off-guard by my response as she turned beat red and was obviously embarrassed in front of her superior, Linda Miller, and fellow SEC investigator Janet Simpson.

After lunch, we returned to the definition of a METALAST customer and client.

"With all due respect," I said, "up until the last few days with the SEC, Ms Nguyen, no one before has ever made an issue of who is or who is not a METALAST customer or client. I believe that this is being blown far out of proportion. You are attempting to make it appear as though there is some type of conspiracy or investor or shareholder misrepresentation that doesn't exist. We're arguing semantics. Ms Nguyen, we are the partner of the United States Navy, R&D partner with the United States

Air Force, and supplier of products and services to the US Army and the US Marine Corp Logistics Command in Albany, Georgia. Our products have been specified or approved by many of the most respected names in America, including BAE Systems, Boeing, General Dynamics, GE Healthcare, Honeywell, Lockheed Martin, and Raytheon. I hardly think we need to misrepresent our professional relationships. We're not engaged in some conspiracy to misinform our shareholders or prospective investors."

> **LIFE LESSON #116:**
>
> "THE DIFFERENCE BETWEEN WINNING AND LOSING IS MOST OFTEN NOT QUITTING."
>
> —WALT DISNEY

Now that their nearly one-year-long investigation had confirmed that I had done nothing wrong, she looked at her watch and wrapped up the deposition.

I thought, *This is it?* I felt relieved.

During our brief walk down Mission Street toward the Hyatt Regency, our attorney told me he thought the SEC interviews couldn't have gone any better. "It's entirely up to the SEC to demonstrate some type of fraud, embezzlement, or corporate wrongdoing," he said. "Judging by their questions, they appear to have nothing more than unsupported allegations of investor misrepresentation. And that's after a year of conducting a forensic audit of the company's and your personal finances. I don't think you have anything to worry about."

We stopped in front of the hotel entrance, and I took a deep breath of the cool, moist air. All I wanted to do was return to the ranch and relax. But I needed to focus on getting back to Newport Beach for a potential investor meeting.

> **LIFE LESSON #117:**
>
> "A DEAL IS NEVER DONE UNTIL IT'S ACTUALLY DONE."
>
> —DAVID SEMAS

CHAPTER 23

THE PERFECT STORM

On Wednesday evening, Susan and I drove seven hours straight from San Francisco through the Altamont Pass to Tracy and then down I-5, arriving at the Balboa Bay Club in Newport Beach after midnight. We checked into the hotel and immediately fell into bed to catch up on some well-deserved sleep before my nine o'clock meeting the next morning.

I met with investors Jack King and Dick Wray of Wes Star Capital in a private meeting room with a fireplace and large bay windows overlooking Balboa Bay. Jack, a METALAST shareholder, had a bubbly personality, while Dick, a successful retired businessman, was more reserved. I brought Dick and Jack up to date on the status of the SEC investigation, recent sales, pending purchase orders, and related operational issues. When they had asked all of their questions, it was my turn to ask about the status of our financing with the Texas partners and whether they had their capital in place to fund the $20 million.

"All is well," Jack assured me. "We think we'll be able to wrap everything up within the next month or so. We're also working with several other groups—hedge funds that would be able to put up the twenty million dollars for us."

The three of us shook hands and parted ways on a high note. I certainly hoped that this would move forward, and we would get the financing worked out. It wasn't like we had other sources. I couldn't make a normal offering because I would never get it approved by the SEC. I had no choice but to find private investors, a single large private investor, or more than likely an investment group. And who better to accomplish it than Jack King? As a longtime shareholder who knew the company inside and out, he was confident in my capabilities and believed we would one day be a very successful company.

I had been working with Dick and Jack since August and had been told on many occasions that the financing was essentially a done deal. All that was left was to dot the i's and cross the t's and have a face-to-face meeting with the other two members of their Senior Loan and Finance Committee.

With the ongoing SEC investigation, our future looked to be in serious jeopardy for the first time in nearly sixteen years. It was so bad that I was once again forced to loan what eventually became millions of dollars to the company so that it could make its payroll and cover the cost of operations. Close friends and board members also stepped up to the plate by providing millions of dollars in capital to help sustain operations. By greatly restricting our ability to bring another private placement offering to market through the broker-dealer community and thus cutting access to capital for METALAST, the SEC was virtually destroying the very people they were sworn to protect: the individual investors who had invested a total of $85 million and put their trust in our company and its management.

We were not a $65 billion Ponzi scheme. Unlike Bernie Madoff, METALAST was in fact the real deal. It offered exciting, environmentally friendly breakthrough technologies, chemicals, and process control products that had been validated by many leading names in American industry. After an intrusive six-month investigation, the SEC could have easily confirmed that I hadn't taken a salary in four years, we never misused investor proceeds in any manner, and we were always fiscally prudent and responsible.

My father had told me many years earlier that you can be discredited and humiliated at any time, by anyone, at the mere drop of a hat. "David, if you and I were running for political office and as a part of our respective campaigns we found ourselves standing before a crowd of say, five hundred people, all I would have to do is turn to you and announce, 'Well, at least I never stole a hundred thousand dollars from my mother.' At that point, you're doomed. If you immediately respond with, 'No, I didn't steal a hundred thousand dollars from my mother,' I can reply by saying, 'I didn't say you did. I said at least I didn't. Are you guilty or hiding something?' If you don't respond at all, you look guilty. In fact, no matter what you say or do in response, the people within earshot will believe that you stole money from your mother. The damage has already been done and the bell has been rung."

About thirty years had passed since the Colonel had shared this insight, and as was the case most of the time, he had been absolutely right.

> LIFE LESSON #118:
>
> "WHAT IS SAID OF A MAN IS NOTHING. THE POINT IS WHO SAYS IT."
>
> —OSCAR WILDE (IRISH POET AND PLAYWRIGHT, 1854–1900)

The first few months of 2010 were a rollercoaster ride of good news and bad. At the beginning of the year, just as our entire world seemed to be crumbling, I was able to arrange more bridge loans to the company. I only owned 20 percent of the business but went ahead and personally guaranteed millions in loans.

Chemical and equipment sales continued to grow, and new companies were joining the METALAST distribution network. But things

> LIFE LESSON #119:
>
> "IT'S A MATTER OF HAVING PRINCIPLES. IT'S EASY TO HAVE PRINCIPLES WHEN YOU'RE RICH. THE IMPORTANT THING IS TO HAVE PRINCIPLES WHEN YOU'RE POOR."
>
> —RAY KROC

took a significant turn for the worse when Jack King died unexpectedly on January 6, 2010, from complications due to a spontaneous coronary artery rupture. Then, in March, as we were finally putting together the deal with Westar Capital, Westar backed out, saying they wouldn't proceed any further due to the lingering SEC investigation. It was devastating but not surprising.

To add to the confusion of the SEC investigation, tragedy struck on February 5, 2010, when Joe Conack, the SEC's star witness and whistleblower, took his life, leaving behind a loving wife and four children. While we'd had our differences and I hadn't been pleased to learn he was one of the co-conspirators behind the SEC investigation, especially after all METALAST had done for him, I still had a great deal of sympathy for his family.

About the same time, the SEC filed a Wells notice alleging six regulatory violations of compliance rules and regulations. They found no evidence to suggest that I had misspent or misused a single penny as manager of the company. As far as I was concerned, the Wells notice was nothing but a weak attempt to justify a wasteful investigation into our company. We filed a forty-page rebuttal in April 2010.

In June, Ms Nguyen reopened the investigation, likely after her superiors found her report to be incomplete and unsupported. METALAST shareholders that she contacted during this time said she appeared to be aggressively attempting to destroy METALAST by making it impossible to raise operating capital, thus fulfilling her prediction that the business was doomed to failure.

Then everything went quiet. We had no way of knowing what might happen next. My attorney cautioned me that at the very least, the SEC would fine us, but they might also file a civil lawsuit against us for the six minor regulatory violations.

At the end of July, a bizarre incident suggested that things were about to change. Greg and I were having lunch at Adele's in Carson City when our waitress came running in with an alarmed expression. "We just got a call. There's been an explosion at the METALAST Tech Center."

Knowing that this could mean fatalities, I jumped to my feet and called my secretary, Jill.

"Everything is quiet here," she said. "There hasn't been an accident, as far as I know. All is quiet on the home front, and people are working away down in the lab."

Perplexed, I called Dr. Alp Manavbasi, our vice president of technology and a terrific employee and loyal department head.

"Everything is fine in the lab," he told me.

I realized the call was a hoax. I asked the waitress if she thought she could recognize the voice of the individual who had called the restaurant to report the explosion.

"I can do better than that," she said and dialed *69 on the restaurant's phone.

Low and behold, the number belonged to none other than Clyde Burger in Riverside, California.

I contacted the Sheriff's Office, and they asked that I come down to MTC and evacuate the building. I found six deputy sheriffs there, and we evacuated my employees. One of the deputies called Burger's number, and he answered. Naturally, being a psychopathic liar, he denied involvement, claiming anyone could have made a call from that phone, even though it was a private line inside his home office. We filed a police report and formal charges with the Sheriff's Office and, since the call had crossed state lines, the FBI.

This was probably the craziest thing Burger had ever done. I wondered if he had heard some news about the SEC investigation. Had it been closed? My attorney warned me that this was wishful thinking, that the SEC very rarely dropped an investigation.

Finally, on September 1, my attorney called. "I have fabulous news. We received a termination letter from the SEC, dated August 30, 2010, saying the investigation is over. They don't intend to recommend the commission take any action."

We hadn't been entirely exonerated in the true sense of the word because governmental bureaucracies don't work that way. Typically, termination letters from the IRS, SEC, or even FBI end with, "You are no longer the subject of an investigation," which basically means you're off the hook for now. The bottom line? They had dropped the investigation. For all intents and purposes, we had been vindicated and cleared of any wrongdoing or corporate malfeasance. Like the IRS, the SEC had responded to bogus claims from a whistleblower but had found no crime had been committed or misrepresentation made to anyone.

Apparently, it's highly unusual for the SEC to drop a case and elect not to take any enforcement action, especially after a costly, sixteen-month-long investigation. Perhaps somebody higher up in the SEC had finally decided that we were a viable small business, and that the investigation was a waste of resources. It had certainly taken its toll, putting our financing on hold and endangering relationships we had been cultivating with large companies.

We would likely never know the reasons behind the SEC's termination, but I was deeply relieved that it was finally over. The announcement had given us a clean bill of health, which I hoped meant our investors would heave a sigh of relief and come forward to help us. All summer, I had been working to secure additional investors. Because of the investigation, we hadn't been able to do a Regulation D private placement offering like we had in the past, yet we still needed to raise as much as $25 million or more to sustain operations and expand the business so we could finally turn the corner.

The best way to bring in the money was to find savvy businessmen that had a real desire to become involved in a green chemical company. Or perhaps we could form an alliance with a defense contractor or possibly a company involved in the aerospace business.

However, we had about $21 million in liabilities against the company, and $16 million of our original bridge loans were past due. We needed to clean up our balance sheet if we were going to bring in new money.

I went to work on the problem, and by December 2010, I had succeeded in converting nearly all $16 million of the bridge lender loans,

> LIFE LESSON #120:
>
> "MOST OF THE IMPORTANT THINGS IN THE WORLD HAVE BEEN ACCOMPLISHED BY PEOPLE WHO HAVE KEPT TRYING WHEN THERE SEEMED TO BE NO HOPE AT ALL."
>
> —DALE CARNEGIE

most of which belonged to shareholders, to METALAST common LLC interest, meaning they had converted from debt to equity, thus eliminating more than 75 percent of MILLC debt. This greatly improved the balance sheet, making it far more appealing to future investors.

Meanwhile, I had to arrange for additional bridge financing or stop-gap funding for METALAST, likely millions of dollars. At this point, our board of directors included Charlie Dell Donne, Jerry Hollander, Arnie Gittelson, Frank O'Bryan, and my dear friend Roger Luby. Each of them had stepped up to the plate time and time again, so unfortunately, it looked as though I was the only person willing to keep the business going. Not having available cash on hand, I would have to figure out some means by which to borrow money against our personal assets to loan the company to sustain its operations until we could move into positive cash flow and turn the corner.

CHAPTER 24

STAYIN' ALIVE—
TRYIN' TO SURVIVE

Knowing I was innocent of any wrongdoing I had nothing to fear. But our shareholders, partners, and customers like Boeing, Ford Motors, Lockheed Martin, Pratt & Whitney, and others had no way of knowing whether I had committed fraud or some type of securities violation. I was relieved that the SEC ordeal was behind me, but I knew the company was still in a perilous financial position. Without a significant infusion of cash, we were destined for failure.

In the summer of 2010, over breakfast at the local Carson City IHOP, I approached Susan with the problem. "Honey, if I don't put significant cash into METALAST, we're going to fail. I know it's a lot to ask, but will you agree to allow me to borrow a multimillion-dollar second mortgage against our ranch? Before you answer, you should know that if I'm unable to arrange for more funding for the company, we could lose it all and may even end up homeless and on the streets."

Susan turned to me, put down her fork, and gave me a cute grin. "David, you're the one who spent the last fifteen years building this business. Without you there would be no METALAST, shareholders would have lost their investment, and all employees would have lost their jobs. If I can't trust and believe in you, then who is it I should put my faith in? Go ahead. Let's do whatever's necessary to get METALAST over the top. In my heart and soul, I believe you will somehow pull this off, but if we fail, at least we will have done the right thing and will have failed for a worthy cause protecting the other shareholders."

No one had to tell me that I would be putting nearly all our life savings in jeopardy when we borrowed more than $5.5 million against our home, ranch, and most of our personal property. Counting previous loans and loan guarantees that I had made on behalf of the company and years of accrued salary, the business owed me more than $7 million, with interest accruing daily.

To alleviate the payroll burden, I didn't take a paycheck and continued to accrue salary and expenses. Despite the stagnant economy, and even though we were limping along and barely making payroll each month, METALAST revenues were still growing, albeit slowly. On the bright side, the METALAST TCP-HF line of product specifications were being issued by a few Fortune 500 companies. Equipment manufacturing contracts were slowly being awarded, and new business alliances were coming together—just not at the pace to move us into black.

We had weathered some of the most difficult challenges anyone could face in the process of building a business and were still in dire financial straits and far from being a successful enterprise. While it was impressive that this upstart and unknown company in the small community of Minden, Nevada was now recognized by some of the largest names in the industry, we were still in the red. We were proud of the green products we offered and the technical services we provided and knew our reputation was growing around the world. Even with a dedicated and determined management team with a proven track record of honesty and integrity, superior products, a market demand for those products, and a brand that is gaining worldwide recognition, no

> **LIFE LESSON #121:**
>
> "IF YOU DON'T BELIEVE IN YOUR COMPANY ENOUGH TO TAKE A FINANCIAL RISK, DON'T EXPECT OTHERS TO."
>
> —DAVID SEMAS

business can survive without a significant infusion of operating capital and adequate cash reserves.

How could I raise at least $25 million of new capital? With the SEC investigation still lingering in our recent past, could another private placement offering even be successful? Considering the lackluster state of the economy, hostile regulatory environment, and aggressive overreach of governmental regulations like the Dodd-Frank Act of 2010, the private equity markets had been greatly diminished. Most of the surviving venture capital companies wouldn't even begin to consider an unprofitable later-stage chemical company like METALAST. An anti-business climate, fueled by the near collapse of Wall Street, meant that registered FINRA (Financial Industry Regulatory Authority) broker-dealers were dropping like flies. When all was said and done, would we be able to get the broker-dealer community to support such an offering? Or would we need to engage the services of an investment banking firm to assist in identifying suitable private equity candidates willing to invest?

On a near daily basis, I worked closely with our longtime money raisers. We sent executive summaries and investment packages to private equity investor prospects around the country. At least weekly, I would have one- to two-hour-long conference calls with prospective investors and get peppered with the same questions again and again.

"Why has it taken so long to become profitable?" they would ask. "If you have so many specifications now, why aren't they converting to products sooner? What prevents a Henkel, Dow Chemical, DuPont, or PPG from undercutting your pricing margins?"

The questions seemed endless, and after I answered every last one, the time-consuming exercise nearly always ended in disappointment.

"We'll get back to you."

LIFE LESSON #122:

"I'M CONVINCED THAT ABOUT HALF OF WHAT SEPARATES SUCCESSFUL ENTREPRENEURS FROM THE NON-SUCCESSFUL ONES IS PURE PERSEVERANCE."

—STEVE JOBS (FOUNDER OF APPLE, INC. AND THE MICROCOMPUTER REVOLUTION, 1955-2011)

"I'll take it up with our partners."

"We wish you good luck, but it's not our type of deal."

We were either too early for their consideration or, in many cases, too late. We were seeking too much capital, or sometimes not enough. They liked our business model but not the length of time it would take to penetrate the market. They wanted to invest in emerging technologies, biotechnologies, renewable energy, and nanotechnologies but not environmentally friendly chemicals. If we were to eventually succeed in arranging for the capital, I would have to follow up on every lead, leave no stone unturned, and ultimately have the patience of Job.

Undaunted, I continued my relentless pursuit of capital with others like Morgan Stanley, Smith Barney, Ampersand Capital Partners, Huntsman Gay Global Capital, Capital Funding Northwest, and a host of others. Over the course of 2011, I spoke with more than one hundred firms, met with senior partners of sixteen companies, and invested countless man-hours in the very time-consuming quest for capital.

The real estate ad for BCR

LIFE LESSON #123:

"SOME PEOPLE MAKE THINGS HAPPEN, SOME WATCH THINGS HAPPEN, AND SOME WONDER WHAT HAPPENED."

—GAELIC PROVERB

Aerial photograph of Buffalo Creek Ranch, Gardnerville, NV

In the spring of 2010, Susan and I decided to list our ranch property for $15.9 million to see if there were any buyers out there. We listed the property with Marsha Tomerlin, a local real estate agent with Coldwell Banker. Marsha and her husband, Bill, had been friends of ours since moving to the Carson Valley. We agreed to only put Buffalo Creek Ranch on the market for six months to see if we could generate an offer.

Covered bridge at BCR

Even though the economy was in the tank and real estate values had significantly declined across the country, a one-of-a-kind ranch estate would prove highly desirable for the right discriminating wealthy buyer. With an eight-acre vineyard, six-acre apple and fruit tree orchard, two year-round creeks, ten ponds, eight waterfalls, and more than three miles of dry-stacked rock walls lining one mile of terra-cotta-stained concrete

> **LIFE LESSON #124:**
>
> **"HOPE FOR THE BEST, BUT ALWAYS PLAN AND PREPARE FOR THE WORST."**
>
> —THE COLONEL

roadway runners bordered with grass edging, our gentleman's ranch property was a unique estate and perfect for a family compound.

The southerly border boasted more than two thousand aspen trees and spectacular views four hundred feet above the lush Carson Valley. Situated at the base of snow-capped Job's Peak and the eastern edge of the Sierra Nevada and located only fifteen miles from the majestic Lake Tahoe, the ranch was a trophy for the right buyer.

The BCR eight-acre vineyard of cold-hardy varietal wine grapes

The main house at Buffalo Creek Ranch

BCR aerial of deer pasture in foreground and vineyard in background

BCR grass-lined roads and three miles of hand-stacked rock walls

Bear and Pow at Buffalo Creek Ranch, 2005

CHAPTER 25

METALAST—DECEIVED BY A FAIR-WEATHER FRIEND

Once again, METALAST was about to run out of operating capital. Our restaurateur friend Gilles Lagourgue introduced me to Dick Madler (not his real name), who had bought $1.3 million of my personal METALAST International, LLC shares in 1999, which was the first time I sold shares since 1994. Later, Dick also lent MILLC about $3 million in total. In those transactions, neither of us raised concerns about the fairness of the terms to both sides of the transaction. Over the years, we had become friends, and he invited Susan and me to attend his wedding to his second wife, Martha (not her real name).

"David," he had told me several times, "if you can't get enough funding in place until you can stabilize MILLC operations, I'll consider investing more with two major conditions. As long as you're willing to invest or loan at least the same amount of money to the company that I have, then I'll consider putting in more capital and convert my loans to equity as well. But in exchange, I'll also get voting control of your management company."

Dick agreed to loan another $400,000 to the company in January and February of 2013, but only if I would show good faith and guarantee $200,000 of it. Considering we were in the process of negotiating a major $3 million equity investment in MILLC with Dick, which would provide the last major capital infusion in the business, I thought a personal loan guarantee would be the right thing to do. On the negative side, the financial transaction required I give up control of the management company. I was its majority shareholder, but under the circumstances, it appeared to be my best option to fund the business and to protect the investment of the members' ownership in MILLC, the operating company.

It became apparent a few weeks later that DIP Partners, comprised of Dick and Martha, had played me for a fool. Dick and his family had owned a regional chain of auto parts stores, which they had sold to a national chain that controlled about 60 percent market share. Although knowledgeable in the auto parts retail field, I saw no evidence that Dick had any knowledge of the metal-finishing, corrosion control, chemicals, or coatings industry. Martha worked in the restaurant industry, yet it appeared to me to have no business related managerial expertise, and also appeared to me to have no knowledge of or experience in the metal-finishing business or specialty chemical businesses. On the surface, she seemed warm and friendly, but gave me the impression that she had an ego the size of Texas and it seemed to me that she wanted to be the next Erin Brockovich by saving the world from the harmful carcinogen hexavalent chromium. I entirely doubted that she'd succeed with that dream, as I'd seen no demonstration that she possessed the ability to build a company from the ground up or even manage one.

The two spouses used several of my candid email communications that confirmed I could no longer make payroll without capital infusion for the business. As alleged in a $90-million class-action lawsuit filed against the Madlers for conspiracy to defraud the investors by former MILLC members, they played along as though they were

> LIFE LESSON #125:
>
> "HE WHO PERMITS HIMSELF TO LIE ONCE FINDS IT MUCH EASIER TO DO A SECOND AND THIRD TIME UNTIL AT LENGTH IT BECOMES HABITUAL."
>
> —THOMAS JEFFERSON

seriously considering the terms we were negotiating. The Madlers cleverly lured me into thinking they were going forward with the $3 million investment, which turned out never to have been the case.

One Thursday afternoon on April 25, 2013, while sitting outside on my patio overlooking the beautiful Carson Valley and taking a break from the near twenty-four/seven stress, I received a telephone call from Frank O'Bryan, my longtime friend and former boss at Shearson/American Express and a member of the MII board of directors.

Carson Valley, 2019

"David," Frank said, "I just got off the telephone with Dick Madler, and he boasted how he was successful in removing you as manager of METALAST."

"No way," I replied. "Not to my knowledge. It's likely Madler's trying to apply leverage to negotiate better terms of the investment."

Upon further investigation, I was shocked to learn that without receiving proper notice, and under the guise of an expedited hearing, a court order had been issued earlier that afternoon removing my company MII and me as the manager.

After twenty years of dedication and commitment, I had been forced out of the company I'd founded two decades earlier. A court-appointed receiver would take 100 percent control of the company effective the very next day. I had trusted Dick and had dealt in good faith with him. Unfortunately, real-world events lead me to view him as unethical, dishonorable, and manipulative, further demonstrating life is filled with twists and turns.

At this point, I was owed $7 million in principal and interest in loans advanced to MILLC and in executive compensation for accrued wages over eight years, plus $5.5 million in personal loan guarantees for a total of $12.5 million. With mounting interest from the mortgages against our property for loans I'd made to the business, I was in a world of hurt.

On the surface, it appeared that the Madlers had outsmarted me at the expense of hundreds of our MILLC members. However, of significance was the fact that my personal company MII, not MILLC, was the legal owner of the METALAST trademark. The US Patent and Trademark Office registration dated back to 1996, although I had first put the trademark into commerce in 1993. I was hopeful I could eventually use the leverage to force Dick to sell back his position in METALAST so I could retake control on behalf of the LLC members.

Considering the company had not paid any of my salary for the last four years, only partially for the proceeding four year period and had not received partial interest payments due me for the millions in loans I'd made to MILLC, I was in the uncompromising position of trying to come up with $40,000 each month. After being removed as the manager, I struggled to make payments in a timely manner. Without a paycheck or interest income from the loans I had made to MILLC, I was unable to make the huge mortgage payments and sustain BCR and other personal financial obligations. To say this was a tremendous challenge would be a gross understatement. I was forced to borrow and sell other assets just to stay afloat.

To make matters even worse, CPA Jack Pimpley (not his real name), the Reno-based court-appointed receiver for MILLC, petitioned the judge to allow a sham sale of MILLC assets to Dick and Martha in November of 2013. Dick had convinced me that he would invest $3 million in the company, but in the end, his actions resulted in hundreds of LLC members losing their $90 million of equity ownership in the company and laid the blame on my supposed mismanagement. Now I would have to come up with the $5.5 million I had borrowed against our ranch to pay off the loans made to MILLC or file for bankruptcy to delay a foreclosure. This would eventually cause the loss of our home and $10 million in equity.

> **LIFE LESSON #126:**
>
> "WHATEVER CAN GO WRONG, USUALLY DOES GO WRONG."
>
> —MURPHY'S LAW

It became obvious that I had been set up as a scapegoat when the Madlers foreclosed on the MILLC assets in November 2013 and placed the blame on the former manager. They claimed without any basis in fact the company had been mismanaged and all the capital invested by the members had been squandered by a self-dealing manager. Not one word to the court about the fact that, as manager, I had lent MILLC $12.5 million or that I had gone without receiving a paycheck for many years. If this information had been disclosed to the judge, it wouldn't have fit with their false narrative and the court would have likely required that the receiver file for a Chapter 11 reorganization. The Madlers didn't want this to happen, since it could have resulted in a "cram down" of their senior loan position, making them vulnerable to new financing like the rest of the creditors, including myself.

This expedited sale petitioned for by MILLC's receiver was granted by the court—without any type of appraisal, business valuation, or advertising of MILLC assets for sale—and cancelled out $23 million of unsecured debt. About 40 percent was Dick's debt, but it was only $3.8 million in actual principal. However, with his exorbitant 18 percent compounded interest, it ballooned to $9 million. My $12.5 million in loans and loan guarantees represented almost 55 percent of the outstanding financial obligations. Another $1.5 million was from smaller creditors. This wiped out $90 million of LLC members' equity, making it a devastating $102 million loss to everyone except but the Madlers.

When the smoke cleared, in addition to wiping out my ownership in the company, the debt owed to me, and LLC member equity, I was still on the hook for $6 million in loans I had personally guaranteed. Out of curiosity, I went back through my personal bank records and confirmed that, since the formation of MILLC in 1994, my salary had averaged a modest $110,000 a year—while my base salary should have been at least triple that amount. That's the risk you take when you're an entrepreneur. It represents free markets and is the definition of capitalism, where only the strongest survive. If it sounds unfair, it's not. It's the way the real world is. In third world countries, you don't lose your money; you lose freedom and sometimes your life.

> **LIFE LESSON #127:**
>
> **"A FRIEND IS ONE WHO WALKS IN WHEN OTHERS WALK OUT."**
>
> —WALTER WINCHELL (AMERICAN NEWSPAPER COLUMNIST AND RADIO NEWS COMMENTATOR, 1897-1972)

Each week, the clock continued to tick, creeping closer to December 11, the BCR scheduled foreclosure sale date, but no one was willing to help us save either BCR or MILLC.

Over the previous two years, my dear friend, former Shearson/America Express boss and MII Board Member, Frank O'Bryan came to my rescue with a substantial loan. Mark Wyman, another good friend, general contractor, and custom homebuilder lent me large amounts of money so I could meet my financial obligations. Mark had grown up on a ranch in Wyoming and had been raised by parents with good ol' Midwestern values and a help-your-neighbor mindset, which Mark had obviously inherited. At 6'5", the cowboy and true craftsman builder was a third cousin of John Wayne. Without close friends like Frank and Mark and his pretty wife, Krista, it can be challenging to make it through difficult times.

By the end of November, we were falling behind on our other monthly financial obligations, including mortgages, property and health insurance, taxes, utilities, auto loans, credit cards, and memberships. So, I decided to start selling some of my assets, and the sale of these assets generated several hundred thousand dollars in cash, which in the long run was certainly not enough to extend the $5.5 million defaulted loan on my ranch. However, the sale of assets provided some breathing room in terms of paying monthly bills and gave me enough to engage Nevada counsel if I had no other means to stop the foreclosure on BCR.

> **LIFE LESSON #128:**
>
> **"MATERIAL THINGS ARE NICE, BUT WITH FISCAL WELLBEING ON THE LINE, DO WHATEVER IS NECESSARY TO CONVERT ASSETS TO COLD, HARD CASH."**
>
> —DAVID SEMAS

The time had come to circle the wagons and do whatever was

necessary to stay afloat. Along with our normal monthly bills and mortgage payments, I was also the primary sibling and the family patriarch that had supported our mother for twenty years (my father had passed away in 1999). Even after including her monthly Social Security check and my father's Navy veteran survivor benefits, it still cost thousands of dollars more per month to keep her in a board and care home in the Sacramento area. Fortunately, my sister Elizabeth stepped up to the plate to help support our mother.

Judith Harkham Semas, 1942-2013

A few months earlier, we had lost my oldest sister, Judy, at age seventy who, unlike my first and only stab at writing a book, was a highly accomplished writer and published business author. Before Judy's death, sadly Susan also lost her oldest sister, Sherry, at age sixty-four.

I don't know how, but even with all the financial stress, Susan was a trooper and stood shoulder to shoulder with me through thick and thin. It was remarkable to see how mentally strong she was during such difficult times. The stress would have taken a major toll on even the most seasoned business professional—and certainly on most people not accustomed to dealing with financial stress. No matter how strong you think you are, if your wife or significant other isn't standing toe to toe with you, it's difficult if not impossible to mentally survive and wake up every morning ready for your next challenge.

When all was said and done, we had little choice but to go ahead and meet with Steve Harris, our bankruptcy counsel, in Reno on Friday, December 6, so that he could prepare to file for a petition for a Chapter 11 reorganization with the US Bankruptcy Court, District of Nevada, the following Wednesday, December 11, 2013.

It's funny how you think you have many friends, but when push comes to shove and money is involved, most run for the hills, don't return telephone calls, and are nowhere to be found. Unfortunately, the lender went ahead with a planned sale of our property. On the final day, the sale was to take place on the Douglas County Courthouse steps at 1:00 p.m., and at 12:45 p.m., with only minutes to spare, Susan and I were forced to file for the Chapter 11 bankruptcy, which stayed the sale and at least it wasn't a full Chapter 7 liquidation. This was going to make our lives difficult, but I was hopeful that it might be short-lived.

We could only hope that things would turn around in 2014. We were in good health, and so was our family. Thus, we had much to be thankful for. I had to remind myself at times to stay the course and continue to follow my career mantra, which was, "It is what it is." No matter what, I will never give in, never give up, and never say quit.

Month after month, throughout 2014, we struggled to come up with enough cash to pay for utilities, insurance, taxes, car payments, and living expenses while at the same time making certain to pay the huge $50,000 monthly mortgages and other expenses or "adequate protection payments" as they are called—something the bankruptcy court required as a prerequisite for remaining in Chapter 11 bankruptcy. If it weren't for Peter Bacchus, another good friend, and a few other MILLC members, we could have never survived. His funding gave me the cash needed to continue to pay mounting legal fees, mortgage, car payments, and living expenses until we could sell BCR.

It became apparent the main problem was that several prospective buyers were sitting on the fence, waiting to see if a trustee would be appointed or if the Chapter 11 stay would be lifted. This would mean the lender could foreclose on the property on the courthouse steps and the buyer could acquire the ranch at a deeper discount in the $6 million range.

After the Madlers filed another absurd lawsuit in the bankruptcy court in Reno falsely claiming I had fraudulently conveyed the METALAST trademark to myself, we reached a settlement agreement mediated by Judge Zive with the devious duo. The agreement allowed them to temporarily use the USPTO-registered trademark until June 10, 2015. The Madlers begrudgingly agreed I always owned the trademark and that they could no longer use the name METALAST "in any fashion or manner whatsoever" after that date.

This appeared to be a good deal for us. I knew it would be nearly impossible for them to change the name of the company in ninety days, which also included removing the name and trademark from all technical literature, marketing materials, and product labels. Ethically I warned the judge, the Madlers, and their attorney that they couldn't meet manufacturer or governmental specifications because it required them to reference the name METALAST in verifying the origin of their 120 chemicals. My warnings went unheeded. They believed I was overstating the significance of the METALAST trademark, which I wasn't.

With a settlement reached that might one day produce a few million dollars when they finally realized they couldn't sell their chemical without the trademark, I was still hoping escrow would close in October. Unfortunately, on June 3, 2015, six days before they were to stop using the name METALAST, the Madlers filed another baseless lawsuit against me and shamefully named Wendi and Greg. This required that I hire a specialized litigation attorney, so I engaged Mike Hoy of Reno to represent Greg, Wendi, my three corporations, and myself.

This time they filed the lawsuit in federal court, hoping to unwind the bankruptcy-court-approved settlement agreement. The baseless lawsuit was entirely unwarranted and lacked factual evidence that would support the absurd allegations.

The Madlers falsely alleged trade-secret disclosures, fraud, copyright violations, and unfair competition. Their thirty-four causes of action were ridiculous. The only thing missing was that I had killed Jimmy Hoffa and knew where he was buried. The nonsense was meant to confuse the federal court and distract from the real issue with mountains of exhibits. But the lawsuit was nothing more than buyer's remorse. They had agreed to a settlement under terms that would be nearly impossible to meet. Instead of renegotiating new terms and paying me for the trademark, they chose to go ahead and use the trademark anyway and then sue me in a different court, which was meant to deplete my remaining assets so they could steal the trademark. This was a clear breach of contract of the settlement agreement requiring their new company, Custom Care Surface Technology, LLC, to stop using my METALAST name and trademark "in any fashion or manner whatsoever" beyond June 10, 2015.

The Madlers terminated the legal services of Ms Chang (not her real name), claiming she had failed to protect their interests by having them agree to the terms of the bankruptcy-court-mediated settlement agreement. They hired a no-holds-barred five-person legal team from a California law firm that had a take-no-prisoners style of doing business. The lead lawyer would stoop to whatever courtroom tactics were required to prevail, although in the end, after several appeals, they lost every single preposterous cause of action. They used one after another underhanded trick in the book, including misrepresenting or omitting material facts, in their unsuccessful attempts time and time again to win any motion before the court. They used hyperbole and, when necessary, concealed evidence that would support our legal position. Now I found myself in another costly lawsuit with a den of thieves in a different federal court, running up more legal expenses that I couldn't afford.

In contrast to the behavior the Madlers' lawyers, my attorney, Mike Hoy, was a professional, behaved ethically, and refused to stoop to opposing counsel's tactics, although at times I wished he had. Mike sometimes chastised their lead counsel but did so in an eloquent manner. Mike used the art of tact, defined by Winston Churchill as "the ability to tell someone to go to hell in such a way they look forward to the trip."

In the initial court, the US Bankruptcy Court, District of Nevada, Reno, we finally received approval for our Chapter 11 reorganization plan, which became a confirmed plan in March 2015. As long as we made our minimum monthly payments to the creditors and filed our reports with the US trustee, we had five years to pay off the debt. This meant we were in post-confirmation Chapter 11, so things were looking much better on that front.

Although we were finally in our Chapter 11 post-confirmation phase, we were still required to pay off the first and second mortgage holders. Finally, a buyer appeared with a close of escrow slated for

> **LIFE LESSON #130:**
>
> "MANY OF LIFE'S FAILURES ARE PEOPLE WHO DID NOT REALIZE HOW CLOSE THEY WERE TO SUCCESS WHEN THEY GAVE UP."
>
> —THOMAS EDISON

November, which was extended to December. Then he gave absolute assurance he would close by February 2, 2016. This date was significant because if the bankruptcy court lifted the automatic stay, the lender could foreclose, and I would be forced to convey title by giving a deed in lieu of foreclosure to the lender.

Unfortunately, the buyer couldn't get his funds in time, and the ranch didn't close escrow. We had prayed this wouldn't happen, but in the end, we had no choice and were forced to convey title to our beautiful agricultural estate property. However, on the positive side, this wiped out about 70 percent of our financial obligations. But thanks to the Madlers' hostile takeover, we still had to pay off the remaining MILLC debt of about $5 million.

At the age of sixty-six, not twenty-six, I was finding it increasingly difficult to once again dust myself off. But as I had done before, I put one foot in front of the other, and with the loving support of Susan and my children, I kept my nose to the grindstone and continued the good fight against the Madlers on the ownership of the METALAST® trademark.

Well, at this point in my life, "never give in, never give up, and never say quit" was no longer simply a canned phrase or state of mind; it was a survival instinct embodied in my heart and soul.

> LIFE LESSON #129:
>
> "LIFE IS NOT ABOUT WAITING FOR THE STORM TO PASS BUT LEARNING TO DANCE IN THE RAIN."
>
> —VIVIAN GREENE (BRITISH AUTHOR, WRITER, AND HUMANITARIAN, 1904-2003)

CHAPTER 26

AN UNEXPECTED CALL AND MEETING A POLITICAL ICON

After Susan and I were forced to convey title and the ownership of our home and ranch in February of 2016, we remained on the property until May 1. We moved to Reno, into the Fleur de Lis complex, a beautiful, security-gated condominium that I had leased for one year.

I was with the movers as they were carrying my office desk upstairs when I heard my cell phone ring.

"David, what the hell are you doing?" It was Marc Harris, an old friend and MILLC member. Marc and I had been through thick and thin for thirty years, with our friendship dating back to the time of American Realty Advisors.

I laughed. "What the hell do you think I'm doing, now that you can hear me huffing and puffing?"

Marc paused a moment before replying. "Take a break for a minute, because I want to ask you something."

I caught my breath. "Okay, you have my attention. So what's up?"

"Remember my land for a proposed Mexican hotel, golf, and residential resort project in San Blas, Mexico, about ninety miles north of Puerto Vallarta?"

"Sure, I remember it well. Over the years, you came to me with several questions about different aspects of acquisition, finance, development, and master planning. It was a twelve-hundred-acre project located in the small Mexican fishing village of San Blas. As I recall, it has something like four miles of beach shoreline on the Pacific Ocean and another five miles of frontage on two rivers."

"David, I need your help and want you to be my partner. You forgot more about construction, real estate development, finance, and hotel operations than I'll ever know. So will you come on board and help me make Las Islitas Resort a five-star destination resort development on the Mexican Riviera Nayarit?"

I was somewhat taken aback. Now that METALAST was behind me, I knew this could be a great opportunity to move forward in a positive direction. Better yet, it was in a business I loved. "Yes, of course."

The potential equity participation and substantial profits would enable me to pay back my outstanding METALAST-related Chapter 11 debt. I would also be able to pay back my friends who had helped Susan and me through tough times.

Other than the ongoing legal battle with the Madlers over the METALAST trademark, we were in post-confirmation in our Chapter 11, and BCR was no longer a concern. Most importantly, with the elimination of a monthly $50,000 nut, I was ready to move on. I told myself that this might be the perfect project for me to sink my teeth into. I wasn't about to slow down. Real estate development, master planning, finance, problem solving—they were in my blood. I couldn't retire even if I'd wanted to. I still thought getting up every morning at four-thirty was invigorating. It was what drove me. It defined me.

In the midst of focusing on new real estate development and financing projects and other opportunities, I received a call from Frank O'Bryan, who told me that on November 22, 2016, Roger W. Luby, his dearest friend and

LIFE LESSON #131:

"MOST PEOPLE MISS 'OPPORTUNITY' BECAUSE IT IS DRESSED IN OVER- ALLS AND LOOKS LIKE WORK."

—THOMAS EDISON

business partner of fifty years and one of my closest longtime friends, had passed away.

I had flown down to Orange County and visited Roger several times in 2015. He had been in and out of Hoag Hospital in Newport Beach while suffering from some serious health problems. After losing his wife, Pam, the year before, Roger had also been in a deep depression, so while it was not unexpected, it was nonetheless a real blow to hear about his passing. Many years earlier, we'd made a habit of calling each other every Friday morning, and the tradition had lasted a decade. His Irish swagger, sense of humor, and booming laughter will be sorely missed. Rest in peace, Roger. You were a great man!

Together with my love of music and being a vocalist, I have long enjoyed writing poetry. My first public effort was when I was asked by the Santa Clara County Board of Supervisors to write a poem reciting the history of our country in celebration of the upcoming US Bicentennial celebration on July 4, 1976. It was more than forty-five years ago when I wrote "America's Fourth of July Poem." It was first presented in July 1976 during the US bicentennial celebration held at the Santa Clara County Fairgrounds. Since that time, every few years thereafter, I would update the poem and write a new stanza and then recite the poem at a Fourth of July event. Beginning in 2001, it became a tradition to present the poem at our annual BCR July Fourth party before a gathering of three hundred friends and family members. With the song "America the Beautiful" playing softly in the background, I continue to this day to recite the poem for friends and family and have also created a musical tribute for YouTube.

DAVID MICHAEL SEMAS

 **AMERICA'S FOURTH OF JULY POEM©**

By David Michael Semas
www.sierradorado.com
July 4, 2021

On that cold, wet, and foggy night of April 18, 1775,
American silversmith Paul Revere mounted his steed,
ready to ride
Atop his trusty horse he traveled village to village
and door to door
While on his midnight ride shouting, "The British are
coming! Prepare for war!"

When the smoke cleared at Concord, Bunker Hill,
and Yorktown too
Many patriots paid the ultimate price defending
our red, white, and blue
The Declaration of Independence set all Americans free
And made the United States of America the Land
of Liberty

Our country marched forward with Thirteen States
And continued to grow—with a few mistakes
Then came June 1, 1812, it seemed such a shame
A second war for independence was said to blame!
In 1836, history tells of Houston, Bowie, Crockett,
and Boone
Two centuries later their courage at the Alamo
will not be forgotten soon
Against the mighty Santa Anna's Army over 4,000 strong
250 courageous "Texians" fought for independence
thirteen days long

MAN IN THE ARENA – NEVER SAY QUIT

Outnumbered by tenfold, these fallen heroes quietly
asked for our trust
And then one by one, gave up their lives for the rest of us
We're all a part of what occurred at this little
Texas mission
This act of bravery is now a part of an American tradition

Then, time marches on, the Industrial Revolution begins
With farms, factories, trains, and even cotton gins
Ruthless men forged empires from this virgin land
At the expense of the plains bison and the
American Indian

On April 12, 1861, with the firing on Fort Sumter
before morning sun
The South against the North and the Civil War
had begun
President Lincoln on one side and General Lee on
the other
Cousin fighting cousin and brother fighting brother
The time had come for the Black Man to be set free
Yet over a century later we're still far from harmony

The American Old West was only
twenty-five years in duration
Folklore and legends born add to the
history of our nation
Wyatt Earp, Pat Garrett, Jessie James, and Billy the Kid
Good guys chasing bad guys, that's what these guys did

The Victorian Era and the turn of the century came next
With Teddy's famous Rough Riders preserved in text
Mark Twain coined the Gilded Age was here to stay
While beautiful maidens adorned in satin and lace seen

DAVID MICHAEL SEMAS

every day
Statuesque ladies and top-hatted gents dressed
ever so neat
Romantically holding hands and strolling down
every Main Street

America seemed to be so peaceful and calm
Until the headlines read, "*Lusitania,* Hit By a bomb"
America had fought from its own shore to shore
But sadly this was its first real World War!

The global conflict ended, and the smoke finally cleared
The Roaring Twenties arrived, and all America cheered
Speakeasies, the Cotton Club, Al Jolson, Elliot Ness,
and Al Capone
Tunney, Valentino, and of course, the Babe Ruth
on the throne
Our country went on with all its daily chores
Never forgetting all those devastating wars
Prosperity reigned, and all looked well
Until the day came when Wall Street fell

Chaos and confusion, a run on the banks
Millionaires to paupers and thousands
fell through the ranks
Torn, tattered, and bruised, America came through
Now stronger than ever and still proud too

But on that seventh day of December in 1941
Pearl Harbor was attacked, and World War II had begun
Eisenhower, MacArthur, and Patton were America's
fury unfurled
Hitler's genocidal killing of six million Jews
shocked the entire world

MAN IN THE ARENA – NEVER SAY QUIT

American soldiers have courage, pride,
and honor—don't you see?
They would give up their lives to keep
other countries free
Men on the front lines and women building ships,
planes, and tanks
It's the Greatest Generation for whom
we all owe our thanks

Most will never forget that solemn day of August 6, 1945
High in the clouds the *Enola Gay* carried
the Atom Bomb inside
This heart-wrenching decision was made
by our President Harry S
Hiroshima and Nagasaki, Japan were the targets,
and we all know the rest

Throughout the world the 38th Parallel
was known by so few
Yet our brave young men lost their lives in Korea too
The invention of the jet engine gave our Air Force a thrill
But 243 courageous American soldiers died
on Pork Chop Hill

The decade of the fifties came and went
Names like Fats, Buddy, Bo, and Elvis cast in cement
The Bristol Stomp, the Twist and the Stroll
Made famous the era of rock 'n roll

The sixties were filled with violence in the streets,
Anti-war demonstrations and flower children's treats
It was certainly a time of doubt, confusion, and unrest,
With Timothy Leary, the Beatles,
and of course—The Rabbit Test

DAVID MICHAEL SEMAS

Our President John F. Kennedy, his brother Bobby
And Martin Luther King Jr. all had a dream
They were lost to us forever in one silent scream
Camelot was over when these leaders died
America was shaken and all throughout the world cried

Vietnam was the war that wasn't a war
Yet it killed and maimed our soldiers score by score
They returned home with no parades or cheers
Forced to cope all alone with their own private tears

Since the Space Age began in the fifties in May
Americans have waited for that very special day
Collins, Aldrin, and Armstrong left on Apollo 11
Leaving the Earth's gravitational pull toward heaven
The Eagle has landed, and people of planet Earth
began to unwind
Armstrong said, "That's one small step for a man,
one giant leap for mankind"

The seventies came in with things hard to handle
President Nixon's resignation and the Watergate scandal
Gerald Ford was appointed president because
he could do no harm
And then Jimmy Carter was elected president off
a peanut farm
Only in the land called America could
all of this take place
With the blessed help of our Lord and his saving grace

The movie star Governor Ronald Reagan then stepped in
Conservative media loved him, with his sense of humor
and famous grin
Despite most of the mainstream media's doubts,

MAN IN THE ARENA - NEVER SAY QUIT

he set a challenging goal
As president he restored pride in America,
like diamonds from coal

The 1980s also saw many forms of greed and corruption
Junk bonds, inflation and the Savings & Loan destruction
Then President George H. W. Bush stepped into
Reagan's shoes
Americans thought, "Not a bad guy—what do we
have to lose?"
A Thousand Points of Light from California to DC
Symbolizing unity of all Americans,
but could it really be?

January of 1991, scuds flew, and Operation Desert Storm
hit the ground
General Schwarzkopf, smart missiles, iron-clad tanks
were all around
American military might moved swiftly on
Saddam's army with pride
Hussein's famous elite Republican Guard had nowhere
to hide
The Gulf War ended a mere six months after it had begun
Mothers and fathers elated with the return of daughter
and son

Do you recall that President Jimmy Carter was
elected off a peanut farm?
20th Century comes to a close with
President Bill Clinton's great deal of charm
Then Dot-Commers became Dot Bombers,
overnight it seemed
Their fortunes were lost as though it had
all been a bad dream

Another George Bush in the White House, many
were glad
Ironically, it was something as innocuous as a
Hanging Chad?
No words could ever describe the horrific
and catastrophic events of 9/11
But we know all those innocent souls now reside
peacefully in heaven

The curse of the Bambino began its reign after
the 1918 World Series year
Something Red Sox fans became accustomed to,
shedding an annual tear
Never had a pennant contender come back from
three down
Until Boston sent the Yankee's Evil Empire tumbling
to the ground

President Ronald Reagan was lost to us in the '04 year
Republicans, Independents, and even a Democrat
or two shed a tear
The assassination attempt failed to silence
His Eminence dearly beloved
But the good Lord saw fit to summon Pope John Paul II
to heaven above
The Pilgrim of Peace was seen by more people
than ever before
A statesman, actor, poet, humanitarian,
world leader, and more

In 2005 Hurricane Katrina collided with
America's Gulf Coast
$25 billion in damage, but loss of life hurt the most
Our highest costly natural catastrophe of all—but
it doesn't end there

MAN IN THE ARENA – NEVER SAY QUIT

The real story was the generosity of fellow man
and all those who care

President Obama was Martin Luther King's dream
come true
The American flag unites our people with its glorious
red, white, and blue
While liberals stand proud and conservatives shout,
"Where's the beef?"
We can all agree on one thing: that Bernie Madoff
is a scoundrel and a thief

The Tea Party made famous in Boston Harbor in 1773
Traveled coast to coast demanding once again
we be set free
Deepwater Horizon was a sight to behold and a drilling
platform to boast
For all the oil executives, but not for the local inhabitants
down on the Gulf Coast
Thick Texas tea, black gold, and sticky crude oil spewin'
out of the sea
Damaging our fragile environment was a
gigantic oil company called BP

On May 2, 2011, Blackhawks had the Abbottabad
compound in site
Culminating a global manhunt, with our courageous
Navy SEALs ready for the fight
Closure never occurs for families of their 9/11 loved ones
viciously stricken down
But a decade later all were relieved when
Osama Bin Laden lay dead on the ground

DAVID MICHAEL SEMAS

Four Americans and Ambassador Stevens were
murdered in Benghazi one night
Our men were told to stand down, but six heroes came
to rescue and to the firefight
By not confronting the reality and taking the fight
to ISIS on their home turf
Inevitably, radical Islamic ideology will fester
and manifest much worse

Political pundits and presidential tracking polls tried
to manipulate the call
Businessman Donald Trump said he'll have Mexico
pay for a Beautiful Wall
He'll Make America Great Again using his experience
and *Art of the Deal*
He intends to serve the highest office in the land
with vigor, zest, and zeal
With GDP performance at all-time lows
and an economy in the tank
It's about time we have a new president outside
The Swamp to thank

On the eighteenth day of March 2020, the US economy
was booming like never before
Then the COVID-19 global pandemic arrived,
said to take 100,000 US lives and more
Small businesses were shut down and families
were devastated from state to state
Great Depression unemployment was dwarfed to 40
million by the June-first date

Americans shouted, "Open the Doors!" so our livelihood
and loved ones can survive
What good is a cure if our families are sheltered, starved,
depressed, and deprived

MAN IN THE ARENA – NEVER SAY QUIT

Entrepreneurial business owners revolted and refused
to comply with Draconian law
Politicians and puppet dictators forced to accept people
had reached the final last straw

Our Constitution was written by those willing to
fight to be free
Back and forth bickering between Congress must stop,
don't you agree?
However, let's not take our eyes off the safety
and security ball
The first obligation of our government is
to protect and serve all

With ruthless villains, anarchy, terrorism,
and worldwide turmoil abound
We still must remember the kind and caring acts
of so many around
Like the two hundred strangers that attended
the funeral of a homeless vet
People every day give and donate much to those
in need they never met

Our military defends life, liberty, and freedom
wherever it may be
We give thanks and God Bless America,
from sea to shining sea
With all our accomplishments, we have a long way to go
We need to feed, shelter, and care for our people,
isn't that so?
Cures for cancer, muscular dystrophy, and autism
must be found
And let's not forget the other afflictions
and diseases that abound

We are strong, determined, and exceptional people,
while some say it ain't so
Just ask the millions around the world who flee
oppression if they know.
America is the bright light of hope, opportunity,
and the land of the free
People of all races and cultures long to stand beneath
our Statue of Liberty!

Most on the far left, mainstream media, Hollywood,
and the university elite
Castigate capitalism, patriotism, religion,
and the common folks of Main Street
But as all of us common folks know, no matter what
the critics might say
The greatest place on earth to live free is still the
good old U S of A

In closing, remember that the future holds
many surprises,
But even with all the uncertainty that it comprises
If we fail to learn from our past, we could make
the same mistakes again
But this time—they could be our last!
Thank you and God Bless America!

Shortly after Marc's call in February of 2016 about helping him raise capital for his Las Islitas hotel resort project in Mexico, I received another telephone call, this time from Marty Cohen, my close METALAST confidant and MILLC member. I brought him up to date on the status of METALAST litigation, and we got caught up in other news.

After I hung up, I was struck by a fond memory of the most memorable afternoon I'd spent with a true American political icon fifteen years earlier. During my brief meeting with this statesman, he reminded me to always be ready, willing, and able to return to my roots, because they're the foundation of our life experiences and make us whole. Ambassador Maxwell Milton Rabb was appointed ambassador to Italy by President Ronald Reagan and served from 1981 to 1989. Max went to his office every Monday through Friday until the day of his untimely demise at the age of ninety-one.

During my never-ending search for capital for METALAST back in 2001, Marty called to inform me that one of the largest private equity firms in the country, the New York office of the Carlyle Group, had inquired to see if I would travel to New York to discuss a sizeable investment in MILLC. Naturally, I said yes, and within a few days, on Thursday, November 15, 2001, I jumped on a plane for Dallas to meet with Marty to learn more about the investment group.

While in Dallas the next day, we had lunch with an old friend of Marty's, Dick Cioffi, who was a real character, a local Fort Worth golf celebrity and motivational speaker known and beloved by famous American politicians, business leaders, Wall Street tycoons, and sports legends around the world.

We spent an afternoon at Dick's favorite watering hole, Fort Worth's Stockyards Hotel, and enjoyed listening to his fascinating stories. The thoroughly enjoyable afternoon began the moment we stepped inside what appeared to be an 1880s-era thirst parlor from the Old West. The belt-driven, old-fashioned ceiling fans were slowly spinning, moving the air around the establishment and doing their job to cool the room. Worn wooden plank flooring stretched toward the gorgeous mahogany Burl Wood bar, which seemed to go on forever. A massive mirror sat behind the bar. Above it a sign read: *Buffalo Butt Beer.*

I took a seat at the bar and had to swing my leg over the stool because it was a Western saddle, which, believe it or not, made me feel right at home.

When Dick saw how comfortable I was, he turned to Marty. "You didn't tell me David was actually a good ol' cowboy at heart."

"David has been around horses and has loved the cowboy way of life since he was a young boy," Marty said. "He's the longtime sponsor of the Reno Rodeo Cattle Drive, which pushes three hundred head of cattle across the high desert beginning sixty miles north of Reno. After swallowing ten pounds of dust, they deliver the herd of Corriente roping steers just in time for the fourth largest rodeo in the country: the Reno Rodeo."

With that introduction, Dick and I became fast friends.

Dick was a great guy with a colorful background. We shared stories of days gone by about our world travels, business meetings, and negotiations with fascinating people from all walks of life. Although he was twenty-five years older, we bonded over golf, hunting, American history, the Old West, and conservative politics. At some point, I mentioned that President Dwight D. Eisenhower had been my father's favorite president.

"David," Dick replied with enthusiasm, "boy, do I have a great surprise for you! When are you leaving for New York City?"

"My flight leaves tomorrow," I said.

"Great! How about I set up a meeting Monday afternoon with my very close friend, Ambassador Maxwell Rabb? He was legal counsel to President Dwight D. Eisenhower in the fifties, more or less his chief of staff, and a friend to all five living presidents, not to mention celebrities, wealthy businessmen, and heads of state all over the world."

"What a fabulous opportunity to meet a living legend who rubbed elbows with many of the modern-day leaders of the free world!" I replied. "Do you actually think he'll want to meet with me?"

"Absolutely," Dick said. "Make certain to tell Max that your father was a Seabee in World War II and that he was from Taunton, Massachusetts, because Max was born in Boston. David, believe me: Max will welcome you with open arms. After lunch each workday, he enjoys seeing old friends and meeting new ones because he says it keeps him young. I'll call Max right now and arrange for the meeting."

Sure enough, Dick returned in fifteen minutes with a big smile on his face.

"You're all set. Max is excited about meeting you and wants you to come to his office at two o'clock Monday afternoon. He's still as sharp as a tack,

MAN IN THE ARENA – NEVER SAY QUIT

but keep in mind that at age ninety he gets a little tired in the afternoon, so the meeting will only last for maybe an hour."

Our luncheon turned into a dinner, after which Marty drove me back to my hotel, The Mansion on Turtle Creek in Dallas. I took a cab to the airport the next day and soon arrived in New York City, where I was welcomed by a chilly fall afternoon. I once again hailed a cab, which navigated the hectic, bustling, taxi-cab-lined streets to my buddy Martin Burke's apartment on Manhattan near Fourteenth Street and Broadway near Union Square.

That night, Martin and his friend and partner, Richard Bren, and I had dinner at a great New York hot spot, after which we stopped at all the local bars and pubs for a fun night on the town. I had met Richard many years earlier. His father, Peter Bren, was the chairman of KBS Capital, a major real estate office building investment and asset management company. Richard's uncle, Donald Bren, is the mega-billionaire owner of the Irvine Company of Orange County, California, and one of the wealthiest real estate developers in the country.

My ten o'clock meeting Monday morning with the investment firm of the Carlyle Group was uneventful, but I looked forward to my meeting with Maxwell Rabb that afternoon. I had lunch by myself in a New York deli just around the corner from the ambassador's offices and then walked down the street to the imposing bronze-framed, tinted-glass entrance doors to the forty-story skyscraper.

Since nearly all the major office buildings in New York City had significantly tightened security after 9/11, the lobby was cordoned off with polished brass crowd-control stanchions with yellow guide rope. Five-armed security guards manned a security checkpoint, which was complete with metal detectors, scanning technology, and motion sensors. After passing through security, I walked over to the expansive mahogany guest services desk and asked which elevator I should take to get to the fortieth floor and Ambassador Maxwell Rabb's office.

LIFE LESSON #132:

"FATE PULLS YOU IN DIFFERENT DIRECTIONS."

—CLINT EASTWOOD (AMERICAN ACTOR, DIRECTOR, PRODUCER, FILMMAKER, AND FORMER MAYOR OF CARMEL, CA, 1930-)

Upon arriving at his posh law offices, I was greeted by Gloria, his secretary. The exquisitely decorated reception area featured rich cherry wood wainscot paneling, crown moldings, and several ornately patterned upholstered walls. Persian throw rugs covered the teakwood floors. When I gave Gloria my name, she came around her desk to shake my hand and to let me know Ambassador Rabb had just called and would arrive in ten to fifteen minutes.

Sure enough, about fifteen minutes later, the immaculately dressed 5'9" statesman and retired Boston barrister walked into the room and extended his hand and said, "Don't tell me: you're David Semas, the former California carpenter that rose from the ranks to become a young real estate developer, entrepreneur, Wall Street executive, and chemical company CEO that my dear friend Dick Cioffi has told me so much about. It's a pleasure to make your acquaintance and welcome you to the Big Apple. Please step into my office so we can chat for a while."

We entered his 1,200-square-foot, three-room office suite, which boasted magnificent cherry-wood paneling and a coffered ceiling with hammered copper inserts. The cozy living room featured large, leather-upholstered, oversize chairs facing each other and a real fireplace in the middle of the room across from his oversized desk.

The telephone rang, and he told me to make myself at home before excusing himself to take an important call. I was so taken aback by the overall design and old-world Victorian style of his surroundings that at first I didn't notice the numerous awards, mounted plaques of appreciation, and his beautiful wood-framed Harvard law degree that prominently hung just inside his hand-carved double entrance doors. Then my eyes were drawn to fifty or more photographs covering the walls.

While he was preoccupied with his telephone conversation, I studied some beautiful works of art and Remington bronze sculptures on his sofa tables. Ornately framed photos hung from his walls. The first one I looked at showed Max sitting in the Oval Office talking with President Eisenhower, John F. Kennedy, Richard Nixon, and Lyndon B. Johnson all intently listening. The next photo showed Max with Martin Luther King Jr., and next to it was a photo of Max with Mohammad Ali. In another picture, Max had his arms around Frank Sinatra and Sammy Davis Jr. In yet another, he appeared to be deep-sea fishing with John and Bobby Kennedy. There were photos of Winston Churchill, Queen Elizabeth, General Douglas MacArthur, Henry Ford, Nelson Rockefeller, and the most famous crime fighter of them all, J. Edgar Hoover. There was one with Barry Goldwater and picture after picture of Max with Prime Minister Margaret Thatcher and even His Eminence Pope John Paul II.

As I was walking around his office, I heard Max conclude his conference call. He stood up from behind his beautiful hand-crafted desk and walked over to where I was standing and began to tell me the story behind the picture I had been studying. We walked around his office for about thirty minutes as he recalled the date, time, and details surrounding each photo.

At the end of the historic tour, Max invited me to sit in one of the large leather chairs next to the fireplace. "Enough about me. Tell me about yourself and your fascinating life thus far. I'm certain you'll have many more years to enjoy."

"Thank you, Max," I said, "but compared with your lifetime of achievements, my business and political career is pretty modest."

"From what I've heard," he replied, "I hardly think so. I heard from Dick that your parents were from Taunton, Massachusetts. Were you born there?"

"No. After serving in World War II, my father returned to Fort Ord in Monterey. I was the first born in California in the town of Carmel-by-the-Sea but was raised in Santa Clara, now better known as Silicon Valley."

"Well," Max said, "did you ever meet the Mayor of Carmel, Clint Eastwood?"

I chuckled. "It's funny you should ask. I only met him one time over a four-hour dinner at Nicky Blair's restaurant on Sunset Boulevard in Hollywood back in 1986. Bobby Roberts, my business partner, was a famous record and motion picture producer and well-known entertainment executive. He invited me to a casual dinner with a few film directors and their wives. When I sat down at the table, five couples

---

LIFE LESSON #133:

"A GREAT MAN IS ALWAYS WILLING TO BE LITTLE."

—RALPH WALDO EMERSON

---

all said hello, but the man seated to my right was steeped in a conversation with his companion and had his back to me. Bobby finished introducing me to the Hollywood directors and their wives and then said, 'David, why don't you tell Clint where you were born?'

"The man seated next to me turned to look just as I turned toward him. To my delight, it was none other than Clint Eastwood and Sondra Locke. We shook hands, and I introduced myself and said, 'Hello, Mr. Mayor. Yes, believe it or not, I was born in Carmel.'

Clint gave a big smile, shook his head from side to side, and in his *Dirty Harry* voice said, 'David, no one was born in Carmel. Only the rich and powerful retire and die there.'

"'Is that right?' I quipped. 'Mr. Mayor, I was born in 1949 in the thirty-bed Carmel Community Hospital, formerly known as Grace Deere Velie Clinic, founded in 1929 by one of the four heirs to the John Deere tractor fortune.'

"Clint sat back, rested his hand on the arm of his chair, and said, 'David, yes, you were, because no one would have known that piece of Carmel history. The Carmel Clinic hasn't been a hospital since 1959.'

"Everyone at the table burst into laughter. As for the rest of the evening, we had a great time hearing stories about the film industry. Clint and I talked about golf, football, boxing, and most everything else but his films. He was a gracious dinner guest. I thoroughly enjoyed the evening and will never forget what a gentleman he was to all present."

I was also reminded to answer Max's question. "Yes, my mother and father were not only from Taunton, but they were both born there. Dad was a Seabee in World War II and was stationed in the South Pacific in and around the Marshall Islands."

Max's eyes lit up. "I know Taunton very well. It's about twenty-five miles or so from Fall River and Providence, Rhode Island, right?"

"Yes, sir. That's funny because my grandparents lived in Fall River and New Bedford before moving to Taunton." I told Max that my mentor in the 1970s was Benjamin Swig, the founder of the Fairmont Hotel chain. Like my parents, he was also born and raised in Taunton.

Max smiled. "Yes, I knew Ben dating back to the 1920s, during his days in Boston as a banker and real estate investor, years before he became a famous hotelier. Over our lifetimes we reacquainted on occasion during the Eisenhower administration in the 1950s and all the way up to Ronald Reagan's run for president."

I asked Max when he'd first met Ronald Reagan.

Max lowered his head, looked to his left and then right, and then scratched the side of his forehead. "The very first time was in 1966, when he was running for governor of California. I met him at the Rancho Mirage estate of Walter Annenberg, the founder of *TV Guide*. I was involved during Governor Reagan's unsuccessful GOP bid against Gerald Ford to run for president in 1976. I was much more active in his successful bid against President Carter in the 1980 campaign, after which it was my good fortune to be appointed as ambassador to Italy, where I served until 1989. At first that presidential assignment was a little dicey. It was based at the US embassy in Rome, and the security detail assigned to me and my family was informed by the CIA of a Libyan plot to assassinate me, which was somewhat alarming. At the request of the White House, my family and I flew back to the US, and after more security measures were put into place a month later, we returned to Rome so I could carry out my duties as ambassador."

After only an hour of talking, Max hesitated and then said, "Although we've only had a brief amount of time to chat, I can see that what Dick Cioffi said rings true. He said you were quite a savvy businessman of integrity, and he was right."

I was honored and didn't know how to respond. "Thank you so much, Max. The pleasure has been truly mine." I assumed our conversation was coming to an end.

"Wait a minute," Max said. "Do you have to be somewhere?"

"No, but I've probably intruded enough on your afternoon. I was planning to take my leave and return to my friend's apartment over by Union Square."

"Did you ever happen to meet Norman Mineta, the former mayor of San Jose, a distinguished congressman, and now the secretary of transportation?"

"Yes, I met Norman many years ago when I was a Santa Clara County planning commissioner and again when I was an employee of Norman's longtime friend, Jack Copple, a San Jose builder and respected civic leader."

It was obvious that Max and I had bonded. We proceeded to talk about my early career and the Century Past project, the Central State Teamsters, and my meeting with the Shah of Iran and President Marcos of the Philippines.

Max got quite a kick out of the fact that I had formed a record company called Alone Star Productions that had produced a record album by Pope John Paul II. Record producer John Fiore, my sister Elizabeth, and I owned the recording, production, distribution, and sale rights to Pope John Paul II's whirlwind American speaking tour in 1979. *The Pilgrim of Peace* contained sixty-nine speeches and sermons given by His Eminence before enormous crowds of faithful Christian followers from six cities across America.

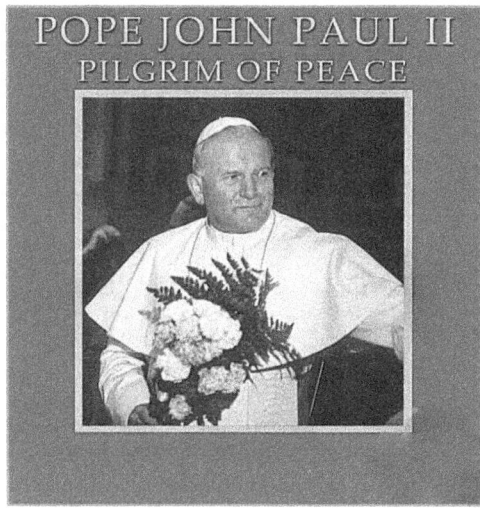

Pilgrim of Peace cover, 1979

Max chuckled. "Did you ever meet His Holiness?"

"No, but it would have been a once-in-a-lifetime experience."

"I was honored and privileged to have known him," Max said, "because as the US ambassador to Italy, I had many occasions to meet him in Rome and break bread together."

I smiled. "Wow! Not too many people in the world can make that statement."

Max asked what had happened after the Pope's album and my real estate projects. I frankly disclosed my embarrassing fall from financial grace in 1980 and how I had been forced to file bankruptcy for $28 million after the prime lending rate skyrocketed from 7.5% to 21.5%. I told Max I rebounded as the executive vice president of construction lending and head of the REO department and real estate investment-banking for Shearson/American Express Development Corporation.

I was amazed that this worldly and distinguished statesman was genuinely fascinated with my stories. As Dick had predicted, Max told me that he admired Sandy Weill, then the chairman of Citigroup, and considered him to be one of the great Wall Street financiers of our time. For the next two hours, we talked about American Realty Advisors, my joint venture partnership with PMRealty Advisors (Pacific Mutual Life), and some of my more interesting projects. We spoke of President Reagan, the astonishing collapse of the Berlin Wall, and Max's thoughts about Presidents George H. W. Bush, Bill Clinton, and George W. Bush. We chatted about METALAST®, the chemical business, and subjects far and wide, from family and golf to politics and big-game hunting and what it had been like to be threatened by Muammar Gaddafi, the ruthless Libyan dictator.

The time flew by, and soon the hands on his ornate nineteenth-century grandfather clock struck four-thirty and the Westminster Abbey chimes resonated in the large office suite. Regrettably, the time had come to leave his company. I felt like I'd met a living piece of history. Sadly, just a few months later, in June 2002, Ambassador Maxwell Rabb passed away at the age of ninety-two after sustaining injuries suffered in a fall while walking to his office.

LIFE LESSON #134:

"WHEN YOU GET A CHANCE TO MEET A LIVING LEGEND, SEIZE THE OPPORTUNITY, BECAUSE YOU DON'T WANT TO EVER SAY, 'I WISH I HAD.'"

—DAVID SEMAS

CHAPTER 27

LITIGATION IN FULL SWING— BACK IN THE SADDLE AGAIN!

On November 16, 2016, on behalf of their company, Dick and Martha filed their fifth frivolous legal action, this time with the United States Patent and Trademark Office (USPTO)'s Trademark Trial and Appeal Board (TTAB). Their relentless and costly litigious attacks continued to take a toll on my dwindling financial resources, which had always been their stated mission. I had already racked up more than $1 million in legal fees.

We had reached agreement in the bankruptcy court, and the lawsuit was settled by mutual agreement on January 28 and approved on March 10, 2015. The Madlers agreed under oath in open court to stop using the name METALAST® by June 10, 2015, yet failed to abide by the agreement. After realizing they couldn't sell their recently acquired chemical products without referencing the name METALAST, they filed their baseless retaliatory lawsuit in the federal court in Reno, six days before they were to have stopped using the name METALAST. Instead of simply honoring the agreement or re-negotiating to pay money to obtain the rights, they invented another set of thirty fabricated phony allegations. By now we were still at least a few years away from a jury trial in the district court case.

I filed my response to the TTAB lawsuit while acting *pro se*, which is Latin for acting as my own attorney. The Madler's attorney was not pleased when my motion to stay the legal proceeding was granted. TTAB continued to suspend the action until the Madler's challenge to all court rulings, including the United States Court of Appeals for the Ninth Circuit.

In October of 2016, the MILLC members or shareholders joined forces, hired several law firms, and filed a $90-million lawsuit against the Madlers, alleging a fraudulent conveyance of assets, gross misrepresentation, conspiracy, bad faith, and breach of contract. It appeared soon I would be the star witness in their pending class-action case.

I was certainly motivated to help, but all I really had to do was tell the truth. The Madlers and their alleged co-conspirators, receiver Jack Pimpley, and their initial attorney, Julie Chang, were in a serious predicament. The overwhelming evidence supported assertions that they had conspired to remove the manager by setting him up as a scapegoat. This was done to gain control of the MILLC assets so that they could wipe out the $12.5 million in Semas debt and the $90 million MILLC members' equity and then hold a sham sale.

As for my original 294 Madler case, Judge Du ruled on March 27, 2018, in favor of Wendi and Greg and granted summary judgments, meaning there wasn't enough evidence to warrant a trial on the frivolous lawsuits filed against them. Three days later, the judge granted summary judgments on all twelve of my motions. The judge also denied all fifteen of the Madlers' motions for summary judgments, further establishing the absurdity of their phony claims. This was great news. It supported my position that the lawsuit was baseless and had been without merit from the start. The only cause of action remaining for trial was the Madlers' unfounded copyright claim and my counterclaim for breach of contract. Once I prevailed, we could proceed with a legal action against Chemetall, BASF, QualiChem and six other distributors for willful and intentional trademark infringement.

The Madlers and their partners and distributors were falsely labeling their chemical products as "formerly Metalast" in a continuing effort to profit from my trademark rights. In November 2018, a lawyer friend filed a lawsuit on my behalf against BASF Corporation, Chemetall US, and the

Madlers' other chemical manufacturing partners and six of their primary distributors for trademark infringement, false designation of origin, trademark dilution, unfair business practices, unjust enrichment, and declaratory relief.

My trademark action against Chemetall, BASF, and the other Custom Care distributors was transferred to the federal district court of Nevada. To lessen the trial burden of the court, and now that my son and daughter and I had won nearly all causes of action, the case was re-assigned to a newly appointed savvy district court magistrate. Judge Carla Baldwin had been a career prosecutor as an assistant US attorney in the criminal division of the US Attorney's Office for the District of Nevada for eight years, prosecuting complex white-collar cases and public corruption. Soon thereafter, Judge Baldwin stayed my trademark infringement case until a final decision, including appeals before the Ninth Circuit Court was handed down in the original Madlers' case. In April of 2022, acting *pro se* I also took control of the trademark case.

For six years prior, Custom Care and their distributors had been infringing on my trademark, trying to run out the statute of limitations. This had created a multimillion-dollar liability exposure because the USPTO-registered METALAST® trademark and brand had been specified by many Fortune 500 companies that were subject to the highly coveted military specifications. This included the extremely difficult-to-obtain QPL (Qualified Product List) certification, which over a two-year period required testing, retesting, and then a twelve-month shelf life. Assuming it qualified, it was eventually validated and issued a QPL certification by the US Navy. Knowingly misrepresenting to governmental regulatory agencies the origin of a chemical was procurement fraud and a false designation of origin.

I believed that if process audit and government compliance departments became aware that thousands of their piece parts and products worldwide were not processed as specified and surface treated with METALAST® over the last five years, this could become more than troublesome for all involved. Threats of lawsuits for a false designation of origin and procurement fraud against Chemetall and BASF will likely come from their powerful and publicly traded multibillion-dollar customers. Many are defense contractors that manufacture sensitive military parts. These products also include their metal finishers processing flight critical components, which might bring them to the settlement table. Sometimes to get someone's attention you may be forced to hit them between the eyes with 2 x 4, metaphorically speaking.

"Let me tell you a real-life story that happened pretty near forty years ago," I said to my attorney friend, Mike Hoy. "It was in the fall of 1978. I was on a hunting trip in Northern British Columbia. Longtime professional guide and outfitter Jim 'Bugs' Haney, who had guided me on many big game hunts, was my outfitter on this particular expedition. My buddy, Gary Plaza, and I spent a few days at his beautiful base camp before Jim and I left for an eight-hour horseback ride to set up a spike camp at the base of a magnificent waterfall next to a high mountain stream with an abundant supply of freshwater salmon. As always, I was right at home on horseback, and Jim knew I could handle just about any steed. But he cautioned me about Devil. This three-year-old colt was full of piss and vinegar. He was mischievous and, quite frankly, a little dangerous. He would rather knock you off his back by running into low-hanging tree branches than let you sit comfortably in the saddle.

After Devil had made several attempts to run me into trees and even buck me off a cliff, I looked over at Bugs and said, 'What the hell?' Bugs said, 'David, have at it, because I've been trying to get him a little more rider-friendly for the last year, but that's like telling a bumblebee to stop liking honey.' I said, 'Jim, as you know, I love horses, but sometimes you just have to get their attention and teach them how to properly behave, so if you don't mind . . .' Again, he said, 'Take your best shot.'

"So, I dismounted, stood right in front of Devil, and in the words of the captain and prison warden in the movie *Cool Hand Luke* said, 'Son, what we've got here is a failure to communicate.' I raised my right arm and slapped his nose. He shook his head and looked me straight in the eye, and I rubbed his forehead, patted him on the neck, and said, 'Now, good buddy, let's become best friends and never let another disagreement come between us.' Over the next five days, Devil and I bonded like a precision equestrian drill team. Jim Haney said he'd never seen anything like it. The point of the story is that sometimes you have to use shock and awe to get the attention of your adversary, but never telegraph the next punch."

In my lawsuit against the Madlers and for the fifth time, the court ordered a settlement conference to be held in March 2020. If the case wasn't settled then, a bench trial before Judge Baldwin was put on the calendar for November 2020. On the morning of March 13th, on my way to attend the court ordered settlement conference I decided to drive to Northern California to visit with my son Greg and daughter Aimee, son-in-law Larry, and grandchildren Houston and Sierra at their home in Gilroy. Their home was about thirty miles south of San Jose and for over a four-hour period, it rained almost nonstop from Los Angeles all the way to Pacheco Pass on Highway 152, about twenty miles from their home. Together with son Greg we had a very enjoyable dinner at a local restaurant.

I left my hotel early the next morning to go back over Pacheco Pass to I-5, only to be met with fog so dense I couldn't see but maybe a few hundred feet in front of me. The thick layer of ground fog—or tule fog, as it's called in the San Joaquin Valley—stayed with me on and off for two hours all the way to Sacramento, where, thank God, the bright sun finally broke through the fog so I could increase my speed to a normal seventy miles per hour.

As I traveled along I-80 past Sacramento, Roseville, and Auburn, Mother Nature threw another curve ball at me. Only a few miles outside of Auburn, I ran smack dab into heavy snow that gradually grew into a snowstorm with fifty-mile-per-hour wind gusts. Light rain had fallen a few hours earlier. Thus, the roads turned into an ice-skating rink. My Jeep Grand Cherokee slid between white lines. Worse, the tractor and semi-trailer in front of me kicked up a small rock, which cracked my windshield. I reduced my speed to twenty-five miles per hour and slowly made my way over the Sierra Nevada. It was a grueling four hours on the slick and slippery interstate before I safely arrived at the valet parking entrance to the

Me on Devil during Haney hunting trip in British Columbia, 1978

Peppermill Hotel & Casino in Reno on South Virginia Street, a few blocks north of the Reno Convention Center.

After checking in and getting a little needed rest, I met my good friends Mark and Krista Wyman for a relaxing Italian dinner at Romanza, one of the six fine-dining restaurants in the Peppermill. The settlement conference was scheduled to begin at one o'clock the following afternoon, and just a few hours beforehand, Mike Hoy, my attorney, called to inform me that the Madlers' attorney had filed a motion with the court to postpone the conference because, at seventy-two years of age, Dick Madler was afraid to leave their $45 million Incline Village estate due to the coronavirus pandemic.

The court granted their motion, and the settlement conference was postponed. After driving ten hours through horrific weather conditions and finally arriving in Reno at the end of the "trip from hell," I was beyond livid. I hung up the phone and noticed a red light was showing on my hotel room telephone. I called the front desk, only to receive a message from the hotel manager. All Peppermill guests were being asked to check out and leave the property by noon the next day. The entire state of Nevada was going into a COVID-19 lockdown, which meant that casinos, hotels, restaurants, bars, and all other "non-essential" businesses would be closed for at least thirty days.

I went downstairs to the Terrace Lounge in the Tuscan Towers and enjoyed a few Jack Daniels to take off the edge so I could go back to my room and go to sleep.

Bright and early the next morning, I packed up my luggage, checked out, and had the valet bring my car around so I could make the eight-hour trek back to our home just a few miles south of Irvine in Aliso Viejo. After what I had been through, I figured it couldn't get much worse, but I was wrong. I pulled into the first Shell gas station around the corner from the

Peppermill at 7:00 a.m. to find that it was closed. I traveled three miles down South Virginia Street to the Shell station that had been our go-to gas station when we'd lived in Reno, filled up, and jumped on I-580 and headed south to Carson City. I thought it a good idea to have breakfast before I left town, so I pulled into IHOP, but they were closed due to COVID-19. Denny's was also closed. At Heid's, the local breakfast stop, the lights were on inside, but a closed sign hung from the locked doors. Before I left town, I stopped at a McDonald's for an Egg McMuffin, hash browns, and orange juice.

With food in my stomach, a full tank of gas, and a cracked windshield, I did okay until I hit another snowstorm just north of Mammoth Lakes. Cars and trucks were sliding all around me as the drivers hit the brakes. There, in the middle of the highway, blocking all three lanes, was an overturned eighteen-wheeler. Police cars, fire trucks, and an ambulance were already on the scene, lights flashing. A Peterbilt tow-truck idled nearby with its amber lights flashing.

After a two-hour delay, I continued over the mountain and down to the town of Bishop for lunch. Up and down Main Street, every restaurant, coffee shop, and donut shop was closed. At the south end of town, I stopped at a Chevron to fill up with gas again and settled for a hamburger, French fries, and a Coke from Burger King. No one was allowed to sit inside, so I had to use the drive-through and park in their lot to eat.

Once I was back on Highway 395, everything went pretty smoothly until the cut-off to the town of Ridgecrest, where wind gusts hit sixty miles per hour. As I made my way to Four Corners, where Highway 395 intersects with Highway 58, the winds subsided. While traveling down Cajon Pass toward San Bernardino, I once again hit dense fog that filled the canyons and drifted across the freeway. I was only an hour from home, but visibility was near zero. What should have been an hour drive home took three hours. My journey had begun at 7:00 a.m. and finished at 10:30 p.m. when I pulled into my driveway. I could barely keep my eyes open, and I hit the sack before I even unpacked. No worse for the wear, I was home safe and sound.

Finally, on November 9, 2020, after more than five tumultuous years of litigation, gamesmanship, and delays, the Madlers sat in court and prepared to deliver their opening statement to Judge Baldwin in the scheduled five-day trial. My two days of testimony were truthful, factual, and cooperative with opposing legal counsel, and theirs was anything but. In the words of Mark Twain, "If you speak the truth, you don't have to remember anything," because the truth always fits like a jigsaw puzzle. On the other hand, Dick delivered evasive answers and suffered convenient memory lapses while proffering material "facts" that did not comport with reality. Martha appeared to have little knowledge about the METALAST business operations and kept repeating how she and Dick believed the settlement agreement only meant they had to take the METALAST name off the building and their stationery. Both spouses contradicted their earlier testimony and attempted to twist the settlement judge's ruling.

Lawrence Lurchman (not his real name), the president of their company, was argumentative, non-responsive, as the court put it, "lacked candor." When shown a label with the name METALAST TCP-HF, he refused to acknowledge the trademark brand and ridiculously repeated that the label only referenced TCP-HF and that the chemical was sold most times without the METALAST brand preceding it. This was absurd on its face and had never happened. In any case, how could he have known? He hadn't been hired by the Madlers until after METALAST International, LLC ceased operations in November 2013. The conduct of the Madlers' attorneys was something to behold as well. Many times, the court warned counsel of their poor conduct, and they were overruled time and time again when they attempted to prevent exculpatory evidence in my favor from being introduced into the record.

The day of reckoning was just around the corner. After the written closing arguments were presented to the court on December 9, 2020, the judge informed the plaintiffs and defendants that her final decision on the breach of contract and the remaining copyright claim would be rendered before the end of January 2021. I was fairly confident that we would prevail, and that Judge Baldwin would issue a permanent injunction against the Madlers that would prevent them from ever using the METALAST trademark, name, and brand in commerce. But I was a little concerned that she might toss them a bone or two and find in their favor on their bogus copyright over the METALAST product label and their questionable trademark claim on their exclusive right to TCP-HF and AA-200, thus preventing me from ever using those sub-marks. I also knew the Madlers would appeal to the Ninth Circuit Court but was relatively certain the circuit court would uphold the decision of the lower court.

Sure enough, on February 23, 2021, at exactly 10:40 a.m. and while driving to a dental appointment, I heard my cell phone ping. I had just received an email from Shondel Seth, the administrative assistant to my attorney, Mike Hoy. She often sent me a legal motion or brief from one of the attorneys or a court filing, like a bench brief, or some type of a judicial notice from the court. The final ruling from Judge Baldwin had been due before the end of January, and here it was three weeks later. We were on pins and needles waiting for her final court order. We anxiously awaited her ruling, hoping she would find in our favor. We prayed that she would grant our motion for an injunction and find against the Madlers. Would Judge Baldwin rule they had been guilty of a breach of contract since June 11, 2015? This would mean that any of the Madlers' distributors that had sold and distributed a Custom Care product labeled "formerly Metalast" or "formerly known as Metalast" after that date was effectively found liable for trademark infringement by a federal judge.

I was almost afraid to open the email, but when I pulled into the parking lot at the dentist's office, I got up the nerve to double-click on the subject line, which read "SEMAS (Custom Care)." I took a deep breath, my heart racing, and just before I opened the email, Mike Hoy sent me a text that read, "We won! I'm calling as soon as I get off my current call."

It was 10:55 a.m. when Mike called. "David, we crushed them. The judge denied all their remaining four causes of action and granted a judgment in your favor on *all* your claims."

Before going to lunch, I glanced at the first two pages and then the conclusion of the scathing forty-three-page court order. After nearly a six-year legal battle, we had finally won the lawsuit. Judge Baldwin had found in our favor on all remaining causes of action, including our breach of contract counterclaim. As I had hoped, the judge had issued an injunction stopping the Madlers from ever using the METALAST trademark, name, or brand in commerce in any fashion or manner whatsoever. The final court order was a judicial masterpiece that referenced in detail the twenty-seven-year history of METALAST International, LLC. It also provided a summary of the last six years of litigation. The Madlers and their legal team must have been shocked when they read the following:

> *VI. CONCLUSION*
>
> ***IT IS HEREBY ORDERED*** *that judgment is granted in favor of Defendants (Semas) on Plaintiff's claims for relief;*
>
> ***IT IS FURTHER ORDERED*** *that judgment is granted in favor of Defendants on Defendants' first and seventh claims for relief;*
>
> ***IT IS FURTHER ORDERED AND ADJUDGED*** *as follows:*
>
> - *Plaintiff's (Custom Care and the Madlers) request for a permanent injunction enjoining Semas and his business entities from using "TCP-HF" or "AA-200" is DENIED;*
>
> - *Plaintiff's request for a permanent injunction enjoining Semas and his business entities from infringing on the Copyright Works is DENIED;*
>
> - *Plaintiff's request for a finding that this is an "exceptional case" under Lanham Act § 47(a) is DENIED;*
>
> ***IT IS FURTHER DECREED*** *that, beginning June 11, 2015, Dick Madler, Martha Madler, and Custom Care Surface Technology, LLC had no right to use "Metalast" in commerce, including, but not limited to, calling itself or its products "formerly Metalast" or "formerly known as Metalast";*

IT IS FURTHER DECREED that Counterclaimants Dick Madler, Martha Madler, and Custom Care are hereby ordered to perform the Settlement by halting all use of "Metalast" on any product labels, advertisements, sales orders, invoices, purchase orders, technical data sheets, safety data sheets, web pages, brochures, or other documents of commerce. This judgment of specific performance may be enforced by contempt proceedings in this court;

IT IS FURTHER ORDERED that Custom Care shall have fourteen (14) calendar days after entry of this order within which to respond to Greg Semas's motion for attorney fees and Wendi Semas's motion for attorney fees (ECF Nos. 466, 469);

IT IS FURTHER ORDERED that Custom Care shall have fourteen (14) calendar days after entry of this order within which to move to retax costs set forth in Wendi Semas's Bill of Costs (ECF No. 467);

IT IS FURTHER ORDERED that any other party may file a motion for attorney fees or bill of costs within fourteen (14) calendar days after entry of this order; and,

IT IS FURTHER ORDERED that the Clerk of the Court ENTER JUDGMENT accordingly and CLOSE this case.

LIFE LESSON #135:

"YOU MAY HAVE TO FIGHT A BATTLE MORE THAN ONCE TO WIN."

—MARGARET THATCHER (PRIME MINISTER OF THE UNITED KINGDOM, 1925-2013)

Granddaughter Indy, husband Taylon, and great grandson Owen

Wendi, husband Ronnie, and grandson Dave at their home in Gardnerville, 2020

We immediately filed a judicial notice with Judge Du and her magistrate, Judge Baldwin, to lift the stay on the trademark infringement case against the Madlers' distributors: Chemetall/BASF, QualiChem, and seven other companies. If granted, this would allow us to proceed with discovery, interrogatories, depositions, and the pending case.

Winning our Madler 294 breach of contract lawsuit was great news, but we needed the judge to lift the stay so I could proceed with litigation against the trademark infringers in the 125 lawsuit. I was suing all of the distributors for disgorgement of profits, meaning every dollar the distributors had made in gross profit since June 10, 2015, plus attorney fees, would be owed to me. This could represent millions in award plus treble damages—or three times that amount if the court found their actions to be intentional, which they were.

The judge didn't lift the stay order, mainly because, as expected, the Madlers' legal team filed an appeal on March 25, 2021 with the Ninth Circuit Court of Appeals in the 294 case.

Considering the scathing forty-three-page court order that had rebuked nearly every phony claim made by the Madlers against my children and me, this undoubtedly would prove to be a futile effort. But it served as another delaying tactic.

After paying off nearly $12.5 million of METALAST International, LLC debt, the good news for Susan and me was in May of 2021 the US Bankruptcy Court issued their ORDER ENTERING FINAL DECREE and dismissed the Chapter 11 bankruptcy and closed the case.

On the home front, Wendi had married a terrific man the previous year. Ronnie Borchert truly loved David, our special-needs grandson. Another happy occasion occurred when our granddaughter, Indy, married Taylon, and the former military couple gave birth to Owen, our first great-grandchild, in February 2020.

From L-R, Houston, Owen, Indy, Larry, Aimee and Sierra, 2021

Marie Gibbs Bodway Semas, 2016

From L-R, RRCD bartender Terry Vanzant and brother Len in the Sierra Dorado Saloon bar trailer, 2014

Granddaughter Sierra entered her sophomore year and was maturing into a beautiful young girl. Grandson Houston was preparing for college, and grandson David had graduated high school. Time flies, I continued to learn, so enjoy each and every moment!

In January of 2020, my youngest sister, Marie, passed away from an illness she had so bravely battled for many years.

My mother had joined my father and the rest of the Semas and Lopes family in heaven right before Thanksgiving of 2020.

A few months later, my only brother, Len, passed away on April 8, 2021. In June we held a beautiful celebration of life for him just days before

Wendi with Grandma Mary Semas at her ninety-third birthday party, 2016

> **LIFE LESSON #136:**
>
> **"PEACE IS NOT ABSENCE OF CONFLICT; IT IS THE ABILITY TO HANDLE CONFLICT BY PEACEFUL MEANS."**
>
> —RONALD REAGAN

the start of the annual Reno Rodeo Cattle Drive, and nearly everyone in the sixty-member crew gathered to share stories of Len's colorful life.

Only my sister, Elizabeth, and I remain of the Semas clan of seven. Our newest addition to the Semas family is a mini-Australian shepherd named Co-Jack, or "CJ" for short, named after our beloved Australian shepherds CoCo and Jack.

Elizabeth "Lizzy" Joan Semas

CJ ready guarding his Christmas tree ready to open presents, December 2021

Susan and I have experienced a lifetime of fantastic moments and heart-wrenching ones too, but that's a reality for most. My father lived to the age of seventy-seven, and my mother lived to the ripe old age of ninety-seven. Never forget those families devastated by the loss of children to illness or affliction, teenagers to auto accidents, and young men and women to war.

LIFE LESSON #138:

"I BELIEVE EVERY HUMAN HAS A FINITE NUMBER OF HEARTBEATS. I DON'T INTEND TO WASTE ANY OF MINE."

—NEIL ARMSTRONG (AMERICAN ASTRONAUT, FIRST PERSON TO WALK ON THE MOON, 1930–2012)

We have been truly blessed to have been given the opportunity to live such a wonderful life.

I vividly remember when, as a youngster, I complained about not having an expensive bicycle I wanted.

Big Leonard turned to me and said, "Davey, you'll learn to be thankful for all you've been given and stop whining about not having material things when you see those that have no food, clothing, or shelter. There is a little boy out there that complained about not having any shoes until he saw the little boy without legs. There are always those far worse off than you. A glass of wine that's filled midway isn't half empty; it's half full."

Thank the Lord for all you've been given.

After eight years of stress, the bankruptcy court was finally behind us, our Chapter 11 was a closed case, and we were finally debt free. Most of the frivolous litigation was coming to a close, my real estate development projects were taking shape, and Susan and I had a bright future before us as we entered the fourth quarter of our lives.

The class-action legal team believed they were making headway when, in May 2020, Judge Miranda Du of the US District Court ruled against both of their lawsuits on a technicality. She determined that even if the Madlers and court-appointed receiver had committed misconduct and fraud, the parties were shielded by litigation privilege under the protection given to a court-appointed receiver. The Judge also ruled the case was "time-barred," meaning the statute of limitations came into play. On Wednesday, May 11, 2022, beginning promptly at nine o'clock a.m. the Ninth Circuit Court of Appeals heard the oral arguments for both Class Action cases. Unfortunately, the Court upheld Judge Du's unfavorable ruling to dismiss the cases. In effect this closed the door on the Class Action members from recovering any portion of their $90 million investment. The Ninth Circuit decision was handed down on June 2, 2022. This was truly a miscarriage of justice, but as I've learned the hard way in protracted litigation, usually, but not always he with the most money wins.

My pending 294 lawsuit counter claim for Breach of Contract against the Madlers in Ninth Circuit Court of Appeals was also heard the same day as the Members Class Action cases in June, but in my case the Ninth Circuit upheld Judge Baldwin's favorable ruling. Chemetall, BASF, Qualichem and the other distributors willfully and intentionally infringed on my METALAST® trademark for more than seven years. Now that the Ninth Circuit upheld Judge Baldwin's Findings of Fact and Conclusions of Law all the Defendants are in serious financial jeopardy. Considering the evidence is prima facie and Judge Baldwin has already ruled the Madlers and their company Custom Care had no authority to use the METALAST name after June 11, 2015, a monetary settlement will likely be reached sometime in the very near future. If not, and considering the facts of trademark infringement are undisputed we will prevail either by a motion for summary judgment or at the time of trial. Soon the day will come to finally move on and focus on the future, not the past. At the end of the day, this painful litigious episode for my wife and family will have taken its toll, but it will also represent another valuable life lesson.

I will always appreciate my father's words when he said, "David, the Lord never gives you more than you can handle. What doesn't break you makes you stronger. Believe in him, and you can overcome any obstacle. If things don't go your way, don't squander it, don't complain about it, don't feel sorry for yourself. Just get up, dust yourself off, move on, and thank the good Lord for your blessings."

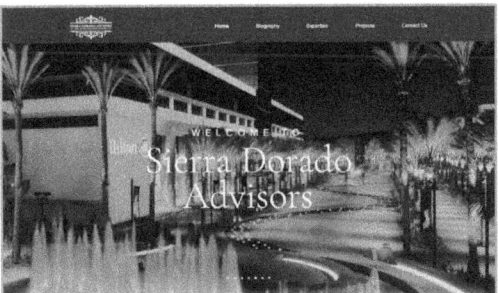

Sierra Dorado website homepage

On a positive note, Sierra Dorado Inc., my real estate development and advisory company, was in full swing. In the summer of 2021, its website design and media consultants, Omar Palma and Patrick Fong, introduced by stepson Derek, transformed the Sierra Dorado website (sierradorado.com) beautifully. I'm working with longtime friends Marc Harris, Martin J. Burke, and Richard Bren on equity and debt financing for our Las Islitas Resort hotel, championship golf course, and exclusive residential community project in San Blas, Mexico. Not being prone to sit idle, I'm always looking for other real estate development and finance opportunities.

With my partners, Jim Kieckhafer and Jeff Mackinen, we closed escrow right before Christmas on December 23, 2020, on a 155-acre property in South Reno near the Summit Mall. The proposed master-planned industrial site is located between I-580 and South Virginia Street (Highway 395), just south of Mt. Rose Highway (SR 431). The property surrounds a Waste Management administrative office building and equipment storage site and includes an Ormat Technologies' geothermal electricity-generating facility, which occupies about twenty-five acres of the land. More than half the project will be set aside as a Conservation Easement and open space to preserve and protect the endangered Steamboat Buckwheat flora species, which is found only at this location.

Another longtime friend, Peter Andrich, senior vice president of CBRE and vice chairman Brett Hartzell of CBRE, the global leader in commercial real estate brokerage, listed the property for sale in December 2021. A bidding frenzy ensued and in March 2022 we executed a Purchase and Sale Agreement with one of the largest industrial building developers in the country and anticipate the close of escrow and sale to be completed before the end of 2022.

LIFE LESSON #137:

"THE BEST REVENGE IS MASSIVE SUCCESS."

—FRANK SINATRA (AMERICAN SINGER, ACTOR, PRODUCER, AND ENTERTAINER, 1915-1998)

Las Islitas Resort logo, San Blas, Nayarit, Mexico

Las Islitas Resort beach

Sierra Dorado Industrial Park aerial rendering, Reno, NV

Sierra Dorado Industrial Park rendering, S. Virginia Street

When you spend a half-century in the real estate development and finance business and private equity investment you will build trust, confidence and usually prosper from many long-term relationships, especially if you haven't burned any bridges along the way.

One Saturday morning, in March of 2022, my telephone rang and on the line were friends Jerry Ottie Thomas and John LiSanti. They presented an opportunity to acquire Nine Mile Hill ranch, a large 3,320 acre ranch in Northern California, two hours north of Sacramento. The pristine rolling hill property had been fully zoned and entitled with a vesting tentative map and Development Agreement for what was to have been a Pulti Del Webb Active Adult Community with 3,700 homes, a championship golf course, 240,000 square feet and thirty two acres of retail commercial. Within a matter of a few weeks my company Sierra

> LIFE LESSON #139:
>
> "HAPPY ARE THOSE THAT DREAM DREAMS AND ARE READY TO PAY THE PRICE TO MAKE THEM COME TRUE."
>
> —LEO JOSEPH CARDINAL SUENENS (ROMAN CATHOLIC ARCHBISHOP OF MECHELEN-BRUSSEL, BELGIUM 1904–1996)

Dorado Development, together with business partners Richard Bren and Martin Burke entered into a purchase contract to acquire the beautiful tree-lined rolling hill acreage with three miles of frontage and two freeway on/off-ramps on California Interstate 5. During our seven-month due diligence period we will determine, which qualified national Active Adult Senior Housing development firm we should align. On the buildout, the entire completed project should generate about $2.5 billion in home sales.

Beginning in 2014, Susan would occasionally remind me that I'm no longer the young cowboy I once was. She would tell me that after being thrown from a horse on occasion over the years, in the future I might come to the realization that I don't bounce well anymore. She suggested I find a more gentleman-type of equestrian adventure rather than pushing three hundred head of corriente roping steers over high desert terrain in the wind, rain, and most times sweltering hot sun. She also reminded me, or should a say challenged me by suggesting my horse would appreciate if I lost thirty pounds. Wearing 38 inch Wrangler Cowboy Cut jeans, a few days later I found a pair of 34 inch Wranglers laid out on the bed, which just happen to be the size I wore when we met in May of 1994. Up for the challenge within three months I weighed in at a trim 215 pounds and squeezed into those 34 inch Wranglers, albeit I needed a pair of plyers to close the zipper.

I took her advice and challenge and thanks to my cowboy friend and sponsor, Myron "My" Galchutt, I was invited to become a member of the Los Caballeros. This equestrian group of gentlemen horsemen from Southern California and around the country were founded by William Wrigley Jr. in 1943. Since September 1949, the group has called Little Harbor on Catalina Island its home for five days of riding, games, competitions at the rodeo, trail class events, and gathering around the campfire for stories, songs, and tall tales. To the Los Caballeros, riding on the island is a unique privilege. I've met many new friends on the annual Catalina Island Trek and on our St. Patrick's Day ride, like cowboy buddies insurance professional Philippe Matta and southern California gas station chain owner and luxury home real estate builder developer David Berri.

With Sierra Dorado Industrial Park, Nine Mile Hill ranch, the fully entitled master planned community, Las Islitas Resort and several other projects in the works I am once again a real estate developer and financier. Between my annual Los Caballeros adventure and real estate projects, I find it all to be fantastic and thoroughly invigorating! I can't help thinking, *I'm back in the saddle again!*

Me and Los Caballeros Gunsel class with kneeling El Presidente Tom Crone (L) and Myron "My" Galchutt (R), 2020

CHAPTER 28
THE MAN IN THE ARENA

Even with all the ups and downs I have faced over a half century, it's been a fabulous journey. As Hans Prager, founder of Gulliver's and The Ritz Restaurant in Newport Beach, would say, "It's my life. I live it, I love it and critics be damned." Or as fictional character Forrest Gump put it, "Life is like a box of chocolates. You never know what you're gonna get." Since my early twenties, I enjoyed singing "My Way" ever since it was first released by Frank Sinatra in 1969. Today, its words and message hold a very special meaning to me now that I'm seventy-three.

I've learned to think on my feet and remain focused in the heat of battle. Fortunately, I've kept my professional conduct above board, have been honest in my business dealings, and have been accountable for my actions. If you stay in business as long as I have, you're going to make a few enemies and countless mistakes, be humbled, and sometimes be humiliated before family and friends. On occasion, you're going to wish you had handled a problem in a different way. As difficult as it might be, honesty is always the best policy. Thanks to keeping a daily diary and accurate books and records since the beginning of my career, I've been able to retrace every step along the way.

Without the meticulous accounting practices of daughter Wendi and the Metalast accounting department, I could have ended up in serious legal trouble with the IRS and the SEC. Should they have found financial improprieties of any kind, either of the unwarranted investigations could have resulted in life-altering grand jury indictments and criminal prosecution. These types of formal inquiries are usually conducted by aggressive and highly experienced government investigators accustomed to dealing with dishonest white-collar criminals.

In the world of the IRS, FBI and SEC, there is no such thing as "you're innocent until proven guilty." In fact, the opposite is true, meaning "you're guilty until proven innocent," which, in the end never happens. If after a forensic and intrusive criminal investigation you have undeniably established your innocence, the IRS, FBI or SEC doesn't exonerate you or declare your innocence. The federal law enforcement agencies unapologetically inform you that you are no longer the subject of an investigation, usually followed with a statement to the affect "this doesn't mean at some future date your case can't be re-opened." So much for fairness, equity and the rule of law and of course the catch phrase, "Justice is Blind." The point being a lying and conniving whistleblower can destroy your career at the blink of an eye without a shred of hard evidence and only mere bogus allegations, rumor and innuendo.

During a deposition under oath, a skilled interrogator can easily set you up for a perjury trap, with you being none the wiser. By the time you're put under oath in a deposition, the investigation team has already reviewed tens of thousands of pages of documents and records. They know the answer to every question they're going to ask you. If you're not experienced in this environment—and most aren't—you could find yourself in handcuffs and under arrest. Just ask Martha Stewart or former US Army Lieutenant General Michael Flynn, both of whom were found guilty of process crimes by the allegation of lying or misrepresenting material facts to the FBI, although in the case of Flynn, several FBI agents testified that he didn't lie.

While it has been a challenge to remain objective, I've done my best to be just as critical of my actions and decisions as I have of others'. I've made my share of mistakes along the way, but if this book can inspire and motivate one person to learn from them, it was well worth writing. The world is filled with excuses, and the more you rely on them, the more you will fail yourself and the weaker you will become in the eyes of others. As a manager or CEO, I was forced to deal with problems head-on, because on the battlefield there is only one general. You either rise to the challenge or run from it, which in my case was never an option.

If I've learned anything in my career, it is that you never know what tomorrow brings. Forecasts are merely guesses—sometimes well founded and other times off the mark. Even one of the world's most valuable company was not immune. Beginning in 1984 (three years behind schedule), Steve Jobs projected Apple would sell 47,000 Macintosh computers per month, but after the initial computer nerds' buying frenzy, sales plummeted by an astounding 90 percent and sales dropped to 5,000 units per month.

As my experiences show, you must plan, strategize, and hope for the best but be prepared for the worst. Solve problems as they occur, and never lose sight of both your short- and long-term goals. Surround yourself with competent, experienced, and loyal people, but accept the fact that this is not easily done if you're a small and undercapitalized company. Everything usually takes twice as long and costs twice as much. Be watchful for that one thing you didn't plan on, because it's likely that one thing will inevitably occur. Be objective and introspective in your decision-making process. If, after careful deliberation, your decisions were correct, great! But if they were wrong, learn and grow from the experience.

Building a business involves a lifetime of solving problems, rising to challenges, making tough decisions, acknowledging failures, and sharing successes with others. If you're to succeed in the long run, you must be demanding yet patient, acknowledge your weaknesses as well as your strengths, and endeavor to improve your performance and those of everyone around you. I believe that you lead by example. You can second-guess all you want, but when all is said and done, the buck stops with the person at the top.

During nearly a half century of running companies, I have never found a shortcut to success. Yes, there have been many who dreamed, planned, worked hard, and rapidly achieved success by being at the right place at the right time in history. However, there have been millions more who have failed while daring greatly, hence "The Man in the Arena." There have been those with great ideas and average management skills who have stumbled, and there have been those with average ideas and great management skills who have succeeded. I am one who would rather bet on the jockey than the horse. I believe you must be prepared to deal in practical reality, not theoretical perception.

While it's fine to admire the accomplishments of business tech icons and billionaire entrepreneurs such as Elon Musk, Jeff Bezos, Michael Dell, Steve Jobs, Phil Knight and Ralph Lauren, please remember that they represent the exception and not the rule. Throughout history, few have built their companies in something less than a lifetime without significant setbacks and even failure along the way. Most are unaware that Thomas Jefferson, Abraham Lincoln, Ulysses S. Grant, P. T. Barnum, Henry Ford, J. C. Penney and Walt Disney filed for bankruptcy protection, so if you're ever forced to, you're in good company.

Like most of us, I didn't inherit wealth, win the lottery, or end up at the right place at the right time. I began my career at the business end of a shovel and joined the United Brotherhood of Carpenters Union when I was eighteen years old. I'm fortunate to have been dealt a pair of twos for most of my life, and I will continue to play the hand I've been dealt. After all, a pair of twos can still be a very good hand. The less fortunate usually are left with only one high card or maybe no cards at all. Be thankful for what the good Lord has given you!

It takes willpower and conviction to succeed, but it also takes courage, mental strength, and character to fail. Like the Man in the Arena, we are given the opportunity with each failure to look inside and see who we are so we can continue on our journey ever wiser, with a heightened sense of awareness of everything around us. True greatness is something most of us never achieve. It requires God-given talent while also demanding self-discipline, self-sacrifice, and dedication to a single purpose. In the relentless pursuit of such greatness, one must reach far beyond the normal physical and mental limitations of mortal man or woman.

A good number of young adults in American society have fallen into an entitlement mentality, and unfortunately, many expect a free ride. The virtues of yesterday, including a good work ethic and a commitment to excellence, dedication, and perseverance, seem to have fallen on deaf ears. A great number of those in the generations behind us baby boomers appear to expect—and sometimes demand—instant gratification but wallow in selfishness, self-indulgence, and non-accountability.

However, I remain optimistic that future generations will eventually learn to be responsible for their actions, like those of the Greatest Generation, who courageously fought in World War II. The future of our country rests in the hands of the youth that follow us. We can only pray that one day, like those before them, they strive to achieve the American Dream and whole-heartedly embrace old-fashioned capitalism, hard work, accountability, pride in teamwork, and personal achievement. It's never too late to change, and most times the pendulum reverses direction. I'm hopeful that future generations will embrace Winston Churchill's famous words, "Those who fail to learn from history are doomed to repeat it."

Republican President Ronald Reagan said, "Government is not the solution to our problem; government *is* the problem." On January 20, 1961, in his inaugural address, Democratic President John F. Kennedy said, "And so, my fellow Americans, ask not what your country can do for you; ask what you can do for your country."

We are a nation of free people. As has been established for more than two centuries, we are the melting pot of all people, races, color, and creeds. If you want to rise to the top, go ahead and step into the arena. If you're willing to risk it all, step up to the plate.

As Teddy Roosevelt stated more than a century ago, if a person fails while daring greatly, ". . . his place

> **LIFE LESSON #140:**
>
> "ALL OUR DREAMS CAN COME TRUE IF WE HAVE THE COURAGE TO PURSUE THEM."
>
> —WALT DISNEY

shall never be with those cold and timid souls who neither know victory nor defeat."

If you look up the word "victim" in Webster's Dictionary my picture is not there. I am not a victim now nor have I ever been. I've always embraced Life Lesson #41, Joe Kennedy's philosophy, "When the going gets tough, the tough get going." I will continue to strive to be the very best I can be and to face the realities of life head-on, and no matter what, I will do my best to never give in, never give up, and never say quit!

Me at Gulfstream restaurant in February 2022

EPILOGUE

When I first started down the path of a business career, little did I know where my life would lead or where my travels would take me. Year by year, I have come to realize I grow and change with each new day, each new experience, and every word heard and spoken. Who I am today is the cumulative sum total of a lifetime of experiences.

Since my earliest exploits as a young businessman, I've been blessed with the opportunity to experience a fascinating career, worldwide travels, and amazing adventures. My life has crossed paths with famous, infamous, and not-so-famous people that could have easily been imaginary characters in a *New York Times* bestselling novel.

Sometimes I suspect my family and friends might think my recollections and colorful stories are reminiscent of the exploits of the fictional character Edward Bloom, played by Albert Finney in *Big Fish*, the 2003 comedy-drama film based on a novel of the same name. In this fabulous story, Edward, a traveling salesman, is terminally ill with cancer and has been taken off chemotherapy. As his life nears an end, he shares flashbacks of fanciful experiences and fascinating characters with Will, his son. Although most of his melodramatic stories took place before Will was born, he begins to piece together an accurate picture of his father, whom he perceives as a kind man with a gentle soul but a penchant for exaggerating and embellishing his tall tales of adventure.

Edward recalls befriending a gentle giant, becoming a respected citizen in a small community, and being given a key to the town by its mayor. He remembers being admired by his high-school coach and hanging out with a famous poet. He even recalls seeing a mermaid through the window of his car after accidentally driving into a lake. Later in his imaginary life, he meets a circus owner and ringmaster who also happens to be, of all things, a werewolf. While working as a hired hand and cleaning elephant pens at the circus, Edward sets his eyes on a local beauty and falls in love at first sight. After many years of searching for her—he knew only that her name began with the letter S—he eventually finds and marries his love. During the Korean War, he rescues conjoined twin sisters who were a singing sensation throughout the land and offers to get them into show business in America. Edward befriends a clumsy bank robber who eventually becomes a wealthy Wall Street tycoon.

At Edward's funeral, Will and his wife, Josephine, are completely caught off-guard when the supposedly fictional characters from Edward's whimsical past arrive. Each is a slightly less fantastical version than his father described, but Will finally comes to appreciate his father's love for life and storytelling.

While my life adventures and global exploits are not nearly as glamorous or grandiose as the fictional character Edward Bloom's, I see the comparison and have come to appreciate that sometimes real life can intersect with fiction. Many executives involved in international business meet famous people and celebrities at one time or another. Some even get a chance

> LIFE LESSON #141:
>
> NANCY ASTOR, THE FIRST WOMAN TO BE SEATED AS A MEMBER OF THE BRITISH PARLIAMENT, SAID TO PRIME MINISTER WINSTON CHURCHILL, "IF I WERE YOUR WIFE, I'D PUT POISON IN YOUR TEA!" CHURCHILL RESPONDED WITH, "MADAM, IF I WERE YOUR HUSBAND, I'D DRINK IT."

to meet a president or a king. However, it's extremely rare to meet a real-life werewolf or a witch.

Certainly, George Haines fits the bill of a famous coach. He didn't greatly admire me, but I respected and admired him. Santa Clara Mayor Gary Gillmor and my dear friend, City Councilman Danny Texera, were local political icons and community leaders, but they never did give me the key to the city. The poet would have been Dennis Lambert of the songwriting duo Potter & Lambert, famous for Glen Campbell's "Rhinestone Cowboy" and the Righteous Brothers' "Rock and Roll Heaven." In 1975, during a ten-day voyage on the *Island Princess* of Princess Cruise Lines, we had a great time in Acapulco, Puerto Vallarta, and Mazatlán.

While I would have loved to have met a mermaid, I never did, other than to say hello to Donna de Varona in the hallways of Santa Clara High School. As a member of the Santa Clara Swim Club, under the tutelage of Olympic swimming coach legend George Haines, she would go on to become an Olympic gold medalist and world-record holder.

I think the closest I ever came to meeting a circus ringleader was when I met the famous artist Brett Livingstone Strong and his famous recording icon partner, Michael Jackson. I guess the big-top circus owner would have been Paul Lowden, owner and operator of the Hacienda Hotel & Casino of Las Vegas (now Mandalay Bay Hotel & Casino). Paul at one time owned the stage performance rights to the world-renowned white tiger master illusionist act of Siegfried & Roy. Paul was also a close friend and associate of Kenny Feld, the CEO and owner of Ringling Brothers. However, to be clear, and to the best of my knowledge, Paul was not then—nor is he now—a werewolf or soothsaying witch. I didn't clean out elephant pens at the circus, but as a young boy, I did clean out Vo-Vô Semas's cow pens at his dairy farm in Taunton, Massachusetts.

Fortunately, I did fall in love with and marry a beauty whose first name began with the letter "S", but it wasn't Sandra Templeton—it was Susan Miller Olsen. I can unequivocally state I never jumped out of a perfectly good airplane and never served in the military or fought in a war. I did spend time in the Philippines with President Marcos just after the Vietnam War on an exciting adventure full of mystery and intrigue. I guess the beautiful non-conjoined twin sisters would have been the voluptuous

> **LIFE LESSON #142:**
> **"LIFE IS A JOURNEY, NOT A DESTINATION"**
>
> —RALPH WALDO EMERSON

identical twins Linda and Wanda Owens, my very close friends and Santa Clara High classmates. I don't think I knew any bank robbers, although Stacey, a pretty female friend of ours from Gardnerville, Nevada, unintentionally married one. As far as a Wall Street tycoon and financier, I know many who could fill that role.

Over my lifetime, I've met a king—the Shah of Iran. I had dinner in 1975 with then-Governor Ronald Reagan, our future President of the United States. Thanks to my dear friend General Marking and his aide-de-camp, Lieutenant Colonel "Kits" Quesada, I was also invited to meet President Marcos of the Philippines. I had the great honor of spending an afternoon with Maxwell Rabb, an ambassador to Italy and chief legal counsel to President Eisenhower. I met and spent time with well-known CEOs, famous entrepreneurs, business icons, politicians, Hollywood entertainers, and showmen from all walks of life.

To be clear, I'm not name-dropping but merely illustrating how anyone's life can be inexplicably altered by a mentor or other people of influence. Chance meetings with business professionals or celebrities might open the door to success for you. In the end, all of these opportunities and chance meetings are really just a part of one's own destiny. Yes, I believe that you make your own destiny by what you do or fail to do, but there's something to be said about fate, divine intervention, timing and a little good fortune.

> **LIFE LESSON #143:**
> **"WHEN YOU COME TO THE END OF YOUR ROPE, TIE A KNOT AND HANG ON."**
>
> —FRANKLIN DELANO ROOSEVELT (THIRTY-SECOND PRESIDENT OF THE UNITED STATES, 1882-1945)

A person's life can't be predicted. One day, by the grace of God, we'll all arrive at the same place. How will you be remembered by those whose lives you touched? What did you contribute to those around you and to those unknown souls in society? Were you a good person?

Did you appreciate the gift of life given to you, and did you do your best to help those less fortunate? At the end of life, all that remains is the indelible mark you left on all those who knew you and how much you unselfishly gave of yourself to others.

There are many parallels that can be drawn between the fictional life of Edward Bloom and the real-life story of David Michael Semas, but in my mind, the only actual "giant" was Big Leonard. While he was just under six feet tall, he was a giant of a father whose steadfast determination, sense of humor, infinite wisdom, and unlimited quotes continue to inspire me to this day. I pay tribute here to a few of his tacky sayings:

- *I can do anything a little man can do but fit in a smaller hole.*
- *What's your name? Oh, I had a dog by that name, but he died on me.*
- *I can dance and spin with the best of 'em. My only problem is stopping.*
- *Dave, I hope you make a million dollars so that one day I can borrow half.*

LIFE LESSON #144:

"YOUTH IS NOT ENTIRELY A TIME OF LIFE; IT IS A STATE OF MIND. NOBODY GROWS OLD BY MERELY LIVING A NUMBER OF YEARS. PEOPLE GROW OLD BY DESERTING THEIR IDEALS. YOU ARE AS YOUNG AS YOUR FAITH, AS OLD AS YOUR DOUBT; AS YOUNG AS YOUR SELF-CONFIDENCE, AS OLD AS YOUR FEAR; AS YOUNG AS YOUR HOPE, AS OLD AS YOUR DESPAIR."

—DOUGLAS MACARTHUR (AMERICAN FIVE-STAR GENERAL AND SUPREME COMMANDER OF THE PACIFIC THEATRE, WWII, 1880-1964)

Now that the METALAST-related litigation is behind me and I've moved on with my life in the real estate development and construction business, Susan and I can enjoy the rest of our days in relative peace and quiet. It's time to take delight in the warm days in sunny Southern California and Palm Springs. Maybe during the afternoon tropical rain showers on the west coast of Mexico along the Riviera Nayarit, with endless evenings grilling "shrimp on the barbie" and telling stories by the fireside. Life is a fantastic experience that should not be squandered. What an incredible joy it will be to watch our grandchildren, great-grandson, and those yet to be born play in the yard or on the beach.

I hope my shared experiences and lifetime adventures bring a smile and inspiration to all those who have taken the time to read this book. We each have a story to tell, and maybe one day you'll tell yours. Who knows? You might turn out to be the next John F. Kennedy, Martin Luther King Jr., or Condoleezza Rice. Or business icons like Elon Musk, Steve Jobs, or Warren Buffett. Maybe your athletic talent will shine, and you'll become another NFL star like Walter Payton, Joe Montana, Jerry Rice, Tom Brady, or Peyton Manning. Or maybe, just maybe you'll choose to be an entrepreneur and live every day of your challenging, yet rewarding life in the arena. Regardless, I hope you'll remember that life is a journey, not a destination, and spend a lifetime seeking your dreams and achieving your goals while enjoying every minute of it with family and good friends. May God Bless you.

ACKNOWLEDGMENTS

Me and Susan at Reno Rodeo, 2012

Many people influenced my life, including radio talk-show host, the Mayor of Market Street and brother Len, entrepreneur sister Elizabeth (Joan), Bill Bennett, Bob Quinn, Freddie Boitano, Jack Aiello, Barry Berman, Danny Texera, Father Walter Schmidt, Russ Frerer, Roger Luby, Frank O'Bryan, Jeff Mackinen, Bobby Roberts, Don Zellner, Jim McWalters, Vic Boyd, Martin Burke and my friend, business partner and CPA of almost thirty years, Jim Kieckhafer.

Certainly, my children had a profound impact on me. I owe my thanks to Wendi, Greg, Aimee, Jordan, and Derek. Son-in-laws Larry and Ronnie. Daughter-in-laws Julie and Kristin. I thank my grandchildren, Indy, Houston, Sierra, and especially Dave as well.

Most importantly, I give my undying gratitude and respect to the mentally strong, steadfast and stand-by-my side Susan, my beautiful, loving wife and soulmate. I owe a great deal of thanks and admiration, for without her continuing support and unwavering encouragement, I might not have had the ultimate willpower to stay the course all these years.

Lastly, I would like to express appreciation to my editor Bill Greenleaf and the staff of FriesenPress, all of whom assisted me in making this book possible.

Son-in-law Ronnie Borchert and Wendi

Wendi Semas Borchert, 2021   Son-in-law Larry Day and Aimee

Aimee Semas Day

Greg Semas at Chaumont-En-Vexin, Picardie, France, in 2016

Greg Semas, AKA General Nelson Miles, 2015

Jordan and Kristen's wedding on Catalina Island, 2019

Jordan and Kristen, 2021

From L-R, Susan, Derek, his wife Julie, and me on Derek's wedding day, 2017

Derek and Julie, 2020

DEDICATIONS

This book is also a tribute to a few very special people. To my father, Leonard, and my mother, Mary, who taught me to stay strong and respect all those around me. To Hank Godwin, who taught the meaning of leadership. To Ben Swig, who asked that one day I would "pay it forward" by passing along his motivational words. To my author sister Judy whom I promised one day I would tell the story of my life. To "Maestro" Coach Haines, for instilling in me a can-do attitude to never give in, never give up, and never say quit. Lastly, and most importantly, to my loving wife Susan Olsen Semas.

Leonard "The Colonel" Semas in 1990

From 1949 until my father's death on January 12, 1999, I was blessed to have shared with him my childhood, my rebellious teenage years, and a great deal of my adult life. Like millions of other brave Americans, he was part of the Greatest Generation. I dedicate this book to my father, Leonard "the Colonel" Semas.

TO THOSE INSPIRED OR ENLIGHTENED BY THESE WRITINGS: HAVE A GREAT LIFE, AND GO OUT AND MAKE IT HAPPEN.

Me and Susan at the Balboa Island Parade June 2022

Me in my home office, 2021

Me and Susan in Aliso Viejo, CA 2020

CPSIA information can be obtained
at www.ICGtesting.com
Printed in the USA
BVHW091348030922
646207BV00005B/5/J